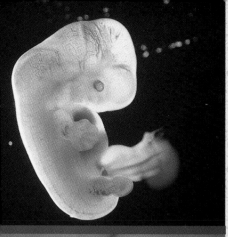

CHILDREN TODAY

Grace J. Craig

University of Massachusetts

Marguerite Kermis

Canisius College

 PRENTICE HALL
Englewood Cliffs, New Jersey 07632

Library of Congress Cataloging-in-Publication Data

Craig, Grace J.
    Children today / Grace J. Craig, Marguerite Kermis.
        p.   cm.
    Includes bibliographical references and index.
    ISBN 0-13-146275-X
    1. Child development. I. Kermis, Marguerite D.,
II. Title.
HQ767.9.C73 1994
305.23'1--dc20   94–13293
                                                  CIP

Editorial/production supervision: Maureen Richardson
Development editor: Marilyn Miller
Acquisitions editor: Pete Janzow
Editor-in-chief: Phil Miller
Interior design and page layout: Kerry Reardon
Cover design: Pentagram
Electronic illustrations: Robin R. Storesund/Storesund Design
Photo research: Ilene Belovin
Manufacturing buyer: Tricia Kenny

© 1995 by Prentice-Hall, Inc.
A Simon & Schuster Company
Englewood Cliffs, New Jersey 07632

Printed in the United States of America

10   9   8   7   6   5   4   3   2   1

ISBN   0-13-146275-X

Prentice-Hall International (UK) Limited, *London*
Prentice-Hall of Australia Pty. Limited, *Sydney*
Prentice-Hall Canada Inc., *Toronto*
Prentice-Hall Hispanoamericana, S.A., *Mexico*
Prentice-Hall of India Private Limited, *New Delhi*
Prentice-Hall of Japan, Inc., *Tokyo*
Simon & Schuster Asia Pte. Ltd., *Singapore*
Editora Prentice-Hall do Brasil, Ltda., *Rio de Janeiro*

CONTENTS

PART TWO

THE BEGINNINGS OF HUMAN LIFE

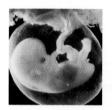

CHAPTER 4

THE PRENATAL PERIOD   132

CHAPTER 5

CHILDBIRTH AND THE NEONATE   172

PART THREE

Infancy: The First Two Years of Life

CHAPTER 6

INFANCY: PHYSICAL, MOTOR, AND COGNITIVE DEVELOPMENT 216

CHAPTER 7

PART FOUR
EARLY CHILDHOOD

CHAPTER 8

CHAPTER 9

**EARLY CHILDHOOD: PHYSICAL
DEVELOPMENT**   **338**

CHAPTER 10

**EARLY CHILDHOOD: DEVELOPING
THOUGHT AND ACTION**   **378**

PART FIVE

MIDDLE CHILDHOOD

CHAPTER 13

MIDDLE CHILDHOOD: COGNITIVE DEVELOPMENT AND SCHOOL TASKS 496

CHAPTER 14

MIDDLE CHILDHOOD: PERSONALITY AND SOCIAL DEVELOPMENT 534

PART SIX

ADOLESCENCE

CHAPTER 15

ADOLESCENCE: A TIME OF TRANSITION   **574**

CHAPTER 16

ADOLESCENCE: SOCIAL AND PERSONALITY DEVELOPMENT **610**

PREFACE

The primary purpose of *Children Today* is to introduce a wide range of college-level students to the exciting and dynamic field of child development. The story of the first two decades of a human life, in any cultural context, is likely to be a rich and compelling drama. The systematic and interdisciplinary study of children in broad cultural contexts is a challenge that puzzles researchers and students alike. This text draws from many fields–anthropology, sociology, history, nursing, public health and, of course, psychology–to present an up-to-date portrayal of the key issues, topics, and contemporary controversies in child development.

Children Today is aimed at a cross section of students varying in academic background, career interests, and past experiences with the social sciences. Many will seek a future in child-related fields, such as social work, education, counseling, nursing, speech therapy, school psychology, program administration and many others. Some students are already coaches, counselors, tutors or parents. Many will be parents at some time. Most have a strong curiosity about their own childhood and adolescence. This text aims to provide a sound, thought-provoking introduction to contemporary child development research and theory, as well as its application.

Children Today represents the collaboration of two authors who bring complementary styles and experiences to the study of child development. Both of us have taught Child Development, to somewhat different audiences, for many years. The book draws substantially from my established life-span text, *Human Development,* now in its sixth edition, but is enriched and expanded by Sherry Kermis. I am most grateful for the energy, insights and perspectives of this younger colleague, who brings a welcome freshness and student-centered stance to the material. Many case studies, examples, tables, figures and study aids are provided from her wealth of classroom tested materials.

Context and Culture. The study of *Children Today* is inextricably embedded in a study of complex and changing cultures. It is impossible to study children developing without taking a close look at those cultural contexts and at the many levels of transactions between child and culture. In this text, we have tried to represent children in many cultural contexts both in the United States and internationally. In the first chapter, we introduce Brofenbrenner's multilevel ecological model to establish a theme of the bidirectional influences of layers of cultural context. Contemporary case study materials and research studies are drawn from majority and minority cultures both here and abroad. Students are encouraged to find themselves within these pages but, alternately, to escape from potentially ethnocentric perspectives into settings that may appear quite foreign.

Chronological Organization. In the field of child development, there is always the question of whether to organize developmental research and theory by topics, such as cognition, genetics and moral development or to present child development as it happens chronologically, emphasizing the holistic interrelated nature of these topics. We have chosen to present child development primarily organized into the classic chronological periods of infancy, early childhood, middle childhood and adolescence. In each age-defined section, there is a balanced presentation of physical, motor, cognitive and social-emotional development. Yet some topics are singled out for special topical emphasis. In the infancy section, there is a full chapter on childbirth and the competence of the newborn. Similarly, in the early childhood section, there is a full chapter on language development, showing the continuity of this crucial area of development from infancy to middle childhood. One central theme in the study of child development is the complex interplay of biological and environmental factors that produce development. Consequently, there is another full chapter on heredity and environment, near the beginning of the text. Here we define the contemporary issues around the processes of development in today's multiple cultural contexts. Up-to-date research helps define the current topics. The topic of developing gender roles is used to illustrate the sequences, processes and interrelationships.

In-text Study Aids. There are a number of features that will help both students and instructors. Each chapter begins with a brief outline and some chapter objectives to help the student focus on what needs to be learned. Throughout each chapter, key concepts or theories are summarized in tables, charts, and mini summaries. A running glossary appears in the margin. At the end of each chapter there is a full summary, some self-test study questions, a list of key terms and some suggested readings. Finally, for each chapter there is an ABC News Video Case that illustrates some issue in the chapter. These cases are summarized in the text or student review.

INSTRUCTOR SUPPLEMENTS

Instructor's Manual
The Instructor's Manual accompanying *Children Today* assembles the relevant teaching material for each chapter and provides lecture outlines, activities, demonstrations, and additional discussion questions to enhance your classroom experience. It also provides a comprehensive "road map" which coordinates by chapter all of the other teaching resources that accompany the text (e.g., transparencies, video segments, New York Times stories, etc.).

ABC News/Prentice Hall Video Libraries
Child Development, 1995
Human Development, 1993
Two video sets Today consisting of feature segments from award-winning programs such as *Nightline, 20/20, PrimeTime Live,* and *The Health Show* accompany *Children Today.* Video Cases at the end of major parts of the book draw upon segments from these series to help instructors link the text material to stories from the world around us.

Test Item File
Prentice Hall offers a comprehensive and extensive Test Item File with more than 2500 questions. A variety of questions are provided, including multiple choice, true-false, short answer, and essay. Questions cover a balance of conceptual, applied, and factual material from the text.

Prentice Hall Test Manager, Version 2.0
Available in 3 1/2" MS DOS and Macintosh formats
Prentice Hall's exclusive computerized testing software allows instructors to easily select, edit, and format their own tests using a personal computer. Features include: full control over printing (with print preview), complete mouse support, on-screen VGA graphics with import capabilities for .TIF and .PCX file formats, and the ability to export files to WordPerfect, Microsoft Word, or ASCII formats. Context-sensitive help is available at all times, and our toll-free technical support line is also available for instructor assistance.

"800-Number" Telephone Test Preparation Service
A toll-free test preparation service is also available for *Children Today.* Instructors may call an 800-number and select up to 200 questions from the Test Item File available with the text. Prentice Hall will format the test and provide an alternate version (if requested) and answer key(s), then mail it back within 48 hours, ready for duplication.

Teaching Transparencies for Human Development
A full set of color transparencies add visual impact to the study of child development. Designed in large format for use in lecture hall settings, many of these high-quality images are not found in the text.

STUDENT SUPPLEMENTS

Study Guide
The comprehensive Study Guide for *Children Today* features a three-part review and self-test format that effectively reinforces learning. Exercises for each chapter progress from basic factual recall to conceptual understanding to application of concepts.

The New York Times Supplement for Human Development
The core subject matter in the text is supplemented by a collection of time-sensitive articles from one of the world's most distinguished newspapers, *The New York Times.* Also included are discussion and critical thinking questions that relate developmental perspectives and topics in the text to issues in the articles.

ACKNOWLEDGMENTS

Children Today incorporates the contributions of many individuals: people of all ages that we have met in classrooms, clinical encounters, and interviews; students and research assistants; colleagues, teachers, and mentors; family members and friends. Their experiences, ideas and insights are reflected in this text. We would like to thank all the reviewers who read earlier drafts of chapters of this text.

We are particularly grateful to Sidney Zimmerman, who prepared a detailed and thoughtful review of every chapter, with extensive comments and suggestions for revisions. Many of his suggestions were followed but all of his efforts are much appreciated.

Special thanks go to the researchers, Jo Hutt, Yumin Meng, and Benjamin Fernandez for their willingness to speedily search out special topics, often with little forewarning. Their cross-cultural perspectives (from England, China and the Philippines), their suggestions and their conscientious search for new material helped make this text reflective of contemporary research trends.

At Prentice Hall, we would like to thank our principle editor, Pete Janzow, who arranged the collaboration, led the general planning, gathered the crew, maintained faith in the end product and talked out many of the rough spots. Particular note should also be made of Grace Janzow, who's sudden arrival (with the help of her mother) gave us all a full realization of what the complex drama of child development is all about. Our production editor, Maureen Richardson, deserves special thanks for her long hours of coordinating, juggling and managing manuscript, art work, photos, and proofs and keeping us all somewhere near the schedule. And finally, a very special thanks is due to our development and copy editor, Marilyn Miller, who made it all work. Her ideas, sense of humor, suggestions, careful editing and, when needed, trouble shooting, made the project a success.

G.J.C.

Part One

HUMAN DEVELOPMENT AN INTEGRATED STUDY

 Child Development: Perspectives, Processes, and Research Methods

"Complex and rich, full of quest and challenge, the process of human development is the product of many strands—the blending of the biological and the cultural, the intertwining of thought and feeling. The process begins with conception and continues through old age."

What, then, is the goal of studying human development?

Amid all the complexities, we seek to discover some consistent common processes and major influences throughout the life span. Beginning with careful observations and descriptions of human growth and behavior, we generate hypotheses, test them, and, in this way, progress to clear explanations and greater understanding.

OF THE LIFE SPAN

2 Theories of Child Development: An Introduction

"Why is it important to understand the theories of human behavior? A broad understanding of various theories creates the detachment that lets us evaluate our own views, actions, and reactions. It is important for us to reexamine the assumptions behind our beliefs to see whether they make sense, whether they fit the evidence, and what follows from them. A familiarity with the major theories, then, allows us to examine, evaluate, and discipline our intuitions and our own 'theories' of human behavior."

A knowledge of the main theories also makes us more eclectic. Learning about different theories allows us to examine behavior from more than one perspective and to see the value of other explanations.

CHAPTER 1

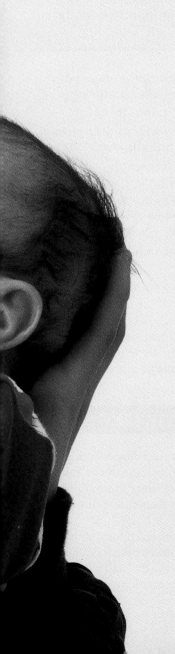

CHILD DEVELOPMENT: PERSPECTIVES, PROCESSES, AND RESEARCH METHODS

OUTLINE

CHAPTER OBJECTIVES

By the time you have finished this chapter, you should be able to do the following:

✔ Discuss the goals of those who study child development.

✔ Explain how historical, socioeconomic, and cultural factors influence our understanding of human development.

✔ Define biological and environmental processes of development, and explain how these two types of developmental processes interact.

✔ Describe the research methodology used in the study of human development.

✔ Describe the major categories of developmental research and explain their similarities and differences.

✔ Discuss the ethical principles that researchers should follow when conducting research with children.

➤ Millions of sperm—fragile and microscopic—swim against great odds to reach the egg cell. Only one unites with it to begin a new human being.

➤ A newborn gasps to fill its lungs and then cries out its own arrival.

➤ Infants form bonds with those who care for them and, as their physical, intellectual, and emotional needs are met, learn to trust the world.

➤ Toddlers touch, taste, pull, push, climb over, under, and through to discover the nature of the world and their powers to affect it.

➤ Preschoolers and kindergartners use the intricacies of words in sequence to command, to inquire, to persuade, to tease, and to attack—all in their efforts to learn more about the world and the people around them.

➤ Schoolchildren, through their new knowledge of rules and order, create and play games of imagination and competition.

➤ Adolescents struggle with choice and decision, with their examination and reassertion of what is important and meaningful in life.

➤ Infants, children, and adolescents discover and rediscover the meaning of relationships. Whether sensitive and fragile, sturdy and supportive, stormy and anxious, or quietly comfortable and comforting, these relationships are a necessary and continuing part of human development.

 AN OBJECTIVE STUDY OF THE LIFE SPAN

Complex and rich, full of quest and challenge, the process of human development is the product of many strands—the blending of the biological and the cultural, the intertwining of thought and feeling, the synthesis of inner motivations and external pressures. The process begins with conception and continues throughout the life of the individual.

In this book, our aim will be to examine developmental trends, principles, and processes across several disciplines as they affect the development of children. We shall investigate the growing child at all ages and stages through adolescence with attention to biology, anthropology, sociology, and psychology.

THE SEARCH FOR AN OBJECTIVE UNDERSTANDING OF DEVELOPMENT

What is the goal of studying child development? Through this study, we seek to discover, amid all the complexities, some consistent common processes and major influences that affect behavior. We begin with careful observations and descriptions of children's growth and behavior. Then we generate hypotheses, test these hypotheses, and, hopefully, progress to clear explanations and greater understanding.

But difficulties in understanding children's behavior are often caused by these very researchers who try to explain and predict it. Whenever we evaluate what people can or cannot do, whenever we try to predict what they should do—in short, any time we judge the behavior of other human beings—we bring to our conclusions an accumulation of values and standards based on our own experiences and environments. It is difficult for us to set aside our subjective judgments and look at others objectively or on their own terms.

In the development of value systems, for example, we find that an American child from one family learns quickly that fighting with her peers is unacceptable behavior and is taught to use words to express anger. A young girl from another family, however, learns to use physical force to demonstrate the same emotions. Whole cultures can, in the same way, encourage either aggressive or cooperative behavior. One culture or socioeconomic group may forbid—or at least strongly disapprove of—the very behavior that another culture or group encourages. Cultural values thus form the basis for the behavior and the judgment of the culture's members. Children gradually learn what is "right" and "normal," and they usually try to behave accordingly.

The same considerations apply to the development of sexual behavior. For instance, much of American culture generally discourages sex play and nudity among young children, frowns on homosexuality at any stage of development, and disapproves strongly of incest and extramarital sex. In contrast, the Marind Anim tribe of New Guinea encourages sexual activity among young children and expects homosexual relations between adolescent boys and older relatives. A bride has intercourse with male members of the husband's family before the husband is permitted access. This culture also encourages tribal women to engage in extramarital sex, as long as they do it with their husband's knowledge and approval (Van Baal, 1966). If we seek to understand human behavior and development without knowing about such cultural variations, we shall be badly misled and our conclusions will be unsound.

Since those who study and work with children are members of various cultures, they carry their own personal values as well as those of their society with them as they design and conduct their research or interventions. Hence, the descriptions of children's behavior by researchers of different periods, cultures, or philosophical views vary.

HISTORICAL, SOCIOECONOMIC, AND CROSS-CULTURAL PERSPECTIVES

The study of child development views both the individual and society as entities that are changed by the passage of time. Societies change over time in response to historical events, like industrialization, and also in response to the population structure, such as the baby boom. Individuals change biologically, personally, and socially over time. In addition to these patterns of change, societies and individuals also interact. For example, children born in different cultures have different experiences.

The cultural and historical experiences individuals are exposed to at various times in their lives affect their attitudes, values and abilities. Perhaps the following two case studies will help illustrate this contention.

> ➤ Al was born in 1915 to immigrant parents. The oldest of three children, he was brought up in a close-knit farm family. Al was too young to experience or understand World War I and too poor to experience the wildness of the "Roaring 20s." The depression of the 1930s hit his family very hard, so he joined the Civilian Conservation Corps during his teens to help out at home. Al enlisted in World War II and returned with awards for bravery. In 1946 he married and he and his wife went on to have four children, one daughter and three sons. The daughter graduated from college; the others were employed as craftsmen. In his beliefs, Al was conservative, religious, and patriotic. He never understood the protests over the Viet Nam conflict. His greatest desires in life were that his children and grandchildren would marry well, be successful financially, and experience happiness.

> ➤ Judy was born in 1948, the youngest of seven children. Her father was a lawyer and her mother, a homemaker. Judy attended private schools and like her father became a lawyer. Asked about her childhood and youth, she remembers fearing the atomic bomb and hiding under the desk during air raid drills in grade school; Judy also recalls the Korean War, the space race, the Civil Rights movement, the assassination of John F. Kennedy, Viet Nam, and Watergate. During the 1960s, she became a student activist— registering voters in the South and protesting the Viet Nam War. While attending law school, she married a fellow activist. Both now have government careers and perform extensive volunteer work. Sometimes Judy wonders if she should have had children before it was too late.

The values and life experiences of Al and Judy have been strongly shaped by the historical events through which they lived. Furthermore, the personal meanings of these historical events are affected by the chronological age and developmental status of the person experiencing them. During the 1960s, for example, the grade-school child perceived student unrest from a very different perspective than the college student (Judy) or the college student's parents (Al). College-age persons not in college also experienced these events differently from their peers who were students.

Historically, attitudes toward childhood have varied widely. In the Middle Ages, European adults largely ignored the period of childhood. They viewed children as infants until age 6 or 7. Older children were considered small adults and treated to adult conversation, jokes, music, food, and other entertainment (Ariès, 1962; Plumb, 1971). Medieval painters did not distinguish between children and their elders except in size. Clothing, hair styles, and activities were the same for all ages.

By 1600, childhood was beginning to be considered a period of innocence, and an effort was made to protect children from the excesses and sins of the adult world. Children were less often seen as anonymous members of the clan or community and more as individuals within an individual family. By the eighteenth century, this attitude received broad support in the upper-middle classes, and children were treated as persons, with a status of their own (Ariès, 1989; Gelis, 1989).

Adolescence as a separate period of childhood is of much more recent origin and to a large degree is limited to developed countries. In the eighteenth, nineteenth, and early twentieth centuries, with unskilled labor in demand, youths capable of working blended into adult society and were accepted as adults. After World War I, advancing technology and rapid social change made it desirable for young people to stay in school longer, thus remaining dependent financially and psychologically on their parents. Clark (1957) has called this extended period of waiting for adult roles "vestibule adolescence." Because adolescents are excluded from active, productive participation in the economy, Clark feels that they stand to lose certain creative abilities that frequently peak at this time.

By the 18th century, children were seen as persons in their own right, with their own interests, as illustrated in John Singleton Copley's painting **Boy with Bow and Arrow.**

CHANGING CHILD-REARING PRACTICES

Methods of disciplining children have also varied throughout history. Harsh physical punishment was the rule in parts of ancient Greece just as it was in nineteenth-century Europe and America, and terrorizing children with stories of ghosts and monsters has long been a popular form of control (DeMause, 1974). In the United States, this century has brought not only a change toward more humane child-rearing practices, often with legal protection for children's rights, but also an increased questioning of all our preconceptions about children and their development. Practices once viewed as dangerous, such as thumb-sucking and masturbation, have generally been accepted as part of a child's normal activity. Rigid schedules for feeding, toilet training, and play have given way to a concern for self-demand, readiness, and self-expression (Wolfenstein, 1955). Parents are encouraged to relax and enjoy their children and to trust the "dialogue" between parent and child.

Attitudes toward children, and the behaviors they give rise to, vary across cultures as well as centuries. For example, Russians traditionally swaddle newborns tightly because they view infants as strong creatures who need to be restrained from injuring themselves. Other cultures, however, regard babies as fragile, vulnerable creatures who need to be protected (Mead, 1972).

ECONOMIC AND CULTURAL CONTEXT OF FAMILIES

Attitudes about family size, structure, and function have also changed over the years. The advice given by "the experts" to parents has altered accordingly (Young, 1990). Until the 1920s, American families were large, usually including members from three or more generations. Grandparents, parents, and children frequently lived under the same roof and shared the same kind of work. Children were expected to stay close to home because their parents needed help in running

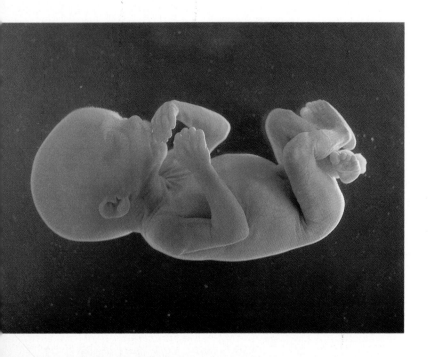

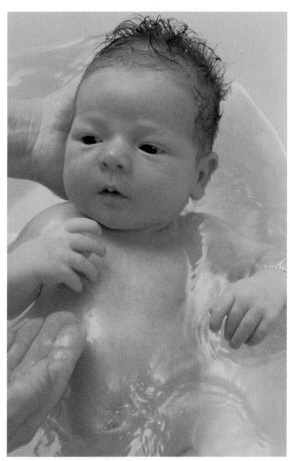

The life span stages depicted in this text are prenatal development, infancy, early childhood, middle childhood, and adolescence.

the farm, store, or household. Parents produced numerous children because birth control was not widely practiced and infectious disease killed off so many children necessary to the economic maintenance of the family.

Since World War II, with the general access to birth control, parents more often have planned the size of their families and shepherded their children through a long period of dependency. Children are now usually in their late teens to mid-20s before they start work and become financially independent. The high cost of raising children to maturity, the general use of contraception, and the growing number of working women have resulted in smaller families. (Whereas 35 percent of American families in the late eighteenth century had seven or more members, today only 3.5 percent do.) Children receive a great deal of individual attention in small families, and parents, in turn, make greater psychological investments in them.

In the past, more children meant, as indicated, a stronger economic base for the family—an additional shelter against poverty. Given our current economic structures and child labor laws, that situation no longer exists. Today, it is the mother who often enters the workforce to provide additional financial support for her family. Since in the typical U.S. family both parents now work, the parenting roles of both mothers and fathers are shifting (Young, 1990). It is important to consider the social circumstances of families in a particular time or place, as well as their contemporary beliefs and values, to begin to understand their child-rearing practices (Jordanova, 1989) and their effect on the child's social, psychological, and biological development.

For example, in families with several children, if the mother has to work outside the home, or there is a low income level, older children often take care of their younger siblings. In these cases, children mainly learn their social roles, values, and competencies from other children. The older children tend to learn nurturant, responsible behavior, while the younger ones tend to develop strong ties to their siblings and a sense of competence among their peers. Family bonds and affiliation usually become stronger (Werner, 1979). In contrast, some children of the wealthy, who are often cared for by non-family staff members, may not develop strong family bonds, as they may have less contact with their parents and siblings (Coles, 1980). The attitudes, values, and expectations of children in these two groups will probably be quite different. In another example, mothers from lower socioeconomic homes have greater numbers of premature babies, that is, babies born before the full-term pregnancy period of 9 months. Premature and low birth weight babies have been found to be at risk for delayed or deficient cognitive development when compared to full-term, normal birth-weight babies.

The typical contemporary American family cycle includes the following realities: husbands and wives spend a longer time together both before the birth of children and after; a shorter segment of their lives is spent in child-rearing, and most commonly parents survive to become grandparents. In some other cultures, couples marry earlier, spend longer at child-rearing, become grandparents at earlier ages, and die earlier because of their shortened life expectancy.

Families develop their own identity, depending on the historical period in which they exist, the cultural norms that shape them, as well as the developmental status of their members. The function of the family changes to meet changing social requirements—as does the family itself.

DEVELOPMENTAL PROCESSES

Central to the concerns of developmental psychologists are the processes by which change takes place. No clear agreement exists on precisely how children acquire a nearly complete grammar of their language by age 5, or how children learn to read or assume a sex role or to express love, grief, or hostility. Nevertheless, some common terms and concepts are used by developmental psychologists—and by sociologists, anthropologists, and educators—to investigate and debate the issues.

Development refers to the changes over time in the structure, thought, or behavior of a person due to both biological and environmental influences. Usually these changes are progressive and cumulative, and they result in increasing organization and function. For example, motor development seemingly progresses from an infant's random waving of arms and legs to purposeful reaching, grasping, creeping, and walking. Developing the ability to use symbols, especially words, is a key step that paves the way for reading, manipulating number concepts, and complex thinking. The development of thinking proceeds from the recognition of concrete objects in infancy to the forming of higher concepts and abstract thought in adolescence.

Some developmental processes, such as prenatal growth, are primarily biological, whereas other types of development depend mainly on the environment. Learning a new language while living in a foreign country or acquiring the speech patterns and accents of one's family, are examples of development strongly influenced by the environment. Most development, however, cannot be so neatly categorized as either biological or environmental, because it involves an interaction of both elements.

The study of child development also seeks to discover and chart the relationship between the chronological age of the individual and the changes observed in that child's response on some dimension of behavior over the course of development to maturity (Wohlwill, 1973). In other words, developmental psychologists may be interested in the approximate timeline on which behaviors emerge in individual's lives. Those who study children's development, therefore, may then compare the timing of the occurrence of similar behaviors in different children, or in children in different cultures or socioeconomic groups.

The establishment of approximate norms for the development of competencies allows us to determine when an individual is advanced or delayed developmentally in relation to peers. This can be useful, for example, in the design of programs to help children who are developmentally delayed.

Development occurs in three areas or domains: the physical, cognitive, and psychosocial. The *physical domain* refers to physical characteristics like size and shape, as well as sensory capacities and motor skills. The *cognitive domain* (from

development The changes over time in structure, thought, or behavior of a person as a result of both biological and environmental influences.

the latin word for "to know") involves all mental abilities, and activities and even the organization of thought. This includes such activities as perception, reasoning, memory, problem solving and language. The *psychosocial domain* refers to personality characteristics and social skills. This includes the child's unique style of behaving, feeling and reacting to social circumstances. For each child, development in these three domains occurs concurrently and interdependently, as in the following example, which is a preview of the children we will be meeting later in this text:

> First, just after birth, Juana visually explores her environment. Her gaze shifts over the stimuli in the room and particular objects capture her attention. As her muscles develop and new motor skills emerge, she will then swipe at, grasp, and place in her mouth the desired object which is near her. Later, she will crawl or toddle toward such objects. It is at this point that environmental feedback begins to teach her that objects exist even if they are out of sight or reach. By 18 months, she starts to search for toys, rattles, and persons—often designing complex strategies to do so. Individuals in her environment now interact differently with her. Parents begin to correct the choice of forbidden objects and substitute safe ones. They encourage or discourage her exploration. Finally, Juana begins to take risks confidently or retreats into safe dependency—because of her temperament but also because of the feedback she receives from the people who care for her.

The various domains of the child's existence interact with each other in complex and unique ways. Development, therefore, is not piecemeal or haphazard; it is rather holistic. Each aspect of development in normal, healthy children involves mutual and interactive changes in all three domains. Table 1–1 summarizes the three domains.

TABLE 1–1 An Overview of the Developmental Domains Organizing Growth and Behavioral Change

The physical domain	Involves the basic growth and changes that occur in the individual's body. Changes include those external changes, such as in height and weight, as well as internal changes in muscles, glands, the brain, and sense organs. Physical health, and motor skills (for example, walking, crawling, and learning to write) are included in this domain.
The cognitive domain	Involves the mental processes related to thinking and problem-solving. Changes include those in perception, memory, reasoning, creativity, and language.
The psychosocial domain	Involves the development of personality and interpersonal skills. These two areas are interrelated and include self-concept and emotions, as well as social skills and behaviors.

BIOLOGICAL PROCESSES OF DEVELOPMENT

All living organisms develop according to a genetic code or plan. In some, like moths and butterflies, the plan is precise and allows for little physical or behavioral alteration. When psychologists refer to the process of growing according to a genetic plan, they use the term **maturation.** The maturation process consists of a series of preprogrammed changes not only in the organism's form, but also in its complexity, integration, organization, and function. Faulty nutrition or illness may delay maturation, but proper nutrition, good health, or even encouragement and teaching will not necessarily speed it dramatically. This seems to be true for the human life span and for such processes as an infant's motor development and an adolescent's development of secondary sex characteristics.

Physical structures and motor capabilities mature at different rates. Any single structure or capability generally has its point of optimal maturity. **Growth** usually refers to the increase in size, function, or complexity to that point of maturity. **Aging** refers to the kind of biological changes that occur beyond the point of optimal maturity. The aging process does not necessarily imply decline or deterioration. Just as aging often improves the qualities of some cheeses and wines, it may also improve human judgment and insight. Furthermore, some tissues start "aging" in adolescence or even childhood.

ENVIRONMENTAL INFLUENCES ON DEVELOPMENT

Our environment influences us every minute of the day. Light, sound, heat, food, drugs, anger, gentleness, severity—these and millions of other influences may fulfill basic biological and psychological needs, cause severe harm, attract our attention, or provide the components for learning. Some environmental influences are temporary and limited to just one situation, for example, a case of chicken pox at age 4. Others may be permanent, such as the sustained interaction with parents, or appear often, as in the case of a troublesome or respected grandparent who periodically enters the child's life. Environmental influences can stunt an organism's growth or promote it, can create long-lasting anxieties, or help to form complex skills.

LEARNING The basic process by which the environment causes lasting changes in behavior is called **learning.** Learning results from experience or practice. It occurs over an enormous range of activities—avoiding hot toasters, factoring algebra equations, running interference in football, falling in love, or losing one's temper. We learn skills and obtain knowledge while forming attitudes, feelings, prejudices, values, and patterns of thought.

Psychologists disagree on the fine points of learning theories, but most agree that *conditioning* is one of the basic learning process. Conditioning involves making associations between various events that occur in an individual's environment. A child, for example, may learn to be afraid of spiders by observing a peer's avoidance response when encountering the leggy arachnids. Some important learning theories—including those that focus on the two major forms of conditioning—are presented in Chapter 2. Throughout the book we shall discuss other aspects of learning, such as modeling and imitation, verbal mediation, and hypothesis testing. We shall also consider the role of insight, discovery, and understanding in children's development.

maturation The physical development of an organism as it fulfills its genetic potential.

growth The increase in size, function, or complexity toward the point of optimal maturity.

aging Biological changes that occur beyond the point of optimal maturity.

learning The basic developmental process of change in the individual as a result of experience or practice.

Through the process of socialization, children everywhere learn the attitudes, beliefs, customs, values, and expectations of their society.

SOCIALIZATION *Socialization* is the general process by which the individual becomes a member of a social group—a family, a community, a tribe, or the like. This includes learning all the attitudes, beliefs, customs, values, roles, and expectations of the social group. It is a lifelong process that helps individuals live comfortably and participate fully in their culture, or cultural group within the larger society (Goslin, 1969).

During childhood, we are socialized into some roles immediately and into others later. A young girl might perform a multitude of roles every day: pupil, neighbor, big sister, daughter, Catholic, team member, best friend, and so forth. When she reaches her teens, she will acquire several more roles. Each new role will require her to adjust to the behavior, attitudes, expectations, and values of the surrounding social groups. Sometimes this process creates stress in an individual who does not find a neat meshing between personal and social values, for example, if this young girl were to become involved with a group of peers during adolescence whose behavior runs counter to what she considers appropriate or correct.

Socialization is generally recognized as a two-way process. In the past, researchers saw children's behavior as almost entirely the result of how parents and teachers behaved. For example, children were believed to passively identify with and then imitate certain influential adults in their life. More recently, a great many studies have focused on how parents and children mutually influence each other's behavior (Hetherington & Baltes, 1988). Infants are socialized by their experience within the family, but their very presence, in turn, forces family members to learn new roles. Perhaps the following example will help to illustrate this point.

Paul and June were a professional couple who had been married for sixteen years before the birth of their first child when they were in their forties. They were happy about the arrival of their daughter but found that having a baby led to many changes in their lifestyle. For example, they could no longer spontaneously decide to go out to dinner and a movie after work. They had to first find a baby-sitter, pick her up, be home by a set time, and then return to the sitter's house before stumbling into bed. To make matters worse, they could no longer sleep in! The days of a carefree "dinc" (double-income-no-children) lifestyle were over. Nevertheless, after several months of adjustment, they could no longer imagine a life without their daughter.

The birth of a baby socializes every other family member into new roles.

The arrival of a child has helped change Paul and June into "parents" with new roles and behaviors that reflect new responsibility and some ability to defer their wants. In this way, current views of socialization stresses the two-directional or shared experience of socialization.

In summary, the socialization process occurs in all stages of life, not just during childhood and adolescence. Adults seek to learn new roles to prepare for expected life changes. A middle-aged man wanting to switch jobs may take a course to expand his vocational skills. A recently divorced woman may have to change her attitudes about not wanting to work and seek training to support herself. However, during childhood, the processes of socialization produce behaviors that persist in later life. Socialization helps to create a core of values, attitudes, skills, and expectations that will shape the adult the child will become.

INTERACTION OF DEVELOPMENTAL PROCESSES   Some psychologists continue to debate how much of our behavior is due to maturation and how much to learning. An infant first sits up, then stands, and finally walks—primarily because of maturational processes. But even this behavior can be obstructed by drugs, poor diet, fatigue, disease, restriction, or emotional stress. Some skills, such as musical or athletic abilities, can be enhanced by extensive practice. Certain other behaviors are more difficult to categorize. In contrast to dogs, for example, children are born with the capacity for speech, but they must *learn* a language. Infants spontaneously show emotions such as anger or distress, but they must *learn* how to handle such feelings (Hebb, 1966).

Behavior, then, is a product of the interaction of maturation and learning. Certain behavioral limitations or characteristics are inherited in the genetic code, however, all behavior develops within a specific environment. Robert Plomin (1990) points out, for example, that an inherited susceptibility to a disease, such as asthma or diabetes, can be triggered by environmental factors. The disease may also affect socialization or intellectual development if it prevents participation in social or athletic events and interferes with school attendance. The same type of interaction can be seen in the relationship between inherited physical characteristics (such as body type, skin color, or height) and a person's self-concept and social acceptance. Behavior may be based on stereotyped expectancies (fat people are jolly, adolescents are awkward) held by the individual as well as by others.

TIMING   The interaction of learning and maturation may depend on exactly when an environmental effect occurs. An example of the crucial nature of such timing is called a **critical period,** a time span when—and only when—a particular environmental factor can have an effect. Several such periods occur during prenatal development, when certain chemicals, drugs, or disease can adversely affect the development of specific body organs. (See Chapter 4.) An example may be seen in exposure to the rubella (or German Measles) virus. If a pregnant woman who

critical period The only point in time when a particular environmental factor can have an effect.

*Before a child can learn to read, he or she must be **ready** to read.*

lacks immunities for rubella is exposed to the virus two months after conception, severe birth defects such as deafness, or even spontaneous abortion (miscarriage) may result. If, however, that same woman were to be exposed six months after conception, absolutely no effects would occur.

Other periods exist during which the individual is more or less sensitive to environmental influences. An *optimal period* is similar to a critical period. It is the particular time span when a specific behavior develops most successfully as a result of the interaction of maturation and learning. But an optimal period does not have the all-or-nothing quality of a critical period. Although there is an optimal time for a behavior to develop, the behavior can be learned at an earlier or later date. **Readiness** refers to a point when individuals have matured sufficiently to learn a specific behavior. They may be unable to learn the behavior fully and efficiently before this maturational point, but it is not crucial that they learn it at the moment of readiness. For example, some children may be optimally ready to learn subtraction at about 7 years of age. If, for some reason, they are not taught to subtract until age 8 or 10, however, the opportunity will not have been lost forever, as would be true of a process for which a critical period exists. The precise nature of timing in human development is still unknown. Are there critical periods for learning certain behaviors? Are there optimal periods for learning to read, to be a gymnast, or to speak a foreign language? These are some of the questions we shall examine in our study of development.

AN ECOLOGICAL MODEL

Today, perhaps the most influential theory of human development is that of the American psychologist, Urie Bronfenbrenner. According to his **ecological systems theory** (1979, 1989), child development is a dynamic and two-directional, that is, mutually reciprocal process. In this model, the growing child actively restructures the multiple levels of environments, or settings, he lives in or encounters, while being simultaneously influenced by these environments, the

readiness A point in time when an individual has matured enough to benefit from a particular learning experience.

ecological systems theory A theory of child development, in which the growing child actively restructures aspects of the four environmental levels he or she lives in, while being simultaneously influenced by them and their interrelations.

interrelations among them, and external influences from the larger environment. Bronfenbrenner pictures the ecological environment as a nested arrangement of four concentric systems (see Figure 1–1).

THE MICROSYSTEM The first level, or *microsystem,* refers to the activities, roles, and interactions of the child and his immediate single setting such as the home, day-care center, or school. For example, in the home, the child's development may be encouraged by the mother's sensitivity to his moves toward independence. In turn, his moves toward independence may encourage the mother to think of new ways to promote this kind of behavior. The microsystem is the environmental level most frequently studied by psychologists.

FIGURE 1–1
The four levels of the environment comprising the ecological systems model of child development.

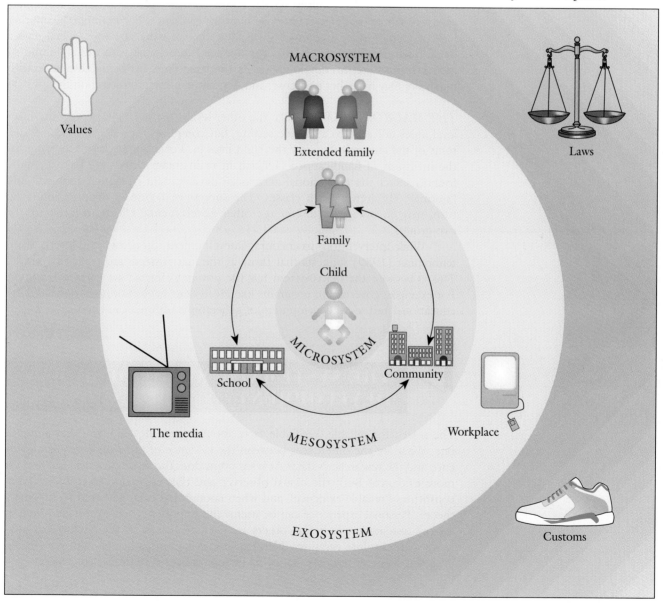

THE MESOSYSTEM   A key feature of the model is that the various microsystems are not isolated from each other. The *mesosystem,* or second level, comprises the interrelations among two or more microsystems. Thus, the child's development is affected by the formal and informal connections between home and school, or among home, school, and his neighborhood peer group. For example, a child's progress at day care may be affected positively by his parents' close communication with the teachers there. Similarly, the attentiveness of his day-care teachers is likely to benefit the child's interactions at home.

THE EXOSYSTEM   The *exosystem,* or third level, refers to the social settings or organizations beyond the child's immediate experience that nevertheless affect him. Examples range from formal settings, such as his parent's workplace and the community health and welfare system, to less formal organizations, like the child's extended family or his parents' social network of friends. For example, his mother may be employed by a company that allows her to work at home several days a week. Such flexibility may enable her to spend more time with her child and so indirectly promotes his development. At the same time, her being able to be with him more may make her less tense, and, therefore, more productive on the job.

THE MACROSYSTEM   Unlike the other levels, the *macrosystem,* or outermost level, does not refer to a specific setting, but comprises the values, laws, and customs of the culture or society the child lives in. For example, laws providing for the inclusion of handicapped children in mainstream classes are likely to profoundly affect the educational and social development of both "disabled" and "normal" children in such classes. The success or failure of mainstreaming, in turn, may encourage or discourage other governmental efforts to integrate the two groups.

While interventions to encourage development can occur at all levels, Bronfenbrenner (1989) suggests that those at the macrosystem are especially critical. This is because the macrosystem has the power to impact on every other level. For example, government programs like Head Start have enormously affected the educational and social development of generations of American children.

THE SYSTEMATIC STUDY OF HUMAN DEVELOPMENT

The search for reliable, verifiable facts about human development is a complex one. What are the differences between the evidence of our own personal experience and the researcher's data? At what point does the researcher stop looking for more evidence? Both the casual observer and the researcher must decide what constitutes "reliable evidence" and when enough has been gathered to support a theory. Personal experience can be useful and important, but it must be tested in a more systematic way before others are likely to believe it. We rarely prove anything with absolute certainty. Nevertheless, if we can gather enough convincing evidence, it is very possible that other people will come to similar conclusions.

ASKING GOOD QUESTIONS

Most breakthroughs in the natural and social sciences have been stimulated by thoughtful questions and astute observation. Someone noticed something intriguing and different, asked probing questions, continued to observe it, and then systematically tested the phenomenon before arriving at some basis for generalization and prediction. Suppose, for example, that we look at the pictures of a house and some human beings as drawn by a 5 1/2-year-old (see Figure 1–2). On closer observation, we notice that the house sits directly on the ground but the chimney leans at a strange angle. Looking at the small figures at the bottom, we notice that the bodies and the heads are combined and that their limbs are out of proportion. (These kinds of human figures are often called "tadpole people.") Are these just common "errors" caused by a child's poor motor coordination? Are they the idiosyncrasies of one particular child?

Jean Piaget, an astute observer of children who developed a comprehensive theory of cognitive development, suggested that children's drawings are not just awkward reproductions of what they see; instead, they are representations of the way children think and construct "reality." After collecting drawings from many children, he proposed that pictures reveal the unique quality of children's under-

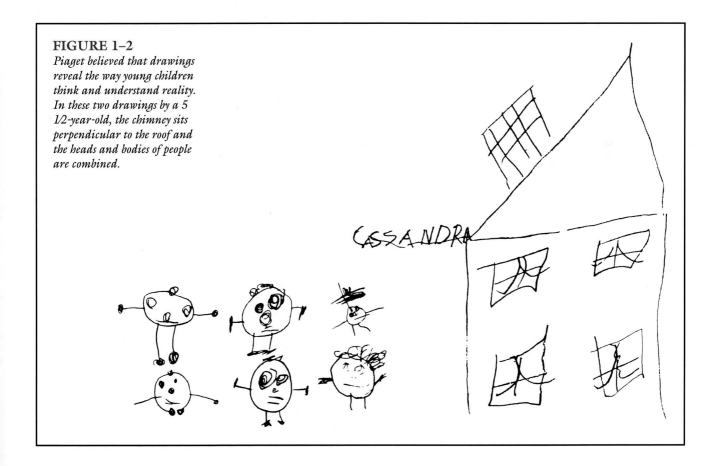

FIGURE 1–2
Piaget believed that drawings reveal the way young children think and understand reality. In these two drawings by a 5 1/2-year-old, the chimney sits perpendicular to the roof and the heads and bodies of people are combined.

standing as well as their lack of understanding about relationships between objects and the world. When compared to adults, young children appear to have cognitive limitations. In fact, these are not deficiencies but differences in the cognitive structures adults and children use. Unlike adults, children may see things only from their own point of view (egocentrism), or they may focus on only one relationship at a time (centration). In the child's experience, things "on" something else are usually related in a particular way. Therefore, their houses sit flat on the ground and their chimneys rise perpendicular to the angle of the roof.

What about the "tadpole people"? Do children really think that people's faces are on their abdomens? "No," say Piaget and some others. This is a representation of the *important* things about people (Freeman, 1980). The child's drawing is not like a photograph; rather, it is the child's symbolic representation of her thinking and understanding of the world. Not all researchers agree with Piaget's interpretation of children's drawings. But Piaget was able to demonstrate certain common features often found in the drawings of children at different age levels, and he was able to stimulate others to do systematic research on children's thinking as expressed in their art (Winner, 1986).

THE SCIENTIFIC METHOD

Research activities serve diverse and important purposes in our daily lives, principally to help us assess the truth of our beliefs regarding others, the nature of the world, and ourselves. Developmental research, in particular, is a means of amassing a body of knowledge regarding child growth and development. It is the main vehicle for determining whether social and educational interventions really work. In short, research and its appropriate methodologies are the sole source of an efficient, verifiable, and accurate study of human development (Kermis, 1984).

Research in child development follows the same scientific method used in any other branch of the social and behavioral sciences. Researchers may differ on what to observe and how best to measure it, but most research essentially consists of four steps:

1. *Define the problem* Determine specifically what you, the researcher, are interested in studying;
2. *Formulate hypotheses as to the suspected causes of the problem* Predict what you think is producing the behavior in which you are interested;
3. *Investigate the hypothesis* (a) Collect the data, and (b) analyze the data, using appropriate statistical measures, and
4. *Draw Conclusions* Demonstrate the causal relations suggested in the hypotheses you formulated initially.

A brief discussion of these steps may help us to understand the way research is designed.

Defining the research problem. The study of child development is full of interesting questions. What does the newborn infant see? How soon does the infant see the garden in the way we see it? Is adolescence necessarily a period of storm and stress, or can it be a smooth transition to adulthood?

What are the differences in moral development demonstrated by middle-school boys and girls? How do these differences manifest themselves in adolescent social behavior? Interesting as they may be, such broad questions are not effective research questions. Before we can conduct a study, we need to narrow the problem to something testable. "How do children learn language?" is too broad. "How does the child begin to understand metaphor, sarcasm, or other forms of nonliteral language?" is a smaller question, but it is not yet testable.

In a recent series of studies, the researchers were interested in how children learn to understand sarcasm. Sarcasm is, after all, a very complicated language form. When the airline loses your luggage and your best friend says, "Well, this must be your lucky day!" he is being sarcastic. The speaker does not literally intend what he says. There is subtlety, irony, and nuance to the meaning of the literal words. There may be humor or cruelty in sarcasm. Adults detect sarcasm using two cues: (1) the context contradicts what the speaker has said, and (2) the speaker often uses tone of voice to signal the meaning. But young children tend to miss these cues; they understand things literally. Researchers can ask, "Which of these cues does the child first understand, and at what age, and in what context?" The researchers have now formulated a testable question (Capelli, Nakagawa, & Madden, 1990).

Develop a hypothesis In most studies, researchers specify their expectations in the form of a hypothesis. They make a prediction about what will happen in the study. In the study on children's understanding of sarcasm, the researchers predicted that children would be able to use intonation or tone of voice much sooner than they would understand the contextual cues. Even very young children listen to vocal expressions as a clue to emotions. But for them to understand the contrast between the context and the literal meaning of the speaker is a much more difficult task.

Test the hypothesis To test whether the hypothesis is correct, researchers choose a specific procedure, decide on a setting, determine a measurement, and select certain aspects of the situation to be controlled. Researchers must be careful to design the observations so that they are measuring the behavior systematically and without bias. In our study on understanding sarcasm, the researchers invented several stories. Each story had two versions: a sarcastic one and a serious one. They tape-recorded these stories in two fashions: Sometimes the punch line was said in a mocking, sarcastic way, sometimes it was said in a neutral tone of voice. Then they played these stories, some serious and some sarcastic, to third graders, sixth graders, and adults, and compared their reactions on a systematic questionnaire (Capelli, Nakagawa, & Madden, 1990).

Draw conclusions Based on the evidence collected, researchers must draw conclusions that neither overstate nor understate what they have found. In our study of sarcasm, the adults clearly identified all sarcastic responses whenever there were context cues (lost luggage), or intonation cues (a mocking tone of voice), or both types of cues available. Sixth graders had considerable difficulty when there was no change in intonation, and third graders almost never understood the sarcasm unless there was a sarcastic tone of voice. The authors concluded that children initially depend much more heavily on intonation than on context to recognize sarcasm (Capelli, Nakagawa, & Madden, 1990).

METHODS OF DATA COLLECTION

Research studies produce widely differing findings, depending on the measurements used and the individuals selected for study. Subjects may be observed in real-life situations, or they may be tested in controlled, contrived situations. They may take written tests to determine their level of achievement, their ability to solve problems, or their creativity. The researchers may observe their behavior directly or ask the participants to report on it. It may be helpful if we examine some of the specific types of measurement.

DIRECT OBSERVATION   Perhaps the most common type of measurement used with infants and young children is to observe the child's behavior directly in a specific situation. The researcher may look at how the child plays with a particular kind of toy or how the child reacts to a stranger. Children may be observed in school settings to see how they work together to solve a problem. Researchers often use recording aids like videotapes to increase the accuracy of the observation. As one begins to study older children, adolescents, and adults, it becomes increasingly difficult to design studies of direct behavior. Teenagers and adults are less willing to be "on stage" for observation and more willing to report their thoughts and feelings to researchers.

CLINICAL, OR CASE STUDY, RESEARCH   Clinical research focuses on case studies of individuals evidencing abnormal behavior or some pattern of behavior in which the researcher is interested. The clinical study method is basically an in-depth interview and/or observation of an individual. An open-ended, exploratory approach to assessing behavior, it has been used extensively in conducting developmental research. One example of such research may be found in the creation of the so-called "baby diaries." Baby diaries represent a poorly controlled and often somewhat haphazard technique. The main method used in their creation is that the observer records characteristics of the developing organism. For example, a summary of one early diary compiled by Moore (1896) follows:

> 5th week: He recognized the human face.
>
> 7th week: He recognized the sounds of the voice.
>
> 9th week: He recognized the breast when he saw it; and the face of his mother
>
> 12th week: He recognized his own hand.
>
> 16th week: He recognized his thumb and the nipple
>
> 17th week: He recognized the ball at a distance of some feet

In the nineteenth century, Charles Darwin, the noted naturalist, kept a detailed account of his eldest son's activities in infancy and early childhood, in search of some understanding of human nature. Part of his account was used recently by John Bowlby (1990), an eminent psychologist, to prepare a detailed retrospective case study of Charles Darwin. Bowlby's intent was to analyze the impact of parental loss in childhood. Case studies are rarely used in research because they involve problems of subjectivity and uncontrolled variables, and they relate to one specific individual. Cause-and-effect relationships cannot be established, nor can generalizations be made to others. But, occasionally, a good case study can stimulate additional research.

In practical settings, such as medicine, education, social work, and clinical psychology, case studies are an important tool for diagnosis and prescription. Short-term case studies, such as the detailed analysis of a child's reactions to war or trauma, can be helpful in creating further understanding. Therefore, although they must be used with caution as a research tool, case studies provide a rich, clinical, descriptive picture of the changing, integrated individual in an environmental context.

ACHIEVEMENT AND ABILITY TESTS Written tests of achievement or ability are a common form of measurement. Yet it is not always easy to construct a good test. To be effective, a good test (or any measurement) must be **reliable** and **valid.** A reliable measure is dependable, consistent, and repeatable. For example, a test of artistic ability must be able to evaluate people in the same way each time or it is useless for research purposes. An unreliable test of artistic ability might be easily influenced by the mood of the participant taking the test or that of the judge assigned to look at the product. Tests also must have validity—that is, they should measure what they intend to measure. In the Peabody Picture Vocabulary Test, for example, the child is shown a booklet containing pictures. For each item, the child hears a word and is asked to point to one of four pictures on a page. This is simply a test of comprehension of English vocabulary, presented orally. Yet researchers sometimes mistakenly employ it as a measure of "intelligence." To do so would be an invalid use of this measure.

SELF-REPORT TECHNIQUES Self-report techniques consist of interviews, surveys, or questionnaires in which the researcher asks questions designed to reveal the subjects' feelings and behavior patterns. Sometimes, subjects are asked for information about themselves—as they are in the present or were in the past. At other times, they may be asked to reflect on, or react to, statements or thoughts about themselves or to rate themselves on some personality traits. In each case, they are expected to try to be as honest and objective as possible. Sometimes such instruments have "lie scales" built in, which repeat questions in slightly different formats designed to "catch" the respondent. Lie scales detect false responses by persons who may not believe the response originally given would be acceptable to the tester.

Although interviews and questionnaires are commonly employed with adolescents and adults, these techniques need considerable adaptation when used with children. In one such study, the researchers wanted to know about children's understanding of themselves and their family. They used a self-report technique called *interactive dialogues.* One of these dialogues was called, "What I'm like and what others in my family are like." The interviewer brought a series of cards with pictures to the interview. Along with answering the questions, the children sorted the cards, indicating which pictures were more like their family and which were less like their family (Reid et al., 1990).

PROJECTIVE TECHNIQUES Sometimes, the researcher does not ask the question directly. In a projective technique, subjects are given an ambiguous pic-

reliability The extent to which a measuring technique will produce the same results each time it is used.
validity The accuracy with which a procedure measures what it is supposed to measure.

ture, or task, or situation. Then they must tell a story, interpret a picture, or guess the outcome of the situation. Because the task is ambiguous and there are no right or wrong answers, it is assumed that individuals will project their own feelings, attitudes, anxieties, and needs into the situation. Rorschach inkblots are probably the most famous projective technique. Another example may be seen in the TAT (Thematic Apperception Test), in which individuals are asked to create a story about a particular ambiguous picture. The tester then examines the themes created by respondents across a series of such pictures.

Word-association exercises and sentence-completion tests are also used. Subjects might be asked to complete a thought, such as "My father always...." Subjects might be shown a series of pictures and asked to interpret, react to, analyze, or arrange them to construct a story. In one study, 4-year-olds participated in a game called *the bears' picnic*. The experimenter told a series of stories involving a family of teddy bears. The child was then handed one of the bears as "your bear" and invited to complete the story (Mueller & Tingley, 1990).

SELECTION OF AN EXPERIMENTAL DESIGN

The design of any social science study structures and defines the type of information that can be collected as well as the manner in which it is analyzed. The growing, changing human organism develops within a changing environmental context. Researchers never capture the whole story. Instead, they must select a particular setting, particular participants, and particular methods of measurement and analysis to highlight the research question posed. This research plan constitutes the **experimental design.**

NATURAL VERSUS EXPERIMENTAL SETTINGS   Research settings may range from highly controlled, standardized laboratories to homes, supermarkets, schools, playgrounds, or hospitals. Some landmark developmental studies have been conducted in natural locations like waiting rooms, athletic events, preschools, and nursing homes. Studies in naturalistic settings have a certain *ecological validity.* They seem true to life. They involve real events and everyday settings. They may seem to be less artificial or contrived. The ongoing interactions between friends or family members can be examined as they really happen. Nevertheless, natural locations permit little control of individuals, events, or conditions, and they may cause some imprecision in measurement. It may be helpful if we look further at the strengths and weaknesses of each approach.

EXPERIMENTAL SETTINGS   In a laboratory setting, the researcher can systematically change some of the conditions (**independent variables**) and observe the resultant behavior (**dependent variables**). For example, children learning vocabulary in the laboratory can do it in a very systematic way. The amount of noise and distraction is limited. The difficulty of the word list is controlled. The expectations and instructions of the experimenter, the reward or punishment, the pace of the presentation, can all be carefully monitored or controlled. Similarly, the behavior being observed can be measured precisely—be it the rate of learning, or forgetting, symptoms of anxiety, or anger. The laboratory is the ideal setting for testing a hypothesis and concluding a cause-and-effect relationship between

experimental design The setting, subjects, and methods of measurement of a behavioral research study that serve to structure the type of information collected.

independent variable The variable that experimenters manipulate in order to observe its effects on the dependent variable.

dependent variable The variable in an experiment that changes as a result of manipulating the independent variable.

Research conducted in natural settings has been criticized for permitting little control of individuals, events, and conditions, resulting sometimes in imprecise measurements of behavior.

the variables. Many studies of learning and memory have been conducted in just such settings, with infants, children, and adolescents.

NATURALISTIC SETTINGS   Studies conducted in natural settings are much less easily controlled. The independent variables are usually controlled solely by selection, not manipulation. The researchers select a particular classroom in a particular school, or compares teachers in Japan, Taiwan, and the United States (Stevenson et al., 1989). Of course, teachers can be trained to use a specific approach, or instructional videotapes can be prepared, but rarely do the events in the classroom follow the script precisely. For some studies in a natural setting, the researchers must wait for the event to occur. In a study in class discipline, for example, they may need to wait until the child misbehaves and then be there with the camera at the right time. Sometimes, in naturalistic studies, the researchers must rely on their notes or films, hoping that they have selected the right details from an ongoing stream of potentially significant events. In some cases, this method has resulted in imprecise observations and unsound conclusions.

Just as some naturalistic studies may be considered uncontrollable and imprecise, some experimental studies may be considered artificial and narrow. This may be due to the unfamiliar setting and isolated circumstances of the laboratory or to the absence of a realistic context in which the behavior makes sense. Bronfenbrenner (1979), has characterized American developmental psychology as "the science of the strange behavior of the child in a strange situation with a strange adult for the shortest period of time (p. 19)." Because of his and other criticisms, researchers are increasingly attempting to combine the precision of the laboratory with the ecological validity of the naturalistic setting. In the research sense, **ecological validity** refers to an understanding of the multiple environmental variables which affect behavior. Ecological researchers therefore create or

FOCUS ON AN ISSUE

A NATURALISTIC STUDY OF CHILDREN'S SOCIAL BEHAVIOR

David E. Day, director of Early Childhood Education at the University of Massachusetts, has used a naturalistic study of children's social behavior to evaluate the effects of the integration of special-needs children and "normal" children in preschool classes. The naturalistic approach is used so that the experiment will not interfere with what the children are doing. Throughout the observation period, the teacher, the teacher's aides, and the children interact the way they normally would in the different activities and areas of the classroom—the block room, the art area, at story time, and so forth.

The evaluation procedure used in the study is a simple one. It begins

> *"The naturalistic approach is used so that the experiment will not interfere with what the children are doing. Throughout the observation period, the teacher, the teacher's aides, and the children interact the way they normally would in the different activities and areas of the classroom. ..."*

with the completion of a profile on each child in the classroom. The profile includes such information as a history of the child's socializing experience, including the number of siblings, birth order, and prior preschool experiences; the child's medical history; the child's family structure, including the parents' reasons for enrolling the child in the program; the child's special needs, based on physical and/or intellectual disability, recorded or threatened abuse, and emotional stress. Various developmental indices, such as the results of developmental tests and psychologists' assessments, are also included.

Once the profiles are completed, the central activity of the study—the observation of the children—starts. Each child is observed several times during a 5- to 10-day observation period. Each observation lasts for

change particular conditions within an ongoing real-life setting. For example, in a middle-school setting, researchers might want to study the effect of using cooperative learning teams to teach science to fourth graders. They would study the performance of the children both before instituting teams and afterward in the classroom where science is taught. In this manner, the teacher's style, the motivation of students, and the physical layout of the classroom, could all be controlled (see the box "A Naturalistic Study of Children's Social Behavior").

LONGITUDINAL AND CROSS-SECTIONAL DESIGNS   As we mentioned earlier, development is a continuous, dynamic, and lifelong process. Therefore, developmental studies, in contrast to other types of research, focus on change over time. Any field of study concerned with *time-associated or age-associated change* is considered a developmental discipline. *Developmental psychology, therefore, focuses on the description, explanation, prediction, and modification of age-associated behavior change.*

But it is not always an easy task to explain or predict behavior change. Why? Mainly because of the nature of "cause" and our differing definitions of age—age as determined by biology, society, history, and so forth. Consider the following example:

just 30 seconds, after which the behavior is coded on a Behavior Checklist Data Sheet. The data sheet is divided into several behavior categories: *Task Involvement, Cooperation, Autonomy, Verbal Interaction, Use of Materials, Maintenance of Activity,* and *Consideration.* The same data sheet is used to study several different kinds of questions, such as: Do "normal" children pay attention to their task, or are they distracted by special-needs children? Are the children task-involved? Do they finish the task? Do they show consideration for other children, both special-needs and "normal"? What is their verbal interaction like? Do "normal" children talk only with "normal" children? Do physically disabled children talk only with physically disabled children? Which disabilities interfere most with normal interactions?

The behaviors coded onto the data sheet by the evaluators are derived from several observations made over the entire program day to ensure that the behavioral profile is a valid reflection of what has happened. The observation data are then summarized on a matrix, which provides a vivid picture of the frequency and location of each behavior. Information regarding the activity or area, number of children present, and the role of the staff in the activity is also recorded during each 30-second observation. This information reveals the range and type of interaction among the children and the adult role in each activity or area.

An analysis of the data from some of the preliminary studies using this procedure has produced a number of interesting findings. Some children with severe physical disabilities had fairly normal communication patterns with other children, but children with minor speech problems often had considerable difficulty in communicating. "Normal" children who had severely disabled classmates frequently showed increased consideration for others, with no reductions in verbal interaction and learning (Day et al., 1979). Much more remains to be discovered. Yet, based on these positive results, integrated preschools with special needs and "typical" children in the same class are becoming more common. Special-needs children benefit from the example and help of their more "typical" peers. "Typical" children benefit from improved social skills and positive attitudes, with no loss of language and learning achievements (Turnbull & Turnbull, 1990).

Jim is 20 years old. He was born and grew up in Ohio. In high school he barely passed his courses but did well in two sports, wrestling and football. He was accepted into a four-year college in Pennsylvania as a special admit student in need of remedial courses and as a starter on the football team. Jim's college has a policy of "academic redshirting" athletes who are at risk for academic difficulty. So he was forced to sit out his freshman year and obtain a C average in his courses in order to play football as a sophomore. Jim attained a B– overall grade-point-average and started to play football on the Division III team. He has maintained a B average overall and is beginning to talk about going to graduate school for athletic training.

There are many questions we can ask about Jim. For example, what will he be like at 30, 40, or 80 years of age? What factors have influenced his academic or social development? Why has he suddenly improved his academic performance? How did the factors that influenced his behavior change as he grew older?

We can see from these questions and concerns that the design of research to answer developmental questions is often challenging at best. But even the most challenging question begins to find its answer in the basic research designs used by developmental researchers: the longitudinal, cross-sectional, and sequential designs. Table 1–2 contrasts these designs.

Longitudinal Designs. In a **longitudinal design,** scientists study the same individuals at different points in their lives. They are measured repeatedly over an extended period of time and compared with themselves. Researchers can plot growth curves, or learning curves, in such areas as language development or cognitive development or physical skills. Children can be followed through adulthood to see which personality characteristics persist and which disappear. Researchers can follow the impact of key life events on the later life course or trajectory (see the box "Personality over the Life Course"). In contrast, a cross-sectional study compares different groups of individuals at different ages at one point in time. In the study of sarcasm presented earlier, for example, the researchers studied third graders, sixth graders, and adults on their understanding of the story dialogues. Both research designs have advantages and disadvantages, and both are necessary to the study of child development.

Longitudinal designs are especially appealing to the developmental psychologist. Because individuals are compared with themselves at different points in time, test subjects do not have to be sorted out and carefully matched. Some developmental processes can be looked at very closely by studying these individuals every week, or even every day. In the study of language development in the second or third year of life, for example, a small group of children can be studied every week for a detailed picture of their emerging language. But longitudinal studies also have several drawbacks. They require a great deal of time from both

TABLE 1–2 Common Developmental Research Designs

Longitudinal designs	Groups of subjects studied repeatedly over time; multiple times of testing occur at different ages. *Assets:* Shows relationships between early and late behaviors. *Liabilities:* Possibility of age changes being interpreted incorrectly because of selective dropout, familiarity with testing materials, and cohort effects.
Cross-sectional designs	Groups of subjects of different ages tested at the same time. *Assets:* Conducted quicker and more efficiently than the longitudinal design. *Liabilities:* Age differences studied rather than age change because of single test time; does not permit study of growth trends; cohort effects may influence age differences.
Sequential designs	Two or more groups of children born at different times tested repeatedly over time. *Assets:* Permits both longitudinal and cross-sectional comparisons of children's performance; allows researchers to measure the existence of cohort effects. *Liabilities:* May have some of the problems of both cross-sectional and longitudinal studies, but the design helps to identify these difficulties; more expensive and longer time frame to collect data.

longitudinal design A study in which the same subjects are observed continuously over a period of time.

researchers and subjects. Subjects may become ill, go on vacation, move away, or simply stop participating in the research project. Some subjects become used to taking the tests and tend to do better than those being examined for the first time. Subjects who stay in the sample tend to be the most cooperative and stable. It has been suggested that subjects who participate in longitudinal studies are healthier, wealthier, and wiser than their peers in society (Friedrich & Van Horn, 1976).

The researchers, too, may move away, lose interest—or even die if the study continues for a long enough period of time. The Berkeley Growth Study, for example, has gone through various principal researchers in its over fifty-year history. Longitudinal studies often require extensive funding; moreover, the original purposes of the study may no longer be considered relevant to today's research needs. As theories and techniques change, it is difficult to incorporate new techniques and ideas into the ongoing design.

Cross-Sectional Designs. **Cross-sectional designs** have the advantage of being quicker, cheaper, and more manageable than longitudinal studies. To ensure that the groups at different age levels are reasonably comparable, cross-sectional designs require careful sampling of participants. In studies of adults of widely ranging ages, for example, it is frequently difficult to find a sample that is matched on variables such as health, education, or cultural and socioeconomic background. Studies of adult intelligence have been plagued by problems of comparable samples. Is the sample of 60-year-olds, for example, as healthy or as well-educated or from the same cultural or socioeconomic background as the sample of those aged forty? Finally, in either longitudinal or cross-sectional designs, it is difficult to separate the effects of chronological age from those of the historical period in which the individual has lived. Our earlier examples of Al and Judy indicate the tremendous impact of historical events on individual development.

Sequential Designs. Some researchers combine both approaches in a **sequential/age cohort design.** Whitbourne (1991) used such a design in a study of personality in young and middle adulthood. In 1968 and again in 1976, she surveyed college seniors on aspects of their self-image, social relationships, and values. She repeated this study in 1984 and 1990, with new groups of college seniors; she also re-surveyed those subjects studied earlier. Each of these age groups was considered an age cohort. The earliest age cohort has now been studied four times. That group can be analyzed for age differences in the same fashion as in a longitudinal design. How did these individuals change as they moved from college students in the late 1960s to starting their careers or marriages in the mid-1970s to parenting in the early 1980s and to re-examining their lives as 40-year-olds in 1990? But this group can also be compared to the other three age cohorts at each age level. In many ways, this group differs from the other three cohorts in their attitudes and values as college students. Perhaps these differences can be attributed to the politically turbulent college campuses of the late 1960s. All cohorts showed a strong interest in achievement and productivity the second time they were surveyed, in their late twenties. This is perhaps an age-appropriate role, both for men and women, as they build their careers. We can see the basic sequential design in Figure 1–3.

Such a combined design is almost essential in the study of adulthood to separate the effects of chronological age from the effects of the particular historical period. The psychological reality of adolescents, or of the parents of adolescents, may differ, depending on whether that person is living in the midst of conflict

cross-sectional design A method of studying development in which a sample of individuals of one age are observed and compared with one or more samples of individuals of other ages.

sequential/age cohort design A combination of cross-sectional and longitudinal research designs in which individuals of several different ages are observed repeatedly over an extended period of time.

FIGURE 1–3
The longitudinal, cross-sectional, and sequential/age cohort research designs. The diagonal rows (see bottom row circled in red) represent longitudinal studies, and the vertical columns (see left column circled in green) represent cross-sectional studies. The complete illustration is of the sequential/age cohort design, and it shows four age cohorts that are being studied at four different times.

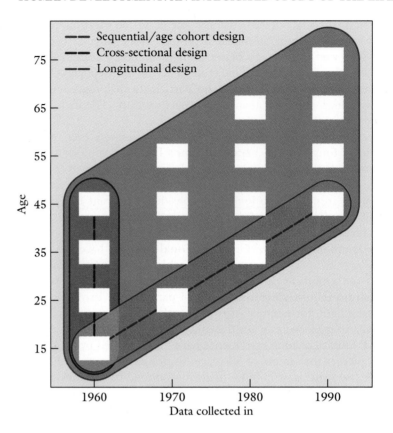

over Civil Rights and the Vietnam War in the late 1960s, or amidst renewed Civil Rights issues and the strong patriotism of the Persian Gulf War of 1991.

INTERPRETING THE EVIDENCE

Three witnesses to a robbery, or to the same research study, may submit three different reports. We do not all interpret evidence in the same way. In the scientific study of child development, it is necessary to establish dependable, repeatable, and consistent procedures that lead to similar conclusions. Otherwise, it becomes impossible for the field to progress and knowledge to expand.

BLOCKS TO GOOD OBSERVATION ***Observer bias.*** Many of us see what we expect to see or what we want to see; this is called *subjectivity*. We either do not notice or refuse to believe whatever conflicts with our preconditions. Whether it results from cultural assumptions, prejudice, stereotyping, or inexperience, a bias will invalidate the conclusions of an observation. Observing without a bias is called *objectivity*. An observer of female athletic skills, for instance, may be incompletely objective if convinced that women either cannot or should not be skilled in this area. In another example, an observer from the United States may report that Finns are highly unfriendly and avoidant when in reality their culture encourages shyness and introspection.

Insensitivity. When we observe the same thing every day, we often become so accustomed to it that we fail to recognize its significance. For example, the seat locations that students choose in a classroom may tell us something about their popularity, leadership, feelings of isolation, and the social groups to which they belong. But if we see these students in the classroom several times a week, we may overlook this readily available information. Another example may be found in our inability to recognize signs of distress in those to which we are closest, or most intimate.

Limits of the hypothesis. Another obstacle to good observation is the tendency to look at too large or too small or too arbitrary a piece of behavior. If, for example, we want to know something about memory in children or adolescents, we can choose a number of different approaches. We may observe some individuals in this group following the routine of a typical day, noting how many times they forget things. But this method is too arbitrary to measure memory functions precisely. Such observations would not reveal, for example, how well the subjects had learned the things they had forgotten or what they did know. A laboratory setting might provide more accurate results.

In some early memory studies, researchers had individuals of different ages (for example, ages 20, 40, 60, and 80) learn lists of nonsense syllables. Then they measured how many of these nonsense syllables subjects could recall 10 minutes later, 30 minutes later, and 24 hours later. In most cases, the older individuals had much more difficulty learning and remembering the nonsense syllables than did the younger subjects. In more recent studies, researchers have asked young adults and older adults to listen to and remember the important facts from selected material. In dealing with this kind of material, the performance of older subjects is much closer to that of younger ones. It seems that older people generally learn to use their memory abilities more selectively. They can learn and remember a good deal of information, provided it is meaningful and useful. In contrast, they apparently screen out useless information (Botwinick, 1984). While these examples deal with adults, they illustrate one type of problem we will find in studies of young children.

LIMITING CONCLUSIONS

It is easy to go beyond the data in an attempt to conclude more than was actually found in a study. This can happen in a number of ways, but we might be particularly on the alert for three of them.

PROBLEMS OF DEFINITION In research, we normally have two different kinds of definitions: a theoretical definition and an operational definition. A *theoretical definition* of a particular variable is based on the theorist's hypothetical construction. For example, a theoretical definition of intelligence might be "the ability to adapt to one's environment." In contrast, an *operational definition* specifies the particular variable in terms of how it is measured. In this case, an operational definition of intelligence might be: "those behaviors that the Stanford-Binet intelligence test measures." Researchers with different ideas of what intelligence means get different results when interpreting the same material. If the researchers want to be sure they are talking about the same thing, they need to agree on a definition that describes the techniques of observation and measure-

FOCUS ON AN ISSUE

PERSONALITY OVER THE LIFE COURSE

The child is father of the man," wrote the English poet William Wordsworth in 1802. Nearly everyone has heard a grandparent comment on the continuity of some relative's temper, stubbornness, or other personality trait. But a social scientist looks for proof of the validity or truthfulness of such statements. Is there essential stability of personality traits over the life course for most people? If so, what are the circumstances, processes, and influences that make this statement more or less true?

"Caspi and Elder (1988) wondered if 'ill-tempered children' became 'ill-tempered' adults, and if inhibited children became inhibited adults."

The obstacles to systematic research on the life course are formidable. Suppose some researchers simply want to know whether or not shy children are likely to be shy as adolescents and as young adults. They might try to design a test of shyness that is appropriate for each age level, give it to some children, and wait to test these same individuals again later on. This is a standard longitudinal design. But what if the researchers also want to know why shyness persists or what the life-course consequences of this behavioral style are? A more complicated and extensive longitudinal study, conducted over several decades, would be required in.

Fortunately for some current researchers, a few extensive and complex longitudinal studies that were started many years ago have amassed a body of information for the examination of some life-course questions. One such study—the Berkeley Guidance Study—tracked the development of every third child born in Berkeley, California, in 1928. In childhood, these children and their parents were monitored on an annual basis. From adolescence on, they were interviewed extensively every 10 years. Remarkably, researchers were able to stay in touch with 139 of the almost 200 initial subjects over a period of 40 years. The individuals in this age cohort were children during the Great Depression, teens during World War II, and young adults in the postwar boom. Yet, as individuals, they experienced these world events very differently. Why? What were some of the key factors in determining their development over the life course? There have been many studies using these data to examine economic factors, parental attitudes, personality factors, educational opportunities, and family crises. Let's look at one of these studies.

Caspi and Elder (1988) wondered if "ill-tempered" children became "ill-tempered" adults, and if inhibited children became inhibited adults. What were the adult consequences of these behavioral styles? What were the life-course patterns for the explosive children and for the withdrawn children, as compared to their peers?

To study these questions, Caspi and Elder selected the individuals in

ment to be employed in their study. That is an operational definition. But their work is more meaningful if they also provide a theoretical definition.

To illustrate, let us consider the problem of studying aggression. We might be able to agree on a theoretical definition of aggression as "behavior that is intended to injure or destroy." But how do we measure intent? What do we observe? To answer these questions, we need an operational definition of our research topic. One researcher might measure hitting, kicking, punching, and other physical acts against another person. A second researcher might measure verbal insults. A third might measure a teacher's rating of the child's aggressiveness on a five-point scale from high to low. A fourth might measure the aggres-

the sample who at ages 8 to 10 were reported by teachers and parents as either the most explosive or the most inhibited. These were the "under-controlled" children, who had frequent outbursts of temper, or the "over-controlled" children, who were anxiously inhibited in their ability to initiate activity. Did these explosive or inhibited behavior patterns persist into adulthood, even though the behavior was often maladaptive? For the most part they did, although there were several exceptions. More importantly, however, the researchers focused on the life trajectory, or the pattern of events over the life course, for individuals with these two different childhood behavior styles.

Children who exhibit problem behavior like an explosive temper or severe withdrawal at age 10 do not experience the same environment as their age mates. Teachers, parents, and peers react to them differently, both when they are children and when they are adults. Explosive behavior—whether expressed in school, in military service, in the workplace, or in dating and marriage—engenders predictable and usually unfavorable reactions in oth-

ers. Consequently, the "explosive" children in the Berkeley Guidance Study, especially the males, fared less well than did other children in many settings. As a group, they attended school for fewer years and earned fewer degrees than did their peers. They were less able to adapt to the educational system's demand for suppression of emotional expression. As adults, the men held lower-level jobs in the workplace and served in lower ranks in the military than did their peers. They changed jobs more frequently and were more likely to divorce. The women married men with lower job status, were more likely to divorce, and became ill-tempered mothers (Caspi et al., 1987).

Those individuals who were shy or withdrawn children had a quite different life-course pattern. Shy boys were likely to avoid or delay decisions about education, dating, marriage, or a career. Consequently, the adult roles of marriage and parenthood and the establishment of a stable career were delayed. Shy girls, who were young adults in the 1950s, were more likely than their peers to accept and follow a conventional pattern of marriage, child

rearing, and homemaking (Caspi et al., 1988).

In both the explosive and the withdrawn patterns, the typical life course shows a progressive accumulation of the consequences of the early behavioral style. The life-course trajectories across 30 or more years are a result of both the continuing interpersonal behavior in numerous situations and the cumulative consequences of these events as well as of particular adult decisions made in work, marriage, and parenting (Caspi & Elder, 1988).

Although Caspi and Elder's findings are impressive, these are general findings. As Professor J. W. Macfarlane and her team at Berkeley found in 1958, "A number [of individuals] who were hostile...in childhood have grown up to become friendly and nurturing parents." Some explosive children also triumphed over their emotional natures to succeed in the educational, military, and work arenas. It remains for future researchers to discover the roots of this success and to determine whether these individuals found socially acceptable outlets for their emotional reactions or learned at some stage to "temper" their emotions.

sive content in a child's storytelling. But the child who scores high in fantasy aggression may be quite low in actual physical aggression as measured by the first researcher. These researchers are measuring different things.

GENERALIZING BEYOND THE SAMPLE   Research is conducted in a particular setting and under particular conditions, with particular individuals from a particular sociocultural context. The results of any study, therefore, must be limited to similar individuals in similar situations. For example, children who experience a great deal of sarcasm in their daily life may learn the cues for this behavior much more quickly than those who grow up in families where sarcasm is a rare event.

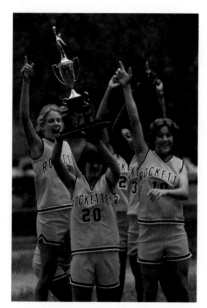

Does height cause weight or weight cause height or are they each the result of some combination of genetic and environmental factors? To measure the relationship between these two variables, researchers use the technique of correlation.

CORRELATION OR CAUSALITY   It is very difficult to establish with any degree of certainty the **cause** of specific behaviors. For example, 8-year-old boys who watch a lot of television engage in more aggressive play with their peers (Liebert & Spraken, 1988). Did the television watching cause the aggression? Perhaps aggressive children watch more television because they like aggression. Several studies indicate that aggressive behavior and seeing acts of aggression on television are related, but we are not sure which causes which or whether the two are, in fact, influenced by a third factor. For instance, height and weight are related to each other. Does height cause weight, does weight cause height, or are they both the result of the genetic plan that interacts with the environmental context provided for growth?

Researchers use a statistical technique called **correlation** to measure the relationship between two variables. In the case of the relationship between television watching and aggression, one might first measure the number of hours a child spents watching violent television shows and then measure her aggressive behavior. Children who view more violent television shows tend to be higher in aggression, while children who view very few violent shows tend to be very low in aggression. When both these factors are found to occur, there will be a strong, positive correlation between watching many hours of violent programming and acting aggressively. If children who watch many violent shows are less aggressive, the correlation would be negative.

When two variables are correlated (either positively or negatively), it is tempting to conclude that one causes the other. For example, parental spanking is positively correlated with children's aggressive behavior; that is, children who are spanked a lot tend to be more aggressive than those who are not. It is logical, on the one hand, to conclude that the child's unruly behavior causes the frequent spanking. Conversely, if one believes that parental behavior usually causes a child's behavior, then perhaps physically aggressive behavior like spanking *causes* the child to imitate such aggression. Both conclusions are logical but not necessarily correct. Correlation does *not* mean causation.

    # RESEARCH ETHICS

It hardly needs to be said that researchers should follow ethical principles when conducting research with human beings. They should never knowingly harm anyone, nor violate basic human rights. This is especially important when conducting research on dependent groups such as children, the aged, or prisoners. Nevertheless, issues of individual rights and what may be harmful to research participants are more complex than they may appear—as the following hypothetical research situation illustrates.

causality A relationship between two variables in which change in one brings about an effect or result in the other.

correlation A mathematical statement of the relationship between two variables.

Three-year-old Emma, who is newly separated from her mother in her first preschool class, sits in a room with an unfamiliar adult in a white lab coat. The researcher asks her to sit on a high chair and place her head into a helmetlike device through which she will look at some pictures. In order to hold her head still, she must place her mouth over a hard rubber bite bar. Emma balks, frowns, and begins to tremble.

Despite the urging of her teacher's aide to do what the "doctor" says, she seems unable to follow the instructions. Soon tears appear on her cheeks.

This scenario could be an example of a research study comparing eye movements and visual processing in preschool boys and girls. The anxiety created by any test situation is familiar to all of us, but it may be more problematic for a child who is relatively unfamiliar with evaluative situations. Such a study raises broad ethical questions. Are the results of this kind of experiment important enough to justify putting vulnerable persons under stress? Is it ethical to test persons without giving them information which they can understand about the purposes of the experimentation?

GUIDELINES FOR ETHICAL RESEARCH PRACTICE

Most of us agree that some experiments using human beings as research subjects are necessary if we are to understand and control the impact of potentially harmful environmental events. These potential benefits must be balanced with the rights of individual research participants.

One of the most basic recommendations needs to be considered in every research project in child development:

> ...(is there)...a negative effect upon the dignity and welfare of the participants that the importance of the research does not warrant. (American Psychological Association, 1973, p. 11)

It is unclear from Emma's story if that research would warrant the potential harm to the young subject.

The basic principles espoused by the Society for Research in Child Development (1990) are fundamental rules that would guide any reputable and honest researcher. They include the following principles:

➤ *Protection from Harm* No treatment or experimental condition given to the child as part of the study should be mentally or physically harmful.
➤ *Informed Consent* Informed consent of the child, if old enough, or from the parents or others who act on the child's behalf (such as school officials) should be obtained for any research involving children. Adults and children should be free to discontinue their participation in the research at any point in time.
➤ *Privacy* Confidentiality of the information obtained in the study must be preserved. No agencies or individuals outside of the researchers will have access to the individual participant's records.
➤ *Knowledge of Results* Children and their parents have the right to be informed of the results of research in terms understandable to them.
➤ *Beneficial Treatments* Each child who participates in the study has the right to profit from beneficial treatments provided to other participants in the study. For example, if a child is in a control group of a study to develop a new vaccine he is entitled to that vaccine at a later time.

A close look at several of these guidelines will help in understanding the ethical principles involved in research with children.

THE RIGHT TO INFORMED CONSENT   All major professional organizations hold that people should participate voluntarily, should be fully informed of the nature and possible consequences of the experiment, and should not be offered excessive inducements such as large amounts of money. Infants and young children do not offer their consent—their parents do. It is hoped that parents have the best interests of their children in mind. Children over the age of 8 and adults should give their own consent. Researchers should be sensitive to other forms of inducement. How easily, for example, can a 9-year-old in school, or a 70-year-old in a nursing home, say "no" to someone who looks like a teacher or an administrator (Thompson, 1990)?

THE RIGHT TO PRIVACY OR CONFIDENTIALITY   We all have a right to privacy; therefore, we have a right to expect researchers to keep confidential information about our private lives, thoughts, and fantasies. Also, test scores must be protected from inappropriate use by those outside the research project. Test scores may be categorized using phrases like "dull-normal intelligence," or "pre-delinquent," or "weak ego control," or "impulsive." Such labels shared with parents, teachers, or employers can easily be misinterpreted. Labels can become self-fulfilling; if teachers are told that a child has limited intelligence, they may treat the child in a way that makes that description come true.

THE RIGHT TO PROTECTION FROM PSYCHOLOGICAL HARM   Everyone agrees that researchers should never knowingly harm their subjects. While physical injury is easily avoided, it is often difficult to determine what is psychologically harmful. For example, in studies of obedience, is it reasonable to give children orders just to see if they will follow them? In the numerous studies of infants' responses to novelty, is it reasonable to expose children for long periods to increasingly novel items?

Another example concerns test failure. Sometimes a researcher wants to demonstrate that a 7-year-old can understand a particular concept but a 5-year-old cannot. All the 5-year-old children, knowingly or unknowingly, experience repeated failure. Should children have to go through the needless confusion of trying to solve what, for them, are unsolvable problems? How does one debrief such children or make them feel that they did well no matter what the outcome?

Most research organizations currently have screening committees to make sure that their studies are not harmful to the participants. Federal guidelines for social and psychological research with children specify that the study should have only minimal risk: that is, risk of harm no greater than that experienced in daily life or in the performance of routine psychological tests (DHS, 1983). These screening committees are becoming more stringent in their protection of the participants. Many committees, for example, feel that they have a responsibility to protect people's rights to self-esteem and to expose them only to test situations that will enhance their self-concept (Thompson, 1990).

BENEFITS TO THE PARTICIPANT   It may not be enough for researchers to seek the voluntary informed consent of their participants, respect their confidentiality, and protect them from physical and psychological harm. Perhaps researchers need to supply some positive benefits to individuals in return for their participation. At the very least, perhaps researchers should try to make participation fun, interesting, or informative, or to create a positive situation in which the person can be heard, supported, understood, and respected. The rights of participants in research are still being explored and defined. Indeed, many studies considered permissible even two decades ago are no longer viewed as ethical.

 ## SUMMARY AND CONCLUSIONS

The goal of studying child development is the discovery and understanding of common processes and major influences from conception through adolescence. Those of us who study child development consider the impact of historical change, socioeconomic factors, and cross-cultural factors on the children who are exposed to them. But the process is complementary. Not only do cultural and social factors affect the children who are exposed to them, but they also help to shape attitudes toward the children. Attitudes toward children, and the child-rearing practices associated with them, have not only changed historically, but vary across different cultural and socioeconomic groups.

Both biology and environment influence development to produce change in the structure, thought, or behavior of a person. Development occurs in three different domains of a child's existence: the physical, cognitive, and psychological domains. Some of the changes are primarily biological in nature, while others are more strongly environmentally determined. In practice, however, much of development involves an interaction between heredity and environment as we shall see in Chapter 3.

For us to be able to fully understand development, we must systematically study it using the Scientific Method. Measures must be reliable and valid to ensure that the results of research are dependable and consistent. Various measures have been used to assess various aspects of development. These include self-reports, such as interviews and questionnaires; such projective techniques reveal an individual's inner feelings and attitudes by asking the person to respond to situations, pictures, and so forth. Case studies have also been found to reveal rich material on development.

Problems with all of these techniques include the subjectivity of their responses, the lack of control of variables, and the fact that they are limited to the study of one individual.

Research designs which allow precise measurement of behavior have evolved in the laboratory and naturalistic settings. Various sorts of designs have evolved to study development: cross-sectional designs, which test people of different ages at one time; longitudinal designs, which test the same people repeatedly at different ages; and time-lag designs, which test people the same chronological age in different years, for example, 5-year-olds in 1950, 1970, and 1990. Sequential/age cohort studies present a combination of these three approaches.

Despite the greater control possible through experimental design, certain barriers still exist to interpreting the data correctly. Factors serving as barriers to good research include the researcher's objectivity, sensitivity to detail, and the selection of an appropriate level of analysis. Furthermore, unless the variables have been operationally defined, conclusions may not be replicable. We must also be careful to avoid confusing correlation (the relationship between two variables) and causation. Sometimes two variables may be very closely related, yet neither causes the other.

Finally, in testing vulnerable individuals such as children, it is essential to keep in mind generally accepted ethical principles. Such principles include voluntary consent, the right to privacy or confidentiality, the freedom from psychological harm, and the right to receive any beneficial results because of the experiment. We need to always safeguard the cognitive, emotional, and physical health of those children we study.

➤ KEY TERMS AND CONCEPTS

aging	dependent-variable	independent variable	reliability
causality	development	learning	sequential/age cohort
correlation	ecological systems theory	longitudinal design	design
critical period	experimental design	maturation	
cross-sectional design	growth	readiness	validity

➤ SELF-TEST QUESTIONS

1. What is meant by the statement, "Difficulties in understanding human behavior are often caused by those who try to explain and predict it"?

2. Compare historical, socioeconomic, and cross-cultural perspectives in terms of their respective contributions to the understanding of human development.

3. What is meant by the term *development,* and what roles do biological processes and environmental influences play in bringing development about?

4. What is the relationship between learning and socialization?

5. How would you explain the relationship between biological and environmental development processes? What roles do timing and readiness play in this relationship?

6. List four basic steps involved in the scientific method.

7. Describe the major categories of developmental research and list their strengths and limitations.

8. List and describe the factors that must be considered in order to interpret evidence.

9. Describe the ethical factors that researchers must consider when conducting research with children.

➤ SUGGESTED READINGS

BOWLBY, J. *CHARLES DARWIN: A new life.* New York: Norton, 1990. A powerful psychological analysis of Darwin's internal struggles and family life as well as his achievements as a naturalist.

COLES, R. *The spiritual life of children.* Boston, MA: Houghton Mifflin, 1990. Through the words and pictures of children, this noted teacher and child psychiatrist shares with the reader some surprisingly profound child understandings of the meaning of life and of human experience.

GIES, F., & GIES, J. *Life in a medieval village.* New York: Harper & Row, 1990. Two skilled historians reconstruct the customs, practices, and social conditions in rural medieval England.

HEWETT, S. *When the bough breaks: The cost of neglecting our children.* New York: Basic Books, 1991. A compelling social commentary on the plight of children in today's United States.

KAGAN, J. *The nature of the child.* New York: Basic Books, 1984. A noted developmental psychologist highlights the research of the last few decades. He editorializes on the effects of early experiences, yet suggests that there are also numerous opportunities for transformations in later childhood and adolescence.

VIDEO CASE: COMPANY HELP WITH CHILD CARE

As the various school vacations roll around, millions of American parents living in households where both adults have full-time jobs but not full-time child care, experience a sense of dread. How are they going to cope with their children during the work day? Richard Feinberg is a magazine editor. His wife Susan works at a nonprofit agency. Usually, they juggle the demands of their jobs and those of their three young sons with a variety of child-care arrangements. However, when this routine is interrupted by school vacations, family life becomes increasingly difficult. Says Richard Feinberg, "If you just look at the math, there's a Christmas break, a February break, and an April break; then there's time before summer camp starts, and again after summer camp, before school begins. I don't have six weeks of paid vacation."

One company, John Hancock Financial Services, has established a program called "Kids to Go" to help parents who find themselves in such a dilemma. Four times a year during a school break of a week or less, the program offers its 5,000 employees supervised activities for their school-aged children. The children "go" to places—movies, museums, roller-skating rinks, and bowling alleys. Parents who can afford to, pay $20 a day. For those unable to pay this amount, John Hancock contributes half. Generally, the company pays as little as $2,000 a year for the program.

Are parents satisfied? Diana Bawn, a Hancock financial analyst who has an 8-year-old son in "Kids to Go," is typical. She says, "It really takes a load off my mind, and it also gives me the freedom to be able to do my work and know that he's well taken care of and not have to field phone calls from babysitters or other things like that." The company benefits also. Officials realize that if they want to keep their best workers, they will have to find ways to assist parents in balancing their jobs and their family. Otherwise, they will have to deal with workers who are distracted by worries about their children.

CASE QUESTIONS

1. Do you believe programs like "Kids to Go" fill a real need? Why or why not?

2. Do you believe companies should develop such programs? Why or why not? Why do you think companies are often reluctant to devise them?

3. Do you think we need a nation-wide system of child care that will encompass the needs of working parents like the Feinbergs and Diana Bawn? Why or why not?

CHAPTER

2

THEORIES OF CHILD DEVELOPMENT: AN INTRODUCTION

OUTLINE

CHAPTER OBJECTIVES

By the time you have finished this chapter, you should be able to do the following:

✔   Describe and compare the major theories of child development.

✔   Be familiar with major terms and concepts employed by each theory of child development.

What of the child? What makes him or her a unique person? How do parents, and teachers, television characters—and even imaginary friends—contribute to the process of development? How do the social, physical, and cognitive realities of children interact to move them toward more advanced skills? These questions and their answers form the basis for theories of development.

What then is the essence of human nature? Are we primarily rational and goal oriented? Or are we driven by passions? How do we learn—by discovery, by insight, or by small sequential steps of increasing complexity? How are we motivated—by reward, pain, curiosity, or inner drives? What is a "conscience," and how does it develop? Do we have control over it? Or is it shaped by external and internal forces that we cannot control? Sometimes we study developmental psychology to seek answers to such basic questions. Any answer that we find will be based on a particular theory of human development—a set of assumptions or principles about human behavior which provides a frame for a particular mass of data.

If you think about the questions raised above, you will probably realize that you have your own "theories" about the answers to them. You lean toward one explanation or another of a specific problem, and the assumptions implicit in your explanation probably have a lot to do with your thoughts about other people. For example, you may view juvenile delinquents either as responsible for their actions or as victims of their environment or early training. You may believe that 6-year-olds are able to decide for themselves what they should study in school, or you may think that at this age they cannot be expected to know what they want. You probably have assumptions about the degree to which each individual is responsible for his or her behavior and the degree to which human rationality can be relied upon to direct our actions wisely.

 ## WHY STUDY THEORIES OF DEVELOPMENT?

Why is it important to understand the theories of human behavior? A broad understanding of various theories creates the detachment that lets us evaluate our own views, actions, and reactions. It is important for us to reexamine the assumptions behind our beliefs to see whether they make sense, whether they fit the evidence, and what follows from them. A familiarity with the major theories, then, allows us to examine, evaluate, and discipline our intuitions and our own "theories" on human behavior.

Theories give shape to otherwise large and unmanageable collections of data. Social scientists use theories to help formulate significant questions, to select and organize their data, and to understand the data within a larger framework. The resulting body of information, together with the broader theory, allows social scientists to make new predictions about future human behavior.

As with any scientific endeavor, not all those who build theories agree with each other. Nor do they all choose the same area of development to explore. Some theorists like Freud or Erikson focus on personality development, while others like Piaget, study the development of thinking in children. Each theorist brings a unique background of training and interests to the study of child development which is then incorporated into the premises of the theories being constructed. Each theory, therefore, becomes a reflection of the personality, thought, and values of the individual who designed it.

THREE CONTROVERSIAL ISSUES

There are three controversial issues which theories of child development address in some fashion: *nature* versus *nurture, continuities* versus *discontinuities,* and the *organismic* versus *mechanistic* nature of human beings. When theories disagree, it is often because of the way they deal with these issues.

NATURE VERSUS NURTURE   Nature versus nurture refers to the question of which factors are most significant in determining development—those related to heredity or to environment? Nature refers to the importance of heredity as the major determinant. Theorists who emphasize nurture, on the other hand, view environmental factors, such as maternal behavior, crowding, temperature and cultural factors, as the major factors underlying the development of behaviors in children. A nature theorist and a nurture theorist would look at the same behavior and describe very different processes by which it developed. For example, a theorist who emphasizes heredity and biology as the determinants of behavior might say that a preschooler's imaginary friends are caused by the level of brain and cognitive maturity of the child. A theorist who emphasizes nurture, might look to environmental factors like isolation, lack of responsive caretakers, or the absence of siblings as the cause of the behavior.

CONTINUITY VERSUS DISCONTINUITY   The question of continuities vs. discontinuities is another crucial question for developmental researchers. Does development occur with behaviors building continually on each other in a quantitative manner? Or does development occur in a stepwise framework, with each stage reflecting the occurrence of qualitatively different behaviors. Learning theorists, as we will see in this chapter, subscribe to the continuous development notion, while stage theorists like Piaget and Freud believe that major discontinuities mark the emergence of new capabilities or behaviors.

ORGANISMIC VERSUS MECHANISTIC   The final question—whether human nature is basically organismic or mechanistic—is derived from philosophy. Organismic theorists believe that humans are active organisms who fully participate in the process of development. Individuals interact with other individuals and events and are changed by these interactions. In turn, they act on the objects and events and change them. Organismic theorists, like Piaget, who study cognition, believe that as we take in information, we are transformed by it.

This makes us able to act more competently in subsequent interchanges. In this theoretical framework, humans are seen as acting on their world. The mechanistic viewpoint, on the other hand, describes humans as passive reactors to environmental events, internal drives, or motivation. This viewpoint is most clearly expressed by the behaviorists, who see humans as being controlled by rewards or punishment.

WHAT IS A THEORY?

Before we begin our discussion of specific developmental theories, a consideration of the definition of key terms is in order. The word *theory* for example has previously been defined as a systematic formulation of principles explaining behavior. Given that definition, developmental theories are logical statements that explain the way in which the behavior of children develops. The word **development** is defined as a process of change involving the physical, psychological, and social spheres of a person's existence. The significant words in this description are *change* and *process*. These words imply that development is not a steady state, nor does it proceed at the same rate at all phases of the life cycle. For example, during the first few days of life, hours are significant; during adulthood, when the main markers of progress are years, months or phases become significant periods for the evolution of behaviors.

Associated with these quantitative differences in development, are those qualitative changes that indicate changes in functioning based on age or developmental levels. These qualitative changes are recognized even by those who never study development per se. Most people realize that concepts and ideas change with age, from birth to death.

THE LIMITATIONS OF DEVELOPMENTAL THEORIES

Our current theories of development, whether biological or psychological, are incomplete. They do not tell us about age-related changes across the lifespan, nor do they tell us about how behaviors can be modified. Many theories only define the development of one area of development such as personality, rather than development in general. But, we do have many good theories that predict and explain limited aspects of behavior or behavior in limited portions of the lifespan. Nevertheless, most developmental psychologists agree that what is needed is a unifying theory of development encompassing biological, behavioral, and social factors—as well as their interactions.

It is unlikely then that any one theory we will discuss will fully explain developmental processes and behaviors. That does not mean that these theories are irrelevant or inadequate. Theories, which usually follow a number of observations, generally play two major roles. First, they systematize the observations into some organized pattern. Second, they develop a rational explanation of how or why the observed phenomenon occurs. Because of the complexity of developmental processes, different theories address discrete aspects of the process. Each of these theories may be valid and worth studying in its own right, but may not explain the cause of the developmental process. Each has its positive and negative aspects, but none is likely to be *the* theory of development. It still remains for some research to successfully integrate the disparate natures of these theories into a core explanation of child development.

As we have seen, the process of human development is very complex and has had many interpretations. Theories of development have been remarkably diverse in their content and underlying beliefs. Why is it important to understand the theories of child behavior? A broad understanding of various theories creates the detachment that lets us evaluate our own views, actions, and reactions. It is vital for us to reexamine the assumptions behind our beliefs to see whether they make sense, whether they fit the evidence, and what follows from them. A familiarity with the major theories, then, allows us to examine, evaluate, and discipline our intuitions and our own "theories" on children's behavior.

Besides helping us understand our own ways of thinking, a knowledge of the major theories makes us more eclectic. By acquainting ourselves with several different theories, we can examine behavior from more than one frame of reference and can see the value of other explanations.

Many psychologists, too, are eclectic. They select from numerous theories those particular aspects that will help them in their work. Almost all psychologists have been influenced by the theories of others. Therefore, in describing the various theories given in this chapter, we do not intend to label or pigeonhole psychologists, but simply to present the basic outlines of some of the most popular beliefs.

LEARNING THEORIES

Learning theories find the key to a person's nature in the way that she is shaped by the environment. According to these theories most behavior is acquired, and it is acquired by learning. *Learning* is a pervasive process. It is not confined simply to formal schooling or instruction; it also includes the acquisition of morality, biases, and mannerisms, such as gestures or even stuttering. Learning, therefore, covers a broad spectrum of behavior. The learning theorist sees child development as a gradual, step-by-step accumulation of knowledge, skills, memories, and competencies. The child becomes an adolescent and then an adult primarily by the gradual, continuous addition of experiences and learning, which lead, in turn, to more skills and knowledge. Based on our earlier discussion of controversial issues in child development, we can see that learning theories emphasize nurture and continuity.

BEHAVIORISM

In the early part of the twentieth century, American psychologists set out to create a "science of human behavior." They were not interested in human thoughts, dreams, or feelings. Instead, they wanted to collect "the facts" by observing what people do. They studied human behavior in much the same way that other scientists studied biology or physics. These researchers carefully defined and controlled the stimuli present in the experimental setting and then observed and recorded their subject's behavioral responses to these stimuli. They did not start from a "grand design," but instead objectively constructed their theory, piece by piece, first by conducting simple experiments and later by designing more complex ones. In this fashion, they inductively built a theory of behavior. Because of their interest in overt, measurable behavior, these researchers were called **behaviorists.**

Behavioral theories derived largely from two major sources: the work in classical conditioning performed by Ivan P. Pavlov (1849–1936) and that conducted in learning by John B. Watson (1878–1958). All of the theories have as their philosophical basis the notion of tabula rasa (clean slate) suggested by the English philosopher John Locke. This notion proposed that all human beings are born without any innate ideas. It is, therefore, up to the environment to structure and teach appropriate behaviors, thoughts, and feelings.

THE NOTION OF REACTIVE BEINGS   Behaviorists assume that human nature is neither bad nor good; people are reactive—they simply respond to their environment. Every individual is shaped by the process of associating stimuli and their responses or associating behaviors and their consequences. Thus the learning process occurs rather automatically. Some say this explanation is **mechanistic,** that it views people as machines that are set in motion by input (a *stimulus*) and then produce output (a *response*). Behaviorists are not concerned with analyzing what happens between the stimulus and the response. The mind itself, particularly its internal stages, cannot be easily observed and described from the outside. Behaviorists do not trust people to give accurate reports of their subjective thoughts and feelings. Consequently, they have not given much attention to the mind. They do not subscribe to any unconscious or genetic determinants of behavior. The areas of greatest impact for the behavioral theories have been on the systematic analysis of behavior, the treatment and management of deviant behaviors, and educational applications.

The behaviorist's model has also been described as **deterministic.** Everything in the individual's behavior, including values, attitudes, and emotional responses, is believed to be determined by either the past or present environment. Therefore, such concepts as blame, respect, and dignity are considered irrelevant. According to behaviorism, because people are products of their past learning history, they deserve neither credit nor blame for their actions. The title of a book by the modern learning theorist, B. F. Skinner, *Beyond Freedom and Dignity* (1971) expresses this idea. In this book, Skinner implies that human behavior is programmed and therefore beyond the individual's control.

CLASSICAL CONDITIONING   As we mentioned previously, behaviorists were especially interested in describing and defining the processes of learning. Perhaps the most basic form of learning is called *conditioning*. There are several famous experiments that demonstrate different types of conditioning.

The experiments of the Russian physiologist Ivan Pavlov (1928) are among the most famous examples of **classical conditioning** (see Figure 2–1). While observing the stomachs of dogs through gastric fistulas (openings directly into the stomach), Pavlov noted that they salivated when meat was placed in their mouths. After several feedings he saw that the dogs had only to hear the bell that marked the feeding period and they would begin to salivate. Pavlov named the meat the *unconditioned stimulus* (**UCS**) since it naturally elicited a particular response, salivation, which he called the *unconditioned response* (**UCR**), since it was naturally associated with the meat.

He began to strike a tuning fork at the same time that he offered food to a dog, and he repeated the pairing of the neutral stimulus (the tuning fork) with

behaviorists Early twentieth-century psychologists who focused their research on overt, measurable, observable behavior rather than on internal medical processes.

mechanistic model In learning theory, the view of human beings as machines that are set in motion by input (stimuli) and that produce output (responses).

deterministic model The view that a person's values, attitudes, behaviors, and emotional responses are determined by past or present environmental factors.

classical conditioning A type of learning in which a neutral stimulus, such as a bell, comes to elicit a response—salivation—by repeated pairings with an unconditioned stimulus, such as food.

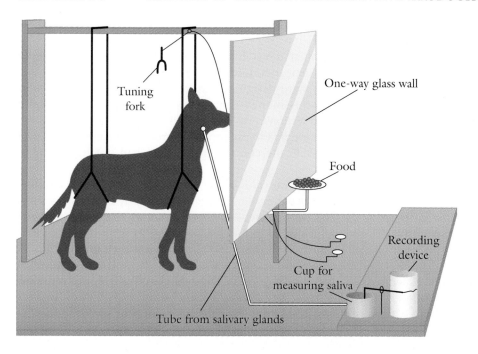

FIGURE 2–1
Drawing of Pavlov's Dog.
See the text for a description of this experiment, the most famous example of the classical conditioning phenomemon.

the food several times. Before long, the sound of the fork alone was enough to make the dog salivate. He did not conclude that the dog "anticipated food when he heard the fork." That would imply thinking. Instead, he and the American learning theorists simply concluded that the dog was now conditioned to salivate at the sound of the tuning fork. Once the tuning fork elicited the salivation, it was called the *conditioned stimulus* (**CS**), since it now stimulated salivation. The salivation was now referred to as the *conditioned response* (**CR**), since it was asso-

Because they assume that people are reactive beings, behaviorists study how individuals respond to their environment rather than investigating what they think or feel about these responses.

ciated with a stimulus that did not naturally produce it. We can see this sequence of conditioning detailed in Figure 2–2.

Others have done similar research with humans. For example, Lipsitt & Kaye (1964) conducted classical conditioning research on twenty 3-day-old infants. Ten of the infants were designated the experimental group and were given 20 pairings of an unconditioned stimulus (a pacifier) and a conditioned stimulus (tone). The desired response was sucking, which was naturally elicited by the pacifier. After the 20 pairings, the experimental group of infants would suck in response to the tone, while the control group, who had not had pairings, would not.

This research suggests the valuable contribution that the behavioral approach can make to understanding development. The study demonstrates that learning occurs in the first days of life. Moreover, it shows that classical conditioning is a technique that allows us to investigate infants' abilities to process sensory information well before they possess language. This is early learning.

Emotional reactions are also thought to be easily classically conditioned. A famous experiment on the conditioning of fear was performed by the American psychologist, John B. Watson, an important early behaviorist. Watson is often associated with a remark he made illustrating the beliefs of behaviorists:

> Give me a dozen healthy infants, well-formed, and my own specified world to bring them up in and I'll guarantee to take any one at random and train him to become any type of specialist I might select— doctor, lawyer, merchant-chief, and yes, even beggar-man or thief, regardless of his talents, penchants, tendencies, vocations, and race of his ancestors. (1930, p. 104)

FIGURE 2–2
The Classical Conditioning Paradigm

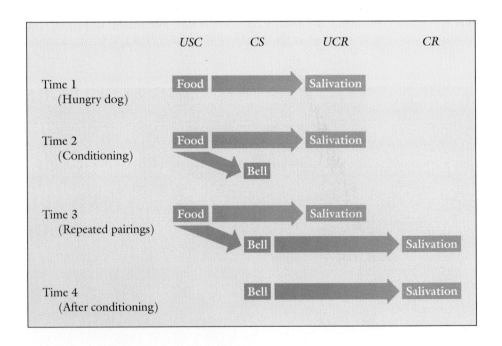

An 11-month-old infant named Albert was the subject of Watson and Rayner's experiment (1920). Albert was confronted with a white rat. At first, he showed no fear of the animal, but then Watson made a loud clanging noise every time he showed the rat to Albert, causing the baby to cry and crawl away. It did not take many pairings of the previously neutral stimulus of the rat with the unpleasant loud noise for Albert to respond with anxiety and fear to the rat alone. Reportedly, Albert was soon frightened by other white or furry objects, even a Santa Claus beard. This spread of a response to other similar stimuli is called **stimulus generalization.**

Albert's case was a dramatic example of conditioning with stimulus generalization—although the experiment was a rather cruel and unethical one and not very precise (Harris, 1979). We can see clear parallels in children's everyday lives. Doctors' white uniforms or medicinal smells may arouse fear in children because they associate these things with unpleasant experiences, such as painful injections. This association of pain of injections with white coats is so well-recognized that many pediatricians have their nurses give the immunizations to small children rather than themselves giving it. In this way, the painful procedures are not associated with the pediatrician. Positive emotional reactions can be conditioned just like negative ones. Reactions of relaxation or pleasure are easily associated with previously neutral stimuli, like an old song that brings back all the memories of a sunny day at the beach or the excitement of a high school dance.

Classical conditioning, therefore, helps us to understand the occurrence of emotional responses, such as fear, in young children. Other learned emotional responses undoubtedly also develop in this manner.

If a person comes to associate a previously neutral stimulus, such as Albert's rat, with an unpleasant emotional state, what can be done to reverse this conditioned response? In **counterconditioning,** the subject is gradually introduced to the once neutral stimulus in the presence of a strong and opposite conditioning stimulus, such as introducing the child to a caged rat while the child eats a favorite ice cream. This soon reverses the conditioned negative response pattern.

Wolpe, Salter, and Reyna (1964) have used **systematic desensitization** to treat common phobias, such as fear of flying or driving, fear of authority figures, and fear of hospitals, where the conditioned stimuli are things like height, uniforms, hospital smells, and "the boss." The most common desensitization technique is relaxation training. Clients are taught to relax deeply, and while in this state, told to imagine themselves approaching the feared situation. Each time clients report tension, they are immediately instructed to stop the image and return to a relaxed state. With repeated pairing, the new relaxation response replaces the old anxiety response, first to the image and finally to the real event or object. Two processes work together in counterconditioning. The old response disappears gradually because it is not actively reinforced. And, in the meantime, the clients learn a new, competing response through the process of classical conditioning.

OPERANT CONDITIONING   The foregoing examples have illustrated classical conditioning. But these procedures do not apply as well to more complex behavior, such as learning to drive a car, playing baseball, or reciting poetry.

stimulus generalization The spread of a response from one specific stimulus to other similar stimuli.

counterconditioning A procedure to eliminate a previously conditioned negative response by replacing it with a new conditioned response in the same stimulus situation.

systematic desensitization In behavior therapy, a technique that gradually reduces an individual's anxiety about a specific object or situation.

These are all examples of predominantly voluntary, or **operant behavior**. The key difference between operant and classical conditioning is that *in operant conditioning, behavior cannot be elicited automatically.* The behavior must occur before it can be strengthened by conditioning, that is, before it can be associated with a reward. In operant conditioning, behaviors that are rewarded or reinforced are likely to reoccur.

Edward Thorndike (1911) conducted experiments on voluntary behavior with cats. Cats placed in a puzzle box learned by themselves to escape from the box or to obtain food by manipulating a latch that opened the door. Thorndike saw in this learning phenomenon what he called the **law of effect:** The consequences of a behavior determine the probability of its being repeated. When first placed in the box, the cats typically explored the inside and pressed the latch only by chance. However, reinforcement in the form of food strengthened the behavior until the cats were opening the door immediately after they were placed in the box. Years later, B.F. Skinner picked up the work of Thorndike and Watson, and, together with other learning theorists, he systematically expanded the laws of behavior.

SKINNER

During his life, Skinner was the main proponent of behaviorism. He had a very full career, with activities ranging from developing pigeon-driven bomb sites during World War II, to designing a self-contained operant conditioning chamber for child-raising, to designing the utopian world presented in his book, *Walden Two.* As can be seen, Skinner was a highly creative individual who liked to invent research equipment that could more carefully measure behavior and could automatically deliver reinforcement. One invention of this type was called a *Skinner box,* which was essentially an animal cage built for a rat or pigeon, though larger animals were sometimes placed in it. The Skinner box contained a movable metal bar, and when the animal pushed this bar, a pellet of food dropped into its feeding tray. With this very simple device, he was able to measure the animal's behavior systematically under different conditions of reinforcement. Rats, pigeons, and sometimes humans were found to be quite predictable as they followed consistent laws of behavior, at least in this kind of situation. In Skinner's experiments (as in Thorndike's), the reinforcement was usually food. But in everyday situations, positive reinforcement may be a nod of approval, a smile, an interesting sight to see, or success in a video game.

As we can see in Figure 2–3, the typical Skinnerian paradigm involves the following components: a *discriminative stimulus,* a *response by the subject* and *reinforcement.* The discriminative stimulus usually serves as a signal to the subject that learning is about to take place. Stimuli such as lights, tones, or words, have served as discriminative stimuli. The response is the operant behavior performed. Skinner called his type of conditioning **operant conditioning** because the response emitted by the subject operated to deliver a reinforcer. Finally, the reinforcing stimulus is delivered for an adequate response. The reinforcer therefore increases the probability an operant behavior will be emitted, that is the subject will show the tendency to repeat the desired response in the presence of the particular discriminative stimulus.

Figure 2–3 presents the typical operant conditioning paradigm. A three-year-old child is looking (response) at books (stimulus). In order to increase this

operant behavior A behavior in which the individual operates on the environment or emits an action.

law of effect A principle of learning theory stating that a behavior's consequences determine the probability of its being repeated.

operant conditioning A type of conditioning that occurs when an organism is reinforced for voluntarily emitting a response. What is reinforced is then learned.

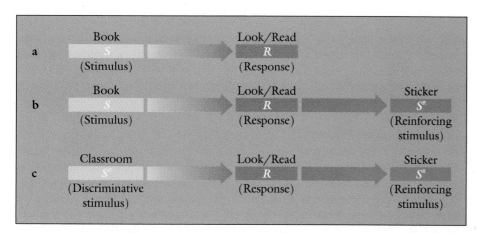

FIGURE 2–3

The Basic Operant
Conditioning Model.
(Source: From N.J. Salkind, 1981, Theo-
ries of Human Development,
New York: D. Van Nostrand, p. 131,
Figure 7–1. Reprinted by permission.

behavior, reinforcement must follow the response. In this case, an effective reinforcer is praise, or perhaps a sticker. A sticker is therefore given to the child when
he looks at the book. Finally, parents or teachers might wish to have the child
associate reading with a particular location, such as a classroom or family room
reading corner. This becomes the discriminative stimulus. The child is only reinforced for looking at books when they are in the appropriate location.

Operant behavior can also be learned by **avoidant conditioning,** in which
the reinforcement consists of the termination of an unpleasant stimulus. For
example, a bright light can be turned off, a loud noise can be stopped, or an
angry parent can be quieted. In operant conditioning, then, one learns a response
to a particular stimulus (or set of stimuli) by repeatedly having that response
paired with a positive reinforcement.

How can operant conditioning be used to teach a complex act? Very often,
the final behavior must be built bit by bit, or shaped. In **shaping,** *successive
approximations* of the final task are rewarded. For example, suppose a child is
learning to put on socks. At first, the parent puts on one sock nearly all the way,
lets the child pull it up, and then praises the child. The next day, the parent may
put the sock on halfway and let the child finish a bit more of the task. It is not
long before the child is putting on socks with no help. Similar principles may be
used to toilet train infants, to teach children to swim, or mold a shy adolescent
into an accomplished public speaker.

Teaching machines introduced by Skinner also applied many principles of
operant conditioning (Skinner, 1968). With these machines, students learned in
small incremental steps, starting with simple problem-solving and building up to
more complex tasks. The desired behavior, or answer, was reinforced at each step
with *feedback* (some form of reward or acknowledgement) from the machine and
by the appearance of a new problem to solve. Eventually, the student succeeded
in mastering fairly complex problems. Now some computer programs called "user
friendly" apply many of the same principles of learning.

As we saw in classical conditioning, while Skinner was not particularly interested in development, his operant conditioning technique has great utility in helping researchers to establish the behavioral capabilities of infants, children, and adolescents as the following study illustrates. Schneider, Trehub & Bull (1979) studied
sound perception and preference in 6-, 12- and 18-month-old infants. They first
rewarded the infants for turning their heads in the direction of a tone. When the

avoidant conditioning A form of
operant conditioning in which the
reinforcement consists of the termination of an unpleasant stimulus.

shaping Systematically reinforcing
successive approximations to a
desired act.

infants had learned to do this, the experimenters varied the intensity of the tones and their frequency. Using this methodology, the researchers were able to determine that infants can detect sounds higher than those typical of speech, and in the high frequencies, their perception approached that of adults. Perception was poorer at the lower frequencies. The researchers therefore determined that most auditory development after infancy takes place in the lower-frequency sounds.

To avoid the unpleasant stimulus of being scolded, this child may behave differently from now on.

CONTEMPORARY BEHAVIORAL ANALYSIS In the 1990s, the systematic study and application of classical and operant conditioning principles is called behavioral analysis. Numerous educational and therapeutic programs have been established to train or retrain individuals to behave in a more appropriate or desirable way. Programs that shape human behavior for therapeutic goals are called **behavior modification.** One effective way to modify behavior is through the use of a *token economy.* Imagine a residential facility for delinquent adolescents. The rewards in this controlled world—like tasty food, time in the gym, a semiprivate or private bedroom, current magazines to read, and, eventually, a weekend pass—can all be bought with tokens. However, these tokens are earned for very precise, carefully defined behaviors in the classroom and in the work setting. The tokens now become effective reinforcement for paying attention and making progress in school, following the rules, and being productive in the workplace. But they are effective only when the trainer remembers operant conditioning principles, such as rewarding small incremental steps toward the achievement of the final goal.

Extensive research has shown that token economies can be used successfully with retarded and autistic people, children in classrooms and at home, and delinquents and psychiatric inpatients (Baker & Brightman, 1989). The aim of training with tokens is to improve a trainee's skills to the point at which these skills are so useful to the trainee in the real world that tokens are no longer required. To this end, any token economy must have a plan for weaning trainees off the tokens as early as possible. Otherwise, they may become so dependent on the token economy that the effectiveness of the behavior modification program is lost.

SOCIAL-LEARNING THEORY Social-learning theorists have tried to enlarge the scope of learning theory to explain complex social patterns. To do so, they have gone well beyond a seemingly "automatic" conditioning process. Albert Bandura (1977), a leading social-learning theorist, points out that in daily life people notice the consequences of their own actions—that is, they notice which actions succeed and which fail or produce no result—and adjust their behavior accordingly. Through such observed **response consequences** they gain information, incentive, and conscious reinforcement. They are able to hypothesize about what is appropriate in which circumstances and to anticipate what may happen as a result of certain actions. Unlike the more mechanistic learning theorists, social-learning theorists give conscious thought a larger role in guiding behavior.

Imitation and Modeling. Just as people learn directly from experiencing the consequences of their own behavior, they also learn by watching another person's behavior and its consequences (Bandura, 1977; Bandura & Walters, 1963). And just as before, they derive basic principles from their observations and formulate rules of action and behavior. All of us (not just children) learn a wide variety of behaviors from observing and imitating (or avoiding) the actions of others

behavior modification A method that uses conditioning procedures, such as reinforcement, reward, and shaping, to change behavior.

response consequences The observed results of one's actions that individuals use to adjust their behavior.

around us. In their early years, children learn the many aspects of a sex-appropriate role and the moral expectations of their community. They also learn how to express aggression and dependency along with prosocial behaviors like sharing. As they grow to adulthood, they will learn career-appropriate attitudes and values, social-class and ethnic attitudes, and moral values.

In a well-known example of modeling, Bandura (1977) conducted a series of experiments in which children watched various levels of aggressive behavior in short films. One group of children saw the aggressive behavior rewarded; another saw it punished; a third group saw a film of nonaggressive behavior play; and a fourth group saw no film at all. The children who saw aggression rewarded were significantly more aggressive in their own play, whereas those who saw the model punished were less aggressive. There is no question that children may learn to express aggression in a particular way from the behavior they see on television programs. (Imitation and modeling are discussed at length in Chapter 10.)

Social Learning and Cognition. Bandura (1986) has compiled an updated summary of social learning theories, which he now calls *social cognitive theory*. Cognition means thinking, and this name change reflects a new emphasis on thinking as part of learning. Social-learning theorists still talk about rewards and punishments, but they recognize that children observe their own behavior, the behavior of others, and the consequences of these behaviors. Children can also anticipate consequences based on past events. They form opinions about themselves and others and then behave in a fashion that is consistent with these opinions (Miller, 1989). This shift in emphasis by social-learning theorists has moved them away from their study of only observable behavior, making them similar to the cognitive theorists, whom we will also discuss.

The earlier extension of learning theory into such areas as *latent learning, incidental learning,* and *observational learning* by psychologists such as Sidney Bijou and Donald Baer, Albert Bandura and others helped to transform learning theory into social-cognitive theory. Latent learning is learning without reinforcement, which is performed later. Incidental learning refers to learning that is not related to a central task the subject is performing but which is, nonetheless, learned. Observational learning refers to learning by observing another perform a task and be reinforced for performing it, for example, the child who sees another child throw a tantrum and be rewarded with attention, is likely to exhibit the behavior later.

All three of these paradigms challenge traditional behaviorism. It is clear in each, for example, that the behaviors include the formation of an internal schema or plan. Moreover, the person involved in the learning has an idea or concept. The learning involved, therefore, occurs at a more complex level than pure stimulus-response association. This learning has created a bridge to the cognitive developmental perspective of Jean Piaget (Berlyne, 1962; Bolles, 1975), which we will discuss later in this chapter.

AN EVALUATION OF LEARNING THEORIES

Learning theories, including behaviorism, contemporary behavioral analysis, and social-learning theory, have made major contributions to our understanding of human development. These theories focus very closely on the situational factors that affect behavior. They specify the situation carefully and make predictions based on past research. In fact, their principles are probably more easily tested than those of any other theory. Some of their predictions have been demonstrated repeatedly. For instance, Skinner and his followers have shown that many types of behavior are indeed affected by reinforcement. Several techniques, such as modeling and various types of behavior modification, have been quite effective in changing behavior when skillfully applied in schools, weight-control programs, and homes for disturbed children.

Despite this precision, learning theorists may be attempting to explain too large an area of human development. For the most part, they have not paid enough attention to thought, emotions, personality, or the understanding of the self. They tend to seek universal processes and to ignore individual differences.

Finally, learning theorists have been baffled by one major human learning achievement. The laws of learning do not adequately account for the complex way in which young children learn a language. More than simple imitation and reward is involved in the development of language. It depends on a complex interaction of the individual child's emerging language-learning abilities and a multifaceted language environment. In explaining language development and the learning of other aspects of one's culture, learning theorists seem unable to describe and account for the complexity of the naturalistic setting. Their behavioral predictions work best in the laboratory, where it is possible to control the stimulus environment closely (Miller, 1989). Table 2–1 presents the key aspects of the behavioral theories.

TABLE 2–1 Key Aspects of the Behavioral Theories

➤ Behavioral theories stress that development follows the laws of learning and is determined largely by environmental events.

➤ Classical conditioning refers to involuntary responses elicited by some naturally occurring stimulus, which is then paired to another unrelated stimulus. Over the course of several pairings, the unconditioned response becomes conditioned to occur in the presence of the second, or conditioned, stimulus.

➤ It is likely that classical conditioning is involved in the learning of fears, emotional responses, and other similar behaviors. Classical conditioning has also been used to condition involuntary, or autonomic, nervous systems responses, such as blood pressure and skin temperature.

➤ The main proponent of modern behaviorism, B. F. Skinner, developed the notion of operant, or instrumental, conditioning.

➤ Skinner's theory states that behavior is a function of its consequences. Operant behaviors are controlled by what follows them.

➤ Reinforcers are stimuli that increase the probability of occurrence of the responses they follow.

➤ Stimuli can be physical, chemical, organismic, or social. They have a measurable impact on behavior.

➤ Skinner developed several innovative methodologies and instruments, including the operant conditioning chamber. He also attempted to apply his principals to both laboratory and real life settings.

➤ Operant conditioning procedures have been very useful in child-raising, education, and clinical practice settings.

COGNITIVE THEORIES

The empirical approach of the learning theorists is considered by some psychologists to be a "typically American" practice. In contrast to it is the comprehensive approach of the eminent Jean Piaget (1896–1984), a Swiss, who dared to weave a complex integrative theory and later test its parts.

Unlike early learning theorists, who saw human beings as passive machines acted upon by the environment, cognitive theorists see human beings as rational, active, alert, and competent. For them, human beings do not merely receive information—they also process it. Thus, each person is a thinker and a creator of his or her reality. People do not simply respond to stimuli—they also give such stimuli structure and meaning. For most cognitive theorists, development consists in the evolving of mental structures or ways of processing information which are in part genetically preprogrammed and based on maturity. These theorists therefore study stage-related or *qualitative* transformations in behavior that occur as the individual grows and matures. Typically, they study qualitative change by observing problem solving during transitional points in development.

Cognitive theorists have appeared relatively recently on the American psychological scene, but their European roots are very old. The European rationalist tradition manifests a respect for the mind and for mental organizing principles. Learning theorists, such as Watson, advised psychologists to ignore such mental concepts because they can not be scientifically observed. Although by no means ignoring behavior, the cognitive theorists have sparked a renewed interest in the mind. They have encouraged research to determine what is in the mind and how the mind develops.

PIAGET

Jean Piaget was a theorist interested in cognitive development. Piaget's interests in the mind were first biological and then philosophical. Because of these interests he decided to integrate biology and epistemology (the field of philosophy that studies the origins of knowledge) in his theory, which is called *genetic epistemology,* that is, the developmental origins of knowledge. Because of his focus, Piaget restored the biological model to psychology. To Piaget, the mind, like any other living structure, does not simply respond to stimuli—it grows, changes, and adapts to the world. Piaget and other cognitive psychologists have been called **structuralists** because they are concerned with the structure of thought (Gardner, 1973b). Three major cognitive theorists are Piaget, Jerome Bruner, and Heinz Werner; here we shall focus on Piaget.

Piaget's investigations grew out of his work with Simon and Binet at their lab in Paris, where he worked on the development of standardized versions of the IQ test which they had developed. The French government had commissioned these two psychologists to create a standardized test to determine the intelligence of school children. While testing children, Piaget became less interested in their right answers than in patterns he found in their wrong answers. These patterns seemed to provide a clue to the way thought processes develop in children. He theorized that the differences between children and adults were not confined to how much they knew, but the *way* they knew. Qualitative as well as quantitative

structuralism A branch of psychology concerned with the structure of thought and the ways in which the mind processes information.

In Piaget's conservation experiment, a child is shown liquid from two identical glasses poured into a short, wide glass and a tall, narrow glass. When asked which has more or less, children under 6 say that the tall glass holds more.

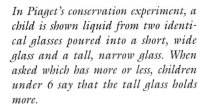

conservation A cognitive ability described by Piaget as central to the concrete operational period. The child is able to judge changes in amounts based on logical thought instead of mere appearances; thus, she judges that an amount of water will remain the same even when it is poured into a glass of a different shape and size.

differences separated the thinking of children from that of adults. It was at this point that he began to diverge from the quantitative, or psychometric, approach to intelligence.

Piaget's approach to intelligence is quite different from the IQ-testing approach with which we are all familiar. Piaget and his colleagues felt that standardized questions frequently led to stereotyped and uninteresting answers. He therefore proposed the use of clinical or probing interview techniques. Such an interview approach reveals the thought processes tapped by a child or adolescent in answering a question rather than the specific knowledge the child has accumulated. The interview accomplishes this by requiring the child to either answer questions or manipulate materials. From interviews, Piaget concluded that logic models can be used to describe the development of integrated thought processes in children.

To illustrate his theory, Piaget devised one of his most famous problems to test **conservation.** Conservation was Piaget's term for the awareness that physical quantities remain constant despite changes in their shape or appearance. In this test, he showed a child two identical glasses, each containing the same amount of liquid. After the child agreed that the amount of liquid in each glass was the same, Piaget poured the liquid from one of the glasses into a tall, narrow glass. He then asked the child how much liquid was in the tall glass—was it more or less than in the original glass, or was it the same amount? Most children aged 6, 7, or older answered that the amount was the same. But children under 6 said that the tall glass held more. Even when these younger children watched the same liquid being poured back and forth between the original glass and the tall glass, they said that the tall glass held more. This experiment has been tried with children of many cultures and nationalities, and the results are nearly always the same.

Piaget reasoned that until they reach a certain stage, children form judgments based more upon perceptual than upon logical processes. In other words, they believe what their eyes tell them. To the younger children, the liquid rose up higher in the tall glass, so there was more of it. Children 6 years or older, on the other hand, barely glanced at the glasses. They knew that the amount of liquid remained the same, regardless of the size or shape of the glass it was in. When children demonstrated this ability, they were said to be able to conserve. They did not base their judgments solely on perception; they also used logic. Their knowledge came from within themselves, as much as from outside sources.

THE ACTIVE MIND   According to Piaget, the mind is neither a blank slate on which knowledge can be written nor a mirror that reflects what it perceives. If the information, perception, or experience presented to a person fits with a structure in his or her mind, then that information, perception, or experience is "understood"—it is assimilated. If it does not fit, the mind rejects it (or if the structure is ready to change, it changes itself to accommodate the information or experience). According to Piaget then, **assimilation** is interpreting new experiences in terms of existing mental structures, without changing them. **Accommodation,** on the other hand, is changing existing mental structures to integrate new experiences.

Piaget proposed a biological model to describe the process by which we adapt to the world. An animal that is eating does two things. It accommodates to the food with a change in the digestive system that produces enzymes and begins the necessary muscular activity. It also assimilates the food, making it part of itself. Human beings gain intelligence, said Piaget, in the same way.

Piaget used the word **scheme** (sometimes translated from the French as "schema," or the plural, "schemata") to designate a mental structure. We shall use the simpler term, *scheme* and *schemes,* here. Schemes are ways of processing information, and they change as we grow and learn more. There are two types of schemes: sensorimotor schemes, or actions, and cognitive schemes, which are like concepts. We adjust our schemes to accommodate new information, but, we simultaneously assimilate new learning into old schemes. On seeing a new object for the first time, we try to fit it into what we know. Is it a weapon? A grooming tool? A cooking implement? If it does not fit our existing concepts (if we cannot assimilate it), we may have to change our concepts or form a new concept (accommodation).

The mind always tries to find a "balance" between assimilation and accommodation, to eliminate inconsistencies or gaps between reality and its picture of reality. This process, called **equilibration,** is basic to human adaptation and, indeed, to all biological adaptation. But then, for Piaget, the growth of intelligence is merely an important example of biological adaptation. Piaget believed that these *invariant functions* of adaptation, assimilation, and accommodation form the basis of the human intellectual adaptation to the environment that allows our species to survive.

PIAGET'S STAGES OF COGNITIVE DEVELOPMENT   The process of intellectual development for Piaget proceeds in this manner. Schemes are organized into operations, which combine to form the qualitatively different stages of cognitive growth which, according to Piaget, occur during the process of development. Therefore, as human beings develop, they use more complex schemes to organize information to understand the outside world. Piaget saw this develop-

assimilation In Piaget's theory, the process of making new information part of one's existing schemata.

accommodation Piaget's term for the act of changing our thought processes when a new object or idea does not fit our concepts.

scheme Piaget's term for mental structures that process information, perceptions, and experiences; individuals' schemes change as they grow.

equilibration Piaget's term for the basic process in human adaptation. In it, individuals seek a balance, or fit, between the environment and their own structures of thought.

ment in four discrete and qualitatively different stages. We may see these stages outlined in Table 2–2.

Piaget's four stages of cognitive development are: the sensorimotor stage (birth to approximately 2 years of age), the preoperational stage (2 years to approximately 7 years), concrete operations (7 years through 11 or 12 years) and formal operations (beginning at age 12 or later).

Infants use comparatively few schemes, many of which involve actions such as looking, grasping, and mouthing. The first period of development is therefore called **sensorimotor** because infant intelligence relies on the senses and on bodily motion for equilibration.

A second stage begins about the time that children start to talk. The **preoperational period** is the time when children know about the world primarily through their own actions. They do not hold broad, general theories about block buildings, grandmothers, or dogs, but they build up specific knowledge about their blocks, their grandmothers, or their dogs. Preoperational children do not make generalizations about a whole class of objects (for example, all grandmothers), and they cannot think through the consequences of a particular chain of events. At the beginning of this stage especially, children will take names so seriously that they cannot separate their literal meanings from the things they represent. If a child decides that a wad of paper is the cake to be served at a party, and the mother unwarily throws the paper "cake" into the garbage, it may be just as upsetting to him as it would be to a bride if someone threw away her wedding cake. At that age the child cannot tell the difference between the symbol and the object for which it stands. By the

TABLE 2–2 Piaget's Stages of Mental Development

STAGE	AGE	ILLUSTRATIVE BEHAVIOR
Sensorimotor	birth to 18 months or 2 years	Infants know the world only by looking, grasping, mouthing, and other actions.
Preoperational	approximately 2 to 7 years	Young children form concepts and have symbols such as language to help them communicate. These images are limited to their personal (egocentric), immediate experience. Preoperational children have very limited, sometimes "magical" notions of cause and effect and have difficulty classifying objects or events.
Concrete operations	approximately 7 to 11 years	Children begin to think logically, classify on several dimensions, and understand mathematical concepts, provided they can apply these operations to concrete objects or events. Concrete operational children achieve conservation.
Formal operations	beginning at 12 years and beyond	Individuals can explore logical solutions to both concrete and abstract concepts: They can systematically think about all possibilities, project into the future or recall the past, and reason by analogy and metaphor.

sensorimotor period Piaget's first stage of cognitive development, lasting from birth to about 2 years. Infants use action schemes—looking, grasping, and so on—to learn about their world.

preoperational period Piaget's second stage of cognitive development (about 2 to 7 years) begins when children are able to use symbols such as language. Their thinking tends to be overly concrete, irreversible, and egocentric, and classification is difficult for them.

end of this period, however, the child has learned that language is arbitrary and that a word can just as easily represent one object as another.

In the next stage of **concrete operations,** children begin to think with some logic. They can classify things and deal with a hierarchy of classifications. They understand mathematical concepts and the principle of conservation. Preoperational children, for example, may have difficulty understanding that a particular animal can be both a "dog" and a "terrier." They can only deal with one classification at a time. But 7-year-olds understand that terriers are a smaller group within the larger group, dogs. They can also see other subgroups, such as terriers and poodles as "small dogs" and golden retrievers and St. Bernards as "large dogs." This kind of thinking shows an understanding of a hierarchy of classification. During the concrete operational period, children master several such logical operations before their thinking is qualitatively like that of adults.

The final stage in Piaget's theory is called **formal operations.** At this point, adolescents can explore all the logical solutions to a problem, imagine things contrary to fact, think realistically about the future, form ideals, and grasp metaphors that younger children cannot comprehend. Formal operational thinking no longer needs to be tied to actual physical objects or events. It allows the individual to ask for the first time "what if" questions..."what if I were to say this to that person?" It allows them to "get inside the head" of other persons and take on their roles or ideals.

PIAGET'S NOTION OF DEVELOPMENT: AN OVERVIEW Piaget believed that intelligence is an example of biological adaptation. It evolves gradually in qualitatively different steps, the result of countless assimilations and accommodations, while the individual attempts to reach new balances. The mind is active, not passive. Piaget's theory stresses the interaction between the biological capacities of each person and the materials encountered in the environment. We all develop through this interaction.

Can the stages of development be speeded up so that, for example, a bright 5-year-old can be taught concrete operations? Piaget called this the "American question" because someone asked it every time he visited the United States. His answer was that even if this were possible, its long-term value was doubtful. Instead, he stressed the importance of giving each child enough learning materials appropriate to each stage of growth, so that no areas of the mind are left undeveloped. Table 2–3 summarizes the key points of the cognitive developmental theory of Piaget.

INFORMATION-PROCESSING THEORY

Piaget has many critics; among them are the *information-processing theorists.* Like Piaget, they are cognitive psychologists because they study thought and the mind. Unlike Piaget, they are skeptical of a theory based on qualitatively different stages. They believe human development, including human cognitive development, is a continuous, incremental progression, not a discontinuous one. These theorists resemble learning theorists because they, too, are trying to develop a science of human behavior. They want to identify basic processes like perception, attention, or memory and to describe precisely how these processes function.

concrete operations Piaget's third stage of cognitive development (7 to 11 years). Children begin to think logically. At this stage, they are able to classify things and deal with a hierarchy of classifications.

formal operations The fourth, and final, stage of Piaget's cognitive theory; it begins at about 12 years and is characterized by the ability to handle abstract concepts.

TABLE 2–3 Key Aspects of Piaget's Theory of Development

➤ Piaget's theory is based on the belief that the child is active, rather than merely reactive, in the process of development.

➤ Development is a biologically based process that results in the addition, modification, and reorganization of psychological structures.

➤ The basic unit of study for Piaget is the scheme. This is a flexible structure which can change quantitatively and qualitatively as the child grows. Schemes are originally sensorimotor but later become cognitive.

➤ Piaget believed that intelligence is a particular example of biological adaptation. He postulates functional invariants which all humans possess—organization and adaptation.

➤ Adaptation is comprised of two complementary processes: assimilation, by which the individual takes information into already existing structures, and accommodation, by which the existing structures are modified to meet the demands of the changing environment.

➤ Piaget postulated that cognitive development is a progression through a series of four qualitatively different stages: the sensorimotor, preoperational, concrete operational, and formal operational stages.

Humans constantly process information. We selectively attend to something—perhaps the letters on this page. We translate the letters into words and the words into ideas. We then store these ideas for later reference. Many information-processing theorists have therefore used the computer as a model of the human brain. The computer has "hardware"—the machine itself—and "software"—the programs that instruct its operation. The mind also has hardware—the cells and organs of the brain—and software—the learned strategies for processing information. The computer must process "input," perform certain operations on the information, store it, and generate "output." The mind, too, must selectively attend and perceive, then associate, compute, or otherwise "operate" on the information. Routinely, information must be stored in the memory and later retrieved. Finally, output in the form of responses—words and actions—must be generated.

Some information-processing theorists have turned their attention to children as a way of studying how these processes develop. Some have been particularly interested in a cognitive activity that they call *encoding*. This is the process of identifying key aspects of an object or event in order to form an internal representation of the event (Siegler, 1986). This internal representation is something like Piaget's "mental image." One developmental question might be: Do children of different ages select different aspects or fewer aspects of an event or object to store in a mental image? Do they select different strategies for encoding or retrieving information? *Retrieval* is the process of receiving information from memory stores.

There are numerous studies on the information-processing capabilities of infants, children, and adolescents. We will be looking at several of these studies throughout the book. Only in recent years have information theorists designed these studies to examine the question of how information processing develops or, in the words of some, how the "computer" reprograms itself to work with new material (Klahr, Langley, & Necher, 1987).

According to Piaget, children learn by actively exploring what is in their environment. If the information obtained fits children's existing concepts, it is assimilated.

COGNITIVE DEVELOPMENT IN SOCIAL CONTEXT   For Piaget, the image of the child is one of an "active scientist" who interacts with her physical environment and forms increasingly complex thought strategies. This active, constructing child seems to be working alone at problem solving. Increasingly, however, psychologists are recognizing that the child is a social being who plays and talks with others and learns from this interaction (Bruner & Haste, 1987). In the psychologist's lab, children may work alone at solving the problem that is given to them by the researcher. Yet, outside of the lab, children will experience real events in the company of adults and older, more experienced peers who will translate or make sense of these events for them. Thus, children's cognitive development is an apprenticeship in which they are guided in their understanding and skill by more knowledgeable companions (Rogoff, 1990). In fact, these more advanced companions, parents, teachers, and others produce disequilibrium in the child's thinking which challenges the child to adopt more complex thought patterns.

VYGOTSKY   The roots of this branch of cognitive psychology are to be found in the work of a noted Russian scholar, Lev Vygotsky (1896–1934). Americans have rediscovered Vygotsky during the past two decades, both revising and expanding his work. Vygotsky was interested not only in the development of the individual mind in social context, but also in the historical development of the community's knowledge and understanding. The central question for him was: How do we, collectively, make sense of our world? He tried to incorporate aspects of sociology, anthropology, and even history to improve his understanding of individual development. Vygotsky concluded that we make sense of our world only by learning the *shared meanings* of others around us.

Together, people construct shared meanings, and these shared meanings are passed down from generation to generation. This is true of simple things like learning how to cook or play sports in the particular style of one's culture. This is also true of more complicated things like the systematic learning of history, math-

Vygotsky believed that adults and older, more experienced peers act as guides by helping children develop their understanding and skills.

ematics, literature, and social customs. We develop understanding and expertise primarily in an apprenticeship with more knowledgeable learners. We are allowed to participate and are guided in this participation, which enables us to understand more and more about our world and to develop an increasing number of skills.

For Vygotsky, a truly interesting questions was: How does the child become what he is not yet? To look at this problem, he defined two levels of cognitive development. The first was the child's actual developmental level as determined by his independent problem solving. The second was the level of potential development determined by the kind of problem solving the child could do under adult guidance or in collaboration with a more capable peer (Vygotsky, 1978). Vygotsky called the distance between these two points the *zone of proximal development* (Rogoff & Wertsch, 1984). He illustrated this concept by studying two children who, on an intelligence test, each had a mental age of 7 years. One child, with the help of leading questions and demonstrations, could easily solve the test items 2 years above his actual level of development. However, the other child, even with guidance and demonstration, could only solve problems a half-year ahead of his actual development. Vygotsky emphasized that we need to know both the *actual and the potential levels of development* in these children to understand fully their cognitive development and to design instruction for them (Vygotsky, 1956).

For Vygotsky and his followers, cognitive development is embedded in life's social and cultural context. The child's best performance demonstrates that what he knows comes from a collaboration with more competent peers or with adults. Barbara Rogoff (1990) describes this process as an "apprenticeship in thinking." Children and other inexperienced learners are allowed *guided participation* in culturally valued activities. The caregivers and companions in these activities structure the child's participation while providing support and a challenge. They build bridges from the child's present understanding to new understanding and skills—thereby gradually increasing the child's participation and responsibility. In short, to understand the child's cognitive development, we must examine the processes that exist in the *social construction of knowledge*.

AN EVALUATION OF COGNITIVE THEORIES

Cognitive theorists criticize learning theory. They find that the emphasis on "repeated practice" and positive reinforcement is too simplistic to explain much of human thought and understanding. According to this view, when people solve problems, they are motivated by their own basic competence, not by a mere stimulus-response reinforcement (Bruner & Haste, 1987).

Cognitive theories respect human rationality and project an optimism absent from learning theories. They consider the human being of any age to be an integrated person who can plan and think through a problem. In addition, they allow us to account for the role that understanding, beliefs, attitudes, and values seem to play in so much of behavior. Many psychologists feel that cognitive theories, in dealing with language and thought, begin where learning theories end.

Cognitive theories have been widely applied to education. They have been especially useful in helping educators plan instruction to fit children's stages of development (see the box "Piaget in the Preschool"). The theories suggest ways to determine when a child is ready for a certain subject and which approaches to it are most appropriate for a specific age. Donaldson (1979), however, suggests that Piaget may have been too distinct in his stages of development, which may make educators too rigid in their ideas of what children can understand.

Cognitive theories are concerned mainly with intellectual development, and thus far they have been unable to explain all of human behavior. Some key areas still to be investigated include social, emotional, and personality development. Although cognitive theorists look chiefly at the development of perceptual abilities, language, and complex thought, they have not yet explored the individual's potentialities for dependence, nurturance, aggression, and sexuality. Psychoanalytic theory has traditionally been concerned with these areas, studying emotions and their relation to personality development.

THE PSYCHOANALYTIC TRADITION

The theories of Sigmund Freud, the neo-Freudians, and the ego psychologists form what we call the **psychoanalytic tradition.** The driving force behind this tradition was the work of Sigmund Freud. The source of data for these theories has been primarily clinical case-study material. Freud's notion of human nature is a deterministic one, resembling the view of the learning theorists, but it emphasizes the determinism of innate drives instead of the determinism of the environment. According to psychoanalytic theory, human beings are driven creatures, constantly trying to redirect or channel potent inner forces. These forces, evident from childhood, are transformed as individuals develop various forms of behavior. The psychoanalytic theories therefore propose that personality development has

psychoanalytic tradition Based on the theories of Freud, whose view of human nature was deterministic. He believed that personality is motivated by innate biological drives.

FOCUS ON AN ISSUE

PIAGET IN THE PRESCHOOL

George Forman and Fleet Hill (1980) have used Piaget's theories to design toys for use in the preschool. The Silhouette Sorter is one of these toys. It is a sorting box designed to improve upon commercially made sorting boxes. A commercially made sorting box consists of a box with various shaped holes cut in it and various shaped blocks to be put through the appropriate holes. These sorting boxes do not encourage children to think about how shapes can change.

The Silhouette Sorter is a box with three holes and one block. Each hole shows a different perspective of the block. In the photo, the child is placing an animal-shaped block through a hole shaped at the side silhouette of the block. The top of the box shows a top silhouette of the same animal-shaped block; the rear of the box has a rear silhouette of the same block. While playing

---

"The Silhouette Sorter is a box with three holes and one block. Each hole shows a different perspective of the block."

---

with the Silhouette Sorter, the child learns that the identity of the animal-shaped block stays the same, whereas the shape or perspective of that block can change.

Some of the points that educators stress when applying the theories of Piaget include the following:

1. Children need to learn through experience.

2. Children need cognitive conflict as part of the process of equilibration.

3. Children need an open environment in which they can pose and test their questions.

4. Children should be helped to construct relationships between objects and the forms the objects can take (Forman & Fosnot, 1982).

The use of the Silhouette Sorter and similar toys helps address these points by providing children with the learning experiences they need to think about objects and their environment.

FIGURE 2–4
The Unconscious.
Freud believed that potent inner forces determine human behavior.

strong ties to the physical maturation of the body. Modern psychologists of the psychoanalytic tradition, such as Erik Erikson, no longer see animal drives, such as sex and aggression, as the sole basis for human behavior, but they still draw heavily from the traditions of Freud and the neo-Freudians.

FREUD

Sigmund Freud (1856–1939), the founder of modern psychoanalysis, was born in Vienna, and conducted most of his work in Europe. Freud's concern was human emotional life, as this was kept well hidden in the society in which he lived. Freud emphasized the unconscious as a determinant of behavior. He believed that the biological, or animal, drives, such as sex and aggression, were the primary forces behind human behavior. Freud's assertion that humans are biologically directed, along with his systematic study of the animal components of human nature, were significant historically in opening the way for a scientific study of human behavior. Much of Freud's theory looked to childhood for clues about the underlying nature of the personality.

Freud's theory is divided into three components: the dynamic, which focuses on the action of psychic energy; the structural, which focuses on the elements of personality; and the sequential, which focuses on the manner in which instincts are gratified across the life cycle. With regards to the dynamic component, Freud believed that *psychic energy*, the energy that operates the different components of development, powered the instincts that drove the whole psychic system (Salkind, 1981; Freud, 1896/1950). These instincts consisted of *thanatos*, the death instinct, and *eros*, the life instinct.

Freud believed that death was unpredictable but was also the only absolute thing in existence. From his medical and biological training he concluded that there was constant conflict between the individual's basic tendency or push towards death and the erotic forces towards life, reproduction, and growth (Maddi, 1980).

The instinctual needs of organisms, according to Freud, are essentially asocial. Society thus attempts to control them. Since needs and goals are found mostly in the external, social world, a person must adapt to society. But that adaptation frequently has costs such as anxiety or neurosis. The drives are, in this case, transformed into slips of the tongue, humor, or dreams. Psychoanalytic theory posits that the early failures of adaptation have long-enduring results. This approach therefore concentrates on the early developmental history of individuals—the period between birth and five years of age—for clues to the underlying nature of the personality.

During the period between birth and entering school, much of the development of the personality occurs, according to Freud's theory. A child is born pure *id*, the primitive, hedonistic component personality structure. The id is based on the *pleasure principle*, that is, the id forces individuals to seek constant, immediate gratification of their impulses. As the child matures biologically, the *ego* develops. The ego is based on rational contact with the external world, or the *reality principle*. The ego encourages the individual to conform to society's directives and to learn to defer gratification in order to achieve broader social goals. Finally, between 3–6 years of age, the *superego* emerges. The superego is the "policeman," or conscience, that thereafter is constantly in conflict with the id, while the ego attempts to achieve a sense of balance for the personality.

According to Freud, the personality develops in several **psychosexual stages.** The first three stages occur well before puberty: In them, children focus their pleasure in different body **erogenous zones.** The **oral stage** is the first, and it occurs in early infancy. Here the child's mouth becomes the center of sensual stimulation and pleasure; infants love to suck things and mouth toys. Later, during the **anal** (ages 1 to 3) and the **phallic stages** (ages 3 to 5), the focus of pleasure moves from the mouth to the genital area.

If children experience too much frustration or too much gratification at any psychosexual stage, they may become fixated on the needs of that stage. Furthermore, the parents' reactions to any of these stages may profoundly affect the child's personality development. For example, if parents are too harsh in treating mistakes in toilet training during the anal stage, the child may develop into a compulsively neat and overcontrolled adult. Parents' reactions at the phallic stage are also critical. At this stage, children generally feel a strong but unconscious sexual attraction to the parent of the opposite sex. This is called the **Oedipal complex** in boys and the **Electra complex** in girls. (The term Electra complex was actually coined by Carl Jung.) Because such desires are clearly inappropriate, they result in anxiety. The child learns to suppress such feelings and reduce the anxiety

psychosexual stages Freud's stages of personality development.

erogenous zones Body areas that serve as the focus of pleasure and that, in Freud's view, change as one moves through the psychosexual stages.

oral stage Freud's first psychosexual stage, during which the infant's sensual pleasure focuses around the mouth.

anal stage Freud's second psychosexual stage, during which the child's sensual pleasure is related to the bodily processes of elimination. The child is concerned with issues of control, such as "holding on" and "letting go."

phallic stage Freud's third stage of psychosexual development (ages 3 to 5), during which the child's sensual pleasure focuses on the genitals.

Oedipal complex A strong but unconscious attraction of boys in the phallic stage to their mothers and their subsequent identification with their father because of their fear of his aggression toward them for this attraction.

Electra complex A strong but unconscious attraction of girls in the phallic stage to their fathers. This attraction culminates in the daughter's realization that she can never be like the father, so she comes to identify strongly with her mother.

by trying to become more like the parent of the same sex. This is known as **identification.**

The oral, anal, and phallic stages are part of the **pregenital period,** in which the child's sexual or sensual instincts are not yet directed toward reproduction. The **latency period,** lasting from about ages 6 to 12, is a time of relative calm. Girls play primarily with girls, boys play primarily with boys, and the focus is on acquiring knowledge and skills. Freud believed that latency was a period during which drives are directed toward the development of social skills and so sexual urges are unexpressed or nonexistent.

Freud's final stage of personality development is the **genital stage,** which begins during adolescence. Due to biological maturation, the old submerged sexual feelings—together with stronger physical drives—emerge. The goal of this stage is the establishment of a mature adult sexuality that will eventually be accompanied by biological reproduction. If things go well, the individual becomes capable of creating a mature balance between love and work. But this stage, like the others, is profoundly shaped by the resolution or lack of resolution of earlier stages. Unresolved earlier conflicts may reemerge periodically as adult neurotic behavior. We may see an overview of stages and possible personality fixations presented in Table 2–4. In Table 2–5 we can see the key aspects of psychoanalytic theory presented.

Freud's theory is far more complex than this short summary suggests. But instead of considering it in any more detail, we shall move on to the neo-Freudians, who have also had a great influence on modern psychology. One of the most interesting and important of the neo-Freudians is Erik Erikson.

identification Taking on the behaviors and qualities of a person whom one respects and would like to emulate.

pregenital period The immature psychosexual development of childhood; it encompasses the oral, anal, and phallic stages.

latency period The fourth of Freud's psychosexual stages of development, characterized by a temporary dormancy in the interest in sexual gratification.

genital stage In psychoanalytic theory, the period of normal adult sexual behavior that begins with the onset of puberty.

TABLE 2–4 An Overview of Freud's Psychosexual Stages

PSYCHOSEXUAL STAGES	ORAL	ANAL	PHALLIC	LATENCY	GENITAL
Approximate ages	Birth to 1 1/2 years	1 1/2 to 3 years	3 to 5 or 6 years	7 through 12 years or puberty	Puberty to death
Erogenous zone	Mouth	Anus	Penis or clitoris	None	Penis, clitoris or vagina
Typical activities	Sucking Biting	*Early* Feces interest Feces play Feces expulsion *Late* Feces retention	Interest in sex differences Masturbation Jealousy Imaginative play	Peer group play Education Skill learning	Interest in the opposite sex Masturbation Sexual experimentation Attempts at adult roles
Fixations	Overeating Overdrinking Smoking Overdependency	*Early* Messiness Rigidity Overscheduling Overneatness *Late* Stubbornness Hoarding Negativism	Sexual identity problems Guilt Preference for much older sex partners Homosexuality	None	None

TABLE 2–5 Summary of Key Aspects of Freud's Psychoanalytic Theory

> ➤ Freud introduced a systematic and global study of personality development.
>
> ➤ Freud's psychoanalytic model of development consists of dynamic, structural, and sequential components.
>
> ➤ Freud postulated that the primary sources of psychic energy derive from the instincts, which are, in turn, based on biological needs of the organism.
>
> ➤ The structural components of the personality consist of: the id, which is the primitive, hedonistic aspect of tension reduction; the ego, which results from the child's interaction with the environment; and the superego, which represents the internalized mores and rules of society.
>
> ➤ Freud postulated that personality development occurred in a sequence of five stages which were based on the erogenous zones of the body: the oral stage (birth to 1 1/2), the anal stage (1 1/2 to 3), the phallic stage (3 to 5 or 6), latency (7 to puberty), and the genital stage (puberty to death).

ERIKSON

Erik Erikson (1904–   ) is a third-generation Freudian. He was introduced into the Vienna Circle, the hand-picked training group for psychoanalysis, by Freud's daughter, Anna. He became a practitioner and originally treated children. Like many others, he left Vienna in the 1930s because of the negative political climate and emigrated to the United States. Erikson taught at the Menninger Foundation, Harvard University, and the University of California at Berkeley. In recent years he became interested in community psychology.

The theory of personality development Erikson developed has much in common with Freud's, but it is marked by some important differences. Erikson became disenchanted with psychoanalytic theory because he believed it dealt with extremes of behavior. He sees the development of the individual as occurring in several stages, many of which correspond to those of Freud. His model, however, is **psychosocial,** not psychosexual. In other words, Erikson believes that personality arises from the manner in which social conflict is resolved during key interaction points in development, for example, feeding during infancy and toilet training. This differs from Freud's emphasis on psychosexual maturation as the determinant of personality.

While Erikson agreed with Freud that early experiences were extremely significant, he saw personality development as a dynamic and continuing process from birth to death as can be seen in Table 2–6. He agreed with Freud that the gratification of instincts was the key force in life, but he saw *ego synthesis,* the ordering and integration of experience, as being equally significant.

Erikson extended Freud's theory of psychosexual development to include what he referred to as *psychosocial development.* This emphasized the cultural or social influences on development rather than the influence of pleasure derived from stimulation of the erogenous zones. The core concept of Erikson's theory is *the acquisition of ego identity,* which he believed was accomplished differently from culture to culture. Erikson believes that for today's youth, development of their ego identity, self-image, and self-concept is more important and has largely superceded Freud's theme of sexuality. Sexuality is important to Erikson, but as

psychosocial stages In Erikson's theory, the phases of development during which the individual's capacities for experience dictate major adjustments to the social environment and the self.

TABLE 2–6 Erikson's Stages of Psychosocial Development

	PSYCHOSOCIAL STAGE	TASK OR CRISIS	SOCIAL CONDITIONS	PSYCHOSOCIAL OUTCOME
Stage 1 (birth to 1 year)	Oral-sensory	Can I trust the world?	Support, provision of basic needs, continuity.	Trust
			Lack of support, deprivation, inconsistency	Distrust
Stage 2 (2 to 3 years)	Muscular-anal	Can I control my own behavior?	Judicious permissiveness, support	Autonomy
			Overprotection, lack of support, lack of confidence	Doubt
Stage 3 (4 to 5 years)	Locomotor-genital	Can I become independent of my parents and explore my limits?	Encouragement, opportunity	Initiative
			Lack of opportunity, negative feelings	Guilt
Stage 4 (6 to 11 years)	Latency	Can I master the skills necessary to survive and adapt?	Adequate training, sufficient education, good models	Industry
			Poor training, lack of direction and support	Inferiority
Stage 5 (12 to 18 years)	Puberty and adolescence	Who am I? What are my beliefs, feelings, and attitudes?	Internal stability and continuity, well-defined sex models, and positive feedback	Identity
			Confusion of purpose, unclear feedback, ill-defined expectations	Role confusion
Stage 6 (young adulthood)	Young adulthood	Can I give fully of myself to another?	Warmth, understanding, trust	Intimacy
			Loneliness, ostracism	Isolation
Stage 7 (adulthood)	Adulthood	What can I offer succeeding generations?	Purposefulness, productivity	Generativity
			Lack of enrichment, regression	Stagnation
Stage 8 (maturity)	Maturity	Have I found contentment and satisfaction through my life's work and play?	Sense of closure, unity, direction	Ego-integrity
			Lack of completeness, dissatisfaction	Despair

Source: Erikson, 1950.

only one of a series of developmental issues to be resolved. We can see the theories of Freud and Erikson contrasted in Table 2–7.

Erikson's stages expand upon the drives within the individual and the way in which these forces are treated by parents and others in society. In addition, Erikson sees the stages as periods of life during which the individual's capacities for experience dictate that he must make a major adjustment to the social environment and the self. Although parental attitudes do affect the way the individual handles these conflicts, the social milieu is extremely important, too. (A good example is the *identity crisis* of many Native Americans today who are confused about the society to which they belong.) Erikson's model expands upon Freud's in another key way. Erikson's eight stages of development encompass all ages of human life.

Erikson's book *Childhood and Society* (1963) presents his model of the eight stages of human development. In Erikson's view, everyone experiences eight crises or conflicts in development. The adjustments a person makes at each stage

TABLE 2–7 Comparison of Freud's and Erikson's Stages of Development

AGE	ERIKSON	FREUD
Birth to 1 year	Trust vs. mistrust	Oral stage
1 to 3 years	Autonomy vs. shame and doubt	Anal stage
4 to 5 years	Initiative vs. guilt	Phallic stage
6 to 11 years	Industry vs. inferiority	Latency stage
Early adolescence	Ego identity vs. ego diffusion	Genital stage
Late adolescence, early adulthood	Intimacy vs. isolation	
Adulthood	Generativity vs. self-absorption	
Late adulthood	Integrity vs. despair	

can be altered or reversed later on. For example, children who are denied affection in infancy can grow to normal adulthood if they are given extra attention at later stages of development. But adjustments to conflicts do play an important part in the development of personality. The resolution of these conflicts is cumulative—that is, a person's manner of adjustment at each stage of development affects the way he or she handles the next conflict.

According to Erikson, specific developmental conflicts become critical at certain points in the life cycle. During each of the eight stages of personality development, a specific developmental task or conflict will be more significant than any other. Yet, although each conflict is critical at only one stage, it is present throughout life. For instance, autonomy needs are especially important to toddlers, but throughout life people must continually test the degree of autonomy they can express in each new relationship. As presented, these stages are extremes. No one will actually become entirely trusting or mistrustful; rather, people will develop varying degrees of trust or mistrust throughout life. Following is a more detailed description of the eight stages.

1. *Trust versus mistrust* From early caregiving, infants learn about the basic trustworthiness of the environment. If their needs are met, if they receive attention and affection and are handled in a reasonably consistent manner, they form a global impression of a trustworthy and secure world. If, on the other hand, their world is inconsistent, painful, stressful, and threatening, they learn to expect more of the same and believe life is unpredictable and untrustworthy.

2. *Autonomy versus shame and doubt* Toddlers discover their own bodies and how to control them. They explore feeding and dressing, toileting, and many new ways of moving about. When they succeed in doing things for themselves, they gain a sense of self-confidence and self-control. But if they fail continually and are punished or labeled messy, sloppy, inadequate, or bad, they learn to feel shame and self-doubt.

3. *Initiative versus guilt* Children at age 4 or 5 explore beyond themselves. They discover how the world works and how they can affect it. For them, the world consists of both real and imaginary people and things. If their explorations, projects, and activities are generally effective, they learn to deal

with things and people in a constructive way and gain a strong sense of initiative. Again, if they are criticized severely or punished, they learn to feel guilty for many of their own actions.

4. *Industry versus inferiority* During the years from 6 to 11, children develop numerous skills and competencies in school, at home, and in the outside world of their peers. According to Erikson, one's sense of self is enriched by the realistic development of such competencies. Comparison with peers is increasingly important. A negative evaluation of one's self compared to others is especially damaging at this time.

5. *Ego identity versus ego diffusion* Before adolescence, children learn a number of quite different roles—the role of student or friend, older brother, Christian, Italian, athlete, or the like. During adolescence, it is important to sort out and integrate these various roles into one consistent identity. Adolescents seek basic values and attitudes that cut across these various roles. If they fail to integrate a central identity or cannot resolve a major conflict between two major roles with opposing value systems, the result is what Erikson calls *ego diffusion*.

6. *Intimacy versus isolation* In late adolescence and young adulthood, the central developmental conflict is that of intimacy versus isolation. The intimacy that Erikson describes concerns more than sexual intimacy. It is an ability to share one's self with another person of either sex without fear of losing one's own identity. Success in establishing this intimacy will be affected by the resolution of the five earlier conflicts.

7. *Generativity versus self-absorption* In adulthood, after the earlier conflicts have, in part, been resolved, men and women are free to direct their attention more fully to the assistance of others. Parents sometimes find themselves by helping their children. Individuals can direct their energies without conflict to the solution of social issues. But failure to resolve earlier conflicts often leads to a preoccupation with one's self—with one's own health, psychological needs, comfort, and the like.

8. *Integrity versus despair* In the last stages of life, it is normal for individuals to look back over their lives and judge them. If one looks back over one's life and is satisfied that it has had meaning and involvement, then one has a sense of integrity. But if one's life seems to have been a series of misdirected energies and lost chances, one has a sense of despair. Clearly, this final resolution is a cumulative product of all the previous conflict resolutions.

The key aspects of Erikson's psychosocial theory are presented in Table 2–8.

AN EVALUATION OF THE PSYCHOANALYTIC TRADITION

Although the psychoanalytic tradition is often thought of in historical terms, it continues to make significant contributions to the study of human behavior. Its basic strength lies in the richness of its holistic approach: its willingness to look at the whole individual—including both conscious and unconscious mental activities—and to deal quite specifically with emotions. Its emphasis on unconscious processes allows it to explore important areas of human behavior that many other traditions barely touch. It is also a rich theory for dealing with interpersonal relationships, particularly the relationships of childhood and those in the primary family unit.

According to Erikson, school provides an environment for children to develop skills and competencies.

TABLE 2–8 Key Aspects of Erikson's Psychosocial Theory of Development

➤ Erikson postulates eight stages that focus on common developmental circumstances occurring during an individual's life.

➤ Each stage is marked by a psychosocial crisis that must be resolved.

➤ Psychological development results from an interaction between the individual's biological needs and societal demands.

➤ Erikson extended the scope of his theory beyond the early years to include young adulthood, middle age, and late life.

➤ The core unifying structure for the personality is the acquisition of ego identity.

➤ While both Freud and Erikson present theories derived from the psychoanalytic tradition, Freud's theory may be called *psychosexual,* while Erikson's is primarily *psychosocial.*

The basic weakness of psychoanalytic theory is inseparable from its strength. Although the theory explores the depths of personality, it is precisely this area that is almost impossible to define or to validate by experiment. The theory draws much of its data from case studies of adults who must subjectively reconstruct their childhoods. Psychoanalytic theory is therefore often described as unscientific, vague, and difficult to test.

HUMANISTIC PSYCHOLOGY AND THE SELF THEORIES

Humanistic psychology developed in the mid-twentieth century as a more optimistic *third force* in the study of personality (Maslow, 1968). It reacted against both the environmental determinism of learning theory and the Freudian determinism of the instincts. Humanistic psychology and the related *self theories* (which center on the individual's self-concept, the perception of personal identity) challenge deterministic learning and psychoanalytic theories. They point out that even those theorists like B.F. Skinner, who deny human freedom, continue to make choices and feel responsible for their actions in everyday life. The stated aim of these theories is to form a picture of human nature that is as close as possible to human experience—people who are more than the sum of the parts and more than a bundle of stimulus-response patterns or animal drives.

Humanistic psychology provides a holistic theory of personality and has close ties to existential philosophy. **Existentialism** is the branch of contemporary philosophy that focuses on an individual's struggle to find meaning in her existence and to exercise freedom and responsibility in the pursuit of an ethical life. Humanists, therefore, reject the determinism of drives, instincts, or environmental programming. They maintain that people can make choices about their own lives. They seek to maximize human potential.

Humans are set apart from other animals by their superior ability to use symbols and think in abstract terms. Although some of the higher primates, such as chimpanzees, are able to learn to employ symbols, their abilities in no way approximate the richness and flexibility of human language and abstract thought. For this reason, humanistic psychologists say that many experiments with other

humanistic psychology According to this theory, humans are spontaneous, self-determining, and creative; it has close ties with existentialism.

existentialism A twentieth-century branch of philosophy that focuses on an individual's struggle to find meaning in his or her existence and to exercise freedom and responsibility in the pursuit of an ethical life.

animals do not tell us much about people. A rat in a maze cannot conceptualize its problem as a human would.

Humanistic psychologists emphasize consciousness, as much as unconsciousness, as a basic human process. They reject the sharp division between the subjective and the objective in psychology. In their view, psychologists must realize that they, too, are subjects and objects of study. People experience themselves, as well as others, as spontaneously self-determining and creatively striving toward goals (May, 1983). This optimism of the humanistic psychologists is in marked contrast to most other theoretical approaches. Let's take a closer look at the humanistic views of Maslow and Rogers.

MASLOW

An important psychologist of the humanist school is Abraham Maslow. His theory of self, proposed in 1954, stresses each person's innate need for **self-actualization**—the full development of potentialities. According to Maslow, self-actualization needs can be expressed or satisfied only after "lower" needs, such as safety, love, food, and shelter, have been met. For example, a child who is hungry most of the day will not attend to reading or drawing in school until properly fed.

Maslow arranged human needs in a pyramid, as shown in Figure 2–5. At the bottom are the most basic physiological *survival needs;* human beings, just as other animals, must have food, warmth, and rest to survive. The next highest are *safety needs;* individuals need to avoid danger and feel secure in their daily lives. They cannot reach higher levels if they live in constant fear and anxiety. When reasonable safety and survival needs are assured, the next most pressing need is to *belong.* Human beings need to love and to feel loved, to be in physical contact with one

FIGURE 2–5
Maslow's Hierarchy of Needs Although higher needs are no less fundamental than lower needs, individuals must satisfy lower needs, such as those for survival and safety, before meeting those for belongingness and esteem. Later in life, adults must work out their needs for self-actualization in order to develop their fullest potential.

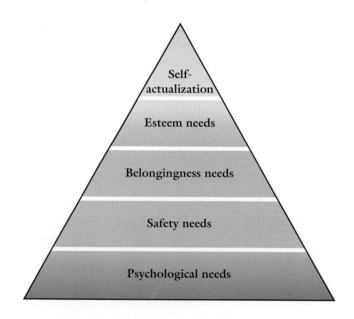

Maslow's theory of self-actualization stresses the importance of achieving the full development of one's potential. Maslow found that self-actualized people are motivated by values that extend beyond their personal needs.

another, to associate with others, and to participate in groups or organizations (May, 1983). Beyond this, they also need to feel *self-esteem;* they need positive responses from others, ranging from simple confirmation of basic abilities to acclamation and fame. All these provide a sense of well-being and self-satisfaction.

When people are fed, clothed, sheltered, established in a group, and reasonably confident in their abilities, they are ready to attempt the full development of their potential, or **self-actualization.** Maslow (1954, 1979) believed that the need for self-actualization was no less important to human nature than these other needs. "What a man can be, he must be." In a sense, the need for self-actu-

self-actualization Realizing one's full potential.

alization can never be entirely satisfied. It involves a "search for truth and understanding, the attempt to secure equality and justice, and the creation and love of beauty" (Shaffer, 1978).

Maslow found that self-actualized people tended to be older (most of the fully self-actualized people that Maslow studied were over age 60). They had satisfied their lower-level needs and now were motivated by values that extended beyond their own personal needs. They tended to be more spontaneous, creative, self-sufficient, and free of cultural stereotypes and limitations than others. Most had formed close relationships with a few friends and were open to others, but they frequently needed privacy and solitude (Maslow, 1968, 1979). Maslow also found that many self-actualized people have "peak experiences"—moments, or even extended periods, of joy from fulfillment and feelings of oneness with the universe.

ROGERS

Another humanistic psychologist, Carl Rogers, has had great influence among educators and psychotherapists. Unlike the Freudians, who believe that human nature is controlled by inner drives, many of them harmful, Rogers (1980) held that the core of human nature consists of positive, healthy, and constructive impulses that come into play from birth onward. Like Maslow, Rogers is primarily concerned with helping people realize their inner potential. But, unlike Maslow, Rogers did not first develop a theory of personality with definite stages and then apply it to his clients. He was more interested in whatever ideas arose first from his practice. He found that the greatest personal growth would occur if he was genuinely and totally involved with his clients and if his clients knew that he accepted them just as they were. He called this "warm, positive, acceptant" attitude **positive regard.** He felt that positive regard from the therapist would foster more self-accepting attitudes in the client and a greater tolerance and acceptance of others (May, 1983).

AN EVALUATION OF HUMANISTIC PSYCHOLOGY

Humanistic psychology has had an impact in several ways. It acts as a spur to other developmental psychology approaches, for it stresses the significance of keeping in touch with real life in all its richness. It has had considerable impact on the counseling of adults and on a generation of self-help programs. It has helped promote child-rearing approaches that respect the child's uniqueness and educational approaches that "humanize" the interpersonal relationships within schools (Weinstein & Alschuler, 1985).

As a scientific or developmental psychology, though, the humanistic perspective is limited. Concepts like self-actualization are loosely defined and not easily used in standard research designs. Furthermore, humanists have been incomplete in their description of these concepts as they apply to different points in the life span. Humanists can define developmental changes over the course of psychotherapy, but they have difficulty explaining normal human development over the course of a life span. The fact remains, however, that humanistic psychology has been an continuing influence in counseling and psychotherapy and

positive regard A "warm, positive, acceptant" attitude toward clients that Rogers found most effective in promoting personal growth.

TABLE 2–9 A Brief Summary of the Theories of Human Development

	ASSUMPTIONS ABOUT HUMAN NATURE	PROCESSES	DOMAINS
Learning theories (Skinner, Pavlov, Watson, Thorndike)	Human nature is neither good nor bad; people simply react and respond to their environment.	Respondent conditioning Operant conditioning Shaping	Behavior modification Conditioned emotional reactions
Cognitive theories (Piaget, Bruner)	Human beings are rational, alert, active, and competent. They do not merely receive information; they also process it.	Assimilation/accommodation Equilibration	Education Moral reasoning
The psychoanalytic tradition (Freud, Erikson)	Human beings are driven creatures, constantly trying to redirect or channel potent inner forces.	Psychosexual development Identification Accomplishment of developmental tasks	Study of human behavior personality, and interpersonal, relationships
Humanistic psychology and the self theories (Maslow, Rogers)	Human beings are more than the sum of their parts and more than a bundle of stimulus-response patterns or animal drives.	Self-actualization Positive regard	Counseling of adults

has provided an alternative holistic perspective that is critical of overly simplistic explanations of human thought and behavior. The various theories of human development are contrasted in Table 2–9.

ETHOLOGY

Ethology is a branch of biology that studies patterns of animal behavior. Among psychologists, it has stimulated a renewed interest in the biological characteristics that humans have in common with animals. Ethologists stress the importance of studying both people and animals in their natural settings. Just as ethologists choose to study the social relationships of baboons in the wild, not in a wire cage, they also insist upon observing children at play during a school recess, not in a contrived laboratory setting.

Ethologists use the same theoretical principles in studying the behavior of humans and animals. They see many similarities between animal and human behavior, and they believe that a similar evolutionary experience has preserved certain behavior traits in humans that are common to animals, too. Ethologists also propose that, like other animals, all human beings demonstrate *species-specific patterns of behavior* that are similar despite cultural differences. Even blind, deaf children smile and babble at the appropriate age, and they demonstrate pouting and laughing throughout their lifetime despite the absence of models to imitate (Eibl-Eibesfeldt, 1989).

The idea that social behavior is largely determined by an organism's biological inheritance is the major feature of **sociobiology,** a branch of ethology. Like ethologists, sociobiologists see similarities between animal and human behavior,

ethology The study of animal behavior, often observed in natural settings and interpreted in an evolutionary framework.

sociobiology A branch of ethology that holds the view that social behavior is largely determined by an organism's biological inheritance.

FOCUS ON RESEARCH

MEASURING ATTACHMENT

An important pattern of behaviors studied by ethologists is attachment. Attachment has been defined as a strong bond of affection between one person and another that connects them in space and time (Karen, 1990). Or we might say that attachment is a long-lasting love between two individuals who want to be together. The quality of an attachment indicates the character of a parent-child relationship and is a good predictor of a child's future behavior. For these reasons, researchers are very interested in measuring the attachment between infants and care-givers.

Attachment can be measured in a number of ways. The classic ethological studies of attachment were conducted by Mary Ainsworth in natural settings. While living in a village in Uganda, Ainsworth observed the way 28 pairs of mothers and infants related to each other. She noted when the babies cried, climbed on their mothers, clung to them, and wandered off on their

own. In turn, she also observed how the mothers reacted when their infants made demands.

"While living in a village in Uganda, Ainsworth observed the way 28 pairs of mothers and infants related to each other. She noted when the babies cried, climbed on their mothers, clung to them, and wandered off on their own."

Ainsworth studied the infant behaviors that "triggered" responses in the mothers and looked at how patterns of nurturance changed over the weeks and months (Ainsworth, 1973). But naturalistic observation has certain drawbacks. Because natural settings are generally uncontrolled from a scientific point of

view, it is difficult to draw firm conclusions from observations. Observed behavior may be open to several interpretations, and causal connections are virtually impossible to establish. For example, is a child's pattern of constant clinging to the mother the result of feelings of love or anxiety about the strange observer?

Laboratory experimentation, which provides a controlled environment for observation, usually offers firmer grounds for making inferences about cause and effect. When Ainsworth returned from Africa, she set up a laboratory experiment, combining aspects of both naturalistic and experimental methodology, known as the *strange situation test*. Her test functions much as a minidrama and is intended to measure the quality of mother-child attachment. The cast of characters in the test is a mother, her 1-year-old baby, and a stranger. The setting is an unfamiliar playroom that contains toys and the test extends

but they go further and claim that complex patterns of social behavior are genetically determined in both animals and humans (MacDonald, 1988; Wilson, 1975). To support this claim, sociobiologists cite examples of birds' nest-building—a complex pattern of behavior that birds play out at the right time without the benefit of learning. Sociobiologists generalize from this and other complex unlearned social patterns of insects, birds, and lower mammals to suggest a similar basis for human behavior patterns. They believe that many human behavior patterns that are used to express dominance, territoriality, nurturance, mating, and aggression show a thin veneer of learned culture on top of a genetically inherited biological pattern of behavior. This has caused vigorous debate among psychologists, most of whom say that human social behavior is learned.

The ethologist's interest in inherited behavior patterns resembles that of the psychoanalyst in drive theory, but there is major difference. The psychoanalyst

through eight scenes.

1. Mother and child enter the room.

2. The pair settle comfortably, and the infant is allowed to roam, explore, and play with the toys.

3. Next, an adult who is unknown to the child enters.

4. The mother leaves unobtrusively, and the adult and infant are now alone in the room.

5. After a few minutes, the mother returns and the stranger leaves.

6. Several minutes later the mother again leaves—this time the baby is alone in the room.

7. The stranger then returns to substitute for the mother.

8. As the mother returns, the stranger leaves.

The entire test runs for about 20 minutes and the interactions, especially the reactions of the infant, are observed through a one-way mirror (Ainsworth et al., 1979; Bretherton & Waters, 1985; Sroufe, 1985).

Prior to the strange situation test, researchers observe the mother and child in the home environment for an extended period. In this way, naturalistic home observations are coupled with more structured laboratory observations to reinforce or complement one another. Even though observation in a natural setting does not yield certainty or hard and fast conclusions, it does provide a realistic frame and often the initial hypothesis can lead to further and more exacting study. Frequently, initial hypotheses based on naturalistic observations are refined in the structured and controlled settings of laboratory experiments. But some laboratory settings may be too contrived or artificial; hence, precision may be gained at the expense of naturalness or reality. By joining field research with laboratory study, investigators hope to obtain the best of both worlds.

In her study, Ainsworth found three basic types of attachment. Between 60 percent and 70 percent of middle-class babies are securely attached. They can separate themselves fairly easily from their mothers, go exploring, and when their mothers are away from them, readily seek and find comfort with others if they need it. Most of the securely attached infants had warm, affectionate, and responsive interactions with their mothers in the 12 months prior to the tests. Follow-up studies indicate that securely attached children are more curious, sociable, independent, and competent than their peers at ages 2, 3, 4, and 5 (Matas et al., 1978; Sroufe et al., 1983; Waters et al., 1979).

Ainsworth found that about 32 percent of the infants were insecurely attached and that this insecure attachment took two forms. In one instance, a child avoided the mother upon her return during the strange situation test. This child was generally very angry. In another case during the test, a child responded ambivalently toward the mother by simultaneously seeking and rejecting affection. The insecurely attached children tended to be heavily dependent on authority figures as they grew older (Sroufe et al., 1983). (See Chapter 7 for further discussion of attachment behavior.)

Adapted from Ainsworth et al., 1979; Bretherton & Waters, 1985; Sroufe, 1985.

sees human drives as remnants of archaic, biological drives that must be restrained if civilization is not to be destroyed. Ethologists and sociobiologists say that such drives and their resulting behavior patterns may be an integral part of civilization itself. Perhaps the successful civilization is the one that does not attempt to restrict human biological heritage (Hess, 1970).

Ethology adds another important dimension of analysis. Most developmental psychologists look at the situational and historical causes of behavior. The ethologist sees these but considers an adaptive function as well—the function of the behavior for the preservation of the individual or the species. For example, a baby cries. The *situational cause* may be that the baby is in pain. The *historical cause* may be that the baby has been rewarded by care after crying in the past. The immediate function is to alert the mother and to "trigger" her nurturance. Crying is an innate behavior pattern directed toward the specific target of nurturance. Finally, the *evolutionary function* is survival of the infant despite its immobility, which makes crying, rather than running to the mother, a dominant response (Hess, 1970). Ethologists emphasize the evolutionary function of many behavior patterns, including things like adult responsiveness to creatures that look babyish, flirting behavior as part of a courtship pattern, or aggressive posturing as part of territorial defense (Bowlby, 1982; Eibl-Eibesfeldt, 1989). The seemingly universal as well as the culture-specific aspects of this behavior are analyzed.

Ethology's way of looking at human nature is making its mark on psychology. The process of infant-caretaker attachment has been extensively examined through this perspective (see the box "Measuring Attachment" in this chapter as well as the further discussion in Chapter 7). Numerous studies have been conducted on peer interaction, with a focus on dominance patterns in human groups. Ethologists suggest that a dominance hierarchy among children may decrease aggressive conflicts in the playground or in the ghetto, much as ethologists have found in other primate groups (Eibl-Eibesfeldt, 1989). Even cognitive development is examined by ethologists, but here they also pay considerable attention to the biological, species-specific component of learning and thinking. Ethologists suggest that the human brain is prepared for certain kinds of learning, but not for others. Complex learning, like that of language, may be done more easily in certain "sensitive periods" of development than it is in others (Bornstein, 1987). Even problem solving is influenced by the human brain's innate sensitivity to only certain aspects of a problem. Studies suggest that 4-year-olds solve problems in a trial-and-error fashion similar to the one used by chimpanzees. Yet, 8-year-old children in all cultures have distinctly human strategies for problem solving (Charlesworth, 1988).

In the 1990s, the research activities of ethologists, both in naturalistic settings and in the laboratory, are challenging and sometimes controversial.

 ## SUMMARY AND CONCLUSIONS

Everyone has a theory about human nature, but not everyone has considered the way in which human nature develops in all its complexity across a variety of domains. For this reason, we study many different theories to enlarge our perspective and to look for ways of integrating their diversity.

Behaviorism is a philosophy that underlies the learning theories. They are therefore based on the belief that the environment is the most significant factor in human development. In classical conditioning, for example, new stimuli are conditioned to be paired with established responses. It is believed that many of our emotional responses are learned in this manner. In operant conditioning, the behavior must occur before it can be strengthened by reinforcement. Much of operant conditioning has been applied to education and to behavior management programs. Social-learning theory applied learning principles to social behavior. Much of this learning occurs through the process of modeling and observation. In this way, children learn sex roles, social attitudes, and moral judgments according to the learning theorists. Overall, while learning theory has much practical utility, it does not explain many complex behaviors, such as language.

The cognitive theories see the mind as active, alert, and possessing innate structures that process and organize information. Piaget's theory of cognitive development is essentially an interactional model that sees intelligence as an example of adaptation to environmental demands. This adaptation occurs through the complementary processes of assimilation (bringing in information with existing structures) and accommodation (changing structures to meet environmental demands). For Piaget, mental structures called schemes form the basis for this incorporation of new knowledge.

Piaget proposed that cognitive development occurred in four stages: the sensorimotor, preoperational, concrete operational, and formal operational stages. In each of these, children use qualitatively different schemata to solve problems.

Information-processing theorists tend to be critical of Piaget's theory. They use computer models to study life-long mental processes such as attention, perception, and memory. They are not, like Piaget, looking for qualitative differences in cognition based on maturity. Vygotsky and his followers also have disagreements with Piaget's theory. Vygotsky tends to see cognitive development as being intrinsically embedded in the social and cultural context. Complex knowledge is therefore acquired by guided participation in culturally meaningful activities. While Piaget would not have disagreed with this, he would have emphasized maturational factors together with social factors as the determinants of cognition.

Freud's psychoanalytic theory is based on principles of determinism. In this theory, behavior and personality are controlled by innate sexual and aggressive drives. Personality develops in several psychosexual stages: the oral, anal, phallic, latency, and genital stages. During each stage, children must solve certain conflicts and reach a balance between frustration and gratification of their needs. The success or failure to resolve each stage will determine a child's future personality.

Erik Erikson disagreed with Freud about the importance of sexuality in determining personality. Erikson believed that the main motivation for personality development is the acquisition of an ego identity. He proposed that this identity seeking is a process that lasts from birth to death and occurs in eight psychosocial stages. The needs of each period are critical at different ages, but the needs are present throughout life.

Humanistic psychology and the self theories reject the determinism of psychoanalytic and learning theorists. These theories view children as being spontaneous, self-determining, and creative. Maslow proposed the concept of self-actualization, which is the development of inner, expressive needs by which humans strive toward a greater understanding of themselves and the world. Rogers, on the other hand, focuses on therapeutic growth through client-centered therapy. According to Rogers the goal of such therapy and personality in general is full development of human potential. Because of this, Rogers sees human nature as basically positive, healthy, and constructive. While criticisms have been made of humanistic psychology—in particular, against its lack of scientific evidence to support its beliefs—it is a growing and active force in developmental psychology.

Finally, ethology, the branch of biology that studies animal behavior, has contributed to developmental psychology. Ethologists study social behavior in natural settings and consider its adaptive function for individuals and groups. Sociobiologists have been criticized for assuming that complex human behavior is as genetically determined as some animal behavior.

The breadth and scope of those theories that address developmental questions is impressive. While none of them presents a comprehensive look at development in general, they all contribute to our greater understanding of the development of individual aspects such as cognition or personality. The future of developmental theories will undoubtedly see more attempts to integrate theories and to combine the biological and environmental components of behavioral determinism. In our following discussion of heredity and environment as they impact on development, we will begin to look at the ways in which this integration might occur.

➤ KEY TERMS AND CONCEPTS

accommodation	deterministic model	law of effect	psychosexual stages
anal stage	Electra complex	learning theory	psychosocial stages
assimilation	equilibration	mechanistic model	response consequences
avoidant conditioning	erogenous zones	Oedipal complex	scheme
behaviorists	ethology	operant conditioning	self-actualization
behavior modification	existentialism	oral stage	sensorimotor period
classical conditioning	formal operations	phallic stage	shaping
cognitive theory	genital stage	positive regard	sociobiology
concrete operations	humanistic psychology	pregenital period	stimulus generalization
conservation	identification	preoperational period	structuralism
counterconditioning	latency period	psychoanalytic tradition	systematic desensitization

➤ SELF-TEST QUESTIONS

1. When studying human development, why is it important to have a broad understanding of the various theories on the subject?

2. What are some of the basic assumptions about human behavior made by learning theorists?

3. Describe the process by which behaviorists attempt to build a "science of human behavior."

4. How would you compare classical and operant conditioning? Be sure to use key terms in formulating your answer.

5. How does behavior modification employ operant conditioning?

6. Explain how social-learning theorists have expanded the scope of learning theory.

7. How are the concepts of imitation and modeling employed in social-learning theory?

8. Explain information-processing theory. How is it similar to other learning theories?

9. What are some criticisms of learning theories?

10. How do cognitive theories differ from learning theories?

11. Describe Piaget's conservation experiment. What is the significance of its results?

12. What does Piaget mean by the "active mind"?

13. Describe Piaget's stages of cognitive development, including his use of schemes, assimilation, accommodation, and equilibration.

14. Compare Vygotsky's contributions to cognitive theory with those of Piaget.

15. What are some limitations of cognitive theories?

16. List some of Freud's assumptions about personality development.

17. Describe Freud's theory of psychosexual stages.

18. How is Erikson's theory of personality development distinguished from Freud's?

19. Name the developmental conflicts which, according to Erikson, become critical at certain points in the life cycle. Discuss the outcomes of these conflicts.

20. What are the strengths and weaknesses of the psychoanalytic tradition?

21. How are humanistic psychology and the related *self theories* distinguished from the theories previously discussed?

22. Explain Maslow's hierarchy of needs.

23. What are some criticisms of humanistic psychology?

24. What contributions has the field of ethology made to the study of human development?

➤ SUGGESTED READINGS

BAKER, B.L., & BRIGHTMAN A.J. *Steps to independence: A skills training guide for parents and teachers of children with special needs,* 2nd ed. Baltimore: Paul H. Brookes Publishing Company, 1989. The basic principles of behavioral analysis are presented in a humane and engaging fashion and in lay terms for use by parents and teachers.

BRUNER, J., & HASTE, H. *Making sense: The child's construction of the world.* London: Methuen, 1987. A slim volume packed full of children's language, problem solving, and social interaction from the perspective of cognitive theorists concerned about the social context of learning.

EIBL-EIBESFELDT, I. *Human ethology.* New York: Aldine DeGruyter, 1989. This compendium of research and related ethological interpretation of human behavior is well worth a few hours of exploration.

KEGAN, R. *The evolving self: Problem and process in human development.* Cambridge, MA: Harvard University Press, 1982. Kegan integrates aspects of several theories—Piaget, Kohlberg, Maslow, Erikson, and others—to define more fully the continued personality development that extends well into adulthood. Although somewhat difficult for the novice, this is probably a landmark theoretical piece for understanding adolescence and adulthood.

LORENZ, K. *King Solomon's ring.* New York: Crowell, 1952. Lorenz, a popular ethologist, provides fascinating descriptions of the ways and habits of various animals and birds. His accounts are humorous, affectionate, and provocative.

MILLER, P. *Theories of developmental psychology,* 2nd ed. New York: W.H. Freeman, 1989. Miller provides an excellent overview of the major developmental theories as well as a useful discussion of the role of theories in developmental psychology.

ROGERS, C.R. *On becoming a person*. Cambridge, MA: Riverside Press, 1961. In very readable style, Rogers presents a perceptive and hopeful model for personal growth throughout the life span.

ROGOFF, B. *Apprenticeship in thinking: Cognitive development in social context*. 2nd ed. New York: Oxford University Press, 1990. An engaging yet scholarly integration of cross-cultural theory and research on the social construction of children's thinking as they participate in cultural activities.

VIDEO CASE: HELPING ABUSED AND NEGLECTED CHILDREN

Most child study experts agree that children who have been abused and neglected have a greater potential than other children to become juvenile deliquents and adult criminals. Is there anything that society can do to change their destiny? One program in Montana attempts to do this with out-of-control abused children. What makes this program in a place called Intermountain unusual is that it relies on personal contact rather than punishment in dealing with such children.

Who goes to Intermountain? Mainly, they are children who would normally be placed in foster care, but because they are so violent, even experienced foster parents are unable to control them. One resident is nine-year-old David who during toddlerhood was left alone in a crib filled with cats in a dark basement. At 7, David had been in four foster homes and had attempted to burn down one of them. Unable to talk, he growled like an animal. Another resident, 4-year-old Hillary, was beaten and molested by the adults in her life.

David and Hillary are typical of the 24 children who stay at Intermountain, where they live in home-like cottages for up to two years. Two counselors stay in each cottage 24-hours a day, offering the children constant attention and guidance.

Many therapy programs treat such children with a system of rewards and punishments or drugs. But Intermountain's treatment program is based on the attachment model of development. Without a critical emotional bond formed during infancy, the directors believe, children grow up emotionally crippled. So the goal is to help Intermountain's children to attach to someone else in order to become emotionally healthy adults. Says clinical director Liz Kohlstadt about the children, "If they feel that this is their home and that the staff are their parents, we've done our job."

Some of the techniques used are extremely unusual. For example, 10-year-old Mary sucks from a baby bottle held by her counselor, Tina. In this way, the counselor "recreated one of the most tender and intimate moments between a mother and child."

Another bonding method is called "holding." On her first day at Intermountain, Hillary tried to escape her counselors because she was afraid they also would beat and molest her. She kicked, fought, and called them names. But the counselors continued to hold on to her. Explains Kohlstadt: "What a holding attempts to do is to contain the child in a safe enough way that the rage becomes part of an interpersonal relationship. It's a bonding process. It's a sense of 'I can help you with this, and I will help you.'" Indeed, after 45 minutes, Hillary calmed down. This marked one of her first steps toward trusting adults.

How successful is Intermountain? In the ten years since this therapeutic approach has been used, about 80 percent of the children have eventually been able to stay with a family and out of an institution. David is an example. He had been placed in foster care and now has a healthy relationship with his foster parents. But Kohlstadt sounds a cautionary note: "We're not curing kids. We're building children. We're not fixing them. Their behaviors will always be a problem."

CASE QUESTIONS

1. In what way is the attachment theory used as the basis of the treatment approach at Intermountain?

2. Do you think this approach is superior to that of rewards and punishments in treating abused or disruptive children? Why or why not?

3. Can you think of other applications of attachment theory that may be useful in dealing with children?

3 Heredity and Environment

"Only rarely can we ascribe a personality or behavioral trait, or even a physical characteristic, to a specific hereditary factor; and it is just as rare that we can be sure that a certain environmental influence is solely responsible for any physical or behavioral trait. Almost any behavior requires *both* inherited capacity and environmental experience. The important issue is not whether nature or nurture has the greater impact on human development; it is how genetics and culture interact in the shaping of the individual."

Thus, there are two starting points. One is the genetic code, or genetic plan, which is present at birth. The other is the environment, or the culture, we live in.

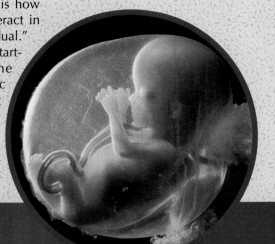

HUMAN LIFE

 4 ▶ **The Prenatal Period**

"Almost from the moment of conception, children are part of an environmental context. The expectations and anxieties, riches and deprivations, stability and disruptions, health and illnesses of the families into which they are born affect not only their life after birth but also their prenatal development."

The moment of conception marks the beginning of the development of the unique human individual. A barely visible, one-celled, fertilized egg carries within itself all the generic information necessary to create a new organism. But first, it must, over the next 9 months, complete a journey that is complex and, at times, perilous.

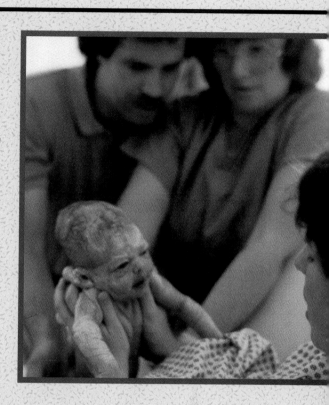

5 ▶ **Childbirth and the Neonate**

"What is the attitude toward childbirth in our own culture? In the United States and in most Western countries, babies are usually born in hospitals, out of view of society."

The reason for this phenomenon is practical. Hospital conditions have greatly diminished the perils of childbirth for both infants and mothers. Indeed, during the last three decades, new medical technology and procedures have dramatically increased the likelihood of saving premature and high-risk infants. But this severing of childbirth from the family and the community has led to the loss of a rich social support system. In response, customs are changing, with a number of other birthing options now available.

It's breeding and training and something much more that drives you and carries you home.

DAN FOGELBERG
RUN FOR THE ROSES

 **CHAPTER**  3

HEREDITY AND ENVIRONMENT

 **OUTLINE**

CHAPTER OBJECTIVES

By the time you have finished this chapter, you should be able to do the following:

✔ Explain the principles and processes of genetic reproduction.

✔ Describe the causes and characteristics of genetic abnormalities, and discuss the application of genetic research and counseling.

✔ Describe contributions and controversies in the field of behavioral genetics.

✔ Discuss various cultural and socialization processes that influence human development.

✔ Describe the relationship between heredity and environment in human development.

✔ Explain the development of gender-role identity and the factors that influence gender-role behavior.

Shortly after Leonardo da Vinci died in 1519 at the age of 67, his younger half-brother Bartolommeo set out to reproduce a living duplicate of the great painter, sculptor, engineer, and author. Since he and Leonardo were related, the father that Bartolommeo chose was himself. He chose as his wife a woman whose background was similar to that of Leonardo's mother: She was young and came of peasant stock, and had also grown up in the village of Vinci. The couple produced a son Piero, who was then carefully reared in the same region of the Tuscan countryside, between Florence and Pisa, that had nurtured Leonardo. Little Piero soon displayed an artistic talent, and at the age of twelve he was taken to Florence, where he served as an apprentice to several leading artists, at least one of whom had worked with Leonardo. According to Giorgio Vasari, the leading art historian of the period, the young Piero "made everyone marvel...and had made in five years of study that proficiency in art which others do not achieve save after length of life and great experience of many things." In fact Piero was often referred to as the second Leonardo.

At the age of 23, however, Piero died of a fever and so it is impossible to predict with certainty what he might have gone on to achieve—though there is some indication in that Piero's works have often been attributed to the great Michelangelo. Nor is it possible to say positively how much of Piero's genius was due to heredity and how much to environment. Full brothers share, on the average, fifty per cent of their genes, but Bartolommeo and Leonardo were half-brothers and so would have had only about a quarter of their genes in common. Piero's mother and Leonardo's mother do not appear to have been related, but in the closely knit peasant village of Vinci it is quite possible that they had ancestors in common and thus shared genes. On the other hand, a strong environmental influence cannot be ruled out. The young Piero was undoubtedly aware of his acclaimed uncle; and certainly his father, Bartolommeo, provided every opportunity that money could buy for the boy to emulate him. But Bartolommeo's efforts to give the world a second Leonardo by providing a particular heredity and environment might, after all, have had little influence. Piero possibly was just another of the numerous talented Florentines of his time. (From Peter Farb, Humankind [Boston: Houghton Mifflin, 1978], pp. 251–252. Reprinted by permission of Houghton Mifflin Co. and Jonathan Cape, Ltd.)

Any parent has inevitably been greeted at some time or other with the statement, "She looks just like her father!" or "You can certainly tell that they are brothers—they look alike, walk alike and even sound alike!". The typical response is generally one of pride: "Yes, there is a certain similarity—she even has some of my movements and mannerisms," which invariably leads to some ruminations on the wonders of genetics. However, like Bartolommeo, if we had attempted to produce "miniclones" of ourselves, we would be at best randomly lucky—and would be unable to tell how much of our success was due to heredity and how much due to environment.

This example illustrates the age-old question of heredity versus environment, which has long fascinated historians and novelists—not to mention developmental psychologists as well as relatives of geniuses. Despite recent success in gene marking, it is still rare that we can ascribe a personality or behavioral trait, or even a physical characteristic, to a specific hereditary factor; it is just as rare that we can be sure that a certain environmental influence is solely responsible for any physical or behavioral trait. Almost any behavior requires *both* inherited capacity and environmental circumstances. The key issue is not whether nature or nurture has the greater impact on human development; it is how genetics and culture interact in the shaping of an individual.

The genetic code, or genetic plan, present at birth is one starting point. From this plan we inherit certain physical and behavioral traits from our parents and ancestors. The unfolding, or maturation, of the genetic plan requires a supportive (or at least not harmful) environment, as we will see in the discussion of the prenatal period in Chapter 4. The environment, or the culture, is the other starting point. Our socialization, or what we learn from our culture and how this learning affects us and every other individual, depends on many cultural factors and on how, when, and by whom we are exposed to these factors.

It is possible, moreover, for the environment to produce devastating effects on the developing fetus that rival those produced by genetic effects. A child, for example, may be born with a cleft lip and palate because of some unknown genetic error or because of steroids the mother took during a crucial period of prenatal development. While one cause is based on heredity and the other on environment, they both produce the same severe malformation.

PRINCIPLES AND PROCESSES OF GENETICS

Cells, chromosomes, genes, DNA, and RNA are all terms which are used when we discuss heredity. Therefore, a brief review of their definition and significance should be helpful before we discuss the processes of inheritance.

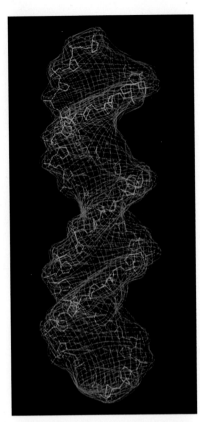

DNA contains the genetic code that regulates the functioning and development of the organism. It is a large molecule composed of carbon, hydrogen, oxygen, nitrogen, and phosphorous atoms.

DNA (deoxyribonucleic acid) A large, complex molecule composed of carbon, hydrogen, oxygen, nitrogen, and phosphorus; it contains the genetic code that regulates the functioning and development of an organism.

mutation An alteration in the strips of DNA and, consequently, in the genetic code.

RNA (ribonucleic acid) A substance formed from, and similar to, DNA. It acts as a messenger in a cell and serves as a catalyst for the formation of new tissue.

FERTILIZATION

We will discuss the process of human fertilization in detail in Chapter 4 as the first step to prenatal development. But it may be helpful to introduce the concept here to facilitate our understanding of genetics and development. Babies are produced from the union of two gametes, or sex cells—the sperm and the ovum. Gametes differ from regular body cells in that they only have 23 chromosomes instead of the normal body cell's 46 chromosomes. When the sperm from the father penetrates the ovum of the mother, fertilization occurs. Once the first sperm has penetrated the ovum, any remaining sperm are turned away. The fertilized cell now becomes the first cell of a new human being. This first cell is called a *zygote.*

GENES AND CHROMOSOMES

Human life therefore begins with a single fertilized cell. Within hours after the sperm penetrates the ovum, the pronucleus of the ovum, containing 23 chromosomes (literally, "colored bodies"), moves slowly toward the center of the ovum; there it joins the pronucleus of the sperm, which also contains 23 chromosomes. The resulting zygote, has 23 *pairs* of chromosomes (a total of 46 chromosomes), half from each parent, the number required to develop a normal human baby.

Once the zygote is formed, the process of cell division begins. The first cleavage, or cell division, produces two cells identical in makeup to the original zygote. As further cell division and cell differentiation take place, each subsequent cell that is formed contains exactly the same number of chromosomes as every other—46. Thousands of genes are strung out in chainlike fashion on a single chromosome. Estimates are that there are tens of thousands of genes on each chromosome and close to 1 million on all 46 chromosomes (Kelly, 1986).

Genes are made up of **DNA (deoxyribonucleic acid),** a large molecule composed of carbon, hydrogen, oxygen, nitrogen, and phosphorus atoms. It has been said that "the human body contains enough DNA to reach the moon and return 20,000 times if all of it were laid out in a line" (Rugh & Shettles, 1971, p. 199). The structure of DNA, as shown in the illustration, resembles a long spiral staircase; two long chains are made up of alternating phosphates and sugars, with cross-links of four different nitrogen bases that pair together. The order in which these paired nitrogen bases appear varies, and it is this variation in order that makes one gene different from another. A single gene might be a chunk of this DNA stairway, perhaps 2000 steps long (Kelly, 1986).

Watson and Crick (1953) suggested that when a cell is ready to divide, the DNA staircase unwinds and the two long chains separate by unzipping themselves down the middle of the paired bases. Each chain then attracts new material from the cell to synthesize a second chain and form a new DNA molecule. Occasionally, there is a **mutation,** or an alteration, in these long strips of nucleic acid. In most cases, this alteration is maladaptive and the cell dies, but a small number of mutations survive and affect the organism.

DNA, then, contains the genetic code, or "blueprint," to regulate the functioning and the development of the organism. DNA is the "what and when" of development, but it is locked in the nucleus of the cell. **RNA (ribonucleic acid)** is a substance formed from, and similar to, DNA and acts as a messenger to the rest of the cell. RNA is the "how" of development. Shorter chains of RNA, patterned from the DNA-like mirror images of the chain, move freely within the cell and serve as catalysts for the formation of new tissue.

Because the genes carry the hereditary potential and operating instructions for all cells, scientists have been eager to discover when, why, and how genes give orders to particular cells. Genes are very specific. The gene that produces insulin is present in every cell in the body, but it functions only within the pancreas. What turns it on or off? What will happen if it produces too little or too much insulin? What triggers cells to divide? In the embryo, genetic programming produces rapid cell division. But what will happen if cells begin to multiply uncontrollably in the adult, as in a cancer? Understandably, cancer researchers are carefully studying the intricate details of how genetic instructions are turned on and off. Genetic discoveries are being made at a tremendous pace. Within a single bacterium, geneticists have constructed synthetic DNA molecules, and they have explored the triggering mechanisms that initiate the sending of a message to a cell. They have even succeeded in the repair or replacement of malfunctioning genes in individual cells (Verna, 1990).

The chromosomes of an individual can be examined with a chart called a **karyotype.** A karyotype is prepared from a photograph of the chromosomes of a single cell (see Figure 3–1). The chromosomes are cut out of the photograph and arranged in matched pairs according to length. These matched chromosomes are then numbered. The first 22 pairs, called **autosomes,** contain genes that determine a variety of physical and mental traits. The 23rd pair contains the *sex chromosomes;* there are two X chromosomes in a normal female (XX) and an X and a Y chromosome in a normal male (XY). These sex chromosomes contain genes that control the development of the primary and secondary sex characteristics and the various other sex-linked traits. Differences between the sexes therefore begin to emerge at conception. More males than females are conceived, as we can see in Table 3–1, but from conception onward, males die in higher numbers than

To develop a normal human baby, the zygote must have 23 pairs of chromosomes, or 46 chromosomes.

TABLE 3–1 Comparative Male to Female Ratios at Various Ages

Conception:	120 to 170 males conceived for every 100 females.
Birth:	106 males are born for every 100 females.
Age 18:	100 males for every 100 females.
25 to 44 years	95 males for every 100 females.
45 to 64 years	92 males for every 100 females.
65+ years	69 males for every 100 females.
85+ years	48 males for every 100 females.

Source: U.S. Bureau of the Census, 1992*a.*

karyotype A photograph of a cell's chromosomes arranged in pairs according to length.

autosomes The chromosomes of a cell, excluding those that determine sex.

FIGURE 3–1

A karyotype showing the chromosomes arranged according to type. Note that there are three number 21 chromosomes, which indicates an individual with Down syndrome.

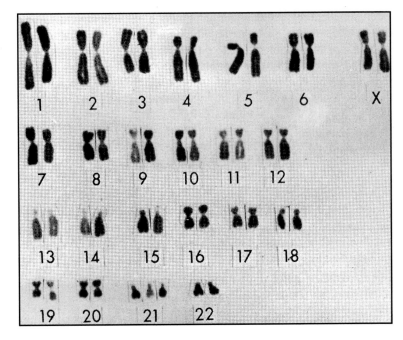

females at each age. Why this occurs has still not been definitively answered. It may be that the X chromosome contains genes that protect the female, the Y chromosome may carry harmful genes, or the mother's body may produce antibodies against the male fetus since it contains the Y chromosome, a foreign element inside her body (Gualtieri & Hicks, 1985).

CELL DIVISION AND REPRODUCTION

In the process of **mitosis,** or ordinary cell division occurring in autosomes, cells divide and duplicate themselves exactly. There are a number of steps in this process. First, the DNA of each gene unzips and replicates itself. Each chromosome then splits and reproduces the former chromosomal arrangement of the first cell. Thus, two new cells are formed, each containing 23 pairs of chromosomes exactly like those in the original cell.

The process of cell division that creates reproductive cells (ova or sperm) is called **meiosis.** The reproductive cells formed during meiosis have only one-half the genetic material of the parent cell—23 chromosomes. The rearrangement of genes and chromosomes resulting from meiosis is like the shuffling and dealing of cards; the chance that any two siblings may receive the same assortment of chromosomes is about 1 in 281 trillion. This figure does not even allow for the fact that the individual genes on a chromosome often make a **crossover** to the opposite chromosome during cell division. It is, therefore, virtually impossible for the same combination of genes to occur twice. We may see the processes of meiosis and mitosis contrasted in Figure 3–2.

mitosis The process of ordinary cell division that results in two cells identical to the parent.

meiosis The process of cell division in reproductive cells that results in an infinite number of different chromosomal arrangements.

crossover A process during meiosis in which individual genes on a chromosome cross over to the opposite chromosome. This process increases the random assortment of genes in offspring.

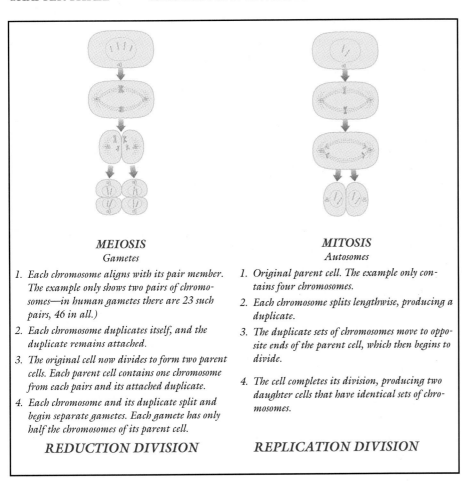

FIGURE 3–2
The contrast between Meiosis and Mitosis.

MEIOSIS
Gametes

1. *Each chromosome aligns with its pair member. The example only shows two pairs of chromosomes—in human gametes there are 23 such pairs, 46 in all.)*

2. *Each chromosome duplicates itself, and the duplicate remains attached.*

3. *The original cell now divides to form two parent cells. Each parent cell contains one chromosome from each pairs and its attached duplicate.*

4. *Each chromosome and its duplicate split and begin separate gametes. Each gamete has only half the chromosomes of its parent cell.*

REDUCTION DIVISION

MITOSIS
Autosomes

1. *Original parent cell. The example only contains four chromosomes.*

2. *Each chromosome splits lengthwise, producing a duplicate.*

3. *The duplicate sets of chromosomes move to opposite ends of the parent cell, which then begins to divide.*

4. *The cell completes its division, producing two daughter cells that have identical sets of chromosomes.*

REPLICATION DIVISION

When the fertilization of an ovum occurs, the sex of the resulting organism is determined by the sperm. All ova carry an X chromosome, whereas sperm have an equal probability of carrying either an X or a Y chromosome. It is the pairing of two X chromosomes that determines the female sex and the union of an X and a Y chromosome that determines the male sex. However, recent research has suggested that the sex of a fetus is also influenced by factors affecting the cervical mucus. This realization arises from work with new reproductive technology in which methods to induce ovulation (such as the use of fertility drugs like Pergonal) are combined with intrauterine insemination, that is, the introduction of sperm directly into the uterus via a cannula. In those cases when ovulation induction is not combined with insemination, and the normal swim by sperm through the cervical mucus into the uterus occurs, an increased number of female babies are conceived (just the opposite of what we indicated in Table 3–1). On the other hand, if the insemination procedure is employed, there is an excess of males since the mucus is bypassed. Researchers have proposed that this may be caused by a thickening of the mucus which slows the passage of the lighter y-chromosome sperm or by changes in the antibodies present in the mucus that may kill off the Y sperm. Interestingly enough, this may be an "environmental" factor that affects sex of the child (Erikssen, 1991).

PATTERNS OF GENETIC TRANSMISSION   Hereditary processes affect a wide range of characteristics each of us possess—the color of our eyes, the shape of our nose, whether or not we can curl our tongue or sit with our legs bent diagonally outward from our knees, our temperament, and other traits both seen and unseen. Much of understanding of the transmission of these genetic traits is based on the work of Gregor Mendel, an Austrian monk who studied plants during the 1860s. Mendel experimented by breeding pea plants that produced green seeds with those that produced only yellow seeds. His resulting plants, which he called *hybrids,* all produced yellow seeds, but 75 percent of the offspring of these hybrids produced yellow seeds, while 25 percent of the offspring produced green seeds. He found the same results when he cross-bred tall and short plants or plants with wrinkled or smooth seeds. He referred to these findings by a law he called *the law of dominant characteristics.* In this law he stated that when two competing traits are inherited, one will be expressed, the dominant trait, while the other will not be revealed, the recessive trait.

Mendel's experiments were groundbreaking in his time and initiated the science of genetics. But we know today that human genetics is far more complex and that human traits are rarely inherited through dominant patterns of transmission.

COMBINATIONS OF GENES   Nearly all of the tens of thousands of genes in an individual occur in pairs. Alternate forms of the same gene pair are called **alleles.** One gene in the pair is inherited from the mother, the other from the father. Some hereditary traits, such as eye color, are carried by a single gene pair. Other traits are carried by a pattern of several interacting gene pairs. For eye color, a child might inherit an allele for brown eyes (B) from the father and an allele for blue eyes (b) from the mother. The child's **genotype,** or gene pattern, for eye color would therefore be *Bb.* But how do these genes combine? What color will the child's eyes be? In eye color, the allele for brown eyes (B) is **dominant** and that for blue eyes (b) is **recessive.** When a gene is dominant, its presence in a gene pair will cause that specific trait to be expressed. Thus, an individual with either the genotype *Bb* or *BB* has brown eyes. The expressed trait, brown eyes, is called the **phenotype.**

In another example, let us assume that the father's genotype is *Bb* (brown eyes) and the mother had blue eyes (which must be the genotype *bb*). All the children of these parents will inherit a recessive gene for blue eyes from the mother. From the father, however, they may inherit either the dominant gene for brown eyes (B) or the recessive gene for blue eyes (b). Therefore, the children will be either blue-eyed *(bb)* or brown-eyed *(Bb).* If we know the genotypes of the parents, we can determine all the possibilities of genotypes and phenotypes— and the probabilities of each—for their children.

Most traits, including eye color, do not usually result from a single gene pair, but from a combination of many gene pairs—with and without dominance—that interact in a number of ways. For the characteristic of height, for instance, several genes or gene pairs seem to combine with others in an additive fashion to create larger or smaller people, with larger or smaller limbs and other parts. Gene pairs may also interact in such a way that one gene pair either allows or inhibits the expression of another gene pair. A system of various types of interaction among genes and gene pairs is called a **polygenic system of inheritance.** Such systems frequently give rise to phenotypes that differ markedly from those of either parent.

alleles A pair of genes, found on corresponding chromosomes, that affect the same trait.

genotype The genetic makeup of a given individual or group.

dominant In genetics, one gene of a gene pair that will cause a particular trait to be expressed.

recessive In genetics, one gene of a gene pair that determines a trait in an individual only if the other member of that pair is also recessive.

phenotype In genetics, those traits that are expressed in the individual.

polygenic inheritance A trait caused by an interaction of several genes or gene pairs.

GENETIC ABNORMALITIES

The majority of babies which are conceived—as a matter of fact, 94 percent of all babies born in the United States—are healthy and normal. Babies born with disabilities of varying levels of severity make up approximately 6 percent of all births and 25 percent of the deaths in the first year of life (Wegman, 1990). Therefore, in the vast majority of cases, when a couple succeeds in conceiving a baby, in all likelihood the outcome will be positive. The baby will be born in good health, possessing all of its physical and mental faculties, and ready to meet the world. Furthermore, when we consider the 6 percent of births resulting in defects, approximately 70 percent of these defects are thought to be due to insults in the prenatal and childbirth periods, and, hence, in many cases, are preventable. We will discuss these preventable aspects of birth defects in greater detail in Chapter 4.

But, for those parents whose babies make up the 6 percent with birth defects, the outcome can be devastating. A child may have overwhelming needs for care or a short life expectancy. In the best-case scenario, the child may have to adjust to different mental or physical abilities than his peers. The likelihood that parents will have an impaired child is affected by factors such as ethnic group membership, parental age, and exposure to certain environmental factors. In the next section, we will see how genetic factors are associated in the transmission of birth defects.

AN OVERVIEW OF BIRTH DEFECTS

Birth defects (also called congenital anomalies) are the leading cause of infant mortality. Those birth defects most likely to be lethal include malformations of the brain and spine (central nervous system), heart defects, and combinations of several malformations. Infant mortality from congenital abnormalities has been declining, although the last decade has seen slight increases in the incidence of some birth defects. In 1985, about 11,000 babies were born nationally with moderate to severe impairments. Congenital anomalies need not only cause death, they may also produce significant disability for the child—often for the remainder of her life. One-fourth of all birth defects are caused by genetic factors, suggesting the need for genetic counseling for both men and women (Behrman, 1992). The remainder of birth defects are caused by environmental agents the mother was exposed to during pregnancy, such as drugs, viruses, radiation and similar factors, or are due to damage caused by accident or the birth process.

When the knowledge of genetics was in its infancy, prospective parents with a family history of inherited disease were faced with a serious dilemma—should they try to have children and risk the possible occurrence of the disease or should they decide against having children at all. This situation occurred because doctors and researchers had little understanding of the manner in which genetic diseases were transmitted. Today, a potential parent asking the question, "Will my child have a genetic defect?" has many more answers, as we will discuss later in this chapter.

TYPES OF GENETIC DISORDERS

The normal human organism needs all 46 chromosomes with their usual complement of gene pairs. Usually, a gross chromosomal abnormality, such as a missing or an extra chromosome, is lethal to the fetus. Classically, genetic disorders have three main causes which have led to their grouping:

➤ Single-gene disorders, in which there is a genetic defect that is passed on to the next generation (for example, Tay-Sachs disease);

➤ Chromosomal disorders, in which the usual orderly chromosomal pattern is disturbed by: the presence of an extra chromosome or chromosome fragment (for example, Down syndrome*), the absence of a chromosome (for example, Turner syndrome);

➤ Multifactorial disorders, in which a number of small mistakes in the genetic information combine to produce a defect, or where the defect has an environmental as well as a genetic origin. Diabetes and Alzheimer's disease may well be examples of such disorders.

Perhaps an example of the way in which one such genetic disorder, Tay-Sachs disease, is believed to occur would be helpful. *Tay-Sachs disease* is a severe genetic disorder that results in early death in those children afflicted with it. The child, who appears normal at birth, begins to show a slight but noticeable physical weakness by 6 months. By 10 months the disorder is readily obvious. Children who had been happy, recognized their parents, ate and slept well regressed. They began to be too weak to move their head, were irritated by sound, and unable to control their eye movements. After age 1, there is a steady physical decline. Convulsive seizures usually begin at 14 months, and by 18 months such children are being tube fed. Their tiny bodies lay limp and frog-legged. Their head starts to enlarge. They usually die of pneumonia somewhere between the ages of 2 and 4. It is a heartbreaking disorder for parents and other loved ones to observe.

In the case of Tay-Sachs disease, there is believed to be one gene that controls the production of one enzyme. This gene is faulty and the enzyme, *hex a enzyme,* does not break down the fatty substances in brain cells (called sphingolipids) as it is supposed to. These substances therefore build up in the cells to lethal concentrations, resulting in subsequent cell death.

Tay-Sachs disease is an autosomal recessive disorder and is therefore very rare. Two individuals possessing the lethal gene must marry. In the general population, this is a rare event and the disorder occurs once in every 200,000 to 500,000 births. However, in the Ashkenazi Jews, one out of 30 are carriers, and one in every 5,000 births is a baby with Tay-Sachs disease.

As we may see from this example, there is a 25 percent risk in *each pregnancy* that the child will have Tay-Sachs disease; a 50 percent risk that the child will be a carrier; and a 25 percent chance that the child will be totally healthy. Since this is the risk for each pregnancy, it is possible for a couple to conceive four diseased children in a row. Thankfully, this disorder is detectable by amniocentesis, a procedure we will discuss later in this chapter. This procedure has assisted couples who carry the gene to make the decision about having or not having children.

---

*A syndrome is a collection of related symptoms.

Some children with such chromosomal abnormalities may have nearly normal intelligence.

GENETIC DISORDERS AND THEIR OUTCOME

While the specific origins of genetic disorders may be helpful to geneticists, those interested in the behavioral effects of such disorders may find it more helpful to categorize genetic defects by their outcome. If we look at the outcomes of such defects, we may better understand the broad scope of genetic defects and their effect on children. Six broad groupings of genetic anomalies (patterns of defects) have been proposed:

1. Severe genetic defects with early death, for example, Tay-Sachs disease
2. Chronic genetic defects with good life expectancy, for example, Down syndrome
3. Remediable genetic defects with improvement of symptoms through medical intervention, for example, Turner's syndrome, Klinefelter's syndrome, and Phenylketonuria (PKU)
4. Treatable genetic defects with recurrent severe episodes, for example, hemophilia, sickle-cell anemia, cystic fibrosis and diabetes
5. Congenital sense deprivation, for example, children born with visual or hearing impairment or loss
6. Genetic anomalies that are mainly behavioral in nature, for example, mental retardation, infantile autism, or childhood schizophrenia (Reed, 1975).

Genetic defects therefore range from those that are life-threatening to those that primarily affect quality of life, from those that are treatable to those that are untreatable, and from those that are primarily biological to those that are primarily psychological. In the next section, we will explore several of these disorders in detail to give a sense of the impact they might have on the lives of children afflicted with them and on those who care for the children.

CHROMOSOMAL DEFECTS

As we have seen, chromosomal abnormalities do occur where individuals survive and exhibit certain characteristic patterns. The most common is *Down syndrome,* which occurs once in 800 births and becomes progressively more common the older the mother. For example, in women 45 and older, the occurrence is once in every 25 births. These individuals have an extra chromosome-21, which either floats freely in the cell nucleus or is situated on top of another chromosome in piggy-back fashion. It causes improper physical and mental development.

Children afflicted with Down syndrome often are severely developmentally delayed and may have serious cardiac and respiratory system problems. Nevertheless, they are often happy children who enjoy music and group play. Recently, there has been a discouraging finding concerning these individuals, however. It appears as though many individuals with Down syndrome develop Alzheimer's disease in adulthood (Kermis, 1986). While this is certainly not good news, it has helped to narrow down the search for the genetic origins of Alzheimer's diseases to chromosome-21, since this is the locus for Down syndrome.

A variation of Down syndrome is known as "mosaic" Down syndrome. It occurs in the following manner: At some point in mitosis, a cell divides improperly, allocating 47 chromosomes to one new cell and only 45 to the other. Cells with only 45 chromosomes cannot survive, but those with 47 do develop alongside normal cells with 46 chromosomes (Koch & Koch, 1974). Children with this genotype have both normal cells and cells with a Down syndrome pattern. Their impaired learning ability and the extent of their other Down syndrome traits, depend on the number of abnormal cells that are produced; these in turn depend on how early the developmental error occurred. Some of these people may have nearly normal intelligence. Even those children with more classic Down syndrome vary in the amount of mental retardation or the number of physical symptoms that they display (Turkington, 1987).

Several abnormalities may occur in the arrangement of the sex chromosomes. One is *Klinefelter's syndrome,* in which individuals have at least one, and possibly more, extra X chromosomes, yielding an XXY arrangement. This occurs 1 in every 1000 live born males. This phenotype usually includes sterility, small external male sex organs, undescended testicles, and breast enlargement. Approximately 25 percent of men with Klinefelter's syndrome have mental retardation. These defects generally worsen as more X's are added to the genotype. This disorder is eased in its physical manifestations by hormonal replacement therapy after the usual age of puberty. This therapy, which involves testosterone (male sex hormone), injections must be continued for the remainder of the individual's life or the secondary-sex characteristics are not maintained.

Another abnormality in the arrangement of the sex chromosomes results in *Turner's syndrome,* which occurs 1 in every 10,000 live born females. In this condition, one X chromosome is either absent or inactive, making an XO arrangement. Individuals with Turner's syndrome usually have an immature female appearance (because they do not develop secondary sex characteristics), and they lack internal reproductive organs. They may be abnormally short and are sometimes mentally retarded. Once the disorder is discovered, usually at puberty, when the girl fails to develop normal secondary-sex characteristics, hormone replacement therapy may be initiated to help her appear more normal. But she will still remain sterile.

A decade ago, popular attention was focused on the XYY pattern, often called the *Supermale syndrome*. This pattern appears in about 1 in 1000 men in the general population, but it is found in about 4 in 1000 men in prison populations. Physically, men with this pattern tend to be taller than average, and they have a greater incidence of acne and minor skeletal abnormalities. In most studies, the average XYY subject has slightly lower intelligence than the XY control group does. It was hypothesized that men in this genotype have a more aggressive personality and develop differently from males with the normal genotype. More extensive examination has indicated that this hypothesis was exaggerated. Although on average these men have a little less impulse control and some are more aggressive with their wives or sexual partners, there is little or no difference between XYY males and XY males in a broad range of aggression measurements (Theilgaard, 1983).

Sometimes, a chromosome may break, and the broken portion may be lost in later cell divisions. At other times, the broken portion may become attached to another chromosome. Environmental effects, such as viral diseases or radiation, may trigger such breaks. Chromosome breakage early in the development of an organism may have a very marked effect on the organism's later growth. Certain parts of the body may fail to develop.

The most serious form of chromosomal breakage occurs in an inherited syndrome called *Fragile X syndrome,* which occurs once in every 1,200 live born males and once in every 2,000 live born females. It is so named because a small portion of the tip of the X chromosome seems to be susceptible to breakage under certain conditions. Individuals with this syndrome may have growth abnormalities. Babies may have large heads, higher-than-normal birth weights, large protruding ears, and long faces. Some have unusual behavioral patterns that may include hand clapping, hand biting, hyperactivity, or poor eye contact. This syndrome is also associated with mental retardation and various forms of learning disorders. It is estimated that fragile X is the second most common chromosomal defect associated with mental retardation. It is second only to Down syndrome.

Because the fragile X disorder is on the X chromosome, it affects males and females differently. As males have only one X chromosome, many more of them are affected. They also suffer much more seriously than do females who have a second X chromosome that is normal and may therefore counter the negative impact of the abnormal X. This particular disability is very curious and is under considerable study by geneticists. It is interesting to note that almost 20 percent of the males who carry the fragile X chromosome do not experience the syndrome. This is very unusual for an X-linked defect (Barnes, 1989).

SEX-LINKED INHERITANCE   The combining of the X and Y chromosomes provides opportunities for some unusual genetic events to occur. Most of the genes on the X chromosome are unable to pair with a corresponding gene on the much shorter Y chromosome. Males therefore express all traits, dominant and recessive alike, that appear on the X chromosome for which there are no mates, or alleles, on the Y chromosome. These single genes are known as sex-linked genes, and the traits that are related to them are called **sex-linked traits.**

Hemophilia, or bleeder's disease, is probably the most dramatic example of a sex-linked genetic abnormality. While it is quite rare, occurring once in every 4,000 to 7,000 male births, it has assumed considerable media prominence because of its association with AIDS. Since hemophiliacs have episodes of bleeding which require transfusions, many hemophiliacs who received transfusions prior to the development of procedures to safeguard the blood supply, developed AIDS. Hemophilia is carried as a recessive gene on the X chromosome. Hemophiliacs are deficient in an element of the blood plasma called Factor VIII which is needed for normal blood clotting. They may bleed for hours from a small wound that would normally clot within 5 minutes; internal bleeding is especially dangerous, as it may go unnoticed and cause death. Hemophilia is a disorder that is recessive on the X chromosome. Females are therefore usually not affected, but their daughters will all be carriers, and 50 percent of their sons will be afflicted.

Hemophilia was common among the royal families of Europe, and it has been traced to the mother of Queen Victoria (1819–1901) of England. Victoria, herself, was not a bleeder, but she transmitted the defect. (Women suffer from the disease in the very rare instance when they inherit the recessive trait from both parents; otherwise, the gene for normal clotting is dominant.) Victoria had four sons and five daughters; the recessive gene was passed to her youngest son, a mild bleeder, and to three of her daughters. As transmitters, the daughters spread the disease throughout the royal families of Europe.

Another example of sex-linked inheritance is *color blindness.* A girl will be color blind only if she receives the same gene from both parents. This means that her father must be color blind and her mother must carry the gene for the defect. A boy will be color blind if he inherits the recessive gene on the X chromosome from his mother. He cannot inherit the trait from his father, because he inherits only the Y chromosome from his father, and none of the traits of color blindness are expressed on it. There are three or four different types of color blindness, some with different patterns of inheritance.

Other kinds of sex-related traits occur as a result of genes on other chromosomes. A beard is an example of a sex-related trait. Women do not normally have beards, but they carry the genes necessary to produce them. Thus, a son inherits traits that determine the type of beard he will grow from both his mother and his father. The dominant traits may actually be inherited through the mother, so that the beards of father and son may be completely different.

NONSEX-LINKED TRAITS   The vast majority of inherited traits are carried not on the sex chromosomes, but on the other 22 pairs, the autosomes. We may see examples of these disorders presented in Table 3–2. Many disorders are carried as single recessive genes. These include *sickle-cell anemia* (a disorder that affects red blood cells and keeps them from transporting oxygen), *cystic fibrosis* (a metabolic disorder that causes an overproduction of mucus throughout the body), *Tay-Sachs disease* (a disorder of fat metabolism that causes mental and physical retardation and early death) and *Phenylketonuria (PKU),* an enzyme metabolism disorder, that produces profound retardation if not treated at birth with dietary intervention. For such disorders to be expressed, a child must inherit the recessive gene from both parents—that is, both parents must be carriers of the **nonsex-linked autosomal trait.** When both parents are carriers of such a disease, approxi-

sex-linked traits Traits carried by genes on either of the sex-determining chromosomes.
nonsex-linked autosomal trait Trait caused by genes on the non-sex-determining chromosomes (autosomes).

TABLE 3–2 Brief Descriptions of Genetic Diseases and Conditions

Cystic fibrosis	Lack of enzyme produces abnormally thick mucous which produces obstructions in lungs and digestive tract; recessive inheritance; 1:2100 Caucasian births; more common in individuals of northern European descent; 10 million Americans are carriers; extensive therapy and immediate treatment of infections allows many to survive into adulthood and reproduce.
Diabetes mellitus	Deficient metabolism of fats and sugar due to body's failure to produce insulin; controllable by insulin, exercise, and restricted diet; two of the main forms of this disease are sex-linked; 1:2500 children are diabetic; polygenic inheritance.
Phenylketonuria	Inability to neutralize a harmful amino acid, phenylalanine, which is contained in many food proteins; causes hyperactivity and severe retardation; treatable by placement on a restrictive diet immediately; 1:8,000 to 12,000 births
Sickle-cell anemia	Abnormal sickling of red blood cells causing oxygen deprivation, pain, swelling, and tissue damage; 50 percent of children die by age 20; recessive inheritance; 1:500 African-American births.
Marfan syndrome	Tall, slender build with thin, long arms and legs; heart defects and eye abnormalities; excessive lengthening of the body leads to skeletal malformations; death from heart failure common in young adulthood; dominant inheritance; 1:20,000 births.
Muscular dystrophy	Degenerative muscle disease causes abnormal gait, loss of ability to walk and eventually most of their motor abilities; occasionally causes death; one type, Duchenne's muscular dystrophy is sex-linked; other types are recessive; 1:4000 males has Duchenne's; 100,000 Americans have inherited some form of musular dystrophy.
Thalassemia (also called Cooley's anemia)	Abnormal red blood cells lead to listlessness, enlarged liver and spleen; retarded physical growth; occasionally death occurs; treatable by blood transfusions; recessive inheritance; 1:500 births to parents of either Mediterranean or subtropical and tropical Asia.

Adapted from McKusick, 1988; and Behrman & Vaughn, 1987.

mately 25 percent of the children will inherit the disorder, 50 percent will be carriers, and another 25 percent will not inherit the recessive genes at all.

An interesting characteristic of these particular disorders is that they occur almost solely within a specific nationality, race, or ethnic group. This is usually because the gene pool has become small enough through intermarriage to allow the risk for carriers to marry to increase significantly. For example, Tay-Sachs disease occurs primarily among Eastern European Jews. Cystic fibrosis is most common among Caucasians. Sickle-cell anemia is found among Africans, African-Americans, and some Mediterranean populations. A disorder called *thalassemia* (or *Cooley's anemia*, a deficiency of hemoglobin in the blood) is prevalent among Italians and other eastern Mediterranean groups.

We have already discussed Tay-Sachs disease earlier in this chapter, so we will now focus on the other disorders. Sickle-cell anemia is a disorder that predominantly affects African Americans in the United States. Because 10 percent of African Americans are heterozygous (carry only one gene for the trait), they thus have the sickle-cell trait which goes undetected unless there is severe oxygen deprivation. Carriers, therefore, possess the sickle-cell trait. However, only 0.2 percent of the African-American population actually have Sickle-cell anemia. They show all the symptoms of the disorder—pain in the joints, blood clots, infections—and may not survive to age 20. Since 10 percent of African Americans are carriers, 1 out of every 100 pregnancies involve two partners who are carriers. This couple has a 25 percent risk of having an afflicted child. A blood test is currently available that determines if an individual is a carrier of the sickle-cell trait. A test using amniocentesis is also available and reliable in 95 percent of cases.

Cystic fibrosis is the most common severe genetic disease of childhood among Caucasian Americans. The symptoms of the disease focus on the function of the exocrine glands, which produce mucous throughout the body, for example, in the lungs, digestive tract, and are also responsible for sweat production to aid in cooling the body. This is a very severe defect, often resulting in death by the time of young adulthood. To survive, such children require extensive physical therapy to loosen mucous several times a day, which is a very fatiguing and time-consuming procedure. Having a cystic child may make it difficult for parents to readily allocate time to other children in the family as well as to each other. Such a child, therefore, requires an incredible family commitment. If the individual survives, fertility is often compromised. For example, most males are sterile and the women, while fertile, have continuing respiratory problems throughout pregnancy that affect fetal health.

Phenylketonuria is an example of the effects of environmental manipulation on the phenotype of a disorder. PKU is a defect in amino acid metabolism caused by an inability of the body to remove phenylalanine from the body—this amino acid has recently received considerable "product recognition" by many of us since it is a component of artificial sweeteners such as Nutrasweet. If you will notice, diet sodas and other such products often have warning labels informing phenylketonurics of the risks associated with their consumption. PKU manifests by the build-up of phenylalanine in the brain which causes cells to become damaged and die. This cell destruction results in a variety of severe neurological symptoms including irritability, athetoid (uncontrollable muscle twitches and movements) motion, hyperactivity, and convulsive seizures. Afflicted children often have an odd reddish-blond coloring in their skin and hair because of the phenylalanine excess.

This disorder is detectable by a blood test given to the baby at birth. If the test is positive, the child is immediately started on a diet to rigidly control phenylalanine. This diet controls the manifestation of the worst symptoms of the disorder—especially, the profound retardation that was its usual end result. Phenylketonurics may have normal life expectancies and the ability to reproduce. However, fertile females with PKU are considered to have very high risk of miscarriage or birth defects because the fetus grows in an abnormal uterine environment.

Some abnormalities are carried by dominant genes instead of by the pairing of recessives. In other words, some abnormalities may be caused by only one gene inherited from one parent. An example is *Huntington's chorea,* which is characterized by progressive dementia, random, jerking movements, and a lopsided, staggering walk. This disorder does not appear until the victims reach middle age or later, after the childbearing years. Those who eventually develop this disease, unaware that they are carrying the defective gene, may produce children who also inherit the dominant gene.

The discovery that one is carrying a defective gene is a rather distressing experience. The possibility of transmitting the disease to future generations should be acknowledged when a carrier is considering marriage or deciding whether to have children. Most people never know what kind of defective genes they carry, although we all probably harbor from five to eight potentially lethal ones at the very least. Most recessive and nonsex-linked genes will probably never be expressed. Still, should the need arise, we can obtain a great deal of information about our genetic inheritance, and about that of a potential partner, to make intelligent and responsible decisions.

 ## GENETIC COUNSELING

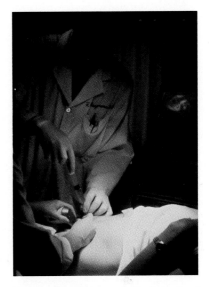

In amniocentesis, a needle is inserted into the mother's abdominal wall to obtain a sample of amniotic fluid. The cells in the fluid are then examined for genetic abnormalities.

Once we know the dangers inherent in certain types of gene pairings and the tragic consequences of various chromosomal abnormalities, what can be done to avoid them? **Genetic counseling** is now a widely available resource that can help potential parents evaluate such risk factors in childbearing and thus enable them to make intelligent decisions (Garver & Marchese, 1986).

Predicting a baby's vulnerability to any of the nearly 5,000 genetic disorders that have been identified so far is frequently a complicated process. The potential parents' complete medical records are examined to uncover diseases that can be traced to a genetic abnormality. Each parent is given a complete physical examination, including biochemical and blood tests. A family pedigree is prepared to show which members of the family have been afflicted by any disorder and whether the inheritance pattern is dominant, recessive, or X-linked. If an inheritable genetic abnormality is found, a genetic counselor evaluates a couple's risk of having a baby with the genetic disorder, puts the risk in perspective, and suggests reproductive alternatives (such as adoption or artificial insemination of donor egg) if the couple decides the risk is too great. Fortunately for many parents, the risk of bearing a child with a disease incompatible with normal life has been considerably reduced by new prenatal-testing methods. Table 3–3 shows the characteristics of persons who are candidates for genetic counseling.

PRENATAL SCREENING

During pregnancy, there are a number of relatively safe screening techniques to detect genetic defects in the fetus. Five types of tests deserve special notice: amniocentesis, ultrasound, chorionic villi sampling, fetoscopy, and maternal blood analysis.

In *amniocentesis,* about half an ounce of the amniotic fluid is withdrawn from the uterus by a syringe inserted through the mother's abdominal wall. The fluid contains fetal cells that can be analyzed for major chromosomal and some genetic abnormalities. This procedure is usually not done until the 15th week of pregnancy, and it takes at least 1 to 2 weeks for all of the tests to be completed. It should also be noted that amniocentesis has an increased risk of miscarriage asso-

genetic counseling Counseling that helps potential parents evaluate their risk factors for having a baby with genetic disorders.

TABLE 3–3 Characteristics of Candidates for Genetic Counseling

> ➤ Anyone who is aware of a family history of inherited genetic disorders or who actually has a genetic disorder, or defect.
>
> ➤ The parents of a child who either has a serious congenital abnormality or genetic defect.
>
> ➤ A couple who has experienced more than three miscarriages or a miscarriage in which the fetal tissue analysis indicated chromosomal abnormality.
>
> ➤ A pregnant woman over age 35 or a father over age 44, who because of age has an increased risk of chromosomal damage.
>
> ➤ Prospective parents belonging to certain ethnic groups that are at high risk for certain disorders, such as Tay-Sachs, sickle-cell anemia or thalassemia.
>
> ➤ A couple who is aware of prenatal exposure to an excessive dose of radiation, drugs, or other environmental agents that can result in birth defects.

Source: Adapted from Lauersen, 1983.

ciated with it. The risk of fetal loss associated with amniocentesis is less than the risk of miscarriage by natural causes at age 35. Obstetricians recommend amniocentesis for women older than 35 on a fairly routine basis because of the increased incidence of birth defects found in babies born to women over this age.

The use of *ultrasound* in prenatal screening provides further information about the growth and health of the fetus. Here, high-frequency sound waves are used to outline the shape of the fetus and to form a picture called a *sonogram*. Sonograms can detect structural problems like a small head or body malformations. This procedure, too, is normally conducted around the 15th week of pregnancy and is offered to about half of the pregnant mothers in the United States. We should note that ultrasound frequently is conducted earlier in high-risk pregnancies; for example, the gestational sac may be visualized to ensure that an ectopic (tubal) pregnancy has not occurred as early as 3 to 4 weeks after a missed menstrual period.

A newer procedure called *chorionic villus sampling (CVS)* can be conducted much earlier than amniocentesis, at around 8 to 12 weeks. In this procedure, cells are drawn from the membranes surrounding the fetal tissue and are analyzed in a fashion similar to that in amniocentesis. Because more cells are collected in this procedure, the tests can be completed within a few days. This procedure involves more risk than either of the other two, however. A small proportion of fetuses abort spontaneously after this procedure (Wyatt, 1985). When this information is given to mothers who are at high risk for a genetic defect, about half choose to wait and use amniocentesis together with ultrasound as a screening technique (Reid, 1990). Recent research has also found limb abnormalities and fetal death associated with CVS done prior to 9 to 12 weeks after the last menstrual period. Moreover, there is greater success in avoiding fetal damage in hospitals that frequently perform the procedure (Kuliev, Modell & Jackson, 1992). If there is a serious likelihood of a genetic defect, it is clearly an advantage to have test results 10 weeks into a pregnancy instead of 18 weeks. Early abortions (before 12 weeks) are much safer and are psychologically easier for the woman.

Fetoscopy is a procedure used to inspect the fetus for limb and facial defects. In this procedure, a needle larger than that employed in amniocentesis and containing a light source is inserted into the uterus to directly view the fetus. This procedure may allow a sample of the fetal blood or tissue to be withdrawn, therefore allowing for the prenatal diagnosis of disorders such as sickle-cell anemia, thalassemia, and hemophilia. Fetoscopy is usually not done before 15 to 18 weeks after conception and involves a risk of miscarriage and infection that is greater than amniocentesis.

Since early in pregnancy, some of the fetus' cells enter the maternal blood stream, *maternal blood analysis* is often a helpful diagnostic tool after 8 weeks post-conception. The substance looked for in this test is *alphafetoprotein,* which is elevated in the presence of kidney disease, abnormal esophagus closure, or severe central-nervous system defects.

A very new and exciting method of prenatal diagnosis has now been developed—*preimplantation genetic diagnosis.* This procedure is associated with *in vitro fertilization (ivf),* in which sperm and ova are mixed together outside of the mother's body and then reimplanted into either the uterus or fallopian tubes. In preimplantation diagnosis, cells are removed from the embryo and analyzed for defects before it is implanted inside the mother's body. Recently, a baby girl was born to parents carrying the cystic fibrosis gene after this procedure (Handyside et al, 1992). The British researchers responsible for her healthy birth suggest that this very costly procedure may be helpful in prenatal diagnosis of such disorders as Duchenne's muscular dystrophy, sickle-cell disease, Tay-Sachs, among others.

PARENTAL DECISION MAKING   The genetic counselor's ultimate responsibility is to help prospective parents digest the information about genetic disorders and then make the right decisions for themselves. The type of advice the genetic counselor gives often depends on the specific disease involved. When a genetic diagnosis shows the possibility of Tay-Sachs disease, the counselor explains that there is a 25 percent chance in each pregnancy that the child will have the disease. For couples who want to have children of their own, the only way currently to avoid the problem is to test for it with amniocentesis.

The counselor's role in advising sickle-cell anemia carriers is less straightforward. In its worst form, the disease causes a general weakening of the body, increased susceptibility to infection, severe pain in the abdomen and joints, deterioration of the heart, kidneys, and bones, and ultimately death. Yet many sufferers lead relatively normal lives—and it is impossible to determine through prenatal testing which form of the disease an unborn child will have.

ADVANCES IN GENETIC RESEARCH

Both the technology of genetics and our understanding of genetic determinants are advancing rapidly. Nearly 5,000 types of genetic defects have been identified and carefully catalogued (McKusick, 1990). Some of the most common are cystic fibrosis, cleft palate, clubbed feet, juvenile diabetes, hemophilia, Alzheimer's disease, and sickle-cell anemia. Over half of the mothers in the United States are given some option for prenatal screening. Furthermore, all 50 states have at least limited genetic screening programs for newborns.

Although several hundred individual genes for specific traits have been located on their respective chromosomes, corrective **gene therapy**—the repair or substitution of individual genes to correct certain defects—is proceeding at a

gene therapy The manipulation of individual genes to correct certain defects.

careful pace. Geneticists have made amazing advances in genetic engineering with respect to plants, bacteria, and even other animals. Scientists can transplant genetic materials from one species into the cell of another species. The result is a hybrid with characteristics of both donors. This *gene-splicing* technique has been used to create new plants. It is also possible to create a strain of bacteria that will produce a human growth hormone (Garber & Marchese, 1986). Through a process called *cloning*, scientists have been able to duplicate some laboratory animals from just one of the *somatic*, or body, cells. But the use of such *genetic-engineering techniques* on humans would involve a number of risks and challenges—physical, psychological, social, and ethical. It is appropriate that most professionals are advancing with extreme caution.

In at least a few cases, however, gene therapy is progressing well and with little public outcry. In the 1970s, a boy named David became famous because he lived in a sterile bubble. He had a severe inherited disorder in his immune system that meant he was liable to die from the slightest infection. This rare condition, called severe combined immunodeficiency (SCID), has now become the target of the first federally approved clinical trials for human gene therapy. In September 1990, a 4-year-old girl with SCID began receiving a billion or so gene-altered immune system cells intravenously in a saline solution. The results have been good—so far. By 1993, the young girl's body was producing its own immunities and she was healthy. Her life comprises activities that all 7-year-olds do. Many other diseases are under study for effective techniques in gene therapy. The most promising candidates are those diseases caused by a single gene that can be isolated, cloned, and transplanted. For cystic fibrosis, the gene treatment may be by an aerosol spray applied directly to the lungs. For sickle-cell anemia, the cure would be a little more complicated. There must be a delivery of the healthy gene to the blood cells along with another gene capable of deactivating the damaged version. Ideally, scientists aim to remove the patient's damaged cells and then alter and return them to the patient. In each case, the genes must reach the right target—for example, the bone marrow, the liver, or cells in the skin. The process is extremely complex (Verma, 1990).

ETHICAL ISSUES IN THE NEW REPRODUCTIVE GENETICS

While tremendous strides are being made in genetic research, many old ethical issues remain to be solved as they relate to this new research in human genetic engineering. The Human Genome Project (Wertz, 1992), a 15-year, $3-billion research effort, is designed to map all the human genes and identify those genes and combinations that cause particular disorders. When we gain this knowledge, what shall we, as a society, do with it? We shall certainly try to prevent such severe disorders, but how? Whose decision will it be, whether a high-risk couple may carry a child with a severe disability to full term? And shall we value such a child less than other children or blame the parents for not preventing the birth? And, what about the use of procedures such as amniocentesis and abortion because of personal preference rather than for health reasons, for example, to selectively abort female babies—a procedure which has been documented as occurring in India, China, and other Asian countries? Is this a justifiable and ethical use of such technology? While we can do nothing about the policies or practices regarding amniocentesis in other countries, the World Health Organization and other similar bodies have issued statements that using prenatal diagnosis for sex selection is an improper use of the technology.

Sex selection, much like genetic engineering, is being affected by advances in medical technology. Procedures such as the sperm separation methods originally developed by Ronald Erikksen for use with cattle breeding are becoming more reliable with humans. Depending upon the father's sperm count, these costly procedures claim an 80 to 90 percent success rate in producing sons or daughters for families willing to undergo the rigorous medical protocals necessary to achieve a child of either sex. The procedure is based on the fact that the y-chromosome-bearing sperm are smaller and faster swimmers, when compared to the larger x-chromosome-bearing sperm. In this methodology, the sperm are first washed and centrifuged to remove faulty sperm and impurities and next allowed to "swim" through a series of solutions. The woman is then artificially inseminated with the man's sperm shortly after ovulation has occurred.

Another ethical issue involves the use of nondirective versus directive counseling by genetic counselors. While the majority of counselors believe in nondirective approaches, for example, "not making decisions for patients, but supporting any decision they make," or "telling patients that reproductive decisions that they make are theirs alone," a majority find this difficult to apply. Many tell patients what others have done in their situation or what the counselor would do. Truly nondirective counseling may even violate the goals of public health programs, as the following remarks indicate:

> Ordinarily, public health targets an at-risk population, for example, heavy smokers, and tries to change their behavior. There is no question of nondirectiveness. The health educator does not say, "I will support whatever decision you make about smoking," but instead says, "Don't smoke." If public health programs in genetics are aimed at prevention, as many appear to be, they come into direct conflict with nondirectiveness. To say to parents at high risk, "Don't have children" could be regarded as a limitation of basic freedom and an insult to human dignity in many societies, but to say, "We support your decision to have children even if there is a high risk for serious disorders" may be going too far in the opposite direction (Wertz, 1992, p. 502).

It may well be that in tampering with human genetics in such a potentially revolutionary way, we may be forced to reconsider the limits of choice.

 ## BEHAVIORAL GENETICS

It is one thing to consider the impact of genetics on the shape of one's nose or the color of one's eyes, but it is quite another to wonder if our short-tempered aggressiveness is, in part, genetically determined. Human behavior seems nowhere near as prescribed or preprogrammed as animal behavior, and what patterns do exist seem highly modifiable, depending on the culture and the circumstance. Nevertheless, the study of the genetic components of behavior has been a highly controversial field for decades. Researchers first look at genetic influences

One research strand behavioral geneticists have focused on is the impact of heredity on individual differences such as in intelligence. However, because the study of intelligence provoked controversy, researchers are now concentrating on analyzing inherited differences in personality traits.

on the development of behavior for the whole human species. These influences include the typical patterns of growth along with perceptual and motor skill patterns. The genetic influence is evident beyond the prenatal period. In fact, genetic programming is involved throughout development. Pubescence, for example, occurs in adolescence as the organism becomes capable of sexual reproduction. There are physical aspects of this change that are genetically programmed, as well as some behavioral tendencies that are part of this sequence. Although certain tendencies can be altered slightly with health care and nutrition, the underlying pattern remains (Scarr & Kidd, 1983).

A second approach to the study of behavioral genetics concentrates on individual differences. Over the years, for instance, researchers have examined individual differences in intelligence: What proportion of variation in intelligence is due to genetic programming? It is clear that intelligence is a measure of both heredity and environment—inherited capacities must be exercised in an environmental context. But the study of intelligence has generated heated debate. Consequently, researchers have shifted recently to the study of personality, where having more of a trait—sensitivity or impulsivity, for example—is not necessarily better. It simply makes a person different. They hope to be able to analyze inherited differences in personality, interests, or even learning style more objectively (Plomin, 1983; Scarr & Kidd, 1983).

ADOPTION STUDIES

One common strategy for attempting to identify genetic influences on behavior is to study adopted children. In the Minnesota Adoption Studies, for instance, adopted children were compared on a number of dimensions with their biological parents, their adoptive parents, and the biological children of their adoptive parents (Scarr & Weinberg, 1983). In addition, the adoptive parents were compared with their biological children. When test scores of adopted children were compared to scores of peers *not* adopted, findings showed that adoptive families were influential—as a group, the adopted children had higher IQs and achieved more in school. But when individual differences within the group were analyzed, test scores were more closely related to the intellectual abilities of biological parents than to the abilities of adoptive parents.

While several other studies have reported similar results (Horn, 1983), there is one area of adoption that points to an unlikely outcome. In the case of Asian children adopted into American homes, for example, they appear to excel in academic areas much the same way in which Asian children raised in their biological families do. This is an unusual outcome given the horrific conditions under which many of these adopted children began their lives. For example, many of them experienced separation, institutionalization, deprivation, malnutrition, and so forth prior to their placement with their American family. These factors are frequently associated with extreme developmental delay, as we will see in subsequent chapters. We might therefore hypothesize that these adopted children would not measure up to American standards—but they actually excelled their American peers (Clark and Honisee, 1982). This study not only pointed out the resiliency of children who have suffered seemingly great environmental damage, but also the impact of the home environment on their recovery. All these children were adopted into homes where they were the main focus of attention and affection from well-educated, middle-class parents who had long-awaited them. Such studies show that the environment is crucial in overcoming the early effects of genetic and environmental damage.

Adoption studies have begun to focus on differences in attitudes, interests, personality, and behavior patterns like alcoholism (Fuller & Simmel, 1986). It might be assumed that such characteristics would be predominantly generated and nurtured within the child-rearing environment—that is, in the adoptive home. Nevertheless, according to several studies, some attitudes, vocational interests, and personality traits seem quite resistant to the adoptive family environment (Scarr & Weinberg, 1983). But the reasons for this are complex and may relate more to the subjects' level of social maturity and moral-reasoning ability at the time of testing.

TWINS AND PERSONALITY

One of the more popular ways of studying genetic influences on personality is to compare differences among identical and fraternal twins. When identical twins are much more similar than are fraternal twins, it is usually assumed that the similarity is due to genetic influence (see the box "Identical Twins Reared Apart").

Repeatedly, studies of twins find that a wide range of personality traits are at least partly inherited. Three frequently inherited characteristics are *emotionality, sociability,* and *activity level*—sometimes called the *EAS traits* (Goldsmith, 1983; Plomin, 1990). *Emotionality* is the tendency to become aroused easily to fear or anger. *Sociability* is the extent to which individuals prefer to do things with others rather than on their own. Traits like emotionality and sociability are usually measured in lengthy questionnaires that are given to the twins during adulthood or to the parents or teachers of twin children. *Activity level* is observed and rated by the researcher or by the parents and teachers. Similarity in emotionality seems to last a lifetime, but the similarity in activity level and sociability diminishes somewhat in later adulthood, probably due to the many different life events twins experience when they are apart (McCartney, Harris, & Bernieri, 1990).

Although these studies offer considerable evidence for a genetic influence on different temperaments and personality styles, they are unable to tell us how the genetic components interact with the environment. A quiet, easygoing child experiences a different environment from the one experienced by an impulsive, angry, assertive child. The child helps shape or trigger the environment which, in turn, limits and molds how the child expresses her feelings. Perhaps examples of the way the environment responds to an easy and difficult child would help to conceptualize this interaction.

Abbie is an aggressive 4-year-old girl. When observed in her Monetessori preschool classroom she is in constant motion—disrupting the work of other children, attempting to start fights with both boys and girls, staring opponents down when the fights are stopped. Most of the attention of the two teachers in the room is directed at undoing the negative effects of Abbie's behavior. Since it is attention she is seeking through her aggressiveness, the teachers' actions only fuel her disruptiveness. The consequence is that the other children are beginning to avoid her and the teachers are losing patience with her antics. Her parents have been asked to withdraw her from the program.

Christopher is a quiet, introspective 4-year-old boy. When observed in his preschool classroom, he is actively involved in working with a teacher on a project. His smiling face reveals his interest and enjoyment. The teacher's enthusiasm is enhanced by his receptiveness. He has made friends with all the children in the room—even the more aggressive ones because of his interest in them and willingness to listen to their stories. The consequence is that he is sought out by teachers and children who value his sense of outgoing enjoyment of his daily activities.

These examples indicate the tremendous impact that the personality of a child can have on the environment in which he or she performs activities. In Christopher's case, the psychosocial environment (the people with whom interaction occurs) facilitates his continued growth by positive stimulation. This in fact allows him to more fully engage in learning from more of the classroom environment. Abbie, on the other hand, persists in such negative behavior that she is minimizing her positive learning experience in the classroom. Moreover, her behavior is beginning to limit future opportunities for growth, as she is labeled as difficult. It becomes clear that temperament and personality help to structure those aspects of the environment that the child experiences, while, in turn, the environment—in terms of people and objects in it—shapes the future capabilities of the child. (In Chapter 1, the box "Personality over the Life Span," illustrates this process.)

Some studies suggest that identical twins are more similar than fraternal twins are in personality traits like sociability, emotionality, and activity level. But how much of this similarity can be attributed to genetic influence and how much to the environment?

CULTURE AND SOCIALIZATION

Although we speak of *a* culture and *a* social environment, we must keep in mind that these are not single, fixed entities. An individual's social environment, already complex at the moment of birth, changes constantly. Infants are born into many social groups—a family, perhaps a tribe, a social class, a racial or ethnic unit, a religious group, and a community. Each of these social entities has some shared ideas, beliefs, assumptions, values, expectations, and "appropriate" patterns of behavior. These shared expectations form the culture of the group.

Although some cultural characteristics are universal—food taboos and funeral rites, for example (Farb, 1978)—we shall focus here on cultural diversity and the rich variety of cultural patterns. In examining differences between cultures, however, many people find it difficult not to be a bit ethnocentric. **Ethnocentrism** is the tendency to assume that one's own beliefs, perceptions, and values are true, correct, and factual and that other people's beliefs are false, unusual, or downright bizarre. For instance, members of "primitive" tribes may be regarded by some as simple and unintelligent, exotic, perhaps, but quite "uncivilized"; others may see them as "noble savages," untainted by the evils of civilization and industrialized society. These oversimplifications miss both the complexity and the richness of unfamiliar cultures. But if it is difficult to be objective about distant cultures, it is even harder to suspend judgment on the cultural diversity close at hand. A visitor from abroad who speaks English with a pronounced accent may be accepted with fascination, but a neighbor who speaks with a regional or ethnic accent may be treated with indifference or even hostility.

ALTERNATE FAMILY STYLES

The type of family into which a child is born can dramatically affect the expectations, roles, beliefs, and interrelationships that he will experience throughout life (Hartup, 1989). Here we shall examine three basic family styles and the cultural patterns that underlie them.

EXTENDED FAMILIES In an extended family (one having many relatives and several generations close by), children may be cared for by a variety of people—uncles, aunts, cousins, grandparents, or older siblings, as well as by parents. Until fairly recently, many American and Western European children were raised in extended families, and people tended to live out their lives in the areas where they were born. As our society became increasingly industrialized, people became economically and physically mobile, often moving away from their family's base to raise their children alone. The extended family, however, is still a common pattern in many cultures, as it was throughout history—from the peoples of India to the Indians of the Americas.

COMMUNAL FAMILIES Communal social systems are found in various forms in Israel, the former Soviet Union, China, and, to a lesser degree, in Europe and the United States. Here the social relationships take a different form from those of the extended family. The peer group is usually an intensely power-

ethnocentrism The tendency to assume that one's own beliefs, perceptions, customs, and values are correct or normal and that those of others are inferior or abnormal.

FOCUS ON AN ISSUE

IDENTICAL TWINS REARED APART

Oskar Stöhr was raised as a Catholic in Hitler's Germany and became a Nazi youth. Jack Yufe grew up in the Caribbean as a Jew and spent many years on an Israeli kibbutz. Identical twins who were separated at birth, Stöhr and Yufe did not meet until they became adults. Their lives, although markedly different in some superficial ways, show some startling similarities. Both men doze off while watching television; love spicy foods, liqueurs, and buttered toast dipped in coffee; have overbearing, domineering relationships with women whom they yell at when they are angry, and think it is funny to sneeze in a crowd of strangers. They also have amazingly similar mannerisms, temperaments, and tempos, and, when tested, showed very similar personality profiles (Holden, 1980).

"When Bridget and Dorothy, both housewives, met for the first time at age 38, each wore seven rings on carefully manicured hands, two bracelets on one wrist, and a watch and bracelet on the other wrist."

Striking similarities have shown up in other pairs of identical twins separated at birth. Kathleen and Jenny sat in the same positions and laughed and wept over the same things. Both Olga and Ingrid stopped menstruating at the age of 18, when each assumed she was pregnant, arranged to marry the man responsible, found out she wasn't pregnant, and started menstruating again around the time of the wedding (Farber, 1981). When Bridget and Dorothy, both housewives, met for the first time at age 38, each wore seven rings on carefully manicured hands, two bracelets on one wrist, and a watch and bracelet on the other wrist (Holden, 1980).

How many of these similarities are pure coincidence? How many are the product of similar backgrounds? And how many are linked in some unknown way to the hereditary code locked in the genes?

ful force in the socialization of young children. Communal societies reinforce conformity and cooperation while discouraging individualism and significant deviance from group standards.

The Israeli *kibbutz* represents one of the most sustained and studied efforts to institutionalize communal child care in any modern progressive society. The kibbutzim were founded by self-declared idealists in open rebellion against their own families. They sought, among other things, to dismantle traditional family structures, to liberate women from sex-stereotyped roles, and to raise children in a collective, unpossessive way. The early kibbutzim were designed to prevent children from identifying strongly with their individual family units. To foster this collective spirit, the kibbutzim relied on a system in which many adults supervised all of the children's activities. In these houses, four to eight children of the same age were cared for according to group-approved child-rearing methods. Boys and girls were treated alike. The children were taught to share, to think of group interests before individual desires, and to value their roles in the kibbutz society. Children benefited from the attention of the child-care specialists and from their relationships with their own parents, whom they saw daily during extended visiting periods.

Although the traditional kibbutz system deemphasized the concepts of private property and private enterprise, it recognized differences in individual poten-

To discover where the truth lies, Thomas Bouchard and his colleagues at the University of Minnesota have been conducting a study of 48 pairs of identical twins who were separated at birth. The researchers have compared the 48 sets of identical twins reared apart to a small group of fraternal twins reared apart and to a large sample of identical and fraternal twins reared together (Tellegen et al., 1988). In most cases, the IQ scores of the identical twins were remarkably similar, and even their brain wave tracings were almost the same (Bouchard, 1987). By comparing these twins with fraternal twins, researchers have concluded that perhaps 50 percent of measured intelligence in adulthood is due to heredity (Plomin, 1990).

Several personality traits were also quite similar in the identical twins who were reared apart. All of the twins in the study answered extensive self-report personality questionnaires. The correlation of traits for the identical twins reared apart was surprisingly high. Traits that were quite similar included sense of well-being, social potency, stress reactions, alienation, aggression, control/caution, harm avoidance, and absorption/imagination. Some traits had lower correlations, including achievement (works hard) and social closeness (intimacy). Whether they had been reared together or apart, the fraternal twins showed far less similarity in all of these traits.

Many of the identical twins also had similar neuroses. Even when they were brought up in totally different emotional environments, they shared mild depressions, phobias, and hypochondriacal traits. These similarities sparked the researchers into thinking about the role that heredity plays in common neurotic illnesses—a role that has already been established for psychoses.

The researchers themselves are the first to warn against drawing too many conclusions from these findings. They point to the problems—the size of their sample and the fact that most of the identical twins grew up in similar environments, so their similarities may not be traceable to their genes alone. Moreover, they warn, there is a tendency among researchers and lay people alike to look for and find similarities in the twins' behavior even when differences are more informative. Bouchard and his colleagues also say these differences show that there is no one answer and that human behavior is a result of both our genetic inheritance and the environment that shapes us (Bouchard, 1987).

tial and need. The peer group, whose members grew up in daily, intimate contact with one another, developed into a closely knit and supportive social unit. Instead of being isolated from the rest of the community, the children who grew up in children's houses were central to the functioning of the kibbutz (Spiro, 1954). Extensive analysis and testing of kibbutz-raised children revealed very strong peer links and positive, but more diffuse, bonds with parents and adult caregivers (Beit-Hallahmi & Rabin, 1977).

Some communal groups in the United States have attempted a modified version of this child-care method; they have considered their children to be a commonly held segment of society, not the property of individual parents. Needless to say, a successful communal arrangement depends on a very high degree of consensus among parents on social values, ideals, and lifestyles. In the United States, communal groups have not had the success that they have had in Israel—perhaps because of our cultural diversity. In addition, the commune has never been considered a part of "mainstream" society. When Americans think of communes they tend to conjure up the flower children of the 1960's, the Manson Family, the tragedy of the Jonestown mass suicide in Guyana, or the fiery end to the standoff with the Branch Davidians in Waco, Texas. Despite these associations, however, there have been successful communal living arrangements in the United States.

Children who are part of an extended family have many more people to interact with and learn from.

NUCLEAR FAMILIES The traditional nuclear family consists of a husband, a wife, and their unmarried children, all of whom live as a unit apart from relatives, neighbors, and friends. The husband and father is head of the household, and he spends much of the day away from home, working for the financial support of the other family members. Virtually all family members depend on the father for their material needs. The wife and mother is responsible for housekeeping, cooking, and most of the care and training of the children. Many people in the Western world assume that this pattern is the "natural" and customary family form. Indeed, many Western countries have constructed legal safeguards to protect it. In the United States, husbands (but not wives) are obligated by law to support their families. As we have seen, however, the nuclear-family pattern is not the norm even in the United States. In the 1990s, nuclear families account for less than half of all American families. Unmarried women now bear a substantial number of children—over 25 percent of the infants born in 1990 were to unmarried women (National Center for Health Statistics, 1992). Many children grow up in single-parent families as a result of the continuing high divorce rate. Even in two-parent families, both parents normally work. In 1992, over 50 percent of the mothers of newborns returned to the labor force within the first year after giving birth (U.S. Bureau of the Census, 1993).

The traditional nuclear family has carried a heavy responsibility for child care: health care, moral training, economic and emotional stability. (Recall the ecological model of child development presented in Chapter 1. In that model, the child and her immediate interactions with the family are nested within three larger levels of the environment.) Parents have been expected to meet all these demands with minimal outside assistance. Children, primarily influenced by family training, were expected to do as their parents told them. Parents were considered responsible for regulating the influence of the outside world on their children (Keniston, 1977). Now, however, they are influenced by a vast network of social institutions that includes television and the public school system. Parents encounter pressure from stressful jobs, the high economic cost of rearing children, and the advice of doctors, teachers, and other professionals. They delegate a tremendous amount of responsibility for child care to these professionals, but most parents lack real authority over these surrogate caregivers.

THE FAMILY AS TRANSMITTER OF CULTURE   Besides integrating the individual child into the family unit, parents or care-givers in all of the family styles discussed also interpret for the child the outside society and its culture. Religion, ethnic traditions, and moral values are conveyed to children at an early age. In a cohesive, homogeneous society like the Israeli kibbutz, people outside the family reinforce and expand parental teachings. There is little contradiction between the family's way of doing things and the customs of the community at large. But a more complex, multiethnic society, many cultural traditions often oppose one another. Some parents struggle to instill their own values so that their children will not become assimilated into the culture of the majority. Parents express many cultural values to their children in their attitudes toward such daily choices as food, clothing, friends, education, and play.

FAMILY SYSTEMS

Families are more than the sum of the individuals within them. They have structure and a hierarchy of authority and responsibility. They have rules for behavior, both formal and informal. They have customs, rituals, and patterns of relationships that persist over time (Kreppner & Lerner, 1989). Each family member may have a specific role in interactions with other family members. An older sibling may be responsible for younger siblings. Each family member may have alliances with some family members, but not with others. Two sisters, for example, may frequently take the same side against their brother. The network of interrelationships and ongoing expectations is a major influence on the child's social, emotional, and cognitive development.

Patterns of mutual influence within the family are extremely complex. This is true even in small families. Siblings in the same family may share many similar experiences, such as an overly strict mother or middle-class suburban family values. Yet there is also a set of *nonshared experiences* and relationships. In one series of studies, the relationships between parents and their firstborn and parents and their second-born were compared over a period of time (Dunn, 1986). As one might expect, the relationships between mother and firstborn were often quite close and intense, at least until the birth of the second child. Things then became more complicated. If the firstborn child had an affectionate relationship with the father, this affection tended to increase, as did the conflict and confrontation between the mother and this firstborn. If the mother gave a good deal of attention to the second child, the conflict between the mother and the first child escalated. In fact, the more the mother played with the second baby at age 1, the more the siblings quarreled with each other a year later (Dunn, 1986).

Clearly, members of the same family do not necessarily experience the same environment. When adolescents are asked to compare their experiences with those of their siblings, they often note more differences than similarities. Although they may see some similarity in family rules and expectations, there are many differences concerning the timing and impact of the events—a divorce, for

Similarity of interests may cause more intimacy between certain family members.

instance. Even larger differences occur in how each sibling is treated by the other siblings (Plomin, 1990). In a recent study, parents and adolescents were asked to rate their family environment. There was some agreement on whether or not the family was well organized, had a strong religious orientation, or was often in conflict. But considerable disagreement existed between parents and their adolescent children on how cohesive the family was, how much expressiveness or independence was allowed, and whether or not there was an "intellectual" family orientation (Carlson, Cooper, & Stradling, 1991). It becomes apparent that as each child enters a family, the nature of the family and consequent interactions within it change as the following comments indicate.

> It became very clear to me that the family into which I was born as the first daughter was very different from that of my fourth sibling. He was ten years younger and had been born when my parents were older. I was the experimental child—didn't have a bicycle until I was in high school, had curfews, and was very responsible for the other children in the family. I had the sense that I had to be the peacemaker and keep my parents happy. I guess today I would say that I always had a strong need for their approval.

> My brother, on the other hand, was different. I thought he got away with murder. He had no curfews, he had a car in high school, my parents were never harsh with him in terms of academic expectations. He is a very engaging guy, but there is something about him that is slow to grow up. He has sort of a Peter Pan quality. He married late, at age 34. He and his wife are definitely socially and materially oriented and are putting off the decision to have children. I was afraid that being the last one home he would have trouble moving off on his own. After my father died, I thought for a time that he would "inherit" Mom. He's just now beginning to come into his own and I'm very proud of him for it. He's finally growing up.

The family may be an important microcosm in which the child learns about the broader cultural community, but the transmission of its culture is not simple. This is due partly to the complex nature of the family system itself—and partly to the complexity of the society in which we live. The more diverse the social fabric, the more pressure on the family system. It also becomes more difficult to transmit values when values are unfocused and in transition. This is perhaps the main challenge American families face today.

 ## SOCIALIZATION PROCESSES

socialization The lifelong process by which an individual acquires the beliefs, attitudes, customs, values, roles, and expectations of a culture or a social group.

Parental influences are just one element in the larger process of socialization. **Socialization** is the lifelong process by which individuals learn to become members of a social group, whether a family, a community, or a tribe. Becoming a member of a group involves recognizing and dealing with the social expectations of others—family members, peers, teachers, and bosses, to name only a few. Whether tense and anxiety-producing or smooth and secure, our relationships with these *socialization agents* determine what we learn and how well we learn it. Socialization also forces individuals to deal with new situations. Infants are born into families; children go to school; families move to new neighborhoods; adolescents begin to date; people marry and raise families; older people retire from jobs; friends and relatives get sick or die. Adapting to the major changes, or milestones, throughout life is an essential part of socialization.

Children actively participate in their own socialization. They have their own personalities and ways of interacting with their families and environments. As children learn, they can modify the behavior of their parents and other socializing agents. Even very young infants are capable of making socialization a two-way process. For example, the "easy" baby who soothes and smiles easily, who sleeps in regular patterns, and cries little facilitates the bonding and attachment by parents. In contrast, the "difficult" baby, who is easily frustrated, cries often, and is inconsolable when upset makes the attachment by parents more problematic. The following comments by a parent indicate the impact on family socialization that a small baby can make.

> My husband and I married late and tried to start a family immediately. Our daughter was born when I was 42, and she has certainly been a handful. From the moment of her birth, she screamed for no apparent reason—and we would find it difficult to calm her. Once she got mobile she never seemed to sit still. She was always into things and would seem to defy me when I asked her to stop doing something. She behaves badly when we are out in public, and we have stopped going out as a family until her self-control improves. I hate to say it, but sometimes I feel as though I don't like my own child.

Sometimes socialization is almost automatic, and sometimes it takes a great deal of effort. But how does it happen in the first place? How do people learn to adapt to new and different situations? To understand the process, we need to consider the various social factors that influence behavior, particularly those that influence the development and control of the emotions.

LEARNING PROCESSES

Depending on the culture, a child can develop a wide range of human behaviors—passive or aggressive, dependent or independent, liberal or conservative, vegetarian or meat-eating. Much of the behavior that children adopt is the behavior that their social, ethnic, or religious group considers appropriate; that is, behavior that will help the child to become an individual who fits into the culture. Let us consider processes by which children become fully participating members of society.

REWARD AND PUNISHMENT It is no secret that most people learn to behave according to what "pays." Reward patterns commonly produce or reinforce behavior patterns. Thus, children who receive attention when they whine are very likely to become chronic whiners. The effects of punishment, on the other hand, are not so easily interpreted. Clearly, punishment is a problematic child-rearing method. Although it seems to be fairly effective in suppressing certain types of behavior, it may cause various far-reaching side effects, some of which may be even less desirable than the original offense. For example, care-givers who use physical punishment to discipline their children actually serve as aggressive models. Their children may learn to imitate the aggression in addition to—or rather than—learning to stop the behavior that provoked the punishment (Parke & Slahy, 1983).

Another effect of punishment involves anxiety—the feeling of fear without an awareness of the cause. If children are punished for aggressive behavior (or for dependent behavior), they often learn to feel anxious not only about those "bad" or "babyish" behaviors, but also about the angry feelings that went with them. They may learn these associations so well that as adults they regularly experience anxiety whenever they feel angry (or dependent), whether their feelings are justi-fied or not. Still another potential effect of punishment is suppression of the wrong response or avoidance of the wrong part of the situation. For instance, if the father is always the one who does the spanking, the child may learn to avoid the father instead of the behavior that brought about the punishment. If this hap-pens, the father will probably have less influence on the child's behavior than the mother.

Of course, punishment may be useful in certain situations. It can be a fairly effective means of suppressing behavior, especially when appropriately combined with rewards for correct behavior. But it must be closely related to the behavior that is being punished and should be carefully and consistently administered. In any event, the dangers of using punishment should always be weighed against the possible benefits.

MODELING   From early childhood on, we observe the actions of those around us and copy whole behavior patterns, frequently down to the most minute detail. *Modeling* (imitation) is also practiced by adults. We see it in the customs and con-ventions that shape many of our thoughts and actions and in the fads, fashions, and trends that regularly sweep whole countries.

The influence of modeling on learning has been the subject of a number of studies. Research has shown that certain models are more influential than others because they possess certain characteristics that invite imitation. The three most important are power, nurturance, and perceived similarity (Bandura, 1977). *Power* is the ability to control desirable resources and to exert influence over oth-ers. Studies involving a relatively powerful adult, a relatively powerless adult, and a child reveal that the child is more likely to imitate the powerful adult (Bandura, 1977). *Nurturance,* or affectionate care and attention, also plays a part. Children imitate the warm, rewarding, affectionate model rather than the cold, punitive, distant one. *Perceived similarity* with the model is a significant factor in the effec-tiveness of modeling. Boys tend to model other boys or men; blacks tend to model other blacks; muscular, athletic children tend to imitate athletes.

Modeling continues through the entire life span. At any level, imitation is a process that constantly shapes and augments our lives. For example, a recent Australian study found that the social skills of kindergartners were very similar to their mother's skills. The mothers of popular children offered effective, sensitive and group-oriented suggestions of how their children might approach two strange children. The mothers of children who were disliked or ignored dis-rupted the group of playing children in order to impose their child on the group—or they gave ineffective help to their child (Russell & Finnie, 1990). In

People choose role models at various stages of the life span.

this way, parents are powerful models to their children in terms of peer and other relationships.

Although training and modeling are responsible for a large portion of social learning, certain complex behavioral phenomena, which develop over time, may not be fully explainable in these terms. Many theorists find the concept of identification useful in explaining such patterns.

SOCIAL CONCEPTS We learn more than just isolated patterns of behavior. With the help of older or more competent peers, we also learn to make sense of social events and social relationships. The preschooler is not able to understand the full meaning of "friendship" or "justice" or a wedding ceremony. But adults and older peers provide a framework, or structure, for interpreting social events as they happen. Every day, children and adults must engage in social problem solving. They define social goals (making a friend), obtain relevant information, select the social strategies (asking, bribing, grabbing), and make some judgment about these strategies (Is it socially acceptable?). Obviously, the success and sophistication of social problem solving depend on the sets of social concepts and social knowledge that a person has (Rose-Krasnor, 1988).

Two kinds of social concepts are essential to social problem solving. First, the child or adult must be able to make accurate *social inferences* about others' motives, emotions, or anticipated actions. Second, the child or adult needs basic *social knowledge* of things like norms, roles, or relationships. When adults visit foreign countries, they often lack many aspects of both kinds of social concepts. Often, they can overcome their lack of knowledge with the tutoring of a more experienced peer. The development of social concepts for children, however, involves the interaction of the child's developing cognitive abilities and the availability of more experienced adults to provide structure for his growing understanding (Hartup, 1989; Rogoff, 1990).

AN INTEGRATIVE SELF-CONCEPT   Most people spend a good deal of time thinking about themselves. They tend to interpret things subjectively, to see the world as it affects them personally. They may also worry about the way they affect others, about their appearance, their health, and their happiness. On another level, people may wonder about "who they are" and "where they are going." Such terms as ego, identity, and self-fulfillment have become part of the popular vocabulary, and the concepts they represent indicate significant personal attitudes toward the self. How do these attitudes develop? How are they maintained? Theories of the self-concept are far too numerous and complex to study here, but we can trace the evolution of self-awareness through various life stages.

Infants are initially unable to differentiate between the self and the world around them. Gradually, however, they develop a body awareness; they realize that their bodies are separate and uniquely their own. Much of infancy is devoted to making this distinction. Later, young children compare themselves with their parents, peers, and relatives. They know that they are smaller than their older brothers and sisters, darker or fairer, fatter or thinner. They can demonstrate their capabilities. Also, they can identify their preferences and their possessions (Harter, 1988).

By middle childhood, self-knowledge expands to include a range of trait labels. A fifth grader may describe herself as popular, nice, helpful, smart in school, and good at sports. These self-attributes are logical, organized, and generally consistent. In adolescence, self-knowledge becomes more abstract, and there is considerable concern about how others regard us. For example, an adolescent is able to analyze the fact that she is usually a sensitive and understanding person who can sometimes be selfish. She is also aware that her selfishness may annoy her family and friends (Harter, 1988).

Adolescents and adults formulate a very real, integrated idea of who they are within the social world. As we learned in Chapter 2, a major task for the adolescent is putting together an identity. It is during adolescence that the intellect becomes capable of formulating philosophies and theories about the way things are and the way they ought to be. With this new mental ability, adolescents begin to develop a sense of "ego identity"—a coherent, unified idea of the self. We may see the various factors which influence our self-concept presented in Figure 3–3.

Self-concept is crucial in the development of an integrated personality. An individual's self-concept, even as a child (and certainly by adulthood), must be fairly consistent, or the personality will be fragmented and the individual will suffer from "role confusion." The self-concept includes both a real and an ideal self—that is, the self we believe we are and the self we think we ought to be (Mead, 1934). The individual who perceives these selves as similar will be better prepared to mature and adapt than the one who sees the real self as much inferior to the ideal one.

As the social context helps to form the individual's self-concept, the self-concept is, in turn, influencing socialization (see the box "Children Who Survive"). We tend to study our own behavior and attitudes and to monitor them according to our ideas about ourselves. If an attitude or value seems to fit in, we

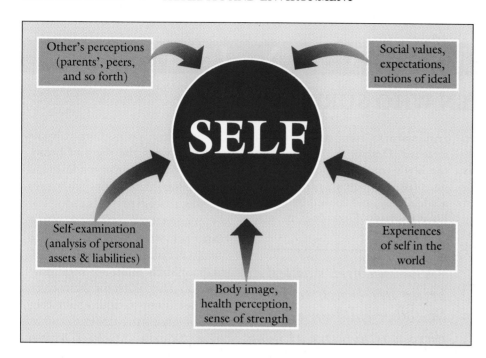

FIGURE 3–3
Factors affecting self-concept in children.

are likely to adopt it. If it is inconsistent with our idea of the self, we will filter it out, no matter how much these inconsistent attitudes are rewarded or how powerful our role models are. In filtering out cultural behavior that is inconsistent with the self-image, a process of *integration* takes place. In other words, when the self-concept becomes strong enough to help dictate our behavior, it becomes an agent of socialization as well as a product of it.

The self-concept may be self-rewarding or self-punishing. When individuals behave in a way that is consistent with their self-image, they do not necessarily need a pat on the back from society; they feel pleased with themselves and are thus rewarded. For example, a boy who considers himself a good athlete will enjoy praise from his peers after playing a good game, but he will also gain satisfaction from performing in a way that is consistent with his self-image, even if he is just practicing alone. Self-concepts can also be self-punishing. People who perceive themselves as failures may unconsciously sabotage their own endeavors in order to maintain that image. Drastic change in an image—even for the better—can be very upsetting. A child with buck teeth may emerge from braces in acute psychological distress despite a radically improved appearance. The reflection in the mirror may no longer be consistent with the homely self-image, and the result may be a new struggle for identity.

THE INTERACTION OF GENETICS AND CULTURE

As mentioned at the beginning of this chapter, the ancient argument of heredity versus environment is still raging and is likely to continue. The real issue is not which influence on the personality is more powerful, but how heredity and environment

FOCUS ON AN ISSUE

CHILDREN WHO SURVIVE

Throughout history children have been forced to grow up in seemingly brutalizing environments. Perhaps the major care-giver is mentally ill, or alcoholic, or abusive. Children may be exposed to oppressive poverty, overcrowding, or criminality. Some children experience repeated losses through war and disasters, whereas others are physically abused or seriously neglected. Usually, these unfortunate children develop lifelong personality scars. They may feel insecure, lonely, and helpless. As adults, they are more likely to become child abusers, criminals, or drug addicts. Some may suffer mental illness, whereas others may be unable to sustain meaningful relationships. But even the casual observer will note that certain children survive such devastating childhood experiences without serious scars—they succeed despite their environment. Why is it that these children seem invulnerable to their oppressive experiences? What factors help to make children *resilient*? How do they learn strategies for coping with enormous stress? Perhaps if we understood these children better we could help other children in less extreme environments to develop more adequate coping strategies.

Norman Garmezy tells of a preadolescent boy growing up in the slums of Minneapolis (Pines, 1979). He lives in a run-down apartment building with his father, an ex-convict who is dying of cancer; an illiterate mother; and seven brothers and sisters, two of whom are retarded. Despite this environment, the boy's teachers report that he is unusually competent, performs well academically, and is liked by most of his classmates. How does he manage?

"A young girl wanted to bring her lunch to school like other children did, but there was nothing at home to put between the slices of bread. Not discouraged, she made bread sandwiches. After this, whenever she was forced to make do, she would tell herself to make bread sandwiches."

After studying hundreds of such children, researchers have identified certain characteristics that these resilient or seemingly invulnerable children share. First, they are socially competent. They seem to be at ease with both peers and adults. Adults often describe them as appealing or charming, and willing to learn from adults. Second, these children are self-confident. They see themselves as effective. They look at problems as challenges, and they believe that they have the ability to master new situations. Garmezy offers an example. A young girl wanted to bring her lunch to school like other children did, but there was nothing at home to put between the slices of bread. Not discouraged, she made bread sandwiches. After this, whenever she was forced to "make do," or she encountered a difficult situation, she would tell herself to "make bread sandwiches." Third, these children often are very independent. They think for themselves, and they listen to adults, but they are not necessarily dominated by them. Fourth, Michael Rutter (1984) emphasizes that these children usually have a few good relationships that provide security (Pines, 1984). These relationships may be with peers, or with a teacher, an aunt, or a neighbor. Finally, these children are achievers. Some children do well scholastically, whereas others become good athletes, artists, or musicians. They enjoy positive experiences of achievement—they learn that they can succeed and that they can affect their environment.

There is still a great deal that we don't know about resilient children. The interplay between these children's temperament and talents and their life circumstances is far more complex than can easily be discovered in one or two studies. Nevertheless, perhaps the research on resilient children will help us understand children in more normal situations as they learn coping strategies for the stress of everyday life (Anthony & Cohler, 1987).

Young children are able to identify their most prized possessions.

interact in the development of human behavior. Studies of adoption and of twins show that to some extent our genes influence social traits like sociability, emotionality, and activity level. These inherited traits, in turn, influence the environments we seek, the things we attend to, and how much we learn.

Children also help tailor their environment in other ways. For example, psychologists Sandra Scarr and Kathleen McCartney believe that children interact with their environment in three different ways, depending on their individual genetic predispositions. In the *passive interaction pattern*, the parents give and the child accepts both the genes and the environment, either favorable or unfavorable, for the development of particular abilities. A musical child in a musical family, for instance, receives an enriched musical environment in which to develop his skills. In an *evocative interaction pattern*, the child evokes particular responses from his parents and others based on his genetically influenced behavior. An active, sociable, extroverted child will demand responses from parents and teachers. A quiet, passive, shy child may be ignored. Finally, Scarr and McCartney (1983) suggest that an *active relationship* may exist between the child and his environment; that is, the child may actively seek specific environments (peers, opportunities) that are compatible with his temperament, talents, or predispositions.

Our physical appearance—whether we are tall or short, dark or light, plain or beautiful—is genetically determined, but the way in which our culture views these physical attributes can profoundly affect personality development. In our culture, for example, people who are tall are frequently given more power and authority, not necessarily because they are worthy of it, but because they literally "stand head and shoulders" above the rest of us. For the same sort of cultural reasons, a beautiful, rugged child with learning disabilities who appears to have no disabling characteristics may be treated as if he has no handicap at all. In other words, inherited traits may be admired or not, depending on current cultural attitudes toward physical appearance. This makes it even more difficult to separate the effects of genetics and culture. For instance, the muscular, handsome boy

If a child's self-concept includes performing well in school, then completing homework may be rewarding in itself.

who is not particularly intelligent may develop more self-confidence and become a more capable person because everyone around him believes that muscular, handsome males must be capable. On the other hand, the beautiful, intelligent blond girl may develop a confused self-concept because everyone around her thinks of her as beautiful but dumb.

The interaction of heredity and environment may begin immediately with the newborn infant. T. Berry Brazelton and his students have spent several years studying individual differences in newborn infants all over the world. They've studied African, Asian, Latin American, European, and American infants. In one study, Brazelton compared Zambian infants and caucasian American infants (Lester & Brazelton, 1982). Many of the newborn Zambian infants were undernourished and dehydrated at birth. Their behavior reflected this physical state. They exhibited poor visual following and less motor activity, and they had poor head control. But because the Zambian culture expects newborns to be vigorous, the parents ignored the limp behavior of their infants and handled them as if they were more responsive than they actually were. The infants were breast-fed frequently and on demand and showed rapid weight gain. Within a couple of weeks, they had become highly responsive, sturdy neonates. The American infants, on the other hand, were considerably stronger at birth. Most stayed in the hospital for 3 days (the Zambian infants went home the day after they were born) and were handled gently at home. The American babies were fed every 3 or 4 hours and were involved in little play activity. They changed very little in their general responsiveness or activity over the first 2 weeks.

It seems apparent, then, that genetic endowment by itself does not determine neonatal behavior. The genetic endowment, the prenatal environment, the mother's reproductive and obstetric history, and the caregiving system all play a role in determining behavior.

The interaction of genetics and culture can perhaps be most clearly seen in the matter of gender. We inherit our gender, but from the point of conception, it is affected by our social environment. A crucial balance of masculinizing hormones at a critical period in prenatal development determines whether a male fetus will develop male or female genitals. If for some reason these hormones are not present at the right time, the fetus will develop female genitals, even if it is a genetic (XY) male. In short, the genetic code is not always followed exactly.

GENDER-ROLE IDENTITY

Orthodox Jewish boys thank God daily that they were not born female. Many of the world's other religions also believe women to be inferior in many ways. But what does being born female imply? Gender is genetically determined, and some suggest that men and women are inherently and dramatically different in intellect, personality, adult adjustment, and style—primarily because of genetic programming. The opposite point of view contends that men and women differ because of the way they are treated by their parents, their teachers, their friends, and their culture throughout life. A third view states that gender identity is determined by both heredity and environment. This view holds that there are significant differences in men and women but there is nothing intrinsically inferior in either gender. When we argue about whether genetics or culture is more important in determining gender-role identity, we are probably addressing the wrong issue.

Genetics and culture may set the outer limits of gender-role identity, but they interact like two strands of a rope in forming personality or psychosexual identity. We need to look more closely at this interplay throughout the life span.

Although gender-role identity is established in early childhood, it remains a developmental issue well into adulthood. Gender-role identity is perhaps our most fundamental self-concept, but it is not a permanent, rigid personality trait. Before we consider how gender-role identity can change because of life situations, let us examine some of the clear differences between the genders and how these genetic "givens" may determine some aspects of behavior.

MALE-FEMALE DIFFERENCES

Studies have shown that male babies, on average, are born slightly longer and heavier than are female babies. Newborn girls have slightly more mature skeletons, and they seem to be a bit more responsive to touch. As toddlers, boys are a bit more aggressive, and girls have a slight edge in verbal abilities. By age 8 or 10, boys are beginning to outperform girls in spatial skills and in mathematics. By age 12, the average girl is well into the adolescent growth spurt and maturation, while the average boy is still considered a preadolescent, physically. By mid-adolescence, the girl's superiority in verbal skills increases, as does the boy's edge in spatial skills and mathematics. By age 18, the average female has roughly 50 percent less muscular strength than the average male. In adulthood, the male body carries more muscle and bone, while the average female body carries more fat as insulation. There are built-in health advantages for women, including more pliable blood vessels and the ability to process fat more efficiently. By middle age, males are succumbing much faster to health hazards, such as emphysema, arteriosclerosis, heart attacks, liver disease, homicide, suicide, or drug addiction. By age 65, there are only 68 men alive for every 100 women; at age 85, women outnumber men almost two to one. At the age of 100, there are five times as many women as there are men (McLoughlin et al., 1988).

Many of these differences between males and females appear to be genetically caused. For example, Maccoby and Jacklin (1980) suggest that the greater aggressiveness in males may be due to their prenatal exposure to higher levels of some sex hormones. Tieger (1980) disagrees, stating that there is no biological predisposition toward aggressiveness in males; rather, the difference in aggressiveness between males and females is due to sex-role socialization. A more recent review (Hyde, 1984) suggests that even these "well-established" differences between males and females in aggression—as well as in mathematical skills and verbal abilities—should be looked at with caution. After examining hundreds of studies, Hyde concluded that the differences noted between the average male and the average female were not found consistently.

Equally significant are the findings in areas where males and females do *not* differ. Ruble (1988) reviewed many studies on sex-role differences, noting areas in which differences were not established. There appeared to be no consistent differences due to gender, for example, in sociability, self-esteem, motivation to achieve, or even in rote learning and certain types of analytical skills.

Furthermore, the differences that actually exist between males and females are small, often less than 5 percent of the full range. In many studies conducted in the mid-1980s, these tendencies were not as strong as previously believed

(Halpern, 1986; Ruble, 1988). Men average only slightly higher in activity level, aggression, or mathematical reasoning, and women score only slightly higher in empathy. Moreover, many of the personality differences that do exist are modifiable with training, with the situation or with changes in cultural expectations.

GENDER AND SOCIALIZATION

There are at least two interrelated components of what the child learns about his or her gender: *gender-related behaviors* and *gender concepts*. Social-learning theorists have focused on how gender-appropriate behaviors are learned and combined into a sex role, or gender role. (Because the term "sex" has many meanings, there is some preference for the use of the word "gender" when we talk about maleness or femaleness. Some major authors, though, continue to use the terms "sex" and "gender" interchangeably [Ruble, 1988].) Cognitive theorists, in contrast, focus on how the child comes to understand gender-related concepts and how she develops a gender identity. Let's begin by looking at the acquisition of the culturally defined behaviors that make up a sex (gender) role.

SEX-TYPED BEHAVIOR   In most cultures, children display clear sex-typed behavior by 5 years of age. Indeed, by age 3 many children have learned some sex-specific behaviors (Weinraub et al., 1984). In nursery schools, for example, girls are often observed playing with dolls, helping with snacks, showing greater interest than boys in art and music. Boys in nursery schools can be found building bridges, roughhousing, and playing with cars and trucks. Pitcher and Schultz (1983) found this clear differentiation among 2- and 3-year-olds, noting that sex-specific behaviors became stronger by the time children reached age 4 or 5.

Sometimes, these sex-typed behaviors are exaggerated or stereotypical. **Gender-role stereotypes** are rigid, fixed ideas of what is appropriate masculine and feminine behavior. They imply a belief that "masculine" and "feminine" are two distinct and mutually exclusive categories and that an individual's behavior must be one or the other. These ideas pervade nearly every culture. In the United

gender-role stereotypes Rigid, fixed ideas of what is appropriate masculine or feminine behavior.

The popularity of Barbie dolls suggests the social pressure for female children to be "real girls."

States, for instance, parents expect their male children to be "real boys"—reserved, forceful, self-confident, tough, realistic, and assertive—and their female children to be "real girls"—gentle, dependent, high-strung, talkative, frivolous, and impractical (Bem, 1975; Williams, Bennett, & Best, 1975). Some children are put under strong social pressure to conform to these gender-role stereotypes, regardless of their natural dispositions.

The learning of gender roles begins in infancy. Kagan (1971) reports that mothers respond more physically to their boys but more verbally to their girls when their infants babble. These differences in how the two sexes are treated are obviously detectable by the time a child is 6 months old, at least in Kagan's Boston-area study. A similar study conducted 20 years later in Montreal finds that the rooms and toys provided for infants of each sex are quite stereotyped. Parents still expect active, vigorous play with objects from their boys, and quieter play with dolls from their girls (Pomerleau et al., 1990). In many cases, however, studies are unnecessary. Many care-givers recognize that their responses toward a 1-year-old boy differ from those used with a 1-year-old girl. It is not simply a matter of pink and blue blankets; often, it is hundreds of little things every day—the way children are held, how often they are picked up, how they are talked to, the kinds of things that are said to them, the amount of help they are given, how care-givers respond to crying. All of these behaviors are frequently subtly influenced by the child's sex.

How are gender roles learned? The processes of reward and punishment and modeling for appropriate or inappropriate behavior begin early in infancy. Society's baby boys are socialized toward a masculine stereotype of physical activity and prowess. Smith and Lloyd (1978) studied the behavior of mothers with 6-month-old infants who were not their own. The babies were "actors": Girls were sometimes presented as boys or boys as girls, as well as being presented as their true sex. Invariably, mothers encouraged the perceived boys more than the perceived girls in walking, crawling, and other physical play. Girls were handled more gently and encouraged to speak. As children get older, parents consistently react more favorably when their children engage in behavior that is appropriate to their sex.

Fathers may be especially important in the development of the child's gender role (Honig, 1980; Parke, 1981). While fathers teach children of both sexes to become more independent and autonomous, they also, more than mothers, teach specific gender roles by reinforcing femininity in daughters and masculinity in sons. It was once thought that fathers were influential only in teaching their sons masculine behavior, and this seems to be somewhat true in the preschool period. Boys whose fathers have left before they reach age 5 are often more dependent on their peers and less assertive (Parke, 1981). For girls, the effect of father absence is more evident during adolescence. Effective fathers help their daughters learn to interact with men in appropriate ways (Lamb, 1979; Parke, 1981).

GENDER CONCEPTS   From the time they are toddlers, children are learning concepts like "boy," "girl," "man," or "woman," and then more specific concepts like "tomboy" and "sissy." Sometimes, these gender-based cultural standards, or stereotypes, are called *gender schemes* (Levy & Carter, 1989). It is generally believed that the development of such gender schemes are partly a result of the child's cognitive developmental level and partly due to the particular aspects of the culture that the child is able to observe. Among the many concepts learned is the child's own *gender identity*. This gender identity develops in a particular sequence over the first 7 or 8 years of life. Children learn to label themselves "boy" or "girl" at an early age. They do not understand that they will be male or female forever or that gender is constant despite the clothes, activities, or hairstyles they may adopt. Gradually, children will understand these factors of gender identification. However, it is not unusual for a preschooler to ask his father whether he was a boy or a girl when he was little. By age 6 or 7, most children no longer make such mistakes. They have achieved what is called *gender constancy* (Stangor & Ruble, 1987).

There is more to learning gender concepts than simply achieving gender constancy, however. Our understanding of gender includes a web of interrelated concepts, attitudes, and expectations about traditional and nontraditional gender roles. Carol Martin studied people's attitudes toward "tomboys" and "sissies." She asked college sophomores whether they approved of certain behaviors of typical girls, typical boys, "tomboys," and "sissies." She asked the students what they would expect of these children when they grew up, and she questioned the students as to whether they would mind if their own child was a "tomboy" or a "sissy." It turns out that women in the study were more accepting of the cross-sex children than were men, and "sissies" were much more negatively evaluated than were "tomboys." It was assumed that "tomboys" would grow out of their cross-gender behavior. "Sissies," in contrast, were thought to be less well adjusted and more likely to grow up still showing inappropriate behavior (Martin, 1990). In another study, Martin tried to discover how these attitudes and expectations were developed. In this study of 4- to 10-year-olds, she found that the younger children could not use the label of "tomboy" or "sissy" to predict interests and behavior of another child. By age 8, however, children had well-developed concepts and possessed the culture's attitudes toward "tomboys" and "sissies" (Martin, 1989).

Children develop gender concepts directly from what they are taught and from the models around them. They also develop them more indirectly from stories, movies, and television. Recent studies of the nature of stereotyped models in television indicate that the sex-role images presented on television over the past 10 to 15 years have been quite stable, traditional, conventional, and supportive of stereotypical roles (Signorelli, 1989). Even studies of children's elementary school reading books in 1972 and again in 1989 indicated that there was a preponderance of sex-stereotyped roles presented to young children in their school books (Purcell & Stewart, 1990). It is not surprising, therefore, that children's concepts about gender are sometimes stereotypical and strongly sex typed.

THE ANDROGYNOUS PERSONALITY

Is it a good thing for children to learn a strong, clear pattern of behavior and set of concepts to define masculine and feminine behavior? Does such learning contribute to better mental health? Is it more "normal"? Two decades ago, parents and teachers were urged to help children establish clear, sex-typed behavior by the time they entered elementary school. Failure to do so might predispose individuals to psychological maladjustment. Now, however, much of the literature suggests that exaggerated sex-typed behavior restricts and limits the emotional and intellectual development of both men and women (Bem, 1985). In fact, several recent studies have provided little support for the traditional view that deviation from sex-role standards—either in personality or in interests—leads to psychological maladjustment (Orlofsky & O'Heron, 1987).

Many psychologists realize that a number of beneficial male and female traits can easily exist in the same person. Both men and women are capable of being ambitious, affectionate, self-reliant, gentle, assertive, and sensitive. This blend of personality traits goes into the makeup of what is called an **androgynous personality.** Yet an androgynous personality is not limited by such deficiencies and narrow abilities. Depending on the circumstances, men with androgynous personalities can be independent and assertive, but able to cuddle an infant or offer a sensitive ear to another person's troubles. Likewise, women who have androgynous personalities are able to be effective and competent in the material world and still be fully expressive and nurturant when necessary.

Contemporary popular literature suggests that rigid sex-role stereotypes tend to restrict emotional and intellectual growth. Women who show a high degree of feminine behavior actually tend to be anxious and insecure. They are less creative and score lower on tests of intelligence and spatial perception than do women with fewer stereotypical feminine traits. Highly masculine men also score lower on tests of intelligence and creativity than do men with more androgynous personalities. Although rigidly masculine personalities assert themselves easily enough, they find it difficult to be playful and spontaneous (Ruble, 1988). Not all researchers agree, however, on the advantages of androgynous personalities for psychological adjustment. In a recent study, there seemed to be little difference in psychological development for men who were high in masculinity as compared to men who were androgynous (that is, men who were high in both masculine and feminine characteristics). Neither group was particularly prone to depression, anxiety, or social maladjustment. In contrast, low-masculinity men seemed to have problems of social maladjustment. For women, the results were more telling. Even women who showed strong masculinity and low femininity were no less well adjusted than were their strongly feminine or their androgynous peers (O'Heron & Orlofsky, 1990). It appears that sex-typing, or androgyny by itself, is not necessarily a ticket to positive psychological adjustment or maladjustment.

The androgynous personality is formed by specific child-rearing practices and parental attitudes that encourage cross-sex behavior. Traditionally, parents have accepted more cross-sex behavior in girls than in boys, as illustrated in the studies of "tomboys" (Martin, 1990). Lifelong androgynous gender identities that combine aspects of both masculinity and femininity are established most often in children when such behavior is modeled and accepted. It helps for the same-sex parent to provide a model of the cross-sex behavior and for the opposite-sex parent to reward this pattern (Ruble, 1988). Often parents may attempt to develop androgynous behavior in their children, but find their efforts stymied by other family members as the following comments by the mother of two young girls indicate.

It's absolutely infuriating. My husband and I have two little girls whom we are attempting to raise in a non-stereotyped way. We read books to them with girls as strong and resourceful characters (even though they are hard to find), we do things with them that encourage the same—scuba diving, fishing, hiking—and then what happens at Christmas? My mother buys them dolls, my sister-in-law buys them kitchen sets, and my sister buys them make-up kits!

androgynous personality A sex-role identity that incorporates some positive aspects of both traditional male and traditional female behavior.

These feelings are echoed in the following comments by the parents of (hopefully) androgynous boys:

> We have never bought into that stereotype that boys must be boys (translate that to mean beasts!). We have always encouraged them to realize that there are other people in the world besides them and that getting along means respect. Our three little boys are all close in age, and they are actually civilized human beings who enjoy life. So, what do our relatives give them for birthdays? GI Joe tanks, guns, and ninja turtles paraphernalia. We wouldn't mind tinker toys, building blocks, and so forth, but our relatives think we are too harsh on the kids...so they try to "help out."

GENDER ROLES OVER THE LIFESPAN

Gender labels and gender identity affect behavior throughout the life span. In adolescence, pressures often intensify for individuals to assume fairly traditional sex-typed behavior. In adulthood, gender-role behavior varies depending on life circumstances and situations. Barbara Abrahams and her colleagues (1978) studied the permanence of sex-role behavior through four major life situations: cohabitation, marriage, anticipation of a first child, and parenthood. The researchers believed that men and women would modify their sex-role behavior in response to the demands of these situations, and they predicted a change toward an androgynous personality style as men and women moved toward parenthood. Quite the opposite occurred.

In cohabiting situations, where unmarried partners live together but are not necessarily committed to a long-term relationship, feminine characteristics (loyalty, compassion, sensitivity) were rated low in self-descriptions by both men and women. In marriage, where a greater commitment may exist for the needs of the partner, feminine characteristics were rated higher by both men and women. Couples expecting their first child were in an ambivalent life situation. Women felt more self-sufficient while simultaneously experiencing a greater need to be cared for. Men often felt a bit "left out"; at the same time, they were increasingly concerned with providing security for their wife and the expected child. Both men and women in this situation said that they felt stronger masculine and feminine impulses than did their married counterparts who were not expecting children.

In the parenting situation, both men and women reported more traditional sex-role characteristics. Shortly after the birth of their first child, men became preoccupied with business and finances. Women were now less independent and more home- and child-centered. The balance swung back to a traditional husband-dominated relationship. In other words, sex-role differences became increasingly traditional across the four situations. Men reported less role change across the situations than did women, probably because the behavioral changes required for women were greater.

SUMMARY AND CONCLUSIONS

The process of human growth and development from conception through adolescence—and beyond to adulthood—is complex and not easily broken down into its component causes. All children are the product of a delicate interaction between genetic material inherited from their parents and cultural behavior patterns. The role of heredity versus environment in child development, which has also been called the nature versus nurture controversy, is not a new one. Similar concerns have been raised by philosophers, scientists, and others as long as human beings have been conscious. We still do not have exact answers; however, it is fairly clear that neither heredity nor environment alone produces human behavior.

In this chapter we have presented the key aspects of reproductive genetics as well as those factors associated with failures of meiosis in germ cells or mitosis in autosomes. Some of these defects produce very severe effects, for example Tay-Sachs disease with its early death, while others produce effects that vary depending on the extent of chromosomal damage, for example Down syndrome. Some of the disorders occur predominantly in males because of their sex-linked origins. They may occur in females, but this is extremely rare. When this happens the woman must have inherited two damaged X chromosomes, an unlikely event. An example of this type of genetic defect is hemophilia. From this overview we can see that genetic defects have various origins. They may be caused by a single gene defect, by chromosomal translocation or breakage, or by multifactorial factors, in which a number of small mistakes combine to produce errors.

Genetic counseling is a new specialty in medicine that apprises potential parents of the risks associated with their planned pregnancy. This is especially suggested for older parents, parents with a recognized genetic defect in their family, or couples that have suffered three or more miscarriages. Genetic counseling has several phases. The couple first receives extensive physicals, blood work and family analysis. Karyotyping is done where the actual genotype of the parents' cells may be visualized. Finally, should pregnancy occur, various prenatal-screening procedures are performed including ultrasound, amniocentesis, or chorionic villi sampling. Recently, when in vitro fertilization procedures are performed, preimplantation embryonic biopsies have been performed which effectively detect certain defects. We should note that the rapid movement of reproductive genetics has lead to concern over ethical dilemmas. Some researchers have suggested that these dilemmas will form a major research and theoretical focus for the first half of the next century.

A child's behavior is not determined solely by genetics, however. The effects of culture and socialization cannot be underestimated. Research on adopted children and twins, for example, have pointed out the strong contributions of both heredity and environment to behavior. Genes establish the codes for human development, but culture dictates how and if the genetic potential will be realized. Different family structures and child-rearing practices produce distinctive values, personalities, and social behaviors in the children raised by them. Because the family is the main socialization agent in society, it must walk a tightrope between the needs of children and the demands of society. In these days of rapid social change, the task of socialization is crucial but challenging for American families.

The interactive effects of genetics and culture are nowhere as visible as in the establishment of gender-role identity. Although the biological and biochemical substrate of sexual identity is laid down prenatally, gender roles and gender identity evolve throughout childhood and adolescence. Societies have notions of appropriate gender roles and attempt to enforce fairly rigid sexual stereotypes on the behavior of children. Children assimilate these stereotypes, as they do other social behaviors, very rapidly and fairly unshakably in early childhood. This conformity to cultural norms of sex-appropriate behavior—as well as conflict over this conformity—may lead to intellectual and emotional damage in both sexes.

As we can see, understanding the development and behaviors from birth through adolescence is a very complex exercise. It has already undoubtedly raised questions in you about the way in which these principles of heredity and environment merge to produce the human child. We shall address these, and other questions, more fully as we move through the chronological journey of the child between conception and maturity in the remainder of this textbook.

➤ KEY TERMS AND CONCEPTS

alleles	ethnocentrism	meiosis	polygenic inheritance
androgynous personality	gender-role stereotypes	mitosis	recessive
autosomes	gene therapy	mutation	RNA (ribonucleic acid)
crossover	genetic counseling	nonsex-linked autosomal	sex-linked traits
DNA (deoxyribonucleic acid)	genotype	trait	sex-typed behavior
dominant	karyotype	phenotype	socialization

➤ SELF-TEST QUESTIONS

1. Describe the process involved in the transmission of an individual's genetic code.

2. What is the difference between mitosis and meiosis?

3. How do genes combine to determine a person's traits?

4. What are some abnormalities caused by chromosomal defects? What is known about the causes and symptoms of these defects?

5. How are sex-linked disorders transmitted? What are some examples of sex-linked disorders, and who is most likely to manifest these disorders?

6. What are some diseases caused by non-sex-linked autosomal traits? Describe the characteristics of these disorders.

7. Explain genetic counseling.

8. What are the latest advances in genetic research? What are the advances we can look forward to in the near future? Are there limitations to this type of research? Explain.

9. Describe the types of studies common to behavioral genetics and the conclusions often reached by these studies. Why are these studies controversial?

10. Compare and contrast three basic family styles and the cultural patterns that underlie them. Are the values of the family and the values of society always consistent with each other? Please explain.

11. What are the various socialization processes that influence behavior? How do these processes operate?

12. Describe the relationship between heredity and environment in human development. Give an example.

13. What are the genetic differences, if any, between male and female behavior patterns?

14. Describe the process by which gender-role behaviors are established.

15. How might gender-role stereotypes inhibit the development of a well-rounded personality? How can this be avoided?

16. In what way do major life situations evoke changes in gender-role behavior?

➤ SUGGESTED READINGS

ANTHONY, E.J., & COHLER, B.J. (Eds). *The invulnerable child*. New York: Guilford Press, 1987. A collection of well-researched articles about the resilient children who seem to do well despite oppressive childhood circumstances.

BROOKS-GUNN, E., & MATTHEWS, W.S. *He & she: Children's sex-role development*. Englewood Cliffs, N.J.: Prentice Hall, 1979. A readable explanation of the development of separate sex roles.

FEATHERSTONE, H. *A difference in the family: Living with a disabled child*. New York: Penguin, 1981. Featherstone, herself the parent of a severely disabled child, presents a well-researched, highly readable, and sensitive view of the family's struggle to cope with the worries, fears, doubts, and day-to-day demands and eventual meanings of life with a handicapped child. An excellent source book for social service personnel as well as parents and grandparents.

HALPERN, D.F. *Sex differences and cognitive abilities*. Hillsdale, NJ: Lawrence Erlbaum, 1986. A detailed, research-oriented summary of sex differences in cognitive abilities. It carefully summarizes the biological as well as the psychosocial hypotheses about such sex differences.

KELLY, T.E. *Clinical genetics and genetic counseling* (2nd ed). Chicago and London: Yearbook Medical Publishers, 1986. A carefully researched yet readable introductory textbook on genetics and its clinical applications.

PLOMIN, R. *Nature and nurture: An introduction to human behavioral genetics*. Pacific Grove, CA: Brooks/Cole, 1990. This brief, easily accessible paperback book translates the technical genetic research for the lay reader without losing the intriguing challenges of the field.

TOBIN, J.J., WU, D.Y.H., & DAVIDSON, D.H. *Preschool in three cultures: Japan, China, and the United States.* New Haven: Yale University Press, 1989. In detailed, case-study fashion, these authors present a vivid and persuasive picture of cultural variation in the way three preschools chose to nurture, educate, and socialize their students.

VIDEO CASE: PRENATAL TESTING

Although prenatal testing was originally developed for older pregnant women with higher risk for fetal abnormalities or for women with particular medical problems such as diabetes, today most young and healthy women will undergo some form of it to see if their baby is healthy. What many women, however, fail to understand is that the three most used tests are not routine, simple procedures. One problem is that the majority of prenatal tests are performed in the average obstetrician's office. Most of these doctors can identify whether the pregnancy is normal. But with high-risk patients or where a problem is suspected, a specialist may be required. In fact, some referral centers for high-risk cases focus on sonography, while others focus on amniocentesis and CVS. But getting prenatal tests done well solves only part of the problems incurred by prenatal testing. The other difficulty is having them accurately interpreted. Actually, experts worry most about the effects of prenatal misdiagnosis, especially when prospective parents are informed that their fetus has a problem for which no help exists.

Because every year hundreds of thousands of women choose to take prenatal tests, there is a large potential for poor choices as a consequence of inaccurate data. For example, 42-year-old June Hinkle was told that her baby would probably not survive pregnancy. However, if he did, his prognosis was poor. So it was suggested that she terminate her pregnancy. Instead, Hinkle asked for a second opinion. Having received more information, Hinkle was able to get a treatment that saved her baby's life. Doctors are concerned that not enough babies are getting such life-saving referrals. Experts say this is because doctors sometimes want to keep their patients rather than lose them to another practitioner.

Slowness to refer can be especially harmful in sonography because doctors tend to mistakenly think they can master it easily. According to Jim Miller, a former salesman of ultrasound equipment, "Whether you buy the equipment outright or whether you lease it because of what you can charge for the exams . . . you've paid for the equipment in six months. After that, it's a profit and a good business."

The answer to such problems lies in the patient herself. She must learn to protect her best interests by not letting the doctors "control" her pregnancy. If they do not answer her questions, then she should consult another practitioner. The best place to go if birth defects are suspected late in pregnancy is a referral center which has the latest equipment, something the average obstetrician usually does not have.

CASE QUESTIONS

1. Do you think that every pregnant woman should choose to undergo prenatal testing? Why or why not?
2. What are the two main problems associated with prenatal testing procedures?
3. Why do these problems arise?
4. What can women do to protect themselves if problems arise relating to the prenatal testing they have undergone?

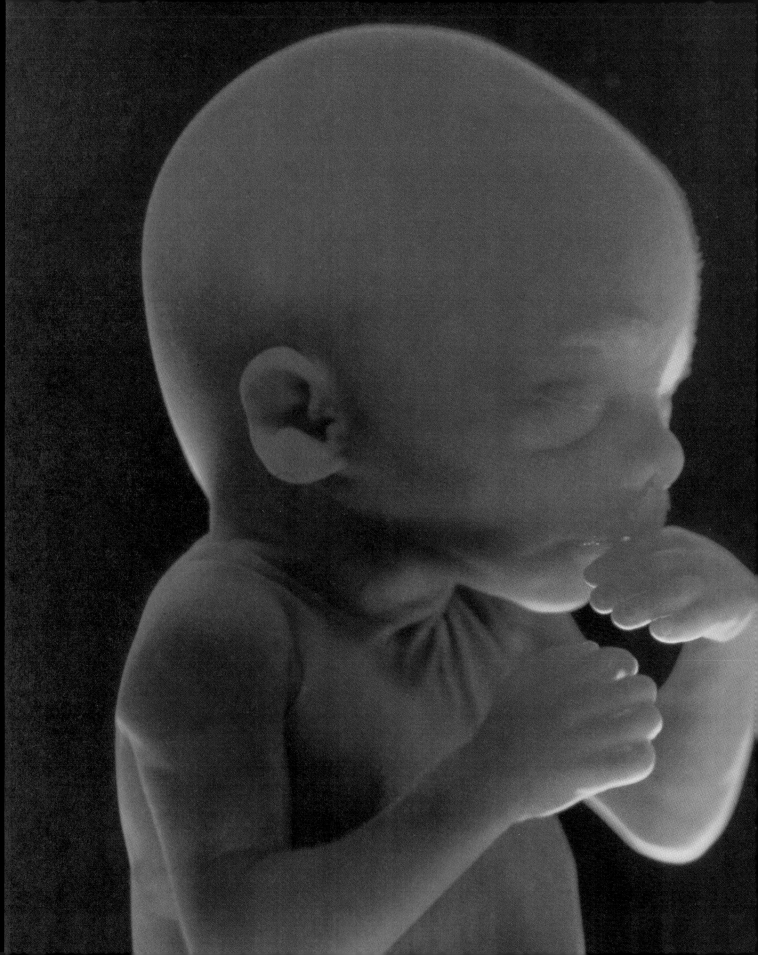

The history of man for the nine months preceding his birth would, probably, be far more interesting and contain events of greater moment than for all the three score and ten years that follow it.

SAMUEL TAYLOR COLERIDGE

THE PRENATAL PERIOD

OUTLINE

CHAPTER OBJECTIVES

By the time you have finished this chapter, you should be able to do the following:

✔ Understand the reasons why couples choose to have or not have children.

✔ Understand factors that affect the likelihood of conception.

✔ Understand the psychological effects of infertility on men and women.

✔ Describe three prenatal developmental periods.

✔ Discuss the reproductive alternatives provided by modern technology, including the emotional, legal, and moral issues they raise.

✔ Describe the general trends that occur in prenatal growth and development.

✔ Explain the importance of critical periods in prenatal development.

✔ Discuss the factors that influence prenatal development.

✔ Discuss physical and emotional adjustments that the family faces during pregnancy.

"Congratulations, Mr. and Mrs. Smith. The test is positive...you can expect a baby in nine months. Let's bring out our charts and figure out the due date." With these or similar words, a couple enters the homestretch of a road they embarked upon once sexual intercourse was undertaken for the purpose of procreation. In this event, the words undoubtedly produce intense joy and excitement in the couple. What they have hoped for during their months of trying has come to pass. At least the initial response is joy. After a day or so the reality of what they are about to experience sets in. The woman begins to worry about the health of her baby and wonders if she can carry it safely to term. She begins to plan for what the baby will need when he or she comes home—clothes, diapers, a nursery. The husband begins to hope he has the financial wherewithal to sustain a secure life for his "family"—what a nice word! But he also worries about his wife and baby's health, wonders if he will still have the companionship of his wife, and feels just a little left out of the special role his wife has in the whole enterprise.

This is only one of many possible scenarios that describe the way a couple may deal with the reality of a pregnancy. In some cases, the couple is not married, the pregnancy is not planned, and the perfect nursery may remain a dream. There are many different ways in which the impending arrival of a baby affects parents-to-be. If the parents have gone through a lengthy period of infertility, for example, the initial response may be disbelief rather than joy—if the parents are teenagers experimenting with sex, the response may be fear. But for most people who have planned on having a baby—regardless of their financial background—the initial response to a positive pregnancy test is happiness and expectation.

As in our chapter on genetics, we shall study here the interaction of heredity and environment—this time in connection with the prenatal period. The fetus inside the womb of the mother is very much affected by the physical environment in which its parents live—the amount and quality of food they consume, the immediate safety of their home and community, the work its mother does, perhaps even the music the parents listen to, and other factors. Prolonged stress which the mother experiences has an effect on the developing fetus—as do viruses, radiation, temperature and other factors. This interaction of heredity and environment is so intimate during the prenatal period that an embryo that is perfect genetically can be terribly damaged by a virus the pregnant woman is exposed to—an environmental factor.

Prenatal development—the unfolding of inherited potential—is one of the most dramatic examples of maturation. The prenatal maturation of human infants occurs within a highly controlled environment—the uterus—and it follows an orderly, predictable sequence. But even in the uterus there are environmental influences that affect development. Almost from the moment of conception, children are part of an environmental context. They do not begin life with a "clean slate." The expectations and anxieties, riches and deprivations, stability and disruptions, health, and illnesses of the families into which they are born affect not only their life after birth but also their prenatal development—these factors may even affect the chances that this baby would be conceived at all. In this chapter, we will explore a couple's decision to have children, and what may happen if they are unable to conceive. We will then examine the biological and maturational processes during the prenatal period as well as the environmental influences on these processes.

 ## BECOMING PREGNANT

Our attitudes toward having children change throughout our lives. Most teenagers who are sexually active want to avoid pregnancy, and this often persists into the early twenties. Even when couples marry, the idea of having children remains remote for many. Other factors get in the way—gaining stable employment, finishing an education, finding a place to live, perhaps becoming successful in their careers. Consequently, for many people the decision to have a child is postponed—until perhaps they realize that their biological clocks are running out of time, or they feel the "time is finally right." To a certain extent, deciding when the appropriate time to start a family is a new possibility for people, a direct consequence of the availability of effective contraception. In the past, families frequently were started very early in a marriage, often in an unplanned or haphazard way. It was just how things were.

Couples who decide to have or not have children do so for a variety of reasons. Hoffman and Hoffman (1973) studied the reasons why couples value the idea of having children. The reasons still persist today. One reason is that society often views the attainment of adult status and mature relationships as culminating in procreation. Society—in the form of institutions, parents, and peers—therefore puts pressure on couples to validate their relationships through children. Others want to have children for the sense of immortality it gives to individuals—"my genes and values will continue on through these children." For others, religious values dictate that their sexuality should culminate in the birth of a child. Some couples want to have children to have family ties with their associated affiliation and togetherness. Another reason why couples choose to become parents is because of the novelty, stimulation and fun they assume having children will entail. Others look to the opportunity to mold another person into their version of an ideal person. In this sense, creativity, accomplishment and the sense of competence are the motivating reasons in the decision to become parents (Hoffman & Hoffman, 1973; US Bureau of the Census, 1993).

For teenagers who have felt powerless much of their lives, becoming pregnant is one way of ensuring that they can dominate at least one other person.

Some reasons are somewhat more negative than the reasons stated above. Having power or influence over others is a reason that some people who have felt helpless during their lives choose to have children. For example, this is one of the main reasons why teenagers choose to become pregnant. It gives them control over another person. In this motivation, the guiding of a child to some ideal is not the goal, the goal is dominance. Children represent the first real opportunity to dominate another person. Social competitiveness is another reason for choosing to have children. This reason is obvious to many people—it is seen in the father who lives vicariously through his son's athletic prowess, the mother who pushes her daughter into modeling and beauty pageants, and in any parent whose child has done well and been recognized at anything. Children can definitely be a source of prestige and status in a community. A final reason for having children is not as relevant in the industrialized countries as it is in agrarian economies—the economic utility of children. Large families in agricultural economies provide more hands to cultivate the field, maintain animals, and perform all the other chores involved in keeping a farm viable.

Today's potential parents are somewhat more ambivalent about having children than were their parents. Because they have a choice as to whether to have children, they tend to weigh factors such as career, lifestyle, and the cost of raising children very heavily. Especially as more women choose professional careers, they are more likely to consider other factors as equally or more important than having children (Neal, Grout & Wicks, 1989).

We can see that the reasons why people choose to have or not have children are complex. They are partly a matter of individual choice, partly a matter of peer or parental pressure, and partly determined by society or culture.

BARRIERS TO ACHIEVING PREGNANCY

The decision to start a family does not necessarily mean that the couple will be successful. Many couples are infertile, others conceive but fail to carry a pregnancy to term, a few deliver a baby only to have it die in the month after birth. Various factors affect these negative outcomes. We shall discuss them in this section of the chapter after we get a sense of the numbers of children and families that are affected by such events.

Birth rates have fluctuated greatly during the past century; for example, they were low during the Great Depression and climbed to their highest during the baby boom of the 1950s. In the 1960s and 1970s, birth rates dropped substantially and have since remained at a low, stable level. Women are currently not having enough daughters to replace them in the next generation. In other words, the overall population of the United States will soon start declining unless the birth rate or immigration increases. In general, the more educated and employed women and those with higher family income tend to have lower fertility (USD-HHS, 1992). This is not a biological phenomenon—it is because these women tend to choose to start families later and have fewer children than less educated, unemployed women.

In 1992, slightly over 100,000 children were adopted, over half by relatives. While this number appears high, it is significantly lower than numbers for the 1970s. One reason for this decline in adoptions is the increase in abortions. In 1992, there were an estimated 1.6 million abortions performed, about 42 abortions for every 100 live births (USDHHS, 1992; Statistical Abstracts of the United States, 1993).

A couple's success in achieving pregnancy is affected by many factors. Their age, overall health—current and past—and their knowledge of their own bodies all act to influence the likelihood of their success.

VENEREAL DISEASE AND FERTILITY If the woman has had venereal disease, such as syphilis or gonorrhea, this may affect the likelihood of her conception and successful carrying of a child. Pelvic Inflammatory Disease (PID),—a consequence of some venereal diseases,—severely scars the fallopian tubes, causes pelvic adhesions (scar tissue which may, for example, link the ovary to the intestine), and may cause infertility. In order to check the health of the tubes in women who have a history of such disease, an x-ray of the fallopian tubes and uterus is performed to visualize any damage that may be there. Other less severe venereal diseases—and even common yeast infections—also affect the ability to conceive. Infections produce acidity in the vagina which may kill sperm outright. Herpes, however, does not affect the ability to conceive, but it may seriously affect the fetus or baby during the birth process (Lauersen, 1983).

PREVIOUS ABORTION AND CHILDBEARING If an abortion was carried out early in pregnancy at a reputable clinic under sterile conditions, it is unlikely that any permanent damage has been done. But if infection, heavy bleeding, or tubal infection occurred as a result of the abortion, there is a significant risk that conception and pregnancy may be difficult. Of course, this risk increases with the number of abortions a women has had because of the trauma and scarring this produces in the uterus. Such a condition may produce an incompetent cervix, a cervix so weakened that it is unable to remain closed as the weight of the fetus increases. A large-scale study is currently underway to determine the long-term effects of abortion on women's physical and mental health.

ENDOMETRIOSIS Endometriosis is a condition in which the menstrual flow (the uterine lining or endometrium) is pushed backward through the fallopian tubes and into the abdomen. Once there, it forms tumorlike growths that attach to the ovaries, intestines, and outside of the tubes. These growths continue to increase in size each month with the normal monthly hormonal stimulation in a woman's body. The result of severe endometriosis is infertility because the growths become large enough to interfere with ovulation and make conception difficult or even impossible.

MATERNAL AND PATERNAL AGE The question of fertility is a real one as a couple moves into their thirties or even forties, as indicated in Chapter 3. For some women, ovulation and menstrual periods begin to be irregular in the late thirties. Since the eggs are the same age as her body, an older menstruating woman may have damaged eggs that are difficult to fertilize or, if fertilized, have errors that result in miscarriage. Some women in this age group may even be premenopausal and already be undergoing the hormonal changes associated with menopause that make an unsupported pregnancy difficult. Older men, too, have concerns. Although it is possible for men to fertilize an egg at any age, that probability decreases with age. Older sperm are less motile, slower swimmers, and more likely to show deformed morphology (or shape). Often couples in their thirties and forties are not really "infertile," but are rather "subfertile," and require considerable medical advice or assistance to achieve pregnancy.

 ## PRENATAL DEVELOPMENT

We have now discussed some general factors that influence a couple to decide to become parents, as well as the individual factors that affect the likelihood of their success. Let us now discuss the prenatal journey of the child they create. The development of each unique human individual begins at the moment of conception. A one-celled, fertilized egg that can hardly be seen carries all of the genetic information needed to create a new organism. But the journey of the next 9 months is complex and, at times, perilous. It is estimated that over 50 percent of all fertilized eggs are lost within the first 2 weeks (Grobestein et al., 1983). As we have seen, another 25 percent may be lost through miscarriage after the mother knows that she is pregnant. We will now look at the process of fertilization and the intricate sequence of development over the next 9 months.

CONCEPTION AND FERTILIZATION

About the 10th day after the beginning of the average woman's regular menstrual period, an **ovum,** or egg cell, that has developed in one of her two ovaries is stimulated by hormones and enters a sudden period of growth that continues for 3 or 4 days. By the end of the 13th or 14th day of growth, the follicle surrounding the ovum breaks, and the ovum is released to begin its journey down one of two **Fallopian tubes.** This release of the ovum from the ovary is called **ovulation.**

In most women, then, ovulation occurs about the 14th day after the onset of menstruation. The mature ovum survives for only 2 or 3 days. A man's **sperm,** deposited in a woman's vagina during sexual intercourse, also survives for as long as 3 days. A viable sperm, moving from the vagina through the uterus and up the Fallopian tube and reaching the ovum during the critical 48– to 72–hour period, can **fertilize** the ovum. Otherwise, the ovum continues down the Fallopian tube to the uterus, where it disintegrates.

The sperm and ovum are single cells, each containing half of the hereditary potential of the individual. The union of the two cells to produce a human being is quite a remarkable achievement. Some 300 million sperm are deposited in the vagina during intercourse, yet only one of these may fertilize an ovum. The sex and inherited traits of the child depend upon which of these millions of sperm cells survives to penetrate the ovum. For the sperm cells, the trip to the ovum is long and difficult. The microscopic sperm cells must work their way upward through a foot-long passage, through acidic fluids that can be lethal to them, through mucus and other obstacles—and finally one arrives at the proper place at the proper time. It is at that moment of fertilization "…when, out of a billion possibilities, the DNA of one individual, specific person is created" (Silber, 1991, p. 73).

ovum The female reproductive cell (the egg or gamete).

Fallopian tubes Two passages that open out of the upper part of the uterus and carry the ova from the ovary to the uterus.

ovulation The release of the ovum into one of the two Fallopian tubes; occurs approximately 14 days after menstruation.

sperm The male reproductive cell (or gamete).

fertilization The union of an ovum and a sperm.

INFERTILITY

For 1 in 12 couples, conceiving a child in the manner described is not possible, but alternatives are now available (Mosher & Pratt, 1990). Fertilization that occurs outside of the womb is called *in vitro* **fertilization.** Ovum and sperm are united in a petri dish (not in a test tube, as implied by the now common phrase, "test tube babies"). This new ovum, which has been fertilized "in solution," grows for the first few days with rapid cell division and then must be promptly implanted in a human uterus to survive.

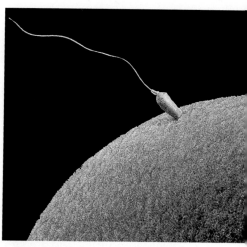

A living human ovum at the moment of conception. Although some sperm cells have begun to penetrate the outer covering of the ovum, only one will actually fertilize it.

We may see a fuller discussion of this new reproductive technology in the box "Reproductive Technology: What are the Options?" These procedures are no longer experimental, but are clinically approved, with established guidelines (OB/GYN News, June 1984). The guidelines insure the safety of the procedure and aid in the selection of couples who can appropriately be helped to achieve fertilization in this fashion. There are now dozens of fertility clinics in the United States and Canada.

We can describe much of what happens in fertilization, and in the development of the fetus that follows, but there are still many things we do not fully understand about the outcome of fertilization. Researchers are working on some rather interesting questions. For instance, for every 100 girls conceived, approximately 160 boys are conceived. Why are more male sperm successful at penetrating the ovum than female sperm? We know, for example, that compared to the female, the male sperm has a smaller, rounder head and a longer tail; it swims faster, is more affected by an acid environment, and tends to live for a shorter period of time (Rosenfeld, 1974; Silber, 1991). While many more boys are conceived, however, only 105 boys are born for every 100 girls. Why do more boys than girls die during the prenatal period? And why do ovulation induction procedures seem to produce an increase in girls unless the sperm is introduced directly into the uterus by an insemination procedure? These are just some of the many challenging questions that are being investigated.

PSYCHOLOGICAL EFFECTS OF INFERTILITY Infertility can be traumatic and may have severely depressing effects on both partners. Although childlessness is more accepted in today's society than previously, there is a distinct group of infertile couples who feel great social and personal pressure to become parents. As the couple realizes that they may never become parents, an emotional state develops which some have called *the crisis of infertility* (Seibel & Taymor, 1982). As recently as thirty years ago, 40 percent to 50 percent of infertility cases were thought to be caused by emotional factors. There is no doubt that emotional factors can worsen the effects of infertility, but it is unlikely that these are a primary cause (Seibel & Taymor, 1982; Silber, 1991).

Infertile men and women have reported experiencing depression, helplessness, and marital strain. Infertile women tend to take greater personal responsibility for infertility and engage in more problem-focused coping behavior than do their husbands. The husbands tend to experience more home-life stress and lower home-life performance than their wives (Abbey, Andrews, & Halman, 1991).

in vitro **fertilization** Fertilization of woman's egg outside the womb.

FOCUS ON AN ISSUE

REPRODUCTIVE TECHNOLOGY: WHAT ARE THE OPTIONS?

In early 1985, William and Elizabeth Stern went to the Infertility Center of New York. They wanted to find a woman willing to carry their child implanted by artificial insemination. Both Sterns were in their late thirties, and a pregnancy was potentially dangerous for Elizabeth. They were among 2 million people who visit fertility centers each year in an effort to have children.

About 10 million people of childbearing age have difficulty conceiving (Lord et al., 1987). Most want children and have tried unsuccessfully for years to have them. Many turn to adoption agencies, only to find that it may be years before they have a chance to adopt a baby. For those on a tight budget, the cost, which can be over $10,000, may make adopting a child prohibitive. Because an increasing number of couples postpone trying for a child until they are in their late twenties or early thirties, many feel a rising sense of desperation as the years go by without having a child.

As couples get older, the rate of infertility increases. In 1988, the last year for which there are figures, about 5 million or 8.4 percent of women between the ages of 15 and 44 had fertility problems. In women ages 15 to 24, this figure drops to 4 percent, but for women 35 to 44 years of age, the figures rises dramatically to 21 percent (Mosher &

"Both Sterns were in their late thirties, and a pregnancy was potentially dangerous for Elizabeth. They were among 2 million people who visit fertility centers each year in an effort to have children."

Pratt, 1990). In many instances, female infertility is caused by a blockage or abnormality in the Fallopian tubes. For 70 percent of women with this problem, microsurgery can restore fertility. Among women with a complete blockage, only 20 percent can successfully conceive (Wallis, 1984). However, today conception is possible using some of the newer techniques which are available in the major fertility research centers.

There are several options available to would-be parents. The first that comes to mind, of course, is adoption. Most infertile couples try this route first, but they find it so time-consuming, costly, and frustrating that they soon look for other possibilities.

Modern advances in reproductive technology have given infertile couples several new alternatives. The oldest and still very widely used technique is *artificial insemination*. Simply stated, artificial insemination is the impregnation of a woman by the artificial introduction of semen. This can take several forms. A woman can be artificially injected with the sperm of her husband, or if the sperm is diseased or weak, with sperm donated by a stranger and kept frozen until used.

Another technique that infertile couples try is *in vitro* fertilization, a technique of fertilizing a woman's egg with a man's sperm in a laboratory dish, then placing the fertilized egg in the woman's uterus (Wallis, 1984). In vitro fertilization, more commonly known as the process of making test-tube babies, is an increasingly popular method of dealing with the infertility problem.

Part of the causes of increased infertility in the United States is the late birthtiming decisions made by many couples. As we can see in Figure 4-1, since 1975 there has been a gradual and steady increase in the number of older women who expect to have a future birth. There has also been an increase in childlessness

However, clinics have long waiting lists for treatment that, at most, offers approximately a 20 percent chance of success (Wallis, 1984).

A newer method of *in vitro* fertilization referred to as the GIFT Protocal has been found to have a 46 percent chance of success. In this procedure too, the egg is fertilized by the sperm in a petri dish (not a test tube at all!), the cells are allowed to grow somewhat, and then the embryo is placed in the *fallopian tube* in the site where fertilization normally occurs. The success rate of this procedure is approximately two times greater than when embryos are introduced into the uterus for implantation.

A recent development of *in vitro* fertilization, known as "donated eggs," involves having the egg donated by a stranger, fertilized by the sperm of the mother-to-be's husband, and then placed in her uterus. The technique of "donated eggs" makes it possible for an otherwise barren woman to have the experience of bearing a child—regardless of her age. With better understanding of the hormonal control of ovulation, it is now possible for postmenopausal women to carry and deliver babies. It is an alternative for couples who cannot conceive but can carry children. In contrast, an option available to couples who might be able to conceive but cannot carry children is to enter into a contract with a surrogate mother who will carry a child to term for them. This was the alternative chosen by the Sterns when they signed a contract with Mary Beth Whitehead to have her bear a child for them.

The unraveling of the arrangements between Whitehead and the Sterns, known as "the Baby M case," brought to prominence the emotional, ethical, and legal issues raised by solutions to the infertility problem. These issues have by no means been resolved. Federal and state legislatures are just beginning to examine the legal dimensions of the problem. Because the technology involved is so new, there is little hard data on the psychological aftereffects of carrying someone else's child or of rearing a child someone else bore at the legal parents' request. Nor does anyone yet know the eventual effects on the child. Most difficult of all are the moral questions raised by reproductive technology and its relation to traditional values. Is it right to hire a woman's uterus or a man's sperm so that some other couple can have a chance to raise a child? What are the implications of raising children for whom only one of the parents is a biological parent? On the other side

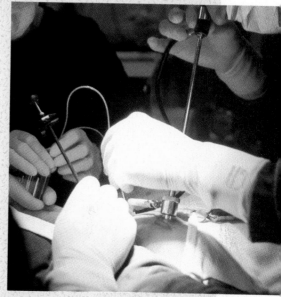

In vitro fertilization.

of the equation: Is it right to deny a childless couple the opportunity to raise children and have a full family life that modern technology makes possible? Finally, we cannot ignore the trauma that infertile couples experience as they deal with miscarriage and innumerable visits to infertility specialists to achieve their goal—a healthy baby (Beck, 1988). As a society, we have not yet resolved these issues, just as we have not yet resolved other issues connected with reproductive rights.

at all ages between 18 to 44 years. Many women are increasingly entering career tracks and choosing to postpone both their first marriage and the birth of their first child. This late birthtiming decision is even more likely in dual-career families. Moreover, research has indicated that often in these dual-career families, if one of the partners has not yet dealt with the issue of childlessness, the decision is delayed until the other partner comes to terms with it (Soloway & Smith, 1987). The inability of such a couple to come to agreement on whether and/or when to become parents may result in their seeking marital counseling. Results of research further indicate that marital partners may have different agendas about child birthtiming and different educational, career, and personal goals. Consequently,

> When either the husband or wife assesses the situation and decides the time is right to have a child, the other partner may not have reached the same conclusion that all the conditions are right for him/her to proceed with childbearing. Even if the issue of having a child has been discussed previously, neither may have anticipated that one might be ready for parenthood before the other marital partner. (Soloway and Smith, 1987, p. 262)

In this situation it is important for the couple to be aware of the psychological problems that may arise if one person forces the other to comply with the request to have a child. Frustration and dissatisfaction with the child's presence after birth may result. Consequently, marital counseling by someone familiar with

FIGURE 4–1
Married Women without Children Who Still Expect a Future Birth.
(Statistical Handbook on the American Family, 19??.)

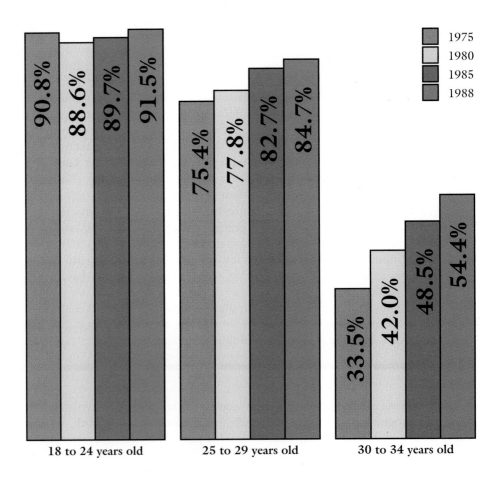

the psychological problems of fertility may assist such couples in their decision-making process.

However, after proper counseling and a full comprehension of their problems by the couple, many fertility problems can be overcome; thus, many couples are eventually helped to achieve pregnancy. In fact, the state of technology has reached the point where postmenopausal women can become pregnant using donor eggs inseminated with their husband's sperm and then implanted in their own uterus. It now appears as though the age of the woman is irrelevant in the process—what is crucial is the age of the eggs put in her. British doctors have achieved a pregnancy rate of 46 percent per cycle in postmenopausal women using donor eggs (Silber, 1991). This is a very high rate since the usual pregnancy rate per cycle in women in their 20s is only 25 percent. Obviously, the 46 percent rate is only possible with the use of new reproductive technologies.

PERIODS OF PRENATAL DEVELOPMENT

As we have seen, the majority of couples who decide to have a child are successful in their efforts. Let us now explore the dramatic biological sequence that marks the time between the egg's fertilization and the baby's birth.

After the ovum is united with the sperm, it is called the **zygote.** It then enters the **germinal period,** a time of very rapid cell division and initial organization of cells that lasts for about 10 to 12 days. This is followed by the **embryonic period,** during which structural development of the embryo takes place. This structural development stage lasts for about 7 weeks. From the beginning of the third month until birth—a time known as the **fetal period** when the embryo is now called a fetus—the organs, muscles, and systems begin to function. Many of the processes that the organism will need to survive at birth are developing during this period.

GERMINAL PERIOD

The process of cell division (cleavage) begins just a few hours after fertilization and produces two cells. The second cleavage, which takes place after about 2 days, produces four cells. A third cleavage then produces eight cells. The rate of cell division increases, and by the end of 4 days, as many as 60 to 70 cells may have been produced.

In some cases, the first division of the zygote produces two identical cells, which then separate and develop into two individuals. The result will be **identical,** or **monozygotic, twins.** Because they develop from the same cell, identical twins always are the same sex, and they share the same physical traits. In other cases, two ova are released and each unites with a sperm; this produces **fraternal,** or **dizygotic, twins.** The genetic traits inherited by fraternal twins can be as different or as similar as those of any siblings conceived at different times. Fraternal twins may be of the same or opposite sex because the ova are fertilized by two separate sperm.

zygote A fertilized ovum.

germinal period After conception, the period of very rapid cell division and initial cell differentiation lasting approximately 2 weeks.

embryonic period The second prenatal period, which lasts from the end of the second week to the end of the second month after conception. All the major structures and organs of the individual are formed during this time.

fetal period The final period of prenatal development, lasting from the beginning of the third month after conception until birth. During this period, all organs, limbs, muscles, and systems become functional.

identical (monozygotic) twins Twins that result from the division of a single fertilized ovum.

fraternal (dizygotic) twins Twins resulting from the fertilization of two separate ova by two separate sperm.

Identical twins share physical traits and are always the same sex; fraternal twins (right) can be as different or as similar as siblings born at different times.

Beyond the early stages of cleavage, the cells continue to divide and form a ball that moves through the Fallopian tube toward the uterus. At this point, the solid ball of cells forms a hollow sphere, or **blastula,** around an accumulation of fluid. During the formation of the blastula, the cells begin the process of differentiation—that is, they separate into groups according to their future function. Some of the cells move to one side of the hollow sphere and start to develop into the embryo, while others develop into a protective covering for the embryo.

At the beginning of the second week, the blastula completes its journey down the Fallopian tube and arrives in the uterus, where it will develop during the coming months. Within a few days, it becomes embedded in the uterine wall, in a process called **implantation.** After a successful implantation, the developing organism enters the embryonic period. Many defective ova are spontaneously aborted at this point, often before the woman even knows she has been pregnant. Such a miscarriage resembles a heavy period that arrives somewhat late. We may see the journey that the egg makes into the uterus depicted in Figure 4–2.

EMBRYONIC PERIOD

blastula The hollow, fluid-filled sphere of cells that forms several days after conception.

implantation The embedding of the prenatal organism in the uterine wall after its descent through the Fallopian tube.

Generally, the embryonic period is considered to extend from near the end of the second week to the end of the second month after conception. It is a crucial time when much that is essential to the baby's further prenatal development and future lifetime development occurs. During the embryonic period, all the tissues and structures that will house, nurture, and protect the embryo (and later the fetus) for the remainder of the 9 months are formed. In addition, the development begins, in form at least, of all organs and features of the embryo itself. During the

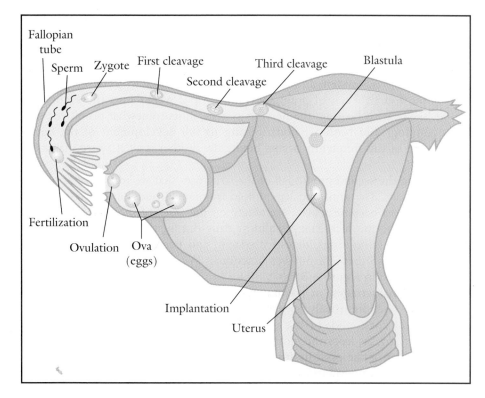

Fallopian tube
Sperm Zygote First cleavage Second cleavage Third cleavage Blastula
Fertilization
Ovulation Ova (eggs)
Implantation
Uterus

FIGURE 4–2

The journey of the fertilized egg is shown as it moves from ovary to uterus. Fetal development begins with the union of sperm and egg high in the Fallopian tube. During the next few days, the fertilized egg, or zygote, travels down the Fallopian tube and begins to divide. Cell divisions continue for a week until a blastula is formed. By this time, the blastula has arrived in the uterus and, within the next few days, will implant itself in the uterine wall.

embryonic period, this very tiny being develops arms, legs, fingers, toes, a face, a heart that beats, a brain, lungs, and all the other major organs. By the end of the embryonic period, the embryo is a recognizable human being.

The embryo develops within an **amniotic sac** filled with amniotic fluid; it is then nourished by means of an organ called the **placenta,** which develops specifically to assist the growth of the new organism. The **placenta** is a disk-shaped mass of tissue growing from the wall of the uterus; it is formed partly from the tissue of the uterine wall and partly by the **chorion,** the outer layer of tissue that surrounds the embryo and the amniotic sac.

The placenta starts to develop at the moment of implantation and continues to grow until about the seventh month of pregnancy. It is connected to the embryo by the **umbilical cord,** a "rope" of tissue containing two fetal arteries and one fetal vein. The placenta provides for an exchange of materials between mother and embryo, keeping out large particles of foreign matter but passing on nutrients. Thus, enzymes, vitamins, and even immunities to disease pass from the mother to the embryo, while the resulting waste products in the embryo's blood are passed to the mother for final elimination. Sugars, fats, and proteins also pass through to the embryo, but some bacteria and some salts do not. It is important to note that the mother and child do not actually share the same blood system. The placenta allows the exchange of nutritive and waste materials across cell membranes without the exchange of blood cells.

During this period, the embryo itself grows rapidly and changes occur daily. Immediately after implantation, the embryo develops into three distinct

amniotic sac A fluid-filled membrane that encloses the developing embryo or fetus.

placenta A disk-shaped mass of tissue that forms along the wall of the uterus through which the embryo receives nutrients and discharges wastes.

chorion The protective outer sac that develops from tissue surrounding the embryo.

umbilical cord The "rope" of tissue connecting the placenta to the embryo; this rope contains two fetal arteries and one fetal vein.

layers. They are the **ectoderm,** or outer layer, which becomes skin and the nervous system; the **mesoderm,** or middle layer, which becomes muscles, blood, and the excretory system; and the **endoderm,** or inner layer, which becomes the digestive system, lungs, and glands. Simultaneously, the neural tube (the beginning of the nervous system and the brain) and the heart start to develop. At the end of the fourth week of pregnancy and only 2 weeks into the embryonic period, the heart is beating; the nervous system, in its somewhat primitive form, is functioning; and both are contributing to the development of the entire embryo. All of this frequently occurs before the mother is even aware that she is pregnant.

During the second month, all of the structures that we recognize as human develop rapidly. The arms and legs unfold from small buds on the sides of the trunk. The eyes become visible, seemingly on the sides of the head, at about a month, and the full face changes almost daily during the second month. The internal organs—the lungs, digestive system, and excretory system—are being formed, although they are not yet functional. We may see the growth of the embryo depicted in Figure 4–3.

Many **miscarriages,** or **spontaneous abortions,** occur during the embryonic period. They are usually caused by inadequate development of the placenta, the umbilical cord, and/or the embryo (Beck, 1988). Because the embryo receives its nutrients from the mother through the placenta, it is obvious that an inadequate diet or the poor health of the mother may adversely affect the developing child. It is important for us to keep these phases of prenatal development in mind when we discuss later in this chapter environmental factors that can affect the embryo and fetus. It becomes obvious that, depending on the timing of exposure, damage will occur to broadly different aspects of fetal development.

FETAL PERIOD

The fetal period lasts from the beginning of the third month until birth—or for about 7 months—versus an average total gestation period of 266 days. It is during the fetal period that the organs, limbs, muscles, and systems become functional. The fetus begins to kick, squirm, turn its head and, eventually, its body. Even with its eyes sealed shut, the fetus starts to squint, frown, move its lips, open its mouth, swallow a little amniotic fluid, suck its thumb, and make sucking motions.

During the third month, the first external signs of sex differentiation become apparent. The penis and scrotum in the male or the beginning of the labia in the female can be detected, although the male organs develop sooner than do those of the female. At the same time, the male fetus develops a prostate gland, vas deferens, and epididymis, while the female develops Fallopian tubes and ovaries with their full complement of approximately 400,000 eggs.

The eyes, still set toward the sides of the head, develop their irises, and all of the nerves needed to connect the eye to the brain are now in place. Teeth form under the gums; ears begin to appear on the sides of the head; fingernails and toenails form. The fetus develops a thyroid gland, a thymus gland, a pancreas, and kidneys. The liver begins to function, and the lungs and stomach begin to respond. By the twelfth week, the vocal cords have developed, the taste buds have

ectoderm In embryonic development, the outer layer of cells that becomes the skin, sense organs, and nervous system.

mesoderm In embryonic development, the middle layer of cells that becomes the muscles, blood, and excretory system.

endoderm In embryonic development, the inner layer of cells that becomes the digestive system, lungs, thyroid, thymus, and other organs.

miscarriage (spontaneous abortion) Expulsion of the prenatal organism before it is viable.

gestation period The total period of time from conception to birth; in humans, this averages about 266 days.

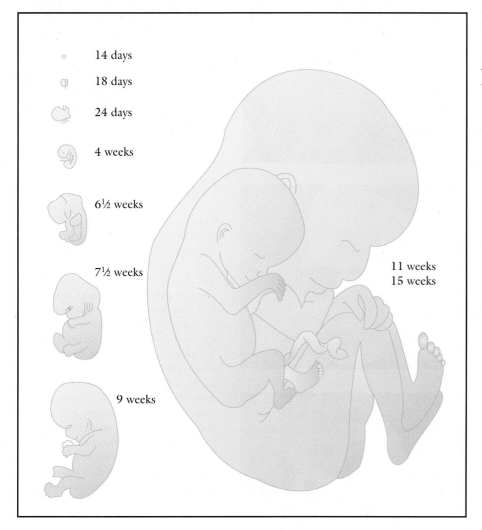

14 days

18 days

24 days

4 weeks

6½ weeks

7½ weeks

11 weeks
15 weeks

9 weeks

FIGURE 4–3
The Embryonic Period.
This is a lifesize illustration of the growth of the human embryo and fetus from 14 days to 15 weeks.

formed, and ribs and vertebrae have begun to ossify (turn from cartilage to bone). The fetus, although unable to survive on its own, has acquired almost all of the systems and functions necessary for a human being. And at this point, it is only about 3 inches long and weighs around half an ounce.

During the fourth to sixth months (the second trimester), all of the processes begun in the first trimester continue. (The 9 months before birth are divided into three equal segments of 3 months each, called **trimesters.**) The body becomes longer, so the head does not look as out of proportion as it did during the preceding month. The face develops lips, and the heart muscle strengthens, beating from 120 to 160 times a minute. In the fifth month, the fetus acquires a strong hand grip and increases the amount and force of its movements. The mother will be able to feel an elbow, a knee, or the head, as the fetus moves around during its waking periods. This feeling of movement is a very important experience for many pregnant women as the following comments indicate:

trimesters The three equal time segments that comprise the 9-month gestation period.

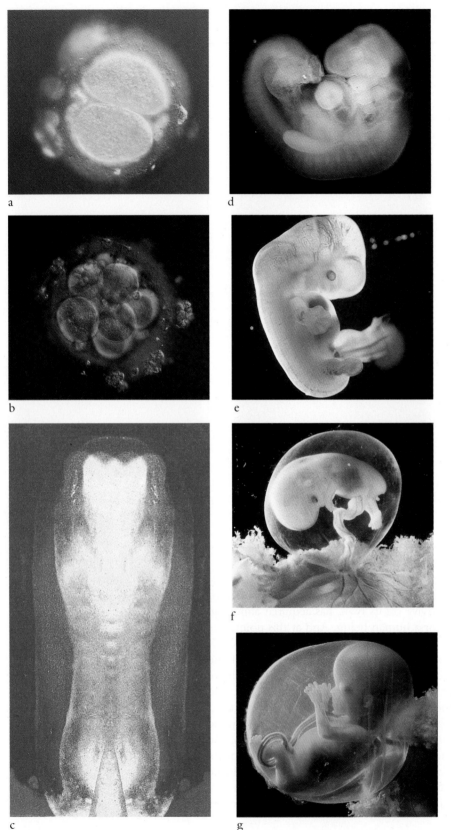

Stages of prenatal development: (a) A two-celled organism showing the first cleavage a few hours after fertilization. (b) The germinal period at 2 days—no cell differentiation exists yet. (c) An embryo at 21 days. Note the primitive spinal cord. (d) A 4-week embryo. One can now distinguish the head, trunk, and tail. The heart and nervous system have started to function by this time. (e) A 5-week-old embryo. The arms and legs are beginning to unfold from the sides of the trunk. (f) A 9-week-old fetus showing the umbilical cord connection with the placenta. (g) A 16-week-old fetus showing the umbilical cord connection with the placenta. All internal organs have formed but are not yet fully functional. (h) A 20-week-old fetus. At this stage, most internal organs have begun to function, and the fetus is able to kick, turn its head, and make facial expressions.

I remember the day I first felt my daughter move inside of me. It was initially a soft, tickling sensation—much like I would imagine a butterfly's wing to feel. It was such a wonderful feeling. As time went by, the movements became more intense...it seemed as though whenever I finally sat down to rest in the evening, she would wake up and want attention. Sometimes I would play with her; I would push in one spot and then she would push back. One time when I was 8 months pregnant and giving a lecture she decided to flip right over. Luckily, I had a podium in front of me or the flip would have been visible.

I remember my sister telling me to watch the movements my daughter made after she was born. I would see her making the movements she had been making inside of me for all those months. Sure enough, I saw her pushing those arms and legs out and squirming around. I'm sure she was glad to finally be out in the open, away from the tight confines of the sac and uterus.

During the fifth month, the fetus is also undergoing a process of skin-cell replacement. Oil glands form and secrete a cheesy coating, called the *vernix caseosa,* that protects the skin from the amniotic fluid. The fetus also develops a hairy covering on its body, referred to as *lanugo hair,* and begins to grow eyebrows and eyelashes.

In the sixth month, the fetus grows to about 12 inches in length and weighs approximately 1 1/2 pounds. The eyes are completely formed, and the eyelids can open. Bone formation progresses, hair on the head continues to grow, and the fetus begins to straighten out its posture so that the internal organs can shift to their proper positions.

By the beginning of the third trimester (that is, after 24 weeks of development in the uterus), a healthy fetus is considered **viable**—it might survive outside the mother's body if it were placed in an incubator and given special, intensive care. With modern medical advances, however, some special care units for premature infants have been able to sustain babies who are born even earlier than this. Perhaps as many as 20 percent of fetuses born at 24 weeks survive, provided they are in the best-equipped neonatal intensive care units in the nation. At 29 weeks, fully 90 percent survive in such units (Kantrowitz, 1988). Such care is very expensive, however, and for very premature infants with multiple problems who must be cared for in *newborn intensive care units (NICU's).*

At 7 months, the fetus weighs about 3 pounds, and its nervous system is mature enough to control breathing and swallowing. During this seventh month, the brain develops rapidly, forming the tissues that localize the centers for all of the senses and motor activities. The fetus is sensitive to touch and can feel pain; it may even have a sense of balance.

A frequently raised question is whether or not a fetus hears. It has long been known that a fetus is startled by a very loud sound occurring close to the mother but hardly at all by a moderate sound. The reason is that the fetus is surrounded by a variety of sounds. There are digestive sounds from the mother's drinking, eating, and swallowing. There are breathing sounds. Also, there are circulatory system sounds that correspond to the rhythm of the mother's heartbeat. Loud conversational speech from outside the body can be heard, but it is muffled. In fact, the internal noise level in the uterus is thought to be as loud as that

viable After 24 weeks of development, the ability of the fetus to live outside the mother's body, provided it receives special care.

of a small factory (Aslin et al., 1983; Armitage et al., 1980). Noise does affect the fetus, however, as the following mother's comment indicates:

> I'll never forget the day we went to a modified sports car race at a local track. We were sitting on metal bleachers in the upper section just under a metal roof. I was seven months pregnant at the time. The noise was absolutely incredible. I finally put ear plugs on to muffle some of the noise. The amazing thing was that our poor baby had no ear plugs. He seemed to be upset by the noise because he was moving very strongly inside of me. I finally had to leave the race because my body hurt from the pummeling he was giving me.

Some researchers suggest that if mothers read to children rhythmically or play certain music before birth, the child prefers those experiences after birth. Studies were done in which certain books, like Dr. Seuss's *The Cat in the Hat*, were read aloud by mothers to their unborn babies. Others played classical music like Vivaldi or Bach. In all cases, the infants preferred these "familiar" patterns to unfamiliar patterns. They were more likely to be soothed by them and sucked a nipple or pacifier more upon hearing them. This demonstrated that prenatal auditory experiences influence postnatal auditory preferences (DeCasper and Spence, 1992). See the box "Does the Fetus Learn?" for a more complete discussion of this type of research.

Researchers have determined that the human organism does much more than just develop physically during the prenatal period. As early as 15 weeks, the fetus can grasp, frown, squint, and grimace. Reflex movements result from the touching of the soles of the feet or the eyelids. By 20 weeks, the senses of taste and smell are formed. By 24 weeks, the sense of touch is more fully developed, and there is response to sound. By 25 weeks, the response to sound grows more consistent. At 27 weeks, a light shown on the mother's abdomen sometimes causes the fetus to turn its head. In any case, a brain scan will show that the fetus has reacted to the light. All of these behaviors—facial expressions, turning, kicking, ducking actions—that occur late in the seventh month occur in the womb and may be purposeful movements that make the fetus more comfortable (Fedor-Freybergh & Vogel, 1988).

In the eighth month, the fetus may gain as much as a half-pound a week and begins to ready itself for the outside world. Fat layers now form under the skin in order to protect the fetus from the temperature changes that it may encounter at birth. Although the survival rate for infants born after 8 months is better than 90 percent in well-equipped hospitals, these babies do face risks. Breathing may still be difficult; initial weight loss may be greater than for full-term babies; and, because their fat layers have not fully formed, temperature control could be a problem. For these reasons, babies born at this developmental stage are usually placed in incubators and are given the same type of care as babies born in the seventh month.

Fetal sensitivity and behavior also develop rapidly in the eighth month. At the middle of the month, it is thought that the eyes open in the uterus, and the fetus may be able to see its hands and environment, although it is quite dark. Some doctors think that awareness starts at about 32 weeks, when many of the

FOCUS ON AN ISSUE

DOES THE FETUS LEARN?

Is the fetus capable of learning? Can we train the unborn child, and can this training give the child a head start on its later learning? What has the fetus already learned about its mother? For centuries, people have wondered about how experiences in the womb may affect the unborn child. The Greek philosopher Aristotle thought the fetus could acquire "sensation" (Hepper, 1989). In medieval Europe, some even believed that the fetus might possess "ideas." If Aristotle and these others are correct, how are these sensations or ideas acquired? Is there evidence that either supports or debunks these beliefs?

First, let us review what we already know about fetal capabilities. Researchers generally agree that the fetus is sensitive to touch and vibration and can hear in the final 2 months before birth (Hepper, 1989; Poole, 1987). It must be noted, however, that sounds coming from outside of the mother must compete with sounds inside the mother's body in order to be heard. Researchers who placed microphones in the wombs of sheep were shocked to discover the rather high volume of noise inside the sheep (Armitage et al., 1980). With the rhythmic noises of the circulatory system, the steady beat of the mother's heart, and the various rumblings of the mother's digestive system, the fetal environment seems to be as loud as a small factory.

Researchers speculate that sounds coming from outside the mother's body must be quite muffled.

The fetus adapts to its noisy environment through a simple form of learning called *habituation*. Quite simply, the fetus learns to respond to certain sounds. Repetitive sounds, such as a steady heartbeat, are soothing. The fetus is startled by sudden new sounds or vibrations but seems to calm down as the sounds continue. Researchers have discovered that after birth, the sound of a metronome set to the pace of the mother's heartbeat is soothing to the newborn.

"With a curriculum that includes the "kick game" and other exercises, Van de Carr's goal is to stimulate the fetal brain."

What does the fetus learn from the outside world? Peter Hepper (1988) created an interesting experiment with a group of expectant mothers in London. Hepper asked these mothers how often they watched Britain's most popular television soap opera, *Neighbours* (BBC1). He selected one group who watched the program nearly every day and another group who virtually never watched it. Within hours of the babies' birth, Hepper

played the theme music from the show to the newborns while they were crying. As soon as they heard the music, the babies in the first group stopped crying and became alert. Newborn babies of the mothers who had not watched the program showed no reaction. There seemed to be little doubt that the newborns who had been habituated to the music of the television program had learned something.

If the fetus can learn in the womb, is it possible for us to give the baby an academic head start before birth? Rene Van de Carr, founder and president of Prenatal University in Hayward, California, believes he can do just that. With a curriculum that includes the "kick game" and other exercises, Van de Carr's goal is to stimulate the fetal brain. Parents are instructed to tap the abdomen where the baby kicks and to speak loud encouraging words while teaching vocabulary to the fetus. Dr. Van de Carr claims that the newborn graduates of Prenatal University are more alert, quicker to develop, and are emotionally closer to their parents than are newborns who do not have these prenatal experiences. Other proponents of fetal training make even more expansive claims (Poole, 1987).

neural circuits are quite advanced. Brain scans show periods of dream sleep. As the fetus moves into the ninth month, it develops daily cycles of activity and sleep, and hearing is thought to be quite mature (Shatz, 1992).

During the ninth month, the fetus continues to grow and begins to turn to a head-down position in preparation for the trip through the birth canal. The vernix caseosa starts to fall away, and the hairy coating dissolves. Immunities to disease pass from the mother to the fetus and supplement the fetus's own developing immune reactions. Approximately 1 to 2 weeks before birth, the baby "drops" as the uterus settles lower into the pelvic area. The weight gain of the fetus slows, the mother's muscles and uterus begin sporadic, painless contractions, and the cells of the placenta start to degenerate—all is ready for birth.

We may see the accomplishments of the various stages of prenatal development presented in Table 4–1.

DEVELOPMENTAL TRENDS

The whole process of prenatal development that we just described seems quite orderly and predictable. Nevertheless, each fetus develops with its own differences—in size and shape, in skin tone, in strength and proportions, in developmental pace, and so on. For example, the gestation period (the time for a full-term pregnancy as measured from the mother's last menstrual flow to the day of childbirth) is usually 40 weeks. But normal full-term infants are born as early as 37 weeks or as late as 43 weeks.

What general trends do we see in this process of prenatal development? Usually—although with some exceptions—development proceeds from the top of the body downward. This "head-to-tail" development is called the **cephalocaudal developmental trend.** (It is not a rule, or a law, or even a principle, but just a trend.) Similarly, development usually proceeds from the middle of the body outward. This "near-to-far" development is the **proximodistal trend.** These trends will be seen again, with a few exceptions, in the development of physical coordination and skill in infants and preschool children. Infants control eye and head movements first, then arms and hands, and finally legs and feet. They reach and grab with the full hand long before they can pick up something like peas with a finger and thumb.

A fetus initially reacts to a poke on the skin with gross, generalized, whole-body movements. At birth and later, the movements become more localized and specific. This is the **gross-to-specific trend.** (Children learning to write often move their whole bodies, including the tongue. Only later can they confine the action to the fingers, the hand, and slight arm motion.)

Finally, there are the developmental processes of **differentiation** and **integration.** In the biology of prenatal development, cells become *differentiated* into distinct and specialized layers. But these layers soon become *integrated* into organs or systems. Later, during the child's development of motor skills, the processes of differentiation and integration frequently work together. Watching a child learn how to skip shows that the individual actions must be mastered and combined as well. Most children's thought is, in fact, a consequence of many discrete or differentiated concepts combined into integrated systems.

cephalocaudal developmental trend The sequence of growth in which development occurs first in the head and progresses toward the feet.

proximodistal developmental trend The directional sequence of development that occurs from the midline of the body outward.

gross-to-specific developmental trend The tendency to react to stimuli with generalized, whole-body movements at first, with these responses becoming more local and specific later on.

differentiation In embryology, the process in which undifferentiated cells become increasingly specialized.

integration The organization of differentiated cells into organs or systems.

TABLE 4–1 Three Stages of Prenatal Development

	TIME	DEVELOPMENT
GERMINAL PERIOD	**0–2 WEEKS**	
Fertilization	0	Ovum impregnated by sperm
Cell division	2 hrs–12th day	Ball of 70+ cells forms
Implantation	12th–14th days	Blastula embedded in wall of uterus
EMBRYONIC	**2 WEEKS–2 MONTHS**	
Nourishing structures	1st–4th weeks	Amniotic sac, placenta, chorion, and umbilical cord form
Cellular structures	1st–4th weeks	Ectoderm, mesoderm, and endoderm evolve
Heart and nervous system	3rd–4th weeks	Start to form and function
Head	3rd–4th weeks	Forms and grows rapidly
Organs and limbs	4th–8th weeks	Arms, legs unfold; lungs and digestive, excretory systems form
Facial features	4th–8th weeks	Eyes move to side of head; mouth, ears form
FETAL PERIOD	**2 MONTHS–9 MONTHS**	
Eyes	8th–12th weeks	Irises and nerves are in place
Teeth	8th–12th weeks	Form under the gums
Ears	8th–12th weeks	Develop
Fingernails and toenails	8th–12th weeks	Appear on limbs
Sex organs	8th–12th weeks	Penis and scrotum in male, labia in female appear
Glands	8th–12th weeks	Thyroid and thymus form
Internal organs	8th–12th weeks	Pancreas, kidneys develop; liver, lungs, stomach start to work
Bone structure	12th week	Ribs and spine begin to change from cartilage
Vocal cords and taste buds	12th week	Are formed
Body	4th–6th months	Lengthens, is covered by hairy fuzz, replaces skin cells, starts moving so mother feels it
Face	4th–6th months	Grows lips, eyebrows, and eyelashes
Heart muscle	4th–6th months	Beats 120–160 times per minute
Hands	5th month	Acquire strong grip
Eyes	6th month	Completely formed, eyelids can open
Head	6th month	Hair grows
Fetus	24th–26th weeks	Viable, may survive outside mother's body if in incubator
Body	7th month	Weighs 3 pounds, nervous system can control breathing and swallowing
Brain	7th month	Forms tissues for sensory, motor activities; can experience pain, touch, and sound
Body	8th month	Increases in length to 17 or 18 inches, weighs 4 to 6 pounds, forms fatty layers under skin for use after birth
Baby	9th month	Continues to grow, turns in head-down position for birth, loses fuzzy body covering, weight gain slows, "drops"
Mother	Last week or two before birth	Uterus settles lower in pelvic area, muscles begin painless contractions, placenta starts to break down

PRENATAL INFLUENCES

At this point in our study of prenatal development, we have described only normal developmental processes. The predictable and predetermined sequence outlined would presumably occur under ideal environmental conditions. These ideal conditions include a well-developed amniotic sac with a cushioning of amniotic fluid; a fully functional placenta and umbilical cord; an adequate supply of oxygen and nutrients; and freedom from disease organisms and toxic chemicals. What we have not considered is the effect on the fetus of any alteration in these conditions.

Most pregnancies in the United States (92 percent to 95 percent) result in full-term, healthy, well-developed babies. In most cases, the protective system of shielding in the uterus and filtering through the placenta works efficiently. However, every year in the United States, some 150,000 or more babies (from 5 percent to 8 percent of the live births) are born with birth defects. These defects range from gross anomalies that spell certain and almost immediate death for the newborn to minimal physical or mental defects that may have little impact upon the future development of the child. Although we might like to assume that birth defects only happen to other people's babies and are probably caused by some inherited traits, they can happen to anyone and only a small proportion are the result of inherited factors. The majority of birth defects are caused by environmental influences during the prenatal period, or during childbirth, or by the interaction of heredity and environmental influences (see Chapter 3).

The study of developmental abnormalities is called **teratology** (derived from the Greek word *tera,* which means "monster"). A teratogenic agent, or **teratogen,** is the specific agent that disturbs the development of the fetus—a virus or chemical, for example. In revealing the causes of abnormalities in infants, teratology also helps us to understand the normal process of development and to prevent defects and abnormalities whenever possible.

CRITICAL PERIODS

During prenatal development, the effects of many environmental conditions depend upon the relative stage of development, that is, the point in the developmental sequence when the change in the prenatal environment occurs. Unfortunately, many environmental effects on prenatal development occur before a woman is even aware of her condition. She may not be particularly concerned about her nutritional needs, not especially worried about minor diseases like rubella (German measles) or influenza, not thinking about the potential harmful effects of any drugs that she may be taking. In short, the damage is often done before a woman knows that there is an unborn child to worry about.

A critical period is the time when an organ, structure, or system is most sensitive to a particular influence. Figure 4–4 illustrates the critical periods in prenatal development, highlighting when specific organs and systems can be most seriously harmed.

The timing and nature of critical periods can be seen in the range of effects of the drug thalidomide. Thalidomide was prescribed as a mild tranquilizer for pregnant women, mostly in Great Britain and Germany in 1959 and 1960. It relieved insomnia and nausea and other symptoms of morning sickness. Within

teratology The study of developmental abnormalities or birth defects.
teratogens The toxic agents that cause these disturbances.

FIGURE 4–4

Critical periods in prenatal development. Green represents highly sensitive periods;
blue represents less sensitive periods.

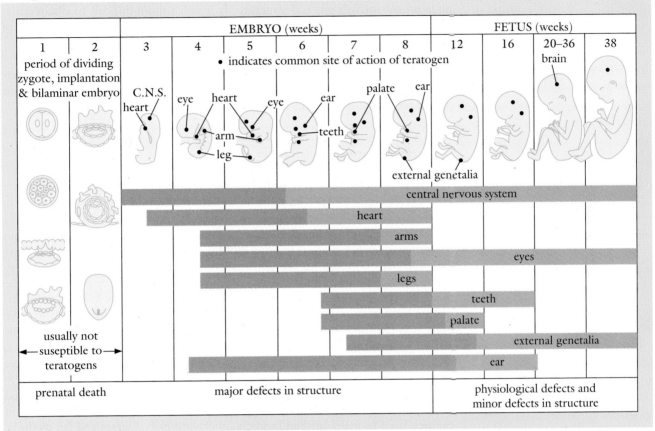

the next 2 years, as many as 10,000 deformed babies were born, and the deformities were attributed to the mothers' intake of thalidomide. A careful study of the history of these pregnancies showed that the nature of the deformity was determined by the timing of the mothers' use of the drug. If the mother took the drug between the 34th and 38th days after her last menstrual period, the child had no ears. If she took the drug between the 38th and 47th days, the child had missing or deformed arms. If she took the drug between the 40th and 45th days, the child had defects in the intestines or gall bladder. If she took the drug between the 42nd and 47th days, the child had missing or deformed legs (Schardein, 1976).

TYPES OF PRENATAL INFLUENCES

The variety of factors that have been found to influence prenatal development is impressive—even frightening. Nutrition, drugs, diseases, hormones, blood factors, radiation, maternal age at the time of conception, stress, and type of prenatal care all play a part in the development of the child. There is some concern that even though we know about the effects of many environmental factors, there are still drugs and other agents whose influences on the fetus have not yet been determined. It is relatively easy to study the direct effects of a drug like thalidomide on the infant's physical structure. It is much more difficult to discover the subtle neurological changes that lead to a learning disability at age 7 as a result of heavy air pollution (Needleman, 1986).

NUTRITION   One of the most important elements of the prenatal environment is nutrition. As the following excerpt points out, the effects of a lack of proper prenatal nutrition can extend throughout an individual's life span:

> A fetus, malnourished in the womb, may never make up for the brain cells and structures that never came properly into being. Malnutrition both before and after birth virtually dooms a child to stunted brain development and therefore to considerably diminished mental capacity for *the rest of his life.*" (Rosenfeld, 1974b, p. 59)

Fetal malnutrition may be caused by a mother's imbalanced diet, a vitamin deficiency, or deficiencies in the metabolism of the mother. In some cases, however, the fetus is unable to use the nutrients supplied by the mother. This may happen because of metabolic disorders, genetic abnormalities, or problems in the placenta. The most notable symptoms of fetal malnutrition are low birth weight, smaller head size, and smaller size overall, as compared to newborns who have been in utero for the same amount of time (Metcoff et al., 1981; Simopoulos, 1983). Malnourished pregnant women also often have spontaneous abortions, give birth prematurely, or lose their babies shortly after birth; even less severe nutritional deficiencies can cause problems that last a lifetime.

In countries ravaged by famine or war, the effects of malnutrition on child development are clear. There are high rates of miscarriages and stillbirths, and children born to malnourished mothers quickly develop diseases and fail to thrive unless immediate dietary adjustments are made. Even in developed societies such as ours, it is estimated that from 3 percent to 10 percent of all live births show indications of fetal malnutrition (Simopoulos, 1983). According to Zeskind and

The effects of malnutrition on child development are painfully apparent in countries ravaged by famine or war.

Ramey (1981), most cases of fetal malnutrition occur in low-income families. The truly unfortunate outcome is that reduced brain development in the late fetal period and early infancy probably is never overcome. If previously well-nourished mothers go through a temporary period of malnutrition during pregnancy, but the baby has a good diet and responsive caregivers after birth, there may be no long-lasting deficits (Stein & Susser, 1976).

Therefore, if the period of malnourishment has been relatively short, it can sometimes be compensated for with infant nutrition programs, or with combined health, nutrition, and child-care programs. H. G. Birch and J. D. Gussow (1970) have cited a range of studies in which carefully controlled "nourishment programs" for expectant mothers resulted in full-term, healthy babies. Research indicates that short-term malnutrition of the mother during pregnancy may have relatively minor effects on the fetus. Evidence of this is based on a study of pregnant women who, during the blockade in Holland in World War II, were on fairly limited rations for as much as 3 months during their pregnancies. Although these women were not starving, they were seriously undernourished. Except for a slight rise in the rate of stillborn and spontaneous abortions, those infants who survived were remarkably healthy once food was readily available, and they made up their initial low weight. Follow-up tests of these individuals at age 19 indicated no apparent reduction in intelligence and no marked behavioral abnormalities (Stechler & Shelton, 1982).

Research with animals also demonstrates that the mother can buffer the fetus from the effects of malnutrition by drawing on her own stored resources, and she can also protect her own tissues from serious long-term drain. Both mother and fetus, therefore, appear capable of recovery from limited malnutrition (Jones & Crnic, 1986). But if the mother becomes pregnant shortly after the birth of the first child, the second pregnancy may further deplete her body's reserves and compromise the health of the second child.

DRUGS AND CHEMICAL AGENTS Drugs administered during pregnancy may adversely affect the developing fetus and neonate. Drugs are a potentially serious problem for expectant mothers for a variety of reasons. Some physicians prescribe drugs for pregnant women without considering the potential effects on the fetus. Narcotic addictions are at high levels in society and large numbers of infants are being born who were exposed to the prenatal stress of illicit drug use by their mothers. In addition to prescription or illicit drugs, Americans use great quantities of non-prescription, over-the-counter medications. Among the sorts of drugs that pregnant women take are vitamins, aspirin, antacids, antihistamines, diuretics, cathartics, antibiotics, and sleeping pills. This does not include the general exposure to environmental chemicals, such as pesticides, paint, alcohol and other substances. We should note that the FDA (Food and Drug Administration), the government agency responsible for drug testing, does not test drugs on pregnant women.

Developing structures are usually more vulnerable to drugs than are structures that are already developed. Furthermore, some drugs may cross the placental barrier only to be trapped in the primitive system of the embryo or fetus. For example, fetal systems may be unable to handle a drug as efficiently as the maternal system can. Instead of being passed as a waste, the drug may accumulate in an organ or system of the fetus. Although a drug has been found "safe" for use by adults, it does not necessarily follow that it will be safe for the tiny developing organism that depends on and shares the environment provided by that adult. It may be true, in fact, that almost no drug is safe for the fetus.

Narcotics.   In general, narcotics like morphine, heroin, and even methadone depress fetal respiration and can cause behavioral disturbances in the infant. Babies born to women who use such drugs regularly are smaller than the norm and less responsive as newborns. More importantly, these babies experience withdrawal symptoms—extreme irritability, shrill crying, vomiting, shaking, and poor temperature control. They have disturbed sleep and have difficulty sucking. After the first few weeks, many continue to suffer from disturbed sleep, poor appetites, and lack of weight gain. At 4 months, they are more tense and rigid, more active, and less well coordinated than are normal babies. Up to 12 months, they have difficulty maintaining attention. Some researchers suspect that these attention deficits may persist well into childhood (Vorhees & Mollnow, 1987). The severity of the symptoms depends on the extent of the mother's addiction, the size of the doses, and how close the last dose was to the time of delivery.

Barbiturates.   Additional research is needed on the effects of barbiturates (a type of sleeping pill) on the developing fetus. Early studies suggested that even though barbiturates seemed to cross the placenta, the most serious effect was that such drugs appeared to cause minor depression in the growing child. Newer findings, however, show a clearly significant rise in the risk of learning disabilities among children whose mothers used barbiturates during pregnancy (Briggs et al., 1986; Gray & Yaffe, 1986, 1983; Nichols & Chen, 1981).

Alcohol.   Until recently, it was believed that light drinking during pregnancy would not adversely affect fetal development. How much is too much is no longer clear, however, and the critical periods regarding alcohol consumption have not been defined. We are certain of the damage that heavy drinking leads to—as many as 32 percent of infants born to heavy drinkers showed congenital abnormalities (Ouellette et al., 1977). A recent study showed that as little as two ounces of alcohol daily taken early in pregnancy was sufficient to produce facial deformities (Astley et al., 1992). These abnormalities have been identified as part of the **fetal alcohol syndrome,** which is more closely examined in the box, "Smoking and Alcohol: The Effects on the Fetus."

Children with the full range of symptoms of fetal alcohol syndrome are usually the offspring of mothers who drank heavily during pregnancy. More moderate drinkers place their infant at risk for less-severe effects commonly called *fetal alcohol effects* (FAE). These children show somewhat milder growth retardation and central-nervous system dysfunction (Vorhees & Mollnow, 1987; Streissguth et al., 1989). In addition, there is a correlation between the amount of alcohol consumed and the severity of birth defects. A recent study found that the more alcohol consumed during pregnancy the poorer the intelligence and motor coordination shown by the child at 4 years of age (Barr et al., 1990; Streissguth et al., 1989). In general, then, the consensus is that it is best for pregnant women to not drink during their pregnancies.

Smoking: Tobacco and Marijuana.   The inhaled products of tobacco or marijuana smoke cross the placenta. Each time the mother smokes a cigarette, the heart of the fetus beats more quickly (Simpson, 1957). Among heavy smokers of either product, there is an increased risk of prematurity, low birthweight, spontaneous abortion, and infant mortality. Cigarette smoking has been thoroughly studied over the past two decades, with the results summarized in the box "Smoking and Alcohol: The Effects on the Fetus." The effects of marijuana use have

fetal alcohol syndrome Congenital abnormalities, including small size, low-birth weight, certain facial characteristics, and possible mental retardation, resulting from maternal alcohol consumption during pregnancy.

been less thoroughly studied. However, researchers recently completed a series of studies in Jamaica, where marijuana is used in somewhat higher doses. Here, the newborn infants with prenatal marijuana exposure have somewhat high-pitched cries and behave in a fashion rather similar to that of infants experiencing mild narcotic withdrawal. It appears that high doses of marijuana affect the central nervous system and, hence, the neurological control of the infant (Lester & Dreher, 1989).

Cocaine. The 1980s saw a dramatic increase in the use of cocaine for "recreational purposes," sometimes sniffed in small amounts and other times smoked in the potent form called "crack." Some of the first studies on the effects of prenatal exposure to cocaine uncovered very few negative symptoms (Madden et al., 1986). Unfortunately, some pregnant mothers, lulled into a false sense of security, consciously used cocaine prior to childbirth, believing the myth that it would produce easier labor. Recent, more extensive research, carefully monitoring the level of use, has demonstrated that not only is this myth false, but also that the risk of severe damage to the newborn infant is considerable.

Mothers using cocaine experience more complications of labor. Their infants suffer from greater risk of growth retardation, prematurity, mental retardation, and even death by cerebral hemorrhage. Newborn infants have difficulty establishing motor control, orienting to visual objects or sounds, and achieving the normal regulation over waking and sleeping. The majority of cocaine-exposed infants can be classified as "fragile" infants, overloaded by normal environmental stimulation. They have few protective mechanisms to avoid overstimulation, and they have great difficulty controlling their overly excited nervous system. These infants cry frantically and seem unable to sleep. Even after a month, and with the help of swaddling and pacifiers, they still have difficulty attending to normal stimulation without losing control and lapsing into frantic, high-pitched cries (Chasnoff, 1989). These infants pay an enormously high price, which may last for months or even years, for their mothers' "recreational" drug use.

Other Drugs. Several studies, such as those cited earlier in this section, have indicated that many women consume a wide range of drugs during pregnancy. In a Michigan study of nearly 19,000 women, it was found that these women averaged three prescription drugs during their pregnancies (Piper et al., 1987). Some of these drugs prescribed by physicians were clearly hazardous to the fetus. For example, tetracycline, an antibiotic, has been demonstrated to have adverse effects on teeth and bones while contributing to other congenital defects. Heart medications, tranquilizers, and vaccines also appear to have a toxic effect on the fetus and cause behavioral difficulties in newborns. Some anticonvulsant medications given to mothers who have epilepsy can cause structural malformations, growth delays, heart defects, or even mild mental retardation or speech irregularities (Vorhees & Mollnow, 1987).

In addition to prescription drugs, pregnant women often use over-the-counter drugs such as aspirin, Tylenol, cough medicine, laxatives, and allergy pills. Yet many of these substances are also not particularly safe. Aspirin in large doses can lead to excessive bleeding and other problems (Briggs et al., 1986). Even large doses of antacid tablets or cough syrups, especially those containing codeine, may not be entirely safe (Brackbill et al., 1985). Stimulants like amphetamines, or even caffeine, readily cross the placenta and stimulate the fetus. Furthermore, these substances do not clear as easily from the fetus's system as they do from the mother's. Research on some of these substances is rather difficult to conduct. But because many of these agents affect the central nervous system, they

FOCUS ON AN ISSUE

SMOKING AND ALCOHOL: THE EFFECTS ON THE FETUS

Few people these days encourage pregnant women to smoke or drink. Since 1957, when the first reports appeared on the effects of cigarette smoking on fetal development, the link between smoking and fetal abnormalities has become increasingly clear. But as recently as the mid–1970s, many doctors advised their patients that moderate drinking was harmless or even good for their mental health. We are now learning that this is not so.

SMOKING

Each time the mother smokes a cigarette, the heart of the fetus beats more quickly. Among heavy smokers, a rate much higher than the norm is found for spontaneous abortions, stillbirths, and prematurity. Babies born to heavy smokers tend to weigh less at birth than those born to nonsmokers (Streissguth et al., 1989; Vorhees & Mollnow, 1987). Richard Naeye (1979, 1980, 1981) has examined the extensive research studies on smoking conducted over the past 25 years, and makes the following points:

1. Newborns whose mothers smoke during pregnancy weigh approximately 200 grams less than newborns whose mothers do not smoke.

2. The more cigarettes a mother smokes per day, the smaller the newborn.

3. This growth disadvantage may continue for several years after birth.

4. Mothers who stop smoking during pregnancy often have normal-sized babies.

5. Smoking during pregnancy can also lead to congenital malformations, neonatal pneumonia, and a higher rate of newborn mortality.

Richard Naeye continues to examine the effects of maternal smoking during pregnancy. In a large follow-up study conducted on thousands of children, he has found that 7-year-olds whose mothers smoked 20 or more cigarettes per day scored lower on tests of spelling and reading and had a shorter attention span than did children of light smokers or nonsmokers (Naeye & Peters, 1984; Vorhees & Mollnow, 1987).

How does smoking damage fetuses? Research points to the placenta. The placenta is the site of an exchange between the blood of the mother and of the fetus. The mother's blood provides nutrients and oxygen to the fetus, along with many other substances. The fetus, in turn, passes waste materials out of its system to the mother's, where they can be dissipated. Some forms of damage to the placenta occur only among women who smoke, and other forms of damage occur often

among women who smoke (Naeye, 1981). Researchers also suggest that smoking can constrict blood vessels in the uterus, reducing the flow of nutrients to the placenta (Fried & Oxorn, 1980). Both effects can reduce the amount of oxygen and nutrients supplied to the fetus, leading to reduced birth weight and possible fetal damage.

In light of the potential for harm, many doctors urge women who are trying to become pregnant not to smoke and those who are already pregnant to stop for the duration of the pregnancy.

ALCOHOL CONSUMPTION

The consumption of alcoholic beverages by pregnant women is also being examined more closely. Since 1968, a growing body of research has indicated a relationship between drinking during pregnancy and problems with spontaneous abortion, birth defects, and learning disabilities. By the mid–1970s, it was obvious that as many as a third of the infants born to heavy drinkers (alcoholics) showed marked congenital abnormalities (Ouellette et al., 1977). These abnormalities have been identified as part of the fetal alcohol syndrome (FAS) and include small size and low-birth weight, possible mental retardation, and neurological abnormalities. Certain distinct facial characteristics also are common, such as a small head, thin upper lip, a poorly developed indentation above the upper lip, a wide space between the margins of the eyelids, and flat cheekbones (Rosett et al., 1981).

> *"Yet, in a carefully conducted study of drug-free, light-drinking women in Dublin, Ireland, some effects on the newborn were found for women who drank as little as three glasses of beer per week."*

FAS may be fairly common, perhaps occurring as often as one in every thousand births. This would make it the third largest cause of mental retardation in this country (Streissguth, 1983; Streissguth et al., 1983). It almost always occurs among mothers who drink heavily. Heavy drinkers consume *4 or more ounces of alcohol daily.* What, then, is the effect of light to moderate drinking on the developing embryo or fetus? (Moderate drinking may be defined as consuming from *1 to 4 ounces per day.*)

Many researchers believe that FAS is simply the worst of many insults and abnormalities that can result from drinking during pregnancy. Similar, yet milder, abnormalities are usually called *fetal alcohol effects,* or *FAE* (Vorhees &

Mollnow, 1987). Since the mid–1970s, Dr. A. P. Streissguth and her colleagues have followed a group of over 1500 children who were born in the Seattle area. They have conducted a longitudinal study to determine the effects of the pregnant mother's drinking and smoking on the child's later behavior. Even in moderate amounts, alcohol seems to be related to the increased occurrence of heart rate and respiratory abnormalities in the newborn, to the newborn's difficulty in adapting to normal sounds and lights, and to lower mental development scores at 8 months. These findings cannot be attributed to nicotine or caffeine because both were carefully controlled in this project. At 4 years of age, the children of moderate alcohol users were less attentive and less compliant with their parents and performed less well on a laboratory test of visual attention than did children of non-drinking mothers (Streissguth et al., 1984). While the subjects were in elementary school, Streissguth and others found evidence suggesting that learning disabilities, attention problems, and hyperactivity may be more common among children born to mothers who were defined as moderate drinkers (Briggs, Freeman, & Yaffe, 1986; Streissguth et al., 1989).

Reviewing all of this evidence, the experts come to different conclusions. The Surgeon General advises abstinence for pregnant

women. In contrast, many doctors still advise that drinking up to one glass of wine or beer each day is safe and is even advisable in some cases as a way of reducing anxiety. Yet, in a carefully conducted study of drug-free, light-drinking women in Dublin, Ireland, some effects on the newborn were found for women who drank as little as three glasses of beer per week (Nugent, Greene, & Mazor, 1990). Many experts now advise that no more than one small glass of beer or wine should be consumed in any single day during pregnancy.

are being studied fairly extensively now for long-term behavioral effects and learning disabilities (Buelke-Sam, 1986).

Hormones. Some hormones ingested by the mother, including oral contraceptives, may cause malformation of the fetal sexual organs. Mothers who took the hormone diethylstilbestrol (DES) to help prevent miscarriages have had daughters with a higher risk of getting vaginal cancer or cervical abnormalities and sons who may be sterile or prone to develop testicular cancer. Hormones produced by both fetus and mother may alter the course of sexual development; in extreme cases, it may result in the development of a body type opposite to the baby's genetic sex (Briggs et al., 1986).

Chemical Agents. Many chemical substances in the mother's environment may be harmful to the fetus. Yet pregnant women have little or no control over some of them. For example, in the late 1950s, an industrial plant in Japan discharged waste containing mercury into the ocean. People living in the surrounding community had children born with profound retardation and neurological impairment. It was found that the mercury had worked its way up the food chain in the ocean's system and had become deposited in the larger fish. Fish was the principal food source for many of these people (Reuhl & Chang, 1979). There are similar stories concerning lead poisoning of mothers and infants. The exposure to moderate levels of lead, either prenatally or after birth, impairs cognitive development of the infant. Affected children have slower reaction time, have difficulty maintaining attention, and are more distractible, disorganized, and restless. Even in the 1980s, when we had reduced the levels of lead in car emissions, infants born in our cities had high enough levels of lead in their blood to produce lifelong behavioral deficits (Vorhees & Mollnow, 1987).

The damaging effects of mercury and lead are well established. Several other chemicals found in the environment are suspected to have negative effects. One study compared newborns whose mothers consumed fish contaminated with PCBs (a common set of compounds found in electrical transformers and paint) during pregnancy with a control group of normal infants (Jacobson et al., 1984). The infants exposed to this toxic substance showed weak reflexes and motor immaturity, and they startled more. Also, more than would be expected were born prematurely or were small for their gestational ages. Research continues on a wide range of other potential environmental toxins, including food preservatives, insecticides, and even some cosmetics and hair dyes.

In summary, then, the effects of drugs are difficult to predict. What may have no effect on animals or women who are not pregnant may be very harmful to a rapidly developing fetus. In addition, there are wide individual differences in infants and mothers in their vulnerability to drugs. It is generally advised that great caution be used in the ingestion of drugs by women during pregnancy—and even while breast-feeding.

DISEASES Many diseases do not appear to affect the embryo or fetus at all. For example, most kinds of bacteria do not cross the placental barrier, so even a severe bacterial infection in the mother may have little or no effect on the fetus. On the other hand, many viruses—particularly rubella, syphilis, herpes, poliomyelitis, and many varieties of viral colds—do cross the placental barrier. The example of rubella (or German measles) has been carefully studied. This disease may cause blindness, heart defects, deafness, brain damage, or limb deformity, depending upon the specific time in the developmental sequence that the mother contracts it.

In general, diseases may produce infections that gain entry to the fetus by one of two routes: the transplacental route—taken by infections such as AIDS and rubella—and the ascending cervical-amniotic route—taken by venereal diseases such as syphilis and gonorrhea. The cervical-amniotic route essentially infects the amniotic fluid first, and then the fetus. Maternal infections may affect the fetus in a variety of ways. They may infect the fetus and produce miscarriage, stillbirth, or severe deformity. They may produce death in infancy or defective or malformed tissues and organs. Or they may also produce no effect at all—especially in women who have immunities for the diseases to which they are exposed. It is important to remember that once an infection reaches the fetus it may produce extremely severe effects, since the fetus lacks an immune system to battle it.

Perhaps the most devastating virus transmitted to the fetus is the human immunodeficiency virus (HIV). This transmits acquired immune deficiency syndrome (AIDS) to the newborn. Although the number of AIDS babies in the United States is small, it is increasing rapidly. In 1989, 547 infants died of AIDS; in 1992, 2,000 babies were born with this disorder. Babies are the fastest-growing group of AIDS sufferers in the country. Pregnant mothers diagnosed as HIV positive often need multiple services for their own physical and mental health, sometimes for drug dependence, and certainly for counseling in anticipation of a very ill and dying baby (Stuver, 1989).

Since the AIDS epidemic was first recognized, there has been geographic clustering of AIDS cases within the United States. Most of this clustering is due to pools of HIV-infected individuals who engage in high-risk behavior such as drug use and certain unprotected sexual practices. A high incidence of HIV babies occurs in the same areas where there are high incidences of low birthweight, low maternal education, and high maternal drug abuse. Based on this and other research, it is clear that most pediatric AIDS cases are associated with intravenous drug use by one or both parents. Many of these HIV babies have low birthweight, in part due to inadequate health care and poor nutritional status. The largest percentage of HIV babies is found among minority groups, primarily as a function of their high rates of intravenous drug use (Morse et al., 1991).

STRESS Regardless of what folklore may say, a mother's momentary thoughts will not affect the fetus. If a woman "thinks bad thoughts," her baby will not be born with some sort of psychic burden; if she is frightened by a snake, a spider, a bat, or some other creature, the child will not begin life with a personality defect or a birthmark. In other words, a mother's grief, worry, surprise, or other short-term emotional problems will not have an effect on her unborn child.

Prolonged and intense emotional stress during pregnancy, however, can affect the developing child. During the prenatal period, the family makes adjustments for the impending birth. Sometimes this stress and change influence the emotional or nutritional state of the mother. Indeed, a family struggling with unemployment, illness, marital discord, or difficult relationships with in-laws may find a new child—especially an unplanned or unwanted one—too much of a burden. Similarly, newly married prospective parents who are still adjusting to each other's needs may not be ready to take on the additional responsibilities of parenthood. Single mothers face particularly difficult problems concerning financial and living arrangements; social support is important at this time, when they feel most alone. Teenage mothers may also face these problems, as well as the equally difficult ones involving interrupted school and social lives, parental disapproval, and having to assume responsibilities for which they are not ready.

Prolonged stress during pregnancy may cause an expectant mother to neglect her diet, become frail or physically ill, ignore medical advice, or take harmful drugs. Furthermore, prolonged and intense emotional stress during pregnancy may cause either chemical changes—secretions of hormones from the endocrine system—or muscular tensions that can affect the environment of the developing child (Montagu, 1950).

RH FACTOR   Sometimes, there is incompatibility between the mother's blood and that of the developing fetus. The most well-known and well-studied component of blood is the *Rh factor*. The Rh factor is a component of the blood found in almost 85 percent of whites and nearly 100 percent of blacks; its presence makes a person's blood "Rh positive," its absence, "Rh negative." The two Rh types are genetically inherited and are incompatible under certain conditions. If a mother's blood is Rh negative and her baby's is Rh positive, the trouble begins.

Some of the baby's blood "leaks" into the mother's system; the mother's body builds up antibodies that then leak back into the baby's system and attack its blood cells. No danger exists for the mother, only for the unborn child. Furthermore, the antibody buildup does not usually happen quickly enough to affect a first child, only those born later. Today, with modern obstetrical care, an Rh-negative mother can be treated after her first Rh-positive pregnancy to prevent future Rh incompatibility problems (Freda, Gorman, & Pollack, 1966; Kiester, 1977; Queenan, 1975).

RADIATION   Excessive doses of radiation in early pregnancy, through the use of repeated X-rays, radium treatment administered to cancer patients, or through high levels of radiation in the atmosphere (resulting from nuclear explosions, for example), have produced marked effects on prenatal development (Sternglass, 1963). Careful review of the evidence in animals as well as humans indicates that moderate levels of radiation cause structural damage during the embryonic period (from 2 to 8 weeks), and tend to cause mental retardation or mild central-nervous system damage in the period from 8 to 15 weeks of pregnancy. The effects of lower levels of radiation are not well established (Jensh, 1986).

The hormonal balance and tissue development in older first-time mothers may be a factor in the higher incidence of prenatal defects or abnormalities reported for this population.

MATERNAL AND PATERNAL AGE   The age of the mother can have an effect upon the prenatal development of the child. The incidence of prenatal defects or abnormalities is higher for first-time mothers over 35 years of age and for teenage mothers than for mothers between these ages. Although the precise reason for this is unclear, it is suspected that the hormonal balance and tissue development in the mother may play a role. For instance, Down syndrome occurs most often in children of mothers over age 35. As we can see in Table 4–2, the risk of Down syndrome is almost ten times greater at age 40 than at 30. Although we understand the cause of the abnormality (an incorrect number and pairing of chromosomes), we do not yet know why it occurs more frequently to mothers in this age group. It may have to do with increasing damage to the eggs because of time for greater exposure to mutating agents, problems with meiosis in older eggs, or other unknown factors (Baird and Sadorvick, 1987).

TABLE 4–2 Risk of Giving Birth to a Down Syndrome Infant by Maternal Age

MATERNAL AGE	FREQUENCY OF DOWN SYNDROME INFANTS AMONG BIRTHS
30	1/885
31	1/826
32	1/725
33	1/592
34	1/465
35	1/365
36	1/287
37	1/225
38	1/176
39	1/139
40	1/109
41	1/85
42	1/67
43	1/53
44	1/41
45	1/32
46	1/25
47	1/20
48	1/16
49	1/12

Source: Baird/Sadovnick, 1987.

Male factors also underlie failure to conceive or bear a healthy child. Older men, like older women, have an increased risk of spontaneous mutations or gene replication errors during meiosis. It may even involve a greater risk for older men since divisions in the male germ cell line occur with greater frequency than in females. For example, the cells lining the testicles divide throughout a man's life to provide the cells necessary for spermatogenesis (sperm production). There are relationships between paternal age and the increased incidence of cleft lip and palate, aneuploidy (abnormal chromosome numbers) and missing X chromosomes. It has also been documented that cytomegalovirus, a virus capable of producing significant birth defects, shows viral transmission through semen (Gunderson & Sackett, 1982). In addition, it has been shown that the sperm carries the extra chromosome in about 25 percent of Down Syndrome conceptions (Magenis et al., 1977).

PERINATOLOGY

A new branch of medicine, **perinatology,** considers childbirth not as a single point in time but as a span of time that begins with conception and goes on

perinatology A branch of medicine that deals with the period from conception through the first few months of life.

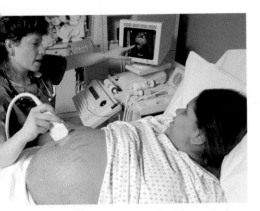

The safety and reliability of ultrasound imagery used to inspect the fetus makes this technique popular among the medical profession.

amniocentesis A test for chromosomal abnormalities that is performed during the second trimester of pregnancy; it involves the withdrawal and analysis of amniotic fluid.

fetoscope A long, hollow needle with a small lens and light source at its end that is inserted into the amniotic sac for observation of the fetus.

ultrasound A technique that uses sound waves to produce a picture of the fetus while it is still in the mother's uterus.

through the prenatal period, delivery, and the first few months of life. In order to deal with the multifaceted health problems of this period, many specialists—including obstetricians, pediatricians, geneticists, endocrinologists, biochemists, surgeons, social workers, and psychiatrists—work in teams. The *perinatologist* is a specialist in the management of high-risk pregnancies and deliveries. In addition to their regular medical training, these physicians must have an additional two years of training that is focused on the latest research and management of high-risk pregnancies.

The perinatologist and perinatal team work intensively with women who have high-risk pregnancies. Because of the need to closely monitor high-risk mothers and fetuses, perinatal teams are usually associated with major hospitals where there are the resources necessary to support and maintain such pregnancies. They often are consulted prior to the pregnancy and then follow the expectant mother and her baby throughout the pregnancy and delivery. They make use of the high technology prenatal-screening procedures described in Chapter 3, which allow for the early diagnosis and prompt medical treatment of potential problems. These techniques include **amniocentesis,** the use of **fetoscopes,** and **ultrasound** pictures. As we discussed in Chapter 3, amniocentesis involves the withdrawal of a small amount of amniotic fluid by means of a long, thin needle with a syringe attachment. This is a relatively painless procedure in which the needle is inserted through the mother's abdominal wall into the amniotic sac. Fetal cells in the fluid can then be examined for various genetic defects. The procedure has a slight risk of miscarriage associated with it. However, if the procedure is performed in conjunction with an ultrasound to visualize the fetus inside the womb, the risk is minimized. A fetoscope is a long, hollow needle with a small lens and a light source at its end. The needle is inserted in the amniotic sac so that a doctor may observe the developing fetus for major structural defects as well as take blood or skin samples. This technique has made it possible to carry out a number of essential tests that cannot be performed by any other prenatal screening technique. Amniotic-fluid tests detect many biochemical disorders, but they are not capable of providing information on the fetal-blood or body-cell type, information that is needed to detect certain genetic diseases prenatally. Fetoscopy can perform this function through fetal-blood sampling and skin biopsies. The geneticist who has a blood sample, for example, can use it to diagnose certain hemoglobin disorders including, sickle-cell anemia, thalassemia, hemophilia, and disorders of the white blood cells and serum proteins (Lauersen, 1983).

Pictures produced by ultrasound mapping show the location, position, size, and movement of the fetus. They can assist in amniocentesis by finding a safe place to insert the needle. As early as 7 weeks after conception, ultrasound pictures can diagnose pregnancy, and they can monitor the heartbeat, breathing, and movements made by the fetus throughout the rest of the pregnancy. Ultrasound images are used to judge the maturity of the fetus by helping to determine whether its size is proper for the number of weeks into the gestation period. They can also be used to identify a number of prenatal conditions, including defects of the fetus's neural tube, abnormal growth or development, and multiple pregnancies (Knox, 1980). As ultrasound pictures are a reliable and safe way to inspect fetuses, physicians and hospitals are using them with increasing frequency.

MATERIAL AND FAMILY ADJUSTMENT

Adjustment to parenthood is a major developmental task for adults, especially so with a first child. The new parents must make economic and social adjustments; often, they must reevaluate and modify existing relationships. Among the factors involved in this adjustment are the cultural attitudes of the family toward pregnancy, childbearing, and child rearing.

Motivations for childbearing vary considerably from culture to culture. In some societies, children are valued as financial assets or as providers for the parents in their old age. Sometimes children represent those who will maintain the family traditions, or they symbolize fulfillment of the parents' personal needs. At other times, children may be regarded as a duty or a necessary burden. Certain cultures accept children as inevitable, a natural part of life about which one does not make conscious decisions. In India, for example, Hindu women want to have children to guarantee them a good afterlife. Sons are needed to carry on the family name, to assist the father and follow in his footsteps, and finally to care for aged and ill parents. Although a daughter is a financial liability because her family must provide a dowry, custom still requires that an Indian man have at least one daughter to give away in marriage (Whiting, 1963).

In all cultures, the pregnant woman must adjust to the physical, psychological, and social changes that come with motherhood. Profound bodily changes occur that can hardly be ignored. Even before the fetus is large enough to create a change in a woman's appearance, she may feel nauseous or experience a fullness or tingling sensation in her breasts. Often she may suffer fatigue and emotional hypersensitivity during the early weeks of pregnancy, but in the middle stage of pregnancy, she frequently experiences a sense of heightened well-being. In fact, increased capacity and functioning of some of the bodily systems occur, such as in the circulatory system. In the last stages of pregnancy, some physical discomfort is usual along with, at times, a feeling of emotional burden. Increased weight, reduced mobility, an altered sense of balance, and a pressure on internal organs from the growing fetus are changes experienced by all pregnant women. In addition, other symptoms such as varicose veins, heartburn, frequent urination, or shortness of breath may contribute to the discomfort that some women feel. Wide individual variation exists in the amount of discomfort, fatigue, or burden experienced during the last few weeks. Some women find this last period of pregnancy much easier than others do.

These physical changes have an impact upon the psychological state of the pregnant woman. She must come to terms with a new body image and an altered self-concept, and she must deal with the reactions of those around her. Some women experience a feeling of uniqueness or distance from old friends or a desire for protection. Pregnancy may also be regarded with uncertainty by some women—they may be unsure about career plans following childbirth, anxious about their ability to handle a child, fearful of the possibility of birth defects, concerned about the financial burden, or simply uncomfortable with a markedly changed self-image. They may be eager to have the child, yet disappointed that they will have to share their time, energy, and husband with someone else (Jess-

Motivations for having children vary from culture to culture.

Although our society pays more attention to the mother during pregnancy, a father tends to experience many of the same pleasures and concerns of expecting a child.

ner, Weigert, & Foy, 1970). With the impending birth of a second child, the woman sometimes wonders if she has "enough love to go around"—whether she will be able to fulfill the expectations of all those who need her—her other child, her husband, the new baby.

Compared to the major physical and emotional changes that the mother undergoes, the father's role seems minor. Fathers may seem to stay in the background, quietly providing for the mother and baby, but a closer look reveals that fathers also experience a major transition to parenthood. In many ways, pregnancy is a "family affair" (Parke, 1981). Both father and mother experience the problems and pleasures of expecting a child. During the first trimester, fathers not only need to cope with the morning sickness, fatigue, and "edginess" of their spouse, but perhaps as many as 65 percent of first-time fathers experience some of the same symptoms themselves (Liebenberg, 1967). In addition, fathers worry about the future as much as mothers do; they are concerned about their ability to support an enlarged family and about what kind of parent they will be. They tend to be just as concerned as mothers over whether the child will like and respect them and whether they will be able to meet the child's emotional demands (Ditzion & Wolf, 1978; Parke, 1981). Some take this opportunity to learn more about children and parenting. Others make new financial arrangements. Many fathers provide increased emotional support for their wives. When there are other children in the family, fathers often spend more time with them and help them to prepare for the new arrival (Parke, 1981).

Both parents' attitudes toward pregnancy are shaped, to a significant degree, by those of the surrounding society. At times in our history—and some remnants of the attitude still remain today—pregnancy was considered to be an abnormal condition or an illness, something neither to be looked at nor discussed. A pregnant woman was confined and protected. She was not out in public, or in school, or in an office carrying on a career. Today, in our culture and in many others, pregnancy is considered a normal condition. In some cultures, it is even revered and accorded a special status as signifying the highest state of feminine fulfillment.

Western cultures have begun to accept pregnancy as "nothing out of the ordinary." Employers often encourage women to work and perform all normal tasks until the time of delivery. Some women experience little or no discomfort, fatigue, or excessive conflict with their other roles. Others take the discomfort and fatigue in stride and go on with their lives, minimizing the dramatic physical changes. Still others feel cheated because they are not given special treatment.

All of these conflicting feelings and social attitudes, when coupled with the parents' personal needs and mixed emotions, result in a major period of stress, change, and adjustment. None of these feelings will harm the unborn child, however, unless the mother suffers severe or prolonged emotional stress. Nevertheless, parental attitudes do help to create the atmosphere of the environment that the child enters at birth. This notion is illustrated in the following story.

> I remember a pair of young parents who told me they made their first priority one of enjoying their child. They were already obviously enjoying each other. That was fifteen years ago. The enjoyment still goes on today. I feel good every time I am around the family. Growth is obvious, and there is pride in accomplishment and good feelings about everything. These are not indulgent parents, incidentally, nor is the family without secure and clearly set down limits.

> Part of the art of enjoyment is being able to be flexible, curious and to have a sense of humor. An episode of a five-year-old spilling milk all over the table can be quite a different experience dependent upon what family he lives in and how matters are approached. (Satir, 1972)

SUMMARY AND CONCLUSIONS

The decision whether to have children is both personal and cultural. Procreation may be understood as a sign of attaining adult status, as an economic necessity, as following religious beliefs or more simply as an exciting creative accomplishment. For some couples, there are barriers to childbearing. Physical barriers include structural problems, venereal diseases and endometriosis. Parental concerns about their genetic inheritance or their age or lifestyle may also be barriers.

The decision whether to have children is one of the most important ones that married couples face. Many factors affect the answer to this question: the family backgrounds of the potential parents, the peer group with which they identify, pressure from society. Other personal goals and agendas also influence the decision, such as where the couple is individually in terms of education, career, and life goals.

Once the decision to start a family is made, the process is far from automatic. Some couples have difficulty conceiving because of congenital problems, past sexual history, disease, hormonal imbalance, or other problems. It has been estimated that as many as 1 in 12 couples may be infertile and require the use of the new reproductive technologies in order to assist their conception. Infertility has been found to have significant psychological stress associated with it for both males and females.

Once fertilization occurs, the new life starts its journey toward birth. During the germinal period, the fertilized egg continues to divide and moves slowly down the fallopian tube and into the uterus. Once implantation occurs, the embryonic period has begun. This lasts until the third month. During the embryonic period, 95 percent of the body parts become differentiated and begin to function. The embryo becomes recognizably human, although very small. Once the fetal bones start to ossify, the fetal stage begins. During this stage, the body of the fetus continues to develop, body parts begin to function, sensation occurs, and the fetus becomes heavier and larger. By 24 weeks after conception, the fetus is able to exist—with tremendous medical support—outside the body of its mother. During the last three months therefore the fetus gains new skills, grows, and starts to process information from its environment, which facilitates the maturation of its nervous system. Usually between 37 to 40 weeks after the mother's last menstrual period, the baby is born. Some obstetricians allow pregnant women to go to 43 weeks if all is well with the baby. At that point they often use drugs to begin labor.

This maturational process is far from automatic. A number of things can go wrong. Environmental factors can work alone or combine to produce malformed or malfunctioning organs. Drugs, radiation, age, disease and various internal factors can affect the fetus. Many do become affected and, if they survive to birth, may face a lifetime of coping and special environments. However, the majority of fetuses will survive to birth and beyond in good health and vitality.

Being pregnant—and then embarking on parenthood—require adjustments of both fathers and mothers. Both sexes respond differently to this period of stress, change, and challenge.

➤ **KEY TERMS AND CONCEPTS**

amniocentesis	Fallopian tubes	integration	sperm
amniotic sac	fertilization	*in vitro* fertilization	teratology
blastula	fetal alcohol syndrome	mesoderm	trimesters
cephalocaudal development	fetal period	miscarriage	
chorion	fetoscope	monozygotic twins	ultrasound
dizygotic twins	germinal period	ovulation	umbilical cord
ectoderm	gestation period	ovum	viable
embryonic period	gross-to-specific development	placenta	
endoderm	implantation	proximodistal development	zygote

➤ **SELF-TEST QUESTIONS**

1. After a woman ovulates, what is the period of time during which she can become pregnant? Describe the process that occurs if the ovum is fertilized, and contrast it to the fate of an unfertilized ovum.

2. What is in vitro fertilization?

3. What is the germinal period, and what important processes do cells begin at this time?

4. What is the embryonic period? How long does it last?

5. What is the fetal period? List and describe the developmental processes of this period.

6. What are some of the advances in reproductive technology? What are the dilemmas they raise?

7. What is the purpose of the vernix caseosa?

8. List and describe the general prenatal developmental trends of a fetus.

9. What is a teratogen or a teratogenic agent?

10. How do environmental factors impact fetal development?

11. What is the relationship between thalidomide and the timing and nature of critical periods?

12. List the factors that have been found to influence prenatal development.

13. What is fetal alcohol syndrome?

14. What is the effect of cigarette smoking on a fetus?

15. How does prolonged and intense stress affect the environment of a fetus?

16. Name some physical and emotional adjustments a mother and father make during pregnancy.

➤ **SUGGESTED READINGS**

BORG, S., and LASKER, J. *When pregnancy fails: Families coping with miscarriage, stillbirth and infant death.* Boston: Beacon Press, 1981. These two authors have themselves lost an infant. Hence, they speak from personal experience as well as from a knowledge of the professional literature about the experience of loss and family adjustment.

COREA, G. *The mother machine.* New York: Harper & Row, 1986. A powerful and controversial examination of the social and ethical implications of the new reproductive technologies.

DORRIS, M. *The broken cord.* New York: Harper & Row, 1989. A sensitive and compelling account of a single father's struggle with raising a child who has fetal alcohol syndrome. Expanded discussion of the complex problem of FAS among the Native American population.

EISENBERG, A., MURKOFF, H. E. & HATHAWAY, S. E. *What to expect when you're expecting.* New York: Workman Publishing, 1988. A popular, practical guide that addresses concerns of mothers- and fathers-to-be from the planning stage through postpartum.

KITZINGER, S. *Birth over thirty*. New York: Penguin Books, 1985. Kitzinger presents a thorough, sensitive discussion of physical, emotional, and social changes during and after pregnancy for the woman over 30.

NILSSON, L. *A child is born*. New York: Delacorte Press, 1990. Vivid full-color photography of the course of prenatal development with up-to-date text on the psychological as well as the medical facts of prenatal development and childbirth. An excellent gift for an expectant couple.

SHAPIRO, H. J. *The pregnancy book for today's woman*. New York: Harper & Row, 1983. This book addresses many current issues of pregnancy, including drug use, herpes, jogging, caesarean sections, and pregnancies in women over age 30.

SILBER, S. J. *How to get pregnant with the new technology*. New York: A Times Warner Book, 1991. This very well-written book combines an excellent review of current research with a readable format. It addresses the normal process of conception and the respective male and female causes of infertility. The new reproductive technology is presented in impressive detail. A positive, upbeat, and understandable treatise on the process of reproduction in today's world.

VIDEO CASE: FERTILITY CLINICS

Sally Pappas is a nurse for the Public Health Department in Long Beach, California. When she and her husband decided to have a child, they discovered that they were infertile. So they turned to *in vitro* fertilization. However, Sally's medical background did not prepare her for what they learned—the emotional and financial toll this process would take on them. Even so, they were willing to undergo almost anything. Says Sally Papas, "If they had asked us to hang upside down from a tree, we would have been delighted, because our focus is a family."

Nevertheless, Mr. and Mrs. Pappas did go through a lot—innumerable blood tests, daily injections of powerful drugs, invasive surgery, and the frustrating wait to find out if Sally was pregnant. After five attempts in six years, they gave up. George Pappas recalls: "Our money was exhausted. We mentally didn't want to go through it anymore...It hurt too much."

How unusual was the Pappas's experience? Not as rare as the public might expect. For the more than 2 million Americans with some kind of infertility, there are nearly 300 American clinics offering *in vitro* fertilization or other methods. The government exerts little if any regulation over this industry. Although many clinics are reliable, ABC news reporters have found that some of these clinics greatly overestimate the number of patients who can have a child. In addition, there is inadequate disclosure about the danger of the treatments and the drugs employed. At seminars conducted at IVF America, one of the biggest chains in the nation, the graphs used indicated that for clients going through four to six treatments costing between $40,000 to $60,000 the chances of becoming pregnant were 80 percent. But what the seminars did not suggest was that many experts advise patients to stop after three tries because the rate of success plummets. According to experts, the usual rate in the industry is only 1 in 10 couples.

As indicated, another problem concerns fertility drugs. Dr. Zev Rosenwacks, a leading IVF practitioner, says that these drugs have potentially unknown side effects. But at an IVF America seminar, the audience was told that these drugs posed no significant risks.

Even if a pregnancy occurs, there are unexpected risks. Dr. Marsden Wagner of the World Health Organization, and a leading authority on infertility, estimates that four times as many IVF babies die around the time of birth as do babies conceived in the usual way. Moreover, "there is a much higher risk of spontaneous abortion early in pregnancy, and there is also a higher risk that these babies will have some kind of a handicap, a permanent neurological handicap."

Despite these problems and the small success rate of *in vitro* fertilization, some people will want to attempt it. What should they know? They need to talk to doctors and perhaps hospitals. They may also want to investigate some societies that have been organized, such as the American Fertility Society.

CASE QUESTIONS

1. What are some of the unexpected problems of *in vitro* fertilization?

2. What are some of the overstated claims some clinics make?

3. What role does the government play in regulating these clinics?

4. What can clients do to protect themselves?

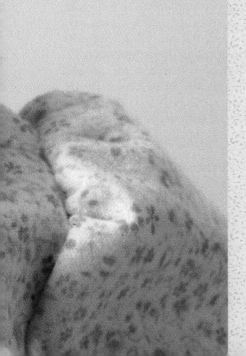

Hold a baby to your ear
As you would a shell:
Sounds of centuries you hear
New centuries foretell
Who can break a baby's code?
And which is the older—
The listener or his small load?
The held or the holder?

E. B. WHITE
"CONCH"

CHAPTER

5

CHILDBIRTH AND THE NEONATE

CHAPTER OBJECTIVES

By the time you have finished this chapter, you should be able to do the following:

✔ List and describe the three stages of childbirth.

✔ Discuss the benefits and liabilities of medical advances in childbirth.

✔ Explain "natural" childbirth.

✔ Describe parent-infant bonding.

✔ Discuss the neonate, including the following: neonatal adjustment, neonatal assessment, infant states, infant capacities, and temperamental differences.

✔ List the special needs of premature infants.

The ways in which parents prepare for the birth of a child show considerable variation. From the teenage mother who awaits the birth in her parents' home, attends special classes in high school for pregnant young women, and gains limited support from the young man who fathered the child to the more affluent couple in their thirties, the diversity of parents and patterns of waiting is impressive. There is one generality, however. For the last month or so prior to the birth of a child—especially a first child—the prospective parents assume that the birth may occur at any moment. The tension associated with waiting inevitably heightens. For many mothers-to-be, fears for the baby's health increase, as does concern over what the labor will be like. For many prospective fathers, the focus shifts to concerns with finances and lifestyle. Perhaps a description of the final weeks prior to childbirth in several families would illustrate this diversity.

➤ Kevin and Jewel are middle-class African-Americans in their early thirties who live in Kansas City. They are both professionals—he is the director of a college career placement office, and she is a contract administrator for a major health insurance company. Jewel's suitcase sits packed by the back door. The nursery is ready for their first child, stocked with much the new baby will need. The Lamaze classes have been completed, the breathing practiced, and Kevin's bag (complete with lotion for back massage, an ice bag, tapes of favorite music) is also sitting by the door. Last week they even arrived at the hospital convinced "this was it," only to find that it was a false alarm. Finally, the moment arrives, they give each other one final kiss, check their watches to see how long it's been since the last contraction, and head out the door.

➤ Eva and Jairo are Mexican-Americans who are also approaching thirty and live in New York City. They have four children under the age of 9,—three girls and a boy. The entire family is anxiously awaiting the arrival of the newest member—their oldest daughter, Raquel, who is almost 9 will serve as *mamacita* ("little mother") to the child. Eva has continued to work at her job in a clothing factory—despite the lateness of her pregnancy—by adding a month to her due date. The family needs her income as well Jairo's to make ends meet. She has carefully washed the baby clothes from their other children and has washed and folded several dozen diapers. She and Jairo are especially excited over the gift of a beautiful baby blanket from the members of their church. When the time comes for the baby's birth, she and Jairo will take the subway uptown to the hospital where the child will be born. Eva plans on returning to work within a week and has arranged for her sister, Maria, who also has a new baby, to care for theirs until Raquel returns home from school.

➤ Angie is 15 and lives with her father in Dade County, Florida. Her mother lives in the mountains of North Carolina. She and her 16-year-old boyfriend are expecting their baby within a month. Both sets of parents have been very supportive. She has even had a shower thrown by her boyfriend's mother who is a nurse and will be her coach during labor and delivery. The young father is not interested in attending the birth—as Wil confessed to a friend, he is really frightened about the whole process. When the baby is born, he or she and Angie will spend several months in her boyfriend's home. Angie will have to take the remainder of the school year off but is planning on attending summer school to make up the incomplete courses. Her boyfriend's sister has volunteered to serve as babysitter. Angie and Wil had originally talked about getting married after the baby's birth but have recently decided that it would not work out. They hope to remain friends in the future, and Wil plans to help support his child.

We can see from these examples that each mother has a childbirth story. How different, for example, the story of Kevin and Jewel is from that of Angie and Wil. While they come from different parts of the country, such differences may be found even within the same city. Differences exist in potential parents based on ethnic group membership, income level, religion, education and parental age. These differences have already affected the baby—even before birth—and will continue to affect him or her throughout development.

Attitudes toward childbirth differ widely from one culture or historical period to another—and even one mother to another, as we have seen above. Among the Jarara of South America, for example, women traditionally gave birth in public with everyone in attendance (Gutierrez de Pineda, 1948). In traditional Laotian culture, relatives and friends dropped by and visited a woman in labor. They played musical instruments, told jokes, and even made licentious comments to divert her attention (Reinach, 1901). In contrast to this public participation in childbirth, some cultures keep childbirth hidden. The Cuna of Panama tell their children that babies are found in the forest between deer horns, and children never witness even the preparations for childbirth (Jelliffe et al., 1961). The cultural ideal among the !Kung-San, a tribal society in northwestern Botswana, is that women tell no one about their initial labor pains and go out into the bush alone to give birth. They deliver the baby, cut the cord, and stabilize the newborn—all without assistance (Komner & Shostak, 1987).

What is the attitude toward childbirth in our own culture? In the United States and in most Western countries, babies are usually born in hospitals, out of view of society. The reason is not because our society dictates extreme modesty, such as we see among the Cuna; rather, it is dictated by the knowledge that hospital conditions have greatly reduced the hazards of childbirth for both infant and

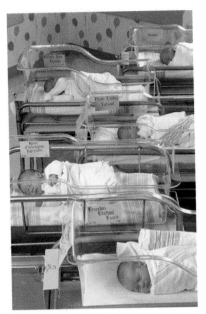

Although the technological sophistication of hospital maternity care has saved many high-risk and premature babies, it has also tended to isolate the mother and newborn from their traditional support system.

mother. The last three decades have witnessed dramatic progress in saving premature and high-risk infants through new medical technology and procedures.

The greater safety of the hospital, however, has had some important social side effects. The removal of childbirth from the family and the community has resulted in the loss of rich social support. The new mother, in many cases separated even from her husband and family except during hospital visiting hours (which are typically extended for fathers), is apt to feel alone, exposed, and unsupported in one of her life's major events. Segregating the mother also means that children grow up knowing little about the birth process except what they learn from second-hand reports. Consequently, new parents are sometimes surprised at the appearance of their newborn infants—small, often wrinkled creatures whose soft-boned heads may be misshapen after the passage through the birth canal.

In the past two decades, much has been written and said in a negative fashion about childbirth as a medical and surgical event, rather than as a natural and family-centered event. As a result, customs are changing. Research indicates that early contact helps promote a deep bond between parents and the new child. Informed parents can make better decisions that balance the need for medical safety with the need for strong family bonds. To assist in this bonding process, birth today is more likely to involve both the mother and father as full partners in the birth process—even siblings are sometimes involved—which also usually to occurs in a comfortable, homelike environment.

In this chapter, we will examine the process of birth, the capabilities of the newborn, and the psychological effects of birth on both the infant and the family.

 CHILDBIRTH

Although the attitudes toward pregnancy and childbirth vary from culture to culture, the birth of a child follows the same biological timetable in every society.

THE SEQUENCE OF CHILDBIRTH

Childbirth is not an isolated event. It is part of a process initiated when the woman first discovers she is pregnant—or even before, in couples who plan pregnancies. Successful labor and delivery begins months before she enters the labor room. In fact, successful childbirth depends on the care the mother takes of herself and the quality of medical attention she receives.

Labor and delivery often involves teamwork by the father, the mother, the midwife (if she is part of the birthing process), the obstetrician, and the obstetric nurse. Labor and delivery, which is most successful from a developmental viewpoint, is done naturally, smoothly and gently, with time to bond closely after the birth. However, since every pregnancy involves individuals, there is therefore room for considerable variation, as the following comment indicates:

> Few pregnancies seem as though they could have been lifted right from the pages of an obstetrical manual—with morning sickness that vanishes at the end of the first trimester, first fetal movements felt at precisely 20 weeks, and lightening that occurs exactly two weeks

before the onset of labor. Likewise, few childbirth experiences mirror the textbook—commencing with mild regular contractions, widely spaced, and progressing at a predictable pace to delivery. (Eisenberg, Murkoff & Hathaway, 1984)

Prior to the onset of labor, there are certain events in the last few weeks that lead up to it. One of the first signs of impending labor is the descent of the baby's head into the birth canal, an event called *lightening*. This term refers to the sensation that the pregnant woman experiences of feeling less burdened. But with this downward movement by the baby comes the increased need for urination, since pressure is now placed on the bladder. One or two days prior to delivery the pregnant woman may experience intermittent contractions. Meanwhile, the baby's movement typically declines significantly. Once its head is engaged in the pelvis, the baby is more constricted. Finally, in response to changes in hormonal secretions, the process of childbirth begins.

We usually describe the process of childbirth as occurring in three stages: labor, the birth itself and the delivery of the afterbirth.

LABOR   **Labor,** the first stage, is the period during which the cervix of the uterus dilates to allow for the passage of the baby. Although labor can last from a few minutes to over 30 hours, it typically takes 12 to 18 hours for the first child and somewhat less for later children. It begins with mild uterine contractions, generally spaced 15 to 20 minutes apart. As labor progresses, the contractions increase in frequency and in intensity until they occur only 3 to 5 minutes apart. The muscular contractions of labor are involuntary, and the mother can best help herself by trying to relax during this period.

Labor is typically divided into three sections also. The first phase, called *latent labor*, is the longest and least intense phase of labor. Gradually, the cervix stretches and becomes dilated, creating an opening to allow for passage of the baby through the birth canal. The second phase, *active labor*, is usually shorter than the first, lasting an average of 2 to 3 1/2 hours for first babies and often less for later born children. During this phase the contractions become stronger and more frequent, usually occurring 3 to 4 minutes apart and lasting 40 to 60 seconds. The final stage, referred to as advanced active or *transitional labor*, is the most demanding and exhausting phase. This may last only 5 to 10 minutes, but the intensity of contractions picks up dramatically. They become very strong, 2 to 3 minutes apart and 60 to 90 seconds long, with intense peaks that continue for most of the contraction. By the end of this phase, the cervix is fully dilated and the final pushing is ready to begin.

Some mothers experience **false labor,** especially with the first child. It is often difficult to distinguish false labor from real labor, but one test that often works is to have the expectant mother walk about. Real labor usually becomes more uncomfortable with simple exercise, but the pains of false labor tend to diminish. In addition to the false labor around the due date, during the last 4 to 6 weeks many women have increasing numbers of usually painless contractions which are caused by the pressure of the heavier baby on the abdominal muscles and its increasing pressure on the pelvis.

During labor, two other events must occur. First, a mucous plug that covers the cervix is released. This process is called *showing* and may cause some bleeding. Second, the amniotic sac, or "bag of waters," which has enclosed the fetus, may

labor The first stage of childbirth, typically lasting 12 to 18 hours and characterized by uterine contractions during which the cervix dilates to allow for passage of the baby.

false labor Painful contractions of the uterus without dilation of the cervix.

break and some amniotic fluid may rush forth. Generally, the rush of water stops when the woman stands up because the baby's head blocks the flow. The rupture of membranes before labor begins is uncommon, and occurs in less than 15 percent of pregnancies.

BIRTH   The second stage of childbirth is the actual birth of the baby. **Birth** is usually distinguished as the period between the time that the cervix is fully dilated and the time when the baby is free of the mother's body. This stage usually lasts from 10 minutes to 40 minutes, and, like labor, it tends to last longest for a first birth. Contractions are regular, with one every 2 to 3 minutes, and they are of greater intensity and longer duration than those occurring during labor. Each birth contraction lasts about 1 minute, and the mother can actively assist in the birth by bearing down with her abdominal muscles during each contraction.

Normally, the first part of the baby to emerge from the birth canal is the head. It *crowns,* or becomes visible, and emerges more and more with each contraction until it can be grasped. The tissue of the mother's **perineum** (the region between the vagina and the rectum) must stretch considerably to allow the baby's head to emerge. In Western cultures, and especially in US hospitals in the United States, the attending doctor often makes an incision, called an **episiotomy,** to enlarge the vaginal opening. It is believed that this can heal more neatly than the jagged tear that might occur if the incision is not made. Episiotomies are much less common in Western Europe. Obstetricians occasionally use a steel or plastic tool, called *forceps,* or a *vacuum extractor* (a cup placed on the baby's head and connected to a suction device) to grasp the head and hasten the birth, should complications arise. Like episiotomies, forceps and vacuum extractor deliveries are more common in the United States than Europe. Recent statistics suggest that 20- to 30 percent of American births use either of these instruments, while only 5 percent of European births do so (Korte and Scaer, 1990).

In most normal births, the baby is born head first in a face-down position. After the head is clear, the baby's face turns to one side so that its body emerges with the least resistance. More difficult births occur when the baby is positioned in a **breech presentation** (buttocks first) or a **posterior presentation** (facing

birth The second stage of childbirth, which is the time between full cervix dilation and the time when the baby is free of the mother's body.

perineum The region between the vagina and the rectum.

episiotomy An incision made to enlarge the vaginal opening during childbirth.

breech presentation The baby's position in the uterus, such that the buttocks will emerge first; assistance is usually needed in such cases to prevent injury to the mother or the infant.

posterior presentation A baby is positioned in the uterus facing the mother's abdomen rather than her back.

Two types of breech presentation. Delivery in this position is difficult for both mother and baby.

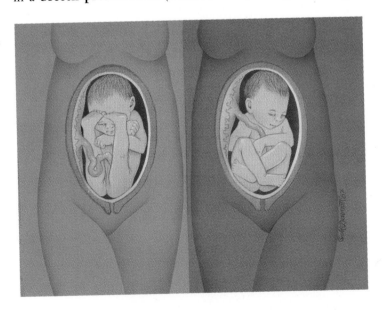

toward the mother's abdomen instead of toward her back). In each of these cases, the baby is usually assisted to prevent unnecessary injury to the mother or the infant.

AFTERBIRTH The expulsion of the placenta, the organ developed especially to nourish the fetus, and related tissues marks the third stage of childbirth, the *delivery of the afterbirth*. This stage is virtually painless and generally occurs within 20 minutes after the delivery. Again, the mother can help the process by bearing down. The placenta and umbilical cord (together known as the afterbirth once they have been expelled from the uterus) are then checked for imperfections that might signal damage to the newborn.

THE MEDICAL TECHNOLOGY OF CHILDBIRTH

In most cases, birth is a safe, natural process. Mother and infant work tremendously hard, and at the very end, a doctor or midwife serves as baby catcher. Some deliveries, however, require major medical intervention due to problems like improper fetal position and prematurity. In the past 20 years, obstetrical medicine has made dramatic progress in dealing with difficult deliveries. Infants that would not have survived in 1960 are now thriving in record numbers. For example, today over 80 percent of premature infants weighing 750 to 1000 gms. (1.6 to 2.2 lbs.) will survive in a well-equipped intensive care unit for newborns (Ohlsson et al., 1987). In 1972, only one out of five such tiny newborns survived (*Newsweek*, 1976). (Premature infants are further discussed later in the box "The 'Kilogram Kids.'")

The new medical advances include drugs, microsurgery, diagnostic tools, and preventive measures. For instance, a vaccine given to an Rh-negative woman immediately after her first delivery can completely prevent blood incompatibility problems in future pregnancies. As we saw in Chapters 3 and 4, procedures like amniocentesis, ultrasound mapping, and the use of fetoscopes can help diagnose conditions prenatally, and steps can then be taken to treat the fetus or the newborn.

The new technology of childbirth is a blessing to many families, especially those facing premature or high-risk deliveries. But some critics argue that it is too frequently applied to deliveries that should be routine. Some consumer advocates point to the increasing rate of Caesarean births as the inevitable result of increased technology in the delivery room.

FETAL MONITORING Many hospitals have routinely measured the fetal heart rate during labor using devices called fetal monitors. These can be applied either externally or internally. The external type of monitor records the intensity of uterine contractions and the baby's heartbeat by means of two belts placed around the mother's abdomen. The internal monitor consists of a plastic tube containing electrodes; it is inserted into the vagina and attached to the baby's head. Besides measuring the fetal heartbeat, it monitors uterine pressure, fetal breathing, and head compression (Goodlin, 1979). Proper interpretation of the data yielded by the monitor can alert the obstetrician to compression of the umbilical cord, poor fetal oxygen intake, and fetal distress (*Pediatrics*, 1979). Typically, the internal monitoring device is used only in high-risk situations when either the mother's or infant's situation warrants it.

afterbirth The placenta and related tissues, following their expulsion from the uterus during the third stage of childbirth.

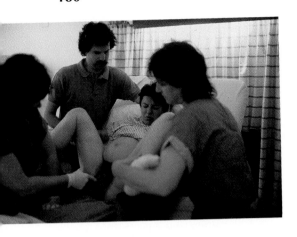

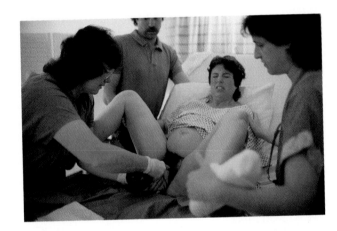
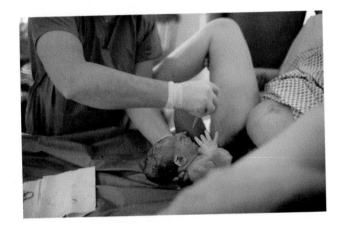
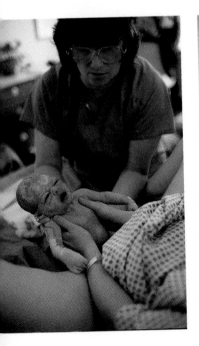
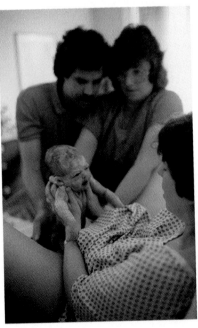
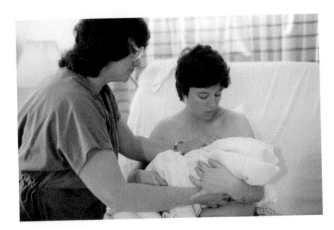

The birth process.

The same type of fetal monitoring is often done prior to birth in high-risk situations or in *postterm* situations when the baby is more than two weeks overdue. Prenatal fetal monitoring provides the same information but is used to make decisions about the following eventualities: drug induced laboring; interventions in the mother's health to assist the baby such as bed rest during the final month, or the advisability of caesarean births due to health factors such as *gestational diabetes* (a type of diabetes that occurs frequently during the pregnancies of older mothers) or **toxemia** (abnormally high blood pressure associated with toxins in the blood) which threatens the life of the mother and baby.

Although fetal monitors can be quite effective in high-risk pregnancies, the routine or continuous use of them with low-risk or healthy mothers is now discouraged. The American College of Obstetrics and Gynecology has changed its standards and no longer considers fetal monitors part of standard care for maternity patients (BIRTH, 1988). These monitors can be easily misread, leading to unnecessary surgical procedures. Also, the monitors restrict movement, requiring the mother to remain in bed, on her back, rather than letting her get up and walk around. But, most importantly, research has not indicated that the routine use of such monitors produces healthier babies and fewer complications (*BIRTH*, 1988; Marieskind, 1989).

MEDICATION As discussed in Chapter 4, drug use during pregnancy can harm the developing fetus. For this reason, physicians avoid giving medication to the expectant mother, especially during the early months of pregnancy (Brackbill, 1979). Parents and physicians try to weigh the use of anesthetics and painkillers for the mother during childbirth against the risk of possible damage to the baby. Recent evidence suggests that the routine use of general anesthetics at birth increases the incidence of brain damage and may delay the development of memory and coordination abilities in the child. Even regional anesthesia designed to block pain in the pelvic area may depress the newborn's early functioning (Murray et al., 1981). Physicians and medical researchers have long known that drugs that reduce the mother's level of awareness and sensitivity affect the infant's alertness and responsiveness at birth. Also, drug residues may remain in the infant's blood and urine for weeks after delivery (Broman, 1986). Are the effects of these drugs only temporary?

There is conflicting evidence about the long-term effects that may result from exposure at birth to powerful anesthetics given to the mother (Brackbill, 1979; *Pediatrics*, 1978). Researchers have discovered that a significant number of children whose mothers were given routine anesthetics during childbirth have been delayed in learning to sit up, stand, walk, and talk (Brackbill & Broman, 1979). Clearly, drugs that slow the birth process increase the danger of **anoxia**, a condition in which an insufficient amount of oxygen reaches the baby's brain. Any lack of oxygen at this time can have serious, long-lasting effects on the child's later mental and motor development—it can result in learning disabilities or even more severe brain damage later in childhood. A few studies suggest, however, that mild anesthetics actually facilitate certain high-risk deliveries, as well as ease pain (Myers & Myers, 1978). Although no one disputes the importance of easing the mother's pain, it is clear that during pregnancy or childbirth any medication should be used with caution (Broman, 1986).

CAESAREAN SECTION Most births, with or without anesthesia, occur through the birth canal as described earlier. But in some cases, delivery through

toxemia Poisoning of a mother's body during pregnancy due to a metabolic disturbance.

anoxia In prenatal development and childbirth, a lack of sufficient oxygen reaching the brain, which can cause irreversible brain damage.

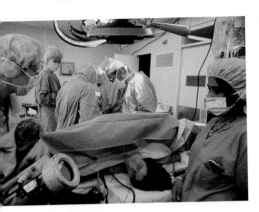

Although most births occur through the birth canal, in cases where this is either difficult or dangerous a Caesarean section is advised.

the birth canal may be dangerous or difficult. A fetus may be too large to pass between the mother's pelvic bones; the mother may have **toxemia;** she may be in danger of excessive bleeding; she may have a disorder, such as diabetes or some other illness, that will put too much stress on the fetus. This can result in fetal distress. Occasionally, despite a lengthy labor, the uterine cervix does not dilate, a condition referred to as dystocia. A prolonged labor places a great strain upon the mother and also increases the danger that the fetus may suffer the serious effects of oxygen deprivation. In addition, multiple births and breech presentations commonly make vaginal delivery dangerous or impossible.

In the United States, **Caesarean section** is usually advised for all of these conditions. This is a surgical procedure used to remove the baby and the placenta from the uterus by cutting through the abdominal wall. After a woman has had one Caesarean delivery, it is often recommended (but not always necessary) that future deliveries also be by this method. Because the procedure involves anesthesia and a long recovery period, it is not recommended for the sake of convenience. Nevertheless, it is no longer uncommon for a mother to have four or more babies by Caesarean section (see the box, "Caesarean Childbirth.")

Since Caesarean section is major abdominal surgery, the active participation by the mother in the delivery of her baby is no longer necessary. She will be anesthetized either by intravenous method, and thus be unconscious for the delivery, or by one of the various nerve block methods such as the spinal or epidural block. In the case of nerve blocks, the mother is fully conscious and is therefore awake to experience the birth of her baby. This allows her to interact fully with her husband and baby during and immediately after the birth.

Since the mother is not actively involved with this sort of surgery, the best thing a couple can do to participate in a Caesarean birth is to prepare for it intellectually and emotionally prior to the actual event. Most childbirth classes, for example, devote some time to what happens during Caesareans and to the actual risk of having one. Sometimes the decision to have a surgical delivery is an emergency; in other circumstances, it follows a long period of active labor.

The most difficult psychological consequence for the mother and father in this situation is the sense of failure at not having "successfully" made it through delivery. As parents increasingly take childbirth classes in the hope of participating more fully in the birth of their child, parents whose births have not matched their plans or expectations often experience a deep sense of disappointment (Lauersen, 1983). (see the box "Caesarean childbirth").

Once a healthy baby is right there in the delivery room and the sense of urgency and questioning is removed, the sense of failure is often mitigated. Women who have been fully informed of why the procedure was necessary have also found it easier to accept than those who feel the decision was involuntarily taken from them when other options were open.

THE EXPERIENCE OF CHILDBIRTH

Caesarean section A surgical procedure used to remove the baby and the placenta from the uterus by cutting through the abdominal wall.

The experience of childbirth varies from generation to generation, mother to mother, and culture to culture. Some cultures consider birth as an illness; for example, pregnant women of the Cuna Indians of Panama visit the medicine man daily for drugs and are sedated throughout labor and delivery. In some cultures, as we have seen, home birthing is the norm, while for most western industrialized cultures hospital births account for the vast majority. But the Jarara of South America have mothers give birth in view of the whole community. In some cultures the father is intimately involved, while in others he is excluded. In some births, a woman who has already had children acts as a coach to the laboring woman, while in others, she labors alone.

Recent research suggests the usefulness of having another woman who had already experienced a normal labor and delivery present to provide low-tech emotional support to the laboring mother. This research found that employing a *doula,* a Greek word meaning, "the experienced mother who guides a new mother in child care," significantly reduced the stress of the new mothers. Most of the subjects came from poor households and had no husband. Prenatal care ranged from good to nonexistent. Hispanic women made up two-thirds of the sample. The doulas were also recruited from the community, spoke English and Spanish, and received approximately three weeks of training about childbirth, hospital policy, and support techniques. Results indicated that the emotional support experimental group needed less medical intervention during their deliveries and that fewer of their infants required prolonged hospital stays than the control group (Bower, 1991).

In general, the mother's experience of childbirth depends on the cultural expectations imposed on her, the knowledge she has of what to expect, and the confidence she has in a successful outcome. This is often affected by the preparations she has made for childbirth.

PREPARED CHILDBIRTH

Concern over the effect of drugs given during pregnancy and childbirth is one of the reasons that **"natural" childbirth** was first suggested by doctors such as Grantly Dick-Read (1953) and Fernand Lamaze (1970). This method has increased in popularity in recent years. Basically, "natural" childbirth (we put the word natural in quotes because here it means a good deal more than having babies naturally) involves three things: preparation, limited medication, and participation. To Dick-Read, the key was preparation. In Western society, women frequently approach childbirth with limited knowledge and exaggerated fear. This fear produces tension, which causes tightening of the muscles and makes labor more difficult and painful than necessary. Dick-Read proposed that if the mother understood the birth process—and knew how to help herself at each stage—she would be more relaxed during labor, the pain would be less intense, and she would probably not need medication. Drawing on Dick-Read's philosophy, Lamaze developed a childbirth preparation program that is taught to both mothers and fathers in classes throughout much of the Western world.

How does prepared childbirth work? The mother, and often the father too, attend from six to eight classes where they learn about pregnancy and the stages of labor. The expectant mother is taught exercises for relaxation, breathing, and muscle strengthening. When the time comes for birth, the mother knows which breathing procedures will minimize the pain. She even knows the most effective way to push so as to help deliver her baby. Often, her husband is encouraged to be with her during labor and delivery to coach her through the process and lend emotional support. If there is no husband, if he does not feel comfortable playing

"natural" childbirth A childbirth method that involves the mother's preparation (including education and exercises), limited medication during pregnancy and birth, and the mother's (and perhaps father's) participation during the birth.

FOCUS ON AN ISSUE

CAESAREAN CHILDBIRTH

Despite the best preparations and expectations for a normal prepared childbirth, many mothers find themselves scheduled for delivery by Caesarean section. Medical procedures have improved sufficiently, making this a reasonably safe operation. It is frequently performed under regional anesthesia, so the mother is awake and aware. Also, because the procedure is completed quickly, very little of the anesthesia reaches the infant. Doctors assure expectant mothers that they can expect an excellent outcome for both themselves and their infants if a Caesarean delivery is advised, given the new procedures.

Nevertheless, many consumer advocates wonder if we have gone too far in increasing our rate of Caesarean births. The rate of Caesarean sections performed in the United States in 1970 was 5.5 percent. The rate increased to 18 percent in 1980, and to 24.4 percent in 1987 (Cohen & Estner, 1983; Marieskind, 1989). Caesarean section is now the most frequently performed major surgery,

---

"...it is estimated that perhaps 60 percent of women who have delivered one child via Caesarean section could safely give birth vaginally in subsequent pregnancies if encouraged to do so."

---

with nearly a million performed each year and with some hospitals performing over 40 percent of childbirths by this method. But, if this is a reasonably safe operation, why is this increase a problem?

First, the procedure is major abdominal surgery. Any major surgery requires a period of recovery that is much longer than recovery from childbirth. Second, not all doctors performing Caesarean sections are sensitive enough to the special problems of these mothers, including the need to arrange early contact with their infants. Third, some consumer advocates argue that the sharp rise in the rate of Caesarean sections is a consequence of the increased use of certain medical procedures that seem to interrupt the natural process of labor. They argue that the use of fetal monitors and the regular administration of four or five different kinds of drugs, such as painkillers and drugs used to induce labor, create situations that lead eventually to the need for surgical childbirth. Perhaps the rapid rise in the rate of Caesarean sections is a signal that we ought to examine some other practices introduced in the past two decades.

The psychological reactions of mothers to Caesarean childbirth can be quite negative. Many mothers report feeling disappointed, disillu-

---

this role, and for a variety of other reasons, other people may be birth partners—mothers, sisters, or friends. In some circumstances, siblings are present. While fathers are often present when babies are born, they are not the only ones who may assist in the birthing process.

The key to natural childbirth is that during the actual birth, the mother is a full participant—awake, alert, working, and in control. Is prepared childbirth as successful as it sounds? Generally, it is. The infant has a quick and safe delivery because the mother is able to help, and drugs are not used. How does preparation help? Recent studies suggest that the mother's active perception of pain and her emotional distress are reduced because she has more accurate expectations and has learned some ways of actively coping. For example, the monitoring of contractions better allows a woman to control and coordinate the timing of breathing and pushing with her expulsive labor contractions (Leventhal et al., 1989).

sioned, or a sense of failure, particularly those who had general anesthesia and "missed the event." Repeated studies report that some mothers who have had a Caesarean section are disappointed or even angry at being cheated, are slow to choose a name for the baby, test lower on self-esteem shortly after giving birth, and have more difficulty feeding their infants (Oakley & Richards, 1990).

And, finally, there appears to be a higher rate of grieving, or mourning, or actual depression following Caesarean sections than following vaginal deliveries (Cohen & Estner, 1983; Kitzinger, 1981). It is common for some mothers to experience mild depression after childbirth. Many factors may contribute to this, including major hormonal changes, the letdown after a long-anticipated event, the fatigue of late pregnancy and childbirth, and the rather insistent day-and-night demands of a new infant. It is not clear why mothers who have given birth surgically often experience more depression than others. Some mothers report that the loss of control, loss of involvement, and loss of participation in a critical life event contribute to a somewhat long, partially unexplained, sense of sadness (Cohen & Estner, 1983). It may also be that since the mother is recovering from major surgery in addition to caring 24 hours a day for a newborn, that fatigue is a factor in her somewhat increased risk of depression.

Physicians, too, have been concerned about the radical increase in the rate of Caesarean births since 1970. At first, they noted the continued drop in infant mortality and maternal mortality rates during this period and the improved health of premature infants. But the increased use of surgical delivery in the 1980s was not accompanied by a major increase in the health of infants or by any related decrease in infant mortality. Alternative ways of coping with these situations are being investigated. For example, it is estimated that perhaps 60 percent of women who have delivered one child via Caesarean section could safely give birth vaginally in subsequent pregnancies if encouraged to do so (Donovan, 1986). This is usually done by giving a trial of labor. In this procedure, rather than automatically scheduling a repeat Caesarean, the obstetrician allows the mother to go into labor and delivery vaginally until she either delivers normally or by Caesarean. The reason that would most preclude such a trial is the type of incision the mother had in her initial Caesarean. Women who have undergone a classical Caesarean cannot attempt a vaginal delivery because of the risk of uterine rupture. Women who had the low-segment, bikini-type incision are candidates for such a procedure (Lauersen, 1983).

The American College of Obstetrics and Gynecology now regularly recommends more complete parent education about the risks and benefits of vaginal versus Caesarean delivery (Marieskind, 1989; DeMott & Sandmire, 1990).

In addition, many childbirth experts emphasize the central role of the father in the coaching of his wife during labor and delivery. Often, he may become overwhelmed by the hospital environment, the competence of the nurses and physicians involved in the actual process rather than in the rehearsal, and his inability to soothe his wife once—or if—she loses control. In this situation, the father is encouraged to persist in his stress management techniques which were taught in the childbirth class.

In general, the woman's perception of pain during labor is affected by various factors. Being alone and being fatigued, hungry, or thirsty can produce a greater sense of pain. Thinking about and expecting pain also serves to increase the perception of pain when it actually occurs. Fear of the unknown, tensing up during contractions, feeling anxiety and stress also enhance pain. Once this happens, the techniques suggested in Table 5–1 are useful to help the woman restore her sense of control.

In "natural" childbirth classes, parents learn to prepare as much as possible for the actual course of birth.

TABLE 5–1 Pain Risk Factors during Labor and Delivery

Being alone	Having the company and support of those you love and/or experienced medical personnel.
Fatigue	Being well rested by attempting not to overdo things during the final month; trying to rest and relax between contractions.
Hunger and thirst	Eating light snacks during early labor and chewing ice chips throughout.
Thinking about and expecting pain	Turning thoughts to other distractions; trying to think of contractions in terms of what they accomplish rather than how much pain they cause; reminding oneself that no matter how great the discomfort, the duration will be relatively short.
Anxiety and stress; tensing during contractions	Employing relaxation techniques between contractions; concentrating on breathing.
Fear of the unknown	Learning as much as possible about childbirth before the event; trying to focus on what is happening now —not in the future.
Self-pity	Turning thoughts to how lucky the person is to be completing the nine months; anticipating the baby to come.
Feeling out of control and helpless	Having good childbirth preparation; understanding enough to feel some sense of control and confidence.

Source: Adapted from Eisenberg, Murkoff, & Hathaway, 1984, p. 270.

CHANGING PRACTICES

The experience of childbirth varies widely, even in Western cultures, depending on where the baby is born, who is present, what medical practices the mother elects, and what practices the doctor requires. In many hospitals, the full-term mother is treated as if she were entering the hospital for some type of surgical procedure. She signs in, her pubic hair is shaved, she is given an enema, and she is allowed nothing to eat or drink. She lies in a hospital bed through much of her labor with a fetal monitor attached to her abdomen, and often an intravenous needle attached to her arm. She is prepared for a Caesarean section, should one be necessary. A husband or coach is with her; they talk quietly, and he or she may offer considerable encouragement and perhaps occasional back rubs, but there is not much activity. If the frequency and duration of contractions decrease, labor may be induced by an injection of a drug like pitocin, or by the artificial rupture of the amniotic membranes. These procedures often result in active, vigorous labor, which may occur quickly and sometimes almost violently. Finally, when the cervix is almost fully dilated, the mother is moved to the delivery room. Her legs are elevated and placed in stirrups. Medication is administered if needed, and the actual birth takes place.

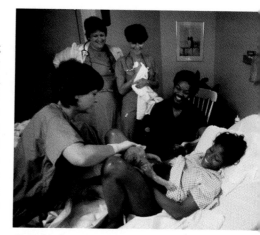

In a birthing center or when delivery takes place at home, the mother is usually attended by a midwife.

Contrast this experience with that of another woman who enters the birthing center adjacent to the local hospital. A pleasant bedroom and lounge are available to her, and there are no standard orders for medical procedures. She and her partner are free to walk, talk, eat a bit, and sip some juice. She may try several positions, crouching down on all fours if it seems more comfortable. The mother is encouraged to walk frequently or to stand so that gravity can help the infant's progress through the birth canal. She is attended through much of the labor and the actual childbirth by a licensed nurse-midwife, who also may have provided childbirth education classes and exercises for the parents during the woman's pregnancy. When the time comes for the actual birth, the mother has a choice of positions—she may lie on her back, sit partly elevated, or sit in a birthing chair (Young, 1982).

Clearly, there are a number of options besides whether or not one has prepared childbirth, whether or not one uses medication, or whether or not one takes advantage of such technologies as fetal monitors.

MIDWIVES Childbirth assistants who remain with a mother throughout her labor are known as **midwives;** they are increasingly relieving obstetricians in supervising births in which no complications are expected. *Nurse-midwives* are usually trained in hospital nursing programs, where they study obstetrics and related subjects, such as nutrition and community health, for a year or more. Some states also permit lay midwives to deliver babies. In America, nurse-midwives are more common than lay midwives. Although the practice of midwifery has had a controversial history in the United States, midwives deliver 80 percent of the world's babies. In Sweden, Denmark, Finland, Holland, and Japan, where deliveries by midwives have been common, the infant mortality rate is consistently lower than that in the United States (Smith, 1987; National Center for Health Statistics, 1990). We should not look on this as a simple cause-and-effect relationship, however. The United States has a much more diverse population. Infant mortality is much higher in minority groups, where prenatal care may have

midwife A childbirth assistant who remains with a mother throughout labor and who can supervise births where no complications are expected; nurse-midwives have had training in hospital nursing programs, where they have studied obstetrics.

FOCUS ON AN ISSUE

NEWBORNS AT RISK: UNTANGLING THE STATISTICS

In the United States, nearly 90 percent of babies are born healthy and on time. In 1990, 89.6 percent of newborns scored a healthy 9 or 10 on the Apgar Scale at 5 minutes after birth. Only 10.6 percent were born preterm, or prior to 37 weeks after gestation. Only 7 percent of newborns weighed less than 5 1/2 pounds, and less than 1 percent died in their first year. Primarily because of medical advances and health education, our infant mortality rate (along with those of most developed countries) has fallen steadily in the last five decades from a rate of 47 deaths per 1,000 births, in 1940, to a rate of 26 deaths per 1000 births in 1960, 12.6 in 1980, 9.2 in 1990, and to an all-time low rate of 8.5 in 1992 (National Center for Health Statistics, 1993*a*; 1993*b*; Children's Defense Fund, 1991). But, despite these optimistic statistics, some infants still face serious risks at birth. Let's take a closer look at the statistics concerning the roughly 10 percent of United States babies who come into the world struggling for health. Who are these at-risk newborns? Can some of their problems be prevented?

"One of the best predictors of low-birth weight is the absence of prenatal care, beginning in the first three months of pregnancy."

Death in the first year of life can strike any baby, but it occurs 2.4 times as often among black infants as to white infants and twice as frequently among babies living below the poverty line than among those above it. Babies born prematurely, or with low-birth weights, or low Apgar Scores can be born in any family, but each of these outcomes is far more common when the mother is under 15 or over 44, when she lives below the poverty line, or when she is unmarried (National Center for Health Statistics, 1993*a*). Are there any common threads in this?

One of the best predictors of low-birth weight is the absence of prenatal care, beginning in the first three months of pregnancy. In nearly a quarter of live births, the mother receives prenatal care late or does not receive it at all. Teen mothers, minority mothers, unmarried mothers, and women living in poverty are far more likely to delay prenatal care than are married, more affluent women over the age of 20 (National Center for Health Statistics, 1993*a*). In some areas, there simply is no adequate access to basic health services for poor families. Yet early prenatal care can often remedy maternal health problems, like high blood pressure, anemia, or poor nutrition before they become risk factors for the infant. Selective educational programs can be initiated to

been limited or nonexistent (see the box "Newborns at Risk: Untangling the Statistics"). In the last decade, however, licensed nurse-midwives have participated in a greater number of hospital births as members of birthing teams and also in birthing centers (Eakins, 1986).

BIRTHING CENTERS   Birthing centers are a popular alternative to traditional hospital maternity care. The philosophy behind birthing centers is that childbirth is a natural, nonpathological event and that technological intervention should be kept to a minimum. They seek to combine the privacy, serenity, and intimacy of a

address potentially harmful behaviors like smoking, alcohol use, and drug use as well as to teach new skills such as basic child care.

Young teens mothers, aged 15 and under, are at particular risk in childbearing. They are usually neither physically nor emotionally mature enough for the stresses of bearing and caring for a child. As a group, their immaturity, nutritional habits, and avoidance of health services places them at greater risk for premature or sickly babies. In addition, they may lack the stamina, patience, and understanding to care for even a healthy child. Often, the absence of even a basic education and isolation from the social support of peers or family make coping with the difficult tasks ahead even more difficult. As one social worker reported:

I will never forget the look of fatigue which I saw on the face of a 14-year-old girl who had given birth to twins, four months previously. She looked old beyond her years as she sat on the stoop of her parents' house in rural South Carolina. Her mother and brother were away at work, her younger siblings in school, while she remained home to care for her babies and her youngest brother. Her father had tried to be supportive, but now, he had moved several hundred miles away to find work, so the bulk of the child care fell on her. At an age when her peers were starting high school, dreaming of their future and beginning to date, it seemed, her future had arrived. She was at home, lonely, chasing a toddler, changing diapers, and soothing two restless babies.

Just as late or absent prenatal care is a predictor of low-birth weight, low-birth weight is often used as a marker or indicator of the greater likelihood of infant disability or even death. Low-birth weight babies are two to three times more likely to suffer from chronically disabilitating conditions than are their peers. In addition, such infants are forty times more likely to die in their first month of life than are normal-weight newborns. Over the past two decades, medical technology has managed to reduce the death rates for these low-birth rate babies, even though their numbers have not been similarly reduced. In fact, the rate of low-birth weight babies has risen from 6.7 percent in 1984 to a stubbornly steady 7 percent in the early 1990s (National Center for Health Statistics, 1993b). Although many communities continue to improve in health statistics, in others, where poverty has increased and drugs and AIDS are widespread, the rates of low-birth weight babies and of infant mortality have increased sharply (Wiener and Engel, 1991). Currently, cities such as Washington, Philadelphia, and Baltimore have low-birth weight rates and infant mortality rates that are higher than those for Bulgaria or Costa Rica (Children's Defense Fund, 1992). Faced with such statistics, Marian Wright Edelman asks: "Is this the best America can do?" (Children's Defense Fund, 1992, p. x).

home birth with the safety and medical backup of a nearby hospital, and they consider the parents' social, psychological, and aesthetic needs as equally important as medical requirements (Allgaier, 1978).

Birthing rooms at these centers are designed to accommodate the entire process from labor through delivery and recovery (Parker, 1980). The delivery itself is most often performed by a midwife rather than by a physician. Most birthing centers encourage prepared childbirth and an early return home, generally within 24 hours. They also encourage mothers to keep their infants in their rooms to help promote early bonding (Allgaier, 1978; Parker, 1980).

Birthing centers are not equipped to handle everybody. They screen out women with high-risk factors or complications. Typical guidelines exclude women over 35 having their first baby, women having twins, women suffering from diseases like diabetes or cardiac problems, and women who have previously had Caesarean deliveries (Lubic & Ernst, 1978).

Most parents find birthing centers deeply satisfying. The centers keep birth focused on the family and give the parents the maximum amount of independence and control (Eakins, 1986). Physicians, too, find that as childbirth becomes more family centered, there is a different role and responsibility for them (Willson, 1990). In many ways, the good obstetrician is skilled in teamwork procedures. He is essentially, the leader of a team composed of the nurse, the midwife, the husband, the wife—and to a certain extent, the baby, who must participate with "birth protocol" or the whole enterprise changes its venue. For some older physicians who were not trained with the expectation that both parents will be participatory partners in childbirth, this new openness and scrutiny of their work is uncomfortable. Others enthusiastically involve the father and mother. As one father was busily photographing the Caesarean birth of his daughter, for example, the obstetrician as laughingly remarked, "It's too bad you don't have a video camera. I'm so much better live!" This sort of interchange goes a long way to reduce the stress and humanize the process of childbirth.

HOME BIRTHS   In the United States, some women are taking the idea of prepared childbirth one step further: They are choosing to have their children at home. There, in familiar surroundings, a woman can share the event with her husband, older children, and close friends. After the birth, she can spend as much time as she wants with her infant, instead of being regulated by a hospital's schedule. Some research indicates that the closeness of family members made possible with home births may greatly enhance early parent-infant attachment (Eakins, 1986).

Although 85 percent to 90 percent of all childbirths are routine and uncomplicated, home birth requires certain precautions. First, high-risk conditions such as prematurity, toxemia, multiple birth, or maternal illness are appropriate for facilities equipped to handle possible complications. Second, a physician or midwife should be on hand during birth, and an emergency plan should be ready if hospitalization is required. Although a great deal of attention has been focused on home births, the rate of such births is low—in fact, it has remained about 1 percent since 1975 (National Center for Health Statistics, 1993).

THE INFANT'S EXPERIENCE

In this discussion on the experience of childbirth, we have almost ignored the infant's experience. If the mother has been heavily anesthetized, the infant, too, will be groggy and may need to be revived. Often, mucus is removed from the nose and mouth with a syringe. Also, it is common for the infant to cry at birth, indicating its vigorous responsiveness. Sometimes, however, things are calmer than this.

Frederick Leboyer (1976), a French obstetrician, has developed a method of childbirth intended to make the birth process less stressful for the infant. He strongly objected to the bright lights, the noise, and the practice of holding the infant upside down and slapping it. He recommended that childbirth take place in a quiet, dimly lit room, that the cord remain connected for several minutes so that breathing would not be rushed, and that the baby be placed on the mother's abdomen, where it could be gently fondled and caressed. After a short time, the baby should be given a warm bath to relax.

Most hospitals still use bright lights and don't use the warm bath. Most place the newborn on the mother's abdomen or chest. The cord is cut more leisurely than in the past, and many infants nurse at the breast within minutes of birth (Young, 1982; Nilsson, 1990).

Even with new hospital procedures, childbirth is a remarkably stressful event for the newborn. Despite this stress, the full-term baby is well equipped to handle the event (Gunnar, 1989). In the last few moments of birth, the infant produces a major surge of adrenalin and noradrenalin, the stress hormones. The adrenalin shock counteracts any oxygen deficiency and prepares the baby for breathing through the lungs. Almost immediately, as the infant experiences the bright, noisy delivery room and the cold air, there is a first cry. The first breaths may be difficult because the fluid that was in the lungs must be expelled, and millions of little air sacs in the lungs must be filled. Yet, within minutes, most infants have established fairly regular breathing, typically with a lusty cry.

What about pain? The newborn has relatively high levels of a natural painkiller called beta-endorphins circulating in its blood system. Perhaps as a result of this, most infants experience a period of unusual alertness and receptivity shortly after birth. Many experts have suggested that this period of extended alertness, which may last an hour or more, is an ideal time for parents and infant to get acquainted (Nilsson, 1990).

PARENT-INFANT BONDING

Within minutes after birth, infant, mother, and father—if he is present—begin the process of **bonding,** or of forming an attachment. After the initial birth cry and filling of the lungs, a newborn calms down with time to relax on the mother's chest. After a little rest, she may struggle to focus her eyes on a face. She seemingly pauses to listen. The parents watch in fascination and begin talking to this new creature. They examine all of the parts—the fingers and the toes, the funny little ears. There is close physical contact, cradling, stroking. Many infants find the breast and almost immediately start to nurse, with pauses to look about. Infants who have had little or no anesthesia may enjoy a half-hour or more of heightened alertness and exploration, as their mother or father holds them close, establishes eye contact, and talks to them. They seemingly want to respond. It has now been clearly established in at least eight different independent laboratories and in five different countries that babies are capable of doing some limited imitation of a parent. They move their heads, open and close their mouths, and even stick out their tongues in response to the facial gestures of their parents (Meltzoff & Moore, 1989).

bonding Forming an attachment; refers particularly to the developing relationship between parents and infant that begins immediately after birth.

It is now known that the baby's physical responses trigger significant physical processes within the mother's body. When the baby licks or sucks on a breast nipple, it causes increased secretion of prolactin, a hormone important in nursing, and oxytocin, another hormone that contracts the uterus and decreases bleeding. The infant also benefits from early breast-feeding. Although milk is not yet available, the mother produces a substance called *colostrum*. This substance appears to help clear the infant's digestive system.

Some psychologists believe that these early parent-infant interactions are psychologically significant in helping to establish a strong parent-infant bond (see the box "Emerging Fatherhood: Changing Roles"). In one study (Klaus & Kennell, 1976) of 28 first-time, low-income, high-risk mothers, the hospital staff provided half of the mothers with 16 extra hours of infant contact in the first 3 days after birth. The two groups of mothers and infants were later examined at 1 month, 1 year, and 2 years. Over the 2-year period, the extra-contact mothers consistently showed significantly greater attachments to their babies. They were more affectionate and attentive. Early extra contact may be particularly useful for teenage mothers or those who have had little or no experience with newborns, and for mothers of premature and high-risk infants who are more likely to experience slow bonding patterns at birth due to the difficulties of accepting their babies' shortcomings. But some researchers feel that early bonding is not quite so essential. They have found that, except for high-risk mothers and infants, the increased contact following birth made little or no difference (Field, 1979).

In general, the initial excitement and bonding is merely a foreshadowing of the depth of emotion that is to come—at least with normal, emotionally sound parents. As one mother comments:

> I am a career woman who has always valued my logical and rational abilities. I was absolutely unprepared for the feeling I felt when I first held my daughter. It was an overwhelming sense of wonder and thankfulness that she was alive and healthy. By the end of the first year, however, the feeling had grown to be all-encompassing. I could not imagine what life had been like before she arrived. I am aware of her every moment during my day—whether at work or with her. My husband has similar feelings. This is truly bonding...what we felt initially was only a tiny portion of our current feelings today.

In any case, mothers and fathers who spend the early period with their babies report more self-confidence in their ability as parents and greater self-esteem. Goldberg (1983) notes the value of these feelings. She points out that because parenthood is a major transition, it is particularly important for parents to be encouraged in their new roles. She also suggests that as parents typically have an idealized image of what their baby will be like, parent-infant contact during the first few hours and days following birth may help them to adjust their expectations concerning the appearance and behavior of their infant. Furthermore, if parents are to become attached to their baby, they need to become acquainted. Why should they delay in getting to know each other? Goldberg concludes, however, that if things do not go well in those first few days, or if the infant is premature or handicapped, or the mother is ill or sedated, the relationship is not doomed—attachments can form later.

THE NEONATE

Until this point, we have been discussing the biological and psychological aspects of childbirth. We have largely focused on the parents who have done the bulk of the work in the relationship to this time. However, once the baby is actually physically present in the parent's world, the nature of the exchange changes. Now in very meaningful ways, the baby is part of the triad. He or she actively—but at first unintentionally—helps to mold the development of the family unit. We will now look at the condition of the new baby at birth and afterward.

During the first month of life, a baby is known as a **neonate.** The first month is a very special period in a baby's life. It is distinguished from the rest of infancy because during this time, the baby must adjust to leaving the closed, protected environment of the mother's womb to live in the outside world. The first month is a period of both recovery from the birth process and adjustment of vital functions, such as respiration, circulation, digestion, and body-heat temperature regulation.

At birth, the average full-term baby weighs between 5 1/2 and 9 1/2 pounds (2.5 and 4.3 kilograms) and is between 19 and 22 inches (48 and 56 centimeters) long. The baby's skin may be covered with the *vernix caseosa,* a smooth and cheeselike coating that developed during the fetal period. This coating is present especially in a Caesarean delivery because it has not been wiped off during the tight passage through the birth canal. The baby's skin also may be covered with fine facial and body hairs that drop off during the first month. Temporarily, the newborn's head may look misshapen and elongated as a result of the process called *molding.* In molding, the soft bony plates of the skull, connected only by cartilage, are squeezed together in the birth canal. Also, the external breasts and the genitals of both boys and girls may look enlarged. This enlargement is temporary, too. It is caused by the mother's female hormones that passed to the baby before birth. The general appearance of the newborn, then, may be a bit of a shock to new parents, who expect to see the plump, smooth, 3- to 4-month-old infant shown in advertisements.

THE PERIOD OF ADJUSTMENT

Despite their appearance, full-term neonates are sturdy little beings who are already making the profound adjustment to their new lives—from having their mothers do everything for them to functioning on their own as separate individuals. Four critical areas of adjustment are respiration, circulation of blood, digestion, and temperature regulation.

The birth cry traditionally symbolizes the beginning of the neonate's life. It also signals a major step in the child's development, for with the first breaths of air, the lungs are inflated for the first time, and they begin to work as the basic organ of the child's own respiratory system. During the first few days after birth, the neonate experiences periods of coughing and sneezing that often alarm the new mother, but they serve the important function of clearing mucus and amniotic fluid from the infant's air passages.

neonate A baby in the first month of life.

FOCUS ON AN ISSUE

EMERGING FATHERHOOD: CHANGING ROLES

George Russell awoke again feeling queasy. Ever since his wife, Kate, became pregnant and has had morning sickness, he too has felt ill in the morning. This morning was no different. George is going through what many other men with pregnant wives have experienced. Studies have indicated that between 10 percent and 15 percent of first-time fathers-to-be mimic some of the symptoms of their pregnant wives. They too occasionally experience nausea, abdominal discomfort, and strange cravings (Parke, 1981).

Some first-time fathers-to-be undergo a fair amount of stress as their wives go through pregnancy. It seems that mild depression, anxiety, and feelings of inadequacy are common. Among the natives of the Yucatan in Mexico, for example, pregnancy is confirmed when the woman's mate has nausea, diarrhea, vomiting, or cramps (Pruett, 1987). Not only do expectant fathers crave dill pickles with ice cream, they also have deeply troubling dreams and

disturbing changes in sexual activity. It is obvious that these husbands have identified with their wives (Pruett, 1987).

"Fathers who develop a strong bond with their infants are usually more sensitive to the child's changing needs and interests in later years."

Certainly, not all fathers experience such symptoms. Yet many fathers find the period of their wife's first pregnancy a time of anticipation, uncertainty, changing attitudes, and changing roles. The definition of an appropriate role for fatherhood in our society has expanded in recent years.

Many fathers are now urged and encouraged by their wives and even their friends to participate directly in their child's birth. In childbirth

classes, they have learned techniques of physical and emotional support for their wives as we saw earlier in this chapter. They can coach the mother through childbirth and then immediately start getting to know the newborn infant. As one mother who had had a Caesarean section commented, "It was amazing. While they were stitching me up, they were taking the baby to the nursery to be bathed, weighed, and so forth. My husband disappeared with her. When he came back two hours later, he had given her first bath, diapered her, and was all set to show me how to take care of babies!"

Fathers who have participated in their child's birth report an almost immediate attraction to the infant with feelings of elation, pride, and increased self-esteem (Greenberg & Morris, 1974). Some studies report that these fathers are more deeply involved with and attached to their infants than those who do not participate in birth and early care (Pruett, 1987). They also feel a

The onset of breathing marks a significant change in the neonate's circulatory system, too. The baby's heart no longer needs to pump blood to the placenta for aeration. Instead, the blood now circulates to the lungs to receive oxygen and to eliminate carbon dioxide (Pratt, 1954; Vulliamy, 1973). To achieve this, a valve in the baby's heart closes to redirect the flow of blood along the changed route. The circulatory system is no longer fetal; rather, it becomes entirely self-contained. The shift from fetal to independent circulatory and respiratory systems begins immediately after birth but is not completed for several days. Lack of oxygen for more than a few minutes at birth or during the first few days of adjustment may cause permanent brain damage.

closer relationship to their wives because of this shared experience. New fathers who do not participate in childbirth and early infant play frequently feel more distant from their wives and somewhat ignored when the baby arrives. Often, the companionship between husband and wife is sharply reduced while the mother's focus is on the infant (Galinsky, 1980).

Many studies report that fathers who have begun a relationship with their newborns continue to provide more direct care and more play to their developing infants. This somewhat newer role of the nurturing father has many benefits for family development. In one study, infants whose fathers were actively involved in care-giving scored higher on motor and mental development tests (Pederson et al., 1979). In another, such infants were found to be more socially responsive than average (Parke, 1979). Couples report less tension, more joint goals, and shared decision making when both of them actively parent the infant. But, in evaluating these studies, we must remember that fathers who choose

to have early contact with their infants may differ in many other ways from those who do not choose such contact (Palkovitz, 1985).

Actively involved fathers generally relate to their infants differently from the way mothers do. More often than not, these fathers play with their babies, while mothers wash them, diaper them, and feed them. Even when these fathers are involved in caretaking activities, they generally play while tending to their infants. Furthermore, the father's style of play is also much different from the mother's. They tend to play vigorously—tossing their babies in the air, moving their arms and legs to-and-fro, and bouncing them on papa's knee. Mothers, on the other hand, tend to coo at their babies, babble baby talk, and usually play more gently. At a very early age infants look to their fathers with great expectations. "At only six weeks of age, babies will hunch their shoulders and lift their eyebrows, as though in anticipation that 'play-time has arrived' when their fathers appear" (Brazelton & Yogman, 1984).

Fathers who develop a strong bond with their infants are usually more sensitive to the child's changing needs and interests in later years. These fathers also tend to have more influence over the child. They are more likely to be looked up to and listened to because of the close, complex relationship established. It becomes clear in the research on fathers and their children in middle childhood and adolescence, that fathers are instrumental in the gender identity of both their sons and daughters, and also in the achievement motivation and drive of both. The new research on father's certainly contradicts Margaret Mead's statement, "Fathers are a biological necessity but a social accident."

Before birth, the placenta provided nourishment as well as oxygen for the infant. Once free of the womb, the infant's own digestive system must begin to function. This change is a longer, more adaptive process than are the immediate and dramatic changes in respiration and circulation.

Another gradual adjustment involves the neonate's temperature regulation system. Within the uterus, the baby's skin was maintained at a constant temperature. After birth, however, the baby's skin must constantly work to provide insulation from even minor changes in external temperature. During the first few days of life, babies must be carefully covered. Soon, they become better able to maintain their own body-heat temperatures, aided by a healthy layer of fat that accumulates during the first weeks of life.

All neonates are not equally equipped to adjust to the abrupt changes brought about by birth, and it is essential to detect any problems at the earliest possible moment. Great advances have been made in this area in recent years. At one time, babies were considered healthy if they merely "looked" healthy. Then, in 1953, Virginia Apgar devised a standard scoring system, and hospitals were able to evaluate an infant's condition quickly. We may see this scoring system, the Apgar score, presented in Table 5–2. The Apgar score is taken at 1 minute and again at 5 minutes after the baby's birth. The attendant observes the pulse, breathing, muscle tone, general reflex response, and color of the skin (or the mucous membranes, palms, and soles for nonwhite babies). A perfect Apgar score is 10 points, with a score of 7 or more considered normal. Scores below 7 generally show that some bodily processes are not functioning fully and require at least watching and perhaps special attention. A score of 4 or less requires immediate emergency measures.

COMPETENCE OF THE NEWBORN

What can newborns do? What can they hear? How much do they see? What can they learn? We are still discovering some of the fascinating capabilities and skills that newborns possess. With the new emphasis on family interaction, parenting and bonding, it is helpful to understand these competencies in order to see the infant as a fully participating partner in the family's social interactions.

Until the 1960s, psychologists thought that neonates were incapable of organized, self-directed behavior. As a matter of fact, it was not uncommon to find the infant's world being described as a "booming, buzzing confusion." It was common to read in psychological literature that infants did not use the higher centers of the brain until they were almost a year old, or that newborns saw light and shadow but not objects or patterns. Behavior in the first weeks of life was considered to be almost entirely reflexive. Later experiments have shown

TABLE 5–2 Apgar Scoring System for Infants

	SCORES		
	0	1	2
Pulse	Absent	Less than 100	More than 100
Breathing	Absent	Slow, irregular	Strong cry
Muscle tone	Limp	Some flexion of extremities	Active motion
Reflex response	No response	Grimace	Vigorous cry
Color*	Blue, pale	Body pink, extremities blue	Completely pink

*For nonwhites, alternative tests of mucous membranes, palms, and soles are used.

Source: From "Proposal for a New Method of Evaluating the Newborn Infant" by V. Apgar, Anesthesia and Analgesia. 1953, 32, 260. Used by permission of the International Anesthesia Research Society.

that we had significantly underestimated newborns. We now know that neonates are capable of organized, predictable responses and mental activity that is more complex than was expected of them. They have definite preferences and show a striking ability to learn. Moreover, they are able to attract attention to their needs. We shall introduce some of these concepts in this chapter but more fully explore them in Chapter 6.

The key to this new understanding of infants lies in the development of more precise and creative ways of observing them. Early studies were poorly designed. They employed inadequate measurements and frequently put the infant at a disadvantage. Even adults who are placed flat on their back to stare at a white ceiling while being covered up to their necks with blankets are not their most perceptive or responsive selves. When infants are placed tummy down on the mother's skin in a warm room, however, they will display an engaging repertoire of behaviors (Prechtl & Beintema, 1965). This and other new study techniques allow infants to respond fully to testing.

INFANT STATES   When we watch sleeping newborns, we notice that at certain times they lie calmly and quietly, and at other times they twitch and grimace, although their eyes remain closed. Similarly, when awake, babies may be calm but are still capable of thrashing about wildly and crying.

By observing infants' activity over a considerable time, P. H. Wolff (1966) was able to separate and identify six newborn behavioral states: *regular sleep, irregular sleep, drowsiness, alert inactivity, waking activity,* and *crying.* Most of the day is spent in either regular or irregular sleep. As the infant matures and the cortex of the brain "wakes up," these percentages shift. For example, by 4 weeks to 8 weeks of age, the typical baby is sleeping more during the night and less during the day. By the end of the first year, the typical baby is sleeping through the

Child development researchers now know that infants are capable of more complex responses and mental activities than was previously believed.

night. Once this occurs, parents begin to relax more and find the experience of parenting far more workable. As one working mother reported, "I no longer feel like a zombie." We can see the behaviors typical of these states presented in Table 5–3.

These states have a regular duration and seem to follow predictable daily cycles of waking and sleeping. The level of responsiveness in newborns depends largely on their particular behavioral state. For example, Wolff found that babies in a state of alert inactivity reacted to stimulation by becoming more active. Babies who were already in an active state had a different response: They seemed to calm down when stimulated. It is very important, therefore, to consider the state of newborns when trying to assess their reactions to outside events. In addition, since newborns spend approximately 70 percent of their time sleeping, research should be timed to their awake and alert phases. As we can see, this may be difficult.

ABILITY TO BE SOOTHED   Crying is the infant state that causes parents and caregivers the most worry; it challenges them to discover the cause and then invent ways to stop it. Of the many techniques used to soothe babies, three stand out in their effectiveness: picking them up, providing constant rhythmic movement, and, for some, reducing the amount of stimulation that they receive from their own bodies by swaddling them in blankets. (This is probably why some

TABLE 5–3 The Classification of Infant States

Regular sleep	The infant's eyes are closed, and he or she is completely relaxed. Breathing is slow and regular. The face looks relaxed, and the eyelids are still.
Irregular sleep	The infant's eyes are closed, but he or she engages in gentle limb movements of various sorts—writhing, stirring, stretching, and so forth. Grimaces and other facial changes occur. Breathing is irregular and faster than in regular sleep. Rapid eye movements occasionally occur.
Drowsiness	The baby is fairly inactive. The eyes are open but often close. Breathing is regular but faster than regular sleep. When the eyes are open they may have a dull, glazed quality.
Alert inactivity	The eyes are open, bright, and shining. They follow moving objects and can make good quality movements together (conjugate movement). The baby is fairly inactive with a face quiet and not grimacing.
Waking activity	The baby frequently engages in motor activity involving the whole body. The eyes are open, and the breathing is highly irregular.
Crying	The baby has crying vocalizations combined with vigorous, disorganized motor activity.

infants sleep so well when wrapped up and taken for a ride in a car. They are getting a combination of physical security and rhythmic movement.)

Newborns differ greatly in how easily they can be soothed and by which methods. Many infants quiet quite easily, either with their own self-comforting methods or to the sounds of an adult voice; other infants require more active soothing (Brazelton, Nugent, & Lester, 1987). Most important, some match must exist between the parents' technique for soothing the baby and the baby's ability to be soothed. When the match is wrong, awkward, or nonexistent, both mother and child may get themselves into behavioral patterns that later are hard to change (Brazelton, Nugent, & Lester, 1987).

REFLEXES Full-term infants confront the world with a number of complex **reflexes** and combinations of reflexes. It is believed that these reflexes have evolutionary survival value and reflect behaviors that have been in the past—and may still be in some ways today—necessary for the infant's ability to survive. Most disappear after 3 or 4 months. A few of them deserve special mention. We may see these reflexes described in Table 5–4.

The *Moro reflex* is the newborn's startle reaction. When newborns are startled, as by a loud sound, they react first by extending both arms to the side, with fingers outstretched as if to catch onto someone or something. The arms are then gradually brought back to the midline. Some have thought the Moro reflex to be a remnant of our ape ancestry—in the event of a fall, infant apes who grasped their mothers' hair were the most likely to survive. Another body reflex is the *tonic neck reflex*. It occurs when babies' heads are turned sharply to one side. They react by extending the arm and leg on the same side while flexing the arm and leg on the other side, in a kind of fencing position. The *stepping reflex* occurs when newborn babies are held vertically with their feet against a hard surface. They lift one leg away from the surface, and, if tilted slightly from one side to the other, they appear to be walking. The *grasping reflex* applies to newborn's toes as well as to their fingers. Babies will close their fingers over any object, such as a pencil or finger, when it is placed on their palm. Some neonates can grasp with such strength that they support their full weight for up to a minute (Taft & Cohen, 1967).

A very useful reflex of the mouth is the *rooting reflex*. When one cheek is touched, babies "root," or move the mouth toward the stimulus. This aids them in finding the nipple. A mother who is unfamiliar with this response may try to push the infant's head toward the nipple. Because the reflex is toward, not away from, the stimulation, the baby will move toward the hand that pushes, thus seeming to reject the breast. The better maternal response to rooting is to hold the nipple and touch the baby's cheek with it. In this way, the baby turns and finds the nipple. The rooting reflex disappears by the third or fourth month (Taft & Cohen, 1967). The *sucking reflex*, like the rooting reflex, is clearly necessary for infant survival. Like some other reflexes, sucking begins in the uterus. Cases have been reported of babies born with thumbs already swollen from sucking.

Newborns' eyes are also capable of several reflex movements and motor patterns. The lids open and close in response to stimuli. The pupils widen in dim light and narrow in bright light; they also narrow when infants are going to sleep and widen when they wake up. Even an infant who is only a few hours old is capable of following a slow-moving object, like a bright red ball, with its eyes (Brazelton, 1969).

reflex An unlearned, automatic response to a stimulus. Many reflexes disappear after 3 or 4 months.

TABLE 5–4 Reflexes of the Newborn

REFLEX	DESCRIPTION
Moro (startle)	When infants are startled by loud sounds or by being suddenly dropped a few inches, they will first spread their arms and stretch out their fingers, then bring their arms back to their body and clench their fingers. Disappears after about 4 months.
Tonic neck	When infants' heads are turned to one side, they will extend the arm and leg on that side, and flex their arm and leg on the opposite side, as in a fencing position. Disappears after 4 months.
Stepping (walking)	When infants are held upright with their feet against a flat surface and are moved forward, they will appear to walk in a coordinated way. Disappears after 2 or 3 months.
Placing	Similar to the stepping reflex. When infants' feet are put against a table edge, they will attempt to step up onto it. Disappears after 2 months.
Grasping (palmar)	When a pencil or a finger is placed in infants' palms, they will grasp it tightly and increase the strength of the grasp if the object is pulled away. Disappears after about 5 months.
Babkin	If objects are placed against both palms, infants will react by opening their mouths, closing their eyes, and turning their heads to one side. Disappears after 4 months.
Plantar	Similar to the grasping reflex. When an object or a finger is placed on the soles of infants' feet near the toes, they will respond by trying to flex their feet. Disappears sometime after 9 months.
Babinski	If the soles of infants' feet are stroked from heel to toes, infants will spread their small toes and raise the large one. Disappears after 6 months.
Rooting	If infants' cheeks are touched, they will turn their heads toward the stimulus and open their mouths, as if to find a nipple. Disappears after 3 or 4 months.
Sucking	If a finger is put in infants' mouths, they will respond by sucking and making rhythmic movements with the mouth and tongue.
Swimming	Infants will attempt to swim in a coordinated way if placed in water in a prone position. Disappears after 6 months.
Ocular neck	Infants will tilt their heads back and away from a light shining directly into their eyes.
Pupillary	The pupils of infants' eyes will narrow in bright light and when going to sleep, and will widen in dim light and when waking up. Reflex is permanent.

Many other reflexes govern the behavior of the newborn. Some, like sneezing or coughing, are necessary for survival. Others seem to be related to the behavior patterns of our ancient ancestors. Still others are not yet understood.

perception The complex process by which the mind interprets and gives meaning to sensory information.

SENSORY AND PERCEPTUAL CAPACITIES Can newborn babies see the details of an object directly in front of them? Can they see patterns? Can they see color and depth? Can they hear a low whisper? Are they sensitive to touch, or are they rather numb? Research indicates that all of the senses are operating at birth, but perception is limited and selective. **Perception** is the active process of inter-

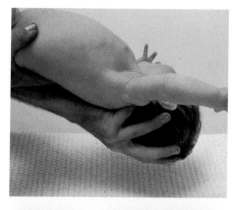

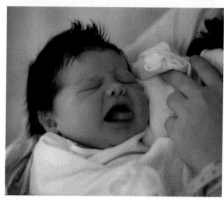

Some reflexes of the newborn: top left, Moro reflex; top right, stepping reflex; bottom left, sucking reflex; and bottom right, rooting reflex.

preting sensory information. Visual perception is not just seeing; for example, it involves giving meaning to what we see. When infants turn their heads to selectively look at one thing and not another, or position themselves to get a better view of something in particular, they are exhibiting some perceptual competence. In Chapter 6, we will discuss the perceptual competencies of infants in greater detail. At this point, let us look briefly at the sensory and perceptual capacities of the newborn.

Vision. From anatomical research, we know that infants are born with a full, intact set of visual structures. Most—but not all—of these structures are immature and need to develop over the next few months before they reach full capacity. However, neonates do have some visual skills. From the first moments, newborns' eyes are sensitive to brightness. Their pupils contract in bright light and dilate in darkness. They have some control over eye movements, and they can visually track an object that moves within their field of vision, such as a face or a doctor's penlight. The eye movements are initially short and jerky and are limited to a short span. Newborns are able to focus optimally within a narrow range of 7 to 10 inches (17.8 to 25.4 centimeters), with objects beyond this appearing blurred. Their visual acuity for distance is estimated to be about 20/600, as compared to a normal adult with 20/20 vision. This means they are nearly blind to details across the room (Banks & Salapatek, 1983) since 20/600 vision translates into seeing an object 20 feet away as though it were 600 feet away. Furthermore, newborns sometimes lack **convergence** of the eyes—they are not able to focus

convergence The ability to focus both eyes on one point.

both eyes on the same point. They will not be able to do so consistently until the end of the second month (Fantz, 1961). Lack of convergence probably limits depth perception.

We know that newborns are able to perceive their environment by the fact that they are selective about what they watch. Newborns clearly prefer to look at complex patterns. They look particularly at the edges and contours of objects, especially curves (Roskinski, 1977). Newborn babies are also exceptionally responsive to the human face (Fantz, 1958). It is not surprising, then, that they develop an early recognition of their mothers' faces. An experiment by Carpenter (1974) showed a newborn's preference for his or her mother's face at 2 weeks. Carpenter presented each infant with pictures of its mother and another woman. At 2 weeks, the infants preferred to look at the familiar face. In some cases, they turned their heads completely away from the strange pictures, perhaps because the stimulus was too strong or too unfamiliar (MacFarlane, 1978).

One of the more startling examples of visual perception in neonates is their seeming ability to imitate facial expressions. A team of psychologists has run a series of experiments with infants, who are sometimes no more than 2 or 3 days old, to demonstrate imitation. First, the researchers find a time when the neonate is in a calm, alert state (a condition that is not always easy to find). The infant and adult look at each other, and the adult goes through a series of expressions in random order. He purses his lips; he sticks out his tongue; he opens his mouth wide; he opens and closes his hand. In between, the adult pauses and wears a neutral expression. Both infant and adult are videotaped. Later, observers view the videotape of both the adult and the baby, and they try to match what the baby was imitating. Meltzoff and Moore (1989) find remarkable consistency. It appears that many of these babies seem to match their expressions and hand movements to those of the adults. However, some researchers find slightly different results or argue that infants open their mouths wide to a variety of stimuli. In any case, the neonate seems to see the stimuli and to respond to them in a somewhat selective fashion.

The visual sensitivity and preferences of newborns depend not only on the objects they are shown but also on their own state of arousal. Most visual preference studies must be done when the infant is awake, alert, and not too hungry. Newborns who have been fed will watch stimulating displays, such as rapidly flashing lights, nearly twice as long as awake, alert newborns who are being tested before their feeding (Gardner & Karmel, 1984).

It is important for us to keep in mind in our later discussion of infant social development, that behavioral competencies such as gazing at familiar objects (like the mother's or father's face), and imitating—or seeming to imitate—facial expressions, are important factors in developing and sustaining attachment between the infant and parents. The baby who alertly explores his or her mother's face, or who soothes when held by a familiar father, is the baby with whom the parents will find it easier to sustain attachment.

Hearing. We are certain that newborns can hear. They are startled by loud sounds, and they often turn toward a voice. Newborns are soothed by low-pitched sounds, such as lullabies, and they fuss after hearing high-pitched squeaks and whistles. Clearly, therefore, babies are responsive to the sounds in their environment. But how well developed is this hearing?

The anatomical structures for hearing are rather well developed in the newborn (Morse & Cowan, 1982). For the first few weeks, however, there is still excess fluid and tissue in the middle ear, and until it is reabsorbed, hearing is believed to be somewhat muffled—much the way you may have heard if you had a bad cold. Moreover, the brain structures for transmitting and interpreting hearing, are not fully developed. In fact, brain structures will continue to develop until the child is about 2 years old (Morse & Cowan, 1982; Aslin, 1987; Shatz, 1992). Despite these limitations, newborns are capable of responding to a wide range of sounds. Even in the first month of life, they are especially sensitive to speech sounds (Eimas, 1975). They also seem to show preference for the human voice. For instance, they will listen to a song sung by a woman rather than the same song performed on a musical instrument (Glen, Cunningham, & Joyce, 1981). Infants also seem to be able to localize sound. Even in their first few days, they will turn their heads toward a sound or a voice. One researcher has found that babies who turn toward a sound in the first few weeks of life seem to lose this ability during the second month and then pick it up again in the third month (Muir & Field, 1979).

The newborn's senses are finely tuned. For example, an infant can recognize his mother by her smell.

Other Senses. We know less about newborns' senses of taste, smell, and touch than we do about seeing and hearing. Some studies suggest that these three senses are finely sensitive. Although evidence indicates that newborns may have reduced sensitivity to pain for the first few days, the senses of taste and smell are operating fully. Newborns discriminate between sweet, salty, sour, and bitter through clearly differentiated facial responses to the four taste groups (Rosenstein & Oster, 1988). Also, newborns react negatively to strong odors, whereas they are selectively attracted to positive odors, such as a lactating female (Makin & Porter, 1989). As early as 6 days, the infant can distinguish the smell of its mother from the odor of another woman. This reaction is based on body odor, not just milk or breast odor, and naturally, the infant shows a preference for the familiar scent (MacFarlane, 1978; Makin & Porter, 1989).

The sense of touch is especially important to the comfort of newborns. The simple act of holding the arms or legs or pressing the abdomen often will be enough to quiet infants. Swaddling, as already mentioned, has a similar effect (Brazelton, 1969).

LEARNING AND HABITUATION   We have already seen considerable evidence of infant learning. The neonate quiets to a familiar sound, song, or lullaby, even to a familiar soap opera theme song (see box in Chapter 4). The neonate's ability to imitate facial expressions demonstrates some learning. Improved methods of observation have yielded useful information about the capacities of infants to learn some fairly complex responses. The newborns' ability to turn their heads has been used in many learning experiments. Some pioneering conditioning studies were conducted by Papousëk (1961). In these experiments, newborns were taught to turn their heads to the left to obtain milk whenever they heard a bell. For the same reward, they also learned to turn their heads to the right at the sound of a buzzer. Then, to complicate the situation, the bell and the buzzer were reversed. The infants quickly learned to turn their heads according to the rules of the new game.

Because sucking is well developed in the neonate, this ability has also been used in studies of neonatal learning and visual preferences. Kalnins and Bruner

(1973), in an expansion of an earlier study by Siqueland and DeLucia (1969), wanted to determine whether infants could control sucking when it was linked to rewards other than feeding. Pacifiers were wired to a laboratory slide projector. If the infants sucked, the slide came into focus; if they did not suck, the picture blurred. Bruner noted that the infants learned quickly to focus the picture and also adapted quickly if conditions were reversed—that is, they learned to stop sucking to get the picture into focus. In other words, the infants—some as young as 3 weeks old—not only coordinated sucking and looking but also effectively controlled the focus of the slide show. Their own reward was clear, rather than blurred, visual stimulation. Bruner concluded that infants had been greatly underestimated in both their perceptual capabilities and their ability to solve problems voluntarily.

Papoušek's (1961) experiments involved more than the buzzers and bells discussed earlier. He also used light to reveal a key facet of newborn behavior. Infants were taught to turn on a light by turning their heads to the left. Infants would turn their heads several times during a short period in order to turn on the light. But then an interesting thing happened—the infants seemed to lose interest in the game. Papoušek found that he could revive their interest by reversing the problem, but they soon became bored again. Papoušek's findings were important for two reasons. They supported Bruner's (1971) belief that competence, instead of immediate reward, motivates much of human learning, and they demonstrated a second learning phenomenon: **habituation.**

Infants habituate—they become accustomed to certain kinds of stimuli and then no longer respond to them. The process of habituation serves an important adaptive function. Infants need to be able to adapt to or ignore nonmeaningful stimuli, like the hissing of a radiator or the light touch of their clothing. Researchers use this process of habituation to find out a number of things about the perceptual capacities of infants. For example, a newborn's response at the onset of a moderately loud sound is a faster heartbeat, a change in breathing, and sometimes crying or general increased activity. As the sound continues, however, the infant soon habituates, or stops responding. When we change the sound stimulus, even by a small degree, and the response begins anew, clearly the infant perceives the change and reacts to the small difference. This habituating ability has been the basis of many experiments that have provided information about the sensory capacities and perceptual skills of newborns.

ASSESSMENT   During the first few days of a baby's life, most hospitals provide an extensive evaluation of the newborn. They may include a neurological examination and a behavioral assessment. Brazelton's (1973) Neonatal Behavioral Assessment Scale has been used increasingly by many hospitals. The 44 separate measures on this test can be grouped into seven behavioral clusters similar to the competencies discussed in this chapter. The seven clusters are presented in Table 5–5 and include *habituation, orientation, motor tone and activity, range of state, regulation of state* (that is, self-soothing ability), *autonomic stability* (that is, does the infant react to stimulation with unusual tremors or startles), and *reflexes.* The scale includes the usual neurological tests, but it is designed primarily to assess the newborn's behavioral capabilities.

Newborns differ in their responses to new, prolonged, or slightly annoying stimuli. Some can easily detect, attend to, and habituate (grow accustomed) to changes in their environment. Others may be less responsive, or they may be

habituation The process of becoming accustomed to certain kinds of stimuli and no longer responding to them.

overly responsive and too easily irritated—behaviors that decrease their attention spans and adaptability to changes. By assessing the newborn's competencies and ways of responding, the Brazelton scale may supply early information about a child's future personality and social development. Parents who observe a physician administer the Brazelton scale become much more sensitive to the capabilities and individuality of their own neonate (Parke & Tinsley, 1987).

THE INDIVIDUALITY OF NEWBORNS

From the moment of birth, infants demonstrate their uniqueness and their variability. Parents with more than one child are usually quite aware of differences in their children's personalities, although all of the children were seemingly "brought up" more or less the same way. Many times these differences can be noted even before a child is born. One fetus may kick actively, whereas another will shift position gently or cautiously. The following infant profiles demonstrate the great differences which may occur.

> Patrick was a very happy and placid baby. He slept in a regular pattern, was very good about feeding, and easily soothed. He had accepted a pacifier and usually relaxed immediately once he started sucking on it. When awake he would often lie in the infant carrier and quietly look around the room. If anyone approached him he would quietly turn to them and appear to be studying them. When picked up, even by new adults, he would mold against them and relax. At bedtime, his mother turned on the music box, turned down the lights, and he promptly fell asleep.

> Megan was temperamentally very different from her twin brother, Patrick. She fussed frequently and had trouble with feeding. She would not stay sucking very long on the breast, so her mother switched her at 6 weeks to a bottle. Even after this change, she took extended periods of time to finish her feeding. She refused to accept a pacifier and was difficult to soothe. She did not sleep in any regular pattern and tended to be up several times a night. In fact, she had trouble going to sleep in the evening. Her pediatrician had suggested to her parents that they let her cry for 15 to 20 minutes at night before picking her up. She sometimes fell asleep before then but often persisted in her crying for extended periods of time.

How profound are these differences in the temperament styles of neonates? What does the newborn's behavior tell us about his or her future personality? What are the dynamics between the baby's personality and the parents', and what are their effects? The individuality of the newborn has been the subject of many studies.

TEMPERAMENT   Most researchers agree that there are strong constitutional differences in temperament that appear early, are probably inherited, and are quite stable through much of the life span. But there is little agreement, on which of these aspects of temperament can be reliably identified in the neonate (Bates, 1987). One of the simpler models of individuality lists just three characteristics that are present at birth—*emotionality, activity level,* and *sociability* (Buss &

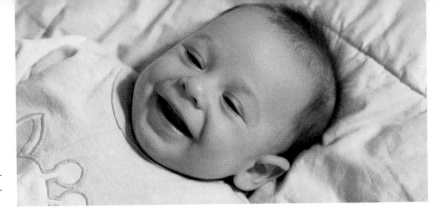

According to Chess, one of the characteristics of "easy children: is their ability to easily adapt to new situations.

Plomin, 1984; Plomin, 1990). Emotionality refers to the ease and strength with which an infant is aroused by a stimulus to a behavior and to emotional expression. Activity level is the amount of energy that the infant expends as a normal part of his waking day and the speed at which this energy is spent. Sociability refers to the infant's preference for being with others and to his ability to be rewarded by this interaction. An extremely high or low level of any of these temperament characteristics is not necessarily an advantage or a disadvantage. These are just ways in which infants differ.

In contrast, Chess (1967) identified nine criteria to differentiate neonatal behavior: *activity level, biological regularity, positive-negative responses to new stimuli, adaptability, intensity of reaction, threshold of responsiveness, quality of mood* (overall amount of pleasure versus displeasure displayed), *attention span and persistence*, and *distractibility.*

Chess used these criteria to study 136 children. She found that children could be divided into three basic types. She also determined that qualities seen as early as 2 or 3 months of age could be traced throughout childhood. The largest of Chess's three groups consisted of the "easy children"—babies (and later, children) who were biologically regular and rhythmical. The easy child has regular sleeping and eating schedules, accepts new food and new people, and is not easily frustrated. The "difficult children" form a smaller group. They withdraw from new stimuli and adapt slowly to change; their mood is often negative. A third type is the "slow-to-warm-up child." Children in this group withdraw from activities quietly, whereas the difficult child does so actively and noisily. Slow-to-warm-up children will show interest in new situations only if they are allowed to do so gradually, without pressure. Chess found no evidence that these temperament types were influenced by parental behavior. On the contrary, children's temperaments seemed to be as much a part of them as the inherited color of their eyes.

Another factor which has received considerable attention is *shyness.* Jerome Kagan and his colleagues at Harvard University have been studying the temperamental quality of shyness for several years via a longitudinal study of some 400 2 to 7-year-old children from intact middle-and upper-class white families (Kagan and Snidman, 1991; Kagan, Reznick and Gibbons, 1989). These researchers define shyness as inhibition to the unfamiliar. Kagan believes that this trait occurs in about 10 percent of the children in the study, developing around 21 months of age and persisting through 7 years of age. The opposite trait, which the researchers call *boldness,* or feeling comfortable in new situations, also occurs in about 10 percent of the children. Most children's behavior falls somewhere between these two extremes.

Kagan and his colleagues believe that shyness and boldness are inborn, genetic traits that are related to certain physiological functions. They appear to be lifelong, and are not related to sex or socioeconomic class. This does not mean that the sort of extreme shyness (or extreme boldness) presented above is cannot be modified. Kagan and others believe that parents can help shy children to become more outgoing and spontaneous. This can be done by orchestrating initial interactions with other children in the shy child's own home, by letting the shy child know it is acceptable to retreat to a safe base, and by teaching him coping skills for stressful situations.

SELF-REGULATION One of the major developmental tasks for the newborn infant is self-regulation. As we have seen, the full-term neonate is well equipped with a variety of ways to respond and adjust to outside stimulation. For instance, infants are capable of habituating to repeated stimuli and of comforting themselves in response to stress. But these self-regulating mechanisms vary with individual temperaments. Some infants are easily overstimulated; others are more difficult to arouse. Some respond best to auditory stimulation, others to touch. Some are hypersensitive to particular types of stimulation. Sensitive caretakers help the babies focus their reactions to sensory experiences and moderate overexcitement or underarousal (Greenspan & Greenspan, 1985).

Although the basis of newborn individuality is not entirely understood, researchers agree generally that widely different personality styles are apparent at birth and that these differences increase over the first few months of life. During this same early period, infants and parents will establish a relationship based on their own unique personalities (Lewis & Rosenblum, 1974). Many studies suggest that infants' temperaments and behavioral styles influence parental behavior and partially determine the quality of early interactions (Bates, 1987).

Researchers regularly find that babies differ greatly in the amount of attention they evoke from their parents, with irritable infants receiving more parental stimulation than overly placid ones. Such attentiveness, however, may be accompanied by feelings of anger, bewilderment, or self-pity in the care-giver when numerous efforts to soothe or amuse the baby have failed. Babies who are easily quieted and amused may cause their parents to feel competent and satisfied in their caregiving (Segal & Yahraes, 1978). Thus, the predictability of an infant's behavior affects the caregiver as well. Mild personality differences between parent and infant are fairly common, and even the most willing and enthusiastic parent needs time and patience to become acquainted with the infant's unique personality. The development of mutuality, reciprocity, and a "symbiotic relationship" between parent and infant is certainly not automatic or instinctive, as we shall see in Chapter 7.

THE PREMATURE INFANT

So far, we have discussed only the development of healthy, full-term babies. A substantial number of newborns, however, are considered to be **premature**—a condition that can pose serious problems for infants and caregivers alike.

Two indicators of prematurity are frequently confused. The first is *gestational time*. The infant born before a gestation period of 37 weeks is considered premature. The second indicator is *low birth weight*. Because the average birth weight is 7 1/2 pounds (3.4 kilograms), an infant who weighs less than 5 1/2 pounds (2.5 kilograms) is usually classified as premature, or in need of special attention, although only half of such infants have a gestation period of less than

premature Having a short gestation period (less than 37 weeks) and/or low birth weight (less than 5 1/2 pounds).

37 weeks. Low-birth-weight babies, even when full term, often have problems resulting from fetal malnutrition, for example. Therefore, both cutoff points—5 1/2 pounds (2.5 kilograms) and 37 weeks—are used in classifying babies as premature (Babson & Benson, 1966). The World Health Organization defines a premature infant as one weighing less than 2.5 kilograms at birth. But it is obvious, that there are significant differences between, for example, a 28-week fetus weighing 3 1/2 pounds and a low-birth weight full-term infant. The 28-week fetus may require intensive care to sustain it. It may have immature lungs and still need considerable development. The low-birth weight full-term infant may have neurological damage but overall should be as mature as other full-term infants. Prematurity can occur for a number of reasons. The most common is a multiple birth, when two or more infants are born at the same time. Other causes include diseases or disabilities of the fetus, the mother's smoking and/or drug taking, and malnutrition. In addition, diseases of the mother, such as diabetes or polio, may lead a doctor to deliver a baby before full term.

Immediately after birth, premature infants usually have greater difficulty making adjustments than do full-term babies. Their adaptation to the basic processes of circulation, respiration, and temperature control is more complicated. Among these, temperature control is a common problem. Premature infants have very few fat cells and thus poorly maintain body heat. Therefore, in industrialized nations, newborns weighing less than 5 1/2 pounds are usually placed in incubators immediately after birth. Another common problem is the feeding of premature infants. In their first few months, they seem unable to catch up in weight and height with full-term infants. It seems almost impossible to match the nutritional conditions of the late fetal period to produce a growth rate outside the uterus comparable to that inside.

It is often believed that the effects of prematurity may last long after infancy. Several studies have indicated that premature infants suffer more illnesses in their first 3 years of life, score lower on IQ tests, and are slightly more prone to behavioral problems than are full-term babies (Knobloch et al., 1959). More recent research seems to indicate that this is true only for a small proportion—less than one-quarter—of premature infants (Bennett et al., 1983; Klein et al., 1985). Researchers have found a high rate of prematurity among children later diagnosed as being learning disabled, having reading problems, or being distractible or hyperactive.

All such reports, however, must be very carefully interpreted. It cannot be concluded, for example, that prematurity causes any of these defects. Although the immature birth condition of babies may make them less able to adjust to the shock of birth, prematurity has a more complex association with problems in later life. For instance, conditions like malnutrition, faulty development of the placenta, or crowding in the uterus may result in a number of symptoms—only one of which is premature birth. In such cases, the prematurity is merely a symptom of a disability or malfunction; it is not a cause of the defect.

PARENT-INFANT BONDING WITH A PREMATURE INFANT

Some of the later problems of premature infants may also arise from the way that they are treated during the first few weeks of life (see the box, "The 'Kilogram Kids'"). Because they are kept in incubators under conditions that are free of harmful microorganisms, they receive less of the normal physical contact experienced by most newborns. There is little opportunity to enjoy the early contact after delivery that Klaus and Kennell found to be so important in promoting bonding. Few premature infants are breast-fed; few are held even while being bottle-fed; and some are unable to suck at all for the first few weeks. These infants miss the social experiences of normal feeding, which establish an early mutuality between the caregiver and the full-term infant. The care-giver may become less responsive because the infant appears unattractive or sickly or has a high-pitched, grating cry. These are great obstacles to effective parent-infant bonding in the early weeks of life.

The consequences of faulty bonding due to prematurity are apparent throughout infancy (Goldberg, 1979). Preterm infants are held farther from the parent's body, touched less, and cooed at less. Later, these infants tend to play less actively than babies born fullterm and have difficulty absorbing as much external stimuli. Many of the differences between premature infants and full-term babies disappear by the end of the first year. This may be due to the efforts of parents who compensate for the infant's lack of responsiveness with more active parenting and intervention (Goldberg, 1979).

In many hospitals, parents are encouraged to become more involved with the care of premature infants. They can put on masks and gowns and enter the intensive care unit to help with feeding, diaper changes, and other care. They can stimulate the baby by gently stroking and talking to it. This promotes better bonding and caretaking when the baby is sent home.

There have been several follow-up studies of premature infants whose parents became actively involved in their care while these infants were in the hospital. The parents learned early to be responsive to the very subtle behavior of their premature infants. As these children grew up, they improved at each stage. As infants, they developed more appropriately at social and intellectual tasks, and, at age 12, these children who showed higher intellectual and social competence than those who missed it in the neonatal intensive care unit (Beckwith & Cohen, 1989; Goldberg et al., 1988).

Some of the potentially detrimental effects of prematurity may be offset by an enriched environment during the first year of life. Zeskind and Ramey (1978) ran a pilot program for infants born premature because of fetal malnourishment. These infants were provided with full-service day care in addition to the necessary medical and nutritional services. Most of them reached normal performance levels by 18 months. Another matched group of fetally malnourished infants received the same medical and nutritional services but were cared for at home, not in the day-care program. These infants were slower to reach normal levels, and deficits in their performance were still apparent at 2 years. Zeskind and Ramey's study shows that with proper medical care, nutrition, and caregiving during their early development, premature infants need not be seriously disadvantaged by the conditions of their birth.

High-risk infants present similar problems in early bonding. They are likely to be segregated from their mothers' room for medical reasons and often have developmental problems that interfere with their ability to signal and reward parents for successful care giving. The result is often a fussy, unresponsive baby and an overattentive mother. Sometimes, bonding patterns and mutual responses improve if the mother imitates her baby's behavior instead of providing completely new stimuli that overwhelm and confuse the infant (Field, 1979).

Bonding between parents and a handicapped infant is extremely difficult. While facing problems similar to those encountered with premature infants, such

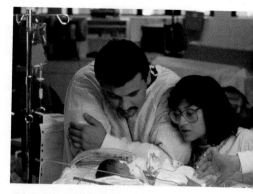

Even though there are obstacles to bonding with the premature infant in the early weeks after birth, many parents try to interact with their newborn as much as possible.

FOCUS ON AN ISSUE

THE "KILOGRAM KIDS"

There is an "elite club" of perhaps 10,000 infants born each year who spend their first few months following birth fighting for their lives. These infants are born 2 1/2 to 3 months ahead of schedule, and they weigh less than 1000 grams (2.3 pounds).

Three decades ago, virtually all of these infants would have died. But, according to a recent government survey, approximately 17,000 infants weighing less than 2 pounds are admitted annually to over 400 neonatal intensive care units around the country. Currently, they have about a 70 percent chance of survival, with the larger ones in this group doing much better than the tiny ones. Slightly larger infants, weighing between 2 and 3 pounds, have a 90 percent survival rate in these special facilities (Kantrowitz, 1988).

But what is the experience of these tiny creatures and their families over the first several months of life? They may lie in a waterbed in an incubator, connected by wires and tubes to banks of blinking lights and digital displays. The several electronic and computerized devices monitor or adjust temperature, respiration and heart rates, blood gases, and brain waves. Parents are encouraged to visit their infants often, and they are usually allowed to stroke and caress their children through the gloved portholes in the incubator. In many of these intensive care units, an effort is made to provide a "homelike," personal atmosphere (Fincher, 1982).

"...according to a recent government survey, approximately 17,000 infants weighing less than 2 pounds are admitted annually to over 400 neonatal intensive care units around the country."

Daily life-threatening crises are not unusual—these tiny beings need nutrients and struggle to function in their alien environment. Excess fluid strains the heart and lungs, yet too little may lead to dehydration and disruption of the sodium and potassium balance. The tiny bones need calcium for bone development, but too much calcium clogs tubes and tiny blood vessels.

For parents, the premature birth of a child is traumatic. According to neonatologist Ron Cohen, the parents are "in shock, mourning, grieving, going through denial, anger" (Fincher, 1982, p. 72). They are forced to deal with one crisis after another and hope that relatively little permanent damage will occur during this period. The staff in the special care units are very much aware of the parents' state and try to help them cope.

Is there any way to avoid the struggle of premature birth and the enormous emotional and financial costs of saving the lives of these tiny newborns? Several studies have demonstrated that over 50 percent of very early births could have been prevented with regular prenatal medical care, beginning at 12 weeks (Knobloch et al., 1982; Monmaney, 1988). Dozens of studies have demonstrated that providing free care to low-income pregnant women dramatically cuts the need for high-tech rescues, and at half the cost (Monmaney, 1988). Even in those cases where very early birth cannot be prevented, the chances of survival are dramatically higher if the mother has had regular medical care.

In one study, 72.7 percent of the mothers of premature survivors had regular medical care, compared to only 25.2 percent of the mothers of nonsurvivors. It is much easier to treat a mother's ill health or poor nutrition early in pregnancy and thus reduce the risk of complex medical problems encountered by the neonate (Rahbar et al., 1985).

as early separation of infant and parents, there are other obstacles that must be overcome. The nature of the handicap may severely impair the baby's ability to respond. Moreover, parents frequently need to go through a period of mourning for the perfect child that did not arrive before they can accept, nurture, and become emotionally attached to the one that did. This is a case in which support groups comprised of other parents with handicapped infants can be very helpful. They help the parents realize that they are not alone in their situation. In addition, others going through similar experiences often have techniques they can suggest that prove helpful.

Let us remember that almost 90 percent of all births go smoothly, without complications in either pregnancy or delivery. Many women consider giving birth as one of the most important and psychologically significant experiences in their lives. They are more likely to have this sense of deep satisfaction if they are involved in choosing various birthing procedures and can be surrounded by loved ones. They appreciate prepared childbirth for the opportunity it offers to be alert and actively engaged with the infant in the first few hours of life. Parents who share the childbirth experience frequently report a deepening of their marriage and a strong sense of elation. Childbirth is indeed a peak experience for many, a time for reaffirming ideals and basic values.

SUMMARY AND CONCLUSIONS

For many couples, childbirth is a peak experience that is the culmination of their commitment to each other. Childbirth itself is a team effort involving the mother, father, nurse, midwife and obstetrician—as well as the baby. Childbirth occurs in three stages: labor, which is the longest segment; the actual birth, which is usually completed in less than two hours; and delivery of the afterbirth, in which the placenta and related tissues are expelled from the uterus.

Modern obstetrical care is highly technological, for example, fetal monitoring during labor. Such technology has made it possible for doctors to save many high-risk babies and mothers who might have died in the past. Critics charge that such technology is too frequently used in the normal labor and delivery and has caused an increase in the number of Caesarean (surgical delivery) births.

The experience of childbirth has changed in this century from an event largely handled at home by the woman, her female relatives and a midwife, to a procedure largely conducted in hospitals. While hospital deliveries were sterile, institutional procedures in the past, the development of more comfortable birthing centers has decreased this negative environmental aspect. Another factor that has made childbirth a less stressful procedure is the increase in prepared childbirth. This is largely the result of parents taking childbirth classes to assist them in

anticipating what childbirth is like and learning techniques to control the pain and stress that may occur. The benefits of prepared childbirth are great. The mother is awake and alert during this peak experience; the father is allowed to participate and begin bonding as soon as possible; the infant is less sleepy.

For the infant, childbirth is also a stressful event. Frederick Leboyer has proposed a gentle method of childbirth which involves low lights, being placed on the mother's abdomen for several minutes before the umbilical cord is cut, and then a warm bath. While not all hospitals use all of these suggestions, many have accepted several, such as the low lighting and the time for bonding after birth.

Once the baby is born, he or she is called a neonate for the first month. Part of this time is spent adjusting to the new world and new functions its body will be responsible for without its mother's assistance—breathing, temperature regulation, digestion, and others. Newborns have behavioral states that regulate their interactions with this new world. Initially, most of the time is spent in sleep. Then gradually more and more time is spent in quiet alertness.

Newborns have well-established sensory capabilities. They see—although not sharply; they hear—although in a somewhat muffled fashion they have well-developed senses of taste and smell. Various assessment instruments have been developed, including Brazelton's Neonatal Behavioral Assessment, to examine the individual infant's responsiveness and receptivity to stimuli from the environment.

Newborns, like the rest of us, are all individuals, with unique approaches to the world. Temperamental qualities also vary. Some newborns are easy, others difficult, and still others slow-to-warm. Researchers have recently begun to study the effects of such temperamental qualities on parental interaction and attachment.

Finally, not all infants are healthy at birth, although the majority are. Some are either born preterm or have low birth weight for term—both classifications of the World Health Organization category entitled prematurity. Premature infants often pose a challenge for parents. They do not look like the "perfect baby" the parents hoped for; they require expensive care that allows little interaction; and once home they frequently require continued special care and attention.

➤ KEY TERMS AND CONCEPTS

afterbirth	convergence	midwife	posterior presentation
anoxia	episiotomy	"natural" childbirth	premature
birth	false labor	neonate	reflex
bonding	habituation	perception	
breech presentation	labor	perineum	toxemia

➤ SELF-TEST QUESTIONS

1. Compare and contrast the attitudes toward childbirth among Western, !Kung-San, and Laotian cultures.

2. Describe the three stages of childbirth.

3. What is the purpose of the fetal monitor? Why is there a debate in the medical community concerning its use?

4. What are some side effects of giving medication during the birthing process? What causes anoxia?

5. Give several reasons why a Caesarean section may be performed during childbirth.

6. List the three fundamental keys to "natural" childbirth.

7. List and describe the available options that a pregnant woman has when delivering her baby.

8. Describe Leboyer's method of childbirth.

9. What is bonding and what do studies find significant concerning this interaction between parent and child?

10. What are the major physical developments that occur in the neonate immediately following birth?

11. Describe the Apgar score and explain what it measures.

12. List the six newborn behavioral states that were identified by Wolff in 1966.

13. What is the Moro reflex? List and describe other infant reflexes.

14. What is infant habituation? How does this ability provide information about the sensory capacities of the newborn?

15. What are two indicators of premature birth? What are the effects of prematurity on the development of the child?

➤ SUGGESTED READINGS

BEAN, C. A. *Methods of childbirth*. New York: William Morrow, 1990. A wealth of practical information covering all aspects of childbirth from late pregnancy and delivery to postnatal treatment.

BRAZELTON, T. B. *Infants and mothers: Differences in development* (rev. ed.). New York: Delta/Seymour Lawrence, 1983. Three infant-mother pairs, all having different personalities and temperamental styles, are described just after childbirth and at selected periods during the children's first 2 years. Written in a highly readable fashion.

EISENBERG, A., MURKOFF, H. E., & HATHAWAY, S. E. *What to expect the first year*. New York: Workman Publishing, 1989. A comprehensive, month-by-month guide which clearly explains everything parents need to know about the first year with a new baby.

GOLDBERG, S., & DEVITTO, B. A. *Born too soon: Preterm birth and early development.* San Francisco: W. H. Freeman, 1983. These infancy specialists examine the many aspects of preterm infants, including carefully developed advice for their care and for aiding their development.

JONES, C. *Sharing birth: A father's guide to giving support during labor.* New York: Quill, 1985. A step-by-step guide, with photographs, to help fathers prepare for their role in childbirth.

KITZENGER, S. *Your baby, your way: Making pregnancy decisions and birthplans.* New York: Pantheon Books, 1987. A positive, helpful guide for expectant mothers and fathers written by a well-known childbirth educator. The physical and psychological facts are clearly presented together with options for decision making.

LEBOYER, F. *Birth without violence.* New York: Knopf, 1976. A classic set of birth procedures that are different from those once used in hospitals. Contains many compelling photographs.

VIDEO CASE: HELPING BABIES BOND

When 8-month-old Jenny was viewed by infant psychiatrist Stanley Greenspan, she was very subdued, rarely smiled, had no interest in the world, showed no joy in any human being, and could not distinguish her mother Joan from other adults. If Jenny were an adult, she would have been diagnosed as depressed. But an infant depressed? Was it really possible? According to Dr. Greenspan, it was. If babies are not touched enough or don't establish eye contact with a special adult—signs of their failure to receive tender loving care—they can become depressed. The reason? Human contact isn't enough for babies; every infant needs to form a human bond. Failure to bond can negatively affect a person's entire emotional life. Infants who have formed an attachment with a "special adult" have a far better chance of feeling emotionally secure as an adult. Therefore, Dr. Greenspan believes that if a baby shows, as Jenny did, signs of bonding improperly, we need to be as concerned as when a baby is not crawling, walking, or talking.

The first thing to do, explains Greenspan, is to discover why the bonding does not occur. Behind a one-way glass, Greenspan watched Jenny's mother interacting with her daughter. The mother seemed depressed and preoccupied. Instead of taking cues from Jenny, Joan reacted inappropriately. For example, when the baby was restless, Joan tried to stimulate rather than soothe her.

Having diagnosed the problem, Greenspan suggested that Joan bring Jenny to him for psychotherapy, and she agreed to do this three or four times a week. This baby psychotherapy consisted of training the mother to interact better with Jenny. Essentially, Joan had to learn to become sensitive to her baby's specific needs and cues. If, for example, Jenny had a favorite stuffed animal, Joan

was instructed to hold it in front of her face as a way of encouraging eye contact between mother and daughter.

For several years Greenspan monitored their progress. By 2 1/2 Jenny showed emotional closeness to her mother for the first time. At 3, she was in most respects like others her age. Then, at age 4 Jenny had a baby brother, Bob. By now Joan had learned to be a better parent. The way Bob looked and "talked" to his mother showed that she "enraptured" him.

Explains Greenspan "Some babies have to be wooed. Every baby has its own thing that gets it in this world." And don't worry about spoiling a baby. "Just love them" he advises. "You can't spoil a baby."

CASE QUESTIONS

1. What symptoms of Jenny's seemed to indicate that she was depressed? What was the cause of her depression? Do you agree that babies can be depressed? Why? Why do babies need to bond with another human being?

2. Stanley Greenspan says that we need to pay as much attention to signs of emotional problems in babies as we do to their not walking or talking. Why is this so important?

3. Describe what Joan learned to do during Jenny's psychotherapy. How did this affect Jenny? Do you think that such training is needed for many parents? Do you think some groups such as teenage parents would especially benefit? Why? Do you agree that it is impossible to spoil a baby? Why?

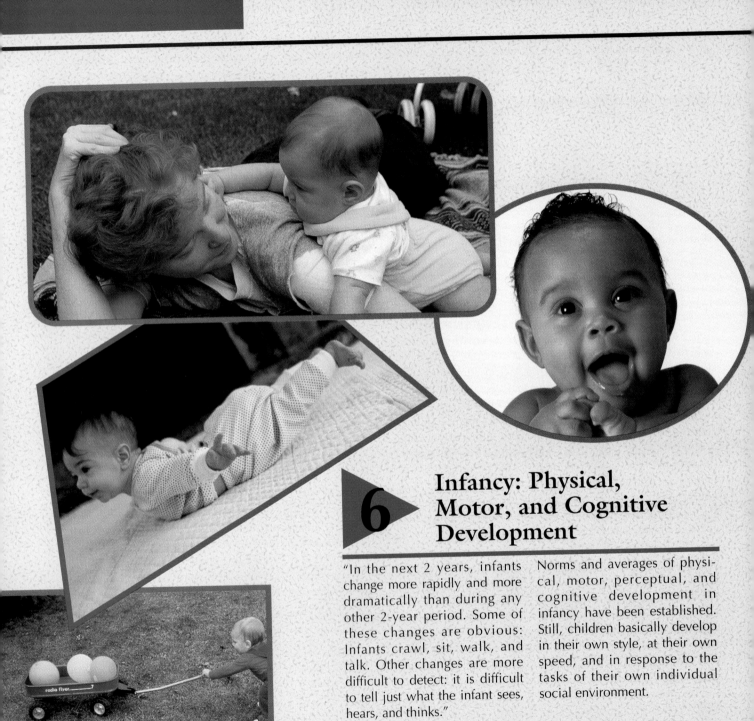

Part Three

INFANCY: THE FIRST TWO YEARS

6 Infancy: Physical, Motor, and Cognitive Development

"In the next 2 years, infants change more rapidly and more dramatically than during any other 2-year period. Some of these changes are obvious: Infants crawl, sit, walk, and talk. Other changes are more difficult to detect: it is difficult to tell just what the infant sees, hears, and thinks."

Norms and averages of physical, motor, perceptual, and cognitive development in infancy have been established. Still, children basically develop in their own style, at their own speed, and in response to the tasks of their own individual social environment.

7 Infancy: Developing Relationships

"Babies come into the world with certain response styles....By age 2, the child has elaborated or restricted these basic response styles within a cultural context to produce what is called a *personality*."

The personality of every infant develops *within relation-* *ships*. Of these, the primary, or first relationships, are the most important for the development of future relationships and for the acquisition of fundamental attitudes, expectations, and behavior.

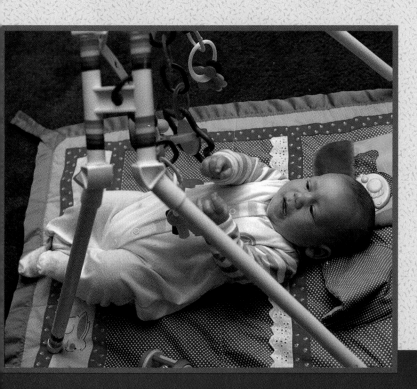

The child is a little inspector
when it crawls
It touches and tastes the earth
Rolls and stumbles toward the
object
Zigzags like a sail
And outmaneuvers the room.
I am learning the child's way
I pick up wood pieces from the
ground
And see shapes into them
I notice a purple velvet bee rest-
ing on a flower
And stop to listen to its buzz
They have included me
And though I will not be put
away to rock alone
And don't roll down the plush
hills
Nor spit for lunch
I am learning their way
They have given me back the
bliss of my senses.

HY SOBILOFF
"THE CHILD'S SIGHT"

CHAPTER 6

INFANCY: PHYSICAL, MOTOR, AND COGNITIVE DEVELOPMENT

OUTLINE

Infant Competencies: An Overview
Nutrition and Malnutrition
Perceptual Competence
Cognitive Development
Environmental Stimulation
    and Infant Competencies
Early Intervention
Summary and Conclusions

CHAPTER OBJECTIVES

By the time you have finished this chapter, you should be able to do the following:

✔ Describe the developing competencies of the infant during the first 2 years.
✔ Contrast breast-feeding and bottle-feeding.
✔ Describe the nutritional needs of the infant.
✔ Describe the infant's perceptual development during the first year.
✔ Explain and critique Piaget's theory of cognitive development in the infant.
✔ Discuss the effect of environmental stimulation on infant competency.

Within a day or two of birth the infant can lift his head in a gentle, bumbling motion and squint at objects close to him. He snuggles against his mother's breast, tasting the warm milk, and smelling the familiar good scents he associates with her. As he sucks, he often seems to softly stroke her breast in the tight-fisted way infants have. As we saw in Chapter 5, neonates come into the world able to sense and respond to their environment. They can see and hear, taste and smell, feel pressure and pain. They are selective in what they like to look at, and they are able to learn. They are still physically immature and dependent, however, and have limited cognitive ability. In the next 2 years, infants change more rapidly and more dramatically than during any other 2-year period. Some of these changes are obvious: Infants crawl, sit, walk, and talk. Other changes are more difficult to detect: It is difficult to see the brain grow and become more specialized; and it is difficult to tell just what the infant sees, hears, and thinks.

In this chapter, we will highlight what we know about physical, motor, perceptual, and cognitive development in infancy. Although norms and averages of growth and behavior have been established for children at various stages of development, children essentially develop in their own style, at their own pace, and in response to the tasks of their specific social context as the following cases illustrate:

> At 12 months of age, Letitia was very active and independent. She had been walking for a month, but she often crawled when she wanted to get somewhere in a hurry. She cried whenever her mother tried to restrain her. From birth on, she was fussy. She slept irregularly and was given to long crying spells. At 8 months, Letitia frequently howled when things did not go as she expected. She knew at an early age which toys, food, and people she preferred, and she did not like changes in her environment.

> Her sister, Kenyatta, born a year later, had developed in a different way. By the end of 12 months, she was quiet and placid, and she was content to sit in her playpen or crib for long periods of time. She had been able to pull herself upright at 7 months. She showed no signs of temper, frustration, or anxiety other than crying when someone unknown to her came near.

From the outset, these sisters differed on the three basic dimensions of temperament that we described in Chapter 5. Letitia is more emotional and intense than is Kenyatta, and she has a higher activity level than her sister does. However, Letitia is also less sociable than Kenyatta is. These individual differences become clearer as the children grow older.

➤ At 18 months, Letitia's active, sensitive, and intense nature became even more distinct. She usually played alone. She enjoyed lining up small sticks, stones, and toys and endlessly rearranging them. She continued to disturb her mother's sleep occasionally, by her sudden waking and howling. Her fussiness and unpredictability began to show in her eating habits; she sometimes refused to eat food that she had always enjoyed. She was often upset when she was taken out of her home, sometimes crying uncontrollably when her mother took her for a visit to friends. Her expressions of surprise, joy, and anger were always intense, which puzzled her mother, who was a quiet, calm person herself. Letitia firmly resisted all attempts at toilet training.

➤ Kenyatta, at 18 months, continued to be an easygoing, gentle child, but she had become more outgoing and friendly. She laughed and smiled whenever she was picked up and played with, especially by those who came to visit. She knew the names of some objects in the room and the parts of the body. She got hungry at regular intervals and would sleep peacefully most nights. She kept her even temper, but she was afraid of loud music or sudden noises. She was easily distracted from whatever she was doing. At 24 months, she had almost toilet trained herself by imitating her older sister.

This brief description of Letitia and Kenyatta at 12 and at 18 months indicates that although common developmental changes occur during the first 2 years of life, great variations exist in temperament, interests, personality, and even in the social context that infants experience. Parent-child relationships will differ based on reactions to numerous events and on each infant's birth order and temperament. The older sister must take the lead in learning new skills. The younger sister has both the advantage of following a more competent model and the disadvantage of losing in competition with her more competent sister.

Even in the same family, the social context of development is not identical. Parents will often wonder, "How did it happen that our children have two such different personalities, when we raised them the same...or, when they were raised in the same family?" The reality is that as more children are added to the same family, the family itself changes.

INFANT COMPETENCIES: AN OVERVIEW

Infancy is a time of perceptual and motor discovery. Infants learn to recognize faces, food, and familiar routines. They explore flowers, insects, toys, and their own bodies. Every day is a discovery of the people, objects, and events that make up their environment. Such discovery is not only exciting but also is helpful in learning how to adapt to one's environment.

For decades, developmental psychologists have carefully studied the characteristics of infants and children. Arnold Gesell, a pioneer in the field, observed hundreds of infants and children over a period of time. He recorded the details of

About half of all 8-month-olds can pull themselves into a standing position.

when and how certain behaviors emerged, such as crawling, walking, running, picking up a small pellet, cutting with scissors, managing a pencil, or drawing the human figure. From the resulting data, he reported the capabilities of "average" children at varying ages. By 15 months, for example, his "average" children were able to walk; by 18 months, they could walk fast and run stiffly; at 21 months, they were able to kick a large ball (Gesell, 1940).

In the healthy, well-nourished children that Gesell observed, these behaviors emerged in an orderly and predictable sequence. By knowing the age of a specific child, he could predict not only the child's approximate height and weight but also what the child knew or was able to do. He concluded that development does not primarily depend on the environment. Instead, Gesell believed that, given a normal environment, most achievements result from an internal biological timetable. Behavior emerges as a function of maturation.

There are weaknesses in Gesell's theory and method. The children studied by Gesell came from one socioeconomic class and one community setting; their similar environments may have influenced their similar behaviors. We now know that children raised in widely different social or historical contexts develop quite differently from those described in Gesell's developmental schedules. Gesell's infants of the 1930s normally walked at 15 months. Contemporary American infants normally walk at around 12 months. Also, infants raised in a Guatemalan village—where they spent their first year confined to a small, dark hut, were not played with, were rarely spoken to, and were poorly nourished—were late on all major developmental milestones. Indeed, they did not begin to speak until the middle or end of their third year (Kagan, 1978). Nevertheless, Gesell's contribution remains substantial. If we use his developmental sequences carefully and do not overinterpret them, we have a useful baseline of common developmental milestones and the order of their emergence—but not the exact timing for modern infants.

Developmental psychologists have gone well beyond the pioneering studies of Gesell and have undertaken a closer analysis of the structure and function of the infant's developing competencies. Perceptual, motor, cognitive, and emotional development go hand in hand in a particular social context. The infant reaches out for an attractive object that he sees and pulls it in for closer inspection. The baby who has just begun to walk toddles precariously toward the outstretched arms of an eager, encouraging parent. If we are to understand fully the infant's developing competencies, we need to look at the rich complexity of these achievements within their social context (Thelen, 1987, 1989). Before we discuss this analysis, let's take an overview of the infant's motor and physical accomplishments during the first 2 years.

THE FIRST 4 MONTHS

At the end of 4 months, most infants resemble the chubby, appealing babies seen in magazine advertisements. Since birth, they have nearly doubled in weight, from 6 to 8 pounds (2.7 to 3.6 kilograms) to somewhere between 12 and 15 pounds (5.4 to 6.8 kilograms), and they have probably grown 4 or more inches (10 or more centimeters) in length. Their skin has lost the newborn look, and their fine

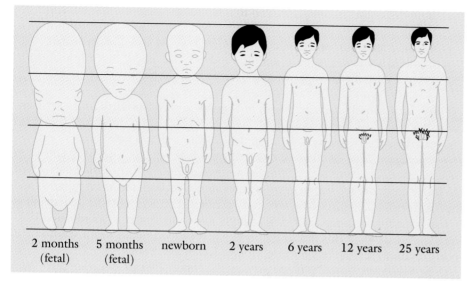

| 2 months (fetal) | 5 months (fetal) | newborn | 2 years | 6 years | 12 years | 25 years |

FIGURE 6–1
The cephalocaudal (head-downward) and proximodistal (center-outward) development that we saw in prenatal growth continues after birth, and the proportions of the baby's body change dramatically during infancy.

birth hair is being replaced by new hair. Their eyes have begun to focus; When awake, they babble contentedly and smile in response to pleasant stimulation.

At birth, the size of an infant's head represents about one-quarter of the total body length. Around the age of 4 months, however, the body starts to grow and lengthen much more rapidly than the head, and these proportions change markedly (see Figure 6–1). By 12 years, a child's head is only one-eighth the length of the body, and by 25 years, only one-tenth of the total body length.

The infant's teeth and bones are also beginning to change. In some children, the first tooth erupts at 4 or 5 months, although the average age for this event is closer to 6 or 7 months. Many bones are not yet hard and heavily calcified but are still soft cartilage. They tend to be pliable under stress and rarely break. Muscles, however, may pull easily and be injured. Occasionally, well-meaning adults have discovered this when hoisting infants up by the arms and swinging them in play (Stone, Smith, & Murphy, 1973).

Much to the delight of parents and caregivers, by 4 months the average baby is usually sleeping through the night. This sleep pattern sometimes begins as early as the second month. Gradually, the baby settles down into the family routine, daytime as well as nighttime. This is not to say that all babies sleep through the night that early. Many continue to awake during the night until they are a year old or more. Each infant has his or her own unique rhythm and pattern of sleep and wake periods as the following comments indicate:

Our first child slept through the night when she was 1 month old and today at 4 she still is a very sound sleeper. Our second child arrived eleven months later and she never slept through the night until she was 14 months old. My friends and pediatrician made many suggestions of ways to get her to sleep—none worked. I was becoming frustrated—and a real zombie at work—since she was up every three hours all night. Finally, I decided to consider the time she was up, and taking a bottle to be "our" special time when our other child was not needing attention at the same time. I really came to enjoy those late evening hours we spent together—and became much more human when I started adjusting my own sleep cycle to fit hers.

When 4-month-olds are placed in a stomach-down position, they can generally hold up their chests as well as their heads. In a sitting position, they hold the head steady and observe very carefully everything that is going on.

Average infants of this age can roll over from stomach to back and from back to stomach (Dargassies, 1986; Stone et al., 1973). Most of the reflexes that are found in the newborn seem to dissolve in the second and third months, and they are gradually replaced by voluntary actions. The well-coordinated stepping reflex, for example, is replaced by seemingly more random, less-coordinated kicking (Thelen, 1989). This is also the time when sudden infant death syndrome is most common (see the box "Sudden Infant Death Syndrome").

Self-discovery usually begins about this time. Infants discover their own hands and fingers and spend several minutes at a time watching them, studying their movements, bringing them together, grasping one hand with the other. Some 4-month-olds also discover their feet and manipulate them in much the same way. It is quite normal, however, for some infants to be 5 or 6 months old before becoming aware of their feet, especially if they reach this age during the winter, when heavily bundled.

FROM 5 TO 8 MONTHS

By 8 months, babies have gained another 4 or 5 pounds (1.8 to 2.3 kilograms) and have grown about 3 more inches (7.6 centimeters), but their general appearance does not differ dramatically from that of 4-month-olds. They probably have at least two teeth, and perhaps a few more. Their hair is thicker and longer. By this time, too, their legs are oriented so that the soles of their feet no longer face each other.

At about 5 months, most infants achieve something called a *visually guided reach*. Before this age, they have possessed many of the component skills, such as a reflex grasp and then a more voluntary grasp, that are needed to perform this visually guided reach. They have been able to reach out toward an attractive object and have visually examined a variety of objects. It is a difficult task, however, to put all of these components together—to look, reach out, and successfully grasp an attractive object. Yet, in some ways, this one achievement transforms the world of the infant. Now begins a period of more systematic exploration of objects—with the hands, the eyes, and the mouth used individually or in combination (Rochat, 1989).

Most 8-month-old babies are able to pass objects from hand to hand, and some are able to use the thumb and finger to grasp. They may delight in filling both hands, and they are usually able to bang two objects together—a feat often demonstrated joyfully and endlessly. Most 8-month-olds can get themselves into a sitting position, and nearly all babies of this age can sit without support once they are placed in position. If they are put on their feet, well over half of the 8-month-olds can stand while holding on to some support, and about half can pull

a

b

c

d

e

(a) At 4 months, infants can lift their chests as well as their heads and can carefully observe what is happening around them.

(b) Many 8-month-olds start to play social games like peekaboo.

(c) By 12 months, many infants are actively exploring their environment.

(d) At 18 months, most toddlers are able to walk alone, and they like to carry or pull toys with them.

(e) Two-year-olds walk, run, and can usually pedal a tricycle.

FOCUS ON AN ISSUE

SUDDEN INFANT DEATH SYNDROME (SIDS)

One of the most shattering events parents may experience is the sudden and unexplained death of their baby. Yet this is the most common cause of death among infants between 1 week and 1 year in age. There are approximately 10,000 deaths annually from what is known as the *sudden infant death syndrome,* or *SIDS.* SIDS is defined as the sudden death of an apparently healthy infant or child in whom no medical cause can be found in a postmortem examination. SIDS has been called a diagnosis of exclusion because its victims can only be identified through an autopsy that rules out all other explainable causes of death. SIDS, sometimes called "crib death," tends to happen without warning, while the child is asleep. The high incidence of SIDS has produced a great deal of concern within the medical profession.

Researchers have been unsuccessful in finding the precise cause but have found circumstances where SIDS is common. Unmarried mothers under 20 years of age who have delayed or not sought prenatal care run a higher than normal risk of having a child with SIDS. This risk is also increased if the mother has been ill during her pregnancy, has a short interval between pregnancies, or has earlier experienced the loss of her fetus. Smoking and the abuse of narcotics by the mother are often

> *"Because of this and other research linking sleeping position and SIDS, the American Academy of Pediatrics now recommends putting babies at risk to sleep on their back or propped on their sides against pillows."*

connected with sudden infant death syndrome. Smoking mothers who are also anemic run a particularly high risk of having a child with SIDS (Bulterys et al., 1990). In a Swedish study of all Swedes born between 1983 and 1985, it was found that smoking doubled the risk of SIDS and that the more the mother smoked, the greater her infant's risk of SIDS. In addition, maternal smoking was found to influence the time of death, as infants of smokers died at an earlier age. The researchers concluded that in countries like Sweden, smoking may be the single most important preventable risk factor for SIDS (Haglund & Cnattingius, 1990).

Recent research by Buck (1989) and her team from the University at Buffalo Medical School found that there was a sevenfold increased risk for SIDS associated with vaginal breech delivery and more than twice the risk for SIDS when mothers were in labor 16 hours or longer. Their research was conducted on 132,948 mothers from upstate New York who gave birth in 1974. It appears as though the majority of breech SIDS infants were single footling deliveries (a rare type of breech presentation with the baby emerging one foot first). The more common form of breech birth was not associated with an increased risk of SIDS. The researchers suggest that an earlier problem in the infant's development, not the breech birth itself, may be the primary causal factor. Buck (1991) observes that SIDS babies may have experienced a previous

themselves into a standing position. A few may even begin to sidestep around the crib or playpen while holding on, and some babies may be walking, using furniture for support. This is a phenomenon referred to as *cruising.*

During the period from 5 to 8 months, most babies develop some form of locomotion. This is the time when the family dog is no longer safe, and all valuables should be placed above the infant's reach. They may learn to crawl (with body on the ground) or creep (on hands and knees). Other infants develop a method called "bear walking," which employs both hands and feet; still others

central nervous system insult in utero since they often show signs of subtle growth retardation including reduced birth weight and length.

Babies who have been born prematurely or were underweight at birth run a higher than average risk of SIDS. They generally have greater than average difficulty breathing and often need support from respiratory devices.

Frequently, in the week prior to the occurrence of SIDS, infants have severe breathing and digestive problems. Second and third children also run more risks of SIDS than the average first born. Babies who are part of multiple births also run above average risks, particularly triplets and the second child in twin births. "Several twin pairs, both [fraternal and identical], have died on the same day. Among 32 twin pairs recorded, 3 were found dead together" (Shannon et al., 1987).

Infants who later died of SIDS have been observed to be less active and less responsive than their siblings. Some have also been described as having had a strange cry. Deaths frequently occur at night when the infant is asleep and lying in any position (Shannon, Kelly, Akselrod, & Kilborn, 1987). Recent research from Tasmania has

indicated, however, that babies put to sleep in a prone position (on their stomachs) may be at greater risk for SIDS (Dwyer, Ponsonby, Newman, & Gibbons, 1991). Because of this and other research linking sleeping position and SIDS, the American Academy of Pediatrics now recommends putting babies at risk to sleep on their back or propped on their sides against pillows (AAP Task Force on Infant Positioning and SIDS, 1992). We should note, however, that the American Academy of Pediatrics believes that the risk is very low for healthy babies who sleep in prone positions.

SIDS seems to occur most often in winter. Although medical researchers have not yet found a physiological cause, they suspect irregularities in the autonomic nervous system, especially as it relates to breathing and heart functions (Shannon, Kelly, Akselrod, & Kilborn, 1987). Recent research has found that some infants apparently are born with a degree of respiratory center immaturity, that in combination with other problems, such as illness, head colds, exposure to cold, air or smoke, may result in cessation of breathing. Vestibular stimulation by rocking has been shown to be beneficial for premature babies in

reducing *apnea* (halting of breathing). There also appear to be other benefits of rocking for premature infants, including more rapid maturation of the nerve cells of the cerebellum which is still developing during the first six months of life. Shannon and his colleagues suggest that SIDS may be reduced by the use of automatically rocking cribs, especially during the night when most deaths occur.

The occurrence of an infant's seemingly unexplained death has a devastating effect on the family and everyone else connected with the child. All those associated with keeping the infant alive experience guilt, loss, and powerlessness (Mandell et al., 1987). The family's grief and loss are often mixed with anger and frustration. "Who is to blame?" "Why did this happen?" The family needs as much information as possible as well as support in their sorrow, and reassurance that there is a 98 percent certainty that later infants will not have SIDS (Chan, 1987). Until we understand the causes of SIDS, we shall still fail to identify many infants at risk and fail to monitor them effectively.

"scoot" in a sitting position. The components of crawling are developing for several months beforehand. The infant is looking at more distant attractive objects and is reaching for them. There is a change in the pattern and flexibility of kicking and in other types of leg activity. Also, just before crawling, many infants have periods during which they rhythmically rock forward and backward. All these pieces of behavior need to be integrated into the task of crawling across the floor toward an attractive distant object (Goldfield, 1989). We may see some of these developmental tasks of infancy depicted in Figure 6–2.

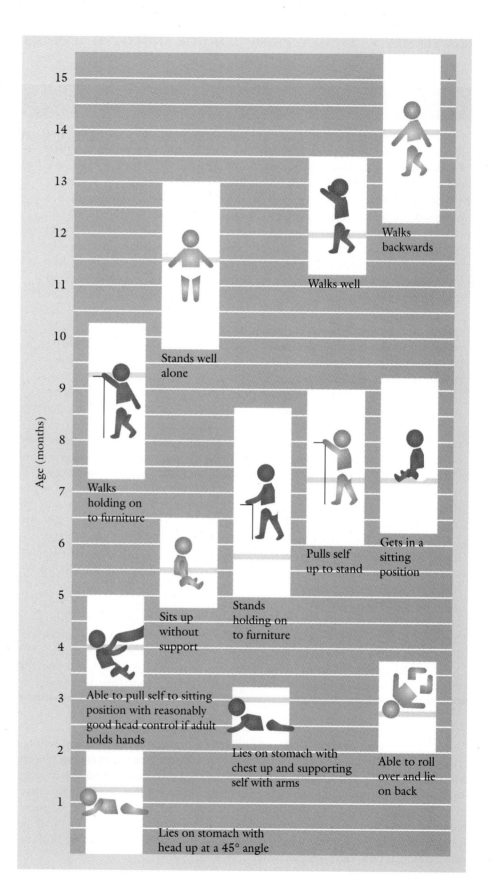

FIGURE 6–2

Examples of developmental tasks in infancy. The lower edge of each box represents the age at which 25 percent of all children perform each task; the line across the box, 50 percent; the upper edge of the box, 75 percent.

Many babies of 8 months begin to play social games, such as peekaboo, bye-bye and patty-cake, and most enjoy handing an item back and forth to an adult. Another quickly learned routine is that of dropping an object and watching someone pick it up and hand it back. This "game" is usually learned accidentally by both baby and adult, but the baby is often the first to catch on to the possibilities for fun.

FROM 9 TO 12 MONTHS

At 12 months, most infants are about three times heavier than they were at birth, and they have grown about 9 or 10 inches (22.9 to 25.4 centimeters) in length. Throughout this first year, girls tend to weigh slightly less than boys do.

By 9 months, most infants have some form of locomotion; most have pulled themselves to a stand, and half of them are beginning to take steps while holding on to furniture. By 12 months, about half are standing alone and are starting to take their first few steps. The age at which free-walking begins varies widely, depending on both individual development and cultural factors. Over 50 years ago, Shirley (1931) and Gesell (1940) found that 15 months was the average age for free-walking to begin. Since 1967, however, researchers have observed that the period between 11 and 13 months is the average for this behavior to begin in healthy, well-fed infants who are given the opportunity and the encouragement to exercise (Frankenburg & Dodds, 1967).

The ability to stand and walk gives the infant a new visual perspective. Locomotion allows for more active exploration. Infants can get into, over, and under things. They can clean out a bureau drawer (in 10 seconds or less) and can follow their mother into the kitchen. Infants of this age placed in "jolly jumpers" or "johnny jump-ups,"—spring supported seats that hang from doorways—will turn to follow their mother as she moves from room to room and will even bounce to whatever music happens to be playing. Their world is broadened once again. The infant's motor development is spurred on by the new and exciting things that he can see and hear. His ability to explore at new levels and with new abilities spurs on his cognitive and perceptual development (Thelen, 1989).

Twelve-month-olds actively manipulate the environment. They are able to undo latches, open cabinets, pull toys, and twist lamp cords. Their newly developed **pincer grasp**—where the thumb opposes the forefinger—allows them to pick up grass, hairs, matches, and dead insects. They can turn on the television set and the stove, and they can explore kitchen cupboards, open windows, and poke things into electrical outlets. Because children are so busy exploring the environment, care-givers must set limits on their explorations. They have to strike a balance between too much restriction and sufficient control in order to keep the baby safe. "No" becomes a key word in the vocabulary of both the child and care-givers—although most pediatricians suggest concentrating on the "major no's" and baby-proofing the house to assist in maintaining the baby's safety. As one parent comments:

> When our son was born, friends gave us a basket of various devices to help make our home safer for him as he grew. There were plugs to block electric outlets, seals for the refrigerator and toilet to prevent prying hands from opening them, locks for the cupboards, a gate for

pincer grasp The method of holding objects, developed around the age of 12 months, in which the thumb opposes the forefinger.

the stairway...and a sign that read "this too shall pass!" We used all of them during his first 18 months!

At 12 months, babies are frequently able to play games and can "hide" by covering their eyes. They can roll a ball back and forth with an adult and can throw small objects, making up in persistence what they lack in skill. Many children of this age begin to feed themselves, using a spoon and holding their own cup for drinking. While this is not the "neatest" process, it contributes to the child's development toward autonomy.

The 12-month-old is on the verge of language. Infants of this age are usually struggling either to walk or to utter their first words—but generally not both. Most infants achieve control of walking first, then they start talking. Some 12-month-old children, however, can manage "mama," "dada," and two to eight other words, such as "no," "baby," "bye-bye," "hi," and "bow-wow." In Chapter 8, we will discuss in detail the infant's acquisition of language.

As they enter the second year, children become aware of themselves as individuals separate from their mothers (or care-givers); they increasingly exercise choice and preference. They may suddenly and vehemently refuse a food that they have always liked. They may protest loudly at bedtime, or they may engage in a "battle of the wills" with someone over a formerly trouble-free event, such as getting into a snowsuit or being placed in a highchair. Infants in their second year of life, once they have begun to walk, are usually referred to as **toddlers.**

AGE 18 MONTHS

The 18-month-old usually weighs between 22 and 27 pounds (9.9 and 12.2 kilograms), an indication that the rate of weight increase has slowed. The average height at this age is about 31 to 33 inches (78 to 83 centimeters). Almost all children at this age are walking alone. When walking, they generally like to push or pull something with them or carry something in their hands. They seldom drop down on all fours now, although walking may actually take more of their time and effort. Some are not yet able to climb stairs, and most have considerable difficulty kicking a ball, because their unsteadiness does not permit them to free one foot for kicking. Children of this age also find pedaling tricycles or jumping nearly impossible.

At 18 months, children may be stacking from two to four cubes or blocks to build a tower, and they can often manage to scribble with crayon or pencil. They have improved their ability to feed themselves and may be able to undress themselves partly. (The ability to put clothes on generally comes later.) Many of their actions are imitative of those around them—"reading" a magazine, sweeping the floor, or chatting on a toy telephone.

Most 18-month-olds have made strides in language and may have a vocabulary of several words and phrases. They usually combine two words to make a single sentence, and they can point to and name body parts and a few very familiar pictures. They may now begin to use words effectively. (For more on language development, see Chapter 8.)

toddler The infant in his or her second year of life who has begun to walk—the child has a somewhat top-heavy, wide stance and walks with a gait that is not solidly balanced or smoothly coordinated.

AGE 24 MONTHS

By their second birthdays, toddlers have added approximately another 2 inches and pounds. Again, the rate of gain is tapering (see Figure 6.3).

Because, until recently, 2-year-olds were usually considered too young for most nursery schools, and yet too old for regular monthly visits to a doctor, relatively few studies had been made on this age group. Toddlers stayed with their families and their care-givers and were seen around the neighborhood, but they were generally out of the range of most research psychologists. Several studies show the 2-year-old as a fascinating active learner, just beginning to break through into new areas of skill, social understanding, and accomplishment (Bronson, 1981).

Two-year-olds not only walk and run, but they can usually pedal a tricycle, jump in place on both feet, balance briefly on one foot, and accomplish a fairly good overhand throw. They climb up steps and, sometimes, come down again with assistance. They crawl into, under, around, and over objects and furniture; they manipulate, carry, handle, push, or pull anything they see. They put things into and take things out of large containers. They pour water, mold clay, stretch the stretchable, and bend the bendable. They transport items in carts, wagons, carriages, or trucks. They explore, test, and probe. All of this exploration provides a vital learning experience about the nature and possibilities of their physical world as the following comments suggest.

FIGURE 6–3

The weight and height of about 50 percent of the infants at a given age will fall in the blue regions; about 15 percent will fall in each of the white regions. Thus, on the average, 80 percent of all infants will have weights and heights somewhere in the blue and white regions of the graphs. Note that as the infants age, greater differences occur in weight and height within the normal range of growth.

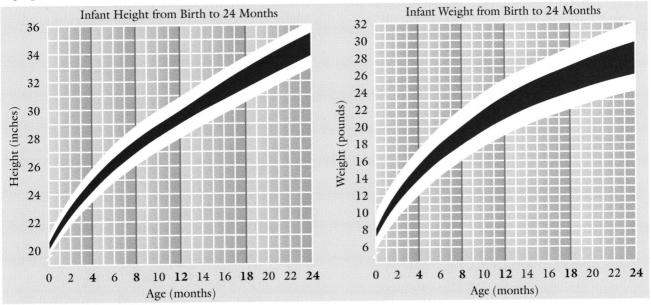

My husband and I were making the final preparations for our sabbatical housing and needed to make a lengthy long-distance telephone call. Our two daughters, aged 2 and 3 needed to be kept busy, so I innocently suggested that they take their bean bag chair up to their bedroom and pretend that their beds were boats and the bean bag was an island. They happily set off upstairs to play.

Forty-five minutes later, we finished our call and noticed that it was surprisingly quiet in the house. My husband went upstairs to check on the kids. He called down, Sherry, you've got to come up here and see this! When I opened the kid's door, the entire room looked like it was filled with fog. Their brown carpet was white, the air was white, and our little 2-year-old looked like a ghost—her hair, clothes, eye lashes, everything was white.

When piecing together what happened, we were told by our 3-year-old that they had been pretending that the bean bag was a water tube and since it was going so fast, they had to put powder (a brand new large bottle of it) on their hands to make their grip better. Once they squeezed the bottle, the powder shot out about four feet. They varied how hard they squeezed and it went farther and shorter. In no time, the whole room—and their bodies—were coated with baby powder! (An unanticipated benefit? The room smelled baby powder fresh for weeks afterward!)

The language development of most 2-year-olds shows some marked gains. They are able to follow simple directions, name more pictures, and use three or more words in combination; some even use plurals. Given a crayon or pencil, 2-year-olds may create "scribbles" and be fascinated briefly with the magical marks. They may stack from six to eight blocks or cubes to build towers, and they can construct a three-block "bridge." Their spontaneous block play shows matching of shapes and symmetry. If they are willing, 2-year-olds can take off most of their own clothing, and they can put on some items.

Physical, motor, and cognitive development during the first 2 years is a complex, dynamic process. For infants to thrive, they must have their basic needs met by their environment. They must get enough sleep, feel safe, receive consistent care, and have appropriate stimulating experiences. Each developing system—perceptual or motor skills, for example—supports the others. A blind child does not crawl or walk as soon as the seeing child does. There is no lure of a distant toy or of a parent's face. There is no visual feedback to guide this child's motor action. Cognitive development, too, depends on the information that the child receives from his actions and his sensory explorations. What is more, these interacting systems are helped or hindered by the social context in which the infant develops (Hazen & Lockman, 1989; Thelen & Fogel, 1989). In the next few sections, we will look at some of these components of infant development.

NUTRITION AND MALNUTRITION

Ours may be considered the best-fed nation in the world, but many Americans still suffer from nutritional deficiencies. R. H. Hutcheson, Jr. (1968) found that 20 percent of a study group of 1-year-olds from poor families in Tennessee suffered from severe anemia (a red blood cell deficiency caused by a lack of iron), and another 30 percent suffered from moderate anemia. In poor areas of Alabama and Mississippi, researchers have found anemia rates to be as high as 80 percent among preschool children.

Two kinds of malnutrition generally occur. One is due to an insufficient total quantity of food, and the other to an insufficiency of certain kinds of food. Starvation or severe lack of food results in a condition called *marasmus*. Children with this pattern of malnutrition have a diet that is deficient in both protein and total calories. Considerable muscle wasting and loss of subcutaneous fat accompanies this type of malnutrition. However, if it lasts for a relatively short period of time, supplemental foods may be introduced and there is no long-term negative impact of the poor nutrition. Another type of severe malnutrition, called *kwashiorkor* (from the Swahili for "deposed child"), is caused by an insufficiency of protein, in relation to total calories. Kwashiorkor more typically occurs in children 18-months of age or older who are no longer breast-feeding. The Swahili word for this type of malnutrition comes from the African tradition of placing a child in the home of relatives for weaning if the mother becomes pregnant. Once removed from the protein-rich breast milk, such children often suffer a deficiency of protein in their diets. The effects of Kwashiorkor have been found to be more damaging in the long run since brain development is significantly affected by the shortage of protein. Children with Kwashiorkor are often presented in media accounts of starvation such as that occurring in Somalia, Ethiopia, or the African Sahel. They have edemous (fluid retention) midsections so their stomachs protrude, but their arms and legs are often extremely thin.

In the United States, these severe forms of malnutrition are rare, but milder malnutrition of both types is quite common. A great many people who can afford a good diet often consume too many "empty calories" in the form of foods high in carbohydrates but low in proteins, vitamins, and minerals. Many people who receive too few calories cannot afford to buy animal proteins, and they take in inadequate amounts of proteins from other sources. The diets of the poor most often lack vitamins A and C, riboflavin, and the mineral iron (Eichorn, 1979). All these substances are required for healthy body functioning, immune system action, and brain development.

BREAST-FEEDING VERSUS BOTTLE-FEEDING

Milk is the major source of nutrients for infants. It is used almost exclusively in the diet for the first 6 months and together with solid foods for the next 6 to 12 months. Many women throughout the world choose to breast-feed their infants. The breast milk of a reasonably well-fed mother contains a remarkably well-bal-

Although breast-feeding is more nutritious than bottle-feeding, many other factors influence a mother's choice.

anced combination of nutrients, as well as antibodies that protect the infant from some diseases. Even a malnourished mother's milk provides nearly adequate nutrients, often at cost to her own health. If breast-feeding goes on for extended periods of time during severe malnutrition, the mother no longer is able to produce milk. In addition, if pregnancies occur in close sequence, with each subsequent child, both mother and child have more nutritional risk. This is the reason why the World Health Organization proposes family planning with a 2- to 3-year break between pregnancies as the ideal situation.

The content of breast milk suits most babies, and breast-fed babies tend to have fewer digestive disturbances. Additionally, breast milk is always fresh and ready at the right temperature, does not need refrigeration, and is absolutely sterile. Unless the mother is very ill, has an inadequate diet, or uses a lot of drugs or alcohol, breast milk is better for a baby's health. Despite these findings, many mothers in the United States and throughout the world have switched from breast-feeding to bottle-feeding (see the box "Trends in Breast-Feeding and Bottle-Feeding").

WEANING AND THE INTRODUCTION OF SOLID FOODS

Some mothers in developed countries begin weaning babies from the breast at 3 or 4 months, or even earlier; others continue breast-feeding for as long as 2 or 3 years. Although such extended breast-feeding is rare among middle- to upper-class mothers in the United States, 2 or 3 years is not rare for certain American subcultures or, as previously indicated for some other cultures.

Normally, at about 3 months of age, infants gradually start to accept some strained foods. Usually, they begin with the simple cereals such as rice, and expand to a variety of cereals and pureed fruits, followed somewhat later by strained vegetables and meats. It is possible that some infants may be allergic to one or a variety of foods, and it is therefore advised that foods be introduced slowly. Others seem to take to almost everything that is offered. By 8 months, most infants are eating a broad range of specially prepared foods, and milk consumption is usually reduced. As they acquire teeth, finger foods are introduced and sometimes even earlier if manual dexterity is sufficient. Foods such as cheese strips, for example, readily dissolve in the mouth even without teeth, and infants seem to enjoy the experience of picking up and placing cheese strips in the mouth.

Weaning is a crucial time for the onset of malnutrition, as we saw earlier in this chapter. Particularly vulnerable are the 1-year-olds, who have already been weaned from the breast and whose families have insufficient money for milk or other nutritious foods. These children may survive on diets composed of potato chips, dry cereals, and cookies—foods that typically provide calories for energy but few nutrients. Even with enough milk or a variety of nutritious foods available, 1-year-olds may be unwilling to drink a sufficient amount of milk from a cup; they may also prefer crackers to more wholesome snacks of cheese and meat. It is important to note that contrary to advertising slogans, children do not require sugared cereals. Children tend to like the crunchiness and taste of whole grain cereals without sugar until they have sugar introduced.

Public health programs in the United States have played an important role in efforts to improve the nutritional status of pregnant women, infants, and young children. In the early 1980s, the WIC program (a special supplemental food program for women, infants, and children) provided food supplements and education for over 3 million individuals monthly. The supplements of milk, cheese, iron-fortified cereals, eggs, and fruit juices have been recognized to improve the health of infants both during and after participation in the program (Ryan et al., 1985). Decreased funding of these programs by 1991 resulted in parallel increases in infant malnutrition (Children's Defense Fund, 1991).

Even in cases of severe malnutrition during infancy, serious remedial programs of food supplementation combined with education can produce dramatic results. In a study done in Bogota, Colombia, children were provided with food supplements for the first 3 years of their lives. The food supplements were accompanied by periodic home visits. These children showed much less growth retardation and all-around better functioning than the control groups—even 3 years after the supplements were discontinued (Super, Herrera, & Mora, 1990).

We have examined the typical development patterns and nutritional needs of infants during their first 2 years. We will now analyze the process of perceptual and cognitive development.

PERCEPTUAL COMPETENCE

As explained in Chapter 5, perception is a complex process of interpreting our sensory environment. This process takes time to develop (Gibson & Spelke, 1983). The whole notion of talking about infant competence reflects a significant change in our view of the infant. Through hard work and the use of imaginative research techniques, psychologists have discovered that human infants are far more complex and have many more competencies than had once been supposed.

FOCUS ON AN ISSUE

TRENDS IN BREAST-FEEDING AND BOTTLE-FEEDING AROUND THE WORLD

Despite the fact that breast-feeding is better for infants than bottle-feeding, studies have shown that mid-twentieth-century mothers both in the developed and less developed countries of the world have shifted from breast-feeding to bottle-feeding in record numbers. Mothers in the United States led this decline in breast-feeding as infant formulas became more available in the 1940s, 1950s, and 1960s. By 1971, less than 10 percent of babies born in the United States were breast-fed after the first 3 months of life. Although it has generally caused no hardship or nutritional problems for the great majority of infants in developed countries, the shift to commercial infant formula has resulted in widespread malnutrition and high-infant mortality in poorer countries. Some recent statistics illustrate this

shift: Over 90 percent of the infants in Chile were breast-fed in 1960; and in 1968, less than 10 percent

---

"Recently, in response to the efforts of major national and world health organizations, many women have returned to breast-feeding their infants."

---

were breast-fed. In Mexico, 95 percent of 6-month-old infants were breast-fed in 1960; in 1966, only 40 percent were breast-fed. In Singapore, 80 percent of 3-month-old infants were breast-fed in 1951; in 1971, only 5 percent were breast-fed. In the poorer countries of the

world, bottle-fed babies had a much higher mortality rate than those who were breast-fed (Latham, 1977). Malnutrition occurs when people lack the money to buy expensive milk substitutes; in addition, many babies die when the commercial formula is diluted with contaminated water, thereby transmitting intestinal diseases to the infants.

Recently, in response to the efforts of major national and world health organizations, many women have returned to breast-feeding their infants. In the United States, over 50 percent of mothers breast-feed their infants for at least a few weeks, and 35 percent continue this practice for at least 3 months (U.S. Department of Health and Human Services, 1989). Yet, even in the 1990s, the levels and trends of breast-feeding vary widely across

---

New technology has helped researchers in their studies. Today, it is possible to measure certain basic physiological reactions of a baby to the environment and to specific stimulation. Heart activity, brain wave activity, and the electrical response of the skin can provide useful information about what infants perceive and how much they understand. Researchers can also gather information from highly refined pictures of an infant's movements—for example, eye movement or hand manipulation. But new technology is only part of the answer. A good research plan, or paradigm, is more important. As we saw in Chapter 2, the classical and instrumental conditioning paradigms have been used to assess infant sensory and memory capabilities. The basic premise is that an infant cannot be conditioned to respond to stimuli he or she cannot perceive.

Another useful strategy to measure infant competence is the **novelty paradigm.** It is well known that babies quickly tire of looking at the same image or playing with the same toy. Infants *habituate* (adapt to) repeated sights or sounds (see Chapter 5). Also, very young infants often show their disinterest by looking away. If given a choice between a familiar toy and a new one, most

novelty paradigm A research plan that uses infants' preferences for new stimuli over familiar ones in order to investigate their ability to detect small differences in sounds, patterns, or colors.

socioeconomic, cultural, and religious groups. Breast-feeding is highest in women who are older, better-educated, and relatively affluent. It is more popular in the western United States and is less popular in the Southeast. Breast-feeding practices are also influenced by family and cultural ideas about how mothers should care for their children, by the amounts of time and money that are available, and by the advice mothers receive from healthcare professionals.

Curiously, the increase in the number of working mothers was not a major cause in the decrease, and then increase, in the trend toward breast-feeding. Breast-feeding declined among women who did not work between births as well as among those who did. In developing countries, where there are high infant mortality rates, the large percentage of bottle-fed babies is still a major public health concern. Here, too, despite extensive educational campaigns by the World Health Organization and other groups, the decision of whether to breast-feed and, if so, for how long, is personal and is embedded in the sociocultural context. In Korea, boys are much more likely to be breast-fed than girls are (Nemeth & Bowling, 1985). In Nigeria, mothers with more education breast-feed less often, and Christian mothers breast-feed for a much shorter period of time than do Moslem mothers (Oni, 1987). In Zaire and many other countries, rural women use breast-feeding as a form of birth control, and, hence, they may continue it for several years (Mock et al., 1986). (It is important to note that this method of birth control is not 100 percent effective.)

Why do some mothers choose to breast-feed, whereas others prefer to bottle-feed? It appears that good nutrition is only one of the many factors that influence this choice. Obviously, cultural factors, personal factors (such as allocating time to

The shift from breast-to-bottle-feeding occurred in less developed countries as well as in Europe and the United States.

work and child care, the social schedule one keeps, and the availability of a peer group that is accepting of breast-feeding, among others) and even national policies may have an effect. For example, until recently, the United States has lacked a family-leave policy. Many women returned to work six weeks after the birth of their child. Combining full-time work and successful breast-feeding is difficult unless a support group of other successful women exists to give advice.

infants will choose the new one. Even if there is only a very small difference in the new toy, the infant will choose it. Researchers have been able to use this information in setting up experiments to determine how small a difference in sound, pattern, or color the infant is capable of detecting.

The **surprise paradigm** is another useful paradigm to study the infant's understanding of the world. Human beings tend to register surprise—through facial expression, physical reaction, or vocal response—when something happens that they did not expect or, conversely, when something does not happen that they did expect. Researchers are able to determine infants' surprise reactions by measuring changes in their breathing, heartbeat, or galvanic skin response or simply by observing their expressions or bodily movements. Researchers can design experiments to test very precisely what infants expect and what events violate their expectations (Bower, 1974). Because of such research techniques, we know that even though newborns have limited sensory and perceptual competence, these abilities improve dramatically during the first 6 months. All of these paradigms allow us to determine infant competencies without their use of language.

surprise paradigm A research technique used to test infants' memory and expectations. Infants cannot report what they remember or expect, but if their expectations are violated, they respond with surprise. For example, if the doll is not under the cloth where the infants saw it hidden, they are surprised.

VISION

Humans are visually oriented organisms. In adults, vision is the most highly developed sense and tends to dominate human environmental interactions. During the first 4 to 6 months, infants' visual abilities develop rapidly. Even before grasping or crawling is possible, they explore the world visually. As we saw in Chapter 5, newborns can visually track a moving penlight and can discriminate between different shapes; however, they prefer to focus on complex patterns and human faces (Fantz, Ordy, & Udelf, 1962). Focusing ability itself improves rapidly during the first few months. Although newborns focus best on objects only 10 inches (25.4 centimeters) away, 3- to 4-month-olds focus almost as well as do adults (Aslin, 1987). Infants' visual acuity increasingly sharpens. Where newborns discriminate stripes 1/8 of an inch (3.2 millimeters) apart and 10 inches (25.4 centimeters) away, 6-month-olds discriminate stripes 1/32 of an inch (.8 millimeters) apart from that same distance (Banks & Dannemiller, 1987; Fantz et al., 1962).

Color discrimination improves steadily over the first year. Even newborns can see bright colors like yellow, orange, red, green, and turquoise. For the first 1 to 2 months, they actually prefer black-and-white patterns over colored ones, probably due to the greater contrast. The color images may appear a bit blurry or washed-out to the infant because of this lack of contrast. By 2 months, the infant picks up more subtle colors like blue, purple, or chartreuse, when compared with gray. Infants' color vision and preference for color improve rapidly. By 4 months, they discriminate between most colors, and, by 6 months, their color perception nearly equals that of adults (Bornstein, 1978; Maurer & Maurer, 1988; Teller & Bornstein, 1987).

Infants are selective in what they look at from the beginning. They look at novel and moderately complex patterns and at human faces. Some changes take place during the first year, however, in exactly what attracts their attention. Newborns look only at the edges of a face. By 2 months they look at the eyes. By 4 months infants prefer a regularly arranged face over a distorted face. By 5 months infants look at the mouth of a person who is talking and by 7 months respond to the whole face and facial expressions. Also, as infants mature, they show increasing preference for greater complexity or contour over simpler designs.

Researchers wonder what causes these changes in selective attention. Are they due partly to the ways in which the neural system matures? Bornstein (1978), for example, discovered that 4-month-old infants prefer "pure" colors to other shades and look for a longer time at perpendicular lines than at slanted lines. He suggests that infants select these colors and lines because they trigger more "neural firing" in the brain. In other words, infants look at the things available that excite the most neural activity.

A number of other improvements in vision occur during the first 6 months. Compared to newborns, older infants are better able to control their eye movements; they can track moving objects more consistently and for longer periods of time (Aslin, 1987). They also spend more time scanning the environment. During the first month of life, only 5 percent to 10 percent of their time is spent scanning, whereas nearly 35 percent is spent scanning at 2 1/2 months (White, 1971). Although newborns are attracted to bright lights and objects, provided the objects are not too bright, 4-month-olds are able to see and respond to dimmer objects.

SEEING OBJECTS   Do infants see objects the way adults see objects? It was once thought that infants had difficulty separating the object from the background. But, in reality, this problem is rare. Infants may not "see" that a cup is separate from a saucer without picking up the cup, but they can "see" that the cup and saucer are separate from the background. By 3 or 4 months, infants have had many visual experiences in which their head moves or the object moves. They will notice, for example, that a milk bottle, from another angle, is still a milk bottle. Infants can use motion as well as space to help define the objects in their world (Mandler, 1990; Spelke, 1988).

DEPTH PERCEPTION   Humans see things in three dimensions. We see that some things are closer and that others are farther away. Even with one eye closed, we can tell the approximate distance of objects. The objects that are close to us appear larger, and they block our view of more distant objects. If we close one eye and hold our heads still, the view resembles a two-dimensional photograph. But, if we move our head, the world comes to life with its three-dimensional aspect. If we use both eyes (binocular vision), we really don't have to move our heads. The left-eye view and the right-eye view slightly differ. The brain integrates these two images, giving us information on distance and relative size.

Do infants have depth perception? Are their brains preprogrammed to integrate the images from two eyes in order to gain information about distance or relative size? Can they use the information that is gathered by moving their heads to see the world in three dimensions?

It appears that the infant's brain can integrate two images in rudimentary form. Because the newborn's eyes are not well coordinated and because the infant has not learned how to interpret the information transmitted by the eyes, depth perception is probably not very sophisticated. It seems to take about 4 months for binocular vision to emerge (Aslin & Smith, 1988).

What is the evidence of developing depth perception? Even infants as young as 6 weeks use spatial cues to react defensively to potentially dangerous situations. Infants seem to dodge, blink, or show some form of avoidance reaction when an object appears to be coming directly at them (Dodwell, Humphrey, & Muir, 1987). By 2 months infants react defensively to an object on a collision, but not near-miss, course. In addition, they prefer three-dimensional to two-dimensional figures. At 4 months, infants are able to swipe with reasonable accuracy at a toy that is dangled in front of them. By 5 months, they have a well-controlled, visually guided reach for objects that are close to them. However, infants at 5 months who are wearing a patch over one eye are slightly less accurate at reaching for objects. Similarly, when given the choice of two objects, one slightly closer than the other, they don't always pick the closer object (Granrud, Yonas, & Pettersen, 1984).

One of the best-known experiments to test infants' depth perception is the **visual cliff.** Gibson and Walk (1960) created a special box to simulate depth. On one side, a heavy piece of glass covered a solid surface. On the other side, the heavy glass was 2 to 3 feet (60 to 90 centimeters) above a floor, simulating a cliff effect. Infants 6 months or older refused to crawl across the surface that appeared to be a cliff. Younger infants who were not yet able to crawl showed interest but not distress, as indicated by heart rate changes, when they were placed on the cliff side of the box (Campos, Langer, & Krowitz, 1970). This heart rate change indicated that younger infants are able to discriminate the spatial cues but do not show a marked fear response to the greater depth.

Even when coaxed by their mothers, infants will not crawl over the edge of the visual cliff.

visual cliff An experimental apparatus that tests depth perception of infants by simulating an abrupt drop-off.

Further studies by Joseph Campos and his colleagues have focused on how children learn not to cross the cliff side. A baby who has just barely learned how to crawl can sometimes be coaxed across the cliff, provided it is not too deep. The same baby will later refuse to cross if his mother has signaled to him that it is dangerous. She may tell him in an anxious voice not to cross, or, much more simply, she may express a look of fear, anxiety, or even horror. If these mothers do not show such a fear response themselves, but are rather encouraging, the babies can be coaxed to cross the deep side to reach their parent (Kermoian & Campos, 1988). It appears that the visual cues for depth perception are developed within the first 4 to 6 months (Yonas & Awsley, 1987). The particular meaning of the information about distance or depth is learned more gradually, especially as the child begins to move about his or her environment. This is an excellent example of the way in which maturation and the psychosocial environment combine to produce the behaviors we observe in infants and children.

HEARING

The anatomical development of the auditory system is virtually complete before the end of gestation. Within the first few months, infants' hearing acuity improves considerably. At birth, the middle ear is filled with fluid and tissue, most of which disappears after the first few weeks. Despite this blockage, newborns show changes in heart rate and respiration in response to moderate sounds (for example, 60 decibels—a normal telephone conversation). At 3 months, they respond to much softer sounds (43 decibels) and to even softer tones at 8 months (34 decibels) (Hoversten & Moncur, 1969). We also know by changes in their heart rates that infants detect fairly large changes in loudness, pitch, and duration of sound. They may even detect much smaller changes or hear much softer tones, although it is difficult to measure this, except under hospital experimentation conditions. This measurement is done by a study of the electrical activity of the brain using EEG (electroencephalogram) readings (Hecox, 1975).

Infants do respond in other ways to sounds. They can be soothed, alerted, or distressed by them. Low-frequency or rhythmic sounds generally soothe infants. Loud, sudden, and high-frequency tones cause them distress. Infants also show—by turning their heads—that they can locate the source of the sound. These and other behaviors indicate that infants have fairly well developed auditory perception within their first 6 months of life.

As with vision, babies also show auditory preferences early in development. Infants are especially attentive to human voices. By 4 months they will smile more in response to their mother's voice than to another female voice. By 6 months they show distress upon hearing their mother's voice if they cannot see her. This is the age at which the mother's mere talking to her baby from another room—perhaps while preparing food or a bottle—no longer is an effective soother. The infant must both see and hear her to stop crying. By 10 months if the infant hears the mother's voice on tape she will look at her; if she hears another female voice, she will look at the other female. Infants this age also vocalize more after hearing their mother's voices (Mandler, 1990).

An important aspect of infants' hearing during the first year is their seemingly inborn ability to differentiate between speech and nonspeech sounds. As early as 1 month, infants can detect subtle differences between speech sounds called *phonemes* (the shortest speech segment in which a change also produces a change in meaning, such as "lip" and "lap" (Eimas, 1975). In fact, one researcher was amazed to find that infants in the first year could pick up differences in language that even she could not pick up. She had borrowed a tape containing sounds used in the Czechoslovakian language. After listening to it repeatedly, she could detect no differences. When she called the language lab to complain, they told her that she was mistaken. She then played this tape to her Canadian babies, who detected the differences immediately (Maurer & Maurer, 1988). It is clear that infants' sensitivity to speech sounds helps them learn how to speak. This sensitivity and their ability to recognize familiar voices help strengthen infants' attachment bond to parents and care-givers.

INTEGRATION

Researchers have generally agreed that at birth an infant's vision, hearing, and senses of touch, taste, and smell are nearly complete and that they improve rapidly over the next 6 months. In contrast, there has been great disagreement as to whether there is integration of these senses during early infancy. How do we ask infants if they know that a particular sound comes from a particular object? How do infants acknowledge that the bumpy thing they just felt is now the same thing they are looking at? It is difficult to design experiments for the first 6 months of life. Recent, imaginative work, however, suggests that either the senses are interrelated at birth or the necessary learning is extremely rapid.

As you recall from Chapter 5, newborns will turn their heads to look at the source of a sound. They don't necessarily know what they will see, but there is a mechanism in place that will help them learn this. Some creative experiments have been done on integration. In one study, infants were allowed to suck on either of two different kinds of pacifiers: One was covered with bumps, and the other was smooth. When the pacifier was removed and the infants were shown both kinds of pacifiers, they *looked longer* at the nipple that they had just *felt* in their mouth (Meltzoff & Borton, 1979). In another experiment, infants at 4 months were shown two films of complex events that they had not seen before and that had only *one* soundtrack. The infants turned to look at the film that matched the sound. Next, the film was simplified so that only two speakers' faces were shown, and it looked as if both speakers were talking at exactly the same time. The infants were still able to pick the speaker's face that matched the soundtrack (Kuhl & Meltzoff, 1988).

Much of this sensory integration must, of course, be learned. Infants must learn which sounds go with which sights, what the soft fur feels and looks like, what the noisy puppy looks like, and so forth. Nevertheless, it appears that infants have a built-in tendency to seek these links. Integration advances rapidly over the first year. In another study, Rose, Gottfried, and Bridger (1981) found that even though 6-month-olds could sometimes visually identify an object that they had touched or were touching, their cross-modal transference (tactual-visual) was not as strong as it was in older infants. Some of the research on the visual cliff makes a similar point about the integration of emotion and perception. Although young infants did recognize the depth in the visual cliff, and they noticed that one side was different from the other, they did not necessarily recognize that it was something unsafe or something not to be crawled across. They were interested more than afraid. Older infants who had a higher level of integration were more wary of the visual cliff. This does not indicate that higher levels of integration cause the older infants to be afraid, but it does demonstrate that behavior and emotions become linked over time—perhaps because of experience, or maturation, or some combination of both.

Integration, then, is a process that becomes increasingly efficient and effective over the first year of the infant's life. One of the milestones in this process is the coordination of vision with reaching; this seemingly simple accomplishment takes several months.

THE VISUALLY GUIDED REACH

If 1-month-old infants are shown a very attractive object, they will do a number of things. Often, they will open and close their hands and wave their arms in a seemingly random way. Sometimes, they will open their mouths as if they are about to suck. They may even look intently at the object. But they cannot coordinate any of these reflexes—reaching out, grasping the object, and bringing it to their mouths. It takes at least 5 months to develop this skill.

Successful reaching requires a number of different abilities: accurate depth perception, voluntary control of grasping, voluntary control of arm movements, and the ability to organize these behaviors in a sequence (Bruner, 1973). Throughout the first 5 months, infants are learning about objects with their mouth and hands, then linking visual information to direct the exploration of the fingers (Rochat, 1989). Finally, in the visually guided reach, infants combine

The coordination of vision with reaching—the visually guided reach—is one of the milestones in development.

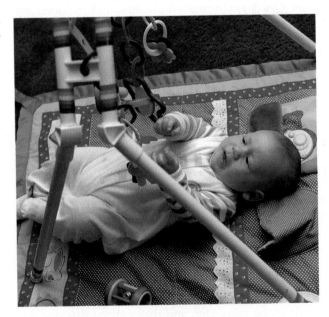

many bits and pieces of behavior; they *functionally integrate* and *subordinate* them to the total pattern. When they are first learning the guided reach, children must attempt individually the acts of reaching, grasping, and mouthing. Later, the reach itself becomes a means to an end, and children can then turn to a larger task—like stacking blocks. Their reaching is then functionally integrated and subordinated to block building.

BRAIN DEVELOPMENT AND EXPERIENCE

Recently, neuroscientists and developmental psychologists have been studying the relationship between sensory, perceptual, and motor experience and the development of certain areas of the brain. Brain growth occurs both as the neurons themselves grow in size and also because the number of connections between them increases (Shatz, 1992). It is clear that the human brain grows considerably in size and complexity during the first 2 years as we saw earlier in this chapter. At birth, it is about 25 percent of the size and weight of the adult brain. By the infant's first birthday, it is double that size. At 2 years, it is at about 75 percent of adult size. In the first few months, there is rapid development in the primary sensory and motor areas of the brain. This corresponds to the time when we know there is rapid development of the perceptual systems.

From numerous animal studies, we know that there are links between sensory and motor experience and actual brain growth. For instance, kittens who are raised in an environment where there are vertical lines but no horizontal lines actually lose the ability to make accurate perceptual judgments about horizontal lines. The kitten who lives in a deprived visual environment actually has fewer brain cells that respond to that kind of visual input after the period of deprivation. The environment, therefore, plays a significant role in early perceptual development. While the visual system is functional at birth, without light, the neural connections between the eye and the brain, which are present at birth, will not be maintained. Moreover, the early learning of skills contributes to further learning and development.

Many theorists believe that the brain is "prewired" for certain basic sensory and motor functions. However, this "prewiring" must be used in order to be "fine tuned" and even, in some cases, to continue to exist. This "wiring" is somewhat redundant, with many connections lost through disuse and others strengthened by use (Bertenthal & Campos, 1987; Greenough, Black, & Wallace, 1987; Shatz, 1992). An adult human brain has more than 100 billion neurons connected with one another in ways that make memory, vision, learning, thought, and consciousness possible. One of the most remarkable features of the adult nervous system is the precision of this wiring. The achievement of such complexity is even more astounding when one considers that in the first few weeks after fertilization many of the sense organs are not even connected to the embryonic processing centers of the brain. During fetal development, neurons must be generated in the right quantity and location so that eventually correct pathways may be formed (Shatz, 1992). This research on brain development gives further support to the view that development is neither purely genetic nor purely environmental but depends on a combination of both factors.

COGNITIVE DEVELOPMENT

Cognition is the process by which we gain knowledge of our world. Cognition encompasses the processes of thinking, learning, perceiving, remembering, and understanding. Cognitive development refers to the growth and refinement of this intellectual capacity. Many theorists believe that infants take an active role in their own cognitive development. The problem is in finding out what infants do know and think about. When subjects cannot talk to you and tell you what they are thinking, how can you study their developing intellects?

The individual most influential in the study of emerging infant intelligence has probably been Jean Piaget. As was discussed in Chapter 2, Piaget was one of the few psychologists who had woven a design large enough to encompass all human intellectual development. Piaget was personally fascinated with the human mind, a passion that fueled his natural talents as an observer of behavior. Part of his work focused on the interaction between heredity and the environment, and part on the ways in which children manipulate the environment to exercise and develop their cognitive abilities.

As detailed in Chapter 2, Piaget saw humans as active, alert, and creative beings who possess mental structures, called schemes, that process and organize information. Over time, these schemes develop into more complex cognitive structures. Intellectual development occurs in four qualitatively different sequential periods that begin in early infancy and go on for the next 12 to 15 years into adolescence and beyond. His first period of intellectual development is called the sensorimotor period.

THE SENSORIMOTOR PERIOD

Infants come into the world prepared to respond to the environment with the perceptual capacities just discussed and with a few ready-made motor patterns—sucking, crying, kicking, and making a fist. For Piaget, these sensorimotor patterns form the infant's schemes—the infant's only way of processing information from the environment.

But what about thoughts and concepts? How do infants develop an understanding of objects, people, or relationships? How do they code and store things in their memory without any words? What, after all, is infant intelligence? According to Piaget, these ready-made schemes—looking, visually following, sucking, grasping, and crying—form the building blocks for cognitive development. They are transformed over the next 18 months into some early concepts of objects, people, and the self. Piaget considered sensorimotor behavior to be the beginning of intelligence. From observing their actions, we can make inferences about infant knowledge of the physical world.

ADAPTATION

cognition The process by which we know and understand our world.

Piaget viewed the sensorimotor period as comprising six fairly discrete stages. Because other researchers have found some variations in the course of events, we will not discuss this period by these discrete stages but rather by some of the processes of development that occur during it.

Infant schemes are elaborated, modified, and developed by a process that Piaget (1962) called **adaptation.** He described how his 7-month-old daughter, Lucienne, played with a pack of cigarettes. Unlike a 2-year-old, who might take out a cigarette and pretend to smoke it, Lucienne had no such behaviors in her repertoire. She treated the pack of cigarettes as if it were any other toy or object that she had been used to handling. Looking, mouthing, grasping, and banging were her only ways of interacting with the world: these were her toy-manipulating schemes. In other words, she *assimilated* the pack of cigarettes into her existing schemes. With each new object, children make minor changes in their action patterns, or schemes. The grasp and the mouth must *accommodate* the new object. Gradually, through assimilation and accommodation, these action patterns become modified and the infant's basic sensorimotor schemes develop into more complex cognitive capacities.

Piaget noted a specific form of adaptation in infancy that he called a **circular response.** Much of what infants learn begins quite by accident. An action occurs, and then infants see, hear, or feel it. For example, some babies may notice their hands in front of their faces. By moving the hands, they discover that they can change what is seen. They can prolong the event, repeat it, stop it, or start it again. Infants' early circular responses involve the discovery of their own bodies. Later circular responses concern how they use their bodies or themselves to change the environment, as in making a toy move.

According to Piaget, at the end of the sensorimotor period, most infants will have achieved a number of simple but fundamental intellectual abilities. These include concepts about the uses of familiar objects, an understanding of object permanence, memory development, and some beginning ways to symbolically represent things, people, and events. Each of the following sections examines a part of this development.

Infants have a limited number of behavioral schemes in their repertoire. Looking, mouthing, grasping, and banging are the ways they interact with their environment.

PLAY WITH OBJECTS

Although they are often unnoticed by parents or care-givers, accomplishments in object play are important to children's cognitive development. By 4 or 5 months, infants generally reach out, grasp, and hold objects. These seemingly simple skills—together with their advanced perceptual skills—equip them for more varied play with objects. In their play with objects, infants and young children demonstrate a memory for repeated events, match their actions appropriately with various objects, and develop their understanding of the social world through pretending and imitation. Play, in other words, lays the groundwork for further complex thinking and language.

Object play goes through definite stages, starting with simple explorations by about 5 months and ending with complex imitative and pretending behavior by the end of 3 years (Garvey, 1977). By 9 months, most infants explore objects; they wave them around, turn them over, and test them by hitting them against something nearby. But they are not aware of the use or function of the things that they are handling. By 12 months, they stop first and examine objects closely before putting them in their mouths. By 15 to 18 months, they try to use objects as they were intended—for example, they might pretend to drink from a cup, brush their hair with a toy brush, or make a doll sit up. By 21 months, they generally use objects appropriately. They try to feed a doll with a spoon, put a doll in

adaptation In Piaget's theory, the process by which infant schemes are elaborated, modified, and developed.

circular response A particular form of adaptation in Piaget's theory, in which the infant accidentally performs some action, perceives it, then repeats the action.

the driver's seat of a toy truck, or use keys to unlock an imaginary door. The play becomes still more realistic by 24 months. Toddlers take dolls out for walks and line up trucks and trailers in the right order. By 3 years, preschool children may make dolls into imaginary people with independent wills. They might have a doll go outdoors, chop wood, bring it back inside, and put it in an imaginary fireplace (Bornstein & O'Reilly, 1991; Fein, 1981).

IMITATION

The object play of 2-year-olds is rich with imitations of their world. Infants' imitations—of actions, gestures, and words—are not as simple as they might appear to adults.

Within the first 3 months, infants do some sporadic imitation in the context of play with the care-giver. For example, an infant may imitate facial expressions, or stick out her tongue and match the sound or pitch of the mother's voice. Normally, mothers begin this game by imitating the infant. In fact, it is sometimes hard to tell who is imitating—mother or child (Uzgiris, 1984). By 6 or 7 months, however, infants are much better at imitating gestures and actions. The first hand gestures to be imitated are those for which they already have action schemes: grasping, reaching, and so on. By 9 months, they can imitate novel gestures, such as banging two objects together. During the second year, infants begin to imitate a series of actions or gestures, even some that they have seen sometime previously. At first, children imitate only those actions they choose themselves. Later, they imitate those who show them how to brush their teeth or how to use a fork or spoon. Some toddlers even train themselves to use the toilet with relatively little struggle by imitating an older child.

Does imitation require a mental representation of the action? Is it thinking? Piaget believed that even simple imitation was a complex match of action patterns. He predicted that infants would not imitate novel action until they were at least 9 months old. *Deferred imitation*—imitating something that happened hours or days before—requires memory of an image or some use of symbolic representation. Piaget predicted that this would not occur until the age of 18 months. But infants seem to be able to imitate novel action somewhat earlier than Piaget predicted. For instance, children of deaf parents begin to learn and use sign language as early as 6 or 7 months (Mandler, 1988). Imaginative researchers, using novel toys, have demonstrated deferred imitation well before 18 months. One such study used a box with a hidden button. If the infant found the button, a beep was heard. There was another box with an orange light panel on top. If the infant leaned forward and touched the light panel with his or her head, a light went on. There was also a bear that danced when jiggled with a string. Infants were shown these actions but were not given an opportunity to play with the toys immediately. Infants at 11 months could imitate these actions 24 hours later and infants at 14 months could imitate them a week later. Infants who had not seen the demonstration did not spontaneously perform these actions (Meltzoff, 1988a; Meltzoff, 1988b). It seems that infants have more ability to remember and imitate an action sequence than we had previously thought.

By 6 or 7 months, infants are greatly improved in their ability to imitate gestures and actions.

OBJECT PERMANENCE

According to Piaget, **object permanence** is the primary accomplishment of the sensorimotor period. This is an awareness that an object exists in time and space regardless of one's own perception of it. Infants do not fully develop object permanence until they are about 18 months old. During the first year, "out of sight, out of mind" seems literally true for them. If they do not see something, it does not exist. Thus, a covered toy holds no interest, even if an infant continues to hold on to it under the cover.

To understand how infants develop the idea of object permanence, Piaget (1952) and other researchers investigated infant search behavior. They found that most infants do not sustain a successful search for an object that they have just seen until 18 months of age. They do, however, form an idea of their mothers' (or care-givers') permanence somewhat before this, but they do not generalize this insight to all other external objects.

The development of object permanence involves a series of accomplishments. First, infants must develop a recognition of familiar objects. They do this as early as 2 months; for example, they become excited at the sight of a bottle or their care-givers. Second, infants about 2 months old may watch a moving object disappear behind one edge of a screen and then shift their eyes to the other edge to see if it reappears. Their visual tracking is excellent and well timed, and they are surprised if something does not reappear. But they do not seem to mind when a completely different object appears from behind the screen. In fact, infants up to 5 months will accept a wide variety of objects with no distress (Bower, 1971).

Infants older than 5 months are more discriminating "trackers." They will be disturbed if a different object appears or if the same object reappears but moves faster or slower than before. Even these older infants, however, can be fooled in this experiment: Imagine two screens side by side with a gap in the middle. An object disappears behind one screen; it does not appear in the gap, but it does reappear from behind the outer edge of the second screen. Not until infants are 9 months old will they expect the object to appear in the intervening gap. In fact, they are then surprised if it does not (Moore, Borton, & Darby, 1978).

As stated earlier, infants do form the complete idea of person permanence somewhat before object permanence, but the first developmental stages remain almost the same as for objects. T. G. R. Bower (1971) arranged mirrors so that infants would see multiple images of their mothers. He found that most infants less than 5 months old were not disturbed at seeing more than one mother; actually they were delighted. Infants older than 5 months or so, however, had learned that they had only one mother, and they were very disturbed at seeing more than one.

Infants learn more about objects when they begin to search for *hidden* objects. Searching behavior proceeds through a predictable sequence of development, and it begins at about 5 months. Infants younger than 5 months do not search or hunt; they seem to forget about an object once it is hidden. Hunting behavior begins somewhere between 5 and 8 months. Infants of this age enjoy hiding and finding games; they like being hidden under a blanket or covering their eyes with their hands and having the world reappear when they take their hands away. As we have seen, they are surprised if one object vanishes behind a screen and another emerges on the other side. If a toy disappears through a trap-

object permanence According to Piaget, the realization in infants at about 18 months that objects continue to exist when they are out of sight, touch, or some other perceptual context.

In Bower's multiple mothers experiment, infants younger than 20 weeks are not disturbed by seeing more than one mother. But older infants become upset at the sight of such images.

door and another reappears when the door is opened again, they are also surprised, but they accept the new toy. Older infants, between 12 and 18 months, are puzzled; they search for the first toy.

Some irregularities occur in 1-year-olds' hunting behavior, however. If a toy is hidden in place A and they are used to finding it there, 1-year-olds will continue looking for it at place A, *even when they have seen it hidden in place* B. Piaget (1952) suggests that infants of this age seem to have two memories—one of seeing the object hidden (the seeing memory) and another of finding it (the action memory). Not everyone agrees with Piaget's interpretation of this "hiding" experiment, however. Mandler (1990) has suggested that there are other explanations for the irregularities in 1-year-olds' hunting behavior.

The final attainment of object permanence occurs at about 18 months and seems to depend on infants' locomotive ability. When infants crawl and walk, they can pursue their guesses and hypotheses more actively. If a ball rolls away, they may follow it and find it. If mother is out of sight, they may go and find her. In this way, they test the properties of the world around them through their own actions.

MEMORY

Most of the sensorimotor abilities discussed so far require some form of memory. We have seen how 4-month-old infants prefer to look at new objects, which shows that they have already established some memory for the familiar (Cohen & Gelber, 1975). An infant who imitates must be able to remember the sounds and actions of another person. Infants who search for a toy where they have seen it hidden are remembering the location of that toy. Although sensorimotor abilities have been studied thoroughly, the role that memory plays in them has not.

Very young infants seem to have powerful visual memories (Cohen & Gelber, 1975; McCall, Eichorn, & Hogarty, 1977). Habituation studies have shown that infants as young as 2 months store visual patterns (Cohen & Gelber, 1975).

Fagan (1977) found that 5-month-olds recognize patterns 48 hours after the first presentation and photographs of faces after 2 weeks. He discovered, too, that 5- to 6-month-olds, who had previously recognized facial photographs after a delay of 2 weeks, had trouble recognizing the photos if they had been shown similar photos in the meantime (Fagan, 1977). This could be reversed, however, by briefly presenting the original image.

A few studies have indicated rather long-term memory in infants, at least for dramatic events. For instance, children who participated in an unusual experiment at a very young age remember the actions that took place when reintroduced to that setting several months later (Rovee-Collier, 1987). Indeed, in one study, children recalled aspects of their experiment 2 years later (Myers, Clifton, & Clarkson, 1987). These children were able to repeat their actions, although four out of five children could not verbally report them. These studies indicate that memory for sights, for actions, and even for events develops early and is relatively robust.

Children generally start pretending between 6 and 12 months.

SYMBOLIC REPRESENTATION

During infancy, some of the earliest forms of representation are actions. Infants smack their lips before their food or bottle reaches their mouths. They may continue to make eating motions after feeding time is over. They may drop a rattle, yet continue to shake the hand that held it. They may wave bye-bye before they are able to say the words. These actions are the simplest forerunners of **symbolic representation**—the ability to represent something not physically present.

Imitating, finding hidden objects, and pretending—all point to an underlying process of symbolic representation (Mandler, 1983). Between 6 and 12 months, children begin *pretending,* that is, using actions to represent objects, events, or ideas. They may represent the idea of sleeping by putting their heads down on their hands. As we have seen in object play, toward the end of the second year children use objects appropriately; they may, for example, have a doll drive a truck, which is represented by a shoe box. Such pretending behavior shows that children of this age create symbols independent of the immediate surroundings—a forward step in cognitive growth.

Pretending behavior, too, develops in a predictable sequence (Fein, 1981; Rubin, Fein, & Vandenberg, 1983). The first stage occurs by about 11 or 12 months; most children of this age pretend to eat, drink, or sleep—all familiar actions. In the next few months, there is a dramatic increase in the range and amount of pretend activities. At first, infants do not need objects to pretend, as when a child pretends to sleep, curled up on a rug. But as they grow older, toys and other objects are used, too. By 15 to 18 months, they feed brothers and sisters, dolls, and adults with real cups and toy cups, spoons, and forks. At this point, children need realistic objects to support their pretend games. By 20 to 26 months, they may pretend that an object is something other than what it is; a broom may become a horse, a paper sack a hat, a wood floor a pool of water. Such forms of pretending represent a further step in cognitive development. By noting the rough similarities between a horse and a broom, children combine a distant concept with a familiar one and thus establish a symbolic relationship between the two. (Language, of course, is the ultimate system of symbolic relationships, as we shall see in Chapter 8.)

symbolic representation The use of a word, picture, gesture, or other sign to represent past and present events, experiences, and concepts.

CRITIQUE OF PIAGET'S THEORY

Piaget's theory of infant cognitive development has fueled 30 years of research and debate. His careful, naturalistic observations of infants have challenged others to look more closely. His emphasis on the interaction of maturation and experience and on the infant's active, adaptive, constructive role in his or her own learning brought a new respect to infant research. For Piaget, the toddler is a "little scientist" who tests and discovers the nature of physical objects and of the social world. The younger infant wiggles and kicks and varies his motions to "make interesting sights last." Or he repeats and extends and varies his voice just to enjoy the sound of his own babbling. For some observers, Piaget made the infant more human—more like us—and definitely worthy of our study.

But Piaget was not correct in everything he found. Many critics feel he emphasized motor development far too much and ignored perceptual development. Some of his stages are probably wrong. It appears, for instance, that infants can imitate much earlier than Piaget would have imagined. Indeed, some newborns appear to imitate an adult sticking out his tongue. Even the development of object permanence may not occur precisely in the fashion that Piaget describes. In fact, some critics suggest that infants may have more sophisticated knowledge of objects based on their perceptual development but that their motor development may lag behind. Hence, young infants might be able to show evidence of object permanence if they are given tests that do not require coordinated actions (Baillargeon, 1987; Gratch & Schatz, 1987; Mandler, 1990).

ENVIRONMENTAL STIMULATION AND INFANT COMPETENCIES

The environment exerts a powerful influence on the development of infant competencies. The presence or absence of stimulation can speed up or slow down the acquisition of certain behaviors. In addition, motivation, timing of stimulation, and the quality of care-giving also affect infant development. A number of questions can be raised about the effects of early experience upon infant competencies. Do normal patterns of behavior—motor, intellectual, and social—emerge in a predetermined fashion—regardless of the nature of the infant's early experiences? Or are there minimal experiential conditions that are necessary for proper development? What about the timing of experience; for example, are early experiences more crucial than later experiences? Can patterns established early be modified later?

Early experience can affect structural development, intersensory coordination and behavioral maturation, as we have already seen. Even motor behaviors whose onset is maturational can be developmentally retarded in severely restricted institutionalized infants. Clearly, malnutrition affects cognitive development. However, most homes provide an adequate enough environment to allow cognitive competencies to grow. There is also a body of research indicating that when deprivation occurs, serious and often permanent damage may be done to the infant's intellectual abilities.

DEPRIVATION

The home environment can have a significant impact upon the well-being and general developmental outcome of children. There is essentially a continuum of environments that exist—ranging from optimal environments to seriously deprived environments, such as barren institutions. As would be expected, the more restricted and deprived the environment, the more profound the developmental delay of the child exposed to it. Being deprived of normal experiences can have a marked and sometimes prolonged effect upon infant development. Wayne Dennis (1960, 1973; Dennis & Najarian, 1957) found that institutionalized children were severely retarded in even such basic competencies as sitting, standing, and walking when they had no opportunities to practice these skills. And because of the almost total lack of stimulation in their environment, these children were also retarded in language, social skills, and emotional expression:

> As babies they lay on their backs in their cribs throughout the first year and often for much of the second year....Many objects available to most children did not exist....There were no building blocks, no sandboxes, no scooters, no tricycles, no climbing apparatus, no wagons, no teeter-totters, no swings, no chutes. There were no pets or other animals of any sort....They had no opportunities to learn what these objects were. They never saw persons who lived in the outside world, except for rather rare visitors. (Dennis, 1973, pp. 22–23)

In a 15- and 20-year-lag follow-up study, Dennis (1973) found that even those children who were adopted showed some developmental retardation in maturity. Those who remained in barren institutions showed marked retardation throughout life.

THE FAMILY ENVIRONMENT

The general effect of environment on the development of children has been demonstrated in several studies. A recent longitudinal study of children with sex-chromosome abnormalities recently contrasted the outcomes of children with such anomalies from competent nondysfunctional families with those from dysfunctional families. In this study, the dysfunctional families had such characteristics as ineffective parenting, and multiple stresses affecting the family such as poverty, drug and alcohol abuse, or death of a family member. In general, both groups of children showed some motor and cognitive problems when compared to their normal siblings. However, the nature and extent of these problems were more pronounced if the child came from a multidysfunctional family. (Bender, Linden, & Robinson, 1987).

Another study followed the entire population of 670 children born on the island of Kauai in the Hawaiian Island in 1955 (Werner, 1989). At birth, 3 percent of the infants showed severe birth complications, 13 percent moderate complications, 31 percent mild complications, and 53 percent no complications. At the age of 2 years, a general assessment was done of their overall functioning. Of these 2-year-olds, 12 percent were rated as deficient in social development, 16 percent deficient in intellectual functioning, and 14 percent deficient in health. As is typical, the more severe the birth complications had been, the lower the developmental level of the children. Of special interest, however, was the relationship between birth complications and environmental factors. In general, the infants coming from dysfunctional families, especially those with low socioeconomic status, showed the greatest negative effect stemming from birth complications. For example, infants born with the most severe birth complications who were living in dysfunctional poor families with mothers of low intelligence showed a 19- to 37-point difference in their average IQ scores when compared to those infants with mild or moderate complications. On the other hand, infants with severe birth complications who were born into stable, higher socioeconomic status families only showed a 5- to 7-point difference when compared with their peers who had been born with mild or moderate deficiencies.

What specifically is there about these environments that produces such a negative effect? Part of the answer lies in the notion of family dysfunction—where there is great stress that tends to be persistent or insoluble in families, the members often tend to focus on their personal needs rather than on the collective good of the family. If such a family is placed in poverty, needed factors such as access to health care, ability to gather information about dealing with problems, and often knowledge of what options might exist to improve the situation of their child with special needs are also removed.

An ongoing study at Buffalo's Children's Hospital lends additional support to this contention. Infants born to cocaine-addicted mothers are being followed extensively by the neurological unit of the hospital. These infants are repeatedly tested for neurological, psychosocial, and emotional problems as they move through early childhood into childhood. The results have been striking to date. Neurological damage appears to be minimal—contrary to what had been expected. However, these children often show adjustment problems and heightened aggression. This appears to be due to the nature of the dysfunctional families in which they are living rather than their neurological problems. In many cases, the father is absent, the mother remains addicted, and there is no semblance of a stable environment to encourage the development of self-control and self-esteem in these children.

NORMAL VERSUS OPTIMAL ENVIRONMENTS

Studies such as those done with institutionalized infants may be criticized on methodological grounds, but the consensus is that deprived early experience has a devastating effect on the developing child. The questions then remain—what about the effects of normal environments? What is there in the normal or even enriched environment that may contribute to the social and intellectual growth of children?

MOTIVATION

The vast majority of infants seem motivated to develop their skills with self-rewarding experiences. For example, children show considerable persistence in learning to walk, for the sheer satisfaction of walking. Infants learn skills not only because they are intrinsically motivated, but also because the environment responds. They learn to push a toy simply to see it move. They practice motor skills to experience and gain mastery of a task.

The responsiveness of the environment is crucial. In one study, three groups of infants were presented with three different types of crib decorations (Watson & Ramey, 1972). Infants in the first group were given a mobile that they could control. The second group was given a stabile, which did not move. The third group was given a mobile, but the wind, not the infants, made it move. Infants in the third group were then allowed to control the mobile; they performed poorly both immediately and 6 weeks later. They had already learned that their behavior had no effect—the environment did not respond.

VARIETY AND TIMING OF STIMULATION

On the other hand, and contrary to the belief of some parents, grandparents, and other care-givers (and most toy manufacturers), infants do not require a vast assortment of toys or a massively enriched environment to develop cognitive skills (Yarrow et al., 1972). Instead, a moderately enriched environment, in which infants are given stimulating objects slightly ahead of the time that they would normally use them, seems to promote optimum growth (White & Held, 1966). The goal is to match the task with the child's development. Slightly accelerated stimulation, therefore, encourages growth and development; greatly accelerated stimulation confuses children. They will ignore or reject a task that is too difficult.

THE CARE-GIVER

A stimulating environment is created by a concerned adult care-giver. As we shall see in Chapter 7, the interpersonal relationship with the care-giver is a major influence on a child's mental development. In the course of feeding, diapering, bathing, and dressing their infants, parents and other care-givers provide a constant source of stimulation; by talking with infants and playing games, they demonstrate relationships between objects as well as between people. Even simple behaviors like imitation occur most often in a rich dialogue of social play between adult care-giver and infant (Uzgiris, 1984). When development goes well, the infant competencies develop at the approximate ages described.

There is great need for children to be raised in a responsive social environment if they are to show optimal developmental outcome. When we contrast the children raised in institutions or dysfunctional families with those raised in optimal family environments, this becomes especially clear. Children raised in institutions or dysfunctional families grow up without a responsive care-giver who adjusts care-taking activities to the unique and special needs of individual children. In both cases, there is likely to be a lack of *contingent feedback*, from care-givers; that is the infant's behavior is not likely to produce immediate results but interaction is more typically done on a schedule. Such infants therefore get little chance to shape and alter their environmental inputs. They receive little direct encouragement in the form of consistent and contingent feedback for emerging social skills and language skills such as smiling, crying, and vocalizing. Many of these infants appear to grow up to be children who have learned that they cannot

A moderately enriched environment seems to promote optimum cognitive growth in infants.

FOCUS ON AN ISSUE

"HOTHOUSE" BABIES

We now know quite a bit about the infant's emerging competence. We know it is important to have a responsive environment and to match the environmental stimulation to the infant's current abilities. We know that infants are learning and making associations from the day they are born, and perhaps even before. Knowing these things, why not create the best possible environment, one that maximizes the opportunity for learning? Why not create a "hothouse" environment that provides early training in academics and other skills with the aim of developing a "superbaby"? Several researchers, in fact, tried. Perhaps the most well-known is Glenn Doman, in his *Better Baby Program* (Moore, 1984). Doman has written several books, such as

How to Teach a Baby to Read (1963), and he provides a week-long course for parents on how to stimulate advanced mental development. He believes that regular and systematic stimulation and early training accelerate brain growth. His program urges brief training sessions in reading and mathematics, beginning at 1 year. These training sessions, with flashcards, are to last 5 or 10 minutes at first and then are to be extended as the child grows older. Later, toddlers and 2-year-olds study Japanese or modern art, or learn to play the violin.

Other programs of infant stimulation are much less intense but instruct parents on how to maximize the learning opportunities in daily routines. You might be surprised, for example, to discover how much

a toddler can learn from kicking, banging toys, or from making a peanut butter sandwich (Lehane, 1976).

What are the results of these training programs? There have been some rather remarkable case studies. Many 3- or 4-year-old children have been taught to read at a second- or third-grade level. There are children who play the violin at 4 years. But the results are not consistent, and there are some dangers. Sometimes an overeager parent teaches a child by the age of 2 to avoid anything that looks remotely like a flashcard. Children who spend a great deal of time in rote learning have less time to explore the world around them, and to initiate activities with other children, as well as with adults. There are less opportunities for sim-

control their environment—and they therefore cease trying. They often become passive or aggressive as the situation and their frustration demand.

 ## EARLY INTERVENTION

Some of the most hopeful and exciting applications of our knowledge of infant development have been the success stories from a number of *early intervention* programs. It is possible now to identify at birth (or even before) infants who fall into certain high-risk groups. Perhaps they are premature, malnourished, or developmentally delayed. Their mothers may be alcoholics, users of crack-cocaine or emotionally disturbed. Also, poverty restricts the diets, health care, and the quality of care some infants are likely to receive. Without help, many of these infants will have persistent learning disabilities or emotional scars. In addition, they may have health problems and are at greater risk for premature death.

Over the past two decades, several programs have offered a variety of supportive services to parents and infants in these high-risk groups. Because adequate

ply discovering. Finally, an overemphasis on cognitive development can have negative effects on social and personality development. Children can become insecure or overly dependent on their parents. Some children may become quite anxious because of the high expectations placed on them at an early age.

> *"...just as tomatoes grown out of season taste flat, perhaps a "hothouse" child will be a flat, unexciting individual."*

Several child development experts have gathered together in a symposium to discuss the challenges and problems of the trend toward "hot housing" infants and young children. One of them defines "hot housing" as "inducing infants to acquire knowledge that is typically acquired at a later developmental level" (Sigel, 1987, p. 212). Most of these experts agreed that structured training of infants and young children too early in academic tasks tended to have serious negative side effects on social and emotional development. They not only lost play time, but they suffered achievement anxiety and limited informal social skills. Some had limited cognitive development as well, with gaps in their understanding of the physical world despite their rote memory for complex definitions or their advanced skills in reading. Professor Sigel suggested that "hot housing" was a wonderful metaphor. It reminded one of the tomato plant in the greenhouse, in an artificial climate, protected and sterile, and with chemicals and alien forces that force growth "out of season." He asked, "Who really likes hothouse tomatoes?" (Sigel, 1987, p. 218). Professor Sigel suggests that, just as tomatoes grown out of season taste flat, perhaps a "hothouse" child will be a flat, unexciting individual. Similarly, early harvesting of hothouse children may stunt full development, depress their emotional range, and limit their ability to explore, create, and even problem solve in new environments. He suggests that parents provide a rich and varied growth environment for children, complete with social supports, and that they make ample room for the child to self-select and self-pace cognitive development, together with social awareness, a strong self-concept, and positive ways of socially interacting (Sigel, 1987).

funding is limited, however, many of these programs serviced less than half of the children who needed them. Thus, it is possible to compare the progress of infants and their families within the programs with others who are not enrolled. By and large, these programs have demonstrated a real difference. They show that an optimal environment is critical for the high-risk child to flourish and thrive (Horowitz, 1982; Korner, 1987).

One of the first major home-based, parent-oriented intervention programs for infants was developed by Ira Gordon in the late 1960s (Gordon, 1969). Working with poverty families in rural Florida, Gordon set the goal of enhancing the intellectual and personality development of the infants and the self-esteem of the parents. He trained women from the immediate community in child development, and they served as weekly home visitors. The women learned about the particular curriculum or activities to be offered at the appropriate developmental time for the infants they visited, and they learned interviewing skills. Those infants who participated in the weekly program on a regular basis for 2 or 3 years demonstrated significantly more advanced development over matched controls, at least as based on intelligence tests. Also, in follow-up measures, fewer children who had participated for at least 2 years were placed in special classes in public schools than children from the control group.

The second, somewhat similar, home-visitors' program was developed in the mid-1970s at Peabody Teachers' College in Tennessee. This set of programs, the Darcee Infant Programs, focused more on assisting the parent, especially the mother, than on the infant. Visitors were trained to participate as partners rather than as trainers. The goals of the program were to help the parents learn general coping skills for daily living, to increase awareness of the child's development, and to encourage certain behaviors in the child. Children in this program, too, performed well on intelligence tests, and the mothers showed improved teaching styles. On the whole, the mothers became less directive and more supportive (Gray, 1976).

Early intervention programs also have been established for children with more severe handicaps (Broussard, 1989; Sasserath, 1983). These programs offer a number of supports to both infant and family. Certainly, they help by demonstrating developmentally appropriate activities to capture the child's attention and to enhance learning. Also, they help parents to be aware of the milestones of development and sometimes the very small milestones of the severely delayed or retarded child. Beyond that, they help parents to be responsive to the child's needs and to the child's discoveries. But such programs must also meet the parents' needs. Parents should be supported in their adjustment to and parenting of a difficult or disabled child. Most experts on infant development would recommend a balanced program—even for the potentially gifted child. The National Association for the Education of Young Children (1988) recommends to parents and infant day-care workers that infants need:

1. A secure, predictable environment so that they can learn to anticipate events and to make choices.
2. An intimate, stable relationship with a warm, responsive care-giver who is sensitive to the child's interests, needs, and rhythms.
3. Respect for the infant as an active participant in the dialogue of living rather than a passive recipient of training.
4. Ample space to explore, objects to handle, and other children to observe, imitate, and with whom to socialize.

When all of these factors are in balance, the child has been provided with a nurturing environment. Such an environment encourages the development of skills and abilities, does not stifle the child's natural inquisitiveness, and provides a sense of active exploration with which to approach learning opportunities throughout life.

These fathers are attending a parent-training camp.

SUMMARY AND CONCLUSIONS

The notion of competencies developing during infancy is relatively new for those who study children to take. It is now recognized that predictable changes occur in the physical and cognitive development of infants and toddlers. However, there is also considerable variability in the timing of these behaviors—associated with varying levels of responsiveness and control of the environment and care-givers to which the child is exposed. There has been disagreement about the causes of such diversity. Arnold Gesell and his colleagues, for example, believed that maturation was the predominant cause, while Piaget saw it as a combination of maturity and experience.

Children grow in their abilities in all the behavioral domains as they grow toward adulthood. Each skill builds on previous actions and experiences, and, in turn, becomes the foundation on which future behaviors grow. Certain environmental factors influence this growth such as malnutrition. It becomes clear that infants require a well balanced diet during the first 2 years. This is essential since early malnutrition can permanently retard growth, particularly in the brain and central nervous system.

The development of sensory and perceptual competence also seems to consist of an interaction between maturation and experience. In general, infants are born with a sensory apparatus that is functional but in need of refinement. This refinement proceeds throughout the remainder of life. It now appears as though the senses of infants are preprogrammed to work together. Immediately after birth, infants begin to link sights, sounds, and touch. Eye-hand integration accelerates after 5 months, once the visually guided reach is achieved.

Cognitive development, according to Piaget and others, begins with the elaboration of sensorimotor schemes. Infants build their own intelligence by elaborating and modifying these schemes in the process of adaptation. Of special interest is the type of adaptation called a circular response. This is the means by which infants discover their bodies and use them to intentionally change the environment. Using this model, infants acquire a number of fundamental intellectual abilities during the first 2 years. These include concepts about the use of familiar objects, imitation, the understanding of object permanence, memory, and symbolic representation.

It is important to realize that while maturation and brain development are vital factors in the acquisition of these competencies, so too is the environment. The environment has a powerful effect on the development of infant competencies. An environment that is responsive to the child's skills and stimulation—timed slightly ahead of the child's developmental level—will accelerate a child's normal progress. Lack of stimulation and an unresponsive environment retard the child's sensorimotor and cognitive development.

➤ **KEY TERMS AND CONCEPTS**

adaptation	novelty paradigm	surprise paradigm	visual cliff
circular response	object permanence	symbolic representation	
cognition	pincer grasp	toddler	

➤ **SELF-TEST QUESTIONS**

1. Describe the developing competencies of the infant during the first 2 years.

2. List two types of malnutrition.

3. List the advantages of breast-feeding.

4. What are the nutritional needs of the infant during the first 2 years?

5. Discuss and compare the novelty paradigm and the surprise paradigm.

6. Discuss the relationship between brain development and sensory and motor experience during the first 2 years.

7. Describe Piaget's theory of cognitive development. What have been some of the major criticisms of this theory?

8. What do studies reveal about the long-term memory of the infant?

9. What is symbolic representation, and what is its significance for infant development?

10. Explain the effect of deprivation on infant development.

11. Describe two intervention programs that provide optimal stimulation for the infant.

➤ SUGGESTED READINGS

CAPLAN, F. *The first 12 months of life*. New York: Grosset & Dunlop, 1973. Written in a style appropriate for parents, this book supplies much practical information drawn from the Princeton Center for Infancy and Early Childhood. Contains monthly growth charts and many photographs.

CAPLAN, F. *The second 12 months of life*. New York: Grosset & Dunlop, 1979. A continuation of the above.

DITTMANN, L. L. (Ed.). *The infants we care for* (rev. ed.). Washington, DC: National Association for the Education of Young Children, 1984. This book is particularly addressed to infant day-care providers. It sensitively surveys the needs and capabilities of infants.

FIELD, T. *Infancy*. Cambridge, MA: Harvard University Press, 1990. Another title in the popular and highly readable Developing Child series. This book surveys the latest infant research and highlights the infant's surprising abilities. It also makes applications to current practical concerns, including day care, maternal drug use, and infants at risk.

HAZEL, R., BARBER, P. A., ROBERTS, S., BEHR, S. K., HELMSTETTER, E., & GUESS, D. *A community approach to an integrated service system for children with special needs*. Baltimore: Paul A. Brooks, 1990. Early intervention services for special needs children from birth to age 3 are now federally mandated. This manual serves as a helpful guide to community service agencies.

OLDS, S., & EIGER, M. S. *The complete book of breast-feeding* (rev. ed.). New York: Bantam, 1987. A well-written, helpful guide for parents and others who work with young infants.

SIEGLER, R. *Children's thinking*. 2nd ed. Englewood Cliffs, NJ: Prentice Hall, 1991. An excellent text that integrates the latest research with central themes from several theoretical perspectives. It presents a coherent picture of cognitive development from infancy to adolescence.

ZIGLER, E. F. & FRANK, M. (eds.). *The parental leave crisis: Toward a national policy*. New Haven, CT: Yale University Press, 1988. A source book for analyzing the problems of those who care for our children in the face of changing family patterns.

VIDEO CASE: TOUGHEST CHOICE

At Florida's New Life Dwelling Place, run by two nuns, mothers who have lost their children to foster care get them back for a six-month parenting course. If they pass, the mothers obtain permanent custody. But if they fail, they have to decide to either give their children up for adoption or return them to foster care.

Most of the mothers in the small program—New Life can take in twelve mothers and their children at a time—are themselves children of abusive parents. Explains one nun, "It's awfully hard to teach them to

cope with a lifetime of grief. Our goal is to begin to help them."

Winning back their children is not easy. The mothers are confined to the grounds except for one trip to the mall each week. No male visitors are allowed. They must attend classes every day. There they learn everything from self-esteem to basics like diapering and dressing their children.

One third of the children at New Life eventually go home with their mothers. For example, Kathy and her three children were at New Life for one year. The nuns decided that she is a good mother and the state welfare department, which has the final say in the matter, approved reunification.

In contrast, after a negative assessment, Betty decided to give her daughter Misty up for adoption. Although she felt as if part of herself was being ripped out, Betty wanted to give her daughter "another chance to live."

New Life is the only program of its kind in Florida supported by state funds. "Without such programs," says its director, "we'll pay later in delinquency, crime, and mental dysfunction."

CASE QUESTIONS

1. Do you believe that parents can be trained to be good parents? Why or why not?

2. Do you agree that we need more programs like New Life? Why or why not? Are there any dangers in such programs? Can you suggest any alternative programs?

3. Why do you think our society funds few programs like New Life?

*Where are you going, my little
one, little one...
Where are you going, my baby,
my own?
Turn around, and you're two...
Turn around, and you're
four...
Turn around and you're a
young girl
Going out of the door.*

INFANCY: DEVELOPING RELATIONSHIPS

CHAPTER OBJECTIVES

By the time you have finished this chapter, you should be able to do the following:

✔ Discuss attachment and separation behaviors.

✔ List six milestones in the emotional development of the infant within the first relationship.

✔ Discuss stranger anxiety and the theory that attempts to explain this behavior.

✔ Describe the effect on emotional development when a child does not form an attachment relationship or when a child's progress toward attachment is interrupted.

✔ Describe the factors that affect the quality of the relationship between the infant and the care-giver.

✔ Discuss adjustments that must be made by a family for a special needs infant.

✔ List different bonding disorders.

✔ Discuss the differences and similarities between father-child interaction and mother-child interaction.

✔ Describe infant emotional development in the context of a family system.

✔ List the problems of mothers who work outside the home.

✔ Compare the effect of different child-rearing patterns on the development of the infant.

Four-month-old Maria lay in her carrier on the sofa and observed the activities in the room. She was the focus of much attention. Her older sister would frequently come over and gently place her nose on her sister's and then give a big smile. The baby would broadly smile back—after an initial wide-eyed startle. Her mother was folding clothes, but often would approach her to stroke her face or quietly say something to her. She too was greeted with a smile. Even the dog was part of the action—he would wander over to give her a friendly sniff. Finally, in walked Dad. The smile she gave to him lit up the room, as well as his face. After greeting the others, he quickly picked her up to cuddle her.

Human infants are born into an environment rich with expectations, norms, attitudes, beliefs, values, traditions, and ways of doing things. A cultural heritage, complete with value systems and standards for social behavior, awaits them. Family members, of course, are already aware of their relationships to the infant, but newborns do not realize their relationships to those around them. At birth, Maria, described above, had no awareness of herself either as an individual or as an organism that can interact with the environment. She could not recognize herself in a mirror. She did not know that her hands were part of her body or that she was actually the agent responsible for her own movement. She had not developed trust or mistrust and had no expectations concerning those who care for her. She was not conscious of being female. Now she is beginning that process of mutual interaction that will lead to trust and a particular understanding of herself and others.

A dramatic series of changes takes place during the first 2 years of human life, as was mentioned in Chapter 6. Within that period, the unaware newborns become toddlers. They become aware of their environment and of the ways in which they can act upon it; aware of whether the world around them is responsive or unresponsive to their needs; aware that they can do some things for themselves or seek help when necessary. They become aware of various family relationships and of what is good and what is bad. They become conscious of being a girl or a boy and begin to learn how a sex designation imposes a certain style of behavior.

Babies come into the world with certain response styles. Some are more sensitive to light or to sudden loud sounds than others. Some react more quickly to discomfort than others. Some infants are fussy; some are placid; some are active, assertive, and vigorous. By age 2, the child has elaborated or restricted these basic response styles within a cultural context to produce what is called a *personality*.

In this chapter, we shall look at how the infant personality develops within relationships. We shall focus on primary, or first, relationships—those that establish patterns for the development of future relationships and for the acquisition of basic attitudes, expectations, and behavior.

ATTACHMENT AND SEPARATION

In the course of a lifetime, most individuals are involved in a number of significant interpersonal relationships. The first, and undoubtedly most influential, bond is the one that immediately begins to grow between the infant and the mother or care-giver. The bond becomes firmly established by the time the child reaches 8 or 9 months of age. Since the mid-1960s, many psychologists have applied the term **attachment** to the process of development of this first relationship. It is characterized by strong interdependence, intense mutual feelings, and vital emotional ties.

Attachments, as well as losses or separations, actually occur and affect us throughout life. The infant's first attachment, however, goes through several phases that lay the groundwork for future development. The process involves a characteristic series of events as the infant progresses from earliest awareness to the development of trust and confidence in the care-giver. Later, an equally characteristic sequence of events takes place in reaction to the loss of the relationship. These first responses to attachment and loss lay the foundation for later relationships, whether with peers, relatives, other adults, spouses, or lovers.

IMPRINTING AND ATTACHMENT BEHAVIORS

The psychologist Mary Ainsworth (1983) defines "attachment behaviors" as those that primarily promote nearness to a specific person to whom the infant is attached. These include signaling behavior (crying, smiling, vocalizing), orienting behavior (looking), movements relating to another person (following, approaching), and active physical contact behavior (clambering up, embracing, clinging).

attachment The bond that develops between a child and another individual as a result of a long-term relationship. The infant's first bond is usually characterized by strong interdependence, intense mutual feelings, and vital emotional ties.

These behaviors indicate attachment only when they are specifically directed toward one or two care-givers, rather than toward human beings in general.

Ainsworth describes these behaviors as the criteria of attachment since without them attachment tends to have difficulty establishing itself. Consider, for example, how difficult it would be to develop the sense of emotional closeness to an infant who constantly stiff-armed the care-giver when she was picked up. Or what if an infant engaged in no smiling or vocalizing in response to the care-giver's appearance? Ainsworth and others (1979) have found that when a disability such as blindness occurs—or when the baby finds touch aversive—bonding between that infant and the care-giver is at risk. Such situations may require special intervention in which pediatric psychologists or psychiatrists suggest alternate ways of developing the first relationships. For example, psychiatrist Stanley Greenspan, whose work we will discuss later in this chapter, has written extensively on the high-risk care-giver/infant pairs he has assisted in developing these crucial first relationships (Greenspan & Greenspan, 1985).

The important point is that the infant must *act* in order for attachment to take place. The infant's initial behavior seems to invite nurturing responses from the care-giver. She (or he) not only feeds, diapers, and generally cares for the infant's physical needs, but also communicates with the baby by talking, smiling, touching, and nuzzling. *The attachment process, then, is a mutual system.* The baby's behavior prompts the care-giver to act in certain ways, and the care-giver's actions set off responses in the baby.

Why does attachment occur? Is it a conditioned response, or is there an innate need to establish a relationship? For a long while, developmental psychologists thought that babies formed attachments to their care-givers only because they fulfilled the babies' primary needs. It was thought that children learned to associate the care-giver's nearness with the reduction of primary drives, such as hunger (Sears, 1963). Much of this early stance derives from Freud's theory, which stated that there was nothing innate in a child's attachment drive. Attachment was merely determined by the child's needs being gratified by a care-giver. Through this process the infant formed a permanent, positive inner image of the mother which he could rely on during short absences. In this process, the infant was a passive recipient of care-giver behaviors. Research—conducted primarily with animals—now indicates that this is only a small part of the situation.

We can probably better understand infants' first relationships with their care-givers if we look at some of the relationships that other animals have with their mothers. This relationship has been studied most extensively in ducks and geese.

IMPRINTING **Imprinting** refers to the process by which newly hatched birds form a relatively permanent bond with the parent in the period immediately following birth. More than 40 years ago, Konrad Lorenz, an Austrian zoologist, observed that goslings began to follow their mother almost immediately after hatching. This bond between goslings and parent was important in helping the mother protect and train her offspring. Interestingly enough, Dr. Lorenz also found that orphaned greylag goslings nurtured by him during their first 24 hours after hatching—the *critical period* for imprinting—developed a pattern of following *him*, not another goose. This pattern was relatively permanent—and sometimes annoyingly persistent. Some of Lorenz's greylag geese much preferred to spend the night in his bedroom than on the banks of the Danube (Lorenz, 1952).

Orphaned goslings nurtured by Konrad Lorenz during the critical imprinting period follow him as if he were their real mother.

The critical period for imprinting occurs after hatching, when the gosling is strong enough to get up and move around, but before it has developed a strong fear of large moving objects. If imprinting is delayed, the gosling will either fear the model parent or simply give up and grow limp, tired, and listless.

Baby birds may be imprinted to objects that differ greatly from the mother. In a laboratory setting, for example, ducks have been imprinted to duck decoys, flashing lights, windup toys, milk bottles, and even to a checkerboard wall (Hess, 1972). The strength of this bond varies, and seems to depend on the activity of the duckling and the type of stimulus. The object should move enough to require some, but not too much, exercise by the baby bird, and, if possible, the stimulus should respond with some kind of sound—like clucking, peeping, or humming.

Ethologists who study imprinting are concerned with distinguishing the types of stimuli necessary to *trigger* or *release* imprinting behaviors. A large moving object may be all that is necessary to release the behaviors of following and vocalizing and, thereby, to begin the process of imprinting. In a natural setting, this triggering or releasing process is mutual. The mother's clucking releases peeping, visual scanning, and following behaviors in the duckling. Similarly, the duckling's peeping triggers the mother's vocalizations (Hess, 1972).

Researchers disagree about the similarities and differences between imprinting on birds and bonding behavior in humans. There is no clear evidence that a "critical period" exists for human bonding. As we saw in Chapter 5, parents and infants may be particularly receptive to bonding in the first few days after birth, but this is hardly a critical period. On the other hand, it is clearly necessary for human infants to establish some kind of relationship with one or more major care-givers within the first 8 months or so in order for adequate personality development to occur. What we know about imprinting in birds provides promising parallels to human development, but they are not identical.

ATTACHMENT IN MONKEYS An important series of studies was done by Harry Harlow (1959) on social deprivation in monkeys. Because monkeys have closer biological ties to humans than birds have, studies of their social development are more relevant to humans than studies of goslings. An important series of observations began somewhat accidentally when Harlow was studying learning and conceptual development in monkeys. When he was setting up his laboratory conditions, he decided that it would be best to rear each young monkey without its mother in order to control the total learning environment. The mother was an uncontrolled variable. She taught the baby certain skills, and she rewarded and punished certain behaviors. She also served as a model for the baby to imitate. Harlow wanted to get at the basic process of learning, and to do this, he felt it necessary to remove the mother from the cage. In doing so, however, he stumbled upon a new and more exciting area of study.

Separation from the mother had a disastrous effect on the young monkeys. Some died. Others were frightened, irritable, and reluctant to eat or play. Obviously, the monkeys required something more than regular feeding to thrive and develop. Harlow experimented with surrogate monkey mothers, wire forms designed to hold a bottle (Harlow & Harlow, 1962). Some of the surrogates were covered with soft cloth while others were bare wire. Regardless of which surrogate supplied the food, all the young monkeys showed a distinct preference for the cloth form, clinging and vocalizing to it, especially when frightened. The infant monkeys developed bonds with their cloth surrogates and would not

imprinting The instinctual learning process by which newly hatched birds form a relatively permanent bond with the parent in a few hours or days.

In Harlow's studies of attachment, young monkeys showed a distinct preference for the cloth-covered surrogate mother over the wire mother regardless of which one supplied food.

accept substitutes. The object they looked at and clung to was the focus of their psychological attachment, regardless of the food source.

Monkeys with cloth surrogates did not exhibit the extremely fearful, neurotic behavior of the completely orphaned monkeys, but they failed to develop normally nonetheless. As adults, they had difficulty establishing peer relationships and engaging in normal sexual activity. They were poor parents to their own offspring as well, despite Harlow's attempt at "psychotherapy"—he put them with "normal" monkeys. Subsequent research found that the improved social interactions of the surrogate-raised monkeys were enhanced by having a moving surrogate, for example, a cloth covered bleach bottle that swung up and down and sideways. Such movement may foster the growth of the cerebellum, a portion of the brain that appears to be involved in emotional development.

Further studies in this series have indicated that peer contact among infant monkeys at least partially makes up for the deprivation of the infant-adult attachment bond (Coster, 1972). Infant monkeys who are raised with surrogate mothers and who have adequate opportunity to play with other such infant monkeys develop reasonably normal social behavior. Thus, mutually responsive social interaction is crucial for normal monkey development. One would suspect that it is true for humans, too, because they are also a social species! In fact, research on twins and orphaned children seems to support this contention. These children often become attached to each other in a manner that may even preclude attachment to adults.

THE ETHOLOGY OF HUMAN ATTACHMENT   Ethological theory, which looks at the similarity between behaviors across species, recognizes that babies contribute actively to the ties established with their parents. Ethologists assume that many of the behaviors that have evolved over time for various species, have done so because they had *survival value*. John Bowlby (1973), who was originally trained as a psychoanalyst, was intrigued by Lorenz's research on imprinting. He believed that human babies were also born with preprogrammed behaviors that functioned to keep parents close by. This would therefore increase the probability of the infant being protected from danger.

Bowlby proposed that attachment was based on built-in behaviors in *both* the infant and caretaker. He believed that attachment was initiated by these preprogrammed behaviors but maintained by pleasurable environmental events, such as physical closeness of the mother and child, the reduction of hunger, and comfort. In this way, his theory combines elements of both heredity and the environment in the development and maintenance of attachment.

Bowlby worked with Mary Ainsworth (1973; 1978) to develop this theory. Ainsworth and Bowlby proposed that the development of attachment went through four phases or periods:

1. *The Presocial or Preattachment Phase*—birth to 6 weeks. During this time, the infant was engaging in those attachment behaviors also described by Ainsworth—gazing, babbling, clinging, smiling, and grasping at the adult. Once these signals are responded to, the baby in effect encourages the adult to remain close to him by continuing to emit those behaviors that serve to "rope the adult in." At this age, such behaviors are directed at all adults even though the infant recognizes the mother's voice, smell, and manner. Since infants at this age are indiscriminate, this phase is not believed by

Bowlby to be true attachment—although many parents believe the behaviors of their infants are directed only at them.

2. *The Social or Attachment-in-the-Making Phase*—6 weeks to 6 to 8 months. During this phase the infant begins to discriminate particular people. The infant learns to trust in the environment and people in it. Along with this comes the expectation that these people will respond to the infant's needs. Generally during this phase, even though infants can distinguish their mother by a variety of means, and are beginning to respond differentially to her, they still will not cry when separated from her.

3. *The Clear-Cut Attachment Phase*—6 to 8 months to 2 years. During this phase, the child will attempt to keep those people whom he has discriminated in proximity or closeness. True attachment to a care-giver is evident in the **stranger, or separation anxiety,** which many infants exhibit when the care-giver leaves. Separation anxiety appears to be a universal phenomenon, occurring around 6 months of age and increasing until about 15 months. This parallels the time in cognitive development when object permanence develops. It appears as though infants who have not yet achieved object permanence fail to show separation anxiety.

This phase is typified by the older infant and toddler actively trying to keep their mother close. They will climb to follow her, turn in a jolly jumper as she moves from room to room, and cry when she leaves. Often infants use their mothers as *secure bases* from which to launch their explorations. Mothers become the emotional support to which they return.

4. *The Reciprocal Relationship or Goal-Corrected System*—18 months to 2 years (and continuing from that time onward). Once the child's cognitive level allows her to understand why mother or father leaves, what factors influence it, and that they will certainly return, the final phase of attachment begins. In this phase, the caregiver and child mutually work out what is appropriate separation behavior and what is not. The mother, for example, indicates that temper tantrums are inappropriate, but she works with her child to create a ritual that eases the separation. A mother might bathe her child and cuddle while reading a story prior to her leaving. A father may have a quiet talk and work a puzzle, and so forth.

Bowlby and Ainsworth believe that the nature of the parent-child interaction that emerges from the development of attachment in the first 2 years of life forms the basis for all future relationships. The new friendships in school, the teen peer structures and the intimate bonding to a spouse all bear the marks of this first relationship between parent and child.

EMOTIONAL DEVELOPMENT IN THE FIRST RELATIONSHIP

As we have seen, in human infants, attachment occurs very gradually. Children go through phases of emotional and social growth that result in the firm establishment of this first relationship. Stanley and Nancy Greenspan (1985), drawing on the observations and research of many others including Ainsworth and Bowlby,

stranger, or separation, anxiety An infant's fear of strangers or of being separated from the caregiver. Both occur in the second half of the first year and indicate, in part, a new cognitive ability to detect and respond to differences in the environment.

describe six milestones in the emotional development of the infant within the first relationship.

1. *Self-Regulation and Interest in the World*—birth to 3 months. In the early weeks, the infant seeks to feel regulated and calm, but at the same time, to use all of his senses and experience the world. The infant seeks a balance between over- and understimulation. Gradually, infants become increasingly socially responsive. Human infants use signaling and orienting behavior—crying, vocalizing, visual following—to establish contact. Infants at this stage, as Ainsworth indicated, do not discriminate between primary care-givers and other people, and they react to everyone in much the same way.

2. *Falling in Love*—2 to 7 months. At 2 months, self-regulated infants become more alert to the world around them. They recognize familiar figures and direct their attention increasingly toward significant care-givers rather than strangers. Infants at this time find the human world enticing, pleasurable, and exciting—and show it. They smile in eagerness and respond with their whole body.

3. *Developing Intentional Communication*—3 to 10 months. This milestone overlaps considerably with the last. Infants now, however, begin to develop a dialogue. The mother and the baby initiate their own playful sequences of communication, of looking at each other, of playing short games, and taking rests. Fathers and babies, and siblings and babies, do this as well.

4. *The Emergence of an Organized Sense of Self*—9 to 18 months. One-year-old infants can do more things for themselves and can take a more active role in the emotional partnership with their mother and father. Infants at this time can signal their needs much more effectively and precisely. They begin to communicate with words. Sometime around 16 to 18 months, they make the startling discovery that they are the baby in the mirror! If there is a red

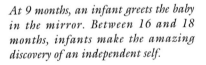

At 9 months, an infant greets the baby in the mirror. Between 16 and 18 months, infants make the amazing discovery of an independent self.

spot on the nose of the baby in the mirror, the infant points to his own nose and looks coy or embarrassed. Before this time, there has emerged a number of emotions, such as anger, sadness, and happiness. But now, when infants can distinguish between themselves and the rest of the social world, they begin to develop the social emotions of pride, guilt, and embarrassment, for example. The infant now recognizes an independent self.

5. *Creating Emotional Ideas*—18 to 36 months. During this period, the infant is able to symbolize, pretend, and form images in his head of people and things. He can learn about the social world through make-believe and pretend play. Now that he has a separate sense of self, he can feel the ambivalent needs of autonomy yet dependency.

6. *Emotional Thinking: The Basis for Fantasy, Reality, and Self-Esteem*—30 to 48 months. Often, the give-and-take of close relationships with significant people now settles into more of a partnership. The young child can discern what the care-giver expects of him, and then try to modify his behavior to meet those expectations and thus achieve his own goals.

STRANGER ANXIETY

One of the developmental landmarks of the attachment relationship, as previously indicated, is the appearance of both stranger anxiety and separation anxiety. Pediatricians and psychologists often make no distinction between the two and refer to both as "7-months anxiety," because they often appear rather suddenly at just about 7 months. Babies who have been smiling, welcoming, friendly, and accepting suddenly become more shy and fearful in the presence of strangers. They become extremely upset at the prospect of being left alone in a strange place, even for a minute. No traumatic event, sudden separation, or frightening encounter is necessary. Children at this stage of attachment cry and cling to their caregivers; they only cautiously turn around to explore a stranger. Stranger anxiety continues through the rest of the first year and much of the second year, with varying degrees of intensity.

THE DISCREPANCY HYPOTHESIS If no event is needed to bring on such anxiety, why does it first occur, almost without fail, in most children at about the same age? Most psychologists see stranger and separation anxieties as a sign of intellectual development in infants. As infant cognitive processes mature, they develop schemes for the familiar and notice anything that is new and strange. They can distinguish care-givers from strangers, and they become keenly aware of the absence of the primary care-giver. When they detect a departure from the known or the expected, they experience anxiety (Ainsworth et al., 1978); this is known as the **discrepancy hypothesis.**

The anxiety is based on the infant's new awareness that the care-giver's presence coincides with safety. Things seem secure with familiar care-givers around, but uncertain when they are not. Thus, anxiety at 7 months can be viewed as a demonstration of the baby's more complex and sophisticated expectations. The infant's anxiety and distress vary a bit, based on a number of factors. Most infants are more distressed if the stranger is a male or if he towers over them. They are less distressed if the mother is close by or if the stranger is a child or a midget (Boccia & Campos, 1989).

Following the development of a separate sense of self infants develop ambivalent needs of autonomy and dependency.

discrepancy hypothesis A cognition theory according to which infants acquire, at around 7 months, schemes for familiar objects. When a new image or object is presented that differs from the old, the child experiences uncertainty and anxiety.

At about 7 months, infants become shy and fearful in the presence of strangers. The stranger anxiety is a landmark in the infant's social development.

Some psychologists believe that, at least by 9 months, the anxiety reaction is complicated by the learning that has already occurred. Bronson (1978) found that 9-month-old babies sometimes cry when they first notice a stranger, and even before the stranger has gotten close. This implies that children may have learned from negative experiences with strangers and may be anticipating another disturbing encounter. But the learning may be more subtle than that. Perhaps the mother signals her baby by her facial expression or tone of voice. In one study, mothers of 8- to 9-month-old babies were carefully trained to knit their eyebrows, widen their eyes, pull down their lips, and demonstrate worry on their faces while greeting the stranger with a worried "Hello." The control group was trained to demonstrate a pleased, smiling face, and a cheery "Hello" to the stranger. As predicted, these 8- to 9-month-old infants picked up their mother's signals quite accurately. Infants whose mothers posed joy were more positive toward the stranger, smiled more, and cried less when they were picked up by the stranger than did those infants whose mothers displayed worry (Boccia & Campos, 1989). This kind of emotional signaling by the mother is called *social referencing.*

It is likely, then, that by the time infants are 1 year old, stranger and separation anxiety are influenced both by their ability to differentiate between the familiar and the strange, and by their past experiences with strangers and with their mother's reactions to strangers. Parents can assist their infants and toddlers in adjusting to strangers by their own emotional reaction and by giving the children time to get to know the strangers (Feiring, Lewis, & Starr, 1984).

Stranger anxiety is a milestone in the attachment process and in social development (Bretherton & Waters, 1985). Once children learn to identify the care-giver as a source of comfort and security, they feel free to explore new objects in the care-giver's reassuring presence. Children who fail to explore, preferring to hover near their mothers, may not feel a secure attachment and thus miss out on new learning. On the other hand, some infants are too readily comforted by strangers or show wariness when returned to their mothers. This is a second kind of social maladjustment; it indicates uncertainty about the care-giver's ability to support the infant (Sroufe & Fleeson, 1986). These children are likely to suffer a more pervasive and unresolved anxiety that interferes with further development.

SEPARATION AND LOSS

If, as was discussed, the attachment relationship is an essential part of normal development—and if that relationship progresses through a series of predictable, nearly universal stages—what happens to the child who does not have such a relationship or whose progress toward attachment is interrupted? What happens to the child who is brought up in an orphanage and is handled by numerous, changing care-givers during the first few years? What happens to the infant who must spend a prolonged period in a hospital? And what about the child who has begun to establish a relationship and is suddenly separated from the care-giver?

In Chapter 6, we saw that prolonged institutionalization retards the development of cognitive and sensorimotor competencies in infants. Social deprivation has an even more devastating effect on the young child's emotional development. Infants who are cared for by continuously changing care-givers who meet only their most basic physical needs are unable to develop an attachment relationship. The mutual responses between child and primary care-giver do not occur consistently; the social interaction that permits expression of emotion is missing (Bowlby, 1973, 1980, 1988). The result is profound apathy, withdrawal, and generally depressed functioning, which in time lead to inadequate personality development.

The child who has formed a full attachment relationship responds quite differently to separation from the primary care-giver than does the child who has never established such a relationship. The "attached" child goes through a series of rather dramatic reactions to both brief and prolonged separation.

John Bowlby (1973) divides the separation reaction of hospitalized fully attached toddlers into three stages: *protest, despair,* and *detachment.* During the protest stage, children refuse to accept separation from the attachment figure. They may cry, scream, kick, bang their heads against their beds, and refuse to respond at all to anyone else who tries to care for them.

During the second stage, which may come a few hours or even several days after the initial reaction, the children appear to lose all hope. They withdraw and become very quiet. If they cry, they do so in a monotonous and despairing tone, rather than with the anger they exhibited earlier.

Eventually, separated children begin to accept attention from the people around them and appear recovered from their misery. If they are visited by the primary care-giver, they react with detachment or even disinterest.

> A child living in an institution or hospital who has reached this state will no longer be upset when nurses change or leave. He will cease to show feelings when his parents come and go on visiting day; and it may cause them pain when they realize that, although he has an avid interest in the presents they bring, he has little interest in them as social people. He will appear cheerful and adapted to his unusual situation and apparently easy and unafraid of anyone. But this sociability is superficial: he appears no longer to care for anyone. (Bowlby, 1960, p. 143)

When faced with the first two stages of a child's separation reaction, well-meaning adults often try to subdue what they see as inappropriate behavior. But such adults underestimate the complexity of young children's reactions. These children need patient understanding and warm nurturance to help weather the stress. In fact, the child's response to separation is a prototype of behavior later in life. It foreshadows the turmoil that adolescents go through over the loss of a first love and the grief that adults experience upon the death of a spouse or a child. Both young children and adults need to "work through" these emotional reactions in order to come to terms with the inevitable separations that occur throughout life. Only if they are allowed to express these feelings can children reach a level of detachment that will permit them to survive emotionally in their new situation and eventually form new attachments.

PATTERNS OF EARLY RELATIONSHIPS

Most children, in most cultures, form a basic attachment within the first year of life. Infants all over the world show similar responses to their social environments; gradually, they establish an attachment relationship with the specific care-

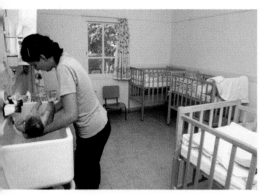

In most cultures children form a basic attachment within the first year of life, but the intensity of bonding and anxiety varies according to specific child-rearing practices. Children reared in a kibbutz (left) are less attached to their care-givers than are children in other cultures who spend much of their infancy strapped to their mother's back.

giver. Although the sequence of development of this first relationship occurs fairly consistently across cultures, the details of it vary dramatically depending upon the personality of the parents, their child-rearing practices, and the unique contribution of the child.

THE QUALITY OF THE RELATIONSHIP

THE SECURELY ATTACHED INFANT How do we judge the quality of the relationship that develops between the infant and the primary care-giver? Look back at the box on "Measuring Attachment" in Chapter 2 for the details of one of the most popular techniques, called the Strange Situation Test, which is also summarized in Table 7–1. There are, of course, other ways to measure the quality of the infant-caretaker relationship. There are rating scales and other types of observation. Yet, the Strange Situation Test is used more often than any other. We should note, however, that while many researchers have used the Strange Situation Test to measure attachment, there have been differences in the classifications of attachment they have derived from it. In general, while researchers agree that there is a continuum of attachment behaviors ranging from secure attachment to failure to attach, different labels may be used to describe these behaviors.

Sroufe and his colleagues measured one group of babies at 12 and 18 months, carefully dividing them into three categories: *securely attached, avoidant,* and *ambivalent* (Sroufe, 1977). Over the years, they followed these babies as they grew to elementary school children. Even at age 2, the differences between the securely attached infants and the others were dramatic. Those children with

TABLE 7–1 Ainsworth's Strange Situation Paradigm[1]

EPISODE	EVENTS	VARIABLES OBSERVED
1	Experimenter introduces parents and baby to playroom and then leaves.	
2	Parent is seated while baby plays with toys.	Parent as a secure base.
3	Stranger enters, seats self, and talks to parent.	Reaction to unfamiliar adult.
4	Parent leaves. Stranger responds to baby, and offers comfort if upset.	Separation anxiety.
5	Parent returns, greets baby and offers comfort if needed. Stranger leaves.	Reaction to reunion.
6	Parent leaves room; baby is alone.	Separation anxiety.
7	Stranger enters and offers comfort.	Ability to be soothed by stranger.
8	Parent returns, greets baby, offers comfort if needed. Tries to reinterest baby in toys.	Reaction to reunion.

Source: Ainsworth et al., 1978.

[1]While each episode lasts about 3 minutes, the separation episodes may be cut short if the baby becomes too distressed.

strong attachment relationships at 18 months had become more enthusiastic, persistent, and cooperative. By age 2, they were also more effective in coping with tools and in peer interactions than were the children in the other two categories. They spontaneously invented more imaginative and symbolic play than the others. These differences still existed when the children were 5 years old (Arend, Gore, & Sroufe, 1979). Later, in elementary school, children who were securely attached as toddlers persisted in their work longer, were more eager to learn new skills, and had more highly developed social skills both with adults and peers (Bretherton & Waters, 1985).

Numerous other studies, some with different methodologies, have quite similar findings (Belsky & Rovine, 1990). It seems that the quality of the relationship between care-giver and infant between 6 and 18 months provides the foundation for most aspects of child development. Securely attached toddlers and preschoolers do simple things, like explore playrooms, better than those children who are not securely attached. They maneuver around the furniture, find their way to interesting toys, and position themselves comfortably for appropriate play with greater ease than those children who have attachment problems (Cassidy, 1986). Also, securely attached 3-year-olds are better-liked by their peers in the nursery school (Jacobson & Wille, 1986).

A warm, supportive relationship between care-giver and infant, with ample verbal interaction, leads to higher levels of cognitive competence and greater social skills (Olson, Bates & Bayles, 1984). It supports active exploration and an early mastery of object play and the social environment. The care-giver/infant attachment, therefore, lays the foundation for future development.

RESPONSIVENESS In her studies of children in Uganda, Ainsworth (1967) found that children who showed the strongest attachment behavior had a highly responsive relationship with their mothers. Back in the United States, she reported that securely attached 1-year-olds had mothers who were more responsive to their cries, more affectionate, more tender, less inept in close bodily contact, and more likely than mothers of insecure 1-year-olds to synchronize their rate of feeding and their play behavior with the baby's own pace (Ainsworth et al., 1978). Since that time, researchers consistently found that infants who were securely attached at age 1 had mothers who were more responsive to their physical needs, their signals of distress, and their attempts to communicate with facial expressions or vocalization (Bornstein, 1989).

Does this mean that a mother must respond to every little thing her infant does? Of course not. Even highly responsive mothers do not respond 100 percent of the time. Bornstein and Tamis-Lemonda (1989) find that mothers' responsiveness is somewhat different depending on whether the infant is in distress or not. When infants are in distress, the average mother responds about 75 percent of the time quite quickly. The majority of mothers are quite consistent in responding to their infants' cries. A small minority, however, are quite unresponsive. In contrast, mothers respond quite differently to bids for attention, vocalization, and smiling. Some mothers respond as rarely as 5 percent of the time to such cues, whereas others respond as often as 50 percent of the time. What is more, mothers respond in a different way—some with physical play, others with vocal imitation, and still others with touching, playing, patting, and feeding. These researchers and others find that mothers who are more highly responsive to their infants' cues, both in the first 6 months and later, tend not only to have more securely attached infants but also to have more cognitively advanced infants.

A warm supportive relationship established in infancy between care-giver and child offers the child a firm base from which to learn competencies.

Clarke-Stewart and Nevey (1981) also studied the interactions of mothers and their children who were either securely or insecurely attached. They noticed that mothers who were more verbally responsive and attentive to their children tended to have children who were more autonomous and communicative. Interactions between the securely attached infant and mother were gentler and warmer, and these interactions drew more compliant and cooperative behavior from the infant (Londerville & Main, 1981). Source and Emde (1981) compared the interactions of mothers who were in a room with their infants and reading with those mothers who were not reading. They reported that the infants whose mothers were reading received less attention and exhibited less pleasure and less exploration of the room; the nonreading mothers gave their infants more sensitive responses as they explored the room. They concluded that the mothers' presence is not enough—the mothers must also be emotionally open to the children.

A MUTUAL DIALOGUE   In studying attachment, it is not enough to look at just the mother's behavior. Infants, too, contribute to the interaction. The behaviors of both evolve gradually, one responding to the other. This emphasis on mutual influence between mother and infant represents a new conceptual approach. Yet, clearly, an infant who is sociable and derives pleasure in close proximal contact can encourage even the most tentative new mother. In contrast, a fussy and irritable baby interrupts a caretaker's best efforts at soothing or verbal give-and-take (Belsky et al., 1984; Lewis & Feiring, 1989).

Schaffer (1977) has investigated the way in which **mutuality,** or interactive **synchrony,** between infant and care-giver is achieved. He observed that most infant behavior followed an alternating on-off pattern—for instance, while visually exploring new objects, babies stared and then looked away. Some care-givers responded to these patterns with more skill than others did. Films of mothers face to face with their 3-month-old infants revealed a pattern of mutual approach and withdrawal; they took turns looking and turning, touching and responding, vocalizing and answering.

It is this rare kind of synchrony between infant and care-giver during the first few months that predicts a secure relationship at age 1 and also more sophisticated patterns of mutual communication at that time (Isabella, Belsky, & Von Eye, 1989).

Care-givers do not merely respond to the behavioral rhythms of the child. They also change the pace and nature of the dialogue with a variety of techniques: introducing a new object, imitating and elaborating on the infant's sounds or actions, or making it easier for the child to reach something of interest. By monitoring the baby's responses, care-givers gradually learn when the child is most receptive to new cues from them. No matter which technique is used, the mutual process takes many months to develop fully.

Some techniques seem to be especially effective in developing synchrony (Field, 1977; Paulby, 1977). Field compared infant reactions to three different maternal behaviors: the mother's spontaneous behavior, her deliberate attempts to catch and hold the child's attention, and her imitation of the child. The infants responded most to the imitations, perhaps because of the slowed-down, exaggerated nature of imitative action. The closer the similarity between maternal and infant behavior, the less discrepancy babies have to deal with, and the more attentive they will be. Furthermore, each mother carefully observed her infant's cutoff,

mutuality (synchrony) The pattern of interchange between care-giver and infant in which each responds to and influences the other's movements and rhythms.

or gaze-away, point. Field suggested that respecting the child's need for a pause is one of the earliest rules of "conversation" that a care-giver must learn.

Some parents frequently overstimulate their infant despite signals from the baby that should indicate this. Babies turn away, hide their heads, close their eyes, and in general try to get a few minutes of pause. Some parents fail to stop the overstimulation until the child actually cries. Other parents frequently understimulate their infant. They ignore their baby's smiles and babbling or other bids for attention. An infant whose cues for attention are ignored will soon give up trying unless he or she really needs it, and then the child is liable to cry. Often, parents have mixed patterns of sensitivity. Sometimes they overstimulate, sometimes they understimulate, and sometimes they misidentify the cues or signals from the infant. This tends to be particularly true of abusive mothers (Kropp & Haynes, 1987), of depressed mothers (Field, 1986), of some adolescent mothers (Lamb, 1987), and of mothers whose temperament is considerably different from that of the infant's (Weber, Levitt, & Clark, 1986).

The behavior of a very sensitive and responsive mother changes as the infant grows older (Crockenberg & McCluskey, 1986). Indeed, some have used the word "scaffolding" to describe the mother's or father's role in progressively structuring the parent-child interaction (Ratner & Bruner, 1978; Vandel & Wilson, 1987). That is, the parents provide the framework around which they and their infant interact. They pick specific games like imitation or peek-a-boo. As the child becomes older, the game becomes more sophisticated. Thus, early turn-taking, games, and free play gradually become structured by the parent. The child learns increasingly complex rules of social interaction—rules of pacing and give-and-take, rules of observing and imitating, how to maintain the game, and so forth.

Early mutuality and signaling lay the foundation for long-standing patterns of interaction. This has been illustrated in studies of maternal responses to crying.

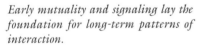

Early mutuality and signaling lay the foundation for long-term patterns of interaction.

Mothers who respond promptly and consistently to infant crying in the first few months are most likely to have infants who cry less by the end of the first year. A quick response gives babies confidence in the effectiveness of their communications and encourages them to develop other ways of signaling their mothers (Bell & Ainsworth, 1972). When maternal care is inconsistent, infants fail to develop confidence and become either insistent or less responsive. Mutuality blossoms into a variety of behaviors in the second year of life. Some toddlers exhibit spontaneous sharing behavior, both with parents and with other children—showing a new toy, placing it in someone's lap, or using it to invite another child to play. Such behavior indicates toddlers' interests in the properties of toys, their delight in sharing, and their realization that others can see the same things that they see.

Children apply skills acquired in the mother-child dialogue to a wider social context. This represents an important developmental stage and suggests that some toddlers are not as egocentric as Piaget believed (Eisenberg, 1989).

MULTIPLE ATTACHMENTS OR EXCLUSIVITY Infants who have a relatively exclusive relationship with a parent or care-giver tend to exhibit intense stranger and separation anxieties. They also show these anxieties at an earlier age than do infants whose relationship with the care-giver has not been that exclusive (Ainsworth, 1967). A child who is constantly with the parent, sleeps in the same room at night, and is carried in a sling on the parent's back during the day experiences a dramatic and intense separation reaction. On the other hand, the child who has had a number of different care-givers from birth tends to accept strangers or separation with far less anxiety (Maccoby & Feldman, 1972).

A question often asked is, "Is the development of attachment impaired if care is distributed among a number of caretakers as well as parents?" This is especially crucial when we consider that there are over 5.5 million children yearly being cared for in day-care centers. If the quantity of attachment is crucial, then children with less time with their parents will suffer—or so it would appear. Research, however, indicates that day care and multiple care-givers may have no adverse effects on attachment. Rather these children often form multiple attachments (Clarke-Stewart & Fein, 1983; Welles-Nystrom, 1988). For example, infants attach not only to mothers, but also to fathers, siblings and peers.

It would appear that the infant's social network is an amazingly complex and diverse one. The power of peers as attachment figures was revealed in a famous study by Anna Freud (Freud & Dann, 1951) of six German-Jewish orphans, who were separated from their parents at an early age during World War II. They were placed in a country home at Bulldog Banks, England, which had been transformed into a nursery for war children. This was their first experience in a small, intimate setting; previously they had been in larger institutions.

Due to their past experiences, the children were either hostile or ignoring toward their adult care-givers, but were solicitous and concerned in their behavior toward each other. For example, a care-giver had accidentally knocked over one of the smaller children. Two of the other children threw bricks at the care-giver and called her names. Moreover, the children resisted being separated from each other, even if for special treats such as pony rides. The children were even able to overcome frightening situations to help each other.

On the beach in Brighton, Ruth throws pebbles into the water. Peter is afraid of waves and does not dare to approach them. In spite of his fear, he suddenly rushes to Ruth, calling out: "Water coming, water coming," and drags her back to safety. (Freud & Dann, 1951, pp. 150–168)

When toddlers first attend a day-care program, they often experience considerable separation distress. This seems to be particularly true when they are between 15 and 18 months old. But, even at this vulnerable age, some toddlers adjust more readily than others. Toddlers who have had an exclusive relationship with only one person have an especially difficult time. Conversely, those who have had too many separations and too many care-givers also experience a good deal of separation distress. Adjustment is easiest for toddlers who have had some experience with other caregivers and who have had a moderate degree of separation experience with several opportunities for reuniting (Jacobson & Wille, 1984).

THE INFANT WITH SPECIAL NEEDS

Infants with special needs frequently cause severe stresses in mutuality. Blind infants cannot search caregivers' faces or smile back. Deaf babies may appear to be disobedient. Infants with other severe handicaps cannot respond to signals as normal babies do. Obvious handicaps that are evident from birth, such as Down syndrome and cerebral palsy, are certain to create serious adjustment problems for all family members. Until recently, we too often ignored the way that an infant affects a care-giver and concentrated instead on the impact of the care-giver's behavior on the child. In the past decade, researchers have begun to devote more attention to the former situation. When we study how infants' behaviors influence the adults around them, we begin to notice all the subtle means by which these small people help in maintaining the fundamental links that seem so essential to their later socialization.

VISUALLY-IMPAIRED INFANTS   Visual communication between caregiver and child is usually a prominent element in the establishment of attachment relationships. Care-givers depend heavily on subtle responses from their infants—looking back, smiling, and visually following—to maintain and support their own behavior. Care-givers often feel, unconsciously, that a blind infant is unresponsive. It is essential for both that they establish a mutually intelligible communication system that overcomes this disability.

In early life, one of the normal infant's best developed resources for learning is the visual-perceptual system. Babies look at and visually follow everything new and have distinct preferences. They particularly like to look at human faces. Blind infants, however, cannot observe the subtle changes in their care-givers' facial expressions or follow their movements. Thus, visually-impaired infants fail to receive information that sighted babies use in formulating their own responses.

Care-givers of sighted infants rely on visual signals of discrimination, recognition, and preference. Otherwise competent blind infants do not develop signals for "I want that" or "Pick me up" until near the end of the first year. Thus, the first few months of life are extremely difficult for both care-giver and infant. The child's seeming lack of responsiveness can be emotionally devastating for the care-givers unless they are wisely counseled by experienced people. The great danger is that communication and mutuality will break down and that the care-giver will start to avoid the child (Fraiberg, 1974).

Blind babies do not develop a selective, responsive smile language as early as sighted children; they do not smile as often or as ecstatically. They have very few facial expressions. Yet they rapidly develop a large, expressive vocabulary of hand signals for their care-givers. Eventually, they are able to direct and relate these signals to unseen people and objects. Training parents and caregivers of visually-impaired infants to watch for and interpret hand signals greatly enhances the parent-child dialogue, attachment formation, and all subsequent socialization (Fraiberg, 1974).

HEARING-IMPAIRED INFANTS   The developmental difficulties of deaf infants follow a pattern that differs from those of blind infants. In the first few months of life, their well-developed visual sense generally makes up for the problems imposed by deafness. These children are visually responsive. After the first 6 months, however, communication between parents and infants begins to break down. The children's responses are not full enough to meet the parents' expectations. Often, the discovery of the child's deafness does not occur until the second year. By this time, the child has already missed a good deal of communication. One of the first indications of hearing impairment in 1-year-olds is seeming disobedience, as well as frequent startling when people approach. (The child does not hear them coming.) In 2-year-olds, there may be temper tantrums, frequent disobedience (or, conversely, severe withdrawal), together with widespread failure to develop normal expectations about the world around them. The diagnosis of deafness may come as a shock to parents who have been "talking to my child all along." Like parents of visually-impaired children, they need special training and counseling to help the child develop fully. Without careful attention during infancy, deafness can result in poor communication during the preschool years and in severe social, intellectual, and psychological deficits later (Meadow, 1975).

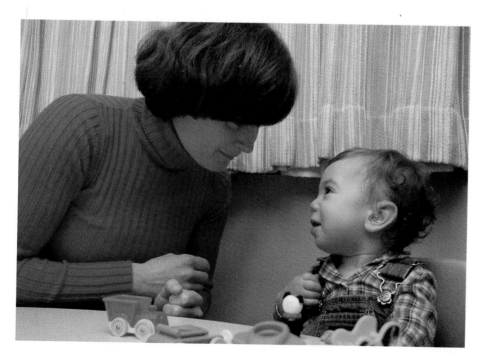

The diagnosis of deafness may come as a shock to parents who have been talking to their children all along. These parents need special training and counseling to help their handicapped children develop fully.

SEVERE HANDICAPS   When an infant is born with a severe handicap, such as cerebral palsy, there is a high risk of maternal rejection, withdrawal, and depression. A severely handicapped infant strains marital ties and may trigger a variety of disturbances in other children in the family. Child-care workers can help almost immediately with a family's early adjustment problems, and they should be consulted at once. Early success or failure in coping with initial traumas will greatly affect parents' abilities to make wise decisions about the care and education of this child (Turnbull & Turnbull, 1990).

BONDING DISORDERS

Occasionally, caregivers and infants encounter serious problems when they try to establish their relationship. Such problems are known as bonding disorders. The *failure-to-thrive* infant and the *abused* or *neglected infant* are products of such relationships. Failure-to-thrive infants are usually small and emaciated. They appear to be quite ill and unable to digest food properly. Sometimes, they start eating very soon after arriving at a hospital; at other times, they are listless and withdrawn, almost immobile. These infants often avoid eye contact by staring with a wide-eyed gaze, actively turning away, or covering their face or eyes. By definition, failure-to-thrive infants weigh in the lower 3 percent for their age group and show no evidence of any disease or abnormality that would explain their failure to grow. Often, disruption in the home and social environment of these infants is indicated. In addition, there is some evidence of developmental retardation among these infants, but it can generally be reversed with appropriate feeding (Barbero, 1983; Drotar, 1985).

In many cases, the mother of failure-to-thrive and abused or neglected infants is mentally or physically ill, depressed, alcoholic, or using drugs. She may have experienced some recent crisis that has had a prolonged emotional impact. An important finding is that the parents of these children have experienced similar deprivations when they were infants. Some studies show that as many as 85 percent of abusive or neglectful parents have had very negative early childhood experiences themselves; that is, they, too, were abused or neglected. Certainly, not all people who were abused as children grow up to abuse their children. But, too often, the cycle repeats itself (Helfer, 1982).

FATHERS, SIBLINGS, AND THE FAMILY SYSTEM

Most research in child development has focused on the relationship between mother and child and has neglected the rest of the family. Evidence shows that infants form strong early attachments to fathers as well as mothers, particularly when they have regular, close contact from birth. The stronger the early attachment, the more influence the father will have on later socialization. Siblings, too, form strong long-term bonds that often last a lifetime. The popular literature frequently highlights the competitive rivalry between siblings. The positive, supportive, mutual-caring roles have often been downplayed. But throughout life, siblings frequently protect and help one another. Many families also have a variety of other family members who play a strong role in the infant's development—including grandparents, aunts, uncles, and cousins. Indeed, most children develop in a social context that allows several early attachments. The strength of certain relationships can make up for some of the inadequacies of others. The infant has an opportunity to choose and discriminate between these relationships. His evolving emotional development is not attendant on the strengths and weaknesses of any one attachment bond.

FATHERS AND FATHERING

During the 1980s, much was learned about fathers and fathering in the American family system. There is some evidence that fathers are spending more time with their infants than they did in the past (Pleck, 1985; Ricks, 1985). Aside from breast-feeding, fathers are quite capable of routine child care. They can bathe, diaper, feed, and rock—sometimes as skillfully as the mother performs these tasks. They can be as responsive to the infant's cues as mothers are (Parke, 1981), and infants can become as attached to them as they are to their mothers. Fathers who spend more time taking care of young children form strong attachments to them, and the children benefit from this extended time (Ricks, 1985). Despite these similarities, however, fathers are not, by and large, taking over the major responsibility for infant care, and the nature of the father's relationship with the infant is different from that of the mother's.

FATHERING The style of interaction between the father and infant differs from the interaction between the mother and infant. Whereas mothers are likely to hold infants for care-taking purposes, fathers are more likely to hold infants just to play with them (Parke, 1981). Fathers are also more often physical and spontaneous. Play between fathers and infants occurs in cycles that have peaks of high excitement and attention followed by periods of minimal activity. Mothers engage their infants in subtle, shifting, gradual play, or they initiate such conventional games as pat-a-cake. Fathers, however, tend toward unusual, vigorous, and unpredictable games, which infants find most exciting (Lamb & Lamb, 1976). The exception to this pattern occurs when the father is the primary care-giver—he then tends to act more as mothers do (Field, 1978).

As infants get older and require less direct care-taking, father-infant interaction is likely to increase. Fathers may engage in more rough-and-tumble play and interact more frequently with the young child in public places, such as zoos or parks (Lewis, 1987).

Fathers who frequently interact with their infants, who are responsive to their signals, and who become significant individuals in their children's world are likely to develop into forceful agents of socialization later on. As the child grows older, the father becomes an important role model. He may also become an admirer and advocate of the child's achievements. There seems to be a link between paternal interaction in infancy and interaction in later childhood. Fathers who are inaccessible to their infants may have difficulty establishing strong emotional ties later on. It is even possible that they will have a negative influence as the child grows older (Ricks, 1985).

As more fathers become more involved parents, infants are increasingly likely to look to them for social referencing.

Fathers who are the most influential in their young children's lives not only spend time with them, but are also sensitive to their wants, cries, and developmental needs (Esterbrook & Goldberg, 1984; Parke, 1981). Indeed, fathers are increasingly taking the time to broaden their parenting role, even when their children are infants (Parke, 1981; Lamb, Pleck, Charnov & Levine, 1987). Because of this greater involvement, infants are more likely to use both their mothers and their fathers for *social referencing*. The term social referencing denotes the process by which infants seek affective cues or signals from an adult figure to help them resolve their uncertainty, form an appraisal, and regulate their subsequent behavior (Hirshberg & Svejda, 1990). The referencing process is an important avenue of parental influence in socioemotional development. It appears from the research, as though fathers play a big role in shaping their infant's responses when the child is uncertain as to what the appropriate behavior should be.

FATHERS AND THE FAMILY SYSTEM There are social and psychological reasons why fathers are usually not equal partners in infant care. In one study, mothers and fathers were recruited from a childbirth class where, at least initially, the fathers were active participants and were expected to continue sharing infant care with their wives. But it did not work out that way (Grossman, Pollack, & Golding, 1988). Very soon after the birth of the child, both mothers and fathers rated the fathers as less competent in most infant-care skills. Fathers were then relegated to the role of "helping" the mother. No father in this study ever talked about the mother "helping" the father take care of the infant. The more competent one—the mother—generally assumed the chief responsibility for the infant and, therefore, got more practice at performing infant care and interpreting the baby's signals. If someone feels incompetent, they do not enjoy doing a job (Entwisle & Doering, 1988). Most families work this out by selecting complementary roles for father and mother. Less successful couples tend to become impatient with each other. In these cases, it is common for the father to play with the infant but to serve as a reluctant and occasional helper. We should note here that sometimes the designated care-giver is the father—because his nurturing skills are better than the mother's.

The father's indirect influence on the infant and, indeed, on the whole family is considerable. Numerous studies have indicated that a father's emotional support of the mother during pregnancy and early infancy is important to the establishment of positive beginning relationships. The absence of a father during infancy creates considerable stress on the whole family system (Lewis, 1987).

Although in our culture the father is often a secondary care-giver, he plays an important part in a complex system of interactions. It is not enough just to study the ways in which a mother and baby or a father and baby interact. We must look at the way the three of them affect one another's behavior. Clarke-Stewart (1978), in her study of the three-way pattern in many families, finds that the mother's influence on the child is usually direct, whereas the father's is often indirect, through the mother. The child usually influences both parents quite directly.

The addition of an infant, especially a firstborn child, to a family affects the marriage itself. Studies have shown that the birth of the first child can create considerable stress on the marital relationship. A newborn makes heavy demands on the time and energy of both mother and father. Complementary roles need to be established. Decisions must be made about child-care arrangements, the mother's return to work, and so forth (Baruch & Barnett, 1986). The stress on the marriage may be greater if the infant is demanding, frequently sick, or handicapped. It is possible for stress to bring the couple closer together (Turnbull & Turnbull, 1990). Yet, if the marriage was vulnerable to begin with, the stress may cause increased dissatisfaction and turmoil.

SIBLINGS

Siblings form significant and long-lasting attachments to one another, beginning in infancy, although younger siblings are often more attached to the older siblings than the reverse (Lewis, 1987). Infants often form very strong attachments to a somewhat older sibling and are upset with the loss of that sibling even when the separation is only overnight (Dunn & Kendrick, 1979). Older siblings become important social models. Children learn how to share, cooperate, help, and empathize by watching their older siblings. They learn appropriate sex roles and family customs and values. In some cultures, the older siblings perform a major caretaking role, sometimes being the principal caretaker of the younger child (Whiting & Whiting, 1975). In many families, the positive aspects of sibling roles—helping, protecting, and providing an ally—last a lifetime. It is somewhat surprising, therefore, that the negative aspects of sibling relationships have received more attention (Lewis, 1987).

Siblings tend to form strong bonds and mutual caring roles that often last a lifetime.

Two negative aspects of sibling relationships are sibling rivalry and the dethroning of the older sibling with the birth of the new infant. It is clear that the birth of the second child makes a profound impact on the first or older sibling (see the box "The Formation of Family Systems"). Parents pay less attention, time, and energy to the first child. The role of the older child must shift. Parents' attitudes in handling this change influence the degree of sibling strife, competition, and rivalry (Dunn & Kendrick, 1980; Lewis, 1987; Lewis, Feiring, & Kotsonis, 1984). For example, if the parents attempt to enlist the older sibling in the care of the newborn from the onset, an alliance is often created both between the siblings, and between the older sibling and the parents. The mother and father may refer to the newborn as "*our* baby." In addition, it is important that special time be created when the first child has his or her own time with the parents. This makes the older child feel special rather than discarded. The following story illustrates this point:

> Our second daughter was born eleven months after our first. When the older one had her first birthday, there was already another child there. We made the decision that we would include her in everything we did for the new baby. She "helped" us change her, feed her, and cuddle her. We talked about "her" baby. Nearly two years later, she announced to the pediatrician on one visit, "My baby has a sore bottom. We need some medicine!" Now at 3 and 4 they are still close. They share a room and play together constantly. When one is upset, the other comforts her.

FOCUS ON RESEARCH

THE FORMATION OF FAMILY SYSTEMS

We know that the birth of a baby creates a lot of changes for a couple. Each parent has to balance the needs of this new family member with the need to maintain a reasonable relationship with one's spouse. But what happens with the introduction of a second child? Kreppner and his colleagues (1982) examined the formation of the family system when it changes from three members to four members after the birth of a second child. They also investigated how family interactions change over a 2-year period as this new infant grows. Are there some developmental events that pressure family members to interact with one another in new ways?

The researchers selected 16 families for observation. Each family, comprised of a mother, father, and one child who was 4 years of age or less, was expecting a baby. The first observations were recorded late in the pregnancies; both parents were interviewed about their individual and family histories and their parental attitudes. Following the birth of the second child, all families were videotaped periodically over a 2-year period, accumulating about 26 videotapes per family, each running 30 or more minutes in length. The observers also visited with the families for at least 2 to 4 hours at the time of each taping, acting in many ways like normal house guests. These observations were supplemented by extensive interviews when the second child was 8 months, and at the end of the 2-year period.

"Immediately after the arrival of the second child, there is a kind of doubling of parental tasks."

What did the researchers conclude from their observations? Although there were many differences in family interaction patterns, they were able to identify three phases in the process of family formation.

Phase One: Initial Integration of the Infant into the Family (birth to 8 months). Immediately after the arrival of the second child, there is a kind of doubling of parental tasks. Parents must care for the new infant and yet not neglect the older child.

GRANDPARENTS AND OTHERS

In many cultures, including our own, grandparents have considerable contact with their adult children and their grandchildren—often on a weekly basis. In families where both parents work, grandparents are frequently the primary care-givers for much of the time. The grandparent's role is usually somewhat different from that of the parent, and a different attachment relationship is formed. Grandparents frequently offer more approval and support, or empathy and sympathy, and less discipline. Sometimes, the relationship is more playful and relaxed (Lewis, 1987). Grandparents also have the time to tell the child the stories of when they—or their parents—were little. This helps to create a sense of family identity and tradition.

 ## MATERNAL EMPLOYMENT

THE SOCIAL ECOLOGY OF CHILD CARE

In modern societies, child care for young children is a complex issue. In 1990, more than half of American mothers with children under age 3 worked outside of

In addition, the first child may be confused about his or her position in the family and may feel the need to compete for attention. This child often needs to reassert her- or himself as "already big," as superior, while still wanting and needing all the attention the baby is receiving. Parents develop different ways to channel, limit, or satisfy this older child's needs.

Often, parents must experiment with different ways of dealing with their various jobs—they divide and delegate child-care and housekeeping tasks in their own fashion, forming a "working team." The researchers observed several different family solutions to these problems.

Phase Two: The Second Child Learns to Crawl and Walk (9 to 16 months). When the second child begins to crawl and to move about, there are new tasks for the family.

The second child can now interact directly with all members of the family—he or she can interrupt the play of the older child, for example. Parents must begin to cope with sibling problems, and hence, be mediators and teachers. Parents frequently state and enforce "the rules." The older child usually tries to maintain his or her leading position in the family. One solution for the child is to take on a parenting role for that second child. Another possibility is to join forces with the father while ignoring the baby.

Phase Three: Differentiation Within the Family (17 to 24 months). When the second child starts to use words somewhat effectively, at 16 to 18 months, a new phase of family interaction begins. The second child seems more fully human now and, hence, a real partner in the family. New alliances form, including one between the

siblings. There is often a clear and distinct boundary between the parents—the adults—and the children. The parents find that verbal rules can now apply to both children. At this stage, new patterns of interaction begin to develop.

There is need for more research in this area as the family group grows even larger. Many parents, for example, report anecdotally that the transition from two to three children is even more difficult than that described above. As one father puts it, "Once you get to three, they outnumber you! You have two laps, two sets of legs to chase them, two sets of arms to hold them. It's infinitely more difficult." This remains a research question that needs to be tested.

the home, compared with approximately 33 percent in 1975 (United States Bureau of the Census, 1993). Another example of this same trend may be found in Sweden, where 85 percent of mothers with children under school age work part time or full time outside of the home. But there is a difference. In Sweden, public child care is provided for every family that requests it. There are day-care centers, or day nurseries, and there are also family day-care providers (so-called day mothers). Both the day-care centers and the day mothers are hired and licensed by the municipalities. There is also a system of open preschools, where mothers or day mothers may take their children to meet and play with other children and receive advice and support in their caring roles. In other words, there is a publicly funded child-care system that provides support to families with infants and young children (Andersson, 1989; Hwang and Broberg, 1992).

In the United States, there is a quite different *social ecology* in most communities for the raising of infants and young children. Parents are often expected to make their own decisions about what type of child care they want and how much of it they will receive. They are financially responsible for providing supplemental child care and are assisted in this responsibility only if they have a low income. Because nearly 60 percent of mothers of infants and toddlers work outside of the home, many families face the difficult decision of finding suitable alternative child care at affordable prices.

In fact, over 8 million preschool and 15 million school-aged children are cared for by someone other than their mothers. Over 40 percent of the children are cared for in someone else's home, 30 percent in their own home, and the remainder in day-care centers and preschools. Based on these statistics, it is clear that American parents are willing to use formal and informal group care arrangements to care for their infants, toddlers, and young children.

Whatever their arrangements, many working mothers are ambivalent about their dual role as worker and mother. Some receive criticism from other family members or from friends in the community. Yet most women work because they need the money, either as single mothers or as part of a dual-income family. After work, they must somehow find the time and energy to care for their children and handle the countless household responsibilities of family management. The stress for both mothers and fathers of juggling parenting and work responsibilities in a social ecology that offers very few supports can be quite considerable. We may see the percentages of working mothers in the United States in selected years between 1975 and 1990 presented in Figure 7–1.

INFANT DAY CARE

In Sweden, employers must provide 9 *months* of parental leave (Welles-Nystrom, 1988). In the United States, however, 6 *weeks* of leave is quite common. Mothers who must or who choose to return to work soon after birth face a number of difficult decisions. They must arrange for safe and reliable supervision of their children while they are at work. Some may hire a relative or friend, others seek licensed family day-care centers, and still others look for a reliable, high-quality day-care center.

In families where both parents work, grandparents are frequently the primary care-givers for much of the time.

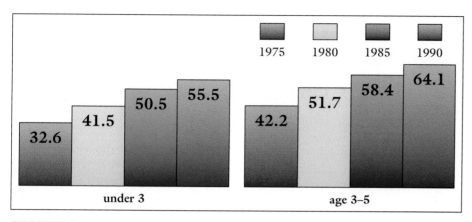

FIGURE 7–1
Labor Force Participation Rates for Wives with Husband Present by Age of Youngest Child from 1975–1990.
Statistical Abstract of the United States (Washington, DC: Department of Commerce, 1992).

Both family day-care homes and well-run day-care centers seem perfectly capable of fostering normal development in infants and toddlers. Several studies, conducted under ideal conditions, show that children ranging in age from 3 months to 30 months developed at least as well in a group care situation as did children with similar backgrounds who were reared at home (Kagan, 1978; Keister, 1970; Clarke-Stewart, 1982). In Sweden, where high-quality day care is the norm, children with early day care (beginning before age 1) were generally rated more favorably and performed better in elementary school than did the average child reared at home by his or her own mother. They were more competent in cognitive tests like reasoning and vocabulary, were rated as better by teachers in school subjects like reading and arithmetic, and were rated as more socially competent than their home-reared peers (Andersson, 1989). Some authors in the United States find similar small positive effects on cognitive or social development for children in group care (Clarke-Stewart & Fine, 1983).

The day-care services available to many families are not ideal, however. Staffs may be poorly trained, poorly paid, and have high turnover. These facilities rarely admit researchers. One study (Vandell & Corasaniti, 1990) looked at 349 third graders in an area of Texas where, it turns out, day care and family day care were of relatively poor quality, and there were few enforced public standards. When these researchers compared children who had extensive day care beginning in infancy with groups who had less day care, they found highly significant, pervasive, negative effects. Those with extensive day care scored lower on peer relations, work habits, emotional health, cognitive skills, and standardized tests. They also earned lower grades in school. Some had serious behavior problems, including excessive aggressiveness. The authors agree that other factors—social factors and family dynamic factors—lead some parents to need full-time infant care, whereas others do not need it. Whether the infant care interrupted attachment and, hence, caused the problematic behavior of the children in this study is difficult to say. Perhaps the problems may have been due to poor preschools, family dynamics, or an interaction of these factors.

FOCUS ON AN ISSUE

EARLY INFANT DAY CARE: A CAUSE FOR CONCERN?

In the fall of 1986, a noted, responsible expert on infant development published a startling warning to infant-care professionals. He had reviewed several studies of infant and preschool development comparing children who had begun day care or other forms of nonparental care in their first year with children who had not begun so early. Although the studies indicated wide variations in the quality of care received, the types of families served, and the consistency of care given, he reached one cautiously stated conclusion: that "entry into care in the first year of life is a 'risk factor' for the development of insecure-avoidant attachments in infancy and heightened aggressiveness, noncompliance, and withdrawal in the preschool and early school years" (Belsky, 1986, p. 7). This one statement produced an

---

The reason for the intense reaction was clear. Was it true that infants were "at risk" when both parents worked and placed their infants in some alternative care arrangement?

---

immediate and intense reaction from many researchers, day-care professionals, and parents.

The reason for the intense reaction was clear. Was it true that infants were "at risk" when both parents worked and placed their infants in some alternative care arrangement? If so, there were implications for the role and rights of women, implications for the profession of infant day care, and implications for the personal decision making of parents. Clearly, a whole lifestyle of dual-working parents was being challenged. Some day-care workers felt personally insulted, but a few others suggested that the possibility of harm due to very early care in less than ideal day-care arrangements deserved close scrutiny (Fitzcharles, 1987; Miringoff, 1987). Other experts

---

Other recent research has found that such results are affected by children's gender, the family's economic status, and the kind of child care. Poor children seem to do better when cared for by their mothers or grandmothers, while, in more affluent families, girls do better with baby-sitters and boys do better with their mothers (Baydar & Brooks-Gunn, 1991). Other studies suggest that the timing of when a mother returns to work is crucial. Some babies whose mothers went back before they were 1, did less well on cognitive and behavioral measures than did infants whose mothers waited until they were 1. Other studies seem to indicate that mothers who returned earlier had children with less impact than those who waited until the second quarter of the first year (Field, 1991; Baydar & Brooks-Gunn, 1991). Additional research is needed to clarify these issues. Indeed, for many parents, who must return quickly to work to support their families after the birth of a child—the results may be irrelevant since they must use whatever care is available when they need it.

What is the process that leads to trouble for some infants who have non-parental care for more than 20 hours per week beginning at age 1? (see the box "Early Infant Day Care: A Cause for Concern?") Jaeger & Weinraub (1990) sug-

warned of a hasty conclusion drawn from diverse studies conducted in complex environmental circumstances (Chess, 1987).

What are the details of this complex warning, and what is the evidence that supports it? Jay Belsky presents his arguments carefully. He is well aware of the past research on the effects of infant day care on development. Prior to 1980, virtually all of this research was done in high-quality, often university-based, research-oriented centers. There was little, if any, evidence to suggest that such nonmaternal care was problematic. In fact, in some instances infants in these high-quality centers did better on social, cognitive, and emotional aspects of development than did similar home-reared infants. But since 1980, researchers have studied infants in a wide range of nonmaternal care arrangements.

The families studied include some single-parent families, some families at risk for abuse or neglect, and a full range of dual-parent families at all economic levels.

When Jay Belsky looked closely at these diverse studies as well as his own, he found disturbing commonalties. Among those children who have had nonmaternal care starting in the first year and for more than 20 hours per week, he found more children with anxious avoidant attachments to their mother. This is the case even when the nonmaternal care-giver is a neighbor or relative at home with her own child. It certainly does not happen to all children, or even the majority of children in these circumstances. But the proportion of infants who are not "securely attached," according to the standard Strange Situation Test,

is nearly double (Belsky, 1986; Belsky & Rovine, 1988, 1990).

Other researchers reach quite different conclusions, even looking at much of the same data. It is clear that the quality of alternative infant care is an even more important factor. Infants who have low-quality care or who experience several changes in their primary caretaker are particularly vulnerable. Also, families who have many stresses in their life and place their infant in a low-quality caretaking arrangement have added risk (Phillips, McCartney, Scarr, & Howes, 1987).

It is clear that age alone is not the only, or even the primary, cause for concern. Yet, because a safe, secure attachment is so basic to later social and personality development, the debate over which factors or combination of factors put infants "at risk" will continue for some time.

gest two models. One model is the *maternal separation model*. According to this model, daily, repeated separations from the mother are experienced by the infant as either maternal absence or as maternal rejection. The infant comes to doubt the mother's availability or responsiveness. It is the absence of the mother that leads to insecurity.

The other model is called the *quality of mothering model*. In this perspective, it is not maternal employment or separation, per se, that determines the infant's outcome, but how maternal employment affects maternal behavior. The employed mother is unable to be as sensitive and responsive a care-giver as she might be if she had more time and practice or if she did not have regular interruptions. It is this change in the maternal behavior that produces insecurity in the infant. Current research based on the quality of mothering model focuses on the competing demands of the mother's work and family, the quality of the child care (and whether she has to worry about it), the characteristics of the infant, and whether the mother thinks that her infant is sturdy, can adjust, and is capable of coping with the situation. What is the general quality of the mother's life? Does she find pleasure in her varying roles, employment status, and maternal satisfaction? How much role conflict is there or marital strain or fatigue? If the mother feels strong separation anxiety when she leaves her child each day, the child tends not to do well (McBride, 1990).

The potential risks of early day care involve many factors, including the quality of day care, family dynamics, the infant's temperament, and the broader social ecology of child rearing in a community.

 ## CHILD REARING AND PERSONALITY DEVELOPMENT

Commonly asked questions about child rearing by both parents and researchers include whether to breast-feed or bottle-feed, when or how to wean, whether to pick up babies immediately when they cry or to let them cry for a while, whether to allow thumb-sucking or blanket carrying, what to do about temper tantrums, when to toilet train and how. If we look at these specific practices separately, we tend to get answers that are contradictory. It is hard to put them together to form a clear theory of good child rearing. We often conclude, for example, that it does not matter much whether children suck their thumbs or carry a blanket.

Yet such practices, when viewed in the context of the total pattern of child-rearing practices, clearly do matter. These patterns have a strong influence on later personality development. The way that we convey our culture to our children, beginning in infancy, is not at all subtle. From birth we try to instill in our children attitudes and values about the nature of their bodies—the acceptability of self-stimulation, the degree of physical closeness that is desirable, the amount of dependency allowed, and the goodness or badness of both their behavior and their basic nature as human beings. These attitudes and values, communicated through many child-rearing practices, have a very wide-ranging effect on personality development.

It is in the context of broad, cross-cultural child-rearing patterns that we shall examine specific child-rearing practices. We shall concentrate on three particular aspects of child-rearing practices during the infancy period. First, we shall study the development of trust and nurturance in infants. As you recall from Chapter 2, this refers to the initial stage of Erikson's theory, and such questions as: What do infants learn about the basic trustworthiness of their social environment? Is the environment consistent and predictable? Is it responsive to the child's needs? Second, we will examine how children's attempts at autonomy are met. When toddlers start to get up and move around, to do things for themselves, to control their bodies, to try to control their environment, how are their needs satisfied? Third, we will look at child-rearing practices during infancy in terms of their effect on growing self-awareness in childhood. Children who are heavily swaddled during the first year or who are bound to a cradleboard, for example, cannot explore their bodies as can children who are relatively free to move about. Children who have no access to a mirror do not discover their own images. But there are pervasive attitudes toward the body and the self that children learn each day.

TRUST AND NURTURANCE

If we look at infant care in other societies, we see quite dramatic differences both in approach and results. One study, for example, suggested a difference between the attitudes of American mothers and Japanese mothers toward their infants (Caudill & Weinstein, 1969). In general, the American mother viewed the infant as passive and dependent. Her goal was to make her child independent. The average Japanese mother held the opposite opinion of her infant. She saw her child as an independent organism who needed to learn about the dependent relationships within the family.

Such differences in attitude have resulted in two different child-rearing practices. American infants are ideally put in cribs in their own rooms, whereas Japanese infants traditionally share a bedroom with their parents. In the study, the Japanese mother tried to respond quickly when the baby cried, and she fed her child on demand. The American mother tended to let her child cry for a short while in the hope of establishing a regular, mature feeding schedule. The Japanese mother felt the need to soothe and quiet her baby often, whereas the American mother wanted to stimulate her baby to smile and vocalize. As a result of these different approaches, the Japanese baby quickly became less vocal and active than the American baby. But some of these differences may be due in part to the infant's initial temperament, as was mentioned in Chapter 5.

FEEDING, WEANING, AND COMFORT Whether or not a mother breast-feeds or bottle-feeds her infant, the important question for psychological development is how the feeding method fits into the total pattern of nurturant care that the infant receives. Feeding time allows for the closeness between mother and child, and it expresses sensitivity and responsiveness between care-giver and child.

In some cultures, the transition period between the infant's birth and separation from the mother lasts for 3 years or more. Feeding is an integral part of this prolonged relationship (Mead & Newton, 1967). Children may sleep close to their mothers, be carried around in a sling during most of the first year, and be breast-fed until the age of 3 (Richman et al., 1988). In other cultures—especially in America—some infants may be separated from their mothers almost immediately—separate bed, separate room, early weaning. Somewhat in jest, Mead and Newton described the transition period for some American babies as lasting less than a minute—until the umbilical cord is cut! In Sweden, maternal leave has been extended to 9 months at 90 percent salary, with an additional 9 months at reduced salary, mandated by law. There is a public campaign that urges mothers to stay home with their children for at least 9 months in order to provide continuity of care and nurturance. Despite the fact that Sweden has perhaps the lowest infant mortality rate in the world, mothers are concerned about the vulnerability of their infants, and both mothers and fathers pay close attention to the diet and health of the infant (Welles-Nystrom, 1988).

In Italy, the nurturance of the infant is a social affair. Mothers and infants are rarely alone. Mothers do most of the feeding, dressing, and cleaning of their infants in an indulgent and caring fashion. The family, friends, and neighbors all contribute to the social interaction with the infant. In one study, 70 percent of the time, although the mother was present, other people were tending to the baby—

hugging, talking, teaching, and even teasing the infants. The American observer was quite surprised at the amount of teasing that occurred, sometimes to the point of tears on the part of the infant. Infants were spanked; pacifiers were held just out of reach; candy was offered and then taken away. Adults said, "Here comes Daddy!" only to laugh and declare "He isn't here anymore!" and then swoop the tearful infant up to hug and kiss him or her amidst the laughter of onlookers. Even naptime was not sacred, as infants were jiggled and pinched to wake up when adults wanted to play with them. Despite this large amount of attention and stimulation, the infants seemed to learn to cope remarkably well (New, 1988).

Considerable research has been devoted to thumb-sucking and other comfort devices, but remarkably few definitive conclusions have been reached about them. For the most part, sucking experience seems to be a natural need. Yet parents have responded to this need in a variety of ways (Goldberg, 1972; Richman et al., 1988). In much of early twentieth-century Europe, thumb-sucking was considered a dirty habit, harmful to a child's general personality development. Elaborate devices, vile-tasting applications, or even simple sleeves were used to cover a child's hand to prevent thumb-sucking. This era, with its strong fear of pleasure and of sense exploration, seems to be over. Today, some children are given a pacifier to suck—on the assumption that they can more easily give up the pacifier than they can give up the thumb. Most children who use either thumbs or pacifiers, however, give them up as regular comfort devices by the end of the preschool years; those who remain avid thumb-suckers or avid comfort seekers generally have other needs that are not being met. Evidence that thumb-sucking causes major damage to the dental arch is inconclusive. Most of this damage seems to occur in children who are still sucking at age 5, 6, or 7, when they are getting their second teeth.

Children use a wide variety of comfort devices and comfort-seeking behaviors. Favorite blankets, toys, and other objects, and twisting and rubbing their hair or skin all provide familiar sensations. Parents and care-givers convey their values and attitudes by their reactions to comfort seeking—attitudes toward the child's body, self-stimulation, and what they feel is an acceptable level of closeness and dependency. From such reactions, children learn whether they are considered good or bad, whether they should feel anxious or guilty, and when to feel comfortable and secure. They learn a great deal more than merely whether they should suck their thumbs or carry a blanket. Some bright children have learned the abstract words their parents use to give meaning to these behaviors, as the following comment indicates.

> A bright 3-year-old who had developed a fondness for her pacifier was asked by the pediatric dentist to stop using the "binky." Her comment to him was, "I can't stop, Doctor, it's a habit!"

SOCIAL REFERENCING AND CULTURAL MEANING

One important avenue of parental influence on the infant is a process called *social referencing*. In situations of uncertainty, infants look to the parent's face to detect an emotional signal as to whether or not this situation is safe or unsafe, good or bad. We have seen the effectiveness of social referencing in encouraging an infant

One of the most popular comfort devices children use is a beloved blanket.

to cross a visual cliff or in deciding whether to become somewhat sociable to a stranger, for instance. But infants seem to look for an emotional signal under a wide range of circumstances, including how much to wander away from mother, or whether or not to explore a strange toy. Infants look at fathers as well as mothers for emotional signals, and, although they look more at mothers than at fathers when both are present, the father's signals seem to be equally effective in regulating the infant's behavior (Hirshberg & Svejda, 1990).

What happens if mother and father give conflicting emotional signals to their infant? What are the consequences of one parent encouraging the child to explore an unusual toy and the other frowning and displaying worry? In a study conducted with 1-year-olds, parents were coached to give consistent or conflicting emotional signals. The infants adapted much more easily to consistent signals, either both parents happy or both parents fearful, than they did to conflicting emotional signals. In fact, when they were given conflicting facial responses— happy from mother and fear from father, for example—the infants expressed their confusion in a wide range of anxious behaviors. Some did agitated sucking or rocking, or avoided the situation altogether. Others wandered aimlessly or seemed disoriented. It seems that 1-year-olds are remarkably sensitive to the emotional signals from their parents. Some infants were much more able to handle the conflict than were others (Hirshberg, 1990).

What are some of the messages that parents are already teaching their children at age 1? In a series of studies, anthropologists have intensely observed the !Kung San, a group of hunters and gatherers in Botswana. In this culture, the sharing of objects is an important value. When the anthropologists looked at mothers and their 10- to 12-month-old infants, they were surprised to find that, in contrast to many American parents, these parents seemed to pay no attention to the infant's exploration of objects. They did not talk about the objects and did not smile—but they neither punished nor frowned as children picked up twigs, grass, parts of food, nut shells, bones, and the like. They used an expression that meant "He's teaching himself." However, there was one activity with objects to which they did pay attention. The adults focused on the sharing and the giving and taking of objects. In fact, grandmothers began symbolic training by guiding the giving of special beads to relatives. When adults paid attention to objects at all, they did it by encouraging sharing with words like "Give it to me" or "Here, take this" (Bakeman & Adamson, 1990). It appears that, through social referencing, games, and selective attention, parents are already teaching their 1-year-olds the values of their culture.

AUTONOMY, COOPERATION, AND DISCIPLINE

By the time infants are 1 year old, their parents or care-givers have taught them some guidelines for acceptable behavior, especially for their dependency needs and their needs for physical closeness. But, in the second year, care-givers cope with a whole new set of issues. Again, their personalities, as well as their cultural backgrounds, will affect their attitudes and methods of dealing with the toddler. To appreciate the diversity of problems facing those who care for toddlers, let us consider some typical 2-year-olds.

> He explores the qualities and possibilities of almost everything in his environment. She discovers the delights of pulling the toilet paper roll—endlessly. He uses pencil and crayon on walls, floors, and furniture. She enjoys picking up small things, from cigarette butts to crumbs to pebbles; many of these things will be given a taste test. He wedges his body into, under, or over any space that looks interesting. She picks up and carries around glass figurines as well as toys. He alternates between clinging dependence and daring exploration, often within the space of a few minutes. She walks and runs and climbs for the sheer feel of walking and running and climbing. He tries to cheer up another child by sharing his bottle, or he willfully refuses to share. She is docile and eager to please one minute, and she challenges authority and routine the next. He wants to feed and dress himself on one occasion and wants everything done for him on the next. She may rebel at bedtime, protest at bath time, refuse to have her shoes or snowsuit put on, or reject a food that she has always enjoyed. He learns to say "No!"

Toward the end of the second year, toddlers experience increased emotional conflict between their greater needs for autonomy and their obvious dependence and limited skills. The changes that occur in children around this age were observed at length by Margaret Mahler and her colleagues (1975). They noted an extraordinary ambivalence in 18-month-old children. The toddlers were torn between a desire to stay close to their mothers and a wish to be independent. Their new sense of being separate beings seemed to frighten them. They tried to deny it by acting as if their mothers were extensions of themselves. For instance, a child might pull the mother's hand in an effort to have her pick up an object that the child desired. In addition, the toddlers appeared to experience a wider range of emotions and were developing new ways of dealing with their feelings, such as suppressing the need to cry.

A new emotional experience—empathy—begins to develop. From 18 to 24 months, toddlers start to engage in *prosocial behavior,* including cooperation, sharing, helping, and responding empathically to emotional distress in others. This new ability to interact with peers does not emerge smoothly. Often, when a toddler sees the distress of others, she is confused. She may laugh or not seem to know how to react. In one series of studies, mothers were asked to make believe that they had just hurt themselves. The toddler at 21 months was confused and anxious about the mother's distress. But mothers who regularly responded with empathy to their own child's distress soon promoted an empathy in their own children so that, 3 months later, some of these toddlers had learned soothing, comforting behaviors (Radke-Yarrow et al., 1983). In studies of cooperation in simple tasks, almost no 12-month-old infants can cooperate with each other. At 18 months, cooperation is infrequent and almost accidental. At 24 months, with a little coaching from adults, nearly all the toddlers were able to cooperate (Brownell & Carriger, 1990).

HARVARD PRESCHOOL PROJECT   Probably no ideal method of child rearing can be used by every family everywhere. For over two decades, however, Burton White and his colleagues at the Harvard University Preschool Project have produced a profile of what they consider one pattern of effective parenting. Effective mothers are not necessarily full-time care-givers (White, 1975). Many have part-time jobs, and the rest are far too busy to spend long stretches of time closely directing their children's activities. They generally allow, and even encourage, a great deal of childhood exploration, provide a safe environment, set clear limits, and do not always drop whatever they are doing to answer a child's request. Yet they provide a rich educational environment and many bits and pieces of information.

Primarily, the effective care-giver acts as a consultant for the child concerning behavior and as an architect of the child's environment. She (or he) is available to explain a new phenomenon, to provide language for a new experience or object, to reinforce exploration and discovery, to set limits designed to protect the child from physical harm, and to help the child adjust to social requirements. At the same time, the care-giver provides an environment that stimulates and promotes both cognitive growth and physical development. Indeed, some researchers have found that a care-giver's reaction to, and interaction with, the child between the ages of 10 months and 2 years has a dramatic and lasting effect upon the child's cognitive and emotional development throughout childhood (White, 1988).

White's profile presents only one pattern of middle-class American child rearing. It applies some broad American cultural values to the actual behaviors of parents interacting with their children. It is certainly not the only effective style. Nevertheless, this child-rearing pattern has some clear advantages. Children raised this way acquire an active, exploratory learning style. They develop confidence in approaching problems, an understanding of limits, self-reliance, and a feeling of competence in learning about the world around them. These feelings, attitudes, and approaches may affect their learning throughout their lives.

TOILET TRAINING   Although much early research, suggested by Freudian theory, focused upon the methods and effects of toilet training, recent studies view it as a part of a cluster of child-rearing issues. Toilet training is just one aspect of behavior affected by adult attitudes toward both children's explorations and the handling of their own bodies as well as toward their need for autonomy.

Those who are severe and harsh in toilet training are usually just as strict about other behaviors requiring self-mastery and independence, such as feeding, dressing, and general exploration. Some adults demand that a child have early and total control of bowel and bladder; they regard "accidents" as intolerable and dirty. Such people are likely to be severe when children break a plate, play in the dirt, explore new places and objects, and attempt to feed themselves (see the box "Successful Toilet Training").

DISCIPLINE   How does a parent or care-giver set limits on a child's behavior? Some, afraid that any kind of control over their children's behavior will prevent creative exploration and independence, helplessly stand by while their 2-year-olds do whatever they please. Discipline, when it comes, is then often harsh, reflecting the adults' own feelings of frustration. Others determined not to "spoil" their children, and convinced that 2-year-olds should act like responsible little citizens, set so many limits on behavior that their children, literally, cannot do anything right. Although it is easy to see the errors in these extremes, it is not quite so simple to provide a set of guidelines that will be effective for every occasion. For example, adults who encourage exploration and manipulation may have to cope, sooner or later, with a child who wants to stick pins into electrical outlets. Obviously, guidelines must be tempered with common sense and must consider children's needs for safety as well as for independence and creative experience. Children permitted to run, jump, and climb can also be taught to walk quietly, to hold someone's hand, or to allow themselves to be carried in public places.

One important technique to help raise a child with a sense of self-discipline is parental feedback. Parents need to reflect back to the children how they are coming across to others. Children need this feedback if they are to become sensitive to the needs of others. Feedback might consist of praise for good behavior, such as, "I like the way you help me set the table." Or it might be in terms of a mild scolding, such as, "I am upset that you opened my purse and took money without my permission." The key to feedback is that behavior is criticized, guidance is given, but the child is never criticized.

Children who have developed a strong attachment relationship, and whose needs are met through loving interaction with an adult, are neither spoiled by lots of attention nor frightened or threatened by reasonable limits. They are stronger and more confident because they have a trustworthy relationship from which to venture forth into independence.

DEVELOPMENT OF THE SELF

At first, infants cannot differentiate between themselves and the world around them. Gradually, however, they begin to realize that they are separate and unique beings. Much of infancy is devoted to making this distinction. From 3 to 8 months there is active learning about the infant's body. First, the child discovers his hands, his feet, and some of the things he can do with them. Later, the child acts on the world and sees what happens. At 7 or 8 months,

FOCUS ON APPLICATION

SUCCESSFUL TOILET TRAINING

Mark, aged 2 1/2, wanted to go to the preschool his older brother was attending. However, Mark had been resisting toilet training.

Current "advice from the experts" to parents about toilet training goes something like this. In general, toilet training should not be undertaken before children show interest in the process, have been dry at night, or show by gestures that they are aware that they are having a bowel movement or urinating. Once these behaviors have arrived indicating readiness, then it is time to begin the process. Buy training pants or the disposable pull-ups. Place the child on the potty frequently initially to help him or her make the association. Give rewards for success—stickers work well, as do pennies or hugs. Often, a reinforcer may be the attainment of something the child must be "big enough" to participate in, as the following examples suggest.

Mark, aged 2 1/2, wanted to go to the preschool his older brother was attending. However, Mark had been resisting toilet training. His mother told him that he would go to school when he was potty trained. He learned within three days.

Mattie, who was 3, desperately wanted to wear "big girl" underpants, like her older sisters. She learned to use the toilet reliably within a day of wearing her first pair.

Ernestine, aged 3 1/2, was still in a crib. She stopped wearing diapers and had no accidents when she was put into her own twin bed.

In each of these examples, the children were physiologically and psychologically ready for toilet training. They were also mature enough to remember to use the toilet when they felt the urge. Despite this, for many children, "accidents" occasionally occur—especially when they are engaged in an activity they do not want to halt. Accidents are best dealt with by quietly cleaning the child, setting him or her immediately on the potty, and then explaining that "we will work on it harder for the next time." Criticism accomplishes nothing except making the child self-conscious and overly stressed about the process. The opportunity to observe and imitate an older child often speeds the learning.

the infant makes a couple of significant advancements. He becomes particularly wary of strangers. That means he is quite discriminating of those he knows well and of those he doesn't. He also becomes able to delay his actions, even for just a short time. This allows him the beginnings of self/other schemes. Infants now become more deliberate in their testing and exploring of their own responses and results. Also, by observing the behavior of those around them, infants learn the beginnings of how they should behave. They can imitate. They begin to know what's expected. In the period from 12 to 18 months, the infant is hard at work learning these social expectations and learning what happens when he tests or explores the social world. By the end of this period, he clearly recognizes himself in pictures and in the mirror. Now he is capable of some of the social emotions, like pride or embarrassment. He is ready for more detailed socialization (Lewis & Feinman, 1991). Finally, from 18 to 30 months, the child is developing considerable knowledge about himself with respect to the social world, about his gender, about his physical fea-

Possibly the sense of ownership that toddlers display is necessary to complete their sense of self.

tures and characteristics, about his goodness and badness, about what he can and cannot do.

At around the age of 21 months an awareness of sex roles has begun to develop (Goldberg & Lewis, 1969). Girls and boys begin to exhibit different behavior. Boys are likely to disengage themselves more dramatically from their mothers, whereas girls demand greater closeness to them and have more ambivalent feelings about being separate. This seems to be linked to the children's awareness of their sexual differences.

By the end of the second year, the child's language has considerable self-reference. Children know their names and use them, often describing their needs and feelings in the third person: "Terri wants water." The words "me" and "mine" assume new importance in the vocabulary. And the concept of ownership is clearly and strongly acted out. Even in families in which sharing is emphasized and ownership is minimized, and despite many spontaneous demonstrations of sharing, toddlers show fairly extensive evidence of possessiveness. It may be that they need to establish a concept of ownership in order to round out their definition of self. Sharing and cooperation come more easily once toddlers are confident about what is theirs.

Self-awareness is a result of self-exploration, cognitive maturity, and reflections about self. Toddlers can frequently be heard talking to and admonishing themselves ("No, Lee, don't touch") and rewarding themselves ("Me good girl!"). They incorporate cultural and social expectations into their reflections, as well as into their behavior, and begin to judge themselves and others in light of these expectations. If they enjoy consistent, loving interaction with the care-giver in an environment that they are free to explore and can begin to control, they learn to make valid predictions about the world around them. Gradually, they establish a perception of themselves—perhaps as acceptable, competent individuals.

SUMMARY AND CONCLUSIONS

During infancy and toddlerhood, the first relationships between the infant and care-giver occur. This first relationship forms the basis for all later personality development. It is not clear how much of the determinants of these first relations are genetic or how much environmental, but in general an interaction is assumed. Ethologists who compare behavior across species have studied imprinting in animals as a possible mechanism to explain attachment in humans. In animals, the timing of exposure to stimulation is crucial. While in humans the development of a trust relationship during the first 6 months of life is important, there does not seem to be the same sort of critical period for its development.

During the first relationship, considerable emotional development occurs. Stanley and Nancy Greenspan describe six milestones in the development of the first relationship: *self-regulation and interest in the world,* *falling in love, developing intentional communication, the emergence of an organized sense of self, creating emotional ideas, and emotional thinking.* These stages mark the beginning of the developmental process of attachment. Attachment culminates in the lifelong process where individuals first discriminate someone they care for and then seek proximity to that person.

As discrimination develops, stranger anxiety also arises. Somewhere between 6 to 8 months of age, the infant gains the cognitive ability to detect discrepancies between the familiar care-giver and all others. At similar ages, separation anxiety and the sense of loss may be experienced when the care-giver is absent. The degree of separation and stranger anxiety in normal children varies according to the exclusivity and intimacy of the early relationships. When the attachment process has been interrupted or is dysfunctional, children may suffer from impaired personality development and subsequent emotional difficulties.

The patterns of early relationships are affected by individual differences in the temperaments and environments in which they occur, whether or not the child is handicapped in some way, and if some sort of dysfunction exists in the bonding of the parent-child pair. When mutuality and interactive synchrony mark the communication between care-giver and infant, the attachment that develops is strong. When there is mutuality between the care-giver and child, the positive dialogue that develops is transferred to the larger social environment in which the child participates. Interactions with peers and other adults show the same trust and prosocial behavior. When something goes wrong in the communication dialogue because of physical or psychological abnormalities, the subsequent difficulties can produce devastating effects on the child's personality and mental health. Special counseling may be needed to compensate for and overcome such developmental problems.

Although much of the research on the development of attachment focuses on mother-child interactions, recent research has focused on the role of fathers. Infants can form strong attachments to a variety of people and objects in the environment. When fathers play a significant role in the lives of infants and toddlers, the attachment may be as strong as that to the mother. The nature of the paternal role tends to be that of playmate rather than care-giver and nurturer. However, when fathers assume the primary caregiver role, they more closely resemble mothers in terms of their smiling, imitating, and vocalizing with the infant.

The entire family changes when an infant is born. Patterns of communication, recreation, and responsibility shift. The way in which the couple handles these new demands either brings the couple closer or disturbs the marriage. If the marriage is strong, and the couple negotiates the new demands with equanimity, humor, and mutual respect, then the relationships between the child and parents—and future children—will also be strong.

One difficult task that many families confront is how to provide infant and preschooler care if the mother works. Over 50 percent of American mothers work, and their children are placed in a variety of day-care situations including home care, care in the home of another, or a formal day-care situation. There is a growing concern that entry into day care in the first year of life may be a risk factor for later child development.

Child-rearing practices reflect cultural beliefs and in turn influence later personality development. The manner in which parents handle such early transitions as feeding, toilet training, discipline, and comfort devices convey fundamental messages to their children. Children learn attitudes about their bodies, such as the acceptability of self-stimulation, or physical closeness. Family patterns in handling dependency and autonomy also have pervasive effects on the child's personality and self-concept. The social experiences—both within and outside the family—to which the child is exposed in the first 2 years, essentially shape the growing understanding about the social world and the attitudes that children have about themselves.

➤ KEY TERMS AND CONCEPTS

ambivalent	discrepancy hypothesis	mutuality
attachment	imprinting	stranger anxiety

➤ SELF-TEST QUESTIONS

1. What are attachment behaviors and what is the significance for the relationship between the infant and the care-giver?

2. What is imprinting and when does it take place?

3. List six milestones in the emotional development of the infant within the first relationship.

4. What is stranger anxiety? When and why does it occur?

5. Compare what happens to a child who does not form an attachment relationship or one whose progress toward attachment is interrupted, with a child who has formed an attachment relationship.

6. How does an exclusive relationship affect the adjustment of the infant?

7. Describe how a responsive environment can affect the development of attachment behavior and emotional development.

8. How did Schaffer define mutuality, or synchrony, and what effect does it have on infant development?

9. Compare and contrast the securely attached infant, the avoidant infant, and the ambivalent infant.

10. How does the special needs infant influence the attitude of the care-giver?

11. List several bonding disorders.

12. Describe the differences and similarities between father-child interaction and mother-child interaction.

13. What are the negative and positive effects of sibling relationships?

14. What is the grandparent's role in the development of the infant?

15. List some problems faced by mothers who work outside the home.

16. Describe the controversy over early infant day care.

17. List several factors to consider when evaluating a day-care center.

18. Describe some of the child-rearing practices that vary from culture to culture, and explain how these different patterns influence later personality development.

➤ SUGGESTED READINGS

ALSTON, F. *Caring for other people's children: A complete guide to family daycare.* Baltimore: University Park Press, 1984. As the title suggests, this handy compendium covers numerous aspects of infant and young child development, activity planning, parent relations, laws and regulations, and more.

BOWLBY, J. *A secure base: Parent-child attachment and healthy human development.* New York: Basic Books, 1988. Bowlby's latest integration of his influential theory presented in a very readable style.

BRAZELTON, T. B. *Toddlers and parents: A declaration of independence.* New York: Delacorte, 1974. A colorful description of the phases of development during the second year. Contains suggestions to parents on how to manage their children's behavior.

CONDRELL, K. N. *How to raise a brat.* Tallahasse, FL: Loiry/Bonner Press, 1985. This very readable book makes extensive use of case studies to illustrate the mistakes parents make as well as some constructive things to do to resolve many common conflicts of infancy and childhood.

LAMB, M. E. *The father's role: Cross-cultural perspectives.* Hillsdale, NJ: Erlbaum, 1987. Descriptions of the role of fathers in diverse cultures. English fathers, Chinese fathers, pygmy fathers, and many others are covered.

PARKE, R. Fathers. Cambridge, MA: Harvard University Press, 1981. Based on solid research, Parke presents the many roles of fathers and their significance with respect to childbirth, infant development, and several other aspects of child development.

SPOCK, B., & ROTHENBERG, M. B. *Baby and child care.* New York: Simon & Schuster Pocket Books, 1985. Spock, now in his mid-80s, has thoroughly revised (with the aid of a coauthor) his classic guide to reflect the changing medical practices and cultural shifts of the 1980s.

ZIGLER, E. F., & LANG, M. E. *Child-care choices: Balancing the needs of children, families, and society.* New York: Free Press, 1991. A thorough overview of children's needs and a comprehensive look at current available child-care options, in light of today's economic and social realities.

VIDEO CASE: PROBLEMS WITH DAY CARE

Mrs. O. wanted to return to college and needed someone to look after her infant son Adam. After visiting various centers in and around New Orleans, she and her husband selected Enchanted World. It seemed to have the right proportion of adults per children to insure that Adam got the attention he needed.

As Adam's parents discovered later–after watching tapes of their baby's first day at the center recorded by hidden cameras from the television program "Prime Time"—Enchanted World was hardly enchanted. With no parents present, the facility was an entirely different place. While the owner stayed in her office, one woman watched more babies than the state of Louisiana required for such facilities. Adam cried unconsoled all day long. Only once did the owner enter the room where he was and help settle him down. Meanwhile, in the toddler area one woman oversaw seventeen children, far below the number of adults required by the state. Moreover, children were locked into highchairs for as long as 1 1/2 hours, with nothing to do. Sanitary conditions were also poor, with adults changing diapers of one child and then, with the same and unwashed hand, feeding another baby.

For 3 1/2 months, "Prime Time" looked into forty moderate-priced day-care centers in eight states. In eighteen facilities, the investigative team used undercover cameras to record conditions. In center after center, they found chaos—hungry children who fell asleep because they were unfed, unsafe changing tables, broken cribs, children running around for hours unsupervised, and children kept in cribs all day long.

Are such conditions the American norm? Although there are many good day-care facilities, experts estimate that in about half of the centers children are not receiving the care they need or that their parents think they are receiving.

One reason is that the state departments responsible for licensing day-care facilities are overburdened. For example, the Louisiana's department has thirteen inspectors for 2,000 facilities. Says one critic, "In a lot of states, dog kennels are inspected more frequently."

"Prime Time" showed the tapes of what happened at Enchanted World to a panel of three well-known child-care experts—Yale's Dr. Edward Zeigler, pediatrician T. Berry Brazelton, and childcare advocate, Dr. Barbara Weinstein. Among their comments: "We have the worst child-care of all industrialized countries" and "If we don't do better, we will lose generations of our country."

But, meanwhile, what about couples like Mr. and Mrs. O.? They observed Enchanted World first-hand and still picked wrong, because alerted to their presence beforehand, the center had "cleaned up its act." The experts advised that to choose a good day-care facility, parents should talk to workers there, rotate days when they unexpectedly drop in at the center, and observe their child carefully for changes. Parents may also consult the National Child Care Referral Agency to identify quality day care in their community.

CASE QUESTIONS

1. Do you believe we have a day-care crisis in the United States? Why or why not? If so, what do you think we can do about it?

2. Can you suggest any alternatives to day care?

3. What do you think the experts meant when they said that unless we do better, we will lose generations of our country?

Part Four

EARLY CHILDHOOD

8 Language: The Bridge from Infancy

"Children must learn a specific language, with all of its cultural ramifications. While they learn syntax and vocabulary, children also absorb social values, such as politeness, obedience, and gender roles."

Thus, the task of acquiring language interconnects with cognitive and social development. For this reason, language acquisition has been called a bridge between infancy and childhood. When children understand and communicate their needs, wants, and observations, the world treats them differently and vice versa.

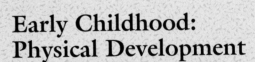

9 Early Childhood: Physical Development

"Almost everything that a child does from birth through the first few years lays the base, in some way, not only for later physical-motor skills, but also for cognitive processes and social and emotional development."

Much of the activity of preschoolers—shaping mud pies, hanging upside down, crawling—seem to be for the sheer pleasure of sensory exploration. Yet all these actions are purposeful; that is, they are directed toward a specific goal.

11 Early Childhood: Personality and Social Development

"There is dramatic growth in the child's self-control and social competence during the four important years from age 2 to age 6."

During this period, young children become socialized. They learn, in other words, within the social context of their community, the rules, norms, and cultural meanings of their society. It is now that they develop a self-concept that well may be permanent.

10 Early Childhood: Developing Thought and Action

"In his pioneering investigation of how logical thinking develops in children, Jean Piaget described the course of development in terms of discrete periods that children pass through on the way to a logical understanding of the world...."

Piaget's theory offers us a way of looking at the dramatic cognitive advances of preschoolers. Newer theories, however, challenge several of Piaget's findings about the cognitive abilities of the young child and how they develop.

*And always behind my eyes
is the image of my daughter at
age three asking
do butterflies have babies—
Or is it the other way round?*

ELSIE MACLAY
"GREEN WINTER"

LANGUAGE: THE BRIDGE FROM INFANCY

Jason: Maria broke the toy, didn't she?

Mother: Yes, dear. She did.

Jason: I don't break toys. I'm a good boy, amn't I?

Mother: I'm a good boy, *aren't* I?

Jason: Nah, You're a *girl!*

The infant's first word is one of the highlights of infancy—indeed, parents rank it alongside the first time the baby sleeps through the night—especially if the first word is "dada" or "mama." Before that first word, however, even newborns, communicate. It doesn't take long for them to discover how to let their parents know that they are hungry, wet, or bored. By about 1 year of age, most children begin to talk; by 4 1/2, most have developed amazing verbal competence. Their vocabulary may be limited and their grammar far from perfect, but their implicit grasp of language structure is remarkable. They not only know the words with which to designate things and communicate thoughts, but they also exhibit a very sophisticated understanding of the rules that govern the combinations and uses of these words. They speak in full sentences with phrases, clauses, and appropriate grammatical constructions, such as proper tenses and plural forms. This is a startling cognitive achievement when we think of the enormous complexity of the underlying rules of syntax and semantics. Language is an elaborate system of symbols. To manipulate the symbols properly, a child must first master basic cognitive concepts.

The complexity and originality of the 4 1/2-year-old's speech are perhaps best illustrated by the *tag question*, which is a direct statement followed by a tag, or request to confirm the statement: "Maria broke the toy, didn't she?" This apparently simple question actually involves a number of grammatical processes. In order to form the tag "didn't she," Jason had to understand several different rules. He had to know how to copy, or supply, the correct subject pronoun for "Maria," how to supply the auxiliary verb (the proper form of "do"), how to negate the auxiliary verb, and how to invert the word order of the auxiliary verb and pronoun. Somewhat younger children may have the general idea of the tag question but may not yet be able to master all of the grammatical processes. Thus, they might say, "Maria broke the toy, unh?"

Language development is more than a purely cognitive achievement, however. It also involves social growth. Children must learn a specific language, with all of its cultural ramifications. While they learn syntax and vocabulary, children also absorb social values, such as politeness, obedience, and gender roles. Therefore, language acquisition involves both cognitive and social development; it is a bridge between infancy and childhood. When children can understand and communicate their wants, needs, and observations, the world deals with them in quite a different fashion.

LANGUAGE DEVELOPMENT

Language involves the use of symbols for communicating information. The acquisition of language is a complex yet natural process. Perhaps better than any other single accomplishment, it illustrates the range and potential of the human organism. For this reason, it is a particularly fascinating area of psychological development. To understand this phenomenon fully, we should first be aware of some of its most basic elements.

ASPECTS OF LANGUAGE

We often think of language as having three major dimensions: content, form, and use (Bloom & Lahey, 1978). **Content** refers to the meaning of any written or spoken message. **Form** is the particular symbol used to represent that content—the sounds, the words, the grammar. **Use** refers to the social interchange, or exchange, between two people: the speaker and the person spoken to. The details of that social exchange depend on the situation, the relationship between the speaker and the listener, and on the intentions and attitudes of the two participants. In the example at the beginning of this chapter, Jason is talking about who broke the toy (content). He is using an especially sophisticated grammatical form—a tag question. Jason is concerned about receiving reassurance from his mother that he is a good boy, whereas his mother is interested in correcting his grammar. In this simple exchange, a great deal has been communicated. The information is conveyed in a particular form, in a fashion that reflects the relationship and intention of both participants. The form and the use, therefore, also contribute to the meaning of the message.

Form can be examined on three levels. **Phonemes** are the basic sounds—the vowels and the consonants—that combine to form words. English has forty-six separate phonemes: vowels (a, e, i, o and u); consonants such as p, m, k and d; and blends of the two consonants like "th." Other languages use different groups of phonemes. Sounds used in one language may even be absent in another. **Morphemes** are the meaning units—the basic words, prefixes, and suffixes. The sentence, "Mommy warmed the bottles" can be divided into six morphemes: *Mommy, warm, ed, the, bottle,* and *s.* Finally, every language has a **grammar**—a complicated set of rules for building words (**morphology**), as well as the rules for combining words to form phrases and sentences (**syntax**). In English, however,

content The meaning of any written or spoken message.

form The particular symbol used to represent content.

use The way in which a speaker employs language to give it one meaning as opposed to another.

phonemes The smallest units of sound—vowels and consonants—that combine to form morphemes and words.

morphemes The minimal units of meaning in language that form basic words, prefixes, and suffixes.

grammar A complicated set of rules for building words, as well as the rules for combining words to form phrases and sentences.

morphology The set of rules for building words that is present in all languages.

syntax The rules for combining words to form phrases and sentences.

Expressing feelings and establishing and maintaining contact with others are some of the uses of speech.

grammar is primarily concerned with syntax, and the two terms are often used interchangeably. The number of combinations of sounds or sentences in English is, for all practical purposes, infinite. It should be noted that aspects of form also convey meaning. "The dog bit the baby" is different from "The baby bit the dog," simply because of word order. Such distinctions are learned at a very early age.

The social use of language is complex. Children learn to be polite and deferential to their elders, to simplify their language for babies, to take turns when they are involved in a conversation, and to understand indirect as well as direct speech. They learn to determine the speaker's intention as well as to understand the actual words. For example, a sentence such as, "What is this?" can have different meanings, depending on the situation. It can serve as a simple request for information, but it also can be an expression of horror.

We use speech for a number of purposes. We use it to satisfy wants and needs; to control others; to maintain contact with other people; to express feelings; to imagine, pretend, or create; and to inquire and describe (Halliday, 1973). Young children are exposed to and implicitly learn these functions of language, as well as specific words and forms.

THE PROCESSES OF LANGUAGE LEARNING

Just how do humans progress from crying to babbling to speaking the infinite forms of adult language? In recent years, a great deal of research has been devoted to this question, both for its own sake and for the insight an answer might give into other areas of learning. There has been much controversy as to precisely how the process works, but it is possible to highlight four components: *imitation, reinforcement, innate language structure,* and *cognitive development.* Imitation and reinforcement are terms associated with B.F. Skinner and the

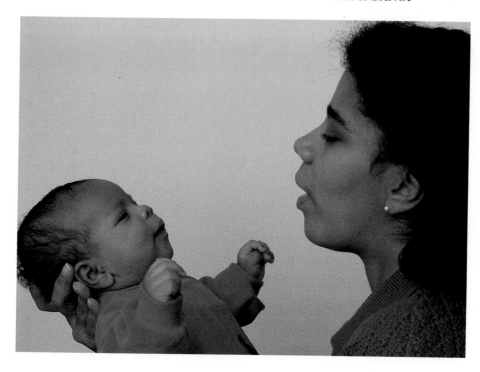

Imitation plays an important part in language learning, particularly in the early stages of development.

behaviorists, whom we discussed earlier in Chapter 2. Innate language structure is associated with Noam Chomsky, and cognitive development is based on the work of Jean Piaget. All four components are probably part of the process.

IMITATION   Imitation plays a large part in language learning. Children's first words—usually simple labels—are obviously learned by hearing and imitating. In fact, most early vocabulary must be learned in this way; children cannot invent words and make themselves understood. But the development of syntax is not so easily explained. No doubt some phrases result from imitation, but a form such as "amn't I" is clearly original. So too is a phrase such as "my want to go." It is unlikely that children have heard anyone speak this way. Even when people use baby talk or attempt to correct children's errors, the children tend to adhere to their own consistent speech patterns, for which there are no immediate models.

REINFORCEMENT   As we have seen in previous chapters, reinforcement is a powerful learning device, and this probably holds true for certain aspects of language acquisition. Certainly, children are influenced by reactions to their speech. Smiles, hugs, and increased attention will encourage learning to some extent. Also, when words produce favorable results, children are likely to repeat them. If an infant calls "Mommy" and she comes or if he says "Cookie" and gets one, he will use these words again. But reinforcement does not seem sufficient to explain the acquisition of syntax. As we know, much of children's speech is original and has never been reinforced. Even if some forms are encouraged and others discouraged, it simply would not be possible to reinforce all correct forms and extinguish all incorrect ones. Also, especially when children first begin to talk, adults tend to reinforce any speech at all, however unintelligible or incorrect. Even when they are more discriminating, they are likely to respond to content instead

FOCUS ON AN ISSUE

MUST ONE BE HUMAN TO LEARN LANGUAGE?

Are humans the only animals capable of using language to express simple and complex thoughts? During the past two decades, a number of chimpanzees and apes have been able to learn at least the rudiments of human communication. Chimps have been able to associate names with objects, put two words together, and use words in a new context. These are definitely aspects of human language that are seen in developing humans. But chimps have been unable to master the complex use of words and grammar that is an essential part of language.

Chimps have limited control of their vocal tract, which makes speech impossible. Researchers made their first breakthrough in teaching human language to chimps when they moved from vocal speech to other forms, such as the manual sign language used by deaf human children. After quickly learning the signs for 200 or more nouns, including concrete nouns for the food, people, and things around them, action verbs, and significant adjectives like "big" and "sweet," the chimps extended the use of

---

A gorilla named Koko invented the following new words: "Finger bracelet" for ring, "eye hat" for mask, and "elephant baby" for a Pinocchio doll.

---

many of these signs to new referents they had never directly learned. Washoe, the first chimpanzee to learn sign language, initially learned the sign for "hurt" in connection with scratches and bruises. When she saw a person's naval for the first time, she signed "hurt." She used the same sign for a decal on the back of a person's hand (Klima & Bellugi, 1973).

Within months of the time their training began, the chimps started to combine signs to express specific thoughts. For example, when Washoe heard the sound of a barking dog, she combined the signs for "listen" and "dog." When she wanted the person with her to continue tickling her, she signed "more" and "tickle," and when she saw a duck she signed "water-bird." A gorilla named Koko invented the following new words: "finger bracelet" for ring, "eye hat" for mask, and "elephant baby" for a Pinocchio doll. Koko also named a kitten "all ball" (Hayes, 1977).

To test the logical and grammatical abilities of chimps, the trainers of

---

of form. If a child says, "I eated my peas," her parents will probably praise her—unless the statement is not true, in which case they will no doubt call her attention to the vegetables remaining on her plate.

INNATE LANGUAGE STRUCTURE   Linguist Noam Chomsky (1959) drew attention to the limitations of reinforcement theory. He believes that every human being is born with a mental structure for acquiring language. This *language acquisition device (LAD)* enables children to process linguistic data selectively from their environment and to formulate a generative grammar, from which they create language. Thus, when children hear people talk, they unconsciously induce rules and form their own language according to these rules. This process follows a developmental sequence; children can assimilate certain data before others. But according to Chomsky, at least some of the basics of language are preprogrammed into the human organism. (To explore whether other animals have the capacity for using language, see the box "Must One Be Human to Learn Language?").

chimp Sarah took a different approach. Sarah learned to associate magnetized pieces of plastic in various colors and shapes with the objects, people, and actions around her and to express her thoughts on a metal board. She learned to use plastic symbols that had no resemblance to the objects they represented (for instance, Δ is the symbol for pear) and to understand the rudiments of grammar, which enabled her to respond to sentence organization. When tested, Sarah correctly understood such complex sentences as, "Sarah banana pail and cracker dish insert" (Sarah put the banana in the pail and cracker dish) 8 out of 10 times. In addition, her ability to form sentences she had never seen before indicated substantial cognitive ability (de Villiers & de Villiers, 1979).

Chimps appear to have the capacity to use symbols to represent objects and events and to communicate their insights. But there is considerable debate as to what this indicates about their cognitive processes and to what extent this use of symbols resembles a human infant's learning of language. Chomsky (1976) points to the fact that there is a vast difference between the language learning of humans and the rudimentary responses of chimps. Chimps, says Chomsky, never learn the subtleties of word order nor do they ever use language in a creative, spontaneous way. It has also been argued that although apes can be trained to produce behaviors that have some of the properties of human linguistic behavior, they do not have the inner motivation for language that a child does. Therefore, the communication of the chimp and the child differ profoundly (Sugarman, 1983).

Other psycholinguists argue that there are no significant differences between young children's use of words and a trained chimp's use. Researchers at the Yerkes Primate Center found that Pygmy monkeys spontaneously learned to relate symbols and objects, presumably exhibiting abilities for abstract thought (Savage-Rumbaugh, Rumbaugh, & McDonald, 1986).

The debate involves more than the potential of chimpanzees and other apes to conceptualize and communicate. It also involves our inability to know what the chimps are really thinking when they employ words and combinations of words. We can only interpret the chimps' use of the symbols to which they are painstakingly exposed by dedicated researchers. To some extent, the same problem exists with our understanding of how human infants learn language. What is the thought process that results in a human infant's early speech? As embodiments of the mysteries of language development, the chimp and the human child are indeed akin.

In order to show that innate language abilities exist, researchers have examined deaf children's ability to develop spontaneous systems of languagelike gestures (Goldin-Meadow & Mylander, 1984). They have also studied children's abilities to link specific ideas with specific words (Gleitman & Wanner, 1982). The theory of innate language structure helps to explain the ability of all peoples to create and transmit language and the natural responsiveness of infants to learn to speak. It takes into account the incredible complexity of human language and points out the inadequacy of simple imitation and reinforcement theories.

While there are good points associated with an innate language structure, as we may see above, there have also been criticisms of Chomsky's work. For example, children do not gain full mastery of grammatical rules until middle childhood, much later than Chomsky proposed (Brown, 1973). In addition, while Chomsky proposed that a common grammar underlies all languages, scientists have been unable to agree on what that grammar is (Moerk, 1989). Finally, Chomsky, critics suggest, does not really explain the process of learning a language. In a sense, his argument, they contend, is circular; he claims children learn

"What's the big surprise? All the latest theories of linguistics say we're born with the innate capacity for generating sentences."

language because they are prewired to do so (Brown, 1973; Maratsos, 1983). Despite these criticisms the theory has been useful and has stimulated considerable study of the development of children's language.

COGNITIVE DEVELOPMENT   The fourth major approach to language acquisition emphasizes the link between language learning and a child's developing concepts and relationships. This view is supported by the fact that basic grammatical structures are not present in earliest speech but develop progressively, leading theorists to conclude that learning them depends on prior cognitive development (Bloom, 1970). Thus, a particular speech pattern will not emerge before the child has grasped the concept behind it. Between the ages of 1 and 4 1/2, children are actively constructing their own grammar, gradually approaching the full grammar of the adults around them. At any given time, however, children are capable of expressing only those concepts that they have mastered.

There are many parallels between cognitive development and language development. About the time that the child is acquiring object permanence and is interested in games of hiding and finding objects, his beginning language reflects these cognitive processes with words like "see," "all gone," or "more?" and "bye-bye." Comings and goings and hidings and findings become the focus of language and of vocabulary. A little later, when children are fascinated with possession and with what is theirs and what is someone else's, this, too, is reflected in their language development. They are, at about this time, learning aspects of syntax that reflect the possessive case—"Daddy sock," "baby bed," and later, "mine," and "Mommy's cup."

Which comes first, the understanding of concepts or the language to express them? Piaget (1962) theorized that the ability to conceptualize an idea precedes the ability to express it in words. Others have observed that very soon after a child begins to understand relationships such as "bigger" or "more than," words help shape, sharpen, and transform conceptual thinking (Vygotsky, 1962; Bruner, 1983). Recent research indicates that the development of language and cognition may go hand in hand. For instance, words expressing concepts may be used productively and symbolically before children solve conceptual problems about how to compare and relate objects. These words are used mainly to categorize objects. Along with the development of the cognitive abilities to comprehend relationships between things, more relational words emerge (Gopnik, 1988). Generally, by the time children begin elementary school, their language and problem-solving skills have been integrated, enabling them to understand and interact with other people in many situations. We may see some milestones in the development of language presented in Table 8–1.

LANGUAGE BEGINNINGS

Language development involves learning to speak or produce oral language, learning the meaning of words, and learning rules of grammar—how words can be combined into sentences to communicate ideas. During the preschool years, there are two key processes involved in language development. **Receptive language** is a

TABLE 8–1 Milestones in Language Development*

AVERAGE AGE	LANGUAGE BEHAVIOR DEMONSTRATED BY CHILD
12 weeks	Smiles when talked to; makes cooing sounds.
16 weeks	Turns head in response to human voice.
20 weeks	Makes vowel and consonant sounds while cooing.
6 months	Cooing changes to babbling, which contains all sounds of human speech.
8 months	Certain syllables repeated (for example, "ma-ma").
12 months	Understands some words; may say a few.
18 months	Can produce up to fifty words.
24 months	Has vocabulary of more than fifty words; uses some two-word phrases.
30 months	Vocabulary increases to several hundred words; uses phrases of three to five words.
36 months	Vocabulary of about a thousand words.
48 months	Most basic aspects of language well established.

*These figures are only *averages;* individual children frequently depart from them in varying degrees.
Source: Baron, *1992, p. 273.*

receptive language The repertoire of words and commands that a child understands, although he or she may not be able to say them.

child's understanding of the spoken or the written word. **Productive language** is what the child says or, later, what the child writes. These interrelated processes evolve simultaneously. Often, receptive language, or language comprehension, develops a little bit ahead of language production. For example, a parent may ask her 14-month-old the following question, "Will you go into the kitchen and bring back the cookies?" The child may return with the cookies but be unable to produce such a sentence—or even the words "bring cookies"—himself.

BEFORE THE FIRST WORDS

The production of language begins with an undifferentiated cry at the moment of birth. Soon after, infants develop a range of different cries and, by about 6 weeks, a variety of cooing sounds. At the time of birth, infants have developed a large area in the left hemisphere of the brain (the hemisphere that controls language) that allows them to listen to and respond to language from the very beginning (Brooks & Obrzut, 1981). By the second or third month, infants are sensitive to speech and can distinguish between such similar sounds as *b* and *p* or *d* and *t* (Eimas, 1974). In the first year of life, then, long before the first words are spoken, infants are able to learn a great deal about language.

THE BRAIN AND LANGUAGE   Even before infants are capable of generating words, their brains are busy recognizing what is familiar and signaling their wants—as well as generating actions to learn more about their worlds, as we discussed earlier in Chapters 5 and 6. All of this occurs prior to their forming one understandable word and long before they structure sentences or truly use their native language. It is believed that the brain processes language by means of three interacting sets of structures:

1. A large collection of neural systems in both the right and left cerebral hemispheres, representing nonlanguage interactions between the body and its environment, that is, all that the person does, perceives, thinks, or feels;
2. A smaller number of neural systems located in the left cerebral hemisphere, representing phonemes, phoneme combinations, and syntactic rules for combining words. (On being stimulated from within the brain, these systems assemble word-forms and generate sentences to be written or spoken; on being externally stimulated by speech or a written text, they initially process visual or auditory language signals);
3. A third set of structures, largely in the left cerebral hemisphere, mediating between the other two structures by taking concepts and producing word-forms or the reverse—by receiving word-forms and forming corresponding concepts (Damasio & Damasio, 1992).

We can see these brain systems presented in Figure 8–1. Furthermore, as we see in Figure 8–2, concepts are complex and involve various sensations and associated actions. Coffee cups are one example of such concepts, but many other things could be substituted. Coffee cups are learned in a variety of ways. There is, of course, the taste of the coffee within; the temperature and warmth of the cup; the shape and designs on the cup. These representations are all stored well before the child possesses the word for "cup" or "mug."

productive language The spoken or written communication of children.

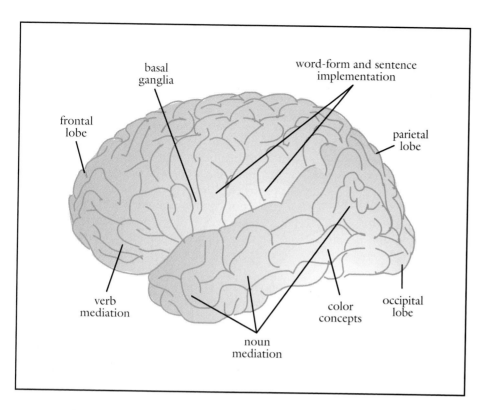

FIGURE 8-1

Brain Systems for Language in the Left Hemisphere.
These systems include word and sentence-implementation structures and mediation structures for various lexical items and grammar. The neural structures representing the concepts themselves are distributed across both the right and left hemispheres in many sensory and motor regions.

In the brain illustration, the following labels appear: frontal lobe, basal ganglia, word-form and sentence implementation, parietal lobe, verb mediation, noun mediation, color concepts, occipital lobe.

FIGURE 8-2

Components of a Concept.
Concepts are stored in the brain in the form of "dormant" records. When reactivated, these records can re-create the various sensations and actions associated with a specific entity or a category of entities. For example, a coffee cup can evoke visual and tactile representations of its shape, color, texture and warmth, along with the smell and taste of the coffee, or the path of the hand and the arm in raising the cup from the table to the lips. Although all these representations are re-created in separate brain regions, their reconstruction occurs fairly simultaneously.

SOCIAL COMMUNICATION   As we learned in Chapters 6 and 7, throughout the first year, infants have been learning nonverbal aspects of communication in the "mutual dialogue" between parent and infant. They have been learning to signal, to take turns, to use gestures, and to pay attention to facial expressions. Infants learn a lot about communication while playing simple games like peekaboo (Ross & Lollis, 1987). Indeed, some parents are very skillful at structuring social games with their infants that help them learn many aspects of the conversation in a most enjoyable fashion. Parents who do this well provide a structure for the game, or a scaffolding, that helps the child learn the rules of give and take and turn-taking (Bruner, 1983). But the social communication with the infant goes far beyond parent games. Certainly, by 1 year of age, most healthy infants are quite alert to the people around them, including strangers, and they respond appropriately to the varied emotional expressions of adults (Klinnert et al., 1986).

BABBLING   From the earliest moments, infants explore a variety of sounds. Often, they start with vowel sounds and front-of-the-mouth consonants: "Ahh, bahh, bahh, bahh." By 6 months, infants have a much more varied and complex repertoire. They string together a wide range of sounds, draw them out, cut them off, and vary the pitch and rhythm. Increasingly, they seem to exert control over these vocalizations. They purposefully repeat sounds, elongate them, and pause in a kind of self-imitating pseudo talk, sometimes called **iteration.**

Early vocalizations involve only a few different sounds, or phonemes. But, by the second month, infants are forming a number of consonant sounds as well as clicks, gurgles, grunts, and other sounds, some of which are outside the range of the parents' native language. Although the number of phonemes expands rapidly during the first year, toward the end of that period phoneme production slows down.

Sometime after 6 months, many parents hear something suspiciously like "ma-ma" or "da-da" and report this as their precocious infants' first words. Usually, however, these are chance repetitions of sounds that have no real meaning. Around this time, babbling takes on inflections and patterns very much like those of the parents' language. In fact, the babbling begins to sound so much like adult speech that parents may strain to listen, thinking that perhaps it is coherent language. This highly developed babbling is what Arnold Gesell has termed **expressive jargon.** Such patterns of babbling appear to be the same for infants in all language groups (Roug, Landberg, & Lundberg, 1989).

Just how important is babbling? In what ways does babbling prepare a baby for speaking? A baby's babbling is an irresistible form of verbal communication, and care-givers throughout the world delight in imitating and encouraging these vocalizations. It appears that in the course of babbling, babies are learning how to produce the sounds they will later use in speaking. Thus, the sounds or phonemes that babies produce are influenced by what they hear before they use words. Although babbling is a means for babies to communicate and interact with other people, it is also a problem-solving activity. Babies babble as a way to figure out how to make the specific sounds needed to say words. This may be why babies do not stop babbling when they start producing words. In fact, new words seem to influence babbling, while babbling in turn affects the preferred sounds babies use in selecting new words (Elbers & Ton, 1985).

Recent research has found that babies are language universalists who can distinguish all the sounds of human language, while adults are language specialists

iteration Infants' purposeful repetition, elongation, and pause in sounds that imitate speech.

expressive jargon A term used to describe the babbling of an infant when the infant uses inflections and patterns that mimic adult speech.

Babbling between care-giver and infant can be a pleasurable experience for both.

who can only perceive and reproduce sounds in their native tongue. The researchers tested six-month-old infants who were taught to look over their shoulders when they heard a difference in pairs of sounds and to ignore sounds that seemed alike. The babies were able to distinguish variations in unfamiliar languages but ignored the familiar similarities of their own language. This study showed that language perception is clearly shaped by experience—but at an earlier age than was originally thought. The study also indicated that the "conversations" between parents and infants are instrumental in producing spoken language (Kuhl et al., 1992). As the researchers suggest:

> Infants demonstrate a capacity to learn simply by being exposed to language during the first half year of life, before the time that they have uttered meaningful words. By 6 months of age, linguistic experience has resulted in language-specific phonetic prototypes that assist infants in organizing speech sounds into categories. They are in place when infants begin to acquire word meanings toward the end of the first year. Phonetic prototypes would thus appear to be fundamental perceptual-cognitive building blocks rather than by-products of language acquisition. (Kuhl et al., 1992, p. 608)

Comparisons of the babbling of hearing babies and deaf babies also indicate how important what the baby hears is for the child's language development, even at the babbling stage. Although the babbling of groups of hearing babies and deaf babies was initially comparable, only the babbling of the hearing infants moved closer to the sounds of words used in their language (Oller & Eilers, 1988). Moreover, the babbling of deaf babies appears to lessen significantly after 6 months, when language production begins to be facilitated by reinforcement.

Babbling appears to play a key role in babies' learning to use the specific sounds needed to speak the language of their care-givers. For example, when the babbling of 10-month-old infants in Paris, London, Hong Kong, and Algiers was analyzed, researchers discovered that differences in how these infants pronounced vowel sounds paralleled the vowel sound pronunciations found in their native languages—French, English, Cantonese, and Arabic (de-Boysson-Bardies, 1989).

What if a baby's babbling is atypical? In specific cases, atypical babbling has been associated with delays in beginning to speak (Stoel-Gammon, 1989). However, there is still much to be learned about the role of babbling in both normal and problematic speech development.

In all cultures, some children develop a fairly extensive vocabulary of *pseudo words*. They use a particular range of specific vocalizations, usually paired with gestures, that have specific meanings (Reich, 1986).

RECEPTIVE VOCABULARY   Care-givers and researchers generally agree very young children understand words before they can say them. Infants as young as 1 year are able to follow some directions from adults and show by their behavior that they know the meaning of words like "bye-bye." Infants' comprehension of speech, however, is a very difficult area for psychologists and linguists to study. Although it is relatively easy to listen to children speak and to record them, it is much more difficult to identify and describe concepts that very young children associate with specific words. Even when the evidence seems clear—for example, when a 1-year-old follows the instruction "Put the spoon in the cup"—the child's understanding may be nowhere near as complete as we conclude. It is, after all, hard to put the cup in the spoon. Also, children may receive clues, such as gestures, that help them to perform tasks correctly. Parents of very young children often say that their children understand far more words at home, in familiar surroundings, than in unfamiliar testing rooms. Although this may be true, it is also true that parents use gestures and context clues to help convey their message. Parents, also will frequently accept vague signals as evidence that their children understand instructions.

By the time children are 3 to 4 years old, they will readily begin to ask what the meaning of sentences, concepts or phrases are—especially, if they have been reinforced and encouraged to ask questions. The following exchange indicates the way in which this proceeds:

Mother *(singing):* Suzanne takes you down to a place by the water....She gets you on her wavelength and lets the river answer....

5-year-old girl: Mommy, what does wavelength mean?

Mother: It means that you and another person have really understood each other...that you've both felt the same way when you were talking to each other. Does that make sense, honey?

5-year-old girl: Sure, Mom. It's like when we were talking about how we couldn't wait for the snow to be gone and the flowers to come up. We both felt really happy.

In this case, a verbal young child has fully engaged in discussion with her mother—and learned a new word in the process.

FIRST WORDS

Most children utter their first words around the end of the first year. They then add single words, slowly at first, and much more rapidly by the middle of the second year. As children approach age 2, single words give way to two-word, and then three-word, sentences.

There is wide individual variation in the rate at which language learning progresses. Toddlers who seem to be progressing rather slowly in this area are not necessarily developmentally delayed; they may be busy with other tasks, as the following example indicates.

> My second child, a boy, was really remarkable. He didn't walk until he was almost 18 months old. But could he talk! He would stand in his crib and yell, "Get me out of here," but he wouldn't try to get out. Our third child, Norma, was just the opposite. She was cruising around the living room at 7 months and walking at 9 months. She didn't talk until she was 14 months old.

Some children start late but catch-up quickly; others seem stuck at particular stages for long periods of time. Regardless of the pace of language learning, the sequence of language development follows a regular and predictable pattern. This pattern appears not only in English but in every language. Analysis of language acquisition in many countries has revealed remarkably consistent patterns (Slobin, 1972).

EARLY WORDS AND MEANINGS   Throughout the world, infants' first utterances are single words—most often nouns and usually names of the people, things, or animals in the immediate environment. In the beginning, children simply do not have the ability to use words in combination. Some psycholinguists feel that despite this restriction in language production, children can conceive full sentences and that their early utterances are actually **holophrastic speech**—single words meant to convey complex ideas. Thus, in different contexts, with different intonations and gestures, "*mama*" may mean "I want my mother" or "Mama, tie my shoe," or "There she is, my mama." Other psycholinguists warn against over-interpreting brief utterances.

What words form an infant's early vocabulary? Because the care-givers of each infant use different words and the process of development is individual, the vocabularies learned by infants differ. But the types of words first used by infants fall into categories. Names—that is, nouns that refer to specific things, such as "dada," "bottie," and "car"—comprise much of a child's early vocabulary (Nelson, 1974). However, children at the one-word stage also use words that indicate function or relationship, such as "there," "no," "gone," and "up," possibly even before they use nouns (Bloom, Lifter, & Broughton, 1985). The individual words and category of words a child uses most may depend on the child's personal speech style. Nelson (1981) identified children with a *referential style* who tended to use nouns, and *expressive* children who learned more active verbs and pronouns.

Katherine Nelson was one of the first researchers to study differences in language-learning styles among children. By the age of 18 months, when children

holophrastic speech In the early stages of language acquisition, the young child's use of single words, perhaps to convey full sentences.

Among the first words infants use are nouns such as "car."

had vocabularies of approximately 50 words, the two distinct groups mentioned above had emerged. The referential children had vocabularies that were dominated by naming words—mostly nouns indicating persons or objects but few actions. The expressive children, on the other hand, had learned the naming words but also knew a higher percentage of words used in social interactions (for example, "go away," "I want it," "give me," and so forth). Thus Rachel, a referential child, had 41 name words in her 50-word vocabulary, but only 2 words in the social interaction or question-asking categories; Elizabeth, an expressive child, had a more balanced vocabulary; with 24 name words and 14 words in the social interaction and question-asking categories. The later language development of expressive and referential children also differs from each other. Expressive children typically have smaller vocabularies and are more likely to use pronouns than nouns when compared to referential children (Nelson, 1981). In addition, expressive children tend to create and use "dummy words"—words with no apparent meaning—to substitute for words they do not know.

Early speech grows out of the prelinguistic gestures that every baby uses to communicate (Gopnik, 1988). A child's first words appear to be social in nature. The child speaks in order to influence other people; he wants his mother's attention, to eat a cookie instead of an apple, or to indicate that he will not sit down in his bath. Later, in the one-word stage, when the child's abilities to think and to remember are more developed, the same types of words have been found to express intrapersonal thoughts and ideas (Gopnik & Meltzoff, 1987).

OVEREXTENSIONS AND UNDEREXTENSIONS   When a child first uses a word, it usually refers to a specific person, object, or situation. The word "Goggy" may apply to a child's own pet. The child may then use it when naming other dogs, or other four-legged animals. But when this child learns new words such as "horsie" or "kitty" she will redefine all of the animal categories she had previously learned (Schlesinger, 1982). This is an example of *overextending* a word. Children tend to overextend, underextend, or overlap the categories they use to determine what words refer to, because they often do not share adults' knowledge of culturally appropriate functions and characteristics of objects. Instead, they may emphasize aspects of objects that adults have come to ignore when categorizing objects (Mervis, 1987). Some interesting examples of overextensions used by children are given in Table 8–2.

As children learn additional contrasting names for objects, such as kitty, cat, lion, and tiger, they reassign words to more specific and increasingly hierarchical categories (Clark, 1987; Merriman, 1987). In other words, a lion and a tiger are different. They are both examples of the more general "cat" category. Over time, the child's linguistic categories take on the language use structure of the adults in that linguistic culture. The process of categorizing language appears to follow the same general pattern as that of intellectual or cognitive development (Chapman & Mervis, 1989).

Children's words and their meanings are closely linked to the concepts the children are developing. A child who applies the word "moon" to everything round has some concept of *round*. But which comes first—the word and its meaning or the concept? Researchers differ on their interpretation of the evidence. Some, including Piaget, believe that most of the time the concept forms first. The child discovers a concept and then finds a name to attach to it, whether learned or of his own creation. Evidence for this theory includes the finding that

TABLE 8–2 The Overextension of Words. Children may apply a word to many objects with common properties or functions.

CHILD'S WORD	FIRST REFERENT	EXTENSIONS	POSSIBLE COMMON PROPERTY
Bird	Sparrows	Cows, dogs, cats, any moving animal.	Movement
Mooi	Moon	Cakes, round marks on window, round shapes in books, tooling on leather book covers, postmarks, letter O.	Shape
Fly	Fly	Specks of dirt, dust, all small insects, his own toes, crumbs, small toad.	Size
Koko	Cockerel crowing	Tunes played on a violin, piano, accordion, phonograph, all music, merry-go-round.	Sound
Wau-wau	Dogs	All animals, toy dog, soft slippers, picture of old man in furs.	Texture

Source: From deVilliers and deVilliers, 1979.

twins have been known to create their own private language, and deaf children create signs or gestures even when they are not taught sign language. This would suggest that concepts come first and words afterward (Clark, 1983). Other researchers believe that words help shape our concepts. When a young child names the family pet "dog," he is simply naming that object. When he extends and refines his categories, he is learning the concept of "dog" (Schlesinger, 1982). In fact, both processes are probably true and serve to complement each other as the child learns language.

TWO-WORD SENTENCES

Toward the end of the second year, most children begin to put words together. Often, the first attempts are simply two words that represent two ideas: "Mommy see," "Sock off," or "More milk." This is a fascinating period in language development because implicit rules of syntax appear. In recent years, psycholinguists have studied the development of language production by recording and analyzing lengthy samples of children's speech, collected at daily or weekly intervals. Valuable insights have been gained about such features as sentence length, the kinds of grammatical rules used, and the types of meanings expressed by children at any given stage.

TELEGRAPHIC SPEECH When children start putting words together, their sentences seem to be sharply limited in length. At first, they seem restricted to two elements, then three, and so on. At each stage, the number of words or thoughts in a sentence is limited—children retain high-information words and omit the less significant ones. The result is what Brown (1965) calls **telegraphic speech.** The informative words, which Brown terms *contentives*, are the nouns, verbs, and adjectives. The less important words are known as *functors*, and are the inflections, auxiliary verbs, and prepositions.

telegraphic speech One- and 2-year-olds' utterances that omit the less significant words and include the words that carry the most meaning.

When children first put two words together, they do it in a consistent fashion. They may say, "See dog" or "See truck" as they point at things. But they never say, "Truck, see." Even in the two-word sentence, we can find certain consistencies. What sort of grammar is being used? A number of models have been identified.

PIVOT GRAMMAR   Among the first significant grammatical analyses was the study by Braine (1963), which identified a **pivot grammar** at the two-word phase. *Pivot words* are usually action words (go), prepositions (off), or possessives (my). They are few in number and occur frequently in combination with *x-words,* or open words, which are usually nouns. "See," for example, is a pivot word that can combine with any number of open words to form two-word sentences: "See milk," "See Mommy," or "Mommy see." Pivot words almost never occur alone or with other pivots (McNeill, 1972). X-words may, however, be paired or used singly. These prohibitions and combinations are not random, but result from children's limited comprehension and production of language. The length restriction is apparently the main barrier to their expression of complex grammatical notions in more adult-sounding forms.

CASE GRAMMAR   Children seem able to express a number of relationships by word order: agent (who did it), patient (to whom), instrument (with what), location (where), and so forth (Fillmore, 1968). They are expressing a **case grammar.** Because of the variety of relationships that a two-word sentence can be used to express, the child's utterance must be interpreted in context. Lois Bloom (1970) noted that a child she was studying said, "Mommy sock" one time to indicate that her mother was putting on a sock and another time to communicate that she had found her mother's sock.

With the help of gestures, tone, and context, children can communicate numerous meanings with a small vocabulary and limited syntax. Dan Slobin (1972) studied the variety of meanings conveyed by two-word sentences spoken by 2-year-olds. Although his young conversants were from different linguistic cultures, speaking English, German, Russian, Turkish, or Samoan, the children used speech in the same ways. Among the concepts that the 2-year-olds were able to communicate by two-word utterances were:

Identification: See doggie.

Location: Book there.

Nonexistence: Allgone thing.

Negation: Not wolf.

Possession: My candy.

Attribution: Big car.

Agent-action: Mama walk.

Action-location: Sit chair.

pivot grammar A two-word sentence-forming system used by 2-year-olds and involving action words, prepositions, or possessives (pivot words) in combination with x-words, which are usually nouns.

case grammar The use of word order to express different relationships.

Action-direct object: Hit you.

Action-indirect object: Give papa.

Action-instrument: Cut knife.

Question: Where ball?

LANGUAGE COMPLEXITIES

Throughout the preschool years, children are rapidly expanding their vocabularies, their use of grammatical forms, and their understanding of language as a social act. We can only look at a sampling of these many accomplishments.

AN EXPANDING GRAMMAR

One of the more influential works in the study of language acquisition was written by Roger Brown (1973). Brown and his colleagues studied many children but recorded at length the speech patterns of three particular young children—Adam, Eve, and Sarah. Taking a developmental approach, Brown identified *five distinct, increasingly complex stages.* He views development in terms of **mean length of utterance (MLU)**—the average length of the sentence that the child produces—instead of age, because children learn at very different rates. Eve, for example, progressed nearly twice as fast as Adam and Sarah. Yet the sequence is similar for most children. Certain skills and rules are apparently mastered before others, and certain errors are peculiar to specific stages.

STAGE 1 The first stage is characterized by two-word utterances, which we have discussed. This is the period in which telegraphic speech and pivot and open words first emerge. Brown, however, goes beyond this structure to focus on the meaning that children are attempting to convey with word order and position—the concepts of existence, disappearance, and recurrence, and of possession, agency, and attribution.

STAGE 2 This stage of language acquisition is characterized by utterances slightly longer than two words. In addition to learning prepositions, articles, and case markers, children begin to generalize the rules of **inflections** to words they already know. Children at this stage are able to form the regular past tense of many verbs such as "play/played," and the regular plurals of many nouns. To determine whether children have reached a more complex language stage and are not just relying on memory, Berko (1958) devised a test using nonsense words (see Figure 8–3). For instance, "This is a wug. Now there is another one. There are two of them. There are two——." The subjects had to supply the correct inflection by generalizing what they knew about plurals. The tests, which have since been given to children even younger than Berko's preschool and first-grade subjects, reveal a surprising grasp of rules for conjugating verbs and forming plurals and possessives. In fact, children often overgeneralize. In spite of the fact that

mean length of utterance (MLU) The average length of the sentences that a child produces.

inflections Changes in form that words undergo to designate number, gender, tense, mood, and case.

This is a wug.

Now there is another one.
There are two of them.
There are two _____ .

FIGURE 8–3
One of Berko's Tests of
Children's Syntax.
Nonsense words are used to avoid
interference from memorization.

they may have already learned the forms of some irregular verbs, such as "go/went/gone," children produce words like "goed." They are applying the rule for forming the regular past tense to every verb. Although technically an error, such usages demonstrate children's extraordinary ability to generalize a complex language principle. This is called **overregularization.**

STAGE 3 In the third stage, children learn to modify simple sentences. They create negative and imperative forms, ask yes-no questions, and depart in other ways from the simple statements of earlier stages. The negative form is an excellent example of how complex language learning can be. It also reveals children's ability to create original forms without depending on a model. The concepts for using negatives seem to exist quite early—long before the third stage. At first, children negate by putting the negative word at the beginning of an utterance; they express concepts such as nonexistence ("no pocket"), rejection ("no more"), and denial ("no dirty"), but cannot use auxiliary verbs or embed a negative form within a sentence. By the third stage, however, children easily say such sentences as, "Paul didn't laugh" and "Jeannie won't let go" (Klima & Bellugi, 1966). In fact, they often use double and triple negatives, throwing them in wherever possible to emphasize a point.

Children also begin to learn the use of active and passive voice during the third stage. Bellugi, Brown, and Fraser (1970) developed a test of children's understanding of these forms. They gave their subjects stuffed animals and asked them to act out "The cat chases the dog" and "The dog chases the cat." The 3-year-old subjects had no trouble demonstrating these simple declarative sentences. However, when shown two pictures illustrating "The boy is washed by the girl" and "The girl is washed by the boy," the children seldom identified the picture that corresponded to the sentence they heard. They had not yet mastered the passive concept. Their comprehension was limited to the more typical word order of agent-action-object.

STAGES 4 AND 5 In the fourth and fifth stages, children learn to deal with increasingly sophisticated structures. They begin to use subordinate clauses and

overregularization The generalization of complex language principles, typically by preschool children rapidly expanding their vocabularies.

This 3-year-old is able to demonstrate the sentence, "The rabbit chases the dog" but not, "The dog is chased by the rabbit." Children of this age have not yet mastered the passive concept.

fragments within compound and complex sentences. By the age of 4 1/2, children have a good grasp of syntax, but they continue to learn for many years. Carol Chomsky (1969) tested subjects between the ages of 5 and 10 and found that children are actively acquiring syntax within those years. Such structures as, "John asked Bill what to do" are learned very late; the subject of "do" was not clearly understood by some 10-year-olds. And, of course, many adults have great difficulty with certain constructions.

MORE WORDS AND CONCEPTS

Throughout the preschool period, children are learning words rapidly—often at a rate of two or three a day. Some words have meaning only in context. For example, "this" and "that." Some words express relationships between objects: "softer," "lower," and "shorter." Frequently, children understand one concept, such as "more," a lot earlier than they know the word or the concept that contrasts directly with it—in this case, "less." A 3-year-old may easily be able to tell you which dish has more candy, but not which dish has less.

Often, children want to say things, but they do not know the right word, or they cannot recall it. At these times, children invent words. They use nouns in place of verbs, as in, "Mommy, needle it" ("Mommy, sew it"). Or a child trying to fold paper might ask, "How do you flat it?" Also, children invent complex words like "sweep-man" (someone who sweeps).

At least through age 3, children also have difficulty with pronouns and their use. By ages 4 to 5, most children have mastered them. For example, a child might say "my want to go out" or "us need to take a nap." Even when corrected, these errors persist for some time as the following conversation between Rachael, aged 3, and her mother indicates:

Rachael: *My need to use the potty, Mommy.*

Mother: *You mean, I need to use the potty.*

Rachael: *Mommy have to go too?*

Mother: *No, honey, but I'll go with you.*

Rachael: *Yeh, Mommy! Us can go together.*

Many parents at times during this phase, find themselves participating in a "who's on first" game that they have absolutely no chance of winning. The three-year-old will invariably wear them down.

Another problem encountered by some children is that they have trouble pronouncing certain words, even though they can often recognize the correct pronunciation; for example, a child may understand that "I smell a skunk" is the correct form but may only be able to say, "I mell a kunk." Another difficult word for children is also one of their favorite foods "pisghetti."

INFLUENCES OF PARENTS' SPEECH

To gain and hold the attention of prelinguistic children, adults often use a particular mode of speaking that has been dubbed "motherese." When using motherese, adults (both men and women) exaggerate their vowels, speak in pitches higher than normal, and create words composed of repeated syllables, such as "bye-bye" and "nighty-night." They use short, simple sentences and talk about what is happening at the moment. While watching her infant try to stand, a mother might verbalize his progress: "Sabir falls down...Bump...Sabir sits up...Can Sabir stand up?" The care-giver exaggerates intonation and stress, pauses between sentences, and often repeats earlier words and sentences (Ferguson & Snow, 1977).

The simple, exaggerated qualities of motherese probably make it easier for young children to understand and learn language. Short sentences are useful because young children have short memories. Simple sentences help children find the important words. Pauses help them separate words and sentences (Hirsh-Pasek, Nelson, Jusczyk, & Wright, 1986).

It was once thought that the frequent use of motherese played a key part in the language development of the young child. But now researchers view motherese as only one of a variety of ways to interact verbally with the child. The simplified speech characteristic of motherese comes naturally to an adult speaking with anyone who does not yet speak fluently. In other words, motherese is not primarily a tool used to teach a baby language. Rather, the simplified way that care-givers speak to the child appears to be a reaction to the child's language abilities, not a strategy to improve them (Bohannon & Hirsh-Pasek, 1984). Looking at how young children learn to speak in other cultures confirms the idea that motherese is not critical to language development. In the Pacific Kaluli (Schieffelin & Ochs, 1983) and the Quicke Mayan cultures (Ratner & Pye, 1984), for instance, children learn to speak without extensive use of motherese.

Yet every culture successfully transmits language to its children. There appear to be many methods of talking and relating to infants that facilitate language development. Each culture has integrated some of these strategies into the patterns of social interaction with children (Snow, 1989). Although children do pick up specific words from their care-giver, the critical aspect of adults' speaking to children is that they provide children with information about language. Children generalize from what they hear, enabling them to understand words and syntax.

Researchers looking at American children found that care-givers ask questions to check for children's understanding, expand children's utterances, and make ritualized use of play speech. Adults often speak for the children; that is, they express children's wants, wishes, and actions in syntactic English. The child's language develops most from everyday communication with adults who seek to communicate—that is, to understand and to be understood (Schacter & Strage, 1982).

It is not clear how the use of language by parents and the child's language development are related (Chesnick, et al., 1983). Of course, it is critical that parents both talk and listen to their children regularly. Differences between individuals in language development have been shown to be inherited to some extent. But they are also influenced by the environment. For example, twins typically have delayed language development. Studies have shown that these children received significantly less verbal input than children who were not twins did from their mothers, because the mothers of twins had to divide their attention between the two children (Tomasello, Mannle, & Kruger, 1986).

When parents speak with their children, however, they communicate far more than words, sentences, and syntax. They are demonstrating how thoughts are expressed and how ideas are exchanged. They are teaching the child about categories and symbols and about how to translate the complicated world into ideas and words. These conceptual tools provide a "scaffold" for the child to create his own form of expression (Bruner & Haste, 1987). Long before they can speak, children are initiated into their culture and language by the speech of their parents and care-giver. For a situation where this interaction went awry, see the box "Is There a Critical Period for Language Learning?"

In all cultures, parents by speaking to infants provide them with information about language.

FOCUS ON AN ISSUE

IS THERE A CRITICAL PERIOD FOR LEARNING LANGUAGE?

In 1970, a 13-year-old girl named Genie was discovered in Los Angeles. Her condition was startling. Since the age of 20 months, Genie had been a virtual prisoner in a small curtained room in her house. For most of her days, she was strapped in a pottychair, where she was only able to move her hands and her feet. At night, she was laced into a kind of straitjacket and enclosed in a cagelike crib. Treated like an animal, Genie had no bowel or bladder control and could not stand erect. She was severely malnourished and was unable to chew solid food. She was also mute: She could neither speak nor understand language.

Since the first days of her imprisonment, Genie was never spoken to—a rule enforced by her father.

She was fed by her brother, whom she saw for only a few minutes a day, but no words ever passed between them. The only sounds she heard were her father's doglike barks on some of the occasions when he beat her for crying or making noise.

Genie knew almost no language and had no understanding of grammar.

After she was removed from this situation, Genie was cared for by doctors at the Los Angeles Children's Hospital, who took care of her immediate bodily needs, nursed her back to health, and calmed her

fears. Psychologists were called in to try to evaluate her mental state and abilities, including how much she understood and how much language she had learned. They next had the task of teaching her language. Many psychologists feel that there is a critical period for learning language—the time during a child's early years when language learning must begin if it is to occur at all. Genie gave researchers a unique opportunity to study this critical period theory.

Genie knew almost no language and had no understanding of grammar. Researchers approached teaching her in much the same way they would approach teaching a younger child—through direct exposure to language during daily activities. She made only one- or two-word utter-

---

As we saw in earlier chapters, some research indicates that children are introduced to the language of their culture even before birth. DeCasper & Spence (1992), for example, reported that *prosody,* which is a combination of rhythm, intonation, and inflection in speech, appears to be recognized and stored prenatally. Babies whose mothers had read *The Cat in the Hat* aloud while they were in the womb, preferred that reading to unfamiliar ones that they heard after birth. They sucked more in response to the familiar story than to unfamiliar readings. Whether further research supports this finding, it is more than likely that reading aloud aids children's introduction to their own languages by showing them the timing and inflections of more formal speech.

LANGUAGE AND GENDER   Language is one means for children to learn who they are and how they should relate to other people. A critical category of identification for the young child is gender. What should a boy do? How does a girl behave? Assumptions about gender appear to be psychologically embedded in mothers' thinking; these ideas cause them to behave differently toward children based on their gender (Lloyd, 1987). When mothers were observed interacting

ances at first, but she soon progressed. Within a year of her release, she began to string two and sometimes three words together to make phrases like "clear white box." She soon began to use these phrases to form simple agent-action-object sentences, and she learned to add the word "no" to the beginning of the sentence to express a negative thought.

Despite this progress, it soon became apparent that Genie's language learning was severely limited. Even after 4 years of training, she had not learned many of the rudiments of grammar or articulation most children learn before the age of 4—rudiments that could transform her garbled messages into easily understood speech. She could not use personal pronouns nor the demonstrative adjectives "this" and "that." In addition, despite her teachers' prodding, she never asked questions in the way a normal 3- or 4-year-old would. And, unlike normal children, she never experienced the explosive spurt of language development that quickly transforms a child's first words into full grammatical sentences. On the contrary, her progress was painfully slow. After 4 years, she could hardly be understood, and after 7 years, she learned as much language as a normal child learns in 2 or 3 years.

Nevertheless, the fact that any progress was made disproved the theory that language can be learned only during a critical developmental period between the age of 2 and puberty. Genie did learn a limited amount of language after this time. Because her language development has fallen far short of that of a normal child, however, it may still be true that optimum language development is tied to this critical period—but there is no way to know this for sure. Due to the severe physical and emotional deprivation Genie experienced in her childhood, it is impossible to determine whether her language difficulties reflect her speech deprivation alone or whether the malnutrition, physical and emotional abuse, and social isolation she suffered also played a part.

By 24 years of age, Genie had received years of special education, rehabilitation, and foster care. She had also been closely observed and tested as psychologists attempted to find other clues to the mystery of language acquisition. Yet, despite this care and attention, her language still lacked many of the aspects of a 5-year-old's. Her case has provided many insights but no answers. Indeed, some believe that it has added even more fuel to the issue of whether a critical period in language development exists (Pines, 1981; de Villiers & de Villiers, 1979).

with babies who were presented to them as either a boy or a girl, the supposed gender affected how the mother played with and spoke to the infant. Babies dressed as boys were offered a toy hammer and were verbally encouraged to play actively. When the same baby was presented as a girl, the mothers picked up a fluffy doll and praised the child for being clever and attractive (Smith & Lloyd, 1978).

How does the social context in which language is used affect language development? Exploration of this complex question is in its early stages. One study has looked at how play preferences may influence children's exposure to language. The language mothers and fathers used while playing with their toddlers with three types of toys—vehicles, dolls, and shape sorters—was analyzed. Playing with dolls elicited the most verbal interaction, whereas play with vehicles involved little talking whether the parents were playing with daughters or sons. These results suggest that children who play frequently with dolls may have more opportunities to learn and practice language than do children who play with other toys. Because boys and girls play selectively with same-sex stereotyped toys starting by age 2, play patterns may contribute to differential language environments for children (O'Brien & Nagle, 1987).

CHILDREN'S CONVERSATIONS

Children do more than say words or sentences. They have conversations—with adults as well as with other children—and even with themselves (see the box "Why Do Children Talk to Themselves?"). Conversations typically follow a certain pattern.

MONITORING THE MESSAGE

First, it is necessary to gain the other person's attention. A child just learning the art of conversation may yank on somebody's clothing. As time passes, the same child may instead say something like, "Know what?" Children then learn that conversations often have a beginning, a middle, and an end. They discover, too, that in conversations people take turns; they talk on the same subject, they make sure the other person listens, or is understanding; and they make sounds or nod to indicate that they understand what the other person is talking about (Garvey, 1984).

By casually listening to children's conversations, one notices that they do not run smoothly. Children often stop to see if the other is listening, and if they are understood. Children pause, repeat themselves, correct themselves. They ask questions. Indeed, this is a normal part of developing effective communication (Garvey, 1984; Reich, 1986). Even school-aged children sometimes have considerable difficulty communicating all of the appropriate information to a listener. First- and second-grade children have difficulty comprehending each other fully, finding the part of the message they don't understand, and asking appropriate questions to help each other repair messages (Beal, 1987).

Finally, children must learn to adjust conversations to reduce friction, conflict, and embarrassment. This means using courtesy markers like "please" and "thank you"; paying attention; and selecting the proper forms of address, phrasing, and suitable topics. This usually means noting the status of the other person. Children spend a good deal of time learning these social refinements, and they are aided with reminders like, "Don't talk to your grandmother like that" (Garvey, 1984). In the next section, we review other ways that children learn to be sensitive to social situations and to people with whom they are talking.

THE SOCIAL CONTEXT OF LANGUAGE

The way that language is used depends on the situations and the intentions of a speaker and a listener who have some kind of social relationship. Social relationships, in turn, involve mutual considerations of both role and status. We show our awareness of another person's status by our tone of voice, grammar, and mode of address, among other things. For example, an elderly neighbor may expect children to be quiet and calm and conveys these expectations in his speech. The neighborhood children, in response, will show deference in their speech by modulating their voices and using polite forms of address. In general, children are quick to learn nuances of speech and to conform to a social role.

They are also quick to perceive degrees of status and the attendant speech behavior in a wide variety of social settings.

Thus, children recognize early that, based on their characteristics, people are meant to be treated in different ways. Being able to interpret the social world accurately is a critical task for children. But in all cultures, commonly accepted social lessons are accompanied by unspoken attitudes that children also absorb. While the child expands her world by comprehending how she relates to others, she is acquiring the particular beliefs that comprise the world view of her culture (Ochs, 1986).

One researcher examined how children between the ages 4 and 7 modify their speech to correspond to different social situations and roles (Anderson, 1979). Twenty-four children were given an opportunity to play out several roles with the use of puppets. Three different situations were used: father-mother-child, physician-nurse-patient, and teacher-student-foreign student. In each setting, the children manipulated two puppets while the researchers worked the third. In improvising the various parts, the children spontaneously revealed how much they had already learned about social relationships and the social and cultural characteristics of speech.

Anderson found that although methods of portrayal varied with age, even the youngest children had a clear understanding of social context and power relationships, and they adjusted their vocabulary and speech accordingly to reflect these notions. Four-year-olds expressed their social understanding mostly by changing the pitch and loudness of their speech. Those who role-played authority figures, such as fathers and physicians, stretched out their vowels and talked at a lower pitch than those who role-played lower-status figures. Children portraying low-status persons, on the other hand, used a higher and softer tone of voice, asked more questions, and deferred politely to the authority figure. "Mothers" spoke in higher, sometimes sing-song voices. And every child, when speaking to a foreign student, spoke in a slow, flat monotone. Those who role-played young children simplified their speech, leaving out consonants and articles.

Slightly older children were able to modify appropriately the vocabulary and context of their speech. "Doctors" used medical terms like "hernia" and "temperature," often without knowing their meaning. A "patient" might say, "Doctor, do I have a hernia?" and the "doctor" might reply, "No, but I'll go out and get you one." Older children who played authority figures had learned techniques for maintaining control of a conversation. They would use floor holders, such as "Well...," "Now...," or "Then...," to prevent others with lower status from talking too much; they also made syntactic changes in their speech. "Fathers" would use imperatives, such as, "Have this done by tomorrow!" "Mothers" would use expressions of endearment and polite forms, such as, "Would you mind if I...?" at least when played by girls. As boys' ages increased, so did their reluctance to play dependent, less authoritative roles, such as young children.

These girls are playing pretend. One of them is having a conversation with the help of the telephone. Through play, children can practice their conversational skills—for example, they learn to take turns speaking.

LANGUAGE AS AN INVITATION TO ACTION

Jerome Bruner (1983) suggests that one of the social purposes that language serves for young children is to invite others to engage in joint actions. This may take three forms:

FOCUS ON RESEARCH

WHY DO CHILDREN TALK TO THEMSELVES?

Josh is alone in his room playing a game in which he tries to fit pieces into a puzzleboard. If we look in on him, we might overhear Josh say to himself, "This piece doesn't fit. Where's a round one? No, it doesn't. It's too big. This one is small...." Children between the ages of 4 and 8 have been observed directing their talk to themselves about 20 percent of the time in school environments that permit it (Berk, 1985). This is a high percentage. Why do they do so?

Psychologists call talking aloud to oneself *private speech.* All people, young and old, talk to themselves. But, unlike adults, young children do so in public situations, such as at school or in a playground. Young children often sing words to themselves about what they are doing...songs they have generated spontaneously rather than the words to group songs. They also talk to themselves far more often than adults do. Some of the early observations of private speech among preschool children were made by Jean Piaget. He suggested that the private speech of young children indicated their immaturity. Social speech was more difficult because it required consideration of the listener's perspective. He called this talking to oneself *egocentric speech* (Piaget, 1926).

Numerous researchers have reported an apparent relationship between intelligence and the amount and quality of children's use of private speech.

Piaget's observation stimulated other researchers to record the way children use social language and private speech. Early findings tended to raise questions about Piaget's explanation. Observers found that the amount of private speech varied a great deal depending on the situation, but even the youngest children used far more social speech to communicate and exchange ideas with others than they used private speech. Perhaps, private speech served a distinct and separate purpose.

A Russian observer suggested the private speech often mirrored adult social speech and served to help in the development of inner thought and self-direction. When observing children engaged in private activity, researchers have found three stages in the development of the children's private speech. In its earliest stage, private speech occurs after an action—"I made a big one." At the second stage, talking to oneself accompanies an action—"It's getting darker and darker with lots of paint." Later, in the third stage, it precedes an action—"I want to make a scary picture with dark paint." Private speech in each of these stages seems to serve the purpose of controlling or guiding a child's behavior in performing a task. The progression corresponds, researchers believe, to the developing thought process in a child's mind. At the final stage, when speech comes before behavior, the child is planning a course of action. The changes in private speech from stage 1 to stage 3 illustrate the development of thought processes in guiding one's behavior and its accompanying linguistic

1. an asymmetrical one, in which the child will be experiencer and the adult will serve as agent, for example, reading books;

2. a parallel one, in which the child and adult share an experience, for example, when a child asks his mother for a cuddle; and

3. an alternating one, in which a child and adult play a game that requires taking turns, for example, the child hides the mother's face, and then the mother hides the child's face, and so forth.

It appears as though none of these occurs earlier or is used more frequently than the others. In addition, Bruner (1983) indicates that 95 percent of chil-

development. The child's use of language progresses from simply mirroring adult speech in stage 1 to internally structuring one's behavior in stage 3.

Many studies have supported the idea that the function of private speech is to guide the child in the performance of a task. But some studies have failed to show a connection between private speech and the development of performance abilities. These studies were done in traditional school environments where children were not encouraged to integrate private speech with their activities. Later research has shown that when children are given verbal tasks and encouraged to speak, they talk to themselves quite a bit (Frauenglass & Diaz, 1985). Other researchers have found that children in comfortable school environments tend to accompany academic tasks with private speech if adults are not present.

Numerous researchers have reported an apparent relationship between intelligence and the amount and quality of children's use of private speech. It seems that the brighter the child, the more private speech is used and the more mature is its content. Talking aloud to one-

self seems to follow a curve. It increases at first as the child develops self-control, peaks at age 4 or 5, and then diminishes drastically by age 8 (Diaz & Lowe, 1987). The private speech of bright children seems to peak at an earlier age than that of average children (Berk, 1986).

Further research has confirmed that there are connections between private speech, behavior, and thought. As children grow older and their speech is internalized, they become quieter and pay more attention to their tasks. This suggests that, as private talk is internalized, behavior is brought under the control of thought. There is now evidence indicating that talking to oneself is related to the quality of performance, especially among brighter children. Impulsive primary school children who have difficulty with self-control and persistence can even be helped by training them to use self-directed verbal commands to regulate their own behavior (Diaz & Lowe, 1987).

Learning to think and self-guidance are not the only functions of private speech. For example, children seem to talk to themselves as a means of playing and relaxing,

Often, young children talk out loud while they work or play. Sometimes the talk is pretend dialogue, but more often it fulfills other functions.

expressing feelings, and absorbing emotions and ideas. Young children take great pleasure in word play, which is an important means of learning language. Children tell themselves fantasies or speak to an imaginary playmate or talk to inanimate objects (Berk, 1985). Private speech is thus a way of expressing one's feelings, of gaining understanding of one's environment, and of developing language, as well as being a tool for developing self-control and inner thought.

dren's invitations up to approximately 18 months of age are accepted and responded to in a supportive manner. After that age, there is an increased likelihood of refusal, perhaps because of growing encouragement for children to become more independent.

 ## LANGUAGE AND CULTURE

Suppose, for a moment, that you are traveling in Mexico for the first time. You have studied Spanish in school for 4 years, you have learned to read it reasonably

In cultures where politeness is valued, children learn polite forms of expression when they are very young.

well, and you have no trouble with menus or street signs. You know when to say "please" and "thank you," and you can even enter a limited conversation. But you feel socially inept because you know that whatever you say, you will still "sound like an American." To behave and feel like a Mexican, you would have to have mastered thousands of behavioral details, such as knowing when to be silent, what form of address to use, and what tone of voice to adopt. In the meantime, you observe 4- and 5-year-old Mexican children expressing themselves effortlessly. As we shall see, children absorb all the behavioral details of their own culture and reflect them in their speech easily and naturally.

The best-known theory about the relationships between language and thought was proposed by Benjamin Whorf (1956). According to his hypothesis of linguistic relativity, language determines or strongly influences thinking. Therefore, language and thinking are culture-specific entities. There are significant differences among the world's languages that reflect this interaction. The Hanuxoo people of the Philippines, for example, have 92 names for different varieties of rice. The Eskimos have dozens of words to describe different snow and ice conditions. As Whorf has noted, it becomes clear that different environmental conditions affect the things that people think about—as well as their linguistic usage.

SOCIAL CLASS AND ETHNIC DIFFERENCES

Every culture defines what to say, when, and to whom, just as it dictates pronunciation, syntax, and vocabulary. In cultures where politeness is esteemed, for instance, children learn polite forms of expression at a very early age. In Java, a child's first word may well be *njuwun,* "I humbly beg for it."

Often, children are presented with more than one form of language usage because of cultural differences within society. This is especially true in America's heterogeneous society. We reflect racial and ethnic differences and distinct social and economic classes in our use of language. These differences become especially apparent in public school classrooms. Schools have traditionally reflected the dominant American culture and may be a minority child's first exposure to these values, including the mainstream patterns of speech.

The status of Black English, a form of English spoken by many African Americans, especially those who live in large cities, has been debated for decades. Some theorists contend that Black English is one of many dialects—just as standard English is one—and that each dialect is a legitimate variation of English. This viewpoint is called the *difference hypothesis* (Williams, 1970). It is a response to an opposing viewpoint, the *deficit hypothesis,* which asserts that language patterns deviating from standard English are deficient and substandard.

Black English was considered to be poor English, growing out of a restricted language code, until linguists began to study it systematically. Labov (1970) cites the richness and complexity of Black English. It has its own rules and is frequently employed in richly expressive ways. Moreover, it is quite similar to standard English and the differences are in general quite superficial. In addition, the speaker can comprehend standard English quite well, even though she does not always produce it.

Linguists have found that the so-called errors committed by speakers of Black English were actually consistent alternative grammatical forms. For example, the word "be" in Black English, as used in the sentence, "I be sick," indicates a repeated action or existential state. In other words, it expresses an ongoing, rather than a transitory, condition. The concept expressed concisely by "I be sick" might be rephrased in standard English as, "I have been and still am feeling sick."

What position should schools assume toward Black English and other dialects differing from standard English? When Black English is the child's original language form, its use can be an important mode of self-expression. But most children who speak Black English will ultimately have to negotiate between the two linguistic codes. Ideally, speakers of Black English—and other dialects—will learn to negotiate between their code and standard English, gaining linguistic access to working and socializing in the larger culture while retaining their own distinct linguistic identity.

BILINGUALISM

Language is not just a means of communication. It is also a symbol of one's social or group identity. Thus, language conveys attitudes and values through its use and nonuse. The child who grows up amidst two languages and becomes *bilingual,* goes through both a linguistic and a socializing process (Grosjean, 1982). It is estimated that by the year 2000, there will be 5 million children in the United States for whom English is not the primary language at home. Although speakers of non-English languages live throughout the United States, they are more heavily concentrated in Hawaii, California, New Mexico, Texas and New York (Bonvillain, 1993).

The status of bilingualism in different nations is strongly affected by issues of social class and political power. In Europe, for example, bilingualism is associated with being a highly cultured "citizen of the world." In the United States, bilingualism is more often a sign of being a recent immigrant who has not become "Americanized." Although our society has moved toward acceptance of cultural pluralism, the millions of American children growing up in bilingual environments may experience overt or subtle pressures to conform. Along with English, they are learning to speak such languages as Spanish, Chinese, Hebrew, Italian, Polish, French, Vietnamese, Arabic, Japanese, Korean, Farsi, or Russian.

Does learning two languages instead of one during the preschool years hinder a child's language learning? Does it interfere with cognitive development? Early studies in the United States and Great Britain concluded that learning two languages at a young age was detrimental to cognitive development. In general, bilingual children scored less well on standardized English tests than did monolingual, English-speaking children.

Most of these studies, however, did not take into account the social class or education level of either the children or their parents. In other words, the scores of bilingual children may have been depressed for reasons other than their bilingualism, such as poverty, parents being uneducated or unfamiliar with a new culture, or poor schooling. In recent research, such social factors are taken into consideration when evaluating the effects of bilingualism.

Most researchers now believe that linguistically, culturally, and probably cognitively, it is an advantage for children to learn more than one language (Diaz, 1985). Evidence from a Yugoslavian study that compared Hungarian and Hun-

Children learning a second language after learning their primary language follow patterns similar to those of children learning two languages simultaneously.

garian/Serbo-Croatian-speaking children at ages 6 and 10 showed that even though the bilingual children appeared to be at a linguistic and cognitive disadvantage at the age when they were still learning the two languages, they caught up linguistically, and sometimes surpassed their monolingual peers cognitively, once they had integrated the two languages (Goncz, 1988).

How does a child master two languages? Learning two languages by the age of 5 is a complex task involving two systems of rules, two sets of vocabulary, special usage, and different pronunciation. Many children who are bilingual in the earliest years, however, show little confusion between the two languages by the age of 3, although they sometimes substitute vocabulary from one language when speaking in the other. This has led linguists to theorize that the young child uses a unitary language system and only later is able to distinguish two separate languages. But there is some evidence that bilingual children make use of two separate language systems even as infants (Genesee, 1989).

Why do some children continue to mix words from two languages? Researchers argue that children are modeling their parents' use of the two languages. When parents consistently speak one language or the other, children's language mixing can be reduced markedly. This suggests that early language mixing does not reflect interlinguistic confusion. Rather, the child is formulating hypotheses about language based on the information she gets from her mother and father.

Bilingual children frequently develop strong person-language bonds. That is, they speak one language with one person and a second language with another person. Young bilingual children often begin translating between their parents and others as soon as they learn to speak—as early as age 2 or 2 1/2. Children, such as recent immigrants, who learn a second language after learning to speak their primary language, also associate their first and second languages with particular people and situations.

Language is a crucial aspect of development. The acquisition of speech enables the child to interact in a more dynamic way with adults and other children in his environment. Ideas may now be freely communicated; emotions shared; dreams described and futures planned by the verbal child. The process of education outside the home can now begin more fully—as can the games and activities shared with peers and parents. The uncaught butterfly observed in the field can now be carried home by the child through words...and the parent, brother, sister, or friend can share the experience.

SUMMARY AND CONCLUSIONS

Human beings are highly verbal creatures. Once the human infant is able to actively engage in language, a whole new developmental phase emerges. Furthermore, once language begins, it soon often explodes into being—with the child's vocabulary by age 3 having several hundred words.

Language is a complex accomplishment. Psycholinguists study three basic elements of language: content, the meaning of written or spoken messages; form, the

particular symbols used to represent the messages; and use which depends on the intention and situation of the speaker. Form itself consists of phonemes, the basic sounds; morphemes, which are basic word forms; and syntax, which is the sentence structure.

Language learning has elements that are shared by all members of the human species, as well as those elements that are individually or environmentally determined. Infants and toddlers learn language initially, according to Noam Chomsky, because of an inborn ability to comprehend and structure language called the language acquisition device (LAD). Chomsky believes that this device enables children to understand grammatical rules and form their own language from these rules. Cognitive development in general also affects and is affected by language growth. For example, object permanence occurs simultaneously with the use of words like "all gone" and "more." In addition, the grammatical structures in children's speech appear to follow certain kinds of cognitive development. Other components of language learning include imitation and reinforcement. It is clear from research that children whose parents engage in speech with them and reinforce them for speech activities are more verbal and gain language earlier than those children who lack this experience.

Language is understood before children can produce it. Many aspects of interpersonal communication exist in infants before they speak. These include signaling, turn-taking, and gesturing. Language production begins with babbling and iteration. Early babbling produces a universal, wide variety of sounds, some of which are outside the parents' native language. After six months, infant babbling takes on the inflection phonemes and patterns of the parents' language. Also, deaf infants babble less than hearing children. At this age, infants' language development becomes more closely linked to the language around them.

Most children are producing some words by one year. All children—regardless of culture—utter single words, usually nouns, first. These words are believed to represent holophrastic speech, that is, they are meant to convey complex ideas. Children commonly make similar errors during language acquisition. Two such errors are overextension and underextension, which deal with the child's notions of concepts and the words to represent them. Following single-word utterances, all children begin to produce two-word sentences. The first use of case grammar, the expression of relationships by using word order, occurs here. During the second and third year, children's speech rapidly begins to form longer sentences. These often are examples of telegraphic speech, in which the child uses high-information words. Pivot words—such as action words and possessives—also are key aspects of language at this age.

Not all theorists emphasize age as the main determinant of language. Roger Brown proposes that language development should be measured by average sentence length. He states that language development occurs in five distinct, sequential stages: two-word utterances; longer phrases, marked by inflection; simple sentences that use negative and imperative forms; and two final stages that involve mastering complex, compound, and subordinate structures. Brown suggests that true mastery of syntax is not complete before age 10.

It is important to note that language occurs in a social context and is therefore strongly affected by factors such as social class and ethnic group membership. Conversation skills, inflection, and gestures are examples of aspects of language that are strongly cultural. Children assimilate social values through language—values such as politeness, obedience, respect, and authority. The first language of some children in ethnic groups may actually be a form of dialect rather than standard English. Many African-American children, for example, who use Black English—a legitimate dialect with its own gramatical rules and modes of expression—may have to learn to negotiate between their spoken dialect and standard English in order to succeed in education and career.

In many parts of the world, including America, many children are bilingual. Such children learn two distinct languages simultaneously as they grow. Although such children may initially mix words from two languages, by age 4 many are truly bilingual—that is, they are able to speak both languages fluently.

➤ KEY TERMS AND CONCEPTS

case grammar	holophrastic speech	morphemes	productive language
content	inflections	morphology	receptive language
expressive jargon	iteration	overregularization	syntax
form	mean length of utterance	phonemes	telegraphic speech
grammar	(MLU)	pivot grammar	use

➤ SELF-TEST QUESTIONS

1. List three major dimensions of language.
2. Differentiate between phonemes and morphemes.
3. Describe four components of language development.
4. Discuss the sequence of language development in infancy.
5. Differentiate between receptive and productive language. How are these processes related, and when do they evolve?
6. What is babbling, and how important is it to the infant's language development?
7. Contrast the language development of twins versus singletons.
8. Describe holophrastic speech.
9. Differentiate between overextensions and underextensions. How are a child's words and meanings closely linked to the concept the child is learning?
10. What is telegraphic speech? What are its two major components? What types of grammar are used in telegraphic speech?
11. Describe the five stages of language acquisition as identified by Roger Brown.
12. Discuss the influence of parents' speech on the infant.
13. Describe the process by which a child's language acquisition develops into conversational skills.
14. Discuss the cultural and social values that children assimilate in language.
15. How do social class and ethnic differences pose a critical issue for teachers?
16. Discuss how bilingualism affects the language development of the child.

➤ SUGGESTED READINGS

CAZDEN, C. (Ed). *Language in early childhood education.* Washington, D.C.: National Association for the Education of Young Children, 1981. A collection of studies and articles about language development during the preschool period. This is of particular interest to individuals working with young children in preschools.

DE VILLIERS, P. A., & DE VILLIERS, J. G. *Early language.* Cambridge, MA: Harvard University Press, 1979. A good, complete summary of early language development from birth to age 6.

GARVEY, C. *Children's talk.* Cambridge, MA: Harvard University Press, 1984. Another selection in The Developing Child series. This book discusses the social and conversational aspects of language learning.

McLANE, J. B., & McNAMEE, G. D. *Early literacy.* Cambridge, MA: Harvard University Press, 1990. An excellent and balanced discussion of the pros and cons of early reading for young children.

PORTER, R. P. *Forked tongue: The politics of bilingual education.* New York: Basic Books, Inc., 1990. A controversial and well-researched, yet highly readable presentation of the successes and failures of the current bilingual education programs in the United States.

SPRADLEY, T. S., & SPRADLEY, J. P. *Deaf like me.* New York: Random House, 1978. The story of a profoundly deaf girl written by her father and uncle. It describes the parents' struggle to communicate with the child and unhelpful professionals, and it encourages total communication, including the early use of sign language.

WINNER, E. *The point of words: Children's understanding of metaphor and irony.* Cambridge, MA: Harvard University Press, 1988. A somewhat advanced analysis of children's growing ability to discover the more subtle and indirect meanings of language.

VIDEO CASE: BREAKING THE SILENCE

Jeff Powell Jr., Ben Lahr, and Lucy Harrison are three teenagers who have something in common: they are among an estimated 350,000 Americans diagnosed as suffering from autism. Autistics were seen as mentally retarded and often hostile. Lucy Harrison's recorded IQ is 45. Ben Lahr's face is covered with self-inflicted bruises. Autism has also erroneously been viewed as an emotional disorder. Thus, a therapist traced Lucy's autism to her mother's coldness. But, whatever its cause, the result was the same: autistics remained locked in a world of silence.

All this began to change recently when the director of the special education program at Syracuse University paid a brief visit to Australia to observe an experimental treatment of people with cerebral palsy. The treatment consisted of someone lightly steadying the hands of such people to the point where they were able to communicate by typing. The researchers believed the same method might work with autistics.

What Dr. Bickland observed in Australia convinced him to review his ideas about autism. What if it were not an emotional disorder but rather a disconnection between what the brain wants and the muscles can do? The implications were enormous: Maybe inside every autistic was someone with something to say. The question then became how to get it out. To help autistics to literally speak was nearly impossible, as speech is a highly complex motor act. But what if someone provided the lightest possible counterweight to their hand, enabling them to make some selections on a typewriter keyboard, each selection only slightly different from another? In terms of motor skills, this was incredibly easy. So Bickland began training facilitators to do just this with teenage autistics. Over time, 800 facilitators were trained and starting working across the country.

It was as if the prison doors opened and the prisoners could speak. Back came a deluge of voices. Jeff typed, "They used to treat me as if I were stupid, but I'm not." Ben typed, "I am a Democrat" and "Anita Hill is telling the truth." Lucy's first sentence was "Autism is frustrating." Later she typed, "I am like everyone else" and "I fear losing my ability to communicate. I fear once again being a clown in a world that is not a circus."

Such responses convinced Dr. Bickland, his facilitators, and the families of the autistics. There are, however, some critics who find it hard to believe that it isn't the facilitators who are producing the answers. Moreover, Bickland has refused to permit objective testing of the teenagers involved. But Bickland brushes such objections aside. "Every parent and facilitator we've talked to says it's the kids' movement and words. Also, the kids tell us information we don't have, like what went on over the weekend or who their siblings are." As for testing, he says that these children are extremely vulnerable to failure, and he doesn't want them to be involved in any situation with this possibility.

Meanwhile, other developments seem to back him up. Lucy now computes numbers like lightning and reads faster than anyone in the family. Ben helps make lunch. Jeff excels in physics, social studies, and poetry, and plans to go to college. Sums up Bickland, "The moral is for us to be very careful how we judge people. To not be able to speak or not able to speak correctly is not the same as not having something to say."

CASE QUESTIONS

1. Do you believe autistic children really can communicate, or are the facilitators guiding them? Why?

2. Do you think that parents of children with disabilities such as autism are exceedingly vulnerable to treatments that produce "miraculous" results? If so, can you suggest any ways they can protect themselves?

3. Do you believe that such children should be objectively tested in order to confirm Dr. Bickland's assertions? Why or why not?

CHAPTER 9

EARLY CHILDHOOD: PHYSICAL DEVELOPMENT

Child art is an art which only the child can produce. There is something that the child can also perform, but it is not art. It is imitation, it is artificial.

FRANZ CIZEK

OUTLINE

Physical Growth and Change
Physical-Motor Development
Environmental Factors Influencing
Physical Development
Health and Illness
Summary and Conclusions

By the time you have finished this chapter, you should be able to do the following:

✔ Discuss the physical development of the preschool child.

✔ Describe brain development during the preschool years and its impact on motor skills.

✔ Describe the changes in motor and fine motor skills during early childhood.

✔ Describe the role of art in children's development.

✔ Discuss the variables influencing physical development, including nutrition and health.

✔ Describe the major types of illness and disabling conditions affecting young children and their impact on children and their families.

✔ Explain the relationships between poverty and health in early childhood.

✔ Discuss the factors that encourage the development of resilient children.

"Mommy, watch me! Watch me!"

"Daddy, did you see me jump off that swing? Wasn't I brave?"

"Come on, Heather, let's slide down the stairs on our tummies—head first!!"

For most adults, it is fascinating to watch young children at play or exploring their world. Their laughter and open smiles are contagious. Their activities may also be heart-stopping to watch at times. Children at this stage are often daredevils—after they overcome their initial fears. Active exploration, climbing, running, awkward skipping, and all the other motor activities performed by young children form the basis for later physical development. Skills learned now are practiced and refined in later periods of life. Future athletes, artists, and musicians arise from the physical explorations of early childhood.

In this chapter, we will concentrate on the dimension of physical development during early childhood. This is the period from 2 years through 5 years of age, during which the physical-motor skills of children rapidly develop. Children also make dramatic discoveries about the world around them by using their growing cognitive abilities.

As we look at each type of physical development, it is important to remember that the different aspects of the process do not really occur separately. For example, when a child begins to walk or skip, she is motivated to do so, she has the information needed, and she has the physical capacity to carry out her idea. Thus, the ways in which a child behaves and thinks can be viewed as an integrated system (Thelen, 1989). Looking carefully at specific aspects of development offers many ways to understand the process by which children grow and change.

As we discussed earlier in Chapter 6, many researchers in physical development such as Esther Thelen (1992) believe that children's motor skills like walking and reaching emerge as the culmination of various component processes and structures that each child assembles to accomplish a particular task—for example, the child crosses the room to grab a desired toy. Some components are in place very early; others emerge more slowly. For the toddler to walk, for example, leg strength must be sufficient to allow him to shift balance and support to a single leg. Until that leg strength is attained, the child will be incapable of independent walking.

The child must learn to adapt his stepping, lifting or throwing patterns to his changing physical body and to the immediate environment (Thelen, 1992). When a child is motivated and ready to practice a specific skill, or to put some of the components together, the child may work at self-paced exploration with considerable persistance. The following example illustrates one such child's skill development through play.

A motor skill like reaching is the culmination of a variety of component processes and structures assembled by the child to perform a specific task.

> One spring afternoon, Tommy, aged 2 1/2, visited the pond on his grandparents' farm. While grandpa repaired the boat, Tommy and his older brother ventured out onto a small dock a few steps away. His brother picked up a large stone and tossed it into the water. Tommy lingered, watching the circular patterns of widening waves while his brother left to play with a neighbor. Tommy started back toward his grandfather (who was watching him carefully) but then stopped to pick up a pebble—returned cautiously to the dock and dropped it into the calm water. Surprise! He too had made the plop sound and that fascinating circle of widening waves. He smiled and watched transfixed until it disappeared. He turned to fetch another stone and then another and another. Most of the afternoon, despite the urging of his grandmother to come inside, he carried one stone after another to the pond. He lifted tiny pebbles and threw them as far as he could into the water. He lifted larger stones he could barely carry and struggled to simply drop them in. His grandfather marveled at Tom's persistance and wondered about the common notion that 2-year-olds have short attention spans.

Thelen and others believe that the key process underlying motor development is *exploration*. She (1992) defines this physical exploration as an active testing or problem solving by the child in order to choose which actions will best match the functional needs. Indeed, many researchers now believe that skill acquisition may involve the selection of appropriate and efficient actions from a larger pool of possible coordinated patterns (Thelen, 1989). We can see from this explanation of children's motor development that motivation and cognition are both involved in the development of motor abilities. It is therefore important for us to remember that while we will focus on physical motor skills in this chapter, this is a somewhat artificial distinction.

 ## PHYSICAL GROWTH AND CHANGE

Those who study the maturation of children have long been interested in variations in their physical size and proportions and shapes of their bodies—as well as variations in the timing of growth. In general, this study has followed one of two different paths: first, and most frequently, it has focused on the measurement of body shape, stature, muscle and fat tissue; second, it has focused on the psychological measurement of motor activities. Studies included in this second category have focused on children's feelings about their bodies, their perceptions of its shape, size, and capacities. But both of these paths often interact to study the efforts growing children make while engaging in physical activities, and the kinds of satisfaction or dissatisfaction this is likely to exert upon their self-concept (Cratty, 1986).

Even our own daily observations of growing children's play and peer interactions suggest the close interaction of mind and body. We have all seen thin, shy, withdrawn children—as we have all seen the stereotypic muscular, confident bully. In general, research has found that children's satisfaction with their bodies and themselves depends on how closely their bodies conform to societal ideals. Furthermore, the literature documents the relationships between athletic prowess and the achievement of social recognition in childhood and adolescence. Young children's changing bodies, and their continual adjustments in how they feel about those bodies, form an inseparable duo. Because of this, we shall present information in this chapter not only on the physical changes in young children's bodies, but also on the psychological adjustments associated with them.

BODY SIZE AND PROPORTION

Interest in the body size and proportion of children and youth has been stimulated by many factors. Extreme deviations in growth rates may be a cause for medical concern and may actually lead to interventions to accelerate or delay unusual rates of change. Physical educators and developmental psychologists have been interested in variations in the physique of young children because of the possible relationships with exercise tolerance, power, and strength—as well as personality and the manner in which the child's body develops. Finally, coaches and scientists interested in high-level athletic performance such as in the Olympic Games often study the highly specialized body builds that seem most associated with success in particular events and their precursors in early childhood (Cratty, 1986).

GROWTH CHANGES The rate of growth in humans is not uniform. For most infants, the first year and a half of life is marked by extremely rapid growth. The growth rate levels off by the ages of 2 through 6 and remains fairly stable until the growth spurt associated with adolescence. Cratty (1986) and others have suggested that this stable pattern of growth is the reason why children in early and middle childhood are able to acquire so many new skills so rapidly.

> ...somehow such children do not have to worry about sudden changes in stature and can concentrate on using their relatively unchanging bodies to full advantage (Cratty, 1986, p. 50).

We get a very different picture of growth, however, when we study *individual* children. Each child's growth is the result of the genes of the parents and their parents, of nutrition, and of the opportunity to play, and exercise. There are also gender differences in growth rates and patterns. These gender differences are small and insignificant in early childhood.

BODY PROPORTIONS During the period of physical growth from birth to maturity, the proportions of body segments to total body size also change dramatically, as we may see in Figure 9–1. At birth, for example, the head comprises one quarter of the body length. By maturity, despite the fact that the head has doubled in size, it only makes up one-eighth the body length. The legs increase fivefold to make up half the body length at maturity. The arms increase their length by four times at maturity, while the body's trunk shows a threefold increase.

Not all parts of the body grow at the same rate. Body segments have their own *growth spurts* at various stages during the growing years. For example, the 3- to 4-year-old's relatively short, stubby fingers begin to grow longer which makes object handling much easier for the 6- to 7-year-old.

Changes in body proportions also affect the location of the body's center of gravity, or weight center. In children, the center of gravity is higher than in adults, since children carry a higher proportion of their weight in their upper body. Boys have a slightly higher center of gravity than do girls. During the school years, the center of gravity descends to the pelvic area as changes in stature occur. Since young children tend to be more top heavy, controlling the body is more difficult. They will lose balance more quickly because of their higher center of gravity. This makes coming to a quick stop without falling quite difficult. Ball-handling, especially with larger balls, may also be negatively affected by this easy loss of balance. For example, when a young child catches a ball, the ball's weight shifts his center of gravity forward and upward, depending on the level at which the ball is received. This movement may result in a loss of balance in the direction of the ball's movement, which causes the child to either fall over backwards or to drop the ball after momentary possession (Nichols, 1990).

SKELETAL MATURATION Bones begin as soft tissue or cartilage and then harden, or ossify, as the body matures. *Ossification* begins before birth and continues until late adolescence. At birth the ossification process has progressed to include the entire shaft of the long bones. At the end of each bone is a cartilagi-

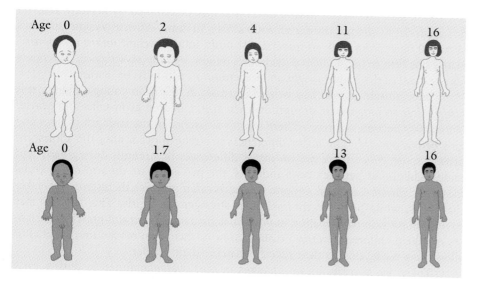

FIGURE 9–1
Changing Body Proportions in Girls and Boys from Birth to Maturity.
(Source: Nichols, B. (1990). *Moving and learning: The elementary school physical education experience.* St. Louis, MO: Times Mirror/Mosby College Publishing.

Their higher center of gravity often causes young children to lose their balance.

epiphysis The cartilaginous growth center at the end of each bone.

nous growth center called the **epiphysis.** Between the epiphysis and the shaft of the bone lies the growth plate, where bone continually grows until maturation. The closure of the growth plate varies depending on the sex of the child. In general, girls mature sooner than boys. During these preschool years, therefore, girls are usually more advanced by a few months in bone maturation than are boys.

Skeletal age, which is determined by bone maturation, is typically measured by x-rays of the bones of the wrists. These x-rays show the degree of ossification, or progress of maturity, of the bones. Skeletal age may vary by as much as four years in children of the same chronological age. For example the skeletal age of 6-year-olds may vary from 4 to 8 years (Nichols, 1990).

While vigorous activity is essential to stimulate normal bone growth, there is growing concern today about potential injury to growing bones during the developing years. This is especially of concern when the damage is to the epiphysis. There is also increasing evidence that the stress of overtraining may have some lasting effect on bone growth. Injuries to mature children may produce little disturbance, but injury to young children may result in greater growth disturbance, since the younger child has many more years of growth before maturity (Nichols, 1990). We shall describe this in greater detail in Chapter 12 when we discuss organized sports in middle childhood.

INTERNAL BODILY CHANGES Besides the obvious changes in height and weight that occur in early childhood, internal bodily changes also affect the child's physical development. These changes include differences in fat and muscle tissue and cardiovascular changes.

The rate at which fatty tissue is deposited in the body increases for a brief period from birth to 6 months and then decreases until 6 to 8 years of age. The decrease is more marked in boys. An increase in the rate of fat deposition for both sexes then occurs just before the adolescent growth spurt. There are also gender differences in the rate and placement of fatty tissues: These account for the differences in contours in boys and girls in middle childhood which become more obvious at adolescence.

During early and middle childhood, muscle tissue increases in length, breadth, and width. The number of muscle fibers is largely determined by heredity and will not appreciably change during an individual's lifetime. Muscle weight increases about 40 times from birth to maturity. At birth, muscle weight makes up approximately one-fifth to one-fourth of the body's weight; by early adolescence, it accounts for one-third of the body's weight and it increases to two-fifths by maturity.

Since muscle growth lags behind increases in height in young children, it is not possible to judge their strength by their size. Children grow taller and heavier before they become stronger. There is little difference in the strength of boys and girls before puberty. The major differences in strength occur after the adolescent growth spurt. Since there are no major differences in strength during early and middle childhood between boys and girls, the two sexes are on a relatively equal footing in physical activity. Despite this, girls often perceive themselves as weaker than boys, while boys see themselves as stronger than girls. This "myth" may have an impact on participation in physical activities. Parents and preschool teachers may help children develop a realistic view of their own maximum potential to allow them to develop to their fullest, whatever their gender.

There are also significant changes in cardiovascular function during early childhood. The *heart rate,* which is the number of heart beats per minute, under-

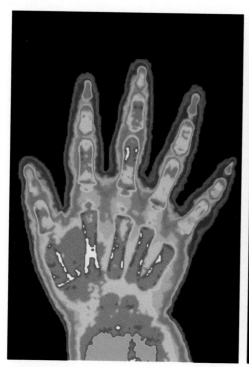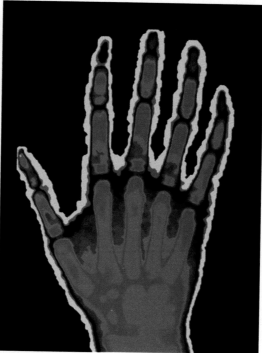

(Left) X-ray of 2-year-old's hand and wrist. (Right) X-ray of 6-year-old's hand and wrist. Note the greater degree of ossification in the older child's bones.

goes considerable change during the life of an individual. At rest, children's heart rates are consistently higher than those of adults. For example, the heart rate of children under 6 years of age averages 100 beats per minute, while for the average adult it is about 70 for men and 80 for women. The higher heart rate of young children is probably due to their smaller *stroke volume,* the amount of blood each contraction of the heart ejects into circulation. Since younger children have smaller hearts and their hearts contract, with less force, their stroke volume is less than that of adults. Because of these differences, *cardiac output* is also lower for children. Cardiac output is the amount of blood that can be pumped out of the heart each minute.

These changes significantly impact on the amount of physical activity that young children can perform. Most children are highly motivated to engage in playing games, running, and other motor activities. They tend to work hard at these activities but also tire easily. Young children seem to handle this well. They play hard, then rest or slow down before returning to full activity again. But they are also more susceptible to the negative effects of heat and cold, so care needs to be exercised by adults when young children engage in vigorous physical activity where there are extremes of temperature (Nichols, 1990).

BRAIN DEVELOPMENT

During early childhood, children develop a broad variety of skills ranging from physical coordination and perception to memory and language. These complex capabilities are closely linked to corresponding aspects of brain development. Brain development supports increasingly complex learning; in turn, perceptual and motor activity as well as problem solving and language learning create and strengthen the child's specific network of neural connections.

DEVELOPMENT OF NEURONS As we have seen in Chapter 4, as early as two weeks after conception, the specialized cells that will form the nervous system differentiate from those cells that will make up the skeleton, muscles, and other organs of the body. During the embryonic and early fetal period, there is rapid production of the basic nerve cells called **neurons.** The human brain has 100 to 200 billion neurons which store and transmit information.

All these basic nerve cells (neurons) are present by the end of the second trimester of prenatal development. However the nerve fibers extending from these neurons will continue to grow and branch or die depending on whether or not they are stimulated. Also, insulating and supporting cells, called **glial cells,** continue to grow rapidly from the second trimester through the second year, and somewhat more slowly thereafter. These glial cells improve the efficiency of transmission of nerve impulses. The rapid multiplication of glial cells and the development of the neural interconnections are responsible for the tremendous increase in brain size and weight in infancy, toddlerhood, and more slowly, in early childhood.

MYELINATION Development of certain areas of the brain persists into the third decade of life, but much of the crucial development occurs during the early childhood period. The process of brain maturation involves **myelination.** This is a process in which insulating cells (the myelin sheath) surround the neurons of the fast-conducting pathways of the central nervous system (Cratty, 1986). These sheaths help transmit nerve impulses with speed and precision across related groups of neurons. Myelinization of pathways for motor reflexes and vision occurs in early infancy. This is then followed by more complex movement pathways, and, finally, the pathways and structures that control attention, self-control, memory, and learning.

LATERALIZATION The cortex, or surface, of the human brain is divided anatomically into two cerebral hemispheres—the left and the right. The hemispheres have different ways of processing information which may be very striking—a phenomena referred to as **lateralization.** Roger Sperry (1970), among others, discovered many of these important properties of the cerebral cortex through surgery designed to reduce epileptic seizures. By cutting the connection between the two hemispheres, he reduced patients' seizures without noticeably impairing their ability to perform daily activities. Subsequent experiments indicated that each hemisphere of the brain was strong in some areas and weak in others. Although Sperry was awarded a Nobel Prize in medicine for his research revealing hemispheric specialization, he also developed life-saving techniques for brain surgery. We may see these areas illustrated in Figure 9–2.

As we can see, the left side of the brain controls the right side of the body, while the right side of the brain controls the left side. The left hemisphere is largely responsible for speech, language, writing, logic, math, and science. The right side is responsible for spatial construction, creative thinking, fantasy, art, and music appreciation (Cratty, 1986; Hellige, 1993). The hemispheres of the

neurons The cells that make up the nervous system. They form prenatally and continue to grow and branch throughout life.

myelination The formation of the myelin sheath covering the fast-acting central nervous system pathways. This sheath increases the speed of transmission and precision of the nervous system.

lateralization The process whereby specific skills and competencies become localized in particular hemispheres of the brain.

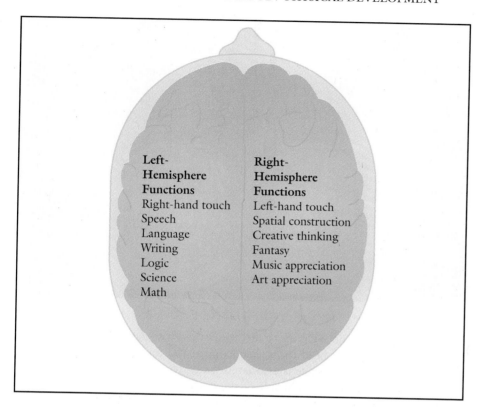

FIGURE 9–2
The Functions of the Right and Left Cerebral Hemisphere.
(Source: Shea, C.H., Shebilske, W.L., and Worchel, S. [1993]. *Motor Learning and Control*. Englewood Cliffs, NJ: Prentice Hall, p. 38.)

brain may therefore be thought of as two general information-processing subsystems with different biases and abilities (Hellige, 1993). But researchers are now beginning to emphasize the way in which the brain "puts itself back together"—to allow these two differently organized subsystems to coordinate their activities. Therefore, while the brain's hemispheres have separate or complementary functions, the main point is that they almost always work together.

When we observe the way in which children's skills develop, it is not surprising to learn that the different hemispheres of the brain develop at different times (Thatcher, Walker, & Guidice, 1987). For example, language develops very quickly during early childhood. Language skills are housed in the left hemisphere—which shows accelerated growth during the period from 3 to 6 years, and then levels off. The right hemisphere, on the other hand, matures more slowly during early childhood, and then accelerates slightly in growth between 8 and 10 years of age. This developmental difference is also reflected in the growth of children's skills in middle childhood. Spatial skills such as drawing, finding directions, and recognizing geometric shapes are slow to develop across childhood and adolescence. Research indicates that lateral specialization continues throughout childhood and into adolescence.

HANDEDNESS Researchers have long been intrigued by the fact that children tend to prefer to use one hand over another. Handedness is not the only asymmetry noted during development. Most children show head-turning responses and foot preferences—and even ear and eye preferences—that favor one side of

Early in development, the act of putting marks on paper is important in and of itself; as a child develops, however, this simple pattern of exploration will give way to more complex skills, including writing and drawing.

the body over the other (Cratty, 1986). For the most part, children exhibit a preference for right-side head turns, handedness, and footedness. For most children, this right-side preference is associated with strong left-sided cerebral dominance. (Remember that the right side of the body is controlled by the left side of the brain, and vice versa.) However, of special concern over the years have been those children who prefer to use their left hand. The left hand has been associated in some cultures with deviancy or evil—hence, the name "sinister," which refers to left-hand usage. However, despite these preferences, there is only a weak relationship between preference in motor functions and the dominant cerebral hemisphere—the hemisphere that possesses greater capacity to carry out skilled motor action.

Research on cerebral dominance has found that for the majority of right-handed people language is localized on the left side of the brain. However, for the remaining 10 percent of the population who are left-handed, language is often shared between the two sides of the brain rather than being located predominantly on one side. This would indicate that the brains of left-handed people may be less strongly lateralized than those of right-handed persons (Hiscock & Kinsbourne, 1987). Furthermore, many left-handed people appear to be *ambidextrous,* or able to use both hands with fairly good dexterity.

For most children there is a gradual acquisition of preferred hand usage which becomes fairly ingrained by early to middle childhood (Gesell & Ames, 1947). Coren and Porac (1980) documented the increased use of the right hand beginning from the nursery school years through adulthood. This may indicate increased pressure or training by parents and teachers to use the right hand, as well as increased brain specialization. A majority of 3- to 5-year-olds show a well-established foot preference. However, in one-third to one-fourth of the children, this growth continues beyond the age of 5. Some researchers have suggested recently that since "footedness" is less culturally influenced than handedness, foot preference may actually be a more sensitive indicator of developmental motor and cognitive delays than degree of handedness (Bradshaw, 1989; Gabbard, Dean, & Haensly, 1991).

While many parents are concerned about what effect left handedness will have on their children, it is important to note that research shows that few left-handed individuals have any developmental problems. They appear to be normal in all respects. In fact, some research suggests that children who have mixed preferences—or at least the ability to use both hands—may best adapt to sports requiring mixed preferences. Examples of this may be the switch-hitting baseball player, the soccer player who uses both feet equally well—or the left-handed baseball pitcher. There is also a tendency for left or mixed preference children to attain greater verbal and mathematical talents than their right-handed peers (Benbow, 1986). Some researchers contend that left-handed children are more creative than right-handers because of the more balanced involvement of both hemispheres in the completion of various tasks. Both Benjamin Franklin and Leonardo da Vinci are examples of highly creative left-handed individuals.

PHYSICAL-MOTOR DEVELOPMENT

Because of changes in their growing bodies and in their abilities to concentrate and refine activities, children's **gross motor skills**—capabilities involving large body movements such as running, hopping, and throwing—improve markedly (Clark & Phillips, 1985). **Fine motor skills,** capabilities involving small body movements, develop more slowly. Nonetheless, children are eventually able to put together a wooden puzzle, draw with a pencil, and use a spoon and fork.

Separating physical-motor and perceptual development from cognitive development in preschool children is a difficult task. Children's understanding of the world depends on the information they receive from their own bodies, perceptions, motor activity, and the ways in which they experience themselves. Almost everything that a child does from birth through the first few years lays the base, in some way, not only for later physical-motor skills, but also for cognitive

gross motor skills Capabilities involving large body movements.
fine motor skills Capabilities involving small body movement.

Although they take longer to develop than gross motor skills, fine motor skills such as those involved in putting together the pieces of a wooden puzzle now emerge.

processes and social and emotional development. Looking, touching, exploring, babbling, bouncing, scribbling—all form the basis for the performance of more complex developmental tasks. Although much of what preschool children do—making mud pies, crawling, or hanging upside down—appears to be sheer sensory exploration, experts in development consider all children's actions to be purposeful, to be directed toward some goal (von Hofsten, 1989). For example, they explore places and objects to find out what they feel like, to see them, and to hear them. Sensory exploration leads to concepts like "up," "down," "straight," and "tight." For instance, when a girl walks on a log at the beach, she learns not only how to balance, but also the cognitive concept "narrow" and the emotional concept "confidence."

Many aspects of development proceed from a physical-motor base. Some developmental sequences are continuous, as in the natural progression from scribbling to writing; others seem somewhat discontinuous. For example, children may explore different textures and weaves of material randomly with their fingers and eyes before they are ready to sort and classify, or compare and contrast, the materials. In similar fashion, they must sort and compare thoughts before they can deal with complex ideas. Another example is the relationship between early infant crawling experience and later motor skill development. Crawling triggers psychological development, especially the perception of spatial concepts, since the experiences associated with crawling provide a foundation for visual-spatial perception (McEwan, Dihoff, & Brosvic, 1991). The process of crawling provides "…a state of eye-hand coordination, vestibular processing, improvement of balance and equilibrium, spatial awareness, tactile input, kinesthetic awareness, and social maturation" (McEwan, Dihoff, & Brosvic, 1991, p. 75).

Some developmental sequences involve **functional subordination.** Actions that at first are performed for their own sake later become part of a more complicated, purposeful skill. For example, a child's simple, fine motor explorations with crayon and paper have value in and of themselves, at first. Later, putting marks on paper becomes functionally subordinated to more complex skills, such as writing, drawing, creating designs, or even carpentry. The roots of complex thought are not always obvious; nevertheless, a look at physical-motor development is a good starting point from which to seek out these roots.

AGES 2 AND 3

Compared with infants, 2-year-olds are amazingly competent creatures. They can walk, run, and manipulate objects. When we see one beside a 4- or 5-year-old, however, we recognize the younger child's limitations. Two-year-olds—and even 3-year-olds—are still rather short and a bit rounded. They walk with a wide stance and a body sway. Although they can climb, push, pull, and hang by their hands, they have little endurance. This is a fact recognized by parents who have spent 15 minutes dressing toddlers in every layer of warm clothing they own in preparation for the ten minutes spent outside. Toddlers also are inclined to use both arms or both legs when only one is required (Woodcock, 1941). Thus, when a 2-year-old's mother offers him one cookie, he is likely to extend two hands.

functional subordination The integration of a number of separate simple actions or schemes into a more complex pattern of behavior.

The gait of 2-year-olds is characterized by a wide stance and a body sway. They love to walk and run but have little endurance. In contrast, the legs of 3-year-olds stay closer together when they run.

By the age of 3, children's legs stay closer together during walking and running, and they no longer need to keep a constant check on what their feet are doing (Cratty, 1970). They run, turn, and stop more smoothly than they did as 2-year-olds, although their ankles and wrists are not as flexible as they will be at ages 4 and 5 (Woodcock, 1941). Three-year-olds are more likely to extend one hand to receive one item, and they begin to show a preference for using either the right or left hand.

AGES 4 AND 5

Four-year-olds are able to vary the rhythm of their running. Many 4-year-olds can also skip rather awkwardly and execute a running jump and a standing broad jump (Gesell, 1940). The average child of 4 is probably able to work a button through a buttonhole and can use a pencil or crayon to draw lines, circles, and simple faces.

Five-year-olds can skip smoothly, walk a balance beam confidently, stand on one foot for several seconds, and imitate dance steps (Gesell, 1940). They manage buttons and zippers and may be able to tie shoelaces. Many children can throw a ball overhand and catch a large ball thrown to them (Cratty, 1970). But accurate throwing and effective catching will show many changes over the next few years (Robertson, 1984).

Whereas 3-year-olds may push a doll carriage or a large truck for the fun of pushing it, 4-year-olds have functionally subordinated their pushing into a fantasy of doll play or a cars-and-trucks game. Where 3-year-olds daub and smear paint with abandon and stack blocks one on top of another, 4-year-olds make a "painting" or use blocks to build houses, space stations, or farms. Four-year-olds are still exploring some physical-motor activities for their own sake—for example, they may accurately pour liquid into tiny cups or operate a syringe and a funnel—but much of their play is embedded in the acting out of complex roles or the purposeful construction of objects or games. We can see the motor development of preschool children presented in Table 9–1.

TABLE 9–1 Motor Development of Preschool Children

2-YEAR-OLDS	3-YEAR-OLDS	4-YEAR-OLDS	5-YEAR-OLDS
Walk with wide stance and body sway.	Keep legs closer together when walking and running.	Can vary rhythm of running.	Can walk a balance beam.
Can climb, push, pull, run, hang by both hands.	Can run and move more smoothly.	Skip awkwardly; jump.	Skip smoothly; stand on one foot.
Have little endurance.	Reach for objects with one hand.	Have greater strength, endurance, and coordination.	Can manage buttons and zippers; may tie shoelaces.
Reach for objects with two hands.	Smear and daub paint; stack blocks.	Draw shapes and simple figures; make paintings; use blocks for buildings.	Use utensils and tools correctly.

FINE MOTOR SKILLS

Fine motor skills involve the refined use of the hand, fingers and thumb. The development of various abilities in which the hands are involved comprises a series of overlapping processes beginning before birth. At the sixth fetal month, a grasp response may be elicited. Near the end of the third year, a new manual ability emerges when the child begins to integrate and coordinate manual schemes with other motor, perceptual, or verbal behaviors. For example, 4-year-olds will be able to run, to watch a ball, and simultaneously position the hands and fingers to catch the ball. Another example may be found in the preschool child's ability to carry on a dinner conversation while successfully manipulating a fork (Cratty, 1986). The development of self-care skills also falls under this set of skills.

The final period of manual activity, lasting from early to middle childhood, is marked by children's efforts to expand their artistic abilities. Musical instruments are played by young children, and they are able to represent their thoughts with increasing sophistication using artistic expression through sculpturing, drawing, and clay modeling (Kellogg, 1969).

SELF-CARE SKILLS As children gain fine motor skills, they become increasingly competent to take care of themselves and complete their daily activities independently. From 2 to 3 years of age, for example, children are able to put on and remove simple items of clothing. They can also zip and unzip large zippers. The average child of this age is able to use a spoon effectively, may string large beads, and can open doors by turning the knob.

The 3- to 4-year-old child can fasten and unfasten large buttons and is able to independently serve food—although still with minor "messes" on occasion. He is also able to use scissors to cut paper and can copy simple shapes using pencil and paper. By the time children are 4 to 5 years of age, they are able to dress and undress themselves without assistance. They can use a fork very well and have sufficient manual dexterity to cut the line of shapes with scissors. The 5-to 6-year-old can use a knife to cut soft food and can tie a simple knot. By age 6, children are able to tie their own shoes—although many of them consider this a very difficult task to learn.

FROM SCRIBBLING TO WRITING Scribbling has been described as a type of "motor babbling" (Cratty, 1986). As the child matures, the forms that arise

Preschoolers often practice tying shoelaces; by age 5, some children are able to complete this task.

from scribbling gradually become transformed into printing and writing—in much the same way as the sounds produced by babbling eventually combine to form words. In Table 9–2, we may see the stages through which children pass between scribbling and learning to write and draw.

CHILDREN'S ART Rhoda Kellogg has extensively studied the development of children's art. In the course of her working as an early childhood educator, she has amassed a collection of over half a million children's drawings from all over the world—tracing their artistic development from age 2 to 8. She has shown that the expressive gestures of children, from the moment that they first may be

TABLE 9–2 The Child's Progression from Scribbling to Writing and Drawing

1. A child may either hold a writing implement or use it to make marks on paper and on other surfaces.
2. Crude scribbling is performed whereby the child makes seemingly random marks without producing any coherent designs.
3. The child reacts to what is drawn; she may produce lines or squares or may balance a scribble on one side of a piece of paper with a figure drawn on the other.
4. The child draws simple geometric figures, beginning first with crude crosses and simple spirals.
5. More exact geometrical figures are drawn; two or more figures are placed in combinations; coloring proceeds with increasing accuracy.
6. More complex designs such as houses, people, and other familiar objects are drawn.
7. Block printing and cursive writing are learned in school.
8. With proper training and/or interest, the complex three-dimensional pictures and figures are drawn.

recorded by crayon or pencil, evolve in universal ways from basic scribbles to consistent symbols. Kellogg (1969) believes that every child, in his or her discovery of a model of symbolization, follows the same graphic evolution.

According to Kellogg, all children begin their artistic life producing a basic set of scribbles. Out of these shapeless scribblings eventually emerge: first, the circle, the upright cross, the diagonal cross, the rectangle, and other common forms. Then two or more of these basic forms are combined into that comprehensive symbol, the *mandala*, a circle divided into quarters by a cross. Over several years of development such basic patterns gradually become the child's conscious representation of familiar objects.

By age 3, the child begins to form "face" shapes, and by age 4, humans. By 4 to 5 years of age, the child achieves a "human" form with arms and legs, and, eventually, the suggestion of a trunk and clothes. By late 4 and 5, some children add other pictorials such as houses, animals, boats, and other objects.

HOW ADULTS AFFECT CHILDREN'S ART Kellogg (1969) sees a crisis of sorts at age 5, with kindergarten training that begins to shape the child's art to the adult's cultural standards. The child begins to produce art that "sells" or elicits adult approval. This is also the point at which many children cease being creative, and only some children are seen as "artists." Kellogg feels that artistic endeavors should be free and spontaneous in contrast to training in mathematical and word symbols which must be arbitrary.

Most art instruction conveys the message that it should be pictorial (or pure design) and functional in some way. Children's drawing is not considered "art" by most adults, and they attempt to shape it into what is considered art. In any event, by the age of 9 or 10, most children have lost the ability to simply produce what aesthetically pleases them. As Kellogg comments, "Adults do not scribble and most adults do not function at all in art. Therefore, the child has difficulty taking seriously his artistic self-education."

MOTOR SKILLS AND OVERALL DEVELOPMENT

Children's early motor experiences vary considerably. For some children, early childhood holds a wealth of motor experiences, including the opportunity to attempt to master diverse locomotor, climbing, and manipulative skills. Other children find their experiences limited during this important phase of development—either because of environmental or physical constraints. Opportunity for balanced and varied activity helps a child effectively and efficiently execute skills. (Nichols, 1990).

Success at performing physical activities also has an impact on young children's self-concept. Children's self-concepts include feelings about their body and their physical skills. Often, physically proficient young children are sought out by peers and become leaders at early ages. This valued skill level may give them the self-confidence and assurance to lead their classmates (Nichols, 1990).

LEARNING PHYSICAL-MOTOR SKILLS

The physical-motor skills that preschool children learn are usually everyday actions, such as tying shoes, cutting with scissors, feeding themselves, buttoning and zipping up clothes, using a crayon or pencil, skipping, and jumping. These skills increase the young child's capability to move around, to take care of herself, and to express herself creatively. They expand the child's world and her ability to act upon it. Some young children also learn more highly skilled activities, such as gymnastics, how to play the piano or violin, and even how to ride a horse. Although there is debate over the value of early training, psychologists have identified the important conditions for physical-motor learning. These conditions are readiness, motivation, activity, attention, and some kind of feedback. It is helpful to look closely at these factors before deciding whether or not to train a young child.

For a young child to learn a highly skilled activity like playing the piano certain conditions have to be in place, including readiness, motivation, and attention.

READINESS Any new skill or learning generally requires a state of *readiness* on the part of the child. A certain degree of maturation, some prior learning, and a number of preliminary skills must be present before the child can profit from training. The classic twin study of Myrtle McGraw (1935) demonstrated that although early training in the normal motor skills, such as cutting, buttoning, or climbing stairs, accelerated the acquisition of those skills, the gains were only temporary. The research method for these studies, called *co-twin* control studies, involved training only one twin in a particular skill. The training itself consisted of daily practice or drill three times a week, with the researcher praising and assisting the child, as well as demonstrating whenever necessary. It was assumed that such a concentrated and enriched training program would produce a permanent advantage in the skill being taught. But, the researchers found that when the untrained twin had reached the proper stage of maturation, or readiness, for the task involved, he or she learned it very quickly and caught up with the trained twin within a few weeks.

The study revealed that early training—training given before the appropriate maturation point has been reached—produces no lasting advantage at least not for those skills that are *phylogenetic* in nature. Phylogenetic skills are behaviors that all normal members of a species possess, for example, crawling, sitting, walking, and so forth. *Ontogenetic* behaviors, which are individually learned behaviors, do appear to be affected by training. These behaviors include roller skating, skiing, bicycle riding and other such activities. The twin who received the specialized training did engage in the ontogenetic activities at an earlier age and continued to outperform his or her twin in these activities.

The difficulty for parents and teachers is to know when children have reached the readiness point. American and Soviet studies have indicated that if children are introduced to new physical-motor learning at the optimal point of readiness, they learn quickly with little training or effort (Lisina & Neverovich, 1971). Children at the optimal readiness point want to learn, enjoy the practice, and get excited over their own performance. Children are frequently the best indicators of when they have reached the point of optimal readiness; they begin to imitate particular skills on their own. Readiness also becomes a factor in the age at which children should start formal academic tasks such as writing.

COMPETENCE MOTIVATION Another strong motive in motor-skill acquisition is **competence motivation** (White, 1959). Children try things out just to see if they can do them, to perfect their skill, to test their muscles and ability, and to enjoy the way it feels. They run, jump, climb, and skip for the pleasure and challenge of these activities. This kind of motivation is *intrinsic;* it comes from within

competence motivation A need to achieve in order to feel effective as an individual.

Activity is essential to motor development—for example, children cannot learn how to climb unless they practice that activity.

the child and is generated by the activity. *Extrinsic* motivation can also play a part in skill development. Parental encouragement, peer competition, and the need for identification can prompt a child to attempt, and then to perfect, a certain skill. Adults can boost the self-confidence of a child if they are encouraging and set goals that the child is able to accomplish.

But what if young children are pushed to develop skills through organized physical activities? Team sports often emphasize competition and may communicate criticism and pressure. Experts in sports medicine recommend avoiding formal sports for young children. They encourage adults to help children to initiate their own active play. Such play experiences lead to a positive attitude toward developing skills. Physical activity becomes associated with well-being and with doing one's best (Rice, 1990).

The best motivation parents can provide may be doing physical activities year-round themselves. Research shows that the level of physical activity of preschool children is significantly related to the amount of time their parents spend in physical exercise (Poest et al., 1989).

ACTIVITY Activity is essential to motor development. Children cannot master stair climbing unless they climb stairs. They cannot learn to throw a ball unless they practice throwing. When children live in limited and restricted environments, the development of their physical-motor skills will lag. Children raised in crowded surroundings often show a delay in the development of skills of the large muscles. They lack strength, coordination, and flexibility in running, jumping, climbing, balancing, and the like. Children who are hampered in their ability to use activity to learn—because they have few objects to play with, places to explore, or tools to use, as well as few people to imitate—may have trouble developing their motor skills. On the other hand, given a rich, meaningful environment full of objects to handle and use, open space to explore, and active people to imitate, children will generally have the necessary stimulation to pace their own learning. They will imitate a task, often repeating it endlessly. They will stack blocks and discover ways to make shapes. They will pour water repeatedly from one container to another to explore the concepts of "full" and "empty," "fast" and "slow," "spilling drops" and "making streams." Such self-designed and self-paced schedules of learning are often more efficient than adult-programmed lessons (Karlson, 1972).

ATTENTION Physical-motor learning is also enhanced by *attention*. Paying attention requires an alert and engaged state of mind. But how can children's attention be increased? Young children cannot just be told what to do and how to do it. Rather, children at age 2 or 3 learn new physical skills most effectively by being led through the activity. In the former Soviet Union, exercises and games were used to teach children to move their arms and legs in a desired fashion. Their techniques show that children between the ages of 3 and 5 frequently can focus their attention most effectively by active imitation. Varying types of follow-the-leader games are fun and reasonably successful. Gradually, the teacher can add verbal reminders to help children focus on a particular aspect of the physical activity. Finally, when children are 6 or even 7, they can attend closely to verbal instructions and follow them reasonably well, at least when participating in famil-iar tasks and activities (Zaporozlets & Elkonin, 1971; Zelazo & Reznick, 1991).

Researchers have recently explored the relationship between children's abil-ity to follow the rules of a game or activity and their developmental age. Previ-ously, researchers had successfully determined the rules which governed chil-dren's behavior, but they had largely ignored the notion of *execution*, which is the translation of knowledge into behavior. Younger children's inability to execute rules may have multiple causes. They may lack the ability to control attention, which therefore impedes rule use. And, even if they have the necessary attention, younger children may have difficulty following rules because they can't inhibit irrelevant responses (Zelazo & Reznick, 1991).

FEEDBACK The course of learning motor skills is also motivated by feedback. **Extrinsic feedback** comes in the form of rewards, such as cookies, candy, or praise given for a task well done. Specific feedback such as "Now you've got a strong grip on the bar" is more useful than general praise. The anticipation or promise of rewards is the extrinsic motivation previously discussed. **Intrinsic feedback** is a crucial monitor for skill development. Children discover that there are certain natural consequences to their actions and that these may be more pre-cise than arbitrary extrinsic feedback. For example, when climbing a jungle gym, they may derive pleasure from a feeling of tension in their muscles or from the experience of being up high, seeing things that cannot be seen from the ground. If they feel a bit wobbly, they will try to stabilize themselves. The "wobble" is intrinsic to the task and is usually more effective in making children aware of their need for safety than being told by an adult to be careful (which is extrinsic). Par-ents and teachers can help to point out the natural consequences of an action, but the learning process is most effective when a child has the experience itself.

In the United States today, early childhood education programs are expected to provide opportunities for daily practice of gross motor and fine motor skills. By and large, this practice is expected to be individual and self-moti-vated, not teacher directed. Considerable research suggests that self-paced and active play results in higher levels of physical-motor development (Johnson,

extrinsic feedback Rewards of praise given for performing a task well.

intrinsic feedback Feedback that comes from experiencing the nat-ural consequences of performing a task.

Christie, & Yawkey, 1987). Furthermore, there is evidence that certain kinds of playgrounds and indoor play environments designed according to these principles support higher levels of play and higher levels of motor development (Frost & Sunderline, 1985). Teachers ideally prepare an environment that allows for active exploration and interaction with other children and with materials. Children are encouraged to express themselves freely and loudly in outdoor environments and to develop small muscle skills and endurance with a wide variety of materials. National guidelines for childhood education programs have been established in accordance with these principles (National Association for the Education of Young Children, 1986).

ENVIRONMENTAL FACTORS INFLUENCING PHYSICAL DEVELOPMENT

Many factors influence the development of physical abilities in infants and young children. These may be separated into two major groups: first, those factors that cause normal variations in physical development such as inherited size and body conformation; and second, environmental influences which produce optimal or abnormal patterns of physical development. This second group includes such factors as nutrition, illness, accidents, or a combination of factors that might, for example, be present for a homeless family. We shall focus on this second set of variables in this section of the chapter.

NUTRITION

Nutritional problems have significant effects on the physical development of children. Poor nutrition may limit the size of children's bodies and brains. As we have seen in earlier chapters, sustained periods of malnutrition during crucial phases of brain development may permanently reduce children's cognitive abilities. Similarly, prolonged deprivation of essential nutrients may have pronounced effects on children's movement capacities and physical development.

Since children often appear to eat very little, parents may worry that their children are not eating enough. Despite this concern, children's nutritional requirements are easily satisfied. The necessary protein may come from milk or meat (including fish, cheese, or eggs). Carrots, green vegetables, or egg yolks supply Vitamin A. Vitamin C can come from citrus fruits, tomatoes, and leafy green vegetables. Calcium may come from cheese, yogurt, milk, figs, or broccoli (Kendrick, Kaufmann, & Messenger, 1991). Providing an assortment of fresh fruits, vegetables, and grains along with low amounts of meat provides enough protein, vitamins, and minerals for young children's health. No one food is essential for a child's diet or health. The key lies in offering attractively presented foods throughout the day—combined with not forcing children to eat when they refuse. Despite the message of television commercials that high sugar and fat foods are "good," high-fat and low-nutrient foods do not provide the most nutritious source for children's growth (see the box "Children's Food Preferences").

FOCUS ON APPLICATION

CHILDREN'S FOOD PREFERENCES

Eating or ingesting of food—except for breathing and excretion—is one of the most frequent human activities. Eating is also a very personal activity. Food is one of the major sources of pleasure for human beings and has great emotion attached to it. We tend to remember tastes and smells with fondness, for example, the scent of warm chocolate chip cookies or cinnamon—or with distaste—for example, the odor of formaldehyde or ammonia. Food selection is also an important human activity. Search, selection, and preparation of food invariably take more time than its ingestion. A good example of this is the time spent preparing a holiday dinner compared to the relatively short time consumed in eating it.

"Toddlers younger than 2 years of age tend to place everything in the mouth."

There are developmental differences in food selection and the individual's ability to make good food selections. For the fetus, for example, the main source of nutriment is placentally delivered blood. After birth—in a relatively abrupt manner—the main food is maternally delivered milk, either from the breast or the bottle. Finally, and more gradually, the wide range of food products available to adults are introduced. In fact, the weaning process is often considered one of life's major transitions. What is of interest to researchers is the manner in which the child after weaning selects foods to consume. In some cases, it is believed that specific instruction into the nature of foods and their appropriateness is provided by parents, while in others modeling, but no specific instruction, is the main determinant (Rozin, 1990).

Another aspect of development is learning which substances are edible and which inedible. Toddlers younger than 2 years of age tend to place everything in the mouth. Researchers offered children ranging from 18 months to 5 years of age a variety of items in a "cafeteria" setting. These items included normal foods, inedible items (sponge and paper), items offensive to adults (a whole dried fish, human hair, imitation dog feces), and dangerous items (imitation soap). Children under 2 years of age placed all of the items, except for hair, in their mouths. By 3 years of age, many of the items rejected by adults were also rejected by the children (Rozin et al., 1986). Given the tendency of young children to mouth any object, we may sometimes wonder how they safely negotiate young childhood without ingesting toxins, sharp objects, and other unsafe items.

There are also cultural differences in food preferences. In American society, for example, many foods are predominantly limited to a breakfast context. Foods such as eggs and grains, which may be present at any meal in developing countries, are limited to breakfast in the United States. Preschool children are also likely to combine foods they like regardless of the appropriateness of the context. For example, many preschoolers believe that if they like two foods, such as beef and whipped cream, then they will like these foods when they are combined. Many parents have suffered through meals where their children put apple sauce on beef or gravy on ice-cream.

In general, various ways have been suggested to encourage good nutrition in early childhood. Offering a well-balanced array of foods, attractively served is helpful. Given the size of young children's stomachs, a combination of small portions at meals and snacks at various times of the day are more likely to provide good nutrition. A pleasant mealtime experience, with little discussion of disliked foods or table manners is beneficial to children's eating patterns. Finally, sugary foods and desserts generally provide calories—with little or no nutritional benefit—at considerable cost. Fruit is a better alternative for snacks or meals (Kendrick, Kaufmann, & Messenger, 1991).

NUTRITIONAL DEFICIENCIES The nature of specific dietary deficiencies vary from country to country. During the past forty years considerable progress has been made in understanding how nutritional deficiencies develop and how to remedy them. Nevertheless, malnutrition exists in many parts of the world. This is because of the complex economic, environmental, social and educational forces that influence food production, distribution and consumption. For example, we may see pictures of starving children from Somalia on the evening news and hear that the United Nations is providing food. However, the food supplies may not be able to reach all those who need them, they may be sold on the black market, or they may give only short-term relief to a long-term problem based on war, drought, or poverty (Hansen, 1990).

Various nutritional diseases currently affect the physical and cognitive development of children around the world.

Protein-Energy Malnutrition. *Protein-energy malnutrition* (also called kwashiorkor and marasmus) is a chronic health problem in poor populations worldwide. In general, the more severe the malnutrition and the longer it lasts, the more impaired the child's physical growth and brain development. Delayed cognitive development and possibly irreversible mental retardation are also potential results (Ricciuti, 1993). Recently, however, researchers have concluded that malnutrition by itself is not the main cause of these lasting physical and cognitive effects. It is rather the "ecology of malnutrition"—poverty and poor housing, health care, and education—that seems to maintain the physical and cognitive losses (Lozoff, 1989; Ricciutti, 1993).

Iron-Deficiency Anemia. Iron-deficiency anemia is one of the most common nutritional diseases found in population surveys within the United States. A number of research studies in the 1970s and 1980s suggested that iron-deficiency anemia was associated with lower levels of cognitive functioning and school performance in preschool and school-age children. Advances in biochemical techniques have made it possible to more precisely determine children's iron status. The physical symptoms of iron-deficiency anemia include fatigue, poor concentration, and breathlessness. However, psychological effects also occur based on altered brain activity associated with a lack of iron. Abnormal information processing and learning are associated with altered iron metabolism. Prior to treatment, children with iron-deficiency anemia have lower IQ scores than nonanemic children. In the case of anemic children younger than 3 years, improving iron status has not generally improved test performance, while there has been more improvement in the test performance of school-age children (Lozoff, 1989; Ricciuti, 1993).

NUTRITIONAL INTERVENTION Recently there has been renewed interest in the question of whether supplements of minerals and vitamins greater than that recommended by public health agencies can enhance brain functioning and increase intelligence in normally nourished children. Research does not seem to support this view. Malnutrition is best viewed as only one of a variety of health and environmental conditions that adversely affect the physical growth, cognitive development, and school performance of children growing up in poor populations (Ricciuti, 1993).

In general, the relationship between nutrition and the later behaviors of children is not always obvious. For example, undernourished children sometimes perform better than adequately nourished children on tests of muscular strength and flexibility (Cratty, 1986). On the other hand, dental health is invariably poor among undernourished populations.

The "ecology of malnutrition" presents environmental factors that must be remedied—in addition to nutritional supplements. Parents may be stressed or ill or fatigued or even depressed. They may need to use all their energies finding adequate housing and keeping their children safe. There is then little opportunity for parent supportive play and education. There is no question that the pressure of economic problems hinder many poor families from providing adequate and appropriate foods for their families.

With respect to health policies, research suggests that *prevention* is preferable to *therapeutic interventions* (Lozoff, 1989). Thus, nutritional supplements and medical care cannot completely reverse behavioral deficiencies once undernutrition has occurred. An example of this is seen in programs to prevent iron-deficiency anemia in the United States. Iron-deficiency anemia has declined radically because of increases in breast feeding, iron fortified formula and cereals, and the Women, Infants and Children (WIC) program, which provides nutritional supplements to women and children who are at risk for poverty. Once iron deficiency anemia occurs, however, therapy does not completely raise the lower school test scores of affected children to those of "normal" children (Lozoff, 1989; Ricciuti, 1993).

ENVIRONMENTAL HAZARDS AND ACCIDENTS

Information about the child's motor development can determine when certain problems may occur and the points at which interventions should be introduced for at-risk children.

> ...the young child (0–3 years) lacks the motor control (e.g., balance, coordination, strength) necessary to ensure his or her safety when riding in an automobile. In addition, the physical development of the infant renders him or her more susceptible to brain injury because of softer brain consistency and skull construction and because a greater proportion of body weight centered in the head pulls the head forward in collisions. Because of these vulnerabilities, it becomes particularly critical that prevention measures be taken by adults for restraining infants and young children in car seats. (Maddux et al., 1986, p. 27)

Because of an awareness of motor development, pediatricians often engage in *anticipatory guidance* with parents—pointing out what sorts of accidents and hazards must be avoided at which ages. In general, the three greatest environmental hazards for preschoolers are automobiles, their own homes, and swimming pools. Each year many young children die in motor vehicle accidents, or from ingesting toxic or caustic substances found in their houses or garages, or by falling into a swimming pool and being unable to swim.

Prevention of these accidental deaths is accomplished quite easily. Infant car seats, fences around pools, and placement of dangerous substances in locked or very high cabinets effectively protect small children from their own inquisitiveness or lack of physical abilities. In addition, young children require careful monitoring during their play—whether indoors or outside—since they lack the cognitive ability to follow safety rules and may let their natural curiosity and urge to explore drive their behavior.

Although preschoolers are especially vulnerable to accidents in the car, their own homes, and swimming pools, all of these can be easily prevented.

LEAD POISONING One specific environmental hazard which has evoked considerable concern is *lead poisoning*. Lead poisoning is damage caused by too much lead in the body. Even small amounts of lead can interfere with children's learning and behavior. In larger amounts, lead causes serious damage to the brain, kidneys, nervous system, and red blood cells. Because of young children's natural tendency to engage in hand-to-mouth activity and their curiosity, they are at the greatest risk of lead poisoning.

The major source of contamination from lead is lead-based paint which becomes chips or dust for children to swallow. Since the mid 1970s, paints have not contained lead, so mainly older homes and buildings may contain layers of lead-based paint. Children become poisoned from eating, chewing, or sucking on objects coated with lead dust or chips. Soil may also be contaminated from paint that has weathered or been sanded or scraped off buildings. In addition, auto exhaust of leaded gasoline may cause lead to accumulate in the soil. When children get contaminated dirt on their hands and then put their hands in their mouth, they may therefore become lead poisoned (Kendrick, Kaufmann, & Messenger, 1991). Children who live in urban areas are at the greatest risk for lead poisoning since the largest concentration of homes with older paint is in cities.

The major psychological and behavioral effects of lead poisoning are only encountered when high levels of lead are present. Since the major contamination from lead has been reduced, the usual effects are subtle behavioral ones detectable only in fairly large studies (Berney, 1993). These include lower intellectual achievement and less appropriate school behavior than that shown by the general population.

THE PROBLEM OF LOW-INCOME AND HOMELESSNESS

One effect of the economic crises of the 1980s and 1990s has been an increase in the number of children living in poverty. By 1991, 1 out of every 4 children under the age of 6 was living in poverty. (According to the Federal Government in 1991, a family of three was defined as living in poverty if its total annual income was $10,860. For a family of four, that amount was $13,924.) This marked a significant increase over the poverty rate in children in 1979. At this point, we need to note that low-income by itself is not a health hazard. Certainly many families confront the challenges of limited income and with the help of friends and the community provide adequate food, health care, supervision, and education for their children.

Yet for some families, the risks of prolonged low income are too high, and they experience the cycle of poverty depicted in Figure 9–3. Poverty often becomes a cycle in which health, poor or inadequate nutrition, and school failure are interrelated, leading in turn to unemployment, environmental inadequacy, and other debilitating conditions which can be passed on to the next generation.

Of particular concern today are the increasing numbers of children who are not only poor, but also homeless. In 1991 only one-third of young families, headed by a parent younger than 30) were homeowners—down from one-half in 1980. For fam-

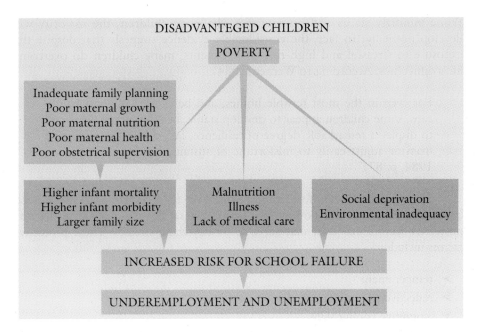

FIGURE 9–3
The Consequences of
Poverty in Children.
Source: Garmezy, N. (1991). Resiliency
and vulnerability to adverse developmental outcomes associated with poverty.
American Behavioral Scientist, 34(4),
p. 419.

ilies with the fewest economic resources, this decline has been disastrous. In 1980, there were virtually no homeless families in America. Now families with young children make up one-third of all homeless people (Children's Defense Fund, 1992). The National Academy of Sciences has estimated that there are 100,000 homeless children in the United States today. These children may sleep each night in emergency shelters, welfare hotels, abandoned buildings, cars, or on the street.

Badly housed or homeless children are at risk for a variety of physical and psychological problems. Lead poisoning and exposure to structural, electrical, and sanitation hazards associated with substandard housing are an example of these risks. Homeless children also face educational disruption as they may move from school to school or school district to school district. Some homeless children are separated from family members in the family's efforts to find shelter. Finally, homeless children are exposed to considerable emotional stress. The results of this sustained emotional stress have been compared with post-traumatic stress disorder. Young homeless children may have short attention spans, weak impulse control, speech delays, or sleep disorders. They may be either withdrawn or aggressive. Many become depressed or anxious or regress to earlier behaviors such as unusual dependency on parents or siblings (Children's Defense Fund, 1992).

Homeless children often have potentially serious health problems. Intestinal parasites causing severe diarrhea, unmet acute and chronic medical needs, hepatitis, and AIDS, have been found in homeless young children—who also exhibited developmental and school problems (Bass, Brennan, Mehta, & Kodzis, 1990). Other studies have found serious psychosocial problems in preschool homeless children. Anxiety, depression, and learning difficulties have been reported (Bassuk & Rosenberg, 1990). Homeless children are three times as likely as other children to have missed immunizations (Bassuk, 1991).

RESILIENT CHILDREN When discussing the effects of low income on children, there is often a tendency to overemphasize the negative impact on children.

While minority status and poverty may challenge children, the majority will develop normally. In fact, the considerable evidence suggests that despite the exposure to stressful and high-risk environments, many children do overcome life's difficulties. According to Werner (1984):

> For even in the most terrible homes, and beset with physical handicaps, some children appear to develop stable, healthy personalities and to display a remarkable degree of resilience, i.e., the ability to recover from or adjust easily to misfortune or sustained life stress. (Werner, 1984, p. 87)

Most research has unfortunately focused on the negative outcomes associated with stresses such as poverty and homelessness. But it is now clear that the protective factors that exist may serve to modify these stresses. These protective factors include:

- temperament
- reflectiveness in meeting new situations
- cognitive coping skills
- positive responsiveness to others
- warmth and cohesiveness of families
- the presence of a caring adult
- the presence of external support, such as a caring teacher or church that fosters ties to the larger community (Garmezy, 1991).

Resilient children—children with these protective factors active in their lives demonstrate unusual psychological strength despite a history of severe or prolonged psychological stress. The following children are typical of these resilient individuals:

> These were children like Michael for whom the odds, on paper, did not seem very promising. The son of teenage parents, Michael was born prematurely and spent his first three weeks of life in the hospital, separated from his mother. Immediately after his birth, his father was sent with the Army to Southeast Asia for almost two years. By the time Michael was eight, he had three younger siblings and his parents were divorced. His mother left the area and had no further contact with the children.

> And there was Mary, born to an overweight, nervous and erratic mother who had experienced several miscarriages, and a father who was an unskilled farm laborer with only four years of education. Between Mary's fifth and tenth birthdays, her mother had several hospitalizations for repeated bouts with mental illness, after having inflicted both physical and emotional abuse on her daughter.

> Yet both Michael and Mary, by age 18, were individuals with high self-esteem and sound values, caring for others and liked by their

resilient children Children who develop normally despite exposure to persistent and/or prolonged stress.

peers, successful in school and looking forward to their adult futures. (Werner, 1984, p. 87).

The presence of at least one caring adult helps children to modify the negative effects of constant stress.

Of the positive attributes displayed by children in poverty, some are instilled by family or schools or other social institutions such as churches. Others appear to be inherently present in children as a function of their temperament or cognitive skills. One persistent characteristic of resilient children is the faith that things will work out. This belief can be sustained if children encounter people who give meaning to their lives and a reason for commitment and caring (Werner, 1984).

The research on resilient children points out the need to avoid categorically labeling poor children as disadvantaged. Many of them, with the appropriate environmental and emotional supports, may well be resilient. Research on these children focuses on the "self-righting" tendencies which appear to move some children to normal development despite even persistently adverse environmental conditions.

 ## HEALTH AND ILLNESS

During the 1980s, every key measure of maternal and child health in the United States worsened, failed to improve, or improved at a slower rate than previous years. As a result, the United States has fallen behind other countries with fewer resources on health indicators such as low birthweight and infant mortality. Every year nearly 1 million infants start life at a disadvantage because their mothers do not receive adequate prenatal care (Children's Defense Fund, 1992). About 1 child in 5—and for very young children, 1 in 4—live in families with incomes below the federal poverty level. Many more live in families marginally above the poverty line. Low income is the major factor responsible for most, if not all, of the other disadvantages found in other high-risk children such as minority group members (Starfield, 1992).

As we can see in Table 9–3, poor children are more likely to become ill and have more serious illnesses. This results from increased environmental risk associated with poor housing, hazardous neighborhoods, poor nutrition, and inadequate preventive care. The higher rates of serious illness and death rates from diseases of childhood also reflect poor access to medical care.

Once children are born, other health concerns are raised. For example, the United States has drastically fallen behind other countries in the rate of immunization for preventable diseases. In many urban areas, fewer than half the toddlers and young children are fully immunized. A recent study of nine urban areas by the Center for Disease Control found that only 10 to 42 percent of children who started school in 1991 had received the necessary preschool vaccinations on time. Compared with other countries, the United States ranks seventeenth in the proportion of children who are immunized against polio. When the proportion of nonwhite American children is compared with the rates of other nations, the United States ranks seventieth behind such impoverished countries as Nicaragua and Trinidad and Tobago (Children's Defense Fund, 1992).

A major cause of the low American rates in preventive care of children is that many American children have little or no health insurance or live in commu-

TABLE 9–3 Relative Frequency of Health Problems in Low-Income Children Compared with Other Children

HEALTH PROBLEM	RELATIVE FREQUENCY IN LOW-INCOME CHILDREN
Low birth weight	double
Delayed immunization	triple
Asthma	higher
Bacterial meningitis	double
Rheumatic fever	double—triple
Lead poisoning	triple
Neonatal mortality	1.5 times
Postneonatal mortality	double—triple
Child deaths due to accidents	double—triple
Child deaths due to disease	triple—quadruple
Complications of appendicitis	double—triple
Diabetic ketoacidosis	double
Complications of bacterial meningitis	double—triple
Percent with conditions limiting school activity	double—triple
Lost school days	40% more
Severely impaired vision	double—triple
Severe iron-deficiency anemia	double

Source: Starfield, 1985.

nities where they lack access to doctors, hospitals, or health clinics. Health care and social services are often too fragmented or inaccessible for many poor families. As a result, children with disabilities, poor children, and children whose parents are less educated or speak little English often lack the necessary support services they need to have good health. Because of this lack of preventive care, many problems exist in the United States that may seriously limit the potential life and its quality for young children. We may see some of these problems presented in Table 9–4.

ILLNESS

Young children are healthy by adult standards because, on the average, they have fewer chronic disabling or life-threatening disorders than adults. But children are also in a different developmental phase than adults. Ill health may be manifested by delays or reversals in development—by delays in the child's achieving developmental milestones. In addition, the implications of labeling are greater for children than for adults. For example, a health status measure that emphasizes handicaps may make children appear to be more disabled than they may be. This is because children have inherently greater developmental potential and greater capacity to adapt or compensate for their infirmities than do adults (Starfield, 1992).

During early childhood, the most common acute conditions are upper respiratory problems. The second most common type of condition is injury. The fre-

TABLE 9–4 Preventable Health Problems in Young Children in the United States

➤ Every 13 seconds an American child is reported abused or neglected (2.7 million a year).

➤ Every 3 hours a child is murdered.

➤ The United States has a higher infant mortality rate than 19 other nations.

➤ The United States has a higher infant mortality for nonwhite infants than the overall rates of 31 other nations, including Cuba, Bulgaria, and Kuwait.

➤ The United States has a higher low birthweight rate than 30 other nations.

➤ The United States has a low birthweight rate among nonwhites higher than the overall rates of 73 other countries, including many Third World and former Communist Eastern Bloc countries.

➤ The United States has a higher death rate among preschool children than 19 other nations.

➤ The United States has a smaller proportion of children immunized against polio than 16 other nations.

➤ The United States has a higher child poverty rate than 7 other industrialized Western countries. One in five American children—14.3 million—are poor, making them the poorest group of Americans.

Source: Children's Defense Fund, 1992.

quencies for both illness and injury are greater for males than females during the preschool years. The most common problem reported by 12 percent of children in a single year is allergy. Ear infections and non-specific symptoms such as skin rashes, headache, or anemia also occur quite frequently. Chronic medical conditions are present in about 7 percent of children. These include asthma, heart conditions, arthritis, epilepsy, and diabetes.

In the past, the common view was that children with severe chronic illness die in childhood. However, current estimates of survival suggest that at least 90

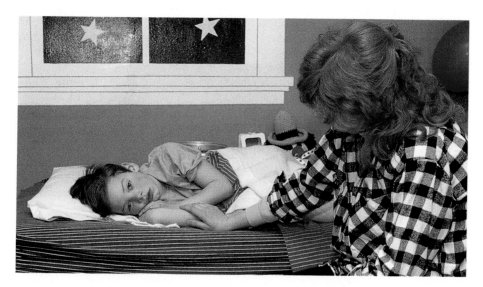

Although young children are healthier than adults, they still get sick. Chronic conditions affecting children include asthma and arthritis.

percent of children—even with very severe long-term illnesses—survive to adult-hood. This change is largely due to improved medical and surgical technologies, as well as the availability of sophisticated medical care (see the box, "Technology-Dependent Children"). The focus of health care for such children today is on improving the quality of their lives, rather than merely insuring their survival. Many of them are not able to participate as active members of most aspects of life.

CHRONIC ILLNESS

The total prevalence of chronically ill or disabled children in the population has been estimated at between 10 percent and 30 percent (Perrin, Guyer, & Lawrence, 1992). The large majority of these conditions are mild and have little impact on children's daily activities or use of health services. About 10 percent of children with *chronic illnesses,* or about 2 million children nationwide, however, have their quality and quantity of life seriously affected by their illness or dis-abling condition. Among this group, only asthma and congenital heart disease occur with any great frequency. Other individual conditions—such as leukemia, epilepsy, kidney failure, or arthritis—are rare. For these children, the low numbers do not accurately reflect the disproportionately greater strain on them and their families imposed by their chronic illness or disability. Diseases such as *leukemia* (cancer of the white blood cells), *muscular dystrophy* (a progressive loss of motor functioning leading to death), *cerebral palsy* (a disorder of muscles producing varying degrees of movement impairment), or disabilities such as *blindness* or *deafness* all occur in less than 1 percent of the population, but their effects may be devastating at worst and challenging at best for the child and his or her family.

Three of the more common chronic illnesses encountered by children include sickle-cell anemia, diabetes, and asthma. In addition to these more com-mon serious disorders, AIDS has also emerged as a concern in early childhood—although the number of affected children remains low. We shall briefly discuss some key aspects of these chronic illnesses and their impact on the children expe-riencing them.

SICKLE-CELL ANEMIA Anemia is a term that refers to a blood disorder caused by too few red blood cells (the cells that carry oxygen) or too little hemo-globin (the pigment that gives red blood cells their color). Because of the decreased oxygen in the blood, people with anemia are often tired or lack energy. In *sickle-cell anemia,* the normal round red blood cells assume a sicklelike shape and lack the proper amount of oxygen. The sickle shape makes it difficult for them to move through small blood vessels, and they consequently become dam-aged or destroyed. Sickle-cell anemia is an inherited disease which tends to occur more frequently among people of Mediterranean descent and African Americans.

Not all children with sickle-cell anemia are affected the same way. Some are able to participate in activities with little negative effect. However, the majority have intermittent periods of pain and fatigue. The main cause of pain for these children is the blockages resulting when the sickle-shaped cells block blood ves-sels. Extreme pain occurs in the place of blockage. Stress or overexertion may bring these crises on, although they may also occur without warning.

Sickle-cell anemia is not curable, but medication may sometimes control its more negative consequences. Children with sickle-cell anemia should avoid

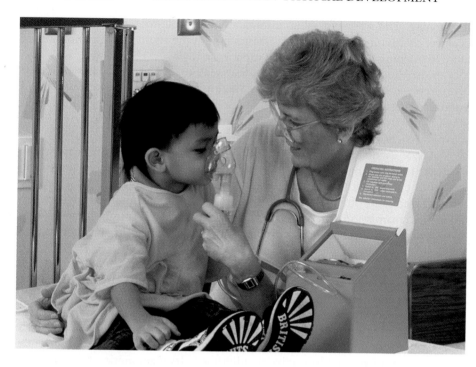

One focus of early intervention with disabled children and toddlers is on proactive planning to help prepare them to join in the activities of other children.

overexertion and infections. They may require hospitalization to treat the painful crises and resulting infections.

DIABETES Diabetes is a disorder of metabolism caused by the failure of the pancreas, a gland located behind the stomach, to produce a chemical called *insulin*. Insulin helps the body store and use glucose (sugar) and metabolize fat. Without insulin, cells in the body cannot use the body's glucose and therefore obtain insufficient nourishment.

When children have diabetes, they usually require adding insulin to their bodies on a daily basis through injections—typically one in the morning and one in the late afternoon. Diabetic children also need to follow a special low sugar, low fat diet, which must be balanced with exercise. Food makes glucose rise in the blood, while insulin and exercise make it decrease. Children with diabetes often have difficulty balancing their blood sugar and may swing between *hypoglycemia* (low blood sugar) and blood sugar levels that are too high. Sugar levels which are too high may result in a diabetic coma. This is rare in children who are being adequately monitored for their sugar levels. The more common hypoglycemic or insulin reaction may result in unconsciousness and convulsions if not treated promptly. The usual treatment is to provide sugar immediately in the form of orange juice or sugar tablets (Kendrick, Kaufmann, & Messenger, 1991).

ASTHMA Asthma is an example of a disorder with relatively minor symptoms in children for the majority of time, but there may be severe episodes—much like as in sickle-cell anemia. Asthma is a chronic lung disease involving the restriction of air flow into the lungs. For most asthmatic children, antihistamines or bronchial dilators successfully control their symptoms most of the time. However, when stress occurs in the child's life, an asthmatic crisis may occur that can become life-threatening. The symptoms of an asthma attack include wheezing, breathing difficulties, coughing, and a feeling of constriction in the chest. These symptoms are quite frightening to the children who experience them.

Most children outgrow asthma as they mature, but may still show evidence of exercise-induced asthma as adults. Since physical activity often brings on asthma attacks, children with asthma have frequently been restricted in their physical activity by their parents and may have anxiety about participating in such activities (Nichols, 1990).

AIDS. Acquired Immune Deficiency Syndrome (AIDS) is a disease whose incidence is increasing in the general population. But its incidence remains low in preschool children for two reasons: first, most infants contract AIDS through their mothers and often die before the age of two; second, the most common mode of transmission for AIDS, sexual activity, is not typically practiced by preschoolers. Nevertheless, AIDS remains a concern for health researchers and planners.

When AIDS does occur in a child, it challenges families, schools, and health services in ways that are similar to some chronic illnesses, but also unique to AIDS. First, children with AIDS are highly concentrated in poor and minority families, as we saw in earlier chapters. In New York State, for example, AIDS is the leading cause of death among Hispanic and African-American children aged 1 to 4 years. Second, AIDS is invariably fatal, so the children who are currently infected are not expected to survive to adulthood. Its main mode of transmission (through the blood of infected mothers) means that the main family care-giver is also likely to be affected and thus may be unable to care for the sick child (Perrin, Guyer, & Lawrence, 1992).

The possibility of transmission of the human immunodeficiency virus (HIV) from infected children to their contacts has been the focus of considerable social fear. Consider the case of Ryan White, a hemophiliac child who contracted AIDS through a blood transfusion. He had difficulty in attending school and maintaining friendships because of his illness. His case, unfortunately, was not an isolated one. The families of infected children, day-care centers, schools, and hospitals themselves have all shown concern over the disease's transmission.

Concern has especially been raised over infected preschoolers who drool, bite, mouth toys, and may be incontinent since body fluids are the main source of contamination. A recent study of 25 infected preschool children and their 89 family members found that no transmission of HIV occurred from infected children to their household contacts. These family members had shared many items, hugged, kissed, slept in the same bed, and bathed together (Rogers et al., 1990). This research offers evidence that there is an extremely low probability of virus transmission through normal daily activity routes. A preschool child has far greater risk in riding without a car seat or playing in a neighbor's pool than in contracting AIDS.

CHRONIC HEALTH PROBLEMS AND THE FAMILY

Families provide the bulk of care for children with chronic and disabling conditions. Mothers of such chronically impaired children are significantly less likely than the mothers of healthy children to be employed outside the home. In the past, these children were likely to be moderately impaired. With today's medical technology, severely impaired children requiring respirators or intravenous or tube feeding are likely to receive care at home. Many of these children require extensive nursing care, monitoring, and the use of complex equipment on a 24-hour basis. It is estimated that 20,000 to 30,000 children in the United States require home care with significant technology dependence.

Serious illness or disability significantly impacts the lives of affected children and their families. The following features have been found in families caring for seriously impaired children:

➤ disruptions in school attendance and achievement for the child and his or her siblings

➤ decreased peer contacts and friendships

➤ adjustment problems in both the child and siblings

➤ depression and anxiety in the mother

➤ marital stress and disruption for the father and mother (Varni & Babani, 1986).

In general, the successful mainstreaming of chronically ill and disabled children depends on their social competence skills and social acceptance. Controlling the level of stress within the family also assists in the child's overall adjustment—both within and outside of the family setting. Self-help or support groups often help families with ill or disabled children to reduce the stress and sense of isolation associated with care-giving.

PSYCHOLOGICAL EFFECTS OF CHRONIC HEALTH PROBLEMS Children with long-term illness or other special needs often are at risk for secondary disabilities such as mental health problems and educational difficulties. Many studies have found that children with chronic health problems have twice the risk of having significant behavioral and psychiatric problems than normal healthy children. These studies have also found that the severity of the chronic disorder does not seem to raise or lower this risk—*any* chronic health problem carries the same relative risk (Perrin, Guyer, & Lawrence, 1992).

Children with chronic illnesses also have difficulty participating in preschool and school activities. In addition, many developmental disabilities create the need for special education services in response to the child's special educational and physical needs. For the most part, however, chronic illnesses do not create a direct impact on the child's actual ability to learn. Their effects are rather indirect and include excessive fatigue or the effect of medication on the child's abilities.

The most common problems chronically ill children face are absence from normal daily activities such as school, preschool, church, or social groups. Children with recurring acute episodes such as those associated with asthma or sickle-cell anemia may often miss extended blocks of activities. As was stated recently:

Many years ago, when the issue for these children was planning for premature death, schooling was considered unimportant; today, with most children surviving to adulthood, there is a great need to improve educational opportunities and to diminish the effects of illness or its treatment on the child's participation in school. (Perrin, Guyer, & Lawrence, 1992, p. 72)

FOCUS ON AN ISSUE

TECHNOLOGY-DEPENDENT CHILDREN: RESIDENTS IN NURSING HOMES

Tricycles, wagons, and dolls are not usually found in a skilled nursing facility or nursing home. However, across the United States nursing homes are expanding their services to care for technology-dependent children. These children, because of advances in medical technology, once would have died but now continue to survive—but only with the assistance of the most sophisticated equipment and intensive nursing care. The numbers of these children is rising at such a rapid rate that in some children's hospitals, the demands of caring for these severely impaired children is disrupting the traditional clinical mission of the hospital (Kettrick & Donar, 1987). Hospitals, which are traditionally geared to quick turnover of patients, are having to cope with large numbers of technology-dependent children occupying beds for extended periods of time, even years.

"Today, given the shortage of hospital beds for acutely ill children, nursing homes have become the main treatment site."

Many of these children are on ventilators, which breathe for them, or require such specialized nursing services as tube feeding, cardiac care, oxygen support, and chemotherapy for childhood cancers. Some of the typical diagnoses of such children are muscular disorders such as muscular dystrophy, asphyxia (shortage of oxygen from birth or other accident such as near drowning), spinal cord injury from sports, motorcycle, or automobile accidents resulting in paralysis or congenital disorders.

Today, given the shortage of hospital beds for acutely ill children, nursing homes have become the main treatment site. They provide the constant monitoring and skilled nursing judgment and intervention these children require. The backgrounds of technology-dependent children vary considerably. Some may be teenagers who were injured in accidents; others are preschoolers or school-aged children with chronic impairments. For example, one nursing home admitted a 4-year-old girl as a patient who was ventilator-dependent. Her family had already exhausted $500,000 in insurance coverage, and she was now on Medicaid (the program for those who are poor). Her parents thought that she would be happier in a less institutionalized setting than the hospitals.

Nursing homes that care for these children often spend consider-

EARLY INTERVENTION As with many social or intellectual problems, prevention is the best way to deal with health problems of children. For example, preventing children from being born with AIDS is a better alternative than treating the child until death. However, since prevention is not always possible, early intervention is the next most desirable alternative.

When children with significant health problems and their families receive early diagnosis and treatment, the child's potential for optimal development is maximized, and she is less likely to suffer developmental delays. The family often becomes part of a support network of health care providers, rehabilitation experts, and lay people that may serve to reduce the stress of family members, while enhancing their care-giving capabilities (see the box "Technology-Dependent Children: Residents in Nursing Homes"). If disabled children and toddlers receive early intervention, the educational costs to society are reduced by mini-

able time planning for their young residents. Rooms are frequently renovated—walls are papered with bright primary or pastel colors. Cribs, mobiles, rocking chairs, games and toys, as well as specially designed pediatric hospital equipment must be purchased. The staff must be specially trained in child growth and development and in the special emotional needs of sick children.

Dietary services may be included to allow for the pizza, burgers, and French fries which children love. Recreational therapy must be tailored to meet the needs of severely disabled children—who are, nonetheless, still children. One nursing home's activities program now encompasses Bert and Ernie puppet shows, trips to the zoo, and photos taken with Santa. The program even includes a specially equipped "tot lot" complete with wading pool, sandbox, and swings.

Family participation is encouraged from the first placement interview through the child's entire stay. Families are free to choose their own level of involvement. Siblings are also encouraged to come to visit the nursing home so that they can see for themselves the care being considered for their sister or brother. The staff are especially sensitive to the emotional pain that the family is going through in this type of situation. The nursing home placement interview may be the first time that the parents realize that their child may not get well—that there may be no quick cure and, possibly, no cure at all. Many nursing homes, therefore, involve parents and family members in the children's direct care and encourage them to become part of the caregiving team. As one nursing home administrator commented: "Families have entrusted us with the care of their loved one. Many of them, relinquishing the secure 'cocoon' of the hospital ICU, experienced apprehension as they transferred their child to a strange new environment. These families are now an extension of our family as we share disappointments, setbacks, and heartaches, as well as birthdays, weddings, and holidays. They are remarkable people, and their love and dedication to their children are an inspiration....Parents tell us their burden now seems lighter. And we are privileged to witness the children's resilience and courage."

References: Reynolds, S.L. (1988). "Technology-Dependent children: new residents of nursing homes." *Long-Term Care Currents, II* (1).

US Congress, Office of Technology Assessment, *Technology-Dependent Children: Hospital vs. Home Care—A Technical Memorandum*, OTA-TM-H-38. Washington: US Government Printing Office, May, 1987.

Kettrick, R.G. & Donar, M.E. (1987). The vent-dependent child: Medical and Social Care. *Critical Care: The State of the Art 1986*. Fullerton, CA: Society of Critical Care Medicine, 1987.

Glick, P.S., Guyer, B., Burr, B.H. & Gorbach, I.E. (1983). "Pediatric nursing homes: Implications of the Massachusetts experience for residential care of multiply handicapped children." *New England Journal of Medicine*, 309:640–646.

mizing the need for special education and related services after they reach school age. Furthermore, early intervention minimizes the likelihood that disabled or seriously ill children will be institutionalized and increases the opportunities for more independent living in society after the child matures. Positive results have been achieved in child-adult interactions when parents have been trained to work with their children. The earlier this positive dialogue occurs, the better the developmental outcome (Gallagher, 1989).

The emphasis of intervention is generally on helping the parent or offering direct help to the child—based on the underlying belief that the child is a capable individual who with effort will succeed at a variety of tasks ranging from the concrete to the abstract. The focus is often on *proactive planning*—planning ahead to prepare the child with basic skills that will allow him or her to successfully participate in various activities both within and outside the family. Another focus is *self-*

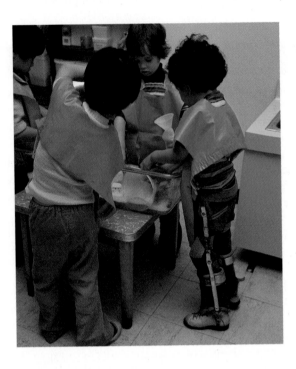

Early intervention helps this child develop the skills to participate fully with his peers.

efficacy, preparing the child to do things alone, with assistance if need be, but with the child as the primary agent. The most effective programs appear to be those involving parent education, long duration of support and follow-up, and tasks that strongly encourage active hypothesis testing by the child so that he or she maintains high levels of motivation and effort (Cratty, 1986).

 ## SUMMARY AND CONCLUSIONS

The period of early childhood is one of expanding skills. An example of this may be found in comparing the relatively incompetent toddler of 2 years to the relatively mature child at 6 years. While there is still a great deal to learn and a long way to go, the 6-year-old is well on his or her way. The average 2- to 3-year-old is embarking on a period of rapid learning and growth. Parents and students tend to expect more of this age child—particularly in terms of physical skills and in understanding the adult world—than they are capable of performing. The achievement of language has a tendency to make many adults view children as slightly smaller versions of themselves.

While this chapter has emphasized the physical development of early childhood, in fact, this is a somewhat arbitrary distinction since children develop holistically. Physical, cognitive and social aspects of child develop are closely linked. The child grows and learns as one "dynamic system." The child's actions reflect her intentions and understandings of the world around her. Conversely, the child's physical size and physical activities, for example, affect her understanding of her world and her social behavior, as well as the reactions of her parents, and the social acceptance by her peers—which in turn affect her physical activities, and so it goes.

In terms of physical growth, early childhood presents the child's transition from a chubby, wide-stance toddler to the taller, more slender 6-year-old. On the average, boys are slightly heavier and taller than girls, and girls naturally have a bit more fatty tissue. However, when size is controlled, both boys and girls show equal strength and overall physical prowess. While girls tend to attribute greater strength to boys, and boys tend to believe this, it is in reality untrue.

Important internal changes also occur during early childhood. Cartilage hardens into bone in many growth areas of the body. New bones are formed in the wrist, hand, ankle, and foot. All this skeletal growth adds protection to the child's growing internal organs and gives the child a firmer shape. Internal organs like the lungs and circulatory system increase in capacity and hence cause the child to have greater stamina and resistance to disease. Muscles and ligaments grow stronger gradually and pace the way for more advanced motor skills.

Considerable growth also occurs in the brain and central nervous system as **glial cells** continue to form and the process of **myelination** continues. As major areas of the brain develop, attention, balance, and the control of body movement also improve.

Growth has slowed for young children, so they usually have smaller appetites than before and often become picky eaters. Because calorie intake is small, the need for a high quality diet for preschoolers is important. Milk and milk products, meat or meat alternatives, vegetables, fruit, bread and cereals are required in a balanced fashion. Poor nutrition is associated with a variety of behavioral symptoms including lethargy, poor memory, attention deficits, and lower IQ. Iron-deficiency anemia and low protein diets are particularly problematic. However, usually children who have poor nutrition also have social and psychological deficits in their environment as well.

Poverty may lead to poor health care, depressed parents, or poorly nourished parents and hence depressed social interaction and stimulation for the child. Efforts to treat the poor nutrition need to treat the parents and social stimulation at the same time to be successful.

Some children are at particular risk for problems in physical development—as well as cognitive and social development. These children include those from low-income families, especially the homeless, and children with chronic illness or disabling conditions. In general, the interventions suggested to enhance these children's overall health and physical functioning are broad based. They include parent education, remedial education for the child, and a network of appropriate agencies to help address the complex needs of the families of children with special needs.

Finally, it is important to note that not all children who are raised in environments of poverty, poor nutrition, or violence will be negatively affected. In many cases, resilient children arise in these settings, that is, children who develop normally despite the various negative conditions around them. These children have strong self-concepts, good coping skills, and warm temperaments. In addition, they have often benefited from an individual—whether teacher, parent, or other—who cared specially for them. Research on resilient children suggests new directions for future interventions with children at risk.

➤ KEY TERMS AND CONCEPTS

epiphysis	myelination	fine motor skills	extrinsic feedback
glial cells	lateralization	functional subordination	intrinsic feedback
neurons	gross motor skills	competence motivation	resilient children

➤ SELF-TEST QUESTIONS

1. Describe the relationship between physical-motor development and cognitive development in preschool children. Distinguish between continuous, discontinuous, and functionally subordinate developmental sequences.

2. Compare and contrast the physical development of 2- and 3-year olds and that of 4- and 5-year olds.

3. What important conditions are required for physical-motor learning?

4. What environmental variables influence physical development in children?

5. How do nutrition and nutritional deficiencies affect growth in early childhood? What sorts of interventions have been proposed to deal with undernutrition? What are their limitations?

6. How do minority status and poverty affect health in early childhood? What sorts of illnesses occur disproportionately among poor children? What effect do they have on physical development?

7. Discuss the impact of homeless on the physical development of young children. What sorts of interventions have been proposed to deal with the problems of homelessness that are unique to childhood?

8. How does serious chronic illness or disabling condition affect young children? What special problems do their families face?

9. Describe the individual and environmental factors that are believed to produce resilient children. How could these factors be used to develop intervention programs for children who are at risk in early childhood?

➤ **SUGGESTED READINGS**

Schorr, L. & Schorr, D. (1988). *Within our reach— Breaking the cycle of disadvantage.* New York: Doubleday. This book presents the way in which broad-based social programs for children can help to break their cycle of poverty.

Shea, C.H., Shebilske, W.L., & Worchel, S. (1993). *Motor learning and control.* Englewood Cliffs, NJ: Prentice Hall. This book presents an excellent overview of the principles involved in motor control and athletic training. It offers excellent case examples of motor training and retraining.

Wagonseller, B.R. & McDowell, R.L. (1979). *You and your child: A common sense approach to successful parenting.* (1979). Champaign, IL: Research Press. This book is a well written and informative guide for parents of young children. It combines a good discussion of physical and cognitive development with helpful suggestions for parents.

VIDEO CASE: JOEY AND FONZIE

Joey Hoagland was born with a rare congenital heart disease that robs his body of oxygen. By the age of 3, he had undergone three open heart operations. After the third surgery, he suffered a stroke and fell into a coma for eight days. When he regained consciousness, he discovered that the left side of his body was paralyzed and he was blind in one eye. Afterwards, Joey refused to cooperate with physical therapists or doctors, some of whom predicted that he would always walk with a limp and never sing. He had lost trust in humans to help him.

Yet, for a severely handicapped child such as Joey, help came—but not in human form. Just when they had almost given up hope for his recovery, his parents heard about Dolphins Plus, a natural dolphin habitat in Key Largo, Florida. Although it is a research center, Dolphins Plus permits a group of properly trained visitors to swim with the dolphins, who the scientists there discovered, worked especially well with handicapped children. Says Betsy Smith, a sociologist at Dolphins Plus, "As soon as I put a handicapped child in the water, this dolphin relaxes, becomes very different, very, very quiet and calm and will stay with and work with that child as long as it takes."

At first, Joey was shy and fearful on seeing the dolphins. A friendly dolphin named Fonzie greeted him, but Joey remained afraid to get in the water. But Fonzie persisted and several days later their swim therapy started. When the 40-pound child couldn't move his leg, the 700-pound dolphin gently moved it for him. In a short while, Joey was practicing unclenching his paralyzed hand in his sleep so that he could grab a fish to feed Fonzie. Fonzie seemed to provide what medicine couldn't—emotional therapy. Studies indicate that dolphins reduce stress in children to such a degree that they become deeply relaxed and therefore much more receptive to teaching.

Their relationship with humans is greatly helped by the dolphins' extraordinary sonar capacity. Says animal behavior expert Doctor John Schull, "They can perceive very fine variations in hardness and texture and size, using their hearing alone." This may allow dolphins to detect certain handicaps in humans. Joey's mother believes that this is exactly what happened with Fonzie in relationship to Joey. "Fonzie," she says, "never concentrated on what Joey couldn't do." As a result, after eight months of therapy, Joey was able to carry a heavy pail of fish to feed his friend. And, although Joey still takes medicine to keep his heart beating properly, he seems as normal as any boy his age.

CASE QUESTIONS

1. How did Joey's development differ from that of other children his age?
2. Do you believe that Fonzie "sensed" that Joey was handicapped? Why was Fonzie able to help Joey?

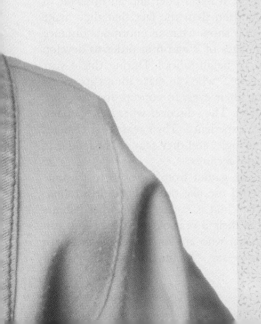

Thou straggler into loving arms,
Young climber up of knees,
When I forget thy thousand ways,
Then life and all shall cease.

MARY ANNE LAMB,
"A CHILD"

CHAPTER 10

EARLY CHILDHOOD: DEVELOPING THOUGHT AND ACTION

OUTLINE

CHAPTER OBJECTIVES

By the time you have finished this chapter, you should be able to do the following:

✔ Describe the aspects and limitations of preparational thought.

✔ Explain how pretend and real play promote cognitive and physical development.

✔ Discuss Piaget's view of preschool children and the strengths and weaknesses of his theory.

✔ Discuss the memory capabilities of preschool children.

✔ Describe the major types of children's play and how they influence childhood development.

✔ Discuss the role of art in childhood development.

✔ Understand the positive role of cognitive immaturity in children's cognitive development.

✔ Describe the different approaches to early education.

"Mother, who was born first, you or I?"

"Daddy, when you were little, were you a boy or a girl?"

"What is a knife—the fork's husband?"

The mother was breast-feeding her newborn daughter. Her 5-year-old son observed her closely and asked with utter seriousness, "Mommy, do you have coffee there sometimes, too?" (Chukovsky, 1963, pp. 21, 22, 24)

Preschool children, relative newcomers in this world, often demonstrate their thinking in ways that are both amusing and thought provoking. The initial comments, collected by Kornei Chukovsky, a Russian poet and an observer of children's behavior, reveal more about children than the fact that they make errors and have limited knowledge. They also show what an enormous distance preschool children must cover between the ages of 2 and 6 in order to develop the thought processes necessary for them to begin school. During this 4-year period, young children change from "magicians," who can make things appear by turning their heads or disappear by closing their eyes, to concept-forming, linguistically competent realists (Fraiberg, 1959). They discover what they can and cannot control. They try to generalize from experience. Their reasoning changes from simple association to the beginnings of logic, and they acquire the language necessary to express their needs, thoughts, and feelings.

Conversations with preschoolers run the gamut from hilarious to frustrating—hilarious, because of questions and word use like those above; frustrating, because of attempting to decipher what the child is saying. Sometimes parents may even have to ask their 4-year-old what their 3-year-old is saying. This can lead to a knowing smile between the children who are somewhat pleased with their alliance. A child may—in all seriousness—say, "Mom, I'm worried because my teacher says I have fossils!" The worried parent, who is looking for any evidence of ossified bony protuberances on her child, suddenly realizes that what he means is freckles! Communication can be challenging for the parents of a young child.

In this chapter, we will concentrate on the different dimensions of developing cognitive competence during early childhood. As we saw in Chapter 9, this is the period during which the physical-motor skills of children rapidly develop. Children also make dramatic discoveries about the world around them by using their growing cognitive abilities. It is often difficult to disentangle the contributions of physical and cognitive development, but in this chapter we shall focus on the growth in cognition that occurs during early childhood.

COGNITIVE DEVELOPMENT

In his pioneering investigation of how logical thinking develops in children, Jean Piaget described the course of development in terms of discrete periods that children pass through on the way to a logical understanding of the world (see Chapter 2). Piaget formulated a theory about how the process of thinking, or cognition, develops. Piaget's theory is based on the premise that human beings actively construct a personal understanding of the world. Children build their own reality based on their level of thinking. For instance, a child's understanding of a particular event, such as her mother's walking out of the front door waving good-bye, will vary depending on whether the child understands that her mother will continue to exist when the child doesn't see her.

Piaget viewed children as little scientists, working diligently to figure out how the world works. According to this view, children do not merely absorb knowledge passively. Instead, they actively explore their surroundings, trying to comprehend new information based on their current patterns of understanding. Piaget called these beliefs about reality *schemes*. Schemes change through two processes, *accommodation* and *assimilation*. If new information conflicts with a child's scheme, she can either modify her beliefs (a process called *accommodation*) or fit the information to her present beliefs (a process called *assimilation*).

Piaget divided intellectual development into four periods which we see presented in Table 10–1. The first, the sensorimotor period of infancy, was discussed in depth in Chapter 6. The infant's intelligence is composed of sensory and action schemes used to explore the world. Toward the end of the sensorimotor period, children begin to show the capacity to understand the world through symbolization. The child's most dramatic use of symbols occurs during the beginning of language use.

Piaget called the second period, which generally spans ages 2 to 7, *preoperational*. During the preoperational period, children continue to expand their understanding of the world, using their increasing language and problem-solving skills. But Piaget theorized—based on his now-famous cognitive experiments— that during this age period children have not yet achieved the mental capacities necessary to understand many basic logical operations needed to correctly interpret reality. These operations include most concepts of number, cause and effect, time, and space. (According to Piaget's cognitive theory, these operations will be accomplished during the third, or *concrete operational,* period.) As children move

TABLE 10–1 Piaget's Stages of Cognitive Development

STAGE OF DEVELOPMENT	RELEVANT AGE RANGE	TYPICAL ACHIEVMENT AND LIMITATIONS OF BEHAVIOR
Sensorimotor	Birth to 2 Years	Infant knows the world by looking, grasping, mouthing, and other actions. At end of stage, child begins to use symbols. Child refines the relationship between thought and action, beginning with the initial necessity to do things to understand them, and at the end of the stage, to do them symbolically.
Preoperational	2 to 7 Years	Child shows continued growth of symbolic activity. Child's language develops and egocentric thought is the rule of behavior.
Preconceptual	2 to 4 years	Child continues development of symbolic activities and language and imagery. Communication is egocentric.
Transitional	5 to 7 Years	Child has good language and imagery skills but lacks ability to represent transformations. Child centers on single features of stimulus arrays.
Concrete operational thought	7 to 12 Years	Child is able to perform true mental operations and transformations based on concrete realities. Child conserves, seriates, and performs categorical thought. Child has difficulty thinking of all possible combinations and in transforming transformations.
Formal operational thought	12 years on	Adolescents think of all possible combinations, think hypothetically and deductively, understand abstract thought, and can perform more complex types of conservation.

Adapted from: Siegler, 1991.

from infancy to early childhood, they interact more smoothly with people and their immediate environment and also improve their internal representations of the world around them. In fact, many researchers believe that the development of internal mental representations of people, objects, and events is the key development of the preoperational period. These internal representations allow children to think about objects when they are absent, the phenomenon called *symbolic representation* which we discussed in Chapter 6.

We shall first discuss the dramatic cognitive advances made by preschool children in terms of Piaget's preoperational stage of development. Then theories will be presented that challenge some of Piaget's conclusions about young children's

symbolic representation The use of symbols in the form of actions, images, or words to represent events or experiences.

cognitive abilities and how they develop. While all researchers may not agree on the exact nature of cognitive development, there is consensus on the tremendous increase in cognitive abilities during early childhood. Children, who enter this period with only rudimentary language and thought abilities, leave it asking questions such as, "Where did grandpa go when he died?," or "Do you see the butterfly lights on the houses at night?" The transition is both exciting and challenging.

ASPECTS OF PREOPERATIONAL THOUGHT

The preoperational period lasts from about ages 2 to 7 and is divided into two parts—the *preconceptual stage* (from ages 2 to about age 4) and the *intuitive,* or *transitional, stage* (from about ages 5 to 7).

The preconceptual stage is highlighted by the increasing use of symbols, symbolic play, and language. Previously, thought was limited to the infant's immediate environment. Now, the use of symbols and symbolic play marks the child's ability to think about something not immediately present. This development gives the mind greater flexibility (Siegler, 1991). Similarly, words now have the power to communicate, even in the absence of the things they name. Children in the preconceptual stage still have difficulty with major categories, however. They cannot distinguish between mental, physical, and social reality. For instance they think anything that moves is alive—even the moon and clouds—a cognitive pattern called *animism.* Children expect the inanimate world to obey their commands, and they do not realize that physical law is separate from human moral law. These traits stem partly from children's self-centered view of the world, or **egocentricity;** they are unable to separate clearly the realm of personal existence and power from everything else (Brown, 1965; Siegler, 1991).

The intuitive, or transitional, stage begins roughly at age 4. The transitional child begins to separate mental from physical reality and to understand mechanical causation apart from social norms. For example, before this stage of development, children may think that everything was created by their parents or some other adult. Now, they begin to grasp the significance of other forces. Intuitive children are beginning to understand multiple points of view and relational concepts, although in an inconsistent and incomplete way. Their comprehension of arrangements by size, numbers, and spatial classification is incomplete. Transitional children are unable to perform many basic mental operations.

One of the critical activities throughout the preoperational period is the development of symbolic representation. Without it, there could be no symbolic play, no language, not even a basic understanding of multiple points of view. Symbolic representation involves the child's taking an external object or event and creating an internal representation of it—in some cases, this may be a sort of "picture" of the person or event, while in others, it may be the creation of something that represents the person or event, such as a word.

REPRESENTATION

egocentricity Having a self-centered view of the world, viewing everything in relation to oneself.

The most dramatic cognitive difference between infants and 2-year-olds is in the use of symbols—that is, the use of actions, images, or words to represent events

Two-year-olds develop the ability to use symbols to represent actions, events, and objects—one of the milestones in cognitive development. This young businesswoman is reading her newspaper during her commute to work.

or experiences. This is seen most clearly in the development of language (covered in Chapter 8) and in pretend, or symbolic, play (Flavell, Miller, & Miller, 1993). Two-year-olds are able to imitate past events, roles, and actions. By gestures in play, preschoolers may act out an extensive sequence that represents a car ride. Given other props, they may act out a family dinner or imitate a mean baby-sitter or a favorite book or television character.

The ability to use numbers to represent the quantity of objects in a particular array is another use of representation which we will discuss in more detail later in this chapter. Still another is the acquisition of skills in drawing and artistic representation that begins during this period.

Although symbolic representation starts at the end of the sensorimotor period, it is a continuing process; a child is much better at symbolization at age 4 than at age 2. In experiments with young children, Elder and Pederson (1978) found that the youngest children (2 1/2 years old) needed props similar to the real object for their pretending games. But the 3 1/2-year-olds were able to represent objects with quite different props or act out a situation without props. For instance, they could pretend that a hairbrush was a pitcher and even pretend to use a pitcher with no props at all.

Once children begin to use symbols, their thought processes become more complex (Piaget, 1950, 1951). They show that they perceive the similarity between two objects or two events by giving them the same name; they become aware of the past and form expectations for the future; and they distinguish between themselves and the person they are addressing. Fein (1981) suggests further that symbolic play may help children in two other ways:

1. It may help children become more sensitive to the feelings and points of view of others, and
2. it may help children understand how an object can change in shape or form and still be the same object.

This increased sensitivity to others helps the child make the transition into more *sociocentric* rather than egocentric thinking in which there is an understanding of what others think or feel. While this requires many more years to mature, it begins in the new symbolic representational abilities of the preschooler.

PRETEND AND REAL

sociocentric Emphasizing the shared or social interpretation of a situation as opposed to an egocentric view which ignores the reality of others.

When children are involved in pretend play, they usually participate in two levels of representation, or meaning—the level of the reality-based meaning of actions and objects, and the level of the pretend meaning of actions and objects. According to Bateson (1955), children must maintain two meaning *frames:* a real frame and a play frame. When in the real frame, children playing cowboys and Indians know that they are actually children and that they are riding broomsticks. But simultaneously, they participate in the pretend frame of the cowboys and Indians story. When there are problems or disagreements, children often "break frame" to resolve their disputes before continuing with their make-believe.

Researchers now studying children's make-believe play find that preschool children in all cultures (see the box "Cultural Variations in the Meaning of Play") become increasingly sophisticated in making pretend-real distinctions (Rubin et

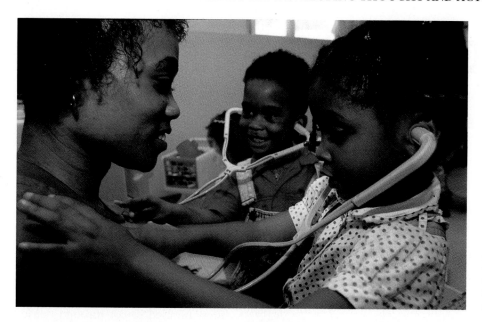

When in the real frame, these children playing doctor know that they are actually children, but at the same time they are participating in the pretend frame of doctor and patient.

al., 1983). They are able to make greater and greater leaps from the real to the pretend meaning of a particular object or action, and they can extend the duration and complexity of their pretend roles and activities. This kind of representation seems to follow a predictable sequence.

THE DEVELOPMENT OF PRETEND PLAY The development of pretend play during early childhood has been fairly well mapped by various researchers (Piaget, 1962; Vygotsky, 1978; Garvey, 1990; Lillard, 1991). Pretend play begins when normal routines and objects are detached from their typical roles and functions and used in an atypical, playful fashion. Earlier in development children make fleeting efforts at pretending, such as the brief tonguing of an empty spoon, but by preschool age, children show clearly that they know they are pretending. They may clearly state so, "We are playing mother and kid!" In addition, older children, as we saw above, are able to step back and forth between play and reality—all the while keeping straight, which world they are in.

Preschoolers are capable of various types of pretense. According to Lillard (1991), they can pretend about either the identity or property of an object, oneself, another person, an event or action, or a situation. As the child becomes older, they rely less on concrete props. Another developmental change involves the growing flexibility at using the self and another as either the actor or recipient. At first the child is both the agent and recipient of actions in solitary play, for example, the child pretends to go to sleep, covers himself, and so forth. Later, he uses the object as the active agent—for example, the doll lies down and goes to sleep as though it were doing this itself.

As the child becomes increasingly socialized, pretend play also does so, as the following observations suggest:

First, role-appropriate actions and objects become standardized or conventionalized. In the child's play, babies drink from bottles, cry and curl up; adults drink from cups, talk on telephones, make dinner,

FOCUS ON DIVERSITY

CULTURAL VARIATIONS IN THE MEANING OF PLAY

It has been recognized for many years that play is a leading activity for cognitive development. Play is also a primary vehicle for practicing the values, behaviors, and roles of society as the child understands them. Through play, for example, children act out the themes, stories, or episodes which express their understanding of the sociocultural events of their society (Nicolopoulou, 1993). Vygotsky, the theorist who was discussed earlier in Chapter 2, proposed that even when children play alone, they act out in a significant way the times or episodes of social drama.

Children in all cultures develop and learn in a social context which includes older peers and adults who pass on the cultural heritage. When children pretend to be such people, therefore, they have certain restrictions placed on their behavior because of the role they adopt—for example, the father in play follows the parent's behavior as the child understands it; so too for the mother, doctor, or cowboy as played by the child. When a little girl plays mother she basically attends to and makes explicit her understanding of the rules embedded in the role of mother (Nicolopoulou, 1993). Given that the role of mother—and other major social roles and values—differs from culture to culture, we would

expect to see the nature of play also vary between cultures. This appears to be the case despite the fact that play itself is a cultural universal.

The appeal of play for a child is undeniable. Even in cultures where there is little time for play, children frequently create play situations by integrating chores and fun. Among the Kipsigis of Kenya, for example, it is common to play tag while watching cows, or climb trees while watching younger siblings (Harkness & Super, 1983). Work songs are common among Amish children as they collectively wash potatoes or shuck peas. Children in areas of the world where violence or war exist most of the time play soccer or play at shooting guns when safe times exist—children have even been found to play act funerals or observed violence (Timnick, 1989).

There are vast differences in the amount and type of play that are observed cross-culturally and within cultures. In some societies, children's games are simple, while in others they are highly complex and elaborate. In some societies, competitive games are virtually nonexistent and cooperative games are the rule. For example, in the day nurseries of the former Soviet Union collective play was emphasized— "not only group games, but special complex toys are designed which require the cooperation of two or

three children to make them work (Bronfenbrenner, 1972)." In simple cultures with limited technological sophistication, where daily survival depends on motor skills, games of physical skill are generally the only forms of competition found. For example, in hunting-and-gathering societies—where sharp instruments must be used to cut through dense undergrowth—playful competition in the speed of machete use is the norm. On the other hand, in hunting societies, foot races, competitive tracking, and spear-throwing contests are the main types of play (Hughes, 1991).

Interestingly enough, in technologically advanced cultures, while children may play games of strategy—such as Monopoly, Nintendo, or charades, they also engage in games of physical skills or competitive games such as team sports. Generally, however, in the complex, more advanced cultures, there is less a sense of community in games and more of an emphasis on individual success—even in the team setting. This mirrors the societies themselves where individuals are expected to compete to ensure the economic survival of their families—hence, the term "breadwinner" which suggests that making a living involves competition (Hughes, 1991).

and wheel baby carriages. Second, solitary pretend play gives way to social sociodramatic play. Even toddlers engage in pretend play with siblings. (Flavell, Miller, & Miller, 1993, p. 83)

The capacity for **sociodramatic play,** in which the child acts out a pretend interchange, increases dramatically beginning at about age 2 to 2 1/2 years. By the age of 5, what started as simple gestures and imitations has begun to comprise intricate systems of reciprocal roles, improvisations of material, coherent plots, and interweaving of themes (Flavell, Miller, & Miller, 1993). This represents a complex and dynamic interplay of cognitive skills—often between two or more children. As Bretherton (1989) states:

Children must become co-playwrights, co-directors, and vicarious actors, without getting confused about which of their roles they or a playmate are momentarily adopting. (Bretherton, 1989, p. 384)

THE APPEARANCE-REALITY DISTINCTION Another type of symbolic representation that contains dual meanings is known as the "appearance-reality distinction." If, for example, a cat wears a dog mask, is he a cat or a dog? When Charlie Brown is dressed as a ghost for Halloween, is he really Charlie Brown or is he really a ghost? And what about a joke store sponge that looks like a solid piece of granite, or a red toy car covered with a green filter that makes it look black? Flavell and his colleagues (1986) showed objects like these to children ages 3 to 7 and asked them, "What is this really and truly?" "Is it a rock or a sponge?" "Is it red or is it black?" They then asked the children "What does this look like?" Three-year-olds were quite confused by such questions. In some situations, the young children insisted that the car looks black and the car is black. In others, they reported that the sponge is a sponge and looks like a sponge. They clearly experienced difficulty with the two kinds of meanings. Most children of 5 or 6, however, are much better at these appearance-reality distinctions.

There seems to be a relationship between pretend play and appearance-reality distinctions. Children who have had a lot of practice with pretend play at 3 and 4 years are better able to understand that objects can look like something else (Flavell, Flavell, & Green, 1987; Flavell, Green, & Flavell, 1986). Some have found that children who have had a lot of experience with pretend play are also better at taking someone else's perspective or understanding someone else's feelings. Researchers suggest that seemingly innocent make-believe play provides important experiences for children's development of structured knowledge (Flavell, 1985; Garvey, 1977).

LIMITATIONS OF PREOPERATIONAL THOUGHT

Even with the development of symbolic representation, preoperational children still have a long way to go before they become logical thinkers. By adult standards, their thought processes are quite limited. First, their thinking is *concrete.* Preoperational children cannot deal with abstractions. They are concerned with the here and now, with physical things they can represent easily (see the box "A Young Child's Conception of Death").

This Inupiat toddler is engaging in sociodramatic play with her older sibling.

sociodramatic play Pretend play in which children take on the persona, actions, and scripts of other persons or objects to play out a temporal drama.

FOCUS ON APPLICATION

A YOUNG CHILD'S CONCEPTION OF DEATH

Imagine a 4-year-old who has just been told that a beloved and recently active, caring grandmother has died. Given what we know about young children's thinking, what reactions can be expected? What aspects of the situation are particularly difficult to understand? Are there specific fears and anxieties the child might experience? Finally, how should care-givers reassure the child?

A number of researchers have studied the differences between young children's understanding of death and how older children and adults view death (Speece & Brent, 1984). They have focused on three major aspects of the death concept:

1. Death is always irreversible, final, and permanent;

2. the absence of life functions is characteristic of death; and

3. death is universal—everyone must die.

The researchers found that children under the age of 5 lack all three of these components in their concept of death. They interviewed children of different ages and asked them a variety of questions. Sometimes, they asked general questions

such as, "What is death?" But more often, they asked specific questions. Such questions might include: "Can a dead person come back to life?" "Can a dead person talk? Or feel? Or see? Or dream? Or think?" "Does everyone die?" "Can you think of someone who might not die?"

Young children frequently see death as a temporary state, like sleeping or "going away." They will sometimes suggest that dead people wake up or come back to life after a while. Is this reversibility? Some authors suggest that it does not mean that children see death as reversible in all cases, but that they have not yet established distinct categories of dead and alive. After all, when one is asleep one is also alive, so why not when one is dead?

Young children also do not seem to understand that all functions cease when one is dead. But they may think that there is reduced functioning. One child suggested "that you can't hear very well when you're dead." Often, children think that the deceased can't do visible things like eating and speaking, but

they can do less visible things like dreaming and knowing. Finally, young children do not yet realize that death is universal. They frequently believe that death can be avoided by being clever or lucky, and that certain people are exempt from death, such as teachers, or members of their immediate family, or themselves. Some believe that you can do fairly magical things to keep from dying—for example, a child may think that if she prays a lot she won't die. Is it any wonder that it is very difficult to explain the death of a friend or relative to a child who is under the age of 5?

Researchers generally agree that the concept of death develops between the ages of 5 and 7. Most 7-year-olds have at least a rudimentary knowledge of the three basic components of death. This seems to parallel the transition in the child from Piaget's stage of preoperational thought to concrete operational thinking (Speece & Brent, 1984).

Explaining the death of a grandmother to a young child does not just involve coping with the child's

Second, their thinking is often *irreversible*. For young children, events and relationships occur in only one direction. They cannot imagine how things would be if returned to their original state or how relationships can go in two directions. Consider the following example of **irreversibility** in a preoperational child's thought:

A 3-year-old girl is asked:

"Do you have a sister?" She says, "Yes."

"What's her name?" "Jessica."

"Does Jessica have a sister?" "No."

irreversibility The belief that events and relationships can occur in only one direction, which is characteristic of preoperational thought.

limited cognitive understanding. The reality of someone's death is difficult for adults as well as children. Adults may intellectually understand the reality of death, its finality and permanence, its absence of life functions, and its universality. But emotionally they must struggle to cope with their loss. Young children, too, face emotional upheaval while trying to understand the realities of death. However, there are a number of factors that further complicate the adjustment for children. First, they are to some extent egocentric—they will be primarily concerned with how situations and events affect them. Second, they have trouble understanding cause and effect. Hence, when a young child asks, "Why did Grandma die?" she may not be asking what we think she is asking. She may not want to know about disease and old age; she may be wondering, instead, why her grandmother left her. Children wonder if they control such situations: "Did she leave because I was bad?" "If I'm good, will she come back?" "Will Mommy or Daddy die and leave me?" They may feel anger or guilt or they may wonder if their own angry thoughts caused the death. Children told that

death is like sleep may be afraid to close their eyes at night in fear that they, too, will die. Children who are told that the angels took someone to heaven may develop other fears as the following example suggests.

Four-year-old Carlos was very attached to his grandfather, who had lived with him. His parents told Carlos that angels had come to take grandpa home. Later that week Carlos became very upset when his parents tried to get him to play outside or go outside with them. He would cry, fall to the ground, and be visibly very frightened. Upon talking with a counselor who worked extensively with children, it turned out that Carlos had become afraid that the angels would come to get him too if he went outside. He felt that he was safe as long as he had a roof over his head that prevented their entry. Within a short period of time with the counselor, he came to accept his grandfather's death and to understand that he was safe outside.

Sometimes, young children will either try to get a deceased loved one to return or attempt to protect

themselves with a variety of magical strategies. They may make a bargain with God that if they are very good, the loved one will return. They may engage in rituals to protect themselves from dying also. These rituals may include positioning toys, stuffed animals, or furniture in special places in their rooms to create a place of safety for themselves.

It becomes clear that parents need to be sensitive in dealing with death when they have young children. Mahler (1950) described grief reactions in children as differing from adult bereavement. Following the initial sorrow from the loss or separation, children may be angry at life, or even at the deceased person—feeling that it is unfair to be left behind.

All of these factors influence children's understanding of death. The preschool child needs simple, correct information combined with ample reassurance and emotional support to cope with the reality of death. Psychologists and pediatricians generally agree that parents must be honest. Children's anxiety is lessened if they know what is going on around them, and if they perceive that people are being truthful.

In this example, the relationship is one-way only; it is irreversible—the younger girl knows she has a sister, but she does not yet recognize that *she* is Jessica's sister. We will see more examples of irreversibility in Piaget's conservation experiment later in this chapter.

Third, preoperational children's thought is *egocentric*—centered on their own perspective so that they are unable to take into account another person's point of view. Preoperational children concentrate on their own perceptions and assume that everyone else's outlook is the same as theirs. Piaget (1954) made an interesting study that demonstrates this limitation of thought in his Three Mountain task. He seated children in front of a plaster model of a mountain range and showed them pictures of the mountain range, each taken from a different angle. He asked them to select the picture that represented their view of the mountains, then to select the picture that represented what a doll would see if seated facing the mountains from another angle. Most children had no trouble picking the picture matching their own viewpoint, but they could not put themselves in the doll's place and imagine the doll's view of the mountains. Based on children's responses in this experimental situation, Piaget concluded that preoperational children assume that their perspective is the only one.

Fourth, preoperational children's thought tends to be *centered* on only one physical aspect or dimension of an object or situation. They cannot hold several aspects or dimensions of a situation in mind at the same time. This limitation—also called **centration**—is best seen in the *class inclusion problem,* a classic task used to study preoperational thought. Young children have difficulty comparing a part with the whole. For example, if they are shown a collection of wooden beads, some red and some yellow, and are asked whether there are more red beads or more *wooden* beads, they will not be able to handle the problem. They cannot simultaneously consider color and the broader category of wooden beads.

Fifth, preoperational children *focus on present states,* not on processes of change or transformation. They judge things according to their appearance in the present, not how they came to be that way.

PIAGET'S CONSERVATION EXPERIMENTS   Several of these preoperational limitations can be seen in one of Piaget's classic experiments on the *conservation of matter.* In Chapter 2, one of these experiments was described. A child is shown two identical glasses holding the same amount of liquid. After the liquid from one of the glasses is poured into a taller glass, the child says the taller glass holds more water. In a second experiment, presented in Figure 10–1, a child is presented with two identical balls of clay. As the child watches, one ball of clay is transformed into various shapes while the other remains untouched. One ball might be rolled into a sausage, broken into five little balls, or flattened into a pancake. At each transformation, the child might be asked which has more clay, the untouched ball or the one that has become a sausage, five little balls, or a pancake. The child might say at one time that the untouched ball has more clay because it is fatter. But the child might also say that the sausage has more because it is longer, or the little balls because there are more of them, or the pancake because it is all spread out. At no time has a child said that the two are identical, although she has witnessed the whole transformation process. Clearly, preoperational children focus on the current state of the object, not on the process of transformation. They center on one dimension at a time, such as either fatness or "spreadoutness." Their thinking is concrete and is based on direct experience in the here and now. Their view of the process is irreversible. All of these cognitive limitations make preoperational children nonconservers.

CLASSIFICATION   Preoperational children have a problem with classification—putting together those events or objects that go together. Young children have trouble with classification tasks because of their relatively short memories and attention spans. They may forget why they are putting things together before they finish a task. A preschooler may move a chair toward a table, then think about a friend to sit in the chair, then think of her hair, and run off to find a comb. Going into the bathroom for it, she sees a bar of soap—she thinks about

centration The focusing or centration on only one aspect or dimension of an object or situation, which is characteristic of preoperational thought.

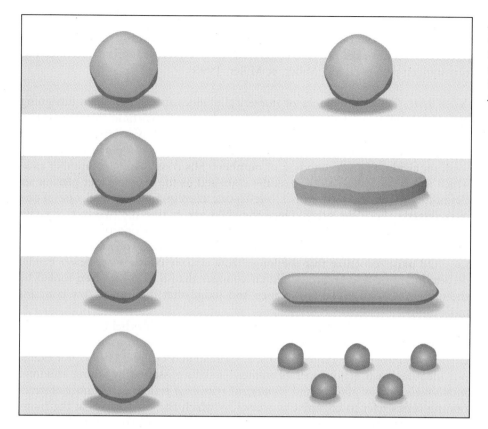

FIGURE 10–1
In this conservation experiment, a child is shown two identical balls of clay. One ball remains the same, while the other is transformed into various shapes.

playing in water, turns on the tap, and remembers that she is thirsty. So she goes to her mother, who wonders what happened to the table-and-chair project. Other problems in classification arise because of the confusing variety of reasons for which things, events, and people can be classified. Use, color, texture, size, sound, and smell are criteria for classification that are readily apparent to an adult; but a child who has no trouble grouping plates, forks, and cups on the basis of use may not see the possibility of grouping plates according to size or cups according to color. One basis, or reason, for classification may block another.

SERIATION Sequences or series of any kind are difficult for young children to manage. For example, when presented with six sticks of graduated length, children can usually pick out the shortest or the longest. They may even be able to divide the sticks into piles, putting shorter sticks in one pile and longer sticks in the other. But young children have considerable difficulty lining the sticks up from shortest to longest because such a task requires a simultaneous judgment that each stick is longer than the next but at the same time is shorter than another (Flavell, 1963).

Early in the preoperational stage, between ages 2 and 4, children have difficulty correctly ordering the sticks. They might arrange two subset, for example, long and short sticks, but have difficulty integrating the subsets. Later in the preoperational stage, between 4 and 7 years, children can correctly order the set of sticks, but have difficulty inserting an additional stick of the same height into the sequence. Piaget proposed that the problem such children had was one of centering on a single dimension of an array. In order to correctly insert an additional stick, the child would have to perceive it as larger than the one just smaller than it, and smaller than the one just larger than it. The preoperational child finds this very difficult to do (Flavell, Miller, & Miller, 1993).

NUMBER The development of numerical abilities in children is an intriguing area—both because of the amount of formal educational time that is spent in teaching about numbers, and also because of the great practical use to which numbers are put throughout an individual's life. Piaget did much of the early work on children's understanding of numbers. His conservation of number task, which is seen in Figure 10–2, basically consisted in the experimenter placing six candies each in two rows, with a one-to-one correspondence, with one of the rows directly above the other. Once the child agrees that the two rows contain the same number of candies, the experimenter shortens one of the rows and removes one of the candies from the longer row. In order to conserve number, the child must recognize that the longer row actually contains one fewer candy, despite the rows' appearance. Children younger than 5 or 6 are often fooled by the misleading perceptual appearance and judge that the longer row contains more candy.

Despite this problem with conservation of number, Rochel Gelman and her colleagues have determined that younger children indeed do have more competencies in number than Piaget proposed. Gelman and Gallistel (1986), for example, identified two major types of numerical skills possessed by young children: *number-abstraction abilities* and *numerical-reasoning principles*. Number-abstraction processes refer to cognitive processes by which the child arrives at the number of an array of objects. For example, a 3-year-old might count the number of

FIGURE 10–2
Piaget's Experiment on the Conservation of Numbers.
When shown the arrangement of candies in the top two rows and asked whether one line has more or both lines are the same, the 4- or 5-year-old will generally answer that both lines contain the same number of candies. Using the same candies, those in the lower row were pushed closer together and one candy was removed from the upper row, but the line was spread out so that it was longer. The child has watched this operation and has been told that he or she may eat the candies in the line that contains more. Even preoperational children, who can count, will insist that the longer line has more, although they have gone through the exercise of counting off the candies in each line.

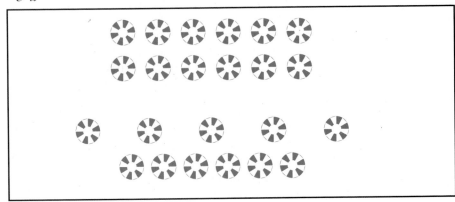

cookies on a table and arrive at the number "four." Numerical-reasoning principles allow the child to determine the correct way to operate on or transform an array (Flavell, Miller, & Miller, 1993). For example, the child might come to realize that the only way that number can be increased in the conservation task presented above is to add an additional object. Simply spreading out the objects is an irrelevant transformation. These two types of numerical skills develop at different rates. Not until the child has gained some understanding of basic reasoning principles is he capable of adding, subtracting, multiplying, and dividing (Becker, 1993).

TIME, SPACE, AND SEQUENCE A 3-year-old may be able to say, "Grandma will come to visit next week." Even a 2-year-old may use words that seem to indicate a knowledge of time and space: "later," "tomorrow," "last night," "far away," "next time." A child of 2 or 3, however, has very little appreciation of what these terms mean. Noon may mean lunchtime, but if lunchtime is delayed an hour, it is still noon to the young child. Waking from a nap, a child may not even know whether it is the same day. The concepts of weeks and months, minutes and hours are difficult for children to grasp; a date such as Wednesday, April 14, is too abstract a concept for them.

Perhaps an example of children's understanding of daily activity sequences would be helpful. Recently, a series of experiments have been conducted to determine children's ability to time sequences related to their daily activities. Three kinds of tasks were used: placing elements in backward order, judging order from changing reference points (for example, if it is lunchtime, what has the child already completed and what activities are still left to do during the day), and estimating the lengths of intervals separating parts of activities.

Even though this preschooler is pointing to a number on the clock, the concepts of minutes and hours is very difficult for her to understand.

When preschoolers were asked to perform these tasks, interesting differences emerged in their behavior. By age 5, for example, children exceeded chance levels on the backward order test—they were able to indicate, beginning at the end of the day what they had accomplished earlier, as well as order their day from multiple reference points. Younger children were unable to do this. By age 4 to 5, children surpass chance levels on the judgment of time intervals (Friedman, 1990).

This study shows how difficult time concepts are for young children. At the age of 5, they have just mastered the ordering of their activities. To teach children to recite the days of the week or months in the year simply involves the rote memorizing of abstract material. Some contend that drilling children on such factors as order of days or months may actually get in the way of the time concept that underlies this knowledge.

> ...when children are repeatedly drilled on a content, these drills may constitute the preponderance of operations that they perform. Thus, recitation of the days of the week and months during the school years probably encourages verbal-list representations of these contents. This might actually delay the development of the more flexible operations that imagery permits....(Friedman, 1990, p. 1411)

With only a limited sense of time, young children have very little idea of cause-and-effect sequences. In fact, their early use of the words "cause" and "because" may have nothing to do with the customary adult understanding of

By crawling under the easel, this preschooler is learning the meaning of such words as "far," "near," "over," "under," "to," "far," "inside," and "outside."

these terms. The same is true of the word "why"—the 4-year-old's favorite question. Children may repeat the question "why?" endlessly, perhaps because they are trying to abstract words or communicate vague feelings. Their associations often are egocentric or unconnected. A child may ask her mother why Daddy isn't home. The mother may answer, "It isn't time" or "He's still working." These may not be the answers the child is looking for because of what she associates with her father's evening arrival—dinner, special games, or even punishment.

Spatial relations are another set of concepts that must be developed during the preschool period. The meanings of words such as "in," "out," "to," "from," "near," "far," "over," "under," "up," "down," "inside," and "outside" are learned directly in the process of the child's experience of his own body (Weikart, Rogers, & Adcock, 1971). Weikart and associates suggest that the usual progression is for children to learn a concept first with their bodies (crawling under a table) and then with objects (pushing a toy truck under a table). Later, they learn to identify the concept in pictures ("See the boat go under the bridge!") and are able to verbalize it.

BEYOND PIAGET: SOCIAL PERSPECTIVES

In recent decades, some of Piaget's conclusions about the mental capabilities of young children have been challenged. His specific conclusions about the limitations of children's thoughts at different ages have been called into question. Critics have disputed his view of the child as a solitary explorer attempting to make sense of the world. Instead, these developmental psychologists argue, learning takes place within a framework of relationships with parents, caretakers, and peers. What's more, such interaction occurs within the context of the beliefs and rules in the child's specific culture. Piaget saw the developing child as an "active scientist," learning as he goes along by experimenting with solutions to problems. Piagetian tasks were purposely devised to isolate ideas, such as conservation of number or quantity, to determine whether the child could use the concept in the experimental condition.

Since Piaget developed his theory about how children think, some developmental psychologists have looked at children from a very different perspective. Rather than the "active scientist" described by Piaget, these psychologists emphasize that a child is a social being. According to these psychologists, a child figures out how to interpret her experiences by interacting with more experienced people—parents, teachers, older children. In the course of daily interaction, the adults in the child's life pass on the rules and expectations of their particular culture (Bruner & Haste, 1987). Some theorists conclude that the process of growth is not strictly divisible into a series of specific stages (Bornstein & Bruner, 1986).

Piaget used complex materials and problems to determine a child's conceptual abilities. If the ability to solve a problem is linked to assessing real situations with the help of clues from the environment and help from adults, a simpler format is needed. Following this reasoning, Piaget's experiment for demonstrating egocentricity was altered in one respect. Instead of asking the child to imagine the juxtaposition of objects and mountain peaks as seen by a doll, the task was changed to the simpler one of determining if a naughty boy could hide so he would not be seen by a police officer. Although none of these children in Edinburgh, Scotland, had hid-

These children have learned to sing "Happy Birthday: through guided participation.

den from a police officer, they had played hide-and-seek games and understood the task immediately. Even 3-year-olds were remarkably successful (Hughes & Donaldson, 1979). When Piagetian problems are presented so that they make "human sense," they are clear to younger children (Donaldson, 1978).

In the following example, Valerie, age 5 1/2, cannot solve Piaget's class inclusion problem with beads, although she can explain the principles of class inclusion to her mother:

> Valerie asked her mother if she loved her more than she loved the kids in her kindergarten. Her mother hesitated, since Valerie's brother was also in the kindergarten, and answered that she loved Valerie and David more than the other kids at the kindergarten. Valerie looked at her mother with a "Silly Mom" kind of look, and explained, "David and I are some of all the kids at the kindergarten—so if you said you loved the kids at the kindergarten you'd be saying you love us too, and you wouldn't have to leave anybody out!" (Rogoff, 1990, p. 5)

The psychologist reports that the next day, Valerie's curious mother tried Piaget's traditional class inclusion problem with Valerie, using red and green wooden beads. When asked to indicate the wooden beads, Valerie pointed to all the beads. But when asked whether there were more red beads or more wooden beads or the same amount, Valerie claimed that there were more red beads (Rogoff, 1990).

Cognitive development is seen as a social and cultural process. The ways that adults demonstrate how a problem is solved are part of learning to think. All cultures initiate children into a myriad of activities through what has been called **guided participation.** When young children learn to help set or clear the table or to sing "Happy Birthday," specific aspects of cultural activity are being transmitted from the more experienced members, adults, to the less experienced members, children.

guided participation The process by which more experienced people transmit cultural information to children.

Katherine Nelson (1986), for example, argues that a knowledge of events is the key to understanding the child's mind. Whereas Piaget tends to focus on what young children don't know, such as categories and numbers, Nelson is interested in what they do know, what they have learned from their own experiences. She believes that a young child's day-to-day experiences become the material for her mental life and problem-solving abilities. Because the child's cognitive processes are based on real-life events, a child's understanding of the world is embedded in social or cultural knowledge.

If development is looked at as a training process, how does a child work toward gaining abilities just beyond reach? To explain this process, Vygotsky provided the concept of the **zone of proximal development (ZPD),** in which children develop through participation in activities slightly beyond their competence, with the assistance of adults or more skilled children (Vygotsky, 1978). Vygotsky used ZPD to refer to the difference between the child's actual developmental level and the potential level that is guided by adults or older peers. In fact, Vygotsky believed play to be a primary means of moving children toward more advanced levels of social and cognitive skills—a leading activity, which becomes a major source of advanced skills (Nicolopoulou, 1993). As Vygotsky stated:

> In play a child is always above his average age, above his daily behavior; in play, it is as though he were a head taller than himself. As in the focus of a magnifying glass, play contains all developmental tendencies in a condensed form; in play, it is as though the child were trying to jump above the level of his normal behavior. (1933/1967, p. 16)

For many researchers, therefore, individual activity develops through social interaction in events that are social or historical practices in particular cultures. Play provides an excellent opportunity to study the way children learn social mores in widely diverse cultures (Rogoff, 1993).

MEMORY

A fundamental aspect of cognitive development is the ability to remember. It allows a person to perceive selectively, classify, reason, and generally form more complex concepts.

THE COMPUTER MODEL To explain how memory functions, some psychologists (such as the information-processing theorists discussed in Chapter 2) have used the computer as a model for the human brain. Memory is an aspect of this computer brain, having storage capacity for information and an array of "associational switches" that gives access to what is stored. The system of associational switches allows the individual to put new items into the memory and take them out in a particular order.

Information theorists think of memory as having three parts:

1. a sensory register that records information received through the senses,
2. a short-term memory that holds what the mind is conscious of at the moment, and
3. a long-term memory that holds items for as long as a lifetime.

zone of proximal development
Vygotsky's concept of children's ability to develop through participation in activities slightly beyond their competence with the help of adults.

Information comes into the system and makes contact with the sensory register, which holds it for a very brief period—around 250 milliseconds. This is sometimes called the "very short-term memory." The information is then either lost or transferred to the short-term memory, often described as the "working" memory. The short-term memory holds the information that a person is consciously aware of at any one time and keeps it longer than does the sensory register. Nevertheless, it loses information fairly rapidly. Our attention is somewhat fleeting, and we are conscious of something for only a short time unless we concentrate on it or rehearse it.

The last type of memory is **long-term memory.** Some theorists believe that nothing in the long-term memory is ever lost (except by damage to the brain). The long-term memory constitutes a person's permanent knowledge base. Information such as one's social security number and birth date are kept there (Atkinson & Shriffrin, 1971; Hagen, Longeward, & Kail, 1975).

The things the memory holds can usually be categorized as images, actions, or words. For this reason, researchers often refer to visual memory, motor memory, and verbal memory. The visual memory, as we saw in infancy, is the first to develop. If adults are asked to remember their very early years, frequently they cannot remember much before the age of 3. Under hypnosis or in psychotherapy, they occasionally recall things earlier than this, but such memories tend to be pictorial. They often recall locations, actions, and nonverbal events as if they were seeing a movie, but they have difficulty putting these images into words. Adults usually have verbally coded recollections after the ages of 4 to 6 and therefore can talk about them. One of the reasons for this is that the development of language in preoperational children may enable them to store new information for longer periods of time. They are no longer as dependent on their visual and motor abilities. Let us consider some other memory tasks and see how well preschool children perform them.

RECOGNITION AND RECALL Studies of preschool children's memory skills have focused on two different behaviors—*recognition* and *recall*. **Recognition** refers to the ability to select from pictures or objects that are currently present or events currently happening only those one has seen or experienced before. For example, children may recognize a picture in a book as something they have seen before but be unable to name it or tell us about it. **Recall** refers to the ability to retrieve data about objects or events that are not present or current. It requires the generation of information from long-term memory without the object in view. For instance, if a child who is looking at a picture book is asked what picture comes next and then names it correctly, he would be recalling the next picture.

Myers and Perlmutter (1978) have found preschool children's performance on recognition tasks to be quite good, but their recall performance is poor; both forms of remembering improve, nevertheless, between the ages of 2 and 5. In a recognition task in which many objects were shown only once to children between the ages of 2 and 5, even the youngest could correctly point to 81 percent of them, and the older children remembered 92 percent. The study showed that preschool children have considerable proficiency in the recognition skills necessary to encode and retain substantial amounts of information. In recall studies, however, when children between the ages of 2 and 4 were asked to name objects that the experimenter had just shown, the 3-year-olds were able to name only 22 percent of the items and the 4-year-olds only 40 percent—a considerable differ-

recognition The ability to correctly identify items previously experienced when they appear again.

recall The ability to retrieve information and events that are not present.

ence from the scores attained in the recognition task. Preschool children are clearly better at recognition than at recall, but children may perform better on such memory tasks if their care-givers routinely ask many questions that test children's memories (Ratner, 1984).

REHEARSAL AND ORGANIZATION Young children's recall difficulties are generally assumed to occur because of their limited strategies for encoding and retrieval (Flavell, 1977; Myers & Perlmutter, 1978). Preschool children do not spontaneously organize or rehearse information that they want to remember, as older children and adults often do. If you give an adult a list to memorize, such as "cat, chair, airplane, dog, desk, car," the adult might first classify the items as "animals," "furniture," and "vehicles" and then repeat (or rehearse) the words quietly before being asked to recall the list. The adult, therefore, has used two memory strategies—**organization** and **rehearsal.** Adults and children, from age 6 on, improve their ability to recall information when taught memory strategies, but it has been found difficult to teach preschoolers to organize and rehearse information.

This does not mean that preschoolers are without any memory strategies. In one study, for example, 18- to 24-month-old toddlers watched an experimenter hide a Big Bird toy under a pillow and were then told to remember where Big Bird had been hidden because they would later be asked where he was. The experimenter then distracted the children with other toys for four minutes. During this time the children frequently interrupted their play to talk about Big Bird, point at the hiding place, stand near it, or even attempt to retrieve the Big Bird toy (DeLoache, Cassidy, & Brown, 1985). The researchers determined that these were attempts by the toddlers to remember—memory strategies at work. The researchers concluded that these activities resemble and may in fact be precursors of more mature strategies for keeping the material alive in short-term memory.

Recently, DeLoache and colleagues determined that preschoolers group spatial—but not conceptual—items into categories when trying to memorize them (DeLoache & Todd, 1988). For example, when very young children were required to remember the location of a hidden object, they frequently used rehearsal-like verbalizations—referring to the hidden toy, the fact that it was hidden, the hiding place, and their having found it. This suggests that preschoolers can be strategic and deliberately change their behavior in certain situations to better remember material. This appears to be a genuine precursor to the complex, generalizable and effective strategies of older children (Flavell, Miller, & Miller, 1993).

Some researchers have focused on teaching memory strategies—such as study-sorting, group-naming, or category-cuing—to preschool children. Preschoolers are able to learn these techniques and to retain them for several days. Then, after a brief time, they no longer used these strategies. This may be because they forgot them or lost interest in repeatedly performing the strategies and tasks. In addition, learning these memory strategies appeared to have little effect on children's recall abilities (Lange & Pierce, 1992). Similar results have been found in the case of memory strategies mothers use to teach children such skills as gift wrapping, names of characters in stories, or the location of zoo animals. While children employed simpler and fewer techniques than their mothers, they do appear to learn about memory strategies in general from them. This indicates that children may, with adult guidance, learn to employ some simple strate-

organization and **rehearsal** Strategies for improving recall used mainly by adult learners.

It is highly unlikely that this father can get away with skipping any parts of the storybook he is reading aloud if it is one of his daughter's favorites.

gies that are not yet within their usual strategy repertoire ((Harris & Hamidullah, 1993).

Such studies demonstrate that with carefully contrived learning experiences and instructional techniques, young children may learn cognitive skills beyond their current repertoire of abilities. But this learning does not endure—either because children cannot fit the skills comfortably into their current hierarchy of abilities or because they are too busy learning about the world in other, more comfortable ways. It may also be that the skills just beyond the child's cognitive reach are more likely to be used, while those well beyond it will require more time before they are integrated into the child's cognitive behaviors.

Preschool children, therefore, remember a great many things. Try skipping a sentence in a child's favorite storybook or adding a new ingredient to her fruit salad. The child will remember exactly how it was before. Experimental tasks that demonstrate memory in adults may not tap the abilities that children use to enhance memory. But when children are given tasks in a context that is meaningful to them, they have demonstrated what may be rudimentary strategies for remembering. These behaviors can be interpreted as evidence of an early natural propensity to keep what must be remembered in mind (DeLoache, Cassidy, & Brown, 1985). When groups of children who were asked to "remember" or to "play with" toys were compared, the children who played with the toys demonstrated a better memory of them. This suggests that the act of playing contributed to the children's mental organization of experiencing the toys. Their memory strategy appears to involve perceiving the items through use (Newman, 1990).

EVENT SCRIPTS AND SEQUENTIAL UNDERSTANDING It is increasingly clear that children are able to remember information that is ordered temporally, in a time sequence. They appear to structure a series of occurrences into an ordered, meaningful whole. In one study, children were asked to describe how they had made clay pieces 2 weeks before. When the children were given the opportunity to remake the same clay pieces, they were able to describe how they had worked step by step. It appears that children are able to organize and remember a sequence of actions after a single experience (Smith, Ratner, & Hobart, 1987).

Young children are aware that an event such as a birthday party is composed of an orderly progression of events: a beginning, when the guests arrive with presents; a series of events in the middle, including playing games, singing "Happy Birthday," blowing out the candles, and eating cake and ice cream; and an end, when each guest gets a favor. Children have good memory abilities for repeated events, such as a family dinnertime, grocery shopping, or a day at nursery school. It is as if they have developed a format or script for these routine events (Mandler, 1983; Nelson et al., 1983; Friedman, 1990). When mothers talk to their young children about objects and events that are not immediately present, such as describing the errands to be done after lunch, they help their children to develop scripts, and thereby remember the events (Lucariello & Nelson, 1987).

In younger children, events can be remembered only in the order in which they occur. The ability to order and remember information with more flexibility develops with familiarity and over time. Only when children have become extremely familiar with an ordered event can they reverse the sequence of steps (Bauer & Thal, 1990). Scripts therefore present a mnemonic to remember the sequence of an event. They provide an oral rehearsal for the child to enact. Children, as we discussed earlier, may even rehearse these scripts out loud when they are alone. As a recent review stated:

> Life is eventful. People and objects in a young child's world do things; children observe these events and enter into them, thus joining the flow of the world around them. They mentally represent these events (*event knowledge*). Some of these event representations are generalized and abstract (*scripts*). This event knowledge, including scripts, of everyday life may be the young child's most powerful mental tool for understanding the world. (Flavell, Miller, & Miller, 1993, p. 85)

 ## PLAY AND LEARNING

Play is children's unique way of experiencing the world. Play satisfies many needs in a child's life: the need to be stimulated and diverted, to express natural exuberance, to experience change for its own sake, to satisfy curiosity, to explore, and to experiment within risk-free conditions. Play has been called the "work of childhood" because of its central role in the young child's development. It promotes the growth of sensory capacities and physical skills and provides endless opportunities to exercise and expand newfound intellectual skills. Play is different from any other kind of activity. By its very nature, playing is not directed toward a goal. As anyone who has observed a busy playground can attest, children expend great energy just for the fun of it. Catherine Garvey (1990) defined play as something that

1. is engaged in simply for pleasure;

2. has no purpose other than itself;
3. players choose to do;
4. requires players to be "actively engaged" in it; and
5. relates to other areas of life—that is, it furthers social development and enhances creativity.

TYPES OF PLAY

How children play changes as they develop. Young preschoolers play with other children, talk about common activities, and borrow and lend toys. But their interaction does not include setting goals or making rules for their play. Older preschoolers, however, can play together and help one another in an activity that has a goal. Preschool children like to build and create with objects, and to take on roles and use props (Isenberg & Quisenberry, 1988). An overview of the types of play in which preschoolers engage, as well as appropriate play materials, is presented in Table 10–2.

TABLE 10–2 General Characteristics and Appropriate Play Materials for the Preschool Child

AGE	GENERAL CHARACTERISTICS	APPROPRIATE PLAY MATERIALS
2	Uses language effectively. Large-muscle skills developing, but limited in the use of small-muscle skills. Energetic, vigorous, and enthusiastic, with a strong need to demonstrate independence and self-control.	Large-muscle play materials: Swing sets, outdoor blocks, toys to ride on, pull toys, push toys. Sensory play materials: Clay, fingerpaints, materials for water play, blocks, books, dolls, and stuffed animals.
3	Expanded fantasy life, with unrealistic fears. Fascination with adult roles. Still stubborn, negative, but better able to adapt to peers than at age 2. Early signs of product orientation in play.	Props for imaginative play (such as, old clothes). Miniature life toys. Puzzles, simple board games, art materials that allow for a sense of accomplishment (for example, paintbrushes, easels, marker pens, crayons).
4	Secure, self-confident. Need for adult attention and approval—showing off, clowning around, taking risks. More planful than 3-year-olds, but products often accidental. Sophisticated small-muscle control allows for cutting, pasting, sewing, imaginative block building with smaller blocks.	Vehicles (for example, tricycles, Big Wheels). Materials for painting, coloring, drawing, woodworking, sewing, stringing beads. Books with themes that extend well beyond the child's real world.
5	Early signs of logical thinking. Stable, predictable, reliable. Less self-centered than at 4. Relaxed, friendly, willing to share and cooperate with peers. Realistic, practical, responsible.	Cut-and-paste and artistic activities. Simple card games (for example, Old Maid), table games (for example, Bingo), and board games (for example, Lotto), in which there are few rules and the outcomes are based more on chance than on strategy. Elaborate props for dramatic play.

Source: Hughes, 1991.

Each type of play has its own characteristics and functions. But the types are not rigidly distinct, and may overlap in any play situation. Some of the major forms of children's play are described below.

SENSORY PLEASURE   The aim of this kind of play is sensory experience in and for itself. Children will endlessly splash water, ring doorbells, chew grass, bang pots, open bottles, and pluck flower petals just to experience new sounds, tastes, odors, and textures. Sensory play teaches children key facts about their bodies, senses, and the qualities of things in the environment.

PLAY WITH MOTION   Running, jumping, twirling, and skipping are just some of the countless forms of play with motion that are enjoyed for their own sake. Play that involves the continually changing sensation of movement is one of the earliest types that infants experience—being lifted up high and swung around by an adult, blowing bubbles with their food, or simply rocking. Infants and adults frequently engage in movement routines that are not only exciting and stimulating for children, but also give them painless practice in body coordination. Play with motion is often begun by an adult and provides infants with some of their earliest social experiences. Children do not usually share this kind of activity with other children until about age 3 (Garvey, 1990).

ROUGH-AND-TUMBLE PLAY   Parents and teachers frequently criticize and try to eliminate the kind of rough-and-tumble mock-fighting play of which young children are quite fond. This is usually an attempt to reduce the amount of aggression and real fighting among children. But rough-and-tumble play is play-fighting, not real fighting. Recent research suggests that it offers real benefits to the child. Not only is it a chance to exercise and release energy, but children learn to handle their feelings, to control their impulses, and to filter out negative behaviors that are inappropriate in a group. What is more, they are learning to make the essential distinction between pretend and real (Pellegrini, 1987).

PLAY WITH LANGUAGE   Children love to play with language. They experiment with its rhythm and cadences. They mix up words to create new meanings. They play with language to poke fun at the world and to verify their grasp of reality. They use it as a buffer against expressions of anger. The primary function of language—meaningful communication—tends to be lost in language play. Children concentrate on the language itself, playfully manipulating its sounds, patterns, and meanings.

Judith Schwartz (1981) has looked at and provided examples of several kinds of language play. Sometimes, children play with sound and rhythm, regularly repeating letters and words in a steady beat: *La la la / Lol li pop / La la la / Lol li pop.* They will also make patterns with words as if they were practicing a grammatical drill or sentences using the same words: *Hit it. / Sit it. / Slit it. / Mit it.* And: *There is the light. / Where is the light? / Here is the light.* In a less frequent kind of play, children play with the meaning of words or invent words to fit meanings. For example: *San Diego, Sandiego, Sandi Ego / San Diego, Sandi Ego / Eggs aren't sandy!* Why do children play with language? Partly because it's funny. It makes others laugh when a young child says something like: "I'm gonna telly 'cause you put jelly in my belly and made me smelly."

a

b

c

d

e

Different types of play satisfy different needs and help promote different aspects of development. Some of the major forms of children's play include; (a) sensory play; (b) play with motion; (c) rough-and-tumble play; (d) language play; (e) dramatic play and modeling; (f) constructive play or play with games and rituals.

f

Playing with language also gives young children a chance to practice and master the grammar and words they are learning. By ages 3 and 4, children are using some basic linguistic rules and structures of meaning. They ask questions such as, "Couldn't table legs be fitted with shoes?" and "Since there is running water, is there sitting water?" (Chukovsky, 1963, pp. 61–62; Garvey, 1977, pp. 59–60).

Finally, children use language to control their experiences. People tend to make order out of their experiences by creating structures and rules around them. Older children similarly use language to structure their play. They create rituals—sometimes very elaborate ones—that must be followed; by following the rituals carefully, they control the experience (Schwartz, 1981).

DRAMATIC PLAY AND MODELING One of the major types of play involves taking on roles or models: playing house, mimicking a parent going to work, pretending to be a firefighter, a nurse, an astronaut, or a truck driver. Such play, called *sociodramatic play,* as we discussed earlier in this chapter, involves not only imitation of whole patterns of behavior but also considerable fantasy and novel ways of interaction. As we shall see shortly, children come to understand various social relationships, rules, and certain other aspects of the culture through imitative play.

GAMES, RITUALS, AND COMPETITIVE PLAY As children grow older, their play involves rules and has a specific aim. They make decisions about taking turns, they set up guidelines about what is and what is not permitted, and they often create situations in which someone wins and someone loses. Although the intricate rules of baseball and chess are beyond most preschoolers, they are beginning to cope with the ritual and rules of tag, hide-and-seek, red rover, and perhaps war games. Such games require, and help to develop, cognitive skills like learning rules, understanding the sequence of cause-and-effect, realizing the consequences of various actions, learning about winning and losing, and learning to fit behavior to certain patterns and rules (Herron & Sutton-Smith, 1971; Kamii & DeVries, 1980; Flavell, Miller, & Miller, 1993).

PLAY AND COGNITIVE DEVELOPMENT

As already mentioned, play promotes cognitive development in many areas. In their play with motion, preschool children become aware of speed, weight, gravity, direction, and balance. In their play with objects, they realize that objects have conventional and appropriate uses and properties. In their play with others, children practice social concepts and roles while learning aspects of their culture.

EXPLORING PHYSICAL OBJECTS When preschool children play with all sorts of physical objects—sand, stones, water, and other kinds of toys and materials—they discover and learn about the properties of these objects and about the physical laws that affect these objects. When playing in a sandbox, for example, a child can learn that different objects make different marks in the sand. When bouncing a ball on the floor, a child can learn that throwing the ball harder will make it bounce higher. When building a house with blocks, a child can learn that blocks must balance and be properly supported before they will stay in place. By engaging in constructive play, then, children acquire bits of information that they can use to build their knowledge. This greater knowledge, in turn, lets them learn at increasingly higher levels of understanding and competence (Forman & Hill, 1980). Gradually, they learn to compare and classify objects, and they develop a better understanding of concepts—for example, size, shape, and texture. In addition, through active play children develop skills that make them feel physically confident, secure, and self-assured (Athey, 1984).

PLAY AND EGOCENTRISM The egocentrism that Piaget ascribes to preoperational children is particularly evident in their play with others. Two-year-olds will watch other children and seem interested in them, but usually they will not approach them. If they do approach them, the interaction usually centers on playing with the same toy or object (Hughes, 1991). Children 2-years-old and younger may seem to be playing together, but they are almost always playing out separate fantasies.

Some have thought that by the time they are 3 years old or more, most children begin to understand another child's perspective on the world. Dramatic play reflects this greater social maturity. The play of 3-year-olds reflects an understanding of other's views which allows them to be successful at role-playing games. In role playing, success depends on cooperation among players—if children do not act out their parts, the game does not work. This supports an earlier study in which children were asked to describe how a playmate might feel in a given situation (Borke, 1971, 1973). Children were asked to guess how another child would react to losing a pet, breaking a toy, or attending a birthday party. By age 4, it seems that some children can reliably identify those situations likely to produce happiness, sadness, fear, and anger.

In another study, Shatz and Gelman (1973) asked 4-year-olds to describe to 2-year-olds how a specific toy worked. According to this study, even 4-year-olds understood the necessity of addressing younger children in simple terms. They found that 4-year-olds spoke slowly, used short sentences, employed many attention-getting words, such as "see," "look," and "here," and often repeated the child's name. Four-year-olds did not speak to older children or adults in this way. The study suggests that preschool children have some appreciation of younger children's needs and are able to modify their behavior to meet those needs.

As with all behaviors, however, social maturity is relative. Children at the age of 3 or even 4 can still be very stubborn and negative. However, by the age of 3, there is a slightly greater tendency for children to be willing to conform to others' expectations. People are more important to 3-year-olds than they were a year earlier, and they therefore seek out social interaction. By now, they are more interested in the effects of their behaviors on the world around them and draw considerable satisfaction from showing their products to others—even if the products were accidental rather than intentional (Hughes, 1991).

DRAMATIC PLAY AND SOCIAL KNOWLEDGE Older preoperational children are testing their social knowledge in dramatic play. The imitating, pretending, and role taking that occur in dramatic play promote the growth of symbolic representation—the transforming of here-and-now objects and events into symbols. Dramatic play also gives children the opportunity to project themselves into other personalities, to experiment with different roles, and to experience a broader range of thought and feeling. This role playing leads to a better understanding of others as well as a clearer definition of one's self (Fein, 1984).

Role playing allows children to experiment with a variety of behaviors and to experience the reactions and consequences of that behavior. For example, children who play hospital day after day with dolls, friends, or alone will play many different roles: patient, doctor, nurse, visitor. In acting out these roles, children may be motivated by very real fears and anxieties of being immobilized in a hospital bed, being dependent on others, and having their bodies acted upon by others. Whatever the dramatic situation, role playing allows children to express intense feelings, resolve conflicts, and integrate these feelings and conflicts with things they already understand.

THE ROLE OF PEERS Children spend far more time interacting directly with one another than with adults (but see the box "Play Tutoring: The Role of Adults in Children's Play"). Children play with siblings and other children at home, in the neighborhood, at school, and most everywhere that children go. In many cultures, the significance of children's interaction with other children is even greater than it is in the American middle class (Rogoff, 1990). Child care in these societies is largely carried out by 5- to 10-year-old children, who tend infants and toddlers (Watson-Gegeo & Gegeo, 1989). Children may carry a younger sibling or cousin around on their backs or hips, thus enabling the younger children to be involved with the sights and sounds of the community (Rogoff, 1990).

Children's groups around the world generally include a mix of ages. In fact, childhood groups based on age—so common in American culture—result from groupings in school and other activities organized by adults that are not part of all cultures. In the United States and throughout the world, informal neighborhood groups include children of various ages. The mixed-age peer group can offer older children the opportunity to practice teaching and child care with younger children, while younger children can imitate and practice role relations with older children (Whiting & Edwards, 1988). Even the youngest children can use other children as models. The playful activities of children may be especially useful for developing new ways of thinking. Playing may suggest novel, creative solutions to problems.

ART AS DISCOVERY AND PROBLEM SOLVING The interdependence of cognitive and motor skills is apparent in children's art. Here, fine motor coordination works with perceptual, cognitive, and emotional development. The degree of development in all these separate areas is evident in the final product. But, no matter how much we examine the end result of the artistic process, the exploratory process itself is what is significant—the daubing, smearing, scribbling, and finally, the representational drawing (Gardner, 1973a). From the moment children take crayons in hand and begin to scribble, at about 18 months, they start working out forms and patterns that will be essential to their later progress. Rhoda Kellogg (1970) has suggested that children start making art by scribbling and by placing their scribbles at different places on the paper. By age 3, they draw shapes in increasingly complex forms. By age 4 or 5, they start to draw representational pictures of houses, people, and other familiar objects.

Once children begin to draw representational objects, their drawings reveal how they think and feel. Goodnow (1977) suggests that children use their draw-

Paintings reveal how children think and feel. Children use art to solve problems, and they follow specific rules and sequences when drawing and painting.

ings as a problem-solving process. They work in specific sequences and have specific rules about space and position of elements in the drawing. For example, when drawing a picture of a girl, they may start at the top by drawing hair; when they have finished that, they move in sequence down to the next part of the figure. If the hair occupies the space that a later-drawn part, such as the arms, would normally occupy, the children may omit the arms, change the shape of them to fit around the hair, or reposition the arms. Only rarely will they invade the space that the hair already occupies. These rules about space and position carry over into all drawings children do.

Children like to handle and manipulate materials in their art. Fingerpaint, clay, mud, sand, and even soapsuds provide opportunities to experiment with a multitude of new shapes, colors, and textures. Children not only gain a fuller sensory experience of combining texture and appearance but also learn directly about thickness and thinness, solidity and fluidity, and concentration and dilution.

THE ADAPTIVE ROLE OF COGNITIVE IMMATURITY

Intelligence is a key aspect of human beings as a species. It allows us to modify our environment to suit our needs and also to adapt ourselves in the process. As with our biological abilities, however, humans undergo a long period of cognitive immaturity—or apprenticeship—in which the young are dependent on adults for care and guidance. It may be that the prolonged period of cognitive immaturity in humans has a specific role in development—a role arrived at through evolution.

FOCUS ON AN ISSUE

PLAY TUTORING: THE ROLE OF ADULTS IN CHILDREN'S PLAY

Imagine several neighborhood children, all 4 and 5 years old, playing "store" in the backyard. The oldest is the self-appointed shopkeeper and leader. The others are customers, cashiers, baggers, and clerks. The "store" extends over much of the backyard, including a table and a few chairs, some doll furniture, and the lower limbs of trees. Items to buy include paper dishes, rocks as shoes, and newspaper pages as clothing. The children have been busily involved in this dramatic activity for nearly an hour—setting up the store, assigning roles, planning situations, and acting out several vignettes. You are surprised at the length of time this activity has held their interest. You are pleased by the level of their language and social skills, and at their ability to solve problems. This activity seems to have considerable educational value. But the children are making lots of "mistakes." They overprice items or give back more

money in change than they receive in payment. They make strange rules like "only boys can buy baseballs," or "you can't buy apples because they aren't good for you." Also, there are numerous disputes among the children about the "right" way to do things.

Adults watching this scene are frequently tempted to get involved in this play or at least to correct some misunderstandings. After all, if this is a good learning experience, why not make it a little better?

Child development experts disagree about the value of direct adult participation in children's sociodramatic play. Many specialists warn that in sociodramatic play, children need time to pose problems as well as test and try problem solutions. They need to create their own storyline and dialogue, not follow someone else's. Adults, these experts suggest, have a tendency to take over the leadership, make the decisions,

solve the problems, and thus limit the educational value of the play activity.

Yet, recently, some psychologists have begun to argue for more direct involvement by grownups, provided it is done carefully. In what way would adults' involvement benefit children? What types of adult involvement in children's play actually help rather than hinder a child's social, linguistic, and cognitive development?

Child psychologists have thus become increasingly interested in the developmental effects of what is called *play training*—the direct and indirect involvement of adults in children's play. Studies indicate that children who frequently engage in sociodramatic play—have higher levels of social and cognitive skills. For example, children who often engage in lengthy, elaborate sociodramatic play also show more persistence in school-related tasks. Elaborate socio-

Why might cognitive immaturity exist in an adaptive sense for children? One explanation is that prolonged cognitive immaturity may allow for a longer time to practice adult roles and socialization—through play and other means. On the other hand, a completely different explanation may be viable. Perhaps some aspects of younger children's cognitive system are qualitatively different from that of older children and adults to permit younger children to attain social-cognitive milestones such as attachment or language (Bjorklund & Green, 1992). For example, the limited motor and sensory skills of infants may keep them close to their mother and reduce the information with which they must deal. This allows them to construct a simple, readily understandable world from which they can gradually build their cognitive skills.

dramatic play appears to be less common among children from lower socioeconomic groups than among middle-class children who have the leisure and materials to develop such play (Feitelson & Ross, 1973; Rubin et al., 1976; Smith & Dodsworth, 1978; Smilansky, 1968). Experiments in play training were undertaken to determine if given materials, experience, and gentle tutoring in longer, more elaborate sociodramatic play, children from lower socioeconomic groups would make gains in linguistic, cognitive, and social skills. In fact, they did. The children who had play tutoring showed significant gains in language, IQ scores, creativity, impulse control, and cooperation (Feitelson & Ross, 1973; Rubin et al., 1976; Smith & Dodsworth, 1978; Smilansky, 1968).

The play-training experiments included both direct and indirect adult involvement. Indirect involvement required an adult to remain outside the drama but offer comments and suggestions to the children playing. Direct involvement required an adult to take a direct part, adopt a role or roles, and show by example what was wanted in the way of play behavior. Both forms of adult participation had beneficial results. Since those experiments, conducted mainly in the 1970s, the value of play training has been confirmed by field observations at both preschool classes and home. Adult involvement in children's play affords the children a number of immediate benefits in addition to the long-term ones of increased cognitive and social skills. Children have the sense that their playing is worthwhile and has the approval of adults. Parents or teachers joining children in their games build rapport both at home and in class. When adults participate in the games, the children are less easily distracted and stick with their games longer than they might have otherwise. Persistence at play may have two very valuable outcomes: (1) The play episodes become richer and more meaningful, and (2) children gain the habit of sustained commitment to an activity, which will prove valuable later in life. But the adults need to use caution and not intervene too much in children's play.

Investigators have suggested three basic modes of adult participation in children's play. *Parallel playing* involves having an adult play alongside a child without directly interacting, as in each constructing a separate object from wooden blocks. *Coplaying* refers to having an adult join children in an ongoing play of which the children remain in control. In this instance, an adult interacts with children but offers only indirect guidance by asking questions. *Play tutoring* involves having an adult teach children new play behaviors.

Sensitive adult participation in children's play can be very beneficial to the children involved. Children enjoy such participation and learn much from the examples, ideas, and support of older people.

Based on James E. Johnson, James F. Christie, and Thomas D. Yawkey, *Play and Early Childhood Development* (Glenview, IL: Scott, Foresman, 1987), pp. 21–25, 30–32.

Young children have an unrealistic optimism in performance expectations and generally overestimate their skills on academic tasks or in comparison with other children. This unrealistic assessment of their abilities would be a handicap in older children or adults, but may well be adaptive in young children. For example, this unrealistic optimism fosters feelings of self-efficacy in children—the belief that they will eventually succeed, perhaps on the next try. This provides the motivation to practice skills because the child firmly expects to master them, or to attempt behaviors they would not otherwise try if they had more realistic conceptions of their own abilities (Bjorklund & Greene, 1992).

Even egocentrism, which is often presented as a liability for young children, may become an asset. Research, for example, has found that young children learn memory strategies and recall materials better when the target information is related to themselves in some way. Egocentrism may actually enhance children's learning in certain situations because they interpret events according to their own perspective which helps them to comprehend and retain these events. Even in terms of language development and play, egocentrism may be perceived as positive. For example, when young children engage in parallel play, they tend to engage in *collective monologues* in which they talk with one another, but not really to one another (Piaget, 1955). If they were not engaged in the social situation of play, they would not be so vocal. In this case, egocentrism serves as a technique that gives them access to more socially oriented activities.

According to this viewpoint, therefore, the preoperational child shows adaptive intelligence, rather than intelligence inferior to that of older children and adults. Preoperational thought provides the necessary components—and time—for the development of a fully integrated cognitive system. Because of this, educators' attempts to intensely instruct young children—sometimes beginning as early as infancy—have been labeled by some researchers as *miseducation* (Elkind, 1987) that may paradoxically reduce their learning performance. For example, an increase in certain cognitive abilities may make language learning more difficult.

The slow maturation of children's cognitive abilities, then, does not merely provide a waiting period for mature cognitive ability; it provides a protracted period of time in which adaptive limitations may actually increase children's learning potential throughout their development. What were once viewed as preschoolers' cognitive liabilities, for example, egocentrism and a poor sense of their overall cognition, may actually be exactly what is needed for their particular period of cognitive development. Indeed, researchers have voiced a caution, "…we should rethink out efforts to hurry children through a childhood that has uses in and of itself" (Bjorklund & Green, 1992, p. 52).

 EARLY CHILDHOOD EDUCATION

Schools and programs for preschoolers have become an integral part of educating American children. The changing role of women, and such social trends as two-income families, divorce, and single parenthood, have accelerated this trend. Early childhood education has been promoted as a way to improve both the early learning experiences of poor children and America's education system in order for it to compete successfully with other countries. In some middle- and upper-class families, the choice of school and formal and informal educational activities of 3- and 4-year-olds become a focus of social competition, as the following exchange illustrates:

> Not long ago an old friend called to congratulate my wife and me on the birth of our son. During the catch-up conversation, he asked about my then three-year-old daughter's progress. Was she taking gymnastics, ballet, or swimming? Was she enrolled in reading, math, and computer classes? Had I succeeded in placing her name on preliminary lists for testing and admission to selective preschools and private kindergartens? "One can never start too early," he assured. "Oh, and how has she done on early tests?" (Piccigallo, 1988)

In the 1960s, the leaders of the reform movement fostering early childhood programs had ambitious ideas about what 3- and 4-year-olds were likely to gain from schooling. They considered children "competent" to improve their intelligence almost from infancy (Bloom, 1964). A prominent educator claimed that "you can teach any child any subject matter at any age in an intellectually honest way" (Bruner, 1960). This found itself translated into instructional efforts beginning in the crib by some educators who claimed that "it is easier to teach a one-year-old any set of facts than it is to teach a seven-year-old" (Doman, 1984).

These views have been criticized for failing to view the young child as a different kind of learner than the older child. It has been argued that formal instruction puts excessive demands on young children (Elkind, 1986; 1987). Young children may actually be harmed by early instruction. Children who are given tasks that are too intellectually demanding are in danger of falling into early patterns of frustration and failure (Ames, 1971). Both short- and long-term risks have been found to be associated with the stresses that formal education places on young children. Fatigue, loss of appetite, decreased efficiency, psychosomatic ailments, and a reduced motivation for learning have all resulted from premature formal schooling (Bjorklund & Green, 1992).

Although some educators believe that 3- and 4-year-olds should be at home where they will, ideally, receive warmth, security, and continuity in the years before starting school, this option is not open to or desirable to many parents. In addition, research has shown that preschool can offer specific advantages to children. Attending nursery school has been found to foster children's social and emotional development. Compared to children at home, preschool students made advances in sociability, self-expression, independence, and interest in the environment (Mussen, Conger, & Kagan, 1974). In another study, children attending preschool surpassed home-staying children on such intellectual tasks as vocabulary, comprehending language, and visual memory (Brand & Welsh, 1989). Long-term gains in ability to learn and in reading have been found in both middle-class and poor children. Some educators feel that a year of preschooling helps many youngsters who would otherwise repeat a grade or require special placement (Featherstone, 1985).

Ultimately, it is the nature of the young child's experience of her surroundings—not whether she attends a formal preschool or spends most of her time at home—that will contribute to her ability to learn. Children learn by observing the consequences of their acts, by putting objects into new forms, and by getting feedback from those around them. Whether they are at home or school, their surroundings are a powerful presence contributing to the enhancement or retardation of their growth. A carefully planned, well-paced early education program can give children the experiences they need for their cognitive development—especially when this program is designed with children's developmental level in mind (Zigler, 1987).

DEVELOPMENTALLY APPROPRIATE CURRICULUM

The key concept in defining quality education is "developmental appropriateness." Because children learn in different ways at different ages, what is acceptable for one age group is inappropriate for another. Obviously, the aim of a developmentally appropriate preschool is to match the school program with the developmental needs and abilities of young children. Within such a setting, the individual needs of each child can be addressed. The developmentally appropriate tasks for 3- and 4-year-olds involve using large- and small-muscle activity to explore their environment. Educators of young children recognize that development cannot be accelerated or skipped. Each stage of development has its own tasks to accomplish (National Association for the Education of Young Children, 1987).

How can educators best match their educational programs for young children with their students' developmental needs? The National Association for the Education of Young Children (NAEYC) appointed a commission to study this question and to make recommendations. Their conclusions, based on research findings, are presented in the form of guidelines for teachers of early childhood classrooms. Their guidelines for developmentally appropriate programs for preschoolers include the following:

> In place of an "academic" program, an educational curriculum should include all areas of a child's development—physical, emotional, social, and cognitive.

> Curriculum plans should be based on observations of each child's interests and developmental progress, not the average of the group.

> A learning environment should allow for active exploration and interaction with adults, other children, and teaching materials. Highly structured, teacher-directed activities are not encouraged.

> In place of workbooks, dittos, or other abstract materials, young children should be offered concrete real activities and materials that are relevant to their lives.

> Adults should respond quickly and directly to children's needs and messages and adapt to children's styles and abilities.

Other guidelines include specific illustrations of appropriate and inappropriate practice for different age levels from infancy to age 8. For example, stimulating children's skills of 4- and 5-year-olds in all developmental areas fosters the growth of self-esteem, social skills, and language abilities. Learning activities that allow them to be "physically and mentally active" are considered to be the appropriate preparation for future learning. In contrast, an emphasis on teaching specific academic skills, such as the rules of reading or mathematics, is considered to be inappropriate. These are tasks that can be mastered at a later, appropriate level of development. It is noteworthy that, given the wide range of programs currently offered, a large national organization of educators could reach such near consensus on basic principles (National Association for the Education of Young Children, 1986).

APPROACHES TO EARLY EDUCATION

A number of models for early childhood education have been created. Some schools follow a specific model closely, but most incorporate elements of various approaches. Following are descriptions of three influential models for teaching preschoolers: the *Montessori method, formal didactic education,* and *open education.* Each model incorporates an approach to how children learn, as well as beliefs about how people think and behave in our culture.

In a Montessori school, there is a focus on the development of motor and sensory skills and the ability to order and classify materials.

MONTESSORI SCHOOLS Although most Montessori schools in the United States and Canada tend to be expensive private schools, the Montessori method took root in quite different surroundings. Dr. Maria Montessori, an energetic and innovative Italian physician, began her experimental educational methods with retarded children and then with socially disadvantaged children from the tenements of Rome. She believed that children who had experienced a difficult, chaotic, or unpredictable home life needed surroundings that emphasized sequence, order, and regularity. The Montessori approach features a *prepared environment* and carefully designed, self-correcting materials. Each child may select a task to work on individually, returning the materials to the shelf when finished. A typical task involves arranging in sequence a set of graduated cylinders, weights, or smooth- to rough-textured pieces of cloth. Some of the cylinders may have handles to facilitate the fine-motor development and finger control necessary for writing. There will be a sound table where children are introduced to letters and phonics. The children may also learn practical tasks, such as washing dishes, making soup, gardening, and painting a real wall. Classrooms are age-mixed, with children from 3 to 7. As we have seen earlier in this chapter, groups of mixed age children provide an excellent atmosphere for learning and growing. The older children assist and teach the younger children.

The atmosphere in a Montessori school is one of quiet busyness and confident accomplishment. The teacher arranges the environment, but avoids interfering with the learning process; teachers especially avoid injecting any "extraneous" elements, such as praise or criticism. The curriculum develops motor and sensory skills, as well as the ability to order and classify materials. These are considered the basic forerunners of more complex tasks, such as reading and understanding mathematics. Many contemporary educational techniques incorporate some Montessori methods—particularly self-teaching materials, individually paced progress, real-life tasks, and the relative absence of both praise and criticism.

FORMAL DIDACTIC EDUCATION The formal "back-to-basics" approach uses carefully structured lessons to inculcate a particular set of skills. It is typified by the Bereiter and Engelmann program (1966) designed for disadvantaged children. To teach the requisite skills in a gradual, sequential order (later known as the Distar program), the two psychologists divided the children into homogeneous small groups of about five members. The teacher asked a question or offered a sentence, and the children responded by answering the question or repeating the sentence in unison. The children also interacted individually with the teacher, receiving immediate feedback and warm praise for success. Positive reinforcement was relied upon extensively. Lessons were taught in 20-minute drill periods, and little time was allowed for free play between periods because it was felt that play distracted the children from learning specific facts, principles, and skills.

Research on the Distar program indicated that these children did learn the specific behavioral objectives quickly and well. Long-term results, however, showed little lasting transfer of learned skills to other educational settings. Again, there are several explanations for these results:

1. The follow-up schools for these disadvantaged children might have been so stifling, socially and intellectually, that they could not encourage success in even the brightest, most motivated child.

2. The difference in expectations between the Distar program and the public school was perhaps so great that the particular behaviors could not be sustained.

3. The children might have become overly dependent on the rewards of praise, hugs, and smiles and failed to derive any intrinsic pleasure from the learning and problem-solving process.

At any rate, children in these programs displayed marked initial success, with kindergartners often reading on a second-grade level. This early advantage disappeared by at least the fourth grade, when these children became indistinguishable from other "disadvantaged" children.

OPEN EDUCATION Open education is an eclectic movement that draws upon the work of such diverse theorists as Piaget, John Dewey (1961), and Susan Isaacs (1930). In contrast to assumptions about the nature of open education, based on its name, "open education" does not signify the absence of structure. Indeed, good open education, as exemplified by the British Infant School, requires extensive planning and preparation. The British Infant School was designed to help children enter the formal English educational structure by age 8 or 9 (Plowden, 1967). Some of its main characteristics are:

The Integrated Day. Instead of discrete periods for each subject, children work at continuing projects that employ several skills at once. Setting up a "business office" may entail a field trip for observation, a written report, group discussion, and some artwork or other visual aids.

Vertical Groupings. Children of different ages are in the same classroom. Within several years, a child can develop from being the youngest, following and learning from others, to a position of leadership and responsibility.

Child Input in Decision Making. Children in open classrooms often choose from a variety of activities, deciding how they want to participate and for how long. A child's ability to make responsible decisions is respected, and such potential incentives as reward and punishment are minimized. We should note that this is the same sort of philosophy that underlies the Montessori program presented earlier.

The achievement of the British Infant School is impressive; the children equal or surpass the performance of students in more traditional programs. But the school's curriculum planning is extensive, and community support must be strong. Some open classrooms in other educational systems are unsuccessful; the difference seems to lie in the skill and forethought of the planners and teachers.

COMPENSATORY EDUCATION

Early childhood education has been seen as a way to reverse the damaging effects of poverty and other social problems in America. In 1965, the federal government initiated Head Start, a large-scale effort to break what was called the "cycle of poverty" that affected children and families in urban, suburban, and rural areas.

Head Start is an early childhood preschool program for targeted children from poor families. It is designed to provide the cognitive, emotional, and social experiences needed to succeed in school. In Head Start programs, children practice the cognitive skills typically fostered in early childhood. These include counting, comparing, learning the parts of their bodies, dancing, and singing, using various materials.

Does this year of compensatory schooling make a difference? The first major evaluative study of the effects of Head Start, the Westinghouse Study (1969), found that although Head Start students entered school with better skills than poor children who had not participated in the year of preschool, within a few years there was no difference between the groups in academic performance as measured by standardized tests. This finding of no lasting gains on test scores has generally been confirmed (Haskins, 1989).

But is performance on standardized tests the appropriate measure of Head Start's effectiveness? Many educators and social scientists feel that it is not. They look to the comprehensive goals of Head Start to evaluate its success. Head Start was initiated with the far-reaching goal of changing the lives of children, families, and communities. Many Head Start parents feel uncomfortable with the schooling of their children. They may have been failures at school themselves. Therefore, the involvement of parents and families was built into the program. Head Start parents are expected to volunteer as aides in the classroom, attend parenting classes and job-training programs, and participate in making policies for the program. The goal is that parents and educators work together to improve the lives of the Head Start families (Lombardi, 1990).

By other criteria Head Start has had positive effects. Although their achievement tests were not higher, high school students who had attended Head Start were better adjusted in school than their classmates (Copple, Cline, & Smith, 1987). They participated more fully in school and were less often identified as children with serious academic problems. They had better attendance and were retained less often. This group of children appeared to have made gains that are not readily measured. They had a commitment to school and could meet its demands. Participating in Head Start may have made their parents more committed to education for their children. By these criteria, Head Start seems to succeed in getting children off to a better start.

In Head Start programs, children work on the cognitive skills associated with early childhood learning such as counting, comparing, and learning the parts of their own bodies.

Head Start is a massive, federally funded effort to break the cycle of poverty in the United States. It is not the only model for helping poor children learn. The results of a small experimental program (Consortium Studies, 1978) indicate the potential of more intensive intervention than Head Start has been able to offer. Educators were able to combine an excellent preschool program with intense parent involvement, training, and assistance. Comprehensive services to meet the job, housing, health, educational, and social needs of families were provided. Besides providing enriched school experiences, the program brought about positive changes in how parents related to their children. It showed that programs conducted with abundant resources and care can benefit educationally at-risk children. Although such intensive intervention programs may prove impossible to develop on a large scale, the success of this pilot project highlights the interdependence of the preschool gains and involving and supporting parents and families.

The positive efforts of Head Start and other compensatory preschool programs cannot operate in a vacuum. They must be linked to children's families, to early educational experiences, and to the schools that children attend after Head Start. Early intervention for poor children includes pre- and postnatal care, parent education, and quality child care (Committee for Economic Development, 1987). Above all, education for young children must be a partnership between schools and parents to foster learning and development.

SUMMARY AND CONCLUSIONS

The Cognitive Development shows significant change during the preschool years. Children from 2 to 6 years of age develop their ability for symbolic representation—the transformation of physical objects, people, and events into mental symbols. Symbols allow the thought processes of children to become more complex. Symbols also permit the developments of concepts such as temporal ordering—past and future.

All learning does occur in the preschool or nursery school classroom. Much competence is gained by pretend play. Play provides the opportunity for motor, social, and cognitive experience in the world. Children who have had a good amount of play are better able to understand how an object can change shape or form and still remain the same object, that is, conservation, and they are more sociocentric, that is, sensitive to the needs and emotions of others. Despite this, however, there are limits to preoperational thought. Preoperational children's thought is *concrete, irreversible, egocentric,* and *centered.* They focus on the present state of things and are not aware of how things may be transformed. They have difficulty with classification, time, sequence, and spatial relationships.

In recent years, researchers have challenged some of Piaget's conclusions about the mental capabilities of young children. These psychologists believe that Piaget underestimated the impact of social experience with adults and other children on the growth of children's thinking. They believe that instruction from adults and solving real problems may well further the development of thinking in children. Piaget's theory focuses on understanding the physical world rather than the social and cultural world.

One common factor in all the research, however, is that the thinking, memory, and problem solving of younger children is qualitatively different from that of older children. In the area of memory, for example, preschoolers show good recognition memories, but poor recall memory. Moreover, it has been found difficult to teach preschoolers strategies to organize and rehearse information. Despite this, however, they do seem to have rudimentary memory strategies that relate to meaning, sequence, and function and to their interrelationships. These strategies serve as precursors to the more complex and comprehensive strategies of older children.

Play offers preschool children opportunities to express themselves freely—without pressure to succeed at something or produce a product. Play is valuable as self-expression and exploration and also furthers social development and fosters creativity. Play takes many forms from rough-and-tumble play to play with language. All of these forms offer children with opportunities to learn socially appropriate behaviors, empathy, rules, and the ability to distinguish pretend from real. Play allows children to manipulate reality, meanings, and their experiences.

Based on a careful review of the skills and abilities of preschool children, cognitive immaturity may be seen as adaptive—rather than as a deficiency. Egocentrism and a lack of awareness of cognition itself may actually allow children to have a longer period of development in which to build and refine developmentally appropriate cognitive skills.

Early childhood programs are becoming very important in the United States. With more women working, and a scarcity of high-quality day care, many parents seek preschools or nursery schools as a safe and stimulating environment for their child. Some educators feel that such programs place excessive demands on children before they are ready; others believe that early childhood programs stimulate intellectual, social, and motor development. While educators are divided over the benefits of early education for children, they all agree that standards and guidelines need to be followed to ensure the optimal environment in which children may grow without stress.

The National Association for the Education of Young Children has developed guidelines for educational curricula that match the developmental needs of young children. In general, these guidelines suggest activities that foster motor development, little structured pre-reading or pre-math activities, an open environment with a diversity of ages to encourage exploration and sensitivity, and responsive, guiding adults.

Several early childhood education models exist. Among these models are three influential ones: the *Montessori method, formal didactic education,* and *open education.* The Montessori model is a discovery oriented, self-correcting environment with teachers as guides and an age-mix ranging from 3 to 7. Montessori tasks feature sequence, order, and regularity. In addition to those activities that develop motor, sensory, and practical life skills, there is an introduction to sounds and number, art and music. Traditional, formal approaches teach specific skills in a gradual, sequential order, but the advantages gained tend not to last. This may be because they emphasize rote learning and drill before the children are ready for the concepts. Open education involves planning and forethought for success to occur. It features integrated activities for children to develop several skills simultaneously, much the way they do in the "real world." Again, children of mixed ages participate in the same class and are involved in deciding what to do and for how long.

Head Start, and other compensatory education programs, were developed to provide a preschool opportunity for children from poverty backgrounds. It was hoped that such programs would reverse the damaging effects of poverty on education. Head Start has not been successful in raising achievement test scores, but it has helped children adjust to school and has involved their parents in the educational process. Earlier and more intensive interventions for poor children and their parents are being implemented. These involve health care, parent education, homemaking skills, and other activities not traditionally the realm of the educational system. Nevertheless, where implemented, they seem to be effective at improving the educational experience for poor children.

> ## ► KEY TERMS AND CONCEPTS

centration	organization	sociocentric
classification	recall	**sociodramatic play**
egocentricity	recognition	symbolic representation
guided participation	rehearsal	zone of proximal development
irreversibility		

➤ **SELF-TEST QUESTIONS**

1. What is the preoperational period of child development? Differentiate between the two stages of preoperational thought.

2. Explain the significance of real and pretend play in the cognitive development of a preschool child.

3. List the limitations of preoperational thought.

4. Discuss the criticisms of Piaget's theory and alternate theories of cognitive development.

5. Describe the memory capabilities of preschool children. Differentiate between recognition and recall. What memory strategies do children use?

6. List the different types of play and the benefits

derived from each.

7. How does play promote cognitive development?

8. How does children's art aid in physical and cognitive development?

9. Discuss the benefits of cognitive immaturity for preschoolers.

10. Discuss different views concerning the benefit of formal education for preschoolers.

11. List and discuss different approaches to early education.

12. List the accomplishments and limitations of compensatory education.

➤ **SUGGESTED READINGS**

BRUNER, J. & HASTE, H. *Making sense: The child's construction of the world.* New York: Methuen, 1987. A concise presentation of Jerome Bruner's current perspective on the social construction of knowledge.

GARVEY, C. *Play.* Cambridge, MA: Harvard University Press, 1990. A concise description of the developmental forms of children's play.

KAGEN, S., & ZIGLER, E. (Eds.). *Early schooling: The national debate.* New Haven, CT: Yale University Press, 1987. A collection of the views from scholars

and practitioners on the wisdom and practice of early schooling.

PALEY, V. G. *Bad guys don't have birthdays: Fantasy play at four.* Chicago: University of Chicago Press, 1988. A delightful book on fantasy in childhood and its role in child development.

TOBIN, J. J., WU, D. Y. H. & DAVIDSON, D. H. *Preschool in three cultures.* New Haven, CT: Yale University Press, 1989. A blend of anthropology, human development, and education enriches this vivid picture of cultural variation in attitudes toward young children.

VIDEO CASE: WILD ABOUT LEARNING

The preschool California classroom is quiet, organized, and neat. The 4-year-olds in it know the rules and follow them. Sound perfect? Not according to the man in charge of the school. So he invited a visitor to observe what was going on. The observer was Bev Bos, a preschool teacher for over thirty years in nearby Sacramento. Her classroom is recognized by many child-care experts to be an ideal learning environment for preschoolers.

What Bos saw disturbed her—children standing in line way too long, teachers doing things for children that they didn't need to do. And perhaps most distressing in Bos's view: the children were not excited. They were not having fun.

Bos's own classroom is entirely different from the one she observed. To the outside observer it may seem chaotic because the main activity is play. Says Bos, "When children are playing, they're learning and in fact they're doing some of the most important learning in their lives." Bos interferes with the children's play only when they hurt themselves or hurt another child or destroy property.

But what about reading and writing? Isn't that what preschool is for? For Bos the answer is no. Learning, she argues, must be age-appropriate. This means that teachers must make sure that what children learn in the classroom is geared to children's play and emotional development. Preschool should encourage a sense of wonder or wanting to know, a sense of discovery, and anything that heightens children's own experience.

Bos has her critics. One of them is Roberta Babb, the director of the Creme de la Creme Preschool in Houston. Creme de la Creme students learn letters at 2 and most can read by the time they leave for kindergarten. In addition, they learn foreign languages and how to use computers. Says Babb, "Children ought to have the opportunity to read when they want to and not wait until first grade. Then it's too late."

Bos disagrees. Adults should read to 4-year-olds, not expect the children to be reading to them. "Spending years teaching children to read is a waste of time" she says. "When they're ready, it takes 24 1-hour sessions to teach them to read. If they're not ready and you try to teach reading, it sets them up for failure. They'll never learn to love reading." Such kids may read newspapers and magazines but, "they never will read a novel."

In sum, for Bos, "Education is not a race. It's not who finishes first but who stays longest."

CASE QUESTIONS

1. Do you agree that children learn most by playing? Why or why not?

2. Do you believe that learning is age-appropriate? Why or why not?

3. In what kind of school do you think that children would learn more—one run by Bev Bos or one run by Roberta Babb?

4. Do you think that Bos's teaching philosophy encourages creativity in students? Why or why not?

5. Why do you think the kind of classroom Bev Bos observed is more typical than her own classroom? Do you think this has contributed in any way to the fact that American children have fallen behind children in countries like Japan in many learning areas? If so how?

CHAPTER 11

*Yesterday a child came out to
wander
Caught a butterfly inside a jar
Fearful when the sky
Was full of thunder
And tearful at the falling of a
star.*

JONI MITCHELL
"THE CIRCLE GAME"

EARLY CHILDHOOD: PERSONALITY AND SOCIAL DEVELOPMENT

OUTLINE

Three Theories Revisited
Developmental Issues and Coping Patterns
Aggression and Prosocial Behavior
Understanding Self and Others
The Family Context
The Effects of Television
Summary and Conclusions

CHAPTER OBJECTIVES

By the time you have finished this chapter, you should be able to do the following:

✔ Discuss the strong feelings and conflicts with which preschool children are faced.

✔ Understand the difference between fear and anxiety, give some of the sources of these emotions, and describe the ways that children cope with them.

✔ Discuss the factors that influence aggressive and prosocial behavior.

✔ Describe the development of gender schemes during the preschool period and the effects they have on the child's behavior.

✔ Discuss the impact of parenting styles, and parent's warmth and control on personality and social development during early childhood.

✔ Discuss some of the ways that brothers and sisters influence social development.

✔ List some guidelines that can help parents achieve our society's current child-rearing goals.

✔ Discuss the pros and cons of the effects of television on child development.

During the preschool period, young children become socialized. They learn what is expected of them in their family and their community—what is good and bad behavior for boys and girls like them. They learn how to handle their feelings in socially appropriate ways. They learn who they are within the social context of their community. In other words, young children learn the norms, rules, and cultural meanings of their society, and they develop a self-concept that may persist throughout their lives. In Chapter 3, we looked briefly at some of these socialization processes. In this chapter, we will examine them in more detail, particularly as they relate to the developmental issues of the preschool period.

There is dramatic growth in the child's self-control and social competence during the four important years from age 2 to age 6. Although 2-year-olds have all the basic emotions of 6-year-olds (or, for that matter, of adults), their expression of these emotions is immediate, impulsive, and direct. They cannot wait to have their desires satisfied. A mother who has promised her 2-year-old an ice-cream cone cannot afford the luxury of chatting with a friend outside the ice-cream parlor—her child's impatience will interfere with any attempts at conversation. Expressions of dependency, too, are direct and physical at this age. In an unfamiliar setting, a 2-year-old stays close to his mother, clinging to her clothing or returning often to her side. If forcibly separated from her, he may throw himself on the floor, howling with anger, protest, and grief. Anger is expressed in direct, physical ways at this age. Instead of expressing themselves verbally, 2-year-olds may kick or bite. They may grab a desired toy instead of asking for it.

In contrast, 6-year-olds are much more verbal and thoughtful; they are a little less quick to anger, and they censor or control their behavior. Their coping patterns are far more diverse than those of 2-year-olds; 6-year-olds can express their anger by kicking a door or a teddy bear rather than a brother or sister. They may have learned to hold in their anger and not express it outwardly at all. They may have developed a special assertive posture to defend their rights or a specific fantasy to see them through unpleasant situations. If Mommy is not where they expect her to be, 6-year-olds are unlikely to kick and howl. Instead, they may talk out their anger or fear, or express it in a highly disguised form—perhaps by becoming uncooperative and grumpy or by building an elaborate tower of blocks and then knocking it down. In short, most 6-year-olds have become quite refined in their abilities to cope and have developed their own distinctive styles. There are far more individual variations in methods of coping among 6-year-olds than among 2-year-olds. The personal style that a child develops in these years may be the foundation of a lifelong pattern of behavior.

THREE THEORIES REVISITED

The socialization of a child during the preschool years is complex, involving the ups and downs of interpersonal relationships and the cumulative effects of countless events. It is no wonder that experts disagree about the major influences and critical interactions and even on the best methods to study the processes. As indicated in Chapter 2, there are at least three major theoretical perspectives:

1. The *psychodynamic perspective* emphasizes the child's feelings, drives, and developmental conflicts. Children must learn to cope with powerful emotions, such as anxiety, in socially acceptable ways. Erikson has described the growth of autonomy and the need to balance it with dependency on parents during this period.

2. According to the *social-learning perspective,* social and personality development are primarily products of the environment. The child's behavior is shaped by rewards and modeling. Sometimes these rewards come from parents or adults in the environment, and at other times—especially as the child matures—the rewards become internalized.

3. Finally, the *cognitive development perspective* emphasizes children's own thoughts and concepts as organizers for their social behavior. Children develop increasingly complex concepts—for example, they learn what it means to be a girl or a boy, a sister or brother, or a friend. These concepts, in turn, play a major role in directing children's behavior.

Each of these perspectives have been influential in shaping our understanding of children's social development.

One of the theorists whose name is strongly associated with children's social development is Erikson, who suggested that there were eight stages of development in the human life cycle. His stage of early childhood, initiative versus guilt, involves young children's exploration of their world and themselves. Initiative refers to the purposefulness of young children as they ambitiously explore their surroundings. They eagerly learn new skills, interact with peers, and seek the guidance of parents in their social dealings. Cries such as, "Look, Dad!" or "Help me cut this picture out, Mom," or "Suzie hit me, make her stop!" are heard frequently during the preschool years as children try to understand the workings of

Preschoolers have intense feelings that they must learn to handle during these early years. Learning that losing a race is not the end of the world may take away some of this child's sadness.

their environment. This is the period of play, when children consume every bit of information possible from their activities.

Erikson based his theory on Freud's psychosexual stages—the stage of initiative versus guilt, therefore, corresponds closely to the Oedipal stage of Freud. Sexuality is thus also a key aspect of social development during this stage—in the form of gender identification and choosing gender-appropriate behaviors and activities. In Freud's theory, the superego, or conscience, develops during this time as the young child deals with sexual feelings and a desire for closeness with parents. When the young child goes against the dictates of the superego, guilt results. Guilt is likely to be especially strong when children go against their parents wishes—an activity which is inevitable in their new drive to explore their world.

Guilt associated with an overly strong superego can dampen the child's initiative, according to Erikson. Parents may assist in this suppression of their children's natural curiosity by being overly harsh or critical in their interactions. When this happens, children's self-confidence and desire for mastery of skills breaks down. Timidity and fearfulness may result which they will carry with them for a potentially long period of time—perhaps for their entire life.

In this chapter, we shall discuss research from all three perspectives in order to offer a broader understanding of social and personality development in the preschool child.

DEVELOPMENTAL ISSUES AND COPING PATTERNS

Children must learn to handle a wide range of feelings in these early years. Some are good feelings, such as joy, affection, and pride. Others—such as anger, fear, anxiety, jealousy, frustration, and pain—are not pleasant at all. Children must also find their own ways of resolving developmental conflicts. They must learn to deal with an awareness of their dependence on others and find ways of relating to the authority figures in their lives. On the other hand, children must also deal with their own feelings of independence or autonomy—their strong drive to do things for themselves, to master their physical and social environments, to be competent and successful. As Erikson suggests, children who are unable to successfully resolve these early psychosocial conflicts may have difficulty coping later in life (Erikson, 1950).

HANDLING FEELINGS

The sense of personal and cultural identity that forms between the ages of 2 and 6 is accompanied by many strong feelings that children must learn to integrate into their own personality structures. Finding outlets for these feelings acceptable to both themselves and their parents is no easy task. Children find many solutions to this challenge, but they also experience conflict while doing so.

FEAR AND ANXIETY   One of the most important forces that children must learn to deal with is the stress caused by fear and anxiety. These patterns of psychological and physiological stress are experienced as unpleasant by both children and adults. The two emotions are not synonymous; a distinction must be made between them. **Fear** is a response to a specific stimulus or situation: for example, a child may fear big dogs or lightning and thunder. In contrast, **anxiety** has a more vague or generalized source. Anxious children experience an overall feeling of apprehension, but they do not know its precise origin. A move to a new neighborhood or a sudden change in parental expectations, such as the beginning of toilet training, may be the indirect cause of tensions that seem to come from nowhere. Many psychologists believe that anxiety inevitably accompanies socialization, since the child attempts to avoid the pain of parental displeasure and discipline (Wenar, 1990).

The Causes of Fear and Anxiety. Fear and anxiety have many causes. Young children may be anxious that their parents will leave them or stop loving them. Parents usually act in a loving and accepting fashion, but sometimes—frequently as a means of punishment—they withdraw their love, attention, and protection. The withdrawal of love threatens children and makes them feel anxious. Anticipation of other types of punishment, especially physical punishment, is another source of anxiety for young children. Two-year-olds see parents as powerful people; they may have no realistic idea of how far their parents will go in punishing them. When an exasperated parent shouts, "I'm going to break every bone in your body!" the child (who has probably witnessed countless such acts of violence on television) has no way of knowing that the parent's threat is an empty one. Fear and anxiety may be increased, or even produced, by the child's own imagination. Children often imagine that the birth of a new baby will cause their parents to reject them. Sometimes anxiety results from children's awareness of their own unacceptable feelings—anger at a parent or teacher, jealousy of a sibling or a friend, or the desire to be held like a baby.

The sources of some fears are easily traced—fear of the doctor who gives inoculations, the dread inspired by the smell of a hospital or the sound of a dentist's drill. Other fears are not so easy to understand. Many preschoolers develop a fear of the dark at bedtime. This type of fear is frequently related more to fantasies and dreams than to any real events in the child's life. Sometimes these fantasies stem directly from developmental conflicts with which the child is currently struggling; for example, imaginary tigers or ghosts may arise from the child's struggle with dependency and autonomy. In a classic study of children's fears, Jersild and Holmes (1935) found that younger children are most likely to be afraid of specific things, like strangers, unfamiliar objects, loud noises, or falling. In contrast, children aged 5 or 6 show an increased fear of imaginary or abstract things—monsters, robbers, the dark, death, being alone, or being ridiculed. Fifty years later, researchers found most of the same fears in preschool children, except that fears of the dark, of being alone, and of strange sights are now appearing at an earlier age (Draper & James, 1985).

In today's world, there are many sources of fear, anxiety, and stress. Some can be considered a normal part of growing up: being yelled at for accidentally breaking something or being teased by a sibling. Others are more serious: internal stresses like illness and pain and the chronic long-term stresses of unfavorable social environments—poverty, parental conflict or alcoholism, dangerous neighborhoods (Greene & Brooks, 1985). Some children must cope with major disasters or terrors, such as earthquakes, floods, and wars. Severe or long-term stressful situations can stagger the resources of even the most resilient child (Honig, 1986; Rutter, 1983).

fear A state of arousal, tension, or apprehension caused by a specific circumstance.

anxiety A feeling of uneasiness, apprehension, or fear that has a vague or unknown source.

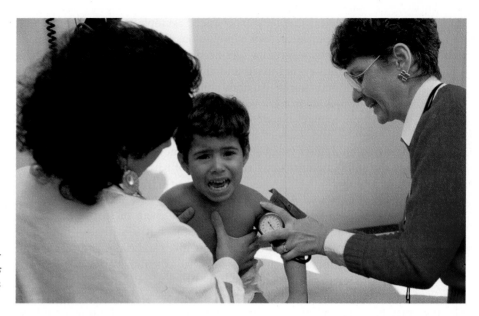

No child really enjoys going to the doctor. Often a trip to the doctor's office is linked in a child's mind with a painful injection.

Although fear and anxiety are emotions that we naturally try to avoid and minimize, they are also normal feelings that are necessary for development. In mild forms, they can be a spur to new learning. Some fears—such as a fear of fast-moving cars—are necessary for our very survival and act as part of our physiological arousal system. But others—such as a fear of the bathtub—interfere with daily life and what our society considers appropriate behavior. Furthermore, very high levels of chronic fear and anxiety are overwhelming and interrupt normal development.

Coping with Fear and Anxiety. How can we help children cope with their fears? Using force or ridicule is likely to have negative results, and ignoring children's fears will not make them go away. With mild fears, children can be gently and sympathetically encouraged to confront and overcome them. With somewhat stronger yet unrealistic fears, children may need some help with desensitization (see Chapter 2).

The best way to help children cope with anxiety and stress is to reduce the amount of unnecessary stress with which they must deal. When children show unusually high levels of tension or frequent temper tantrums, it is often useful to simplify their lives for a few days by sticking to a routine, specifying clearly what is expected, and helping the child to anticipate coming events. Other helpful strategies include reducing exposure to parental fighting or violent television shows and protecting children from the teasing and tormenting of neighborhood bullies or gangs. But not all major life stresses can be avoided. Sometimes children must cope with the stress of common events like the birth of a sibling, moving to a new home, or entering day care, as well as less common stresses like death, divorce, or natural catastrophes. Under these circumstances, parents and teachers should try to accomplish the following (Honig, 1986):

1. Learn to recognize and interpret stress reactions in children.
2. Provide a warm, secure base for children to renew their confidence.
3. Allow opportunities for children to discuss their feelings—a socially shared trauma is easier to handle.

4. Allow immature or regressive behavior, such as thumb-sucking, cuddling a blanket, fussing, or sitting on laps.

5. Help children to give meaning to the event or circumstance by an explanation.

Defense Mechanisms. In response to more generalized feelings of anxiety—especially those generated in the intense emotional climate of the family, involving issues of morality or sex roles—children learn strategies called **defense mechanisms.** A defense mechanism is an indirect way to disguise or reduce anxiety. By the age of 5 or 6, most children have learned how to hide or disguise their feelings with defense mechanisms. They continue to do so when they are adults: We all employ defense mechanisms (Freud called them "classical ego defenses") as strategies for reducing tensions. The following list summarizes the most common defense mechanisms learned by children:

➤ *Withdrawal* A very common defense mechanism in young children is **withdrawal.** It is the most direct defense possible: If a situation seems too difficult, the child simply withdraws and goes away from it, either physically or mentally.

➤ *Identification* This is a more positive defense mechanism than withdrawal. As we noted in Chapter 3, **identification** is the process of incorporating into oneself the values, attitudes, and beliefs of others. Children adopt the attitudes of powerful figures, such as parents, in order to become more like these figures—more lovable, powerful, and accepted. This helps reduce the anxiety that children feel about their own relative helplessness.

➤ *Projection* **Projection** involves a distortion of reality. Children attribute their own undesirable thoughts or actions to someone else. "She did it, not me" is a projective statement that we have all heard and perhaps used. "She doesn't like me" may seem more acceptable than "I don't like her." Projection is more complicated than withdrawal. In withdrawal, children usually know what they are trying to escape. In projection, they may actually have become confused in their own minds about what really happened. This confusion is a defense against the source of the anxiety.

➤ *Displacement* Substitution of something or someone else for the real source of anger or fear is termed **displacement.** For example, Tyler may be angry with his baby sister, but he can't hit her—perhaps he can't even admit to himself that he wants to hit her—so instead he torments the dog. A child who is afraid of his father, but who finds that fear unacceptable (because he also loves his father), might displace that fear onto something else—for example, he might develop a fear of horses or of imaginary tigers.

➤ *Denial* **Denial** is the refusal to admit that a situation exists or that an event happened. Children may react to an upsetting situation, such as the death of a pet, by pretending that the pet is still living in the house and sleeping with them at night.

➤ *Repression* **Repression** is an extreme form of denial in which children completely erase a frightening event or circumstance from their conscious awareness. There is no need to rely on fantasy, because the child literally does not remember that the event ever occurred.

➤ *Regression* **Regression** is a return to an earlier or more infantile form of behavior as a way of coping with a stressful situation. Eight-year-old Ashley

defense mechanisms Any of the techniques individuals use to reduce tensions that lead to anxiety.

withdrawal A defense mechanism in which the individual physically runs away from, or mentally withdraws from, unpleasant situations.

projection A defense mechanism in which the individual attributes his or her own undesirable thoughts or actions to someone else.

displacement A defense mechanism in which a less threatening person or object is substituted for the actual source of anger or anxiety.

denial The refusal to admit that an anxiety-producing situation exists or that an anxiety-producing event happened.

repression An extreme form of denial in which the individual completely erases an anxiety-producing event or situation from consciousness.

regression Coping with an anxiety-producing situation by reverting to earlier, more immature behavior.

suddenly reverted to sucking her thumb and carrying around her "blankie"—behaviors given up years before—when her best friend was badly injured in an accident.

➤ *Reaction formation* **Reaction formation** occurs when children have thoughts or desires that make them anxious, and they react to such thoughts by behaving in a contradictory way. For example, they would like to cling to their parents, but instead they push them away and behave with exaggerated independence and assertiveness.

➤ *Rationalization* This is a very common adult defense mechanism, used less commonly by children because it requires advanced verbal skills and knowledge of social rules. With **rationalization,** children make unacceptable behaviors or thoughts "respectable" by inventing a socially approved explanation for them. For example, if Tyler gives in to his impulse to hit his baby sister, he might explain, "I had to hit her because she was being bad! She had to be taught a lesson."

Most preschool children use several of the defense mechanisms we have mentioned. Very rarely does a child choose a single one and use it exclusively. Withdrawal and denial are generally most common in younger children. Greater maturity is needed to manage reaction formation or rationalization. Some defense mechanisms are learned by observing the behavior of parents or siblings, but most are learned directly, through the child's own experience of what defenses work best to reduce anxiety without causing other problems. The defense patterns that children adopt are learned thoroughly during the preschool years and may stay with them throughout their lives.

As a result of differences in cultural and family backgrounds, children feel fear and anxiety about different things. A hundred years ago, children feared wolves and bears. Fifty years ago they worried about goblins and bogeymen. Now their nightmares are populated with extraterrestrials and killer robots. There are also striking cultural differences in the way children express their fears, or how free they are to express them at all. In contemporary Western culture, showing fear is frowned upon—children (especially boys) are supposed to be brave, and most parents worry about a child who is unusually fearful. But this attitude is not universal. Navajo Indian parents believe it is healthy and normal for a child to be afraid; they consider a fearless child to be ignorant or foolhardy. In a recent study, Navajo parents reported an average of 22 fears in their children, including fears of supernatural beings. In contrast, a group of Anglo-American parents from rural Montana reported an average of 4 fears in their children (Tikalsky & Wallace, 1988).

DISTRESS AND ANGER   Western society not only frowns on the expression of fear, but also expects children to inhibit the display of other negative emotions, such as anger, jealousy, frustration, and distress. Children learn, from a very early age, that open displays of such feelings are unacceptable in public places—and day-care centers and nursery schools count as public places (Dencik, 1989). Although freer displays of emotion are usually permitted at home, most parents expect their children to learn what Kopp (1989) calls *emotion regulation:* the process of dealing with their emotions in socially acceptable ways. As children grow older, their parents' expectations for emotion regulation increase: It is all right for babies to cry loudly when they are hungry, but it is not all right for 6-

reaction formation A defense mechanism in which the individual unconsciously masks his or her anxiety over unacceptable thoughts or desires by behaving in an extremely contradictory fashion.

rationalization A defense mechanism in which an individual explains unacceptable thoughts or behavior by inventing a socially acceptable reason for them.

Different cultures often elicit anxiety about different things as well as sanctioning different ways of expressing it. This Korean child tries to hide her tearful anxiety rather than "let it all hang out."

year-olds to wail bitterly if they must wait a few minutes for a snack. Children who do not learn such lessons at home are at risk of being socially rejected outside the home. Preschoolers who cry too frequently are likely to be unpopular with their peers (Kopp, 1989). Learning to manage anger is even more important. Some children who were still having "temper tantrums" at the age of 10 were followed in a longitudinal study. The researchers found that these children tended to be unsuccessful in adult life as a result of their outbursts of anger: They had difficulty holding jobs and their marriages often ended in divorce (Caspi, Elder, & Bem, 1987).

Learning to manage negative emotions is not the same as never having them. Children can come to accept their angry feelings as a normal part of themselves, yet learn to control or redirect their reactions to such feelings. They may use anger as a motivating force, as a way of overcoming obstacles, or as a means of standing up for themselves or others. Whether they choose to accept or to reject their negative feelings, and the way in which they express that choice, will have significant consequences in later years.

Kopp (1992) refers to children's growing ability to control their behavior as **self-regulation.** In self-regulation, children adopt and internalize a composite of specific kinds of standards for behavior, such as safety concerns, respect for the property of others, and similar rules. Compliance, which is also a component of self-regulation, refers to the child's following the caregivers' requests, such as not to cross the street or run in parking lots. During toddlerhood, parents' requests to perform an action such as "pick up your toys" may be met with cries. By the third year, however, cries occur very infrequently, but resistance behavior increases—such as refusals or off-task negotiations. By the time the child is 4-years-old, there are fewer instances of resistance. Kopp (1992) believes that resistance in itself does not disappear as language skills develop; rather, the child is able to introduce self needs in a more socially satisfactory and less emotional way. This is impressive growth in self-regulatory behavior.

Young children are very open about showing positive feelings like joy. But by the age of 6 they have learned to somewhat mask even these feelings.

AFFECTION AND JOY   In our culture, children must restrain not only their negative feelings but also their positive emotions. Spontaneous feelings, such as joy, affection, excitement, and playfulness, are dealt with quite differently by 2-year-olds and 6-year-olds. Just as 2-year-olds are direct in expressing distress, they are also likely to be very open in showing positive feelings—they hug people, jump up and down, or clap their hands in excitement. During the course of preschool socialization, we manage to teach children to subdue such open expressiveness. Spontaneous joy and affection become embarrassing; because they are considered "babyish," most children learn to control them. On the other hand, special circumstances, such as birthday parties or baseball games, demand types of emotional expression that are considered inappropriate for everyday life. Children learn all of these social norms.

SENSUALITY AND SEXUAL CURIOSITY   Two-year-olds are very sensual creatures, deriving great pleasure from sensory experience. They like the feel of messy, gooey things. They are conscious of the softness or stiffness of clothes against their skin. They are fascinated by sounds, lights, tastes, and smells. In infancy this sensuality was centered on the mouth, but the toddler has a new awareness and fascination with the anal-genital area. Masturbation and sex play are quite common during the preschool period. As children discover that such self-stimulation is pleasurable, some may gradually increase this behavior; most develop an active curiosity about their bodies and ask many sex-related questions.

   The ways in which the culture and the family react to this developing sensuality and curiosity will have a powerful effect on children, just as the reactions of others affect the way that children handle hostility and joy. Until recently, mothers in our society were advised to prevent their children from engaging in this kind of exploration (Wolfenstein, 1951). The result was anxiety and guilt in the children, which led them to adopt the various defense mechanisms described by Freud. But sensual exploration is a natural and vital part of every child's experience. Severe restriction of children's sensual feelings and behavior is likely to cause unnecessary anxiety, guilt, and conflict during adolescence and adulthood.

DEVELOPMENTAL CONFLICTS

Trying to fit their feelings into the structure of acceptability imposed on them by the outside world is not the only task young children must face during the preschool years. Developmental conflicts also arise as they adjust to their own changing needs. Dependency, autonomy, mastery, and competence are pressing issues in their lives. As Erikson (1950) stated, the period of early childhood involves an overall psychosocial conflict between the child's initiatives to explore the world and guilt over causing parental displeasure. During this period, children are pulled between their own autonomy needs and the emotional pull toward dependency on their parents. Clearly, during early childhood, issues relating to dependency and autonomy are still being worked out.

DEPENDENCY   *Dependency* may be defined as any type of activity demonstrating that one person derives satisfaction from another person (Hartup, 1963). It includes the wish or need to be aided, nurtured, comforted, and protected by another, or to be emotionally close to or accepted by that person. Such wishes and needs are normal in people of every age, despite the connotation of weakness or inadequacy that they often carry in American society. Dependency is necessary for the very survival of the young child, who must look to older people for the satisfaction of both physical and psychological needs.

Infants and toddlers show dependency by crying for attention and by seeking close physical contact. By age 4 or 5, children have developed more indirect ways of showing their need for others: Now they seek attention by asking questions, by offering to help, by showing off, or even by outright disobedience. A study by Craig and Garney (1972) traced developmental trends in expressions of dependency by observing the ways that children at ages 2, 2 1/2, and 3 maintained contact with their mothers in an unfamiliar situation. The 2-year-olds spent most of their time physically close to their mothers, staying in the same part of the room and looking up often to make sure that their mothers were still there. The older children (2 1/2- and 3-year-olds) neither stayed as close to their mothers nor checked as often to see if their mothers had left the room. The older the children, the more they maintained verbal contact instead of physical contact. All three age groups made a point of drawing attention to their activities, but the older children were more inclined to demonstrate them from afar. Other studies have shown similar patterns: Distress caused by separation from the mother declines from ages 2 to 3, while "distal" attachment behavior, such as showing things to the mother from across the room, increases (Maccoby & Feldman, 1972). Note, though, that wide individual differences are always found in every age group.

Dependence and independence are commonly considered opposite types of behavior. But this is not necessarily the case for the young child. Although children become less dependent—less clingy—as they become older, their independence (or autonomy) follows a more complex trajectory. Infants are usually fairly cooperative; for example, they will hold out their arms when their parents are trying to dress them. This changes abruptly at about the age of 2, when many children suddenly become quite uncooperative—parents call this stage the "terrible twos." Two-year-olds fight to "do it myself," and temper tantrums are frequent when they find that they cannot manage buttons and the sleeve is inside out. When 2-year-olds are asked to do something, they show their independence by saying "No!" As they get older, they become more compliant and cooperative. Three-year-olds are more likely to do what their parents tell them to and less likely to break rules when their parents are not looking (Howes & Olenick, 1986).

AUTONOMY, MASTERY, AND COMPETENCE   As discussed in Chapter 2, the drive toward autonomy marks the second stage in Erikson's theory of personality development. Toddlers are discovering their own bodies and learning to control them. If they are successful in doing things for themselves, they become self-confident. If their efforts at autonomy are frustrated by criticism or punishment, they think that they have failed and feel ashamed and doubtful about themselves. Although autonomy, mastery, and competence are slightly different drives, they are all part of the same behavior complex that influences our behavior throughout life (Erikson, 1963; Murphy, 1962; White, 1959).

Initiative versus Guilt. Erikson suggests that the primary developmental conflict of the years from 3 to 6 is *initiative versus guilt*. In some ways, this conflict is an extension of the toddler's struggle with autonomy. Toddlers gain control and competence starting with their own bodies—feeding, dressing, toileting, handling objects, and getting around. The preschooler is learning how things work, the meaning of social situations and relationships, and how to influence people in constructive and appropriate ways. Concepts of right and wrong, good and bad, become important; labels such as "sissy," "baby," or "brat" can have devastating effects. The job of the parent or teacher is to guide and discipline the child without creating too much anxiety or guilt. In the confusing and complex social world of the preschool child, initiative can lead either to success and feelings of competence, or to failure, frustration, and guilt.

Another aspect of the initiative versus guilt conflict is associated with the child's sexuality. Exploring the world also involves learning gender appropriate behaviors. Erikson spoke of the little boy's *intrusive* initiative, whereas he felt that little girls engaged in *catching* behaviors. In other words, society acts on young children to teach them socially acceptable gender behaviors. Little boys are often allowed or even encouraged to be aggressive and physical, while little girls are often taught a "waiting mode"—they observe or engage in more passive explorations. As we shall see in Chapter 12 with regard to rough-and-tumble play, rough play is encouraged in boys, but girls who engage in rough play are labeled by teachers as antisocial (Pellegrini, 1988).

Some children—and adults—are more gender-schematic than others. If children come from families that are highly "genderized," then their parents sex-typed attitudes and behaviors lead to similar sex-typing in their children. This can lead to differences among children in the patterns of autonomy and mastery they use to explore the world.

Nearly everyone derives satisfaction from changing the environment to suit himself or herself. For a 3-year-old, this may mean crayoning on a wall or retrieving a toy from a baby sister. Preschoolers are just as pleased with their creations as adults are with theirs. Unfortunately, a youngster's desire to use creativity or ini-

All children need to feel a sense of mastery over their environment. This feeling of mastery may lead to chaos at times but it is still a key aspect of development.

tiative sometimes interferes with other people's plans. A little boy's discovery that he can "improve" the vacuum cleaner by filling its tubes with clay does not fit in with his mother's need to keep the house clean. These opposing needs produce conflicts between parent and child and within the child himself.

Learning Competence. What happens when children's attempts at mastery or autonomy meet with constant failure or frustration? What happens when they have little or no opportunity to try things on their own, or when their environment is so chaotic that they cannot see the consequences of their acts? All children have a need for autonomy, a need to master the environment, and a need to feel competent and successful. If these needs are repeatedly blocked, their personality development is likely to be adversely affected. If their efforts at mastery cause too much trouble, they may give up and become passive. Several studies show that such children fail to develop an active, exploratory, self-confident approach to learning, which White and Watts (1973) called the development of *learning competence*. Beyond this, what happens to children who are constantly punished for their independent behavior and attempts at mastery? Or to children whose parents discourage or frighten them whenever they venture into new activities? When children are made to feel anxious about their autonomy needs, they generally learn to deny, minimize, or disguise these needs. In some cultures, such induced anxiety about autonomy is especially common among young girls.

Some children are necessarily restricted in their drive toward autonomy. Children who are physically handicapped or chronically ill may have little opportunity to test their skills in mastering the environment (Rutter, 1979). Children who grow up in dangerous or crowded surroundings and who have to be restrained for their own safety, or who are supervised by excessively vigilant caregivers, may also learn exaggerated passivity or anxiety (Zuravin, 1985).

AGGRESSION AND PROSOCIAL BEHAVIOR

Much of the research on aggression and prosocial behavior derives from the social-learning theoretical perspective. Social-learning research tends to focus on the social processes of reinforcement and modeling which give rise to specific behaviors. Therefore, much of the research will be directed at studying the effects of parents, siblings, peers, and others on producing and maintaining children's social behaviors.

The young child's interactions with others can be either positive or negative. At one point, children may seek closeness or be anxious to help or share. A short time later, they may become angry and hostile. A principal task of socializing young children is to teach them socially acceptable ways to channel aggressive feelings, and at the same time to encourage positive behaviors such as helping and sharing. Many factors influence the development of aggressive behavior and of positive or prosocial behavior.

Psychologists define **aggression** as behavior intended to hurt or destroy. Aggressive behavior may be verbal or physical. It may be directed at people or displaced toward animals or objects. **Assertive behavior,** on the other hand, does not involve an intent to injure others. It is forthright, direct behavior, such as calmly stating one's rights or initiating vigorous activity, and it need not damage others.

Prosocial behavior is defined as actions intended to benefit others without the anticipation of an external reward (Eisenberg, 1988). These actions often entail some cost, sacrifice, or risk to the individual. Helping, sharing, cooperation, sympathy, and altruism (the unselfish concern for the welfare of others) are examples of prosocial behavior. These actions are frequently a response to positive motivational and emotional states—that is, people behave this way when they feel happy, secure, and empathetic. Aggression, on the other hand, is a common response to anger and hostility.

Whether behavior is considered socially appropriate depends on the situation and on the standards of the culture and the family. Aggression is not always bad, and altruism is not always appropriate. Unaggressive soldiers would be useless in combat, and altruistic football players would never win a game. Moreover, someone who is constantly altruistic may intrude on our privacy. Bryan (1975) suggests that an overly helpful person may be intrusive, moralistic, and conforming.

Considerable research has been devoted to aggressive and prosocial behaviors in an attempt to discover how each originates and what factors control them. We shall look at some of the explanations that have been given for children's anti-social and prosocial actions.

FRUSTRATION AND AGGRESSION

Psychologists from several different perspectives have hypothesized a direct relationship between frustration and aggression. An extreme form of this viewpoint was the *frustration-aggression hypothesis* (Dollard et al., 1939); it stated that all aggression is derived from frustration, and that all frustration, sooner or later, results in some direct or disguised forms of aggression. **Frustration** was defined

aggression Hostile behavior that is intended to injure.

assertive behavior Forthright, direct behavior, such as stating one's rights, that does not harm others.

prosocial behavior Helping, sharing, or cooperative actions that are intended to benefit others.

as the blocking of a goal; this results in angry feelings that "mediate" the aggression. The aggression might be expressed directly, toward the source of frustration, or displaced onto another person or object. It might be physical or verbal, or it might be disguised and channeled outward, as in some form of art, or turned inward, as in an ulcer. Nevertheless, it is there somewhere if you look for it carefully enough.

The frustration-aggression hypothesis was called into question by a well-known study (Barker, Dembo, & Lewin, 1943) of the behavior of preschool children in a frustrating situation. The children were given a number of attractive toys, which were then removed and placed behind a wire screen—the toys were visible, but the children could not reach them. They reacted in a number of different ways to the frustration they felt. A few were aggressive toward their peers, toward the investigators, or toward the wire screen. Others tried to escape from the room or regressed to earlier behaviors, such as thumb-sucking. Some just patiently waited or turned their attention to something else. Although some critics claimed that aggression could have been disguised as avoidance or regression, this experiment is more often interpreted as showing that aggression is by no means the only reaction, or even the dominant one, to frustration.

Doubt has also been cast on the other half of the frustration-aggression hypothesis—the idea that all aggression is derived from frustration (Dollard & Miller, 1950). Some aggression may simply be learned or imitative behavior. For example, soldiers and football players are trained to be aggressive whether or not they feel angry or frustrated. As we saw in Chapter 3, children behave more aggressively after observing an aggressive model. Rewarding children for aggression also results in their becoming more aggressive (Cowan & Walters, 1963; Lovaas, 1962).

PUNISHMENT AND AGGRESSION   Although research indicates that rewards encourage aggression, the case for using punishment to discourage aggression is not so clear. True, if children are punished for aggressive acts, they will very likely inhibit this behavior—at least in the presence of the punisher. But they may channel their aggressive feelings and acts into other outlets instead. For example, their aggression at home may decrease, but they may become more aggressive at school. They may express their aggression in different ways, such as tattling or name-calling. Punishment may even backfire and cause the child to be more aggressive in general. People who use physical punishment to curb a child's aggression may actually be encouraging it because they are providing a very obvious model of aggressive behavior.

REWARDS, PUNISHMENT, AND MODELING   Just as aggression may not always derive from frustration, helping and sharing may not always derive from empathy. Rewards and punishments, and the observation of models, strongly influence both antisocial and prosocial behavior.

Our culture offers different models and systems of reward and punishment to members of different segments of society. For example, the models and rewards available to boys differ considerably from those available to girls. On the average, females of all ages tend to express more concern for the feelings of others than do males (Eisenberg, 1989). Although both sexes are equally adept at understanding how another person feels, females are more apt to express their empathy because our culture allots to females the role of expressing such feelings.

frustration The blocking of a goal, causing angry feelings which, according to some, results in aggressive behavior.

Similarly, children who live in neighborhoods where many children are aggressive are more likely to be rewarded for aggressive behavior than those who do not have to fight for their rights.

Experiments on both antisocial and prosocial behavior have also shown that imitation of models is more likely to occur when the observers sense a similarity between themselves and the model, or when the model is perceived as powerful or competent (Eisenberg, 1988). Thus, boys are more likely to imitate other boys than to imitate girls. Children are also more likely to imitate other children who have "dominant" personalities—that is, children who are socially powerful and who engage in the most interesting activities (Abramovitch & Grusec, 1978). These are well-liked children who dominate their peers through the force of their personalities, not through physical aggression. In fact, preschool children dislike overly aggressive playmates (Ladd, Price, & Hart, 1988).

The modeling process is more effective when a model is perceived as nurturant or is someone who has a special relationship with the child. Consequently, parents are generally the child's most influential models. However, the influence works in a variety of ways. For example, a girl may model herself after her father because he is powerful, or because she and her father have a strong nurturant relationship, or because other people comment on the father's and daughter's similar tempers or senses of humor.

PROSOCIAL BEHAVIOR   A number of studies have demonstrated the influence of modeling on prosocial behavior. In a typical experiment, a group of children observe a person performing a prosocial act, such as putting toys or money into a box designated for "needy children." Other children in a control group watch a model who does not exhibit prosocial behavior. After watching the generous model, each child is given the opportunity to donate something. The researchers usually find that children who witness another person's generosity become more generous themselves (Eisenberg, 1988).

Because rewards and punishment affect aggression, it is assumed that they also affect helping and sharing. However, this is difficult to prove. Researchers are understandably reluctant to do experiments in which prosocial behavior is punished, and experiments in which it is rewarded are inconclusive because the results may be due to modeling: When experimenters give a reward, they are also modeling "giving" (Rushton, 1976). The role of learning in prosocial behavior is better demonstrated by a recent experiment that showed that 4-year-old children who were given many chores to do at home were more likely to be helpful outside of the home. Interestingly, the most helpful children in this study were black males. The experimenters hypothesized that, because the black children were more likely to come from fatherless homes, their mothers had turned to their sons for help and emotional support. Thus, these children had learned helping and comforting behaviors very early in life (Richman et al., 1988).

Two other procedures that influence prosocial behavior are **role playing** and **induction**. In role playing, children act out other roles as a way of seeing things from another's point of view. In induction, children are given reasons for behaving in certain ways—for example, they may be told what consequences their actions will have for others. Staub (1971) used both procedures in an experiment with groups of kindergarten children. He subsequently tested them to determine the effectiveness of these procedures. He found that role playing increased the willingness of the children to help others and that its effects lasted for as long as a

role playing The acting out of a role in order to see things from the perspective of another person.

induction Giving children reasons for behaving in socially desirable ways or for not behaving in undesirable ways.

week. However, induction had little or no effect on the children in Staub's experiment, perhaps because children are unlikely to pay much attention to a lecture from an unfamiliar adult. Induction is more effective when used by parents. Parents who use inductive forms of discipline—for example, who explain to their children the reasons for behaving in certain ways—are more likely to foster prosocial behavior in their children (Eisenberg, 1988).

Cooperation is also regarded as a form of prosocial behavior. Madsen (1971; Madsen & Shapira, 1970) found that American children become less cooperative (or more competitive) as they grow older. When playing a game that can be won only if the two players cooperate (see Figure 11–1), 4- and 5-year-olds often cooperated. Older children, however, tended to compete with each other; as a result, neither player won. Compared to American children, Mexican children and children raised on Israeli kibbutzim were more likely to cooperate, evidently because their cultures place more importance on group goals and less on individual achievement. Madsen suggested that American children are raised to be competitive and that they learn this value so completely that they are often unable to cooperate.

Angry or empathetic feelings, rewards and punishment, and modeling all play a part in the aggressive or altruistic behavior that children learn; all of these factors are present in family life. They may work together—the child may be rewarded for nonaggressive acts and mildly punished for aggressive ones. Or they may work against one another—the child may be continually subjected to frustrating situations but be severely punished when reacting aggressively. In any case, even the most careful parents cannot shelter a child completely from opportunities to imitate negative behavior.

PEERS AND SOCIAL SKILLS

Children influence one another in significant ways. They provide emotional support for one another in a variety of situations. They serve as models, they reinforce one another's behavior, and they encourage complex, imaginative play. In these ways, children help one another to learn a variety of physical, cognitive, and social skills (Asher et al., 1982; Hartup, 1983). Young boys playing aggressively, for example, may first imitate characters seen on television and then imitate one another. They continue to respond and react to one another in a fashion that

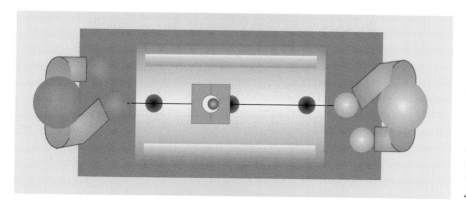

FIGURE 11–1

In Madsen's game, two children sit at opposite ends of a game board that features a cup at each end, a gutter down each side, and a marble holder with a marble inside. To play the game, the children move the marble holder by pulling on strings; if the marble holder is moved over a cup, a child earns the marble as it drops into the cup. The children must cooperate to earn marbles—if the both pull on the strings at the same time, the marble holder comes apart and the marble rolls into the gutter.

Although these children are sharing materials they are not yet at the level where they cooperatively play together.

supports and escalates the play—this is sometimes called **social reciprocity** (Hall & Cairns, 1984).

THE ROLE OF PLAY IN SOCIAL SKILL DEVELOPMENT   An early study on peer relations (Parten, 1932–33) identified five different levels of social interaction in young children:

1. *solitary play;*
2. *onlooker play,* in which the child's interaction consists merely of observing other children;
3. *parallel play,* in which the child plays alongside another child and uses similar toys but does not interact in any other way;
4. *associative play,* in which children share materials and interact somewhat, but do not coordinate their activities toward a single theme or goal; and
5. *cooperative play,* in which children engage in a single activity together, such as building a house with blocks or playing hide-and-seek with a common set of rules.

Different modes of play predominate at given age levels. Two-year-olds mostly engage in onlooker and parallel play, whereas 4- and 5-year-olds show increasing amounts of associative and cooperative play. In optimal surroundings, 5-, 6-, and 7-year-olds can interact for relatively long periods of time while sharing materials, establishing rules, resolving conflicts, helping one another, and exchanging roles. Unfortunately, some children have trouble interacting with peers even when conditions are optimal. We see these social interactions contrasted in Table 11–1.

social reciprocity The continued interaction between individuals as they respond and react to each other in a manner that encourages the prevailing behavior.

TABLE 11–1 Levels of Social Interaction and Age in Preschoolers

TYPE OF PLAY	CHARACTERISTICS OF INTERACTION
Solitary play	Children play alone or observe other children playing. Occurs often during period from 2–6 years; makes up 1/3 to 1/2 of play time for preschoolers; 2-year-olds spend more time observing other children playing than playing themselves. Usually, the older the child, the more likely that solitary time will be spent actually in play activities.
Parallel play	Children play alongside other children and use similar toys but interact in no other way. Children frequently engage in social dialogues during this type of play but do not jointly perform play activities. This makes up a fairly low amount of preschoolers' play time.
Associative play	Children share materials and interact somewhat but do not coordinate activities toward a common goal. They may comment on each other's behavior or activities but do not join efforts to achieve a shared end.
Cooperative play	Children share materials for prolonged periods, follow established rules, resolve conflicts, mutually assist one another and in a group, and share roles. This is true social interaction since children play with other children rather than alongside them. As children mature, more of their play is true cooperative play.

When we observe children in nursery schools, day-care centers, or kindergartens, it is apparent that some children are popular with their peers while others are not. These patterns tend to be remarkably stable over the years: Children who are rejected by their peers in kindergarten are likely to be rejected in elementary school as well. Later, they are more likely to have adjustment problems in adolescence and adulthood (Parker & Asher, 1987). It is helpful, then, to determine who these children are—those regularly chosen by their peers and those rejected. It has been repeatedly shown that popular children are more cooperative and exhibit more prosocial behavior during play with their peers. Unpopular children may either be more aggressive or more withdrawn, or they may simply be "out of sync" with their peers' activities and social interactions (Rubin, 1983).

Which comes first: Do rejected children adopt these negative behaviors because they are rejected, or are they rejected because of their behavior? One researcher videotaped kindergarten boys as they tried to join a play group (Putallaz, 1983). The social skills they demonstrated were used to predict each child's social status in first grade. In this and other studies, popular children were found to have a variety of social skills. They initiate activity with others by moving into the group slowly, making relevant comments about what's going on, and sharing information. They seem sensitive to the needs and activities of others. They don't force themselves on other children but are content to play beside another child. In addition, popular children have strategies for maintaining relationships. They show helpful behaviors; they are good at maintaining communication and sharing information; and they are responsive to other children's suggestions. Finally, children who are destined to be popular have strategies for conflict resolution. Popular children do not necessarily give in when faced with conflict, but they are less frequently involved in aggressive or physical solutions (Asher, 1983; Asher et al., 1982). We see these features presented in Table 11–2.

TABLE 11–2 Characteristics of Popular Children in Kindergarten

➤ Possess a variety of social skills.
➤ Initiate activity by moving into the group slowly, making relevant comments, and sharing information.
➤ Sensitive to the needs and activities of others.
➤ Don't force themselves on other children.
➤ Content to play alongside other children.
➤ Possess strategies for maintaining friendships.
➤ Show helpful behavior.
➤ Are good at maintaining communication.
➤ Are good at sharing information.
➤ Are responsive to other children's suggestions.
➤ Possess strategies for conflict resolution.
➤ When faced with conflict, are less likely to use aggressive or physical solutions.

Source: Asher, 1983; Asher et al., 1982.

If peer relations are a significant socializing influence in the lives of children—at least by middle childhood—and if the success of these relationships depends on the development of social skills, then it is probably important to help children develop these skills during the preschool period. Adults can help in two ways. First, they can teach social skills directly, by modeling and by induction. Second, they can offer opportunities for successful social experiences with peers. Children need opportunities to play with other children, as well as appropriate space and materials to support this play. Dolls, clothes for dress-up activities, toy cars and trucks, blocks, and puppets support cooperative play and offer opportunities for interaction. With preschoolers, adult care-givers must be available to help initiate activities, negotiate conflicts, and provide information (Asher et al., 1982).

THE ROLE OF IMAGINARY COMPANIONS IN SOCIAL SKILL DEVELOPMENT   During the preschool years, many children create imaginary companions who become a regular part of their daily routines. Imaginary companions are invisible characters, named and referred to by children in their conversations, who are played with directly for a period of time. These companions appear to be "real" to the child but do not exist objectively (Taylor, Cartwright, & Carlson, 1993), as the following example indicates.

> Jimmy, aged 4, loved to listen to records. His favorite song was "Casey Jones," and he would play it over and over again. Jimmy was the youngest in his family, with two older sisters, and there were few other children in the neighborhood. So, one day, Crazy Tones came to visit.

> Crazy Tones was Jimmy's imaginary companion. They did everything together. Jimmy took him for rides in his cart, they sat on the stairs and had conversations for extended periods—Jimmy always saved

room for Crazy Tones at supper and in bed. The whole family heard about Crazy Tones at mealtimes and came to accept him as a sort of "ghostly" member of the family. He was around for almost a year, before vanishing when Jimmy started kindergarten.

Recent research shows that as many as 65 percent of preschoolers have imaginary friends. While some children with imaginary companions have clinical problems as adults, the creation of such friends is associated with positive characteristics. For example, in comparison with children who don't have imaginary companions, those who do are more sociable, less shy, have more real friends, are more creative, and participate in more family activities (Mauro, 1991). Imaginary companions also seem to help children in learning social skills and practicing conversations. They are powerful predictors that children will play happily in nursery school and will be cooperative and friendly with peers and adults (Singer & Singer, 1990).

Finally, there may be cognitive as well as emotional benefits to possessing an imaginary companion. It is possible that children who are adept at fantasy have experiences that help them master the relationship between symbolic representation and the real world. Pretending may facilitate children's understanding of their mental images as being distinct from external objects. Once this distinction is practiced and mastered through pretend play—with or without imaginary companions—children may be more prepared to handle this distinction in other situations and settings.

UNDERSTANDING SELF AND OTHERS

So far, we have been talking about how children learn the bits and pieces of behavior—how they learn to share or be aggressive or handle their feelings. Children, however, act in a more comprehensive way. They put together all the bits and pieces to form whole patterns of behavior appropriate for their culture, gender, and family. Experts disagree on just how this integration of patterns of social behavior occurs. Most agree that as children grow older they become less dependent on the individual rules, expectations, rewards, and punishments of others, and more able to make judgments and to regulate their own behavior. Cognitive developmental theorists hold that the child's integration of patterns of social behavior coincides with the development of a concept of self, along with certain social concepts. These concepts then help to mediate the child's behavior in social situations. The preschool period is an important time for building some of these basic concepts.

THE SELF-CONCEPT

Even the 2-year-old has some self-understanding. As we discovered in Chapter 7, by 21 months the child is able to recognize herself in the mirror; if she sees a red mark on her nose she shows some self-conscious embarrassment. The language of the 2-year-old is full of assertions of possession. In one study of 2-year-olds playing in pairs, most of them began their play with numerous self-assertions. They

Preschoolers are fascinated with themselves. They love to compare themselves with other children excitedly noting how they are different and how they are similar.

defined their boundaries and their possessions—"my shoe, my doll, my car." The author of this study asserts that this is a cognitive achievement, not necessarily selfishness: The children are increasing their self-understanding and their understanding of the other child as a separate being (Levine, 1983). A review of other studies of children's self-concepts and social play concluded that children who are most social also have a better-developed self-concept (Harter, 1983). Thus, self-understanding is closely linked to the child's understanding of the social world.

During the preschool years, children develop certain kinds of generalized attitudes about themselves—a positive sense of well-being, for example, or a feeling that they are "slow" or "bratty." Many of these ideas begin to emerge very early, at a nonverbal level. Children may develop strong anxieties about some of their feelings and ideas while being quite comfortable with others. They also develop a set of ideals during these years, and they learn to measure themselves against what they think they ought to be. Often, children's self-evaluation is a direct reflection of what other people think of them. John, for example, was a lovable 2-year-old with a talent for getting into mischief. His older brothers and sisters called him "Bad Buster" whenever he got into trouble. By the age of 7, John was making an effort to maintain his "Bad Buster" reputation. These early attitudes eventually become basic elements of a person's self-concept, but they are difficult to explore later on because they are learned at a less sophisticated verbal level.

Preschool children are fascinated with themselves, and many of their activities and thoughts are centered on the task of learning all about themselves. They compare themselves to other children, discovering differences in height, hair color, family background, and likes or dislikes. They compare themselves to their parents, learn that they share common traits, and discover behaviors to imitate. As part of their drive to find out about themselves, preschool children ask a variety of questions about where they came from, why their feet grow, whether they are good or bad, and so on.

An awareness of how one appears to others is a key step in the development of self-knowledge. Young preschoolers tend to define themselves in terms of their physical characteristics ("I have brown hair") or possessions ("I have a bike"). Older preschoolers are more likely to describe themselves in terms of their activities: "I walk to school," "I play baseball" (Damon & Hart, 1982).

As children learn who and what they are and begin to evaluate themselves as active forces in their world, they are putting together a cognitive theory or *personal script* about themselves that helps to integrate their behavior. Human beings need to feel that they are consistent. They do not act randomly: They try to bring their behavior into line with their beliefs and attitudes. The strongest influence on children's developing self-image is usually their parents because they provide children with the definitions of right and wrong, the models of behavior, and the evaluations of actions on which children base their own ideas.

SOCIAL CONCEPTS AND RULES

internalization Making social rules and standards of behavior part of oneself—adopting them as one's own set of values.

Preschool children are busy sorting, classifying, and struggling to find meaning in the social world, just as they are in the world of objects. Central to the development of social concepts and rules is a process called **internalization**: Children learn to make the values and moral standards of their society part of themselves.

Some of these values relate to appropriate sex-role behavior, some relate to moral standards, and some simply relate to the customary way of doing things.

How do children internalize these rules? At first, they may simply imitate verbal patterns: Jennifer says "No, no, no!" as she crayons on the wall. She is doing what she wants to do, but at the same time she is showing the beginnings of self-restraint by telling herself that she shouldn't be doing it. In a few more months, she may have the self-control to arrest the impulse she is presently unable to ignore. Cognitive theorists point out that children's attempts to regulate their own behavior are influenced not only by their developing self-concept, but also by their developing social concepts. Such concepts reflect increased understanding about others as well as increased understanding about oneself. For example, a preschool child may be learning what it means to be a big brother or sister, or to be a friend. He or she is also learning about concepts such as fairness, honesty, and respect for others. Many of these concepts are far too abstract for young children, but they struggle to understand them.

FRIENDSHIP   One area that has been studied a great deal is children's concepts of friendship. A clear cognitive understanding doesn't occur until middle childhood—notions of mutual trust and reciprocity are too complex for the preschool child. Nevertheless, preschool children do behave differently with friends from the way they behave with strangers, and some 4- and 5-year-olds are able to maintain close, caring relationships over an extended period of time. They may not be able to verbalize what friendship is, but they follow some of its implied rules (Gottman, 1983).

Character Attribution. Young children learning about social concepts often ask the question, "Why did they do that?" A common answer is based on character attribution. For example, the question, "Why did Kevin give me his cookie?" may be answered with, "Because Kevin is a nice boy." As children get older, they are more and more likely to see other people, and also themselves, in terms of stable character attributes (Miller & Aloise, 1989). Some experts believe that care-givers can encourage children to be helpful or altruistic by teaching them that they are kind to others because they want to be—because they are "nice"—and not just because such behavior is demanded of them (Eisenberg et al., 1984; Grusec & Arnason, 1982; Perry & Bussey, 1984).

CHILDREN'S DISPUTES   Recently, researchers have been paying attention to children's social conflicts or disputes. Their verbal arguments with peers, with siblings, and with parents often demonstrate a surprisingly sophisticated level of social understanding and an ability to reason from social rules and concepts. Children as young as 3 years are able to justify their behavior in terms of social rules ("Now it's my turn!") or the consequences of an action ("Stop, you'll break it if you do that!") (Dunn & Munn, 1987). In fact, a close look at children's verbal disputes over the preschool years demonstrates a systematic development in their understanding of social rules, their understanding of another person's perspective, and their ability to reason from social rules or from the consequences of their actions (Shantz, 1987).

GENDER SCHEMES

Among the more significant sets of social concepts and social rules that preschool children learn are those related to gender-appropriate behavior. As we saw in

Chapter 3, some aspects of children's gender roles are learned by modeling themselves after significant individuals in their lives and by being reinforced for gender-appropriate behavior. But this is not the whole story. Children are selective in what they imitate and internalize. Research suggests that children's developing understanding of gender-related concepts—their *gender schemes*—help to determine what attitudes and behaviors are learned. Moreover, these gender-related concepts develop in predictable ways over the preschool period.

By the age of 2 1/2, most children can readily label people as boys or girls, men or women, and they can also answer the question, "Are you a girl or a boy?" (Thompson, 1975). But even though they can divide the human race into male and female, they may be confused about what that means. Many 3-year-olds believe, for instance, that if a boy puts on a dress, he becomes a girl. They may not realize that only boys can become daddies and only girls can become mommies. But by age 6 or 7, children understand that their gender is stable and permanent for a lifetime, despite superficial changes. The first level of understanding, the one that is achieved between the ages of 2 and 6, is called **gender identity.** Later on, between ages 5 and 7, children are thought to acquire **gender constancy**—the understanding that boys invariably become men and girls become women, and that gender is consistent over time and situations (Kohlberg, 1966; Shaffer, 1988).

Recent research has found that 4-year-olds who understand labels for boys and girls displayed more knowledge of gender stereotypes than children who did not. Moreover, the mothers of children who mastered these labels endorsed more traditional roles for women as well as for sex roles within the family. These same mothers also initiated and reinforced more sex-typed play with their children (Fagot, Leinbach, & O'Boyle, 1992).

It becomes clear that during early childhood children acquire some sense of the meaning underlying gender stereotypes. When given the opportunity in research settings, 4-year-olds give fierce bears to boys and fluffy kittens to girls. This suggests that cultural associations of objects and qualities with one sex or the other do not depend solely on observing or being taught specific associations, such as dolls are for girls and trucks are for boys. As the researchers concluded:

> Few men keep bears, and cats do not belong only to women. Rather it appears that children, like the rest of us, make inferences on the basis of what they see or know about the nature of things. Children, even at these early ages, may have begun to connect certain qualities with males and other qualities with females. (Fagot, Leinbach & O'Boyle, 1992, p. 229)

gender identity The knowledge that one is male or female, and the ability to make that judgment about other people.

gender constancy The concept that gender is stable and stays the same despite changes in superficial appearance.

Many developmental psychologists believe that children are intrinsically motivated to acquire the values, interests, and behaviors consistent with their own gender. This process is known as *self-socialization*. Children develop concepts of "what boys do" and "what girls do" that might be quite rigid and stereotyped: For example, boys play with cars and don't cry; girls play with dolls and like to dress up. A child will pay more attention to the details of the kinds of behavior that are gender-appropriate and little attention to sex-inappropriate behaviors (Martin & Halverson, 1981).

Do young children actually attend to some things more than to others, and do they remember some things better than others, because they are consistent with their gender schemes? Several studies have indicated that they do. In memory tests, for example, boys tend to remember more of the items that are labeled "boy items" and girls remember more "girl items." Children also make memory errors when a story violates their gender stereotypes. They may remember that a boy was chopping wood when, in fact, a girl was chopping wood in the story. Such results indicate that children's developing gender concepts have a powerful influence on their attention and learning (Martin & Halverson, 1981). During the period when concepts of gender stability and consistency are being developed, children tend to have particularly rigid and stereotyped concepts of sex-appropriate behavior. These concepts and rules become organizers that structure the child's behavior and feelings. If they are violated, children may feel embarrassed, anxious, or uncomfortable. Table 11–3 describes the development of gender schemes during early childhood.

 ## THE FAMILY CONTEXT

Children's developing understanding of gender-appropriate behavior and gender schemes often involves modeling and dramatic play.

The processes described in this chapter do not happen in a void. Rather, they are affected by the immediate household, social forces, and cultural beliefs (Bronfenbrenner, 1979). For most children, the strongest force is the family in which they grow up. Many of the dynamics within the family—interactions with siblings, parenting techniques, the number and spacing of children—have an effect. In addition, social learning will be affected by the structure and circumstances of the family: whether there are two parents or only one, and whether they are employed; whether grandparents or other relatives reside in the household; whether the family lives in a luxurious house in the suburbs or a crowded apartment in the city. If the circumstances of the family undergo major changes or disruptions, a child's social experiences may be markedly altered.

TABLE 11–3 The Development of Gender Schemes Across Early Childhood

LEVELS OF SCHEMES	APPROXIMATE AGE	CHARACTERISTICS OF BEHAVIOR
Gender identity	2 to 5 years	By 2 1/2, children can label people as boys or girls; confusion about the meaning of being a boy or girl; believe gender is changed by surface appearance, for example, changing clothes changes gender.
Gender constancy	5 to 7 years	Understanding that gender is stable and permanent; boys grow up to become daddies or men, girls grow up to become mommies or women; gender is consistent over time and situations.

STYLES OF PARENTING

Parents use a variety of child-rearing techniques, depending on the situation, the child, and the child's behavior at the moment. Ideally, parents limit the child's autonomy and instill values and self-control, while taking care not to undermine the child's curiosity, initiative, or competence. To do this, they must balance the parenting dimensions of control and warmth.

Parental control refers to how restrictive the parents are. Restrictive parents limit their children's freedom to follow their own impulses; they actively enforce compliance with rules and see that children fulfill their responsibilities. In contrast, nonrestrictive parents are less controlling, make fewer demands, and place fewer restraints on their children's behavior and expression of emotions.

Parental warmth refers to the amount of affection and approval the parents display. Warm, nurturing parents smile frequently and give praise and encouragement. They try to restrict their criticisms, punishments, and signs of disapproval. In contrast, hostile parents criticize, belittle, punish, and ignore. They only rarely express affection or approval.

These general styles of parenting affect children's aggression and prosocial behavior, their self-concepts, their internalization of moral values, and their development of social competence (Becker, 1964; Maccoby, 1984).

AUTHORITATIVE, AUTHORITARIAN, AND PERMISSIVE PARENTS
Many researchers in child development have found Diana Baumrind's (1975, 1980) description of parenting styles to be helpful. Baumrind has identified three distinct patterns of parental control: authoritative, authoritarian, and permissive. Although the names "authoritative" and "authoritarian" sound very similar, and despite the fact that both of these types of parents exert firm control over their children's behavior, these styles are markedly different from each other. Both are also radically different from permissive parenting.

Authoritative parents encourage the developing autonomy of their children while at the same time setting reasonable limits.

Authoritative parents combine a high degree of control with warmth, acceptance, and encouragement of the growing autonomy of their children. Although these parents set limits on behavior, they also explain the reasoning behind these limits. Their actions do not seem arbitrary or unfair, and as a result, their children are willing to accept these actions. Authoritative parents are willing to listen to their children's objections and to be flexible when it is appropriate. For example, if a young girl wants to stay out beyond the customary hour, authoritative parents would probably ask her about her reasons for wanting to stay out late, what the circumstances will be (such as, will she be at a friend's house, and will the friend's parents be there?), and whether it will prevent her from carrying out her responsibilities (such as homework or household chores). If her responses meet their standards, authoritative parents would probably allow their daughter the freedom to stay out later than usual.

Authoritarian parents are controlling and adhere rigidly to rules. They tend to be low on warmth, although this is not always the case. In the situation that we just described, these parents would probably refuse their daughter's request with a statement like "A rule is a rule." If the child continued to argue or began to cry, the parents would become angry and might impose a punishment—perhaps even a physical punishment. Authoritarian parents issue commands and expect them to be obeyed; they avoid lengthy verbal exchanges with their children. They behave as if their rules are set in concrete and they are powerless to change them. Trying to gain some independence from such parents can be very frustrating for the child.

Permissive parents are at the opposite extreme from authoritarians: Their parenting style is characterized by few or no restraints placed on the child's behavior. The issue of staying out later than usual would probably not even arise, because there are no curfews in this house, no fixed times for going to bed, and no rule that the child must always keep her parents informed of her whereabouts. Rather than asking her parents if she can stay out later than usual, the young girl might simply tell her parents what she plans to do, or perhaps just let them find out about it afterward. She has plenty of freedom but very little guidance. When permissive parents are annoyed or impatient with their children, they often suppress these feelings. According to Baumrind (1975), many permissive parents are so intent on showing their children "unconditional love" that they fail to perform other important parental functions—in particular, setting limits for their children's behavior.

INDIFFERENT PARENTS Baumrind's permissive parents tend to be warm and accepting of their children. Maccoby and Martin (1983) have defined a fourth parenting style, consisting of parents who are low in restrictiveness and also low in warmth: the **indifferent parents.** These parents don't set limits for their children, either because they just don't care, or because their own lives are so stressful that they don't have enough energy left over to provide guidance for their children. Table 11–4 summarizes the four parenting styles on the basis of parental control and parental warmth.

EFFECTS OF DIFFERENT PARENTING STYLES As shown by Baumrind (1972, 1975) and by a number of later researchers, parenting styles have an impact on the personality of the developing child. Baumrind found that authoritarian parents tend to produce withdrawn, fearful children who exhibit little or no indepen-

authoritative parenting A pattern of parenting that uses firm control with children but encourages communication and negotiation in rule setting within the family.

authoritarian parenting A pattern of parenting that adheres to rigid rule structures and dictates to the children what these rules are; children do not contribute to the decision-making process in the family.

permissive parenting A pattern of parenting in which parents exercise little control over their children but are high in warmth; this can produce negative results in children who may have trouble inhibiting their impulses or deferring gratification.

indifferent parenting A pattern of parenting in which parents are not interested in their role as parents or in their children; indifferent parents exercise little control and demonstrate little warmth toward their children.

TABLE 11–4 Parenting Styles Combining Warmth and Control

Authoritative	High control High warmth	Accept and encourage the growing autonomy of their children Open communication with children; flexible rules; children found to be the best adjusted—most self-reliant, self-controlled, and socially competent; better school performance and higher self-esteem.
Authoritarian	High control Low warmth	Issue commands and expect them to be obeyed; have little communication with children; inflexible rules; allow children to gain little independence from them; children found to be withdrawn, fearful, moody, unassertive, and irritable; girls tend to remain passive and dependent during adolescence; boys may become rebellious and aggressive.
Permissive	Low control High warmth	Few or no restraints on child; unconditional love by parents; communication from child to parent; much freedom and little guidance for children; no setting of limits by parents; children tend to be aggressive and rebellious; also tend to be socially inept, self-indulgent, and impulsive; in some cases, children may be active, outgoing, and creative.
Indifferent	Low control Low warmth	Set no limits for children; lack affection for children; focused on stress in their own lives; no energy left for their children; if indifferent parents also show hostility (as in neglectful parents), children tend to show high expression of destructive impulses and delinquent behavior.

dence and are moody, unassertive, and irritable. In adolescence, these children—particularly the boys—may overreact to the restrictive, punishing environment in which they were reared and may become rebellious and aggressive. The girls are more likely to remain passive and dependent (Kagan & Moss, 1962).

Although permissiveness in parenting is the opposite of restrictiveness, permissiveness does not necessarily produce opposite results: Oddly enough, the children of permissive parents may also be rebellious and aggressive. In addition, they tend to be self-indulgent, impulsive, and socially inept. In some cases, they may be active, outgoing, and creative (Baumrind, 1975; Watson, 1957).

Children of authoritative parents have been found to be the best adjusted. They are the most self-reliant, self-controlled, and socially competent. In the long run, these children develop higher self-esteem and do better in school than those reared with the other parenting styles (Buri et al., 1988; Dornbusch et al., 1987).

The worst outcome is found in the children of indifferent parents. When permissiveness is accompanied by high hostility (the neglectful parent), the child feels free to give rein to his most destructive impulses. Studies of young delinquents show that in many cases their home environments have had exactly this combination of permissiveness and hostility (Bandura & Walters, 1959; McCord, McCord, & Zola, 1959).

NEGOTIATION OR SHARED GOALS   Eleanor Maccoby (1979, 1980) has looked at styles of parenting from a perspective that is similar to Baumrind's, but she has expanded the dimensions of this model. She is concerned not only with the effects of parental behavior on children but also with the effects of children's behavior on parents. Parents, of course, are in a better position than children to control the home environment. But the nature of the interaction between the two affects the climate of family life. In some families, parents are highly controlling. At the other extreme, the children are in control. Neither extreme is healthy.

Ideally, neither parents nor children dominate the family all of the time. Maccoby (1980) focuses on the ways that parents and children interact so as to achieve a balanced relationship. She points out that as children get older, parents need to go through a process of negotiation with them in order to make decisions. It does not always help to be authoritarian or to be permissive. It is better to help the child develop ways of thinking through problems and of learning the give-and-take of getting along with others. This can be done in a warm, supportive atmosphere.

Maccoby is talking about the evolution from parental control to more self-control and self-responsibility by children as they get older. Warmth and emotional support from the parents are important to this evolving relationship because parents engender such feelings in their children. This makes interactions between them easier, even in situations requiring the exercise of authority. As Maccoby (1980) expressed it:

> Parental warmth binds children to their parents in a positive way—it makes children responsive and more willing to accept guidance. If the parent-child relationship is close and affectionate, parents can exercise what control is needed without having to apply heavy disciplinary pressure. It is as if parents' responsiveness, affection, and obvious commitment to their children's welfare have earned them the right to make decisions and exercise control.

Ideally, parents and children come to agree—through long-term dialogue and interaction—on what Maccoby calls *shared goals*. The result is a harmonious atmosphere in which decisions are reached without much struggle for control. Families that enjoy this balance have a fairly high degree of intimacy, and their interaction is stable and mutually rewarding. Families that are unable to achieve shared goals, however, must negotiate everything—from what to have for supper to where to go on vacation. Despite the need for constant discussion, this too can be an effective family style. But if either the parents or the children dominate the situation, there will not be any negotiation, and the family atmosphere will be very unstable. If a parent is highly controlling, preadolescent children soon learn various ways of avoiding the domination. They stay away from home as much as possible. When the children are in control (the parents are permissive and the children are aggressive), the parents avoid the family situation—perhaps by working late. Both of these extremes weaken the socialization process during middle childhood and adolescence; they make it more difficult for children to effect a smooth transition from the family to independence and close peer friendships. As we shall see later in this chapter, peer ties are very important agents of socialization during middle childhood.

Families provide a powerful context for learning attitudes, beliefs, and appropriate behavior—sometimes down to the last detail of posture and dress.

sibling status Birth order.

SIBLINGS

The first, and probably the closest, peer group that affects children's personality development is their siblings (their brothers and sisters). Sibling relationships provide experiences for the child that are different from parent-child interactions—they are like "living in the nude, psychologically speaking" (Bossard & Boll, 1960, p. 91). The down-to-earth openness of brothers and sisters gives siblings a chance (whether they want it or not) to experience the ups and downs of human relationships on the most basic level. Siblings can be devotedly loyal to one another, despise one another, and/or form an intense love-hate relationship that may continue throughout their lives. Even when children are far apart in age, they are directly affected by the experience of living with others who are both equal (as other children in the same family) and unequal (differing in age, size, competence, intelligence, attractiveness, and so on). Indeed, siblings are important in helping one another to identify social concepts and social roles by reciprocally prompting and inhibiting certain patterns of behavior (Dunn, 1983, 1985).

What influence do brothers and sisters have on one another? And how does birth order, or **sibling status,** affect each child's personality? Although previous generations of psychologists have devoted much speculation to the effects on personality of being oldest, youngest, or in the middle, current research does not consistently support these views. In fact, no consistent personality differences have been found solely as a consequence of birth order. This does not mean, however, that the children in a family are similar in personality. In fact, siblings raised in the same family are likely to have very different personalities—almost as different as unrelated children (Plomin & Daniels, 1987). One reason for this is that children have a need to establish distinct identities for themselves (Dreikurs & Soltz, 1964). Thus, if an older sibling is serious and studious, the younger one may be boisterous. A girl who has four sisters and no brothers may carve out her own niche in the family by taking on a masculine role. We can see some of the interactions between personality and birth order presented in Figure 11–2.

Although birth order seems to have few clear, consistent, and predictable effects on personality, many studies have found effects on intelligence and achievement; here, the oldest child clearly has the edge. On the average, oldest children have higher IQs and achieve more in school and in careers. Only children are also high achievers, although their IQs tend to be slightly lower, on the average, than the oldest child in a family of two or three children (Zajonc & Markus, 1975). One explanation for this finding is that only children never have the opportunity to serve as teachers for their younger siblings. Serving as a teacher may enhance a child's intellectual development (Zajonc & Hall, 1986). We should note here that this will become significant when we discuss cooperative learning in the next chapter. In cooperative learning, children of all intellectual abilities work jointly on classroom projects. As the children serve as teachers for each other, it is believed that intellectual development is stimulated.

Nonetheless, differences in IQ based on birth order tend to be small. Larger and more consistent differences appear when researchers look at family size. The more children there are in a family, the lower are their IQs and the less likely they are to graduate from high school. This is true even when other factors, such as family structure and income, are taken into account (Blake, 1989). But note that family structure (whether there are two parents or one) and income do have

FIGURE 11–2
Personality Characteristics and Birth Order

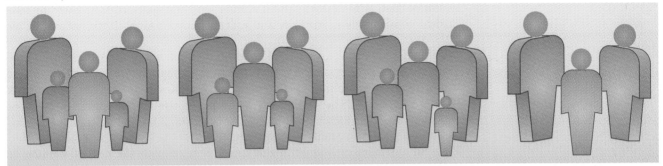

First-born (oldest) child	Second-born (middle) child(ren)	Last-born (youngest) child	Only child
TYPICAL FAMILY ENVIRONMENT			
Has parents' undivided attention; is dethroned by second-born and shares attention.	*Has model or pace-setter in older siblings; must share attention from the beginning.*	*Has several models; receives much attention; has many helpers; although she must share, she is not displaced and is often pampered.*	*Receives parents' undivided attention; in absence of siblings, is often pampered.*
POTENTIAL FAVORABLE OUTCOME			
Assumes responsibility; protects and cares for others.	*Is ambitious; has social interests; is likely to be more sociable than oldest or youngest— but may become a "black sheep."*	*With much stimulation and many chances to compete, often outperforms other siblings.*	*Takes more responsibility earlier.*
POTENTIAL UNFAVORABLE OUTCOME			
Feels anxious and insecure; is afraid of reversals of fortune; is overly conservative and concerned with rules and laws.	*Is rebellious and envious; attempts to surpass others.*	*Feels inferior to everyone; because of indulgence may become problem child.*	*Wants to be the center of attention; is afraid of competition with others; feels own position is right and any challenge is unfair.*

strong effects on IQ and achievement—effects that are noticeably greater than those of birth order or number of siblings (Ernst & Angst, 1983).

Firstborns are only children for a year or more; they have their parents' exclusive attention. Then a baby sibling comes along, displacing them from their position of unique importance. Although reactions to the new baby vary, few children show outright hostility to the newcomer—at least at first. They are likely to be very curious about the baby and to direct any hostility toward the mother, often by getting into mischief just when she is feeding or diapering the baby (Dunn, 1985). They may also regress to infantile behavior such as thumb-sucking or wetting their pants. This reaction has been interpreted by psychoanalysts as a defense mechanism, indicating disguised anxiety. More recently, theorists have interpreted it as simple imitation, reflecting interest in the baby, or as a way of competing with the baby for the mother's attention. In any case, the infantile behavior is only temporary. By the end of the new baby's first year, it is the younger child who is doing the imitating, and the older child is likely to have gained considerably in maturity and independence (Dunn, 1985; Stewart et al., 1987).

Older siblings are powerful models; research suggests that children with older siblings of the same sex tend to show stronger sex-typed behavior than those with older siblings of the opposite sex (Koch, 1956; Sutton-Smith & Rosenberg, 1970). The spacing between siblings also has an important effect on sibling status. The closer in age, the more intense is the influence of the sibling relationship (Sutton-Smith & Rosenberg, 1970).

In any case, each child in the family is faced with the task of forming an individual self-concept.

DISCIPLINE AND SELF-REGULATION

In different cultural groups and in different historical periods, techniques of discipline have varied widely. There have been periods of harsh physical punishment and periods of relative permissiveness. Methods of disciplining children—setting rules and limits and enforcing those limits—are subject to changes in fashion just like other aspects of culture.

The child-rearing literature of the 1950s and early 1960s warned against strong, overbearing disciplinary methods; parents worried about stifling their children's emotions and turning them into anxious, repressed, neurotic people. The literature of the 1970s and 1980s, in contrast, pointed out that children need a sufficient amount of external social control, firmness, and consistency in order to feel safe and secure.

So far, the 1990s seem to be continuing the trend toward firm parental control. Of course, children's need for affection and approval is also recognized. Six guidelines have been offered to achieve current child-rearing goals (Perry & Bussey, 1984). Parents are advised to:

1. Foster an atmosphere of warmth, caring, and mutual support among family members. Affection, like other social behaviors, tends to be reciprocated. Children who are generally happy and content show more self-control and behave in more mature and prosocial ways;
2. concentrate more on promoting desirable behaviors than on eliminating undesirable ones. They should make a deliberate attempt to suggest, model, and reward children's helping and caring behaviors;
3. set realistic expectations and demands, firmly enforce their demands, and be consistent;
4. avoid the unnecessary use of power assertion—the use of force and threats to control children's behavior. Power assertion fosters similar behavior in children and may cause anger, bitterness, and resistance;
5. help children gain a sense of control over themselves and their environment;
6. use verbal reasoning (induction) to help children develop an understanding of social rules.

Children need to know the consequences of their behavior, including how other people will feel. They should also have the opportunity to discuss or explain their actions to their parents. This helps them develop a sense of responsibility for their behavior. In the long run, self-regulated behavior is determined by children's understanding of the situation.

Balancing children's need for firmness and consistency with their need for warmth and approval is a difficult job for a parent. In Chapter 14 we will look more closely at this issue.

THE EFFECTS OF TELEVISION

Television is not simply an electronic toy or one of many forms of entertainment: It is a pervasive influence in the lives of children—one that has had a major impact on family relationships and traditions. In 1950, only 1 family in 20 had a television set. Ten years later, television was found in about 90 percent of American homes. Today 98 percent of families have at least one television set; some have three or four. Children now spend more time watching television than doing anything else, except sleeping (Fabes et al., 1989; Huston et al., 1989). In 1993, the average child watches approximately 7 1/2 hours of television per day (Bennett, 1993).

Given how much time children spend watching television, many authorities have wondered what effects this is having on their development. Concern has focused on three aspects of television viewing: the content of programs and commercials, the rapid-fire visual format, and the way in which television is used in the home (Rubinstein, 1983).

PROGRAM CONTENT

Television is a major socializing force in our society. Many have concluded that by exposing children to a large amount of casual violence on the screen, we are teaching them to think of aggression as a commonplace and acceptable outlet for their own frustrations. Others have taken the opposite view: They have argued that viewing violent acts on television may serve as a substitute for overt aggression, with the result that actual aggression is diminished rather than increased (Feshbach & Singer, 1971). Although this second theory is appealing, research does not support it. A large number of studies have shown that exposure to televised violence produces a small but significant *increase* in the aggressiveness of viewers (Huston et al., 1989; Heath, 1989).

The effects of television, however, are not that simple. Children frequently do not understand everything they see on television, and they do not pay attention to or absorb shows they do not understand (Anderson et al., 1981). Some of the effects of what children do see and seem to understand may be moderated if a parent or other adult explains and comments on what is happening (Collins et al., 1981). Additionally, children are not merely watching "meaningless violence." Every cartoon and drama has a variety of characters, scenes, and situations.

Let us consider a single child fascinated by a single program. A Mickey Mouse cartoon, for example, shows a tiny mouse somehow managing to outwit

Does television teach that aggression is an acceptable response to frustration? Both parents and the government are becoming increasingly concerned about the effects of television violence on children.

the big bullies of the world. In a western show, the marshal usually gets the troublemakers and justice prevails. Violence in the service of the simple themes of such programs—provided children understand the themes—does very little damage to most children. But for some children, habitual television viewing of aggressive programs may be combined with an environment in which many of the available role models—parents, siblings, or friends—are also aggressive or antisocial. This combination seems to escalate aggressive behavior, especially in children with certain personality traits or emotional problems (Huesmann et al., 1984; Heath, 1989).

Many other aspects of program content will affect children. Often, certain kinds of people are presented in a stereotyped fashion: Members of minority groups may be depicted in unfavorable ways, women may be shown in passive, sexualized, or subordinate roles, and old people may be made to appear senile or burdensome. As a result, children can develop unrealistic social beliefs and concepts. Even their overall view of the world may be affected. One study found that heavy television viewing caused people to see the world as a mean and scary place—probably because there are more frightening incidents on television than occur in most children's everyday experience (Rubinstein, 1983). Much of this data prompted the American Academy of Pediatrics in 1993 to suggest that children younger than age 5 should watch *no* television. Children from 5 to 10 should watch limited amounts, and only in the company of a parent who interprets the program's message.

Despite the numerous studies that have shown negative effects of television viewing, the medium can also have a positive influence on children's thoughts and actions. Television can teach children many forms of prosocial behavior. Carefully designed children's programs are able to interweave many different themes, such as cooperation, sharing, affection, friendship, persistence at tasks, control of aggression, and coping with frustration. Children who have seen these programs for even relatively short periods of time become more cooperative, sympathetic, and nurturant (Stein & Friedrich, 1975). Gender-role stereotyping is beginning to decrease in television programming. Some shows now depict men and women in nontraditional roles—women working outside the home, men doing housework. Children who watch such shows have been found to have more flexible gender-role concepts (Rosenwasser et al., 1989).

TELEVISION FORMAT

Unlike other "members of the family," the television set is not responsive or interactive. Television is characterized by rapid-fire visual and auditory stimulation, and visual techniques like zooms, cuts, and special effects. These techniques can be used creatively to capture the child's attention and to structure an educational message, or they can bombard the senses, demanding little thoughtful response on the part of the child. One reviewer suggests that children pay attention to minor superficial impressions but fail to follow much of the storyline or understand much of the content (Winn, 1983). Others have found that the format can be quite stimulating—it can capture children's attention and create heightened arousal (Rubinstein, 1983; Wright & Huston, 1983).

Both the content and the format of television may influence children's development.

Although many critics have claimed that the fast-paced, attention-getting stimulation shortens children's attention span and makes them less able to pay attention in other environments, such as the classroom, there is as yet no solid evidence to support this view (Anderson & Collins, 1988). However, too much television takes up time children would otherwise spend reading, playing, and interacting with adults in their environments. In this way, especially with its multisensory stimulation, it may encourage passive learning and limit thinking, which is damaging to children's intellectual abilities in the long-run.

In some ways, and for some children, television might actually advance cognitive development. The children who watch the most television tend to be from low-income or minority-group families. For such children, television can serve as a source of information that they would otherwise have no way of obtaining. If they watch shows like "Sesame Street" and "Mr. Roger's Neighborhood," they will pick up many of the skills, concepts, facts, and vocabulary taught on these shows (see the box "Programs Designed for Young Viewers"). As one review summed up, "Even a skeptical interpretation of the data concluded that children learned letter and number skills from unaided viewing" (Huston et al., 1989, p. 425).

Some authorities are concerned that the stimulating format of television might capture children's attention so completely that they sit mesmerized in front of the screen. This fear, too, appears to be exaggerated for most preschoolers. Although some sources claim that children watch as much as 30 hours of television a week, this figure is misleading because it refers to the amount of time the television set is turned on. Preschoolers sit in front of the television for 2 to 3 hours per day. However, during this time preschoolers generally do not sit and stare at the screen; in fact, they are looking at the screen only about half the time. The rest of the time they are in and out of the room, engaging in other activities, and talking to parents and siblings. Much of this talk is about the program they are watching (Anderson & Collins, 1988; Huston et al., 1989). The bigger problem with time spent in front of the television—at least in terms of cognitive development—is for older children who actually do watch the television for greatly extended periods of time.

FOCUS ON AN ISSUE

PROGRAMS DESIGNED FOR YOUNG VIEWERS

Across the nation, 1- to 4-year-old children sit in front of their television sets every day watching the rapid-fire sequences of "Sesame Street" flash before their eyes. They see Big Bird on roller skates one minute, Cookie Monster counting to 10 the next, and Ernie and Bert singing a duet the next. Some developmental psychologists have expressed concerns about the effects of these constantly changing sequences. They fear that a regular diet of this kind of viewing may shorten children's attention span and lessen their ability to reflect on and retain new information.

> *"One study found that children have negative attitudes toward parents who refuse to buy them a heavily advertised toy."*

There is, at present, no evidence that watching these shows has any harmful effects on children's cognitive development. On the contrary, it has been shown that children can learn a great deal from them. Shows like "Sesame Street" and "Mr. Roger's Neighborhood" are carefully designed for the cognitive capacities of young children. These programs use the same kind of language that mothers use when they speak to toddlers and preschoolers:

simple sentences, frequent repetitions, a restricted vocabulary, and an emphasis on the here and now (Rice & Haight, 1986). Television programs designed for teenagers or adults are likely to go over the heads of younger children, but preschoolers are quite capable of understanding the programs that are designed for their own age group (Anderson & Collins, 1988). Watching "Sesame Street" is associated with improved vocabulary and prereading skills in preschoolers. Watching "Mr. Roger's Neighborhood" has been found to increase prosocial behavior and imaginative play. A program called "Reading Rainbow," designed for school-age children, has been successful in encouraging reading and the use of libraries (Huston et al., 1989).

Those are examples of television at its best. Television at its worst frightens children and gives them nightmares, provides them with models for aggressive and irresponsible behavior, and exploits children's naiveté in order to turn them into greedy little consumers. Because older children and adults have learned not to believe everything they see on television, many commercials are expressly aimed at younger children. Preschoolers are often unable to distinguish commercials from the programs that precede and follow them, and they do not understand that the purpose of commercials is simply to sell them

something. They are easily deceived by misleading advertising (Huston et al., 1989). When a commercial succeeds in motivating the child to say, "I want one of those" or "I want some of that," many parents wisely say no. This often leads to a conflict between the parent and the child. One study found that children have negative attitudes toward parents who refuse to buy them a heavily advertised toy (Fabes et al., 1989).

Many children are frightened by horror programs they see on television; the effects of such experiences may be short-lived or may last for days or months. Older children can be helped to deal with frightening material by being reminded, "It's not real—it's only a show." However, this technique does not work with preschoolers, perhaps because they are unable to hold onto the idea "It's not real" at the same time that they are watching a highly arousing program (Cantor & Wilson, 1988). Generations of children have listened with a mixture of delight and fear to scary stories like "Little Red Riding Hood" and "Hansel and Gretel," and have suffered no permanent psychological harm. But horror movies shown on television may be too graphic—too visually compelling—for children who are not old enough to understand that films are "not real." For this age group, the Cookie Monster is scary enough.

At its best, television can be an educational tool that can expand the horizons of children and encourage them to break away from stereotyped images. The attention-getting, high-action, rapid-pace techniques can help children focus on the information to be learned and seem to do no harm to their cognitive development (Greenfield, 1984; Wright & Huston, 1983). However, these compelling techniques cannot be duplicated in the classroom and many teachers find themselves frustrated by children who passively wait for education to occur.

SUMMARY AND CONCLUSIONS

Three theoretical perspectives—the psychodynamic, social learning, and cognitive development perspectives—provide frameworks for the study of personality and social development during early childhood. The period between 2 to 6 years of age is associated with major transitions in the child's socialization. Children learn norms and rules of their culture or society; they develop a self-concept which will sustain them throughout life; and they form a set of defense mechanisms which they will use when confronting stress or anxiety.

A key developmental issue of the preschool years is that of handling emotions or feelings. These defense mechanisms assist them in exhibiting the emotions their culture deems appropriate. By the age of 5 or 6 most children use a mixture of defense mechanisms when under stress. A danger of such defenses, however, is that they can isolate the child from reality. During the preschool years, it is the role of parents to assist their children in limiting stress. When stress is unavoidable, parents provide a secure base for their children.

In general, our society frowns on uninhibited displays of either positive or negative emotions. Children need to learn to control their joy, as well as their anger. In addition, they must balance their need for autonomy and independence with the dependency and love needs that they have for their parents. Socialization is a process which naturally produces anxiety in the involved parties.

Aggressive and prosocial behaviors are learned as complex patterns during the preschool years. One of the primary goals of socialization is to teach children ways to channel their aggressive feelings. Frustration, for example, may lead some children to become aggressive. But aggression is also learned by imitating or identifying with models (either powerful role models or parents who use physical punishment), or through parents, peers, or others who reward a child's aggressive behavior.

Prosocial behavior, which includes sharing, helping, and so on, is also learned from identifying with models or through a system of rewards and punishments. Some theorists believe that gender differences in prosocial behavior occur because girls are more likely to be rewarded for nurturing. Therefore, they become more sensitive to the needs and concerns of others. Modeling is most effective in producing prosocial behavior when the model is perceived as similar by the children or when the model is powerful, competent, and supportive. Induction and role playing are other manners by which prosocial behavior develops.

Children also learn behaviors from each other. In peer relationships, children model and reinforce each other for what they consider appropriate behaviors. Children who are popular with their peers during the preschool years are likely to remain so in later childhood; children who are bullies in preschool become aggressive older children. Children who lack social skills in early childhood may be aggressive or withdrawn in later childhood and adolescence.

Socialization is also designed to teach children the concepts and rules of the society in which they live. Children absorb moral standards and values by internalizing society's rules. As these rules are internalized, children develop the self-control necessary to regulate their own behavior. As children mature, their disputes are characterized by the ability to take another's perspective and by the use of words rather than physical intervention to resolve conflicts.

Gender schemes are derived from socialization and genetically based sex differences. By the age of 2 1/2, most children can identify themselves and others as male or female. By the age 5 to 7, the child acquires the notion of gender as fixed for a lifetime, despite appearances. Gender schemes help children organize which behaviors they will remember and choose to imitate.

Children also grow and develop in the context of families. Siblings and parents form the first reference group for children. The warmth and control exercised by parents, as well as the basic style of parenting they use affects the child's personality and social development. The child's position in the family structure, the number of children in the family, and the child's basic personality all influence his or her IQ and achievement level. Children from the same family may show widely differing personalities because of their individual efforts to assert their own uniqueness.

Parents and the discipline they employ in raising their children also have a significant impact on the child's personality, self-esteem, and desire to achieve. An atmosphere of warmth, caring, and firm control within the family—with the parents serving as authoritative guides for the child's behavior—appears to be most conducive to a child's learning self-discipline and self-regulation. Parents use of verbal reasoning also encourages children to develop an understanding of social rules and expectations.

One key ingredient in the cognitive and interpersonal skills of today's children is television. Recent research suggests that toddlers watch 2 to 3 hours of television per day, with older children watching over 7 hours on the average. Exposure to televised violence increases aggression, but certain programming has been found to increase prosocial behavior and also assist in developing school-related skills. Recently, however, the American Academy of Pediatrics has suggested drastically limiting children's television watching because of its contribution to violence, passive learning, and decreased reading ability. Nevertheless, for children from disadvantaged homes, television can become a good source of information, as well as increase their vocabularies and letter and number skills.

As with any aspect of the social environment, moderation appears to be the key in parental control, television watching, and peer interactions during the preschool years. Children need time for the growth of self and social understanding to take place—and a safe base from which their initial explorations of the world may occur.

➤ KEY TERMS AND CONCEPTS

aggression	dependency	induction	regression
anxiety	displacement	internalization	repression
assertive behavior	fear	permissive parenting	role playing
authoritative parenting	frustration	projection	sibling status
authoritarian parenting	gender constancy	prosocial behavior	social reciprocity
defense mechanisms	gender identity	rationalization	withdrawal
denial	indifferent parenting	reaction formation	

➤ SELF-TEST QUESTIONS

1. List three main theories that address the socialization of the child.

2. Discuss the sources of anxiety. Compare and contrast fear and anxiety in the preschool child.

3. What are defense mechanisms? List several different types employed by children.

4. Discuss different strategies that children might use to cope with anxiety and stress.

5. List several of the strong feelings that preschool children begin to deal with and the ways they learn to handle these feelings.

6. Discuss the developmental conflicts that children must resolve during the preschool years.

7. Compare aggressive, assertive, and prosocial behavior. Discuss several of the explanations that have been given for these types of behavior.

8. What is social reciprocity?

9. List six different levels of interaction in young children. At what age do these levels apply?

10. What is internalization, and how does it relate to a child's developing self-regulation?

11. What are gender schemes, and how do they apply to socialization?

12. How do parenting styles used by parents affect children's personality and social development during middle childhood?

13. How do sibling relationships affect the personality development of a child?

14. List six guidelines that help to achieve current child-rearing goals.

15. How is television a major socializing force in our society?

➤ SUGGESTED READINGS

DAMON, W. *The moral child: Nurturing children's natural moral growth*. New York: Free Press, 1991. Approaches to moral education, both at home and in the community, are clearly and concisely linked to the normal course of moral development as it is formed in infancy through adolescence.

LEWIS, M. *Shame: The exposed self*. New York: Free Press, 1991. This "history of shame" as a human response during infancy and early childhood looks at the many ways in which shame is induced and expressed, reacted to, and handled.

LIEBERT, R. M., & SPRAKEN, J. N. *The early window: Effects of television on children and youth* (3rd Ed.). Elmsford, NY: Pergamon, 1988. An updated readable review of the theory and research on the positive and negative effects of television.

PALEY, Y. G. *The boy who would be a helicopter: The uses of storytelling in the classroom*. Cambridge. MA: Harvard University Press, 1990. An engaging account of one boy's odyssey from social isolation to integration woven within an insightful essay on excellent early childhood education.

SINGER, D. G., & SINGER, J. L. *The house of make-believe: Children's play and the developing imagination*. Cambridge, MA: Harvard University Press, 1990. A comprehensive review of children's evolving fantasy play and its function in child development.

VIDEO CASE: TELEVISION CARTOONS—A SPECIAL CASE?

Under a new system agreed to by the television networks on June 30, 1993, listings in newspapers and magazines will include a violence warning for certain specific programs. These warnings will also be listed in the body of a show when appropriate, for example, after a station break. But one type of show is not covered in this agreement—cartoons—although it is estimated that while there are five acts of violence per hour during prime time, there are fifteen acts of violence per hour on Saturday morning cartoons. Why then did the networks exclude cartoons from their agreement?

In the view of Christine Hikawa, ABC television vice president, cartoons are a special case. Explains Hikawa:

> We have child development experts on our staff who tell us a couple of things about cartoons. One, when children see animation, they distance themselves from it a little bit. It's comedic, it's fantasy to them. Our cartoon characters are primarily animals, Sylvester the cat chasing Tweety Bird—it's a cat and a bird. Children understand that in nature cats chase birds. The same with Tom and Jerry—a cat chasing a mouse. They also understand that they are not superheroes, that they can't see

through metal and they can't fly. And that is why we believe cartoons are not part of this.

But what about Saturday morning television's Darkwing Duck and the Wild West cowboys of Moo Mesa? Aren't they far more violent than Tom and Jerry?

No, says Ms. Hikawa. "Well the cowboys of Moo Mesa are cows," she notes, "and their guns shoot stars. We don't consider this to be realistic violence that is both very upsetting and desensitizing to children."

Nevertheless, some effort has been made to deal with cartoon violence. According to the Children's Television Act, stations will lose their license if they fail to reduce the number of cartoons and increase their educational and informational programming. However, as one critic pointed out, in forty-five years of television, only one station ever lost its license. In other words, it is highly doubtful that Congress or the FCC will enforce this law.

CASE QUESTIONS

1. Do you believe that television cartoons negatively affect young children? Why or why not?

2. Has enough been done to limit the possible negative effects on young children of television cartoons? Why or why not? What do you suggest should be done?

12 ▶ Physical Development in Middle Childhood

"The rapid spurt of physical growth that we saw in infancy and toddlerhood slows in the preschool period and remains slow during middle childhood; it doesn't speed up again until early adolescence."

Still, children continue to develop the speed, strength, and coordination that are necessary for gross motor skills. This is the period when many children seem to become obsessed with sports and stunts showing off their newfound physical prowess. Fine motor skills are also growing quickly during middle childhood. Indeed, most of the skills needed for writing develop during the sixth and seventh years.

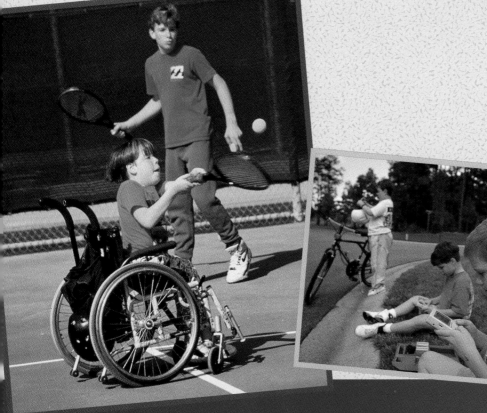

13 Middle Childhood: Cognitive Development and School Tasks

"The fact that so many cultures have chosen the ages from 5 to 7 years for beginning the systematic education of their young is probably no historical accident. Between ages 5 and 7, many of children's cognitive, language, and perceptual-motor skills mature and interact in a way that makes some kinds of learning easier and more efficient."

During this period, children make the transition from preoperational to concrete operation thought. This developmental task requires years of manipulating and learning about the materials and objects in their environment. From this experience, children acquire a more sophisticated form of thinking.

14 Middle Childhood: Personality and Social Development

"Perhaps the rituals and rules of middle childhood are practice for adulthood, exercises in learning the detailed behavior that is expected of adults."

Although experts may be unsure about the precise reasons for the traditions of middle childhood, they do know that in nearly every society a special culture of childhood apparently exists. Clearly, parenting styles and peer group relationships affect the development of a child's personality within the specific culture of childhood.

Then the child turned ten times
round the seasons
Skated over ten years frozen
streams
Words like "when you're older"
must appease him
...and promises of someday
make his dreams.

JONI MITCHELL,
"THE CIRCLE GAME"

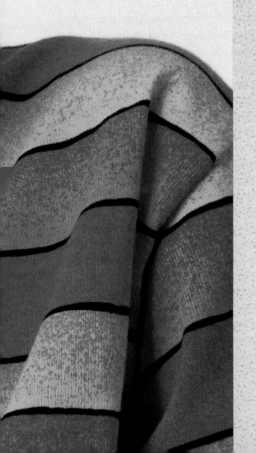

PHYSICAL DEVELOPMENT IN MIDDLE CHILDHOOD

CHAPTER OBJECTIVES

By the time you have finished this chapter, you should be able to do the following:

✔ Discuss the physical development of the school-aged child.

✔ Describe the changes in fine motor and gross motor skills during middle childhood.

✔ Describe the role of vigorous play in child health and motor development.

✔ Explain rough-and-tumble play and its role in social development for boys.

✔ Identify the major health and safety concerns for school-aged children.

✔ Explain the causes and consequences of obesity in middle childhood.

✔ Discuss appropriate accommodations schools can make to provide an effective educational and social environment for the physically challenged student.

✔ Identify some key goals for physical education in the elementary school.

Juan and Jimmy, best friends aged 10, are on summer vacation. As soon as Jimmy is up in the morning he runs up the stairs to Juan's apartment, and they are out the door in seconds. They go down the block to the black-topped playground where a basketball game is already underway. The older boys playing refuse to let them into the game. Somewhat dejected, they wander away but find water gushing from an open fire hydrant. They decide to spend some time playing there. In the afternoon, there is the flag pole by the factory whose rope children have for years used as a ride—first, you grab the rope and climb to the roof of the one story building; then you hold the rope and jump, and swing round and round the pole until you fly off. They manage to complete one revolution before the security guard angrily chases them away. They run all the way home when they see older gang members beginning to gather on the corners. Finally, very tired, they climb the stairs to their apartments just as the street lights are coming on.

School-aged children have considerable energy and creative capacities with which to explore their world. Middle childhood refers to the period from 6 to 12 years—the play and industry years during which children refine their motor and cognitive abilities and become more independent. They begin to branch out from their families and interact more with peers. Friendship patterns become more established and valued. Children are able to plan and carry out activities in sequence that easily fill their days—as Juan and Jimmy presented above do. In addition, given appropriate training, school-age children are able to learn to swim, ski, dance, or play a musical instrument—as well as many other difficult motor abilities they are given the opportunity to learn.

Middle childhood is also a time of increased responsibility. In societies around the world, children of this age are introduced to the tasks and roles of the adult world in a more formal way. In industrial societies, this means school and academic learning for several hours each day. In tribal cultures, the "schooling" may mean an apprenticeship in the gender-specific roles of hunting, gathering, cooking, or weaving (Rogoff, 1990).

School-aged children have new physical abilities and coordination they constantly use. Running, jumping, and hopping skills become more mature. New sports such as soccer, baseball, or tennis are now open to children because of their motor skills. Group sports assume significance since sufficient numbers of individual children now have the talent to participate—both boys and girls. Many children show an intense interest in acquiring and improving the skills necessary to participate in such team sports.

The environments where children live give them the opportunity to learn and practice motor skills. Some children during middle childhood have had a wealth of experiences behind them which have allowed them to develop diverse skills. Special classes and activities such as dance, music, art, or organized sports may have also provided them with instruction and feedback which have made their efforts more efficient and effective. Other children may have spent time running and playing without instruction or organized activities. They may have developed stamina and the ability to plan their own activities and create their own fun which the more formal experiences have not encouraged. In either case, the physical development of middle childhood provides children with the readiness to move into more complex or group activities for which their early childhood experiences prepared them.

As we mentioned, in Chapter 9, it is important for us to remember that physical, cognitive, and social factors interact to produce individual development. For purposes of clarity, we are focusing in this chapter on physical development, but the various domains of development cannot really be disentangled. When we look at Juan and Jimmy—or other school-aged children—building a fort, or working on building a model, or painting a picture, it is difficult to determine if their growing cognitive skills allow them to plan daily activities or if their new physical abilities allow them to think of new things to do. Because of their new cognitive abilities, for example, they are able to focus their attention for longer periods of time, anticipate the next moves others will make, and monitor the strategies each uses. These skills clearly influence the activities in which they may successfully engage. In either case, the interaction of thinking and action during these years is clear.

In this chapter, we shall present the changes in physical characteristics and motor skills exhibited by children in these middle years of childhood. We shall discuss the special health and nutrition needs of school-aged children and the psychological impact of problems in these areas. Rough-and-tumble play as a special form of children's vigorous play will then be presented. Finally, we shall discuss the physical environment of the school as it reflects—or in some cases frustrates—children's motor development.

Their enhanced motor skills and coordination open the door for school-aged children to participate in sports such as tennis.

 ## PHYSICAL GROWTH AND CHANGE

As we look at the various aspects of physical development during middle childhood, we can recognize that children follow a similar sequential process. However, each also emerges as a unique individual. Not all children mature at the same rate. Great variation exists in individual development, and this variability increases with age and experience throughout the school years. Some children may be more mature in certain areas than others. For example, one child may have mature physical and motor development for her age and yet be functioning socially at a less advanced level. Another may be socially and cognitively advanced but lag behind peers in motor skills.

PHYSICAL GROWTH DURING MIDDLE CHILDHOOD

In tracing growth changes in children during middle childhood, the variation in rate of growth of various parts and systems of the body that were initially presented in Chapter 9 during early childhood continue. At certain times the growth rate is accelerated while at other times it is relatively steady. We see the typical profile of growth for one boy presented in Figure 12–1. In general, there is a fairly steady increase in height during middle childhood which varies from the more rapid pace of growth during infancy and adolescence. From year to year, for the individual child, spurts and slower growth periods alternate. Annual gains are high during infancy, decreasing to a relatively stable 2 to 3 inches a year during middle childhood. From 5 to 6 years, for example, there is a stretching up in height and loss of baby fat. During adolescence, a growth spurt occurs that establishes the individual's final height, which stays uniform throughout adulthood.

Variability occurs in the timing and extent to which growth occurs during childhood. This may be influenced by the environment in which children live, their nutrition, their gender, and basic characteristics inherited from their parents and grandparents. Girls, for example, are slightly shorter and lighter than boys until age 9, when girls' growth accelerates because of hormonal changes that occur earlier in girls than boys. A girl's growth begins to outpace a boy's growth at that age. We also see that some girls are structurally smaller than other girls. These overall differences in height may affect the child's body image and self-concept—another way in which physical, social, and cognitive development interact.

During middle childhood, therefore, as we can see, growth is slower and more regular than during the first 2 years of life. The average 6-year-old weighs 45 pounds and is 3 1/2 feet fall. As children enter school, they are in a steady

FIGURE 12–1
The Height of a Boy at Various Ages.
(Source: Cratty, B. (1986). Perceptual and Motor Development in Infants and Children. Englewood Cliffs, NJ: Prentice Hall, p. 52.)

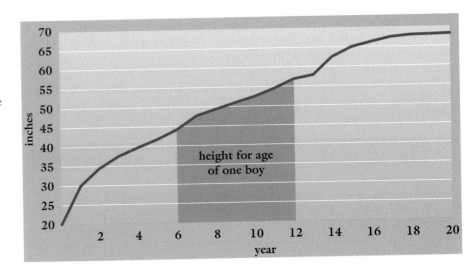

period of growth that continues to around 9 years of age for girls and 11 years for boys, when the adolescent growth spurt begins. Figure 12-2 shows pictorially the changes in body size and proportion typical of middle childhood.

This period of fairly stable increase in height and weight during middle childhood is associated with a parallel increase in the performance of motor skills. All children will become less awkward and more accomplished in activities such as running, jumping, and hopping during this period. However, children who are taller in stature will gain the mechanical advantage of their longer limbs, which may account for some of the variability observed in children's motor skill performance (Nichols, 1990).

INTERNAL CHANGES

As the body grows in the observable dimensions of height and weight, there are also internal changes associated with this growth. During middle childhood, for example, skeletal maturation continues. The long bones of the body lengthen and broaden, and ligaments grow but are not yet firmly attached to the bone. This gives school-aged children considerable flexibility in their body movements— although recent research has found that children are less flexible from 5 to 8 years than they were from 3 to 4. In addition, girls are slightly more flexible than boys at all times during childhood (Koslow, 1987). Many adults have marveled at the 8-year-old who is able to sit on the floor with her feet casually hooked around her neck, or the 9-year-old boy who can sit with legs bent out from the knees at a 45-degree angle.

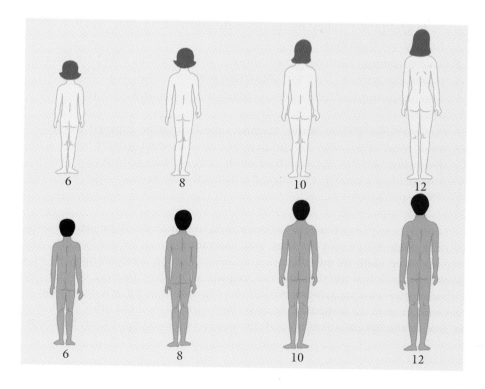

FIGURE 12–2
During middle childhood, there are tremendous variations in growth patterns, but these changes in body size and proportion are typical of this period.

Although both boys and girls of school age show considerable flexibility in their body movements, girls are slightly more flexible than boys.

SKELETAL MATURITY   In middle childhood, bones grow longer as the body lengthens and broadens. But the ligaments are not yet firmly attached. Since the skeleton is not yet mature, early physical training which is overly rigorous may have negative consequences. Many Little League pitchers, for example, have injured their shoulders and elbows. Other young children have suffered wrist, ankle, and knee injuries in their sports or jungle gym activities. Other children suffer from growing pains. These episodes of stiffness and aching caused by skeletal growth are particularly common at nighttime and may be quite painful. Some rapidly growing children experience these as early as 4 years of age. For others they emerge at adolescence. In either case, they are normal physical responses to growth, which should be explained to children in that manner (Sheiman & Slomin, 1988; Nichols, 1990).

Another area of skeletal growth more obvious in school-aged children occurs in their teeth. Beginning at 6 to 7 years of age, children lose all 20 of their primary teeth. When the first few permanent teeth grow in, they often look too big for their mouths until facial growth catches up. Two of the more noticeable landmarks of middle childhood are the toothless smile of a 6-year-old, followed by the "beaver-toothed" grin of an eight-year-old.

As was mentioned earlier with regard to height and weight, there is considerable variability in children's rate of skeletal maturity. Falkner (1962), for example, proposed six different patterns of maturation which are still discussed today. These include:

1. An average child who will closely approximate the mean curve for height and weight at stated ages.
2. Early-maturing children who are tall in childhood only because they are more mature than the average; they will not become unusually tall adults.
3. Early-maturing children who are also genetically taller than average from early childhood. They mature rapidly and remain taller than average throughout their lives.
4. Late-maturing children who are short in childhood but who later evidence reasonable growth. They will not remain unusually small in adulthood.
5. Late-maturing children who are genetically short and who remain short adults.
6. An indefinite group, whose members must often be exposed to medical evaluation. They may be children whose adolescent growth spurt starts unusually early, by the eighth or ninth year, or their growth may evidence unusual delay and be the cause for parental and medical concern (Cratty, 1986, p. 58).

From these patterns we may see that skeletal maturity may be used to assess not only children's present maturity, but also future problems and benefits. The early-maturing child in middle childhood may become a valued member of a sports team and therefore become the recipient of adult's coaching efforts. This early start may increase self-esteem and serve as the basis for self-motivation to train hard in order to sustain this success. Late maturers, on the other hand, may not receive this special attention and may rather be discouraged from participating in sports or athletic training during middle childhood. This also may have long-term consequences as the following quote indicates:

> These youngsters are far less likely to persist in sports and games, and may instead turn toward more sedentary endeavors likely to elicit recognition, including music, scientific efforts, computers, and other forms of academics. Less acceptable social compensations than these are also often acted out by the youngster who is immature and inept physically (Cratty, 1986, p. 66).

Certainly not all children will either become star athletes or scholars. Many lack outstanding talent in either arena. However, when children are encouraged to follow one path and discouraged from following another, such diverse patterns may develop. Research has found that children as young as 8 years of age have already begun to assign favorable and unfavorable social attributes to various body types, including their own. They are therefore aware at this age that various body types exist and how to rate them. Furthermore, they were found to show some signs of social retardation if they believed their own body type was not the most socially acceptable—typically, lean and muscular (Cratty, 1986).

FAT AND MUSCLE TISSUE Fat deposition increases briefly between birth and 6 months. It then decreases until children are 6 to 8 years of age, with a more marked decrease in boys. During the adolescent growth spurt, boys show a decrease in fat deposition while girls show an increase—which accounts in part for the differing body contours of adult men and women.

During middle childhood, muscles increase in length, breadth, and width (Nichols, 1990). The relative strength of girls and boys is similar during middle childhood but again diverges at adolescence with boys' strength surpassing that of girls.

BRAIN DEVELOPMENT DURING MIDDLE CHILDHOOD Between 6 and 8 years, the forebrain undergoes a small growth spurt. By age 8, the brain has achieved 90 percent of its adult size. During middle childhood the corpus callosum, which is the main connecting link between the hemispheres of the brain, also becomes more mature in both structure and function. Interestingly enough, as we will see in Chapter 13, this is also the time when the child moves from one Piagetian stage to another in cognitive development. It is intriguing to note that children typically achieve concrete operations at the same time their brains are growing more rapidly in substance and connections.

During middle childhood, brain development appears to involve more efficient functioning of various structures in the brain, for example, the *frontal lobe* of the cortex. The frontal lobe is responsible for thought and consciousness. This part of the brain slightly increases in its surface area because of continuing myelination, which was described in Chapter 9. In addition, lateralization of the brain's hemispheres becomes more pronounced during the school years (Thatcher, Walker, & Guidice, 1987). We now know much about the brain's development—and are on the verge of an explosion of knowledge about brain function and anatomy—because of the development of various medical technologies that allow scientists to explore the brain in increasingly fine detail. (See the box "How Researchers Look at the Brain".)

FOCUS ON RESEARCH

HOW RESEARCHERS LOOK AT THE BRAIN

Our knowledge of the brain and nervous system has grown greatly over the past two decades—largely because of the availability of computer-assisted medical technology which enables us to study the brain's functioning in considerable detail. Health sections of newspapers and magazines are filled with articles using the current alphabet of brain investigation—CAT, PET, MRI, and now MSI. It is helpful for us to be familiar with some of these methods and the way they help us to study the brain's function.

In the past, doctors learned much about the action of the brain by observing the effects of brain damage. For example, if a person suffered some sort of trauma, such as a bullet or projectile wound, doctors would observe the patient's behavior (at least those who lived) for any abnormalities. In this century, brain surgery and stimulation with electrodes were instrumental in our beginning to map the specialization of the cerebral hemispheres. In the 1920s the *electroencephalogram*

> *In this century, brain surgery and stimulation with electrodes were instrumental in our beginning to map the specialization of the cerebral hemispheres.*

(EEG) was invented. EEG's were essentially amplified recordings of the waves of electrical activity that were picked up by electrodes attached to the head. An EEG provides a simple way of measuring brain waves during problem solving or particular activities.

A *CAT scan (Computerized Axial Tomography)* is a computer-generated interpretation of brain structures. While an x-ray beam scans the brain, a computer records how much of the beam is absorbed. The density of the tissues, fluids, and bones scanned determine the amount of absorption. The computer is programmed to interpret the pattern of absorption and to then display it in a color-image on a monitor. This technique is appreciated by patients since it involves no injected dies or special risks or discomfort to the patient (Shea, Shebilske, & Worchel, 1993).

A *PET Scan (Positive Emission Tomography)* is also a computer-

MOTOR SKILL DEVELOPMENT

Throughout middle childhood, children continue to grow in the strength, speed, and coordination needed for gross motor skills. This newly acquired physical ability is reflected in their interest in sports and daredevil stunts. They climb trees, use logs as balance beams to cross streams, jump from beam to beam in the skeleton of an unfinished house. Numerous studies demonstrate the progress of motor development during this period. According to Keogh (1965), at age 7 a boy can throw a ball approximately 34 feet. By the time he is 10, he will probably be able to throw it twice as far, and three times as far by the time he is 12—and his accuracy will improve as well. Girls make similar progress in throwing and catching skills, although at every age their average throwing distance is shorter than that of boys (Williams, 1983). Sex differences are noted in many other physical skills: All through middle childhood, boys can run faster than girls. After age 11, the difference in running speed widens because boys continue to improve, whereas girls do not (Herkowitz, 1978). However, girls tend to outperform boys in skills that require agility or balance—for example, girls are better at hopping. These sex differences are closely linked to the specific activities

generated representation of brain activity. However, PET scans involve the administration of a radioactive sugar, after which the brain is scanned to discover where the sugar is absorbed. More active areas of the brain absorb more sugar since sugar fuels cell activity. The computer then interprets and displays its interpretation of brain activity in a color-coded image on a display monitor. PET scans have been used by researchers to determine which portions of the brains are most active during activities such as listening to music or performing math computations. They have also been employed to map the maturation of different brain structures.

MRI (Magnetic Resonance Imaging) currently presents the most detailed views of brain structures commonly available today. In magnetic resonance imaging, the head is put in a magnetic field that aligns the axis on which atoms rotate. A radio frequency then makes the atoms spin. When the frequency is turned off, a computer monitors the electromagnetic energy emitted when the atoms stop spinning. The computer then interprets and displays its interpretation of energy released in a color-coded image.

The newest technology to study brain function is the *MSI (Magnetic Source Imaging)*. This technology is only available in the United States at the Scripps Foundation Center in La Jolla, California, and the Veterans Administration Hospital in Albuquerque, New Mexico. The development of MSI was based on the knowledge that every electrical signal creates a magnetic field around it. This is also true with regard to electrical signals in the brain and central nervous system. However, in the body, magnetic fields are infinitesimally small—a billionth of the earth's gravitational pull in the base of the brain. A device that measures magnetic fields is pressed against the skull for several seconds. Sensors collect data from 37 points—then the head is moved slightly and the process repeated. A complete scan takes approximately an hour. The computer-generated image is then overlaid on an MRI scan. The resulting image shows both tumors or brain structures from the MRI—plus the sensory and motor functions from the MSI.

Researchers are on the verge of more detailed study of the brain's language center, and of identifying what pattern of brain signals results in dyslexia or attention-deficit disorder in children. Given this new technology, researchers will be able to determine not only the size and shape of brain structures, but also monitor their functions. This may well significantly increase the role of neuroscience in medicine and psychiatry.

practiced. Girls in Little League baseball develop longer, more accurate throws. Boys and girls who play soccer develop skills at a similar pace.

When we carefully study the make-up of basic movements, such as jumping, the movements of adults and school-age children are not different. The magnitude of the jump or the position from which the individual takes off, differs for adults and children, but the jump itself is remarkably uniform (Clark, Phillips, & Peterson, 1989). This research offers support for the view that environmental constraints may affect observed motor behaviors, just as maturation of the central nervous system may affect them (Thelen, 1988). As children mature, they acquire new ways to jump and jump higher and farther—this may be partly because of increased muscle strength or practice. Despite these changes in magnitude, however, the structure of the jump remains unchanged.

Sex differences in motor skills before the onset of puberty are more a function of opportunity and cultural expectations than of any real physical differences between boys and girls (Cratty, 1986; Nichols, 1990). In general, because of social expectations, girls do better at activities that are expected of girls and boys do better at skills considered more masculine.

A 12-year-old girl can throw a ball 3 times as far as she could at the age of 7—one sign of the rapid development of gross motor skills that occurs during this period.

The school-age child is capable of controlled purposeful movement (Nichols, 1990). By the time she enters formal school—usually around 5 years of age—various locomotor skills such as running, jumping, and hopping are well in place. They are executed with even rhythm and relatively few mechanical errors—for example, in foot placement or use of the arms. When we consider the developmental sequence for running, it is amazing to consider how far children have come from tottering 18-month-olds.

FINE MOTOR SKILLS   Fine motor skills—those skills that enable children to use their hands in increasingly sophisticated ways—also develop quickly during this period, starting even before a child enters first grade. In nursery schools, teachers help build writing readiness as they offer preschoolers the opportunity to draw, paint, cut, and mold with clay. As their teachers guide them through these activities, children discover how to draw circles, squares, and, finally, triangles. (Children who cannot draw a triangle have difficulty with more complex writing skills.) Each increasingly complex shape requires the improved hand-eye coordination children need to learn in order to write. Most of the fine motor skills required in writing develop during a child's sixth or seventh year. However, some even some perfectly normal children cannot draw a diamond or master many letter shapes until the age of 8.

The mastery that children develop over their own bodies during this period gives them feelings of competence and self-worth that are essential to good mental health (see also the box "Children's Concepts of Their Bodies"). Controlling their own bodies also helps them win the acceptance of their peers. Awkward, poorly coordinated children are often left out of group activities; they may continue to feel unwanted long after their awkwardness disappears. We see an overview of the physical characteristics of school age children presented in Table 12–1.

BASIC MOVEMENT QUALITIES   In general, virtually all motor performance data for school-age children reflects continuous improvement. Plateaus some-

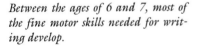

Between the ages of 6 and 7, most of the fine motor skills needed for writing develop.

TABLE 12–1 Characteristics of Physical Development during Middle Childhood

5- TO 6-YEAR-OLDS

➤ Steady increases in height and weight.
➤ Steady growth in strength for both boys and girls.
➤ Awareness of large body parts.
➤ Increased use of all body parts.
➤ Gross motor skills improving.
➤ Perform motor skills singly.

7- TO 8-YEAR-OLDS

➤ Steady increase in height and weight.
➤ Steady increase in strength for both boys and girls.
➤ Increased use of all body parts.
➤ Gross motor skills refined.
➤ Fine motor skills improving.
➤ Increasing variability in motor skill performance but still performed singly.

9- TO 10-YEAR-OLDS

➤ Growth spurt begins for girls.
➤ Increase in strength for girls accompanied by loss of flexibility.
➤ Awareness and development of all body parts and systems.
➤ Combine motor skills more fluidly.
➤ Balance improved.

11-YEAR-OLDS

➤ Girls generally taller and heavier than boys.
➤ Growth spurt begins for boys.
➤ Accurate judgments in intercepting moving objects.
➤ Continued combination of more fluid motor skills.
➤ Continued improvement of fine motor skills.
➤ Continued increasing variability in motor skill performance.

times appear—or even some deceleration—from 7 to 9 years. As motor skills improve, the activities of children also grow to reflect their new physical maturity. Vigorous play develops in intensity as we will see in subsequent sections of this chapter. Hobbies and crafts also become part of the child's repertoire of behaviors. Arts and crafts, carpentry materials, and the more complex construction sets begin to fill the child's "wish list". No longer are simple legos desired, for example, but legos with motors built in. Train layouts become more elaborate.

All of these changes in the quality of movements which the child performs are affected by seven factors: balance, agility, body build, throwing ability, speed, hand precision, and strength and power (Cratty, 1986).

Balance. Balance is a combination of several abilities: balancing objects, balancing the body in one position on one foot, and dynamic balance, which involves children maintaining balance while crossing a narrow balance beam. An

FOCUS ON AN APPLICATION

CHILDREN'S CONCEPTS OF THEIR BODIES

Remember when you thought your heart was shaped like the classic box of valentine chocolates, or when you were sure, if you tried hard enough, you could look through one ear to see the other? During the early school years, all children conceptualize their internal body organs and functions in a concrete way. They are vitally interested in the workings of their bodies, and based on their observations and the little information they receive, they actively construct what is going on inside. As they grow older and acquire more knowledge and understanding, they learn to describe their bodies in a more sophisticated and abstract way. As you will see, many of their thoughts are remarkably accurate, whereas others are totally outrageous.

In a fascinating study of the thoughts that 6- to 12-year-old children have about the inside of their bodies, Cathleen Crider (1981) found that the typical grade-school child first identifies the brain, bones,

---

One 9-year-old described his organs in a very global way: "The heart," he said, "is what you breathe in."

---

heart, blood, and blood vessels. As you can see from the drawing (Figure 12–3) by a 7-year-old girl, the stomach is absent, but the vegetables that she ate for dinner are present. In the child's mind, nothing is certain about the body interior except the foods she puts into it (Schilder & Wechsler, 1935).

Children's perceptions give them their first clues of their internal organs. They can feel their heart beating; they can feel the hardness of their bones under their skin; they can identify their brain from the inner speech that accompanies thought. Other organs, like the nerves and liver, are not as easy to understand. After having liver for dinner, children may wonder if they have a liver, too. They will be satisfied with their parents' simple answer that they do, and they may feel no need for more information. Similarly, children may understand their bodies' nerves only in terms of the emotional problems of a nervous relative. Even with considerable instruction, it is difficult for them to comprehend other hidden functions of nerves.

Children often use the little information they have about their bodies in a very inventive way. For instance, they think of body organs, like the stomach and brain, as con-

---

additional skill involves maintaining body position in any of the above positions while the child's eyes are closed.

Body Agility. Agility is measured in a variety of ways. It may be the rapidity with which children change direction while running, rhythmic hopping, getting up quickly from a sitting or laying position, or vertical jumps of various types. Agility is related to flexibility by the child, but is also a function of strength and muscle development.

Body Build. Movement is also affected by the child's particular body build. Body build is a combination of height, weight, and physique. This is partly affected by maturation since, as we have already seen, the nature of the body's composition changes as children grow.

Throwing Abilities. Children's skill with balls—both in catching and throwing—affects the quality of the movement they perform. Throwing improves as children grow, as does the nature of the hand position they use to catch balls. In general, boys seem to possess better throwing ability than do girls. However,

tainers. A child who has already become aware of his stomach describes it in this way: "The stomach is a round thing in our body for holding food. The food goes in your mouth, down your neck, to your stomach. If we didn't have a stomach, the food would go everywhere and it would be a mess" (p. 54).

Like every other aspect of development, conceptualization of this kind occurs at different rates for different children. One 9-year-old described his organs in a very global way: "The heart," he said, "is what you breathe in. It goes like this. [Child breathes in and out.] The lungs are to breathe in too. Food goes in the stomach, and then it comes in your heart, and then it makes you breathe air....Your heart moves your stomach." A second 9-year-old had much more sophisticated ideas: "Your heart works by pumping blood out to the vessels," said the child. "Blood goes through your body, some to your head. It

doesn't stop. It keeps on going, but I don't know where it goes" (Crider, 1981, p. 57).

This does not imply that any single child has an equal grasp of all his body systems. On the contrary, a child's understanding may be sophisticated in one area and very simplistic in another. For example, at the same time that a child explains how her stomach "mashes" food and turns it into blood that moves throughout the body, she may conceive of the muscles only in a very global sense: Muscles "make you strong."

Until children learn to think abstractly—to conceptualize the things they cannot directly perceive—they will continue to construct explanations of what's inside their bodies in these concrete terms. In a child's mind, it makes sense that food collects in the little toe, that the lungs are in the throat, and that the heart is for love. Only when their thought processes pass into the

FIGURE 12–3
Drawing of body interior by a 7-year-old girl.

formal operational stage described by Piaget will they be able to understand the real picture of their inner bodies.

girls who play baseball or softball, and therefore practice throwing and catching skills, appear to do as well as boys in middle childhood.

Hand Precision. Children's ability to engage in fine motor skills associated with hand precision are also a primary factor in evaluating their overall quality of movement. A typical measure of this sort of motor skill might involve asking children to drop pennies with precision and speed into a small opening.

Strength and Power. Measures of strength and power are difficult to obtain on children since it is difficult to convince children of 5 to 7 years to exert themselves in ways that may cause even momentary discomfort. A painless way to measure strength in young children is to measure the pressure exerted on a hand dynamometer.

Studies using these seven measures of movement qualities find that between 5 and 12 years of age, children generally show increments in all areas—moreover, there is considerable overlap in these skills. For example, both strength and flexibility contribute to many tasks. As children get older, they become stronger. This

By the age of 7, many children become interested in arts and crafts, reflecting the continuous expansion of their motor skills.

improvement may be due to factors other than maturation such as experience, improvement in skills through practice, or increased willingness to undergo an all out effort (Cratty, 1986). This is true in tests of muscle strength as well as in activities such as sustained running, jumping, or competitive swimming.

In general, in tests of strength during middle childhood, there are few, if any, sex differences until the seventh to eighth year, when boys, because of their physical activities, may slightly exceed girls. However, by the end of childhood, the strength of girls may exceed that of boys because girls have already begun their adolescent maturation. Similar finds occur in tests of flexibility, jumping, and throwing.

In general, school-age children show yearly improvements in a variety of skills including measurable improvements in strength, agility, balance, and velocities in which running and throwing occur. There are also measurable improvements in body mechanics. Body parts become more coordinated (Roberton & Halverson, 1988). These changes result in both the actions themselves improving, as well as their outcomes, for example, balls are thrown harder and distances are run faster.

The increased muscle strength of school-aged children may not only be the result of maturation but of practice in sports such as competitive running or swimming.

VIGOROUS PHYSICAL ACTIVITY

It is important for children to engage in vigorous activity if they are to have normal growth and development. With our current social emphasis on sedentary activities such as television watching and video game playing, as well as busing to school as opposed to walking or cycling, many children are physically unfit. For them, physical education classes in school or organized sports activities are the only real exercise they get.

In Table 12–2, we see the activities physical educators may conduct to help children engage in vigorous activity. These range from equal-strengthening activities for school-age boys and girls to teaching specific motor skills or the use of particular types of equipment for exercise. In general, such physical education activities should be designed to improve children's self-perceptions and the use of their bodies to perform various motor movements. While physical educators working with young children may teach only one skill at a time, those working with children in middle childhood emphasize activities involving the combination of skills.

During middle childhood, children have fairly short attention spans. Therefore, organized activities and instruction need to be of short duration with few rules. Instruction should build sequentially, with children being given the opportunity to practice small "subsets" of the skills before being asked to perform the whole activity or movement.

In addition to these cognitive requirements for motor performance, there are social aspects of children's worlds that influence their ability to participate in sports or organized vigorous play. For example, one observer of middle childhood notes:

> Socially an egocentric kindergarten child is transformed into a group-centered participant by the fifth or sixth grade. Dependence upon adults is replaced by the growing importance of the peer group for establishing patterns of behavior. Girls and boys may have developed some perceptions or expectations regarding the suitability of some activities for each sex. (Nichols, 1990, p. 27)

Teacher and adults in general must continue to encourage all children to develop a variety of skills and to design activities where girls and boys together may engage in vigorous physical activity together. In this way all children may achieve optimal physical development.

ROUGH-AND-TUMBLE PLAY

As we have said throughout this chapter, moderate to vigorous physical activity are instrumental to refining and strengthening motor activities during middle childhood. Rough-and-tumble play is one vehicle where this vigorous activity occurs. The term **rough-and-tumble play** refers to vigorous, playful, and nonaggressive interchanges between children. Examples of this type include play fighting and chasing, as well as somewhat antagonistic behaviors such as teasing, hitting at, poking, pouncing, sneaking-up, carrying another child, piling on top of

rough-and-tumble play Typically playful and nonaggressive activity involving vigorous interchanges between children; examples include play fighting and chasing.

TABLE 12–2 Age Characteristics of Physical Development during Middle Childhood

	5–6 YEARS	7–8 YEARS	9–10 YEARS	11 YEARS
GROWTH				
Characteristics	Steady increases in height and weight.		Growth spurt begins for girls.	Girls generally taller and heavier than boys. Growth spurt begins for boys.
	Steady growth in strength for boys and girls		Increase in strength for girls.	
	Flexibility good		Loss in flexibility.	
The student needs	Vigorous physical activity to enhance fitness, growth, and development			
	Equal expectations for strength of boys and girls			
The teacher provides	Running, climbing, supportive activities			
	Equal strengthening activities for boys and girls			
			Stretching activities to enhance increased understanding of fitness	
AWARENESS OF BODY PARTS				
Characteristics	Aware of large body parts	Aware of all large and small body parts		
				Accurate judgments in intercepting, moving objects
The student needs	Increased use of all body parts		Awareness and development of all body parts and systems	
The teacher provides	Movement challenges to explore location and possible movements of body parts			
	Knowledge of how body parts are used to perform motor skills			
	Activities for total body development			

each other, holding, and pushing (Pellegrini, 1988). These behaviors are also accompanied by smiling and laughter.

Clearly, this list of behaviors does not necessarily suggest "nonaggressive" activity. In fact, research has found that the nature of rough-and-tumble play differs depending on certain social or personality factors in the participating children. Since aggressive or socially rejected children have a tendency to interpret social provocations such as those presented above as aggressive, they will turn playful episodes into aggression. Popular, confident children, however, tend to correctly interpret these activities as play and do not turn them into aggression (Pellegrini, 1988). In fact, when popular children engage in rough-and-tumble play it soon is transformed into games-with-rules, where protections are devel-

TABLE 12–2 Age Characteristics of Physical Development during Middle Childhood (cont.)

	5–6 YEARS	7–8 YEARS	9–10 YEARS	11 YEARS
MOTOR SKILLS				
Characteristics	Gross motor skills improving	Gross motor skills refined Fine motor skills improving Increasing variability in motor skill performance		
	Perform motor skills singly		Combine motor skills more fluidly Balance improved	
The student needs	Opportunity to refine and use gross motor skills	To use gross motor skills in a variety of situations Opportunity to refine manipulative and other fine motor skills		
	Opportunity to work with medium-sized objects	To work with equipment varying in size and weight		
			To use motor skills in a variety of sports and dance activities To develop combinations of skills into movement sequences or routines	
The teacher provides	A variety of experiences in using skills	A variety of experiences to challenge each child and requiring greater body and object control		
	Experiences to explore the use of equipment such as ropes, hoops, balls, and wands			
		Activities to further develop skills in ball handling	Activities requiring greater accuracy Activities combining motor skills and beginning sports and dance skills	

Source: Nichols, 1990.

oped to avoid hurting children. When rejected or aggressive children engage in this play, however, it soon deteriorates into aggression. Popular children therefore use rough-and-tumble play groups as opportunities to model and practice **prosocial behaviors**—behaviors that encourage social exchanges between children—with other popular children (Pellegrini, 1988).

GENDER DIFFERENCES IN ROUGH-AND-TUMBLE PLAY

Interesting gender differences emerge in teachers' and peers' responses to rough-and-tumble play. Boys' rough play is associated with social problem solving and

For popular boys, rough play is a way to sharpen their already considerable social skills of negotiating and forging alliances.

social preference, while that of girls is associated with their being considered anti-social by their teachers (Pellegrini, 1989). Popular boys often engage in rough play to have fun and interact cooperatively with peers. Therefore, for these boys, rough play is a way of practicing and developing social skills that are related to their popularity—such as negotiations and alliances. Aggressive boys tend to be excluded from rough play by those boys who are popular. For different reasons, girls too are often discouraged from participating in these behaviors. Girls who engage in rough play may be labeled by teachers and peers as antisocial because they engage in what is seen as a male-oriented behavior.

Finally, while rough-and-tumble play may be perceived somewhat nega-tively by adults who view it as progressing to aggression, it serves a valuable edu-cational purpose. Rather than leading to increased aggression, rough play often leads to children's engagement in cooperative games with rules. Enhanced social problem solving and popularity are also an outcome for boys who participate. Popular boys can engage in rough-and-tumble play, while unpopular boys can-not, because they lack the necessary social skills to participate. Disliked or unpop-ular boys usually cannot discriminate between play and aggression.

 HEALTH IN SCHOOL-AGED CHILDREN

The health profile of American children has changed markedly in the past fifty years. Widespread immunization has eliminated many of the major infectious dis-eases that threatened children such as polio, diptheria, and measles. But new dis-eases, such as AIDS, have arisen, and some infections and respiratory illnesses remain problems for children, such as influenza and ear infections. Asthma has also been increasing in recent years in children who live in cities (U.S. Dept. of Health and Human Services, 1992).

During middle childhood, some school-related disabilities become more apparent. Mental retardation, learning disorders, emotional and behavioral problems, and vision and hearing impairment are frequently diagnosed more accurately.

Violence toward children has also become a national concern because of rapidly rising rates of child deaths due to violence. For example, in 1986, nearly 2 percent of children—more than 1,000,000—were demonstrably harmed by abuse or neglect. Still others are the victims of gang violence or drug wars in inner cities (see the box "Children Living in Danger").

HEALTH AND ILLNESS

Minor illnesses such as ear infections, colds, and upset stomachs are very prevalent in the preschool period. During the years from 6 to 12, most children experience fewer of these illnesses. This is partly a result of greater immunity due to previous exposure. Also, most school-age children know and practice somewhat better nutrition, health, and safety habits (O'Connor-Francoeur, 1983; Starfield, 1992). Nevertheless, fairly frequent minor illnesses occur. During this period, nearsightedness, or myopia, is often first diagnosed. For example, 25 percent of white, middle-class sixth graders have some myopia and have been fitted with glasses.

One author suggests that minor illnesses such as colds are actually of some benefit to the child's psychological development. Although common illnesses certainly disrupt children's school progress, as well as family social roles and work schedules, they and their families generally recover rather quickly from these interruptions. In the process, children learn to cope with minor stress and to increase their knowledge of themselves. They develop a bit more empathy and a realistic understanding of the role of "being sick." Hence, children's illnesses can be seen as a normal part of social and behavioral development (Parmelee, 1986). We shall now briefly discuss two of the more common health problems of middle childhood.

OTITIS MEDIA   *Otitis media,* or inflammation of the middle ear, is a common disease of infancy and childhood. Many children experience multiple episodes of the disease prior to their third birthday and then continue to have them throughout childhood. Otitis media is associated with a set of symptoms including fever, pain, and fluid in the ear. It is also often associated with transient conductive hearing loss, in fact, repeated episodes may lead to chronic auditory impairment (Lonigan et al., 1992). Several studies have found a relation between an early or continued history of Otitis media and later problems in language development including expressive language disorder and poor narrative skills.

While not all children have severe effects of Otitis media, persistent middle-ear infections are a common cause of mild hearing loss—temporary or permanent—and of consequent language delays and disorders (Friel-Patti, 1990). Children who are most at risk to suffer hearing loss are those children who may lack access to health care or early treatment to reduce the risk of fluid accumulation in the middle ear.

FOCUS ON DIVERSITY

CHILDREN LIVING IN DANGER

The morning after a 19-year-old gang member was gunned down at a phone box at 103rd and Grape Streets in Watts, his lifeless body lay in a pool of blood on the sidewalk as hundreds of children walked by, lunch boxes and school bags in hand, on their way to the 102nd Street Elementary School. A few months later, during recess, kindergartners at the school dropped to the ground as five shots were fired rapidly nearby, claiming another victim. On still another occasion, an outdoor school assembly was disrupted by the crackle of gunshots and wailing sirens as students watched a neighborhood man scuffle with police officers. (Timnick, 1989, p. 132)

Unfortunately, experiences such as these are no longer rare for children living in central cities such as Los Angeles. Children often fall asleep in these areas to the sounds of gunshots. Children as young as 6 are recruited as drug-runners. Some babies' first words and gestures are the names and signs of their parents' gangs (Timnick, 1989). Researchers

When young children experience an initial trauma before age 11, they are significantly more likely to develop psychiatric symptoms during adolescence.

have found that children growing up in war-zone environments like South-Central Los Angeles often become anxious or depressed. Children who have either directly experienced violence or who have witnessed, for example, the brutal murder of a parent or sibling, are especially likely to experience severe psychological distress.

The concept of *Post-Traumatic Stress Disorder* was first suggested to describe the psychological problems exhibited by returned Viet Nam War veterans. These individuals were suffering the aftermath of war. They had flashbacks to combat, often had difficulty sleeping, vivid nightmares, difficulty in concentrating, difficulty in controlling their impulses, and were either withdrawn, aggressive, or alternating between the two behaviors. Recent research has suggested that children living in inner-city "war zones" exhibit similar patterns of behavior. Many children relive the violent experiences they have been exposed to in aggressive play, nightmares, and sudden memories that intrude during class or other activities.

OBESITY Obesity—defined as weighing at least 20 percent more than one's ideal weight—is becoming increasingly common among American children: About one-quarter of school-age children are now overweight (Gortmaker et al., 1987). What makes this particularly worrisome is that so many of these children will still be overweight when they reach adulthood: Nearly 70 percent of obese 10- to 13-year-olds will become obese adults (Epstein & Wing, 1987). Their obesity will predispose them to a number of medical problems, such as heart disease, high blood pressure, and diabetes.

Genetic factors play an influential role in obesity. The child of one obese parent has a 40 percent chance of becoming obese; the odds leap to 80 percent if both parents are obese. If the child is adopted, it is the weight of her biological parents, rather than of her adoptive parents, that will have the greatest influence on her adult weight (Rosenthal, 1990; Stunkard, 1988).

obesity Weighing at least 20 percent more in body weight than would be predicted by one's height.

The chronic situations of ongoing violence existing in many inner city areas produce a state of sustained stress for children. These young children who live in such environments are fearful, depressed, anxious, and distressed (Garbarino, Kostelny, & Dubrow, 1991). Research with families of these children suggests that mothers were likely to underestimate the extent of psychological distress their children were experiencing. This may be because the children do not talk about their fears with their parents—or because the parents cannot acknowledge the emotional pain in their children, which they may feel helpless to remedy (Elkind, 1981). Also, some of these children may witness violence at home as well as at school or in the streets. Thus, they may endure abusive family relationships and then watch hours of romanticized violence on television (Timnick, 1989).

When young children experience an initial trauma before age 11, they are significantly more likely to develop psychiatric symptoms during adolescence. Those children who live under multiple threats in their environments are also more likely to experience significant developmental delays over other children.

In addition to the violence they are experiencing on a daily basis, some of these children also experience poor housing, schools, and medical care. Their parents may be so overwhelmed by their own stress and difficulties that they may not always be emotionally unavailable to care for their children. Families may split up over the stress—or children may experience inadequate or neglectful parenting.

The psychological consequences of being in an environment of ongoing violence include poor concentration and school-related problems. These children are often fearful of being abandoned or may become overly aggressive and cocky to disguise their fears. Many of them develop blunted emotions since they are afraid to care for people who may be killed or abandon them. In some cases, art therapy has helped when combined with discussions of the violence. As we can see in Figure 12–4, even when children can't verbalize their feelings, their art often reveals much about what is on their minds. Therapists may then be able to get the children to tell a story about their picture that makes a connection to the trauma they have suffered.

The American Psychological Association's Committee on Violence and Youth recommends that a community approach be taken with children living in violence. Programs involving health care, recreation, and vocational training should be built around children's developmental needs. Role models from the community and peer support groups should be available to assist children in finding alternate pathways to violence and drug use.

The fact that childhood obesity is more common now than it was 20 years ago proves that environmental factors are also important because genes do not change that quickly. One environmental factor that has been blamed is television viewing, which has increased steadily over this period. Today, an average child watches television for 23 hours a week, and those who watch more tend to be heavier than those who watch less. There are two reasons for the connection between television viewing and obesity: too little physical activity and too much snacking on junk food (Dietz, 1987). Children who sit in front of a television set are not getting the exercise they need to develop their physical skills and to burn off excess calories. At the same time, if they spend their viewing hours munching on potato chips and drinking sweetened beverages, their appetite is diminished for more nutritious (and less caloric) foods.

Television watching has been linked to the increase in numbers of obese children. Children who watch more than 23 hours of television a week tend to weigh more than children who watch less.

Children should not be placed on drastic weight-loss programs even if they are seriously overweight, because they need a balanced, nutritious diet to support energy levels and proper growth. Instead of trying to lose weight quickly, they must develop better eating habits that they can maintain over time. In particular, they should increase their intake of healthy foods like fruits and vegetables and decrease their intake of foods that are high in fats, for example, pizza. Equally important, they must increase their physical activity. As we noted earlier, obesity often runs in families, and because of this, successful weight-loss programs frequently involve treating the parents as well as the children (Epstein et al., 1990).

Although overweight children face fewer medical risks than overweight adults do, there are serious social and psychological consequences of their obesity. Peers may reject them because of their physical appearance and because they are less adept at sports. The result can be a negative self-image that may make the child even more reluctant to interact with age-mates or to engage in physical activities.

PHYSICAL FITNESS

Health is often measured by what it is not, or illness. However, an index of positive health is the degree of physical fitness individuals achieve. The human body was built for movement. Vigorous physical activity is required for the development of a healthy body (Nichols, 1990). The progressively more demanding physical activities performed by most school-aged children—combined with physical education classes they take in school—ideally promote favorable attitudes toward an active life whose components include vigorous, fun-filled activities. Furthermore, an increasing body of research links health problems such as cardiovascular disease to inactivity during the childhood years. The beginnings of clogged blood vessels, a symptom of cardiovascular disease, have been found in autopsies of children as young as 2 years of age. High cholesterol and triglycerides (a type of fat) have also been found in sedentary children (Nichols, 1990). Exercise reduces all three of these characteristics which are major risk factors for adult cardiovascular disease. This finding reinforces the need for children to be active and exercise regularly.

Physical fitness, which refers to the optimal functioning of the heart, lungs, muscles, and blood vessels—does not require children to become master athletes. In order for children to be physically fit, they must engage in sport or exercises that involve four different aspects of conditioning—flexibility, muscle endurance, muscle strength, and cardiovascular functioning. Needless to say, some activities in which children participate are better for accomplishing this than are others. Soccer, tennis, bicycling, and swimming, for example, exercise the whole body, while baseball does not (Nichols, 1990). In baseball, for the most part one player moves at a time and then for only a brief time.

Given the high average number of hours children spend in front of television during middle childhood, or working video games, it is not surprising that many American children live relatively sedentary lives. In addition, if they are latchkey children who must care for themselves between coming home from school and their parents' return home from work, they may have been warned to

Soccer is a good sport for children because it exercises the whole body in contrast to a sport like baseball.

stay inside the house or apartment for safety reasons. This further increases the number of hours spent in inactivity.

A recent national survey of 8,000 children from 10 to 18 years of age found that children in the 1990s are generally less physically active and fit, and more obese than children were in the 1960s. In addition, the survey found that most middle-aged joggers were cardiovascularly more fit than most children—that more than half of the children surveyed participated in no physical activity—and that many children did not even learn at school about activities to perform to improve their physical fitness. For such children, a well-designed physical education program that requires regular exercise and teaches good nutrition would be very beneficial.

ACCIDENTS AND INJURIES

Children's motor development changes both their exposure to hazards and their ability to protect their personal health. As children become more mobile, for example, they are able to interact with their physical environment in ways that increase their risk of accidents and exposure to illness. During infancy it is fairly easy to safeguard children. However, as children grow in coordination, size, and strength, they begin to engage in increasingly more dangerous activities including the use of skateboards and bicycles—as well as to participate in team sports involving potentially deadly projectiles and potentially crippling bodily contact (Maddux et al., 1986). Generally, from infancy onward, children's need to perform their newfound skills often conflicts with their need for protection against risks to their health. In addition, their ability to harm themselves often exceeds their ability to foresee the consequences of their actions (Achenbach, 1982). Many children, for example, have been warned against riding their bicycles out into the street without looking, but in the excitement of play may forget—and be seriously injured.

An understanding of motor development and its relationship to accident risk is important since accidents are the leading cause of death and disability among children. Injuries cause more deaths in children than the six next frequent causes combined (cancer, congenital anomalies, pneumonia, heart disease, homicide, and stroke). About half of all deaths in children result from injuries and accidents. We may see a listing of the causes of death due to accidents and injuries presented in Table 12–3.

For example, while 1- to 4-year olds are particularly at risk for poisoning; children from 5 to 9 have higher rates of pedestrian accidents; older children and

TABLE 12–3 Causes of Accidental Death and Injury in Children

Motor vehicle accidents	Each year 4,600 children die, and for every death approximately 40 children become disabled. 1 out of 20 infants born in the United States will become seriously injured in a motor vehicle accident by adulthood. 2,000 children a year die while crossing the street. 700 children between 5 and 14 years of age die in bicycle accidents.
Drowning	1/3 of all drowning victims in the United States are children younger than 15 years old.
Burns and fire deaths	800,000 children under 15 are burned each year.
Asphyxiation	Aspiration is the most common cause of household deaths in children under 6—choking on food or nonfood products. Approximately 700 children died in 1992 from asphyxiation.
Firearms	1/5 of all those killed by firearms are children under 15; males are more likely than females to be killed by firearms.
Falls	Falls are the 5th leading cause of accidental death in children; each year about 500 children under 14 years of age are killed from falls; in 1978 147,000 children were injured in falls down stairs.
Sports and recreational injuries	1.8 million children were injured in 1992 in injuries related to sports and recreation; football is the leading cause, followed by wrestling and gymnastics.
Poisonings	Each year 80 children under 5 die from poisoning; for every death, 1,000 ingestions are reported to poison control centers.
Fireworks	Approximately 3,200 children under 15 are injured by fireworks each year.
Animal bites	Children receive between 450,000 to 750,000 animal bites annually; 60,000 of these result in serious injuries such as facial disfigurements or psychological problems.

Source: Cataldo, Dershewitz, Wilson, Christophersen, Finney, Fawcett, and Seekins, (1986).

adolescents are more likely to be injured on recreational equipment such as swings, bicycles, and skateboards. They are also more likely to be injured in sports-related activities.

Motor development is not the only determinant of the increased accident risk of school-age children. Young children often are unable to control impulses sufficiently to "listen to" internal rules and statements. Because of this, children at play may not follow rules such as, "Look both ways before you cross the street." They may also be exposed to or take part in environmental hazards such as drugs or violence.

Since their improved mobility exposes school-aged children to greater accident risk, they often need guidance on ways to protect themselves from injury.

DRUG USE AMONG SCHOOL-AGED CHILDREN   We tend to associate drug use with adolescence, but recent studies have found that elementary school children below the age of 12 test and try abusable substances such as alcohol, cigarettes, and marijuana. This is especially likely to be true in urban areas where drugs are more readily available. Early use of alcohol, tobacco, and marijuana is associated with alcohol and other drug abuse in adolescence and adulthood. Although the average age of first use of alcohol and marijuana is 13, pressure to initiate use begins even earlier. Elementary school students report peer pressure to try beer, wine, and liquor, and many succumb to this pressure.

In surveys of children of fourth graders in the District of Columbia public schools in both 1988–89 and 1990–91, considerable drug use was reported. In 1990–91, for example, approximately 43 percent of fourth graders reported trying alcohol, 13 percent without parental knowledge. 18 percent reported smoking cigarettes, and 2 percent reported smoking marijuana. Several students reported trying crack cocaine, but usage was infrequent (Bush & Iannotti, 1993).

The reasons children gave for trying these substances included: having a family member who used the substance, having a friend who used the substance, having been offered the substance by peers, and having seen a friend, peer, or family member selling the substance. For example, almost 60 percent of those who tried cigarettes lived with a smoker—a factor which may account for their increased experimentation. In addition, the majority of children surveyed indicated that they were not bothered if their best friends used any of these substances.

In general, this research indicates a tendency for young children to try substances that may produce negative health effects—especially on growing bodies. The research also suggests the effects of modeling behavior on school-aged children—children who try these substances have often seen either peers or family members using them. In addition, this early use of potentially harmful substances suggests the need for education and intervention during middle childhood. By adolescence, habits may be well established.

PHYSICAL DEVELOPMENT AND THE SCHOOL ENVIRONMENT

We generally think of school in terms of its effect upon children's cognitive or social development, forgetting that schools must also provide for children's physical and motor needs. The effect of the standard American classroom was aptly

"Just think of it as a brief interlude in, as opposed to a major disruption of, your life.

summarized by a first grader after her first day at school. When asked how she liked her new school, she replied, "Oh, you mean sit-down school?" She was reacting not to the difference in teachers and schedules, but to being confined to a desk and chair for a whole day. There is no evidence that children learn best by sitting in straight-backed chairs for long periods of time—on the contrary, many studies have shown the limitations of passive, receptive learning.

An elementary school in Massachusetts may set an example for the type of design that will be used in the future. Besides desks and tables, the classrooms have cubicles and caves built into the walls at varying heights. Each nook is large enough for one or two children and is furnished with rugs and cushions. The cubicles are special places to which the children can retreat to read, study, or hold problem-solving discussions. These quiet, busy classrooms offer a relaxed atmosphere and promote good achievement.

Another example of a positive, open environment may be found in Montessori classrooms where various stations designed for particular activities are placed about the classroom. There may be a reading corner complete with pillows, a section for carpentry, one for water activities, and so forth. This design allows small children to move around the classroom and integrate activity with learning. Rugs are used as transportable "desks" to make space for children to work individually.

Six-year-old children are still learning with their bodies, still integrating physical and intellectual knowledge. It is artificial to divorce the body from the mind and personality, using it only in gym or at recess. A school can be responsive to a child's physical needs in many ways. In a math class, for example, children might measure a corridor in yards or in meters, and then measure it again in terms of their own footsteps or the time it takes them to walk its length. In this way, their knowledge would be both abstract and concrete, both general and personal. Schools might also stress physical expression for its own sake. For example, some British primary schools have set aside a special period for movement expression and exploration (Evans, 1975).

School-aged children still use their bodies as a way of gaining physical and cognitive knowledge.

COPING WITH PHYSICAL CHALLENGES

A number of physical conditions that require special considerations in the school environment may affect children during middle childhood. We need to be sensitive to the issue of labeling for children with various physical conditions. The term **physically challenged** is more acceptable today than are the terms handicapped or physically disabled. While physically challenged may be seen by some as a euphemism, it more accurately reflects the environment that such children confront. It also directs the efforts of the educational system to changing the environment to meet the needs of such children. Many efforts in special education are therefore focused on talking about the environmental challenges facing children, and, consequently, avoiding laying the blame on the particular child's special needs. Building ramps or providing children with adaptive equipment such as language boards or Braille scanners is effective environmental intervention that enhances their ability to learn.

In some cases, the child's special needs may make participating in classroom activities difficult. Peer relations and friendships may be difficult to initiate or sustain. In addition, developmental delays may limit the child's ability to effectively interact with more advanced peers. In today's school environment, because of legislation on behalf of children with special needs, most physically challenged children are **mainstreamed** or taught in the least restrictive setting possible.

What sorts of special needs do physically challenged children have? These problems run from low fitness associated with obesity or poor nutrition, to severe *cerebral palsy.* Cerebral palsy is a neuromuscular condition caused by damage to areas of the brain. Children with cerebral palsy often are multiply disabled—with uncontrollable body movements and difficulty in producing language. Those children with severe cerebral palsy often require the use of a wheelchair to control their body movements. Some of these children are also learning disabled, while others may be highly intelligent, as the following case indicates:

physically challenged A term emphasizing the environmental factors that serve to limit a disabled child's access to goods and services; rather than dealing with handicapping conditions themselves, the emphasis is on changes in the environment such as ramps or language boards which help the child to adapt.

Although children now learn such activities as dancing in physical education classes, even here, much of the time they are engaged in sedentary activities such as watching.

Mike was a feisty 9-year-old. He had severe cerebral palsy which required his placement in a wheelchair someone else had to push. Speech was difficult for him, and he had to go through extreme body contortions to push the words out. It was difficult for others to watch him. Despite this, he participated fully in classroom discussions. He had a good sense of humor and often laughed at himself. His peers, with the help of sensitive teachers, became comfortable with his condition and vied to help push his wheelchair.

Other physically challenging conditions elementary schools experience include blindness and deafness, diabetes, and asthma. Children with special needs, like other children, are expected to develop life skills in school that will help them become more independent and as fit as possible. It is also an educational goal that they will develop a good self-concept and learn socially appropriate behaviors that will enable them to optimally interact with peers and adults.

PHYSICAL EDUCATION

Elementary schools have as their main goal to optimize learning for all children—and to build a foundation of skills that will prepare children for lifelong learning. *Physical education* is defined as a process of carefully planned and conducted motor activities that prepare students for skillful, fit, and knowledgeable performance (Nichols, 1990). Physical education may be carried out in a series of settings in the school: classrooms, gymnasium, multipurpose room, the playground, or playing fields.

Physical education is included is traditional elementary school curriculum because physical activity in childhood is associated with a range of beneficial health and fitness outcomes. In addition, childhood physical activity often fosters attitudes and habits that increase the likelihood of individuals engaging in regular exercise in adulthood.

Because of poor fitness performance over the past twenty years, current national health objectives call for increasing the numbers of children participating in daily physical education classes and performing regular physical activity (U.S. Dept. of Health and Human Services, 1992). Because 80 percent of elementary school children are enrolled in physical education classes, these classes may assist in increasing the overall physical activity and interest in lifelong fitness of American children. A national health objective, therefore, calls for physical education classes to engage students in actual physical activity—preferably lifetime sports such as tennis and jogging—for at least 50 percent of class time (U.S. Dept. of Health and Human Services, 1992).

A recent study found that during the weekly schedule of 140 minutes of physical education in the elementary schools studied, less than 10 percent of class time was spent on moderate to vigorous physical activity, approximately 24 percent was spent in minimal activity and 68 percent was spent in sedentary activity (Simons-Morton, et al., 1993). Traditional team sports and games accounted for the bulk of class time, but lifetime activities such as dancing, calisthenics, jogging, and jump roping were also represented. In all activities, however, much of the time spent was sedentary, as children often were waiting to participate or watching, rather than actually participating.

Other researchers observed schools, however, where children arrived on the field promptly and became active immediately. In these situations, teachers provided rapid transitions between activities, students were organized into small groups, which maximized equipment sharing and participation, and received extensive individual instruction and reinforcement. Given this model, it is possible—with appropriate organization—to achieve the national goal of 50 percent of classroom time spent on moderate to vigorous activity (Simons-Morton, et al., 1991).

THE STATUS OF PHYSICAL EDUCATION IN ELEMENTARY SCHOOLS

Today most states have some mandate regarding physical education instruction in elementary schools. However, for the most part, these mandates are general in nature and give individual school districts considerable autonomy in determining physical education time and curriculum. But several national laws passed in the past twenty years have had a serious impact on physical education.

One of the most important laws passed was *Title IX of the Educational Amendments of 1972.* This law stated:

> No person in the United States shall on the basis of sex, be excluded from participation in or be denied the benefits of, or be subjected to discrimination under any educational program or activity receiving federal financial assistance.

This act provided greater equity of opportunity for girls and women in interscholastic and intercollegiate sports, as well as physical education classes.

Another important law was *Public Law 94-142, the Education of All Handicapped Children Act,* commonly known as the *mainstreaming act,* which was passed in 1976. This law required that education be provided for all children with special needs in the least restrictive setting. Because of this law, such children—who were formerly excluded from physical education classes—have the opportu-

mainstreaming Requiring that all handicapped should have access to all education programs provided by schools in the least restrictive setting; this includes physical education classes.

Title IX opened the way for girls to participate in all school sports programs and physical education classes.

Since 1976, federal law has required that handicapped children be allowed into physical education classes with nonhandicapped peers.

nity to participate in physical education classes, often with nonhandicapped class-mates.

In 1987, the U.S. House of Representatives and U.S. Senate jointly passed resolutions requiring states to require daily physical education for all children from kindergarten through high school.

Finally, in 1990, Congress passed *PL 101-336, the Americans with Disabilities Act*, which became effective in January, 1992. This law extended the Rehabilitation Act to prohibit discrimination based on disabilities in public housing and transportation, as well as in institutions, such as schools, which are designed to serve all citizens.

These mandates have yet to be fully accomplished, but they have raised the level of concern for the importance of physical education in the education of all children. Physical education, when performed appropriately and involving a significant proportion of moderate to vigorous regular physical activity, has been found to produce the following benefits to some degree in children who participate:

1. improvement of mental alertness, academic performance, readiness to learn, and enthusiasm for learning;
2. greater health and physical fitness;
3. improved overall health by increasing cardiovascular endurance, muscular strength, power, flexibility, weight regulation, better bone development, and posture, and more skillful movement, active lifestyle habits, and constructive use of leisure time (Nichols, 1990).

Children enjoy being physically active. They are challenged by progressively more difficult movement sequences. By meeting this challenge and succeeding, children may develop healthful habits which will be sustained throughout their lives. In actuality, it does not matter what specific activities or sports children learn. It is what they learn about their bodies and themselves in performing the activity that is paramount.

SUMMARY AND CONCLUSIONS

During middle childhood, a pattern of stable physical growth persists which culminates in the adolescent growth spurt. Not only do children grow taller and heavier, but their bodies undergo accompanying internal changes. Bones continue to grow and mature—at different rates in different children. Some children are early-maturers who will go through a fairly rapid growth spurt before their growth halts. Others are late-maturers whose growth period will last for a longer time, and they will therefore end up taller when their growth halts. Still others more closely resemble the average pattern of growth.

Muscles tend to grow larger and stronger. This increases children's physical strength and endurance. These changes allow the child to engage in progressively more complex, coordinated motor activities. The motor activities of children in middle childhood resemble those of adults in terms of their actual processes—what differs are environmental constraints such as positioning and outcome—for example, the actual distance a ball is thrown.

For each child, the quality of movement is based on some combination of various factors including balance, body agility, body build, throwing abilities, hand precision, strength, and power. The overall maturity of movement therefore varies in children of the same chronological age since each child will have differing skill levels for each of these factors.

While much of today's children's activities is performed in the school environment, children also engage in vigorous play, including rough-and-tumble play. This rough play also offers an opportunity for vigorous physical exchange between children. While rough play might appear to resemble aggression, it differs in many ways. Rough-and-tumble play also offers boys a chance to practice prosocial skills such as negotiation and alliance building. It has more positive attributes for boys than for girls, who are perceived as antisocial if they participate in rough play.

Health is an important factor in children's physical development. Healthy children are better able to optimally participate in the physical, cognitive, and social activities of the world around them—including the school environment. Children with disabling conditions may require special interventions to take full advantage of their learning opportunities. Some children have significant health problems such a cerebral palsy, blindness, deafness, or diabetes. Other children have difficulties associated with their behaviors, for example, obesity, lack of physical fitness, or learning disabilities. Still others have acute illnesses which require their temporary adaptive efforts. This final category includes disorders such as influenza, Otitis media, and other similar problems.

As children's motor skills develop and become refined, their world expands commensurably. The entire house and neighborhood are now open to school-aged children. This significantly increases the hazards and risks to which they are exposed. A rise in accidents and injuries during this period reflects children's greater mobility and independence. Unfortunately, children's cognitive ability and impulse control during this period is not as mature as their physical abilities. This also contributes to their increased risks.

School environments often reflect an awareness of the physical needs of elementary school students. Physical education classes, for example, have as their goals in elementary school to increase the motor skills of children—as well as their self-concept and social skills. In the past twenty-five years, the benefits of physical education and athletic competition have been extended to both boys and girls, as well as to physically challenged students by virtue of various legislative mandates and recommendations.

In general, children enter this period of middle childhood as "little people", but by its end they more closely resemble adults in size and abilities. Their strength, endurance, and ability to compete now allow them to participate fully in the physical world around them.

KEY TERMS AND CONCEPTS

rough-and-tumble play
prosocial behaviors

obesity
mainstreaming

physically challenged
mainstreaming

➤ SELF-TEST QUESTIONS

1. Discuss the development of gross and fine motor skills in middle childhood.

2. How do the different patterns of skeletal maturity affect children's eventual adult height?

3. What environmental and biological factors influence motor skill development during middle childhood?

4. Discuss the factors contributing to the development of basic movement qualities in school-age children?

5. How are children's illnesses a part of normal behavioral development?

6. What is the primary cause of childhood obesity? What is the most advisable treatment for this condition?

7. How does children's motor development influence exposure to hazards and risks in middle childhood?

8. What factors lead to drug use by school-age children?

9. Describe the components of rough-and-tumble play. How does this play differ from aggression?

10. Discuss the gender differences in response to rough-and-tumble play.

11. How should the school environment reflect the physical development of children during middle childhood?

12. What sorts of physical challenges do disabled children face in the school environment? What sorts of illnesses and disabilities affect school-age children?

13. What sorts of legislative mandates have shaped the design of physical education and sports participation in elementary schools?

14. What difficulties are associated with attempts to design physical education programs that will serve all children in an equitable manner?

➤ SUGGESTED READINGS

HUGHES, F. (1991). *Children, Play and Development.* Englewood Cliffs, NJ: Prentice Hall. This book presents an excellent overview of the interactions of play and development during childhood. Not only theory and research, but also applications are presented.

KREMENTZ, J. (1992). *How it feels to live with a physical disability.* New York: Simon and Schuster. This book presents fifteen children and adolescents presenting in their own words what living with a disability means to them. Beautiful photographs strengthen the book's

presentation of the normal lives these children live. While this book was intended for a late childhood audience, it is appropriate for readers of all ages.

U.S. Dept. of Health and Human Services. (1992). *Healthy People.* Boston, MA: Jones and Bartlett. Recent proposals to move the United States toward a nation of optimally healthy people are presented in this readable set of recommendations. This also contains informative background material on the origins of the recommendations.

VIDEO CASE: SEXUAL HARASSMENT IN SCHOOLS

In middle childhood, physical development can begin to cause problems. According to Nan Stein, who runs the Sexual Harassment in Schools Project at Wellesley College, "I can't tell you how many parents of 6-year-olds have told me about...attempts to put sand in somebody's pants...or pull down pants, or to flip up skirts, or to lift sons up by their underwear." Moreover, a survey she did

showed widespread problems and few attempts by school authorities to intervene. When girls try to speak up about harassment, adds Stein, they are "interrogated, demeaned, or the event is trivialized."

Is what these children are going through a form of sexual harassment? Stein believes it is, according to the laws covering sexual harassment, which define it as unwanted and unwelcomed behavior of a sexual nature that interferes with your work or your education. However, in dealing with young children it may be inappropriate to apply the words "sexual harassment." Instead, she prefers to use the language that they employ like "bullying" or "teasing." But whatever such behavior is called, asserts Stein, a lot of children are clearly bothered by it. For example, in one school, little girls are afraid to wear skirts on Friday because the boys in the schoolyard are flipping up their skirts.

But Stein has her critics. Professor Christina Hoff Sommers of Clarke University believes that there is an epidemic of rudeness which researchers like Stein are determined to put a gender bias spin to. That is, they want to show that girls are primarily the victims. So they expand the meaning of terms to encompass behavior that few people have ever identified as harassment. What they've done is taken behavior ranging from sexual teasing to schoolyard horseplay and have been calling it harassment.

In response, Stein counters that there is a real problem as indicated by what children themselves are saying. Junior high school principals have come to her and suggested it is a problem and one that is widespread.

CASE QUESTIONS

1. How does Stein define sexual harassment in school? Do you agree or disagree? Why?

2. What examples of the behavior of boys toward girls does Stein cite? Do you think these are examples of sexual harassment?

3. In a recent survey of 1,800 boys and girls in the eighth through the eleventh grades, four out of five said they had experienced sexual harassment in their schools, including being the object of sexual taunts, jokes, insults, or being sexually touched, grabbed, or pinched. In light of this data, do you think that some preventative education should be undertaken with younger children? Why or why not?

And so we discovered that education is not something which the teacher does, but that it is a natural process which develops spontaneously in the human being.

MARIA MONTESSORI,
THE ABSORBENT MIND

CHAPTER 13

MIDDLE CHILDHOOD: COGNITIVE DEVELOPMENT AND SCHOOL TASKS

OUTLINE

CHAPTER OBJECTIVES

By the time you have finished this chapter, you should be able to do the following:

✔ Compare preoperational thought with concrete operational thought.

✔ Describe how Piaget's concepts of thinking in middle childhood could be applied to education.

✔ Discuss cognitive development during middle childhood as it is described by information-processing theorists.

✔ Describe some of the developmental challenges that middle childhood presents for children, parents, and teachers.

✔ Discuss the ongoing controversy regarding definitions of intelligence and the uses and abuses of intelligence testing.

✔ Explain the two main types of learning disabilities and the various views on their causes and treatments.

For most children, middle childhood is a time for settling down, for developing more fully those patterns that have already been set. It is a period for learning new skills and refining old ones—from reading and writing to playing basketball, dancing, or skateboarding. Children focus on testing themselves, on meeting their own challenges as well as those imposed by the environment. The child who is successful in these tasks will probably become even more capable and self-assured; the one who is unsuccessful is more likely to develop a feeling of inferiority or a weaker sense of self.

Erikson has referred to middle childhood as the period of *industry*. The word captures the spirit of this period, for it is derived from a Latin term meaning "to build." In this chapter, we shall sample some of the ways in which children build cognitive competencies. We shall also look at school tasks and problems encountered in middle childhood, including the ways in which intelligence and achievement tests are administered and interpreted and some current approaches used in understanding learning disabilities.

The development of physical and cognitive competencies and an increased mastery of the environment are only part of a child's developmental tasks during this period. For school-age children, "belonging" is of critical importance. They become very concerned about their status among their peers. This status depends increasingly on the competence and capabilities discussed in this chapter.

 ## CONCRETE OPERATIONAL THOUGHT

The thinking of a 12-year-old child is very different from that of a 5-year-old. This difference is due not only to the much larger body of knowledge and information that the 12-year-old has accumulated, but also to the different ways in which the two children think and process information. For Piaget, the elementary school child is in a period of developing concrete operational thought.

COGNITIVE ABILITIES OF THE SCHOOL BEGINNER

A large part of intellectual development takes place in formal schoolrooms. It is at school that children learn to think like adults, and for this reason alone, starting school is a milestone in the life of any child. The fact that so many cultures have chosen the ages from 5 to 7 years for beginning the systematic education of their young is probably no historical accident. Between ages 5 and 7, many of children's cognitive, language, and perceptual-motor skills mature and interact in a way that makes some kinds of learning easier and more efficient.

In Piaget's theory, the years between ages 5 and 7 mark the transition from preoperational to *concrete operational thought:* Thought becomes less intuitive and egocentric, and more logical. In Chapter 10, we discussed some of the limitations of preoperational thought when compared to concrete operational thought. However, we also saw that many of these differences relating to cognitive immaturity are actually adaptive for young children. Before age 7, children tend to focus on one aspect of a problem at a time. They focus on the here-and-now and on perceptual evidence, rather than on logical reasoning. Their ability to find relationships between the events and things around them is limited.

Toward the end of Piaget's preoperational stage, the rigid, static, irreversible qualities of children's thought begin to "thaw out," to use Piaget's own terminology. Children's thinking begins to be reversible, flexible, and considerably more complex. They begin to notice one, then another aspect of an object and can use logic to reconcile differences between the two. They can evaluate cause-and-effect relationships, especially if they have the concrete object right in front of them and can see changes occur. When a piece of clay looks like a sausage, they no longer find it inconsistent that the clay was once a ball or that it can be molded into a new shape, such as a cube. This emerging ability to leap mentally beyond the immediate situation or state lays the foundation for systematic reasoning in the concrete operational stage and, later, in the formal operational stage. We may see the properties of preoperational and concrete operational thought contrasted in Table 13–1.

One difference between preoperational and concrete operational thought can be illustrated by school-age children's use of **logical inference** (Flavell, 1985). Recall Piaget's liquid conservation experiment (Chapter 2). In this experiment, preoperational children consistently judge that a tall, narrow glass holds more liquid than a short, wide one, although both quantities of liquid were shown to be identical at the start. Concrete operational children, in contrast, know that both containers hold the same amount of liquid. They can make logical inferences from what they have seen. Concrete operational children begin to think differently about states and transformations. They can remember how the liquid appeared before it was poured into the tall, thin container. They can think about how its shape changed as it was poured from one glass into the other and can imagine what shape the liquid would have if it were poured back. Concrete operational children, then, not only include the process of transformation in their thinking, but also are aware that the fluid may assume other shapes in different containers, including the original. Their thinking is *reversible*.

In addition, concrete operational children know that differences between similar objects can be quantified, or measured. In Piaget's (1970) matchstick

logical inference A conclusion reached through "unseen" evidence; concrete operational children are capable of this type of thinking.

TABLE 13–1 A Comparison of Preoperational and Concrete Operational Thought

STAGE	AGE	THE CHILD'S THINKING IS
Preoperational	2 to 5–7 years	Rigid and Static
		Irreversible
		Focuses on the here-and-now
		Centered on one dimension
		Egocentric
		Focused on the perceptual evidence
		Intuitive
Concrete Operational	5–7 to 12 years	Flexible
		Reversible
		Not limited to the here and now
		Multidimensional
		Less egocentric
		Uses logical inferences
		Seeks cause and effect relations

problem, children are shown a zigzag row of six matchsticks and a straight row of five matchsticks placed end to end (see Figure 13–1). When asked which row has more matchsticks, very young children center only on the distance between the end points of the rows and thus pick the "longer" row with five matchsticks. Concrete operational children, however, can take into account what lies between the end points of the rows and therefore will choose the one with six matchsticks.

Finally, unlike preoperational children, concrete operational children can theorize about the world. They think about and anticipate what will happen; they make guesses about things and then test their hunches. They may estimate, for example, how many more breaths of air they can blow into a balloon before it pops and will keep blowing until they reach or surpass this mark. *This ability to theorize is limited to concrete objects and social relationships that children can see and test.* Children do not develop theories about abstract concepts, thoughts, or relationships until they reach the stage of formal operations, which begins around age 11 or 12.

FIGURE 13–1
Piaget's Matchstick Problem.
Concrete operational children realize that the six matchsticks in the zigzag top row will make a longer line than the five matchsticks in the bottom row. Younger children will say that the bottom row is the longest because they tend to center only on the end points of the two lines and not what lies between them.

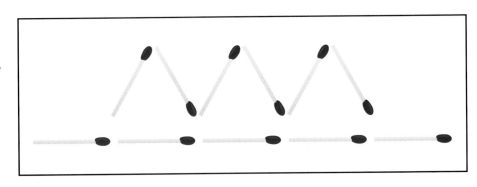

Piaget defined *operation* as a reversible mental action. The concrete operational period, therefore, means that children are able to perform reversible mental actions on real, concrete objects but not on abstract ideas.

The transition from preoperational to concrete operational thought does not happen overnight. It is a developmental task that requires years of experience in manipulating and learning about the objects and materials in the environment. To a large extent, children learn concrete operational thought on their own. As they actively explore their physical environment, asking themselves questions and finding the answers, they acquire a more complex, sophisticated form of thinking (see the box "Children's Humor: 'Why Did the Cookie Cry'?").

PIAGET AND EDUCATION

As we saw in Chapter 6, infants benefit from stimulation that is presented slightly ahead of their developmental level. Such stimulation promotes cognitive growth. Some researchers believe that appropriate training can also accelerate the cognitive development of preoperational children, hastening their entrance into the level of concrete operations. Training is most effective when children have reached a state of *readiness,* an optimal period that occurs just before they make the transition to the next stage (Bruner, Olver, & Greenfield, 1966).

Many of the basic concepts presented by Piaget have been applied to education, especially in the areas of science and math. One such application includes the use of concrete objects for teaching 5- to 7-year-olds. By combining, comparing, and contrasting concrete objects (for example, blocks and rods of different shapes and sizes, seeds that grow in sand, water, or soil), children discover similarities, differences, and relationships.

One method for using objects is to arrange them into simple patterns (see Figure 13–2). Many children who are 5 to 7 years old may still be centering on one par-

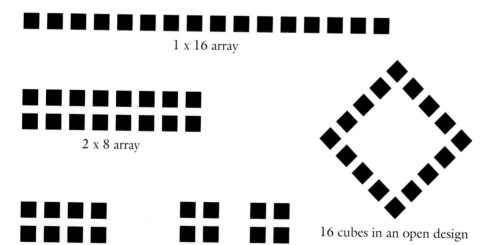

1 x 16 array

2 x 8 array

4 x 4 array

Two "towers" of 8

16 cubes in an open design

FIGURE 13–2

Some possible spatial arrays of 16 cubes. By arranging the cubes in different ways, a teacher can help young schoolchildren understand the number concept of 16.

FOCUS ON AN ISSUE

CHILDREN'S HUMOR: "WHY DID THE COOKIE CRY?"

Children's humor is definitely different—different from adult humor, and often, unique to the child. It is often difficult for adults to see why children find something funny, as the following example indicates:

One father came home from work to find his 4-year-old son, Corey, dissolved in laughter. Corey would sober himself up and then would repeat "ping pong balls falling on your head" and dissolve into laughter again. He was unable to convey what had been so funny so the father asked the mother what had happened.

It turned out that Corey had been watching "Captain Kangaroo" and one of the characters walked into a room where ping pong balls fell on his head from the ceiling. Everytime the character tried to get up, more balls would fall. Corey thought this was very funny and had been trying to

share his experience with his father—to no avail.

This sort of slapstick humor does not appeal to every adult—or even every child. However, when it does, it is very effective at producing laughter.

What makes something funny? One view is that humor is associated with the *discovery and resolution of incongruity* (Shultz, 1976). For example, a child might be asked which of two endings to a question is funnier: *Q:* Why did the cookie cry; *A:* Because its mother was a wafer, or *B:* Because its mother was a wafer so long. For most young children, the question itself is funny without a "punchline" because the notion of a cookie crying is incongruous—it is unexpected.

Other factors involved in the creation of humor are cognitive complexity (for example, the Tom Swifties which were popular in the 1960's—"I've always liked the status of Venus di Milo," Tom said disarmingly) and the creation of a play frame or mood. Pretend play

and the development of imagery are prerequisites to humor.

Humor changes developmentally. During the preschool years, play and humor are often linked. For example, the sheer enjoyment of bouncing on a trampoline or jumping into the water may evoke shouts of laughter—even though nothing truly "funny" is occurring. Children during this age may also find play with words to be funny. For example, 3- and 4-year-olds love to produce such rhymes as "shoe, boo, foo, poo, and so forth—or use forbidden words such as "poop" in public (McGhee, 1979).

During middle childhood, children have learned that words are sometimes ambiguous in meaning. Therefore, jokes and riddles such as "Why did the cookie cry?" become a staple of humor. Third graders usually appreciate jokes like the following:

Judge: Order! Order in the court.

---

ticular aspect of objects. Yet a teacher or care-giver may want to teach an abstract concept (say, the number 16), an operation (subtraction), or a relationship (equality). In introducing second graders to the number concept of 16, for example, a teacher might present several different spatial arrays of 16 cubes—grouped into two towers of 8, one row of 16, four rows of 4, and so on. The teacher could also give verbal cues to the concept of conservation, pointing out, for instance, that the number of cubes remains the same even though the length and width of the rows may change.

There are many other applications of Piaget's concepts. For example, addition and subtraction involve an understanding of reversibility *(5 + 8 = 13, and 13 - 5 = 8)*. Again, children can best learn about these processes by manipulating real

Defendent: Ham and cheese on rye, your honor. (McGhee, 1979)

After the age of 11 or 12, children become increasingly bored with riddles and engage in more sophisticated humor—play with social expectations, illogical behavior and events or play-on-words. An example of more sophisticated adolescent humor is:

Three women had gone to the medicine man for help in having a baby. The witch doctor told the first woman to sit on the hide of an antelope and she would have a baby. He told the next woman that she should sit on the hide of a buffalo to have a baby. The final woman was told to sit on the hide of a hippopotomous. It came to pass that all three had baby boys, but the woman who sat on the hippopotomous hide had twins. Why? Because the sons of the squaw of the hippopotomous hide are equal to the sons of the squaws of the other two hides.

During middle childhood children love riddles; then, at age 11 or 12, they discover humor in playing with social expectations or in illogical behavior or events.

Humor may be seen as a form of intellectual play that reflects the cognitive skills and level of thinking of the children engaging in it. Pleasure in cognitive mastery is also involved in more sophisticated types of humor. Finally, the nature and intensity of children's reactions to potentially humorous events is tied to the context in which they occur. For example, children may laugh at an adult's fall—but only when it isn't their own parent, and only when it is clear there is no real injury. At that point, they may not only laugh, but also imitate. Other contextual factors that affect humour are gender—boys tell more jokes and engage in more physical humor than do girls, and family exposure—if parents tell jokes and engage in humorous activities, then children do also (McGhee, 1979).

The various types of children's humor are evidence of their growing cognitive capacities, combined with their own creativity. With each advancing stage, children become aware of more incongruities that tickle them. They play with language, tease, tell jokes, and clown. A playful frame of mind often helps growing children resolve tension, become more creative—or just plain have fun—as they learn to negotiate the complexities of their world.

objects. Many concepts of time and distance are quite abstract, or they involve the understanding of the relationship between different units of measure. For example, telling time from a clock requires the understanding of the relationship between minutes and hours. Understanding the basic principles of Piaget's theory of cognitive development makes it easier to develop effective educational lessons and to organize these lessons into a logical sequence. Indeed, Piagetian concepts have been applied to a wide range of curriculum projects, including social studies, music, art, math, and science.

Some educators have noted that Piaget seems to have a philosophy of learning as well as a theory of cognitive development. They point to the Piagetian

Following Piaget, some educators stress that children's interest in learning is encouraged when they have the intrinsic satisfaction of solving a problem or discovering a principle rather than looking to a teacher for praise.

principles that children are active learners, that they construct their own theories about how the world operates, and that they themselves are motivated to change these theories when pieces of information do not fit (Bruner, 1973). These educators warn against structuring education in ways that encourage children to seek praise from the teacher rather than to solve problems for their own sake. They emphasize that children's interest in learning depends on the intrinsic rewards they find in the encounter with the subject matter itself. Children gain confidence from mastering a problem or discovering a principle.

These educators also point out that, too often, teachers instruct young children by *telling* them instead of *showing* them. They remove the real-life, concrete context of many subjects. They present rules and items for children to memorize by rote without motivating the children to develop an understanding of these rules. Children are then left with an arid body of facts without the structure to connect them and without the ability to apply these facts and principles to other settings. Children, they contend, need to learn by doing, by actively exploring ideas and relationships, and by solving problems in a realistic context. We may see the key aspects of Piagetian's principles of education presented in Table 13–2.

Piaget was a remarkable observer of the young child; he offered a number of key insights into the child's cognitive development. But there are some aspects of cognitive development that he did not describe and that are important for school learning. Many of these come under the heading of what is called the information-processing perspective.

TABLE 13–2 Piaget's Principles Applied to Education

> ➤ Children are active learners who construct their own theories about how the world operates.
> ➤ Children are motivated to change their theories when pieces of information do not fit.
> ➤ Children's interest in learning depends primarily on the intrinsic rewards gained from contact with the subject matter itself. Teachers' praise may be detrimental to optimal learning.
> ➤ Teachers should *show* rather than *tell* children what to do.
> ➤ Children need to learn by doing, by actively exploring new ideas and relationships, and by solving problems in a realistic format.

INFORMATION PROCESSING

As you recall, information-processing theorists view the human mind as something like a computer, except that the mind's processes change somewhat as the child develops. In information-processing theory, the different components of the mind—attention, memory, problem solving, and the like—can be studied separately. During middle childhood, many of these processes show considerable development.

MEMORY

A number of significant developments occur in the memory abilities of concrete operational children. Recall from Chapter 10 that preoperational children do well in recognition tasks but do poorly in recall tasks; they have trouble using memory strategies like rehearsal. The ability to recall lists of items improves significantly, however, between the ages of 5 and 7. At this time, most children consciously begin the task of memorizing. They look at the material to be remembered and begin to rehearse it—repeating it over and over to themselves. Later, they may also organize the material into categories, and, still later, they may create little stories or visual images to help them remember. This increasingly deliberate use of strategies makes the older child's recall more effective and efficient (Flavell, 1985).

Elementary school children learn different strategies to help them remember things. These strategies are sometimes called *control processes*. Let's look at how some of these memory control processes develop.

1. *Rehearsal* At first, children rehearse simply by saying the items to be memorized over and over to themselves. Gradually, their rehearsal becomes more efficient. Finally, starting at about age 9, children change their rehearsal strategies; instead of rehearsing each item one at a time, they begin to rehearse several items together in a group (Ornstein, Naus, & Liberty, 1975; Ornstein, Naus, & Stone, 1977).

2. *Organization* Another major development in the use of memory strategies is the ability to organize. Whereas younger school-age children tend to relate words by simple association, depending upon the closeness of the words in a presented list, older children organize groups of words by common features—apples, pears, and grapes are "fruit." Children who group words into categories are able to remember more items in memory tasks than those who do not. However, they seldom use this strategy on their own before age 9 (Bjorklund, 1988).

3. *Semantic elaboration* When we study a child's memory for sentences or paragraphs, it is clear that children can often remember what is actually said to them as well as what they infer from a statement. In a series of studies by Scott Paris and his colleagues, children were given sentences like "Her friend swept the floor." They would then be asked if the friend had a broom. Eleven-year-olds but not 7-year-olds were able to infer the presence

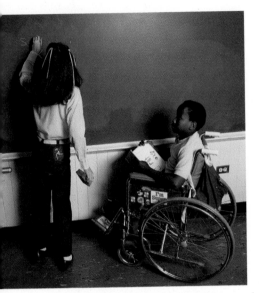

When spelling a word, children usually need to retrieve the proper letters from their memory.

of a broom (Paris, Lindauer, & Cox, 1977). It seems that this kind of memory is active; it requires semantic elaboration. It is a process of reconstruction, rather than an unedited copy of what is stored in memory. It is more like putting the bits and pieces together and making some logical inferences (Flavell, Miller, & Miller, 1993).

4. *Mental imagery* Sometimes, children can be taught to remember unusual material by constructing a mental image. Older children are more likely to construct such images than are younger children, and their images tend to be more vivid and memorable (Siegler, 1986).

5. *Retrieval* Often, when children try to spell a word, they must search their memory for the proper letters. They may know the letter with which the word begins, but they need to sound out several possibilities using all of the vowels. Older children are better than younger ones at these retrieval strategies (Flavell, Miller, & Miller, 1993).

6. *Scripts* Memory for routine events may be organized in the form of scripts. An event that occurs over and over again need not be stored separately in memory each time; it can be remembered in the form of a standard sequence of events, along with "slots" for the variable items. For example, a "school morning script" might specify the events that typically occur on school mornings: get up, get dressed, eat breakfast, and so on. The slots would be filled with variable items, such as which clothes were put on, what was eaten for breakfast, and the conversation at the breakfast table (Nelson & Gruendel, 1986).

METACOGNITION

There are several other information-processing components that become more sophisticated during middle childhood. Children become better able to focus their attention on what they're doing and to keep it focused despite distractions. They gradually improve their problem-solving strategies. They also develop higher-order control processes. Children become better able to monitor their own thinking, memory, knowledge, goals, and actions. They become better able to plan, to make decisions, and to select which memory strategy or problem-solving strategy they want to use. These higher-order processes are called meta processes, or **metacognition.**

In his description of metacognition, Flavell (1985) cites the following example: Preschool and elementary schoolchildren were asked to study a group of items until they were certain they could remember them perfectly. After studying the items for a while, the elementary school children said they were ready, and they usually were. When they were tested, they remembered each item without fail. The preschool children did not perform as well, even though they assured the researchers that they knew every item.

Despite the good intentions of the preschoolers to remember and understand the things they studied, they did not have the cognitive ability to do so; they could not monitor their own intellectual processes. This ability to monitor one's own thinking and memory is just beginning at about age 6. These abilities emerge between ages 7 and 10. For example, most fourth graders, when contrasted with second graders, are capable of deliberately and efficiently using category organization as a memory strategy. However, their use of these strategies

metacognition The process of monitoring one's own thinking, memory, knowledge, goals, and actions.

seems to occur more efficiently when the material to be learned is typical or familiar (Hasselhorn, 1992).

Like other aspects of cognitive ability, metacognitive skills develop gradually during middle childhood and adolescence. Just as a 9-year-old has greater metacognitive ability than a 4-year-old, a 15-year-old's self-monitoring skill far surpasses that of the 9-year-old. Because children use these self-monitoring skills in oral communication, reading comprehension, writing, and other cognitive abilities, they are a critical part of cognitive development.

GENDER DIFFERENCES IN COGNITION

In their pioneering review of the literature on sex differences, Maccoby and Jacklin (1974) concluded that there was a gender difference favoring girls in verbal ability, and there were differences favoring boys in quantitive and spatial abilities. There has been considerable support for gender differences in problem-solving tasks. Women tend to perform better than men on tests of perceptual speed, in some tests of fluency in ideas and words, and on tasks involving manual precision. Women also do better than men on mathematical calculations. Men tend to perform better on certain spatial tasks, target-directed motor skills, and on disembedding tests (tests that involve finding a shape hidden in a more complex array). Men also tend to do better than women on tests of mathematical reasoning (Kimura, 1992).

Recent research has found that while these gender differences do emerge in standardized aptitude testing, the differences have been declining in recent years. For example, in studying results of the Preliminary Scholastic Aptitude Test (PSAT) between 1960 and 1983, researchers found that significant gender differences did exist. Girls scored higher than boys on scales of grammar, spelling, and perceptual speed; boys had higher means on measures of spatial visualization, high school mathematics, and mechanical aptitude. No differences were found in verbal reasoning, arithmetic, and figural reasoning. In addition, over the years studied, gender differences declined precipitously (Feingold, 1988). However, the gender gap in the upper levels of performance on high school mathematics has remained constant since 1960.

Gender differences in cognitive abilities—like many of the other differences we have observed in comparing groups of people based on age, income level, or ethnic/racial background—have multiple causes. For example, while there may be sex differences in brain development (Kimura, 1992), different social expectations for boys and girls may be more influential in shaping actual behavior. As Gilligan (1987) has pointed out, girls who had been well-established in terms of self-confidence and personal identity during middle childhood, sometimes confront major obstacles to their intellectual development during the preadolescent and adolescent period. During this time, when their bodies are maturing, they must reconcile their notions of what it means to be woman with what society and the media propose. Attractiveness and "fitting in" may become more important than academic achievement. The broader society may define mathematics and science as more male-oriented than literature and languages. In addition, many adults—even teachers—may assume that boys will do better in math and therefore put more effort into their math learning than into that of girls, as this example shows:

Girls who do well in mathematics during middle childhood may put less effort into this subject when they become preadolescents or adolescents because of implicit societal pressures for women to put attractiveness ahead of academic achievement, especially in "male-oriented" subjects like mathematics.

I remember the day in sixth grade when it happened. We were in a part of the math curriculum where algebra and geometry were just being introduced. Up until that time I had always done fine in math. That year our teacher was a single woman in her late forties who definitely favored the boys in class. She spent more time answering their questions and working with them in and out of class. Well, one day she announced in class that girls had no business doing math (except for her). She said that boys found it easier and that she would rather teach them. From that day, I always had trouble with math. To this day, when I try to help my own kids do their homework, I feel as though a grey curtain covers my eyes when math comes up.

Experiences such as these, combined with widely accepted stereotypes of males and females, may do more to produce sex differences than any actual brain physiology. As we saw in the discussion of motor development in Chapter 9, while there are no significant differences in strength between preschool and elementary school boys and girls, they often believe there are. Both boys and girls believe boys to be stronger. As with physical strength, it is important that all children be exposed to the necessary stimulation and teaching to allow their optimal intellectual development.

 ## LEARNING AND THINKING IN SCHOOL

Most children enter primary school between the ages of 5 and 7. Once in school, they encounter a number of demands and expectations that differ markedly from those in the home. Children vary greatly in how well they adapt to these demands.

NEW DEMANDS AND EXPECTATIONS

Whether schooling starts with nursery school at age 3 or not until first grade at age 6, children must adapt to some changes immediately. They are separated from their parents or care-givers, perhaps for the first time, and must begin to trust unfamiliar adults to ensure their safety and satisfy their needs. At the same time, they must start to become independent and learn to do certain things for themselves. No longer can a little boy sit down and yell, "Put on my boots!" It is time for him to put on his own boots. Even with a favorable student-teacher ratio, children must compete for adult attention and assistance.

The social rules of any classroom are complex. Relationships with classmates involve discovering the right balance between cooperation and competition; relationships with the teacher involve a compromise between autonomy and obedience. One educator has described the schoolchild's situation this way:

> Assigned to classes that may contain strangers, perhaps even adversaries, students are expected to interact harmoniously. Crowded together, they are required to ignore the presence of others. Urged to cooperate, they usually work in competition. Pressed to take responsibility for their own learning, they must follow the dictates of a dominant individual—the teacher. (Weinstein, 1991, pp. 493–494)

Some schools have elaborate codes of behavior: Children must listen when the teacher speaks, line up for recess, obtain permission to go to the bathroom, and raise a hand before speaking. A great deal of time may be spent on enforcing these rules. Psychology students sometimes observe public school classrooms and measure how much time teachers spend on the following activities: (1) teaching a fact or concept; (2) giving directions for a particular lesson; (3) stating general rules of appropriate classroom behavior; (4) correcting, disciplining, and praising children; and (5) miscellaneous. The results are revealing: In a half-hour lesson, it is not unusual for a teacher to spend only 10 percent to 15 percent of the time on

Attending school makes new demands on children. Now they must follow complex codes of behavior such as lining up when traveling in the hallways.

the first and second categories (Sieber & Gordon, 1981). Research indicates that children learn more in classes where "time on task" is maximized—that is, where the teacher spends at least half the time on actual teaching and less on things like keeping order (Brophy, 1986).

Nonetheless, a considerable amount of time and energy may be put into socializing the children to the highly specific demands of the classroom, demands that are only vaguely connected to intellectual or social growth. Of course, these demands may differ radically from one time or place to another, depending upon nationality, customs, and educational philosophy. Almost twenty-five years ago, Bronfenbrenner (1970) described the code of behavior for 7-year-olds in the then Soviet Union:

> *In school:* All pupils are to arrive at school and in the classroom on time, wipe their feet upon entering, greet the teacher and all technical staff by name, give a general greeting by name to one's seat mate, keep one's things in order, obey all instructions of the teacher, learn rules of class conduct (standing when spoken to, proper position in listening, reading and writing). (p. 28)

Compare this kind of regimentation with the "open classroom" that was popular at around the same time in the United States. In the open classroom, children could stand, sit, or lie down anywhere in a decentralized room, select their own work for the day, and interact with the teacher and other children mainly in small groups. This approach assumed that children are motivated to learn on their own and that they learn best when they are free to choose their own subject matter. The open classroom, in its purest form, gradually went out of style after research showed that children were spending much of their time chatting with one another or moving around aimlessly, and that they were actually learning less than they would have learned in a traditional classroom (Bennett, 1976). In other words, they were spending too little "time on task."

Regardless of the kind of school that children enter, there is always a tremendous gap between what is acceptable at home and the new demands of the classroom. The greater the gap, the more difficult the adaptation will be. Although children at this age have just begun to internalize the rights and wrongs of family life, they are suddenly expected to adapt to a whole new set of standards. The success with which they make this transition depends upon family background, school environment, and the variables of individual development. How well have the children previously coped with dependency, autonomy, authority relationships, the need to control aggression, and the prompting of conscience? Their inner resources may be shaky; nevertheless, we require a flexibility from school beginners that is rarely required of adults.

DEVELOPING COMPETENT LEARNERS AND CRITICAL THINKERS

Learning has been defined as "an activity of the brain, under the direction and control of the individual, that must result in additions to and modifications of long-term memory" (Letteri, 1985). In a rapidly changing world, there is much to learn and too little time to learn it. Knowledge may now become obsolete in a decade or less, and because of this, today's children will have to become lifelong learners in order to adapt to a changing world. Meanwhile, these children need to integrate and organize the barrage of information that comes at them from all sides. They must find order and consistency in the complex and sometimes unstable experiences of their lives. To help children adapt and become lifelong learners, many educators urge teachers to avoid focusing on too many disconnected facts, principles, and rules. Instead, they emphasize that teachers should focus on instructing children how to become self-directed, competent learners and critical thinkers.

One approach that teachers can use is derived directly from what we know about information processing. Children can be taught to be competent learners by learning control processes. For example, problem solving often involves many component control processes, such as focusing on relevant details or analyzing a problem into component parts. Each of these strategies might be taught by using simple exercises. Some educators have had rather remarkable success in as little as 15 or 20 hours of training with initially poor students. The students become more analytical and focused, less impulsive, and they earn better grades (Letteri, 1985).

The development of strategy use and cognitive processing skills during middle childhood are significantly affected by children's school experiences. Teachers seem to be responding to children's developing abilities, as well as guiding this development, when they make frequent strategy suggestions to second and third graders. Teachers also give direct metamemory guidance to older students. Especially for low and moderate achievers, exposure to a high-strategy teacher is related to better comprehension and use of cognitive processing instruction. However, the infrequent use of strategy suggestions, and the limited efforts made by most teachers to instruct children in metacognition, suggests that most children could benefit by receiving more instruction in the use of strategy (Moely et al., 1992).

What sorts of strategies might teachers instruct children in? Educators and psychologists recommend a range of teaching strategies to develop student thinking. According to Costa (Costa et al., 1985), children need to develop six kinds of thought. We might call these the "six R's":

1. *Remembering*—recalling a fact, idea, or concept.
2. *Repeating*—following a model or procedure.
3. *Reasoning*—relating a specific instance to a general principle or concept.
4. *Reorganizing*—extending knowledge to a new context for an original solution.
5. *Relating*—establishing a connection between new knowledge and past or personal experience.
6. *Reflecting*—exploring the thought itself and how it occurred.

Developing these thinking skills requires special teaching strategies. To develop reasoning, teachers need to present interesting problems and materials. The goal is to increase curiosity, to foster questioning, to develop related concepts, to encourage evaluation of alternatives, and to help students construct hypotheses and devise methods of testing them. Teaching students to develop critical thinking is more difficult than simply imparting facts and principles (Costa, 1985).

In the past decade, there has been an attempt in U.S. schools to teach learning and thinking skills, to individualize instruction to the learning style and developmental level of the child, and to foster independent, self-regulated, self-paced learning. Often, this results in an increased number of small-group projects and activities. When small-group instruction is done effectively, children experience *cooperative* rather than *competitive* learning activities. Cooperative learning techniques have been found to increase overall performance for children from both the general population and minority groups (*Johnson, Stanne, & Garibaldi*, 1992). Cooperative learning has been found to raise the perceived status of female students in the classroom significantly more than when individualistic teaching strategies were employed (Petersen, Johnson, & Johnson, 1992). In addition, children exposed to cooperative learning techniques achieve high levels of skill in standard areas like math and reading (Costa, 1985). Unfortunately, such classes are hard to manage well. (See the box "The Math Gap: An Educational Dilemma.")

SUCCESS IN SCHOOL

The schoolroom is the most important stage on which children perform during middle childhood. It is at school that children test their intellectual, physical, social, and emotional competencies to find out if they can equal the standards set for them by their parents and teachers and by society as a whole. It is also at school that children gain confidence in their ability both to master their world and to develop social relationships with their peers. The school, in other words, plays a critical role in the healthy development of the child. Unfortunately, how well the school meets the challenge placed before it—to help children maximize all of their personal resources—is open to question.

The educational literature of the late 1960s was filled with biting criticism of our school system. Such books as *How Children Fail* (Holt, 1964), *36 Children* (Kohl, 1968), and *Death at an Early Age* (Kozol, 1970) came to the dismaying conclusion that the majority of our schools are overwhelming failures. Instead of offering intellectual excitement and teaching children how to think independently, schools stifle curiosity. They breed conformity and mediocrity by emphasizing discipline and demanding the "right" answers. In short, these books claimed, school is boring, and it is no wonder that so many students are frustrated and unhappy. The situation was summarized by one 9-year-old student:

> In school we waste time until it's over. I do what I have to. I don't
> like the place. I feel like falling off all day, just putting my head down
> and saying good-bye to everyone until three. We're out then, and we
> sure wake up. (Coles, 1968, p. 1322)

In the 1980s, schools were still getting negative reviews. This time they were also criticized for not teaching basic skills and for being too unstructured and undisciplined (Goldberg & Harvey, 1983).

Even in mediocre school systems, some children not only succeed but also excel. According to David McClelland (1955), the reason why some children achieve more than others may relate to the values of the culture in which they are reared. After comparing several periods of history in several different cultures, McClelland concluded that *achievement motivation*—the drive to attain success and excellence—is a cultural value. Within any given society at any time, some groups value achievement more highly than other groups do (deCharms & Moeller, 1962). Different cultures or subcultures may also value different *kinds* of achievement—one group may stress educational goals, whereas another may place more value on financial or social success. Children whose parents stress values that are different from those of the school may bring less motivation to academic tasks. Such children may simply be channeling their need for achievement into other areas.

Underachievement is a widespread problem in the United States, with prevalence estimates ranging from 15 percent to 50 percent (Carr, Borkowski, & Maxwell, 1991). In many schools, underachievement has been pinpointed as early as the third grade. For both achievers and underachievers, attributions (beliefs), self-esteem, and megacognition interrelate to predict reading achievement. Underachievers have qualitatively different beliefs about themselves in the classroom than do achievers. They seem to possess the same metacognitive strategies, but they do not hold the same expectations of success for themselves as achievers do. As the researchers state, "It is as if their knowledge and abilities were disassociated from their beliefs about instrumentality, a key characteristic of metacognition in achievers" (Carr, Borkowski, & Maxwell, 1991, p. 113). Achievers believe they will succeed, and use the strategies necessary to do so; underachievers do not make the connection between their prior knowledge and internal beliefs about self-efficacy, the ability to succeed at a task.

Success in school is influenced by many other factors. For example, children who are in poor health, who do not get enough to eat, or who are preoccupied with problems at home may do poorly at school tasks. Self-esteem is another important factor. Children's own judgments of their competence seriously affect their performance in school. In one study, 20 percent of school-age children underestimated their actual abilities. These children set lower expectations for themselves and were surprised at their intermittent high grades (Phillips, 1984).

More recently, research has found that children's perceived academic competence was related to the warmth and quality of interaction with their fathers. For boys, fathers tended to be increasingly less easygoing and put more pressure

In order to do well in school, children need to eat well.

FOCUS ON DIVERSITY

THE MATH GAP: AN EDUCATIONAL DILEMMA

We have known for some time that college students coming from Japan and Taiwan to study in the United States outperform their American peers in math and science. Why is this so? Were these students a select group—the gifted, the elite, the highly motivated? What was the mathematics achievement of the average student in these countries in high school or in junior high school?

The general impressions of Asian superiority in mathematics and science were confirmed by studies that were conducted in the late 1960s and early 1970s (Comber & Keeves, 1973; Husen, 1976). These studies documented the average achievements of Asian junior-high and high-school students as being consistently higher than those of American students. Later studies showed similar accomplishments in math for children as young as kindergartners (Stevenson et al., 1986). In these studies, the average score of American kindergartners was below the Japanese average. In first grade, the difference increased, and by fifth grade, it was very large. It was so large that when 60 fifth-grade classes in Japan, Taiwan, and the United States were compared, the average math score of the highest-

scoring American classroom was below that of all the Japanese classrooms and all but one of the Taiwanese classrooms.

Why is this so? Are the Asian students innately smarter? Are they more highly motivated? Are they better educated in math than Americans? A series of studies in 1986 and 1987 addressed these questions, and their findings seem to point the finger at differences in educational practices. Although the American and Asian school systems have certain features in common, there are also highly significant differences. Some of the similarities are that children in each country—Taiwan, Japan, and the United States—start kindergarten at the same age. Almost all school-age children in each country attend elementary school and continue at least through the junior high level. Also, the eventual success of the children in each country depends to a large extent on their educational achievement.

The differences are striking, however. Test scores on nationwide examinations determine entry into high school in Japan, Taiwan, and many European countries, but not in the United States. Career paths, too, are more closely linked to educational achievement in these two

Asian countries. As a result, enormous pressure is exerted on even very young children in Japan and Taiwan: They are told that they must study hard and succeed in school. Far less pressure is put on young children in the United States. The national exams of Japan and Taiwan influence their educational curricula and practices, which are nationally standardized from the elementary grades through high school. America's national or statewide exams (for example, the Regents exams in New York State) influence educational placement only in the last few years of high school and in college.

There are also striking differences in classroom instruction. American children spend far less time in school than their counterparts in Japan and Taiwan, and when they are in school, they spend less "time on task." For example, American fifth graders were observed as spending an average of only 19.6 hours per week in academic activities, exclusive of lunch, physical education, transitions, and the like. The Taiwanese and Japanese children spent 40.4 and 32.6 hours per week, respectively, in academic activities. What is more, the American children spent less of their acad-

on sons who had high rather than low perceived academic competence. For girls, fathers put more pressure on daughters with low perceived academic competence but assumed a "hands-off" policy with their daughters whose expectations were high. Another finding was that children with lower perceived academic competence do not trust their own ideas and often turn to adults for guidance and assistance in homework (Wagner & Phillips, 1992).

emic time on mathematics. By fifth grade, the U.S. classrooms averaged 3.4 hours per week on math compared to 11.4 hours in Taiwan and 7.6 hours in Japan.

These time differences alone might be enough to explain the differences in performance, but classroom organization, teacher behavior, and child behavior differed as well. Classes in the United States were smaller, and the children tended to work alone or in small groups rather than in whole class instruction. The Asian children spent most of their math class working, watching, and listening together as a class. The U.S. approach allowed the teacher the opportunity to individualize assignments and to tutor individuals and small groups. It also encouraged individual problem solving. But there were inefficiencies. Much of the time, the children's work was not closely supervised. Correction and guidance were delayed or absent. The researchers found American children to be out of their seats 21 percent of the time and to be engaged in inappropriate (off-task) activities 17 percent of the time. Compare this to the Taiwanese and the Japanese, who were out of their seats only 4 percent and 2 percent of the time, respectively. Teachers in the Taiwanese and Japanese classes appeared better pre-

A classroom's organization and style of presentation may mirror the goals and values of the educational system. For example, these children in Japan are expected to study long and hard and to work together as a class.

pared, more intensely involved in their subject matter, and more lively in their presentation. Student attention and involvement were higher (Stigler, Lee, & Stevenson, 1987).

Is it any wonder that Japanese and Taiwanese children do better than American youngsters on mathematics tests? Certainly, different educational practices can account for much of the difference in performance on math tests.

Should U.S. schools change their educational philosophy, which emphasizes individualized instruction and small, cooperative learning groups? The researchers suggest simple changes like increasing the percentage of elementary school time spent on mathematics and decreasing transitional and irrelevant activities. Further, they recommend more direct teacher-student communication and better math preparation for teachers.

(The material in this box has been adapted from James W. Stigler, Shin-ying Lee, and Harold W. Stevenson. (1987). Mathematics Classrooms in Japan, Taiwan, and the United States. *Child Development*, 58, 1272–1285.)

PARENTAL INFLUENCES ON SCHOOL SUCCESS

In correlational studies, poverty, gender, ethnicity, and family composition have all been linked to poor school performance. Being male, of minority status, poor, and coming from a single-parent family have been especially linked with high risk for school failure. Yet, as we noted in Chapter 1, it is inappropriate to assume that because two factors are correlated that one causes the other. It is almost always more complicated than that. For example, in correlational studies, inner-city males have been found to be especially at risk for school failure. This may be because inner-city children often grow up in cultural environments where academic achievement and other types of scholastic success may be devalued (Patterson, Kupersmidt, & Vaden, 1990); or where violence produces stress which makes learning difficult (Timnick, 1989); or where effective male role models are unavailable (Garibaldi, 1992). But certainly many inner-city males succeed in school, especially if one or more of these circumstances is absent.

Parents play a large role in providing a supportive environment and in encouraging the development of the specific skills that help children succeed. On the negative side, children from homes where there is severe marital distress, paternal criminality, maternal psychiatric disorder, overcrowding, or where children are intermittently placed in foster care, are at special risk for school failure. These children lack the appropriate safe environment in which learning optimally occurs (Sameroff, et al., 1993).

In contrast, if we look at the parents of children who succeed in school, we find behaviors that almost any parent can accomplish regardless of economic circumstances. Reviews of the research on school success point to three types of parental variables (Hess & Holloway, 1984):

1. Parents of successful children have realistic beliefs about their child's current abilities yet high expectations for the future. They encourage their children to master age-appropriate tasks both in school and at home. These parents believe in their children and help the children to have confidence and high expectations for themselves.
2. Parent-child relationships are warm and affectionate, and parents have discipline and control strategies that are authoritative rather than authoritarian. Children have limits on their behavior but feel safe and accepted.
3. Finally, and perhaps most importantly, these parents talk to their children. They spend time with them, read to them, listen to them, tell them stories, and have lots of conversations with them. They model interest in the world around them and provide some of the conceptual frameworks for understanding social and physical phenomena. They support and enrich the child's exploration and inquiry.

Despite poor English skills, poverty, and early traumas—as well as attendance at urban schools with their often disruptive environments—many of the children succeed academically because of the support and guidance of their parents and siblings. These Southeast Asian parents have created an environment where learning and teaching was valued, as they believe that their children could succeed at any task with hard work (Kaplan, Choy, & Whitmore, 1992).

These factors are not unique to Southeast Asian families. In general, families where children are academically successful are those that possess similar patterns of parent-child relationships. For example, most African-American children who excel academically have parents who stress the importance of education, as well as encourage the development of their self-esteem and belief in personal efficacy—in addition to acknowledging that they may encounter racial bias. The message from these parents is that "you are wonderful" and "ignore the words and behaviors of

Children who perform well in school tend to have parents who strongly value education and encourage their child's self-esteem.

others who try to tell you otherwise" (Patterson, Kupersmidt, & Vaden, 1990). As one educational consultant recently commented:

> Recognizing that teachers alone cannot be expected to raise the achievement and aspirations of African-American male children, the parents of these young men must motivate, encourage and reinforce their sons so that they will use their talents and ability to perform successfully in the classroom....They should also be taught why they should resist peer pressure and why success in school must be reinforced. (Garibaldi, 1992, p. 149–150).

While poverty and minority status may be major factors lowering children's intellectual performance, it is not only poor, minority children who have school problems. Middle- and upper-income families may also have underachieving children. Parents who attributed greater importance to their children's fun, excitement, and socialization, or who emphasized material possessions, were found to have children who performed more poorly in school than families where these values were not as prized. (Kaplan, Choy, & Whitmore, 1992). Other research has found that when family and culture are emphasized, children succeed academically. Where immediate gratification and material possessions are emphasized, children do not do as well.

Proposals to reform the American educational system focus on the demand that the educational system deal with urgent social service needs—poverty, drugs, teenage pregnancy, violence, and other serious social problems. Since families provide the immediate environment and values in which children derive their academic expectations, recent recommendations urge that schools reach out and involve families meaningfully in the education of their children. Culturally compatible values, behaviors, and strategies for success that will enhance children's academic achievement are currently being formulated by educators and researchers.

TECHNOLOGY IN THE SCHOOL ENVIRONMENT

Today's learning environments are in transition as new technology impacts on the way teaching is—and will be—conducted. While those who were children thirty years ago may have arrived in the classroom relatively unaffected by the then new technology of television, today's children have been extensively exposed to it. As one educator commented:

> For the contemporary child who is just learning to read, it is not television that is new. It is the linear and sequential nature of print on the page that is alien. As Marshall Mcluhan pointed out, one can be absorbed by the glowing screen of television in a way that is not possible with books....Most children experience the rhythm and tempo of a world vastly different from the one presented in a typical classroom. Compare the excitement of watching a wide screen version of "Batman" to a classroom discussion on history or geography. The disparity of such experiences creates very real tensions. (Kaha, 1990, p. 46)

Although estimates of children's viewing times vary widely from 11 to 28 hours a week, they all indicate that American children spend more time watching television than in any other activity except sleep. Home observations indicate that by age 4 children look at the television set for half the time it is on, and that their viewing time increases steadily until late childhood when it peaks at around 80 percent of the time spent actually observing what is on the screen. In addition, children from low income and minority families watch television more than their more affluent peers do. For these children, it is extensively used as a source of news and social information (Huston, Watkins, & Kunkel, 1989).

As we saw in earlier chapters, television has the potential for teaching basic skills and for expanding the social and educational horizons of all children. Large-scale evaluations have consistently demonstrated the effectiveness of such educational television programs as "Sesame Street," "Reading Rainbow," and "Freestyle" (Huston, Watkins, & Kunkel, 1989). The educational value of much of commercial television has been more controversial. We have yet to make full and effective educational use of commercial television at home or in the classroom.

COMPUTERS, LEARNING, AND THINKING   Computers have arrived in the classroom as well as in homes and in businesses. Now that most schools have computers, educators are struggling to decide how to use them to enhance learning and thinking. As with many new technologies, controversy surrounds the use of computers by children.

> To many, the computer seems a beneficent genie, a powerful tool with the capacity to transform our schools and revolutionize children's learning. To others, the computer seems a potentially menacing device, more likely to undermine than improve our educational system, more likely to control than serve children. (Lepper & Gurtner, 1989, p. 170)

How are computers likely to affect the lives of children in the future? First, computers may well become personal tutors and make learning more efficient, effective, and highly motivating for students. With a computer, learning is more individualized to the needs and abilities of the student. Second, computers will serve as multipurpose tools for writing and communication skills. Computers may indeed become a boon to students who do not normally succeed in today's schools. Since computers are machines, they are always fair and impartial. This will minimize any pernicious effects of teacher prejudice or favoritism which may occur in classroom learning situations (Lepper & Gurtner, 1989).

Compared to television, computers have one major advantage in the classroom: They permit an ongoing interaction between student and machine. But the nature of the interaction depends on the kind of program that is used. Reviews of available programs suggest that as few as 1 in 10 computer programs are good educational devices (Hassett, 1984). Let's look at some of the ways in which computers can be employed in the school environment.

A key aspect of the computer's arrival in the classroom is the interaction between student and machine. How well this interaction works is a function of the particular program being used.

First, computers have been used for *programmed learning,* or *computer-assisted instruction.* In this mode, the computer serves as a surrogate teacher. The computer program structures learning in sequential steps and adjusts the size of the steps to the ability of the individual child. A child who learns quickly can progress rapidly through the program, whereas one who learns more slowly can be given extra opportunities for review. The programs correct children and provide immediate feedback. If they are well designed, children can learn skills like addition and subtraction or typing. However, this kind of program often is not well written, and children may tire of the repetitive format (Greenfield, 1984).

A second use of computers in the classroom is to foster creativity and inventiveness. One way of doing this is to teach children how to program computers themselves, so that they are responsible for what the computer does. In a programming language called LOGO, children can create complex geometric constructions. They are no longer simply repeating programmed drills; by doing the programming themselves, children discover principles, construct new forms, and analyze structures (Papert, 1980).

Programming at the elementary school level, however, is not always effective—in one study, only about 25 percent of the children remained interested after the initial instruction (Hawkins et al., 1982). It may be that computer programming requires too much abstract thinking from children who are still at the concrete operational level.

Another way of enhancing creativity is to let children use computers for writing stories. Children can be taught to type and to use a word-processing program. Once they gain the basic skills, they can edit their stories with relative ease. For younger children, there are programs that allow them to construct stories without writing. Even preschoolers can use computer graphics to develop sequences of action for stories and then play back their own creations (Forman, 1985).

INTERACTIVE VIDEO AND LEARNING The combined technologies of television and computers make possible a range of new educational media. With the advent of interactive video displays, for example, it is possible to teach a person to ski or fly in a very realistic manner. Compact disk players together with computers also make possible multimedia exposure to encyclopedias, not only presenting a paragraph and picture of a dinosaur to a child, but showing it moving, creating its roar and, if the child is not yet reading, telling the child about that dinosaur.

What will the classrooms of the twenty-first century be like? Some have suggested that the textbook and the teacher will no longer hold center stage, supplemented by a few audio-visual aids. Instead, interactive video displays, extended computer networks and multiple modes of communication will be the norm, in the classroom as well as in the broader world of work. This may well change the nature of what is taught and the skills and abilities that are valued, both in the classroom and in the work place. The memorization of facts from the textbook may become even less important than they are now. Instead, a range of strategies for analysis, synthesis and evaluation of readily available visual, auditory and print materials may need to be taught.

When elementary students can see the morning TV weather report in the form of time-lapsed global photos, their classroom study of the weather takes on new dimensions. With interactive video displays, concepts that were previously abstract and theoretical become concrete, or at least pictoral. The actual events of a science or social studies topic can be played in the classroom, then replayed, dissected, analyzed and reassembled. Children can make predictions and test them on their interactive video display. Already sophisticated computer games like "Civilizations" or "Simcity" offer just those opportunities. Can it be long before there are programs in each subject area that offer a range of simulations of real situations?

The classrooms of tomorrow may well teach a different package of knowledge and skills.

ASSESSING INDIVIDUAL DIFFERENCES

Schools measure children's ability and achievement in order to determine their level of development and their readiness to learn new skills. This is accomplished through various forms of intelligence, diagnostic, and achievement tests.

In the 1940s and 1950s, a great effort was made in the United States to administer tests to schoolchildren—IQ tests, achievement tests, personality tests, and career aptitude tests. School files were—and in many cases still are—filled with test scores of varying degrees of accuracy and significance. In the 1960s, many parents and educators reacted against what they considered the abuse of diagnostic tests. More recently, there has again been an increase in the use of diagnostic and achievement tests. But most teachers are now more aware of the dangers of misinterpreting (or overinterpreting) test results and of pinning labels on children. Consequently, they are using the tests with greater caution.

The rationale behind testing is that schools must assess student abilities in order to plan efficient educational programs. But all too often, the scores have been misused. Teachers and administrators have employed test results to pigeonhole children or to deny some of them access to certain educational opportunities. Almost as frequently, the test results have not been used at all. More than one child has experienced the frustration of entering first grade with reading test scores at the third-grade level, only to be assigned to a class in beginning reading because he or she "has not had that subject yet."

In an approach known as **diagnostic-prescriptive teaching,** however, tests and informal assessments can be a vital aid to education. The idea behind this kind of teaching is that if educators know precisely what an individual child can

diagnostic-prescriptive teaching A system of teaching in which tests and informal assessments inform educators as to a child's abilities so that they may prescribe appropriate instruction.

do, they will be better able to prescribe the next step. The diagnosis does not apply a generalized label but measures a specific, observable behavior or skill. The child is assessed for what he or she can do. The testers do not call the student "superior" or "mildly retarded" or "a slow learner"—they simply identify the child's particular knowledge, skills, and abilities at that point in time. Sometimes, the diagnosis is based on classroom observation or a diagnostic lesson; other times, it is based on formal tests called **criterion-referenced tests** (Glaser, 1963).

Because criterion-referenced tests focus on the achievements of an individual, they differ radically from the more familiar **norm-referenced tests,** which are concerned with how one child's score compares with that of another child. Most standard IQ tests, achievement tests, and scholastic aptitude tests are norm referenced. They compare one child's score with the scores of a large number of other children. In other words, a criterion-referenced math test describes a child's accuracy and speed in several specific math skills, whereas a norm-referenced test shows that a child is performing at a level higher or lower than the average for her grade or age. Thus, a norm-referenced test might identify a child as being in the bottom 10 percent of her class in arithmetic skills, but it will say little or nothing about what she does know, why she fails specific items, or what specific skills she needs to acquire so that she may progress. Also, the test reveals nothing about the child's pattern of attention, her level of anxiety when she faces a math question, or any of a number of things that the teacher may need to know in order to help her. The test may merely label the child, in a general way, as a good student or a poor one.

INTELLIGENCE TESTING

In the field of developmental psychology, perhaps no issue has been more controversial than that of intelligence and intelligence testing. The academic debate has become a public one largely because of the broad impact that intelligence test scores have on educational and social opportunities. When young children are labeled on the basis of IQ scores, the results can be far reaching. IQ scores may affect the extent and quality of children's education, determine the jobs they may have as adults, and put a lasting imprint on their self-image. IQ tests are administered more widely and taken more seriously in the United States than anywhere else. The emphasis on testing, especially at the elementary and secondary school levels, has resulted in the grouping and rating of students based solely on their test performances. Children, too, are taught to take these tests seriously.

Why do we hold intelligence in such high regard? What are we actually trying to measure? In this section, we shall explore the concept of intelligence, beginning with some early attempts to measure and thus to define it.

ALFRED BINET The first comprehensive intelligence test was designed in the late nineteenth century by Alfred Binet, a French psychologist. He was commissioned by the French government to devise a method of identifying those children who would not profit from a public education. Binet needed a scale that would yield an index of the educability of children. His concept of intelligence focused on such complex intellectual processes as judgment, reasoning, memory, and comprehension. To measure these capabilities, he used test items involving

criterion-referenced test A test that evaluates an individual's performance in relation to mastery of specified skills or objectives.

norm-referenced test A test that compares an individual's performance with the performances of others in the same age group.

Some form of diagnostic and achievement tests are important because the school must assess student abilities in order to plan efficient educational programs.

problem solving, word definitions, and general knowledge. Binet believed that intelligence does not remain static but grows and changes throughout life. Test questions, therefore, had to be carefully arranged to reflect this growth. A good test item differentiated between older and younger children. If more than half of the 5-year-olds were able to define the word "ball," and fewer than half of the 4-year-olds were able to do so, then the definition of ball was included on the test for 5-year-olds (Binet & Simon, 1905, 1916). This empirical basis for selecting and ordering items was a landmark in the testing movement. The resulting test score was called a **mental age.**

THE INTELLIGENCE QUOTIENT According to the concept of mental age, a 4-year-old who could answer most of the questions on the test for 5-year-olds would have a mental age of 5. Later psychologists found a way of conveniently expressing the relationship between mental age and chronological (or "real") age: the **intelligence quotient,** or IQ. *Intelligence quotient is calculated by dividing mental age by chronological age and multiplying the result by 100.* Thus, our bright 4-year-old with a mental age of 5 would have an intelligence quotient of 5/4 times 100, or 125. Any child whose mental age and chronological age are equal—in other words, a child whose intellectual development is progressing at an average rate—will have an IQ of 100.

In 1916, an English version of Binet's test, revised by Lewis Terman at Stanford University, was introduced in the United States. The concept of IQ testing won wide acceptance in the United States and was much used during the 1940s and 1950s. In contrast to Binet, who believed that intelligence was modifiable, many American psychologists believed that as mental and chronological ages increased during development, the ratio between them remained fixed—it was innate (Weinberg, 1989).

Today, with a few exceptions, the ratio IQ that was described earlier has fallen into disuse in favor of a norm-referenced **deviation-IQ test,** which assigns an IQ score by comparing a child's performance on the test with performances of

mental age An intelligence test score showing the age group with which a child's performance most closely compares.

intelligence quotient An individual's mental age divided by chronological age, multiplied by 100 to eliminate the decimal point.

deviation IQ An IQ score derived from a statistical table comparing an individual's raw score on an IQ test with the scores of other subjects of the same age.

other children of the same age. This measure carries no automatic assumption about whether intelligence is fixed or modifiable. The current Stanford-Binet test, which is widely used, is the direct descendant of Binet's 1905 test.

THE NATURE OF INTELLIGENCE

The development of sophisticated models for testing and measuring intelligence has stimulated inquiry, both popular and scientific, into the nature of intelligence itself. We shall briefly consider some of the highlights of this continuing debate. Notice that some of the following arguments might be applied equally well to other human characteristics, such as aggressiveness, self-confidence, and even physical beauty.

INNATE AND LEARNED INTELLECTUAL ABILITIES   The nature-versus-nurture controversy still sparks fireworks in academic journals and in the popular press. Arthur Jensen (1969) generated a great deal of controversy when he stated his belief that 80 percent of what is measured on IQ tests is inherited, and only 20 percent is determined by a child's environment. Criticism of Jensen's paper (and the data upon which it was based) was widespread; some psychologists even took the view that there was no good evidence for *any* genetic effect on IQ (Kamin, 1974). The current view is a more balanced one: The consensus seems to be that genetic and environmental factors are about equally potent in determining how well a child will do on an IQ test (Weinberg, 1989). But the pendulum may once again be tipping toward the side of those who think that intelligence is largely innate: A recent paper on identical twins who were reared apart claims that the heritability of IQ (how much is inherited) is 70 percent (Bouchard et al., 1990).

GENERAL AND SPECIFIC ABILITIES   Several early theorists, most notably Spearman (1904), believed that intelligence was a single central attribute, reflected in the ability to learn. He drew this conclusion from the fact that children who did well on one kind of test item usually did well on other kinds of test items, too. For example, a child who has a high score on the vocabulary test is also likely to be above average in solving puzzles or doing math problems (Hunt, 1961). Other theorists (Guilford, 1959; Thurstone, 1938) have contended that intelligence is a composite of many different abilities, such as perceptual speed, word fluency, memory, and others. An individual may be good at remembering facts or perceiving similarities, but this does not necessarily mean that he will also do well on tasks involving spatial relationships.

Intelligence tests differ on whether they define intelligence as a unitary attribute or as a composite of several abilities. The Wechsler Intelligence Scale for Children has separate subtests for information, comprehension, mathematics, vocabulary, digit span, picture arrangement, and others. This test yields a verbal IQ score, a performance (nonverbal) IQ score, and a full-scale score that represents a combination of the two. The current version of the Stanford-Binet test, on the other hand, yields a single score that indicates an overall intelligence level, although individual test items measure a variety of abilities and skills.

One proponent of the view that intelligence is made up of several independent abilities is Howard Gardner (1983). Gardner reviews the literature of neurology, psychology, and even that of human evolutionary history and comes up with seven "frames of mind"—seven different kinds of intelligence. These are divided into two groups. In the first group are *linguistic intelligence*, *musical intelligence*, *logical-mathematical intelligence*, and *spatial intelligence*. The second group includes *kinesthetic intelligence*, *interpersonal intelligence*, and *intrapersonal intelligence*. Each of these forms of intelligence works with different information and processes the information in different ways. Although a child may be below average in the kinds of intelligence measured by IQ tests (mainly linguistic and logical-mathematical), she may be high in other kinds of intelligence—for example, interpersonal intelligence (the ability to understand the feelings and motivations of others).

Another current view is that of Robert Sternberg (1985). Sternberg has a "triarchic" (three-part) concept of intelligence. The first kind is *contextual intelligence*, which involves adaptation to the environment. If the environment is poor, a person who is high in this type of intelligence may modify the environment or find a better one. The second type is *experiential intelligence*, which involves the capacity to cope with new tasks or situations as well as with old ones. Coping with new tasks involves the capacity to learn quickly, and coping with old ones involves the capacity to automatize performance so that a minimum of thought and energy is spent on these tasks. Finally, the third type is *componential intelligence*, which corresponds roughly to the abilities measured by IQ tests.

DIAGNOSTIC AND ACHIEVEMENT TESTS

As mentioned earlier, the purpose of tests is to help schools assess the capabilities of students so that educators can design programs to fit individual needs. Because many capabilities cannot be measured by an IQ test, educators must find other ways to assess the diverse skills and strengths of each individual.

BEYOND ACQUISITION OF KNOWLEDGE   What kind of test to give and how the results should be used depend on educational priorities and how the learning process is viewed. Some theorists believe that the American educational system has focused too much on "intelligence" and "achievement" and has ignored a number of equally significant abilities. For example, of the six different cognitive abilities defined by Bloom and Krathwohl (1956), only the first two are regularly measured in school. Beginning with the simplest, the six categories are as follows:

1. *Knowledge of facts and principles* refers to the direct recall of information. Such knowledge frequently involves the rote memorization of dates, names, vocabulary words, and definitions—items that are easy to identify and test. Perhaps because of its convenience, this cognitive ability has long been the focus of education.
2. *Comprehension* entails the understanding of facts and ideas. Unfortunately, tests that are successful in measuring recall of facts or principles are often unsuccessful in assessing how well the student actually understands the material.

3. *Application* refers to the need to know not only rules, principles, or basic procedures but also how and when to use them in new situations. This ability is less frequently taught and measured than the previous two.

4. *Analysis* involves the breaking down of a concept, idea, system, or message into its parts, then seeing the relationship between these parts. This ability may be taught in reading comprehension, math, or science classes. Often, however, the end product of the analysis is taught, but the analytical process itself is not.

5. *Synthesis* refers to the putting together of information or ideas: integrating or relating the parts of a whole.

6. *Evaluation* entails judging the value of a piece of information, a theory, or a plan in terms of some criterion, or standard.

In schools today, skills that are not easily measured, like the ability to appreciate art, tend to be ignored.

Most testing—and most teaching—focuses on ability 1, with occasional attention given to ability 2. Very rarely do teachers give tests that require a student to use the thinking abilities listed in categories 3 through 6. Indeed, many teachers avoid category 6, although, without evaluation, much information may be hollow and superficial.

LIMITATIONS OF INTELLIGENCE TESTING   In a world where new problems arise and "facts" change every day, it is increasingly important for children to be taught the skills needed to deal with the unknown as well as the known. Thus, some researchers feel that schools should teach children not *what* to think but *how* to think. Children can be taught how to generate new ideas, how to look at an issue in a new way, and how to identify the key aspects of a problem. These skills, it is claimed, are more useful than the facts and principles that are generally taught and measured (Olton & Crutchfield, 1969).

Some skills or abilities—such as a sense of humor—may be ignored because they are not especially valued in the elementary school. Other skills are ignored because the behavior involved is too difficult to define. Teachers may feel, for example, that they cannot measure a student's ability to enjoy classical music or to appreciate art. Recent research has suggested that skills that are learned in group educational settings will inevitably provide a less than accurate portrayal of individuals' capacities—they do not adequately or equally challenge all children in the group to learn. The brightest children may not be fully stimulated, while those who have difficulty may be overwhelmed. Furthermore, appropriate assessment of children's abilities requires an understanding of the cultural constraints regulating their use of concepts and reasoning processes (Miller-Jones, 1989).

The tendency of schools to concentrate on measurable abilities reflects the popularity of **behavioral objectives.** These objectives describe the kinds of knowledge and skills expected of a student after a specified amount of instruction. In a sense, they provide a way of testing *schools,* not students. Each June, schools are expected to demonstrate in a tangible way what their students have learned. As valuable as this approach is, great concern with a school's success often means that children spend most of the school day acquiring competencies that can be easily measured. As a result, less tangible competencies, ways of thinking, and personality traits are often overlooked. How does one objectively measure kindness, courage, curiosity, sensitivity, or openness to new experiences?

behavioral objectives The kinds of knowledge and skills expected of a student after a specified amount of instruction; they provide a demonstration of the school's adequacy as well as the student's.

CULTURAL BIASES AND TEST ABUSES

Psychologists, educators, and parents have criticized diagnostic and achievement tests for various reasons. We have shown that tests do not provide the whole story and that some personal qualities and skills are difficult or impossible to measure using conventional testing methods. In addition, there is the question of the cultural bias of the tests themselves. To show the absurdity of culturally linked intelligence tests, Stephen Jay Gould (1981) gave a class of Harvard students a nonverbal test of innate intelligence designed for World War I army recruits. (A sample of the test is shown in Figure 13–3.) He found that many of his students could not identify a horn as the missing part of a Victrola despite the test-makers' claim that the subjects' "innate" intelligence would guide them to the correct answer.

FIGURE 13–3

Segment of the Army Beta Mental Test.

This is Part 6 of the Army Beta mental test given to recruits during World War I. They were asked to find the missing parts in the following images. (Answers: 1. mouth; 2. eye; 3. nose; 4. spoon in right hand; 5. chimney; 6. left ear; 7. filament; 8. stamp; 9. strings; 10. rivet; 11. trigger; 12. tail; 13. leg; 14. shadow; 15. bowling ball in man's right hand; 16. net; 17. left hand; 18. horn of victrola; 19. arm and powder puff in mirror image; 20. diamond.)

Some minority groups resent being measured by tests that assume wide exposure to the dominant white culture; they feel that the tests are unfair to those who have different cultural experiences. Support for this view is provided by a study of black and interracial children who were reared by white middle-class adoptive parents. The IQ scores and school achievements of these adopted children were well above average—and well above those of children with similar genetic backgrounds but with different cultural experiences (Weinberg, 1989).

Research also suggests that minority groups may be victims of a **self-fulfilling prophecy:** They have acquired low expectations about their academic performances on tests designed by the white community, and these low expectations further lower their self-confidence and thus their test scores.

Not only minority children fall victim to the self-fulfilling prophecy, however. Imagine the effect that being labeled "below average" or "a slow learner" has on a child's self-image. Such labeling of students may also affect the administrators of the tests—the teachers. In a famous study, teachers were told that a few children, actually selected at random, possessed previously undetected high abilities and potential. At the end of the school year, it was found that these children showed significantly better achievement than their classmates. Presumably, the teachers had in some way conveyed their expectations to these students that they were especially bright and would do well in school (Rosenthal & Jacobson, 1968). Although this study has been criticized for its methodological faults, the basic finding has been supported by many later studies. People will respond according to the expectations of others.

It is dangerous to underestimate the complexity of the student-teacher relationship and the effect of labeling on children's performances. Labels do persist, and children do tend to live up to them, whether they be "class clown," "good child," "underachiever," or "bright." Insofar as teachers' expectations affect their own behavior toward children, these expectations apparently do have an influence on children's learning.

It is not always necessary to use tests to assess children's progress. Teachers, parents, and care-givers can learn a good deal about how to proceed by informally observing what children do and say. By merely giving the child a book and listening to him read, a skilled teacher can determine many of the skills that he still has to learn. Perhaps the most dramatic example of the need for caution in the use and interpretation of tests is in the area of learning disabilities.

 ## LEARNING DISABILITIES

The term **learning disability** is used to identify the difficulties of a broad category of children who often have no more in common than the label itself. In school systems today, children are described as "learning disabled" when they require special attention in the classroom—that is, when they have trouble learning to read, write, spell, or do arithmetic, despite having normal intelligence. In the absence of any obvious sensory or motor defect (such as poor vision, deafness, or cerebral palsy), these children are described as having learning disabilities. Of learning-disabled children, 80 percent are boys.

Day after day, learning-disabled children face their own inability to do things that their classmates seem to accomplish effortlessly. With each failure, these children become increasingly insecure about their ability to perform. Some-

self-fulfilling prophecy An expectation that helps to bring about the predicted event, which consequently strengthens the expectation.

learning disability Extreme difficulty in learning school subjects such as reading, writing, or math, despite normal intelligence and absence of sensory or motor defects.

times, this insecurity leads to a growing sense of hopelessness or helplessness. Classmates tend not to choose the child who does not succeed. Children with learning disabilities have difficulty with social skills as well as with academic skills. They may become increasingly isolated from peers or even from family members. Some become shy and withdrawn, some boastful, whereas others strike out with impulsive or angry outbursts. Academic confidence is central to the school-age child's self-esteem. It is difficult to find ways in which the learning-disabled child can develop feelings of confidence and, as a result, experience success in other areas.

The study of learning disabilities has been a challenging puzzle with a confusing array of expert opinions on symptoms, causes, and treatments. Many of the classic controversies of child development are evident in the questions raised. Is this child abnormal, deficient, or disabled, or is she just different in temperament and style? Is her problem due to organic dysfunction or due to her environment at home or at school? Should she be "treated" medically, "managed" with behavioral management programs, or "educated" creatively?

Before the 1950s, there were "slow readers" and children who did poorly on school tasks, but they were not labeled as learning disabled. If they had no obvious emotional or physical problems, it was assumed that they were simply "dumb." Teachers then began to notice that some children who appeared to be quite bright in other respects nonetheless had trouble with school tasks, especially reading. To explain this, the concept of "minimal brain dysfunction" was introduced. It was assumed that there was something wrong with the child's brain but that the abnormality was too subtle (or "minimal") to show up in other ways. Although many authorities still believe that learning disabilities are caused by some kind of subtle brain abnormality, the term "minimal brain dysfunction" is now seldom used (Silver, 1990).

There are two main groups of learning-disabled children. The first group includes children with **dyslexia** (difficulty in learning how to read); many of these children also have **dysgraphia** (difficulty with writing). Others may have **dyscalculia,** difficulty with math.

The second main group of learning-disabled children has **attention-deficit disorder (ADD),** the inability to focus attention on anything long enough to learn it. Many of these children are also **hyperactive**—they can't sit still, and they are constantly getting into trouble. This combination is called ADHD (attention-deficit hyperactivity disorder). Children with attention-deficit disorder, with or without hyperactivity, are likely to do poorly in a variety of school subjects, for the simple reason that they are not spending enough "time on task."

DYSLEXIA

Because dyslexic children often confuse letters such as *b* and *d*, or read *star* as *rats*, it was believed for a long time that these children simply "see things backward." But very few of them have anything wrong with their eyes. In other contexts, dyslexic children have no perceptual problems—for example, they have no trouble finding their way around (so they are not deficient in spatial relationships), and they may be exceptionally good at putting together puzzles. Why, then, do they make errors like confusing *b* and *d*? The answer is that this is a very common kind of error for beginning readers. Most children make reversal errors

dyslexia A learning disability involving reading; unusual difficulty in learning how to read.

dysgraphia A learning disability involving writing.

dyscalculia A learning disability involving mathematics.

attention-deficit disorder (ADD) An inability to keep one's attention focused on something long enough to learn it.

hyperactive Overly active; exhibiting poor impulse control.

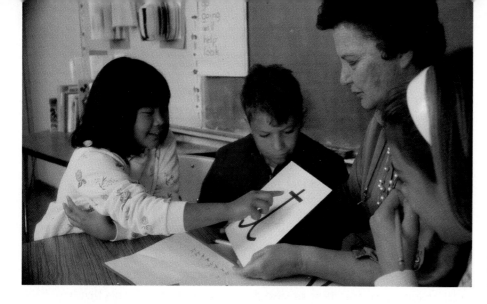

Some learning disabilities may be helped by educational management that works on improving specific skills.

when they are first learning how to read, but most get through this stage quickly. Dyslexic children remain stuck in the early stages of reading (Vogel, 1989; Richardson, 1992).

Dyslexic children also have problems outside of the school context. In fact, many have a pervasive problem involving the use of language. Many of these children were delayed in learning how to speak, or their speech is at a lower developmental level than that of their age-mates. Their difficulty in naming letters and written words is matched by a similar difficulty in naming objects or colors—it takes them longer than usual to pull an ordinary word like *"key"* or *"blue"* out of their memory. They also have difficulty in "hearing" the two separate syllables in a two-syllable word, or in recognizing that the spoken word *"sat"* starts with an *s* sound and ends with a *t* sound (Shaywitz et al., 1991; Wagner & Torgerson, 1987).

Although the hypothesized "brain dysfunction" that underlies dyslexia has still not been identified, it is clear that heredity plays a role in the disorder. Many dyslexic children have a parent who had trouble learning how to read as a child or a sibling with the same problem (Scarborough, 1989). It is also interesting to note that dyslexia tends to run in the same families that exhibit left-handedness. However, left-handedness itself is only weakly associated with dyslexia—most dyslexics are right-handed (Hiscock & Kinsbourne, 1987).

The treatment of dyslexia generally involves intensive remedial work in reading and language. Many educational programs for learning-disabled children provide carefully sequenced tutorial instruction in reading. Some programs emphasize high-interest materials; others emphasize early success. Stanton (1981) emphasizes the need to build the child's confidence in any approach. The teacher must first simplify the problem for the child in order to reduce anxiety about the unknown. He or she must then respond to the child with an attitude of genuineness, unconditional acceptance, and empathy, all of which make the child believe in and expect success. Although no single educational plan seems to work with all children, most programs have some record of success. The graduates of one especially successful program—a British residential school for dyslexic children—are generally able to go on to college. In contrast, the children who attend the least successful programs generally become high school dropouts (Bruck, 1987). People who were dyslexic as children but who manage to overcome this handicap may emerge with renewed self-confidence and may go onto be notably successful in adult life. Thomas Edison, Nelson Rockefeller, and Hans Christian Andersen were all dyslexic as children.

ATTENTION-DEFICIT DISORDER

For every symptom in the broad category of learning disabilities, there is a variety of possible causes. Just as people experience headaches for a number of reasons, an inability to focus attention may arise from any one of several conditions. Some of the suggested causes of ADD include malnutrition, lead poisoning, organic brain damage, heredity, intrauterine abnormalities, prenatal exposure to drugs like "crack," and lack of oxygen during fetal development or childbirth. Many children with symptoms of learning disabilities are known to have had some irregularity at birth; premature births are common among these children (Buchoff, 1990).

Just as there are differences of opinion on the causes of attention-deficit disorder and hyperactivity, there are also differences in the treatments that have been recommended. There is no one correct answer to the problems of a learning-disabled child. Some of the "answers" have been learned quite by accident, as illustrated by the history of one type of drug treatment.

Several years ago, it was discovered that some children who displayed symptoms of hyperactivity responded to the drug *Ritalin,* a stimulant in the amphetamine family. These hyperactive children, whose symptoms had not improved with tranquilizers or depressants, actually calmed down in response to this drug, which ordinarily speeds up behavior. This unusual response gave rise to the hypothesis that these children were either understimulated or were unable to focus on any single task because all stimulation came in at equal levels. Perhaps their high activity levels were attempts to seek more stimulation from the environment. Ritalin lowered their threshold of sensitivity to events around them and allowed them to focus consistently on one task. Although not all ADD and ADHD children improve by taking Ritalin, for those who do improve, the benefits can outweigh the risk of possible side effects *when the treatment program is monitored carefully.* Not only does their school work get better but also their relationships with family members and peers improve (Campbell & Spencer, 1988).

An alternate form of treatment for children with ADD is *educational management,* which takes place both at home and at school. In most cases, this method makes an attempt to restructure a child's environment by simplifying it, reducing distractions, making expectations more explicit, and, in general, reducing confusion. The specific educational plan depends on the theoretical position of the therapist or educator. Cruickshank (1977) advocates an instructional program involving various training tasks that require specific skills. Diagnostic tests are used to identify any deficits that the child demonstrates. The program consists of careful, systematic, and progressively more difficult exercises to correct the problems. A program by Ross (1977) focuses more on the development of selective attention. The specific task does not really matter. Instead, by careful management of the instruction and the rewards, the teacher helps the child to listen and to observe more precisely. The child might work on perceptual exercises or on other general skills.

A part of any treatment program is concern for the child's emotional well-being. Learning-disabled children rarely experience success in school, nor do they develop the feelings of competence and self-worth that go along with it. They may become shy and withdrawn, or they may strike back at society by engaging in delinquent behavior. Early diagnosis of the condition is important, as are patience and understanding.

For children with attention-deficit disorder and hyperactivity, there is no single treatment or approach that "solves" the problem.

Because so many questions about learning disabilities remain unanswered, students studying these disorders should approach them with a healthy amount of skepticism. They should carefully evaluate each diagnosis, each proposed program, and each suggested theory. It requires skillful interpretation to ensure that social and emotional difficulties are not mistaken for neurological problems.

 ## SUMMARY AND CONCLUSIONS

During middle childhood, Piaget proposed that children enter the concrete operational period of cognitive development. Children are therefore able to make **logical inferences,** think about physical transformations, perform reversible mental operations, and, in general, form hypotheses about the physical world. Children are able to theorize about persons, objects, and events in their immediate experience. If children are given specific instruction in concrete operational skills when they reach a state of readiness, it appears as though they will move out of the preoperational stage earlier.

Piaget proposed that education should recognize and respond to the unique character of thinking in middle childhood. Since children are active learners, he proposed that hands-on, discovery learning should occur. Teachers should guide students and structure the learning experience so that learning itself becomes an intrinsic reward for the child. External reinforcement, such as praise from the teacher, may not produce the most optimal motivation for learning. Children should be encouraged to make inferences about objects and their relationships in the world by themselves—rather than have them made for them.

Piaget did not offer the only theory of cognitive growth in middle childhood. Information-processing theorists—by comparing the human mind to the information-processing components of a computer—describe the children's control processes that provide memory strategies, as well as the higher-order control processes such as **metacognition.** Metacognition is similar to the executive programs that act to coordinate all programs running on a computer. Information-processing theories have given us much information about the growth of memory in middle childhood. Children gain strategies such as rehearsal, organization, semantic elaboration, mental imagery, retrieval, and scripts during this time. Metacognition also becomes more developed now. The child's monitoring of his or her own thinking, memory, knowledge, goals and actions becomes more developed during middle childhood. This in turn leads to more skills in thinking, learning, and understanding which change the way the child can deal with the world.

Schools are a primary site of formal learning for middle childhood. Entry into school presents many challenges for children—it is the first time they must establish a trust relationship with another adult; they must also start to be independent and learn to do things for themselves. American educators have attempted to determine the optimal ways to encourage competency and critical thinking in learning. Teachers must help children learn control processes and thinking skills, rather than be encouraged to memorize rote lists of unrelated facts. Success in school depends on the child's achievement motivation and the values of the culture in which the child is reared. If the child's subculture or culture emphasizes success in areas other than academics, the school will not be an important arena for competition for that child. Computers are another tool that educators are employing to teach children. Computer-assisted instruction and the use of computers for programming logic and writing skills are common. The combined technologies of television make possible a range of new educational media, such as interactive video displays.

The assessment of individual differences in intelligence and the ability to profit from schooling is a longstanding concern in developmental psychology. In the nineteenth century, for example, the French psychologist Alfred Binet developed the first intelligence tests. This test was later imported to America and translated into English by Lewis Terman, who called his test the Stanford-Binet. The early psychometricians believed that intelligence was a fixed, inherited characteristic. The contemporary view of IQ testing makes no such assumption but rather believes that children's intelligence is determined by a mix of heredity and environment.

Researchers have also disagreed on the nature of intelligence. Some, like those who designed the Stanford-Binet test, represent IQ as a single attribute—while others, such as the Wechsler IQ test, measure abilities in multiple areas of cognition. In general, today's theorists suggest that intelligence is not unitary and may consist of as many as seven discrete competencies. They also believe that all aspects of human thinking and problem solving are not tested on standard tests of intelligence.

Intelligence tests often come under fire because of the cultural biases and test abuses associated with them. In general, scores are higher for white, middle class students and lower for members of minority groups. Moreover, placing children in labeled-ability categories may create a **self-fulfilling prophecy,** because of teacher's expectations for their performance.

As with physical and motor development during middle childhood, some children are challenged by learning disabilities. **Dyslexia** and **Attention-Deficit Disorder** (with or without **hyperactivity**) are two such problems. Dyslexia causes great difficulty for children in learning to read—despite the fact that they have normal intelligence and no sensory or motor defects. It is believed that dyslexia results from some subtle type of brain abnormality which may be inherited. The basic problem for children with ADD or ADHD is an inability to focus their attention on material long enough to learn it. Drug therapy using *Ritalin* has been found helpful for many of these children.

➤ **KEY TERMS AND CONCEPTS**

attention-deficit disorder	diagnostic-prescriptive teaching	hyperactive	metacognition
behavioral objectives	dyscalculia	intelligence quotient	norm-referenced test
criterion-referenced test	dysgraphia	learning disability	self-fulfilling prophecy
deviation IQ	dyslexia	logical inference	
		mental age	

➤ **SELF-TEST QUESTIONS**

1. How would you best describe a good environment for learning?

2. How does Piaget's preoperational stage differ from the concrete operational stage characteristic of middle childhood?

3. Explain how Piagetian concepts of learning and cognitive development would be applied to educational practices.

4. How do information-processing theorists view the human mind? Explain some control processes and higher-order control processes that are important in middle childhood as they are defined by information-processing theorists.

5. Describe the new demands and expectations that children face when they enter school, and discuss some of the factors that determine how well they adjust to this transition.

6. What are some strategies that teachers can use to help students become competent learners and critical thinkers?

7. Describe different ways in which computers can be used as educational devices in the classroom.

8. Name several factors that determine a child's success in school.

9. What are some of the uses and abuses of intelligence testing?

10. Compare and contrast a criterion-referenced test and a norm-referenced test.

11. Compare and contrast the varying definitions of intelligence.

12. What types of competencies are not usually measured by diagnostic and achievement tests?

13. What are behavioral objectives, and in what sense do they test schools rather than students?

14. Discuss different types of learning disabilities, including their symptoms, causes, and treatments.

➤ **SUGGESTED READINGS**

CAHILL-FOWLER, M. *Maybe you know my kids.* New York: Carroll Publishing Group, 1990. A personal account of the disruptive impact that a child's attention-deficit disorder has on his family, his classmates, and his own learning activities. Offers helpful suggestions and resources to parents and teachers.

FARNHAM-DIGGORY, S. *Schooling.* Cambridge, MA: Harvard University Press, 1990. An excellent review and discussion of several key aspects of schooling today's children. Another selection in the popular Developing Child series.

GARDNER, H. *Frames of mind.* New York: Basic Books, Inc., 1983. A challenging, readable, well-developed presentation of a new way of thinking about intelligence.

GARDNER, H. *To open minds: Chinese clues to the dilemma of contemporary education.* New York: Basic Books, Inc., 1989. A thoughtful discussion of two radically different approaches to education that is done in their respective social contexts.

KIDDER, T. *Among schoolchildren.* Boston: Houghton Mifflin Company, 1989. Chronicles one courageous and determined teacher and one urban fifth-grade classroom. The book also deals with the social and emotional problems that are part of these children's lives.

PAPERT, S. *Mindstorms: Children, computers, and powerful thinking.* New York: Basic Books, Inc., 1980. In this influential book, Papert presents ways of using computers to develop thinking rather than traditional, programmed learning styles.

VIDEO CASE: WHEN YOU CAN'T PAY ATTENTION

Explains Devora Aroesty: "I have a hard time paying attention. When I'm reading a book, I can't remember at the end of the page what I've read. When I'm watching a movie, I can't remember the beginning of the movie... " Because Devora showed no hyperactivity to suggest that she suffered from attention-deficit disorder (ADD)— a biologically based disorder in which the brain is less active than the normal brain and so can't focus attention or control physical or emotional impulses—her teachers assumed that she had a lower level of intelligence than the other children. After a teacher put her in the lowest reading group and Devora returned home crying, Hannah Aroesty refused to accept the school's assessment. Determined to discover why her daughter had such problems concentrating, she finally found that Devora was suffering from ADD.

Devora was lucky because, without a proper diagnosis, parents and teachers often become frustrated and angry with such a child's behavior. These children are viewed as stubborn, lazy, willful underachievers. Consequently, they may experience diminished self-esteem. But for Devora and others where ADD has been diagnosed, there is effective treatment which includes taking the drug Ritalin. After she began treatment, Devora's next school report showed a complete academic turnaround. To experts this was not surprising, as there is no correlation between ADD and intelligence. Says ADD expert Dr. Ned Hallowell, "In fact, many people with ADD are very smart, very creative." Devora's striking improvement prompted her mother to learn more about ADD. The first thing Hannah Aroesty discovered was that she had the same symptoms as Devora. Was it possible that she too had ADD?

For years it was believed that children only had ADD because no one thought to look for it in adults. However, it is now understood that at least half the children who have ADD do not outgrow it and, moreover, it often runs in families.

It is estimated that there are probably 10 to 15 million American adults who are unaware that they have ADD. Hannah Aroesty, it turned out, was one of them. For these people, it can often destroy a life, causing business and interpersonal problems. Bill Garnett's marriage almost broke up because his wife mistakenly believed that his inability to pay attention to what she said indicated that he didn't care about her.

Adult ADD can be detected only by knowing the patient and his or her history. If, since childhood, there is a history of chronic and intense underachievement, trouble with organization, problems in mood regulation, low-level anxiety, and a tendency to procrastinate, then the person may have ADD. And his or her children could have it too.

CASE QUESTIONS

1. What problems does an ADD child have in the classroom? If undiagnosed, what do teachers tend to believe about such a child's abilities? What is the effect on the child?

2. What is the link between childhood ADD and adult ADD?

3. Why is adult ADD difficult to diagnose? How can undiagnosed ADD negatively affect a person's entire life?

Then the child moved ten times
round the seasons
Skated over ten clear frozen
streams
Words like when you're older
must appease him
And promises of someday make
his dreams.

JONI MITCHELL
"THE CIRCLE GAME"

CHAPTER 14

MIDDLE CHILDHOOD: PERSONALITY AND SOCIAL DEVELOPMENT

CHAPTER OBJECTIVES

By the time you have finished this chapter, you should be able to do the following:

✔ Describe different styles of parenting and their effects on children's personality and behavior.

✔ List several factors that affect a child's ability to cope with stressful events.

✔ Discuss the effects of divorce on children.

✔ Describe the factors that can lead to child abuse and list the various types of psychological abuse.

✔ Discuss the development of social cognition and moral reasoning during middle childhood.

✔ Summarize the characteristic features of childhood friendships and peer groups.

✔ Explain how children develop racial awareness and how their attitudes toward members of other groups change as they grow older.

✔ Describe the relationship between a child's academic ability, popularity in the peer group, and self-esteem.

It may seem a bit dramatic to say that children have their own culture, but in many ways it is true. The world of the preadolescent child at play is not the world in which adults live. The child's world has its own customs, language, rules, games—even its own distinctive beliefs and values. What is this "culture of childhood," and what role does it play in a child's development?

Many times, children seem to caricature adults. We have seen how a 2-year-old's fierce demands for autonomy resemble those of a tyrannical adult. A 4-year-old's jealousy and rage may strike an all-too-familiar chord. The customs and rituals of middle childhood sometimes mirror elaborate adult social conventions; in some ways, childhood rituals are even more strict and demanding. A child may pay almost superstitious attention to rituals, such as not stepping on sidewalk cracks for fear of breaking someone's back. Rhymes must be said just so, and rigid rules dictate the one right way to play each game. Peer relationships may also be ritualized. Children may make lifelong pledges in private clubs and in "blood brother" fraternities.

Children adopt the rhymes, rituals, stunts, and customs of childhood without help from adults. Some of their games and rituals have been transmitted from older to younger children for countless generations; this occurs in almost every culture. Many childish chants can be traced to medieval times, and some games, such as jacks, go back to the Roman era (Opie & Opie, 1959).

Children seem to derive potency from mastering the bits and pieces of a culture, from learning how to do things correctly. Perhaps the rituals and rules of middle childhood are practice for adulthood, exercises in learning the detailed behavior that is expected of adults. Perhaps they are a form of security, a familiar framework of rules that allows the child to feel both at home and competent in an otherwise bewildering world. These rules may help children to master intense emotions or to defuse intense peer relationships, such as victim and conqueror. Perhaps they also teach complex social concepts like justice, power, or loyalty.

Although we are not certain of the precise purpose of middle childhood's traditions, the phenomenon of a special culture of childhood exists in almost every society.

THEORETICAL OVERVIEW

We have discussed the three major theories that have shaped child development—the psychodynamic, cognitive developmental, and social learning theories—repeatedly throughout this book. In middle childhood, much of the research and theory construction has also been stimulated by them. Freud wrote about middle childhood—what he called the period of **latency.** He believed that latency was a period during which children turned their sexual energies toward cooperative play, creative efforts, and learning in school.

Erikson echoed this in his stage of middle childhood which focused on a social conflict, that of **industry versus inferiority.** Erikson states that during middle childhood, much of the child's time and energy is directed toward education and skill development. Children begin to interact strongly and meaningfully with adults outside the family and peers during this time. They also start to channel their energies into learning. When children are able to learn effectively, they integrate a sense of industry into their personality—they realize that hard work produces desired outcomes and continue to try to master their environment. For children who do not succeed at school work, they may begin to feel inferior when compared to their peers. This inferiority may stay with them for the remainder of their lives—especially in evaluative contexts. If, however, they are able to succeed at something—sports, music, art, or some other alternative—then they may still retain a sense of industry and a desire to accomplish things.

The cognitive developmental framework has been increasingly applied to social development. Piaget and Harvard's Lawrence Kohlberg, for example, have written extensively on moral development in children from a cognitive developmental perspective. Researchers like Susan Harter study the importance of the child's self-concepts as mediators of his behavior.

Finally, social-learning theory has made major contributions to the understanding of how specific behaviors are learned in the family and the peer group. Peers increasingly serve as models and reinforce such behaviors.

All three of these theoretical perspectives have helped us to understand how children become socialized into their own culture. The way in which they interact with peers, adults, and family members changes between early childhood and adolescence—the tyrannical four-year-old becomes the cooperative 8-year-old, who in turn becomes the rebellious 13-year-old. A variety of factors combine to produce these changes. While no one of the three theoretical perspectives adequately explains all social development during middle childhood, together they help us to understand how children become mature social beings.

In this chapter, we shall look at how a child's personality continues to develop during the school years. In Chapter 11, we examined some of the ways in which the younger child develops a personality—that is, a consistent pattern of social and emotional behavior. Here, we shall describe the influence of family and peer group relationships, as they affect the child and as the child affects them.

latency The period during middle childhood during which Freud believed sexual energies were diverted toward achieving social, cooperative, creative and educational endeavors.

industry versus inferiority Erikson's psychosocial conflict during middle childhood, in which children work industriously and are rewarded for their efforts in school, or fail and develop a sense of personal inferiority.

CONTINUING FAMILY INFLUENCES

Families continue to be one of the most important socializing influences for school-age children. Children acquire values, expectations, and patterns of behavior from their families, and they do so in a number of ways (see also Chapters 3 and 11). Parents and siblings serve as models for appropriate and inappropriate behavior, and they reward and punish children's behavior. Expanding cognitive abilities allow children to learn a wide range of social concepts and rules, both those that are explicitly taught and those that are only implied. Finally, social learning takes place in the context of relationships. Relationships are sometimes close and secure, sometimes anxiety provoking, and sometimes full of conflict.

In this section, we will examine the family as a context for development. We will also examine how families are changing and how stress in the family influences personality development in children.

PARENT-CHILD INTERACTIONS AND RELATIONSHIPS

In the elementary school years, the nature of parent-child interactions change. Children express less direct anger toward their parents, and they are less likely to whine, yell, or hit than when they were younger. For their part, parents are less concerned with promoting autonomy and establishing daily routines and more concerned with children's work habits and achievement (Lamb et al., 1993). School-age children need less—but more subtle—monitoring of their behavior than previously, although parental monitoring is still important. Researchers find, for example, that well-monitored boys receive higher grades than those less monitored (Crosler et al., 1990).

Parents teach the value of warmth and affection by their own behavior.

What might be considered optimal parenting? The experts have differed over the years. Contemporary research emphasizes that one primary goal of parental socialization practices is the increase of **self-regulated behavior** in the child. As discussed in Chapter 11, authoritative discipline practices are more successful than authoritarian practices in the development of self-regulation. When a parent relies on verbal reasoning and suggestions, the child tends to negotiate rather than react with defiance (Lamb et al., 1993).

Parental reasoning with the child (or using induction) is related both to prosocial behavior and to compliance with social rules. Parents who use other-oriented induction—who remind their children of the effect of their actions on others—tend to have children who are more popular and who manifest internalized moral standards. In contrast, when parents use power-assertive socialization, their children do not develop internalized standards and controls. In several studies, for example, children who comply with adult demands when adults are present but not when they are absent were more likely to have parents who used power-assertion. Out-of-sight compliance is associated with parents who use other-oriented induction (Maccoby, 1992).

Parents are more successful in developing self-regulated behavior if they gradually increase the child's involvement in family decisions. In a series of studies on parental dialogue and discipline, Eleanor Maccoby (1992) concluded that children are best adjusted when their parents foster what she calls **co-regulation.** These parents build cooperation and shared responsibility. They look forward to the teenage years, when they expect their children will make most decisions for themselves. In preparation, they engage in frequent discussions and negotiations with their children. These parents see themselves as building the framework for responsible decision making.

When we look at parents who are sensitive to the developmental stages of their children the concept of *scaffolding* is useful (see Chapter 7). Children learn about the social world in complex social contexts accompanied by parents or other more competent partners (Rogoff, 1990). Imagine a family attending a large wedding. Socially competent parents help their children anticipate what will happen and discuss expected events and behaviors before arrival. They may discuss the meaning of the event and/or of specific practices. After arrival, parents cue their children on age-appropriate behavioral expectations. Only small parts of the broad set of shared meanings for "marriage and weddings" are conveyed at any one time. Of course, children also learn by observing the behaviors of their parents, older siblings, and other more socially advanced wedding guests.

As children grow and mature, the quality of the on-going parenting relationship continues to be of key importance. Family relationships are not one-way, but reciprocal. Families have a history of shared goals, shared meanings, and familiar linked streams of behavior. This view suggests that children become socialized by participating in the interaction within close relationships.

> When a parent-child pair are able to engage in noncoercive joint activity, their streams of behavior become interwoven, so that the smooth continuation of one person's behavior depends on the partner's performing the reciprocal portion of the action. Partners develop joint expectations concerning each other's behavior, joint goals, shared scripts from which each acts, and shared meanings that make fuller coordination of their activities possible. (Maccoby, 1992, p. 1014)

Youniss (1983) argues that socialization should not be viewed as a process in which control shifts from parents to child as the child becomes more autonomous and self-regulating. It is rather a process of mutual or shared coregulation throughout the remainder of the participants' lives—until one or the other ends the relationship. In fact, Maccoby (1992) suggests that enduring parental influence stems from the strength and health of relationships parents and children have jointly constructed during middle childhood. In some cases, parents' contributions to the coregulation inhibits their children; in other cases, it enables them to grow in autonomy within the relationship. In addition, interactions with parents allow children to practice and refine social skills that will later improve their peer interactions.

In general, when family members have joint goals, and shared meanings, or scripts, the family as a whole grows and shows optimal development. Coregulation is not a function of any particular cultural group, but is rather something that occurs in diverse family settings. In some cases, it produces beneficial results; in others, the results are more mixed. When coregulation does not exist within a family, the outcome is likely to be more negative. Children in such a family may be at risk for a variety of social and behavior problems.

THE CHANGING NATURE OF THE FAMILY

The research on parenting and parenting styles we have described was based primarily on the "typical American family": mother, father, and two or three children. But this family is no longer so typical. Having children is not going out of style—over 4 million babies were born in the United States in 1990. What may be going out of style, however, is getting married first or staying married afterward. The trend toward single parenthood continues to grow: About one-quarter of all births are now to unmarried mothers. In African-American families, the percentage approaches 65 percent (Bennett, 1993). In 1988, 4.3 million American children were being raised by unmarried mothers, and another 8 million were living with just their mothers as the result of separation or divorce. The number of children living with just their fathers also continues to grow; it is now close to 1 million (Zill, 1991).

The American family has also undergone rapid change with regards to mothers working. Once children enter school, the majority of American mothers enter the workforce. In 1948 only 26 percent of the mothers of school-aged children (ages 6 to 17) worked, in 1975 that percentage was 51 percent and in 1991 it was over 74 percent (U.S. Bureau of Labor Statistics, 1992). Since the early 1950's, the mothers of school-aged children were more likely to work than married women without children. This is undoubtedly due to the greater economic needs of families with children, as well as the greater preponderance of single-parent women who must work to support their families (Scarr, Phillips, & McCartney, 1989).

Let us examine how children are affected by these trends.

POVERTY AND HOUSEHOLDS HEADED BY MOTHERS Only 10 percent of American families with two parents have incomes below the poverty line, but half of all families headed by a mother, are living in poverty (McLanahan &

Booth, 1989). If the mother has not graduated from high school, the likelihood that the family's income will be below the poverty line is almost 90 percent (Children's Defense Fund, 1992).

Children who grow up in poverty, in a home headed only by a mother, experience a multitude of deprivations (McLoyd & Wilson, 1990). Not having a father lowers a family's social status as well as its economic status. Housing is likely to be crowded; frequent moves are common. Meals may be skimpy and nutritionally poor. Medical care may be lacking. Also, the women who head these homes are often psychologically distressed as a result of their struggle for survival. Many suffer from depression or anxiety, which interferes with their ability to be supportive and attentive parents.

The children who grow up in these homes may be handicapped in a number of ways: Both their psychological health and their intellectual development tend to be affected. As a result, they are less likely than other American children to move upward in socioeconomic status—in other words, their economic deprivation is likely to continue into adulthood. They are also more likely to become single parents themselves. Thus, the problems are passed on to the next generation (McLanahan & Booth, 1989).

Children in close-knit adaptable families generally tend to be the best-equipped to cope with stressful situations.

FAMILIES AND STRESS Poverty is a source of stress for both parents and children, but there are other life events that are stressful for children and their families—for example, moving to a different town, being left back in school, or suffering a serious illness or injury. What are some of the factors that determine whether or not a child is able to cope constructively?

One factor is the sheer number of stressful situations in a child's life—a child who can deal successfully with a single stressful event may be overwhelmed if she is forced to deal with several all at once (Hetherington, 1984). A second factor is the child's perception or understanding of the event. For example, the first day of school is a major event in a child's life. A child who knows what to expect and who can use this milestone as a sign of her increasing maturity will have less difficulty dealing with this new experience.

The research literature clearly indicates that close-knit, adaptable families with open communication patterns and problem-solving skills are better able to weather stressful events (Brenner, 1984). Social support systems, such as neighbors, relatives, friendship networks, or self-help groups are also valuable.

Stress and coping do not always occur as single events; instead, they often exist as ongoing or transitional processes. A young child who is moving to a new neighborhood may experience anticipatory anxiety before the move. Immediate short-term adjustments to the new setting will then have to be made, and some long-term coping skills will be needed to deal with establishing new relationships and recovering from the loss of old ones.

Many personality traits influence children's ability to cope with stressful environments. Over the past 30 years, Emmy Werner (1989) has studied a group of what she calls **resilient** children. These children, who were born on one of the Hawaiian islands, lived in family environments marred by poverty, parental conflict or divorce, alcoholism, and mental illness. Yet they developed into self-confident, successful, and emotionally stable adults. Most children reared under such conditions do not do well, so Werner was interested in learning how these children managed to thrive in spite of an unfavorable environment. She found that they had

resilient children Children who overcome difficult environments to lead socially competent lives.

been temperamentally "easy" and lovable babies who had developed a close attachment to a parent or grandparent in the first year of life. Later, if that parent or grandparent was no longer available, these children had the ability to find someone else—another adult or even a sibling or a friend—to give them the emotional support they needed (see the box "Children Who Survive" in Chapter 3).

CHILDREN OF DIVORCE

Nearly half of all marriages now end in divorce (O'Leary & Smith, 1991), which means that each year about a million children experience the breakup of their families. Due to divorce, single parenthood, or the death of a parent, only 40 percent of the children born today will reach the age of 18 in an intact, two-parent home (Otto, 1988). Even with changing custody rules, the majority of the children of divorced parents will have only occasional contact with their fathers, or no contact at all.

The breakup of the family affects children in a number of ways. We have seen that both parents have strong effects on the development of their children; yet a divorce means that both parents will no longer be equally available to their children. These children are also part of a family that has been under tension for a long period of time. They may have heard the word "divorce" spoken aloud (or shouted) in their homes for months or even years. They know that relationships have been disturbed, and they may wonder what will happen to them. They have seen one parent leave and may fear that the other parent will also abandon them. They may feel sad, confused, angry, or anxious; they may become depressed or disruptive, or they may do poorly in school. Many children (particularly younger ones) feel that they are to blame for the divorce—that if only they had been better, maybe their parents would not have split up. They may try to bring their parents back together, perhaps by being very good or by fantasizing about a reconciliation (Hetherington et al., 1989; Hetherington, 1992; Wallerstein et al., 1988). The following case study presents the acting-out behavior that can accompany hostility between parents.

> Bridget was 12-years-old—the middle of three sisters. Her parents had gotten married when the mother discovered she was pregnant. They had fought throughout the marriage, and lately the fighting was constant. Divorce and threats of leaving were regularly heard in the family. Bridget had been an honor student. She began to have serious difficulty with her studies and started to cut classes. Things worsened at home. She left school with three older boys, borrowed her mother's car without permission; the same afternoon and the four were picked up for speeding—100 miles away from home. The state police called the parents to come and pick up their children.

> Before Bridget's parents saw their daughter, the police youth counselor said: "You are angry now and what she did was wrong, but you must remember that when children do things like this they are crying for your attention, guidance, and help."

Relationships with both parents change during and after a divorce. Children may become defiant and argumentative; in adolescence, they may emotionally disengage themselves from their families. Or children may often be forced to become a sounding board for their parents, listening to each parent describe the faults of the other. They may be at the center of a custody battle and may be asked to choose between parents. The parents may compete for the affection of the children and may try to bribe them with gifts or privileges. The parents themselves are often under considerable stress right after the divorce and may be incapable of providing either warmth or control—they may be less affectionate, inconsistent with discipline, uncommunicative, or unsupportive. Also, children may become upset when their parents start dating or establishing relationships with others. A boy who is living with his mother may take over the role of "man of the house" and may feel threatened when a rival appears on the scene (Hetherington et al., 1989).

The way that children respond to divorce is influenced by a number of factors. Perhaps the three most important ones are:

1. *The amount of hostility accompanying the divorce* If there is a great deal of hostility and bitterness preceding or following a divorce, it is harder for children to adjust to the situation. Ongoing legal battles (over custody, for example) or squabbles over the division of property or child care make the situation much more difficult for everyone involved (Rutter & Garmezy, 1983).

2. *The amount of actual change in the child's life* If the child continues to live in the same home, attends the same school, and has the same friends, there tends to be less difficulty in adjusting to separation and divorce. In contrast, if the child's daily life is disrupted in major ways—moving back and forth from one parent's household to the other's, losing old friends, entering a new school—it will be difficult for the child to build self-confidence and to have a sense of order in his or her world. The more changes there are, particularly right after the divorce, the more difficult the adjustment will be (Hetherington & Camara, 1984).

3. *The nature of the parent-child relationship* Long-term involvement and emotional support from a parent—or better still, from both parents—help the child to make a successful adjustment. In fact, the nature of the ongoing parent-child interaction is much more important than whether or not both parents are present in the home (Rutter & Garmezy, 1983).

BREAKDOWN OF RULES   Immediately following a divorce, children—especially school-age children of 5, 6, or 7 years—often appear confused; they exhibit behavioral difficulties, not only at home but also in school and in other places. When children experience a severe disruption in their lives, especially if it occurs suddenly, their understanding of the social world is upset. It may seem to them that the script for ongoing daily life has been torn up—that the old rules no longer apply. The long-established patterns of the family have broken down under the pressure of divorce and separation. In the past, the world was predictable: Daddy came home from work every evening, the entire family sat down to dinner, and bedtime was at 8:00. Suddenly, these patterns are disrupted and the script for understanding the social world no longer seems to apply. Consequently, children often test the rules to see if the world still works the way it did before. They may have to be told by their mothers: "I know it's upsetting that Daddy's not coming home anymore. But that doesn't mean you don't have to go to bed at 8:00. You still have to get up early in the morning and go to school. And you still need your rest." Teachers also need to be helpful in gently reestablishing the rules and expectations of the school situation as well as being emotionally supportive of a child who is going through considerable inner turmoil. Some children almost have to relearn the social script.

STEPFAMILIES   The problems that surface during a divorce may not disappear when one or both parents remarry. Although some children welcome the arrival of a stepparent, for others, the remarriage is another major adjustment that must be made after their adjustment to the divorce. Children may see their dreams of reuniting their parents shattered; they may resent the step-parent's attempt to discipline them or to win their affection. They may see themselves as having a divided loyalty to their parents, or they may worry about being left out of the new family that is forming. Children may also be unhappy about having to share the attention of the custodial parent with his or her new partner, or they may feel guilty about "abandoning" the noncustodial parent by giving affection to the new stepparent. In some cases, children may have the additional problem of having to get along with step-siblings (Hetherington et al., 1989).

In most cases, the major adaptations associated with divorce and with stepfamilies subside in about two years. By that time, children and parents may have adjusted to the new situation and are moving ahead with their lives. While they exist, however, these problems may seriously interfere with a child's social and emotional development.

While some children adjust to a stepparent and step-siblings, others greet the family reconfiguration with emotions like anger, anxiety, or guilt.

CHILD ABUSE

As we discussed earlier in Chapter 7, one of the most serious and dramatic examples of family breakdown is the phenomenon of **child abuse.** Instead of encouraging and reinforcing the bond between parent and child, the child abuser destroys the expectations of love, trust, and dependence so essential to the young child. Severe developmental problems frequently result.

We shall define child abuse, and distinguish it from neglect, by using the term to refer only to physical and psychological injuries that are *intentionally* inflicted on a child by an adult (Burgess & Conger, 1978). *Neglect,* in contrast, is unintentional; it results from parents' or caregivers' failures to act rather than from their injurious actions. The consequences can be equally tragic: Children die of neglect as well as of abuse. Here, however, we shall discuss only the physical and emotional damage that is intentionally inflicted on children: extreme psychological punishment, such as constant ridicule or criticism; violent physical punishment resulting in injury or death; and sexual abuse.

It can be difficult to distinguish between child abuse and ordinary punishment. What qualifies as child abuse is a relative question and must be viewed in light of community standards. Historically, many cultures have condoned and even encouraged physical mistreatment that we consider shocking and brutal. It was used to discipline and educate children, to exorcise evil spirits, or to placate the gods. Furthermore, some cultures imbued certain forms of physical cruelty, such as foot binding, skull shaping, or ritual scarring, with a deep symbolic meaning. Traditionally, children were viewed as the property of their parents, and parents had the legal right to treat them in any way they saw fit. Infanticide or the abandonment of unwanted babies was a time-honored method for desperate adults trying to cope with hunger, illegitimacy, or birth defects (Radbill, 1974). In general, we have different standards now: Causing injury or death to a child is considered to be a serious crime. But, sadly, it is not an uncommon one.

THE INCIDENCE OF CHILD ABUSE In the United States, official reports of child abuse and neglect now number almost 1 million a year; three children die every day as a result of physical abuse or neglect. These figures may be shocking, but they are not unique to the United States; similar rates have been noted in Canada, Australia, Great Britain, and Germany (Emery, 1989).

More than half of physically abused children are abused by their own parents, with mothers and fathers implicated in approximately equal numbers. When someone other than a parent is responsible for the abuse, however, male abusers outnumber females by four to one. For sexual abuse, the proportion of abusers who are male is even higher—nearly 95 percent. You may be surprised to learn that the sexual abuse of a little girl is usually not committed by the child's own father. It is estimated that a stepfather is five times more likely to abuse his stepdaughter than a father is to abuse his daughter (Sedlack, 1989; Wolfe, Wolfe, & Best, 1988).

Although the victim of sexual abuse is likely to be a girl, physical abuse is more often inflicted on a boy. Also, younger children sustain more serious injuries than older ones do; about half of the serious injury or death cases involve children under the age of 3 (Rosenthal, 1988).

Sexual and physical child abuse have long-term effects on the child's emotional well-being. The child's self-esteem has been irreparably damaged, and he

child abuse Intentional psychological or physical injuries inflicted on a child.

or she may find it difficult ever to trust anyone again. Adults who were abused as children are at greater risk of many psychological problems, including depression and alcoholism (Schaefer et al., 1988).

APPROACHES TO UNDERSTANDING CHILD ABUSE   The large amount of research that has been done in this area has been centered on three main theoretical explanations of child abuse: psychiatric, sociological, and situational (Parke & Collmer, 1975).

Psychiatric Explanations. The psychiatric model focuses on the personality of the parents. It assumes that abusive parents are sick and require extensive psychiatric treatment. Early theorists looked for psychotic traits in adults who abused children, but they failed to find any. They discovered that clear cases of adult psychosis, such as schizophrenia, account for only a very small percentage of incidents of child abuse. Other researchers have attempted to find a cluster of personality traits that might indicate a tendency toward abuse. This search, too, has failed to produce any helpful conclusions.

One fact that researchers have discovered about child abusers is that many of them were themselves abused as children (Ney, 1988). Although psychologists are not certain why child abuse patterns are passed on from one generation to the next, one plausible explanation is that people who were abused as children had abusive adult models to follow. Their parents may have taught them that needs like dependency or autonomy are unacceptable—that crying or asking for help is useless, inappropriate, or evidence of an evil nature. One child whose parents were going through therapy to halt their abuse, even became distressed when his father no longer beat him. He poignantly asked the social worker, "How come daddy doesn't love me anymore?" Children absorb such lessons deeply and thoroughly at an early age. Many abused children, once they become parents, apply these lessons to their own children.

Sociological Explanations. The sociological model, as defined by Parke and Collmer, focuses *not* on individual differences but on social values and family organization. One American social value significantly related to child abuse is violence. The United States ranks higher in murders and other violent crimes than other industrialized nations do. Some suggest that the endless display of brutality and hostility on television teaches parents and children alike that violence is an acceptable way to resolve conflicts. If physical aggression occurs in some family disputes, especially those between husband and wife, it is also likely to occur in parent-child relationships. Physical punishment is a widely used disciplinary technique in the United States; 93 percent of all parents use it, although the majority use it sparingly. Comparisons with more peaceful societies that rely more on love-oriented discipline reveal less violence in general and less abuse of children in particular (Parke & Collmer, 1975).

Poverty, unemployment, and overcrowding also play a role in child abuse. Although physical abuse of children is found at all socioeconomic levels, it is almost seven times more likely to be reported in homes where the annual income is below $15,000 (Sedlack, 1989). This statistic may result partly from the fact that abuse in middle-class homes is less likely to come to the attention of authorities. But it is also true that any kind of family stress—and poverty is unquestionably a source of family stress—increases the risk that a child will be abused. Unemployment is also a source of stress. A parent who is suddenly and unexpectedly out of work may become abusive toward his or her children. Aside from the

Because it causes family stress, poverty increases the risk of child abuse.

financial problems, unemployment also lowers the parent's social status and self-esteem. An unemployed father may try to compensate by wielding authority at home through physical domination. In periods of high unemployment, male violence against both wives and children rises.

Another characteristic that is observed in many families troubled by child abuse is social isolation. Parents who abuse their children are often isolated from relatives, friends, and community support systems. They have difficulty sustaining friendships and rarely belong to any formal organizations. Thus, they have no one to ask for help when they need it, and they turn their frustration and rage against their children. Some of this isolation is self-imposed. Abusive parents, with their low self-esteem, feel so guilty and unworthy that they avoid contact with others. They also obstruct their children's attempts to form meaningful bonds and relationships with people outside the home.

Situational Explanations. The situational model of child abuse, like the sociological model, seeks causes in environmental factors. The situational model concentrates on interaction patterns among family members (Parke & Collmer, 1975). This model recognizes children as active participants in the interaction process. It tries to identify the situations in which abusive patterns develop and to find the stimuli that trigger the abuse. One study attempted to discover distinctive patterns in the everyday interactions of families with incidence of child abuse. The study showed that abusive parents had less verbal and physical interaction with their children than did nonabusive parents. Abusive parents were also more negative and less willing to comply with the requests of other family members (Burgess & Conger, 1978).

Abusive parents also tend to be inconsistent in the behavioral demands they make on their children. They may punish their children for coming home late one day, but they ignore it the next—or they may punish them long afterward, so that the children feel they are being punished for no apparent reason. These parents also tend to have trouble in defining their marital roles. They often fail to allocate responsibility between themselves for important tasks, including discipline of the children. Thus, their children may be confused by parental inconsistencies and may lack a clear idea of what kind of behavior will be tolerated. When, in addition, the parents are members of a culture that does not frown on violence, the patterns of abuse are set in motion. Once the pattern is begun, it tends to perpetuate itself. The parents may justify the abuse as a way of "building character" and may play down the injuries sustained by the child. They may shift the blame to the child and justify their behavior on the grounds that the child is "hateful" or "stubborn" (Belsky, 1980; Parke & Collmer, 1975).

Finally, let us look at the role of the child in abusive families. Parents are usually selective in their abuse, singling out one child for mistreatment. Infants and very young children are the most frequent targets. Those with physical or mental abnormalities, or who are unusually difficult to take care of, are at greatest risk. Infants who cry constantly can drive parents to the breaking point. In other cases, there may be a mismatch between the parent's expectations and the child's characteristics—this is basically a problem of incompatibility between parent and child. For example, a physically demonstrative mother may find that her infant does not like to be touched. In other cases, the parent has an unrealistic expectancy of behavior in the children. For example, a mother may believe her 1-month-old's crying is being done to be nasty or because she hates her mother. A father may become angry when his 2- and 3-year-olds fail to take responsibility for the family garden. Such misconceptions may lead to abuse (Parke & Collmer, 1975; Vasta, 1982).

Some children may be singled out for abuse because they serve as an uncomfortable reminder of their parent's own flaws. Many parents have still not come to terms with the unresolved conflicts from their own childhood years. If their child has a characteristic that they regard as unacceptable in themselves, they may punish this child harshly. These unfortunate children tap a wellspring of self-hatred in their parents. We may see these three explanations contrasted in Table 14–1.

All three of these approaches shed some light on the causes of child abuse. None of them, unfortunately, tells us how to stop it. Programs for preventing child abuse focus on providing parents with social support and teaching them better methods for controlling their children. Although such programs usually succeed in reducing the level of abuse, around 25 percent of the participants continue to abuse their children (Ferleger et al., 1988). Sometimes, criminal prosecution of the offenders and removal of the child from the home are the only safe alternatives.

PSYCHOLOGICAL ABUSE   Physical or sexual abuse is always accompanied by a psychological component. Mistreatment exists in the context of an interper-

TABLE 14–1 Approaches to Understanding Child Abuse

Psychiatric explanations	Parents as causes	Focuses on personality of the parents as being sick and in need of extensive psychotherapy; most child abusers were themselves abused as children; presence of poor parenting models leads to family cycles of violence
Sociological explanations	Society as cause	Views American families as living in a culture of violence reflected in television programming; physical punishment is widely used and can get out of control when the family is under stress; social isolation increases the risk the family will have poor parenting skills; socio-economic conditions such as unemployment, overcrowding, and poverty increase stress and, therefore, encourage abuse.
Situational explanations	Immediate circumstances and patterns or interaction as causes	Seeks environmental causes for the abuse such as dysfunctional family interaction patterns; often, the abused child has some trait considered by the parents as undesirable and thus becomes the focus for abuse.

sonal relationship, and this relationship has become psychologically abusive—manipulative, rejecting, or degrading. One researcher states that the psychological accompaniments of child abuse may be even more damaging than the abuse itself (Emery, 1989).

Psychological abuse comes in various forms and may be committed by various people, such as parents, teachers, siblings, and peers. The significant characteristic of these people is that they have power in situations in which the child is vulnerable (Hart et al., 1987). For instance, most of us have encountered, at some point in our lives, the sadistic teacher who picks out one particular student in the class and makes this student the victim of a continuing campaign of cruelty.

Psychological abusers have a wide range of techniques. Hart, Germain, and Brassard (1987) have specified six types of psychological abuse used by parents, teachers, siblings, or peers:

1. *Rejection* This involves refusing the request or needs of a child in such a way as to imply strong dislike for the child. Active rejection rather than passive withholding of affection is involved here.

2. *Denial of Emotional Responsiveness* This is the passive withholding of affection. Detachment, coldness, or failing to respond to the child's attempts at communication are examples of this.

3. *Degradation* Humiliating children in public or calling them "stupid" or "dummy" is degrading. Children's self-esteem is lowered by frequent assaults on their dignity or intelligence.

4. *Terrorization* Being forced to witness violence to a loved one, or being threatened with violence to oneself, is a terrifying experience for a child. A child who suffers regular beatings or who is told, "I'll break every bone in your body if you don't behave," is being terrorized. A more subtle form of terrorism is demonstrated by the parent who simply walks away from a misbehaving child while they are out in the street, leaving the child unprotected from danger.

5. *Isolation* Refusing to allow a child to play with friends or to take part in family activity is to isolate that child. Some forms of isolation, such as locking a child in a closet, may also be terrorization.

6. *Exploitation* Taking advantage of a child's innocence or weakness is exploitation. The most obvious example of exploiting a child is sexual abuse.

Isolating a child from other children is a form of psychological abuse.

Psychological abuse is so common that virtually no one grows up without experiencing some form of it. But in most cases, the abuse is not intense enough or frequent enough to do permanent damage (Hart et al., 1987). The important distinction between the psychologically abused child and the rest of us is that the abused child is caught in a damaging relationship and is not being socialized in a positive, supportive way. As a consequence, the child may not be able to satisfy his or her dependency needs, may have to be overly adaptive in order to escape abuse, and may develop neurotic traits or problem behaviors. What is more, the child has learned to exploit, degrade, or terrorize, and to expect that relationships are often painful. These are pervasive, long-term consequences.

SOCIAL KNOWLEDGE

As we have seen, children are continually learning how to deal with the complex social world that exists both inside and outside the family. In middle childhood, they must come to terms with the subtleties of friendship and authority, with expanding or conflicting sex roles, and with a host of social rules and regulations. One way they do this is by the process of direct socialization: getting rewards for desirable behavior and punishments for undesirable behavior, and observing and imitating models. Social learning helps children to acquire appropriate behaviors and attitudes. Another way children learn about the social world involves psychodynamic processes. Children develop anxious feelings in certain situations, and they learn to reduce this anxiety by using a number of defense mechanisms (see Chapter 11).

A third way that children learn about the social world is called **social cognition.** Just as children's understanding of the physical world changes as they mature, so does their understanding of the social world. Social cognition is thought, knowledge, and understanding that involves the social world.

THE DEVELOPMENT OF SOCIAL COGNITION

As children develop during middle childhood and adolescence, social cognition becomes an increasingly important determinant of their behavior. It is in middle childhood that children must learn how to deal with some of the complexities of friendship and justice, social rules and manners, sex-role conventions, obedience to authority, and moral law. Children begin to look at the social world around them and gradually come to understand the principles and rules that it follows (Ross, 1981). This process has been studied by cognitive theorists, who believe that all knowledge, whether scientific, social, or personal, exists as an organized system or structure, not as unrelated bits and pieces. The understanding of the world does not develop in a piecemeal fashion; rather, it occurs in a predictable sequence (see, for example, the box "Discovering Our Economic System"). The development of social cognition progresses in a way that is similar to other kinds of cognitive development.

As we saw in Chapter 10, preschool children's understanding of the world is limited by their egocentrism. Although by age 7 children have reached "the age of reason" and are able to perform some logical operations, they are still somewhat hampered by their inability to see another person's point of view. Many children in early middle childhood still do not recognize that their point of view is limited to themselves. They are not fully aware that other people have different points of view because of their different backgrounds, experiences, or values. This fact only gradually becomes apparent to the young child.

A first component of social cognition, therefore, is **social inference**—that is, guesses and assumptions about what another person is feeling, thinking, or intending (Flavell, 1985; Flavell, Miller, & Miller, 1993). A young child, for example, hears his mother laughing and assumes that she is happy. An adult might hear something forced about the mother's laughter and infer that the woman is covering up her feelings. Although young children cannot make such a sophisticated inference, by age 6 they can usually infer that another person's

social cognition Thought, knowledge, and understanding that involve the social world.

social inference Guesses and assumptions about what another person is feeling, thinking, or intending.

thoughts may differ from their own. By age 8 or so, they realize that another person can think about their thoughts. By age 10, they are able to infer what another person is thinking while at the same time inferring that their own thoughts are the subject of another person's thoughts. A child might think, "Johnny is angry with me, and he knows that I know he is angry." The process of developing fully accurate social inference is gradual and continues into late adolescence (Shantz, 1983).

A second component of social cognition is the child's understanding of **social relationships.** Children gradually accumulate information and understanding about the obligations of friendship, such as fairness and loyalty, the respect for authority, and the concepts of legality and justice. A third aspect of social cognition is the understanding of **social regulations,** such as customs and conventions. Many of these conventions are first learned by rote or imitation. Later, they can become less rigid, depending on the child's ability to make correct social inferences and to understand social relationships.

Psychologists who study social cognition find that it develops in a predictable sequence—some even call the steps in this sequence "stages." Most researchers agree that children overcome the worst of their egocentrism by age 6 or 7: They stop centering on only one aspect of a situation and gradually get better at making social inferences. As we will soon see, these advances make it possible for a child to form lasting and satisfying friendships with other children. They also affect the child's ability to think about moral issues. We may see these aspects of social cognition presented in Table 14–2.

MORAL JUDGMENT

Moral judgment—making decisions about right and wrong—is another area of social cognition. In the process of growing up, most children somehow learn to tell "good" from "bad" and to distinguish between kindness and cruelty, generosity and selfishness. Mature moral judgment, then, involves more than the rote learning of social rules and conventions.

There is considerable debate as to how children develop morality. Social-learning theorists believe that children learn it by being rewarded or punished for

TABLE 14–2 Aspects of Social Cognition

Social inference	Child makes guesses and has assumptions about what another is feeling, thinking, or intending; by age 6, can infer the thoughts of others differ from theirs; by age 8, realizes that another person can think about their thoughts; by age 10, can infer what another is thinking—as well as infer that their thoughts may be the subject of another's thoughts.
Social relationships	Child accumulates information and understanding about obligations of relationships, such as fairness and loyalty, respect for authority, and the concepts of legality and justice.
Social regulations	Child articulates and understands the customs and conventions of society; first learned by imitation and rote; later they become less rigid.

social relationships Relationships that involve obligations such as fairness and loyalty. The knowledge of these obligations is a necessary part of social cognition.

social regulations The rules and conventions governing social interactions.

moral judgment The process of making decisions about right and wrong.

FOCUS ON APPLICATION

DISCOVERING OUR ECONOMIC SYSTEM

Money has an important place in the world of children. Some of their earliest memories include shopping for groceries and clothing with their parents and, when they are older, buying special treats for themselves. The formal rules that are part of the process of exchanging money for goods and services reflect the order of society itself. When children learn these rules, they are well on their way to understanding how society operates.

To find out exactly how children's understanding of money evolves, Hans Furth (1980) interviewed approximately 200 British children ranging in age from 5 to 11. He asked them questions about money and commerce and about such social institutions as stores,

schools, and government. His findings point to the dynamic growth of knowledge and understanding during middle childhood. At each stage of growth, children are confronted

"By wondering about things, asking questions, and being given more details, children gradually learn what the real world and the world of money are all about."

with information that is inconsistent with their present way of thinking about the world. By wondering about things, asking questions, and

being given more details, children gradually learn what the real world and the world of money are all about.

Furth identified four separate stages that children pass through in their growing awareness of money as a medium of exchange.

In the first stage, children believe that money is freely available. The exchange of money for goods or services is totally meaningless to them. In fact, they believe that one of the ways people get money is by buying something and receiving change. Thus, said one of Furth's young subjects: "Sometimes [the storekeeper] gives you four p[ence] for the sweets back and sometimes he gives you more when you want

various kinds of behavior and by imitating models. Psychodynamic psychologists believe that it develops as a defense against anxiety over the loss of love and approval. Cognitive theorists believe that, like intellectual development, morality develops in progressive, age-related stages. Let us take a closer look at cognitive approaches to moral development.

COGNITIVE VIEWS OF MORAL DEVELOPMENT   Piaget defined *morality* as "an individual's respect for the rules of social order and his sense of justice"—*justice* being "a concern for reciprocity and equality among individuals" (Hoffman, 1970). According to Piaget (1965), children's moral sense arises from the interaction between their developing thought structures and their gradually widening social experience. The moral sense develops in two stages. At the **moral realism stage,** children think that all rules should be obeyed because they are real, indestructible things, not abstract principles. A child at this stage judges the morality of an act in terms of its consequences and is incapable of weighing intentions. For example, a young child will think that the girl who accidentally breaks 12 dishes while setting a table is much guiltier than the girl who intentionally breaks 2 dishes because she is angry with her sister.

moral realism stage Piaget's term for the first stage of moral development, in which children believe in rules as real, indestructible things.

some bigger things" (Furth, 1980, p. 27).

In the second stage, children understand that money is used as a medium of exchange to buy goods and services, but their understanding stops here. In their limited view of the world, they do not understand that shopkeepers must use the money they receive to pay for the goods they eventually sell. Those few children who actually understand a merchant's use of money never relate it back to their own purchases. Children may believe that the money storekeepers collect is their personal property to do with as they wish, not realizing that store-keepers actually have to pay for the things they sell in the store. One child had a very altruistic view of where the money finally winds up: "The money the lady collects," said the child, "she gives it to the blind or something, the poor people" (p. 28).

In the third stage, there is a major leap in children's understanding: They know that storekeepers use the money they receive from customers to stock their stores. However, children cannot understand the profit motive behind a sale, nor can they understand the storekeepers' need to earn money for themselves and for their families. In fact, many children expressed a kind of a moral concern that the storekeepers might be taking money that really didn't belong to them. The children echoed phrases they had heard from their parents but did not fully understand: "Keep the hand out of the till," said one child. "Don't use business money for private affairs" (p. 28).

In the final stage, which, according to Furth, most children reach when they are 10 or 11 years old, children understand the concept of profit. They understand that store-keepers earn money by selling goods for more than they paid for them and that these profits allow them to run their stores and pay their personal expenses.

At each stage, information that conflicts with children's existing view of the world requires a readjustment of thinking. The process of cognitive growth is gradual; concepts that do not fit into the child's cognitive world at an early age are disregarded until a later time, or only parts of them are used. This understanding develops from that of a 5-year-old who asks Daddy for an allowance of a million dollars to that of the sophisticated 11-year-old who charges a quarter for 5 cents' worth of lemonade.

Later, children reach the **moral relativism stage.** At this point, they realize that rules are created and agreed upon cooperatively by individuals and that rules can be changed as the need arises. This leads to the realization that there is no absolute right or wrong and that morality depends not on consequences, but on intentions. We can see these two aspects of morality presented in Table 14–3.

Kohlberg's Six-Stage Theory. Piaget's two-stage theory of moral development was extended by Lawrence Kohlberg (1981, 1984). Kohlberg presented his subjects (children, adolescents, and adults) with a series of morally problematic stories and then asked them questions about the stories. The leading character in each story was faced with a moral dilemma, and the subject being interviewed was asked to resolve this dilemma. Kohlberg was less interested in the specific answers to the problem than in the reasoning behind the answers. Here is one of his stories, which has become a classic:

In Europe, a woman was near death from a special kind of cancer. There was one drug that the doctors thought might save her. It was a form of radium that a druggist in the same town had recently discovered. The drug was expensive to make, but the druggist was charging

moral relativism stage Piaget's term for the second stage of moral development, in which children realize that rules are agreements that may be changed, if necessary.

TABLE 14–3 Piaget's Concept of Moral Development

Moral realism	Ages 4 to 6	Child believes that rules should be obeyed because they are real, indestructible things—not abstract principles; morality of an action is judged by its consequences—a person is guiltier who commits more damage than a person who commits less.
Moral relativism	Ages 7 and older	Child believes the rules are created and agreed upon cooperatively; rules can be changed by consensus as the need arises; there is therefore no absolute right or wrong; morality of an action is determined by the intention rather than consequences of action.

10 times what the drug cost him to make. He paid $200 for the radium and charged $2,000 for a small dose of the drug. The sick woman's husband, Heinz, went to everyone he knew to borrow the money, but he could only get together $1,000, which is half of what it cost. He told the druggist that his wife was dying and asked him to sell it cheaper or let him pay later. But the druggist said, "No, I discovered the drug, and I am going to make money from it." So Heinz got desperate and broke into the man's store to steal the drug for his wife. (Kohlberg, 1969, p. 379)

Developing a sense of right and wrong involves understanding social rules and gaining experience in social relationships.

The person being interviewed was then asked: "Should Heinz have stolen the drug?" "Why?" "Was the druggist right to have charged so much more than it cost to make the drug?" "Why?" "Which is worse, letting someone die or stealing if it will save a life?" "Why?"

The ways that different age groups answered these questions led Kohlberg to the theory that moral reasoning develops in distinct stages. He defined three broad levels of moral reasoning and subdivided these levels into six stages (see Table 14–4). Support for his theory was provided by several studies that showed that young boys, at least in Western societies, generally went through these stages in the predicted fashion. In one 20-year longitudinal study of 48 boys, Kohlberg and his associates found remarkable consistency with these stages (Colby et al., 1983).

Kohlberg's theory has raised many objections. Some researchers have found that it is very difficult to follow Kohlberg's procedures exactly and to agree on how a child's response to the test should be scored (Rubin & Trotten, 1977). Others have attacked Kohlberg's theory on the grounds of **moral absolutism:** It disregards significant cultural differences that determine what is moral in other societies (Baumrind, 1978). Kohlberg (1978) himself acknowledged that it is necessary to take into account the social and moral norms of the group to which a person belongs. He has concluded that his sixth stage of moral development may not apply to all people in all cultures.

Power and Reimer (1978) find other weaknesses in Kohlberg's theory. They point out that Kohlberg's scale measures attitudes, not behavior, and that there is a great difference between thinking about moral questions and behaving morally.

moral absolutism Any theory of morality that disregards cultural differences in moral beliefs.

TABLE 14-4 Kohlberg's Stages of Moral Development

STAGE	ILLUSTRATIVE REASONING
Level I. Preconventional (based on punishments and rewards)	
Stage 1. Punishment and obedience orientation.	Obey rules in order to avoid punishment.
Stage 2. Naive instrumental hedonism.	Obey to obtain rewards, to have favors returned.
Level II. Conventional (based on social conformity)	
Stage 3. "Good-boy" morality of maintaining good relations, approval of others.	Conform to avoid disapproval or dislike by others.
Stage 4. Authority-maintaining morality.	Conform to avoid censure by legitimate authorities, with resulting guilt.
Level III. Postconventional (based on moral principles)	
Stage 5. Morality of contract, of individual rights, and of democratically accepted law.	Abide by laws of land for community welfare.
Stage 6. Morality of individual principles of conscience.	Abide by universal ethical principles.

Source: From *Stages of Moral Development* by Lawrence Kohlberg (unpublished doctoral dissertation, University of Chicago, 1958). © 1958 by Lawrence Kohlberg. Used by permission. Also adapted from *The Philosophy of Moral Development* by Lawrence Kohlberg (New York: Harper & Row, 1981).

Moral decisions are not made in a vacuum; instead, they are usually made in "crisis situations." No matter how high our moral principles may be, when the time comes to act on them, our behavior may not reflect our thoughts or beliefs.

Gilligan's Objections. Carol Gilligan (1982) claims that Kohlberg based his theory entirely on his work with male subjects and failed to consider the possibility that moral development might proceed somewhat differently in females. In other words, she accuses Kohlberg of sex bias. Gilligan found that girls and women generally score lower than males do on Kohlberg's moral dilemma test. But, she says, this does not mean that their thinking is at a lower level—only that they use different criteria for making moral judgments.

According to Gilligan (1982), girls and boys are taught from early childhood to value different qualities. Boys are trained to strive for independence and to value abstract thinking. Girls, in contrast, are taught to be nurturing and caring and to value their connectedness to others. Gilligan believes that there are two distinct types of moral reasoning: One is based on concepts of abstract justice, and the other is based on human relationships and caring for other people. The justice perspective is characteristic of male thinking, whereas caring for others is more common in females. Men often focus on rights, whereas women see moral issues in terms of concern for the needs of others. However, Gilligan notes that sex differences in moral reasoning (like other sex differences) are not absolute. Some women make moral judgments from a justice perspective, and some men make them from a caring one.

Gilligan's subjects were mostly adolescents and young adults. Other researchers have looked at younger children and have failed to find a sex difference in moral judgments made by children younger than age 10. However, some 10- or 11-year-old boys give rather aggressive responses to the questions that are asked on these tests—the sort of responses that are hardly ever given by girls. For example, in one study the children listened to a story about a porcupine that, needing a home for the winter, moved in with a family of moles. The moles soon found that they were constantly being pricked by the porcupine's sharp needles. What should they do? Only boys responded to this question with suggestions like "Shoot the porcupine" or "Pluck out his quills." Girls of this age tended to look for solutions that would harm neither the moles nor the porcupine—in other words, caring solutions (Garrod, Beal, & Shin, 1989).

Eisenberg's View. Nancy Eisenberg (1989a, 1989b) feels that Kohlberg's mistake was not in placing too much emphasis on abstract justice; it was in making the stages too rigid and absolute. She feels that children's moral development is not quite this predictable and narrowly determined. Many factors go into children's moral judgments, ranging from the social customs of the culture in which they are reared to how they feel at a particular moment. Children are capable of making moral judgments at a high level one day and at a lower level the next. They may even make judgments at a higher level for some issues (for example, whether they would help someone who was injured) than for others (for example, whether they would invite someone they didn't like to their birthday party).

With regard to sex differences, Eisenberg also finds that girls between ages 10 and 12 give more caring and empathetic responses than do boys of this age. However, she thinks this stems mainly from the fact that girls mature more rapidly than boys do. By late adolescence, boys have caught up. Eisenberg and her colleagues find few sex differences in the responses of older adolescents (Eisenberg, 1989a; Eisenberg et al., 1987).

PEER RELATIONSHIPS AND SOCIAL COMPETENCE

As the previous discussion indicates, the ability to make moral decisions on the basis of empathy and concern for others is something that develops as children mature. Girls mature a little faster; therefore, they develop empathy at a somewhat earlier age than boys do. Empathy is based on social inference because if you do not know what someone else is feeling, you cannot empathize with him or her. Social inference and empathy are the foundation upon which friendships are based.

CONCEPTS OF FRIENDSHIP

The ability to infer the thoughts, expectations, feelings, and intentions of others plays a central role in understanding what it means to be a friend. Children who can view things from another person's perspective are better able to develop strong, intimate relationships with others.

Using a social cognition model, Selman (1976, 1981) studied the friendships of children aged 7 to 12. His approach was similar to Kohlberg's: Tell children a story involving a social dilemma and then ask them questions designed to measure their concepts about other people, their self-awareness and ability to reflect, their concepts of personality, and their ideas about friendship. Here is an example of the kind of story that Selman used:

> Kathy and Debby have been best friends since they were 5. A new girl, Jeannette, moves into their neighborhood, but Debby dislikes her because she considers Jeannette a showoff. Later, Jeannette invites Kathy to go to the circus on its one day in town. Kathy's problem is that she has promised to play with Debby that same day. What will Kathy do?

This story raises questions about the nature of relationships, about old versus new friendships, and about loyalty and trust. It requires children to think and to talk about how friendships are formed and maintained and to decide what is important in a relationship. In other words, Selman's method provides a way of assessing a child's concepts and thought processes—how the child decides what is important.

Selman (1981) described four stages of friendship. At the first stage (below age 7), friendship is based on physical or geographical considerations and is rather self-centered. A friend is just a playmate—someone who lives nearby, who goes to the same school, or who has desirable toys. At this stage, there is no understanding of the other person's perspective.

At the second stage (ages 7 to 9), the idea of reciprocity and an awareness of another person's feelings begin to form. Friendship is seen mostly in terms of the social actions of one person and the subjective evaluation of these actions by the other. A child at this stage might say that Kathy could go to the circus with Jeannette and remain friends with Debby only if Debby did not object to the change in plans.

At the third stage (ages 9 to 12), friendship is based on genuine give-and-take; friends are seen as people who help each other. Children realize that they can evaluate the actions of their friends and that friends can evaluate their actions in return. The concept of trust appears for the first time. Children at the third stage might realize that the friendship between Kathy and Debby is different from the friendship between Kathy and Jeannette because the older friendship is based on long-standing trust.

At the fourth stage, which occured only rarely among the 11- and 12-year-olds he studied, children see friendship as a stable, continuing relationship that is based on trust. Children are now capable of looking at the relationship from the perspective of a third party. A child at this level might comment, "Kathy and Debby should be able to understand each other." Selman argues that the key to developmental changes in children's friendships is perspective taking ability. We can see these stages of friendship presented in Table 14–5.

Not all researchers agree with Selman's model. For example, there is evidence that young children implicitly know more of the rules and expectations of being a friend than they are able to tell an interviewer (Rizzo & Corsaro, 1988). Also, real friendships are quite complicated and are constantly changing. They may involve mutuality, trust, and reciprocity at one time and independence, competitiveness, or even conflict at another. Certain types of conflict may be intrinsic to the nature of friendship. Such complexities are not easily handled by a model that looks only at the cognitive aspects of children's friendships and ignores the emotional aspects (Berndt, 1983).

FUNCTIONS OF FRIENDSHIP

Children and adults alike benefit from having close, confiding relationships. Through friendships, children learn social concepts and social skills, and they

TABLE 14–5 Selman's Stages of Friendship Development

Stage 1	Ages 6 and under	Friendship is based on physical or geographic factors; children are self-centered, with no understanding of the perspectives of others.
Stage 2	Ages 7 to 9	Friendship begins to be based on reciprocity and an awareness of other's feelings; it begins to be based on social actions and evaluation by each other.
Stage 3	Ages 9 to 12	Friendship is based on genuine give-and-take; friends are seen as people who help each other; mutual evaluation of each other's actions occurs; concept of trust appears.
Stage 4	Ages 11–12 and Older	Friendship is seen as a stable, continuing relationship that is based on trust; children can observe the relationship from the perspective of a third party.

Source: Selman, 1981.

develop self-esteem. Friendship provides a structure for a child's activity in games; it reinforces and solidifies group norms, attitudes, and values; it serves as a backdrop for individual and group competition (Hartup, 1970a).

Friendship patterns shift during childhood (Piaget, 1965). The "egocentric" pattern of Selman's first stage, typical of preschoolers and younger school-age children, changes during middle childhood when children begin to form closer relationships, frequently with a few "best" friends. These friendship ties are very strong while they last, but they tend to be short-lived. In late childhood and adolescence, group friendships become common. The groups are generally large, with several boys or girls regularly sharing activities.

Two children who are friends may satisfy different needs in each other. One may be dominant, and the other may be submissive. One child may use her friend as a model, and the other child may enjoy teaching her friend the "proper" way to play or dress. In still another case, the relationship may be egalitarian, with neither friend playing a clear or consistent role. The pattern depends upon the dominance, dependency, and autonomy needs of each child.

With a friend, children can share their feelings and fears and every detail of their lives. Having a best friend in whom one can confide teaches a child how to relate to others openly and unselfconsciously. However, this pattern of friendship is more common in girls. Boys tend to play in larger groups and to reveal less of themselves to their friends (Maccoby, 1990; Rubin, 1980).

Friendship pairs allow children to share feelings and fears and to reinforce activities, values, and norms.

Friendship can also be a vehicle of self-expression. Children sometimes choose friends whose personalities are quite different from their own. An outgoing or impulsive child may choose a more reserved or restrained child as a close friend. The relationship gives each a maximum of self-expression with a minimum of competition, and the pair, as a unit, demonstrates more personality traits than either child could alone (Hartup, 1970a, 1970b). Of course, friends are rarely complete opposites. Friendship pairs that last over a long period of time usually have many shared values, attitudes, and expectations, both within the pair and in relation to others.

Some childhood friendships last throughout life, but more often friendships change. Best friends may move away or transfer to another school, and children may feel a real sense of loss—until they make a new friend. Sometimes, friends become interested in other people who meet their needs in new and different ways, and, sometimes, friends just grow apart or develop new interests. As children mature, they turn to new partners who can provide more satisfactory relationships (Rubin, 1980).

Finally, not all children have friends. Some are consistently unsuccessful in their attempts to form friendships. Children who are rejected by their peers are at risk for later maladjustment. But we should note that not all children who are rejected by peers are, in fact, friendless. Some research suggests that even a single close friend helps children cope with the negative effects of being disliked and isolated from most of their peers (Rubin & Coplan, 1992).

THE PEER GROUP

What is a **peer group?** When we use this term, we are not talking about just any "bunch of kids." The size of a peer group is limited by the fact that all of its members must interact with one another. In addition, a peer group is relatively

peer group A group of two or more people of similar status who interact with each other and who share norms and goals.

stable, and it stays together for a period of time. Its members share many values, and common norms govern interaction and influence each child. Finally, some degree of status differentiation governs the group's interaction; there is at least a temporary division into leaders and followers.

DEVELOPMENTAL TRENDS IN THE PEER GROUP   Peer groups are important throughout middle childhood, but a general shift occurs both in their organization and in their significance to the child during the years from 6 to 12.

In early middle childhood, peer groups are relatively informal. They are usually formed by the children themselves, and they have very few operating rules and a rapid turnover in membership. It is true that many of the group's activities, such as playing games or riding bikes, may be carried out according to precise rules. But the structure of the group itself is quite flexible.

The group takes on a more intense significance for its members when these children reach the ages 10 to 12. Group conformity becomes extremely meaningful to the child, who may be showing an almost religious reverence for rules and norms in other areas of social interaction. Peer pressures assume a coercive influence on the child. Groups also develop a more formal structure. They may have special membership requirements, club meetings, and initiation rites. At this time, division of the sexes becomes very important. Groups are now almost invariably composed of one sex, and each sex maintains different interests and activities and has different styles of interaction (Maccoby, 1990). These strict attitudes about rules, conformity, and sex segregation are common to children's interaction through the latter part of middle childhood, and they are usually not relaxed until mid-adolescence.

Peer groups form wherever children with common values, interests, or goals are thrown together.

GROUP FORMATION   Children are constantly being thrown together by circumstances—in schools, in camps, and in neighborhoods. In each case, and generally within a very short time, groups form. Role differentiation develops within the group. Common values and interests emerge. Mutual influences and expectations grow, and a feeling of tradition takes shape. The process is almost universal, and some interesting studies have recorded exactly how it happens.

One classic experiment was called the "Red Rover" study (Sherif & Sherif, 1953). The subjects were fifth-grade boys with similar backgrounds who were attending a summer camp. In the first phase of the study, the boys lived in two separate groups for a few days and were watched carefully as they began to form friendships. Just as these budding friendships were starting to solidify, the experimenters split up the friends by dividing the groups along new lines. The second stage of the study lasted for 5 days. The observers saw that in-group friendships soon formed in the new groups, and a clear hierarchy of leadership—not necessarily related to popularity—emerged very quickly. Group names were chosen (the "Red Devils" and the "Bulldogs"), and group rules and norms were developed.

In the final stage, the two groups were brought into direct competition in games that were rigged so that one group was almost never allowed to win. At first, the competition resulted in the quick development of animosity and even open hostility between the groups, with powerful feelings of in-group exclusivity. But the frustrated group's structure soon fell apart. Leadership disintegrated, and intragroup disharmony developed.

A second study, sometimes called the "Robber's Cave" experiment (Sherif et al., 1961), duplicated the circumstances and findings of the first study, with one substantial change. The competition between the groups was now equal. The results showed some interesting things about group structure. Equal competition intensified in-group solidarity in both groups, reinforcing norms and expectations. Feelings of exclusivity within each group and a sense of hostility toward the opposing group also grew stronger, just as the experimenters had hypothesized. Another finding was that the hierarchical structures of both groups changed. Leadership shifted as the boys who did best in the current competition rose to new leadership positions. In other words, group roles were shown to be related quite strongly to group goals. When the goals changed, so did the leaders.

In both of these studies, the experimenters had created openly hostile situations, and in each case, they tried to "undo the damage before the boys were sent home from camp. In the highly frustrating "Red Rover" condition, the hostility was never completely erased. In the second study, however, the experimenters were better able to control the situation. They theorized that if the two groups were brought together with a common goal, the hostility would break down. This theory was proven to be true when both groups were forced to cooperate on a camp project that involved fixing the food truck so that both groups could eat.

Why are these older classic studies still worth describing? They were conducted in natural settings, the kinds of situations that almost every child experiences. They also tell us a lot about groups. As the experimenters predicted, the groups formed quickly, and status differentiation seemed to develop almost automatically. Group members found common values and had shared norms; they even named their groups. Most important, when groups were put into competition against each other, feelings of exclusivity and hostility quickly developed. But when the groups were required to cooperate, hostility was reduced. These findings are typical of the way in which groups form and compete in classrooms, in athletic competitions, and in neighborhood or ethnic rivalries.

STATUS WITHIN THE PEER GROUP   If we watch schoolchildren at lunchtime or at recess, we can observe the "natural selection" of roles that takes place in every group. One girl is surrounded by children eager to get her attention. Another, ignored, stands on the fringes of the group. Three boys run by, shouting. A muscular child grabs a smaller child's toy, and the smaller one cries. This kind of scene occurs all over the world, wherever there are children.

Each peer group has some members who are popular and others who are not. Several factors seem to contribute to this difference in social status; we have already discussed several of these factors in Chapter 10. Peer acceptance is often related to an individual's good overall adjustment—enthusiasm and active participation, ability to cooperate with others, and responsiveness to social overtures. This kind of attunement (or lack of it) tends to reinforce itself in a circular pattern, due to its effects on self-esteem and social self-confidence. The good adjustment of well-liked children is bolstered by their popularity; inept children become even more ill at ease when they are ignored or rejected by the group (Glidewell et al., 1966).

Academic performance and athletic ability also influence popularity. In general, popular children are brighter than average and do well in school. Slow learners are often made fun of or are ignored. Athletic ability is particularly important in settings like camps or playgrounds, where the whole group is involved in sports.

Popularity is affected both by extreme aggressiveness and extreme timidity. No one likes a bully, so the overly aggressive child is shunned. This leads to another kind of circular pattern because this child may become even more aggressive out of frustration or in an attempt to win by force what he or she cannot win by persuasion. As for the timid, anxious child, he or she is at risk of becoming a chronic victim, picked on not just by bullies but even by average children (Dodge et al., 1990; Perry et al., 1990).

Unpopular children often have some trait that makes them different from their classmates—obesity, skin of the "wrong" color, or even an unusual name (see the box "Nicknames"). These traits can reduce children's level of conformity to group standards—and conformity, as we have seen, is very important during middle childhood. How insistent is the pressure to conform to group standards, and who are the children most influenced by these pressures?

PEER GROUP CONFORMITY   Conforming to the peer group can be a normal, healthy, and often desirable behavior. As part of their daily behavior, children conform to peer group standards as well as to adult expectations. But children sometimes conform excessively to group norms, even when these standards are not helpful to the individual child, to the group as a whole, or to outsiders.

Which children are most strongly influenced by group pressures? There are a few characteristics that appear to be common in high-conforming children. They have feelings of inferiority and low "ego strength" (Hartup, 1970a). They

FOCUS ON RESEARCH

NICKNAMES

Remember the good old days in grade school when you were called everything but the name your parents gave you? You may have been lucky enough to have borne the nickname "Chief" or "Coach" or "Ace," or unfortunate enough to be called "Dumbo" or "Four-Eyes" or even "Sewage." These labels may seem amusing to adults, but they are a serious matter to children. Recent research has shown that nicknames may teach children about social status, friendship, morality, and about the adult world itself.

"Children who have no nicknames are considered too insignificant to bother with."

To get to the bottom of the nickname puzzle, Rom Harré and his colleagues (1980) surveyed thousands of youngsters and adults in the United States, Great Britain, Spain, Mexico, Japan, and the Arab countries. What they found is that children between the ages of 5 and 15 often create separate and secret worlds for themselves and that nicknames may perform important social functions in these worlds.

One of the main reasons children bestow nicknames on one another is to separate "us" from "them." Children who have no nicknames are considered too insignificant to bother with. They tend to be low in popularity and to be isolated from the rest of the group. As Harré and his colleagues (1980) point out, "To be nicknamed is to be seen as having an attribute that entitles one to social attention, even if that attention is unpleasant. Thus, it may be better to be called 'Sewage' than merely John" (p. 81).

The "Fatties" and "Lamebrains" of the group are used as examples by group leaders to show how people are not supposed to be. They are walking advertisements of violated group standards. These group standards are the children's attempts to internalize society's norms. Through nicknames, children loudly proclaim what is acceptable to society and what is not. Any behavior, style, or physical characteristic that does not meet society's standards can become the source of a nickname. Thus, when children call others "Stinky," "Pimples," or "Eagle Nose," they are trying to internalize the accepted adult norms for cleanliness and appearance.

Unfortunately, for the recipients of these nicknames, the process can be very painful. However, as the researchers found, these children are often willing victims: "It is not necessarily the fattest, stupidest, and dirtiest who acquire the names 'Hippo' or 'Tapeworm-Woman,' but those who willingly bear the humiliation of being symbols of childhood greed, improvidence, and aversion to washing" (Harré, 1980, p. 81).

Nicknames also express children's own sense of "class" consciousness, social separateness, and hidden knowledge. Nicknames that are understood by only a small circle of friends make outsiders of those who do not know their meaning. In some cases, nicknames communicate secret information that may be unknown to the children who actually bear the names. In one school, for example, the boys labeled the sexually available girls "Dragoon One," "Dragoon Two," and so on, even though the girls had no idea what these names meant.

Children use nicknames differently in various cultures. Nicknames like "The Lame One" or "The Three-Legged One," which poke fun at physical deformities, are much more common in Arab countries than in England or Japan. The Japanese are more likely to use animal and insect analogies. In any culture, it seems that nicknames help children to build the social reality they take with them into adulthood.

What's in a name? In the case of nicknames, there is a lot more than you might expect.

Conformity within a peer group is normal and often desirable behavior.

tend to be more dependent or anxious than other children and are exceptionally sensitive to social cues. Children who have these characteristics also tend to monitor their own behavior and verbal expressions very closely. They are especially concerned with how they appear to others and are constantly comparing themselves to their peers. Watching what others do or say and then adapting to the group norm is common to *self-monitoring children* (Graziano et al., 1987).

Peer pressure can be positive as well as negative: For example, a child who belongs to a group of high academic achievers might feel pressured to complete homework assignments. In fact, children are more likely to conform to peer pressure when it is positive than when it involves antisocial acts, such as drinking, smoking, or stealing. When peer pressure actually involves antisocial acts, boys are more likely than are girls to yield to it (Brown et al., 1986). Children who are unsupervised after school also tend to conform to antisocial peer pressure more than those who are monitored by adults (Steinberg, 1986).

Conformity is especially meaningful to children during late middle childhood, when they are moving away from the security of family life. Preadolescents have a strong need to belong, to feel accepted, and to feel that they are part of a social setting larger than themselves. These needs coexist with an equally strong need for autonomy or mastery. Children try to exert some control over their social and physical environments, to understand the rules and limits, and to find a place within these limits. For this reason, they become very involved in making rules and learning rituals.

At several points in human development, this coexistence of autonomy and acceptance needs is especially important. It is critical for 1 1/2-year-olds, who are just beginning to learn what they can do for themselves. During late middle childhood, these two opposing needs again become paramount. But the balance that the preadolescent works out is different from that of the toddler. For the older child, the peer group often satisfies both the need for acceptance and the need for autonomy.

PREJUDICE

What happens to children as they move away from their families during middle childhood and discover that the norms of the broader culture differ from those at home? Children have this experience when they learn, for example, that their friends do not like spinach or do not go to church. The difference in attitudes can lead to special problems for minority group children, as they must reconcile their own self-image with the unpleasant stereotypes and prejudices that they may encounter. This can affect their behavior, their school achievement, and their relationships with others. As we saw in our discussion of the "self-fulfilling prophecy" (Chapter 13), people tend to live up (or down) to the expectations of others (Howard & Hammond, 1985).

prejudice A negative attitude formed without adequate reason and usually directed toward people because of their membership in a group.

Prejudice means a negative attitude directed toward people because of their membership in a group, with the group being targeted on the basis of race, religion, national origin, language, or any other noticeable attribute. We tend to think of prejudice as an adult attitude, but racial awareness begins to develop early, during the preschool years. Just as a child learns that she is a girl or that he is a boy (see Chapter 11), an African-American child learns that he or she has darker skin than some of the other children seen on television or in the neighborhood. Also, just as the little girl learns that her body differs from that of a boy before she understands what it means to be female in our society, an African-American child learns about the differences in skin and hair before she understands what it means to be an African-American. Thus, she must learn, first, that she is different in appearance from white children; and second, she must learn that these differences may make her unwelcome or may be held against her. The same would hold for a white child in a predominantly minority setting. Prejudice flows in two directions in our society. What the child does not understand is why being a member of this group results in social discrimination. Her efforts to answer this question could be a life-long task (Spencer, 1988).

The understanding of group differences and of what it means to be a member of a group is an aspect of social cognition. Social cognition, in turn, depends on overall cognitive development. Thus, a child whose thought is still egocentric, and who can focus on only one dimension at a time, will assume that people who are similar in one dimension (for instance, skin color) must be similar in other dimensions as well. As children grow older, they become better at seeing people as multidimensional. In an experiment with English-speaking and French-speaking Canadian children, it was found that older children had more flexible attitudes about members of the other language-speaking group. Children who had entered the period of concrete operations were less likely to attribute negative characteristics to the members of the other group than were those subjects who were still in the preoperational period (Doyle, Beaudet, & Aboud, 1988).

This improved ability to see people as multidimensional is opposed by the strong tendency of older school-age children to conform to group standards and to reject those who are different from them in any way. A study done in a California town where the schools were about 50 percent Afro-American and 50 percent white found that children in the older grades were less likely than were younger children to have a friend of a different race. In fact, interracial friendships declined steadily from the fourth grade through the seventh. The researchers concluded that, as children grow older, similarity becomes a more and more powerful basis for friendship. There may also be a fair amount of pressure from other members of a child's group to avoid forming friendships with members of the other group (Hallinan & Teixeira, 1987). This pressure can come from either side. Afro-American children who become friendly with white children may be pressured to give up such friendships because they are being "disloyal" to their race (Schofield, 1981). Recently, studies have also found that African-American children who succeed at school are perceived as being disloyal. They are actively taunted by their peers and are excluded from group activities (Reuter News Service, 1993).

Racial awareness is an important issue for children during middle childhood because it is the time when a child "does or does not sign a 'contract' with society" (Comer & Poussaint, 1975, p. 116). Children absorb the cultural attitudes of those around them. In return for "swearing allegiance" to the standards of society, children must get from society a sense of belonging to a larger, more powerful group. But Afro-American parents have had to accommodate themselves to a majority culture that does not reward them as it does whites. African-American parents are expected to teach their children the values of a society that holds them in low esteem. The children naturally sense this conflict, and it affects their attitudes toward society.

Peer pressures aggravate the conflict. Minority peer groups often have norms that differ widely from those of white, middle-class peer groups. An African-American child growing up in an inner city environment belongs to a culture different from that of most middle-class whites or blacks. The degree of acceptance that African-American children find in the larger society often depends upon their ability to conform to its norms. When minority children get together with other members of their racial or ethnic group, this makes their adjustment easier during middle childhood. It tends to improve their self-esteem and to increase both in-group solidarity and out-group hostility. But minority children eventually face the problem of integrating their own self-concept with society's image of them as members of a specific group, and this can cause conflict, anxiety, or anger at any age.

 SELF-CONCEPTS

As children grow older, their developing social cognition enables them to form a more accurate and complex picture of the physical, intellectual, and personality characteristics of other people. At the same time, they are able to form a more accurate and complex picture of their own characteristics. They compare themselves with their age-mates, and they conclude, "I'm better than Chris at sports, but I'm not as good in math as Kerry," or "I may not be as pretty as Courtney, but I'm better at making friends." Children's emerging self-concepts in turn provide a "filter" through which they evaluate their own social behavior and that of others (Harter, 1982).

SELF-IMAGE AND SELF-ESTEEM

Self-image refers to seeing oneself as an individual with certain characteristics. **Self-esteem** means seeing oneself as an individual with positive characteristics—as a person who will do well in the things that he thinks are important. During the school years, self-esteem is significantly correlated with academic self-confidence (which, in turn, is significantly correlated with academic achievement). The children who do well in school have higher self-esteem than those who do poorly (Alpert-Gillis & Connell, 1989). In view of the key part that school plays in a child's life, this is not surprising.

The correlation between self-esteem and academic self-confidence, however, is far from being a perfect one: Many children who do not do well in school nevertheless manage to develop high self-esteem. Depending on how their parents have treated them and what their friends think of them, children who are not good in one thing can find something else at which they are good. Additionally, if they come from a cultural background that says "school is not important," their self-esteem may not be related at all to their academic achievement. How well one is thought of by one's parents and by one's peer group is far more important than how well one does in the eyes of the larger society. This is why Afro-American children, despite their daily encounters with racial prejudice, generally manage to develop healthy levels of self-esteem (Spencer, 1988).

self-image Seeing oneself as an individual with certain characteristics.

self-esteem Seeing oneself as an individual with positive characteristics—as one who will do well in the things that he or she thinks are important.

The development of self-esteem is a circular process. Children tend to do well if they are confident in their own abilities; their success leads to further increases in self-esteem. On the other side of this coin are the children who do poorly because they lack self-esteem (perhaps due to the kinds of psychological abuse described earlier in this chapter) and whose self-esteem therefore continues to fall. Personal successes or failures in different situations can lead children to see themselves as leaders or losers, as champions or chumps. Fortunately, these experiences do not automatically create a closed circle, and many children who start off with social or academic handicaps eventually find something that they can do well.

Given the close links between self-esteem and achievement, many teachers try to build self-esteem in their students by offering frequent praise. In moderation, praise can be quite helpful. However, critics have suggested that too much praise, without the appropriate links to achievement or to ethical behavior, creates children who do not have a real sense of their own strengths and weaknesses. They may begin to think "I am great no matter what I do". This can create confusion and problems for them in peer and school relations (Damon & Hart, 1992), as the following example indicates:

Realistic praise—that is, praise linked to achievement—encourages the growth of self-esteem in children.

> Early in my son's kindergarten year, he returned home with a three-by-five index card containing two words: 'I'm terrific.' Every child in his class had been given a similar card with the same two words. My son told me that his teacher had asked all the children to recite the words in class, to remember them, and to keep the cards for a further reminder. I asked my son what it all meant. He said that he was terrific and this his friends were terrific. He had no particular ideas about why, how, or what they were terrific at. (Damon, 1991, p. 12)

Children cannot be quickly inoculated with self-confidence through facile phrases such as "I'm great" or "I'm terrific." Researchers have recently raised concerns that when children are told that the most important thing in the world is how highly they think of themselves, they are clearly being sent a message that they are at the center of the universe. This emphasis has been accused of possibly pushing children toward social insensitivity—or self-love. Furthermore, critics contend that without an objective moral referent beyond themselves, children cannot acquire a stable sense of right and wrong—for example, children who deny a misdeed even when caught red-handed because they are convinced of their rightness (Damon. 1991). Teachers are therefore encouraged to link praise to behavior to encourage children to develop *realistic* self-esteem.

ASPECTS OF SELF

A mature internally evaluated self-concept does not come into play until later in middle childhood or, in some children, not until adolescence. Greenwald and Becker (1984), for example, believe that children's self-concept evolves in a series of phases:

1. the *diffuse self,* which is basically the pre-self that exists in infants and toddlers; a condition of not distinguishing between self and others; behavior is oriented toward approval and affection of others;

2. the *public self,* which is the beginning of a coherent sense of identity, but which is sensitive to the evaluation of others and seeks to win the approval of parents, peers, and authorities;

3. the *private self,* which is directed toward individual achievement, measured by meeting the child's own internal standards; usually does not begin to develop until middle childhood or adolescence; and

4. the *collective self,* which focuses on the collective achievement of the child's reference groups; success is measured by how well the internalized goals of the reference group are met.

The self, is therefore seen as a complex, highly individual, attitudinal framework which forms early and is continually refined throughout the person's life. Since it requires considerable social feedback to develop, one's sense of self is highly sensitive to the culture and historical period in which one lives.

SUMMARY AND CONCLUSIONS

A "culture of childhood" exists during middle childhood which is composed of customs, rules, games, and rituals. Distinctive beliefs and values also emerge through social play. These games and rituals help children to understand and adapt to the demands of the society in which they live.

The American family has undergone considerable change in the past twenty years. Many children today are being raised in households headed by mothers due to the effects of divorce and single parenthood. In many instances, these families live in poverty and are subject to multiple dimensions of stress and deprivation. The mothers in these families are often under extreme stress as they attempt to feed, clothe, and shelter their children. They may be unable to provide supportive, guiding parenting for their children.

Children—just as adults—can often effectively handle a single source of stress in their lives but may begin to show the negative effects of stress when multiple situations deteriorate. Various factors have been found to help children cope with multiple stresses. They include knowing what to expect, having a supportive and adaptable family, and having a **resilient personality.** For many children, unfortunately, these factors do not exist in their lives and they may fall victim to the stress that overwhelms them.

Divorce is a stress that significantly affects the lives of children who are exposed to it. They may feel guilty, sad, angry, or anxious. In addition, divorce changes their relations to their parents—they may have to adjust to the loss of one parent, the addition of stepparents, and altered attention from the remaining parent. A child's adjustment to divorce is affected by the amount of hostility shown by the parents before the divorce, how much the child's life actually changes because of the divorce, and the nature of the relations with parents after the divorce.

Another factor which has affected American families in increasing numbers in recent years is **child abuse.** This is the intentional inflicting of physical or psychological harm on a child. Many child abusers were themselves abused as children. People who experienced abuse as children are much more likely to experience psychological problems as adults—as well as to continue the abuse they experienced as children.

There are three main explanations for child abuse: psychiatric, sociological, and situational. All of these attempt to explain the dynamics in families where abuse occurs. The psychiatric explanation focuses on parents as the cause of abuse, the sociological focuses on the social forces that foster abuse, and the situational looks at the interaction between parents and abused child as the prime causal factor. None of these explanations has clearly established a cause or found a workable solution to the multiple problems associated with child abuse.

Psychological abuse also occurs in children. The various sorts of psychological abuse include: *rejection, denial of emotional responsiveness, degradation, terrorization, isolation* and *exploitation.* Exploitation is most clearly seen in cases of sexual abuse.

In addition to the changes in family dynamics and the nature of play, middle childhood also brings considerable advance in **social cognition** to the child. Social cognition is thought, knowledge, and understanding of the social world in which the child lives. Social cognition includes **social inference**—assumptions about the feelings of another, **social relationships,** and **social regulations**—an understanding of the rules of justice and respect that underlie social functioning.

Moral judgment is also an aspect of social cognition. This refers to the process of making decisions about right and wrong. Piaget and Kohlberg are cognitive theorists who suggest that moral thinking develops in stages during childhood. According to Piaget, children are first **moral realists** who believe that rules are physical things and that goodness or badness is determined by an action's consequences, and later are **moral relativists,** who believe that rules are made by people and therefore may be changed by consensus. Children at this stage believe that an act's goodness or badness is determined by the intentions of the person who committed it.

Kohlberg describes three broad levels of moral development, which may be further divided into six stages. The first level, *preconventional,* is based on rewards and punishments; the second, the *coventional,* is based on social conformity; and the third, the *postconventional,* is based on self-chosen ethical principles. Kohlberg's theory has been accused of being culturally and gender specific. It has been described as a white, male, American morality. Gilligan states that the morality of boys and girls differs. She argues that boys are justice oriented, while girls are oriented toward caring and empathy in their moral choices.

Peer relationships and social competence are also powerful factors influencing social development during middle childhood. Selman has studied the development of friendship patterns during childhood. In the first stage, ages 6 and under, friendships are self-centered and based on proximity or convenience. In the second stage, ages 7 to 9, friendships become more reciprocal and are based on an awareness of each other's feelings. In the third stage, ages 9 to 12, children begin to include trust and the evaluation of each other's actions as the basis for friendship. Finally, in the fourth stage, which begins at age 12, children see friendships as stable, continuing relationships based on trust.

Friendships serve many purposes during middle childhood. Children learn social concepts and skills, as well as develop self-esteem through friendships. Friends may be complementary to each other, for example, outgoing and introspective; often, they share revelations about themselves. This is more likely to be true for girls than boys. In addition to friendships, as children move through middle childhood, the peer group becomes more important. **Peer groups** imply shared norms and goals. Group conformity, therefore, becomes increasingly important. Peer groups often form hierarchies based on leadership and followership. When groups compete, feelings of exclusivity and hostility toward the opposing group develop. Cooperative activities undertaken by the competing groups seem to help reduce these negative outcomes.

The status of children within peer groups is based on their overall adjustment. Children who are enthusiastic, cooperative, and responsive tend to be the most popular. Intelligence, school achievement, and athletic ability may also be factors influencing popularity—depending on what the group values. A child who is different in any way tends to be unpopular—this may, in turn, affect the child's self-esteem.

The children most susceptible to group pressure are those with low self-esteem who are anxious and monitor themselves very closely. They are more likely to identify with the group's norms as a way of enhancing their self-esteem. Group membership and conformity become especially meaningful to children during late middle childhood.

Prejudice and racial awareness develop early, although a full understanding of these concepts may be a lifelong task. As children get older, their attitudes toward children of other groups tend to be less rigid. However, in contrast to this cognitive change, older children are more likely to form friendships based on similarity.

Most children, including members of minority groups, develop a good sense of **self-esteem** if their parents or peers think well of them. Often, a child who is not good at one thing, such as school subjects, will find something else, such as art, music, or athletics, at which he or she can excel. These also contribute to the overall self-esteem they will develop.

➤ KEY TERMS AND CONCEPTS

child abuse   moral relativism   self-image
latency   peer group   social cognition
moral absolutism   prejudice   social inference
moral judgment   resilient children   social regulations
moral realism   self-esteem   social relationships

➤ SELF-TEST QUESTIONS

1. List several factors that affect children's ability to cope with stressful events.
2. What are the factors that influence the way a child responds to divorce?
3. Discuss three different explanations for child abuse.
4. List different forms of psychological abuse.
5. Explain social cognition and its significance for middle childhood. Include in your discussion three important components of social knowledge.
6. Describe the sequence of the development of social cognition during middle childhood.
7. Explain Kohlberg's cognitive theory of moral development and describe its connection to Piaget's theory of development.
8. List some criticisms of Kohlberg's model.
9. Discuss Gilligan's two methods of moral reasoning.
10. Describe the importance of friendship pairs during middle childhood.
11. Discuss developmental trends in peer groups.
12. Describe some characteristics of peer group formation.
13. List two factors that contribute to status development within a peer group.
14. Discuss some of the problems children must face as a result of racial and ethnic prejudices. Why is racial awareness a particularly significant issue for children in middle childhood?
15. Describe the relationship between a child's self-image and his or her developing social competence.

➤ SUGGESTED READINGS

COLES, R. *The moral life of children*. Boston: Houghton Mifflin Company, 1986. Children tell a sensitive interviewer of the moral challenges that they face in their complex lives as a result of poverty, prejudice, war, family disputes, and the like.

DUNN, J. *Sisters and brothers*. Cambridge, MA: Harvard University Press, 1985. In a challenging review of the literature, Dunn examines the intensity of the sibling relationship as it develops through childhood and into adulthood.

FURTH, H. *The world of grown-ups*. New York: Elsevier, 1980. A descriptive study of children's thinking about various aspects of society.

GILLIGAN, C. *In a different voice: Psychological theory and women's development*. Cambridge, MA: Harvard University Press, 1982.

HELFER, R. E., & KEMPE, R. S. (Eds.). *The battered child* (4th edition). Chicago: University of Chicago Press, 1987. One of the standard references on child abuse, now thoroughly revised and expanded.

KOZOL, J. *Rachel and her children: Homeless families in America*. New York: Crown Publishers, 1988. A highly readable documentary of life on the edge of society.

RUBIN, Z. *Children's friendships*. Cambridge, MA: Harvard University Press, 1980. A delightful book that explores the roles and effects of friendships on children.

VIDEO CASE: INCEST REDEFINED?

At the age of 15, Ginger Tucker fell in love with her mother's second husband. "We talked a lot, and we started getting along," explains Tucker, "and eventually, one thing led to another, and it became physical." In the view of Maggie Scarf, an expert in modern relationships, in most families the Electra complex, which Freud named after the Greek myth of a girl who hated her mother and loved her father, is just a phase a young girl quickly passes through. However, in stepfamilies, there is a much higher risk that the fantasies will be acted out, just as in Ginger's case. Says Scarf, "You think of the young girls in these families coming into bloom with men who have not, perhaps, been there all the time, who have not been committed to protecting their innocence, who maybe get turned on. He's supposed to love this child, but not too much. He's supposed to caress and kiss this child, but not in a certain way, and so I think the boundaries are trickier in that kind of situation."

Is this incest? In the United States, twelve states have a narrow legal definition of incest, in which only blood-related members of an immediate family can be accused of this crime. This definition is extended in fifteen other states to include steprelations and adopted children. In all the remaining states, the laws fall somewhere in between.

Because experts predict that during the 1990s more American children will live with stepfamilies than with both biological parents, family counselor Jeanette Lofus believes that traditional definitions and current laws are outdated. Says Lofus, "The family in America today is a family of divorce, where divorced people have friends, and stepfamilies, where people bring children from other relationships into these marriages, and we must extend that incest taboo to the stepfamily."

The research data, Richard A. Gardner believes, support such a view. "The best studies" he notes, "seem to indicate that stepfathers are about eight times more likely to have a sexual relationship with a stepchild than a natural father with a natural child." Adds Scarf: "These boundary violations just destroy, obviously, the mother/daughter relationships, but they blow the family system apart because what you have, where you had rules, is chaos."

CASE QUESTIONS

1. Why do you think that stepfathers are more likely to have a sexual relationship with a stepchild than a natural father with his natural child?

2. Why and in what ways do such boundary violations "blow the family system apart"?

3. Should the evolving family be left alone to "police" itself? Or should the traditional legal definition of incest be expanded? If so, how?

Part Six

ADOLESCENCE

15 Adolescence: A Time of Transition

"Some theorists view the period of adolescence as a time of restricted rights and opportunities and rigidly prescribed roles. Others take a more positive view, seeing adolescence as a time when the individual is allowed to explore and experiment with various roles before settling into a social and occupational niche."

Despite their differences, both views take into account that the social and personal experiences of teenagers as they physically and cognitively mature and develop their sexual identity are a consequence of their particular historical and cultural content.

16 ▶ Adolescence: Social and Personality Development

"The ways that adolescents cope with the stresses of new bodies and new roles are based upon their personality development in earlier years."

To deal with internal and external pressures evolving from relations with families, peers, friends, and the wider social environment, adolescents develop coping strategies, including choosing values and forming loyalties that lead to the development of a more mature self.

The young...
are full of passion, which
excludes fear;
and of hope, which inspires con-
fidence.

ARISTOTLE,
RHETORIC BOOK II

CHAPTER

15

ADOLESCENCE: A TIME OF TRANSITION

OUTLINE

CHAPTER OBJECTIVES

By the time you have finished this chapter, you should be able to do the following:

✔ Include cultural and historical factors as part of a discussion of adolescent development.

✔ Discuss physical maturation during adolescence and describe the way in which cultural ideals influence an adolescent's adjustment to these changes.

✔ Discuss the factors that influence an adolescent's emerging sexuality and gender identity.

✔ Describe the cognitive changes that occur during adolescence and explain how these changes affect the scope and content of adolescent thought.

In our culture, adolescence, or the period of transition between childhood and adulthood, stretches over the better part of a decade, often this period has an ambiguous beginning and end. On one hand, we may see a precocious beginning to adolescence that seems to predate overt signs of puberty. Children frequently begin to act like adolescents before physical changes begin. At the other end of this growth period, the difficulty is obvious. How does one define the moment when a child has become a true adult? Of course, the best indicator of adulthood is emotional maturity rather than more obvious but often misleading criteria, such as completing an education, earning a living, marrying, or becoming a parent (Baldwin, 1986).

Despite the uncertainty over defining its boundaries, experts agree that this prolonged transitional period from childhood to adulthood is a modern phenomenon. The period of change is more condensed in "primitive" societies. In such societies, the young person goes through a symbolic ceremony, name change, or challenge at puberty. These symbolic events are referred to by anthropologists as **rites of passage,** or "transition rituals." An apprenticeship of a year or two follows, and, by age 16 or 17, the young person achieves full, unqualified adulthood. This rapid transformation is partly because the skills necessary for adult life in less complex cultures can be mastered without lengthy education. Still, the need for some period of transition is recognized by all; no society demands that a child turn into an adult overnight, and no society fails to recognize the significance of attaining adulthood.

In previous centuries, the physical maturation of puberty occurred later than it does now. In the United States today, a girl has her first menstrual period at an average age of 12 1/2; in the 1880s, the average age was 15 1/2 (Frisch, 1988). When puberty occurred at 15 or 16, the social transition from youth to adult followed closely on the heels of physical change. Now, in the United States and in other industrialized countries, there is an interval of several years between attaining biological maturity and making the social transition to adulthood. Thus, young people who are mature in a physical sense are nonetheless considered too young for the privileges and responsibilities of full adulthood.

In a technologically advanced society where complex jobs go to adults, adolescents experience prolonged dependence. In most cases, the jobs available to them are neither intrinsically interesting nor financially rewarding. This situation

rite of passage A symbolic event or ritual to mark life transitions, such as the one from childhood to adult status.

In technologically advanced societies adolescents must wait until they're old enough to obtain jobs that are interesting and financially rewarding. One ritual of "waiting" is hanging out with friends.

prolongs adolescents' dependence on their parents, delays the time when they can fully use their capabilities, and increases their frustration and restlessness. Some theorists view the period of adolescence as a time of restricted rights and opportunities and rigidly proscribed roles (Farber, 1970). Others, like Erikson, take a more positive view, seeing adolescence as a time when the individual is allowed to explore and to experiment with various roles before settling into a social and occupational niche. Erikson, for example, stated that adolescence should be a time of *moratorium* (a time-out), when the adolescent can explore his or her world before committing fully to relationships or work.

Clearly, the social and personal experiences of adolescents are a function of the historical and cultural context in which they live.

DEVELOPMENT IN A CULTURAL AND HISTORICAL CONTEXT

Although there are patterns in human development that are common to all societies and to all eras, the process of development is always deeply affected by the social and economic forces of the times. This is especially true of adolescence, when the individual tries to come to terms with social pressures and to strike a balance between internal and external values.

Adolescents are highly sensitive to the society around them—its values, its political and economic tensions, its unwritten rules. They are in the process of forming plans and expectations about their own future, and these expectations will depend in part on the cultural and historical setting in which they live. For example, adolescents who spent their earlier years in a period of economic expansion, when jobs were easy to get and family incomes were increasing, tend to expect similar conditions when they enter the job market. They expect their standard of living to be at least as good as that of their parents. They may be unprepared if the economic conditions that prevailed during their childhood worsen around the time that they enter adulthood (Greene, 1990).

Economic and cultural conditions can also have an impact on the timing of the milestones of growing up. Adolescence may be a brutally short prelude to independence, or it may involve prolonged dependence on the family. In nineteenth-century Ireland, for example, potato famines caused widespread poverty and suffering. Young men stayed at home because their labor was needed to keep the families alive. Their growth to adult independence was stunted by terrible economic need. In the United States, the Great Depression of the 1930s altered the plans and conferred unexpected responsibilities on young people coming of age during this period. There was a tendency to grow up as quickly as possible: Young people took on adult tasks and entered the job market sooner than they might have otherwise. This can be seen in the following case study.

> Pete was the oldest of three children in a family of Dutch immigrants. When the Great Depression reached its peak he was 16 years old. His father had been working on a public works project building a bridge and had fallen, severely injuring his back. He was unable to work after that for two years. Pete's mother went to work cleaning people's houses and taking in laundry. Pete dropped out of school and joined the Civilian Conservation Corps. He was immediately transported to Montana, where he was assigned the task of building roads and buildings in Glacier National Park. For this work he received room and board and his wages were sent home to his family. Between his and his mother's efforts, the family survived the Great Depression. Pete never returned to finish high school.

Elder (1980) compared developmental patterns of contemporary teenagers with those of adolescents living in the late nineteenth-century. Five different life events were measured: completion of education, entry into the job market, separation from the parental household, first marriage, and establishment of a new household. Elder found both differences and similarities between the two groups. Although both experienced the same life events, the timing of the events varied. Nineteenth-century adolescents left school earlier and had less formal education. They were quicker to enter the job market but slower to leave the family household, to marry, and to establish their own homes. Although today's young people spend more time in school, they break away from their parents sooner. Nineteenth-century adolescents made a rapid transition to adult occupational status as workers, but they took more time to achieve social independence. Interestingly, neither group experienced the period of youth as a clearly ordered sequence in which everyone left childhood and entered adulthood at approximately the same age.

Cultural and historical factors can be a source of psychological stress during adolescence. The 1960s were an especially difficult era for young people because they lived in a world characterized by ideological ferment and by the constant threat of nuclear annihilation. In earlier times, adolescents could look to adults and to a body of tradition for answers to many of their questions. When the youth of the 1960s looked to authority figures, they found uncertainty, conflicting values, and a vivid sense of the breakdown of the social order. Some turned to drugs, sexual permissiveness and away from what they perceived to be "the establishment." Others came through adolescence with a minimum of stress and did not subscribe to the youth culture of the 1960's. But the turbulence affected everyone in that age group, as we can see in the following case:

> I graduated from college in 1970 and so was a college student during the 1960's. This was a time of considerable unrest on college campuses. Protests frequently occurred; faculty and students were politically polarized; long hair was in and anything to do with the military or police was out.
>
> I was a relatively straight arrow during college. I was the commander of my ROTC unit and several days a week wore my uniform to class. We were also required to have very short hair. Needless to say, I stood out in a campus crowd. I was often hastled in class by both my teachers and fellow students for my appearance. I was in the ROTC house once when a protest surrounded it and shouted to burn it down.
>
> From that time on I realized that all people were not the same—didn't dance to the same music—and that keeping faith with your own beliefs was most important.

Keniston (1975) saw the problems of adolescents as arising from a "tension between self and society"—a lack of fit between who they feel they are and what they feel society wants them to be. According to Keniston, adolescents feel ambivalent not only toward the social order but also toward themselves. They may realize how deeply they have been influenced by the surrounding culture and may feel uncomfortable with this realization. They may feel that society is too rigid and confining, and they may try to break away from it by assuming temporary identities and roles. They may attempt to redefine and transform themselves through introspection, the use of drugs, meditation, or psychoanalysis.

According to Keniston adolescents use introspection as a way of redefining and changing themselves in order to escape what they feel to be society's too constricting views of them.

ADOLESCENCE IN CONTEMPORARY WESTERN SOCIETY

In our society, adolescents experience a phenomenon called *age segregation*. Partly because of choices they make and partly due to circumstances over which they have no control, adolescents tend to remain apart both from younger children and from adults. Their separation from younger children deprives them of opportunities to guide and tutor those who are less knowledgeable than themselves. Their separation from the adult world means that they rarely have the opportunity to serve apprenticeships—to learn jobs by working alongside experienced people in responsible positions. Instead, adolescents are separated for many hours every day from the major activities, customs, and responsibilities of the rest of society. Of course, age segregation is not total: Adolescents interact with younger children by baby-sitting, caring for younger siblings, or working as camp counselors. They also help parents with household chores and may hold after-school jobs that, if nothing else, teach them something about the world of work and commerce.

GLOBAL CRISES Every historical age has had its wars, religious movements, and economic ups and downs, and today is no exception. Although the current period may be less explosive than previous ones, people continue to be distressed by crises at home, in the Middle East, Asia, Eastern Europe, and Africa. Adolescents are—and always have been—especially vulnerable and susceptible to such crises. In general, the state of the world affects adolescents much more than it does younger children. After all, it is primarily adolescents and young adults who fight in wars, participate in riots, and sustain movements for social reform. It is primarily adolescents and young adults who support radical political and religious movements with their idealism, who lose their jobs during economic downturns, and who are hired during economic booms. The effects of events in the broader society are screened from young children by their families and local communities. These children feel the impact of economic recessions or wars only in a second-hand way, perhaps through their parents' unemployment or long-term absence. But many events of the time have a direct impact on adolescents, who must confront, absorb, and react to them. Other events have an indirect effect, through the mass media.

A MASS MEDIA SOCIETY The mass media provide a flood of information and sensations—blending trivial advertising, sensationalized drama, and pressing world issues. Most advertising is meant to sell, not to inform. Television news programs are, to a large extent, a form of entertainment. It is hard even for adult viewers to know what to believe. There is little opportunity for critical analysis of the information or interpretations that are presented.

Most theories of human development emphasize the importance of having an emotionally supportive and responsive environment to promote learning. Individuals of any age learn best when they can act on their environment, perceive the consequences of their actions, and have some power to effect change. But there is no way to alter the events on television, radio, or the movie screen. Some critics suggest that teenagers, with their rapidly developing physical and cognitive capacities, are particularly vulnerable to the passive role of consumer of the mass media. Perhaps they learn casual acceptance of tragedy or brutality or they develop a thirst for excessive raw stimulation. Perhaps they model their behavior on the trite or bizarre events they see portrayed in movies or on television. We still know very little about the complex effects of becoming an adult in a mass media society.

 PHYSICAL MATURATION

Physiologically, adolescence ranks with the fetal period and the first 2 years of life for sheer rate of biological change. Unlike infants, however, adolescents have the pain and pleasure of observing the whole process; they watch themselves with alternating feelings of fascination, delight, and horror as the biological changes occur. Surprised, embarrassed, and uncertain, adolescents constantly compare themselves with others and continually revise their self-image. Both sexes anxiously monitor their development, or lack of it, with knowledge and misinformation, pride and fear, hope and trepidation. Always, there is comparison with the prevailing ideal; trying to reconcile differences between the real and the ideal is one of the problems that adolescents experience during this period of transformation.

BIOLOGICAL CHANGES

The biological hallmarks of adolescence are a marked increase in the rate of growth, rapid development of the reproductive organs, and the appearance of secondary sex characteristics. Some changes occur in both boys and girls—increased size, improved strength and stamina—but most of them are sex specific.

HORMONES The physical changes are controlled by **hormones,** which are biochemical substances secreted in very small amounts by the endocrine glands. The hormones affecting adolescent growth are present in trace amounts from fetal life on, but their output is greatly increased during puberty (see the box "Are Adolescents the Victims of Raging Hormones"?). "Male" hormones and "female" hormones are present in members of both sexes, but males have more of the hormones called *androgens,* the most important of which is *testosterone,* and females have more of the hormones called *estrogen* and *progesterone* (Tanner, 1978).

Each hormone influences a certain set of targets or receptors. For example, the secretion of testosterone causes the penis to grow, the shoulders to broaden, and hair to grow in the genital area and on the face. Similarly, estrogen causes the uterus and the breasts to grow and the hips to broaden. The cells in the target area have the ability to respond selectively to some of the hormones circulating in the bloodstream and not to respond to others: The uterus, for example, selectively responds to estrogen and progesterone. Targeted cells are exquisitely sensi-

hormone A biochemical secretion of the endocrine gland that is carried by the blood or other body fluids to a particular organ or tissue and acts as a stimulant or an accelerator.

The onset of puberty requires considerable adaption whether to a suddenly crackly voice, longer legs, or unfamiliar passions or feelings.

ARE ADOLESCENTS THE VICTIMS OF RAGING HORMONES?

The adolescent period in most Western cultures is marked by changes in behavior and appearance. Historically, most of these changes have been described as negative and were often attributed to changes in biological factors—especially hormones. Many authors and parents have claimed that adolescents were the victims of their *raging hormones.* But is this actually true?

From a physiological perspective, hormones act on the brain in two ways. First, sex hormones can influence personality and behavior by their early influence on brain development. These effects are permanent and therefore are not affected by the change in hormone levels during pubescence. Second, hormones may activate specific behaviors through their effects on the nervous system. These effects tend to be immediate or slightly delayed. Physical and sexual maturation result from an interaction of the hormonal levels, health factors, and the genetics of the developing person. However, there is little support for any direct relationship between levels of hormones during adolescence and the following behaviors (Buchanan, Eccles, & Becker, 1992):

➤ moodiness
➤ depression
➤ restlessness and lack of concentration
➤ irritability
➤ impulsiveness
➤ anxiety
➤ aggression and behavior problems

All adolescents do not exhibit dramatic changes in these behaviors even though all experience hormone increases. Therefore, it is likely that other factors may be involved in producing these behaviors. These factors have been suggested to include changing roles, social or cultural expectations, environmental situations in the home or school, and even the media.

> *"Many authors and parents have claimed that adolescents were the victims of their* raging hormones.*"*

Where family problems exist during early and middle childhood, for example, family dysfunction increases during adolescence. In dysfunctional families, problems with inappropriate sexual behavior, running away, aggression, and drug use may occur. However, where parent-child relationships are good before adolescence, relationships generally continue to be good through adolescence as well, and parents continue to have a major positive influence on their children (Buchanan, Eccles, & Becker, 1992).

This is not to say that hormones have no affect on behavior. But their effect is often mediated by existing psychological or social factors in the home environment. For example, Udry (1988) reported that the level of testosterone was generally a strong predictor of sexual involvement among 12-to 16-year-old girls. However, its effect was

Evidently the famous raging hormones of adolescence do not produce moodiness directly as commonly believed.

reduced or eliminated by having a father in the home or by the girl's participation in sports. Fathers who are present tend to raise girls' self-esteem in ways that lessen their need to be sexually active. They are also more likely to create, with the mother's guidance and role-modeling, situations that stress relationships rather than sexual behavior in itself. These environmental variables may reduce the potential for sexual involvement and thus override any hormonal effects on behavior.

The researchers conclude that, while additional research is needed in this area, the explanation of raging hormones as a direct cause of adolescent behavior is a myth. Other cognitive and social factors including social inference, moral judgment, and a sense of the future may override any of the immediate, short-term effects of hormones during adolescence. For adolescents, then, biology, or more specifically, hormones, are not destiny.

tive to minute quantities of the appropriate hormones, even though the hormones are present in such small amounts that it is like detecting a pinch of sugar dissolved in a swimming pool (Tanner, 1978).

THE NEGATIVE FEEDBACK SYSTEM FOR HORMONES   The endocrine glands secrete a delicate and complex balance of hormones, the maintenance of which is the job of two areas of the brain: the *hypothalamus* and the *pituitary gland*. The hypothalamus is the part of the brain that initiates the processes of growth and reproduction during adolescence. In the hypothalamus there are minute quantities of chemicals called releasing and inhibiting factors. There is a releasing and inhibiting factor for each of the pituitary's trophic (growth-stimulating) hormones. When the hypothalamus receives a blood-borne chemical message telling it that some hormone is too low, then it secretes the appropriate releasing factor into the bloodstream which, in turn, causes the pituitary gland to produce the hormone. When sufficient quantities of the hormone are detected in the blood, the hypothalamus secretes an inhibiting factor that tells the pituitary gland to stop producing the hormone.

The pituitary is located on the underside of the brain. This gland produces several varieties of hormones, including growth hormone, which controls the overall growth of the body, and some secondary trophic hormones. The trophic hormones stimulate and regulate the functioning of a number of other glands, including the sex glands—the testes in the male and the ovaries in the female. The sex glands have two jobs: to produce sperm or eggs and to secrete androgens or estrogens. The hormones secreted by the pituitary gland and by the sex glands have emotional as well as physical effects upon adolescents.

We can see that there are complex chemical messages constantly being sent through the blood stream among the hypothalamus, pituitary, and the target organs such as the sex glands. Levels of hormones in the body are controlled by the *negative feedback system* described above. When low levels of a specific hormone return to the hypothalamus, the appropriate releasing factors are produced and the pituitary secretes the hormone. When sufficient levels are reached, inhibiting factors from the hypothalamus signal the pituitary to stop producing the hormone. In this way, a balance of hormones is achieved within the body. Without this balance, our height, weight, gender characteristics, and reproduction would be seriously affected.

PUBESCENCE   **Puberty** refers to the attainment of sexual maturity in males and females. This is marked in females by the first menstrual period, or **menarche,** and by the first *seminal emission* in males. The period of time which precedes puberty—during which a physical growth spurt occurs—is referred to as *pubescence*. We therefore say that a person is "going through pubescence" but "attains puberty."

The changes of puberty are usually preceded by an increase in body fat; some preadolescents become noticeably pudgy at this time. Both males and females also have fat deposited in the breast area. In females this will be permanent. In males this is a passing phase. This is followed, in late childhood or early adolescence, by a large increase in height. Growth of this magnitude has not occurred since infancy and toddlerhood. Both bones and muscles increase in size, triggered by the same set of hormones. In the course of this growth spurt, boys generally lose most of the extra fat that they acquired at its beginning. Girls, how-

puberty The attainment of sexual maturity in males and females.

ever, tend to keep most of the fat that they have acquired, although it ends up being distributed in different places.

During early adolescence, different parts of the body develop at varying rates. The head has pretty much stopped growing by now, most of its development completed in the first 10 years of life. Next to reach adult size are the hands and feet; then there is an increase in leg and arm length. The gangly physique that frequently results at this time may make adolescents feel awkward. The growth of the extremities is followed by growth in body width, with full development of the shoulders coming last.

Another change is the increase in size and activity of sebaceous (oil-producing) glands in the skin, which causes the teenager's face to break out in acne. A new kind of sweat gland also develops in the skin, causing a stronger body odor.

SEX DIFFERENCES IN PUBESCENCE   The sexes develop at different rates. On the average, girls experience the growth spurt and the other biological changes of pubescence about 2 years before boys do (see Figure 15–1). However, there is a great deal of variation in the rate of development among members of the same sex. A late-maturing boy or girl may still look like a child, whereas another boy or girl of the same chronological age will have the appearance of a full-grown man or woman. In contrast, once the sequence of sexual maturation has begun, it progresses in a fairly predictable order. Keeping in mind the wide individual differences in timing, let us look at the general schedule of physical changes that characterize adolescence.

Sexual Maturation in Males. After the growth spurt, the second major biological change is development of the reproductive system. In males, the first indication of puberty is the accelerating growth of the testes and scrotum. Approxi-

FIGURE 15–1
Growth rates and sexual development during pubescence.
The peak in the line labeled "height spurt" represents the point of most rapid growth. The bars below represent the average beginning and end of the events of pubescence.

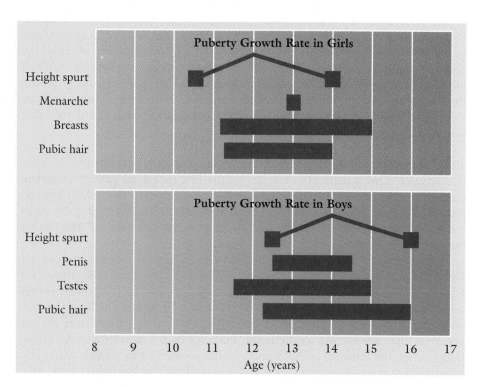

mately 1 year after this has begun, the penis undergoes a similar spurt in growth. In between these two events, pubic hair begins to appear, but it does not attain full growth until after the completion of genital development. During this period, there are also increases in the size of the heart and lungs. Due to the action of the male sex hormone, *testosterone,* boys also develop more red blood cells than girls do. This extensive production of red blood cells may be one factor—although certainly not the only one—in the superior athletic ability of the male adolescent over the female.

The first seminal emission (expulsion of semen from the penis) may take place as early as age 11 or as late as age 16. The initial ejaculation usually occurs during a boy's rapid period of growth and may come about during masturbation or in a "wet dream." These first emissions generally do not have enough semen to be fertile (Money, 1980).

Any unflattering description of the adolescent boy invariably includes his awkwardly cracking voice. However, the actual voice change takes place relatively late in the sequence of pubertal changes, and in many boys, it occurs too gradually to be significant as a developmental milestone (Tanner, 1978).

Sexual Maturation in Females. In girls, the "breast buds" are usually, but not always, the first signal that puberty has begun. There is simultaneous development of the uterus and vagina, with enlargement of the labia and clitoris.

Menarche (the first menstruation), which is probably the most dramatic and symbolic sign of a girl's changing status, actually occurs late in the sequence, after the peak of the growth spurt. Menarche may occur as early as age 9 1/2 or as late as age 16 1/2; the average for American girls is about 12 1/2. As we said, previous generations of Americans matured more slowly than girls do today. The acceleration in sexual development is apparently due to improved nutrition and health care. In other parts of the world, menarche still occurs considerably later: The average Czechoslovakian girl has her first period at age 14, among the Kikuyu of Kenya the average age is 16, and for the Bindi of New Guinea it is 18 (Powers et al., 1989). Menarche generally occurs when a girl has nearly reached her adult height and when she has managed to store a minimum amount of body fat. For a girl of average height, this landmark generally occurs when she weighs around 100 pounds (Frisch, 1988).

The first few menstrual cycles vary tremendously from one girl to another; they also tend to vary from one month to another. In many cases, the early cycles are irregular and anovulatory—an egg is not produced (Tanner, 1978). But it is unwise for a young teenage girl to count on her infertility, as many pregnant 13-year-olds can attest. (We will return to the subject of teenage pregnancies later in this chapter.)

We may see the typical physical changes during pubescence presented in Table 15–1.

One reason girls often feel more mature than boys their own age is that the female growth spurt during puberty occurs about 2 years before the male growth spurt.

BODY IMAGE AND ADJUSTMENT

Young adolescents are frequently fascinated with, and continually appraising, their bodies. Are they the right shape, the right size? Are they coordinated or clumsy? How do they compare with the ideal? Sociologists consider adolescents to be a "marginal group," either between cultures or on the fringe of a dominant culture. Typically, such groups tend to exhibit an intensified need for conformity.

menarche The time of the first menstrual period.

TABLE 15–1 Typical Changes in Adolescence

CHANGES IN GIRLS

➤ Breast development
➤ Growth of pubic hair
➤ Body growth
➤ Menarche
➤ Underarm hair
➤ Increased output of oil- and sweat-producing glands

CHANGES IN BOYS

➤ Growth of testes and scrotal sac
➤ Growth of pubic hair
➤ Body growth
➤ Growth of penis
➤ Change in voice
➤ First ejaculation of semen
➤ Facial and underarm hair
➤ Increased output of oil- and sweat-producing glands

For this reason, adolescents can be extremely intolerant of deviation, whether it be a deviation in body type, such as being too fat or too thin, or a deviation in timing, like being a late maturer. The mass media manipulate this tendency by marketing stereotyped images of attractive, exuberant youths who glide through adolescence without pimples, braces, or awkwardness. Because adolescents are often extremely sensitive about their own physical appearance and spend a lot of time scrutinizing themselves and their friends, the discrepancies between their less-than-perfect self-images and the glossy ideals they see in magazines and on television are often a source of considerable anxiety.

During middle childhood, children become aware of different body types and ideals, and they gain a fairly clear idea of their own body type, proportions, and skills. But in adolescence, body type receives much closer scrutiny. In our society, some young people subject themselves to intense dieting, whereas others embark on rigorous regimens of physical fitness and strength training—weight lifting, athletics, or dancing. In general, girls worry about being too fat or too tall, whereas boys are concerned about being too scrawny (not muscular enough) and too short. The reason weight is important to girls is that they are extremely concerned about social acceptance; and plumpness is frowned on in our society. There are many perfectly normal, even lean, adolescent girls who are medically healthy but who consider themselves obese and wish to lose weight (see the box "Anorexia and Bulimia"). Yet, other cultures consider plumpness to be a feminine ideal and view thinness in women as unhealthy or indicative of poor family circumstances.

For boys, the primary concern is with physical power that can be exerted on the environment (Lerner et al., 1976). Therefore, height and muscles are important to young males. There are some other interesting differences in the changes that are desired by the two sexes. Girls want very specific changes: "I would make my ears lie back," or "I would make my forehead lower." Boys do not articulate

Young adolescents seem to be in love with the image they see in the mirror. In reality they are often very critical of their bodies and can become extremely anxious if they do not conform to an ideal set forth by either their peer group or the wider culture.

their dissatisfactions this precisely. A typical boy's response is: "I would make myself look handsome and not fat. I would have wavy black hair. I would change my whole physical appearance so that I would be handsome with a good build." Both sexes worry about their skin: Almost half of all adolescents voice concerns about pimples and blackheads.

Height, weight, and complexion are the major sources of concern for 10th graders. About two-thirds wish for one or more physical changes in themselves (Peterson & Taylor, 1980). Self-consciousness about one's body diminishes in late adolescence. As shown in a recent longitudinal study, body-image satisfaction is lowest for girls at age 13 and for boys at age 15; after these ages it rises steadily. At every age from 11 to 18, however, it is lower for girls than it is for boys (Rauste-von Wright, 1989).

GIRLS' REACTIONS TO MENARCHE   Menarche is a unique event, a milestone on the path to physical maturity. It occurs suddenly and without warning and is heralded by a bloody vaginal discharge. In some parts of the world, it has major religious, cultural, or economic significance. It may trigger elaborate rites and ceremonies in some cultures, but in the United States, there is no such drama. Nevertheless, for the individual girl it holds considerable significance (Greif & Ulman, 1982).

A study of adolescent girls found menarche to be a memorable event. Only those who were ill prepared or who experienced menarche early described it as especially traumatic or negative. Most often these were girls who had not discussed the onset of menstruation with their mothers or with other women. Some who had a negative experience had received their information from men. But most girls had been prepared by their mothers or female relatives for menstruation and reported a positive reaction to menarche—a feeling that they were coming of age (Ruble & Brooks-Gunn, 1982).

FOCUS ON AN ISSUE

ANOREXIA AND BULIMIA

ANOREXIA NERVOSA

Sufferers of *anorexia nervosa* (anorexia means the absence of appetite while nervosa means of "nervous" origin) literally starve themselves to death. Obsessed by thoughts of food and an unattainable image of "perfect" thinness, they refuse to eat. Even though they may feel that they are becoming increasingly attractive, they actually become emaciated and physically ill. In the United States, where there are now more than 100,000 anorexics (10 times as many as there were a decade ago), 10,000 to 15,000 will die because of the medical problems related to their lack of food.

Almost all anorexics are women under the age of 25. Although there is no one cause, many anorexics are victims of our society's weight obsession. Hearing the repeated message that thin is beautiful and fat is repugnant, they fear that the curves and added weight that come with adolescence will make them undesirable and unattractive. Family pressures to remain thin or to be attractive may make matters worse. A father who teasingly tells his daughter that she is putting on a few extra pounds

around the waist may increase her negative self-concept.

"Everyday she planned a menu for the next day and got up several times to repunch the calorie total on her calculator, fearful that it might have become larger."

Many experts believe that puberty and its accompanying body changes and sexual drives may trigger the symptoms of anorexia nervosa in some of its victims. Fearing womanhood, the anorexic stops eating, thereby putting a halt to her body's development. She loses her body curves and sexual desire and, when her body fat falls below approximately 17 percent of her total body weight, she stops menstruating.

Parents of anorexics are often amazed when the first symptoms of the disease appear. Up until then, their daughters are usually timid, reserved perfectionists who do everything their parents ask and who rarely show any signs of anger, selfishness, or normal rebellion. Instead

of demanding attention, they may slip into the background of the family, perhaps allowing their siblings to receive the bulk of their parents' attention. Often considered "model" children, pre-anorexics willingly accept adult responsibilities, which they perform with uncomplaining efficiency. Unfortunately, these behaviors mask anorexics' neurotic feelings of worthlessness—feelings that are the precursors of a need "to diet away" their bodies.

Ironically, most anorexics are not fat when they begin to diet. They may be no more than 10 pounds overweight, but they see themselves as grossly fat and blame food for their problems. To rid themselves of their self-perceived excess poundage, they may eat smaller and smaller amounts of food, make themselves vomit after meals, take enormous quantities of diuretics and laxatives (some anorexics have reportedly swallowed up to 300 Ex-Lax tablets at a time), and exercise at a frantic pace. They may also turn eating into a ritual, requiring a specific arrangement of food on a specific plate. They lose their ability to see what they look like and may still consider themselves to be obese when they look like skeletons.

EARLY AND LATE MATURERS   Timing in maturation—whether development is early or late—has engrossed researchers almost as much as adolescence itself. Ill-timed maturation is most likely to be a problem for the late-maturing boy. Because girls mature, on the average, 2 years earlier than boys do, the late-maturing boy is the last to reach puberty and the last to experience the spurt in growth. Thus, he is smaller and less muscular than his age-mates, which puts him

Anorexia nervosa has devastating effects on its sufferers and their families. Increasingly isolated in their own fantasies of thinness, most anorexics drop all social contact with their peers. Food becomes the center of their every thought, as you can see from the following passage describing the behavior of an anorexic teenager:

Every night she planned a menu for the next day and got up several times to repunch the calorie total on her calculator, fearful that it might have become larger. She weighed everything she ate, kneeling in front of the food scale in order to make sure its contents were absolutely level. Every morning at exactly 7 a.m. she weighed herself on both her mother's scale and on a doctor's scale...which registered weight in quarter-pound increments....She drew up tables that listed the number of calories in every Weight Watchers frozen dinner, every flavor of Dannon, Colombo, and Sweet 'n Low yogurt, and every variety of Del Monte frozen vegetables. She kept a food diary in which she recorded everything she ate. (Fadiman, 1982, p. 74)

The parents of anorexics frequently worry that their children are going to die of their self-imposed starvation. Powerless to force their children to eat, they may resort to begging, crying, cajoling, and screaming. They also turn to the psychiatric community for help. Unfortunately, psychiatrists have not found a cure for anorexia nervosa. Indeed, there is no single accepted method of treatment. Some therapists take a behaviorist approach, rewarding their patients when food is eaten; others concentrate on analyzing childhood problems that they believe caused the disease; and still others focus on the patient's feelings about food and eating. However, regardless of the theoretical orientation of the therapist, often hospitalization with intravenous feeding is required in order to reverse the life-threatening weight loss anorexics often experience. The goal of all therapy with anorexics is to help them learn to separate their feelings about food from their feelings about themselves and to develop in them a sense of self-worth and autonomy.

BULIMIA

Bulimia is similar in many ways to anorexia nervosa, but it is a different ailment. The bulimic personality is also terribly anxious about weighing too much but has an uncontrollable need to eat, especially sweets. To compensate for overeating, bulimics make themselves vomit. Thus, bulimia is often described as a binge-and-purge pattern of eating.

As with anorexia, most bulimics are female. Bulimia usually afflicts someone in late adolescence, whereas many anorexics are in early or mid-adolescence. Some researchers estimate that about 20 percent of college-age women have engaged in bulimic eating patterns (Muuss, 1986). Several psychologists believe that bulimia is so prevalent among college women that it might indicate difficulty in adjusting to life away from home. Others contend that bulimics binge on sweets in an attempt to alleviate depression.

Women suffering from bulimia consume huge quantities of carbohydrates in a very short time frame, usually an hour or two. They then feel despondent and out of control. Although bulimia does not have fatal consequences, it is nevertheless highly self-destructive and requires treatment. Fortunately, bulimics tend to be more responsive to treatment than anorexics are. The fact that antidepressant drugs are often useful in the treatment of this disorder—even among patients who show no signs of depression—suggests to some researchers that a biochemical abnormality may be involved (Walsh, 1988).

at a disadvantage in most sports. Other children and adults tend to treat a smaller child as though he were a younger child; therefore, the late maturer has lower social status among his peers and is perceived as being less competent by adults (Brackbill & Nevill, 1981). Sometimes, this perception becomes a self-fulfilling prophecy, and the boy reacts with childish dependency and immature behavior. In other cases, he may overcompensate and become very aggressive. At any rate,

There is a great variation in the timing of maturation. Very early or late maturation affects an adolescent's status in his or her peer group.

late-maturing boys have a far more difficult adjustment than early-maturing males, who tend to accrue all sorts of social and athletic advantages among their peers. From middle childhood on, early-maturing males are likely to be the leaders of their peer groups (Weisfeld & Billings, 1988).

Longitudinal studies reveal interesting, continuing differences related to the timing of maturity's arrival. In their 30's, the early-maturing males still enjoy poise and social success. They tend to be responsible, cooperative, and self-controlled. In contrast to this, they may also be rigid, humorless, and unoriginal. The late maturers show a different pattern. They still show signs of immaturity and overcompensation by being impulsive and assertive, but they are also more perceptive, creative, and tolerant of ambiguity. By the forties, the conspicuous success of the early maturers has significantly diminished. Early maturing males tend to have relationship problems and are more likely to experience divorce. Late maturing males, on the other hand, are more self-accepting and have strong relationships with their spouses and children (Jones, 1965). Livson and Peskin (1980) speculate that because late maturers have to learn how to deal with anxiety over their self-image, they develop more flexibility and better problem-solving skills in adolescence, skills that serve them well when they reach adulthood. Their greater success at relationships may come from the fact that, since they were often excluded when young, they attach greater value to relationships as they mature and work harder to keep them.

If early maturity is an asset for teenage boys, it is a mixed blessing for girls. In girls, the initial advantage is attached to late maturity. The late maturing girl matures at about the same time as most of her male peers. She shares the same interests and dating activities with them. She is more popular with her peers than the early maturing girls are. The early-maturing girl, on the other hand is taller, develops breasts sooner, and goes through menarche as much as 6 years before a few of her peers. As a result, she has fewer opportunities to discuss with her friends the physical and emotional changes she is undergoing. There are, however, compensations. The early-maturing girl frequently feels more attractive, is more popular with older boys, and goes out on dates more frequently than her late-maturing age-mates (Blyth et al., 1981). In her 30's, the early-maturing girl seems to reap the benefits of her teenage experiences. She is more confident and self-directed and is better able to meet social, intellectual, and emotional challenges than peers who matured late (Livson & Peskin, 1980).

PARENTAL REACTIONS TO ADOLESCENT DEVELOPMENT

As adolescents develop physically, their relations with their parents undergo marked changes. Some of these changes result from the teenager's striving for greater independence, which generally causes stress within the family, especially during the early stages of adolescence. Often, young people press against the limits previously established by their parents, while their parents grant greater autonomy only with reluctance and anxiety.

Parental anxiety over their maturing children is frequently compounded by other concerns as well. Just as adolescents are preoccupied with their appearance, parents also become concerned about the way they look as they are aging. Parents are reaching middle age, their hair is falling out or turning gray, their bodies are thickening, and their skin is getting wrinkled. They have less energy than they did when they were younger. But most of all, they are beginning to see that what used to be their future is now behind them. Middle-aged parents contrast their declining potential with the developing potential of their offspring and are unhappy with the contrast. Young people can look forward to the future with hope and optimism. Their parents look back on their past and try to assess how much of their early hopes they have achieved, sometimes with a sense of disappointment (Hill, 1980; Steinberg, 1980, 1981).

▷ GENDER IDENTITY AND SEXUAL PRACTICES

The biological changes that occur during adolescence lead to an interest in and the development of a sexual identity.

Directly related to the biological changes that adolescents must face is the issue of a mature gender identity. This includes the expression of sexual needs and feelings and the acceptance or rejection of sex roles. In Chapter 3, we saw how sex roles and sex-role stereotypes are forged long before adolescence, with one crucial period being the preschool years. During middle and late childhood, children associate mostly in same-sex peer groups in a sexually neutral way. With the attainment of puberty and adolescence, the biological changes of physical maturation bring a new interest in members of the opposite sex and a new need to integrate sexuality with other aspects of the personality. During adolescence, young people start entering into relationships in which sex plays a central role.

DEVELOPING SEXUAL BEHAVIOR

The development of sexual consciousness and behavior is different for girls than it is for boys. In adolescence, girls spend more time fantasizing about romance; boys are more likely to use masturbation as an outlet for their sexual impulses. However, masturbation and fantasizing are common in both sexes. According to one study, about half of adolescent girls and three-quarters of boys masturbate (Hass, 1979). Social-class differences play a part here, or at least they did in the past. The ability to develop a rich fantasy life during masturbation was reportedly more prominent in the middle-class male. Guilt over the "unmanliness" of masturbation was of greater concern to the working-class male. These differences seem to be gradually disappearing. In sexual behavior, at least, the young middle-class male no longer seems to differ much from the young working-class male (Dreyer, 1982).

Class differences in sexual behavior have traditionally been less significant among females, partly because of the limited roles that were available to women in the past. Girls were discouraged from overt sexuality; instead, they received early training in enhancing their own desirability and in evaluating potential mates. Dating and courtship provided the setting for each sex to swap its expertise and to train the other in desires and expectations. In our society, femininity connoted passivity, nurturance, and the ability to fit in. Girls had to remain flexible enough to conform to the value systems of potential spouses. But now girls are encouraged to acquire skills to enrich and support themselves, regardless of their future marital plans, and sexuality for both sexes is encouraged through advertising and the mass media.

The expression of sexuality for both sexes is always dependent on the prevailing norms; it changes as these norms change (see the box "Gender and the Media"). Some societies reserve sexuality exclusively for procreation. Others view such restrictions as silly or even as a crime against nature.

CHANGING SEXUAL ATTITUDES   Historical changes in social attitudes are perhaps most clearly seen in our responses to our developing sexuality. In large part, adolescents view themselves, as do adults, according to the cultural norms of the time in which they live. Therefore, sexual practices and the quality of sexual relationships vary over time.

Prior to the mid-1960s, most young people felt that premarital sex was immoral, although older adolescent males were under some pressure to acquire sexual experience. Females, in contrast, were under pressure to remain virginal until marriage. By the late 1960s and early 1970s, sexual attitudes had changed considerably. Sorensen (1973) reported the findings of a study on adolescent sexuality. He stated that the majority of adolescents who completed his questionnaires did not think of sex as being inherently right or wrong, but instead judged it in terms of the relationship between the participants. The reactions of both partners to a sexual experience were thought to be equally important; most considered it immoral for one person to force another into a sexual relationship. A majority rejected the traditional "double standard" that gave a great deal of freedom to boys but very little to girls. Almost 70 percent agreed that two people should not have to get married to live together. A surprising 50 percent approved of homosexuality between two consenting individuals—although 80 percent stated that they had never engaged in homosexual acts and would never want to. The subjects in this study clearly distinguished their own attitudes from those of their parents. Although most of the subjects had considerable respect for their parents, they felt that they differed from them a great deal in attitudes toward sex.

By the late 1970s, the sexual revolution was in full swing. In 1979, Chilman reviewed the findings of numerous studies and reported an increasing trend toward sexual liberalization, reflected both by an increase in sexual activity among

FOCUS ON APPLICATION

GENDER AND THE MEDIA

In their music videos shown on MTV which has a wide adolescent audience the members of En Vogue have reinforced stereotypic views of women.

At pubescence, young adolescents are increasingly aware of their appearance. They watch with a mixture of curiosity, fascination, and at times dismay at the changes in their body and the fluctuations in their less predictable feelings. As they try to integrate these new images and feelings into an emerging gender role, they look around them for role models—in the family, among friends, at school, and in the media.

> *"Adolescents who watch more television have more stereotypic attitudes about sex roles than peers who watch little television."*

The role of the media in the development of gender roles has been studied extensively. Researchers suggest that the most problematic area is the portrayal of women in American television programming and commercials—and its subsequent impact on young adolescent girls' gender concepts.

When television commercials are studied, for example, certain trends emerge over the past twenty years. A lower percentage of female than of male figures are depicted as employed, but males are presented in increasing numbers as spouses and parents. Women are most likely to be seen in domestic settings, advertising products used in the home. The most striking differences is in the narrators of commercials despite the fact that viewers of both sexes attribute the same credibility to both men and women, 90 percent of all commercial narrators are men (Bretl & Cantor, 1988).

Adolescents who watch more television have more stereotypic attitudes about sex roles than peers who watch little television (Morgan, 1987). Year after year, male characters outnumber female characters three to one in television programs and five to one in children's programs. Female television characters age faster than male characters and mainly appear in romantic parts. Few female characters mix marriage and career with much success; if they work, female characters often have lower-status occupations.

MTV (Music Television), one of the newer entries into television programming, is especially guilty of sex-role stereotyping. In MTV music videos, both male and female characters were shown in sex-typed occupations. Male characters were more adventuresome, domineering, aggressive, violent, and victimized than female characters. Females were more affectionate, dependent, nurturing, and fearful than males. More female characters wore revealing clothing and were more likely to initiate and receive sexual advances than were males. African-American males and females were more sexually active than their white counterparts. In general, females of both races were denigrated as "sex objects" or as "second-class citizens" in the working world (Seidman, 1992).

The contribution of television to creating adolescents' conceptions of social reality—including gender roles—seems to be mediated by their relationship with their parents. When parents and children act as a cohesive unit—when they show affection, engage in shared activities, and find satisfaction in the time spent together—then parents assume a greater role in helping develop their children's social values. When parents exercise little control over their children's television watching, and offer no comments or guidance on what is viewed, then television assumes more importance in value creation (Rothschild & Morgan, 1987).

As more and more time is spent by children of all ages in front of television screens, the role of television in shaping their values and gender identities becomes greater. Researchers have suggested that because of this, television has contributed to the more negative self-concepts found in adolescent girls than boys—largely because of its perpetuating sexual myths and stereotypes. Adolescents' exposure to television's repeated lessons about sex-roles leads to more stereotyped ways of thinking.

adolescents and by a change in societal attitudes. Society had become more accepting of a wide range of sexual activities, including masturbation, homosexuality, and unmarried couples living together (Dreyer, 1982). Hass (1979) reported that 83 percent of the boys he interviewed, and 64 percent of the girls, approved of premarital intercourse; however, only 56 percent of the boys and 44 percent of the girls had actually experienced sexual intercourse. Note that there was not much difference between boys and girls in sexual activity. This statistic reflects the continuing decline in the double standard. The sexual revolution affected girls' behavior much more than it did boys': Even in the 1940s, 1950s, and 1960s, somewhere between one-third and two-thirds of teenage boys had already lost their virginity. During a similar span of years, the proportion of 16-year-old girls who had lost their virginity rose from 7 percent in the 1940s to 33 percent in 1971 and to 44 percent in 1982 (Brooks-Gunn & Furstenberg, 1989).

The sexual revolution was not without problems. Although large numbers of adolescents were having sexual intercourse, many of them did not use birth control. As a result, the rate of pregnancies among teenage girls tripled in the 35 years from 1940 to 1975. Another problem was the spread of sexually transmitted diseases—first syphilis, gonorrhea, and genital herpes, and then, more recently, **AIDS (Acquired Immune Deficiency Syndrome)**. Although AIDS is still rare among adolescents, mainly because it often takes years for the symptoms to appear, they have a high rate for other sexually transmitted diseases (Ehrhardt, 1992). In the United States, for example, one in seven teenagers now has a sexually transmitted disease (Quadrel, Fischoff, & Davis, 1993).

The sexual revolution began to decline by the early 1980s. Young people started being more cautious about sexual activity, and monogamy became fashionable again. During the 1980s, when asked what they thought of the sexual attitudes of the 1960s and 1970s, a sizable proportion viewed these attitudes as "bad." College students in 1980 were more likely than those in 1975 to consider sexual promiscuity "immoral" (Leo, 1984; Robinson & Jedlicka, 1982).

The late 1980s saw a continuation of the trend toward more conservative attitudes in sexual matters, as in other areas of life (Murstein et al., 1989). Although young people still see sex as an essential part of a romantic relationship, they are generally not in favor of casual sex (Abler & Sedlacek, 1989). Also, the majority of college students—of both sexes—now say that they would prefer to marry a virgin. Attitudes toward homosexuality have also become more negative again (Williams & Jacoby, 1989). The trend toward monogamous relationships and the increase in **homophobia** (fear or dislike of homosexuals) is probably related in part to the increasing fear of sexually transmitted diseases, especially AIDS.

The sexual revolutionaries of the 1960s and 1970s have grown older, formed families, and raised children of their own. Their children have a more sober—and perhaps a more realistic—outlook on sexual relationships.

SEXUAL RELATIONSHIPS   Although society as a whole has become somewhat more conservative with regard to sexual behavior, teenagers continue to be highly active sexually. The age at which they begin this activity still varies by gender; it also varies by racial and cultural group. In 1990, the Center for Disease Control reported on a national school-based survey of high school students in the United States. The median age of first intercourse was found to be 16.1 years for boys and 16.9 years for girls (Ehrhardt, 1992). Among whites, 60 percent of the boys have had intercourse by age 18; 60 percent of the girls have had intercourse

AIDS Acquired immune deficiency syndrome—a fatal disease caused by a virus. Anyone can be infected through sexual contact or through exposure to infected blood or needles.

homophobia Fear or dislike of homosexuals.

by age 19. Sexual activity begins at a somewhat earlier age for African-American teens (Brooks-Gunn & Furstenberg, 1989).

Boys start having sex earlier and tend to have a somewhat different attitude toward it than girls do. For boys, sexual initiation is more likely to be with a casual partner, and they receive more social approval for their loss of virginity than girls do. Boys are also more likely to seek a second experience soon afterward, more likely to talk about their activity, and less likely to feel guilty than girls are (Zelnick & Kantner, 1977).

Several factors influence adolescent sexual behavior. Chilman (1979) cites education, psychological makeup, family relationships, and biological maturation as being important. Let us consider these four factors in more detail.

Education is related to sexual behavior partly because those who attain higher levels of education most frequently come from the mainstream middle- and upper-middle classes, which tend to hold a more conservative attitude toward sex. This is especially true for adolescents who emphasize careers, intellectual pursuits, and educational goals. Another factor is the relationship between sexual behavior and academic success or failure in high school: Good students are less likely to initiate sexual activity at an early age (Miller & Sneesby, 1988). Perhaps adolescents who are failing academically turn to sexual activity as a way of gratifying their need for success. In the past, this may have been true more for girls than for boys because girls had fewer opportunities for achievement in other areas, such as sports. With the current emphasis on opportunities for women in all aspects of society, including sports, this situation may be changing.

To some extent, the psychological factors associated with early sexual experience for males are different from that for females. Sexually experienced male adolescents tend to have relatively high self-esteem, whereas sexually experienced females tend to have low self-esteem. However, for both sexes, early sexual activity is associated with other problem behavior, such as drug use and delinquency (Donovan, Jessor, & Costa, 1988).

In the area of family relationships, a number of studies have found that parent-child interactions are related to adolescent sexual behavior. Both overly restrictive and overly permissive parenting are associated with earlier sexual activity in adolescents; moderate restrictiveness tends to work best with this age group (Miller et al., 1986). Another significant factor is communication between parents and offspring: Adolescents who are sexually active are more likely to report poor communication with their parents. Chilman (1979) is quick to point out, however, that good parent-child relationships will not necessarily prevent young people from experimenting with sex.

Recent research has suggested that the changing structure of the American family influences adolescent sexual behavior. The higher divorce rate and increased prevalence of single-parent families are social realities that have an effect on teenage sexual activity. In general, teenagers from two-parent families have less sexual experience than those from single-parent families. For both males and females, the two-parent family is associated with later entry into sexual experience (Young, Jensen, Olsen, & Cundick, 1991). It may be that two-parent homes offer two adult role models for guidance, emotional support, and greater financial stability. In addition, adult models of nonmarital sexual behavior may be more common and acceptable to teenagers from single-parent homes.

According to Chilman, the biological factors that influence early sexual behavior constitute an important area of research, but these factors are the most

Despite the more conservative attitudes of society toward sex adolescents are still very active sexually.

frequently overlooked. She argues that adolescents may have become sexually active at an earlier age because of the decline in the average age of puberty. This hypothesis is supported by the fact that individuals who mature early are likely to engage in sexual activity at a younger age than those who mature late. Note, however, that boys reach sexual maturity about 2 years later than girls do, yet they lose their virginity about a year earlier (Brooks-Gunn & Furstenberg, 1989).

SEXUAL ABUSE   Unfortunately for a significant number of children and adolescents, their first sexual experiences occur without their consent and in an abusive fashion. Cases reported to the police probably represent only a small fraction of the actual number of incidents. In one study, a large, random sample of women was interviewed about childhood and adolescent sexual experiences (Russell, 1983). The results revealed that 32 percent had been sexually abused at least once before the age of 18, and 20 percent had been victimized before the age of 14. Fewer than 5 percent of these women had reported the incidents to the police.

The impact of sexual abuse on children depends on a wide variety of factors—the nature of the abusive act, the age and vulnerability of the victim, whether the offender is a stranger or a family member, whether there was a single incident or an ongoing pattern of abuse, and the reactions of adults in whom the child confides (Kempe & Kempe, 1984). The impact on the individual's sense of identity and level of self-esteem often lasts well into adulthood.

The most common form of sexual abuse occurs between a young adolescent girl and an adult male relative or family friend (Finkelhor, 1984). A stepfather or the mother's boyfriend is more likely to be involved than the girl's natural father is (Wolfe et al., 1988). The mother is usually unaware of the abusive relationship, and the abuse often continues over a period of time and becomes a "secret" between the abuser and the victim.

Adolescent girls who are involved in this kind of sexual abuse may have many symptoms. They often feel guilt and shame, yet are powerless to break loose from the relationship. They may feel isolated—alienated from their peers and distrustful of adults. Some have learning problems, others have physical complaints, and still others turn to sexual promiscuity. Some girls turn their anger on themselves, and they become depressed or contemplate suicide (Brassard & McNeill, 1987). In any case, their attitudes about intimate relationships have been distorted. Later, as adults, it is difficult for these victims of sexual abuse to establish normal sexual relationships; they may even have difficulty in establishing normal parent-child relationships with their own children.

TEENAGE PARENTS

A special topic of concern to researchers studying adolescent sexuality is the incidence of young unmarried mothers. Although the birthrate in the United States for all adolescents has declined slightly, the proportion of babies born outside of marriage has increased. Every day approximately 2,700 teenage girls in the United States become pregnant. The rate of babies born to unmarried American teenagers quadrupled between 1940 and 1985 (National Center for Health Statistics, 1987). More than 1 million adolescent girls now become pregnant each year; over 65 percent of these girls are not married. About 40 percent of these pregnancies end in abortion, and 10 percent end in miscarriage. The other 50 percent of these girls complete their pregnancies and bear children (Brooks-Gunn & Furstenberg, 1989; Sonenstein, 1987). During the 1980s the proportion of unmarried teens who have a child has increased significantly.

We can see the outcome of pregnancy for all women contrasted with 15- to 19-year-olds in Table 15–2. As we can see, teens are significantly more likely to experience unintended pregnancies, miscarriages, and abortions than are nonadolescent women.

Sexual activity among American teenagers is high, but teenagers in most Western European countries are equally active, although the pregnancy rates in these countries are much lower (Hechtman, 1989). The reasons why so many American girls become pregnant are a cause of great concern. One probable factor is that there is now less social stigma attached to illegitimate births. In the past, pregnant teenagers were usually expelled from high school, but today many school systems have developed special programs to help young mothers complete their high school education. In some cultural groups, the unmarried mother may get sustained support both from her family and from the father of her child (Chilman, 1979). Finally, some teenage girls wish to have and keep children because of their own need to be loved. These young mothers have usually been deprived of affection and expect children to supply what they have missed (Fosburgh, 1977).

Many sexually active adolescents do not use contraceptives. The most common reasons for this are ignorance of the facts of reproduction, an unwillingness to accept responsibility for sexual activity, or a sense of passivity about life (Dreyer, 1982). The double standard continues to play a role here: Both sexes tend to view the male as the sexual aggressor and tend to see the female as the one who is responsible for setting limits on sexual activity. At the same time, adolescents also believe that it is more proper for a female to be swept off her feet by passion than it is for her to take contraceptive precautions (Goodchilds & Zellman, 1984; Morrison, 1985).

What is the impact of early parenthood on the teenage girl's later development? There are a number of potentially negative effects. Teenage mothers usu-

TABLE 15–2 Estimated Pregnancy Rates for Women of Reproductive Age by Pregnancy Intention and Outcome (per 1,000 women)

PREGNANCY INTENTION AND OUTCOME	WOMEN AGED 15–44	WOMEN AGED 15–19
Total	109.2	126.8
Births	66.3	64.0
Abortions	26.9	45.5
Miscarriages	16.0	17.3
Intended	47.8	24.7
Births	39.9	20.5
Miscarriages	8.0	4.1
Unintended	61.3	102.1
Births	26.5	43.4
Abortions	26.9	45.5
Miscarriages	8.0	13.2

(Source: Statistical Handbook on the American Family, 1992)

It is generally difficult for teenage mothers to care for the needs of an infant as well as their own developmental needs.

ally drop out of school prematurely; on the average, they work at lower-paying jobs and experience greater job dissatisfaction. They are more likely to become dependent on government support. Adolescent mothers must deal with their own personal and social development while trying to adapt to the 24-hour needs of an infant or small child (Rogel & Peterson, 1984).

The effects of parenthood on the lives of teenage boys may also be negative and long-lasting. Due to pressures that many feel to support their new families, teenage fathers tend to leave school and generally acquire less education than their peers who have not fathered children. They are also more likely to take jobs that require little skill and offer little pay. As the years pass, they are more likely to have marital problems, which often lead to divorce (Card & Wise, 1978).

Often, adolescents who become pregnant encounter strong disapproval at home, or they may already be in conflict with their parents. Yet, if they do not marry, they may have no choice but to continue to live at home in a dependent situation during and after their pregnancy. Thus, some teenagers are motivated to get married in order to escape this situation and to set up their own households (Reiss, 1971). But teenage marriage is not necessarily the best solution to an adolescent mother's problems. Some researchers believe that even though early motherhood is an obstacle to adult growth, it is in many cases preferable to early motherhood combined with early marriage. Adolescent marriage is more likely to lead to dropping out of high school than is adolescent pregnancy. Similarly, those who marry young are more likely to divorce than those who bear a child and then marry later (Furstenberg, 1976).

The children of teenage parents are also at a disadvantage, compared to children of older parents. They may suffer from their parents' lack of experience in handling adult responsibilities and in caring for others. Because these young parents suffer from considerable stress and frustration, they are more likely to neglect or to abuse their children (see Child Abuse in Chapter 14). Children of

Many teenage fathers have an especially hard time because of the pressures they feel to drop out of school to support their new family. Often in such situations only low-paying jobs are available.

teenage parents more often exhibit slow behavioral development and cognitive growth (Brooks-Gunn & Furstenberg, 1986). If adverse factors like poverty, marital discord, and poor education all exist in one family, the child's chances of developing these problems increase.

Some teenage parents, however, do an excellent job of nurturing their young while continuing to grow toward adulthood themselves. To do this, they almost always need assistance. Helping young parents and their offspring to thrive and to become productive remains an overriding social concern and challenge.

 ## COGNITIVE CHANGES IN ADOLESCENCE

Although physical maturation and adjustment to sexuality are major steps that take place during adolescence, important cognitive developments also occur at this time. An expansion in capacity and style of thought broadens adolescent awareness, imagination, judgment, and insight. These enhanced abilities also lead to a rapid accumulation of knowledge that opens up a range of issues and problems that can complicate—and enrich—adolescents' lives.

ABSTRACT THINKING

In Piaget's developmental theory, the hallmark of adolescent cognitive change is the development of *formal operational thought*. This new form of intellectual processing is abstract, speculative, and free from the immediate environment and circumstances. It involves thinking about possibilities as well as comparing reality with things that might or might not be. Whereas younger children seem to be more comfortable with concrete, empirical facts, adolescents show a growing inclination to treat everything as a mere variation on what could be (Keating, 1980). Formal operational thought requires the ability to formulate, test, and evaluate hypotheses. It involves not only manipulation of known, verifiable elements but also manipulation of those things that are contrary to fact ("Now let's just suppose for the sake of discussion that...").

Adolescents also show an increasing ability to plan and think ahead. In a recent study (Greene, 1990), a researcher asked 10th graders, 12th graders, college sophomores, and college seniors to describe what they thought might happen to them in the future and to say how old they thought they would be when these events occurred. The older subjects could look farther into the future than the younger ones could, and the narratives of these older subjects were more specific.

Formal operational thought can therefore be characterized as a *second-order process*. The first order of thinking is discovering and examining relationships between objects. The second order involves thinking about one's thoughts, looking for relationships between relationships, and maneuvering between reality and possibility (Inhelder & Piaget, 1958). Three characteristics of adolescent thought are:

1. the capacity to combine all variables and find a solution to a problem,
2. the ability to conjecture what effect one variable will have on another, and
3. the ability to combine and separate variables in a hypothetical-deductive fashion ("If X is present, then Y will occur") (Gallagher, 1973).

In contrast, information-processing theorists, emphasize the adolescent's improvement in those skills refered to as *metacognition*. Metacognition includes several skills such as the ability to think about thinking, strategy formation, and the ability to plan. Because of these new cognitive skills, teenagers learn to examine and consciously alter their thought processes. For example, they may repeat a number of facts until they have thoroughly memorized them, or they may silently warn themselves not to jump to conclusions without proof.

Teenagers also become extremely introspective and self-absorbed. At the same time, they begin to challenge everything, to reject old boundaries and categories. In so doing, they constantly discard old attitudes and become more creative thinkers (Keating, 1980). In addition to encouraging creativity, thinking about thinking encourages the development of role-taking skills and empathy. True empathy is only possible when persons can imagine what is going on inside the mind of another. In that way, the impact of words, thoughts, and deeds that the other experiences can be understood from his or her perspective.

Adolescents gain cognitive skills that assist their overall problem-solving and decision-making competencies, for example:

A high school student settles down at her desk to do her homework. She may plan in what order to do the assignments, test herself on a few of the vocabulary items on tomorrow's test to see how much she has to study, check whether the vocabulary flash cards actually are helping her, and switch to a strategy of using each word in a sentence....Her knowledge that she often makes careless errors leads her to double-check her solutions to some problem. In the opposite direction, her monitoring and self-regulation can lead to new knowledge, as when she learns that her own memory for word meanings is helped more by a meaning-based strategy than rote memorization. (Flavell, Miller, & Miller, 1993, p. 153)

The behaviors described above are essentially monitoring and self-regulation activities. The main function of such strategies is to provide persons with information about cognitive tasks and their progress in completing them. Metacognitive skills are monitoring strategies that evaluate the effectiveness of the problem-solving strategies individuals use. Adolescents make greater use of these skills than do younger children because of their increased cognitive ability.

The notion of a dramatic, qualitative shift as described by Piaget is not shared by all developmental theorist today. Some psychologists contend that the transition is much more gradual, with shifts back and forth between formal operational thought and earlier cognitive modes. For example, Daniel Keating (1976, 1988) believes that the lines drawn between the thinking of children, adolescents, and adults are artificial. He sees cognitive development as a continuous process and suggests that children may have formal operational abilities in some latent form. He asserts, for instance, that some children have the ability to handle abstract thought. Perhaps better language skills and more experience with the world, instead of new cognitive equipment, are responsible for the appearance of these abilities in adolescents.

It is generally agreed that not all individuals are able to think in formal operational terms. Furthermore, adolescents and adults who attain this level do not always maintain it consistently. For example, many people who find themselves facing unfamiliar problems in unfamiliar situations are apt to fall back on a much more concrete type of reasoning. A certain level of intelligence seems to be necessary for the development of formal operational thought. Cultural and socioeconomic factors, particularly education level, also play a role (Neimark, 1975). The fact that not all individuals achieve formal operational thought has led some psychologists to suggest that it should be considered an extension of concrete operations, rather than a stage in its own right. Piaget (1972) has even admitted that this may be the case. Nevertheless, he emphasized that elements of this type of thought are essential for the study of advanced science and mathematics.

INFORMATION PROCESSING AND INTELLIGENCE

Many theorists differ in their definitions of the nature of intelligence. Is intelligence what we know, or is it our ability to acquire knowledge? Is intelligence an accumulation of facts and conclusions, or is it the cognitive processes that we use to arrive at these conclusions? In Chapter 10, we discussed current theories of intelligence and ways of measuring intelligence. Many critics of intelligence testing have charged that these tests measure the product, rather than the process, of intellectual behavior. Piagetian theorists suggest that intelligence tests fail to measure qualitative changes that occur when a child enters a new stage of thought.

In the standard intelligence test, for example, it is difficult to capture the shift from concrete operational thinking to formal operational thinking. Information-processing theorists make a similar argument. They argue that intelligence tests fail to measure process components like attention, memory, problem solving, or decision making.

One major theorist, Robert Sternberg (1984, 1985), has attempted to analyze intelligence into three information-processing components that can be measured separately. For Sternberg, each of these components has a different function:

1. *Meta components* the higher-order control processes for planning and decision making. An example of such processes is the ability to select a particular memory strategy or to monitor how well one is memorizing a list (metamemory).
2. *Performance components* the processes used to carry out problem solving. These include selection and retrieval of relevant information from stored memory.
3. *Knowledge acquisition* (or *Storage*) *components* the processes used in learning new information.

Essentially, "the metacomponents serve as a strategy construction mechanism, orchestrating the other two types of components into goal-oriented procedures" (Siegler, 1991, p. 69). All of these processes are thought to increase gradually throughout childhood and adolescence. We may see Sternberg's theory as conceptualized by Siegler (1991) presented in Figure 15–2.

Actually, cognitive development and, hence, the growth of intelligence involve both the accumulation of knowledge and the growth of information-processing components. The two are definitely related. Problem solving is more efficient and effective when one has a larger store of relevant information. Individuals with more efficient storage and retrieval strategies develop a more complete knowledge base.

FIGURE 15–2
A diagram of Sternberg's theory of intelligence as adapted by Siegler (1991).
(Source: Siegler, R.S. (1991). *Children's Thinking* (Second Edition). Englewood Cliffs, NJ: Prentice Hall.)

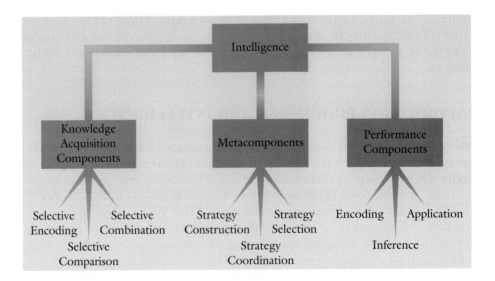

Adolescents are more efficient and effective at solving problems and making inferences than are school-age children. But they also have a broader range of scripts or schemes on which to call. As you recall, preschool children develop simple scripts for everyday activities. Adolescents develop more complicated scripts for special circumstances (a football game) or procedures (the election of a president). When they attempt to solve a problem or to understand a social event, they can make inferences about the meaning of such things by drawing from their more elaborate social scripts.

What, then, are the cognitive advances of adolescence? To information-processing theorists, cognitive development in this period includes the following:

1. a more efficient use of separate information-processing components, such as memory retention, and transfer components;
2. the development of more complex strategies for different types of problem solving;
3. more effective ways of acquiring information and storing it symbolically; and
4. the development of higher-order (meta) executive functions, including planning, decision making, and flexibility in choosing strategies from a broader base of scripts (Sternberg, 1988).

CHANGES IN SCOPE AND CONTENT OF THOUGHT

Basic academic skills and abilities, such as reading comprehension or rote memory, often reach optimal or near-optimal functioning levels during adolescence. Rote memory for simple lists of material, for example, reaches adult levels at about age 12 to 14 in most individuals. In contrast, vocabulary continues to improve well into adulthood. Nevertheless, because of greatly improved cognitive skills and the ability to use abstract thinking, adolescents develop a much broader scope and richer complexity in the content of their thoughts. It influences not only the study of science and math but also how adolescents examine the social world.

Since the adolescent can now deal with contrary to fact situations, reading and viewing science fiction often becomes a new hobby for many teens. Even experimentation with the occult, cults, or even altered states of consciousness caused by anything from meditation to drug-induced states, intrigues adolescents. The ability to understand contrary to fact situations also affects the parent-child relationship during adolescence. Adolescents contrast their "ideal" parent with the "real" parent they see on a daily basis. The adolescent becomes highly critical of institutions, including the family, in general and then specifically criticizes parents.

Family bickering is therefore bound to escalate during early adolescence, as we discussed earlier in this chapter. Many researchers feel that the "battles" that rage over such daily activities as chores, dress, schoolwork, and family meals serve a useful purpose. They allow the adolescent to test his or her independence in the safety of home, over relatively minor issues. Indeed, negotiation has become one of the prime words in the psychology of adolescence. Many researchers, instead of talking about rebellion and the painful separation of teenagers from their family, now prefer to describe adolescence as a time in which parents and teenagers

During middle and late adolescence teenagers exhibit a growing concern about the social political and moral issues of their society.

negotiate new relationships with one another (Flaste, 1988). The teenager must gain more independence in his or her life; the parents must learn to see their child as more of an equal, with a right to a differing opinion. For most adolescents, the interplay between these competing needs is conducted within a caring, close relationship with their parents. In a recent study, for example, teenagers who had the strongest sense of themselves as individuals were raised in families where the parents offered guidance and comfort—but also permitted their children to develop their own points of view (Flaste, 1988).

Particularly during middle and late adolescence, there may be an increasing concern with social, political, and moral issues. The adolescent begins to develop holistic concepts of society and its institutional forms along with ethical principles that go beyond those that he or she has experienced in specific interpersonal relationships. The rational processing of issues is also employed in an effort to achieve internal consistency, as individuals evaluate what they have been in the past and what they hope to become in the future. Some of the swings and extremes of adolescent behavior occur when young people start taking stock of themselves intellectually. There is a desire to restructure behavior, thoughts, and attitudes, either in the direction of greater self-consistency or toward greater conformity with a group norm, a new and individualized image, or some other cognitive model.

The improved cognitive abilities that develop during adolescence certainly help young people to make vocational decisions. They are able to analyze options, both real and hypothetical, and to analyze their talents and abilities. Ginsburg (1972) suggests that it is not until late adolescence that vocational choices become realistic, based in part on candid self-appraisal and valid career options.

ADOLESCENT SELF-INSIGHT AND EGOCENTRISM   One aspect of formal operational thought is the ability to analyze one's own thought processes. Adolescents typically use this ability a great deal. In addition to gaining insight about themselves, they also gain insight into others. This ability to take account of others' thoughts, combined with the adolescent's preoccupation with his or her own metamorphosis, leads to a peculiar kind of egocentrism. Adolescents tend to assume that others are as fascinated about them and their behavior as adolescents are about themselves. They may fail to distinguish between their own concerns and the concerns of others. As a result, adolescents tend to jump to conclusions about the reactions of those around them and to assume that others will be as approving or as critical of them as they are of themselves. Research findings indicate that adolescents are far more concerned than younger children are about having their inadequacies discovered by other people (Elkind & Bowen, 1979).

The adolescent's idea that he or she is constantly being watched and judged by other people has been called the **imaginary audience** (Elkind, 1967). Adolescents use this imaginary audience as an internal sounding board "to try on" various attitudes and behaviors. The imaginary audience is also the source of much adolescent self-consciousness—of feeling constantly, painfully on display. Because adolescents are unsure of their inner identity, they overreact to others' views in trying to figure out who they really are (Elkind, 1967).

At the same time that they fail to differentiate the feelings of others, adolescents are also very absorbed in their own feelings, believing that their emotions

imaginary audience Adolescents' assumption that others are focusing a great deal of critical attention on them.

are unique and that no one has ever known, or will ever know, such personal agony or rapture. As part of this type of egocentrism, some adolescents come to believe in a **personal fable**—a feeling they are so special that they must be exempt from the ordinary laws of nature and that they will live forever. This feeling of invulnerability and immortality seems to be the basis for some of the risk-taking behavior that is so common during this period (Buis & Thompson, 1989). Another type of personal fable is the *foundling fantasy* (Elkind, 1974). Armed with new critical insights, the adolescent suddenly becomes aware of a great number of failings in his or her parents—and then has trouble imagining how two such ordinary and limited individuals could have possibly produced this sensitive and unique individual. All of this self-absorption can be a great obstacle in learning to see eye to eye with the rest of the world. Fortunately, egocentrism begins to recede by the age of 15 or 16, as adolescents begin to realize that their imaginary audience is not really paying very much attention to them and that they are subject to the laws of nature just like everyone else.

Nonetheless, adolescence is an intellectually intoxicating experience. New powers of thought are turned inward to one's own cognitive processes and outward to a world that has suddenly grown more complex. Included in this growth is the capacity for moral reasoning.

MORAL DEVELOPMENT   In Chapter 14, we discussed Kohlberg's theory of the development of moral reasoning. Earlier thinkers, of course, have observed moral development and studied the changes that occur as children grow, especially during adolescence. Kohlberg drew on the developmental theories of J. M. Baldwin (1906), George Mead (1934), and, most directly, Jean Piaget (1965). Although Kohlberg was directly influenced by Piaget, it is Kohlberg's model that has generated the most interest and research.

By looking at individuals in Western society, one can find some validation for many aspects of Kohlberg's theory. By the time they reach their teens, most children in our society have outgrown the first level of moral development (the preconventional level) and have arrived at the conventional level, which is based on social conformity. They are motivated to avoid punishment, are obedience oriented, and are ready to abide by conventional moral stereotypes. They may stay at this "law-and-order" level for the rest of their lives, especially if they receive no stimulation to think beyond it. The final two stages of moral development—morality by social contract and morality as derived from self-chosen ethical principles—require the thought processes of adolescent development. But what is the process of change? Can one teach more advanced moral thought?

Kohlberg and others have set up experimental "moral education" classes for children who come from a variety of social backgrounds. The results, even with juvenile delinquents, suggest that moral judgment can indeed be taught. The classes center on discussions of hypothetical moral dilemmas. The child is presented with a problem and is asked to give a solution. If the answer is argued at level 4, the discussion leader suggests a level 5 rationale to see if the child thinks it is a good alternative. The students almost always find that this slightly more advanced reasoning is more attractive, and through repeated discussions like this, sooner or later they begin to form judgments at level 5. At this point, the discussion leader might start suggesting level 6 reasoning as an alternative (Kohlberg, 1966).

Kohlberg's model and his experiments with "moral education" show several things. An adolescent's set of values depends partly upon cognitive development.

Adolescence is a time of self-absorption and self-reflection. Sometimes adolescents feel terribly alone and may believe that no one else has ever thought or felt the way they do.

personal fable Adolescents' feeling that they are special and invulnerable—exempt from the laws of nature that control the destinies of ordinary mortals.

FOCUS ON AN ISSUE

ADOLESCENT DEPRESSION

I am worthless, I am of no use....Vivienne's diary entry, April 11, 1973. (Mack & Hickler, 1981)

Vivienne wrote these words in her diary a full 8 months before she hanged herself in the basement of her home. At the time of her death, she was an attractive, well-liked, intelligent 9th grader. Her suicide shocked both family and friends. But the signs of serious depression had been present for at least 18 months in the poetry, school essays, and diary entries as well as in the behavior of this sensitive and empathetic young girl (Mack & Hickler, 1981).

It is often easy to miss what ought to be obvious signals of serious depression in children and adolescents. We tend to think of children as happy and carefree—as though children don't have reasons to be depressed. Furthermore, the word "depression" is used to describe many emotional states in everyday life, and, yet, the common understanding of this term is different from actual clinical depression. *Depression* can be defined as an affective (emotional) disorder with a characteristic set of symptoms. The individual experiences a prolonged period of sadness, sorrow, hopelessness, or emptiness. He or she loses interest in usual activities or pastimes. This may be accompanied by physical symptoms like poor appetite and weight loss (or overeating and weight gain), abnormal sleeping patterns (either insomnia or a tendency to sleep too much), loss of energy, and agitation. The depressed individual may have feelings of self-reproach, worthlessness, and inappropriate guilt; may be unable to think clearly or to concentrate; and may have a repetitive preoccupation with thoughts of catastrophe, death, or suicide. Depression can begin after an experience of loss or a stressful event. But the normal feelings of grief and disappointment are exaggerated and prolonged. There may be periods of weeping, but often there are no tears—only hopeless apathy, self-blame, and withdrawal (McKnew et al., 1983).

> *"It is often easy to miss what ought to be obvious signals or serious depression in children and adolescents."*

Clinical depression is more difficult to diagnose in children than it is in adolescents and adults because it may have somewhat different symptoms, depending on the age and developmental level of the child. Some authors believe that when depression occurs in middle childhood, it is really just prolonged and intense sadness in reaction to a loss or tragic event. It lacks the distorted thinking, self-blame, and guilt that are more common in adolescents and adults. Nevertheless, the emotions may be just as intense, and the child may have prolonged periods of physical symptoms—poor appetite, weakness, sleep difficulties, and the like—as well as feelings of helplessness, loneliness, loss, and guilt (Garber, 1984).

The incidence of depression increases dramatically in adolescence: The two peak onset times for serious depression are ages 15 to 19 and ages 25 to 29 (Judd, 1991). Although depression in childhood occurs equally often in girls and boys, depression in adolescence and adulthood is about twice as common in females. Researchers have not yet determined the precise reasons for this sex difference—it seems to result from a combination of social, cultural, and biological factors (APA Task Force on Women and Depression, 1991).

The adolescent's newly developed ability to be critical and analytical can be focused on the social realities of the world or directed inward. In normal adolescence, there is often an intensification of self-consciousness and a preoccupation with the self that may be relentlessly critical. These thought processes, combined with the adolescent's relatively limited life experiences, tend to increase the risk of depression and suicide.

In understanding depression, like other pathologies, it is helpful to have some knowledge of the development of normal processes.

These values are, in part, a product of the adolescent's experiences in making moral judgments. If he receives challenging, yet safe, opportunities to consider moral dilemmas at higher levels, adolescence may then be a time of considerable moral development.

Educators, in particular, are concerned with how the moral sense develops during childhood and adolescence. These educators feel that if they could understand it better, they could do something about the rising rates of delinquency and help to create a better social order. Even though Kohlberg has provided useful descriptions of the stages of moral development, he has not adequately described how a child progresses from one level to another. According to Kohlberg's framework, which is derived from that of Piaget, presenting a child with increasingly complex moral issues creates a disequilibrium in his mind. It would then seem that the consideration of moral paradoxes and conflicts sets up a disturbance that forces the child to make increasingly more mature analyses and judgments about social situations. However, it is not entirely clear if superior moral judgments necessarily lead to superior behavior, and very little research has been done to date on the relationship between the two.

What we do know is that adolescents are highly receptive both to the culture that surrounds them and to the behavior of the models they see at home, in school, and in the mass media (see the box "Adolescent Depression"). We cannot expect them to behave morally if those who serve as their models do not provide an example of moral behavior.

SUMMARY AND CONCLUSIONS

Adolescence in contemporary Western society has two key aspects. First, adolescents tend to live in age-segregated societies. They often rely heavily on peers and have little contact with either older adults or younger children. A second characteristic is the significant exposure to the mass media that molds adolescent thinking and behavior. Both of these factors play an important role in the experiences and attitudes of adolescents.

Significant biological changes occur during adolescence which culminate in physical and sexual maturity. These changes for both boys and girls include rapid growth, the development of reproductive organs, and the appearance of secondary sex characteristics. Since body image is in part a function of appearance and the individual's response to his or her body, when the body is altered in major ways, the self-image also changes. Teenagers are both fascinated and concerned by the changes their bodies are undergoing. They constantly compare their bodies to the cultural ideal. Early-maturing boys have definite advantages over late-maturing boys, while for girls early maturity is a mixed blessing.

Sexuality is one of the major issues that adolescents must resolve. The development of sexual culture and behavior shows considerable gender variability. It is also influenced by prevailing cultural or subcultural norms and values. The sexual revolution of the 1960s and 1970s has largely affected women. Increasing numbers of teenage girls are becoming sexually active, while the percentage of boys who are sexually active has remained fairly constant. In the 1980s and 1990s, adolescents are again becoming more conservative in their sexual attitudes—due to changes in cultural norms, but also due to the advent of **AIDS.** American teenagers continue to be very active sexually and also to have the highest rate of teenage pregnancies when compared to European teens.

Sexual abuse is recognized to occur in many children and adolescents. When children are abused, their self-esteem, sense of identity, and ability to form meaningful relationships may be affected—even into adulthood.

Another aspect of a more active sexual lifestyle can be found in teenage pregnancy. More than a million teenagers a year become pregnant. Almost half of these pregnancies end in abortion. For those who chose to give birth to a child, early parenthood puts many pressures on both the mother and father.

Associated with the new biological maturity and social experiences of the adolescent are increases in cognitive skills. Cognitive changes in adolescence are characterized by the development of formal operational thinking. This type of thinking allows for abstract thinking that is not tied to the immediate, concrete environment. Because of the growth of metacognitive skills such as monitoring and self-regulation, adolescents are able to think about their own thought processes—and those of others. Information-processing theorists also state that adolescents gain metacognitive skills which in turn influence the effectiveness of their cognitive strategies.

As cognitive skills improve and broaden, adolescents develop the capacity for broader and more complex content to their thoughts. These skills also cause adolescents to become more introspective and self-critical, which leads to a new form of egocentrism during early adolescence. During this period, some adolescents see themselves performing before an imaginary audience and may believe that a **personal fable** or script guides their daily path. This egocentrism diminishes in middle and late adolescence, when individuals find that they are not the center of the world's attention. The **imaginary audience** becomes, in a sense, a hypothesis about the world, which the young adolescent must test.

Also associated with improved cognitive skills is the ability to develop advanced moral reasoning. Older adolescents are more likely to use conventional arguments or self-chosen ethical principles to judge the morality of actions than are younger adolescents. In general, however, it does not follow that superior moral reasoning necessarily leads to superior moral behavior.

Adolescence is a crucial transition period during which the child grows into an adult. Many issues adolescents confront regarding sexuality, morality, commitments, and careers will shape the remainder of their lives. The adolescent is now uniquely able to look to past behaviors, integrate them with present realities, and project into the future the person he or she will become.

➤ KEY TERMS AND CONCEPTS

AIDS	hormone	menarche	puberty
homophobia	imaginary audience	personal fable	rite of passage

➤ SELF-TEST QUESTIONS

1. Give several examples of how cultural and historical factors influence the development of adolescence.

2. List the biological changes of males and females during adolescence.

3. What are some examples of how cultural ideals affect body image and adjustment during adolescence?

4. Discuss how the physical changes that are occurring during adolescence can affect parental self-image.

5. Compare and contrast early- and late-maturing males. How does this compare to the early and late maturity of females?

6. Discuss the way in which attitudes toward male and female sexuality in our society have changed.

7. List several factors that influence adolescent sexual behavior.

8. Describe the sexual revolution and changes in sexual attitudes and behavior that have since taken place.

9. Describe the impact of sexual abuse on one's sense of identity.

10. Discuss the negative impacts of early parenthood on teenage boys and girls.

11. What is formal operational thought? How did Piaget view the adolescent's cognitive changes?

12. How do information-processing theorists describe cognitive development?

13. Describe the impact of cognitive development on changes in the scope and content of adolescent thought.

14. Explain adolescent egocentrism.

15. Discuss Kohlberg's model of moral development and why it does not adequately describe how a child might progress from one stage of moral development to another.

16. List several cultural factors that shape adolescence in Western society.

COLES, R., and STOKES, G. *Sex and the American teenager*. New York: Harper & Row, 1985. Presentation and discussion of a detailed, interview-based survey of American teenage sexual attitudes and behavior.

COLMAN, W. *Understanding and preventing AIDS*. Chicago: Children's Press, 1988. A detailed, well illustrated overview for teenagers and their parents, including clear presentation of the immune system and realistic profiles of young AIDS patients.

ERIKSON, E. *Identity: Youth & crisis*. New York: Norton, 1968. A full discussion of adolescent identity formation with many examples taken from case studies.

FELDMAN, S. S. and ELLIOTT, G. R. *At the threshold: The developing adolescent*. Cambridge, MA: Harvard University Press, 1990. Results of the extensive Carnegie Foundation study of adolescent development in social context, presented for professionals and nonprofessionals alike.

KEMPE, RUTH S. and KEMPE, C. HENRY. *The common secret: sexual abuse of children and adolescents*. New York: W. H. Freeman, 1984. A hard-hitting, statistics-packed presentation of the range, extent and impact of sexual abuse in America.

ROSENBERG, E. *Growing up feeling good*. New York: Beaufort Books, Inc., 1983. One of the best self-help guides for early adolescents, it is also valuable for parents of adolescents and for teachers.

SHENGOLD, LEONARD. *Soul Murder: The effects of childhood abuse and deprivation*. New Haven, CT: Yale University Press, 1989. This psychiatrist explores the adult results of the psychological trauma of childhood abuse. The lives of Dickens, Kipling, Chekhov and Orwell are examined along with contemporary less well known victims of abuse.

VIDEO CASE: HOW TO CONVINCE TEENAGERS NOT TO HAVE CHILDREN

With over one million females under twenty becoming pregnant each year, child-care advocates are searching for preventative programs that work. One with a high success rate is a small program run by the Children's Aid Society in a drug-infested New York City project. In a community where 70 percent of girls become pregnant before the age of twenty, only 2 young women of the 300 teenagers who have participated over the years have become pregnant. The program works, experts suggest, because "it concentrates on what happens above the waist, not below." Says Philip Coltoff, the executive director of the Children's Aid Society, "When you offer children options—a good education, a job, a family in the future, a sense of belonging, and an opportunity to get out of a neighborhood that's not so nice now—these kind of options are not only cheap, they're the best contraceptive in the world."

The program's emphasis is on developing self-esteem and responsibility. Standards are rigorous. For five years, teenage participants must meet for two-hour classes, six days a week. Homework must be done. Junior League volunteers are available to assist. Two times a week boys and girls separate into two groups to talk about their bodies, sexual responsibility, and postponing sex. But for those who are sexually active, a staff doctor not only monitors health but dispenses contraceptives–even to boys as young as 14. The input of parents is not neglected. They are required to attend group sessions two days a week, where they learn to be better parents.

The cost for each child in the program is $1,500 a year. Although this may seem relatively expensive, supporters argue that it is cheap when compared to the billions spent on combating the effects of teenage pregnancy on society.

If a teenager stays in the program, graduates from high school, and holds a summer job, the reward is enormous. He or she is guaranteed a four-year scholarship to Hunter College. In sum, the program gives these teenagers a chance to achieve their dreams. Says one alumni, now at Hunter College, "I want to be a successful social worker, to get a house in Connecticut, and then start to have two or three kids."

CASE QUESTIONS

1. What in your opinion are some of the worst costs of teenage pregnancy to our society?

2. What kinds of measures seem to work best in preventing teenage pregnancy? Why? What measures do not seem to work? Why?

3. Why do you think this program is successful? Why do you think there are not more programs like it?

Don't laugh at a youth for his affectations; he is only trying on one face after another to find a face of his own.

LOGAN PEARSALL SMITH,
AFTERTHOUGHTS (1931)

CHAPTER 16

ADOLESCENCE: SOCIAL AND PERSONALITY DEVELOPMENT

OUTLINE

CHAPTER OBJECTIVES

By the time you have finished this chapter, you should be able to do the following:

✔ Discuss the major developmental conflicts that adolescents must resolve in order to make a successful transition to adulthood.

✔ Explain the concept of identity status.

✔ Describe the factors and processes that help to shape moral development and the selection of guiding values during adolescence.

✔ Discuss patterns of drug use during adolescence.

✔ Describe how parenting styles and family dynamics continue to influence a child's behavior during adolescence, and identify key characteristics of successful family functioning during an adolescent's increasing independence.

✔ Name some reference groups that might be important during adolescence and explain their significance.

✔ List the purposes of dating and explain how attitudes toward dating change between early and late adolescence.

In moving from childhood to the status of young adulthood, adolescents frequently display a curious combination of maturity and childishness. This mixture is awkward, sometimes even comical, but it serves an important developmental function. The ways that adolescents cope with the stresses of new bodies and new roles are based upon their personality development in earlier years. To meet new adult challenges, they draw on the skills, resources, and strengths that they developed in earlier periods of their lives.

In the preceding chapter, we mentioned that the transitional period between childhood and adulthood varies from culture to culture. In some societies, adult skills are easily mastered; new adult members are urgently needed and promptly recruited by the larger community. In our society, successful transition to adult status, especially occupational status, requires lengthy training. Adolescence in modern societies is prolonged, stretching from puberty through the second decade of life. Despite their physical and intellectual maturity, adolescents live in limbo, excluded from the meaningful problem-solving work of the larger social group.

On the one hand, prolonged adolescence gives the young person repeated opportunities to experiment with different adult styles without making irrevocable commitments. On the other hand, a decade of adolescence generates pressures and conflicts of its own, such as the need to appear independent and sophisticated when one is in fact still economically dependent on one's parents.

Some psychologists argue that adolescents are also under pressure from their parents, who have transferred to them their own compulsions to succeed and to attain a higher social status (Elkind, 1988). The adolescent must cope with all of these inner and outer pressures, confront and resolve significant developmental tasks, and weave the results into a coherent, functioning identity. In this chapter, we will look at the coping patterns commonly used to meet the dilemmas of adolescence and at the triumphs and tragedies that result. We shall examine how the young person selects values and forms loyalties and, as a consequence, how the young person presents a more mature self to society.

DEVELOPMENTAL TASKS IN ADOLESCENCE

Each period in life presents developmental challenges and difficulties that require new skills and responses. Most psychologists agree that adolescents must confront two tasks:

1. achieving a measure of independence or autonomy from one's parents, and
2. forming an identity, creating an integrated self that harmoniously combines different elements of the personality.

Adolescence has traditionally been seen as a period of "storm and stress," a dramatic upheaval of the emotions. The term storm and stress is derived from the name of a German literary movement of the late eighteenth and early nineteenth centuries (Sturm und Drang). It was adopted by Anna Freud, the daughter of Sigmund Freud, as a label for the emotional state of adolescents. Anna Freud (1958) went so far as to say, "To be normal during the adolescent period is by itself abnormal" (p. 275). The Freudians argue that the onset of biological maturation and increased sexual drive produce conflicts between adolescents and their parents, adolescents and their peers, and adolescents and themselves.

INDEPENDENCE AND INTERDEPENDENCE

According to the prevailing view, adolescents use conflict and rebelliousness as the principal way to achieve autonomy and independence from their parents. The media, especially since the mid-1960s, has focused on the "generation gap" and the turbulent conflict between parents and their children. Stories on this topic may have high drama and great interest, but they have limited support in research. Most of the research literature indicates that the degree of conflict and turbulence in adolescent relations with the rest of the family has been exaggerated.

Just as emotional turmoil is not an inevitable part of growing up, neither is conflict between adolescents and their parents. Although the emotional distance between teenagers and their parents tends to increase in early adolescence as they go through the physical changes of puberty (Steinberg, 1988), this does not necessarily lead to rebellion or to rejection of parental values. Bandura (1964) interviewed adolescent boys from middle-class families. He found that by the time the boys reached adolescence, they had already internalized their parents' values and standards of behavior so thoroughly that there was actually less need for parental control than had been expected. The process of emancipation was substantially complete by the time the boys reached adolescence because the parents had encouraged their sons' independent behavior starting in early childhood. Note, however, that Bandura's subjects were all middle-class American males; his results may not be applicable to a wider range of adolescents. Socioeconomic and cultural factors will have a large influence on the degree of tension and conflict each teenager experiences. Nevertheless, findings such as Bandura's call into question the Freudian view of inevitable conflict stemming from biological drives.

Clearly, definitions of autonomy that stress freedom from parental influence need to be reconsidered. The concept of independence must take into account

Contrary to popular belief, adolescence is not inevitably marked by rebellion against parents.

the continuing influence of parents on their children during and after adolescence. One theorist (Hill, 1987) has suggested an interesting approach to adolescent independence-seeking: Hill defines *autonomy* as self-regulation. Independence involves the capacity to make one's own judgments and to regulate one's own behavior. "Think for yourself," we often say when we want someone to be independent. Many adolescents go through a process in which they learn to do precisely that. They reevaluate the rules, values, and boundaries that they previously learned at home and in school. Sometimes, they encounter considerable resistance from their parents, which may lead to conflict. More often, parents work through this process with their children, minimizing the areas of conflict and assisting their adolescents to develop independent thought and self-regulated behavior (Hill, 1987).

Becoming an adult is a gradual transformation. It requires the ability to be simultaneously independent and interdependent. Interdependence can be defined as reciprocal dependence. Social relationships are interdependent, as for example, in the traditional marriage. The husband is dependent on his wife to cook, keep house, and mend his clothes. In turn, the wife is dependent on her husband to earn an adequate income and to protect her from danger. At work, bosses are dependent on their workers to produce goods, and workers are dependent on their bosses to manage the enterprise so that they all have an income. *Interdependence* involves long-term commitments and interpersonal attachments that characterize the human condition (Gilligan, 1987). Over time, adolescents develop the ability to combine a commitment to others that is the basis of interdependence with a sense of self that is the basis of independence.

IDENTITY FORMATION

Before adolescence, we view ourselves according to a collection of different roles—for example, daughter, older sister, friend, student, church member, and flute player. In adolescence, our new cognitive powers of formal operational thought allow us to analyze these roles, to see inconsistencies and conflicts in some of the roles, and to restructure them in order to forge a new identity. This process sometimes requires abandoning old roles and establishing new relationships with parents, siblings, and peers. Erikson (1968) sees the task of identity formation as the major hurdle that adolescents must cross in order to make a successful transition to adulthood.

Teenagers may be drawn to and adopt the values, behaviors, attitudes, and even mannerisms of a friend or peer they look up to.

SOURCES OF IDENTITY   Adolescents derive many of their ideas of suitable roles and values from **reference groups.** Reference groups may consist of individuals with whom adolescents are close and whom they see every day, or they may be broader social groups with whom adolescents share attitudes and ideals—such as religious, ethnic, generational, or interest groups. Individuals compare themselves to a reference group, whether broad or narrow, and find their values either confirmed or rejected.

Adolescents must come to terms with a variety of reference groups. Groups that were automatic in childhood—such as the family, the neighborhood gang, the church youth group—are no longer as comfortable or fulfilling. There may be conflicting loyalties between an adolescent's family, ethnic group, and peer group.

Sometimes, adolescents are drawn to the values and attitudes of one person, rather than to those of an entire group. This person, called a **significant other,** might be a close friend, an admired teacher, an older sibling, a movie or sports star, or anyone whose opinions are highly valued. Although the influence of a significant other may be felt at any stage of life, it often has its greatest impact during adolescence, when the individual is actively seeking models.

Thus, adolescents are surrounded by a bewildering variety of roles offered by a multitude of reference groups and significant others. These roles must be integrated into a personal identity, and the conflicting ones must be reconciled or discarded. The process is made more difficult when there is conflict between roles (for instance, between being a member of a funloving peer group and being a good student) or between significant others (for instance, between a boyfriend and an older sister).

ERIKSON'S CONCEPT OF IDENTITY   Erik Erikson, a clinical psychologist, spent much of his professional life working with adolescents and young adults. His work on the process of establishing "an inner sense of identity" has had an enormous impact on developmental psychologists and on the general public. According to Erikson, the process of self-definition, called *identity formation,* is lengthy and complex. It provides continuity between the individual's past, present, and future. It forms a framework for organizing and integrating behaviors in diverse areas of one's life. It reconciles the person's own inclinations and talents with earlier identifications or roles that were supplied by parents, peers, or society. By helping the person to know where he or she stands in comparison to others in society, it also provides a basis for social comparisons. Finally, an "inner sense of identity" helps to give a direction, a purpose, and a meaning to one's

reference group A social group or collection of people with whom an individual shares attitudes, ideals, or philosophies.

significant other Anyone whose opinions an individual values highly.

future life. It is a rich and full concept presented with numerous examples drawn from personal case studies (Erikson, 1959, 1963, 1968; Waterman, 1985).

The richness of Erikson's concept is somewhat lost when we translate it into research. Unfortunately, as one researcher observed, a lengthy autobiographical interview on an individual's vocational plans, religious beliefs, political ideology, and social roles is too often translated into a one- or two-word categorical label. (Archer, 1985).

MODES OF IDENTITY FORMATION In a theory based on Erikson's developmental scheme, James Marcia (1980) has defined four different states or modes of identity formation. The four modes, or *identity statuses,* are **foreclosure, diffusion, moratorium** and **identity achievement.** These statuses are defined according to two factors: whether or not the individual has gone through a decision-making period called an **identity crisis;** and whether or not the individual has made a commitment to a selected set of choices, such as a system of values or a plan for a future occupation.

Adolescents who are in *foreclosure status* have made a commitment without going through a decision-making period. They have chosen an occupation, a religious outlook, or an ideological viewpoint, but the choice was made early and was determined by their parents or teachers rather than by themselves. The transition to adulthood occurs smoothly and with little conflict.

Young people who lack a sense of direction and who seem to have little motivation to find one are in *diffusion status.* They have not experienced a crisis, and they have not selected an occupational role or a moral code. They are simply avoiding the issue. Some seek immediate gratification; others experiment in a random fashion with all possibilities (Coté & Levine, 1988).

Adolescents or young adults in *moratorium status* are in the midst of an ongoing identity crisis or decision-making period. The decisions may concern occupational choices, religious or ethical values, or political philosophies. Young people in this status are preoccupied with "finding themselves."

Identity achievement is the status attained by people who have passed through the crisis and have made their commitments. As a result, they pursue work of their own choosing and attempt to live by their own individually formulated moral code. Although there are healthy and pathological dimensions to all four identity statuses, identity achievement is usually viewed as the most psychologically desirable (Marcia, 1980). We may see these various identity statuses contrasted in Table 16–1.

foreclosure The identity status of those who have made commitments without going through an identity crisis.

diffusion The identity status of those who have neither gone through an identity crisis nor made commitments.

moratorium The identity status of those who are currently in the midst of an identity crisis.

identity achievement The identity status of those who have gone through an identity crisis and have made commitments.

identity crisis A period of making decisions about important issues—of asking "Who am I and where am I going?"

TABLE 16–1 Marcia's Model of Identity Formation

	UNDERGOING IDENTITY CRISIS OR DECISION MAKING PERIOD	COMMITMENT TO CHOICES CAREER
Foreclosure status	No	Yes
Diffusion status	No	No
Moratorium	Ongoing	Ongoing
Identity achievement	Completed	Completed

EFFECTS OF IDENTITY STATUS Research indicates that identity status profoundly influences an adolescent's social expectations, self-image, and reactions to stress. Moreover, cross-cultural research in the United States, Denmark, Israel, and other societies suggests that Marcia's four statuses are part of the developmental process in several related cultures. Let us look at how the four identity statuses interact with some of the problems of adolescence.

Anxiety is a dominant emotion for young people in moratorium status because of their unresolved decisions. They struggle with a world of conflicting values and choices and are constantly faced with unpredictability and contradictions. These adolescents are often tied to their parents with ambivalent bonds of love and hatred; they struggle for freedom, yet they fear and resent parental disapproval. Among college students, there are many in the moratorium status. These are the people who are actively seeking information and making decisions.

Adolescents in foreclosure status experience a minimum of anxiety. These adolescents hold to more authoritarian values than those in other statuses, and they have strong, positive ties to significant others, who sometimes follow untraditional paths. They generally operate in a pattern of continuity and stability, although in some areas of life, they may experience uncertainty. Young men in foreclosure status tend to have less self-esteem than do those in moratorium status, and they are more susceptible to the suggestions of others (Marcia, 1980).

Diffusion status is seen most frequently in teenagers who have experienced rejection or neglect from detached or uncaring parents. These adolescents may become society's dropouts, perhaps turning to drug or alcohol use as a way of evading responsibility. Baumrind (1991) has shown that drug and alcohol abuse is most common in the offspring of what she refers to as "unengaged parents."

In comparison to young people in moratorium, foreclosure, or diffusion status, those who have attained identity achievement have the most balanced feelings toward their parents and family. Their quest for independence is less emotionally charged than that of the moratorium youths, and it is not tainted with the fear of abandonment that bothers individuals in the identity diffusion status (Marcia, 1980).

The proportion of people in identity achievement status increases with age. In junior high and high school, there are far more individuals in diffusion and foreclosure statuses than in moratorium and identity achievement statuses. Identity status may also vary according to the aspect of life that is being considered: A high school student may be in foreclosure status in regard to sex-role preference, moratorium status in regard to vocational choice or religious beliefs, and diffusion status in regard to political philosophy.

SEX DIFFERENCES Marcia and other researchers have noticed a marked difference between males and females in the behavior and attitudes associated with the various identity statuses. Males in identity achievement and moratorium statuses seem to have a great deal of self-esteem, whereas females in these statuses appear to have more unresolved conflicts, especially regarding family and career choices. Later studies have partially confirmed some of these earlier findings but have presented a more complex picture.

Sally L. Archer (1985), for example, found that for family and career choices, girls of senior high school age were most likely to be in foreclosure status, whereas boys were most likely to be in diffusion status. Furthermore, girls in foreclosure and moratorium statuses expressed a great deal of uncertainty about reconciling conflicts due to their family and career preferences. Although both boys and girls said that they planned to marry, have children, and pursue careers, it was primarily the girls who expressed concern about possible conflicts between family and career. When asked how much concern they had, 75 percent of males and 16 percent of females said *none,* 25 percent of males and 42 percent of females said *some,* and 0 percent of males and 42 percent of females said they felt *a lot* of concern about potential conflicts between family and career.

In the other major areas of interest—religious and political beliefs—studies indicate a mixed result. In religion, research indicates that there are no significant differences between the genders. But with respect to political beliefs, there seems to be a significant difference in identity status between older male and female adolescents. Males are more often in identity achievement status than females are, and females are more often in foreclosure status than males are (Waterman, 1985).

ADOLESCENCE AND THE FAMILY

Adolescents are very much influenced by their families, even though the old ties may be strained in some instances. Studies over the past 20 years have consistently shown that there is much less conflict between adolescents and their families than was previously believed.

> Survey studies are consistent in reports of conflict in only 15% to 25% of families....When conflicts do occur, mundane issues predominate. Family chores, hours, dating, grades, personal appearance, and eating habits are the matters of concern....Study after study has confirmed that parent-adolescent conflicts about basic economic, religious, social, and political values are rare. (Hill, 1987.)

The relatively few adolescents who form independent opinions about ideological matters generally do so late in their high school or college years (Waterman, 1985). Moreover, there appears to be a definite time frame to when conflict is likely to occur. Generally, early adolescence is more conflict laden than is later adolescence, by which time both parents and teens have come to grips with potentially difficult autonomy and separation issues. It is important for families to realize that if they can keep open communication and shared views during adolescence, the difficult times will be successfully negotiated.

IMPACT OF THE FAMILY ON ADOLESCENTS

Parents continue to influence not only teenage beliefs—they also influence teenage behavior (see the box "Family Relationships: Shared Views or Conflict"). However, mothers and fathers influence their teenagers in different ways. Although there seems to be little difference between the way adolescent males and females report their family relations (Hauser et al., 1987; Youniss & Ketterlinus, 1987), there seems to be considerable difference between the behavior and roles of mothers and fathers in adolescent family relations (Steinberg, 1987a). Fathers tend to encourage intellectual development and are frequently involved in problem-solving activities and discussions within the family. As a result, both boys and girls generally discuss ideas with their fathers (Hauser et al., 1987). Adolescent involvement with mothers is far more complex. Mothers and adolescents interact in the areas of household responsibilities, schoolwork done at home, discipline in and out of the home, and leisure-time activities (Montemayor & Brownlee, 1987). This may cause greater strain and conflict between mothers and their children. However, it also tends to create greater closeness between mothers and adolescents than between adolescents and their fathers (Youniss & Ketterlinus, 1987).

In Chapter 11, we discussed the influence that different parenting styles (Baumrind, 1975, 1980) have on children's psychological makeup. This influence continues into adolescence. Baumrind's concept of three categories of parenting styles has had considerable support in the research literature. The authoritative parenting style is most likely to yield "normal" or "healthy" adolescent behavior (Baumrind, 1991; Hill, 1987). We may speculate that the warmth coupled with the sense of confident control administered by the authoritative parent is reassuring for most adolescents. In this instance, the parent provides the experimental adolescent with a "safety net." The consequences of failure are not irreparable, because the parents will pick up the pieces.

Family dynamics and alliances also play a powerful role. Like parenting styles, these elements begin to shape behavior long before adolescence. An older brother who dominated his younger brother in childhood will probably have the same influence on his sibling in adolescence; a daughter who was "Daddy's girl" at age 6 will probably still be close to her father when she is 16. Although alliances between various family members are natural and healthy, it is important that parents maintain a united front and a distinct boundary between themselves and their children. Parents need to work together to nurture and to discipline their children. A close bond between a child and one parent that excludes the other parent can disrupt development. The excluded parent loses stature as a socializing agent and authority figure. Problems also can arise from other kinds of imbalances, such as the absence of one parent due to divorce or separation. When an adolescent is testing new roles and is struggling to achieve a new identity, parental authority may be severely tested in a home where there is only one parent.

In general, the greater involvement of mothers in their adolescent children's daily life activities such as homework tends to make this relationship more complex.

THE ADOLESCENT LEAVES HOME: THE IMPACT ON THE FAMILY

Families must make adjustments as adolescents become increasingly independent and prepare to leave home. This is not an easy task. Parents and children must renegotiate roles. Adolescents require a different support system than younger children do, primarily because adolescents are actively exploring their independence. Separateness and self-assertion are not harmful characteristics for adolescents—they are age appropriate and crucial to development. Some families encourage this development, whereas others oppose it.

Researchers identify three dimensions in family functioning: *cohesion, adaptability,* and *quality of communication* (Barnes & Olsen, 1985). In most cases, it helps during the separation process if families have moderate but not extreme lev-

FOCUS ON APPLICATION

FAMILY RELATIONSHIPS: SHARED VIEWS OR CONFLICT

Researchers increasingly look at family discourse and conflict both from a social cognition and a family process framework. As the adolescent matures, he or she quite reasonably has shifting views or social understandings about the social world. At times of rapid individual or family change, such as early adolescence or divorce, there are more instances of divergent points of view. Open communication helps refine and shape shared meanings within the family and, where necessary, define areas of difference or of change such as increased autonomy or responsibility. The more families can successfully view some of these dialogues as progress in their "soon to be adult" progeny, and help shape or change with the times, the better.

Some evaluations of the family environment are shared, while others are subjective and distinct for individual family members. Adolescents' perceptions of their families may therefore diverge from that of their parents with regard to their emerging emotional and intellectual autonomy, but be shared in areas that potentially threaten the family's cohesiveness—for example, conflict or stable family values such as achievement orientation or religion (Carlson, Cooper, & Spradling, 1991).

Holding distinct perceptions of family cohesiveness has different consequences for adolescent boys than for girls. Divergent views of family cohesion are associated with increased self-competence for boys, for example, while girls have more positive self-evaluations when they are in greater agreement with their parents regarding family cohesion. This supports research suggesting that the family provides a major sense of social support and connectedness for adolescent girls, while too great a sense of family cohesion lowers adolescent boys' sense of self-competence.

"Loss of maternal support may be too threatening to adolescents, while fathers are more likely to encourage independence and disagreement."

Shared values also affect adolescents differently depending on which parent the values are shared with. For example, disagreements with the mother undermine the adolescent's perceived social competence beyond the family. On the other hand, disagreements with the father provide opportunities for the adolescent to experience relational challenges that actually strengthen his or her social competence outside the family. Loss of maternal support may be too threatening to adolescents, while fathers are more likely to encourage independence and disagreement (Holmbeck & O'Donnell, 1991).

Mothers tend to have more frequent and extensive contacts with their children than do fathers. Mothers, therefore, acquire more information about their children's changing characteristics and self-perceptions than do fathers (Collins, 1991). Because of this, during adolescence mothers and adolescents may have more congruence between the mother's and adolescent's self-evaluation of competence than do fathers and children. Fathers tend to lag behind their adolescent children's self-evaluation of their competence. This may lead to disagreement or discussion of issues relating to autonomy and responsibility, which tend to be key issues for adolescents.

In general, then, the research on family process and shared views during adolescence tends to find it a period of *transformation,* rather than of *disruption* or *disagreement.* Parent-child relations during this time demonstrate a combination of stability and change with continuity and discontinuity, as all family members work to maintain affective bonds while adapting their interaction patterns. In families where functioning has been good throughout the childrens' lives, new forms of interdependency emerge that build on existing strengths. However, when communications have been haphazard or closed, already existing family dysfunction may worsen. But for most families, adolescence is a time when both families and teenagers mature and gain new insights.

As adolescents grow more independent and prepare to leave home families have to adjust to the separation.

els of cohesion and adaptability. It is best if families are somewhat flexible and adaptable but not so loosely structured that they seem chaotic. Also, members should be cohesive without smothering one another. Families adapt best if they can negotiate the changes in a rational fashion, taking into consideration each member's wants and needs. Family cohesiveness can be maintained when parents and the departing adolescent are able to approach one another as equals and to establish a reciprocal relationship (Grotevant & Cooper, 1985). Open communication, which enables family members to talk things out without friction, helps to preserve the cohesion of the family.

Facilitation of adolescent identity formation and separation may be more difficult in single-parent households (see the box "Teenage Runaways"). Some studies indicate that the involvement of another adult—for example, a grandparent, aunt, or teacher—makes the transition easier for parent and adolescent (Dornbush et al., 1985).

VALUES, IDEALS, AND MORAL DEVELOPMENT

Selection of a set of guiding values is a key task during adolescence. This process is hardly new to the adolescent, however. The development of a conscience and moral standards begins very early in the socialization process, when the toddler is taught not to pull hair, tell lies, or take toys away from others. Throughout childhood, social-learning techniques—particularly imitation of parental models and receiving rewards and punishments—play an essential role in the child's moral development.

This early training forms only part of the value system of a mature adult. Many psychologists believe that processes like modeling, identification, and

FOCUS ON AN ISSUE

TEENAGE RUNAWAYS

Each year in the United States, somewhere between 750 thousand and 2 million teenagers run away from home (Shane, 1989). Many are trying to escape from abuse or oppression by parents or stepparents. Others feel alienated from their environment, family, and friends. Some are "throwaways"—adolescents who are forced to leave their homes due to stress within the family (perhaps resulting from divorce, remarriage, or economic hardship) or because of behavior that is unacceptable to their parents.

Runaways and throwaways come from all socioeconomic classes and from all types of families. However, they are more likely to come from homes that are headed by a single parent or a stepparent and where there are many siblings or stepsiblings. Poverty, alcohol and drug abuse, family violence, and sexual abuse are common in the homes from which adolescents run away (Shane, 1989).

Many runaways turn to crime—prostitution, drug dealing, or robbery—in order to survive. They are at risk for a multitude of mental and physical disorders and for death from street violence, drug overdose, or AIDS. Even if they do not fall victim to these hazards, they still have less chance than do other young people of getting the kind of education or training they need for a successful adult life.

> "*Runaways and throwaways come from all socioeconomic classes and from all types of families.*"

A number of programs have been developed to help teenage runaways. Many large cities have houses where they can get food, shelter, and help with their problems. The Department of Health and Human Services operates a national switchboard that runaways can call to receive information on services and psychological counseling. This switchboard also helps runaways get in touch with their parents.

Youth in Need is one example of a program designed to help runaways (Lourie et al., 1979). It is a private, community-based program that offers crisis services to teenagers and their families, and it gives teenagers a place to live while they receive counseling. This enables them to see their home situation from a better perspective and to make plans for the future.

Unfortunately, some teenagers do not have homes to return to. Perhaps their parents cannot be located, are mentally ill or in prison, or are unable to provide a home due to economic circumstances. In a recent sample of homeless and runaway youth, only 36 percent were eventually able to go home again (Shane, 1989).

Whether or not they have a home to go back to, these young people need help and understanding. Unless we can make their future brighter than their past, they will remain alienated from a society that they feel has rejected them.

rewards and punishment, which teach the young child to distinguish right from wrong, can only go so far. They are satisfactory only as a means of teaching an external morality, which the child then internalizes. But in order to become a mature adult, the individual must eventually reassess and analyze these principles to build a coherent set of values.

REASSESSMENT IN ADOLESCENCE

Preadolescent children may be unable to construct their own value system, even if they should want to do so. As we saw in our review of middle childhood, cognitive

The moral growth that occurs during adolescence helps teenagers recognize the value of community action and concern for others. These Texas teenagers have volunteered to clean up trash on Gulf coast beaches.

theorists point out that the individual must have the ability to make relative judgments about what is right in order to form a mature system of morality. The 5-year-old, or even the 11-year-old, simply does not have the mental capacity to form a systematic framework of these principles. It is necessary for a person to have the ability to consider all of the possible alternatives, to reason from the specific to the general, to use cause-and-effect logic, to think about the past and the future, and to consider hypothetical alternatives. The ability to perform all of these cognitive tasks is not fully reached until adolescence—or perhaps later, or perhaps not at all. The newly acquired intellectual abilities of adolescents make the transition to adulthood a period that is marked by changes in ideals, values, and attitudes.

According to Hoffman (1980), moral development occurs in three different, overlapping ways. The first is *anxiety-based inhibition*—socially acceptable behavior that is induced by fear of punishment. Children learn to associate punishment at the hands of parents and others with unacceptable behavior. Eventually, children master this fear of punishment by refraining from the forbidden act. Thus, they have internalized the rules; actual punishment is no longer necessary. Second, as children grow older, they also learn *empathy-based concern* for others. This moral perspective combines the human capacity to share feelings with the growing cognitive ability to figure out how someone else is feeling, as well as how our behavior may alter other people's inner states. Third, children and adolescents undergo moral development through exercising *formal operational thought*—testing hypotheses, reevaluating information, and reformulating concepts. (This is a model developed by Kohlberg, which we discussed in Chapters 12 and 13.)

These three types of moral growth are not chronological stages, nor are they mutually exclusive. According to Hoffman, they usually coexist in all adults. But in adolescence, the three types may shift in importance. For example, anxiety-based morality can be severely undermined in the antiauthoritarian, peer-dominated college environment. At the same time, empathy may be eroded by exposure to some of life's harsher realities, leading to moral cynicism in adolescents. In contrast, empathy-based morality may be strengthened through exposure to inspiring leaders and teachers and through intense debates that stimulate intellectual support of empathic views. Finally, some adolescents may make the transition to adulthood with little or no moral development. This is often true of foreclosure types and of those who remain in sheltered, homogeneous environments, such as military schools. In such cases, childhood morality may take on the guise of political conservatism (Hoffman, 1980).

SOCIAL CONTEXT

The substance of adolescents' values depends heavily on the cultural context and historical period in which they live. At many points in history, there have been groups of older adolescents who have taken on the role of the conscience of society. In our own recent history, we can see this phenomenon in the civil rights and antiwar movements, in the feminist struggle for equality, and in the environmental crusades. Adolescents participated in these social movements for many reasons, both altruistic and selfish. Some carefully thought out their moral positions and endeavored to implement them; others just wanted to be part of the group.

In each decade, young people, particularly college students, have been among the first to reject the old values and to adopt the new. How many of these new values represent a youthful flirtation with ivory-tower idealism? How deeply do the new values affect the rest of society? Some of the values and attitudes with which college students startled the world in the 1960s were later adopted by working-class youth. Mainstream Americans began to show widespread dissatisfaction with the political system and with big business, to reflect relaxed attitudes about sex, and to place less emphasis on formal religion. The outlook and attitudes of a few adolescents in the 1960s became more widely popular in the early 1970s. There is little question that young people's receptivity to new ideas and values has acted as a force in changing the value structure of society. Since the late 1970s, adolescents have participated in the trend toward conservatism in religion and in political attitudes.

Although young people are more conservative today than they were in the 1960s and 1970s, they continue to hold the value systems of the earlier decades. Most older adolescents still believe, for example, in the right to engage in premarital sex or to have an abortion. Many are still willing to run risks in thinking and moral reasoning—to question and to oppose the settled beliefs of an era, whether liberal or conservative. According to Baumrind (1987), "Adolescents may construct a moral vision of an ideal world in which inequities are resolved justly and peers nourish and care for each other in mutual love and interdependence." Unfortunately, there is little practical support for such a vision in the real world. Young people who are strongly committed to this view may feel rejected, or they may feel that there is no place in society for moral action. The risk is that these individuals may become cynical, alienated, or hostile.

DECISIONS ABOUT DRUG USE

During the transitional period of adolescence, individuals are exposed to a variety of behaviors and lifestyles. They adopt certain behaviors and avoid others. A major decision that they must make is whether or not to participate in patterns of drug use and abuse.

Sedatives and stimulants have been used for centuries in the United States, but drug use became particularly widespread in the 1970s. Today, as in the past, alcohol, nicotine, and many other drugs are legally and illegally used by millions of Americans. If all the users of psychoactive compounds that are prescribed and unprescribed—sleeping pills, diet pills, stimulants, alcohol, caffeine, and nicotine—were counted, one would have to conclude, as did Keniston (1968–69), that "the American who has never 'used' drugs is a statistical freak."

Every drug has an abuse potential. In moderate doses, drugs like painkilling opiates or small amounts of alcohol may have beneficial effects. However, when taken in amounts beyond what is required for the relief of pain or more frequently than is necessary, substance abuse occurs. Of all the legal and illegal drugs that are widely available in this country, nicotine, in the form of tobacco, and alcohol have the highest potential for abuse. They are easily and legally obtained and are widely used by adults in this country. In fact, the conspicuous use of alcohol and tobacco is, regrettably, a hallmark of adulthood to a great many adolescents.

ALCOHOL   Alcohol acts as a depressant; its effects are similar to those of sleeping pills. In small amounts, the psychological effects include lowered inhibitions and self-restraint, heightened feelings of well-being, and an accelerated sense of time. Many drinkers use alcohol to ease tension and to facilitate social interaction. The effects of larger doses include distorted vision, impaired motor coordination, and slurred speech; still larger doses lead to loss of consciousness or even to death. These effects depend not only on the amount of alcohol consumed, but also on individual tolerance. Long-term habitual use of alcohol increases tolerance but eventually causes damage to the liver and the brain.

Probably the most powerful factor in teenage alcohol use is the view that alcohol consumption is a symbol of adulthood and social maturity. Teenagers are constantly reminded by their parents and by the adults they see in advertising, television, and movies that drinking is an activity indulged in by the sophisticated and worldly. By early adolescence, more than half of American teenagers have used alcohol; the proportion grows to 92 percent by the end of high school (Newcomb & Bentler, 1989). Although only 1 in 20 high school seniors reports drinking every day, weekend heavy drinking has become quite common among adolescents. Fully 35 percent of high school seniors report having had five or more drinks in a row at least once in the past 2 weeks, and 32 percent report that most or all of their friends "get drunk" at least once a week. Slightly older teenagers and young adults, many of whom can drink legally, generally consume more alcohol because they tend to drink more informally and more regularly at bars and social gatherings. These patterns of alcohol consumption have remained relatively stable for the past 10 years, with only a slight decline since the peak around 1980 (National Institute on Drug Abuse, 1989).

The patterns of alcohol consumption in young people vary according to age, ethnic and religious groups, locality, and gender. For example, the pattern of occasional heavy drinking is highest for those in the 4 years immediately after high school (above 40 percent), for males (50 percent versus 26 percent for females), for noncollege youth, and for those who live in cities rather than in rural areas (National Institute on Drug Abuse, 1987).

Alcohol is the most widely used drug among adolescents and young adults. Participating in heavy drinking binges during spring break is a popular ritual for many college students.

Many cigarette ads now target teenagers. Adolescent girls smoke more frequently than boys.

Males are more likely both to use and to abuse alcohol than are females. The typical alcoholic is a male with low academic grades and a family history of alcoholism. He is likely to have friends who also drink; he may also take a variety of other drugs. Many alcoholics have serious psychological problems, such as depression, a poor sense of identity, a lack of inner goals, or a personality oriented toward a constant search for new sensations and experiences.

TOBACCO   Tobacco use is another habit that the adult world encourages by example. Cigarettes are still a powerfully alluring symbol of maturity to some teenagers. However, as national mortality statistics show and as medical science has long known, cigarette smoking is a serious health hazard. Smoking increases the heart rate, causes shortness of breath, constricts the blood vessels, irritates the throat, and deposits foreign matter in sensitive lung tissues. Years of smoking lead to premature heart attacks, lung and throat cancer, emphysema, and other lung diseases. Moderate smoking shortens a person's life by an average of 7 years (Eddy, 1991).

In the past, boys began to smoke both earlier and in greater numbers than girls did. Since 1977, however, more adolescent girls than boys report daily smoking. For both boys and girls, over half begin smoking by 9th grade. In the years just after high school, many light smokers convert to heavier smoking. Most adult smokers start in their teens and do so as a result of peer pressure. One in four young adults is a daily smoker, and one in five (20 percent) smokes a half-pack of cigarettes or more per day (National Institute on Drug Abuse, 1987). Adults continue to smoke because withdrawal from nicotine addiction is difficult.

Today, tobacco smoking as a sign of youthful rebellion seems to have been largely superseded by other drugs. The incidence of cigarette smoking among American adolescents fell sharply during the period from 1977 to 1981, as more young people recognized the health risks. Daily smoking among high school seniors dropped from 29 percent to 20 percent, and the number who smoked a half-pack or more per day dropped from 20 percent to 13 percent. However, the decline leveled off during the 1980s. In 1988, 18 percent of high school seniors smoked daily, and 11 percent smoked a half-pack or more per day (National Institute on Drug Abuse, 1989).

MARIJUANA   After alcohol and nicotine, marijuana is the most widely used drug in the United States. This drug is not a narcotic or a hallucinogen, although it does build tolerance and produce mild physical and psychological withdrawal symptoms in some who use it regularly (Witters & Venturelli, 1988). It is *not* a totally benign drug. A report by the National Academy of Sciences states that marijuana has definite undesirable short-term effects but that little is known as yet about serious long-term effects. The short-term effects include impaired coordination and perception, along with a rise in heart rate and blood pressure and the possible occurrence of respiratory ailments (Reinhold, 1982).

Marijuana is, of course, an illegal drug in the United States. Illegal drug use over the past two decades has been primarily a phenomenon of youth, despite the fact that adults also use illegal drugs. But patterns of drug use do not remain constant—they change from year to year and from decade to decade. The use of marijuana by adolescents and young adults went up sharply during the 1970s but is now on the decline. The proportion of college seniors who used marijuana at least once a week was 18 percent in 1969; the proportion went up to 29 percent in 1978 and then down to only 6 percent in 1989 (Pope et al., 1991).

Attitudes about marijuana use have also changed; people are now more aware of the negative health effects associated with the drug. Adolescents report that their peers disapprove of illicit drug use, and many strongly object to daily use. These changing peer attitudes match the trend toward less use of marijuana (National Institute on Drug Abuse, 1989).

COCAINE AND OTHER ILLEGAL DRUGS   Cocaine is an extract of the coca plant and is officially classified as a stimulant, not a narcotic. It is highly addictive. The full range of physical and psychological risks has not been fully studied, but they include death from strokes, heart attacks, or respiratory failure (Kaku et al., 1991; Witters & Venturelli, 1988).

Fortunately, the use of this dangerous drug has now begun to decline, after a period of increased use that began in the late 1970s. In 1987, only 15 percent of high school students had ever used cocaine. More important, adolescents' attitude toward cocaine use has undergone a striking change: 97 percent now disapprove of regular cocaine use (Newcomb & Bentler, 1989). The decline in cocaine use can also be seen in college students: In 1978, 30 percent of college seniors had used this drug at least once; the proportion declined to 20 percent in 1989 (Pope et al., 1991).

One troublesome finding in the mid-1980s was the shift to the use of "crack" cocaine—an inexpensive, purified, smokable form of the drug. Although only 5.6 percent of high school seniors have ever tried this drug (Newcomb & Bentler, 1989), the proportion may be higher among high school dropouts. It is more likely for crack addicts to be young adults than to be adolescents; most are members of minority groups living in big cities (*New York Times*, 1989).

Hallucinogen use has also been declining in the high school and college population. The proportion of college seniors who had used LSD at least once went from 20 percent in 1978 to 12 percent in 1989 (Pope et al., 1991).

In contrast to the general downward trend in drug usage, a few drugs have recently shown an increase in popularity. One shift has been in the kind of stimulants that are used. Although the use of amphetamines like "speed" has dropped dramatically, the use of over-the-counter "stay awake" pills, whose major ingredient is usually caffeine, nearly doubled in the 4-year period from 1982 to 1986. The use of inhalants has also increased. Although it is no longer fashionable to sniff glue, there has been a rise in the use of amyl and butyl nitrites, whose more common street names are "poppers" and "snappers" (National Institute on Drug Abuse, 1987). Finally, and most worrisome, is what might be the beginning of a new trend: the use of crystal methamphetamine, or "ice." This drug is smoked like crack; it produces a similar sensation of euphoria and has similar risks (for example, death due to heart attack). Ice has been popular in East Asia for several years and now seems to be gaining in popularity in the United States (Hong, Matsuyama, & Nur, 1991).

Although the use of most illegal drugs has declined, 24 percent of high school seniors continue to use marijuana at least occasionally (Newcomb & Bentler, 1989). However, very few of these adolescents go on to use other drugs (only 9 percent use inhalants, 6 percent use stimulants, and less than 1 percent use heroin)—a finding that would seem to undermine the long-standing belief that marijuana use inevitably leads to the use of more powerful, addictive drugs.

In summary, even though familiarity with drug use continues to be part of adolescent culture, teenage opposition to drug use seems to be growing. Perhaps this is a form of adolescent protest. We may see the changing trends in drug use among high school seniors presented in Table 16–2.

RISK TAKING IN ADOLESCENCE

As we have seen, some adolescents engage in a variety of risk-taking behaviors—as a matter of fact, some have called adolescence a time of risk taking. Many adolescents engage in unprotected sex—sometimes with multiple partners—abuse drugs, drive too fast, perhaps engage in violent activities and/or generally experiment with a variety of dangerous activities. Often, they engage in these high risk activities in combination. Adolescents, 10 through 19 years old, represent the only segment of the United States population in which mortality rates have not declined rapidly during the past two decades (USDHHS, 1991).

Naturally, some teens engage in more of these activities than do others, often accumulating an increasing repertoire as they age (Jessor, Donovan, & Costa, 1992). For other teens, however, the natural increase in energy and intellectual curiosity that accompanies adolescence is harnessed, perhaps in sports or put to constructive, rather than potentially destructive use. For example, many teens become involved in social activism by engaging in environmental clean-ups, or building houses with Habitat for Humanity, or working with children who are sick or experiencing violence in their lives. Just as in our discussion of depression, which follows, adolescents who engage in high-risk behaviors for destructive purposes are in the definite minority of all adolescents.

When adolescents engage in high-risk behaviors, however, there are various reasons that could be advanced to explain why they do so. For example, adoles-

TABLE 16–2 Drug Use: Changing Trends Among High School Seniors, 1978–1988

	DAILY USE			EVER USED		
	1978	1983	1988	1978	1983	1988
Marijuana	10.7	5.5	2.7	59.2	57.0	47.2
Inhalants	0.1	0.1	0.2	12.0	13.6	16.7
Hallucinogens	0.1	0.1	0.0	14.3	11.9	8.9
Cocaine	0.1	0.2	0.2	12.9	16.2	12.1
Heroin	0.0	0.1	0.0	1.6	1.2	1.1
Other Opiates	0.1	0.1	0.1	9.9	9.4	8.6
Stimulants	0.5	1.1	0.4	N/A	16.9	19.8
Sedatives	0.2	0.2	0.1	16.0	14.4	7.8
Tranquilizers	0.1	0.1	0.0	17.0	13.3	9.4
Alcohol	5.7	5.5	4.2	93.1	92.6	92.0
Cigarettes	27.5	21.2	18.1	75.3	70.6	66.4

Source: National Institute of Drug Abuse, 1989.

cents get into trouble because they do not understand the risks they are taking; either because they have too little information or the message about risks was incomprehensible or not presented convincingly enough. A final explanation is that adolescents actually understand the risks but choose to ignore them. Depending on which of these beliefs one holds, the answer to dealing with high-risk behavior may be very different.

A ready explanation for why adolescents take risks is that they underestimate the likelihood of bad outcomes—in other words, they see themselves as *invulnerable*. Because of this belief, they focus mainly on the benefits of such high-risk behaviors—the status gained with peers, or the exhilarating loss of inhibitions for example. This explanation ties in with Elkind's (1967) views on imaginary audience and personal fable. Elkind argued that adolescents' personal fables endowed them with a uniqueness so strong that they became convinced they could not die—or become addicted—or get pregnant.

Over two decades of research on adolescent risk-taking behavior has determined that there are multiple causes for such behaviors. We may see these presented in Figure 16–1. In general the factors producing high-risk behaviors may be divided into five domains: biology/genetics, the social environment, the per-

FIGURE 16–1

A Conceptual Framework for Adolescent Risk Behavior

Note: From "Risk Behavior in Adolescence: A Psychosocial Framework for Understanding and Action" (p. 27) by Richard Jessor, 1992, in *Adolescents at Risk: Medical and Social Perspectives,* edited by D.E. Rogers and E. Ginzberg, Boulder, CO: Westview Press. Copyright 1992 by Westview Press. Reprinted by permission.

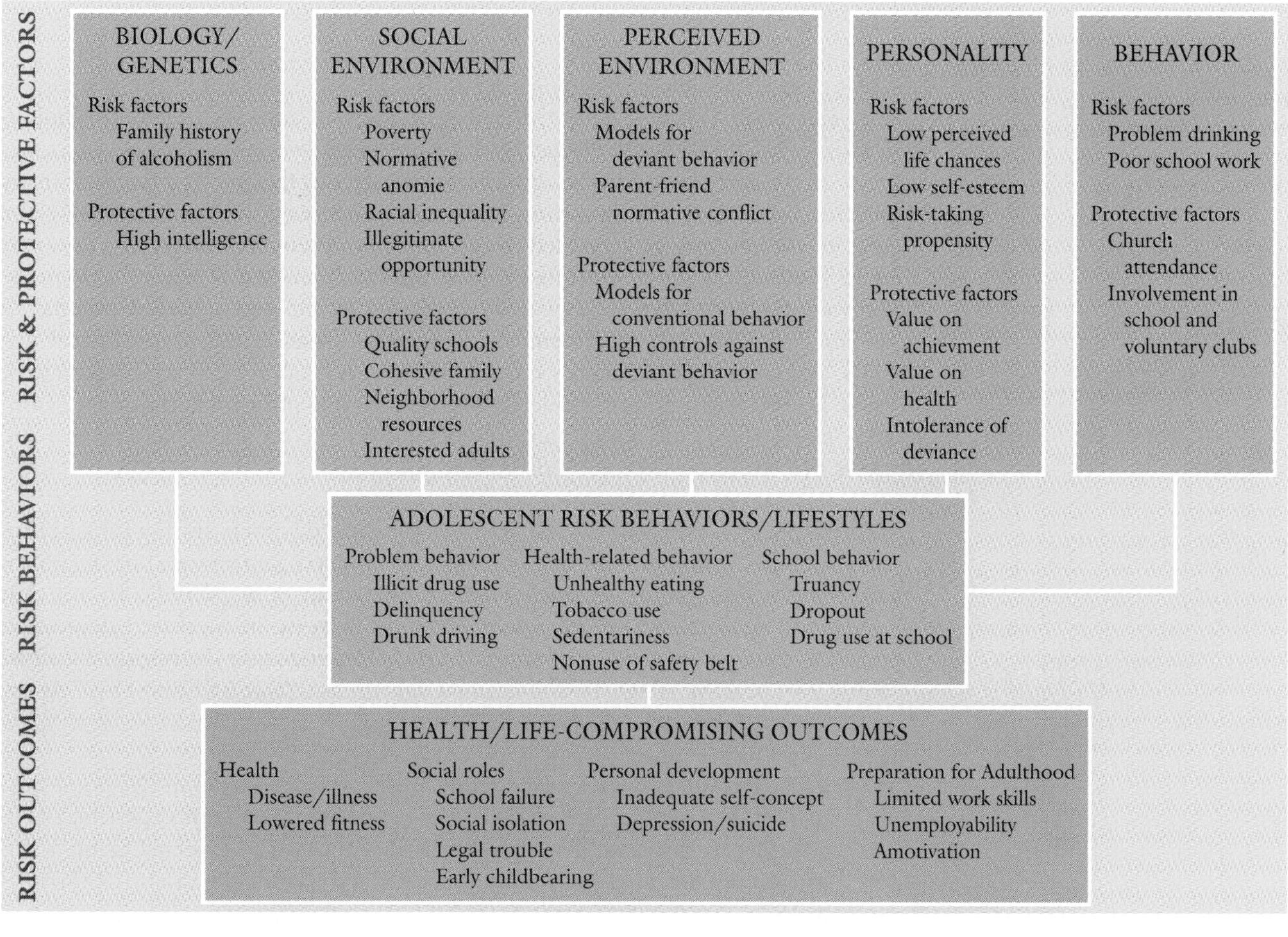

RISK & PROTECTIVE FACTORS				
BIOLOGY/ GENETICS	**SOCIAL ENVIRONMENT**	**PERCEIVED ENVIRONMENT**	**PERSONALITY**	**BEHAVIOR**
Risk factors Family history of alcoholism Protective factors High intelligence	Risk factors Poverty Normative anomie Racial inequality Illegitimate opportunity Protective factors Quality schools Cohesive family Neighborhood resources Interested adults	Risk factors Models for deviant behavior Parent-friend normative conflict Protective factors Models for conventional behavior High controls against deviant behavior	Risk factors Low perceived life chances Low self-esteem Risk-taking propensity Protective factors Value on achievment Value on health Intolerance of deviance	Risk factors Problem drinking Poor school work Protective factors Church attendance Involvement in school and voluntary clubs

RISK BEHAVIORS

ADOLESCENT RISK BEHAVIORS/LIFESTYLES

Problem behavior	Health-related behavior	School behavior
Illicit drug use	Unhealthy eating	Truancy
Delinquency	Tobacco use	Dropout
Drunk driving	Sedentariness	Drug use at school
	Nonuse of safety belt	

RISK OUTCOMES

HEALTH/LIFE-COMPROMISING OUTCOMES

Health	Social roles	Personal development	Preparation for Adulthood
Disease/illness	School failure	Inadequate self-concept	Limited work skills
Lowered fitness	Social isolation	Depression/suicide	Unemployability
	Legal trouble		Amotivation
	Early childbearing		

ceived environment, personality, and actual behavior. These factors interrelate to produce the various adolescent high-risk behaviors or lifestyles. Such behaviors and lifestyles in turn produce negative or compromising outcomes for the adolescents who engage in them.

What sorts of factors protect adolescents from engaging in such high-risk behavior? First, it appears that many families use strategies to protect their adolescents from the risks, dangers, and illegitimate opportunities encountered in many high-risk settings. They garner resources, badger public officials and teachers when their child is having difficulty, and provide monitoring against drug use or other destructive behaviors. Often, the family may move their child to a safer niche, such as a local parochial school, rather than give in to dangerous neighborhood elements (Jessor, 1993). Enlisting parental involvement in public schools has also been found to be a successful strategy. In general, when self-esteem, a sense of competence, and a sense of belonging to a stable family and social order develop within adolescents they are less likely feel the need to engage in high-risk behaviors (Jessor, 1993; Quadrel, Fischhoff, & Davis, 1993).

STRESS AND COPING IN ADOLESCENCE

Are adolescents a troubled group of people? The answer is some are, but most are not. The majority are well adjusted and have no major conflicts with their parents, peers, or themselves. But an estimated 10 percent to 20 percent have psychological disturbances that range from mild to severe. Although this proportion may seem high, it is no higher than the proportion of adults who have psychological disturbances (Powers, Hauser, & Kilner, 1989).

It is often the case that dramatic and extreme rhetoric characterize many articles and discussions involving adolescents—for example, articles may claim that *all* adolescents are depressed or rebellious or potential runaways; articles may state "wait until your child turns 12, then the storm and stress begin." Two problems arise as a consequence of this overstating of the psychological traumas of adolescence. First, all adolescents are viewed as experiencing psychological distress; and second, adolescents who need help are not taken seriously because their behavior and feelings are considered part of a normal phase of adolescence (Connelly et al., 1993). It is important to distinguish between normal adolescents and those who are in psychological distress.

DEPRESSION   In general, studies of psychiatric disorders during adolescence have found a fairly low incidence of moderate to severe depression, but symptoms may be life-threatening in those affected (Peterson et al., 1993). In a recent study, for example, while the results show an increase in measured depression over the teenage years, the percentage of those experiencing depression is consistently low, peaking at age 16 and again at age 19, as we see in Table 16–3. As the authors conclude:

> The relatively low rates of moderate and severe depression in this population indicate that the large majority of teenagers do not experience difficulty in this area. The corollary is that those who evidence symptomatology need to be identified and helped. (Connelly et al., 1993, p. 157)

TABLE 16–3 Percentage of Students by Age and Gender Experiencing None to Mild and Moderate to Severe Depression

MALES				AGE				
Depression	13	14	15	16	17	18	19	Total
None to mild	96%	97%	93%	88%	93%	94%	89%	93%
Moderate to severe	4%	3%	7%	12%	7%	6%	11%	7%
FEMALES				AGE				
Depression	13	14	15	16	17	18	19	Total
None to mild	93%	90%	89%	84%	87%	87%	82%	88%
Moderate to severe	7%	10%	11%	16%	13%	13%	18%	12%

Note. N = 2,698

Source: Connelly, Johnston, Brown, Brow, Mackay, and Blackstock, 1993.

For the adolescents who have problems, the symptoms tend to vary according to gender. Troubled teenage boys are likely to engage in antisocial behavior like delinquency and substance abuse. Troubled teenage girls are more likely to direct their symptoms inward and to become depressed (Ostrov, Offer, & Howard, 1989). As we noted in the box on adolescent depression (Chapter 15), depression is about twice as common in female adolescents and adults as it is in males. Psychologists have not reached an agreement on the reason for this sex difference, but it may be related to the substantial drop in self-esteem that has been found to occur in girls—but not in boys—around the time they enter junior high school (Bower, 1991). This is an effect of sex role socialization that accompanies puberty in adolescent girls—girls are pressured by peers and the media to become more attractive and to value relationships above achievements (Connelly et al, 1993). In general less effective coping styles and more challenges may increase the likelihood of depression among girls as they move through adolescence. This may account for the 16- and 19-year peaks in depression in adolescent girls.

There have also been found to be ethnic group differences in the incidence of depression in adolescence. For example, Causasian and Asian Americans are more likely to show symptoms of depression after stress than are African Americans or Hispanic Americans. Native American teenagers were found to have elevated rates of depression in adolescence. Homosexual youth also show higher rates of depression, as well as a a two- to threefold risk of suicide than heterosexual adolescents (Connelly et al, 1993).

DEPRESSION AND THE CO-OCCURRENCE OF OTHER DISORDERS
Depression in adolescence has been well-documented to occur simultaneously with other disorders. Thus, depression and anxiety disorders often occur together; also depression and conduct disorders, involving acting-out behavior. Boys are more likely to have disruptive disorders and depression, while girls are more likely to have eating disorders such as anorexia or bulimia with depression (Connelly et al, 1993). A high proportion of those attempting suicide are

depressed, at least after the attempt. Depressed mood, thoughts of suicide, and substance use are also related (Kandel, Ravels, & Davies, 1991).

For girls, poor body image may lead to eating disorders and then to depression. Elevated risk of depression has been found to be associated with medical illness—the assumption being that depression makes one vulnerable to medical illness. Depression may also cause other problems because of its impact on interpersonal functioning. Poor social functioning may worsen the parent-child relationship during adolescence and may also affect romantic relationships. For example, there is a threefold increase in teen pregnancy among depressed teenage girls (Horwitz et al., 1991).

DEVELOPMENTAL PROCESSES: RISK AND PROTECTIVE FACTORS
As we have said in Chapter 15, adolescence is a time of great transition. The biological changes of puberty as well as the social changes related to the move from elementary school to middle and high schools all demand adjustment by adolescents. Factors that place adolescents at risk for depression and stress responses include the following:

➤ Negative body image, which is believed to lead to depression and eating disorders.

➤ Increased capacity to reflect on the developing self and the future, which is believed to lead to an increased risk of depression as adolescents dwell on negative possibilities.

➤ Family dysfunction or parental mental health problems, which are believed to lead to stress responses and depression, as well as conduct disorders.

➤ Marital discord or divorce, and economic hardship, which lead to depression and stress.

➤ Low peer popularity, which is related to depression in adolescence and is among the strongest predictors of adult disorder.

➤ Poor school achievement, which leads to depression and disruptive behavior in boys but does not appear to affect girls.

While these factors predict risk for stress, there are counterbalancing factors that help adolescents to cope with the transitions of this period. Good relationships with parents, and by middle adolescence with peers, serve as buffers against the stress of life transitions. The importance of protective, supportive relationships during this difficult time cannot be overestimated, as the following comments indicate:

> Once on a depressed trajectory in development, an individual becomes more likely to stay on this course because of the tendency to both alienate and withdraw from the very social supports that can minimize negative effects. The effects are likely to be especially devastating to a developing adolescent. Imagine the 13-year-old, hospitalized for depression following the death of a parent. The hospitalization removes the adolescent from the peer group and school; family members are likely to visit, but the context is certainly not the same as home. (Connelly et al, 1993, p. 161)

This adolescent experiences unusual—and perhaps stigmatizing—treatment, but also misses important developmental experiences at school with peers. The longer an adolescent is removed from peers, the more difficult is the reintegration process. It may become so stressful in itself that a more isolated, less socially competent, depressed approach to life may be the result.

ADOLESCENTS' COPING RESPONSES   Adolescents use a variety of coping responses to deal with the stress of their daily lives (see the box "Adolescent Suicide"). In general, research has found that substance use, diversionary responses, and rebellious responses are the major ways adolescents cope with stress. Students at all levels report drinking alcohol, smoking cigarettes, and using drugs as a means of reducing stress. We have already discussed substance use earlier in this chapter. Diversionary responses are also frequently employed. These include shopping, taking a hot bath or shower, going out with friends, sleeping, watching television, and eating. These activities do not directly deal with problems being confronted, but rather divert attention away from them. The final category, rebellious responses, includes rebelling against the rules or resorting to violence. Few adolescents who are really stressed out view dealing with the stress "head on" as an option (Mates & Allison, 1992). In this, they different little from adults in similar situations.

PEERS, FRIENDS, AND THE SOCIAL ENVIRONMENT

During adolescence, the importance of peer groups increases enormously. Teenagers seek support from others in order to cope with the physical, emotional, and social changes of adolescence. Understandably, they are most likely to seek this support from others who are going through the same experience. These "others" are their peers. Studies have shown that adolescents spend at least half of their time with their peers—friends and classmates—and much less time with their families (Csikszentmihalyi & Larson, 1984).

THE INFLUENCE OF PEERS

Peer networks are essential to the adolescent's development of social skills. The reciprocal equality that characterizes teenage relationships also helps develop positive responses to the various crises these young people face (Epstein, 1983; Hawkins & Berndt, 1985). Teenagers learn from their friends and age-mates the kinds of behavior that will be socially rewarded and the roles that best suit them. Social competence is a major element in a teenager's ability to make new friends and to maintain old ones (Fischer et al., 1986).

Most adolescents are members of an adolescent peer group. There are two basic types of groups, distinguished by size: The larger, which has between 15 and 30 members, is called a *crowd;* the smaller, which has as few as 3 members or as many as 9, is called a *clique.* The average crowd consists of several cliques. Because of their small number, cliques are highly cohesive. Their members share

Peers serve as audience, critic, and emotional support for their friends' ideas innovations and behavior.

FOCUS ON AN ISSUE

ADOLESCENT SUICIDE

In recent years, growing public concern over the increased rate of adolescent suicide has resulted in suicide prevention activities at the local, state and federal level. This public concern is justified. In 1988, a total of 2,059 adolescents from 15–19 and 243 children under age 15 committed suicide (National Center for Health Statistics, 1991). As we can see in Figure 16–2, suicide is the third leading cause of adolescent death, following motor vehicle accidents and natural causes. It ranks fairly close to violence and homicide, which show considerable racial differences. For example, homicides are the leading cause of death for African-American males between 15 and 24 years of age.

> *"Between 6 percent and 13 percent of adolescents have reported that they attempted suicide at least once in their lives."*

We should note that the statistics on suicide tend to be low estimates of the true prevalence. Suicides have always had a tendency to be underreported because of religious implications, concern for the family, and financial considerations regarding insurance payment restrictions (Garland & Zigler, 1993).

Between 6 percent and 13 percent of adolescents have reported that they attempted suicide at least once in their lives (Gallup Organization, 1991). However, in high school samples, 54 percent to 62.6 percent of students surveyed reported either suicidal behavior or thoughts about suicide (Meehan et al., 1992).

Figure 16–3 illustrates that the suicide rate is higher among males than among females, and higher for whites than for other ethnic groups. The increase in suicide in the past 30 years occurs most strikingly among white males. Explanations for this are complex. Antisocial, aggressive behavior is highly correlated with suicidal behavior. Negative cultural values about suicide may inhibit the behavior in certain ethnic groups. On the other hand, the highest suicide rates of any ethnic group occur in Native Americans, although there is considerable variability across tribes—for example, Apache groups have the highest rates while Navajos rate close to the national average (Berlin, 1987).

What are the risk factors for adolescent suicide? Research has studied suicide attempters and has also conducted *psychological autopsies* of successful suicides in order to determine risk factors for suicide. Many adolescents will experience some or all of these risk factors and never commit suicide. However, while individuals may not always conform to these predictions, they prove useful in designing suicide intervention programs. The generally accepted risk factors for adolescent suicide include the following:

➤ Psychiatric illness, such as conduct disorder, antisocial personality, depression, or substance abuse.

➤ A previous suicide attempt (the best single predictor).

➤ High amounts of depression, hopelessness and helplessness.

➤ Drug and alcohol abuse.

➤ Stressful life events such as serious family turmoil, divorce, or separation.

➤ Increased accessibility and use of firearms.

Elkind (1988) attributed the dramatic increase in adolescent suicide to increased pressure on young children to achieve and be responsible at an early age. Others have blamed the mass media since there is a significant increase in adolescent suicidal behavior following television or newspaper coverage of suicides. Fictional stories about suicide have also been found to be associated with an increase in suicidal behavior (Garland & Zigler, 1993). In general, social imitation—the "copycat suicides"—appear to occur particularly in adolescence, when individuals are most vulnerable to the belief that the future is not in their control, or is unlikely to meet their dreams.

PREVENTION EFFORTS

The most prevalent types of suicide prevention efforts are *crisis intervention services*. Telephone hotlines are the most popular of these services. There are currently over 1,000 suicide hotlines that offer services to adolescents. A relatively new approach to suicide prevention is curriculum-based prevention or education programs. These programs are most commonly directed at secondary school students, their parents, and educators.

The content of a typical suicide prevention program for students includes a review of the statistics on suicide, a list of warning signs, a list of community resources and how to contact them, and a list of listening skills peers can use to assist friends in gaining help (Garland & Zigler, 1993).

Recently, the American Psychological Association has developed a multiple-front prevention program for teen suicide (Garland & Zigler, 1993). This includes the following recommendations:

1. Professional education for educators, health and mental health care workers.

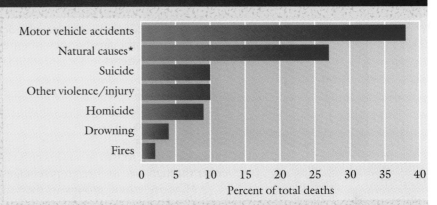

FIGURE 16–2

Major Causes of Adolescent Mortality, 1985
Source: Fingerhut, L., and Kleinman, J. Trends and Current Status in Childhood Mortality, U.S., 1900–1985. *Vital and Health Statistics*. Series 3, No. 26 (DHHS Pub No. 89-1410). Hyattsville, MD: National Center for Health Statistics, 1989.
* *Including neoplasms, congenital anomalies, and a number of relatively rare conditions.*

2. Restricting access to firearms by passing strict gun control laws.

3. Suicide education of the media to ensure correct information and appropriate reporting.

4. Identification and treatment of at-risk youth.

Given the severity of this problem, a comprehensive program such as this, while undoubtedly costly, may offer the best means of preventing adolescent suicide.

FIGURE 16–3

Suicide rates for 15–19-Year-Olds by Race and Gender Group.

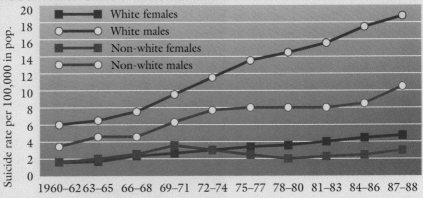

similar characteristics or reputations: for example, the jocks, the populars, the brains, and the druggies (Brown & Lohr, 1987; Dunphy, 1963).

Sometimes, cliques are based on elements of adult society, such as socioeconomic status or ethnic origin. In joining them, adolescents are seeking another component of identity—the group identity. Interestingly enough, in seeking autonomy from the family, they often end up substituting a group that is quite similar to their parents.

ETHNIC CULTURAL PATTERNS IN ADOLESCENCE   In many parts of the United States, the youth culture contains numerous ethnic subgroups. For these adolescents, ethnic differences form the basis for one important reference group. Although everyone in our culturally pluralistic society has an ethnic heritage, less than a fourth of adolescents report that they belong to an ethnic group, either through race or foreign parentage (Havighurst & Dreyer, 1975).

Minority ethnic groups in the United States range in size from the fairly large—Mexicans, Puerto Ricans, Chinese, Native Americans, and African-Americans—to the very small—Amish, Hutterites, and Mennonites. An adolescent's identification with an ethnic group can create conflicts of allegiance between the group's values and those of the larger society. Some special problems face certain groups. African-American youths, for example, must decide whether they want to try to succeed in society on "white" terms or on their own terms. Mexican and Puerto Rican youths must consider whether it is better to try to preserve their own customs and language or to accept the culture of their new society. Chinese, Japanese, Jews, Italians, Irish, and immigrants from many other nations have faced this same problem, and many still encounter it every day.

Demographic trends suggest that increasing numbers of adolescents will come from single-parent, low-income minority families as the century comes to an end (Otto, 1988). This raises the possibility that an increasingly large number

A teenager's identification with an ethnic peer group may result in conflicts in allegiance.

of adolescents will be alienated from the mainstream culture. It is possible, however, that social and cultural norms may shift to incorporate a broader spectrum of youth.

SOLITUDE AND LONELINESS Although 80 percent of adolescents join peer groups, a significant 20 percent do not. Generally, we think of nonjoiners as loners. Most of us think of being alone as a sad state of affairs that no one would willingly choose. However, this is not necessarily the case. Ancient hermits and modern mystics have sought solitude for purposes of contemplation or to deepen their religious experience. Creative work—in painting, music composition, or writing, for example—is solitary. Creative people often seek to be alone, both to create and to think. Solitude may have many other positive attributes as well. Some people experience a sense of renewal or healing when they are alone. Also, many seek solitude for the same reasons as the artist or writer—they can think best when alone and can work through their problems at this time (Marcoen et al., 1987).

Yet there is also a negative side to being alone. This condition can bring on severe feelings of rejection, isolation, depression, and boredom. Hence, there are two ways of experiencing solitude. One is *involuntary aloneness,* which is perceived as an unhappy state of affairs; the response to involuntary aloneness is to seek the company of others or to turn away from them because of feeling rejected. The other way of experiencing solitude is *voluntary aloneness,* which is seen as a relief from the pressures of the world—an opportunity for creativity or psychological renewal.

As young people move from late childhood into early adolescence, some experience a feeling of loneliness. Others do not have this experience at any age-specific point in the transit through adolescence, but they feel lonely after arguing with friends or sensing rejection by other peers (Marcoen et al., 1987). Still others voluntarily withdraw from extensive socializing for a period so that they can deal with personal concerns without experiencing public pressure.

THE NEED FOR SUPPORT Adolescence can be a time of stress. Part of the ability to handle stress grows from finding support in at least one area of engagement. If the changes of adolescence occur in too many areas at one time, they become too difficult to deal with and are a cause of great discomfort. Adolescents who can find security in some environments or relationships are better equipped to deal with discomforts in other aspects of their lives. Gradual changes—in relation to parents and siblings, school, or the peer network—are much easier to deal with than are changes in all of these arenas at the same time (Simmons et al., 1987).

DELINQUENCY The criminal acts of delinquency range in seriousness from shoplifting and vandalism to robbery, rape, and murder. Persons under the age of 16 or 18 who commit criminal acts are called **delinquents;** the age cutoff varies by state and also by the nature of the crime. Although people under the age of 18 make up only 38 percent of the U.S. population, they commit more than 50 percent of the serious crimes (Garbarino et al., 1984).

At some point in their lives, many, if not most, children engage in some kind of behavior that could be called delinquent. Shoplifting, for example, is very common, as are minor acts of vandalism—that is, damage to property performed

delinquency Criminal acts committed by individuals under the age of 16 or 18 (age cutoff varies by state and by nature of the crime.)

for the pleasure of destruction. The labeling of individuals as delinquents depends on whether they are arrested and the frequency of these arrests. To some extent, it also depends on race, socioeconomic status, and family composition.

Statistically, delinquency rates are highest in poor urban areas. Delinquency is more likely to occur among ethnic groups recently assimilated into urban life, either from other cultures or from rural areas. Young males from single-parent homes headed by a mother are especially likely to engage in delinquent behavior, and this is true both at higher and lower socioeconomic levels. It is not merely the absence of a male role model that is responsible for this statistic, because the presence of a stepfather in the home does not seem to improve the situation. An adolescent boy with a stepfather is as likely to get into trouble as one who is living only with his mother (Steinberg, 1987b).

Sociologists and psychologists offer quite different explanations for delinquent behavior. Sociological statistics and theories help to link delinquency to environmental factors, but they do not explain individual psychological factors. A psychological theory of delinquency would maintain that environmental factors do not, in themselves, explain why people commit crimes. Individuals are not delinquent because they are poor or city dwellers. They may be delinquent because, as individuals, they have repeatedly been unable or unwilling to adjust to society or to develop adequate impulse controls or outlets for anger or frustration.

Perhaps the distinction between sociological and psychological causes of delinquency is artificial (Gibbons, 1976). As we have previously seen, sociological factors often lead to psychological consequences, and vice versa. The sociological influences of crowding, mobility, rapid change, and impersonality contribute to psychological problems. Like the other patterns we have studied in this chapter, delinquency is a form of adjustment to the social and psychological realities of adolescence—an extreme adjustment of which society disapproves. Delinquency satisfies certain special needs for self-esteem; it also provides acceptance within the peer group and a sense of autonomy. For some delinquents, the thrill of high-risk behaviors is the compelling factor. The kinds of personality disturbances we have discussed seem to predispose certain adolescents to delinquent behavior.

In addition to these individual factors, research has also implicated the media in the development of violent or delinquent behaviors among some especially vulnerable teenagers. Film viewing, for example, may affect the potential juvenile delinquent through the processes known as social learning and instigation. Identification by the adolescent with the movie and its characters also provides a vehicle by which similar behaviors may occur, as the following example indicates:

> On March 24, 1984, a teenager from Rochester, New York, died after shooting himself with a .38 caliber handgun while playing Russian roulette. The movie *The Deerhunter* recently had been shown in the neighborhood. It was known that the youth had a fascination with films, especially violent ones. On the night of the shooting, he was holding a high school beer-drinking party at his home and had been drinking himself. At least 43 deaths have been attributed, at least in part, to the movie, with all victims being male and 20 victims under the age of eighteen. (Snyder, 1991, p. 127)

Delinquency satisfies certain special needs for self-esteem and is a way of gaining acceptance within the peer group.

FRIENDSHIPS AND RELATIONSHIPS

In late childhood, friendship patterns are often based on sharing specific activities, such as playing ball, riding bikes, or using computers. During adolescence, friendships assume a more crucial significance. As individuals become more independent of their families, they depend increasingly upon friendships to provide emotional support and to serve as testing grounds for new values (Douvan & Adelson, 1966; Douvan & Gold, 1966). With close friends, the younger adolescent is working out an identity. To be able to accept this identity, the adolescent must feel accepted and liked by others.

Adolescents tend to select friends who are from a similar social class and who have similar interests, moral values, and academic ambitions (Berndt, 1982). They become increasingly aware of peer groups and are very concerned about whether their group is "in" or "out." Adolescents know to which group they belong and are usually aware of its effect on their status and reputation. The social status of their group has a measurable effect on their self-esteem: Teens who belong to high-status groups tend to have high self-esteem (Brown & Lohr, 1987).

Between ages 12 and 17, adolescents develop the capacity to form closer and more intimate friendships. Over this period of time, they are increasingly likely to agree with statements like "I feel free to talk with my friend about almost anything," and "I know how my friend feels about things without his or her telling me." This increased intimacy is reported both by girls (in regard to their friendships with other girls) and by boys (in regard to their friendships with other boys). At the same time that the intimacy of same-sex friendships is increasing, friendships with members of the opposite sex are beginning to occur. Close relationships with opposite-sex friends are reported at an earlier age by girls than by boys (Sharabany et al., 1981).

"Hanging out" or working in a pizzeria is typical teenage behavior.

During early adolescence, most interactions with the opposite sex take place in group settings. Many 14- or 15-year-olds prefer this group contact to the closer relationship of dating. "Hanging out" (sitting around and chatting in a pizzeria, on a street corner, or in some other public place) is a popular pastime throughout adolescence, and it becomes increasingly "coeducational" as adolescence progresses. This type of interaction is often the first step in learning how to relate to the opposite sex. Early adolescence is a stage of testing, imagining, and discovering what it is like to function in coeducational groups and pairs. It gives adolescents a trial period when they can collect ideas and experiences with which to form basic attitudes about sex roles and sexual behavior without feeling pressured to become too deeply involved with someone of the opposite sex (Douvan & Adelson, 1966).

For some teenagers, however, dating starts early: In one sample from a small town in the Midwest, 13 percent of sixth graders had already started to date. The proportion rose to over 90 percent in mid- and late adolescence. Bruce Roscoe and his colleagues (Roscoe et al., 1987) have listed seven functions that dating serves:

1. *Recreation*—an opportunity to have fun with a member of the opposite sex.
2. *Socialization*—an opportunity for members of the opposite sex to get to know each other and to develop appropriate techniques of interaction.
3. *Status*—an opportunity to raise one's status within one's group by being seen with someone who is considered desirable.
4. *Mate selection*—an opportunity to associate with members of the opposite sex for the purpose of selecting a husband or wife.
5. *Sex*—an opportunity to engage in sexual experimentation or to obtain sexual satisfaction.
6. *Companionship*—an opportunity to have a friend of the opposite sex with whom to interact and share activities.
7. *Intimacy*—an opportunity to establish a close, meaningful relationship with a person of the opposite sex.

Roscoe and his colleagues questioned adolescents of different ages about their attitudes toward dating. They found that younger adolescents tend to think in terms of immediate gratification; they consider recreation and status to be important reasons for dating. Young adolescents look for dates who are physically attractive, dress well, and are liked by others. Older adolescents are less superficial in their attitudes toward dating; they are less concerned about appearance and more concerned about personality characteristics and the person's plans for the future. Older adolescents consider companionship and mate selection important reasons for dating. For both younger and older adolescents, an interesting sex difference emerged: Females consider intimacy to be more important than sex, whereas males consider sex to be far more important than intimacy (Roscoe et al., 1987).

PERSONALITY INTEGRATION

Throughout this chapter, we have talked about the needs of adolescents and the different patterns that they create to fill these needs. During early adolescence, teenagers usually feel intense pressure to conform to the norms and expectations of a few or several reference groups. Their self-image is affected by how well they fit in with a group or measure up to their peers. Their value systems often depend on the values of other people (Douvan & Adelson, 1966).

Early adolescence is an especially difficult time for young girls. Girls emerge from early adolescence with a poor self-image, relatively low expectations from life and much less confidence in themselves and their abilities than do boys (American Association of University Women, 1991). At the age of 9, a majority of girls felt positive about themselves, but by the time high school was reached, less than a third felt that way. While boys lose some self-esteem during the middle school years, their loss is not as great as that of girls.

Interestingly, there are significant racial differences in this loss of self-esteem. It appears to be largely a white phenomenon. When African-American girls were surveyed, they seemed to derive their self-esteem from their families and communities, rather than from the school system. African-American girls may well be surrounded by strong women whom they admire. In addition, African-American parents often teach their children that there is nothing wrong with them, only with the way the world treats them. White girls, on the other hand, may overly respond to social cues in schools where boys are favored, as we saw in earlier chapters. By the age of 15 or 16, many white girls tend to be filled with self-doubt. When they have problems with subjects in school, such as math, they are more likely to blame personal failure, whereas boys are more likely to blame failure on the fact that the course was "not useful" (Daley, 1991).

This research points out the significance of social cues and expectations during adolescence. As Carol Gilligan commented,

> This survey makes it impossible to say that what happens to girls is simply a matter of hormones....If that was it, then the loss of self-esteem would happen to all girls and at roughly the same time. This work raises all kinds of issues about cultural contributions and it raises questions about the role of the schools, both in the drop of self-esteem and in the potential for intervention. (Quoted by Daley, 1991)

As adolescents grow older, the measuring stick by which they evaluate themselves and those around them changes. Their ideas about the way they fit into the world may come more from their own discoveries about themselves than from other people. Their evaluations may reflect a sincere, idealistic, long-term commitment to certain values, instead of short-term commitments to friends. The development of this new idealism is the reason why the first 2 years of college are often a period of significant transformation. In part, this change in how youths see themselves and others is caused by their exposure to, and reaction to, the college atmosphere. Much of the change is also caused by the maturing of their rational processes—the new cognitive tools that they can use to evaluate themselves.

Noncollege youths often go through the same dramatic transformation during the first few years after high school. In part, their change is also the result of adjusting to a new way of life: being socialized into a particular occupation, learning new rules and norms, and watching their old circle of friends dissolve. Yet, at the same time, older adolescents who enter the workforce frequently develop a more objective and independent outlook. Their measuring stick, like that of the college student, may become more individualistic.

Although many noncollege, working youths do not have to face the awkward, artificial period of dependence that confuses college students, the adjustment process is just as complex. Specific problems center on teenage unemployment and the dull, repetitive jobs that adolescents are usually given. Cognitive maturity makes meaningful and significant work particularly important at this point of development (Dansereau, 1961; Goodman, 1960). Unemployment or meaningless work offers no challenge and denies individuals the opportunity to see the consequences of their efforts. The lack of significant work can be demeaning and demoralizing because the contrast between an optimal state of biological, cognitive, and social maturity and seemingly trivial tasks is disorienting. Often, adolescents have no armor of numbness or carelessness for protection against frustration and lack of fulfillment. Needs for personality integration, identity, and self-fulfillment are especially insistent during these years. Thus, working adolescents, like college students, are vulnerable and sensitive to an impersonal, technological society.

SUMMARY AND CONCLUSIONS

Adolescence, as a period of transition, is prolonged in Western society, mainly because of the length of time it takes to learn adult roles. Adolescents must complete developmental tasks in order to achieve the status of adults. These tasks include the establishment of an integrated identity or self, and appropriate independence or interdependence. In the completion of these tasks, emotional turmoil may occur—but need not. Storm and stress are not inevitable aspects of adolescence. For many teenagers, conflicts occur over relatively superficial matters, and most disagreements are successfully negotiated with parents.

In many instances, the adolescent uses rules and values they have learned from their parents. Since parental standards have been internalized, little direct instruction or monitoring is needed.

Occasionally during adolescence, individuals may have problems coping with stress. Depression, acting out, rebellion, substance abuse, or suicide may result. Depression is a fairly low prevalence problem among adolescents, but is serious in its implications and often occurs in combination with other problems such as eating disorders or rebellion. More females than males are apt to show the symptoms of depression, and there are significant ethnic differences in the occurrence of depression.

As cognitive development moves into formal operations during adolescence, teenagers are able to see the inconsistencies and conflicts in the roles they play, as well as in the roles others—including parents—play. The resolution of these conflicts helps the individuals to carve out

a new identity for themselves, that they will carry throughout the remainder of their lives. Erikson believed that this establishment of an **ego identity** was the crucial task of adolescence.

In addition to introspection, adolescents draw their identity from reference groups and significant others. It is challenging at best for adolescents to integrate the diverse messages they receive about themselves into one coherent personality.

James Marcia modified Erikson's work to define four identity statuses that adolescents may pass through in developing their identity. In the first, if adolescents have made commitments without going through an identity crisis, they are said to be in **foreclosure** status. If the adolescent has neither completed an identity crisis, nor made any commitments, the **diffusion** status occurs. Those who are going through both an **identity crisis** and answering questions about commitments, are said to be in **moratorium** status. Finally, those who have successfully resolved their identity crisis and made their commitments are said to be in **identity achievement** status. Individual identity statuses are influenced by a variety of factors including social expectations, self-image and reactions to stress.

Part of the resolution of the identity crisis is the attainment of a personal moral code. In order to choose a set of moral values, formal operational thought must be reached. Without it, the adolescent is unable to consider alternatives, use cause-and-effect logic, or think about the past and future. Hoffman proposes that the development of morality is affected by different factors at different ages. In young children, for example, morality develops through anxiety-based inhibition. In middle childhood, empathy-based concern for others is the key factor. Finally, in adolescence, the use of formal operational thought with its introspection and hypothetical thinking completes the process. Hoffman believes that it is possible for all three types of moral growth to function in an individual simultaneously.

Drug use and other high-risk behaviors often occur in adolescence for various reasons. They are in part attempts to reduce stress; in other aspects they are shaped by cognitive functioning. High-risk behavior may result from cognitive experimentation—or from something diametrically opposed, the pursuit of raw pleasure. Psychoactive drugs from caffeine to crack are used in the United States. Adolescents often see their consumption as an index of adulthood. Despite this, the use of most illegal drugs appears to be declining among adolescents today.

Families must adjust to the increasing independence of teenagers as they prepare to move out on their own. Most families get through this transition by renegotiating roles while maintaining cohesion, flexibility, and open communication. As the role of the family declines, the role of peers and **significant others** increases. The emotional support gained from such relationships is essential for the development of social skills. Peer groups generally take two forms: larger ones are referred to as *crowds,* while smaller groups are called *cliques.*

Not all groups are positive. It is possible for adolescents to get in with the "wrong crowd" and move into **delinquency.** Juvenile delinquency is more common in adolescent males who live in urban areas, are members of minority groups, and who come from single-parent homes. Delinquency is also associated with psychological characteristics such as the need for affiliation and the unwillingness to learn how to control impulsive actions. In general, delinquency is considered to be a personality disturbance that occurs in individuals who are unable to cope with the rapidity of social change in the world in which they live.

Friendships and relationships become the adolescent's lifeline. Adolescents generally choose friends who are similar to them and share their values. Friendships and dating patterns during early adolescence are usually based on superficial characteristics such as appearance and status. By late adolescence, commitments and choices are taken more seriously and are more likely to reflect the values of the individual. Dating is likely to occur first in group settings and then move to more intimate settings without a large number of peers.

By the end of adolescence, the individual has established an identity and has either made—or is prepared to make—the commitments to work and love that will sustain his or her identity during adulthood.

➤ KEY TERMS AND CONCEPTS

delinquency	foreclosure	identity crisis	significant other
diffusion	identity achievement	moratorium	

➤ SELF-TEST QUESTIONS

1. What are the major developmental challenges of adolescence?

2. Describe the processes of achieving independence and interdependence as they relate to adolescent development.

3. What is the impact of reference groups on the adolescent? How does a significant other influence the teen years?

4. Describe Erikson's concept of identity formation.

5. List and describe four identity strategies that adolescents use to meet the challenge of establishing an identity.

6. Explain why it is important to look at one's cognitive development when discussing one's moral development.

7. Describe three different types of moral growth.

8. Describe the way in which open communication and shared goals may help all members of a family

negotiate the difficulties that may develop during adolescence.

9. In which risky behaviors do adolescents engage, and how can such high-risk activities be reduced?

10. What sort of coping skills do adolescents use to deal

with stresses which they encounter in their daily lives?

11. What are the symptoms of depression in adolescents?

12. What should be done to deal with depression in adolescents?

➤ SUGGESTED READINGS

CARY, L. (1991). *Black ice.* New York: Knopf. Lorene Cary presents a compelling autobiographical account of her journey at age 15 from the black ghetto of Philadelphia, through the pioneering experience of integration, into the privileged world of an exclusive prep school.

ELKIND, D. (1984). *All grown up and no place to go: Teenagers in crisis.* Reading, MA: Addison-Wesley. Drawing from research and clinical practice, David Elkind looks at the pressures placed on adolescents now as compared to the 1950s and 1960s. He warns of the dangers to mental health from overstimulation and exaggerated expectations in childhood.

GILLIGAN, C. (1983). *In a Different voice: Psychological theory and women's development.* Cambridge, MA:

Harvard University Press. A thoughtful and compelling discussion of the different roots of moral thought in women as compared to men. The author contrasts theories and draws from her own research, particularly with adolescent girls.

GREENBERGER, E., and STEINBERG, L. (1986). *When teenagers work.* New York: Basic Books. A controversial examination and analysis of the impact of working on the teenager. There are hidden costs as well as advantages.

HAUSER, S. (1991). *Adolescents and their families: Paths of ego development.* New York: The Free Press. Scholarly, readable, and filled with case studies. Hauser presents four main "paths" through adolescence and the ways parents subtly guide their teenagers.

VIDEO CASE: THE ROLE OF GENDER IN DEVELOPMENT

Are most of the main theories of development gender-blind? Harvard's Carol Gilligan thinks so. According to Gilligan, in contrast to boys, girls lose self-esteem during adolescence. As they mature sexually, girls receive the culturally transmitted message that the ideal woman is "is seen more than heard." Is Gilligan right?

To find out, ABC reporter Carol Simpson observed younger and adolescent girls at Washington DC's Georgetown Day Middle School. The fourth-grade girls followed Gilligan's pattern: they were self-confident and articulate. Says 9-year-old Lee McClain, "I get really aggravated when people tell me that I can't do something."

But when Simpson spoke with eighth-grade girls, she noted that they showed less self-esteem both inside and outside the classroom. Explains 13-year-old Dawn Mason: "There's this voice in my head telling me, 'You know the answer and you can verbalize it well and you know you can do it,' and then there's this other voice saying, 'Well, it's not going to come out right, and it's not going to sound as good as what someone else has said.'"

The effects of this loss of self-esteem may be far reaching. Some experts believe, for example, that the fear of being unable to fulfill unrealistic expectations is contributing to the increase among adolescent girls of eating disorders, depression, and suicidal tendencies, as well as

disorders, depression, and suicidal tendencies, as well as to the high rate of teenage pregnancies.

Is it possible to protect a girl's self-esteem as she becomes an adolescent? Experts contend that mothers can play a major role in building their daughter's confidence. For example, Hila Richardson has a 9-year-old daughter. Like many girls her age, Rebecca has good self-esteem. Hila is trying to avoid teaching Rebecca what women generally have learned from their mothers—that females must be quiet, nice, and pretty. Instead, she is giving Rebecca messages to show "how much she's valued and how important she's been in my life." This mother then is teaching her daughter "to be herself."

CASE QUESTIONS

1. Do you agree that the major personality theories neglect the role of gender in development? Why or why not?

2. Can you suggest any reasons why the role of gender may have been omitted in developmental theories?

3. How do you think that gender affects development?

4. Do you believe that mothers are the key to raising their daughters' self-esteem? Why or why not? What other factors might help?

BIBLIOGRAPHY

AAP Task Force on Infant Positioning and SIDS. (1992). Positioning and SIDS. *Pediatrics, 89(6)*, 1120-1126.

Abbey, A., Andrews, F. M., & Halman, L. J. (1991). Gender's role in responses to infertility. *Psychology of Women Quarterly, 15*, 295-316.

Abler, R. M., & Sedlacek, W. E. (1989). Freshman sexual attitudes and behaviors over a 15-year-period. *Journal of College Student Development, 30*, 201-209.

Abrahams, B., Feldman, S. S., & Nash, S. C. (1978). Sex role self-concept and sex role attitudes: Enduring personality characteristics or adaptations to changing life situations? *Developmental Psychology, 14(4)*, 393-400.

Abramovitch, R., & Grusec, J. E. (1978). Peer imitation in a natural setting. *Child Development, 49*, 60-65.

Achenbach, T. M. (1982). *Developmental psychopathology*. New York: Wiley.

Ainsworth, M. D. (1967). *Infancy in Uganda: Infant care and the growth of love*. Baltimore: Johns Hopkins University Press.

Ainsworth, M. D. (1973). The development and infant-mother attachment. In B. M. Caldwell & H. N. Ricciuti (Eds.), *Review of child development research* (Vol. 3). Chicago: University of Chicago Press.

Ainsworth, M. D. S. (1983). Patterns of infant-mother attachment as related to maternal care. In D. Magnusson & V. Allen (Eds.), *Human development: An interactional perspective*. New York: Academic Press.

Ainsworth, M. D. S., Blehar, M. C., Waters, E., & Wall, S. (1979). *Patterns of attachment: A psychological study of the strange situation*. Hillsdale, NJ: Erlbaum.

Ainsworth, M. D., Blehar, M. C., Waters, E., & Wall, S. (1979). *Patterns of attachment*. New York: Halsted Press.

Ainsworth, M. D., Blehar, M., Waters, E., & Wall, S. (1978). *Patterns of attachment*. Hillsdale, NJ: Erlbaum.

Alan Guttmacher Institute. (1987). *Blessed Events and the Bottom Line: Financing Maternity Care in the United States*. New York: Alan Guttmacher Institute.

Allgaier, A. (1978). Alternative birth centers offer family-centered care. *Hospitals, 52*, 97-112.

Alpert-Gillis, L. J., & Connell, J. P. (1989). Gender and sex-role influences on children's self-esteem. *Journal of Personality, 57*, 97-113.

American Psychological Association. (1973). *Ethical principles in the conduct of research with human participants*. Washington, DC: APA.

Ames, L. B. (December 1971). Don't push your preschooler. *Family Circle*.

Anderson, D. R., & Collins, P. A. (1988). The impact on children's education: Television's influence on cognitive development. Washington, DC: U.S. Department of Education, Office of Educational Research and Improvement.

Anderson, D. R., Lorch, E. P., Field, D. E., & Sanders, J. (1981). The effects of TV program comprehensibility on preschool children's visual attention to television. *Child Development, 52*, 151-157.

Anderson, E. S. (March 1979). *Register variation in young children's role-playing speech*. Paper presented at the Communicative Competence, Language Use, and Role-playing Symposium, Society for Research and Child Development.

Andersson, B-E. (1989). Effects of public day-care: A longitudinal study. *Child Development, 60*, 857-866.

Anthony, E. J., & Cohler, B. J. (Eds.). (1987). *The invulnerable child*. New York: Guilford.

APA Task Force on Women and Depression. (Winter 1991). APA study finds no simple explanation for high rate of depression in women. *Quarterly Newsletter of the National Mental Health Association*, p. 5.

Apgar, V. (1953). Proposal for a new method of evaluating the newborn infant. *Anesthesia and Analgesia, 32*, 260-267.

Archer, S. L. (1985). Identity and the choice of social roles. *New Directions for Child Development, 30*, 79-100.

Arend, R. A., Gore, F. L., & Sroufe, L. A. (1979). Continuity of individual adaptation from infancy to kindergarten, *Child Development, 50*, 950-959.

Ariäs, P. (1962). *Centuries of childhood*. (R. Baldick, Trans.). New York: Knopf.

Armitage, S. E., Baldwin, B. A., & Vince, N. A. (1980). The fetal sound environment of sheep. *Science, 208*, 1173-1174.

Asher, S. R. (1983). Social competence and peer status: Recent advances and future directions. *Child Development, 54*, 1427-1434.

Asher, S. R., Renshaw, P. D., & Hymel, S. (1982). Peer relations and the development of social skills. In W. W. Hartup (Ed.), *The young child: Reviews of research* (Vol. 3). Washington, DC: National Association for the Education of Young Children.

Aslin, R. (1987). Visual and auditory development in infancy. In J. Osofsky (Ed.), *Handbook of infant development* (2nd ed.). New York: Wiley.

Aslin, R. N. (1987). Motor aspects of visual development in infancy. In P. Salapatek & L. Cohen (Eds.), *Handbook of infant perception: Vol. 1 From sensation to perception: Vol. 1*. New York: Academic Press.

Aslin, R. N., & Smith, L. B. (1988). Perceptual development. *Annual Review of Psychology, 39*, 435-473.

Aslin, R. N., Pisoni, D. V., & Jusczyk, P. W. (1983). Auditory development and speech perception in infancy. In P. H. Mussen (Ed.), *Handbook of child psychology* (Vol. 2). New York: Wiley.

Astley, S. J., Clarren, S. K., Little, R. E., Sampson, P. D. & Daling, J. R. (1992). Analysis of facial shape in children gestationally exposed to marijuana, alcohol and/or cocaine. *Pediatrics, 89*, 67-77.

Atchley, R. (1992). *The Social Forces in Late Life*. Belmont, CA: Wadsworth Publishing.

Athey, I. J. (1984). Contributions of play to development. In T. D. Yawkey & A. D. Pellegrini (Eds.), *Child's play*. Hillsdale, NJ: Erlbaum.

Atkinson, R. C., & Shiffrin, R. M. (1971). The control of short-term memory. *Scientific American, 225(2)*, 82-90.

Babson, S. G., & Benson, R. C. (1966). *Primer on prematurity and high-risk pregnancy*. St. Louis: Mosby.

Baillargeon, R. (1987). Object permanence in three-and-a-half- and four-and-a-half-month-old infants. *Developmental Psychology, 23(5)*, 655-674.

Bakeman, R., & Adamson, L. B. (1990). !Kung infancy: The social context of object exploration. *Child Development, 61*, 794-809.

Baker, B. L., & Brightman, A. J. (1989). *Steps to independence: A skills training guide for parents and teachers of children with special needs* (2nd ed.). Baltimore: Paul H. Brookes.

Baldwin, B. A. (October). Puberty and parents: Understanding your early adolescent. *PACE*, pp. 13, 15-19.

Baldwin, J. M. (1906). *Mental development in the child and the race: Methods and processes* (3rd ed.). New York: Macmillan.

Bandura, A. (1964). The stormy decade: Fact or fiction. *Psychology in the Schools, 1*, 224-231.

Bandura, A. (1977). *Social learning theory*. Englewood Cliffs, NJ: Prentice Hall.

Bandura, A. (1982). The psychology of chance encounters and life paths. *American Psychologist, 37*, 747-755.

Bandura, A. (1986). *Social foundations of thought and action*. Englewood Cliffs, NJ: Prentice Hall.

Bandura, A., & Walters, R. H. (1959). *Adolescent aggression*. New York: Ronald Press.

Bandura, A., & Walters, R. H. (1963). *Social learning and personality development*. New York: Holt, Rinehart & Winston.

Bandura, A., Ross, D., & Ross, S. A. (1963). Imitation of film-mediated aggressive models. *Journal of Abnormal and Social Psychology, 66*, 3-11.

Banks, M. S., & Salapatek, P. (1983). Infant visual perception. In P. H. Mussen (Ed.), *Handbook of child psychology* (4th ed.). New York: Wiley.

Banks, M., & Dannemiller, J. (1987). Infant visual psychophysics. In P. Salapatek & L. Cohen (Eds.), *Handbook of infant perception: Vol. 1. From sensation to perception*. New York: Academic Press.

Barbero, G. (1983). Failure to thrive. In M. Klaus, T. Leger, & M. Trause (Eds.), *Maternal attachment and mothering disorders*. New Brunswick, NJ: Johnson & Johnson.

Barker, R. G., Dembo, T., & Lewin, K. (1943). Frustration and regression. In R. G. Barker, J. S. Kounin, & H. F. Wright (Eds.), *Child behavior and development*. New York: McGraw-Hill.

Barnes, D. M. (1989). ``Fragile X'' syndrome and its puzzling genetics. *Research News*, pp. 171-172.

Barnes, H. L., & Olsen, D. H. (1985). Parent-adolescent communication and the circumplex model. *Child Development, 56*, 438-447.

Baruch, G. K., & Barnett, R. C. (1986). *Consequences of fathers' participation in family work: Parent role strain and well-being* (Working Paper No. 159). Wellesley, MA: Wellesley College Center for Research on Women.

Bass, J. L., Brennan, P., Mehta, K. A., & Kodzis, S. (1990). Pediatric problems in a suburban shelter for homeless families. *Pediatrics, 85(1)*, 33-37.

Bassuk, E. L. & Rosenberg, L. (1990). Psychosocial characteristics of homeless children and children with homes. *Pediatrics, 85(3)*, 257.

Bassuk, E. L. (December 1991). Homeless families. *Scientific American*, 66-74.

Bates, E., O'Connell, B., & Shore, C. (1987). Language and communication in infancy. In J. D. Osofsy (Ed.), *Handbook of infant development* (2nd ed.). New York: Wiley.

Bates, J. E. (1987). Temperament in infancy. In J. D. Osofsky (Ed.), *Handbook of infant development* (2nd ed., pp. 1101-1149). New York: Wiley.

Bateson, G. (1955). A theory of play and fantasy. *Psychiatric Research Reports, 2*, 39-51.

Bauer, P. J., & Thal, D. J. (1990). Scripts or scraps: Reconsidering the development of sequential understanding. *Journal of Experimental Child Psychology, 50*, 287-304.

Baumrind, D. (1972). Socialization and instrumental competence in young children. In W. W. Hartup (Ed.), *The young child: Reviews of research* (Vol. 2). Washington, DC: National Association for the Education of Young Children.

Baumrind, D. (1975). *Early socialization and the discipline controversy*. Morristown, NJ: General Learning Press.

Baumrind, D. (1978). A dialectical materialist's perspective on knowing social reality. *New Directions for Child Development, 2*.

Baumrind, D. (1980). New directions in socialization research. *American Psychologist, 35*, 639-650.

Baumrind, D. (1987). A developmental perspective on adolescent risk-taking in contemporary America. *New Directions for Child Development, 37*, 93-125.

Baumrind, D. (1991). The influence of parenting style on adolescent competence and substance use. *Journal of Early Adolescence, 11(1)*, 56-95.

Baydar, N. & Brooks-Gunn, J. (1991). Effects of maternal employment and child-care arrangements on preschoolers' cognitive and behavioral outcomes: Evidence from the children of the National Longitudinal Survey of Youth. *Developmental Psychology, 27(6)*, 932-945.

Bayley, N. (1965). Research in child development: A longitudinal perspective. *Merrill-Palmer Quarterly, 11*, 183-208.

Bayley, N. (1969). *Bayley scales of infant development*. New York: Psychological Corporation.

Beal, C. R. (1987). Repairing the message: Children's monitoring and revision skills. *Child Development, 58*, 401-408.

Beck, M. (August 15, 1988). Miscarriages. *Newsweek*, pp. 46-49.

Becker, J. (1993). Young children's numerical use of number words: counting in many-to-one situations. *Developmental Psychology, 29(3)*, 458-465.

Becker, W. C. (1964). Consequences of different kinds of parental discipline. In M. L. Hoffman (Ed.), *Review of child developmental research* (Vol. 1). New York: Russell Sage Foundation.

Beckwith, L., & Cohen, S. E. (1989). Maternal responsiveness with preterm infants and later competency. In M. H. Bornstein (Ed.), *New Directions for Child Development; Vol. 43. Maternal responsiveness: Characteristics and consequences*. San Francisco: Jossey-Bass.

Behrman, R. E. (1992). Introduction. *The future of children: U.S. health care for children. 2(2)*. Los Angeles, CA: The David and Lucile Packard Foundation.

Beit-Hallahmi, B., & Rabin, A. (1977). The kibbutz as a social experiment and as a child-rearing laboratory. *American Psychologist, 32*, 532-541.

Belknap, P. & Leonard, W. M. (1991). A conceptual replication and extension of Erving Goffman's study of gender advertisements. *Sex Roles, 35(3/4)*, 103-120.

Bell, S. M., & Ainsworth, M. D. (1972). Infant crying and maternal responsiveness. *Child Development, 43*, 1171-1190.

Bellugi, U. (December 1970). Learning the language. *Psychology Today*, pp. 32-38.

Belsky, J. (1980). Child maltreatment: An ecological integration. *American Psychologist, 35*, 320-335.

Belsky, J. (1984). *The psychology of aging: Theory and research and practice*. Monterey, CA: Brooks/Cole.

Belsky, J. (1986). Infant day care: A cause for concern? *Zero to Three, 6*, 1-7.

Belsky, J. (February 1987). Risks remain. *Zero to Three*, pp. 22-24.

Belsky, J., & Rovine, M. (1988). Nonmaternal care in the first year of life and the security of infant-parent attachment. *Child Development, 59*, 157-167.

Belsky, J., & Rovine, M. (1990a). Q-sort security and first-year non-maternal care. In *New Directions for Child Development: Vol. 49. Child care and maternal employment: A social ecology approach* (pp. 7-22).

Belsky, J., & Rovine, M. (1990b). Patterns of marital change across the transition to parenthood: Pregnancy to three years postpartum. *Journal of Marriage and the Family, 52,* 5-19.

Belsky, J., Rovine, M., & Taylor, D. (1984). The Pennsylvania infant and family development project III. The origins of individual differences in infant-mother attachment: Maternal and infant contributions. *Child Development, 58,* 718-728.

Bem, S. (1985). Androgyny and gender schema theory: A conceptual and empirical integration. In T. B. Sondegegger (Ed.), *Nebraska Symposium on Motivation, 1984: Psychology and gender.* Lincoln: University of Nebraska.

Bem, S. L. (September 1975). Androgyny vs. the tight little lives of fluffy women and chesty men. *Psychology Today,* pp. 59-62.

Benbow, C. P. (1986). Physiological correlates of extreme intellectual precocity. *Neuropsychologia, 24,* 719-725.

Bender, B. G., Linden, M. G. & Robinson, A. (1987). Environment & developmental risk in children with sex chromosome abnormalities. *Journal of the Academy of Child and Adolescent Psychiatry, 26,* 499-503.

Bennett, N. (1976). *Teaching styles and pupil progress.* Cambridge, MA: Harvard University Press.

Bennett, S. C., Robinson, N. M., & Sells, C. J. (1983). Growth and development of infants weighing less than 800 grams at birth. *Pediatrics, 7*(3), 319-323.

Bereiter, C., & Engelmann, S. (1966). *Teaching disadvantaged children in the preschool.* Englewood Cliffs, NJ: Prentice Hall.

Berk, L. E. (1986). Relationship of elementary school children's private speech to behavioral accompaniment to task, attention and task performance. *Developmental Psychology, 22*(5), 671-680.

Berk, L. E. (July 1985). Why children talk to themselves. *Young Children,* pp. 46-52.

Berko, J. (1958). The child's learning of English morphology. *Word, 14,* 150-177.

Bernard, J. (1981). The good-provider role: Its rise and fall. *American Psychologist, 36,* 1-12.

Berndt, T. (1983). Social cognition, social behavior and children's friendships. In E. T. Higgins, D. Ruble, & W. Hartup, *Social cognition and social development: A socio-cultural perspective.* Cambridge, MA: Cambridge University Press.

Berndt, T. J. (1982). The features and effects of friendship in early adolescence. *Child Development, 53,* 1447-1460.

Berndt, T. J., Cheung, P. C., Lau, S., Hau, K-L., & Lew, W. J. F. (1993). Perceptions of parenting in mainland China, Taiwan and Hong Kong: Sex Differences and Societal Differences. *Developmental Psychology, 29(1),* 156-164.

Berney, B. (1993). Round and round it goes: The epidemiology of childhood lead poisoning, 1950-1990. *The Milbank Quarterly, 71(1),* 3-39.

Bertenthal, B. I., & Campos, J. J. (1987). New directions in the study of early experience. *Child Development, 58,* 560-567.

Binet, A., & Simon, T. (1905). Methodes nouvelles pour le diagnostic du niveau intellectuel des anormaux. *L'Annee Psychologique, 11,* 191-244.

Binet, A., & Simon, T. (1916). *The development of intelligence in children.* (E. S. Kite, Trans.). Baltimore: Williams & Wilkins.

Birch, H. G. & Gussow, J. D. (1970). *Disadvantaged children: health, nutrition, and school failure.* New York: Harcourt, Brace and World.

Birch, H. G., & Gussow, J. D. (1970). *Disadvantaged children: Health, nutrition and school failure.* New York: Harcourt Brace Jovanovich.

BIRTH. (June 1988). Report for American College of Obstetricians and Gynecologists. *BIRTH, 15*(2), 113.

Bjorklund, D. F. & Green, B. L. (1992). The adaptive nature of cognitive immaturity. *American Psychologist, 47*(1), 46-54.

Bjorklund, D. F. (1988). Acquiring a mnemonic: Age and category knowledge effects. *Journal of Experimental Child Psychology, 45,* 71-87.

Blake, J. (1989). Number of siblings and educational attainment. *Science, 245,* 32-36.

Blendon, R. J. & Edwards, J. N. (Eds.), *The future of American health care, system in crisis: The case for health care reform.* Vol. 1. Washington, DC: Faulkner & Gray.

Bloom, B. S. (1964). *Stability and change in human characteristics.* New York: Wiley.

Bloom, B. S., & Krathwohl, D. R. (1956). *Taxonomy of educational objectives: Handbook I: The cognitive domain.* New York: McKay.

Bloom, L. (1970). *Language development: Form and function in emerging grammars.* Cambridge, MA: MIT Press.

Bloom, L., & Lahey, M. (1978). *Language development and language disorders.* New York: Wiley.

Bloom, L., Lifter, K., & Broughton, J. (1985). The convergence of early cognition and language in the second year of life: Problems in conceptualization and measurement. In M. Barrett (Ed.), *Children's single-word speech.* New York: Wiley.

Blyth, D., Bulcroft, A. R., & Simmons, R. G. (1981). *The impact of puberty on adolescents: A longitudinal study.* Paper presented at the annual meeting of the American Psychological Association, Los Angeles.

Boccia, M., & Campos, J. J. (1989). Maternal emotional signals, social referencing, and infants' reactions to strangers. In N. Eisenberg (Ed.), *New Directions for Child Development: Vol. 44. Empathy and related emotional responses.* (pp. 25-50).

Bohannon, J. N., Jr., & Hirsh-Pasek, K. (1984). Do children say as they're told? A new perspective on motherese. In L. Feagans, C. Garvey, & R. Golinkoff (Eds.), *The origins and growth of communication.* Norwood, NJ: Ablex.

Bonvillain, N. (1993). *Language, culture and communication.* Englewood Cliffs, NJ: Prentice-Hall.

Borke, H. (1971). Interpersonal perception of young children: Egocentrism or empathy. *Developmental Psychology, 5,* 263-269.

Borke, H. (1973). The development of empathy in Chinese and American children between 3 and 6 years of age: A cross-cultural study. *Developmental Psychology, 9,* 102-108.

Bornstein, M. (Ed.). (1987). *Sensitive periods in development: Interdisciplinary perspectives.* Hillsdale, NJ: Erlbaum.

Bornstein, M. H. (1978). Chromatic vision in infancy. In H. W. Reese & L. P. Lipsett (Eds.), *Advances in child development and behavior* (Vol. 12). New York: Academic Press.

Bornstein, M. H. (Ed.). (1989). *Maternal responsiveness: Characteristics and consequences.* San Francisco: Jossey-Bass.

Bornstein, M. H., & Bruner J. (1986). *Interaction in human development.* Hillsdale, NJ: Erlbaum.

Bornstein, M. H., & Tamis-LeMonda, C. S. (1989). Maternal responsiveness and cognitive development in children. In M. H. Bornstein (Ed.), *New Directions for Child Development: Vol. 43. Maternal responsiveness: Characteristics and consequences* (pp. 49-62).

Bossard, J. H. S., & Boll, E. S. (1960). *The sociology of child development.* New York: Harper & Brothers.

Botwinick, J. (1977). Intellectual abilities. In J. Birren & K. W. Schaie (Eds.), *Handbook of the psychology of aging.* New York: Van Nostrand Reinhold.

Botwinick, J. (1984). *Aging and behavior: A comprehensive integration of research findings* (3rd ed.). New York: Springer.

Bouchard, R. J., Jr. (June 25, 1987). Environmental determinants of IQ similarity in identical twins reared apart. Paper presented at the 17th annual meeting of the Behavior Genetics Association, Minneapolis, MN.

Bouchard, T. J., Jr., Lykken, D. T., McGue, M., Segal, N., & Tellegen, A. (1990). Sources of human psychological differences: The Minnesota study of twins reared apart. *Science, 250,* 223-228.

Bower, B. (1991). Emotional aid delivers labor-saving results. *Science News, 139*, 277.

Bower, T. G. R. (1974). *Development in infancy*. San Francisco: Freeman.

Bower, T. G. R. (October 1971). The object in the world of the infant. *Scientific American*, pp. 30-38.

Bowlby, J. (1960). Separation anxiety. *International Journal of Psychoanalysis, 41*, 89-113.

Bowlby, J. (1973). *Attachment and loss: Vol. 2. Separation*. New York: Basic Books.

Bowlby, J. (1980). *Attachment and loss: Vol. 3. Loss, sadness and depression*. New York: Basic Books.

Bowlby, J. (1982). *Attachment and loss: Vol. 1. Attachment* (2nd ed.). New York: Basic Books.

Bowlby, J. (1988). *A secure base*. New York: Basic Books.

Brackbill, Y. (1979). Obstetrical medication and infant behavior. In J. Osofsky (Ed.), *Handbook of infant development*. New York: Wiley.

Brackbill, Y., & Nevill, D. (1981). Parental expectations of achievement as affected by children's height. *Merrill-Palmer Quarterly, 27*, 429-441.

Brackbill, Y., McManus, K., & Woodward, L. (1985). *Medication in maternity: Infant exposure and maternal information*. International Academy for Research on Learning Disabilities. Monographs, Series Number 2. Ann Arbor: University of Michigan Press.

Bradshaw, J. (1989). *Hemispheric specialization and psychological function*. New York: Wiley.

Braine, M. D. S. (1963). The ontogeny of English phrase structure: The first phase. *Language, 39*, 1-13.

Brand, H. J., & Welch, K. (1989). Cognitive and social-emotional development of children in different preschool environments. *Psychological Reports, 65*, 480-482.

Brassard, M. R., & McNeill, L. E. (1987). Child sexual abuse. In M. Brassard, R. Germain, & S. Hart (Eds.), *Psychological maltreatment of children and youth*. New York: Pergamon.

Brazelton, T. B. (1969). *Infants and mothers: Differences in development*. New York: Dell.

Brazelton, T. B. (1973). *Neonatal behavioral assessment scale*. London: Heinemann.

Brazelton, T. B., Nugent, J. K., & Lester, B. M. (1987). Neonatal behavioral assessment scale. In J. Osofsky (Ed.), *Handbook of infant development* (2nd ed., pp. 780-817). New York: Wiley.

Brazelton, T. B., Yogman, M., Als, H., & Tronick, E. (1979). The infant as a focus for family reciprocity. In M. Lewis & L. A. Rosenblum (Eds.)., *The child and his family*. New York: Plenum.

Brenner, A. (1984). *Helping children cope with stress*. Lexington, MA: D. C. Heath.

Bretherton, I., & Waters, E. (Eds.). (1985). Growing points of attachment. *Monographs of the Society for Research in Child Development, 50*(1-2), Serial 209.

Bretl, D. J. & Cantor, J. (1988). The portrayal of men and women in U.S. television commercials: A recent content analysis and trends over 15 years. *Sex Roles, 18*, 9-10.

Briesemeister, L. A., & Haines, B. A. (1988). The interactions of fathers and newborns. In K. L. Michaelson (Ed.), *Childbirth in America: Anthropological perspectives*. South Hadley, MA: Bergin & Garvey.

Briggs, G. C., Freeman, R. K., & Yaffe, S. J. (1986). *Drugs in pregnancy and lactation* (2nd ed.). Baltimore: Williams & Wilkins.

Briggs, J. L. (Winter 1992). Mazes of meaning: How a child and a culture create each other. *New Directions for Child Development, 58*, 25-49.

Broman, S. (1986). Obstetric medication: A review of the literature on outcomes in infancy and childhood. In Michael Lewis (Ed.), *Learning disabilities and prenatal risk*. Urbana: University of Illinois Press.

Bronfenbrenner, U. & Crouter, A. C. (1983). The evolution of environmental models of developmental research. In P. H. Mussen, (Ed.), *The Handbook of child psychology*. New York: John Wiley.

Bronfenbrenner, U. (1970). *Two worlds of childhood: U.S. and U.S.S.R.* New York: Russell Sage Foundation.

Bronfenbrenner, U. (1972). *Two worlds of childhood: U.S. and U.S.S.R.* New York: Simon and Schuster.

Bronfenbrenner, U. (1979). *The ecology of human development*. Cambridge, MA: Harvard University Press.

Bronfenbrenner, U. (1979). *The ecology of human development: Experiments by nature and design*. Cambridge, MA: Harvard University Press.

Bronfenbrenner, U. (1989). Ecological systems theory. In R. Vasta (Ed.), *Annals of Child Development*. (Vol. 6, pp. 187-251). Greenwich, CT: JAI Press.

Bronson, G. (1978). Aversion reactions to strangers: A dual process interpretation. *Child Development, 49*, 495-499.

Bronson, W. C. (1981). Toddlers' behavior with agemates: Issues of interaction and cognition and affect. In L. P. Lipset (Ed.), *Monographs on Infancy* (Vol. 1). Norwood, NJ: Ablex.

Brooks, R. L., & Obrzut, J. E. (1981). Brain lateralization: Implications for infant stimulation and development. *Young Children, 26*, 9-16.

Brooks-Gunn, J., & Furstenberg, F. F., Jr. (1986). The children of adolescent mothers: Physical, academic, and psychological outcomes. *Developmental Review, 6*, 224-251.

Brooks-Gunn, J., & Furstenberg, F. F., Jr. (1989). Adolescent sexual behavior. *American Psychologist, 44*, 249-257.

Brophy, J. (1986). Teacher influences on student achievement. *American Psychologist, 41*, 1069-1077.

Broughton, J. (1977). Beyond formal operations: Theoretical thought in adolescence. *Teacher's College Record, 79*, 88-97.

Broussard, E. R. (1989). The infant-family resource program: Facilitating optimal development. *Prevention in Human Services, 6*(2), 179-224.

Brown, B. B., & Lohr, M. J. (1987). Peer-group affiliation and adolescent self-esteem: An integration of ego-identity and symbolic-interaction theories. *Journal of Personality and Social Psychology, 52*, 47-55.

Brown, B. B., Clasen, D. R., & Eicher, S. A. (1986). Perceptions of peer pressure, peer conformity dispositions, and self-reported behavior among adolescents. *Developmental Psychology, 22*, 521-530.

Brown, J. D. & Newcomer, S. F. (1991). Television viewing and adolescents' sexual behavior. *Research on Adolescent Sexual Socialization*.

Brown, R. (1965). *Social psychology*. New York: Free Press.

Brown, R. (1973). *A first language: The early stages*. Cambridge, MA: Harvard University Press.

Brown, R. W. (1973). *A first language: The early stages*. Cambridge, MA: Harvard University Press.

Brownell, C. A., & Carriger, M. S. (1990). Changes in cooperation and self-other differentiation during the second year. *Child Development, 61*, 1164-1174.

Bruck, M. (1987). The adult outcomes of children with learning disabilities. *Annals of Dyslexia, 37*, 252-263.

Bruner, J. (1983). *Child's talk*. New York: Norton.

Bruner, J. S. (1960). *The process of education*. Cambridge, MA: Harvard University Press.

Bruner, J. S. (1971). *The relevance of education*. New York: Norton.

Bruner, J. S. (1973). *Beyond the information given: Studies in the psychology of knowing*. New York: Norton.

Bruner, J. S., & Olver, R. R., & Greenfield, P. M. (1966). *Studies in cognitive growth*. New York: Wiley.

Bruner, J., & Haste, H. (Eds.). (1987). *Making sense: The child's construction of the world*. London & New York: Methuen.

Bryan, J. H. (1975). Children's cooperation and helping behaviors. In E. M. Hetherington (Ed.), *Review of child development* (Vol. 5). Chicago: University of Chicago Press.

Buchanan, C. M., Eccles, J. S., & Becker, J. B. (1992). Are adolescents the victims of raging hormones: Evidence for activational effects of hormones on moods and behavior at adolescence. *Psychological Bulletin, 111*(1), 62-107.

Buchoff, R. (Winter 1990). Attention deficit disorder: help for the classroom teacher. *Childhood Education, 67*(2), 86-90.

Buck, G. M., Cookfair, D. L., Michalek, A. M., Nasca, P. C., Standfast, S. J., Sever, L. E., & Karmer, A. A. (1989). Interuterine growth retardation and risk of sudden infant death syndrome (SIDS), *American Journal of Epidemiology, 129*, 874-884.

Buis, J. M., & Thompson, D. N. (1989). Imaginary audience and personal fable: A brief review. *Adolescence, 24*, 773-781.

Bulterys, M. G., Greenland, S., & Kraus, J. F. (1989). Cigarettes and pregnancy. *Pediatrics, 86*(4), 535-540.

Bulterys, M. G., Greenland, S., & Kraus, J. F. (October 1990). Chronic fetal hypoxia and sudden infant death syndrome: Interaction between maternal smoking and low hematocrit during pregnancy. *Pediatrics, 86*(4), 535-540.

Burgess, R. L., & Conger, R. D. (1978). Family interaction in abusive, neglectful, and normal families. *Child Development, 49*, 1163-1173.

Buri, J. R., Louiselle, P. A., Misukanis, T. M., & Mueller, R. A. (1988). Effects of parental authoritarianism and authoritativeness on self-esteem. *Personality and Social Psychology Bulletin, 14*, 271-282.

Bush, P. J. & Iannotti, R. J. (1993). Alcohol, cigarette and marijuana use among fourth-grade urban schoolchildren in 1988/89 and 1990/91. *American Journal of Public Health, 83*(1), 111-114.

Buss, A. H., & Plomin, R. (1984). *Temperament: Early developing personality traits.* Hillsdale, NJ: Erlbaum.

Butler, R. N. (1968). The life review: An interpretation of reminiscence in the aged. In B. L. Neugarten (Ed.), *Middle age and aging.* Chicago: University of Chicago Press.

Caldas, S. J. (1993). Current theoretical perspectives on adolescent pregnancy and childbearing in the United States. *Journal of Adolescent Research, 8*(1), 4-20.

Campbell, M., & Spencer, E. K. (1988). Psychopharmacology in child and adolescent psychiatry: A review of the past five years. *Journal of the American Academy of Child and Adolescent Psychiatry, 27*, 269-279.

Campos, J. J., Langer, A., & Krowitz, A. (1970). Cardiac responses on the visual cliff in prelocomotor human infants. *Science, 170*, 196-197.

Canino, I. A. Canino, G. (1980). Impact of stress on the Puerto Rican family: treatment considerations. *American Journal of Orthopsychiatry, 50*, 535-541.

Cantor, J., & Wilson, B. J. (1988). Helping children cope with frightening media presentations. *Current Psychology: Research and Reviews, 7*(1), 58-75.

Capelli, C. A., Nakagawa, N., & Madden, C. M. (1990). How children understand sarcasm: The role of context and intonation. *Child Development, 61*, 1824-1841.

Card, J. J., & Wise, L. L. (1978). Teenage mothers and teenage fathers: The impact of early childbearing on the parents' personal and professional lives. *Family Planning Perspectives, 10*, 199-205.

Carlson, C. I., Cooper, C. R. & Spradling, V. Y. (Spring 1991). Developmental implications of shared versus distinct perceptions of the family in early adolescence. *New Directions for Child Development, 51*, 13-30.

Carlson, C. I., Cooper, C. R., & Spradling, V. Y. (1991). Developmental implications of shared versus distant perspectives of the family in early adolescence. *New Directions in Child Development, 51*, 13-31.

Carpenter, G. (1974). Mother's face and the newborn. *New Scientist, 61*, 742-744.

Caspi, A. (1987). Personality in the life course. *Journal of Personality and Social Psychology, 53*, 1203-1213.

Caspi, A., Elder, G. H., Jr., & Bem, D. J. (1987). Moving against the world: Life-course patterns of explosive children. *Developmental Psychology, 23*, 308-313.

Cassidy, J. (1986). The ability to negotiate the environment: An aspect of infant competence as related to quality of attachment. *Child Development, 57*, 331-337.

Cataldo, M. F., Dershewitz, R. A., Wilson, M., Christophersen, E. R., Finney, J. W., Fawcett, S. B., & Seekins, T. (1986). Childhood injury control. In N. A., Krasnegor, J. D., Arasteh, & M. F. Cataldo, (Eds.), *Child health behavior: A behavioral pediatrics perspective.* New York: Wiley-Interscience, 217-253.

Caudill, W., & Weinstein, H. (1969). Maternal care and infant behavior in Japan and America. *Psychiatry, 32*, 12-43.

Chan, M. (1987). Sudden Infant Death Syndrome and families at risk. *Pediatric Nursing, 13*(3), 166-168.

Chapman, K. L., & Mervis, C. B. (1989). Patterns of object-name extension in production. *Journal of Child Language, 16*, 561-571.

Charlesworth, W. (1988). Resources and resource acquisition during ontogeny. In K. B. MacDonald (Ed.), *Sociobiological perspectives on human development.* New York: Springer-Verlag.

Chasnoff, I. J. (1989). Cocaine, pregnancy and the neonate. *Women and Health, 5*(3), 33.

Chesnick, M., Menyuk, P., Liebergott, J., Ferrier, L., & Strand, K. (April 1983). *Who leads whom?* Paper presented at the meeting of the Society for Research in Child Development, Detroit.

Chess, S. (1967). Temperament in the normal infant. In J. Hellmuth (Ed.), *The exceptional infant* (Vol. 1). Seattle: Special Child Publications.

Chess, S. (February 1987). Comments: ``Infant day care: A cause for concern.'' *Zero to Three*, pp. 24-25.

Children's Defense Fund. (1991). *The state of America's children, 1991.* Washington, DC: Children's Defense Fund.

Children's Defense Fund. (1992). *The State of America's Children 1992.* Washington, DC: Children's Defense Fund.

Children's Safety Network. (1991). *A data book of child and adolescent injury.* Washington, DC: National Center for Education in Maternal and Child Health.

Chilman, C. (1979). *Adolescent sexuality in changing American society.* Washington, DC: Government Printing Office.

Chomsky, C. (1969). *The acquisition of syntax from 5 to 10.* Cambridge, MA: MIT Press.

Chomsky, N. (1959). Review of *Verbal Behavior* by B. F. Skinner, *Language, 35*, 26-58.

Chomsky, N. (1975). *Reflections on language.* New York: Pantheon.

Chukovsky, K. (1963). *From two to five.* (M. Morton Ed. & Trans.). Berkeley: University of California Press.

CìtÇ, J. E., & Levine, C. (1988). A critical examination of the ego identity status paradigm. *Developmental Review, 8*, 147-184.

Clark, E. A. & Honisee, J. (1982). Intellectual and adaptive performance of Asian children in adoptive American settings. *Developmental Psychology, 18*, 595-599.

Clark, E. V. (1983). Meaning and concepts. In P. H. Mussen (Ed.), *Handbook of child psychology* (4th ed., Vol. 4). New York: Wiley.

Clark, E. V. (1987). The principle of contrast: A constraint on acquisition. In B. Macwhinner (Ed.), *Mechanisms of language acquisition.* Hillsdale, NJ: Erlbaum.

Clark, J. E., & Phillips, S. J. (1985). A developmental sequence of the standing long jump. In J. E. Clark & J. H. Humphrey (Eds.), *Motor development: Current selected research.* Princeton, NJ: Princeton Book Company.

Clark, J. E., Phillips, S. J. & Peterson, R. (1989). Developmental stability in jumping. *Developmental Psychology, 25*(6), 929-935.

Clark, K. (May 31, 1957). *Present threats to children and youth.* Draft Report, manuscript in the office of the National Committee on the Employment of Youth, New York City.

Clark-Stewart, A. (1988). Parent's effects on children's development: A decade of progress? *Journal of Applied Developmental Psychology, 9*, 41-84.

Clarke-Stewart, A. (1982). *Daycare.* Cambridge, MA: Harvard University Press.

Clarke-Stewart, K. A. (1978). And daddy makes three: The father's impact on mother and young child. *Child Development, 49,* 466-478.

Clarke-Stewart, K. A., & Fein, G. C. (1983). Early childhood programs. In M. Haith & J. Campos (Eds.), *Handbook of child psychology: Vol. 2. Infancy and developmental psychobiology* (4th ed.). New York: Wiley.

Clarke-Stewart, K. A., & Nevey, C. M. (1981). Longitudinal relations in repeated observations of mother-child interaction from 1 to 2-1/2 years. *Developmental Psychology, 17,* 127-145.

Cohen, L. B., & Gelber, E. R. (1975). Infant visual memory. In L. B. Cohen & P. Salapatek (Eds.), *Infant perception: From sensation to cognition* (Vol. 1). New York: Academic Press.

Cohen, N. & Estner, L. (1983). *Silent knife: Caesarean prevention and vaginal birth after Caesarean.* South Hadley, MA: Bergin & Garvey.

Colby, A., Kohlberg, L., Gibbs, J., & Lieberman, M. (1983). A longitudinal study of moral development. *Monographs of the Society for Research in Child Development, 48* (1-2 Serial No. 200).

Coles, R. (1968). Like it is in the alley. *Daedalus, 97,* 1315-1330.

Coles, R. (1980). *Children of crisis: Privileged ones.* Boston: Atlantic-Little, Brown.

Collins, W. A. (Spring 1991). Shared views and parent-adolescent relationships. *New Directions for Child Development, 51,* 103-110.

Collins, W. A., Sobol, B. L., & Westby, S. (1981). Effects of adult commentary on children's comprehension and inferences about a televised aggressive portrayal. *Child Development, 52,* 158-163.

Comber, L. C., & Keeves, J. (1973). *Science achievement in nineteen countries.* New York: Wiley.

Comer, J. P., & Poussaint, A. F. (1975). *Black child care.* New York: Simon & Schuster.

Committee for Economic Development. (1987). *Children in need.* Washington, DC: Committee for Economic Development, Research and Policy Committee.

Connelly, B., Johnston, D., Brown, I. D. R., Mackay, S., & Blackstock, E. G. (1993). The prevalence of depression in a high school population. *Adolescence, 28*(109), 149-158.

Copple, C. E., Cline, M. G., & Smith, A. N. (1987). *Path to the future: Long-term effects of Head Start in the Philadelphia school district.* Washington, DC: Office of Human Development Services.

Coren, S. & Porac, C. (1980). Birth factors and laterality: The effect of birth order, parental age, and birth stress on four indices of lateral preference. *Behavioral Genetics, 10,* 123-138.

Costa, A. (Ed.). (1985). *Developing minds: A resource book for teaching thinking.* Washington, DC: Association for Supervision and Curriculum Development.

Costa, A., Hanson, R., Silver, H., & Strong, R. (1985). Building a repertoire of strategies. In A. Costa (Ed.), *Developing minds: A resource book for teaching thinking.* Washington, DC: Association for Supervision and Curriculum Development.

Coster, G. (November 1972). *Scientific American,* p. 44.

Council of Economic Advisers. (1987). *The economic report of the president.* Washington, DC.

Council of Economic Advisers. (1990). *The economic report of the president.* Washington, DC.

Cowan, P. A., & Walters, R. H. (1963). Studies of reinforcement of aggression: I. Effects of scheduling. *Child Development, 34,* 543-551.

Craig, G. J., & Garney, P. (1972). *Attachment and separation behavior in the second and third years.* Unpublished manuscript. University of Massachusetts, Amherst.

Cratty, B. (1986). *Perceptual and motor development in infants and children.* Englewood Cliffs, NJ: Prentice-Hall.

Cratty, B. J. (1970). *Perceptual and motor development in infants and children.* New York: Macmillan.

Crawford, J. W. (1982). Mother-infant interaction in premature and full-term infants. *Child Development, 53,* 957-962.

Crider, C. (1981). Children's conceptions of body interior. In R. Bibace & M. E. Walsh (Eds.), *Children's conceptions of health, illness, and bodily functions.* San Francisco: Jossey-Bass.

Crockenberg, S. (1981). Infant irritability, mother responsiveness, and social support influences on the security of infant-mother attachment. *Child Development, 52,* 857-865.

Crockenberg, S., & McCluskey, K. (1986). Change in maternal behavior during the baby's first year of life. *Child Development, 57,* 746-753.

Crowell, J., Keener, M., Ginsburg, N., & Anders, T. (1987). Sleep habits in toddlers 18 to 36 months old. *Journal of the American Academy of Child and Adolescent Psychiatry, 26*(4), 510-515.

Cruickshank, W. M. (1977). Myths and realities in learning disabilities. *Learning Disabilities, 10*(1), 57-64.

Csikszentmihalyi, M., & Larson, R. (1984). *Being adolescent.* New York: Basic Books.

Cutrona, C., & Troutman, B. (1986). Social support, infant temperament, and parenting self-efficacy: A mediational model of postpartum depression. *Child Development, 57,* 1507-1518.

Daley, S. (January 9, 1991). Girls self-esteem is lost on the way to adolescence, new study finds. *New York Times Magazine.*

Damasio, A. R., & Damasio, H. (1992). Brain and language. *Scientific American, 9,* 89-95.

Damon, W., & Hart, D. (1982). The development of self-understanding from infancy through adolescence. *Child Development, 53,* 841-864.

Dansereau, H. K. (1961). Work and the teen-ager. *Annals of the American Academy of Political and Social Sciences, 338,* 44-52.

Dargassies, S. S. (1986). *The neuromotor and psychoaffective development of the infant* (English language edition.). Amsterdam, the Netherlands: Elsevier.

Darling, N., & Steinberg, L. (1993). Parenting style as context: An integrative model. *Psychological Bulletin, 113*(3), 487-496.

de Boysson-Bardies, B., Halle, P., Sagart, L., & Durand, C. (1989). A crosslinguistic investigation of vowel formants in babbling. *Journal of Child Language, 16,* 1-17.

de Villiers, P. A., & de Villiers, J. G. (1979). *Early language.* Cambridge, MA: Harvard University Press.

Dean, P. G. (1986). Monitoring an apneic infant: Impact on the infant's mother. *Maternal-Child Nursing Journal, 15,* 65-76.

DeCasper, A. J., & Spence, M. (1992). Auditorily mediated behavior during the perinatal period: A cognitive view. In *Newborn attention: biological constraints and the influence of experience.* Norwood, NJ: Ablex.

DeCharms, R., & Moeller, G. H. (1962). Values expressed in American children's readers: 1800-1950. *Journal of Abnormal and Social Psychology, 64,* 136-142.

DeLoache, J. S., Cassidy, D. J., & Brown, A. L. (1985). Precursors of mnemonic strategies in very young children's memory. *Child Development, 56,* 125-137.

DeLuccie, M. F. & Davis, A. J. (1992). Father-child relationships from the preschool years through mid-adolescence. *The Journal of Genetic Psychology, 152*(2), 225-238.

DeMause, L. (Ed.). (1974). *The history of childhood.* New York: Psychohistory Press.

DeMott, R. K., & Sandmire, H. F. (1990). *The Green Bay Caesarean section study: The physician factor as a determinant of Caesarean birth rates.* Presented at the fifty-seventh annual meeting of the Central Association of Obstetricians and Gynecologists, Scottsdale, AZ.

Dencik, L. (1989). Growing up in the post-modern age: On the child's situation in the modern family, and on the position of the family in the modern welfare state. *Acta Sociologica, 32,* 155-180.

Dennis, W. (1960). Causes of retardation among institutional children: Iran. *Journal of Genetic Psychology, 96,* 47-59.

Dennis, W. (1966a). Causes of retardation among institutional children: Iran. *Journal of Genetic Psychology, 96,* 47-59.

Dennis, W. (1973). *Children of the creche.* New York: Appleton-Century-Crofts.

Dennis, W., & Najarian, P. (1957). Infant development under environmental handicap. *Psychological Monographs, 717* (Whole No. 436).

Dewey, J. (1961). *Democracy and education.* New York: Macmillan.

Diaz, R. M. (1985). Bilingual cognitive development: Addressing three gaps in current research. *Child Development, 56,* 1376-1388.

Diaz, R. M., & Lowe, J. R. (1987). The private speech of young children at risk: A test of three deficit hypotheses. *Early Childhood Research Quarterly, 2,* 181-184.

Dick-Read, G. (1953). *Childbirth without fear.* New York: Harper & Brothers.

Dietz, W. H., Jr. (1987). Childhood obesity. *Annals of the New York Academy of Sciences, 499,* 47-54.

Ditzion, J. S., & Wolf, P. W. (1978). Beginning parenthood. In Boston Women's Book Collective (Ed.), *Ourselves and our children.* New York: Random House.

Dixon, R. A. & Lerner, R. M. (1988). A history of systems in developmental psychology. In M. Bornstein & M. Lamb (Eds.), *Developmental psychology: an advanced textbook* (2nd Edition). Hillsdale, NJ: Erlbaum.

Dodge, K. A., Coie, J. D., Pettit, G. S., & Price, J. M. (1990). Peer status and aggression in boys' groups: Developmental and contextual analyses. *Child Development, 61,* 1289-1309.

Dodwell, P., Humphrey, G. K., & Muir, D. (1987). Shape and pattern perception. In P. Salapatek & L. Cohen (Eds.), *Handbook of infant perception.* New York: Academic Press.

Dollard, J., & Miller, N. E. (1950). *Personality and psychotherapy: An analysis in terms of learning, thinking, and culture.* New York: McGraw-Hill.

Dollard, J., Doob, L. W., Miller, N. E., Mowrer, O. H., & Sears, R. R. (1939). *Frustration and aggression.* New Haven: Yale University Press.

Doman, G. (1963). *How to teach your baby to read.* New York: Random House.

Doman, G. (1984). *How to multiply our baby's intelligence.* Garden City, NY: Doubleday.

Donaldson, M. (1978). *Children's minds.* New York: Norton.

Donaldson, M. (1979). The mismatch between school and children's minds. *Human Nature, 2,* 158-162.

Donovan, B. (1986). *The Caesarean birth experience.* Boston: Beacon Press.

Donovan, J. E., Jessor, R., & Costa, F. M. (1988). Syndrome of problem behavior in adolescence: A replication. *Journal of Consulting and Clinical Psychology, 56,* 762-765.

Donovan, R. (February-March 1984). Planning for an aging work force. *Aging,* pp. 4-7.

Dornbusch, S. M., Carlsmith, J. M., Bushwall, S. J., Ritter, P. L., Leiderman, H., Hastorf, A. H., & Gross, R. T. (1985). Single parents, extended households, and the control of adolescents. *Child Development, 56,* 326-341.

Dornbusch, S. M., Ritter, P. L., Leiderman, P. H., Roberts, D. F., & Fraleigh, M. J. (1987). The relation of parenting style to adolescent school performance. *Child Development, 58,* 1244-1257.

Douvan, E., & Adelson, J. B. (1966). *The adolescent experience.* New York: Wiley.

Douvan, E., & Gold, M. (1966). Modal patterns in American adolescence. In L. W. Hoffman & M. L. Hoffman (Eds.), *Review of child development research* (Vol. 2). New York: Russell Sage Foundation.

Doyle, A. B., Beaudet, J., & Aboud, F. (1988). Developmental patterns in the flexibility of children's ethnic attitudes. *Journal of Cross-Cultural Research, 19*(1), 3-18.

Draper, T. W., & James, R. S. (1985). Preschool fears: Longitudinal sequence and cohort changes. *Child Study Journal, 15*(2), 147-155.

Dreikurs, R., & Soltz, V. (1964). *Children: The challenge.* New York: Duell, Sloan & Pearce.

Dreyer, P. H. (1982). Sexuality during adolescence. In B. Wolman (Ed.), *Handbook of developmental psychology.* Englewood Cliffs, NJ: Prentice Hall.

Drotar, D. (Ed.). (1985). *New directions in failure to thrive: Implications for research and practice.* New York: Plenum.

Dunn, J. (1983). Sibling relationships in early childhood. *Child Development, 54,* 787-811.

Dunn, J. (1985). *Sisters and brothers.* Cambridge, MA: Harvard University Press.

Dunn, J. (1986). Growing up in a family world: Issues in the study of social development of young children. In M. Richards & P. Light (Eds.), *Children of social worlds: Development in a social context.* Cambridge, MA: Harvard University Press.

Dunn, J., & Kendrick, C. (1979). Interaction between young siblings in the context of family relationships. In M. Lewis & L. Rosenblum (Eds.), *The child and its family: The genesis of behavior* (Vol. 2). New York: Plenum.

Dunn, J., & Kendrick, C. (1980). The arrival of a sibling: Changes in interaction between mother and first-born child. *Journal of Child Psychology, 21,* 119-132.

Dunn, J., & Kendrick, C. (1982). *Siblings: Love, envy and understanding.* Cambridge, MA: Harvard University Press.

Dunn, J., & Munn, P. (1987). Development of justification in disputes with mother and sibling. *Developmental Psychology, 23,* 791-798.

Dunphy, D. C. (1963). The social structure of urban adolescent peer groups. *Sociometry, 26,* 230-246.

Dwyer, T., Ponsonby, A. B., Newman, N. M. & Gibbons, L. E. (1991). Prospective cohort study of prone sleeping position and sudden infant death syndrome. *The Lancet, 337,* 1244-1247.

Eakins, P. S. (Ed.), (1986). *The American way of birth.* Philadelphia: Temple University Press.

Eccles, J. S., Midgley, C., Wigfield, A., Buchanan, C. M., Reuman, D., Flanagan, C., & MacIver, D. (1993). Development during adolescence: the impact of stage-environment fit on young adolescents' experiences in schools and families. *American Psychologist, 48*(2), 90-101.

Edelstein, L. (1984). *Maternal bereavement.* New York: Praeger.

Edwards, C. P., & Gandini, L. (1989). Teachers' expectations about the timing of developmental skills: A cross-cultural study. *Young Children, 44*(4), 15-19.

Ehrhardt, A. A. (1992). Trends in sexual behavior and the HIV Pandemic. *American Journal of Public Health, 82*(11), 1459-1461.

Eibl-Eibesfeldt, I. (1989). *Human ethology.* New York: Aldine de Gruyter.

Eichorn, D. (1979). Physical development: Current foci of research. In J. D. Osofsky (Ed.), *Handbook of infant development* (pp. 253-282). New York: Wiley.

Eimas, P. D. (1974). Linguistic processing of speech by young infants. In R. L. Schiefelbusch & L. L. Lloyd (Eds.), *Language perspectives: Acquisition, retardation, and intervention.* Baltimore: University Park Press.

Eimas, P. D. (1975). Speech perception in early infancy. In Lin L. B. Cohen & P. Salapatek (Eds.), *Infant perception: From sensation to cognition* (Vol. 2), New York: Academic Press.

Eisenberg, A., Murkoff, H. E., & Hathaway, S. E. (1984). *What to expect when you're expecting.* New York: Workman Publishers.

Eisenberg, N. (1988). The development of prosocial and aggressive behavior. In M. Bornstein & M. Lamb (Eds.), *Developmental psychology: An advanced textbook* (2nd ed.). Hillsdale, NJ: Erlbaum.

Eisenberg, N. (1989). Empathy and sympathy. In W. Damon (Ed.), *Child development today and tomorrow* (pp. 137-154). San Francisco: Jossey-Bass.

Eisenberg, N. (1989a). *The development of prosocial moral reasoning in childhood and mid-adolescence.* Paper presented at the April meeting of the Society for Research in Child Development, Kansas City.

Eisenberg, N. (1989b). The development of prosocial values. In N. Eisenberg, J. Reykowski, & E. Staub (Eds.), *Social and moral values: Individual and social perspectives.* Hillsdale, NJ: Erlbaum.

Eisenberg, N., Fabes, R. A., Carlo, G., & Karbon, M. (Spring 1992). Emotional responsivity to others: Behavioral correlates and socialization antecedents. *New Directions for Child Development, 55,* 57-73.

Eisenberg, N., Pasternack, J. F., Cameror, E., & Tryon, K. (1984). The relation of quantity and mode of prosocial behavior to moral cognitions and social style. *Child Development, 55,* 1479-1485.

Eisenberg, N., Shell, R., Pasternack J., Beller, R., Lennon, R., & Mathy, R. (1987). Prosocial development in middle childhood: A longitudinal study. *Developmental Psychology, 23*(5), 712-718.

Elbers, L., & Ton, J. (1985). Play pen monologues: The interplay of words and babbles in the first words period. *Journal of Child Language, 12,* 551-565.

Elder, G. H. (1980). Adolescence in historical perspective. In J. Adelson (Ed.), *Handbook of adolescent psychology.* New York: Wiley.

Elder, J. L., & Pederson, D. R. (1978). Preschool children's use of objects in symbolic play. *Child Development, 49,* 500-504.

Elder, L., Caspi, A., & Burton, L. (1988). Adolescent transition in developmental perspective: Sociological and historical insights. In M. Gunnar & W. Collins (Eds.), *Minnesota Symposia on Child Development: Vol. 21. Development during the transition to adolescence* (pp. 151-179). Hillsdale, NJ: Erlbaum.

Elkind, D. (1967). Egocentrism in adolescence. *Child Development, 38,* 1025-1034.

Elkind, D. (1974). *Children and adolescents: Interpretive essays on Jean Piaget.* New York: Oxford University Press.

Elkind, D. (1981). *The hurried child.* Reading, MA: Addison-Wesley.

Elkind, D. (1984). *All grown up and no place to go: Teenagers in crisis.* Reading, MA: Addison-Wesley.

Elkind, D. (1987). *The miseducation of children: Superkids at risk.* New York: Knopf.

Elkind, D. (May 1986). Formal education and early childhood education: An essential difference. *Phi Delta Kappan,* pp. 631-636.

Elkind, D., & Bowen, R. (1979). Imaginary audience behavior in children and adolescents. *Developmental Psychology, 15,* 38-44.

Ellwood, D., & Crane, J. (1990). Family change among black Americans: What do we know? *Journal of Economic Perspectives, 4,* 65-84.

Emery, R. E. (1989). Family violence. *American Psychologist, 44,* 321-328.

Entwisle, D. (1985). Becoming a parent. In L. L'Abate (Ed.), *The handbook of family psychology and therapy.* (Vol. 1, pp. 560-578). Homewood IL: Dorsey.

Entwisle, D. R., & Doering, S. (1988). The emergent father role. *Sex Roles, 18,* 119-141.

Epstein, J. L. (1983). Selecting friends in contrasting secondary school environments. In J. L. Epstein & M. L. Karweit (Eds.), *Friends in school.* New York: Academic Press.

Epstein, L. H., & Wing, R. R. (1987). Behavioral treatment of childhood obesity. *Psychological Bulletin, 101,* 331-342.

Epstein, L. H., Valoski, A., Wing, R. R., & McCurley, J. (1990). Ten-year follow-up of behavioral, family-based treatment for obese children. *Journal of the American Medical Association, 264,* 2519-2523.

Erikksen, R. (1991). Personal communication with M. D. Kermis. *Protocols for sex selection.*

Erikson, E. (1985). *Young man Luther.* New York: Norton.

Erikson, E. H. (1959). The problem of ego identity. In E. H. Erikson (Ed.), Identity and the life cycle: Selected papers. *Psychological Issues Monograph,* No. 1.

Erikson, E. H. (1963). *Childhood and society* (2nd ed.). New York: Norton.

Erikson, E. H. (1968). *Identity, youth, and crisis.* New York: Norton.

Erikson, E. H. (1981). On generativity and identity. *Harvard Educational Review, 51,* 249-269.

Erikson, E. H., & Erikson, J. M. (1981). Generativity and identity. *Harvard Educational Review, 51,* 249-269.

Erikson, E. H., Erikson, J., & Kivnick, H. (1986) *Vital involvement in old age.* New York: Norton.

Ernst, C., & Angst, J. (1983). *Birth order: Its influence on personality.* New York: Springer-Verlag.

Esterbrook, M. A., & Goldberg, W. A. (1984). Toddler development in the family: Impact of father involvement and parenting characteristics. *Child Development, 55,* 740-752.

Evans, E. D. (1975). *Contemporary influences in early childhood education* (2nd ed.). New York: Holt, Rinehart, & Winston.

Fabes, R. A., Wilson, P., & Christopher, F. S. (1989). A time to reexamine the role of television in family life. *Family Relations, 38,* 337-341.

Fadiman, A. (February 1982). The skeleton at the feast: A case study of anorexia nervosa. *Life,* pp. 63-78.

Fagan, J. F., III. (1977). Infant recognition memory: Studies in forgetting. *Child Development, 48,* 66-78.

Fagot, B. I., Leinbach, M. D., & O'Boyle, C. (1992). Gender labeling, gender stereotyping, and parenting behaviors. *Developmental Psychology, 28*(2), 225-230.

Falkner, F. (1962). The development of children: a guide to interpretation of growth charts and developmental assessments: A commentary and future problems. *Pediatrics, 29,* 448-486.

Fantz, R. L. (1958). Pattern vision in young infants. *Psychological Record, 8,* 43-47.

Fantz, R. L. (May 1961). The origin of form perception. *Scientific American,* pp. 66-72.

Fantz, R. L., Ordy, J. M., & Udelf, M. S. (1962). Maturation of pattern vision in infants during the first six months. *Journal of Comparative and Physiological Psychology, 55,* 907-917.

Farb, P. (1978). *Humankind.* Boston: Houghton Mifflin.

Farber, J. (1970). *The student as nigger.* New York: Pocket Books.

Farber, S. (January 1981). Telltale behavior of twins. *Psychology Today,* pp. 58-64.

Featherstone, H. (June 1985). Preschool: It does make a difference. *Harvard Education Letter,* pp. 16-21.

Fedor-Freybergh, P., & Vogel, M. L. V. (1988). *Prenatal and perinatal psychology and medicine.* Carnforth, Lanc: Parthenon.

Fein, G. G. (1981). Pretend play in childhood: An integrated review. *Child Development, 52,* 1095-1118.

Fein, G. G. (1984). The self-building potential of pretend play, or ``I gotta fish all by myself.'' In T. D. Yawkey & A. D. Pellegrini (Eds.), *Child's play.* Hillsdale, NJ: Erlbaum.

Feingold, A. (1988). Cognitive gender differences are disappearing. *American Psychologist, 43*(2), 95-103.

Feiring, C., Lewis, M., & Starr, M. D. (1984). Indirect affects and infants' reactions to strangers. *Developmental Psychology, 20,* 485-491.

Feitelsen, W., & Ross, G. S. (1973). The neglected factor—play. *Human Development, 16,* 202-223.

Ferguson, C., & Snow, C. (1977). *Talking to children: Language input and acquisition.* Cambridge, UK: Cambridge University Press.

Ferleger, N., Glenwick, D. S., Gaines, R. R. W., & Green, A. H. (1988). Identifying correlates of reabuse in maltreating parents. *Child Abuse and Neglect, 12,* 41-49.

Feshback, S., & Singer, R. D. (1971). *Television and aggression: An experimental field study.* San Francisco: Jossey-Bass.

Field, T. (1977). Effects of early separation, interactive deficits, and experimental manipulations on infant-mother face-to-face interaction. *Child Development, 48,* 763-771.

Field, T. (1978). Interaction behaviors of primary vs. secondary caretaker fathers. *Developmental Psychology, 14*(2), 183-184.

Field, T. (1986). Models for reactive and chronic depression in infancy. In E. Tronick & T. Fields (Eds.), *New Directions for Child Development, 34. Maternal depression and infant disturbance.*

Field, T. (1991). Quality infant day-care and grade school behavior and performance. *Child Development, 62,* 863-870.

Field, T. M. (1979). Interaction patterns of pre-term and term infants. In T. M. Field (Ed.), *Infants born at risk.* New York: Spectrum.

Fillmore, C. J. (1968). The case for case. In E. Bach & R. T. Harms (Eds.), *Universals of linguistic theory*. New York: Holt, Rinehart & Winston.

Fincher, J. (July/August 1982). Before their time. *Science 82 Magazine*, p. 94.

Finkelhor, D. (1984). *Child sexual abuse: New theory and practice*. New York: Free Press.

Fischer, J. L., Sollie, D. L., & Morrow, K. B. (1986). Social networks in male and female adolescents. *Journal of Adolescent Research*, 6(1), 1-14.

Fitzcharles, A. (February 1987). Model versus modal child care. *Zero to Three*, p. 26.

Flaste, R. (October 1988). The myth about teenagers. *New York Times Magazine*, pp. 19, 76, 82, 85.

Flavell, J. H. (1963). *The developmental psychology of Jean Piaget*. Princeton, NJ: Van Nostrand Reinhold.

Flavell, J. H. (1977). *Cognitive development*. Englewood Cliffs, NJ: Prentice Hall.

Flavell, J. H. (1985). *Cognitive development* (2nd ed.). Englewood Cliffs, NJ: Prentice Hall.

Flavell, J. H., Flavell, E. R., & Green, F. L. (1987). Young children's knowledge about the apparent-real and pretend-real distinctions. *Developmental Psychology, 23*, 816-822.

Flavell, J. H., Green, F., & Flavell, E. R. (1986). Development of knowledge about the appearance-reality distortion. *Monographs of the Society for Research in Child Development, 212*.

Flavell, J. H., Miller, P. H. & Miller, S. A. (1993). *Cognitive Development*. Englewood Cliffs, NJ: Prentice Hall.

Ford Foundation Project on Social Welfare and the American Future. (1989). *The common good: Social welfare and the American future*. New York: Ford Foundation.

Forman, G. (June 1985). The value of kinetic print in computer graphics for young children. In E. L. Klein (Ed.), *Children and Computers*, and issue of *New Directions for Child Development*. San Francisco: Jossey-Bass.

Forman, G. E. (April 1972). *The early growth of logic in children: Influences from the bilateral symmetry of human anatomy*. Paper presented at the conference of the Society for Research in Child Development, Philadelphia.

Forman, G. E., & Fosnot, C. (1982). The use of Piaget's constructivism in early childhood education programs. In B. Spodek (Ed.), *Handbook on early childhood education*. Englewood Cliffs, NJ: Prentice Hall.

Forman, G. E., & Hill, F. (1980). *Constructive play: Applying Piaget in the preschool*. Monterey, CA: Brooks/Cole.

Fosburgh, L. (August 7, 1977). The make-believe world of teenage pregnancy. *New York Times Magazine*.

Fraiberg, S. H. (1959). *The magic years*. New York: Scribner's.

Fraiberg, S. H. (1974). Blind infants and their mothers: An examination of the sign system. In M. Lewis & L. Rosenblum (Eds.), *The effect of the infant on its caregiver*. New York: Wiley.

Frankenburg, W. K., & Dodds, J. B. (1967). The Denver developmental screening test. *Journal of Pediatrics, 71*, 181-191.

Frauenglass, M. H., & Diaz, R. M. (1985). Self-regulatory functions of children's private speech: A critical analysis of recent challenges to Vygotsky's theory. *Developmental Psychology, 21*, 357-364.

Freda, V. J., Gorman, J. G., & Pollack, W. (1966). Rh factor: Prevention of isoimmunization and clinical trial on mothers. *Science, 151*, 828-830.

Freeman, N. H. (1980). *Strategies of representation in young children*. London: Academic Press.

Freud, A. (1958). Adolescence. In *Psychoanalytic study of the child* (Vol. 13). New York: International Universities Press.

Freud, A., & Dann, S. (1951). An experiment in group up-bringing. In R. S. Eisler, A. Freud, H. Hartmann & E. Kris (Eds.), *The Psychoanalytic study of the child* (Vol. 6). New York: International Universities Press.

Freud, S. (1933). *New introductory lectures on psychoanalysis*. New York: Norton.

Fried, P. A., & Oxorn, H. (1980). *Smoking for two: Cigarettes and pregnancy*. New York: Free Press.

Friedrich, D. D., & Van Horn, K. R. (1976). *Developmental methodology: a revised primer*. Minneapolis, MN: Burgess.

Friel-Patti, S. (1990). Otitis media with effusion and the development of language: a review of the evidence. *Topics in Language Disorders, 11*(1), 11-22.

Frisch, R. E. (March 1988). Fatness and fertility. *Scientific American*, pp. 88-95.

Frost, J. L., & Sunderline, S. (Eds.). (1985). *When children play*. Proceedings of the International Conference on Play and Play Environments, Association for Childhood Education International, Weaton, MD.

Fuller, J., & Simmel, E. (1986). *Perspectives in behavioral genetics*. Hillsdale, NJ: Erlbaum.

Furstenberg, F. (1976). *Unplanned parenthood: The social consequences of teenage childbearing*. New York: Free Press.

Furstenberg, F. F., Jr. (1987). The new extended family: The experience of parents and children after remarriage. In K. Pasley & M. Ihinger-Tallman (Eds.), *Remarriage and stepparenting: Current research and theory* (pp. 42-64). New York: Guilford.

Furth, H. G. (1980). *The world of grown-ups: Children's conceptions of society*. New York: Elsevier.

Gabbard, C., Dean, M., & Haensly, P. (1991). Foot preference behavior during early childhood. *Journal of Applied Developmental Psychology, 12*, 131-137.

Galinsky, E. (1980). *Between generations: The six stages of parenthood*. New York: Times Books.

Gallagher, J. J. (1989). A new policy initiative: infants and toddlers with handicapping conditions. *American Psychologist, 44*(2), 387-391.

Gallagher, J. M. (1973). Cognitive development and learning in the adolescent. In J. F. Adams (Ed.), *Understanding adolescence* (2nd ed.). Boston: Allyn & Bacon.

Gandini, L., & Edwards, C. P. (1988). Early childhood integration of the visual arts. *Gifted International, 5*(2), 14-18.

Gans, J. E., & Blyth, D. A. (1990). *America's adolescents: How healthy are they?* (AMA Profiles of Adolescent Health Series). Chicago: American Medical Association.

Garbarino, J., Kostelny, K., & Dubrow, N. (1991). What children can tell us about living in danger. *American Psychologist, 46*(4). 376-383.

Garbarino, J., Sebes, J., & Schellenbach, C. (1984). Families at risk for destructive parent-child relations in adolescence. *Child Development, 55*, 174-183.

Garber, J. (December 1984). The developmental progression of depression in female children. In D. Chicchetti & K. Schneider-Rosen (Eds.), *New Directions for Child Development, 26*.

Garber, K., & Marchese, S. (1986). *Genetic counseling for clinicians*. Chicago: Year Book Medical Publishers.

Gardner, H. (1973). *The quest for mind: Piaget, Levi-Strauss, and the structuralist movement*. New York: Random House.

Gardner, H. (1973a). *The arts and human development: A psychological study of the artistic process*. New York: Wiley-Interscience.

Gardner, H. (1983). *Frames of mind*. New York: Basic Books.

Gardner, J. M., & Karmel, B. Z. (1984). Arousal effects on visual preference in neonates. *Developmental Psychology, 20*, 374-377.

Garland, A. F., & Zigler, E. (1993). Adolescent suicide prevention: Current research and social policy implications. *American Psychologist, 48*(2), 169-182.

Garmezy, N. (1991). Resiliency and vulnerability to adverse developmental outcomes associated with poverty. *American Behavioral Scientist, 34*(4), 416-430.

Garrod, A., Beal, C., & Shin, P. (1989). *The development of moral orientation in elementary school children*. Paper presented at the April meeting of the Society for Research in Child Development, Kansas City.

Garvey, C. (1977). *Play*. Cambridge, MA: Harvard University Press.

Garvey, C. (1984). *Children's talk*. Cambridge, MA: Harvard University Press.

Garvey, C. (1990). *Play*. Cambridge, MA: Harvard University Press.

Gelis, J. (1989). The child: From anonymity to individuality. In R. Chartier (Ed.), *A history of a private life: Vol. 3. Passions of the Renaissance* (pp. 309-325). Cambridge, MA: Belknap Press of Harvard University Press.

Gelman, R., & Gallistel, C. R. (1986). *The child's understanding of number*. Cambridge, MA: Harvard University Press.

Genesee, F. (1989). Early bilingual development: One language or two? *Journal of Child Language, 16*, 161-179.

Gesell, A. (1940). *The first five years of life: The preschool years*. New York: Harper & Brothers.

Gesell, A., & Ames, L. B. (1947). The development of handedness. *Journal of Genetic Psychology, 70*, 155-175.

Gibbons, D. C. (1976). *Delinquent behavior* (2nd ed.). Englewood Cliffs, NJ: Prentice Hall.

Gibson, E. J., & Spelke, E. S. (1983). The development of perception. In P. Mussen (Ed.), *The handbook of child psychology: Vol. 3. Cognitive development* (pp. 2-60). New York: Wiley.

Gibson, E. J., & Walk, R. D. (April 1960). The ``visual cliff.'' *Scientific American*, pp. 64-71.

Gilligan, C. (1982). *In a different voice: Psychological theory and women's development*. Cambridge, MA: Harvard University Press.

Gilligan, C. (1987). Adolescent development reconsidered. *New Directions for Child Development, 37*, 63-92.

Ginsburg, E. (1972). Toward a theory of occupational choice: A restatement. *Vocational Guidance Quarterly, 20*, 169-176.

Glaser, R. (1963). Instructional technology and the measurement of learning outcomes: Some questions. *American Psychologist, 18*, 519-521.

Gleitman, L., & Wanner, E. (1982). Language learning: State of the art. In E. Wanner & L. Gleitman (Eds.), *Language learning*. Cambridge, UK: Cambridge University Press.

Glidewell, J. C., Kantor, M. B., Smith, L. M., & Stringer, L. A. (1966). Socialization and social structure in the classroom. In L. W. Hoffman & M. L. Hoffman (Eds.), *Review of child development research* (Vol. 2). New York: Russell Sage Foundation.

Gold, M. (1985). The baby makers. *Science, 6*(3), 26-38.

Goldberg, M., & Harvey, J. (September 1983). A nation at risk: The report to the National Commission on Excellence in Education. *Phi Delta Kappan*, pp. 14-18.

Goldberg, S. (1972). Infant care and growth in urban Zambia. *Human Development, 15*, 77-89.

Goldberg, S. (1979). Premature birth: Consequences for the parent-infant relationship. *American Scientist, 67*, 214-220.

Goldberg, S. (1983). Parent-infant bonding: Another look. *Child Development, 54*, 1355-82.

Goldberg, S., & Lewis, M. (1969). Play behavior in the year-old infant: Early sex differences. *Child Development, 40*, 21-31.

Goldberg, S., Lojkasek, M., Gartner, G., & Corter, C. (1988). Maternal responsiveness and social development in preterm infants. In M. H. Bornstein (Ed.), *New Directions for Child Development: Vol. 43. Maternal responsiveness: Characteristics and consequences*. San Francisco: Jossey-Bass.

Goldfield, E. C. (1989). Transition from rocking to crawling: Postural constraints on infant movement. *Developmental Psychology, 25*(6) 913-919.

Goldin-Meadow, S., & Mylander, C. (1984). Gestural communication in deaf children: The effects and noneffects of parental input on early language development. *Monographs of the Society for Research in Child Development, 49* (3-4, Serial No. 207).

Goldsmith, H. H. (1983). Genetic influence on personality from infancy to adulthood. *Child Development, 54*, 331-355.

Goncz, L. (1988). A research study on the relation between early bilingualism and cognitive development. *Psychologische-Beitrage, 30*(1-2), 75-91.

Goodchilds, J. D., & Zellman, G. L. (1984). Sexual signalling and sexual aggression in adolescent relationships. In N. M. Malmuth & E. D. Donnerstein (Eds.), *Pornography and sexual aggression*. New York: Academic Press.

Goodlin, R. C. (1979). History of fetal monitoring. *American Journal of Obstetrics and Gynecology, 133*, 323-347.

Goodman, P. (1960). *Growing up absurd*. New York: Random House.

Goodnow, J. (1977). *Children drawing*. Cambridge, MA: Harvard University Press.

Gopnik, A. (1988). Three types of early word: The emergence of social words, names and cognitive-relational words in the one-word stage and their relation to cognitive development. *First Language, 8*, 49-70.

Gopnik, A., & Meltzoff, A. N. (1987). The development of categorization in the second year and its relation to other cognitive and linguistic developments. *Child Development, 58*, 1523-1531.

Gordon, I. (1969). Early childhood stimulation through parent education. *Final Report to the Children's Bureau Social and Rehabilitation Services Department of HEW*. ED 038-166.

Gortmaker, S. L., Dietz, W. H., Jr., Sobol, A. M., & Wehler, C. A. (1987). Increasing pediatric obesity in the United States. *American Journal of Diseases of Children, 141*, 535-540.

Goslin, D. A. (Ed.). (1969). *Handbook of socialization theory and research*. Chicago: Rand McNally.

Gottman, J. M. (1983). How children become friends. *Monographs of the Society for Research in Child Development, 48*(3).

Gould, S. J. (1981). *The mismeasure of man*. New York: Norton.

Granrud, C. D., Yonas, A., & Petterson, L. (1984). A comparison of monocular and binocular depth perception in 5 and 7 month old infants. *Journal of Experimental Child Psychology, 38*, 19-32.

Gratch, G., & Schatz, J. (1987). Cognitive development: The relevance of Piaget's infancy books. In J. Osofsy (Ed.), *Handbook of infant development* (2nd ed.). New York: Wiley.

Grattan, M. P., DeVos, E., Levy, J., and McClintock, M. K. (1992). Asymmetric action in the human newborn: Sex differences in patterns of organization. *Child Development, 63*, 273-289.

Gray, D. B., & Yaffe, S J. (1983). Prenatal drugs. In C. C. Brown (Ed.), *Prenatal Roundtable: Vol. 9. Childhood learning disabilities and prenatal risk*. (pp. 44-49). Rutherford, NJ: Johnson & Johnson.

Gray, D. B., & Yaffe, S. J. (1986). Prenatal drugs and learning disabilities. In M. Lewis (Ed.), *Learning disabilities and prenatal risk*. Urbana: University of Illinois Press.

Gray, S. (1976). *A report on the home-parent centered intervention programs: Home visiting with mothers of toddlers and their siblings*. DARCEE, Peabody College.

Greenberg, M., & Morris, N. (July 1974). Engrossment: The newborn's impact upon the father. *American Journal of Orthopsychiatry, 44*(4), 520-531.

Greene, A. L. (1990). Great expectations: Constructions of the life course during adolescence. *Journal of Youth and Adolescence, 19*, 289-303.

Greene, A. L., & Brooks, J. (April 1985). *Children's perceptions of stressful life events*. Paper presented at the Society for Research in Child Development, Toronto, Canada.

Greenfield, P. (1984). *Mind and media: The effects of television, video games and computers*. Cambridge, MA: Harvard University Press.

Greenough, W. T., Black, J. E., & Wallace, C. S. (1987). Experience and brain development. *Child Development, 58*, 539-559.

Greenspan, S., & Greenspan, N. (1985). *First feelings*. New York: Penguin.

Greenwood, S. (1984). *Menopause, naturally: Preparing for the second half of life*. San Francisco: Volcano Press.

Greif, E. B., & Ulman, K. J. (1982). The psychological impact of menarche on early adolescent females: A review of the literature. *Child Development, 53*, 1413-1430.

Grobestein, C., Flower, M., & Mendeloff, J. (1983). External human fertilization: An evaluation of policy. *Science, 22,* 127-133.

Grosjean, F. (1982). *Life with two languages: An introduction to bilingualism.* Cambridge, MA: Harvard University Press.

Gross, T F. (1985). *Cognitive development.* Monterey, CA: Brooks/Cole.

Grossman, F. K., Pollack, W. S., & Golding, E. (1988). Fathers and children: Predicting the quality and quantity of fathering. *Developmental Psychology, 24*(1), 82-91.

Grotevant, H. D., & Cooper, C. R. (1985). Patterns of interaction in family relationships and the development of identity exploration in adolescence. *Child Development, 56,* 415-428.

Grusec, J. E., & Arnason, L. (1982). Consideration for others: Approaches to enhancing altruism. In S. Moore & C. Cooper (Eds.), *The young child: Reviews of research* (Vol. 3). Washington, DC: National Association for the Education of Young Children.

Gualtieri, T., & Hicks, R. E. (1985). An immunoreactive theory of selective male affliction. *Behavioral and Brain Sciences, 8,* 427-441.

Guilford, J. P. (1959). Three faces of intellect. *American Psychologist, 14,* 469-479.

Gunderson, V., & Sackett, G. P. (1982). Paternal effects on reproductive outcome and developmental risk. In M. E. Lamb and A. L. Brown (Eds.), *Advances in developmental psychology* (Vol. 2). Hillsdale, NJ: Erlbaum.

Gunnar, M. R. (1989). Studies of the human infant's adrenocortical response to potentially stressful events. *New Directions for Child Development, 45.* San Francisco: Jossey-Bass.

Gutierrez de Pineda, V. (1948). Organizacion social en la Guajira. *Rev. Institute etnolog., 3.*

H. C. Triandis, W. W. Lambert, J. W. Berry, W. J. Lonner, A. Heron, R. W. Brislin, & J. Draguns, (Eds.), (1980). *Handbook of Cross-Cultural Psychology* (Vols. 1-6). Newton, MA: Allyn and Bacon.

Hagen, J. W., Longeward, R. H. J., & Kail, R. V., Jr. (1975). Cognitive perspectives on the development of memory. In H. W. Reese (Ed.), *Advances in child development and behavior* (Vol. 10). New York: Academic Press.

Haglund, B. & Cnattingius, S. (1990). Cigarette smoking as a risk factor for sudden infant death syndrome: A population-based study. *American Journal of Public Health, 80,* 29-32.

Hall, W. M., & Cairns, R. B. (1984). Aggressive behavior in children: An outcome of modeling or social reciprocity? *Developmental Psychology, 20,* 739-745.

Halliday, M. (1973). *Exploration in the functions of language.* London: Edward Arnold.

Hallinan, M. T., & Teixeira, R. A. (1987). Students' interracial friendships: Individual characteristics, structural effects, and racial differences. *American Journal of Education, 95,* 563-583.

Halpern, D. F. (1986). *Sex differences in cognitive abilities.* Hillsdale, NJ: Erlbaum.

Halsey, N. A., Boulos, R., Holt, E., Ruff, A. B., Kissinger, P., Quinn, T. C., Coberly, J. S., Adrien, M., & Boulos, C. (October 1990). Transmission of HIV-1 infections from mothers to infants in Haiti. *Journal of the American Medical Association, 264*(16).

Handyside, A. H., Lesko, J. G., Tarin, J. J., Winston, R. M. L., & Hughes, M. R. (1992). Birth of a normal girl after *in vitro* fertilization and preimplantation diagnostic testing for cystic fibrosis. *New England Journal of Medicine, 327*(13), 905-909.

Hansen, J. D. L. (1990). Malnutrition review. *Pediatric Review. Communication 4,* 201-212.

Harkness, S., & Super, C. M. (1983). *The cultural structuring of children's play in a rural African community.* Paper presented at the annual meeting of the Association for the Anthropological Study of Play, Baton Rouge, LA.

Harlow, H. F. (June 1959). Love in infant monkeys. *Scientific American,* pp. 68-74.

Harlow, H. F., & Harlow, M. K. (November 1962). Social deprivation in monkeys. *Scientific American,* pp. 137-146.

Harre, R. (January 1980). What's in a nickname? *Psychology Today,* pp. 78-84.

Harris, B. (1979). Whatever happened to Little Albert? *American Psychologist, 34*(2), 151-160.

Harrison, A., Wilson, M., Pine, C., Chan, S., & Buriel, R. (1990). Family ecologies of ethnic minority children. *Child Development, 61,* 347-362.

Hart, S. N., Germain, R. B., & Brassard, M. R. (1987). The challenge: To better understand and combat psychological maltreatment of children and youth. In M. R. Brassard, R. Germain, & S. N. Hart (Eds.), *Psychological maltreatment of children and youth* (pp. 3-24). New York: Pergamon.

Harter, S. (1982). The perceived competence scale for children. *Child Development, 53,* 87-97.

Harter, S. (1983). Developmental perspectives on the self system. In P. H. Mussen (Ed.), *Handbook of child psychology* (4th ed., Vol. 4). New York: Wiley.

Harter, S. (1988). Developmental processes in the construction of the self. In T. D. Yawkey & J. E. Johnson (Eds.), *Integrative processes and socialization: Early to middle childhood.* Hillsdale, NJ: Erlbaum.

Hartup, W. W (1970a). Peer interaction and social organization. In P. H. Mussen (ed.), *Carmichael's manual of child psychology* (3rd ed., Vol. 2). New York: Wiley.

Hartup, W. W (1970b). Peer relations. In T. D. Spencer & N. Kass (Eds.), *Perspectives in child psychology: Research and review.* New York: McGraw-Hill.

Hartup, W. W. (1963). Dependence and independence. IN H. W. Stevenson, J. Kagan, & C. Spiker (Eds.), *Child psychology.* Chicago: National Society for the Study of Education.

Hartup, W. W. (1983). Peer relations. In P. H. Mussen (Ed.), *Handbook of child psychology* (4th ed., Vol. 4). New York: Wiley.

Hartup, W. W. (1989). Social relationships and their developmental significance. *American Psychologist, 44*(2), 120-126.

Haskins, R. (1989). Beyond metaphor: The efficacy of early childhood education. *American Psychologist, 44*(2), 274-282.

Hass, A. (1979). *Teenage sexuality: A survey of teenage sexual behavior.* New York: Macmillan.

Hassett, J. (September 1984). Computers in the classroom. *Psychology Today, 18,* 9.

Hauser, S. T., Book, B. K., Houlihan, J., Powers, S., Weiss-Perry, B., Follansbee, D., Jacobson, A. M., & Noam, G. (1987). Sex differences within the family: Studies of adolescent and operent family interactions. *Journal of Youth and Adolescence, 16,* 199-220.

Havighurst, R. J., & Dreyer, P. H. (1975). Youth and cultural pluralism. In R. J. Havighurst & P. H. Dreyer (Eds.), *Youth: The 74th yearbook of the NSSE.* Chicago: University of Chicago Press.

Hawkins, J. A., & Berndt, T. J. (1985). *Adjustment following the transition to junior high school.* Paper presented at the biennial meeting of the Society for Research in Child Development.

Hawkins, J., Sheingold, K., Gearhart, M., & Burger, C. (1982). Microcomputers in schools: Impact on the social life of elementary classrooms. *Applied Developmental Psychology, 3,* 361-373.

Hayes, H. T. P. (June 12, 1977). The pursuit of reason. *New York Times Magazine.*

Hazen, N. L., & Lockman, J. J. (1989). Skill in context. In J. J. Lockman & N. L. Hazen (Eds.) *Action in social context: Perspectives on early development* (pp. 1-22). New York: Plenum.

Hebb, D. O. (1966). *A textbook of psychology.* Philadelphia: Saunders.

Hechtman, L. (1989). Teenage mothers and their children: Risks and problems: A review. *Canadian Journal of Psychology, 34,* 569-575.

Hecox, K. (1975). Electrophysiological correlates of human auditory development. In L. B. Cohn & P. Salapatek (Eds.), *Infant perception: From sensation to cognition* (pp. 151-191). New York: Academia.

Helfer, R. (1982). The relationship between lack of bonding and child abuse and neglect. In *Round Table on Maternal Attachment and Nurturing Disorder* (Vol. 2). New Brunswick, NJ: Johnson & Johnson.

Hellige, J. B. (1993). Unity of thought and action: Varieties of interaction between the left and right cerebral hemispheres. *Current Directions in Psychological Science, 2*(1), 21-25.

Hepper, P. (1989). Foetal learning: Implications for psychiatry? *British Journal of Psychiatry, 155*, 289-293.

Herkowitz, J. (1978). Sex-role expectations and motor behavior of the young child. In M. V. Ridenour (Ed.), *Motor development: Issues and applications*. Princeton, NJ: Princeton Book Co.

Hess, E. H. (1970). Ethology and developmental psychology. In P. H. Mussen (Ed.), *Carmichael's manual of child psychology* (3rd ed., Vol. 1). New York: Wiley.

Hess, E. H. (August 1972). ``Imprinting'' in a natural laboratory. *Scientific American*, pp. 24-31.

Hess, R. D. & Holloway, S. D. (1984). Family and school as educational institutions. In R. D. Parke (Ed.), *Review of Child Development Research 7: The Family* (pp. 179-222). Chicago: University of Chicago Press.

Hetherington, E. M. (1989). Coping with family transitions: Winners, losers, and survivors. *Child Development, 60*, 1-14.

Hetherington, E. M. (June 1984). Stress and coping in children and families. In A. Doyle, D. Gold, & D. Moskowitz (Eds.), *New Directions for Child Development, 24*.

Hetherington, E. M., & Baltes, P. B. (1988). Child psychology and life-span development. In E. M. Hetherington, R. Lerner, & M. Perlmutter (Eds.) *Child development in life-span perspective* (pp. 1-20). Hillsdale, NJ: Erlbaum.

Hetherington, E. M., & Camara, K. A. (1984). Families in transition: The process of dissolution and reconstitution. In R. D. Parke (Ed.), *Review of child development research* (Vol. 7). Chicago: University of Chicago Press.

Hetherington, E. M., Cox, M., & Cox, R. (1982). Effects of divorce on parents and children. In M. L. Lamb (Ed.), *Nontraditional families: Parenting and child development*. Hillsdale, NJ: Erlbaum.

Hetherington, E. M., et al. (1978). The aftermath of divorce. In J. H. Stevens & M. Athews (Eds.), *Mother-child, father-child relationships*. Washington, DC: National Association for the Education of Young Children.

Hetherington, E. M., Stanley-Hagan, M., & Anderson, E. R. (1989). Marital transitions: A child's perspective. *American Psychologist, 44*, 303-312.

Hill, J. P. (1980). The family. In M. Johnson (Ed.), *Toward adolescence: The middle school years. The seventy-ninth yearbook of the national society for the study of education*. Chicago: University of Chicago Press.

Hill, J. P. (1980). *Understanding early adolescence: A framework*. Carrboro, NC: Center for Early Adolescence.

Hill, J. P. (1987). Research on adolescents and their families past and present. *New Directions for Child Development, 37*, 13-32.

Hines, P. M., Garcia-Preto, N., McGoldrick, M., Almeida, R., & Weltman, S. (June 1992). Intergenerational relationships across cultures. *Families in Society: The Journal of Contemporary Human Services. CEU Article 23*, 323-338.

Hirsh-Pasek, K., Nelson, D. G., Jusczyk, P. W., & Wright, K. (April 1986). *A moment of silence: How the prosaic cues in motherese might assist language learning*. Paper presented at the International Conference on Infant Studies, Los Angeles.

Hirshberg, L. (1990). When infants look to their parents: II. Twelve-month-olds' response to conflicting parental emotional signals. *Child Development, 61*, 1187-1191.

Hirshberg, L. M., & Svejda, M. (1990). When infants look to their parents: I. Infants' social referencing of mothers compared to fathers. *Child Development, 61*, 1175-1186.

Hiscock, M., & Kinsbourne, M. (1987). Specialization of the cerebral hemispheres: Implications for learning. *Journal of Learning Disabilities, 20*, 130-142.

Hiscock, M., & Kinsbourne, M. (1987). Specialization of the erebral hemispheres: Implications for learning. *Journal of Learning Disabilities, 20*. 130-143.

Hoffman, J. (1984). Psychological separation of late adolescents from their parents. *Journal of Counseling Psychology, 31*, 170-178.

Hoffman, L. W., & Hoffman, M. L. (1973). The value of children to parents. In J. T. Fawcett (Ed,). *Psychological perspectives on population*. New York: Basic Books.

Hoffman, M. L. (1970). Moral development. In P. H. Mussen (Ed.), *Carmichael's manual of child psychology* (3rd ed., Vol. 2). New York: Wiley.

Hoffman, M. L. (1977). Sex differences in empathy and related behaviors. *Psychological Bulletin, 84*(4), 712-722.

Holden, C. (1980). Identical twins reared apart. *Science, 207*, 1323-1328.

Holmbeck, G. N. and O'Donnell, K. (Spring 1991). Discrepancies between perceptions of decision making and behavioral autonomy. *New Directions for Child Development, 51* 51-70.

Holt, J. (1964). *How children fail*. New York: Dell.

Honig, A. (May 1989). Quality infant/toddler caregiving: Are there magic recipes? *Young Children*, pp. 4-10.

Honig, A. S. (May 1986). Stress and coping in young children. *Young Children*, pp. 50-63.

Honig, A. S. (October 1980). The importance of fathering. *Dimensions*, pp. 33-38, 63.

Horn, J. M. (1983). The Texas adoption project: Adopted children and their intellectual resemblance to biological and adoptive parents. *Child Development, 54*, 268-275.

Horowitz, F. D. (1982). The first two years of life: Factors related to thriving. In S. Moore & C. Cooper (Eds.), *The young child: Reviews of research* (Vol. 3). Washington, DC: National Association for the Education of Young Children.

Horowitz, S. M., Klerman, L. V., Sungkuo, H., and Jekel, J. F. (1991). Intergenerational transmission of school age parenthood. *Family Planning Perspective, 23*, 168-177.

Hospice. *Aging, 5*(3), 38-40.

Hoversten, G. H., & Moncur, J. P. (1969). Stimuli and intensity factors in testing infants. *Journal of Speech and Hearing Research, 12*, 687-702.

Howard, J., & Hammond, R. (September 9, 1985). Rumors of inferiority. *The New Republic*, pp. 17-21.

Howes, C., & Olenick, M. (1986). Family and child care influences on toddler's compliance. *Child Development, 57*, 202-216.

Huesmann, L. R., Lagerspetz, K., & Eron, L. D. (1984). Intervening variables in the TV violence-aggression relation: Evidence from two countries. *Developmental Psychology, 20*, 746-775.

Hughes, F. P. (1991). *Children, play, and development*. Newton, MA: Allyn and Bacon.

Hughes, M., & Donaldson, M. (1979). The use of hiding games for studying the co-ordination of viewpoints. *Educational Review, 31*, 133-140.

Hunt, J. M. (1961). *Intelligence and experience*. New York: Ronald Press.

Husen, T. (1967). *International study of achievement in mathematics: A comparison of twelve countries*. New York: Wiley.

Huston, A. (1983). Sex typing. In P. H. Mussen (Ed.), *Handbook of child psychology* (Vol. 4). New York: Wiley.

Huston, A. C., Watkins, B. A., & Kinkel, D. (1989). Public policy and children's television. *American Psychologist, 44*(2), 424-433.

Huston, A. C., Watkins, B. A., & Kunkel, D. (1989). Public policy and children's television. *American Psychologist, 44*, 424-433.

Hutcheson, R. H., Jr. (1968). Iron deficiency anemia in Tennessee among rural poor children. *Public Health Reports, 83*, 939-943.

Hwang, C. P., & Broberg, A. (1992). The historical and social context of child care in Sweden. In M. E. Lamb, & K. J. Sternberg (Eds.). *Child care in context*. Hillsdale, NJ: Erlbaum, 27-53.

Hyde, J. S. (1984). How large are gender differences in aggression? A developmental metaanalysis. *Developmental Psychology, 20*, 722-736.

Inhelder, B., & Piaget, J. (1958). *The growth of logical thinking: From childhood to adolescence*. (A. Parsons & S. Milgram, Trans.). New York: Basic Books.

Inkeles, A., & Smith, D. H. (1974). *Becoming modern: individual change in six developing countries.* Cambridge, MA: Harvard University Press.

Isaacs, S. (1930). *Intellectual growth in young children.* London: Routledge & Kegan Paul.

Isabella, R. A., Belsky, J., & Von Eye, A. (1989). Origins of infant-mother attachment: An examination of interactional synchrony during the infant's first year. *Developmental Psychology, 25*(1), 12-21.

Isenberg, J., & Quisenberry, N. L. (February 1988). Play: A necessity for all children. *Childhood Education.*

Jacobson, A. L. (1978). Infant day care: Toward a more human environment. *Young Children, 33,* 14-23.

Jacobson, J. & Wille, D. (1986). The influence of attachment pattern on developmental changes in peer interaction from the toddler to the preschool period. *Child Development, 57,* 338-347.

Jacobson, J. L., & Wille, D. E. (1984). Influence of attachment and separation experience on separation distress at 18 months. *Developmental Psychology, 70,* 477-484.

Jacobson, J. L., Jacobson, S. W., Schwartz, P. M., Fein, G., & Dowler, J. K. (1984). Prenatal exposure to an environmental toxin: A test of the multiple effects model. *Developmental Psychology, 20,* 523-532.

Jaeger, E., & Weinraub, M. (Fall 1990). Early nonmaternal care and infant attachment: In search of progress. In *New Directions for Child Development, 49,* 71-90.

Jelliffe, D. B., Jelliffe, E. F. P., Garcia, L., & De Barrios, G. (1961). The children of the San Blas Indians of Panama. *Journal of Pediatrics, 59,* 271-285.

Jensen, A. R. (1969). How much can we boost IQ and scholastic achievement? *Harvard Educational Review, 39,* 1-123.

Jensh, R. (1986). Effects of prenatal irradiation on postnatal psychophysiologic development. In E. P. Riley & C. V. Vorhees (Eds.), *Handbook of behavioral periontology.* New York: Plenum.

Jersild, A. T., & Holmes, F. B. (1935). *Children's fears.* (Child Development Monograph No. 20). New York: Teachers College Press, Columbia University.

Jessner, L., Weigert, E., & Foy, J. L. (1970). The development of parental attitudes during pregnancy. In E. J. Anthony & T. Benedek (Eds.), *Parenthood: Its psychology and psychopathology.* Boston: Little, Brown.

Jessor, R. (1993). Successful adolescent development among youth in high-risk settings. *American Psychologist, 48*(2), 117-126.

Jessor, R., Donovan, J. D., & Costa, F. (1992). *Beyond adolescence: Problem behavior and young adult development.* New York: Cambridge University Press.

Johnson, J. E., Christie, J. F., & Yawkey, T. D. (1987). *Play and early childhood development.* Glenview, IL: Scott, Foresman.

Johnston, L. D., O'Malley, P. M., & Bachman, G. J. (1987). *National trends in drug use and related factors among American high school students and young adults, 1975-1986.* Rockville, MD: U.S. Department of Health and Human Services, National Institute on Drug Abuse.

Jones, A. P., & Crnic, L. S. (1986). Maternal mediation of the effects of malnutrition. In E. P. Riley & C. V. Vorhees (Eds.), *Handbook of behavioral teratology.* New York: Plenum.

Jones, M. C. (1965). Psychological correlates of somatic development. *Child Development, 36,* 899-911.

Jordanova, L. (1989). Children in history: Concepts of nature and society. In G. Scarr (Ed.), *Children, parents, and politics* (pp. 3-24). Cambridge, UK: Cambridge University Press.

Judd, L. J. (Winter 1991). Study finds mental disorders strike youth earlier than thought. *Quarterly Newsletter of the National Mental Health Association,* p. 4.

Kagan, J. (1971). *Change and continuity in infancy.* New York: Wiley.

Kagan, J. (1978). The baby's elastic mind. *Human Nature, I,* 66-73.

Kagan, J., & Moss, H. A. (1962). *Birth to maturity: A study in psychological development.* New York: Wiley.

Kagan, J., & Snidman, N. (1991). Temperamental factors in human development. *American Psychologist, 46,* 856-862.

Kagan, J., Reznick, J. S., & Gibbons, J. (1989). Inhibited and uninhibited types of children. *Child Development, 60,* 838-845.

Kalnins, I. V., & Bruner, J. S. (1973). Infant sucking used to change the clarity of a visual display. In L. J. Stone, H. T. Smith, & L. B. Murphy (Eds.), *The competent infant: Research and commentary.* New York: Basic Books.

Kamii, C., & DeVries, R. (1980). *Group games in early education.* Washington, DC: National Association for the Education of Young Children.

Kamin, L. (1974). *The science and politics of IQ.* Hillsdale, NJ: Erlbaum.

Kammerman, S., Kahn, A., & Kingston, P. (1983). *Maternity policies and working women.* New York: Columbia University Press.

Kandel, D. B., Raveis, V. H., & Davies, M. (1991). Suicidal ideation in adolescence: Depression, substance use, & other risk factors. *Journal of Youth and Adolescence, 20,* 289-309.

Kantrowitz, B. (May 16, 1988). Preemies. *Newsweek,* pp. 62-67.

Kaplan, L. J. (1984). *Adolescence: The farewell to childhood.* New York: Touchstone.

Kaplan, N., Choy, M. H., and Whitmore, J. K. (February 1992). Indochinese refugee families and academic achievement. *Scientific American,* 36-42.

Karen, R. (February 1990). Becoming attached. *The Atlantic Monthly.*

Karlson, A. L. (1972). *A naturalistic method for assessing cognitive acquisition of young children participating in preschool programs.* Unpublished doctoral dissertation, University of Chicago.

Keating, D. (1976). Intellectual talent, research, and development: Proceedings. In D. Keating (Ed.), *Hyman Blumberg Symposium in Early Childhood Education.* Baltimore: Johns Hopkins University Press.

Keating, D. P. (1980). Thinking processes in adolescence. In J. Adelson (Ed.), *Handbook of adolescent psychology.* New York: Wiley.

Kegan, R. (1982). *The evolving self: Problem and process in human development.* Cambridge, MA: Harvard University Press.

Keister, M. E. (1970). *The good life for infants and toddlers.* New York: Harper & Row.

Kellogg, R. (1969). *Analyzing children's art.* Palo Alto, CA: National Press Books.

Kellogg, R. (1970). *Analyzing children's art.* Palo Alto, CA: National Press.

Kelly, T. (1986). *Clinical genetics and genetic counseling* (3rd ed.). Chicago: Year Book Medical Publishers.

Kempe, R. S., & Kempe, C. H. (1984). *The common secret: Sexual abuse of children and adolescents.* San Francisco: Freeman.

Kendrick, A. S., Kaufmann, R., & Messenger, K. P. (1991). *Healthy young children: a manual for programs.* Washington, D.C.: National Association for the Education of Young Children.

Keniston, K. (1975). Youth as a stage of life. In R. J. Havighurst & P. H. Dreyer (Eds.), *Youth: The 74th yearbook of the NSSE.* Chicago: University of Chicago Press.

Keniston, K. (1977). *All our children: The American family under pressure.* Report of the Carnegie Council on Children. New York: Harcourt Brace Jovanovich.

Keogh, J. F. (1965). *Motor performance of elementary school children.* Monograph of the Physical Education Department, University of California, Los Angeles.

Kephart, W. M. (1966). The Oneida community. In W. M. Kephart (Ed.), *The family, society, and the individual* (2nd ed.). Boston: Houghton Mifflin.

Kermis, M. D. (1984). *The psychology of human aging: Theory, research and practice.* Newton, MA: Allyn and Bacon.

Kermis, M. D. (1986). *Mental health in late life: The adaptive process.* Boston, MA: Jones and Bartlett.

Kermoian, R., & Campos, J. J. (1988). Locomotor experience: A facilitation of spacial cognitive development. *Child Development, 59,* 908-17.

Kiester, E., Jr. (October 1977). Healing babies before they're born. *Family Health*, pp. 26-30.

Kimura, D. (September 1992). Sex differences in the brain. *Scientific American*,

Kitzinger, S. (1981). *The complete book of pregnancy and childbirth*. New York: Knopf.

Klahr, D., Langley, P., & Necher, R. (Eds.). (1987). *Production system model of learning and development*. Cambridge, MA: MIT Press.

Klein, N., Hack, N., Gallagher, J., & Fanaroff, A. A. (1985). Preschool performance of children with normal intelligence who were very low birth weight infants. *Pediatrics, 75*, 531-37.

Klima, E. S., & Bellugi, U. (1966). Syntactic regularities. In J. Lyons & R. J. Wales (Eds.), *Psycholinguistics papers*. Edinburgh: University of Edinburgh Press.

Klima, E. S., & Bellugi, U. (1973). As cited in P. de Villiers & J. de Villiers, *Early language*. Cambridge, MA: Harvard University Press, 1979.

Klinnert, M. D., Emde, R. N., Butterfield, P., & Campos, J. J. (1986). Social referencing: The infant's use of emotional signals from a friendly adult with mother present. *Developmental Psychology, 22*, 427-432.

Knobloch, H., Malone, A., Ellison, P. H., Stevens, F., & Zdeb, M. (March 1982). Considerations in evaluating changes in outcome for infants weighing less than 1,501 grams. *Pediatrics, 69*(3), 285-295.

Knobloch, H., Pasamanick, B., Harper, P. A., & Rider, R. V. (1959). The effect of prematurity on health and growth. *American Journal of Public Health, 49*, 1164-1173.

Knox, S. (1980). Ultra-sound diagnosis of foetal disorder. *Public Health, London, 94*, 362-367.

Koch, H. L. (1956). Sissiness and tomboyishness in relation to sibling characteristics. *Journal of Genetic Psychology, 88*, 213-244.

Koch, R., & Koch, K. J. (1974). *Understanding the mentally retarded child: A new approach*. New York: Random House.

Kohl, H. (1968). *36 children*. New York: Norton.

Kohlberg, L. (1966). A cognitive developmental analysis of children's sex-role concepts and attitudes. In E. Maccoby (Ed.), *The development of sex differences*. Stanford: Stanford University Press.

Kohlberg, L. (1966). Moral education in the schools: A developmental view. *School Review, 74*, 1-30.

Kohlberg, L. (1969). Stage and sequence: The cognitive-developmental approach to socialization. In D. A. Goslin (Ed.), *Handbook of Socialization Theory & Research* (pp. 347-480). Chicago: Rand McNally.

Kohlberg, L. (1978). Revisions in the theory and practice of moral development. *New Directions for Child Development, 2*.

Kohlberg, L. (1981). *Essays on moral development: Vol. 1. The philosophy of moral development*. New York: Harper & Row.

Kohlberg, L. (1984). *Essays on moral development: Vol. 2. The psychology of moral development*. New York: Harper & Row.

Komner, M., & Shostak, M. (February 1987). Timing and management of birth among the !Kung: Biocultural interaction and reproductive adaptation. *Cultural Anthropology, 2*(1), 11-28.

Kompara, D. R. (1980). Difficulties in the socialization process of step-parenting. *Family Relations, 29*, 69-73.

Kopp, C. B. (1989). Regulation of distress and negative emotions: A developmental view. *Developmental Psychology, 25*, 343-354.

Kopp, C. B. (Spring 1992). Emotional distress and control in young children. In N. Eisenberg & Fabes, R. (Eds.), *New Directions for Child Development*. San Francisco: Jossey Bass Education Series.

Korner, A. F. (1987). Preventive intervention with high-risk newborns: Theoretical, conceptual, and methodological perspectives. In J. Osofsky (Ed.), *Handbook of infant development*. New York: Wiley.

Korte, D., & Scaer, R. (1990). *A good birth, a safe birth*. New York: Bantam.

Koslow, R. E. (1987). Sit and reach flexibility measures for boys and girls aged three through eight years. *Perceptual and Motor Skills, 64*, 1103-1106.

Kozol, J. (1970). *Death at an early age*. New York: Bantam Books.

Kreppner, K., & Lerner, N. (Eds.). (1989). *Family systems and life-span development*. Hillsdale, NJ: Erlbaum.

Kreppner, K., Paulsen, S., & Schuetz, Y. (1982). Infant and family development: From triads to tetrads. *Human Development, 25*(6), 373-391.

Kropp, J. P., & Haynes, O. M. (1987). Abusive and nonabusive mothers' ability to identify general and specific emotion signals of infants. *Child Development, 58*, 187-190.

Kuhl, P. K., & Meltzoff, A. N. (1988). Speech as an intermodel object of perception. In A. Yonas (Ed.), *The Minnesota Symposia on Child Psychology: Vol. 20. Perceptual development in infancy* (pp. 235-266). Hillsdale, NJ: Erlbaum.

Kuhl, P. K., Williams, K. A., Lacerda, F., Stevens, K. N., & Lindblom, B. (1992). Linguistic experience alters phonetic perception in infants by 6 months of age. *Science, 255*, 606-608.

Kuliev, A. M., Modell, B., & Jackson, L. (1992). Limb abnormalities and chorionic villus sampling. *The Lancet, 340*, 668.

Labov, W. (1970). The logic of nonstandard English. In F. Williams (Ed.), *Language and poverty*. Englewood Cliffs, NJ: Prentice Hall.

Labov, W. (1972). *Language in the inner city: Studies in the black English vernacular*. Philadelphia: University of Pennsylvania Press.

Labov, W., Cohen, P., Robins, C. & Lewis, J. (1968). *A Study of the non-standard English of Negro and Puerto Rican speakers in New York City*. Final Report, U.S. Office of Education Cooperative Research Project No. 3288.

Ladd, G. W., Price, J. M., & Hart, C. H. (1988). Predicting preschoolers' peer status from their playground behaviors. *Child Development, 59*, 986-992.

Lamaze, F. (1970). *Painless childbirth: The Lamaze method*. Chicago: Regnery.

Lamb, M. E. (1979). Paternal influences and the father's role. *American Psychologist, 34*, 938-943.

Lamb, M. E. (1987). *The father's role: Cross-cultural perspectives*. New York: Wiley.

Lamb, M. E., Ketterlinus, R. D., & Fracasso, M. P. (1992). Parent-child relationships. In M. H. Bornstein, & M. E. Lamb (Eds.), *Developmental Psychology: An Advanced Textbook*. Hillsdale, NJ: Lawrence Erlbaum.

Lamb, M., & Lamb, J. (1976). The nature and importance of the father-infant relationship. *Family Coordinator, 4*(25), 379-386.

Lang, A. (1987). Nursing of families with an infant who requires home apnea monitoring. *Issues in Comprehensive Pediatric Nursing, 10*, 122-133.

Laosa, L. M. (1980). Maternal teaching strategies in Chicano and Anglo-American families of varied educational and socioeconomic levels. *Child Development, 51*, 759-765.

Laosa, L. M. (1981). Maternal behavior: sociocultural diversity in modes of family interaction. In R. W. Henderson (Ed.), *Parent-child interaction: Theory, research and prospects* (pp. 125-167). New York: Academic Press.

Laosa, L. M. (1984). Ethnic, socioeconomic, and home language influences upon early performance on measures of abilities. *Journal of Educational Psychology, 76*, 1178-1198.

Latham, M. C. (1977). Infant feeding in national and international perspective: An examination of the decline in human lactation, and the modern crisis in infant and young child feeding practices. *Annals of the New York Academy of Sciences, 300*, 197-209.

Laursen, N. H. (1983). *Childbirth with love*. New York: Berkley Books.

Leboyer, F. (1976). *Birth without violence*. New York: Knopf.

Lehane, S. (1976). *Help your baby learn*. Englewood Cliffs, NJ: Prentice Hall.

Lehman, D., & Nisbett, R. (1990). A longitudinal study of the effects of undergraduate training on reasoning. *Developmental Psychology, 26*, 952-960.

Leo, J. (April 9, 1984). The revolution is over. *Time*, pp. 74-83.

Lepper, M. R., & Gurtner, J. L. (1989). Children and computers: Approaching the twenty-first century. *American Psychologist, 44*(2), 170-178.

Lerner, R. M., Orlos, J. B., & Knapp, J. R. (1976). Physical attractiveness, physical effectiveness and self-concept in late adolescence. *Adolescence, 11*, 313-326.

Lester, B. M., & Brazelton, T. B. (1982). Cross-cultural assessment of neonatal behavior. In D. Wagner & H. Stevenson (Eds.), *Cultural perspectives on child development.* San Francisco: Freeman.

Lester, B. M., & Dreher, M. (1989). Effects of marijuana use during pregnancy on newborn cry. *Child Development, 60,* 765-771.

Lester, B. M., Als, H., & Brazelton, T. B. (1982). Regional obstetric anesthesia and newborn behavior: A reanalysis toward synergistic effects. *Child Development, 53,* 687-692.

Letteri, C. A. (1985). Teaching students how to learn. *Theory into Practice,* pp. 112-122.

Leventhal, E. A., Leventhal, H., Shacham, S., & Easterling, D. V. (1989). Active coping reduces reports of pain from childbirth. *Journal of Consulting and Clinical Psychology, 57*(3), 365-371.

Levine, L. E. (1983). Mine: Self-definition in two-year-old boys. *Developmental Psychology, 19,* 544-549.

Levy, G. D., & Carter, D. B. (1989). Gender schema, gender constancy and gender-role knowledge: The roles of cognitive factors in preschoolers' gender-role stereotype attributions. *Developmental Psychology, 25*(3), 444-449.

Lewis, M. (1987). Social development in infancy and early childhood. In J. Osofsky (Ed.), *Handbook of infant development.* New York: Wiley.

Lewis, M., & Feinman, S. (Eds.) (1991). *Social influences and socialization in infancy.* New York: Plenum.

Lewis, M., & Feiring, C. (1989). Infant, mother, and mother-infant interaction behavior and subsequent attachment. *Child Development, 60,* 831-837.

Lewis, M., & Rosenblum, L. (Eds.) (1974). *The effect of the infant on its caregiver.* New York: Wiley.

Lewis, M., Feiring, C., & Kotsonis, M. (1984). The social network of the young child: A developmental perspective. In M. Lewis (Ed.), *Beyond the dyad: The genesis of behavior.* New York: Plenum.

Lewit, E. M. (Winter 1992). Child indicators: teenage childbearing. In R. E. Behrman, (Ed.), *The Future of Children: U.S. Health Care for Children. 2,* 186-191.

Liebenberg, B. (1967). Expectant fathers. *American Journal of Orthopsychiatry, 37,* 358-359.

Liebert, R. M., & Sprafkin, J. (1988). *The early window: Effects of television on children and youth.* New York: Pergamon Press.

Lipsitt, L. P., & Kaye, H. (1964). Conditioned sucking in the human newborn. *Psychonomic Science, 1,* 29-30.

Lisina, M. I., & Neverovich, Y. Z. (1971). Development of movements and formation of motor habits. In A. Z. Zaporozlets & D. B. Elkonin (Eds.), *The psychology of preschool children.* Cambridge, MA: MIT Press.

Livson, N., & Peskin, H. (1980). Perspectives on adolescence from longitudinal research. In J. Adelson (Ed.), *Handbook of adolescent psychology.* New York: Wiley.

Lloyd, B. (1987). Social representations of gender. In J. Bruner & H. Haste (Eds.). *Making sense: The child's construction of the world. London: Methue.*

Lombardi, J. (September 1990). Head Start: The nation's pride, a nation's challenge. *Young Children,* pp. 22-29.

Londerville, S., & Main, M. (1981). Security of attachment, compliance, and maternal training methods in the second year of life. *Developmental Psychology, 17,* 289-299.

Lonigan, C. J., Fischel, J. E., Whitehurst, G. J., Arnold, D. S. & Valdez-Menchaca, M. C. (1992). The role of otitis media in the development of expressive language disorder. *Developmental Psychology, 28*(3), 430-440.

Lord, L. J., Scherschel, P. M., Thornton, J., Moore, L. J., & Quick, B. E. (October 5, 1987). Desperately seeking baby. *U.S. News & World Report,* pp. 58-64.

Lorenz, K. Z. (1952). *King Solomon's ring.* New York: Crowell.

Lourie, I. S., Campiglia, P., James, L. R., & Dewitt, J. (1979). Adolescent abuse and neglect: The role of runaway youth programs. *Children Today, 8,* 27-40.

Lovaas, O. I. (1962). Effect of exposure to symbolic aggression on aggressive behavior. *Child Development, 32,* 37-44.

Lozoff, B. (1989). Nutrition and behavior. *American Psychologist, 44*(2), 231-236.

Lubic, R. W., & Ernst, E. K. (1978). The childbearing center: An alternative to conventional care. *Nursing Outlook, 26,* 754-760.

Lucariello, J., & Nelson, K. (1987). Remembering and planning talk between mothers and children. *Discourse Processes, 10,* 219-235.

Maccoby, E. E. (1980). *Social development: Psychological growth and the parent-child relationship.* New York: Harcourt Brace Jovanovich.

Maccoby, E. E. (1984). Socialization and developmental change. *Child Development, 55,* 317-328.

Maccoby, E. E. (1990). Gender and relationships: A developmental account. *American Psychologist, 45,* 513-520.

Maccoby, E. E. (1992). The role of parents in the socialization of children: An historical overview. *Developmental Psychology, 28*(6), 1006-1017.

Maccoby, E. E. (March 15, 1979). *Parent-child interaction.* Paper presented at the biennial meeting of the Society for Research in Child Development.

Maccoby, E. E., & Feldman, S. S. (1972). Mother-attachment and stranger-reactions in the third year of life. *Monographs of the Society for Research in Child Development, 37*(1, Serial No. 146).

Maccoby, E. E., & Jacklin, C. N. (1974). *The psychology of sex differences.* Stanford: Stanford University Press.

Maccoby, E. E., & Jacklin, C. N. (1980). Sex differences in aggression: A rejoinder and reprise. *Child Development, 51,* 964-980.

Maccoby, E. E., & Martin, J. A. (1983). Socialization in the context of the family: Parent-child interaction. In P. H. Mussen (Ed.), *Handbook of child psychology: Vol. 4. Socialization, personality, and social development.* New York: Wiley.

MacFarlane, A. (February 1978). What a baby knows. *Human Nature, 1,* 81-86.

MacGregor, S. N., Keith, L. G., Chasnoff, I. J., Rosner, M. A., Chisum, G. M., Shaw, P., & Minogue, J. P. (1987). Cocaine use during pregnancy: Adverse perinatal outcome. *American Journal of Obstetrics and Gynecology, 1*(57), 66-90.

Mack, J., & Hickler, H. (1981). *Vivienne: The life and suicide of an adolescent girl.* Boston: Little, Brown.

Mackenzie, C. (1978). Gray panthers on the prowl. In R. Gross, B. Gross, & S. Seidman (Eds.), *The new old: Struggling for decent aging.* Garden City, NY: Anchor Press/Doubleday.

Madden, J. D., Payne, T. F., & Miller, S. (1986). Maternal cocaine abuse and effect on the newborn. *Pediatrics, 77,* 209-211.

Maddux, J. E., Roberts, M. C., Sledden, E. A., & Wright, L. (1986). Developmental issues in child health psychology. *American Psychologist, 41*(1), 25-34.

Madsen, M. C. (1971). Developmental and cross-cultural differences in the cooperative and competitive behavior of young children. *Journal of Cross-Cultural Psychology, 2,* 365-371.

Madsen, M. C., & Shapira, A. (1970). Cooperative and competitive behavior of urban Afro-American, Anglo-American, Mexican-American, and Mexican village children. *Developmental Psychology, 3,* 16-20.

Magenis, R. E., Overton, K. M., Chamberlin, J., Brady, T., & Lorrien, E. (1977). Parental origin of the extra chromosome in Down's syndrome. *Human Genetics, 37,* 7-16.

Mahler, M., Pine, F., & Bergman, A. (1975). *The psychological birth of the human infant: Symbiosis and individuation.* New York: Basic Books.

Main, M., & Solomon, J. (1986). Discovery of an insecure-disorganized/disoriented attachment pattern. In T. B. Brazelton & M. K. Yogman (Eds.), *Affective development in infancy.* Norwood, NJ: Ablex.

Makin, J. W., & Porter, R. H. (1989). Attractiveness of lactating females' breast odors to neonates. *Child Development, 60,* 803-810.

Mandell, F., McClain, M., & Reece, R. (1987). Sudden and unexpected death. *American Journal of Diseases of Children, 141,* 748-750.

Mandler, J. M. (1983). *Representation.* In J. H. Flavell & E. M. Markham (Eds.), *Handbook of child psychology: Cognitive development* (Vol. 3). New York: Wiley.

Mandler, J. M. (1988). How to build a baby: On the development of an accurate representational system. *Cognitive Development, 3,* 113-136.

Mandler, J. M. (May-June 1990). A new perspective on cognitive development in infancy. *American Scientist, 78,* 236-243.

Maratsos, M. (1983). Some current issues in the study of the acquisition of grammar. In J. H. Flavell and E. M. Markham (Eds.), *Handbook of child psychology:* Vol. 3: *Cognitive Development.* New York: Wiley.

Marcia, J. (1980). Identity in adolescence. In J. Adelson (Ed.), *Handbook of adolescent psychology.* New York: Wiley.

Marcoen, A., Goossens, L., & Caes, P. (1987). Loneliness in pre-through adolescence: Exploring the contributions of a multidimensional approach. *Journal of Youth and Adolescence, 16.*

Marieskind, H. I. (1989). Caesarean section in the United States: Has it changed since 1979? In *An evaluation of Caesarean sections in the United States.* U.S. Department of Health, Education, & Welfare.

Martin, C. L. (1989). Children's use of gender-related information in making social judgments. *Developmental Psychology, 25*(1), 80-88.

Martin, C. L. (1990). Attitudes and expectations about children with nontraditional and traditional gender roles. *Sex Roles, 22*(3/4), 151.

Martin, C. L., & Halverson, C. F., Jr. (1981). A schematic processing model of sex-typing and stereotyping in children. *Child Development, 52,* 1119-1134.

Maslow, A. H. (1954). *Motivation and personality.* New York: Harper & Brothers.

Maslow, A. H. (1968). *Toward a psychology of being* (2nd ed.). Princeton, NJ: Van Nostrand Reinhold.

Maslow, A. H. (1979). *The journals of A. H. Maslow.* (R. J. Lowry & B. G. Maslow, Eds.). Monterey, CA: Brooks/Cole.

Masters, W. H., Johnson, P. E., & Kolodney, R. C. (1982). *Human sexuality.* Boston: Little, Brown.

Matas, L., Arend, R. A., & Sroufe, L. A. (1978). Continuity of adaptation in the second year: The relationship between quality of attachment and later competence. *Child Development, 49,* 547-556.

Mates, D., & Allison, K. R. (1992). Sources of stress and coping responses of high school students. *Adolescence, 27*(106), 463-474.

Maurer, D., & Maurer, C. (1988). *The world of the newborn.* New York: Basic Books.

Mauro, J. (1991). *The friend that only I can see: A longitudinal investigation of children's imaginary companions.* Unpublished doctoral dissertation. University of Oregon.

May, R. (1986). *Politics and innocence: A humanistic debate.* Dallas, TX: Saybrook, & New York: Norton.

McBride, A. (1990). Mental health effects of women's multiple roles. *American Psychologist, 45,* 381-384.

McBride, S. L. (Fall 1990). Maternal moderators of child care: The role of maternal separation anxiety. *New Directions for Child Development, 49,* 53-70.

McCall, R. B., Eichorn, D. H., & Hogarty, P. S. (1977). Transitions in early mental development. *Monographs of the Society for Research in Child Development, 42*(3, Serial No. 171), 1-75.

McCartney, K., Harris, M. J., & Bernieri, F. (1990). Growing up and growing apart: A developmental meta-analysis of twin studies. *Psychological Bulletin, 107,* 226-237.

McClelland, D. C. (1955). Some social consequences of achievement motivation. In M. R. Jones (Ed.), *Nebraska symposium on motivation* (Vol. 3). Lincoln: University of Nebraska Press.

McCord, W., McCord, J., & Zola, I. K. (1959). *Origins of crime.* New York: Columbia University Press.

McCune-Nicolich, L. (1981). Toward symbolic functioning: Structure of early pretend games and potential parallels with language. *Child Development, 52,* 785-797.

McGhee, P. E. (1979). *Humor: Its origin and development.* San Francisco: W. H. Freeman.

McGoldrick, M. (1980). The joining of families through marriage: The new couple. In E. A. Carter & M. McGoldrick (Eds.), *The family life cycle.* New York: Gardner Press.

McGraw, M. (1935). *Growth: A study of Johnny and Timmy.* New York: Appleton-Century.

McKnew, D. H., Jr., Cytryn, L., & Yahraes, H. (1983). *Why isn't Johnny crying? Coping with depression in children.* New York: Norton.

McKusick, V. A. (1988). *Mendelian inheritance in man: Catalogs of autosomal dominant, autosomal recessive, and X-linked phenotypes* (7th edition). Baltimore: The Johns Hopkins University Press.

McKusick, Y. (1986). *Mendelian inheritance in man* (7th ed.). Baltimore: John Hopkins University Press.

McLanahan, S., & Booth, K. (1989). Mother-only families: Problems, prospects, and politics. *Journal of Marriage and the Family, 51,* 557-580.

McLoughlin, M., Shryer, T. L., Goode, E. E., & McAuliffe, K. (August 8, 1988). Men vs. women. *U.S. News & World Report.*

McLoyd, V. C., & Wilson, L. (1990). Maternal behavior, social support, and economic conditions as predictors of distress in children. *New Directions for Child Development, 46,* 49-69.

McNeill, D. (1972). *The acquisition of language: The study of developmental psycholinguistics.* New York: Harper & Row.

Mead, G. H. (1934). *Mind, self, and society: From the standpoint of a social behaviorist.* Chicago: University of Chicago Press.

Mead, M. (January 1972). A new understanding of childhood. *Redbook,* pp. 49ff.

Mead, M., & Newton, N. (1967). Cultural patterning of perinatal behavior. In S. A. Richardson & A. F. Guttermacher (Eds.), *Childbearing: Its social and psychological aspects.* Baltimore: Williams & Wilkins.

Meadow, K. P. (1975). The development of deaf children. In E. M. Hetherington (Ed.), *Review of child development research* (Vol. 5). Chicago: University of Chicago Press.

Meltzoff, A. N. (1988a). Infant imitation and memory: Nine month olds in immediate and deferred tests. *Child Development, 59,* 217-225.

Meltzoff, A. N. (1988b). Infant imitation after a 1-week delay: Long-term memory for novel acts and multiple stimuli. *Developmental Psychology, 24*(4), 470-476.

Meltzoff, A. N., & Borton, R. W. (1979). Intermodel matching by human neonates. *Nature, 282,* 403-404.

Meltzoff, A. N., & Moore, M. K. (1989). Imitation in newborn infants: Exploring the range of gestures imitated and the underlying mechanisms. National Institute of Child Health and Human Development (HD-22514).

Merriman, W. E. (1987). *Lexical contrast in toddlers: A re-analysis of the diary evidence.* Paper presented at the biennial meeting of the Society of Research in Child Development, Baltimore.

Mervis, C. B. (1987). Child-basic object categories and early lexical development. In U. Neisser (Ed.), *Concepts and conceptual development: Ecological and intellectual factors in categorization.* London: Cambridge University Press.

Metcoff, J., Costiloe, J. P., Crosby, W., Bentle, L., Seshachalam, D., Sandstead, H. H., Bodwell, C. E., Weaver, F., & McClain, P. (1981). Maternal nutrition and fetal outcome. *American Journal of Clinical Nutrition, 34,* 708-721.

Milgram, S. (1963). Behavioral study of obedience. *Journal of Abnormal and Social Psychology, 67,* 371-378.

Miller, B. C., & Sneesby, K. R. (1988). Educational correlates of adolescents' sexual attitudes and behavior. *Journal of Youth and Adolescence, 17,* 521-530.

Miller, B. C., McCoy, J. K., Olson, T. D., & Wallace, C. M. (1986). Parental discipline and control attempts in relation to adolescent sexual attitudes and behavior. *Journal of Marriage and the Family, 48,* 503-512.

Miller, P. (1989). *Theories of developmental psychology* (2nd ed.). New York: Freeman.

Miller, P. H., & Aloise, P. A. (1989). Young children's understanding of the psychological causes of behavior: A review. *Child Development, 60,* 257-285.

Miller-Jones, D. (1989). Culture and testing. *American Psychologist, 44*(2), 360-366.

Miringoff, N. (February 1987). A timely and controversial article. *Zero to Three,* p. 26.

Mock, N. B., Bertrand, J. T., & Mangani, N. (1986). Correlates and implications of breastfeeding practices in Bas Zaire. *Journal of Biosocial Science, 18,* 231-245.

Moerk, E. L. (1989). The LAD was a lady and the tasks were ill-defined. *Developmental Review, 9,* 21-57.

Money, J. (1980). *Love and love sickness: The science of sex, gender differences and pair-bonding.* Baltimore: Johns Hopkins University Press.

Monmaney, T. (May 16, 1988). Preventing early births. *Newsweek.*

Montagu, M. F. (1950). Constitutional and prenatal factors in infant and child health. In M. J. Senn (Ed.), *Symposium on the healthy personality.* New York: Josiah Macy Jr. Foundation.

Montemayor, R., & Brownlee, J. R. (1987). Fathers, mothers and adolescents: Gender-based differences in parental roles during adolescence. *Journal of Youth and Adolescence, 16,* 281-292.

Moore, G. (June 1984). The superbaby myth. *Psychology Today,* pp. 6-7.

Moore, M. K., Borton, R., & Darby, B. L. (1978). Visual tracking in young infants: Evidence for object permanence? *Journal of Experimental Child Psychology, 25,* 183-198.

Morgan, M. (1987). Television, sex-role attitudes, and sex-role behavior. *Journal of Early Adolescence, 7*(1), 269-282.

Morrison, D. M. (1985). Adolescent contraceptive behavior: A review. *Psychological Bulletin, 98,* 538-568.

Morse, D. L., Lessner, L., Medvesky, M. G., Glebatis, D. M., & Novick, L. F. (May Supplement 1991) Geographic distribution of newborn HIV seroprevalence in relation to four sociodemographic variables. *American Journal of Public Health, 81,* 25-29.

Mosher, W. D., & Pratt, W. F. (1990). Fecundity and infertility in the United States, 1965-88. *Advanced Data from Vital and Health Statistics, 192.* Hyattsville, MD: National Center for Health Statistics.

Mueller, E., & Lucas, T. (1975). A developmental analysis of peer interaction among toddlers. In M. Lewis & L. A. Rosenblum (Eds.), *Peer relations and friendship.* New York: Wiley.

Muir, D., & Field, J. (1979). Newborn infants orient to sounds. *Child Development, 50,* 431-436.

Murphy, L. B. (1962). *The widening world of childhood: Paths toward mastery.* New York: Basic Books.

Murray, A., Dolby, R., Nation, R., & Thomas, D. (1981). Effects of epidural anaesthesia on newborns and their mothers. *Child Development, 52,* 71-82.

Mussen, P. H., Conger J. J., & Kagan, J. (1974). *Child development and personality.* New York: Harper & Row.

Muuss, R. E. (Summer 1986). Adolescent eating disorder: Bulimia. *Adolescence,* pp. 257-267.

Myers, N. A., & Perlmutter, M. (1978). Memory in the years from two to five. In P. Ornstein (Ed.), *Memory development in children.* Hillsdale, NJ: Erlbaum.

Myers, N. A., Clifton, R. K., & Clarkson, M. G. (1987). When they were very young: Almost-threes remember two years ago. *Infant Behavior and Development, 10,* 123-132.

Myers, R. E., & Myers, S. E. (1978). Use of sedative, analgesic, and anesthetic drugs during labor and delivery: Bane or boon? *American Journal of Obstetrics and Gynecology, 133,* 83.

Naeye, R. L. (1979). Weight gain and the outcome of pregnancy. *American Journal of Obstetrics and Gynecology, 135,* 3.

Naeye, R. L. (1980). Abruptio placentae and placenta previa: Frequency, perinatal mortality, and cigarette smoking. *Obstetrics and Gynecology, 55,* 701-704.

Naeye, R. L. (1981). Influence of maternal cigarette smoking during pregnancy on fetal and childhood growth. *Obstetrics and Gynecology, 57,* 18-21.

National Association for the Education of Young Children. (1986). *NAEYC position statement on developmentally appropriate practice in early childhood programs: Birth through age eight.* Washington, DC: NAEYC.

National Center for Health Statistics. (1984). Trends in teenage childbearing, United States 1970-81. *Vital and Health Statistics* (Series 21, No. 41). U.S. Department of Health and Human Services.

National Center for Health Statistics. (1990). *Health, United States, 1989.* Washington, D.C.: United States Government Printing Office.

National Center for Health Statistics. (1991a). Births, marriages, divorces, and deaths for January 1991. *Monthly Vital Statistics Report, 40*(1). Hyattsville, MD: Public Health Service.

National Center for Health Statistics. (1991b). Advance report of final divorce statistics, 1988. *Monthly Vital Statistics Report, 39*(12, Supplement 2). Hyattsville, MD: Public Health Service.

National Center for Health Statistics. (1993a). *Health, United States, 1992.* Washington, D.C.: United States Government Printing Office.

National Center for Health Statistics. (1993b). Advance Report of Final Natality Statistics, 1990. *Monthly Vital Statistics Report, 41*(9).

National Center for Health Statistics. (August 1990). Advance report of final natality statistics, 1988. *Monthly Vital Statistics Report, 38*(4 Supplement). Hyattsville, MD: Public Health Service.

National Center for Health Statistics. (June 29, 1989). *Monthly Vital Statistics Report, 38*(3). Washington, DC: National Center for Health Statistics.

National Center for Health Statistics. (November 28, 1990). Advance report of final mortality statistics, 1988. *Monthly Vital Statistics Report, 39*(7). Hyattsville, MD: Public Health Service.

National Commission to Prevent Infant Mortality. (1992). *Troubling trends persist: Short-changing America's next generation.* Washington, DC: U.S. Government Printing Office.

National Institute on Drug Abuse. (1987). *National trends in drug use and related factors among American high school students and young adults, 1975-1986.* U.S. Department of Health & Human Services.

National Institute on Drug Abuse. (1989). *National trends in drug use and related factors among American high school students and young adults, 1975-1988.* U.S. Department of Health & Human Services.

Neal, A. G., Grout, H. T., & Wicks, J. W. (1989). Attitudes about having children: A study of 600 couples in the early years of marriage. *Journal of Marriage and the Family, 51,* 313-328.

Needleman, H. L., Schell, A., Bellinger, D., Leviton, A., & Allred, E. N. (1990). The long-term exposure to low doses of lead in childhood. *New England Journal of medicine, 322,* 83-88.

Neimark, E. D., (1975). Intellectual development during adolescence. In F. D. Horowitz (Ed.), *Review of child development* (Vol. 4). Chicago: University of Chicago Press.

Nelson, K. (1974). Concept, word and sentence: Interrelations in acquisition and development. *Psychological Review, 81,* 267-285.

Nelson, K. (1981). Individual differences in language development: Implications for development and language. *Developmental Psychology, 17,* 170-187.

Nelson, K. (1986). *Event knowledge: Structure and function in development.* Hillsdale, NJ: Erlbaum.

Nelson, K. (September 1987). What's in a name? Reply to Seidenberg and Petitto. *Journal of Experimental Psychology, 116*(3), 293-296.

Nelson, K., & Gruendel, J. M. (1986). Generalized event representations: Basic building blocks of cognitive development. In A. Brown & M. Lamb (Eds.), *Advances in developmental psychology* (Vol. 1). Hillsdale, NJ: Erlbaum.

Nelson, K., Fibush, R., Hudson, J., & Lucariello, J. (1983). *Scripts and the development of memory*. In M. T. C. Chi (Ed.), *Trends in memory development research*. Basil, Switzerland: Carger.

Nemeth, R. J., & Bowling, J. M. (1985). Son preference and its effects on Korean lactation practices. *Journal of Biosocial Science, 17,* 451-459.

New York Times. (March 4, 1991). Schools are not families. Editorial, p. A16.

New, R. (1988). Parental goals and Italian infant care. In R. B. LeVine, P. Miller, & M. West (Eds.), *New Directions for Child Development: Vol. 40, Parental behavior in diverse societies* (pp. 51-63). San Francisco: Jossey-Bass.

Newcombe, N., & Huttenlocher, J. (1992). Children's early ability to solve perspective-taking problems. *Developmental Psychology, 28*(4), 635-643.

Newman, L. S. (1990). Intentional and unintentional memory in young children: Remembering vs. playing. *Journal of Experimental Child Psychology, 50,* 243-258.

Newsweek. (February 11, 1980). The children of divorce, pp. 58-63.

Newsweek. (November 15, 1976). New science of birth, pp. 62-64.

Ney, P. G. (1988). Transgenerational child abuse. *Child Psychiatry and Human Development, 18,* 151-168.

Nichols, B. (1990). *Moving and Learning: The elementary school physical education experience*. St. Louis, MO: Times Mirror/Mosby College Publishing.

Nichols, P. L., & Chen, T. C. (1981). *Minimal brain dysfunction: A prospective study*. Hillsdale, NJ: Erlbaum.

Nicolopoulou, A. (1993). Play, cognitive development, and the social world: Piaget, Vygotsky, and Beyond. *Human Development, 36,* 1-23.

Nilsson, L. (1990). *A child is born*. New York: Delacorte.

Nock, S. (1982). The life-cycle approach to family analysis. In B. Wolman (Ed.), *Handbook of developmental psychology* (pp. 636-651). Englewood Cliffs, NJ: Prentice Hall.

Nugent, J. K., Greene, S., & Mazor, K. (October 1990). *The effects of maternal alcohol and nicotine use during pregnancy on birth outcome*. Paper presented at Bebe XXI Simposio Internacional, Lisbon, Portugal.

Nutrition Today. (1982). Alcohol use during pregnancy: A report by the American Council on Science and Health. Reprint.

O'Brien, M., & Nagle, K. J. (1987). Parents' speech to toddlers: The effect of play context. *Journal of Language Development, 14,* 269-279.

O'Connor-Francoeur, P. (April 1983). *Children's concepts of health and their health behavior*. Paper presented at the meeting of the Society for Research in Child Development, Detroit.

O'Heron, C. A., & Orlofsky, J. L. (1990). Stereotypic and nonstereotypic sex role trait and behavior operations, gender identity and psychological adjustment. *Journal of Personality and Social Psychology, 58*(1), 134-143.

Oakley, A., & Richards, M. (1990). Women's experiences of Caesarean delivery. In J. Garcia, R. Kilpatrick, & M. Richards (Eds.), *The politics of maternity care*. Oxford: Clarendon Press.

OB/GYN News. (June 15-30, 1984). In-vitro fertilization comes of age: Issues still unsettled, *19*(12), 3.

Ochs, E. (1986). Introduction. In B. B. Schieffelin & E. Ochs (Eds.), *Language socialization across cultures*. Cambridge, UK: Cambridge University Press.

Ohlsson, A., Shennan, A. T., & Rose, T. H. (1987). Review of causes of perinatal mortality in a regional perinatal center, 1980-84. *American Journal of Obstetrics and Gynecology, 1*(57), 443-445.

Oller, D. K., & Eilers, R. E. (1988). The role of audition in infant babbling. *Child Development, 59,* 441-449.

Olson, S. L., Bates, J. E., & Bayles, K. (1984). Mother-infant interaction and the development of individual differences in children's cognitive competence. *Developmental Psychology, 20,* 166-179.

Olton, R. M., & Crutchfield, R. S. (1969). Developing the skills of productive thinking. In P. H. Mussen, J. Langer, & M. Covington (Eds.), *Trends and issues in developmental psychology*. New York: Holt, Rinehart & Winston.

Oni, G. A. (October 1987). Breast-feeding pattern in an urban Nigerian community. *Journal of Biolosocial Science, 19*(4), 453-462.

Opie, I., & Opie, P. (1959). *The lore and language of school children*. London: Oxford University Press.

Orlofsky, J. L., & O'Heron, C. A. (1987). Stereotypic and nonstereotypic sex role trait and behavior orientation: Implications for personal adjustment. *Journal of Personality and Social Psychology, 52,* 1034-1042.

Ormond, C., Luszc, M. A., Mann, L., & Beswick, G. (1991). The metacognitive analysis of decision making in adolescence. *Journal of Adolescence, 14,* 275-291.

Ornstein, P. A., Naus, M. J., & Liberty, C. (1975). Rehearsal and organizational processes in children's memory. *Child Development, 46,* 818-830.

Ornstein, P. A., Naus, M. J., & Stone, B. P. (1977). Rehearsal training and developmental differences in memory. *Developmental Psychology, 13,* 15-24.

Otto, L. B. (1988). America's youth: A changing profile. *Family Relations, 37,* 385-391.

Ouellette, E. M., et al. (1977). Adverse effects on offspring of maternal alcohol abuse during pregnancy. *New England Journal of Medicine, 297,* 528-530.

Paikoff, R. L. (1991). Shared views in the family during adolescence. *New Directions for Child Development, 51,* San Francisco: Jossey-Bass.

Palkovitz, R. (1985). Fathers' birth attendance, early contact and extended contact with their newborns: A critical review. *Child Development, 56,* 392-406.

Papert, S. (1980). *Mindstorms: Children, computers and powerful thinking*. New York: Basic Books.

Papousâk, H. (1961). Conditioned head rotation reflexes in infants in the first three months of life. *Acta Paediatrica Scandinavica, 50,* 565-576.

Paris, S. C., Lindauer, B. K., & Cox, G. I. (1977). The development of inferential comprehension. *Child Development, 48,* 1728-1733.

Parke, R. D. (1972). Some effects of punishment on children's behavior. In W. W. Hartup (Ed.), *The young child: Reviews of research* (Vol. 2). Washington, DC: National Association for the Education of Young Children.

Parke, R. D. (1979). Perceptions of father-infant interaction. In J. Osofsky (Ed.), *Handbook of infant development*. New York: Wiley.

Parke, R. D. (1981). *Fathers*. Cambridge, MA: Harvard University Press.

Parke, R. D., & Collmer, C. (1975). Child abuse: An interdisciplinary analysis. In E. M. Hetherington (Ed.), *Review of child development research* (Vol. 5). Chicago: University of Chicago Press.

Parke, R. D., & Tinsley, B. J. (1987). Family interaction in infancy. In J. D. Osofsky (Ed.), *Handbook of infant development* (2nd ed., pp. 579-641). New York: Wiley.

Parke, R., & Slahy, R. (1983). The development of aggression. In P. H. Mussen (Ed.), *Handbook of child psychology* (Vol. 4). New York: Wiley.

Parker, Herdt & Carballo (1991)

Parker, J. G., & Asher, S. R. (1987). Peer relations and later personal adjustment: Are low-accepted children at risk? *Psychological Bulletin, 102,* 357-389.

Parker, W. A. (1980). Designing an environment for childbirth. In B. L. Blum (Ed.), *Psychological aspects of pregnancy, birthing, and bonding*. New York: Human Sciences Press.

Parmelee, A. H., Jr. (1986). Children's illnesses: Their beneficial effects on behavioral development. *Child Development, 57,* 1-10.

Patterson, C. J., Kupersmidt, J. B. & Vaden, N. A. (1990). Income level, gender, ethnicity, and household composition as predictors of children's school-based competence. *Child Development, 61*, 485-494.

Paulby, S. T. (1977). Imitative interaction. In H. R. Schaffer (Ed.), *Studies of mother-infant interaction.* London: Academic Press.

Pavlov, I. P. (1928). *Lectures on conditioned reflexes.* (W. H. Gantt, Trans.). New York: International Publishers.

Pederson, F., et al. (1979). Infant development in father-absent families. *Journal of Genetic Psychology, 135*, 51-61.

Pediatrics. (1978). Effect of medication during labor and delivery on infant outcome, *62*, 402-403.

Pediatrics. (1979). The fetal monitoring debate, *63*, 942-948.

Pellegrini, A. D. & Perlmutter, J. C. (January 1988). Rough-and-tumble play on the elementary school playground. *Young Children,* 14-17.

Pellegrini, A. D. (1987). Rough-and-tumble play: Developmental and educational significance. *Educational Psychologist, 22*(1), 23-43.

Pellegrini, A. D. (1988). Elementary-school children's rough-and-tumble play and social competence. *Developmental Psychology, 24*(6), 802-806.

Pellegrini, A. D. (1989). Elementary school children's rough-and-tumble play. *Early childhood Research Quarterly, 4*, 245-260.

Perkins, S. A. (1977). Malnutrition and mental development. *Exceptional Children, 43*(4), 214-219.

Perrin, J., Guyer, B. & Lawrence, J. M. (1992). Health care services for children and adolescents. In R. E. Behrman, (Ed.). *The future of children.* Los Angeles, CA: Center for the Future of Children of the David and Lucile Packard Foundation.

Perry, D. G., & Bussey, K. (1984). *Social development.* Englewood Cliffs, NJ: Prentice Hall.

Perry, D. G., Williard, J. C., & Perry, L. C. (1990). Peers' perceptions of the consequences that victimized children provide aggressors. *Child Development, 61*, 1310-1325.

Peterson, A. C., & Taylor, B. (1980). The biological approach to adolescence: Biological change and psychological adaptation. In J. Adelson (Ed.), *Handbook of adolescent psychology.* New York: Wiley.

Peterson, A. C., Compas, B. E., Brooks-Gunn, J., Stemmler, M., Ey, S., and Grant, K. E. (1993). Depression in adolescence. *American Psychologist, 48*(2), 155-168.

Phares, V., & Compas, B. E. (1992). The role of fathers in child and adolescent psychopathology: make room for Daddy. *Psychological Bulletin, 111* (3), 387-412.

Phillips, D. (1984). The illusion of incompetence among academically competent children. *Child Development, 55*, 2000-2016.

Phillips, D., McCartney, K., Scarr, S., & Howes, C. (February 1987). Selective review of infant day care research: A cause for concern! *Zero to Three*, pp. 18-20.

Phillips, J. L., Jr. (1969). *The origins of intellect: Piaget's theory.* San Francisco: Freeman.

Piaget, J. (1926). *The language and thought of the child.* London: Kegan, Paul, Trench & Trubner.

Piaget, J. (1950). *The psychology of intelligence.* (M. Percy & D. E. Berlyne, Trans.). New York: Harcourt Brace.

Piaget, J. (1951). *Play, dreams and imitation in childhood.* New York: Norton.

Piaget, J. (1952). *The origins of intelligence in children.* (M. Cook, Trans.). New York: International Universities Press. (Originally published 1936)

Piaget, J. (1954). *The construction of reality in the child.* (M. Cook, Trans.). New York: Basic Books.

Piaget, J. (1955). *The language and thought of the child.* New York: World.

Piaget, J. (1962). *Plays, dreams, and imitation.* New York: Norton.

Piaget, J. (1965). *The moral judgment of the child.* (M. Gabain, Trans.). New York: Free Press. (Originally published 1932)

Piaget, J. (1970). Piaget's theory. In P. H. Mussen (Ed.), *Carmichael's manual of child psychology* (3rd ed., Vol. 1). New York: Wiley.

Piaget, J. (1972). Intellectual evolution from adolescence to adulthood. *Human Development, 15*, 1-12.

Piccigallo, P. R. (Fall 1988). Preschool: Head Start or Hard Push? *Social Policy, 1988*, 45-48.

Pines, M. (1979). Superkids. *Psychology Today, 12*(8), 53-63.

Pines, M. (1984). PT conversations: Resilient children. *Psychology Today, 12*(8), 53-63.

Pines, M. (September 1981). The civilizing of Genie. *Psychology Today,* pp. 28-34.

Pitcher, E. G., & Schultz, L. H. (1983). *Boys and girls at play: The development of sex roles.* New York: Praeger.

Pleck, J. H. (1985). *Working wives, working husbands.* Beverly Hills, CA: Sage.

Pleck, J. H., & Staines, G. L. (1982). Work schedules and work family conflict in two-earner couples. In J. Aldous (Ed.), *Two paychecks: Life in dual-earner families.* Beverly Hills, CA: Sage.

Plomin, R. (1983). Developmental behavioral genetics. *Child Development, 54*, 25-29.

Plomin, R. (1990). *Nature and nurture: An introduction to human behavioral genetics.* Pacific Grove, CA: Brooks/Cole.

Plomin, R., & Daniels, D. (1987). Why are children in the same family so different from one another? *Behavioral and Brain Sciences, 10*, 1-60.

Plowden, B. (1967). *Children and their primary schools: A report of the Central Advisory Council for Education in England* (Vol. 1). London: Her Majesty's Stationery Office.

Plumb, J. H. (Winter 1971). The great change in children. *Horizon,* pp. 4-12.

Poest, C. A., Williams, J. R., Witt, D. D., & Atwood, M. E. (1989). Physical activity patterns of preschool children. *Early Childhood Research Quarterly, 4*, 367-376.

Pomerleau, A., Bolduc, D., Malcuit, G., & Cossette, L. (1990). Pink or blue: Environmental gender stereotypes in the first two years of life. *Sex Roles, 22*(5/6), 359-367.

Poole, W. (July/August 1987). The first 9 months of school. *Hippocrates*, pp. 66-73.

Power, C., & Reimer, J. (1978). Moral atmosphere: An educational bridge between moral judgment and action. *New Directions for Child Development, 2.*

Powers, S. I., Hauser, S. T., & Kilner, L. A. (1989). Adolescent mental health. *American Psychologist, 44*, 200-208.

Pratt, K. C. (1954). The neonate. In L. Carmichael (Ed.), *Manual of child psychology* (2nd ed.). New York: Wiley.

Prechtl, H., & Beintema, D. (1965). *The neurological examination of the full term newborn infant* (Clinics in Developmental Medicine Series No. 12). Philadelphia: Lippincott.

Purcell, P., & Sewart, L. (1990). Dick and Jane in 1989. *Sex Roles, 22*(3/4), 177-185.

Quadrel, M. J., Fischhoff, B., and Davis, W. (1993). Adolescent (in)vulnerability. *American Psychologist, 48*(2), 102-116.

Queenan, J. T. (August 1975). The Rh-immunized pregnancy. *Consultant*, pp. 96-99.

Racine, A. D., Joyce, T. D., and Grossman, M. (1992). Effectiveness of health care services for pregnant women and infants. *The future of children: U.S. health care for children 2*(2). Los Angeles, CA: The David and Lucile Packard Foundation.

Radbill, S. (1974). A history of child abuse and infanticide. In R. Helfer & C. Kempe (Eds.), *The battered child.* Chicago: University of Chicago Press.

Radkey-Yarrow, M., Zahn-Waxler, C., & Chapman, M. (1983). Children's prosocial dispositions and behavior. In E. M. Hetherington (Ed.), *Handbook of child psychology: Vol. 4. Socialization, personality and social development.* New York: Wiley.

Rahbar, F., Momeni, J., Fumufod, A. K., & Westney, L. (1985). Prenatal care and perinatal mortality in a black population. *Obstetrics and Gynecology, 65* (3), 327-329.

Ramey, C. T. (1981). Consequences of infant day care. In B. Weissbound & J. Musick (Eds.), *Infants: Their social environments.*

Washington, DC: National Association for the Education of Young Children.

Ratner, N. B., & Pye, C. (1984). Higher pitch in BT is not universal: Acoustic evidence from Quiche Mayan. *Journal of Child Language, 11,* 515-522.

Ratner, N., & Bruner, J. S. (1978). Games, social exchange and the acquisition of language. *Journal of Child Development, 5,* 1-15.

Rauste-von Wright, M. (1989). Body image satisfaction in adolescent girls and boys: A longitudinal study. *Journal of Youth and Adolescence, 18,* 71-83.

Reich, P. A. (1986). *Language development.* Englewood Cliffs, NJ: Prentice Hall.

Reid, M. (1990). Prenatal diagnosis and screening. In J. Garcia, R. Kilpatrick, & M. Richards (Eds.), *The politics of maternity care* (pp. 300-323). Oxford: Clarendon Press.

Reid, M. (1990). Prenatal diagnosis and screening. In J. Garcia, R. Kilpatrick, & M. Richards (Eds.), *The politics of maternity care.* Oxford: Clarendon Press.

Reid, M., Ramey, S. L., & Burchinal, M. (1990). Dialogues with children about their families. In I. Bretherton & M. W. Watson (Eds.), *New Directions for Child Development, 48,* 5-28.

Reiss, I. L. (1971). *The family system in America.* New York: Holt, Rinehart & Winston.

Reuhl, K. R., & Chang, L. W. (1979). Effects of methylmercury on the development of the nervous system: A review. *Neurotoxicology, 1,* 21-55.

Ricciuti, H. N. (1993). Nutrition and mental development. *Current Directions in Psychological Science, 2*(2), 43-46.

Rice, M. L., & Haight, P. L. (1986). ``Motherese'' of Mr. Rogers: A description of the dialogue of educational television programs. *Journal of Speech and Hearing Disorders, 51,* 282-287.

Rice, S. G. (1990). *Putting the play back in exercise.* Unpublished.

Richardson, S. O. (1992). Historical perspectives on dyslexia. *Journal of Learning Disabilities, 25*(1), 40-47.

Richman, A. L., LeVine, R. A., New, R. A., Howrigan, G. A., Welles-Nystrom, B., & LeVine, S. E. (Summer 1988). Maternal behavior to infants in five cultures. In R. A. LeVine, P. M. Miller, & M. M. West (Eds.), *New Directions for Child Development: Vol. 40. Personal behavior in diverse societies* (pp. 81-98).

Richman, C. L., Berry, C., Bittle, M., & Himan, K. (1988). Factors relating to helping behavior in preschool-age children. *Journal of Applied Developmental Psychology, 9,* 151-165.

Ricks, S. S. (1985). Father-infant interactions: A review of empirical research. *Family Relations, 34,* 505-511.

Rizzo, T. A., & Corsaro, W. A. (1988). Toward a better understanding of Vygotsky's process of internalization: Its role in the development of the concept of friendship. *Developmental Review, 8,* 219-237.

Roberton, M. A., and Halverson, L. E. (1988) The development of locomotor coordination: longitudinal change and invariance. *Journal of Motor Behavior, 20*(3), 197-241.

Robertson, M. (1984). Changing motor patterns during childhood. In J. R. Thomas (Ed.), *Motor development during childhood and adolescence.* Minneapolis, MN: Burgess.

Robinson, I. E., & Jedlicka, D. (1982). Change in sexual behavior of college students from 1965-1980: A research note. *Journal of Marriage and the Family, 44,* 237-240.

Rochat, P. (1989). Object manipulation and exploration in 2- to 5-month-old infants. *Developmental Psychology, 25*(6), 871-884.

Rogel, M. J., & Peterson, A. C. (1984). Some adolescent experiences of motherhood. In R. Cohen, B. Cohler, & S. Weissman (Eds.), *Parenthood: A psychodynamic perspective.* New York: Guilford.

Rogers, C. (1980). *A way of being.* Boston: Houghton Mifflin.

Rogers, M. F., White, C. R., Sanders, R., Schable, C., Ksell, T. E., Wasserman, R. L., Bellanti, J. A., Peters, S. M. & Wary, B. B. Lack of transmission of human immunodeficiency virus from infected children to their household contacts. *Pediatrics, 85*(2), 210.

Rogoff, B. (1990). *Apprenticeship in thinking: Cognitive development in social context.* New York: Oxford University Press.

Rogoff, B. (1993). Commentary. *Human Development, 36,* 24-26.

Rogoff, B., & Wertsch, J. (1984). Children's learning in the ``zone of proximal development.'' *New Directions for Child Development, 23.* San Francisco: Jossey-Bass.

Roscoe, B., Diana, M. S., & Brooks, R. H., II. (1987). Early, middle, and late adolescents' views on dating and factors influencing partner selection. *Adolescence, 12,* 59-68.

Rose, S. A., Gottfried, A. W., & Bridger, W. H. (1981). Cross-modal transfer in 6-month-old infants. *Developmental Psychology, 17,* 661-669.

Rose-Krasnor, L. (1988). Social cognition. In T. D. Yawkey & J. E. Johnson (Eds.), *Integrative processes and socialization: Early to middle childhood* (pp. 79-95). Hillsdale, NJ: Erlbaum.

Rosel, N. (1978). Toward a social theory of dying. *Omega, 9*(1), 49-55.

Rosenfeld, A. (March 23, 1974b). Starve the child, famish the future. *Saturday Review,* p. 59.

Rosenfeld, A. (September 7, 1974a). If Oedipus' parents had only known. *Saturday Review,* 49f.

Rosenstein, D., & Oster, H. (1988). Differential facial response to four basic tastes in newborns. *Child Development, 59,* 1555-1568.

Rosenthal, E. (January 4, 1990). New insights on why some children are fat offers clues on weight loss. *New York Times,* p. B8.

Rosenthal, J. A. (1988). Patterns of reported child abuse and neglect. *Child Abuse and Neglect, 12,* 263-271.

Rosenthal, R., & Jacobson, L. (1968). *Pygmalion in the classroom: Teacher expectation and pupil's intellectual development.* New York: Harper & Row.

Rosenwasser, S. M., Lingenfelter, M., & Harrington, A. F. (1989). Nontraditional gender role portrayals on television and children's gender role perceptions. *Journal of Applied Developmental Psychology, 10,* 97-105.

Rosett, H. L., et al. (1981). Strategies for prevention of fetal alcohol effects. *Obstetrics and Gynecology, 57,* 1-16.

Roskinski, R. R. (1977). *The development of visual perception.* Santa Monica, CA: Goodyear.

Ross, A. O. (1977). *Learning disability, the unrealized potential.* New York: McGraw-Hill.

Ross, H. S., & Lollis, S. P. (1987). Communication within infant social games. *Developmental Psychology, 23,* 241-248.

Ross, H., & Sawhill, I. (1975). *Time of transition: The growth of families headed by women.* Washington, DC: Urban Institute.

Rossi, A. S. (1979). Transition to parenthood. In P. Rossi (Ed.), *Socialization and the life cycle.* New York: St. Martin's Press.

Rossi, A. S. (Spring 1977). A biological perspective in parenting. *Daedalus.*

Rossman, I. (1977). Anatomic and body-composition changes with aging. In C. E. Finch & L. Hayflick (Eds.), *Handbook of the biology of aging.* New York: Van Nostrand Reinhold.

Rothschild, N. & Morgan, M. (1987). Cohesion and control: Adolescents' relationships with parents as mediators of television. *Journal of Early Adolescence, 7*(3), 299-314.

Roug, L., Landberg, I., & Lundberg, L. J. (February 1989). Phonetic development in early infancy: A study of four Swedish children during the first eighteen months of life. *Journal of Child Language, 16*(1), 19-40.

Rovee-Collier, C. (1987). Learning and memory in infancy. In J. Osofsky (Ed.), *Handbook of infant development* (2nd ed.). New York: Wiley.

Rowland, T. W., Donnelly, J. H., Landis, J. N., Lemoine, M. E., Sigelman, D. R., & Tanella, C. J. (1987). Infant home apnea monitoring. *Clinical Pediatrics, 26*(8), 383-387.

Rozin, P. (1990). Development in the food domain. *Developmental Psychology, 26*(4), 555-562.

Rozin, P., Hammer, L., Oster, H., Horowitz, T., & Marmara, V. (1986). The child's conception of food: Differentiation of categories of rejected substances in the 1.4 to 5-year age range. *Appetite, 7,* 141-151.

Rubin, K. H. (1983). Recent perspectives on social competence and peer status: Some introductory remarks. *Child Development, 54,* 1383-1385.

Rubin, K. H., & Coplan, R. J. (1992). Peer relationships in childhood. In M. H. Bornstein, and M. E. Lamb, (Eds.), *Developmental psychology: An advanced textbook.* Hillsdale, NJ: Lawrence Erlbaum.

Rubin, K. H., Fein, G. C., & Vandenberg, B. (1983). In P. H. Mussen (Ed.), *Handbook of child psychology* (Vol. 4). New York: Wiley.

Rubin, K. H., Maloni, T. L., & Hornung, M. (1976). Free play behaviors in middle- and lower-class preschoolers: Partner and Piaget revised. *Child Development, 47,* 414-419.

Rubin, K., & Trotten, K. (1977). Kohlberg's moral judgment scale: Some methodological considerations. *Developmental Psychology, 13*(5), 535-536.

Rubin, Z. (1980). *Children's friendships.* Cambridge, MA: Harvard University Press.

Rubinstein, E. A. (1983). Television and behavior: Conclusion of the 1982 NIMH report and their policy implications. *American Psychologist, 38,* 820-825.

Ruble, D. (1988). Sex-role development. In M. Bornstein & M. E. Lamb (Eds.), *Developmental psychology: An advanced textbook* (2nd ed., pp. 411-460). Hillsdale, NJ: Erlbaum.

Ruble, D. N., & Brooks-Gunn, J. (1982). The experience of menarche. *Child Development, 53,* 1557-1577.

Rudd, P., & Balaschke, T. (1982) Antihypertensive agents and the drug therapy of hypertension. In A. Gilman, L. Goodman, T. Rall, & F. Murad (Eds.), *Goodman and Gilman's the pharmacological basis of therapeutics* (7th ed., pp. 784-805.)

Ruebsaat, H. J., & Hull, R. (1975). *The male climacteric.* New York: Hawthorn Books.

Rugh, R., & Shettles, L. B. (1971). *From conception to birth: The drama of life's beginnings.* New York: Harper & Row.

Rushton, T. P. (1976). Socialization and the altruistic behavior of children. *Psychological Bulletin, 83*(5), 898-913.

Russell, A., & Finnie, V. (1990). Preschool children's social status and maternal instructions to assist group entry. *Developmental Psychology, 26*(4), 603-611.

Russell, D. (1983). The incidence and prevalence of intrafamilial and extrafamilial sexual abuse of female children. *Child Abuse and Neglect, 7,* 133-146.

Rutter, M. (1979). Protective factors in children's responses to stress and disadvantage. In M. W. Kent & J. E. Rolf (Eds.), *Primary prevention of psychopathology: III. Social competence in children.* Hanover, NH: University Press of New England.

Rutter, M. (1983). Stress, coping and development: Some issues and questions. In N. Garmezy & M. Rutter (Eds.), *Stress, coping and development in children.* New York: McGraw-Hill.

Rutter, M. (1984). PT conversations: Resilient children. *Psychology Today, 18*(3), 60-62, 64-65.

Rutter, M., & Garmezy, N. (1983). Developmental psychopathology. In P. H. Mussen (Ed.), *Handbook of child psychology* (Vol. 4). New York: Wiley.

Ryan, A. S., Martinez, G. A., & Malec, D. J. (Spring 1985). The effect of the WIC program on nutrient intakes of infants, 1984. *Medical Anthropology,* p. 153.

Salkind, N. (1981). *Theories of human development.* New York: D. Van-Nostrand.

Salthouse, T. (1985). Speed of behavior and its implications for cognition. In J. E. Birren & K. W. Schaie (Eds.), *Handbook of the psychology of aging* (2nd ed.). New York: Van Nostrand Reinhold.

Salthouse, T., & Mitchell, D. (1990). Effect of age and naturally occurring experience on spatial visualization performance. *Developmental Psychology, 26,* 845-854.

Salthouse, T., Babcock, R., Skovronek, E., Mitchell, D., & Palmon, R. (1990). Age and experience effects in spatial visualization. *Developmental Psychology, 26,* 128-136.

Sasserath, V. J. (Ed.). (1983). *Minimizing high-risk parenting.* Skillman, NJ: Johnson & Johnson.

Satir, V. (1972). *Peoplemaking.* Palo Alto, CA: Science and Behavior Books.

Savage-Rumbaugh, S., Rumbaugh, D. M., & McDonald, K. (September 1986). Spontaneous symbol acquisition and communicative use by pygmy chimpanzees. *Journal of Experimental Psychology, 115*(3), 211-235.

Scarborough, H. S. (1989). Prediction of reading disability from familial and individual differences. *Journal of Educational Psychology, 81,* 101-108.

Scarr, S. and Weinberg, R. (1976). IQ performance of black children adopted by white families. *American Psychologist, 44*(11), 1402-1409.

Scarr, S., & Kidd, K. K. (1983). Behavior genetics. In M. Haith & J. Campos (Eds.), *Manual of child psychology: Infancy and the biology of development* (Vol. 2). New York: Wiley.

Scarr, S., & McCartney, K. (1983). How people make their own environments: A theory of genotype/environmental effects. *Child Development, 54,* 424-435.

Scarr, S., & Weinberg, R. A. (1983). The Minnesota adoption studies: Genetic differences and malleability. *Child Development, 54.* 260-267.

Scarr, S., Phillips, D., & McCartney, K. (1989). Working mothers and their families. *American Psychologist, 44*(11), 1402-1409.

Scarr, S., Phillips, D., & McCartney, K. (1989). Working mothers and their families. *American Psychologist, 44,* 1402-1409.

Schacter, F., & Strage, A. (1982). Adult's talk and children's language development. In S. Moore & C. Cooper (Eds.), *The young child: Reviews of research* (Vol. 3, pp. 79-96). Washington, DC: National Association for the Education of Young Children.

Schaefer, M. R., Sobieraj, K., & Hollyfield, R. L. (1988). Prevalence of childhood physical abuse in adult male veteran alcoholics. *Child Abuse and Neglect, 12,* 141-149.

Schaffer, H. R. (1977). *Studies in mother-infant interaction.* London: Academic Press.

Schardein, J. L. (1976). *Drugs as teratogens.* Cleveland, OH: Chemical Rubber Co. Press.

Schieffelin, B. B., & Ochs, E. (1983). A cultural perspective on the transition from prelinguistic to linguistic communication. In R. M. Golinkoff (Ed.), *The transition from prelinguistic to linguistic communication.* Hillsdale, NJ: Erlbaum.

Schilder, P., & Wechsler, D. (1935). What do children know about the interior of the body? *International Journal of Psychoanalysis, 16,* 355-360.

Schlesinger, J. M. (1982). *Steps to language: Toward a theory of native language acquisition.* Hillsdale, NJ: Erlbaum.

Schneider, B. A., Trehub, S. E., & Bull, D. (1979). The development of basic auditory processes in infants. *Canadian Journal of Psychology, 33,* 306-319.

Schofield, J. W. (1981). Complementary and conflicting identities: Images and interaction in an interracial school. In S. R. Asher & J. M. Gottman (Eds.), *The development of children's friendships.* New York: Cambridge University Press.

Schwartz, J. I. (1981). Children's experiments with language. *Young Children, 36,* 16-26.

Sears, R. R. (1963). Dependency motivation. In M. R. Jones (Ed.), *The Nebraska symposium on motivation* (Vol. 11). Lincoln: University of Nebraska Press.

Sedlak, A. J. (1989). *Supplementary analyses of data on the national incidence of child abuse and neglect.* Rockville, MD: Westat.

Segal, J., & Yahraes, H. (November 1978). Bringing up mother. *Psychology Today,* pp. 80-85.

Seibel, M. M. & Taymor, M. L. (1982). Emotional aspects of infertility. *Fertility and Sterility, 37*(2), 137-145.

Seidman, S. A. (Spring 1992). An investigation of sex-role stereotyping in music videos. *Journal of Broadcasting and Electronic Media,* 209-217.

Selman, R. L. (1976). The development of interpersonal reasoning. In A. Pick (Ed.), *Minnesota symposia on child psychology* (Vol. 1). Minneapolis: University of Minnesota Press.

Selman, R. L. (1981). The child as a friendship philosopher. In S. R. Asher & J. M. Gottman (Eds.), *The development of children's friendships*. Cambridge, UK: Cambridge University Press.

Shaffer, D. R. (1988). *Social and personality development* (2nd ed.). Pacific Grove, CA: Brooks/Cole.

Shaffer, J. B. P. (1978). *Humanistic psychology*. Englewood Cliffs, NJ: Prentice Hall.

Shane, P. G. (1989). Changing patterns among homeless and runaway youth. *American Journal of Orthopsychiatry, 59*(2), 208-214.

Shannon, D., & Kelly, D. (1982). SIDS and near-SIDS. *New England Journal of Medicine, 306*, 961-962.

Shantz, C. (1983). Social cognition. In P. H. Mussen (Ed.), *Handbook of child psychology* (Vol. 3). New York: Wiley.

Shantz, C. U. (1975). The development of social cognition. In E. M. Hetherington (Ed.), *Review of child development research* (Vol. 5). Chicago: University of Chicago Press.

Shantz, C. U. (1987). Conflicts between children. *Child Development, 51*, 283-305.

Shapiro, M. (1978). Legal rights of the terminally ill. *Aging, 5*(3), 23-27.

Sharabany, R., Gershoni, R., & Hoffman, J. E. (1981). Girlfriend, boyfriend: Age and sex differences in intimate friendship. *Developmental Psychology, 17*, 800-808.

Shatz, C. (1992). The developing brain. *Scientific American (9)*, 61-67.

Shatz, M., & Gelman, R. (1973). The development of communication skills: Modifications in the speech of young children as a function of the listener. *Monographs of the Society for Research in Child Development, 38*(152).

Shaywitz, S. E., Shaywitz, B. A., Fletcher, J. M., & Escobar, M. D. (1991). Reading disability in children. *Journal of the American Medical Association, 265*, 725-726.

Sheiman, D. L., & Slomin, M. (1988). *Resources for middle childhood*. New York, NY: Garland.

Sherif, M., & Sherif, C. W. (1953). *Groups in harmony and tension*. New York: Harper & Brothers.

Sherif, M., Harvey, O. J., White, B. J., Hood, W. B., & Sherif, C. W. (1961). *Intergroup conflict and cooperation: The robber's cave experiment*. Norman: University of Oklahoma Press.

Shirley, M. M. (1931). *The first two years: A study of twenty-five babies* (Institute of Child Welfare Monograph No. 7, Vol. 1). Minneapolis: University of Minnesota Press.

Shirley, M. M. (1933). *The first two years: A study of twenty-five babies* (Institute of Child Welfare Monograph No. 7, Vol. 2). Minneapolis: University of Minnesota Press.

Shock, N. W. (1977). Biological theories of aging. In J. E. Birren, and K. W. Schaie, (Eds.), *Handbook of the psychology of aging*. New York: VanNostrand Reinhold.

Shultz, T. R. (1976). A cognitive-developmental analysis of humour. In A. J. Chapman, and H. C. Foot, (Eds.), *Humour and laughter: Theory, research, and applications*. London: Wiley.

Sieber, R. T., & Gordon, A. J. (1981). Socialization implications of school discipline or how first graders are taught to listen. In *Children and their organizations: Investigations in American culture*. Boston: G. K. Hall.

Siegler, R. S. (1986). *Children's thinking*. Englewood Cliffs, NJ: Prentice Hall.

Siegler, R. S. (1991). *Children's Thinking*. Englewood Cliffs, NJ: Prentice Hall.

Sigel, I. (1987). Does hothousing rob children of their childhood? *Early Childhood Research Quarterly, 2*, 211-225.

Signorella, M. L. (1987). Gender schemata: Individual differences and context effects. *New Directions for Child Development, 38*, 23-38.

Signorielli, N. (1989). Television and conceptions about sex roles: Maintaining conventionality and the status quo. *Sex Roles, 21*(5/6), 341-350.

Silber, S. J. (1991). *How to get pregnant with the new reproductive technology*. New York: Warner Books.

Silver, L. B. (October 1990). Learning disabilities. *Harvard Mental Health Letter*, pp. 7, 3-5.

Simmons, R. G., Burgeson, R., Carlton-Ford, S., & Blyth, D. A. (1987). The impact of cumulative change in early adolescence. *Child Development, 58*, 1220-1234.

Simons-Morton, B. G., Parcel, G. S., Baranowski, T., O'Hara, N. and Forthofer, R. (1991). School promotion of healthful diet and exercise behavior: An integration of organizational changes and social learning theory intervention. *American Journal of Public Health, 81*, 986-991.

Simopoulos, A. P. (1983). Nutrition. In C. C. Brown (Ed.), *Prenatal Roundtable: Vol. 9. Childhood learning disabilities and prenatal risk* (pp. 44-49). Rutherford, NJ: Johnson & Johnson.

Simpson, W. J. (1957). A preliminary report on cigarette smoking and the incidence of prematurity. *American Journal of Obstetrics and Gynecology, 73*, 808-815.

Singer, D. G. & Singer, J. L. (1990). *The house of make believe: Children's play and developing imagination*. Cambridge, MA: Harvard University Press.

Siqueland, E. R., & DeLucia, C. A. (1969). Visual reinforcement of nonnutritive sucking in human infants. *Science, 165*, 1144-1146.

Skinner, B. F. (1968). *The technology of teaching*. New York: Appleton-Century-Crofts.

Skinner, B. F. (1971). *Beyond freedom and dignity*. New York: Knopf.

Slobin, D. (Ed.). (1982). *The cross-cultural study of language acquisition*. Hillsdale, NJ: Erlbaum.

Slobin, D. I. (July 1972). They learn the same way all around the world. *Psychology Today*, pp. 71-74ff.

Smilansky, S. (1968). *The effects of sociodramatic play on disadvantaged children: Preschool children*. New York: Wiley.

Smith, C., & Lloyd, B. (1978). Maternal behavior and perceived sex of infant: Revisited. *Child Development, 49*, 1263-1265.

Smith, P. K., & Dodsworth, C. (1978). Social class differences in the fantasy play of preschool children. *Journal of Genetic Psychology, 133*, 183-190.

Smith, W. (1987). *Obstetrics, gynecology, & infant mortality*. New York: Facts on File Publications.

Snow, C. (1989). Understanding social interaction and language acquisition: Sentences are not enough. In M. Bornstein & J. Bruner *Interaction in human development* (pp. 83-104). Hillsdale, NJ: Erlbaum.

Snyder, S. (1991). Movies and juvenile delinquency: An overview. *Adolescence, 26*(101), 121-132.

Snyder, S. (1991). Movies and juvenile delinquency: an overview. *Adolescence, 26(101)*, 121-132.

Society for Research and Child Development. (1973). *Ethical standards for research with children*. Chicago: Society for Research and Child Development.

Society for Research and Child Development. (1990). *Ethical standards for research with children*. Chicago: Society for Research and Child Development.

Soloway, N. M. and Smith, R. M. (1987). Antecedents of late birthtiming decisions of men and women in dual-career marriages. *Family Relations, 36*, 258-262.

Sonenstein, F. L. (1987). Teenage childbearing . . . in all walks of life. *Brandeis Review, 7*(1), 25-28.

Sorenson, R. C. (1973). *Adolescent sexuality in contemporary America: Personal values and sexual behavior, ages 13-19*. New York: World.

Source, J. F., & Emde, R. N. (1981). Mother's presence is not enough: Effect of emotional availability on infant exploration. *Developmental Psychology, 17*, 737-745.

Speece, M. W., & Brent, S. B. (1984). Children's understanding of death: A review of three components of a death concept. *Child Development, 55,* 1671-1686.

Spelke, E. S. (1988). The origins of physical knowledge. In L. Weiskrantz (Ed.), *Thought without language* (pp. 168-184). Clarendon Press.

Spencer, M. B. (1988). Self-concept development. In D. T. Slaughter (Ed.), *New Directions for Child Development, 42. Black children and poverty: A developmental perspective.* San Francisco: Jossey-Bass.

Sperry, R. (1970). Perception in the absence of neocortical commissures. In *Perception and its disorders (Research Publication A.R.N.M.D.,* Vol. 48). New York: Association for Research in Nervous and Mental Disease.

Spiro, M. E. (1954). Is the family universal? The Israeli case. *American Anthropologist, 56,* 839-846.

Sroufe, L. A. (1977). Wariness of strangers and the study of infant development. *Child Development, 48,* 731-746.

Sroufe, L. A. (1985). Attachment classification from the perspective of infant-caregiver relationships and infant temperament. *Child Development, 56,* 1-14.

Sroufe, L. A., & Fleeson, J. (1986). Attachment and the construction of relationships. In W. W. Hartup & Z. Rubin (Eds.), *Relationships and development* (pp. 51-72). Hillsdale, NJ: Erlbaum.

Sroufe, L. A., Fox, N. E., & Paneake, V. R. (1983). Attachment and dependency in a developmental perspective. *Child Development, 54,* 1615-1627.

Stangor, C., & Ruble, D. N. (1987). Development of gender role knowledge and gender consistency. *New Directions for Child Development, 38,* 5-22.

Stanton, H. E. (1981). A therapeutic approach to help children overcome learning difficulties. *Journal of Learning Disabilities, 14,* 220.

Starfield, B. (1992). Child and adolescent health status measures. In R. E. Behrman, (Ed.), *The Future of Children* (25-39). Los Angeles, CA: Center for the Future of Children of the David and Lucile Packard Foundation.

Staub, E. (1971). The use of role playing and induction in children's learning of helping and sharing behavior. *Child Development, 42,* 805-816.

Stechler, G., & Shelton, A. (1982). Prenatal influences on human development. In B. Wolman (Ed.), *Handbook of developmental psychology.* Englewood Cliffs, NJ: Prentice Hall.

Stein, A. H., & Friedrich, L. K. (1975). Impact of television on children and youth. In E. M. Hetherington (Ed.), *Review of child development* (Vol. 5). Chicago: University of Chicago Press.

Stein, Z. A., & Susser, M. W. (1976). Prenatal nutrition and mental competence. In Lloyd, Still, J. D. (Ed.), *Malnutrition and intellectual development.* Littleton, MA: Publishing Sciences Group.

Steinberg, L. (1980). *Understanding families with young adolescents.* Carrboro, NC: Center for Early Adolescents.

Steinberg, L. (1981). Transformations in family relations at puberty. *Developmental Psychology, 17,* 833-840.

Steinberg, L. (1986). Latchkey children and susceptibility to peer pressure: An ecological analysis. *Developmental Psychology, 22,* 433-439.

Steinberg, L. (1987a). Recent research on the family at adolescence: The extent and nature of sex differences. *Journal of Youth and Adolescence, 16,* 191-198.

Steinberg, L. (1987b). Single parents, stepparents, and the susceptibility of adolescents to antisocial peer pressure. *Child Development, 58,* 269-275.

Steinberg, L. (1988). Reciprocal relation between parent-child distance and pubertal maturation. *Developmental Psychology, 24,* 122-128.

Steinberg, L., Fegley, S., & Dornbusch, S. M. (1993). Negative impact of part-time work on adolescent: evidence from a longitudinal study. *Developmental Psychology, 29*(2), 171-180.

Stephens, W. N. (1963). *The family in cross-cultural perspective.* New York: Holt, Rinehart & Winston.

Sternberg, R. J. (1984). Mechanisms of cognitive development: A componential approach. In R. J. Sternberg (Ed.), *Mechanisms of cognitive development.* New York: Freeman.

Sternberg, R. J. (1985). *Beyond IQ: A triarchic theory of human intelligence.* Cambridge, UK: Cambridge University Press.

Sternberg, R. J. (1988a). Lessons from the life span: What theorists of intellectual development among children learn from their counterparts studying adults. In E. M. Hetherington, R. N. Lerner, & M. Perlmutter (Eds.), *Child development* (pp. 259-276). Hillsdale, NJ: Erlbaum.

Sternberg, R. J. (1988b). Intellectual development: Psychometric and information processing approaches. In M. H. Bornstein & M. E. Lamb, (Eds.), *Developmental psychology: An advanced textbook* (2nd ed.). Hillsdale, NJ: Erlbaum.

Sternberg, R. J. (Ed.). (1982). *Advances in the psychology of human intelligence.* Hillsdale, NJ: Erlbaum.

Sternglass, E. J. (1963). Cancer: Relation of prenatal radiation to development of the disease in childhood. *Science, 140,* 1102-1104.

Stevenson, H., Azuma, H., & Hakuta, K. (Eds.). (1986). *Child development and education in Japan.* New York: Freeman.

Stewart, R. B., Mobley, L. A., Van Tuyl, S. S., & Salvador, M. A. (1987). The firstborn's adjustment to the birth of a sibling: A longitudinal assessment. *Child Development, 58,* 341-355.

Stigler, J. W., Lee, S., & Stevenson, H. W. (1987). Mathematics classrooms in Japan, Taiwan, and the United States. *Child Development, 58,* 1272-1285.

Stoel-Gammon, C. (1989). Prespeech and early speech development of two late talkers. *First Language, 9,* 207-223.

Stone, L. J., Smith, H. T., & Murphy, L. B. (Eds.). (1973). *The competent infant: Research and commentary.* New York: Basic Books.

Streissguth, A. P., Barr, H., & MacDonald, M. (1983). Maternal alcohol use and neonatal habituation assessed with the Brazelton scale. *Child Development, 54,* 1109-1118.

Streissguth, A. P., Sampson, P. D., Barr, H. M., Darby, B. L., & Martin, D. C. (1989). I. Q. at age 4 in relation to maternal alcohol use and smoking during pregnancy. *Developmental Psychology, 25*(1), 3-11.

Stuber, M. L. (August 1989). Coordination of care for pediatric AIDS. *Journal of Developmental and Behavioral Pediatrics, 10*(4), 201-204.

Stunkard, A. J. (1988). Some perspectives on human obesity: Its causes. *Bulletin of the New York Academy of Medicine, 64,* 902-923.

Sugarman, S. (December 1983). Why talk? Comment on Savage-Rumbaugh et al. *Journal of Experimental Psychology, 112*(4), 493-497.

Super, C. M., Herrera, M. G., & Mora, J. O. (1990). Long-term effects of food supplementation and psychosocial intervention on the physical growth of Colombian infants at risk of malnutrition. *Child Development, 61,* 29-49.

Sutton-Smith, B., & Rosenberg, B. G. (1970). *The sibling.* New York: Holt, Rinehart & Winston.

Taft, L. I., & Cohen, H. J. (1967). Neonatal and infant reflexology. In J. Hellmuth (Ed.), *The exceptional infant* (Vol. 1). Seattle: Special Child Publications.

Takanashi, R. (1993). The opportunities of Adolescence—Research, interventions, and policy. *American Psychologist, 48*(2), 85-87.

Tanner, J. M. (1978). *Foetus into man: Physical growth from conception to maturity.* Cambridge, MA: Harvard University Press.

Taylor, M., Cartwright, B. S., & Carlson, S. M. (1993). A developmental investigation of children's imaginary companions. *Developmental Psychology, 29*(2), 276-285.

Tellegen, A. D. T., Lykken, D. T., Bouchard, T. J., Wilcox, K., Segal, N. L., & Rich, S. (1988). Personality similarity in twins reared apart and together. *Journal of Social and Personality Psychology, 59,* 1031-1039.

Teller, D., & Bornstein, M. (1987). Infant color vision and color perception. In P. Salapatek & L. Cohen (Eds.), *Handbook of infant perception* (Vol. 1). New York: Academic Press.

Terman, L. M., & Merrill, M. A. (1960). *Revised Stanford-Binet Intelligence Scale* (2nd ed.). Boston: Houghton Mifflin.

Thatcher, R. W., Walker, R. A., & Guidice, S. (1987). Human cerebral hemispheres develop at different rates and ages. *Science, 236,* 1110-1113.

Theilgaard, A. (1983). Aggression and the XYY personality. *International Journal of Law and Psychiatry, 6,* 413-421.

Thelen, E. (1987). The role of motor development in developmental psychology: A view of the past and an agenda for the future. In N. Eisenberg (Ed.), *Contemporary topics in developmental psychology.* New York: Wiley.

Thelen, E. (1988). Dynamical approaches to the development of behavior. In J. A. S. Kelso, A. J. Mandell & M. F. Shlesinger, (Eds.), *Dynamic patterns in complex systems.* Singapore: World Scientific Publishers, 348-369.

Thelen, E. (1989). The (Re)Discovery of motor development: learning new things from an old field. *Developmental Psychology, 25*(6), 946-949.

Thelen, E. (1989). The rediscovery of motor development: Learning new things from an old field. *Developmental Psychology, 25*(6), 946-949.

Thelen, E. (1992). Development as a dynamic system. *Current Directions in Psychological Science, 1*(6), 189-193.

Thelen, E., & Fogel, A. (1989). Toward an action-based theory of infant development. In J. J. Lockman & N. L. Kazen (Eds.), *Action in social context: Perspectives on early development* (pp. 23-64). New York: Plenum.

Thompson, R. A. (1990). Vulnerability in research: A developmental perspective on research risk. *Child Development, 61,* 1-16.

Thompson, S. K. (1975). Gender labels and early sex-role development. *Child Development, 46,* 339-347.

Thorndike, E. L. (1911). *Animal intelligence.* New York: Macmillan.

Thurstone, L. L. (1938). Primary mental abilities. *Psychometric Monographs,* No. 1.

Tieger, T. (1980). On the biological basis of sex differences in aggression. *Child Development, 51,* 943-963.

Tikalsky, F. D., & Wallace, S. D. (1988). Culture and the structure of children's fears. *Journal of Cross-Cultural Psychology, 19*(4), 481-492.

Timnick, L. (September 3, 1989). Children of violence. *Los Angeles Times Magazine,* 6-12, 14-15.

Tomasello, M., Mannle, S., & Kruger, A. C. (1986). Linguistic environment of one- to two-year-old twins. *Developmental Psychology, 22,* 169-176.

Turkington, C. (1987). Special talents. *Psychology Today, 21*(9), 42-46.

Turnbull, A. P., & Turnbull, H. R., III. (1990). *Families, professionals and exceptionality: A special partnership* (2nd ed.). Columbus, OH: Merrill.

Turnbull, C. M. (1972). *The mountain people.* New York: Simon & Schuster.

U.S. Bureau of the Census. (1988). *Statistical Analysis of the U.S.: 1988.* Washington, DC: Government Printing Office.

U.S. Bureau of the Census. (1990). *Current Population Reports.* Series P-25, Nos. 519, 917.

U.S. Congress Office of Technology Assessment. (1991). *Adolescent Health: Vol. 1: Summary and policy options.* (Publication No. OTA-H-468). Washington, DC: U.S. Government Printing Office.

U.S. Department of Commerce. (1987). *Statistical Abstract of the U.S.: 1987.* Washington, DC

U.S. Department of Commerce. (1990). *Statistical Abstract of the U.S.: 1990.* Washington, DC

U.S. Department of Health and Human Services. (1983). Regulations on the protection of human subjects. *45CFR, 46,* Subparts A & D.

Udry, J. R. (1988). Biological predispositions and social control in adolescent sexual behavior. *American Sociological Review, 52,* 841-855.

United Nations. (1990). *Demographic Yearbook, 40th issue.* New York: United Nations.

United States Bureau of the Census. (1993). *Statistical Abstracts of the United States.* Washington: U.S. Government Printing Office.

United States Department of Health and Human Services (USDHHS). (1992). *Health People 2000: National health promotion and disease prevention objectives.* Boston, MA: Jones & Bartlett.

United States Department of Health and Human Services. (1989). *Health*United States*1988.* Washington, DC: U.S. Government Printing Office.

Uzgiris, I. C. (1984). Imitation in infancy: Its interpersonal aspects. In M. Perlmutter (Ed.), *Minnesota Symposia on Child Psychology: Vol. 17. Parent-child interaction and parent-child relations.* Hillsdale, NJ: Erlbaum.

Van Baal, J. (1966). *Dema: Description and analysis of Marind Anim culture, South New Guinea.* The Hague: Martinus Nijhoff.

van IJzendoorn, M. H., & Kroonenberg, P. M. (1988). Cross-cultural patterns of attachment: A meta-analysis of the Strange Situation. *Child Development, 59,* 147-156.

Vandell, D. L., & Corasaniti, M. A. (Fall 1990). Child care and the family: Complex contributions to child development. *New Directions for Child Development, 49,* 23-38.

Vandell, D. L., & Wilson, C. S. (1987). Infants' interactions with mother, sibling and peer: Contrasts and relations between interaction systems. *Child Development, 58,* 176-186.

Varni, J. W., & Babani, L. (1986). Long-term adherrence to health care regimens in pediatric chronic disorders. In N. A., Krasnegor, J. D. Arasteh, and M. F. Cataldo, (Eds.), *Child health behavior: A behavior pediatrics perspective.* New York: Wiley Interscience.

Vasta, R. (1982). Physical child abuse: A dual-component analysis. *Developmental Review, 2,* 125-149.

Verma, I. M. (November 1990). Gene therapy. *Scientific American,* pp. 68-84.

Vogel, J. M. (1989). *Shifting perspectives on the role of reversal errors in reading disability.* Paper presented at the April meeting of the Society for Research in Child Development, Kansas City.

von Hofsten, C. (1989). Motor development as the development of systems: comments on the special section. *Developmental Psychology, 25*(6), 950-953.

Vorhees, C., & Mollnow, E. (1987). Behavioral teratogenesis. In J. Osofsky (Ed.), *Handbook of infant development* (2nd ed.). New York: Wiley.

Vulliamy, D. G. (1973). *The newborn child* (3rd ed.). Edinburgh: Churchill Livingstone.

Vygotsky, L. (1962). *Thought and language.* Cambridge, MA: MIT Press (Originally published 1934)

Vygotsky, L. S. (1956). *Selected psychological investigations.* Moscow: Izdstel'sto Akademii Pedagogicheskikh Nauk SSR.

Vygotsky, L. S. (1967). Play and its role in the mental development of the child. *Soviet Psychology, 12,* 6-8.

Vygotsky, L. S. (1978). *Mind in society: The development of higher psychological processes.* (M. Cole, Y. John-Steiner, S. Scribner, & E. Souberman, Eds.). Cambridge, MA: Harvard University Press.

Wagner, B. M., & Phillips, D. A. (1992). Beyond beliefs: Parent and child behaviors and children's perceived academic competence. *Child Development, 62,* 1380-1391.

Wagner, R. C., & Torgerson, J. K. (1987). The nature of phonological processing and its causal role in the acquisition of reading skills. *Psychological Bulletin, 101,* 192-212.

Wallerstein, J., Corbin, S. B., & Lewis, J. M. (1988). Children of divorce: A ten-year study. In E. M. Hetherington & J. Arasteh (Eds.), *Impact of divorce, single-parenting, and stepparenting on children.* Hillsdale, NJ: Erlbaum.

Wallis, C. (September 10, 1984). The new origins of life. *Time,* pp. 46-50, 52-53.

Walsh, B. T. (1988). Antidepressants and bulimia: Where are we? *International Journal of Eating Disorders, 7,* 421-423.

Waterman, A. S. (1985). Identity in the context of adolescent psychology. *New Directions for Child Development, 30,* 5-24.

Waters, E., Wippman, J., & Sroufe, L. A. (1979). Attachment, positive affect and competence in the peer group: Two studies in construct validation. *Child Development, 50,* 821-829.

Watson, G. (1957). Some personality differences in children related to strict or permissive parental discipline. *Journal of Psychology, 44,* 227-249.

Watson, J. B. (1930). *Behaviorism.* New York: Norton.

Watson, J. B., & Rayner, R. (1920). Conditioned emotional reactions. *Journal of Experimental Psychology, 3,* 1-14.

Watson, J. D., & Crick, F. H. C. (1953). Molecular structure of nucleic acids. *Nature, 171,* 737-738.

Watson, J. S. (1972). Smiling, cooing, and ``the game.'' *Merrill-Palmer Quarterly, 18,* 323-339.

Watson, J. S., & Ramey, C. T. (1972). Reactions to response-contingent stimulation in early infancy. *Merrill-Palmer Quarterly, 18,* 219-227.

Watson-Gegeo, K. A., & Gegeo, D. W. (1989) The role of sibling interaction in child socialization. In P. Zukow (Ed.), *Sibling interaction across cultures: Theoretical and methodological issues.* New York: Springer-Verlag.

Watts, W. D., & Wright, L. S. (1990). The relationship of alcohol, tobacco, marijuana, and other illegal drug use to delinquency among Mexican-American, Black, and White Adolescent Males. *Adolecence, 25*(97), 171-181.

Weber, R. A., Levitt, M. J., & Clark, M. C. (1986). Individual variation in attachment security and strange situation behavior: The role of maternal and infant temperament. *Child Development, 37,* 56-65.

Wegman, M. E. (1990). Annual summary of vital statistics—1989. *Pediatrics, 86*(6), 835-847.

Weinberg, R. A. (1989). Intelligence and IQ: Landmark issues and great debates. *American Psychologist, 44*(2), 98-104.

Weinberg, R. A. (1989). Intelligence and IQ: Landmark issues and great debates. *American Psychologist, 44,* 98-104.

Weinraub, M., Clemens, L. P., Sockloff, A., Ethridge, T., Gracely, E., & Myers, B. (1984). The development of sex role stereotypes in the third year: Relationships to gender labeling, gender identity, sex-typed toy preference and family characteristics. *Child Development, 55,* 1493-1503.

Weinstein, C. S. (1991). The classroom as a social context for learning. *Annual Review of Psychology, 42,* 493-525.

Weinstein, G., & Alschuler, A. (1985). Educating and counseling for self-knowledge development. *Journal of Counseling and Development, 4,* 19-25.

Weisfeld, G. E., & Billings, R. L. (1988). Observations on adolescence. In K. B. MacDonald (Ed.), *Sociobiological perspectives on human development.* New York: Springer-Verlag.

Welles-Nystrom, B. (Summer 1988). Parenthood and infancy in Sweden. In R. A. LeVine, P. M. Miller, & M. M. West (Eds.), *New Directions for Child Development, 40. Parental behavior in diverse societies* (pp. 75-78).

Werner, E. E. (1979). *Cross-cultural child development.* Monterey, CA: Brooks/Cole.

Werner, E. E. (1989). Children of the garden island. *Scientific American, 260*(4), 106-111.

Werner, E. E. (1989). High-risk children in young adulthood: A longitudinal study from birth to 32 years. *American Journal of Orthopsychiatry, 59,* 72-81.

Werner, E. E. (November 1984). Resilient children. *Young Children,* 68-72.

Wertz, D. C. (1992). Ethical and legal implications of the new genetics: issues for discussion. *Social Science and Medicine, 35*(4), 495-505.

Westinghouse Learning Corporation. (1969). *The impact of Head Start: An evaluation of the effects of Head Start experience on children's cognitive and affective development.* Columbus: Westinghouse Learning Corporation, Ohio State University.

Whitbourne, S. K. (February 20, 1991). *Adult development: Life span perspective.* Talk given at the Human Development Colloquium Series, University of Massachusetts, Amherst.

White, B. L. (1971). *Human infants: Experience and psychological development.* Englewood Cliffs, NJ: Prentice Hall.

White, B. L. (1975). *The first three years of life.* Englewood Cliffs, NJ: Prentice Hall.

White, B. L. (1988). *Educating the infant and toddler.* Lexington, MA: Lexington Books.

White, B. L., & Held, R. (1966). Plasticity of sensorimotor development in the human infant. In J. F. Rosenblith & W. Allinsmith (Eds.), *Causes of behavior: Readings in child development and educational psychology.* Boston: Allyn & Bacon.

White, B. L., & Watts, J. (1973). *Experience and environment: Major influences on the development of the young child.* Englewood Cliffs, NJ: Prentice Hall.

White, R. W. (1959). Motivation reconsidered: The concept of competence. *Psychological Review, 66,* 297-333.

Whiting, B. B. (Ed.). (1963). *Six cultures: Studies of child rearing.* New York: Wiley.

Whiting, B. B., & Edwards, C. P. (1988). *Children of different worlds: The formation of social behavior.* Cambridge, MA: Harvard University Press.

Whiting, B. B., & Whiting, J. W. M. (1975). *Children of six cultures: A psychocultural analysis.* Cambridge, MA: Harvard University Press.

Whorf, B. (1956). A linguistic consideration of thinking in primitive communities. In J. B. Carroll, (Ed.), *Language, thought and reality* (pp. 65-86). Cambridge, MA: MIT Press.

Williams, B. C., & Miller, C. A. (1992). Preventive health care for young children: findings from a 10-country study and directions for United States policy. *Supplement to Pediatrics, 89*(5), Part 2, 983-998.

Williams, F. (1970). Some preliminaries and prospects. In F. Williams (Ed.), *Language and poverty.* Chicago: Markham.

Williams, H. G. (1983). *Perceptual and motor development.* Englewood Cliffs, N.J.: Prentice Hall.

Williams, J. E., Bennett, S. M., & Best, D. (1975). Awareness and expression of sex stereotypes in young children. *Developmental Psychology, 5*(2), 635-642.

Willson, J. R. (May 1990). Scientific advances, societal trends and the education and practice of obstetrician-gynecologists. *American Journal of Obstetrics and Gynecology, 162*(5).

Wilson, E. O. (1975). *Sociobiology, the new synthesis.* Cambridge, MA: Belknap Press of Harvard University Press.

Windle, M. (1991). The difficult temperament in adolescence: associations with substance use, family support, and problem behaviors. *Journal of Clinical Psychology, 47*(2), 310-316.

Winick, M., & Brasel, J. A. (1977). Early manipulation and subsequent brain development. *Annals of the New York Academy of Sciences, 300,* 280-282.

Winn, M. (1983). *The plug-in drug* (2nd ed.). New York: Viking.

Winner, E. (1986). Where pelicans kiss seeds. *Psychology Today, 8,* 25-35.

Witters, W., & Venturelli, P. (1988). *Drugs and society* (2nd ed.). Boston: Jones & Bartlett.

Wohlwill, J. F. (1973). *The study of behavioral development.* New York: Academic Press.

Wolfe, D. A., Wolfe, V. V., & Best, C. L. (1988). Child victims of sexual abuse. In V. B. VanHasselt, R. L. Morrison, A. S. Bellack, & M. Herson (Eds.), *Handbook of family violence.* New York: Plenum.

Wolfenstein, M. (1951). The emergence of fun morality. *Journal of Social Issues, 7*(4), 15-25.

Wolfenstein, M. (1955). Fun morality: An analysis of recent American child-training literature. In M. Mead & M. Wolfenstein (Eds.), *Childhood in contemporary cultures* (pp. 168-178). Chicago: University of Chicago Press.

Wolff, P. (1966). The causes, controls, and organization of behavior in the neonate. *Psychological Issues, 5*(No. 1, Monograph 17).

Wolpe, J., Salter, A., & Reyna, L. J. (Eds.). (1964). *The conditioning therapies: The challenge in psychotherapy.* New York: Holt, Rinehart & Winston.

Woodcock, L. P. (1941). *The life and ways of the two-year-old.* New York: Basic Books.

Wright, J., & Huston, A. (1983). A matter of form: Potentials of television for young viewers. *American Psychologist, 38,* 835-843.

Wyden, B. (December 7, 1971). Growth: 45 crucial months. *Life,* p. 93ff.

Yarrow, L. J., Rubenstein, J. L., Pedersen, F. A., & Jankowski, J. J. (1972). Dimensions of early stimulation and their differential effects on infant development. *Merrill-Palmer Quarterly, 18,* 205-218.

Yonas, A., & Owsley, C. (1987). Development of visual space perception. In P. Salapatek & L. Cohen (Eds.), *Handbook of infant perception* (Vol. 2, pp. 80-122). New York: Academic Press.

Young, D. (1982). *Changing childbirth: Family birth in the hospital.* Rochester, NY: Childbirth Graphics.

Young, E. W., Jensen, L. C., Olsen, J. A., & Cundick, B. P. (1991). The effects of family structure on the sexual behavior of adolescents. *Adolescence, 26(104),* 977-986.

Young, K. T. (1990). American conceptions of infant development from 1955 to 1984: What the experts are telling parents. *Child Development, 61,* 17-28.

Youngs, G. A., Rathge, R., Mullis, R., and Mullis, A. (1990). Adolescent stress and self-esteem. *Adolescence, 25(98),* 333-341.

Youniss, J. (1983). Social construction of adolescence by adolescents and parents. H. D. Grotevant, & C. R. Cooper (Eds.), *Adolescent development in the family: New directions for child development* (no. 22). San Francisco: Jossey-Bass, 93-109.

Youniss, J., & Ketterlinus, R. D. (1987). Communication and connectedness in mother and father adolescent relationships. *Journal of Youth and Adolescence,* 265-280.

Zajonc, R. B., & Hall, E. (February 1986). Mining new gold from old research. *Psychology Today,* pp. 46-51.

Zajonc, R. B., & Markus, G. B. (1975). Birth order and intellectual development. *Psychological Review, 82,* 74-88.

Zaporozlets, A. V., & Elkonin, D. B. (Eds.). (1971). *The psychology of preschool children.* Cambridge, MA: MIT Press.

Zelnick, M., & Kantner, J. F. (1977). Sexual and contraceptive experience of young unmarried women in the United States, 1976 and 1971. *Family Planning Perspectives, 9,* 55-71.

Zeskind, P. S., & Ramey, C. T. (1978). Fetal malnutrition: An experimental study of its consequences on infant development in two caregiving environments. *Child Development, 49,* 1155-1162.

Zigler, E. F. (1987). Formal schooling for four-year-olds? No. *American Psychologist, 42*(3), 254-260.

Zill, N. (1991). U.S. children and their families: Current conditions and recent trends, 1989. *Newsletter of the Society for Research in Child Development,* pp. 1-3.

Zuravin, S. (1985). Housing and maltreatment: Is there a connection? *Children Today, 14*(6), 8-13.

ACKNOWLEDGMENTS

FIGURES

CHAPTER 1

Figure 1-2: Reprinted from *Analyzing Children's Art* by permission of Mayfield Publishing Company. Copyright 1969, 1970, by Rhonda Kellog.

CHAPTER 2

Figure 2-3: From N.J. Salkind, 1981, Theories of Human Development, New York: D. Van Nostrand, p. 131, Figure 7-1. Reprinted by permission. Figure 2-5: From *Motivation and Personality, 3rd Ed.*, by Abraham Maslow, revised by Robert Frager et al. Copyright 1954, ©1987 by Harper & Row, Publishers, Inc. Copyright © 1970 by Abraham Maslow. Reprinted by permission of Harper Collins Publishers. Inc.

CHAPTER 4

Figure 4-1: Statistical Handbook on the American Family.

CHAPTER 6

Figure 6-3: Adapted from *Growth and Development of Children, 5th Ed.*, by E.H. Watson and G.H. Lowrey (Chicago: Year Book Medical Publishers, 1967).

CHAPTER 8

Cartoon (p. 311): © 1992 by Sidney Harris. Figure 8-3: From "The Acquisition of Language" by U. Bellugi and R. Brown, *Monographs of the Society for Research in Child Development*, 1964, 19 (1), 43-79. Copyright © 1964 by the Society for Research in Child Development, Inc.

CHAPTER 9

Figure 9-1: Nichols, B. (1990). *Moving and Learning: The Elementary School Physical Education Experience.* St. Louis, MO: Times Mirror/Mosby College Publishing.)

CHAPTER 12

Cartoon (p.488): Jack Zeigler.

CHAPTER 13

Figure 13-3: *S.J. Gould (1981). The Mismeasure of Man.* New York: W.W. Norton & Co.

PHOTOS

2 Pentagram 8 (a) James Stevenson/Science Photo Library (b) Taeke Henstra/Petit Format (c) Myrleen Ferguson (d) Myrleen Ferguson 9 (e) Frank Siteman (f) Elizabeth Crews (g) M. Greenlar (h) Tony Freeman (i) Bob Daemmrich 14 Photo Researchers 15 Photo Researchers 16 Photo Reseachers 25 Bob Daemmrich 34 Nancy J. Pierce 40 Pentrgram 47 Photoedit 52 Shirley Zeiberg 56 (a) Wayne Behling, psilanti Press (b) Monkmeyer Press 61 Laima Druskis 62 Richard Hutchings, Photo Researchers 70 Conklin, Monkmeyer Press 73 Gianni Giansanti, Sygma 84 Pentagram 88 Jean Claude Revy, Phototake 89 Photo Researchers 95 Bruce Roberts, Photo Research 101 Photo Researchers 106 Frank Siteman, Picture Cube 108 Elizabeth Crews, The Image Works 112 Daemmrich, The Image Works 113 Gale Zucker, Stock Boston 117 The Bettman Archive 121 (top) Lori Morris-Nantz (bottom) Spencer Grant, Picture Cube 124 John Yurka, Picture Cube 134 W. Hill, Jr./The Image Works 136 Will & Deni McIntyre/Photo Researchers 139 Francis Leroy, Biocosmos/Science Photo Library/Photo Research 141 Alexander Tsiaras/Science Source/Photo Researchers 144 (left) Porterfield-Chickering/Photo Researchers (right) Bruce Roberts/Photo Researchers 148 (c) A. Lennart Nilsson Being Born (b) C. Lennart Nilsson A Child is Born (c) Dr. Landrum B. Shettles (d)-(h) C. Lennart Nillson Being Born 156 United Nations 161William McCoy/Rainbow 164 David Young-Wolff/Photoedit 166 Gaye Hilsenrath/Picture Cube 168 W. Hill. Jr./The Image Works 172 Pentagram 174 Jim Corwin/Stock Boston 176 Griffin/The Image Works 180 Heinz Kluetneier/DOT Pictures 182 Catherine Ursillo/Photo Researchers 186 Lawrence Migdale/Stock Boston 187 Jim Olive/Peter Arnold 195Lawrence Migdale/Photo Researchers 197 Jim Corwin/Stock Boston 201(top left) Format/Science Source/Photo Researchers (top right) Petit Format/J.M. Steinlein/Photo Researchers (bottom right) Tucker/Monkmeyer Press 203 Crews/The Image Works 206 Alan Carey/The Image Works 209 Mark Richards/Photoedit 216 Pentagram 218 E. Crews/The Image Works 220 M. Siluk/The Image Works 223 (a) E. Crews/The Image Works (b) Tony Freeman/Photoedit (c) Crews/The Image Works (d) Suzanne Szasz/Photo Researchers (e) Mary Jane Denny/Photoedit 232 Prentice Hall Archives 235 C. Errath/Explorer/Photo Researchers 237 Dr. Joseph J. Campos 240 Shirley Zeiberg 243 John Eastcott 244 Kramer/The Image Works 246 Dr. T.G.R. Bower/"Scientific American," October 1971, page 38 247 Crews/The Image Works 251 Jeffrey W. Myers/Stock Boston 254 Spencer Grant/Photo Researchers 258 Pentagram 260 National Institute on Aging 262 Thomas McAvoy/Life Magazine, Time Warner 264 Courtesy Harry F. Harlow, University of Wisconsin Primate Laboratory 266 Ray Ellin/Photo Researchers 267 J.R. Holland/Stock Boston 268 Crews/The Image Works 270 (left)Zen Radovan/Photoedit (right) United Nations 272 Robert Brenner/Photoedit 274 Shirley Zeiberg 277 J. Berndt 280 Rhoda Sidney 281 Crews/The Image Works 284 National Institute on Aging 291 Peter Southwick/Stock Boston 296 Corroon/Monkmeyer Press 302 Pentagram 306 David Young-Wolff/Photoedit 307 Carol Palmer/Picture Cube 315 Charles Gupton/Stock Boston 318 Ed Malitsky/Picture Cube 323 Alice Kandell/Rapho/Photo Researchers 325 Shostak/Anthro Photo 329 Joseph Schuyler/Stock Boston 331 Robert Brenner/Photoedit 332 Paula M. Lerner/Picture Cube 338 Pentagram 341 David Young-Wolff/Photoedit 344 David Young-Wolff/Photoedit 345 Scott Camazine/Photo Researchers 348 George Goodwin/Monkmeyer Press 349 George Goodwin/Monkmeyer Press 351 Shirley Zeiberg 353 Shirley Zeiberg 355 Greeman/Grishaber/Photoedit 356 Rhoda Sidney/Monkmeyer Press 362 George Zimbel/Monkmeyer Press 365 Bob Daemrich/Stock Boston367 Robert Brenner/Photoedit 369 Larry Milvehill/Photo Researchers 376 Freda Leinwant/Monkmeyer Press 378 Pentagram 384 Teri Stratford 385 A. Griffiths/Woodfin Camp & Associates 387 Lawrence Migdale/Stock Boston 393 Tony Freeman/Photoedit 394 Lew Merrim/Monkmeyer Press 395 Bohdan Hrynewych/Stock Boston 399 Bill Eppridge/DOT 403 (a) George Goodwin (b) Jim Corwin (c) Elizabeth Crews (d) Myrleen Ferguson (e) David Young-Wolff (f) George Goodwin 407 Lawrence Migdale/Photo Researchers 413 George Goodwin/Monkmeyer Press 415 N. Rowan/The Image Works 420 Pentagram 422 Rameshwar Das/Monkmeyer Press 424 Robert

Brenner/Photoedit **426** Sarah Putnam/Picture Cube **429** Michael Newman/Photoedit **430** Robert Brenner/Photoedit **433** Anthony Jalandoni/Monkmeyer Press **438** L. Kolvoord/The Image Works **442** B. Daemmrich/The Image Works **445** Carol Palmer/Picture Cube **446** Tom Prettyman/Photoedit **450** Rameshwar Das/Monkmeyer Press **454** Teri Stratford **455** Elizabeth Hathon/Stock Market **462** Pentragram **465** Tony Freeman **472** (top)David Young-Wolff/Photoedit (bottom) Myrleen Ferguson/Photoedit **476** (top) Jeff Isaac Greenberg/Photo Researchers (bottom) Tony Freeman/Photoedit **480** Elizabeth Zuckerman/Photoedit **484** Michael Newman/Photoedit **485** Tony Freeman/Photoedit **487** Renee Lynn/Photo Researchers **489** Margot Granitsas/Photo Researchers **490** Lawrence Migdale/Photo Researchers **491** Tom McCarthy/Rainbow **492** David Young-Wolff/Photoedit **496** Pentagram **504** Laima Druskis **506** Will McIntyre/Photo Researchers **508** Ken Kerbs/DOT **509**Frank Siteman/Picture Cube **513** Bob Daemmrich/Stock Boston **515** Kat/Nicol/Woodfin Camp & Associates **517** Michael Newman/Photoedit **522**Bob Daemmrich/Stock Boston **519** Prentice Hall Archives **525** Dan McCoy/Rainbow **529** Stephen McBrady/Photoedit **530** George Goodwin/Monkmeyer Press **534** Pentagram **536** Myrleen Ferguson/Photoedit **538** Myrleen Ferguson **541** David Young-Wolff/Photoedit **544** John Coletti/Photoedit **546** Tony Freeman/Photoedit **549** Myrleen Ferguson/Photoedit **554** Richard Smith/Monkmeyer Press **559** Frank Siteman/Rainbow **560** Myrleen Ferguson/Photoedit **564** Robert W. Ginn/Photoedit **567** Bob Daemmrich/The Image Works **574** Pentagram **579** Richard Hutching/Photoedit **581** Rhoda Sidney/Monkmeyer Press **582** Billy Barnes/Photoedit **585** David Young-Wolff/Photoedit **587** Willie Hill/The Image Works **590** John Elk. III/Stock Boston **591** Steven Frame/Stock Boston **593**Bruce Malone/Retna **595** George Goodwin/Monkmeyer Press **598** Charles Harbutt/Actuality **599** Tony Freeman/Photoedit **604** Rhoda Sidney/Stock Boston **605** Willie Hill, Jr./The Image Works **610** Pentagram **614** Rhoda Sidney/Photoedit **615** Bob Daemmrich/Stock Boston **619** Rhoda Sidney/Monkmeyer Press **621** Richard Pasley/Stock Boston **624** Bob Daemmrich/The Image Works **626** Evan P. Schneider/Monkmeyer Press **627** Tony Freeman/Photoedit **634** Monatiuk/Eastcott/Woodfin Camp & Associates **637** Bob Daemmrich/The Image Works **640** Mike Kogan/Monkmeyer Press **641** E. Crews/The Image Works